Y0-BOA-724

A CLOSER LOOK

The Writer's Reader

permission to write
nd for a writer this is
actly equal to the
ower to write) is a gift,
en what of the lack of
rmission? • A few
ars ago I revisited
ombay, which is my lost
y, after an absence of
mething like half my
e. • What concerned
e now was how a sub–
t was constituted, how
anguage could be
rmed—writing as a
nstruction of realities
at served one or
other purpose instru–
entally. • The first
apbox orator I ever saw
s haranguing a crowd
side the Greyhound
ation in Providence,
hode Island, about the
ils of fluoridated water.
his is the picture I see
en I write. These are
e secrets I was supposed
keep. These are the
men who never let
e forget why stories
ed to be told. • What
e black Southern
iter inherits as a nat–
al right is a sense of
munity. Something
ple but surprisingly
rd, especially these
ys, to come by. • Art
n our bones: We all
e by narrative and

A CLOSER LOOK
The Writer's Reader

Sidney I. Dobrin
University of Florida

Anis S. Bawarshi
University of Washington

Boston   Burr Ridge, IL   Dubuque, IA   Madison, WI   New York
San Francisco   St. Louis   Bangkok   Bogotá   Caracas   Kuala Lumpur
Lisbon   London   Madrid   Mexico City   Milan   Montreal   New Delhi
Santiago   Seoul   Singapore   Sydney   Taipei   Toronto

The McGraw-Hill Companies

Mc Graw Hill Higher Education

A CLOSER LOOK: THE WRITER'S READER
Published by McGraw-Hill, a business unit of The McGraw-Hill Companies, Inc., 1221 Avenue of the Americas, New York, NY, 10020. Copyright © 2003 by The McGraw-Hill Companies, Inc. All rights reserved. No part of this publication may be reproduced or distributed in any form or by any means, or stored in a database or retrieval system, without the prior written consent of The McGraw-Hill Companies, Inc., including, but not limited to, in any network or other electronic storage or transmission, or broadcast for distance learning.
Some ancillaries, including electronic and print components, may not be available to customers outside the United States.

This book is printed on acid-free paper.

1 2 3 4 5 6 7 8 9 0 FGR/FGR 0 9 8 7 6 5 4 3 2

ISBN 0-7674-1743-7

President of McGraw-Hill Humanities/Social Sciences: *Steve Debow*
Executive editor: *Lisa Moore*
Developmental editor: *Renée Deljon*
Director of development: *Carla Kay Samodulski*
Senior marketing manager: *David S. Patterson*
Senior media producer: *Todd Vaccaro*
Lead project manager: *Susan Trentacosti*
Lead production supervisor: *Lori Koetters*
Designer: *Sharon Spurlock*
Manager, photo research: *Brian J. Pecko*
Art editor: *Cristin Yancey*
Cover design: *Joan Greenfield*
Interior design: *Linda Robertson*
Typeface: *11/12 Bembo*
Compositor: *Thompson Type*
Printer: *Quebecor World Fairfield Inc.*

Library of Congress Cataloging-in-Publication Data
A closer look : the writer's reader / [compiled by] Sidney I. Dobrin, Anis S. Bawarshi.
   p. cm.
Includes bibliographical references (p.) and index.
   ISBN 0-7674-1743-7 (acid-free paper)
   1. College readers.   2. English language—Rhetoric—Problems, exercises, etc.   3. Report writing—Problems, exercises, etc.   I. Dobrin, Sidney I., 1967–   II. Bawarshi, Anis S.
PE1417.C6313 2003
808'.042'0711—dc21   2002038662
www.mhhe.com

This one's for
HAT, NCS, VWC, ODU, & USF

To My Parents
Mona Bawarshi and Sami Bawarshi
With Love

Preface

In our combined 25 years of teaching composition, we have asked our students to read the work of professional writers, as most instructors do, to help them improve their own writing. But what does it mean to read in a writing course? What might be a better way for student writers to read, one that would give students a clearer sense of how to examine and practice reading as integral to writing, and writing, in turn, as rhetorical? With these questions in mind, we developed the rhetorical approach of *A Closer Look* to help composition students learn how to read as writers, so they develop the ability to read their own writing rhetorically. This text's primary goal, then, is to teach students how to make more effective choices as writers by teaching them how to look more closely (that is, rhetorically) at texts as readers—in other words, to teach them how to examine and compare different rhetorical strategies and effects.

We believe that this kind of rhetorical approach conveys to students an important message about writing itself. Because we treat reading and writing as rhetorical activities, we help students see that a written text is the result of complex choices made by its writer—and that they, the student writers, have more choices than they may be aware of when they sit down to write. By teaching students how to examine and compare different rhetorical strategies with different rhetorical effects, we hope to heighten students' awareness of the choices writers make, why they make them, and how these choices inform what texts mean and do. Students can then apply their rhetorical reading skills to their own writing, learning over time how to predict and assess the effects of their own writing choices on readers. In sum, we believe that helping students see the range of rhetorical options available to them when they write will help them expand their rhetorical repertoire so they become more agile and astute writers, writers who are better prepared to write effectively and creatively in a range of situations, in school and beyond.

To achieve this book's goal, we selected four essays by each of the 21 professional writers included in the book so students can see how the same writer made a range of rhetorical choices in response to different rhetorical situations. The writers we selected are among the most important of our time, and all but one (Stephen Jay Gould, who, sadly, died while this book was in production) are currently living and writing. The 84 essays by these writers, along with the 7 additional essays by student writers (which appear in a section following the professional writers' section), are presented within their rhetorical contexts: Substantial overviews introduce each writer and extensive questions for reading and writing follow all but one of the four essays by each writer. The apparatus is designed to encourage students to consider the following key questions:

- What can we know about the writer and his or her rhetorical situation that can help us understand why he or she wrote a given text the way it appears?

- What are the consequences, the effects, of the writer's choices?

- What can we, as readers, learn about writing as a result of looking closely at how and why the writer wrote a particular essay the way she or he did—why did the writer make those choices?

- What other choices could the writer have made? How and why would the alternate choices have been effective in the same rhetorical situation? (We provide opportunities for students to practice such alternatives in their own writing.)

A Closer Look, therefore, focuses not only on *what* an essay means but also on *how* the writer crafted its meaning in the context of a rhetorical situation.

HIGHLIGHTED FEATURES

Multiple Essays by 21 of Today's Most Important Writers

Four essays represent each writer, so that students can analyze how the individual writer's rhetorical choices change from essay to essay (that is, from rhetorical situation to rhetorical situation). The collected essays, organized alphabetically by the writers' last names, cover a wide range of audiences—from readers of *Ms.* magazine to readers of *Golf* magazine—and a range of subjects—from breast implants to political exile, from censorship to naps. The essays also represent various subgenres, including personal, academic, and political essays. Rick Bass, Annie Dillard, Barbara Ehrenreich, Henry Louis Gates, Jr., Stephen Jay Gould, Barry Lopez, Salman Rushdie, Amy Tan, John Updike, and Alice Walker are among the featured writers.

Essays about Writing

The first essay by each professional writer is about an aspect of writing (found under the heading "[writer's last name] on Writing"), so that students encounter different ways of thinking about and discussing writing, as well as a context for rhetorically analyzing the writers' work.

Substantial Editorial Apparatus

Each writer's section opens with an introduction that discusses the writer's life, body of work, the essays that follow, and initial rhetorical considerations to keep in mind. A contextualizing note with questions for reading ("At First Glance") precedes each selection, and "Double Take" questions for discussion and writing follow the first three essays. Each writer's section concludes with "A Closer Look at [writer's name]" discussion and writing questions that address all of the selections by that writer; "Looking from Writer to Writer" questions that address other writers in the text in addition to the writer immediately at hand; and "Looking Beyond," brief listings of publications by the writer.

One Essay by Each Writer without Reading and Writing Questions

The last essay by each writer appears with only an "At First Glance" note, so students can be challenged to read closely and write on their own.

Seven Essays about Writing by Student Writers

Essays by seven student writers are included in the text, appearing after the last professional writer section. All the student essays have writing as their topic and each one is preceded by a brief note about the student writer, as well as an "At First Glance" note to guide students' reading. Each student essay is followed by "Double Take" questions, just as the professional writers' essays are.

General Introduction That Includes a Brief History of the Essay

The general introduction prepares students for the work ahead by providing key information. It covers the importance of connecting reading and writing; concepts of rhetoric and the rhetorical situation; the nature of rhetorical choices; an overview of *A Closer Look's* structure and editorial apparatus; and a brief history of the essay, including a detailed portrait of the contemporary essay.

PRINT AND ELECTRONIC SUPPLEMENTS

Website to accompany *A Closer Look* at www.mhhe.com/Dobrin

Offering abundant links relevant to the authors, their rhetorical choices in the book's selections, and their topics, and organized to follow the book's alphabetical order, this site provides online resources for student projects, including research papers.

Resources for Teaching *A Closer Look*

This substantial instructor's resource manual, available both in print and online, provides further background information for the writers and the essays, sample answers to the questions, sample syllabi for both 10- and 16-week courses, and additional activities/considerations.

Teaching Composition Faculty Listserv at www.mhhe.com/tcomp

Moderated by Chris Anson at North Carolina State University and offered by McGraw-Hill as a service to the composition community, this listserv brings together senior members of the college composition community with newer members—junior faculty, adjuncts, and teaching assistants—through an online newsletter and accompanying discussion group to address issues of pedagogy, both in theory and in practice.

PageOut

McGraw-Hill's own PageOut service is available to help you get your course up and running online in a matter of hours—at no cost. Additional information about the service is available online at http://www.pageout.net.

Webwrite

This online product, available through our partner company MetaText, makes it possible for writing teachers and students to, among other things, comment on and share papers online.

For further information about these and other electronic resources, contact your local McGraw-Hill representative, visit the English pages on the McGraw-Hill Higher Education website at www.mhhe.com/catalogs/hss/english/, or visit McGraw-Hill's Digital Solutions pages at www.mhhe.com/catalogs/solutions.

ACKNOWLEDGMENTS

As we hope this book demonstrates, writers and writing do not function in isolation. Writers and writing take place in relation to other writers and writing in contexts of interaction. Such is the case with this book, which could not have been completed without the assistance, advice, and support of many people. We are deeply grateful to the following people for their input during the process of constructing this book: Trish Ventura, Chris Keller, Carla Blount, and Christine Jean Hong who helped us gather and compile materials. We would also like to thank the students from around the country who submitted essays for this book. And for her unfailing support and patience, we thank Amy Feldman. We are also indebted to the reviewers who made suggestions for revisions during the many drafting stages:

G. Douglas Atkins, *University of Kansas*

Nancy Backes, *Cardinal Stritch University*

Monica Barron, *Truman State University*

Kelly Belanger, *University of Wyoming*

Nick Capo, *Pennsylvania State University*

Rebecca Faery, *Massachusetts Institute of Technology*

Ed Frankel, *University of California, Los Angeles*

Lynee Lewis Gaillet, *Georgia State University*

Douglas Hesse, *Illinois State University*

Joy Marsella, *University of Hawaii*

Amy Pawl, *Washington University*

John Ramage, *Arizona State University*

Leslie Ullman, *University of Texas at El Paso*

We would also like to thank the folks at Mayfield Publishing Company for their support, support that has continued after Mayfield became McGraw-Hill. At McGraw-Hill, we have enjoyed and appreciated the expert contributions of Lisa Moore, executive editor; Alexis Walker, sponsoring editor; David Patterson, marketing manager; Susan Trentacosti, project manager; Sharon Spurlock, designer; Lori Koetters, production supervisor; Brian Pecko, photo research manager; Cristin Yancey, art editor; and Todd Vaccaro, media producer. Finally, and with great affection, we wish to thank and acknowledge Renée Deljon (first our sponsoring and then our development editor) for her support, encouragement, and genius. She is, by far, the greatest (and coolest) editor in the textbook business.

S.I.D. Gainesville, Florida
A.S.B. Seattle, Washington

Contents

hat my dentist cried
t one day after finally
moving an unsuspected
urth nerve from one of
y molars comes to
ind each time I try to
derstand myself as a
riter. • Voice is modu-
ed almost entirely by
stance: how close are
u to this subject? And
is one? And this one?
d will this subject *let*
u come closer? • In
any ways writing is the
t of saying *I*, of impos-
g oneself upon other
ople, of saying *listen to*
, see it my way, change
ur mind. • When you
rite, you lay out a line
words. • It comes to
e, in a surge of revolu-
nary insight, that our
es—meaning whatever
is that continues to
ppen when the TV is
f and even when the
wer has failed—are
her and vastly more
rious than anything we
ll find in the flickering
lm of image and spec-
cle. • As more and
ore of my illusions
out myself continue to
l away—to name just a
v among them: that I
s a fine little athlete,
t a bad dancer, a pretty
ious lover, an elegant

INTRODUCTION
A Closer Look at
A Closer Look

This book is about writing. It is designed to give you the opportunity to examine other writers' essays and to consider the choices they made in writing them. Unlike other collections of readings that you may have used, this book not only focuses on what writers write about, but also on how they write about those subjects—the strategies writers use to communicate their subjects. By this, we mean that this book asks you to consider not just what subjects writers write about, but the historical and political contexts in which those subjects are addressed, the words through which writers address those subjects, the ways in which writers position themselves in their writing, the structure of their writing, the logic of their arguments, the audiences that might read these essays, and all of the other factors that shape why and how writers write about various subjects. In asking you to consider not only how to interpret the meanings of the essays gathered here but how these meanings have been produced, this book encourages you to begin seriously considering how you can produce meaning in your own writing. Throughout this text, we will ask you to pause and think about why the writers whose work is represented here have made the choices they have and how those choices affect their writing, and we will ask you to consider how similar choices affect your own writing, both academic and public.

The title of this book, *A Closer Look,* suggests a visual metaphor, one of looking at, examining, viewing. Throughout this book, we turn to this idea of viewing and ask you to take several glances and several in-depth looks at the kinds of choices writers make. This kind of close looking at writing is not unlike other kinds of inquiry you already know how to do. We come to know and act in the world through shared processes of inquiry, which involve the examination of what things and phenomena are, what they do, how they work, what they mean, and what effects they have. For instance, when you were a child and your parents showed you objects and told you what they were, they were teaching you how to make sense of them and how to use them. At school, teachers showed you ideas, facts, concepts, phenomena, and, along with others, you came to understand, question, and eventually apply them. The same holds true for writing. We can observe, speculate on, and examine the act of writing. We can discuss it with others. By doing so we learn what writing is and how to be effective writers. Then we put that knowledge to work, becoming more effective writers by producing writing. This book asks you to look closely at the writing of others, to discuss and consider that writing, so that you can consider the choices you make when you produce your own writing.

CONNECTING READING AND WRITING

Writing is about making choices. Among the various choices they have to make, writers frequently have to decide how to begin their texts; how to organize their ideas; what content to include, what to exclude, and how to order it; what sorts of examples to use and how to present them; how to structure different sentences; what tone to use; and which words to choose. Writers make decisions and these decisions have consequences. The more appropriate these decisions are, the more likely it is that readers will respond favorably to the writing—the more likely, that is, that they will be convinced by the writer's argument or that they will have the kind of reaction that the writer had intended or that they will perform the action the writer is requesting. In this book, we will help you learn how to make more effective choices as a writer by showing you how to look more closely at texts as a reader. The more critically you are able to read and recognize the decisions other writers make in their writing, the more likely you will be able to make effective decisions in your own writing.

The choices writers make when they write are called **rhetorical choices. Rhetoric,** as it was defined by the ancient Greek philosopher Aristotle, refers to the art of persuasion, to the way writers and speakers use language to get something done, whether it be to change someone's mind, to persuade someone to see your side of things, or to get someone to do something. Rhetoric, then, is the deliberate use of language to create some kind of effect. But since rhetoric is an art, as Aristotle was aware, there really isn't a precise formula that writers and speakers can use to help them communicate effectively in every situation and with every audience. Rather, rhetoric involves the art of making choices. It involves having to decide the best way to communicate in this given situation, on this given subject, and for this given audience. The decisions writers and speakers make when they are trying to accomplish something with language constitute their rhetorical choices.

Every time we communicate, we make rhetorical choices. We have to decide what tone to use in addressing our audience, what examples to use, what words to select, and so on. We do this all the time. Think, for example, about the rhetorical choices you make when you are talking to your best friend compared to the rhetorical choices you make when you are talking to your boss or even your parents. The choices you make and the way you act depend on the situation you are in and on the subject you are addressing. Certainly, you are likely to communicate and act differently at the gym from the way you communicate and act as a student in class, and how you communicate and act will depend on the subject you are addressing. Some subjects demand more serious treatment than others, while others require the use of specific words—what is referred to as *jargon*—as in academic and professional settings. The more appropriate your rhetorical choices are to your situation and subject, the more effective you will be in using language to communicate and accomplish what you want.

The same holds for writers. Writers make rhetorical choices and their choices shape the way their writing is read. But how do writers make these choices? How do they know which way to begin, how to organize their ideas, what examples and words to use? Although there is no exact formula you can use to answer these questions, there are strategies you can learn that will help you make your writing more appropriate and effective. If there is one thing we can say with certainty, it is that the choices writers make are not made randomly or arbitrarily. Effective writers, in other words, do not guess. Rather, they make calculated rhetorical decisions. Sometimes, of course, they make wrong decisions, even after multiple revisions; as a result, their writing does not succeed the way they had hoped. But more often than not, effective writers are making thoughtful decisions as they write and it is those decisions that ensure their writing will be successful.

UNDERSTANDING RHETORICAL CHOICES

So how do writers make effective rhetorical choices? They do so by looking closely at their **rhetorical situation.** Basically, the rhetorical situation is made up of a reader or readers, the writer's goal(s), and the context of writing. All three combine to form a situation that the writer must consider when he or she writes. For example, say you have been involved in a minor traffic accident and your car has sustained $500 worth of damage. And say you decide to write three letters regarding the accident, one to your insurance company, one to your parents back home, and one to your best friend away at school. In each case, you are writing in a different rhetorical situation: in a different context, with a different goal, and for a different audience. Even though you are addressing the same subject in all three letters, your goals for each letter will likely differ. So too will your style of addressing the reader, your tone, your choice of words, and even your organization. For example, you might begin the letter to the insurance company by writing: "At 4:30 P.M. on February 15th, I was involved in a minor automobile accident, for which I was not at fault." But in the letter to your parents, you might begin by assuring them that you are not hurt, perhaps beginning: "Before you get too upset, let me assure you that I am OK." The letter to your best friend, on the other hand, might be more cavalier, perhaps beginning: "Dude, you won't believe what happened last week. This horrible driver . . ." In each case, the rhetorical situation (the combination of your goals, audience, and context) shapes the rhetorical choices (the language use, structure, and content) you make as a writer, so looking closely at the situation is an important step in learning how to make your writing work effectively.

Each of the essays we have collected in this book is a result of choices made by its writer, and these choices are partly shaped by the demands of the writer's perception of his or her rhetorical situation. Our argument in this book is that you can learn something of importance about writing by looking closely at the choices other writers make. This is why we repeatedly ask you to locate and examine the writers' rhetorical choices. Before each essay, we provide a brief description of its rhetorical situation, including information about where and when the essay was published, and in some cases what the essay's writer was responding to, who its likely audience might have been, and what its writer's goal(s) might have been. We also direct your attention to certain rhetorical features of that essay. Following each essay, we encourage you to look back at the writer's rhetorical choices, asking you to examine and assess how these choices relate to the rhetorical situation. We do this throughout the book and from different angles, looking closely at each essay by itself, then at each writer's essays as a whole, and then at different essays by different writers. Our goal throughout the book is to heighten your awareness of *what* choices writers make and *why* and *how* they make them.

Such awareness will not only help you become a more critical reader, but it will also help you become a more reflective writer, one who is more likely to predict the effects of your own writing. Paying attention, for example, to how different writers rhetorically construct and communicate their writing goals in relation to their audience and context will help make you more aware of the range of rhetorical options available to you, options that you can use later in your own writing. In addition, looking closely at the choices writers make will enable you to assess the effects of these choices on their readers and in their contexts, effects that you can then use to your advantage when you write for your readers and in your contexts. Finally, learning how to locate and examine the rhetorical choices of other writers will allow you to locate and examine more closely your own rhetorical choices, to ask yourself the same critical questions we are encouraging you to ask of the essays and their writers in this collection. In this way, reading (looking closely not only for the meaning but at how writers make meaning) and writing (producing meaning) are most dramatically connected.

In our culture, a popular and romantic notion exists that writers write in isolation, but this is by and large a misconception. Most of the time writers write within rhetorical situations that affect and limit the decisions they can make. This should not be treated, however, as a denial of a writer's freedom. Think about how difficult (and perhaps even impossible) it would be to write if such limitations did not exist. How would writers make decisions if there were no factors on which to base them? Almost paradoxically, these very limitations produced by rhetorical situations prompt and enable writers to make creative writing choices. Looking closely at the rhetorical strategies other writers use to navigate various rhetorical situations and then practicing these strategies in your own writing will make you a more agile and astute writer, one who is better prepared to write effectively and creatively in a range of situations, in school and beyond.

A BRIEF HISTORY OF THE ESSAY

We have chosen the contemporary essay as our main genre in this book because of its rhetorical range. As we will discuss in more detail in the next few sections, the essay is difficult to define. It is many things to many people. While this flexibility at times frustrates attempts to categorize it, this very flexibility nonetheless makes the essay a useful genre for examining rhetorical choices and effects, as we are doing in this book. The essays collected here are written for a wide range of audiences, from readers of *Ms.* magazine to readers of *Golf* magazine, and on a range of subjects, from political exile to breast implants, from gardens to naps. They are written in various subgenres, from personal essays to academic essays to political essays. This range gives you a chance to examine and compare very different rhetorical strategies with very different rhetorical effects.

The word "essay" comes from the French word *essai,* which Michel de Montaigne first used in 1580 to describe his prose writing. *Essai* literally means an attempt, a testing out of something. The word itself is derived from the French verb *essayer,* which means "to try, taste, or test the fitness of a thing or idea" (Miller 1997, 44). To write an essay, as Montaigne suggested, is to work through something, with the resulting essay a product of that working through. It is not surprising that the essay as a genre manifests itself in various forms. After all, the very thing or idea that the essayist is working through will in part determine how he or she writes about it, and essayists as you will see write about many subjects. And then, of course, different writers have different ways of working through ideas and things. As a result, the essay is a dynamic genre, its resulting form depending on the particular contingencies of the writer's subject, ways of seeing, and rhetorical situation. Looking closely at the essays collected in this book will give you a chance to consider a wide variety of rhetorical strategies writers have used to address these contingencies.

Some scholars have traced the history of the essay before Montaigne, locating its origins in classical Greece and the works of Cicero and Seneca in Rome. Other scholars, including Shirley Brice Heath, have noted the relationship between the essay and the classical epistles or letters, while still others have traced a connection between essays and journals, diaries, and commonplace books (Heilker 1996, 15). By all accounts, however, Montaigne is acknowledged as the inventor of the essay. We must look to his ideas about the essay as well as the cultural conditions that helped him form these ideas in order to more fully understand the history of the essay.

As Paul Heilker has chronicled, the essay as a genre emerged alongside cultural phenomena taking place in the late 1500s and early 1600s, namely the Renaissance spirit of discovery, which perceived knowledge not as fixed and already ordered but in flux and requiring exploration; the rise of antischolasticism, which resisted the idea that the world could be neatly and precisely categorized into disciplines and specializations; and the rise of the baroque style, which rejected the symmetry, polish, and order of the classical "Ciceronian" style and became more irregular and spontaneous (Heilker 1996, 16–20). These cultural developments conspired to create the conditions that gave rise to the essay. Indeed, many of the essay conventions we use to this day—conventions first articulated and practiced by Montaigne—arose as a result of and in relation to these cultural developments. Heilker, for instance, made the following generalizations about essays, all of which can be attributed to the above phenomena: First, essays by their very nature are skeptical, questioning received truths in an increasingly uncertain universe. They are driven by a spirit of discovery, "an exploration of a world in flux that leaves old, inadequate orders behind in its quest for new ideas, new insights, and new visions of the truth" (p. 17). Second, essays do not present experience and ideas in discrete and separated units; rather, they bring "together contrasting and incongruous points of view in an attempt to more fully and deeply address whole problems of existence" (p. 19). Finally, essays rhetorically record the movement of the writer's mind in the process of working through ideas and things. Stylistically, then, essays follow the motion of the mind as it contemplates, digressing at times to make spontaneous connections and to trace consequences (p. 20–21).

Locating the origins of the essay in its historical context allows us to see that the essay emerged as a challenge to traditional ways of knowing and perceiving the world. After Montaigne, other writers took up this challenge. In England, Francis Bacon used *Essays* for the title of his collection of writings in 1597, thus helping establish the genre in English. Bacon's essayistic style differs from Montaigne's in being less self-expressive and conversational and more unadorned, but in both we notice the same meditative quality of the writer drawing on his experience in the process of making knowledge. Following Bacon, English essayists such as Richard Steele, Joseph

Addison, and Samuel Johnson in the 18th century; Charles Lamb, William Hazlitt, Leigh Hunt, Thomas De Quincey, and others in the 19th century; and G. K. Chesterton, A. C. Benson, and George Orwell in the early part of the 20th century all contributed to the complex evolution of the essay, an evolution that saw the emergence of humorous, personal, argumentative, informal, conversational, expository, and critical essays. You will notice even more variations of the essay in the more recently published essays collected in this book.

Today, the notion persists that essays represent *thinking* more than *thought*. As Montaigne described his experience of writing essays, "I cannot keep my subject still. It goes along befuddled and staggering, with a natural drunkenness. I take it in this condition, just as it is at the moment I give my attention to it. *I do not portray being: I portray passing*" (Montaigne 1957, 610). Although Montaigne's reference to drunkenness suggests that essays are somehow rambling or out of control, this is actually not the case. Montaigne's essays do have an order; they are driven by a certain logic and by certain rhetorical choices. Heilker calls this essayistic logic "chrono-logic," a logic that refers to "an arrangement based on the linearity of time" as well as the movement of thought on a subject associated through time (Heilker 1996, 23). It would be a mistake, then, to assume that essays have historically given writers unbridled freedom of expression. Writing about Montaigne, Heilker noted, "He must stay attentive to his subject and not lose it . . . continually offering the attentive reader some 'sufficient word' that allows her to see how his ideas follow one another" (p. 27). The contemporary essayist inherits the same burden. "In fact," Douglas Hesse reminded us, "one characteristic quality of the contemporary essay is the attempt to cast the widest net of associations possible, then struggle to bring the gathered ideas into some meaningful relation" (p. 36). As you look at this collection of essays, pay attention to how the writers gather their ideas into a meaningful relation, a relation that balances the writers' goals and the demands of their readers' expectations.

THE CONTEMPORARY ESSAY

The contemporary essay has become one of the most widely used genres for writers. Few magazines, newspapers, and journals are not filled with essays each month written by some of the most noted writers in the country and some of the most promising new writers. As Donald Hall, a well-known scholar of the essay, has written, "we live in the age of essay" (p. 1). This is perhaps because essays can be so many things and because writers can write in so many ways when they produce essays. As a result, defining the contemporary essay can be difficult. You may notice immediately in reading the selections that the essays cannot be identified by their length; some may be as short as a few paragraphs and others may take up many pages. You may be interested to note that in the book *Art and Answerability: Early Philosophical Essays* by M. M. Bakhtin, the table of contents lists the book as being comprised of three essays, yet the first one is only a page long, while the second is 230 pages long. Both are essays. Regardless of their length, all of the readings here are also essays since they share some of the essayistic qualities we described in the previous section. Yet in the 21st century those same qualities are being questioned, blurred, rewritten. Essays may be expository, they may be personal, they may be critical, they may be political. Essays may be intellectual, they may be scientific, they may be personal narrative.

In many ways, the essays in this book together offer a definition of what the contemporary essay can be. The writers represent the diverse and rich ways in which the essay can be and is written today; as such they contribute to an ongoing definition of the genre as some writers uphold while others stretch the boundaries of the essay. As you read these essays—all of them or only a handful—consider the ways in which they are all essayistic, especially the degree to which they share similar and different characteristics. Also, when those moments arise—as they often do in the essays gathered here—in which the writers address the essay as a subject, consider how writers think about essays. But primarily pay attention to the essays as processes, as parts of larger conversations—conversations grounded in historical and political contexts. And consider at all times the choices the writer makes to enter into that process of engagement. Then ask yourself how you can enter into that process and can produce essays as a way of thinking through things, presenting ideas, and answering questions.

THE STRUCTURE OF *A CLOSER LOOK*

A Closer Look is divided into 22 writer-chapters. Each chapter presents four essays from a single writer and an apparatus that will assist you in looking at the work of each writer. Each writer-chapter begins with an introduction to the life and writing of that writer. One of the things that makes the gathered works here so exciting is that all of the writers anthologized here are living, active writers who write about a range of subjects in a variety of genres and forums: novels, children's books, poetry, nonfiction books, magazines, essay collections, online articles, and so on, yet they all also write essays.* These introductions provide some information not only about the writers' lives, but about facets of their writing and some initial suggestions for things to look for in their essays.

Following the introduction, each writer-chapter contains four essays representing the body of work of the writer addressed in the chapter. Of the four essays, the first is always about writing; that is, the first essay provides an opportunity for you to see how each writer views writing and how that writer expresses those views through writing.

Prior to each of the four essays, "At First Glance" provides short suggestions for things to look for in the essay. When we see things for the first time, we often see details that we might overlook as we become more familiar with them. For instance, think about the first time you saw the room that you sleep in now. Think about seeing it before you added your furniture, your pictures and posters, the little details

---

*Unfortunately, Stephen Jay Gould died during the final production of this book, but he was an active writer until his death.

that make you comfortable in it. Chances are you noticed every run in the paint, each crack in the wall, every spot on the carpet. But chances are that as you became more familiar with that room, those details began to fade into the background and become a part of the way the room always looks. Often, too, when we first encounter something like a new room or a new piece of writing, it helps to have someone give us advice about what we should look for and pay attention to. The "At First Glance" sections before each essay do exactly that: They help to guide our eyes to pay attention to specific strategies that the author has used in the essay and suggest ways we might think about using those same strategies in our own writing.

After the first three essays in each writer-chapter, you will find a series of questions that ask you to do a "Double Take," to glance back at the essay you have just read and to consider some specifics about it. When we see something for the first time, we often do not get a full or accurate picture, and sometimes we do a quick double take to see if we really saw what our eyes indicated we saw. Think, for instance, how many times you have seen something while walking, driving, or riding your bike, and snapped your head around to get a quick second look. The "Double Take" sections of each writer-chapter function in much the same way, asking you to look back to consider the details of the piece you have just read. These questions address only the essay you have just read and the rhetorical strategies used in that essay.

The fourth essay is preceded by the same kinds of "At First Glance" information as the other essays in the writer-chapter; however, unlike the other essays in each writer-chapter, the fourth essay is not followed by a "Double Take" section. Often when we observe an object or a phenomenon, we may clutter our view of that object with too much apparatus. Hence, the fourth essay in each writer-chapter is a "Seeing for Yourself" section, not cluttered by any apparatus. The fourth essay in each writer-chapter should be carefully examined, discussed, and analyzed, but these discussions and examinations should be guided by what you see as important, by your growing rhetorical awareness and curiosity.

Since writers often make similar and different rhetorical choices throughout their body of work, it is also important to consider a writer's choices and strategies by examining a number of essays together rather than by looking only at individual essays. Following all of the essays in each writer-chapter, we ask you to take "A Closer Look" at the writer's works, to consider the patterns that emerge in her or his work, why each writer makes the rhetorical choices she or he does, how those choices affect his or her writing, and what we all, as writers, might learn from this writer's choices. "A Closer Look" also asks you to consider how you might make similar rhetorical choices in your writing.

After looking at each individual writer's body of work, we then encourage you to consider "Looking from Writer to Writer" to compare and contrast the strategies of different writers. Often we don't see the details of a thing, or the effectiveness or weakness of a strategy, until we see it in relation to another like thing. By "Looking from Writer to Writer," we can more readily enter into that process of essaying by examining essays in conjunction with, in contrast to, and in comparison with other essays.

Finally, because we do not want to limit our views of these writers to simply four essays each, we should consider "Looking Beyond" the essays gathered here to each writer's larger body of work. To help you find more works by each of these writers, we have included a list of some of their other works. We encourage you to read more by each writer and to examine his or her rhetorical strategies in a variety of writing scenarios.

The final writer-chapter includes essays by students from around the country writing essays about writing. With each essay, we include a "First Glance" of each of these student writers and some suggestions for reading their essays, with a particular focus on looking at the choices these writers make in their writing. We also include several questions that ask you to take "A Closer Look" at the writers' essays and to consider the rhetorical choices they make.

We would like to conclude where we began, by reminding you that this book is about writing, about the choices writers make when they write. We have organized this book and its apparatus to help you examine the essays closely: to look before each essay at the rhetorical situation the writer had to deal with and to look after each essay at the choices the writer has made in relation to that rhetorical situation. Our goal throughout the book is to encourage you to look before and after at rhetorical choices and their effects—both in the writing that you read and the writing that you produce.

FOR FURTHER READING

To learn more about the essay and to read more essays, you may want to read these books when you finish *A Closer Look.*

The Eloquent Essay, edited by John Loughery (2000)

The Essayist at Work, edited by Lee Gutkind (1998)

WORKS CITED

Hall, Donald. *The Contemporary Essay.* 3rd ed. Boston: Bedford Books, 1995.

Heilker, Paul. *The Essay: Theory and Pedagogy for an Active Form.* Urbana, IL: National Council of Teachers of English, 1996.

Hesse, Douglas. "Saving a Place for Essayistic Literacy." *Passions, Pedagogies, and 21st Century Technologies.* Gail E. Hawisher and Cynthia L. Selfe, eds. Logan: Utah State University Press, 1999, pp. 34–48.

Miller, Thomas. *The Formation of College English.* Pittsburgh, PA: University of Pittsburgh Press, 1997.

Montaigne, Michel de. *The Complete Works of Montaigne.* Donald M. Frame, trans. Stanford, CA: Stanford University Press, 1957.

la—the one that I can't
ake is that I am a fast
orker. • 'Race' as a
eaningful criterion
thin the biological sci-
ces has long been rec-
nized to be a fiction.
hen we speak of the
hite race' or the 'black
ce,' the Jewish race' or
'Aryan race,' we
ak in misnomers, bio-
ically, and in meta-
ors, more generally. •
course I yearn for
wers to all the puzzles,
at and small, that build
order (and wondrous
order) of nature 'out
re'—an order that our
ellectual ancestors
ld only read (under-
ndably) as proof of
d's existence and
evolent intent. •
ays, though sprinkled
h subordinated mem-
es, are written mostly
the present tense and
n't primarily narra-
s. • Even though
ting is a solitary act,
en I sit with words
t I trust will be read
someone, I know that
n never be truly
ne. There is always
eone who waits for
rds, eager to embrace
m and hold them
se. • I grew up in a

The WRITERS
and THEIR ESSAYS

André Aciman

Most introductions and headnotes to André Aciman's work mention early on that "he was born in Alexandria, Egypt." This is perhaps an important thing to mention in introductions and headnotes because Aciman's writing generally addresses his exile from Egypt. He was born, incidentally, in 1960. When Aciman was in high school, he and his family were forced to leave Egypt for the simple reason that they were Jewish. As Aciman writes, after Israel defeated the Arabs in 1948 and became allies with France and Great Britain during the Suez crisis in 1956, most French, British, and Jewish residents were forced out of Alexandria. As he explains about his family, "Some, like us, simply waited, the way Jews did elsewhere when it was already too late to hope for miracles." His exile, and subsequent return to Alexandria as a visitor, has been the subject of most of his work. In much of his work, he also addresses questions of what it means to be Jewish.

André Aciman holds a PhD in comparative literature from Harvard University. Aciman moved to New York in 1968, where he currently lives and teaches at Bard College. He has also lived in Italy and France. Issues of place are crucial to Aciman's writing. As he explains:

> I begin my inward journey by writing about place. Some do so by writing about love, war, suffering, cruelty, power, God or country. I write about place, or the memory of place. I write about a city called Alexandria, which I'm supposed to have loved, and about other cities that remind me of a vanished world to which I allegedly wish to return. I write about exile, remembrance and the passage of time. I write—so it would seem—to recapture, to preserve and return to the past, though I might just as easily be writing to forget and put that past behind me.

As you read Aciman's essays, think about how he accomplishes this in his writing, because it is at the core of his reason for writing.

Aciman's writing is also a quest for meaning, often meaning in his own life. At times his writing can be philosophic, and at times it can be playful, but at all times it is engaging. In a short essay called "The Folio Method,"★ Aciman considers meaningful moments in his life. He writes:

> Perhaps life is what happens not before, but after we miss the boat. What comes before is a shuffling of cards—learning to say yes instead of no, learning to ask when, in fact, it's hiding that comes naturally. No one's supposed to pick the right card the first time. Some miss more than one boat. Others miss a fleet. And some keep missing the point. Perhaps "learning to live" is not just learning to promise never to make the same mistake twice but learning to understand that the boats we missed are boats we never really wished.

As you read the essays gathered here, consider the ways in which Aciman makes use of personal experience to situate these kinds of larger philosophical positions.

Aciman's writing has earned him both a Whiting Writer's Award and a Guggenheim fellowship. His writing has appeared in the *New York Times,* the *New Yorker,* and the *New York Review of Books.* He has written two books, both of which consider his exile from Egypt: *Out of Egypt: A Memoir* and *False Papers.* He has also edited the collection *Letters of Transit: Reflections on Exile, Identity, Language, and Loss,* which includes essays by Aciman, Eva Hoffman, Bharati Mukherjee, Edward W. Said, and Charles Simic. He is currently writing a novel called *Over the Footbridge* which, he says, is about love.

★Posted at http://slate.msn.com/Diary/98-11-03/Diary.asp

Aciman on Writing

At First Glance

André Aciman's "A Literary Pilgrim Progresses to the Past" begins with a series of questions about writers in general. He then tries to tell us a bit about himself as a writer and, though he claims not to know how to categorize himself as a writer, he acknowledges that his writing is primarily couched in issues of place. In the same breath, Aciman also acknowledges that he writes "to recapture, to preserve, and return to the past," though he also says he may "just as easily be writing to forget the past and put that past behind me." As you read this essay, think not only about how memories and pasts affect Aciman's work, but how he chooses to represent those pasts and places. Is there a connection between his representations of pasts and places and how he claims writers choose to represent themselves?

A Literary Pilgrim Progresses to the Past

What my dentist cried out one day after finally removing an unsuspected fourth nerve from one of my molars comes to mind each time I try to understand myself as a writer. Do I, as a writer, have what he called a "hidden nerve"?

Don't all writers have a hidden nerve, call it a secret chamber, something irreducibly theirs, which stirs their prose and makes it tick and turn this way or that, and identifies them, like a signature, though it lurks far deeper than their style, or their voice or other telltale antics?

A hidden nerve is what every writer is ultimately about. It's what all writers wish to uncover when writing about themselves in this age of the personal memoir. And yet it's also the first thing every writer learns to sidestep, to disguise, as though this nerve were a deep and shameful secret that needs to be swathed in many sheaths. Some don't even know they've screened this nerve from their own gaze, let alone another's. Some crudely mistake confession for introspection. Others, more cunning perhaps, open tempting shortcuts and roundabout passageways, the better to mislead everyone. Some can't tell whether they're writing to strip or hide that secret nerve.

I have no idea to which category I belong.

As for a sheath, however, I'd spot mine in a second. It is place. I begin my inward journey by writing about place. Some do so by writing about love, war, suffering, cruelty, power, God or country. I write about place, or the memory of place. I write about a city called Alexandria, which I'm supposed to have loved, and about other cities that remind me of a vanished world to which I allegedly wish to return. I write

15

about exile, remembrance and the passage of time. I write—so it would seem—to recapture, to preserve and return to the past, though I might just as easily be writing to forget and put that past behind me.

And yet my hidden nerve lies quite elsewhere. To work my way closer to it, I'd have to write about loss and feeling unhinged in provisional places where everyone else seems to have a home and a place, and where everyone knows what he wants, who he is and who he's likely to become.

My Alexandrians, however, have an unsteady foothold wherever they stand; they shift time zones, life passions, loyalties and accents with the unwieldy sense that the real world swims before them, that they are strangers in it, that they're never quite entitled to it. Yet peel this second sheath, and you'll find another.

I may write about place and displacement, but what I'm really writing about is dispersion, evasion, ambivalence: not so much a subject as a move in everything I write. I may write about little parks in New York that remind me of Rome and about tiny squares in Paris that remind me of New York, and about so many spots in the world that will ultimately take me back to Alexandria. But this crisscrossed trajectory is simply my way of showing how scattered and divided I am about everything else in life.

I may never mention dispersion or evasion by name. But I write around them. I write away from them. I write from them, the way some people write around loneliness, guilt, shame, failure, disloyalty, the better to avoid staring at them.

Ambivalence and dispersion run so deep that I don't know whether I like the place I've chosen to call my home, any more than I know whether I like the writer or even the person I am when no one's looking. And yet the very act of writing has become my way of finding a space and of building a home for myself, my way of taking a shapeless, marshy world and firming it up with paper, the way the Venetians firm up eroded land by driving wooden piles into it.

I write to give my life a form, a narrative, a chronology; and, for good measure, I seal loose ends with cadenced prose and add glitter where I know things were quite lusterless. I write to reach out to the real world, though I know that I write to stay away from a world that is still too real and never as provisional or ambivalent as I'd like it to be. In the end it's no longer, and perhaps never was, the world that I like, but writing about it. I write to find out who I am; I write to give myself the slip. I write because I am always at one remove from the world but have grown to like saying so.

Thus I turn to Alexandria, the mythical home of paradox. But Alexandria is merely an alibi, a mold, a construct. Writing about Alexandria helps me give a geographical frame to a psychological mess. Alexandria is the nickname I give this mess. Ask me to be intimate, and I'll automatically start writing about Alexandria.

I'll write about diaspora and dispossession, but these big words hold my inner tale together, the way lies help keep the truth afloat. I use the word *exile,* not because I think it is the right term, but because it approximates something far more intimate, more painful, more awkward: exile from myself, in the sense that I could so easily have had another life, lived elsewhere, loved others, been someone else.

If I keep writing about places, it is because some of them are coded ways of writing about myself: like me, they are always somewhat dated, isolated, uncertain, thrust precariously in the middle of larger cities, places that have become not just stand-ins for Alexandria, but stand-ins for me. I walk past them and think of me.

Let me turn the clock back 30 years.

It is October 1968, and I've just arrived in New York City. Mornings are nippy. It's my second week here. I have found a job in the mailroom at Lincoln Center. During my rounds at 10:30 every morning the plaza is totally empty and its fountain silent. Here every day I am always reminded of my very early childhood, when my mother would take me for long walks along a quiet plantation road far beyond our home.

There is something serene and peaceful in this memory. I go out every morning knowing that as soon as I get a whiff of a nippy Manhattan breeze, I'll encounter the memory of those plantation mornings and the hand that held mine along these long walks.

Fast-forward more than two decades. It is 1992. On certain warm summer days at noon I go to pick up my mother on 60th Street, where she still works as an office clerk. We buy fruit and sandwiches on Broadway and walk awhile until we find a shady stone bench at Lincoln Center's Damrosch Park. At times I bring my two-year-old son, who'll scamper about, eating a spoonful, then run back to hide in between raised flowers beds.

Afterward he and I walk my mother back to her office; we say goodbye, then head toward Broadway to catch the bus across from a tiny park where Dante's statue stands. I tell him of Paolo and Francesca, and of cruel Gianciotto, and of Farinata the exile and Count Ugolino who starved with his children.

Dante's statue still reminds me of the tales I told my son then; it reminds me of this park and of other small parks I've since written about, and of how I felt guilty as a son, letting my mother hold so menial a job in her 70's, taking her out for a walk when it was clearly too warm for her, and how, to write a memoir about our life in Egypt, I had hired a full-time baby-sitter who was only too glad to have the time off whenever I'd take my son to lunches that I resented sometimes because they'd steal me from my desk. I think back to that summer and to my explosive snubs whenever my mother complained I'd arrived too late again.

One day, after losing my temper and making her cry at lunch, I went home and wrote about how she would sit in our balcony in Alexandria smoking a cigarette, and of how the wind had fanned her hair on the day she came to pick me up at school after someone had called home saying I had been suspended that day. Together we rode the tram downtown, naming the stations one by one.

Now, whenever I look back to those hot afternoons at Lincoln Center, I see two boys, me and my son, and I see my mother both as she was during those summer lunches in the early '90s and as I remembered her on our walks along the plantation road two and a half decades earlier. But the one mother most clearly limned on those stone benches at Damrosch Park is the one riding the tram with me: serene, ebullient, carefree, catching the light of the sun on her face as she recited the name of the stations to me.

I did not lie about the names of the tram stations, but I did make up the scene about her coming to school that day. It doesn't matter. For this scene's hidden nerve lay somewhere else: in my wanting to stay home and write, in not knowing which mother I was writing about, in wishing she could be young once more, or that I might be her young boy again, or that both of us might still be in Egypt, or that we should be grateful we weren't.

Perhaps it had something to do with my failure to rescue her from work that day, which I'd inverted into her rescuing me from school; or perhaps with my reluctance to believe that an entirely invented scene could have so cathartic an effect, and that lies do purge the mind of mnemonic dead weight.

I don't know. Perhaps writing opens up a parallel universe into which, one by one, we'll move all of our dearest memories and rearrange them as we please.

Perhaps this is why all memoirists lie. We alter the truth on paper so as to alter it in fact; we lie about our past and invent surrogate memories the better to make sense of our lives and live the life we know was truly ours. We write about our life, not to see it as it was, but to see it as we wish others might see it, so we may borrow their gaze and begin to see our life through their eyes, not ours.

Only then, perhaps, would we begin to understand our life story, or to tolerate it and ultimately, perhaps, to find it beautiful; not that any life is ever beautiful, but the measure of a beautiful life is perhaps one that sees its blemishes, knows they can't be forgiven and, for all that, learns each day to look the other way.

Double Take

1. Twice in this essay, Aciman uses short, one-sentence paragraphs. What are the effects of these two paragraphs? Are they really paragraphs? That is, can a single sentence of eight or nine words make up an entire paragraph?
2. We know that place and time are important to Aciman. In this essay he addresses several places at various times. How does he manage to keep us located in those times and places? In other words, what choices does he make to move us as readers from one place and time to another?
3. The final four paragraphs of this essay are dominated by the word "perhaps." What effect does Aciman gain by couching these final four paragraphs in a term as indefinite as "perhaps"?
4. What might Aciman mean when he says, "Writing about Alexandria helps give me a geographical frame to a psychological mess"?
5. Aciman's title makes allusion to a well-known piece of literature. Do you know what that piece of literature is? What might Aciman be suggesting by making such an allusion? What effect does the allusion have on your reading of the title?

At First Glance

Like "A Literary Pilgrim Progresses to the Past," André Aciman writes about Alexandria in his essay "The Capital of Memory." In this essay, however, Aciman takes us through Alexandria in a tour of the city. He writes of two Alexandrias, the one of his memory and the one he visits. He describes the first of these—the Alexandria of memory—in the past tense, something gone. But he takes us to see the contemporary Alexandria in the present tense. As you read, consider how Aciman describes Alexandria and what he sees in the present tense. Consider also that Aciman wrote this piece in 1996. What does he accomplish by having us read the piece many years after he wrote it in the present tense, as if the events were unfolding before us rather than as a story of the past? What might his title suggest if anything about the choice of writing in the present tense?

The Capital of Memory

Alexandria, 1996.

To those who asked, I said I went back to touch and breathe again the past, to walk in shoes I hadn't worn in years. This, after all, was what everyone said when they returned from Alexandria—the walk down Memory Lane, the visit to the old house, the knocking at doors history had sealed off but might pry open again. The visit to the old temple, the visit to Uncle So-and-so's house, the old school, the old haunts, the smell of the dirty wooden banister on days you almost glided downstairs on your way to a movie. And then, of course, the tears, the final reckoning, the big themes: the return of the native, the romance of the past, the redemption of time. All of it followed by predictable letdowns: the streets always much narrower than before, buildings grown smaller with time, everything in tatters, the city dirty, in ruins. There are no Europeans left, and the Jews are all gone. Alexandria is Egyptian now.

As I step onto the narrow balcony of my room at the Hotel Cecil and try to take in the endless string of evening lights speckling the eastern bay, I am thinking of Lawrence Durrell and of what he might have felt standing in this very same hotel more than fifty years ago, surveying a magical, beguiling city—the "capital of memory," as he called it, with its "five races, five languages. . . . and more than five sexes."

That city no longer exists; perhaps it never did. Nor does the Alexandria I knew: the mock-reliquary of bygone splendor and colonial opulence where my grandmother could still walk with an umbrella on sunny days and not realize she looked quite ridiculous, the way everyone in my family must have looked quite ridiculous, being the last European Jews in a city where anti-Western nationalism and anti-Semitism had managed to reduce the Jewish population from at least fifty thousand to twenty-five hundred by 1960 and put us at the very tail end of those whom history shrugs aside when it changes its mind.

The Alexandria I knew, that part-Victorian, half-decayed, vestigial nerve center of the British Empire, exists in memory alone, the way Carthage and Rome and Constantinople exist as vanished cities only—a city where the dominant languages were English and French though everyone spoke in a medley of many more, because the principal languages were really Greek and Italian, and in my immediate world Ladino (the Spanish of the Jews who fled the Inquisition in the sixteenth century), with broken Arabic holding everything more or less together. The arrogance of the retired banker, the crafty know-it-all airs of the small shopkeeper, the ways of Greeks and of Jews, all of these were not necessarily compatible, but everyone knew who everyone else was, and on Sundays—at the theater, in restaurants, at the beach, or in clubs—chances were you sat next to each other and had a good chat. My grandmother knew Greek well enough to correct native Greeks, she knew every prayer in Latin, and her written French, when she was vexed, would have made the Duc de Saint-Simon quite nervous.

This is the Alexandria I live with every day, the one I've taken with me, written about, and ultimately superimposed on other cities, the way other cities were originally sketched over the Alexandrian landscape when European builders came, in the middle of the nineteenth century, and fashioned a new city modeled after those they already loved. It was this Alexandria I came looking for—knowing I'd never find it. That did not bother me. For I had come not to recover memories, nor even to recognize those I'd disfigured, nor to toy with the thought that I'd ever live here again; I had come to bury the whole thing, to get it out of my system, to forget, to hate even, the way we learn to hate those who wouldn't have us.

I am, it finally occurs to me, doing the most typical thing a Jew could do. I've come back to Egypt the way only Jews yearn to go back to places they couldn't wait to flee. The Jewish rite of passage, as Passover never tells us, is also the passage back to Egypt, not just away from it.

Until the mid-1950s, Jews had done extremely well in Egypt. They had risen to prominence and dominated almost every profession, and they were among the major financiers who brokered Egypt's passage from a European to a national economy, serving as important conduits for foreign investors. Jews managed a significant share of Egypt's stock exchange and owned some of the biggest banks and almost all of the department stores; the country boasted the greatest number of Jewish multimillionaires in the Middle East. Jews, though very few in number, held seats in the Egyptian parliament.

These were, for the most part, observant Jews, but in a cosmopolitan city like Alexandria, where overzealous piety was derided and where friendship was almost never based on creed, many of these Jews were quite relaxed when it came to religion, particularly since most of them, educated in Catholic schools, tended to know more about the religions of others than about their own. Seders, I remember, were rushed affairs; no one wanted to inflict Passover on Christians who happened to be visiting and had been induced to stay for dinner.

Following the Israelis' 1948 defeat of the Arabs, anti-Semitism rose sharply in Egypt, and there were some deadly incidents in the wake of the war. Matters became worse after 1956, when Israel joined forces with France and England in a tripartite attack on Egypt after Nasser nationalized the Suez Canal. British and French residents of Alexandria were summarily expelled from Egypt, as were many Jews; everyone had assets, businesses, and properties seized by the state. Aunts and uncles, friends, grandparents, some of whom hadn't been expelled, read the writing on the wall and left within a few years of the 1956 war, abandoning everything they owned. Most settled in Europe, others in America.

Some, like us, simply waited, the way Jews did elsewhere when it was already too late to hope for miracles. We saw the city change and each year watched European shop names come down and be replaced by Egyptian ones, and heard of streets being renamed, until—as is the case now—I didn't know a single one.

The only street whose name hasn't changed is the waterfront road known as the Corniche, al-Corniche, a thick bottleneck mass of tottering loud vehicles emitting overpowering gas fumes.

I try to rest both arms on the balustrade outside my hotel room, as I'd envisioned doing on receiving the glossy brochure with the Cecil's picture. But the small, Moorish/Venetian-style balcony is entirely taken over by a giant compressor unit; it's impossible to maneuver around it. Bird droppings litter the floor.

Two men are speaking in Arabic downstairs. One is telling the other about his very bad foot and his pain at night. The other says it might go away. They don't know how surreal ordinary mundane talk can seem to someone who's been away for thirty years.

On the main square facing the hotel stands the ungainly statue of the Egyptian patriot Sa'ad Zaghlul, one leg forward in the manner of ancient Egyptian statues, except that this one wears a fez. I used to pass by here every morning on my way to school by bus.

Beyond Sa'ad Zaghlul is a villa housing the Italian consulate, and farther yet is the city's main tramway station and to its right the Cinema Strand, all unchanged, though worn by age. To my right is Délices, one of the city's best pastry shops. It hasn't moved either. Nothing, I think, is unfamiliar enough. I haven't forgotten enough.

Across the bay sits the fortress of Kait Bey, its ill-lit, brooding halo guarding the Eastern Harbor. The fortress is said to occupy the site of the ancient Pharos lighthouse, one of the Seven Wonders of the Ancient World. Some say that the fort was built with stones taken from the old lighthouse itself. A French archaeological company has been commissioned to dig here. The area is cordoned off and considered top secret.

Not far from the dig lies the Western Harbor, which the ancients used to call the Harbor of Safe Return, Portus Eunostos, from the Ancient Greek *eu,* meaning good, safe, and *nostos,* meaning return. Nostalgia is the ache to return, to come home; *nostophobia,* the fear of returning; *nostomania,* the obsession with going back; *nostography,* writing about return.

So this is Alexandria, I think, before shutting the window, feeling very much like Freud when, in his early forties, he had finally achieved his lifelong dream of visiting Athens and, standing on the Acropolis, felt strangely disappointed, calling his numbness derealization.

I look at my watch. It is one in the afternoon New York time. I pick up the telephone to call America. After a short wait, I hear my father's voice. In the background, I make out a chorus of children, mine probably—or is it the clamor of a school recess down his block?

"How is it?" he asks. I describe the view from my window.

"Yes, but how is it?" he presses. What he means is: Has it changed and am I moved? I can't find the right words.

"It's still the same," I reply. "It's Egypt," I finally say, all else failing.

Each year the city sees many ex-Alexandrians return and wander along its streets. Like revenants and time travelers, some come back from the future, from decades and continents away, A.D. people barging in on B.C. affairs, true anachronoids drifting about the city with no real purpose but to savor a past that, even before arriving, they know they'll neither recapture nor put behind them, but whose spell continues to lure them on these errands in time. The Portuguese have a word: *retornados,* descendants of Portuguese settlers who return to their homeland in Europe centuries after colonizing Africa—except that they are African-born Europeans who return to Africa as tourists, not knowing why they come, or why they need to come again, or why this city that feels like home and which they can almost touch at every bend of the street can be as foreign as those places they've never seen before but studied in travel books.

The first thing I want to do tonight is roam the streets by myself. The downtown shops are still open, and people are literally spilling out into the streets, an endless procession of cars going up the rue Missallah (Obelisk), renamed Rue Saffeyah Zaghlul after the patriot's wife. The same stores stand in exactly the same spots, the same pharmacies, bookstores, restaurants; and everywhere the unbroken chain of shoe stores and third-tier haberdasheries with wares dangling over the sidewalks, and always that muted spill of lights which reminds me of Cavafy's nights and Baudelaire's Paris. I manage to recognize the Gothic-Venetian window sashes of an old restaurant. When I walk into Flückiger's, the pastry shop, and tell the cashier that I am just looking around, she smiles and says, as she must have done to hundreds like me, *"Ah, vous êtes de nos temps,"* as if time could ever belong to anyone. Do I want to buy cakes? I shake my head. "They're still the same. We're still Flückiger," she adds. I nod. One would have thought that I shopped there every day and had stopped now on my way from work, only to change my mind at the last minute. The idea of eating cake to summon my past seems too uncanny and ridiculous. I smile to myself and walk out through the beaded curtain. It hasn't changed either. Nor have the buildings. They are far more beautiful than I remember, the architecture a mix of turn-of-the-century French and floral Italian. But they are also grimier, some of them so run-down it's impossible to tell how long they've got. It's no different with cars here. Many are rickety thirty-plus patched-up jobs, part rust, part tin, part foil; soldered and painted over with the sort of Egyptian ingenuity that knows how to preserve the old and squeeze residual life out of objects which should have perished long ago but whose replacement will neither come from abroad nor be manufactured locally. These are not really cars but, rather, elaborate collages of prostheses.

I turn right and walk into a murky street that used to be called Rue Fuad. Next to the Amir Cinema looms a strange, large structure I have never seen before. It is the newly dug-up Roman amphitheater I've been reading about. I ignore it completely and turn left, where I spot Durrell's pastry shop, and walk down a narrow street, where I find the Cinema Royale and, right across from it, the old Mohammed Ali known as the Sayyed Darwish Theater, the pride of Alexandria's theater elite.

And then it hits me. The Mohammed Ali is my last stop tonight; I now have nowhere else to turn but the Hotel Cecil. To my complete amazement, I have revisited most of my haunts in Alexandria in the space of about eight minutes!

Once on the crowded streets again, I walk the way I have come, along the edge of the sidewalk, my eyes avoiding everyone else's, my gait hurried and determined, everything about me trying to discourage contact with a city that is, after all, the only one I think I love. Like characters in Homer, I want to be wrapped in a cloud and remain invisible, not realizing that, like all revenants, I am perhaps a ghost, a specter already.

The next morning, I head out on another exploratory walk. But in fifteen minutes I have already reached Chatby, the very place I was meaning to see last. This is where most of the cemeteries are located. Perhaps I should pay a visit to my grandfather's tomb now.

I try to find the Jewish cemetery, but I am unable to. Instead, I head in a different direction and decide to visit my great-grandmother's house. As soon as I near her neighborhood, I find myself almost thrust into the old marketplace. It, too, hasn't changed since my childhood. The pushcarts and open shops are still in place, as is the unforgettable stench of fish and meat, and always the screaming and the masses of people thronging between stacks of food and crates of live chickens.

I could go upstairs, I think, once I reach the building on rue Thèbes, but people are watching me fiddle with my camera, and someone actually pops his head out of the window and stares. I decide to leave. Then, having walked to the next block, I change my mind and come back again, trying to let the building come into view gradually, so as to hold that magical moment when remembrance becomes recovery. I am resolved not to be intimidated this time and make my way straight to the main doorway.

A woman appears with a child in her arms; she is the caretaker's wife: the caretaker died a few years ago; she is the caretaker now. A man also shows up. He lives on the street floor, he says in English, and has lived there since the early fifties. I tell him I, too, lived here once, at number 15. He thinks for a moment, then says he doesn't remember who lives there now. I tell the caretaker that I want to knock at apartment 15. She smiles and looks at me with suspicion. She is thinking. "Sit Vivi," she says. Mme. Vivi. I am almost on the verge of shaking. Vivi was my great-aunt. "They left," she says. Of course they left, I want to shout, we all left thirty years ago! "May I knock at the door?" I ask. "You may," she replies, with the same smile, "but no one is there." When will they be back? She looks at me with a blank stare. No one has occupied the apartment since.

I know that if I push the matter and tip her well, I might persuade her to show me the apartment. But the thought of a dark apartment where no one's been for three decades frightens me. Who knows what I'd find creeping about the floor, or crawling on the walls. It's all well and good for a German to go digging for the ghost of Troy or sifting through Helen's jewels. But no Trojan ever went back to Troy.

When I point to the elevator and ask her whether *it* still works, she laughs. *It* had died long ago. And she adds, with inimitable Egyptian humor, "*Allah yerhamu.*" May God have mercy on its soul.

I step into the main courtyard and look up at our old service entrance: I can almost hear our cook screaming at the maid, my mother screaming at the cook, and our poor maid's heartrending yelp each time the tumor on her liver pressed against her spine. I am trying to decide whether I should insist and ask to be taken upstairs, or perhaps she could show me another apartment in the same line. I see a cat playing in the foyer; next to it is a dead mouse. The caretaker does not notice it. Even the man from the first floor doesn't seem to notice, doesn't care.

I know I'll regret not insisting, and also that this is typical of my perfunctory, weak-willed attempts at adventure. But I am tired of these ruins, and the smell of the old wood panels in the foyer is overpowering. Besides, this is how I always travel: not so as to experience anything at the time of my tour, but to plot the itinerary of a possible return trip. This, it occurs to me, is also how I live.

Outside, I spot an old woman with a shopping basket; she looks European. I ask her whether she speaks French. She says she does. She is Greek. I am almost ready to tell her about my entire life, everything about my grandparents, my mother, our apartment that has never been lived in since the day we left so many years ago, and all these ruins scattered everywhere, but I break in midsentence, hail a cab, and ask to be taken to the museum—by way of the Corniche, because I want to see the water.

The Corniche always breaks the spell of monotonous city life, the first and last thing one remembers here. It is what I think of whenever I sight a beckoning patch of blue at the end of a cross street elsewhere in the world. The sky is clear and the sea is stunning, and my cabdriver, who speaks English, tells me how much he loves the city.

The Graeco-Roman Museum was where I would come to be alone on Sunday mornings in 1965, my last year in Alexandria.

I pay the fee and, as usual, rush through the corridors and the quiet garden, where a group of Hungarian tourists are eating potato chips. The Tanagra statuettes, the busts of Jupiter and of Alexander, the reclining statue of a dying Cleopatra, all these I pass in haste. There is only one thing I want to see, a Fayoum portrait of a mummified Christian. I linger in the old, musty room. The painting is exquisite indeed, more so than I remember. But I am astonished that this bearded man looks so young. There was a time when he was older than I. Now I could almost be his father. Otherwise, nothing has changed: I'm standing here, and he's lying there, and it's all as if nothing has happened between one Sunday and the next.

I want to buy his picture in the museum shop. There are no postcards of Fayoum portraits. I want to buy E. M. Forster's guide to the city, but they haven't had it in a long time. I ask whether they have any of the Durrell books. They haven't carried those in a long time either. There is, in fact, really very little to buy. And very little else to see. I have seen everything I wanted to see in Alexandria. I could easily leave now.

An entire childhood revisited in a flash. I am a terrible nostographer. Instead of experiencing returns, I rush through them like a tourist on a one-day bus tour. Tomorrow I must try to find the cemetery again.

Outside the museum, I am reminded of my grammar school nearby. I remember coming here in high school hoping to pay a quick visit to my old school and getting lost instead. I know I've strayed into the once-affluent Greek neighborhood. But I also know that I'm lost exactly where I lost my way thirty years earlier. The thought amuses me. I used to come here for private English lessons twice a week. I remembered the teacher, and her sumptuous home, and the luxurious china in which I, at the age of seven, would have to drink tea. I remember a poem by Wordsworth, the dim-lit living room with many flowers and perfumes, and my father coming to pick me up after tutorial, discussing books with her. I would sit and listen, and watch them talk, as other guests kept arriving.

I thought I recognized her building and decided, why not, Mademoiselle Nader might still be there. I look at the names on the mailboxes, but there is no Nader. I see the name *Monsieur et Madame E. Nahas* and assume they are Syrian-Lebanese. Perhaps they might tell me where she lives. As I am ascending the stairs, I happen upon a name on a brass plate; it's the name of a very old school friend. I ring his bell. The Filipino maid speaks good English; I explain I used to know her employer. He is in Europe, she replies. She shows me into a living room streaming in daylight. I sit on the sofa and scribble a note for him, leaning over to the tea table. Then I hand it to her and ask whether she knows of a certain Mademoiselle Nader. Never heard of her. I say goodbye and continue climbing the stairs until I've reached the Nahas residence. They're not home either, and their maid has never heard of the Naders. A delivery boy, who happens to be coming up the stairs, seems to remember something and asks me to knock at another apartment. An old woman, speaking impeccable French, says that of course she remembers Marcelle Nader, whom she calls Lola. Lola died two years ago, totally alone, impoverished, and broken-spirited. Her family had lost everything during the mass nationalizations of 1961. She and her sister would rent out rooms in their large home, but even then, that hardly constituted an income. When her sister left for Switzerland, Lola was forced to give private lessons to businessmen who, it seems, had other things in mind but who settled for English the more she aged. In the end, she sold her apartment to, of all people, my old school friend downstairs. I hadn't recognized the apartment at all. Perhaps it was on the same sofa and at the same tea table that I'd learned English.

Turb'al yahud, Alexandria's Jewish cemetery, is located at the opposite end of the Armenian cemetery and lies only a few steps away from the Greek Orthodox. Farther down the quiet, dusty, tree-lined road is the Catholic cemetery. Magdi, a native Alexandrian who is employed by the American school I attended as a child, swears that Turb'al Yahud must be somewhere close by but can't remember where. "I come here only once a year for my mother," he explains, pointing to the Coptic cemetery not far along the same road.

Magdi double-parks and says he will ask directions from the warden of the Armenian cemetery. We have been driving around for more than two hours in search of my parents' old summer beachside home, but here, too, without luck. Either it's been razed or lies buried in a chaos of concrete highrises and avenues built on what used to be vast stretches of desert sand. Soon Magdi comes out looking perplexed. There are, as it turns out, not one but two Jewish cemeteries in the area.

"Which one has a gate on the left?" I say, remembering my very early childhood visits to my grandfather's grave four decades ago. "That's the problem," says Magdi, drawing on his cigarette. "Both have gates to the right."

I am dismayed. I can situate the grave only in relation to the left gate. We decide to try the nearest cemetery.

Magdi starts the car, waits awhile, then immediately speeds ahead, leaving a cloud of dust behind us. In a matter of minutes, we have parked on a sidewalk and ambled up to a metal gate that looks locked. Magdi does not knock; he pounds. I hear a bark, and after a series of squeaks, a man in his early fifties appears at the door. I try to explain in broken Arabic the reason for my visit, but Magdi interrupts and takes over, saying I have come to see my grandfather's grave. The warden is at a loss. Do I know where the grave is, he asks? I say no. Do I know the name then?

I say a name, but it means nothing to him. I try to explain about the gate to the left, but my words are getting all jumbled together. All I seem to remember is a pebbled alleyway that started at the left gate and crossed the breadth of the cemetery.

The warden has a three-year-old son wearing a very faded red sweatshirt bearing the initials CCCP—not unusual in a place where ancient relics come in handy. Their dog, fleeced from the neck down, has a large bleeding ulcer on his back.

"Oh, *that* gate," the warden responds when I point to another, much smaller gate at the opposite end of the cemetery. "It's locked, it's never been used." Indeed, the gate at the end of the alleyway looks welded in place. I am almost too nervous to hope. But I pick my way to the end of the path and, having reached the area near the left gate, climb over a wild bush whose dried leaves stick to my trousers, turning with a sense of certainty that I am trying to distrust, fearing the worst.

"Is this it?" asks Magdi.

I am reluctant to answer, still doubting that this could be the spot, or this the marble slab, which feels as warm and smooth to the touch as I knew it would each time I rehearsed this moment over the years. Even the name looks dubious.

"Yes," I say, point to the letters, which I realize Magdi can't read.

The warden knows I am pleased. His son trails behind him. A fly is crawling around his nose. Both of them, as well as the warden's wife, are barefoot. Bedouin style.

I take out my camera. Everyone is staring at me, including the warden's ten-year-old daughter, who has come to see for herself. It turns out that no Jew ever visits here. "No one?" I ask. "*Walla wahid,*" answers the daughter emphatically. Not one.

There are, it occurs to me, far more dead Jews in this city than there will ever again be living ones. This reminds me of what I saw in a box at the main temple earlier this morning: more skullcaps than Jews to wear them in all of Egypt.

The warden asks whether I would like to wash the tombstone. I know Magdi has to go back to work; he is a bus driver and school ends soon. I shake my head.

"Why?" asks the warden. "*Lazem.*" You must.

I have lived my entire life outside rituals. Now I am being asked to observe one that seems so overplayed and so foreign to me that I almost want to laugh, especially since I feel I'm about to perform it for them, not for me. Even Magdi sides with the warden. "*Lazem,*" he echoes.

I am thinking of another ritual, dating back to those days when my father and I would come on quiet early-morning visits to the cemetery. It was a simple ritual. We would stand before my grandfather's grave and talk; then my father would say he wished to be alone awhile and, when he was finished, hoist me up and help me kiss the marble. One day, without reason, I refused to kiss the stone. He didn't insist, but I knew he was hurt.

I pay the warden's family no heed and continue to take pictures, not because I really want to, but because in looking through the viewfinder and pretending to take forever to focus, I can forget the commotion around me, stand still, stop time, stare into the distance, and think of my childhood, and of being here, and of my grandfather, whom I hardly knew and scarcely remember and seldom think of.

I am almost on the point of forgetting those present when the warden appears, lugging a huge tin drum filled with water. He hoists it on a shoulder and then splashes the dried slab, flooding the whole area, wetting my clothes, Magdi's, and the little boy's feet, allowing the stone to glisten for the first time in who knows how many decades. With eager palms, we all go about the motions of wiping the slab clean. I like the ritual. Magdi helps out silently, but I want it to be my job. I don't want it to end. I am even pleased that my clothes are wet and dirty.

I still can't believe I was able to find my grandfather's grave so quickly. Memories are supposed to distort, to lie. I am at once comforted and bewildered.

In the distance I can hear the tireless drone of Alexandria's traffic, and farther off the loud clank of metal wheels along the tramway lines—not obtrusive sounds, for they emphasize the silence more—and I am reminded of how far Grandfather is from all this: from all these engines; from the twentieth century; from history; from exile, exodus, and now return; from the nights we spent huddled together in the living room, knowing the end had come; from our years in cities he had never visited, let alone thought some of us might one day call home. Time for him had stopped in the early fifties on this dry, quiet, secluded patch of dust that could turn into desert in no time.

I look around and recognize famous Jewish names on tombstones and mausoleums. They, too, like my grandfather, were lucky not to have seen the end. But they also paid a price: No one ever comes here. The opulent mausoleums, built in Victorian rococo, were meant to house unborn generations that have since grown up elsewhere and don't know the first thing about Egypt.

"Are you happy now?" I want to ask my grandfather, rubbing the stone some more, remembering a tradition practiced among Muslims of tapping one's finger ever so gently on a tombstone to tell the dead that their loved ones are present, that they miss them and think of them. I want to speak to him, to say something, if only in a whisper. But I am too embarrassed. Perhaps this is why people say prayers instead. But I don't know any prayers. All I know is that I cannot take him with me—but I don't want to leave him here. What is he doing here anyway? In a hundred years, no one will even know my grandfather had lived or died, here or elsewhere. It's the difference between death and extinction.

I pretend to want to take another picture and ask Magdi, the warden, and his family to pose in front of one of the palm trees, hoping they will stay there after the picture and leave me alone awhile. I can feel my throat tighten, and I want to hide the tears welling up inside me, and I am, once again, glad to cover my eyes with the viewfinder. The warden's daughter comes closer. She wants a picture by herself. I smile and say something about her pretty eyes. I give her father a good tip.

Everyone thinks it's been a good visit. Perhaps all cemetery visits are.

On my last evening in Alexandria, I and a group of young teachers from the American school have gathered at a pizzeria to celebrate someone's birthday. We've parked on a narrow alleyway, halfway on the sidewalk, exactly where my father would park his car. Everyone at the party orders pizza, salad, and beer. It occurs to me that we might easily be in Cambridge or New Haven.

By eleven the party breaks up. Before getting into the car, we take a stroll toward the Church of St. Saba. The streets are very dark, and after spending time in the American bar, I am suddenly confronted with the uncanny thought that we are, after all, very much in Egypt still. Maybe it's the alcohol, but I don't know whether I'm back in Egypt or have never left, or whether this is all a very cruel prank and we're simply stranded in some old neighborhood in lower Manhattan. This, I realize, is what happens when one finally comes home: one hardly notices, and it doesn't feel odd at all.

Later that night, as I'm looking out from my balcony, I think of the young man from Fayoum, and of the young man of fourteen I used to be back then, and of myself now, and of the person I might have been had I stayed here thirty years ago. I think of the strange life I'd have led, of the wife I would have, and of my other children. Where would I be living? I suppose in my great-grandmother's apartment—it would have fallen to me. And I think of this imaginary self who never strayed or did the things I probably regret having done but would have done anyway and don't wish to disown: a self who never left Egypt or ever lost ground and who, on nights such as these, still dreams of the world abroad and of faraway America, the way I, over the years, have longed for life right here whenever I find I don't fit anywhere else.

I wonder if this other self would understand about him and me, and being here and now and on the other bank as well—the other life, the one that we never live and conjure up when the one we have is perhaps not the one we want.

This, at least, has never changed, I think, my mind drifting to my father years ago, when we would stop the car and walk along the Corniche at night, thinking of the worst that surely lay ahead, each trying to give up this city and the life that came with it in the way he knew how. This is what I was doing now as well, thinking of the years ahead when I would look back to this very evening and remember how, standing on the cluttered balcony at the Cecil, I had hoped finally to let go of this city, knowing all the while that the longing would start again soon enough, that one never washes anything away, and that this marooned and spectral city, which is no longer home for me and which Durrell once called "a shabby little seaport built upon a sand reef," would eventually find newer, ever more beguiling ways to remind me that here is where my mind always turns, that here, to quote this century's most famous Alexandrian poet, Constantine Cavafy, I'll always end up, even if I never come back:

> For you won't find a new country,
> won't find a new shore,
> the city will always pursue you,
> and no ship will ever take you away from yourself.

And then I remembered. With all the tension in the cemetery that afternoon, I had forgotten to ask Magdi to show me Cavafy's home. Worse yet, I had forgotten to kiss my grandfather's grave. Maybe next time.

Double Take

1. Following the title, "The Capital of Memory," André Aciman includes a byline that reads "Alexandria, 1996"). Why has the author chosen to identify the date and place in this fashion, even when he immediately tells us where he is in the essay?
2. At several points in this essay, Aciman provides historical background, both about Alexandria and about the exodus of the Jews from the city. What purpose do these histories have in the larger goal of his essay? That is, how do these histories tie into Aciman's present tense description of Alexandria?
3. In the final sentence of this essay, Aciman writes, "Maybe next time," and suggests to us that he may return again to Alexandria. Besides this obvious sort of return that he alludes to, what else might Aciman be suggesting in this final sentence?

At First Glance

André Aciman's essay, "A Late Lunch" is about Aciman meeting his father for lunch. One of the striking things about this essay is the way that Aciman has fashioned his sentences. Notice, for instance, that the subjects of almost all of the sentences in this essay are either "I" (referring to Aciman) or "he" (referring to Aciman's father). Rarely do we see a sentence with any other subject. Think about what this consistency in the use of the two subjects does for the essay. Consider what such a choice emphasizes and also de-emphasizes. Also, think about how the repetition of these two subjects affects the sound, the tone of this essay.

A Late Lunch

My father comes fifteen minutes early. I arrive forty minutes late. He says he doesn't mind waiting. He always has something to read. I can see him sitting quietly behind the large window inside the Museum of Modern Art's lobby, seemingly unaware of the crowd of tourists milling around the gift shop and the information desk. I rush out of the taxicab with my five-year-old son, Alex. It's raining. I'll blame the rain, I think.

We're barely in time for a late lunch. We wait in line at the cafeteria and decide to share the same tray. My father likes the chili here; I order some, too; Alex doesn't know what he wants, so we pick up a fruit platter and a handful of bread sticks. We argue over who is to pay. My father relents and offers to find a table while I wait in the cashier's line. He reminds me not to forget his coffee. I nod and watch his small figure dart into the dining hall. He stops, scans the crowd once more, then scurries toward an empty table by the window at the far corner and proceeds to lay our raincoats down on the chairs.

He is pleased with himself. Our corner overlooks the gleaming wet patio, which on rainy days always reminds me of Alexandria. The storm patters on the large glass pane. It feels snug inside. I look at him again and know he has thought of Alexandria, too.

And as I watch him slowly scoop up the first spoonful of chili, followed by a piece of bread, which he always butters with the scrupulous devotion of men who know the good things in life, I catch a fugitive look on his face that seems to ask, "What's the matter, why aren't you eating?" I shrug, as if alleging a stray thought. I look down at my food and look up again, realizing that I, too, am happy today—happy to be with him, to see him with my son, to know, as I catch him avoiding my eyes, that what matters to me now is not his love but his willingness to be loved, to come because I called.

We're interrupted by the apparition of two women advancing slowly to a table nearby. He stares at them. "I like to come here . . ." he begins. I am reminded of how thoroughly and desperately he likes women! "There are days when every woman is beautiful," he says, as though speaking of fruits that ripen everywhere on the same day. I know he wants to talk about women. As always, I steer the conversation away and ask about my mother instead. "What's there to say?" he replies. "Your mother . . ."

I am about to deflect this as well, when it dawns on me that perhaps our improvised lunch is nothing more than an uncomfortably staged affair between a father eager to say a few things to his son and a son who doesn't want to regret one day having failed to let him say them.

I take a first, shy, tentative step and ask, "Why did you ever marry her?"

"Whoever remembers?" he replies. Why did he have children? "Because I had to."

But who ordered you? "No one," he says, "it was just to make her happy."

He looks around again. "All I wanted was to read books," he adds. "On the second night of our honeymoon, while she slept, I opened the balcony door, and staring at the beachfront facing our hotel, I knew it was wrong. I wanted to study Greek, I wanted to write and travel and be free to love as I pleased. I wanted to leave our bedroom and go downstairs and keep walking past the empty garden and go away, but I didn't dare." Silence. "I forced myself to love her," he says. "Then one day it was over. Or at least someone else made me see it was over."

There is a strained pause in our conversation.

"Who?" I ask.

"You know who," he says without hesitating, almost grateful I had made it easy for him.

He calls her *That one*. I say nothing and, instead, play the open-minded, free-thinking grown-up who knows how to listen to such tales.

"She still calls me."

This I can't believe. More than thirty years later?

"In the middle of the night, when it's daylight over there, she calls."

"And what does Mother say?"

He shrugs.

I can just see him tiptoeing into the living room at three in the morning, tying his bathrobe, whispering in the dark to a woman halfway across the world and at the other end of time, who is probably irritated he's mumbling and can't speak any louder on the phone.

"She has a grown-up daughter. She misses me, she says. She thinks I'm still forty-five; I tell her I'm almost twice that. She doesn't understand, she wants to come, she wants a picture of me."

He stares at me, as if to ask, Can you figure women out?

And suddenly I find myself saying something that is more shocking to me than news of the woman's existence.

"Instead of pictures, why don't you just go back for a few weeks. I'll take care of the rest." By the rest I mean my mother.

"But I've grown old, I'm a grandfather." He turns to my son. "Besides, she says she's fat now."

"Just go," I say, mocking his feigned reluctance.

My father sits quietly. There is no more coffee in his cup; he says he will get some for me as well.

"Everyone is allowed five good years in their life. I've had my five. Everyone meets a dangerous woman in his life. I've met mine."

"Go to Egypt," I interrupt without even looking at him.

"I need more coffee," he says, standing up. "Anyway, first find me a decent picture and then we'll see." He throws a hand in the air to mean he doesn't care, that he's far too old for this, that the whole idea is one big nuisance.

The dining room is almost empty now, and as I watch him head for the coffee machine and disappear into the serving area, I am thinking of the years ahead when I'll come here alone, or with my son, and remember this one day when we sat together as if posing for a mental photograph, thinking of Alexandria, listening to this cheerless tale of two lovers cast adrift in time. We'll sit at this very table and wait for him, and think he's only gone for coffee and is coming back shortly, carrying two fresh cups and dessert on a tray as he did that day when he returned to the table and asked almost casually: "By the way, do you happen to have a picture of me? I mean, a good one?"

Double Take

1. As noted in the "At First Glance" section before André Aciman's essay "A Late Lunch," a majority of the sentences in the essay contain the subjects "I" or "he." However, Aciman makes use of a few other subjects, as well, including "we" five times. What does Aciman accomplish by using the plural subject these five times? When does he choose to use "we"? Why?
2. How does Aciman use dialogue in this essay? Does the dialogue help or hinder the larger focus and structure of this essay? How and why?
3. For whom might Aciman have written this essay? What makes you think so? That is, what clues does Aciman leave in his writing about whom he might be thinking of when writing?

Seeing for Yourself

At First Glance

Like many of his essays, "Shadow Cities" addresses the issue of exile—an important subject for André Aciman. Yet Aciman's exile is to New York, a city with which many of us are familiar, if not directly, then through our cultural identification with New York City—that is, even if we have never been to New York, we are acquainted with it through what we have heard or read about it for most of our lives. Yet, for Aciman, New York is a new place, not familiar. It is a place to be exiled to, not from. As you read this essay, think about how Aciman addresses a place as familiar to us as New York in a way that makes that place seem distant to us. Also, keep in mind that Aciman is writing in English, not his home language. What consequences does this have for how he writes about an American city as a foreign place?

Shadow Cities

On a late-spring morning in New York City four years ago, while walking on Broadway, I suddenly noticed that something terrible had happened to Straus Park. The small park, located just where Broadway intersects West End Avenue on West 106th Street, was being fenced off. A group of workers, wearing orange reflector shins, were manning all kinds of equipment, and next to what must have been some sort of portable comfort station was a large electrical generator. Straus Park was being dismantled, demolished.

Not that Straus Park was such a wonderful place to begin with. Its wooden benches were dirty, rotting, and perennially littered with pigeon droppings. You'd think twice before sitting, and if you did sit, you'd want to leave immediately. Also, it had become a favorite hangout for the homeless, the drunk, and the drug-addicted. Over the years the old cobblestone pavement had turned into an undulating terrain of dents and bulges, mostly cracked, with missing pieces sporadically replaced by tar or cement, the whole thing blanketed by a deep, drab, dirty gray. Finally, the emptied basin of what used to be a fountain had turned into something resembling a septic sandbox. Unlike the fountains of Rome, this one, like the park itself, was a down-and-out affair. Never a drop flowed from it. The fountain had been turned off decades ago.

Straus Park was, like so many tiny, grubby parks one hardly ever notices on the Lower East Side, a relic of a past that wasn't ancient enough to have its blemishes forgiven or to feel nostalgic about. One could say the same of the Art Nouveau–style statue of what I took to be a reclining Greek nymph lost in silent contemplation, looking inward, as it were, to avoid looking at what was around her. She looked very innocent, very Old World, and very out of place, almost pleading to be rescued from this ugly shrub that dubbed itself a park. In fact, the statue wasn't even there that day. She had disappeared, sold no doubt.

The thing I liked most about the square was gone, the way so many other things are gone today from around Straus Park: the Olympia Restaurant, the Blue Rose, the Ideal Restaurant, Mr. Kay's Barbershop, the Pomander Bookshop, the Siam Spice Rack, Chelsea Two, and the old Olympia Theater, drawn and quartered, as all the theaters are these days, plus the liquor store that moved across the street but really disappeared when it changed owners, the flower store that went high tech, and La Rosita, which went from down-and-out to up-and-coming.

Why should anybody care? And why should I, a foreigner, of all people, care? This wasn't even my city. Yet I had come here, an exile from Alexandria, doing what all exiles do on impulse, which is to look for their homeland abroad, to bridge the things here to things there, to rewrite the present so as not to write off the past. I wanted to rescue things everywhere, as though by restoring them here I might restore them elsewhere as well. Seeing one Greek restaurant disappear, or an old Italian cobbler's turn into a bodega, I was once again reminded that something was being taken away from the city, and therefore, from me—that even if I don't disappear from a place, places disappear from me.

I wanted everything to remain the same. Because this, too, is typical of people who have lost everything, including their roots or their ability to grow new ones. They may be mobile, scattered, nomadic, dislodged, but in their jittery state of transience they are thoroughly stationary. It is precisely because you have no roots that you don't budge, that you fear change, that you'll build on anything, rather than look for land. An exile is not just someone who has lost his home; he is someone who can't find another, who can't think of another. Some no longer even know what home means. They reinvent the concept with what they've got, the way we reinvent love with what's left of it each time. Some people bring exile with them the way they bring it upon themselves wherever they go.

I hate it when stores change names, the way I hate any change of season, not because I like winter more than spring, or because I like old store X better than new store Y, but because, like all foreigners who settle here and who always have the sense that their time warp is not perfectly aligned to the city's, and that they've docked, as it were, a few minutes ahead or a few minutes behind earth time, any change reminds me of how imperfectly I've connected to it. It reminds me of the thing I fear most: that my feet are never quite solidly on the ground, but also that the soil under me is equally weak, that the graft didn't take. In the disappearance of small things, I read the tokens of my own dislocation, of my own transiency. An exile reads change the way he reads time, memory, self, love, fear, beauty: in the key of loss.

I remembered that on summer days many years earlier when I was doing research on my dissertation, I would sometimes leave the gloomy stacks of Butler Library at Columbia and walk out into the sun down to 106th Street, where I'd find a secluded shaded bench away from the drunks and sit there awhile, eat a sandwich, a pizza, occasionally smiling at some of the elderly ladies who sat, not in the park, but along the benches outside, the way they did on Saturday afternoons around Verdi Square on Seventy-second Street and had probably learned to do on sunny, windy summer days in Central Europe, and as they still do in those mock-English spots in Paris that the French call *petits squares,* where people chat while their children play. Some of these ladies spoke with thick accents. I pictured their homes to myself: lots of lace, many doilies, Old World silverware, mannered Austro-Hungarian everything, down to the old gramophone, the black-and-white pictures on the wall, and de rigueur schnapps and slivovitz.

They made me think of 1950s pictures of New York, where it seems to grow darker much sooner in the evening than it does nowadays, where everyone wears long gray overcoats because winters were always colder then, and when the Upper West Side teemed with people who had come from Europe before the war and then stayed on, building small, cluttered lives, turning this neighborhood into a reliquary of Frankfurt-am-Main—their Frankfurt-away-from-home, Frankfurt-on-the-Hudson, as the old joke goes, but not an inappropriate name for a city which, in Germany today, dubs itself Mainhattan, and which is, ironically enough, a far stranger city to them, now that it imitates Manhattan, than their adopted Manhattan imitating old Frankfurt. There I met old Mrs. Danziger with the tattoo on her arm. Eighty-three-year-old Kurt Appelbaum, a concert pianist in his day, was sitting on such a bench; we spoke; we became friendly; one night, without my asking, he offered to play the *Waldstein Sonata* and *Rhapsody in Blue* for me. "But do not tape," he said, perhaps because he wished I would, and now that I think of it, I wish I had, as I sat and listened on a broken chair he said had been given to him by Hannah Arendt, who had inherited it from an old German colleague at the New School who had since died as well.

That was the year I rediscovered the Busch Quartet's 1930s recordings of Beethoven, and I imagined its members playing everywhere in those Old World, prewar living rooms around Straus Park. And by force of visualizing them there, I had projected them onto the park as well, so that its benches and the statue and the surrounding buildings and stores were, like holy men, stigmatized by Beethoven's music as it was played by a group of exiles from Hitler's Reich.

I would come every noon, for the statue mostly, because she was, like me, willing to stand by in this halfway station called Straus Park. She reminded me of those statues one finds everywhere in Rome, springing on you from their niches when you least expect them in the evening.

It is difficult to explain what seclusion means when you find it on an island in the middle of Broadway, amid the roar of midday traffic. What I was looking for, and had indeed found quite by accident, was something that reminded me of an oasis—in the metaphorical sense, since this was a "dry" fountain—but an oasis of the soul, a place where, for no apparent reason, people stop on their various journeys elsewhere. Straus Park, it seemed, was created precisely for this, for contemplation, for restoration—in both its meanings—for retrospection, for finding oneself, for finding the center of things.

And indeed there was something physically central about Straus Park. This, after all, was where Broadway and West End Avenue intersected, and the park seemed almost like a raised hub on West 106th Street, leading to Riverside Park on one side and to Central Park on the other. Straus Park was not on one street but at the intersection of four. Suddenly, before I knew why, I felt quite at home. I was in one place that had at least four addresses.

Here you could come, sit, and let your mind drift in four different directions: Broadway, which at this height had an unspecified Northern European cast; West End Avenue, decidedly Londonish; 107th Street, very quiet, very narrow, tucked away around the corner, reminded me of those deceptively humble alleys where one finds stately homes along the canals of Amsterdam. And 106th, as it descended toward Central Park, looked like the main alley of a small town on the Italian Riviera, where, after much trundling in the blinding light at noon as you take in the stagnant odor of fuel from the train station where you just got off, you finally approach a cove, which you can't make out yet but which you know is there, hidden behind a thick row of Mediterranean pines, over which, if you really strain your eyes, you'll catch sight of the tops of striped beach umbrellas jutting beyond the trees, and beyond these, if you could just take a few steps closer, the sudden, spectacular blue of the sea.

To the west of Straus Park, however, the slice of Riverside and 106th had acquired a character that was strikingly Parisian, and with the fresh breeze which seemed to swell and subside all afternoon long, you sensed that behind the trees of Riverside Park, serene and silent, flowed an elusive Seine, and beyond it, past the bridges that were to take you across, though you couldn't see any of it yet, was not the Hudson, not New Jersey, but the Left Bank—not the end of Manhattan, but the beginning of a whole bustling city awaiting beyond the trees—as it did so many decades ago, when as a boy in Alexandria, dreaming of Paris, I would go to the window, look out at the sea at night, and think that this was not North Africa at all, but the Ile de la Cité. Perhaps what lay beyond the trees was not the end of Manhattan, or even Paris, but the beginnings of another, unknown city, the real city, the one that always beckons, the one we invent each time and may never see, and fear we've begun to forget.

There were moments when, despite the buses and the trucks and the noise of kids with boom boxes, the traffic light would change and everything come to a standstill, and people weren't speaking, and the unrelenting sun beat strong on the pavement, and then one could almost swear this was an early-summer afternoon in Italy, and that if I really thought about it, what lay behind Riverside Park was not just an imaginary Seine, but perhaps the Tiber as well. What made me think of Rome was that everything here reminded me of the kind of place all tourists know so well: that tiny empty piazza with a little fountain, where, thirsty and tired with too much walking all day, you douse your face, then unbuckle your sandals, sit on the scalding marble edge of a Baroque fountain, and simply let your feet rest awhile in what is always exquisitely clear non-drinkable water.

Depending on where I sat, or on which corner I moved to within the park, I could be in any of four or five countries and never for a second be in the one I couldn't avoid hearing, seeing, and smelling. This, I think, is when I started to love, if "love" is the word for it, New York. I would return to Straus Park every day, because returning was itself now part of the ritual of remembering the shadow cities hidden there—so that I, who had put myself there, the way squatters put themselves somewhere and start to build on nothing, with nothing, would return for no reason other than perhaps to run into my own footprints. This became my habit, and ultimately my habitat. Sometimes finding that you are lost where you were lost last year can be oddly reassuring, almost familiar. You may never find yourself; but you do remember looking for yourself. That, too, can be reassuring, comforting.

On a hot summer day I came looking for water in a place where no water exists, the way dowsers do when they search for trapped, underground places, seeking out the ghost of water, its remanence. But the kind of water I was really looking for was not fountain water at all, Roman or otherwise. I remembered my disappointment in Rome years ago when, dunking my feet in the turtle fountain early one afternoon, it occurred to me that these surreptitious footbaths in the middle of an emptied Rome in August and all this yearning for sunlight, heat, and water amounted to nothing more than a poor man's simulated swim at the beaches of my childhood, where water was indeed plentiful, and where all of your body could bathe, not just your toes.

At Straus Park, I had discovered the memory of water. Here I would come to remember not so much the beauty of the past as the beauty of remembering, realizing that just because we love to look back doesn't mean we love the things we look back on.

There is a large fountain in Rome at Piazza Navona, where the four great rivers of the world are represented: the Ganges, the Nile, the Plate, and the Danube. I knew it well, because it stood not far from a small bookstore where, years ago, as a teenager, I would go to purchase one Penguin book a week—a small, muggy, and sultry shop, of which I recall the sense of bliss on first coming out into the sun with a new book in my hand. As I surveyed these four rivers, the question was which do I splash my face in?

There is no frigate like a book, says Emily Dickinson. There is nothing I have loved more than to take a good book and sit somewhere in a quiet open spot in Rome with so many old things around me, open up to any page, and begin traveling back sometimes, as when I read Lawrence Durrell and Cavafy, thinking of time, of all that retrospection—to quote Whitman—or eagerly looked forward to the New World, as when I learned to love Eliot and Pound. Does a place become one's home because this is where one read the greatest number of books about other places? Can I yearn for Rome when I am finally standing where I longed to stand when I was once a young man in Rome?

All this, if it hadn't already, begins to acquire absurd proportions when I realize that, during that dissertation summer of many years ago, I had applied for and gotten a job to teach in an American high school in Rome. So that as I sat there in Straus Park, going through my usual pickup sticks and cat's cradles of memories, I had discovered something unique: I didn't want to go to Rome, not for a year, not for half a year, not even for a month, because it finally dawned on me that I didn't very much like Rome, nor did I really want to be in France, or Egypt for that matter—and though I certainly did not like New York any better, I rather enjoyed my Straus Park–Italy and my Straus Park–Paris much more, the way sometimes I like postcards and travel books better than the places they remind me of, art books better than paintings, recordings better than live performances, and fantasies more than the people I fantasize about—some of whom are not only destined to disappoint, but can't even be forgiven for standing in the way of the pictures we originally had of them. Once in Rome, I would most certainly long to be in Straus Park remembering the Rome where I'd once remembered the beaches of my childhood. Italy was just my way of grafting myself to New York.

I could never understand or appreciate New York unless I could make it the mirror—call it the mnemonic correlative—of other cities I've known or imagined. No Mediterranean can look at a sunset in Manhattan and not think of another sunset thousands of miles away. No Mediterranean can stand looking at the tiny lights speckling the New Jersey cliffs at night and not remember a galaxy of little fishing boats that go out to sea at night, dotting the water with their tiny lights till dawn, when they come back to shore. But it is not New Jersey I see when I watch the sunset from Riverside Drive.

The real New York I never see either. I see only the New York that either sits in for other places or helps me summon them up. New York is the stand-in, the ersatz of all the things I can remember and cannot have, and may not even want, much less love, but continue to look for, because finding parallels can be more compelling than finding a home, because without parallels, there can't be a home, even if in the end it is the comparing that we like, not the objects we compare. Outside of comparing, we cannot feel. One may falsify New York to make it more habitable; but by making it more habitable in that way, one also makes it certain it remains a falsehood, a figment.

New York is my home precisely because it is a place from which I can begin to be elsewhere—an analogue city, a surrogate city, a shadow city that allows me to naturalize and neutralize this terrifying, devastating, unlivable megalopolis by letting me think it is something else, somewhere else, that it is indeed far smaller, quainter than I feared, the way certain cities on the Mediterranean are forever small and quaint, with just about the right number of places where people can go, sit, and, like Narcissus leaning over a pool of water, find themselves at every bend, every store window, every sculptured forefront. Straus Park allowed me to place more than one film over the entire city of New York, the way certain guidebooks of Rome do. For each photograph of an ancient ruin there is a series of colored transparencies. When you place the transparency over the picture of a ruin, the missing or fallen parts suddenly reappear, showing you how the Forum and the Colosseum must have looked in their heyday, or how Rome looked in the Middle Ages, and in the late Renaissance, and so on. But when you lift all the plastic sheets, all you see are today's ruins.

I didn't want to see the real New York. I'd go backward in time and uncover an older New York, as though New York, like so many cities on the Mediterranean, had an ancient side that was less menacing, that was not so difficult to restore, that had more past than present, and that corresponded to the old-fashioned world I think I come from. Hence, my obsession with things that are old and defunct and that seep through, like ancient cobblestones and buried rails from under renewed coats of asphalt and tar. Sealed-off ancient firehouses, ancient stables turned into garages, ghost buildings awaiting demolition, old movie theaters converted into Baptist churches, old marketplaces that are now lost, subway stops that are ghost stations today—these are the ruins I dream of restoring, if only to date the whole world back a bit to my time, the way Herr Appelbaum and Frau Danziger belonged to my time. Going to Straus Park was like traveling elsewhere in time. How frugal is the chariot that bears a human soul!

How uncannily appropriate, therefore, to find out fifteen years later that the statue that helped me step back in time was not that of a nymph, but of Memory herself. In Greek, her name is Mnemosyne, Zeus' mistress, mother of the Muses. I had, without knowing it, been coming to the right place after all. This is why I was so disturbed by the imminent demolition of the park: my house of memories would become a ghost park. If part of the city goes, part of us dies as well.

Of course, I had panicked too soon. Straus Park was marvelously restored. After spending more than a year in a foundry, a resurrected statue of Memory remembered her appointed place in the park and resumed her old position. Her fountain is the joy of children and of all people who lean over to splash their faces on a warm summer day. I go there very often, sometimes to have coffee in the morning after dropping my children off at school. I have now forgotten what the old Straus Park looked like. I do not miss it, but somehow part of me is locked there, too, so that I come here sometimes to remember my summer of many years ago as well, though I am glad those days are gone.

My repeated returns to Straus Park make of New York not only the shadow city of so many other cities I've known, but a shadow city of itself, reminding me of an earlier New York in my own life, and before that of a New York which existed before I was born and which has nothing to do with me but which I need to see—in old photographs, for example—because, as an exile without a past, I like to peek at others' foundations to imagine what mine might look like had I been born here, where mine might be if I were to build here. I like to know that Straus Park was once called Schuyler Square, and before that it was known as Bloomingdale Square, and that these are places where everything about me and the city claims a long, continuous, call it a common, ancestral, imaginary past, where nothing ever bolts into sudden being, but where nothing ever disappears, not those I love today, nor those I've loved in the past, that Old World people like Herr Appelbaum, who played Gershwin for me on 105th Street one night when he could have played Schubert instead, and Mrs. Danziger, who never escaped the Nazis but brought them with her in her dreams at night, might still sit side by side with Ida Straus, who refused to board the lifeboats when the *Titanic* sank, and stayed on with her husband—that all these people and all these layers upon layers of histories, warmed-over memories, and overdrawn fantasies should forever go into letting my Straus Park, with its Parisian Frankfurts and Roman Londons, remain forever a tiny, artificial speck on the map of the world that is my center of gravity, from which radiates every road I've traveled, and to which I always long to return when I am away.

But perhaps I should spell the mystery out and say what lies at the bottom of all this. Straus Park, this crossroad of the world, this capital of memory, this place where the four fountains of the world and the four quarters within me meet one another, is not Paris, is not Rome, could not be London or Amsterdam, Frankfurt or New York. It is, of course, Alexandria.

I come to Straus Park to remember Alexandria, be it an unreal Alexandria, an Alexandria that does not exist, that I've invented or learned to cultivate in Rome as in Paris, so that in the end the Paris and the Rome I retrieve here are really the shadow of the shadow of Alexandria, versions of Alexandria, the remanence of Alexandria, infusing Straus Park itself now, reminding me of something that is not just elsewhere but that is perhaps more in me than it ever was out there, that it is, after all, perhaps just me, a me that is no less a figment of time than this city is a figment of space.

A CLOSER LOOK AT ANDRÉ ACIMAN

1. André Aciman has made it clear that writing about place is important to him. As you look back over these four essays, think about how Aciman has addressed place. How has he described places? How has he contextualized places? Does he write about places differently than he writes about people? In an analytical essay, address how Aciman considers place in his writing.

2. Each of the four essays contained here by André Aciman begins with an identification of time: "What my dentist cried out one day after, . . ." "To those who asked, I said I went back to touch and breathe again the past," "My father comes fifteen minutes early," and "On a late spring morning almost two years ago." For a writer so bound up in issues of place, it seems that Aciman is also acutely aware of the role of time in his writing. What do you suppose his strategy might be for identifying moments of time in his first sentences? Why might he be so consistent in this identification? Write an analysis in which you explain how Aciman negotiates between time and place in his writing. Be sure to offer several examples from the Aciman essays to support your explanation.

3. Each of these four essays mentions Aciman's home city of Alexandria, Egypt. Aciman even notes in "A Late Lunch" that his son's name is Alex, and we can only assume that the name is perhaps a tribute to the city. After having read

these four essays and seen the prominence of Alexandria in Aciman's writing, consider what effect this consistency has in establishing the writer's voice and persona. That is, might we assume that Aciman returns again and again to writing about Alexandria in order to intentionally create a particular feel to his writing? What might the consequences of such a strategy be? Write an essay in which you address the role of Alexandria not only in Aciman's writing, but in the establishment of his voice and the feeling of his writing.

Looking from Writer to Writer

1. André Aciman grounds much of his work in remembering a place from where he was exiled as a Jew. Like many Jews, Aciman can be described as a "wanderer," one looking for a place to call home. Similarly, Annie Dillard's writing exemplifies characteristics of wandering. Consider how each of these authors addresses wandering.
2. As has been noted, André Aciman is intrigued with the idea of place, and his writing exemplifies this fascination. Likewise, Scott Russell Sanders's writing also addresses issues of place. Compare Sanders's approach to discussing place with that of Aciman's. How do they each describe and address different places?
3. Much of André Aciman's writing addresses issues of his exile, his Judaism, and his displacement. In many ways, his writing about his cultural situation might be seen as similar to the ways in which Henry Louis Gates writes about African-American culture and its difference from white culture. Look to the essays included here by Gates and consider how each of these authors describes their home culture and the ways in which that culture comes into contact with other cultures.

Looking Beyond

NONFICTION:
False Papers: Essays on Exile and Memory. New York: Farrar Straus & Giroux, 2000.
Out of Egypt: A Memoir. 1994. New York: Riverhead Books, 1996.

EDITED COLLECTIONS:
Letters of Transit: Reflections on Exile, Identity, Language, and Loss. New York: New Press, 2000.

Rick Bass

An important and respected nonfiction and fiction writer as well as environmental activist, Rick Bass is best known for his insight into Nature and reverence for the wild. One reviewer writes that Bass has "a built-in wildness sensor" and, as Bass himself admits, he was drawn with something like an instinct to wild places from a very early age. Born in Fort Worth, Texas, in 1958, the oldest of three brothers, Bass grew up in the suburbs of Houston, where he sought out wild places, the few that remained, while also frequenting the Houston Zoo and the Museum of Natural History. His most lasting and formative impressions of wild places, however, developed from the time he spent camping and hunting with his family on their thousand-acre deer lease in the Texas Hill Country. It was there he learned to recognize the "necessity and holiness of wildness." There he also learned about the connection between place and story; that is, how wild places leave their mark on people in the form of stories they share.

Bass left Houston to attend Utah State University where, in addition to majoring in petroleum engineering and studying essay writing, he played junior varsity football. After graduating in 1980, Bass moved to Mississippi to work for a petroleum company, but maintained a desire to write and continued to teach himself by reading the works of Barry Hannah, Jim Harrison, and Eudora Welty. In 1985 he published his first book, *The Deer Pasture,* an essay collection commemorating his experiences in the Hill Country. This was followed in 1987 by the publication in the *Paris Review* of his first major work of fiction, a story called "Where the Sea Used to Be." This story later became the novel Bass published under the same name nearly 10 years later. Also in 1987, Bass published his second book of nonfiction, *Wild to the Heart.* In addition to celebrating wild places, the essays in this book exhibit the early signs of what would later become Bass's conservationism. Around this time, Bass, his girlfriend, and two dogs left Mississippi in search of wildness, finding it finally in the Yaak Valley in the northwest corner of Montana, near the Canadian border. It is in his beloved Yaak Valley—a place he chronicles, celebrates, and fights to preserve in his nonfiction and fiction (short stories, novels and novellas, essays, journals, and chronicles)—that Bass still lives and writes.

"More and more," Bass explains, "I think a style of writing is not a trait or characteristic you have . . . but rather, a place you go to." Indeed, Bass does not so much write *about* places as he writes *from* places. Forests, prairies, and deserts are the "place-sources" from which his writing is generated. As he expressed it in his essay "On Willow Creek" (reprinted here), "when we run out of country, we will run out of stories." In Bass's writing there is a sense that the life-world and art-world not only relate to one another, but also sustain one another. His writing emerges from his deep affinity with a place, particularly wild places, and in turn much of his writing works to preserve wild places such as the Yaak Valley or the Hill Country of Texas. In Bass, there emerges an almost symbiotic relationship between writing and place. Bass's art and his activism are deeply interrelated.

Bass not only writes about different places, but his writing has also appeared in different forms of print: books, newspapers, magazines, and journals ranging from the *Paris Review* to *Esquire,* the *Seattle Post-Intelligencer, Sports Afield, Sierra,* and *Sports Illustrated.* As a writer, he displays a wide range as he sometimes covers similar subjects but in different genres (fiction and nonfiction) and writes to different audiences, having to make different rhetorical decisions in each case about what kinds of evidence and arguments to make, as well as what voice, tone, and organization to use. As a nonfiction writer, however, Bass is engaged most seriously in the work of conservation and activism. He writes: "I think we tend, as writers, to write fiction when we have time to dally—to look ahead, and muse, or to cast back, and reminisce, or to figure things out, secret things—mystery—but when the stakes are high, when the world's caving in and the food and air and water are being poisoned, we turn instinctively to the nonfiction." As you read the essays that follow, pay attention to how Bass constructs his essays, in particular to how Bass devises his arguments for why he hunts, for example, or why we should save natural places. Decide if you think his strategies as a writer work for his given audiences and why. And see if you can start to think about such strategies in your own writing.

Bass on Writing

At First Glance

In this essay about writing, "Without Safety: Writing Nonfiction," Bass describes how non-fiction writing is riskier and demands more maturity and responsibility than fiction writing. The essay was published in a literary magazine whose focus is both poetry and prose, and whose readers also tend to be writers. As you read the essay and the advice and recommendations it gives, think about how the fiction writers reading it would react to Bass's claims. Also, think about what makes an effective essay according to Bass. Consider whether or not you agree with Bass's assessment and, just as importantly, try to imagine if Bass's advice to writers applies to your own writing in this class.

Without Safety: Writing Nonfiction

This essay, "Without Safety: Writing Nonfiction," is taken from a talk given at the Sandhills Writers Conference in Augusta, Georgia, in the spring of 1989, where I read, before beginning the talk, Joy Williams's essay, "Save the Whales, Screw the Shrimp," to illustrate various points of the talk about nonfiction—about good, or great nonfiction—but because of space limitations, for this essay I have only excerpted from Williams's essay. "Save the Whales, Screw the Shrimp" appeared in the February 1989 issue of *Esquire,* and should be read in its entirety, must be read, please read it—February 1989, *Esquire.* It's a truly phenomenal essay, and shows brilliantly and heartbreakingly all that nonfiction can hope to do, all that it can achieve.

I don't want to talk about me of course, writes Joy Williams, *but it seems as though far too much attention has been lavished on you lately—that your greed and vanities and quest for self-fulfillment have been catered to far too much. You just want and want and want. You haven't had a mandala dream since the '80s began. To have a mandala dream you'd have to instinctively know that it was an attempt at self-healing on the part of Nature, and you don't believe in Nature anymore. It's too isolated from you. You've abstracted it. It's so messy and damaged and sad. Your eyes glaze as you travel life's highway past all the crushed animals and the Big Gulp cups. You don't even take pleasure in looking at nature photographs these days. Oh, they can be just as pretty, as always, but don't they make you feel increasingly . . . anxious?* (I have to leave some of the essay out here, and then pick back up again, for reasons of space: but you must read this essay).

. . . Hidden from immediate view in the butterfly-bright meadow, in the dusky thicket, in the oak and holly wood, are the surveyors' stakes, for someone wants to build a mall exactly

there—some gas stations and supermarkets, some pizza and video shops, a health club, maybe a bulimia treatment center. Those lovely pictures of leopards and herons and wild rivers, well, you just know they're going to be accompanied by a text that will serve only to bring you down. You don't want to think about it! It's all so uncool. And you don't want to feel guilty either. Guilt is uncool. Regret maybe you'll consider. Maybe. Regret is a possibility, but don't push me, you say. Nature photographs have become something of a problem, along with almost everything else. Even though they leave the bad stuff out—maybe because you know they're leaving all the bad stuff out—such pictures are making you increasingly aware that you're a little too late for Nature. Do you feel that? Twenty years too late, maybe only ten? Not way too late, just a little too late? Well, it appears that you are. And since you are, you've decided you're just not going to attend this particular party.

As I think we can see wonderfully in this example, voice is the most important aspect of nonfiction: it's the controlling force of the writing. Do you want your piece to have the voice of a man's hollow shouts in an empty basketball gym? Or the call of a woman coming across an empty field at dusk, to her sister who has gone down to the creek for a walk? Voice is modulated almost entirely by distance: how close are you to this subject? And this one? And this one? And will this subject *let* you come closer? Is the subject affable, or standoffish, or just plain loony?—or, as in the case of Joy Williams's essay, dangerous as hell? In all instances, there is one perfect and proper voice, and it's determined half by the subject—how close it lets you come—and half by your *feeling* for this subject. That's where the creativity of writing nonfiction can play its largest role. To find a good voice for your essay, you simply need to ask yourself those two questions: How do I feel about this subject? How does this subject feel about me?

The release of information in nonfiction, I feel, must be more momentous. You can't be sly or subtle—and yet you can't (rarely, anyway) lay your heart out on the line, either. What you can do, though, is control your release of information. Observation of detail—detail that will give characterization to your subject, or subjects—must be acute. There's almost no room for ambiguity. Observation of detail—what you choose to see, and more importantly, talk about—is the only way you have to sway the story, to show your beliefs, your hopes—which, though it may sound immoral, or unfair, I believe is fair—it's *your* article, you're writing it . . .

This is the time of machines and models, hands-on management and master plans. Don't you ever wonder as you pass that billboard advertising another MASTER-PLANNED COMMUNITY just what master they are actually talking about? Not the Big Master, certainly. Something brought to you by one of the tiny masters, of which there are many. But you like these tiny masters and have even come to expect and require them. In Florida they've just started a ten-thousand-acre city in the Everglades. It's a megaproject, one of the largest ever in the state. Yes, they must have thought you wanted it. No, what you thought of as the Everglades, the Park, is only a little bitty part of the Everglades. Developers have been gnawing at this irreplaceable, strange land for years. It's like they just hate this ancient sea of grass. Maybe you could ask them about this sometime. Roy Rogers is the senior vice-president of strategic planning, and the old cowboy says that every tree and bush and inch of sidewalk in the project has been planned. Nevertheless, because the whole thing will take twenty-five years to complete, the plan is going to constantly change. You can understand this. The important thing is that there be a blueprint. You trust a blueprint. The tiny masters know what you like. You like a secure landscape and access to services. You like grass—that is, lawns. The ultimate lawn is the golf course, which you've been told has "some ecological value." You believe this!

This essay gets fiercer, harsher and better, but we skip ahead: *The Tiny Masters are willing to arrange Nature for you. They will compose it into a picture that you can look at at your leisure, when you're not doing work or something like that. Nature becomes a scenery, a prop. At some golf courses in the Southwest, the saguaro cacti are reported to be repaired with green paste when balls blast into their skin. The saguaro can attempt to heal themselves by growing over the balls, but this takes time, and the effect can be somewhat . . . baroque. It's better to get out the paste pot. Nature has become simply a visual form of entertainment, and it had better look snappy.*

Green paste over errant golf balls? And the mangled, tortured attempts of the saguaro cacti to claim the golf balls? This is an amazingly vivid detail—and it serves perfectly the double purpose of marshalling our disgust in the direction that Williams wants it to go. She is in control.

Humor goes further in nonfiction than in fiction. I believe we're all a little afraid of the truth, the pure truth, in any form, and humor can be an alleviation, a relief, from the even subliminal dread of that approaching truth, a truth that is so inherent in the reading of any nonfiction piece. It's like being sent to the principal's office—you know that what's coming is for real, and so quite often, you're anxious about it. Humor can help dilute the truth. In reading fiction, on the other hand—no matter how riveted we are, or how wonderful the story is—we can rarely approach that level of belief that exists, inherently, in reading "nonfiction": and so we are willing—in fiction—to take risks, willing to commit a little harder, fall a little harder in love, to believe a little more fully that all will work out (or that nothing will work out), because there is that safety net below us: the safety net of fiction. Humor is nice, in fiction, but not as important, because we'll rush pell-mell (or plod diligently) to the end of fiction—but in nonfiction, I believe our hearts beat a little differently: always at least just a little bit, there's that echo of fear—fear of the truth, advancing. A little humor is a blessing, and goes a long way, in nonfiction.

The paradox, of course, is that if you force it, the piece falls apart, collapses.

But you can watch for humor, as you're interviewing your subject, or taking your trip: you can take notes, and when you see it, jot it down, and even plan parts of your article around that gem of humor, the way you would plan a dinner around a beautiful guest who was coming from a long way off.

All right, you say, wow, lighten up will you? Relax. Tell about yourself.

Well, I say, I live in Florida . . .

Oh my God, you say. Florida! Florida is a joke! How do you expect us to take you seriously if you still live there! Florida is crazy, it's pink concrete. It's paved, it's over. And a little girl just got eaten by an alligator down there. It came out of some swamp next to a subdivision and just carried her off. That set your Endangered Species Act back fifty years, you can bet.

I . . .

Listen, we don't to hear any more about Florida. We don't want to hear about Phoenix or Hilton Head or California's Central Valley. If our wetlands—our vanishing wetlands—are mentioned one more time, we'll scream. And the talk about condors and grizzlies and wolves is becoming too de trop. We had just managed to get whales out of our minds when those three showed up under the ice in Alaska. They even had names. Bone is the dead one, right? It's almost the twenty-first century! Those last condors are pathetic. Can't we just get this over with?

Aristotle said that all living beings are ensouled and striving to participate in eternity.

Oh, I just bet he said that, you say. That doesn't sound like Aristotle. He was a humanist. We're all humanists here. This is the age of humanism. And it has been for a long time.

There is so much that is important in nonfiction. You can be disproven at almost any step along the way—you're dealing almost entirely in the rather black-and-white, linear world of facts—and so you've got to keep punching home the theme, in almost every paragraph. Notice how in Joy Williams's essay there's an almost violent attention being paid to the theme—a relentlessness, to the theme of apathy.

If you drift or wander in fiction, it's called "moody" and "mystical." If you drift in nonfiction, it's called "unfocused." You shouldn't confuse the two: fiction and nonfiction.

I'm really getting out on a limb here, but I believe the nonfiction writer deals less with lyricism—with *poetry*—and more in concepts, ideas and scenes: almost literally, the hammering together of a house. You can't have any open doors, open breezes, blowing through a house, no rain blowing in. These things are fine and moody and okay for the safeties of fiction, but for the rock-hard certainties of nonfiction—the If-I-catch-you-in-a-lie-you're-dead basis of nonfiction—you can't afford these things, and so you tend to be less daring with language. There is less room for ambiguity. And lyricism often tends to bring the voice in too close . . .

Instead, you make up for it—this loss of lyricism—with your scenes: you must hear the perfect dialogue, and feel the perfect feelings. Sometimes, if you have to, you, the narrator, must come into the picture, into the story—and don't be afraid to. Suppose you're writing a piece about a visit to a weight-reduction center, and the manager tells you that the average weight loss, per patient, is forty-five pounds. You don't have to just sit there and take this rather interesting but still nonetheless mathematical and therefore potentially dry fact like a little mouse. Step in at the end of the paragraph—don't be shy—and say something like, "And I thought about how much weight forty-five pounds was. I pictured the noise forty-five pounds of iron would make, being thrown out a third-story window. I pictured the sound it would make, when it hit."

You do what you can, to keep fresh water moving over the gills of the story. Maybe only one story in your life will ever write itself. Chances are it is not the one you are working on. Chances are it's going to keep rolling over and dying, turning white belly up. Sometimes the best way to keep it alive, and keep it fresh, is to roll up your sleeves and enter the story—the nonfiction—yourself. Don't be afraid to. Do whatever it takes. ("Well, I say, I live in Florida . . .")

I like to think of novels as being about fate, while stories are about mystery. I think that nonfiction is more like a novel in this regard than even a novel: nonfiction is about nothing if not fate. Again, you've got, throughout your essay, or your article, the voice, the hammering home of the theme that things could not have turned out any differently than how you are reporting them. They may have *tried* to turn out differently, but there was no way—not a one-in-a-hundred chance—that it would, or could, occur differently. It's not just fate that you're writing about in nonfiction, but a sort of Super fate. Beating home that theme.

You can, however, use many of the short story's devices. There are those you cannot use, should not use—foreshadowing, for instance, which is too cute in nonfiction, and even plot, which is too devious—even metaphors seem too cute for nonfiction, because in nonfiction you're a semigod, bringing the truths down off the mountains (whereas in fiction, you're a peasant, toiling down in the dirt with the rest of the common people, just trying to figure things out, just trying to see things). But one of the devices that you *can* take from short story writing is the idea of a final discovery, at the end—an epiphany, if you will.

Epiphanies in short stories are beginning to come under slight attack, and will continue to be increasingly critiqued, I predict—and not always without cause or reason, because it's true, we've just had so damn many of them, there really are more than enough to go around, and we're just getting too used to them, so that only do the very best ones pack any punch any more—but an epiphany in nonfiction is a much more balanced and logical creation, and very often, should be the thing you are writing for.

In the summer, particularly in the industrial Northeast, you did get a little excited. The filth cut into your fun time. Dead stuff floating around. Sludge and bloody vials. Hygienic devices—appearing not quite so hygienic out of context—all coming in on the tide. The air smelled funny, too. You tolerate a great deal, but the summer of '88 was truly creepy. It was even thought for a moment that the environment would become a political issue. But it didn't. You didn't want it to be, preferring instead to continue in your politics of subsidizing and advancing avarice. The issues were the same as always—jobs, defense, the economy, maintaining and improving the standard of living in this greedy, selfish, expansionistic, industrialized society.

You're getting a little shrill here, you say.

You're pretty well off. You expect to be better off soon. You do. What does this mean? More software, more scampi, more square footage? You have created an ecological crisis. The earth is infinitely variable and alive, and you are killing it. It seems safer this way. But you are not safe. You want to find wholeness and happiness in a land increasingly damaged and betrayed, and you never will. More than material matters. You must change your ways.

What is this? Sinners in the Hands of Angry God?

The ecological crisis cannot be resolved by politics. It cannot be solved by science or technology. It is a crisis caused by culture and character, and a deep change in personal consciousness is needed. Your fundamental attitudes toward the earth have become twisted. You have made only brutal contact with Nature, you cannot comprehend its grace. You must change. Have few desires and simple pleasures. Honor nonhuman life. Control yourself, become more authentic. Live lightly upon the earth and treat it with respect. Redefine the word progress and dismiss the managers and masters. Grow inwardly and with knowledge become truly wiser. Make connections. Think differently, behave differently. For this is essentially a moral issue we face and moral decisions must be made.

A moral issue! Okay, this discussion is now toast. A moral issue . . . And who's this we now? Who are you is what I'd like to know. You're not me, anyway. I admit, someone's to blame and something should be done. But I've got to go. It's getting late. That's dusk out there. That is dusk, isn't it? It certainly doesn't look like any dawn I've ever seen. Well, take care.

Think of it as a final proof, in nonfiction—this epiphany, even an unspoken one—a simple (or complex), visual epiphany. In the initial section of your essay or article, you sound the theme, for the first time—the initial theme of Joy Williams's essay being that you want and want and want, and yet you don't feel guilty—and as the essay progresses, you, the essayist, should sound that theme again and again, from various angles—always from new angles, to give the theme *dimension,* and therefore life—and finally, when the proof or discovery is created—when the picture takes shape, when it becomes indisputably evident that what you are saying is true—in Joy Williams's essay, for instance, the epiphany being discovered or revealed that this may not be so much the dawn of a new environmental consciousness, but rather, the dusk of an environment—then your essay or article has finished itself, and the end has been achieved.

The mental attitudes with which one approaches nonfiction are daunting to consider. It's why I can't write too much of it at one time. As I've mentioned, there's no safety net in nonfiction. As you're writing it, and equally daunting, after the piece is finished, you may be tempted to wonder—if you're human: "Did I do this the best that could be done? Did I do the subject justice?" and even, "Could someone else have done this same story better?" I think once more this falls into the area of safety, or lack thereof—with a short story, your creation—something that comes from your heart—only you know it—but with the nonfiction—the profile of an ex-president, for instance—the whole world can see, in real life, what you're up to, what you're writing about—and they can judge you and will.

Another problem with nonfiction is "How much fiction can I put into it?" If it's journalism, precious little—though if it's an essay, the answer is as much as you need to, or as much as you can get away with. I don't believe I've ever been able to write a nonfiction piece entirely straight, with no untruths. I'll invent a quote, or see something that might not have happened—not on the same day, at any rate. It could be something as insignificant as a man clearing his throat when in reality he blew his nose. Who'll know the difference? Though sometimes I make up big lies, too, just to see how they look on paper; and sometimes, if I really like them, I cannot help but leave them in. No one will ever know.

I remember writing about a restaurant up in north Alabama, a backwoods place that served plenty of good hot coffee, and ham the size of license plates. I went into the bathroom to wash my hands, and I looked out the window and saw that there was a mule standing out in the field. In my essay, I had that mule come over to the window (which was open), stick his head through it, and begin chewing on the roll of toilet paper that was on the spindle. Everyone, up until now, believed me.

The question may be raised, "Is this right, or is it wrong—to write nonfiction this way?" I think it's right—that's why I do it. I mean, I think the only true wrong there is, aside from harming someone or speaking poorly of someone who has done nothing to deserve such, is to write a boring or unentertaining piece of nonfiction—because no reader deserves that.

What makes nonfiction be either boring or exciting? If you can't always rely on the old standbys of fiction—plot, metaphor, symbolism—pretty, in art, but a little too cute, a little too intrusive, in the rushed world of reality—then what do you have to rely on? What's the single best tool, the single best crutch, if you will, to get you across that narrow catwalk that spans the abyss of boredom?

I believe that, along with voice, the best tool you have in this regard is characterization. It's not just enough to have an interesting subject or situation: the people moving in or through the situation must rival, even exceed the strength of fictional characters (again, because there's no gauze, no fuzzy pastel mist, no safety—the edges of your nonfiction are hard, and will be judged hard, because life is hard)—and your nonfiction characters' hopes must be more tenuous, or desperate, or threatened, or secure—more *immediate,* more everything—than even in fiction.

Speed is everything; you've got to get right to the story, right to the point in nonfiction, and every careless lift of a character's hand, every sentence uttered, must thunder toward the end of the article, helping to bring about—as soon as possible— that end. Every line of dialogue should have about it the illumination into that subject's character that a condemned man's last words would carry.

Even with such a wonderful nonfiction writer as Annie Dillard—in my opinion, the best—who *seems* to move in ellipses, and gauzes, toward the discovery—as does another great essayist, Barry Lopez—there is not so much the mystical, sometimes ambiguous wandering toward the subject and its end or discovery that characterizes great fiction as there is the feeling that a sheet has been pulled away from the subject, revealing it—the discovery—to have been there all along.

What I am saying is that you can use mysticism, and gauze, in nonfiction—lyricism, too—but you've got to be damned good, and plenty confident, because nothing would be worse than to circumlocate and circumlocate, chanting and digressing, musing, and then to pull away that sheet, and have there be nothing there.

The question was brought up to me once about covering an event, or a person, for the purpose of nonfiction: "How long do you stay out with the subject—or how long do you interview?" I think that you should stay out with your subject long enough to see the end of the story, and then—mentally, at least—you should make a note when you see that end, or what you hope will be the end. Sometimes you are lucky enough to see the end while you are still out in the field—though other times—the scary times—it is not until you're at your desk, poring over pages and pages of rapidly cooling, increasingly indecipherable notes—what to leave in, and what to take out—that you see the end; and at that point, you put the story down on paper, working toward that end in the manner we've described—with speed, or at least steadiness, and voice and characterization.

It's a kind of genius, a commonplace, to begin a short story, not quite knowing where you'll end up—but it's madness, and foolishness, to set out on such a journey in nonfiction.

I'm reminded of the quote in the front of Edward Abbey's novel, *Good News,* a quote by B. Traven: "This is the real world, muchachos, and you are in it." Nonfiction demands a greater responsibility, a greater maturity, sometimes—more discipline— than any other form of writing—and, as in real life, it's easier to foul up.

This may be a typically and sadly male attitude, but I always view going out on a nonfiction assignment like, I suppose, going into battle, or at least into a high-stakes athletic event: I try to get psyched weeks beforehand, and get up for it, and to go sailing into it at full excitement, full sensitivity, full receptivity, or what-have-you—a heightened alertness, trying to notice everything, trying to put everything down on paper, trying to see everything (I'll sort it out back at home) because often there's only going to be that one chance, that one situation. You're going to see the world differently, on a different day, and so is your subject, or subjects. This is why the idea for the story sometimes gets flatter and flatter, upon return trips to pick up "loose ends." It's rarely as alive to you as that first time, and if you don't get it that first time, chances are you may not get it: *it* being the most lively, entertaining version of the story—the truth—that you can capture—and for that reason, I like to hit the story running at full tilt, with nothing else mattering in the world: a sort of do-or-die attitude.

Again, this contrasts markedly with the somewhat luxuriant practice, in fiction, of being able to pause, and let things ferment, waiting for lightning to strike, all the while building up your ideas and themes with the encrustations of time. In nonfiction, you've got to strike while the iron's hot. There's extra pressure, as a result, but there's also extra gratification, from having performed under that pressure, and performed well.

I had a wonderful nonfiction writing professor—the naturalist Tom Lyon—who inadvertently nearly stopped me from writing anything one semester by saying, "Before you sit down to write anything, always remember that you are going to have to make what you are about to say be worth the life of the tree that was cut down in the forest to give you the paper you are writing on."

This is the same man who had this to say about writing nonfiction: "Before you start, sit alone in a dark room for a while, and listen to your heart beating, try to feel the blood moving through your body."

Perhaps he was, and is a pantheist, a mystic. But nonfiction deserves this: on the one hand it can be viewed as being more mundane and ordinary—more *everyday* than fiction—but on the other hand, it can be viewed as being more sacred, because it deals with the here-and-now, without disguise, without safety. It can be about the brutalities and wonders of *real* lives—our lives, and our friends' lives, not just art-conjured lives—and to show these illuminations and wonders can be at least as challenging to the writer and as satisfying to the reader as any other medium. It's the easiest to fail at, I believe, and yet also—or perhaps therefore—can be the most important. I think we tend, as writers, to write fiction when we have time to dally—to look ahead, and muse, or to cast back, and reminisce, or to figure things out, secret things—mystery—but when the stakes are high, when the world's caving in and the food and air and water are being poisoned, we turn instinctively to the nonfiction: and for this reason, we need to learn how to be able to do it well. Sometimes there are not second chances to say the most important things.

Double Take

1. Bass writes, "voice is the most important aspect of nonfiction; it's the controlling force of the writing." What does "voice" in writing mean to you? How would you describe your own writing voice? What does it sound like? Why do you think it sounds that way?

2. What makes nonfiction essay writing riskier than fiction writing, according to Bass? Why is it more suited to high-stakes, serious subjects?
3. What can you learn about writing, your own and that of others, from reading this essay? What sticks with you as useful advice about writing, advice you might keep in mind when you write? What advice do you find less useful or do you disagree with?
4. Alone or in groups, think about which qualities of good essay writing that Bass describes most apply to the kind of writing you are doing in this class or other classes you are currently taking. Be prepared to discuss why (or why not) these qualities apply.

At First Glance

"On Willow Creek" was first published in the Los Angeles Times Magazine, *which most likely means it was read by people who live in the city and whose lives are to some extent removed from the wild places Bass cherishes. Given that this essay is in part a plea for the preservation of wild places such as the Texas Hill Country, consider whether or not Bass's arguments for such preservation are effective. Try to imagine how readers would have reacted to Bass's examples and arguments. Think about what would make them work or not. Think about what sort of persona Bass creates, especially at the beginning of the essay, and how that persona works for or against the credibility he is trying to create.*

On Willow Creek

I don't know how to start, but perhaps that's no matter. I am only thirty-five years old, and the land is over a billion; how can I be expected to know what to say beyond "Please" and "Thank you" and "Ma'am"? The language of the hill country of Texas, or of any sacred place, is not the language of pen on paper, or even of the human voice. It is the language of water cutting down through the country's humped chest of granite, cutting down to the heart and soul of the earth, down to a thing that lies far below and beyond our memory.

Being frail and human, however, memory is all we have to work with. I have to believe that somewhere out there is a point where my language—memory—will intersect with the hill country's language: the scent of cedar, the feel of morning mist, the blood of deer, glint of moon, shimmering heat, crackle of ice, mountain lions, scorpions, centipedes, rattlesnakes, and cactus. The cool dark oaks and gold-leaved hickories along the creeks; the language of the hill country seems always to return to water. Along the creeks is where most of the wildlife is found. It is along a creek that the men in my family built a hunting cabin sixty years ago. We have lived in

Texas for a hundred and twenty years, and the men in my family have always hunted deer—hunting them in Tennessee before that, and Mississippi, and perhaps all the way back to the dawn of man, to the first hunter—perhaps that link across the generations is completely unbroken, one of the few unfragmented systems remaining in this century—*The Basses hunt deer*—a small thing, but still whole and intact.

It is only for the last sixty years, however, that we've hunted deer—once a year, in November—on this thousand acres deep in the hill country.

Sixty years. The land changes so much more slowly than we do. We race across it, gathering it all in—the scents, the sounds, the feel of that thousand acres. Granddaddy's gone, now; Uncle Horace, John Dallas, Howard, gone too: already I've lived long enough to see these men in my family cross that intersection where they finally learn and embrace the real language of the earth—the language of granite, and history—leaving us, the survivors, behind, still speaking of them in terms of memory.

We have not yet quite caught up with the billion-year-old land we love and which harbors us, but as we get older, we're beginning to learn a word or two, and beginning to see (especially as we have children) how our own lives start to cut knifelike down through all that granite, the stone hump of the hill country, until we are like rivers and creeks ourselves, and we reach the end and the bottom, and *then* we understand . . .

Water. The cities and towns to the south and east of the hill country—Austin, San Antonio, Houston, La Grange, Uvalde, Goliad—I could chart them all, thousands of them, for they are all my home—these towns, these cities, and these people drink from the heart of the hill country. The water in their bodies is the water that has come from beneath the hills, from the mystical two-hundred-mile-long underground river called the Edwards Aquifer. The water is gathered in the hill country by the forces of nature, percolates down through the hills and mountains and flows south, underground, toward the ocean.

That water which we don't drink or pump onto our crops or give to our livestock—that tiny part which eludes us—continues on to the Gulf Coast, into the bays and estuaries, where delicate moisture contents, delicate salinities are maintained for the birds, shrimp, and other coastal inhabitants that at first glance seem to be far away from and unrelated to the inland mountains.

A scientist will tell you that it's all connected—that if you live in Texas you must protect the honor and integrity of that country's core, for you are tied to it, it is as much a part of you as family—but if you are a child and given to daydreaming and wondering, I believe that you'll understand this by instinct. You don't need proof that the water moving through those shady creeks up in the wild hills and mountains is the same that later moves through your body. You can instead stand outside—even in the city, even in such a place as Houston, and look north with the wind in your face (or with a salt breeze at your back, carrying your essence back to the hill country like an offering), and you can feel the tremble and shimmer of that magic underground river, the yearning and timelessness of it, just beneath your seven-year-old feet. You can *know* of the allegiance you owe it, can sense this in a way that not even the scientists know. It is more like the way when you are in your mother's arms, or your grandmother's, that you know it's all tied together, and that someday you are going to understand it all.

Of course that's the point of this story, that I was one of those children, and that I am here to say thank you to the country in which I was birthed, and to ask "please" that the last good part of it not be divided into halves and then quarters and then eighths, and on, then, further divided into the invisibility of neglect or dishonor . . .

The men would go north in the fall—my father and his brother Jimmy, driving up to the hill country from Houston, while Granddaddy—only barely a granddaddy then, which now seems unimaginable—came down from Fort Worth.

They would meet up in the high hills and low mountains, in the center of the state. I'd stand there on the back porch in Houston with my mother and watch them drive off—it would often be raining, and I'd step out into the rain to feel it on my face—and I'd know that they were going to a place of wildness, a place where they came from. I'd know it was an act of honor, of ritual, of integrity. I was that boy, and knew these things, but did not seriously believe that I would ever be old enough to go in the fall myself.

Instead, I sought out those woods I could reach. We lived out near the west edge of Houston, near what is now the Beltway, a few hundred yards from the slow curls of Buffalo Bayou. While the men in my family went up to the hill country (and at all other times of the year), I would spend my time in the tiny de facto wilderness between outlying subdivisions. Back in those still-undeveloped woods was a stagnating swamp, an old oxbow cut off from the rest of the bayou; you had to almost get lost to find it. I called it "Hidden Lake," and I would wade out into the swamp and seine for minnows, crawdads, mud puppies, and polliwogs with a soup strainer. In those woods, not a mile from the Houston city limits, I saw turtles, bats, skunks, snakes, raccoons, deer, flying squirrels, rabbits, and armadillos. There were bamboo thickets too, and of course the bayou itself, with giant alligator gars floating in patches of sunlit chocolate water, and Spanish moss hanging back in the old forest, and wild violets growing along the bayou's banks. A lot of wilderness can exist in a small place, if it is the right kind of country: a good country.

That country was of course too rich to last. The thick oaks fell to the saws, as did the dense giant hickories and the sun-towering, wind-murmuring pines. It's all concrete now; even the banks of the bayou have been channeled with cement. I remember my shock of finding the first survey stakes, out in the grasslands (where once there had been buffalo) leading into those big woods along the bayou's rich edge. I remember asking my mother if the survey stakes meant someone was going to build a house out there—a cabin, perhaps. When told that a road was coming, I pulled the stakes up, but the road came anyway, and then the office buildings, and the highway, and the subdivisions.

The men would come back from the woods after a week. They would have bounty with them—a deer strapped to the hood of the car, heavy with antlers (in those days people in the city did not have trucks), or a wild turkey. A pocket of blackjack acorns; a piece of granite. An old rusting wolf trap found while out walking; an arrowhead. A piece of iron ore, red as rubies. A quartz boulder for my mother's garden. And always, they brought back stories: more stories, it seemed, than you could ever tell.

Sometimes my father or uncle would have something new about him—something that I had not seen when he'd left. A cut in the webbing of his hand from where he'd been cleaning the deer. Or a light in his eyes, a kind of *easiness*. A smell of woodsmoke. Beard stubble, sometimes. These were men who had moved to the city and taken city jobs, who drove to work every morning wearing a suit, but they came back from the hill country with the beginnings of beards. There was always something different about them. The woods had marked them.

Because my parents could see that I had an instinctive draw to the animal world— to be more frank, because they could see that I was aflame with the wild—they did their best to keep me nourished, there in the city. My mother took me to the zoo every week, where I'd spend hours looking at the animals with a joy and an excitement, looking at exhibits which would not crush me with sadness. We went to the Museum of Natural History every Saturday. I heard lectures on jumping spiders and wolf spiders. I breathed window fog against the aquarium panes as I watched the giant soft-shelled turtles paddle slowly through their underwater eerie green light. I bought a little rock sample of magnetite from the gift shop. The little placard that came with the magnetite said it had come from Llano County, Texas. That was one of the two counties my father and uncle and grandfather hunted (the thousand acres straddled Llano and Gillespie counties). This only fueled the fire of my love for a country I had not even seen—a country I could feel in my heart, however, and could feel in my hands, all the way to the tips of my fingers: a country whose energy, whose shimmering life-force, resonated all the way out into the plains, down into the flatlands.

All that sweet water, just beneath our feet. But only so much of it: not inexhaustible. We couldn't, or weren't supposed to, take more than was given to us. That was one of the rules of the system. My father, and the other men who hunted it, understood about this system, and other such systems; for them, the land—like our family itself—was a continuum. Each year, each step hiked across those steep slickrock hills cut down deeper into the rocks, deeper into memory, gave them more stories, more knowledge, and at the same time, took them ever closer to the mystery that lay at the base of it.

I'd grip that rough glittering magnetite like a talisman, would put my fingers to it and try to feel how it was different from other rocks—would try to feel the pull, the affinity it had for things made of iron. I'd hold it up to my arms and try to feel if it stirred my blood, and I believed that I *could* feel it . . .

I'd fall asleep listening to the murmur of the baseball game on the radio with the rock stuck magically to the iron frame of my bed. In the morning I would sometimes take the rock and place it up against my father's compass. I'd watch as the needle always followed the magnetite, and I felt my heart, and everything else inside me, swing with that compass needle, too.

When we run out of country, we will run out of stories.

When we run out of stories, we will run out of sanity.

We will not be able to depend on each other for anything—not for friendship or mercy, and certainly not for love or understanding.

Of course we shouldn't protect a wild core such as the Texas hill country because it is a system still intact with the logic and sanity that these days too often eludes our lives in the cities. We should instead protect the hill country simply for its own sake, to show that we are still capable of understanding (and practicing) the concept of honor: loving a thing the way it is, and trying, for once, not to change it.

I like to think that in the sixty years we've been hunting and camping on that rough, hidden thousand acres—through which Willow Creek cuts, flows, forks, and twists, with murmuring little waterfalls over one- and two-foot ledges, the water sparkling—that we have not changed the humped land one bit.

I know that it has changed us. My grandfather hunted that country, as have his sons, and now we, my brothers and cousins, hunt it with them, and in the spring, we now bring our young children into the country to show them the part, the huge part, that is not hunting (and yet which for us is all inseparable from the hunting): the fields of bluebonnets and crimson paintbrushes, the baby raccoons, the quail, the zonetail hawks and buzzards circling Hudson Mountain, the pink capitol domes of granite rising all through the land as if once here lived a civilization even more ancient than our parents, grandparents, and great-grandparents.

A continuous thing is so rare these days, when fragmentation seems more than ever to be the rule. I remember the first time I walked with my daughter on the thousand acres, on the land our family calls the "deer pasture." The loose disintegrating granite chat crunched under her tiny tennis shoes and she gripped my finger tight to keep from falling, and the sound of that gravel underfoot (the pink mountains being worn away, along with our bodies) was a sound I'd heard all my life at the deer pasture, but this time, this first time with my daughter gripping my finger and looking down at the loose pink gravel that was making that sound, it affected me so strongly that I felt faint, felt so light that I thought I might take flight. . . .

A country, a landscape, can be sacred in an infinite number of ways. The quartz boulders in my mother's garden: my father brought her one each year, and I thought, and still think, it was one of the most romantic things I'd seen, that even while he was in the midst of wildness that one week each year, he was still thinking of her.

Other families had store-bought Doug fir or blue spruce trees for Christmas; we had the spindly strange mountain juniper ("cedar") from the deer pasture. Even though we lived to the south, we were still connected to that wild core, and these rituals and traditions were important to us, so fiercely felt and believed in that one might even call them a form of worship. We were raised Protestants, but in our hearts' and bodies' innocence were cutting a very fine line, tightroping along the mystical edge of pantheism. When Granddaddy was dying, just this side of his ninetieth year, and we went to see him in the hospital room in Fort Worth, I took a handful of arrowhead fragments from the deer pasture and put them under his bed. It seemed inconceivable to me that he not die as he had lived, always in some kind of contact with that wildness, and the specificity of that thousand acres.

When Mom was sick—small, young, and beautiful, the strongest and best patient the doctors had ever had, they all said—and she was sick a long time, living for years solely on the fire and passion within, long after the marrow had left her bones and the doctors could not bring it back, and when she still never had anything other than a smile for each day—my father and brothers and I would take turns bringing her flowers from the deer pasture.

One of us would walk in through the door with that vase from the wild. There would be store-bought flowers, too, but those splashes of reds, yellows, and blues, from lands she'd walked, lands she knew, are what lit up her face the most. The specificity of our lives together, and of our love: those colors said it as well as the land can say anything—which is to say, perfectly. Indian paintbrushes. Bluebonnets. Liatris. Shooting stars. I'm certain those flowers helped her as much as did our platelets, the very blood and iron of ourselves, which we also shared with her. She really loved wildflowers, and she really loved the hill and brush country of Texas, and she really *loved us.*

My mother loved to drink iced tea. Sometimes she and my father and brothers and I would go up to the deer pasture in the dead sullen heat of summer, in the shimmering brightness. We'd ride around in the jeep wearing straw hats. We'd get out and walk down the creek, to the rock slide: a stream-polished half-dome of pink granite with a sheet of water trickling over it, a twenty-foot slide into the plunge pool below, with cool clear water six feet deep, and a mud turtle (his face striped yellow, as if with war paint) and two big Midland soft-shelled turtles living in that pond. An osprey nest, huge branches and sticks, rested up in the dead cottonwood at the pool's edge.

My brothers and I would slide down the half-dome and into the pool again and again. A hundred degrees, in the summer, and we'd go up and down that algae-slick rock like otters. We'd chase the turtles, would hold our breath and swim after them, paddling underwater in that lucid water, while our parents sat up in the rocks above and watched. What a gift it is, to see one's children happy, and engaged in the world, loving it.

We'd walk farther down the creek, then: a family. Fuller. My mother would finish her tea; would rattle the ice cubes in her plastic cup. She'd crunch the ice cubes, in that heat. She always drank her tea with a sprig of mint in it. At some point on one of our walks she must have tossed her ice cubes and mint sprig out, because now there are two little mint fields along the creek: one by the camp house, and one down at the water gap. I like to sit in the rocks above those little mint patches for hours, and look, and listen, and smell, and think. I feel the sun dappling on my arms, and watch the small birds flying around in the old oak and cedar along the creek. Goshawks courting, in April, and wild turkeys gobbling. I like to sit there above the mint fields and feel my soul cutting down through that bedrock. It's happening fast. I too am becoming the earth.

Seen from below as it drifts high in the hot blue sky, a zonetail hawk looks just like the vultures it floats with, save for its yellow legs. (Vultures' legs are gray.) The zonetail's prey will glance up, study the vultures for a moment, and then resume nibbling grass. Then the zonetail will drop from that flock of vultures like a bowling ball.

Afterwards, if there is anything left of the prey, perhaps the vultures can share in the kill.

Golden-cheeked warblers come up into this country from Mexico, endangered, exotic blazes of color who have chosen to grace the hill country with their nests in the spring. They place their hopes for the future, for survival, deep in the cool shade of the old-growth cedars, in only the oldest cedars whose bark peels off in tatters and wisps like feathers, the feathery old bark which the warblers must have to build their nests. But as the old-growth cedar is cut to make way for more and more rangeland, the brown cowbird, a drab bully that follows the heavy ways of cattle, lays its eggs in the warblers' delicate nests and then flees, leaving the warbler mother with these extra eggs to take care of. The cowbird nestlings are larger, and they outclamor the warbler babies for food, and push the beautiful gold-cheeked warbler babies out of the nest.

Why must the ways of man, and the things associated with man, be so clumsy? Can't we relearn grace (and all the other things that follow from that: mercy, love, friendship, understanding) by studying the honor and integrity of a system, one of the last systems, that's still intact? Why must we bring our cowbirds with us, everywhere we go? Must we break everything that is special to us, or sacred—unknown, and holy—into halves, and then fourths, and then eighths?

What happens to us when all the sacred, all the *whole* is gone—when there is no more whole? There will be only fragments of stories, fragments of culture, fragments of integrity. Even a child standing on the porch in Houston with the rain in his face can look north and know that it is all tied together, that we are the warblers, we are the zonetails, we are the underground river: that it is all holy, and that some of it should not be allowed to disappear, as has so much, and so many of us, already.

Sycamores grow by running water; cottonwoods grow by still water. If we know the simple mysteries, then think of all the complex mysteries that lie just beneath us, buried in the bedrock: the bedrock we have been entrusted with protecting. How could we dare do anything other than protect and honor this last core, the land from which we came, the land that has marked us, and whose essence, whose mystery, contains our own essence and mystery? How can we *conceive* of severing that last connection? Surely all internal fire, all passion, would vanish.

Stories. On my Uncle Jimmy's left calf, there is a scar from where the wild pigs caught him one night. He and my father were coming back to camp after dark when they got between a sow and boar and their piglets. The piglets squealed in fright, which ignited the rage of the sow and boar. My father went up one tree and Uncle Jimmy up another, but the boar caught Jimmy with his tusk, cut the muscle clean to the bone.

Back in camp, Granddaddy and John Dallas and Howard and old Mr. Brooks (there for dominoes, that night) heard all the yelling, as did their dogs. The men came running with hounds and lanterns, globes of light swinging crazily through the woods. They stumbled into the middle of the pigs, too. My father and Uncle Jimmy were up in the tops of small trees like raccoons. There were pigs everywhere, pigs and dogs fighting, men dropping their lanterns and climbing trees . . . That one sow and boar could have held an entire *town* at bay. They ran the dogs off and kept the men treed there in the darkness for over an hour, Uncle Jimmy's pants leg wet with blood, and fireflies blinking down on the creek below, and the boar's angry grunts, the sow's furious snufflings below, and the frightened murmurs and squeals of the little pigs. The logic of that system was inescapable: *don't get between a sow and boar and their young.*

The land, and our stories, have marked us.

My father and I are geologists. Uncle Jimmy and his two youngest sons manufacture steel pipe and sell it for use in drilling down through bedrock in search of oil, gas, and water. Our hunting cabin is made of stone. We have a penchant for building stone walls. Our very lives are a metaphor for embracing the earth: for gripping boulders and lifting them to our chest and stacking them and building a life in and around and among the country's heart. I've sat in those same boulders on the east side and watched a mother bobcat and her two kittens come down to the creek to drink. There used to be an occasional jaguar in this part of the world, traveling up from Mexico, but that was almost a hundred years ago. Granddaddy would be ninety this October. He and the old guy we leased from, Howard, were born in the same year, 1903, which was the number we used for the lock combination on the last gate leading into the property. It's one of the last places in the world that still makes sense to me. It is the place of my family, but it is more: it is a place that still abides by its own rules. The creeks have not yet been channeled with concrete. There is still a wildness beating beneath the rocks, and in the atoms of every thing.

Each year, we grow closer to the land. Each year, it marks us deeper. The lightning strike that burned the top of what is now called the Burned-Off Hill: we saw firsthand how for twenty years the wildlife preferred that area, but finally the protein content has been lowered again, and it is time for another fire.

The dead rattlesnake my cousin Rick and I found out on the highway two years ago: we put it in the back of the truck along with the wood for that night's campfire: put it down there in the middle of all that wood. That night Russell and Randy unloaded the wood, gathering great big armloads of it. Rick and I shined the flashlights in Russell's face then, and he realized he'd gathered up a great big armload of rattlesnake. We yelled at him to drop that snake, but he couldn't, it was all tangled up everywhere, all around his arms.

The land and its stories, and our stories: the time Randy and I were picking up one of what would be the new cabin's four cornerstones, to load into the truck. August. Randy dropped his end of the sandstone slab (about the size of a coffin) but didn't get his hand free in time. It might have been my fault. The quarter-ton of rock smashed off the end of his left pinky. No more tea sipping for Cousin Randy. He sat down, stunned in the heat, and stared at the crushed pulpy end of that little finger. I thought strangely how some small part of it was already mashed in between the atoms of the rock, and how his blood was already dripping back into the iron-rich soil. Randy tried to shake off the pain, tried to stand and resume work, but the second he did his eyes rolled heavenward and he turned ghost-white in that awful heat and fell to the ground, and began rolling down the steep hill, to the bottom of the gulch. All the little birds and other animals back in the cool shade of the oaks and cedars were resting, waiting for night to cool things off. What an odd creature man is, they had to be thinking. But we couldn't wait for night, or its coolness. We were aflame with a love for that wild land, and our long, rock-sure history on it: our loving place on it.

Granddaddy knew the old Texan's trick of luring an armadillo in close by tossing pebbles in the dry leaves. The armadillo, with its radar-dish ears, believes the sound is that of jumping insects, and will follow the sound of your tossed pebbles right up to your feet before it understands the nearsighted image of your boot or tennis shoe and leaps straight up, sneezes, then flees in wild alarm.

There is a startling assemblage of what I think of as "tender" life up there, seemingly a paradox for such a harsh, rocky, hot country. Cattails along the creeks, tucked in between those folds of granite, those narrow canyons with names like Fat Man's Misery and boulder-strewn cataclysms such as Hell's Half Acre. Newts, polliwogs, bullfrogs, leopard frogs, mud turtles, pipits and wagtails, luna moths and viceroys, ferns and mosses . . .

The old rock, the beautiful outcrops, are the power of the hill country, but the secret, the mystery, is the water; that's what brings the rock to life.

It's so hard to write about such nearly indefinable abstractions as yearning or mystery, or to convince someone who's not yet convinced about the necessity and holiness of wildness. It's hard in this day and age to convince people of just how tiny and short-lived we are, and how that makes the wild more, not less, important. All of the hill country's creatures had helped me in this regard. It was along Willow Creek where as a child of nine or ten I had gone down with a flashlight to get a bucket of water. It was December, Christmas Eve, and bitterly cold. In the creek's eddies there was half an inch of ice over the shallow pools. I had never before seen ice in the wild.

I shined my flashlight onto that ice. The creek made its trickling murmur, cutting down the center of the stream between the ice banks on either side, cutting through the ice like a knife, but in the eddies the ice was thick enough to hold the weight of a fallen branch or a small rock, a piece of iron ore.

There were fish swimming under that ice! Little green perch. The creek was only a few yards wide, but it had fish in it, living just beneath the ice! Why weren't they dead? How could they live beneath the surface of ice, as if in another system, another universe? Wasn't it too cold for them?

The blaze of my flashlight stunned them into a hanging kind of paralysis; they hung as suspended as mobiles, unblinking.

I tapped on the ice and they stirred a little, but still I could not get their full attention. They were listening to something else—to the gurgle of the creek, to the tilt of the planet, or the pull of the moon. I tapped on the ice again. Up at the cabin, someone called my name. I was getting cold, and had to go back. Perhaps I left the first bit of my civility—my first grateful relinquishing of it—there under that strange ice, for the little green fish to carry downstream and return to its proper place, to the muck and moss beneath an old submerged log. I ran up to the cabin with the bucket of cold water, as fresh and alive as we can ever hope to be, having been graced with the sight and idea of something new, something wild, something just beyond my reach.

I remember one winter night, camped down at the deer pasture, when a rimy ice fog had moved in, blanketing the hill country. I was just a teenager. I had stepped outside for a moment for the fresh cold air; everyone else was still in the cabin, playing dominoes. (Granddaddy smoked like a chimney.) I couldn't see a thing in all that cold fog. There was just the sound of the creek running past camp; as it always has, as I hope it always will.

Then I heard the sound of a goose honking—approaching from the north. There is no sound more beautiful, especially at night, and I stood there and listened. Another goose joined in—that wild, magnificent honking—and then another.

It seemed, standing there in the dark, with the cabin's light behind me (the *snap! snap! snap!* sound of Granddaddy the domino king playing his ivories against the linoleum table), that I could barely stand the hugeness, the unlimited future of life. I could feel my youth, could feel my heart beating, and it seemed those geese were coming straight for me, as if they too could feel that barely controlled wildness, and were attracted to it.

When they were directly above me, they began to fly in circles, more geese joining them. They came lower and lower, until I could hear the underlying readiness of those resonant honks; I could hear their grunts, their intake of air before each honk.

My father came out to see what was going on.

"They must be lost," he said. "This fog must be all over the hill country. Our light may be the only one they can see for miles," he said. "They're probably looking for a place to land, to rest for the night, but can't find their way down through the fog."

The geese were still honking and flying in circles, not a hundred feet over our heads. I'm sure they could hear the gurgle of the creek below. I stared up into the fog, expecting to see the first brave goose come slipping down through that fog, wings set in a glide of faith for the water it knew was just below. *They were so close to it.*

But they did not come. They circled our camp all night, keeping us awake; trying, it seemed, to *pray* that fog away with their honking, their sweet music; and in the morning, both the fog and the geese were gone, and it seemed that some part of me was gone with them, some tame or civilized part, and they had left behind a boy, a young man, who was now thoroughly wild, and who thoroughly loved wild things. And I often still have the dream I had that night, that I was up with the geese, up in the cold night, peering down at the fuzzy glow of the cabin lights in the fog, that dim beacon of hope and mystery, safety and longing.

The geese flew away with the last of my civility that night, but I realize now it was a theft that had begun much earlier in life. That's one of the greatest blessings of the hill country, and all wildness: it is a salve, a twentieth-century poultice to take away the crippling fever of too-much civility, too-much numbness.

★★★

The first longing years of my life that were spent exploring those small and doomed hemmed-in woods around Houston sometimes seem like days of the imagination, compared against my later days in the hill country. It seemed, when I went to Hidden Lake, or to the zoo, or the arboretum, or the museum, that I was only treading water.

I fell asleep each night with my aquariums bubbling, the postgame baseball show murmuring on the radio. That magic rock from Llano County, the magnetite, stuck to the side of my bed like a remora, or a guardian, seeing me through the night, and perhaps filling me with a strange energy, a strange allegiance for a place I had not yet seen.

Finally the day came when I was old enough for my first hunting trip up to the deer pasture. My father took me up there for "the second hunt," in late December. I would not go on the first hunt, the November hunt, until after I was out of college, and a hunter. The "second hunt" was a euphemism for just camping, for hiking around, and for occasionally carrying a rifle.

My father and I drove through the night in his old green-and-white 1956 Ford— through country I'd never seen, beneath stars I'd never seen. My father poured black coffee from an old thermos to stay awake. The trip took a long time, in those days— over six hours, with gravel clattering beneath the car for the last couple of hours.

I put my hand against the car window. It was colder, up in the hills. The stars were brighter. When I couldn't stay awake any longer—overwhelmed by the senses—I climbed into the back seat and wrapped up in an old Hudson's Bay blanket and lay down and slept. The land's rough murmur and jostling beneath me was a lullaby.

When I awoke, we had stopped for gas in Llano. We were the only car at the service station. We were surrounded by a pool of light. I could see the dark woods at the edge of the gravel parking lot, could smell the cedar. My father was talking to the gas-station attendant. Before I was all the way awake, I grabbed a flashlight and got out and hurried out toward the woods. I went into the cedars, got down on my hands and knees, and with the flashlight began searching for the magnetite that I was sure was all over the place. I picked up small red rocks and held them against the metal flashlight to see if they'd stick.

When my father and the attendant came and got me out of the woods and asked where I had been going and what I'd been doing, I told them, "Looking for magnetite." How hard it must be, to be an adult.

We drove on: an improbable series of twists and turns, down washed-out canyons and up ridges, following thin caliche roads that shone ghostly white in the moonlight. I did not know then that I would come to learn every bend in those roads, every dip and rise, by heart. We clattered across a high-centered narrow cattle guard, and then another, and were on the property that we'd been leasing for thirty years— the thousand acres, our heart.

It was so cold. We were on our land. We did not own it, but it was ours because we loved it, belonged to it, and because we were engaged in its system. It dictated our movements as surely as it did those of any winter-range deer herd, any migrating warbler. It was ours because we loved it.

We descended toward the creek, and our cabin. The country came into view, brilliant in the headlights. Nighthawks flittered and flipped in the road before us, danced eerie acrobatic flights that looked as if they were trying to smother the dust in the road with their soft wings. Their eyes were glittering red in the headlights. It was as if we had stumbled into a witches' coven, but I wasn't frightened. They weren't bad witches; they were just wild.

Giant jackrabbits, with ears as tall again as they were, raced back and forth before us—leaped six feet into the air and reversed direction mid-leap, hit the ground running: a sea of jackrabbits before us, flowing, the high side of their seven-year cycle. A coyote darted into our headlights' beams, grabbed a jackrabbit, and raced away. One jackrabbit sailed over the hood of our car, coming so close to the windshield that I could see his wide, manic eyes, looking so human. A buck deer loped across the road, just ahead. It was an explosion of life, all around us. Moths swarmed our headlights.

We had arrived at the wild place.

Double Take

1. What sort of persona does Bass create at the beginning of the essay? Why do you think he chooses to begin this way? What does such a rhetorical move do for the essay and its subject? Is it effective?
2. What evidence does Bass give to support his argument for the preservation of the Texas Hill Country? Describe some of the evidence and explain why you think it might or might not work given his audience and his purpose.
3. Bass writes, "it's so hard . . . to convince someone who's not yet convinced about the necessity and holiness of wildness." In which parts of the essay do you think Bass demonstrates the most awareness of his audience who might not yet be convinced? That is, in which places do you think Bass is most clearly directing his argument to those people who are not convinced? How can you tell?
4. What is the relationship for Bass between wild country, stories, and sanity? How does his essay exhibit this relationship? What does this relationship mean to you?

At First Glance

Bass wrote "Why I Hunt" for Esquire *magazine. As you read this essay, think about what that means. Who reads* Esquire? *What shared values and assumptions might these readers hold? To help you understand the context for this essay, and also to help you account for how and why Bass wrote it the way he did, go to your school library and browse through some issues of the magazine. Use the information you gather to help you account for the nature of Bass's argument and to assist you in anticipating how readers would have reacted to it. Certainly, hunting is a sensitive issue for some people. As you read through Bass's defense of hunting, think about whether Bass is careful in his treatment of the subject (whether or not he demonstrates awareness of the sensitive nature of the subject). Regardless of your view of the subject, do you find his argument compelling?*

Why I Hunt: A Predator's Meditation

In the fall, it's what I want to do. It would be unnatural and dishonest to sit on my hands; I'm a hunter, a predator (in the fall), with eyes in front of my head, like a bear's, or a wolf's, or even an owl's. Prey have their eyes on the sides of their heads, in order to see in all directions, in order to be ready to run. But predators—and that's us, or at least some of us—have our eyes before us, out in front, with which to focus, to a single point. For two months of the year—or until I have killed one deer and one elk—that's what I do. I want to be out in the woods, walking quietly, walking slowly—or not walking at all but just sitting in some leaves, completely hidden and motionless—waiting, and waiting. To not pursue the thing one wants would be a waste of one's life.

In the fall, I can do things I couldn't do in my normal, civilized life. I can disappear into the woods, and over the next mountain, the next ridge. My roaming has meaning—it's no longer just roaming, but *hunting.* The year's meat supply is in question. My meat, my family's meat—not some rancher's heifer from Minnesota. Meat from my valley, where I hope to live and die—where I cut firewood, where I pick huckleberries, where I walk, where I watch the stars—my valley.

For those two months, I am *after* something: something tangible, something that's moving away from me, and something that I must have, for the coming year. It's as simple as that.

Over the next ridge. The new life of stores and towns falls away, and the old life returns. There's a loveliness to looking ahead—looking *straight* ahead—that only hunting brings out.

The other ten months are okay, too—I can be the artist, can loll around eating grapes and reading poetry, but the fall comes like a splash of water to my face on a hot, dusty day; and the dust, and my new ways, new feelings—the ones bound by rules—are washed away, leaving the old ways revealed.

I keep eating those lovely candlelit dinners—grouse and potatoes, and the red, almost *purple* heartthrob steaks from elk; fried trout for breakfast, and homemade huckleberry jam. . . . I feel alive. . . . I draw immense strength from those meals, strength to live my life, and it feels *good.* I eat about a pound and a half of meat a day. The cancer studies for this kind of diet alarm me, but I have to trust that they apply to fatty steroid beef, and cattle that must have been raised in pesticide fields. I was seven miles into the mountains when I shot last year's elk, and I carried him out in three trips over a twenty-four-hour period.

Into those same dark woods I go each year, looking straight ahead, and stopping, and listening, and turning my head. . . .

Of course, it's possible that there's a greater life force that judges us; and of course, sometimes I feel guilty about being a hunter, a killer—a killer of deer and elk, though not moose, because they're too easy, and not bears, because . . . well, bears themselves are meant to hunt. During part of the year they're predators, not prey. It seems unnatural to hunt predators.

I'm scared, sometimes, that all the animals I've killed—few as they are—add up, and that I'm liable for them.

I wouldn't mind paying for them with my life someday—we must all give up our lives—but sometimes I get scared I may have to pay afterward, in the afterlife, for my gluttony, my insatiable hunger for clean meat, and so much of it.

Nonetheless, I've studied it, and have come up with this: I am who I am, and I've come from the place we all come from—the past—but I still remember, and love, that place. Some of us are glad to be away from that place, but I'm not one of those people—not in the fall.

The worst day I ever had hunting was when I shot an elk in the neck, where I was aiming, but it made me feel strangely ashamed, after it was over. I broke the elk's neck, the way I always try to do—that instant drop—but he groaned when I walked up to him. He couldn't have been feeling anything, and I hope it was just air leaving his lungs—but it was still a groan.

For a fact—or rather, for me—hunting's better than killing. It takes a while, after it's over—sometimes a long while—before you can think of it as meat. You can't go straight from a living animal to 250 pounds of elk steaks. There's too much knife and ax work involved—and you're the one who has to do it—skinning the animal, and pulling the hide back to reveal your crime, the meat—and already, sometimes, the call of ravens drifting in, black-winged shapes flying through the treetops, past the sun. . . .

Instead of trying to make that instantaneous conversion—which I cannot do—life to meat—what I do is pray, sort of. I give heartfelt, shaky thanks to the animal as I clean it—ravens calling to ravens—and I do this with deer and grouse too, and even, if I can remember—which I don't always—with fish. A man or a woman who apologizes for hunting is a fool. It's a man's, or a woman's, choice, and he or she must live with it.

I don't do it for profit or gain; and rarely do I tell anyone about it after I've done it.

I watch ravens in the off-season. I think ravens have more of a soul than humans—and I think ravens understand the hunt better than I ever will. Sometimes ravens, in Alaska, lead hunters—wolves, or humans—to prey, and then they eat the pickings from the kill.

Ravens, black as coal, shiny and greasy, flying in the sun, like winged, black devils. . . I feel as if I'm on their side, and it scares me, but it would be a lie, in the fall, to switch sides: to pretend that I'm not. I'm a killer, sometimes. I wish I weren't, but I am. I've wrestled with it but can't escape it, any more than—until death—one can escape one's skin.

Double Take

1. Why do you think Bass chose to make the first part of his title so direct? Do you think it was a smart choice? What about the second part? What effect does the word "meditation" evoke?

2. Bass seems to build his argument on certain premises such as "to not pursue the thing one wants would be a waste of one's life." Do you think his readers would accept this premise? What happens to his argument if they do not?

3. What do you think are Bass's most effective, compelling arguments in this essay? What makes them so?

4. As a writer you will be asked to write lots of argument-based papers in school. What can you learn about developing written arguments from reading this essay? Does Bass have a clear claim? Are his examples appropriate? Does the essay demonstrate a clear organization? Does he anticipate counterarguments? Use examples from the essay in formulating an overall evaluation, similar to one your teacher might write in response to your own writing.

Seeing for Yourself

At First Glance

Of all the essays we have collected here, "Thunder and Lightning" is the most overtly "activist." It has the most explicit agenda: to expand the wilderness protected area of the Rocky Mountains to include the Yaak Valley and its low-level rainforest. It is also the most directly connected to an organization, the Sierra Club, and published in the club's magazine, Sierra. *Before you begin to read the essay, think about what it means to be an activist. Then, as you start to read, examine if your assumptions are borne out in the essay. In particular, consider what makes the essay "activist." What of Bass's style, voice, choice of examples, and argument makes this essay especially political?*

Thunder and Lightning

I am hovering like an outlaw up on the Canada/Montana border, over on the east side of the Divide, the Front Range, where I have just made a fool of myself, have been rude and socially unacceptable. I've come over from the deep woods of the west side—the wet, clearcut-riddled side—to read at a benefit for a nonprofit organization from Hollywood that's trying to raise dollars to purchase critical habitat for the grizzlies and the wolves—the beautiful, glossy creatures that have been so kind to Hollywood in the past. The reading has been advertised to the public as an evening of "bears, wolves, and writers"—implicit is the notion that it will be an evening of fun and celebration. Everyone's all duded up; everyone's eating and drinking and merrymaking. As luck would have it, I'm first up at the mike. They're trapped now, everyone in their seats, smiling and expecting poetry about the muscled hump of the grizzly and the night-howl of the wolfpack.

Instead, I ambush them. Instead of giving them a nice reading, I ask for something. I read them a shrill diatribe about the Yaak Valley—the most northwestern valley in the U.S. Rockies, a vital cornerstone to the health of the entire West. I harangue my tender, sweet-smelling audience with a request for letters to Congress to designate the last few roadless areas in the Yaak as wilderness. I point to the raggedy-ass, ink-smudged mimeographs that will be on the table on their way out.

I don't read any pretty poems that day, but instead tell them the harsh facts—about the low-elevation rainforest of the Yaak, the only one like it in the United States; about how it grows big trees, and about how those trees have been clearcut by corporations that are abandoning the area now that most of the big trees are gone. I tell about the thousands of miles of road that the Forest Service has built for the timber industry throughout the valley, and of the nobility of the animals that are hanging on there. I spell out the names of the senators and representatives to write to; I spell out the addresses. The audience shifts, squirms, yawns, rolls eyes, checks watches. No shit, Sherlock, who's up next? We all know the Rockies are being lost, they're thinking. But what I'm thinking is, if we all know it, then why is it happening?

The good thing about my breach of etiquette is that at the cocktail party afterward I have lots of space to myself. Beware the zealot.

I know I've been behaving badly, passing out my little Yaak-flyers at all social gatherings—weddings and christenings included, everywhere except funerals—but I can't help it. Time is so short, and the land, the entire West, is no longer being cut up into halves or quarters or even eighths, but into sixty-fourths now, and one-hundred-twenty-eighths next year, and then into thousandths, and millionths, while we sit complacently idle, or at best strap on our roller blades and hitch up our sagging Lycra. I see too much play in the Rockies these days, and not enough work. I am damn near frantic over what is being lost.

The four largest national parks in the Rockies—Yellowstone, Waterton/Glacier, Banff, and Jasper—are currently of no real or lasting importance to the region's biological health. They are like the large, showy muscles of a bodybuilder who has ceased to work out. They're not going to last; the cardiovascular system's been ignored. The wild, fresh blood can't get from one big muscle to the next.

We're losing the big animals first. In the Yaak Valley, for instance, the animals that we most think of as defining the American wilderness are now down to single- or at most double-digit populations. That means nine or ten grizzlies. Two or three wolves. A single woodland caribou. Perhaps three or four lynx. A handful of black-hearted, uncompromising wolverines.

Some creatures can adapt and move through, across, or around our exponentially increasing fragmentation. But not wolves. Unlike salamanders and woodpeckers, wolves will be shot by our own species whenever we see them. And certainly the grizzlies need the space that's being lost. Down to less than 2 percent of their former range, they simply will not barter with humans.

Conservation and ecosystem biologists refer to grizzlies and wolves as "umbrella species"—meaning that they are animals whose charisma and habitat requirements can help humans save broad, intact ecosystems. If grizzlies and wolves are present, everything else in a system will be present.

When it is raining, I want an umbrella—and believe me, it is pouring, and there aren't enough to go around. The spirit of the Rockies and its wildness is getting soggy, is tattering, falling apart.

Sixty million years ago, the earth not too far from the Yaak Valley got up and left: It was folded and pressed and thrust about 70 miles eastward, up over the Continental Divide and into what would much later become the Blackfeet Indians' sacred grounds, the Badger-Two Medicine region of northern Montana. A pattern of big things traveling great distances was set in motion. And the pattern only got stronger. With the new mountains in place, the frigid hearts of glaciers began to form, sliding up and down the mountains, cutting and shaping them for the species that existed then, and for the ones that would come later.

With sharp, loving teeth, the glaciers sculpted hideaway cirques, hanging valleys, fast, wild rivers, and then eased, groaning, down onto the plains, dumping moraines and clacking boulders and cobbles, stopping at the edge of what is now called the Front Range of the Rockies—where the mountains meet the plains.

There was also a great glacier out on the plains, and a narrow band of open ground between the two ice sheets, a corridor running north and south along the Front Range. This was a corridor for humans, bear, bison, and mammoths—big animals, even giant mammals, always moving.

Paleontologist Jack Horner (the guy who was advisor to the movie *Jurassic Park,* but who is not responsible for its fictions) has discovered 75-million-year-old fossils along the Front Range of a previously unknown dinosaur he calls a myosaur, which he believes traveled in great herds like bison. *Tyrannosaurus rex,* the terrible 16,000-pound "lizard king," followed them, feeding on the bodies of the drowned, the sick, and the diseased, much as grizzlies move down low in spring to feed on green-up grasses and the carcasses of winter-killed deer, elk, and moose.

Once there were hundreds of thousands of individuals, even millions, in the herds of Rocky Mountain megafauna, but due to a lack of intact systems, and a lack of predators to drive the herds into large groups and keep them moving, our herds—elk and antelope, now—are much smaller and more spread out.

Yet the essence of the emerging science of conservation biology, beyond the recognition that all of nature is interconnected, is that a habitat must not become fragmented, cut off from other wildlands. Should it be made into an "island," then it will be able to support fewer species, and some stranded populations will go extinct.

To avoid such losses, you protect the richest ecosystems first, along with places strategically located between them, to allow genetic transfer between the systems.

Which—surprise!—brings me back to the Yaak, up on the Canadian border. Like some wild species hiding out in the dense, wet timber, I seem unable to leave, in my frantic heart, this one relatively small but cornerstone valley: among the most biologically diverse in the Rockies, and one that is totally unprotected, with not a single acre of designated wilderness. Not a single protected wildlife refuge, park, nothing. It's just open season.

If the Yaak falls, then the wild creatures in British Columbia will lose an important link to the Bitterroot Range along the Montana/Idaho border and the Salmon Mountains to the south (where they would have a straight shot into Yellowstone to the southeast, or into Oregon's Blue Mountains to the southwest).

The Yaak similarly connects the Northern Continental Divide ecosystem—Glacier National Park, the Bob Marshall Wilderness, Badger-Two Medicine country, and the Swan Valley—to the Selkirks of northern Idaho, and to the North Cascades, which connect to the Central Cascades and the Coast Range.

Because the Yaak so strategically links north to south and west to east, it has the combined, teeming diversity of all these systems. Not just grizzlies and wolves, but wolverines, woodland caribou, snowy owls, and sculpin.

If the Yaak is not saved, if we allow it to fall, we might as well cut open the body of the Rockies and reach in and grab the hot, bloody, steaming red heart and twist it free, yank it out. Steam will rise from the empty carcass. Blood-flow will stop. The brain and body might function a few more seconds—five or ten years. But then no more.

Am I asking people to flock to see this place? I am not—not until there is some system of preservation, some plan, in place. It frightens the hell out of me to be focusing on it. But the Yaak is so much at the edge—so heavily fragmented—that if we do not draw attention to it, it will surely be lost. The populations of the big creatures are dwindling, and yet the lushness, the biodiversity, is still here. Even as I write these words, in the early fall, the chitter of a kingfisher is mixing with the caws of ravens. Earlier this morning, I heard coyotes; last night, elk. There is still a symphony, still a harmony—but the big guys are in trouble, and when places like the Yaak are in trouble, then so too is the West: Jasper, Banff, Glacier, Yellowstone, and Rocky Mountain National Park. All of it.

On a visit to India last year, a friend explained the Buddhist ceremonies to me—how the high priest, before each service, would grip a bell symbolizing thunder, or force, in one hand, and a dorje, a rattle, symbolizing lightning, or direction, in the other. He would ring the bell and shake the dorje, thunder and lightning, the dorje's lightning giving direction and purpose to the brute power of the bell's thunder, heaven's message to the earth that we need both. For me it all came back to the symbolism of the disappearing bear and wolf in my own country, our own form of holiness: The great berry-grazing, thunderous, brute power of the grizzly, drawing his or her strength from a single mountain year-round—sleeping inside the mountain, in the winter—and the dorje of the wolves, traveling single-file sometimes, on the hunt, or on the move, searching—always, it seems—for a new valley where they might be safe, where they might rest, even if only for a while. Thunder and lightning. Never mind that grizzlies once gathered in great numbers on California beaches to feast on the carcasses of washed-ashore whales, or that they roamed the deserts of Texas and Mexico, the prairies of Kansas, and the forests of Minnesota. All we are talking about right now is trying to hold on to what we've got. If grizzlies don't have cores of pristine wildness, and if they cannot move from core to core, then they're gone.

One summer day I find myself sitting barefoot in a field up in the Yaak with local conservationists Chip Clark and Jesse Sedler, and Evan Frost of the Greater Ecosystems Alliance in Bellingham, Washington. Evan has come all the way over here because he recognizes the vital location of the Yaak.

We're talking about how absolutely critical it is to have corridors; we're naming creeks in the Yaak, elk-wintering flats, grizzly-denning areas, wolf runways. We must sound like modern versions of the old trappers and mountain men who first came to this country almost 200 year ago. Like them, we're describing routes and passes; special, shining places that are a long journey away, through wild, rugged country. Evan is listing the valleys to cross, the rivers to get from here to the Pacific Northwest. It's a short list, and you're there: fresh, new genes. Meanwhile, Jesse and I are diagramming how a wandering wolf could come out of Canada, down through the Yaak, and head all the way to Mexico. If.

The Bull River Valley and Trout Creek country, through the Ninemile, then straight down into the Salmon/Bitteroot. A day's or two-days' journey into Yellowstone, and down to Bear Lake in northern Utah, near the Cache Valley, where a grizzly bear once leapt up out of the marsh and chased Jim Bridger and bit Bridger's horse in the ass. Into the high Uintas, then, where grizzlies and wolves may still be secretly holed up. Down into the Weminuche Wilderness in the San Juan Mountains of Colorado, and into New Mexico. Down the ridge of the Sangre de Cristos toward Mexico.

Except it's not quite like the old mountain men's talk must have been. We're sitting here in the late-summer sun, surrounded by cool, dark trees. Clearcuts have scarred our valley, made it unattractive to humans. Evan and Chip and Jesse are spreading out Mylar sheets on top of maps of the Yaak, computer-generated overlays that show remaining stands of old growth—stability—and grizzly-radio-collar telemetry locations, and polygon mapping of elk herd movements. Some of these data, put together by Jesse in his spare time on a borrowed computer, were gathered while he was cruising the valley on his old motorcycle with a busted-out headlight, like Easy Rider, dodging deer in the dusk; some are from Chip and Jesse's work measuring trees for the Forest Service.

We have more data, and less hope.

I can barely even talk about woodland caribou. They used to be all through the upper part of this valley, but now we have only one lonely bull that wanders over every few years during breeding season, sniffing the ancient scent of the soil, old migration corridors, where so many of his kind once lived.

He's sort of an embarrassment, the way he keeps hanging on. (One year he showed up on the golf course at Bonners Ferry, Idaho.) Neither the state nor the feds will list the woodland caribou as an endangered species, and I get the feeling they're all wishing he'd hurry up and die, and that another two dozen in the Idaho Panhandle would go ahead and kick the bucket too, so that the problem would just go away. The bull trout, a little-known migratory fish found in northern Montana and Idaho, is also vulnerable to habitat fragmentation. It lives in rivers or lakes, and in the fall travels as far as 160 miles upstream to spawn (when anglers and dams will allow it). But it doesn't die after spawning, like a salmon does; it returns to its home. Some live to be as old as ten years, and as large as 25 pounds.

Some bull trout spawn every other year, while others spawn every third year, so that if there is a drought or a fire, a whole lake's population will not be lost; there'll be some survivors back in camp who didn't make the journey that year. Once they've made that great cruise up through the forest, beneath the cool cedars and across the shallows (their huge, humped backs tingling with fear, perhaps, at the knowledge of ospreys and eagles above—traveling up toward the Yaak at night, perhaps, under the moon, past otters, wolves, and bears; past coyotes, lions, lynx, and wolverines)—once they've made it up to the creek's headwaters, each female excavates a redd (spawning ground) roughly the size of a pickup bed and buries her eggs a foot and a half deep.

The eggs are fertilized; and then, beneath gold larches, red maples, and aspenblaze, with the days growing colder, the bull trout head back downstream, coasting, to their home.

The fry are born around the first of the year, like good thoroughbreds. They don't come out of the gravel after hatching; they'll wait until spring for that. But such is their fury, their lust to enter the system, that even as immature fry they are predators.

They hang out in their river, then, for one to three years before beginning their migration down to the lake or larger river they have never seen or been to, but which is their home. These days there is an introduced species, lake trout, in those lakes, that will eat the young bull trout with a vengeance, but still the trout migrate.

Beyond lake trout, what's hurting the bull trout? Dams. Eroded soil from road-building, overgrazing, and clearcutting that washes straight into the creeks and rivers, preventing fertilization of their eggs. Even though the Yaak River is still clear, there's about a quarter inch of sediment covering the best spawning riffles. What the giant trout need is habitat protection.

There are fewer than 20 bull trout in the Yaak. One creek where they are making a last stand is a place with scabrous, lunar-gray clearcuts perched on steep slopes. Those 20 bull trout—maybe only ten or so each year—cut off by Libby Dam to the north, and by sedimentation downstream—are still moving back and forth through the autumns, as they have through the millennia—back and forth, back and forth, being big, being wild, in nature—but with the nature around them getting smaller and smaller.

I've got this theory that even though the populations in the Yaak are down, they're maybe a hundred times more important, genetically, than denser populations. For these individuals to have survived, in the face of such heavy development, they must have supergenes, survivors' genes—and should be saved at all costs. I believe their genes can save the other populations. In other words, the fish up in that creek are high-grade ore, as good as gold.

The wolf biologist Mike Jimenez tells of a lone, male wolf he followed in Idaho, the first known wolf in that state in a long damn time. Jimenez refers to that wolf as "a super-individual," one with survivors' genes. Hunting on his own, the wolf was bringing down adult moose, something I had not thought possible and which I don't readily understand, when deer and elk were also available.

A wolf killed in Yellowstone two years ago, the first known wolf to make it back to the park in more than 60 years, was DNA-tested and discovered to have come directly from a valley near the Yaak, Ninemile—or, if not, then from that pack's ancestors, which started out in Canada and Montana's Glacier/Pleasant Valley country, up in this dark, wooded part of the state.

The animals are not resting. If they're not resting, why should we, who claim to be bound up with them in the weave? Any good work that is going to be done must happen now, this year, these next few years. We can rest only after we make a good resting spot.

Wendell Berry writes in his poem, "The Peace of Wild Things,"

When despair for the world grows in me,
and I wake in the night at the least sound
in fear of what my life and my children's lives may be,
I go and lie down where the wood drake
rests in his beauty on the water, and the great heron feeds,
come into the peace of wild things
who do not tax their lives with forethought
of grief: I come into the peace of still water.
And I feel above me the day-blind stars
waiting with their light. For a time
I rest in the grace of the world, and am free.

I take a hike up a steep, timbered hill to a special spot in the Yaak. It's at the edge of one of the roadless areas that we have to save if any wilderness—any thunder and lightning—is going to survive. It's springtime, and I am in some old-growth cedars at about 5,000 feet, when I hear the sound of frogs. I have been looking for bear sign, but I move quietly toward the sound, toward a little alder-bench on the side of the mountain.

I've just read David Quammen's disturbing essay on amphibians' mysterious, worldwide demise. The cause may not be ultraviolet radiation or global warming, but something more basic: fragmentation. It's never really occurred to me before, how frogs and salamanders maintain genetic vigor. A grizzly or a wolf can always try, at least, to get up and go. But how far, really, can a frog go, over the dam's spill-way, or down the sedimented creek, or across the road? It's a whole new problem to brood about.

I'm tired from hiking all day. I find the little pond where they're calling. It's not even a pond so much as a rain puddle, a snowmelt catchment, about the size of some-one's living room. I've been on this mountain a hundred times, but never knew it was here, ephemeral. The frogs grow silent, even at my stealthy approach.

How long will this little high-elevation marsh last? How long do its inhabitants have to find it, lay their eggs, and then hatch? And then where do they go? What kind of frogs are these? I don't even know their damn name. They're not leopard frogs, or green frogs; they're kind of funky-looking, tiny, but with big heads, as if for shoveling, burying themselves.

All any wild thing wants is a place to settle, a sanctuary with the freedom to roam if it wants or needs to. I take Berry's poem to heart: I curl up on the hillside and rest, very still, waiting for the frogs to forget about me, and to start up again. I've heard frogs singing so loudly during breeding season in southern Utah that the din made me nauseous. But when this little chorus starts back up, it's nowhere near as thunderous. This pond is not that crowded.

Earlier in the afternoon, farther back into the roadless area, I'd heard a grizzly flipping boulders just above me, looking for ants. It was right up at snowline, and the boulders were immense. I feel certain it was a grizzly. There was no way I could go higher to see, though; I was afraid it might be a sow with cubs. I turned and went back down the mountain, having heard only the music of those boulders.

Now I lie here in the spring grass like a child, listening to the frogs, and thinking about the future: thinking about grizzly music, wolf music, elk music, trout music, and frog music. I try to feel the old earth stretching beneath me, whispering, or singing.

"I listen to a concert in which so many parts are wanting," Thoreau wrote, in the springtime, in 1856. "Many of those animal migrations and other phenomena by which the Indians marked the season are no longer to be observed . . . I take infinite pains to know all the phenomena of the spring, for instance, thinking that I have here the entire poem, and then, to my chagrin, I hear that it is but an imperfect copy that I possess and have read, that my ancestors have torn out many of the first leaves and grandest passages, and mutilated it in many places. I should not like to think that some demigod had come before me and picked out some of the best of the stars. I wish to know an entire heaven and an entire earth."

The music of the predators and their prey: big predators and big prey are heard most easily and clearly. Yet we are learning to hear other, subtler harmonies, too, even as they grow fainter in the Rockies: the beetles and the rotting logs, the mosses and the frogs.

As blue dusk comes sliding in, I'm sitting there curled up like a child on a warm spring night, up on the mountain, a long way from home, listening to frogs. I'm on the side of the mountain that faces civilization. Two miles away, below me, there is a logging road, and someone's been cutting firewood; I just heard his saw shut off. I imagine it's already dark, down there.

I picture the woodcutter, a neighbor, sitting on a stump, resting from his day's work, mopping his brow, and also listening—hearing the silence after his saw is shut off, and then the sound of the night.

After a while I hear his truck start up, and he drives away. I watch the yellow of his headlights wind far down into the valley as he heads home, where he will sleep, and rest, that night, as will I.

We will not hear anything as we sleep, but the frogs will keep singing, the elk will keep bugling, and the wolves will keep howling, until the fire within them goes out. We are still part of their song, too, but we just are not hearing it yet.

We should not rest much longer. We should only take naps. We should listen more closely. We should save a few places, like the Yaak, that have never been saved. It's simple; it's what we've known all along. We need to put the pieces back together.

CORE VALUES

When a vase shatters, you begin to mend it by picking up the largest pieces. In the shattered Rockies, those pieces are the Glacier/Waterton, Great Yellowstone, and Salmon/Selway ecosystems in the north, and the San Juan and northern New Mexico ecosystems in the south. At the core of these regions are the wilderness as a national parks that the Sierra Club has worked so hard to establish protect in the past.

But preserving existing cores is no longer enough. It is the smaller pieces of public and private land around these protected wildlands that will determine whether the Rockies can continue to support such uncompromising, wide-ranging creatures as wolves and grizzlies. If these pieces continue to be fragmented by roads and clearcuts and mines and second homes, the Rockies' rocks will remain, but not the wild creatures and processes that make up its living, breathing ecosystem.

The Sierra Club's Ecoregion Program aims to protect and expand the Rockies' existing cores of wildness. Some of the places that could make the range whole, such as the Yaak Valley in Montana, need official wilderness designation. Others, such as Colorado's Piceance Basin (where energy companies have dominated in recent years), need restoration.

Here are some of the projects the Club is currently pursuing in the Rockies:

- Helping to shape a Clinton administration study of the Columbia River watershed, which includes a huge portion of the Northern Rockies. Because President Clinton has declared at least outward allegiance to protecting ecosystems, the Columbia initiative could provide a chance to move land management still anchored in 19th-century plunder into the 21st century.

- Challenging the environmentally and economically disastrous Animas–La Plata water project, which would pump water out of the Animas River near Durango, Colorado, to a storage reservoir 1,000 feet uphill.

- Working for passage of statewide wilderness bills for Idaho and Montana, as well as on an expanded Northern Rockies Ecosystem Preservation Bill, which made its debut in Congress last year.

- Working locally to prevent destructive grazing, mining, and logging, and to protect biodiversity (by obliterating unneeded roads in grizzly bear habitat, for instance).

One overarching principle guides these activities. From Jasper to the Rio Grande, the Sierra Club is driven by the belief that permanent preservation—particularly the designation of wild areas—should lie at the heart of its efforts to mend the Rockies ecosystems. In a superlative mountain range long beleaguered by those who would chop it to pieces for profit, that would be a salutary step forward. "We are not fighting progress," said Howard Zahniser, a principal author and advocate of the 1964 Wilderness Act three decades ago. "We are making it."

A CLOSER LOOK AT RICK BASS

1. One of the recurring arguments Bass makes on behalf of protecting wild places is that such places give us stories to tell that also teach us how to depend on one another; they teach us about friendship, mercy, love, and understanding. Choose an audience, one that might be inclined to agree or disagree with you, and write an essay in which you argue for or against protecting wild places. If you do not think wild places need protection, then develop an argument explaining why.

2. Imagine that *Esquire* magazine is soliciting responses to Bass's "Why I Hunt." Write an essay, with *Esquire* readers in mind, in which you argue against hunting. Make sure to situate your strategy in the context of the readers' assumptions.

3. In "Without Safety: Writing Nonfiction," Bass writes: "Humor is nice, in fiction, but not as important, because we'll rush pell-mell (or plow diligently)

to the end of fiction—but in nonfiction, I believe our hearts beat a little differently: always at least just a little bit, there's that echo of fear—fear of the truth, advancing. A little humor is a blessing, and goes a long way, in nonfiction." In the essays you have read by Bass, locate moments of humor and examine how they function. Does humor work in Bass's essays in the ways he says it does here? Develop your argument with examples and analysis.

4. In the introduction to this chapter, we described the symbiotic relationship between writing and place that Bass's essays exhibit. Having read some of Bass's essays, explore this relationship. What does it mean, for example, when we write, "Bass does not so much write *about* places as he writes *from* places"?

Looking from Writer to Writer

1. In the essay "We Are Shaped by the Sound of Wind, the Slant of Sunlight," Barry Lopez writes about the tradition of nature writing. In the essay, Lopez makes some important and emphatic claims about the role of nature writing. For instance he writes, "The real topic of nature writing, I think, is not nature, but the evolving structure of communities from which nature has been removed." In other words, though Lopez is writing about nature writing, he is also addressing larger issues of ethics and morality. To what extent can we say the same of Bass's writing? Looking at what Lopez says about nature writing in his essays, how do you think he would assess Bass's essays? Does Bass's work live up to the standard that Lopez describes?

2. Compare the more visual and less directly argumentative approach in John Updike's essays to the more direct activism in Rick Bass's essays. Bass makes arguments while Updike prefers to create impressions or scenes. Which approach (or some combination of the two) do you consider more effective? To what extent does the approach depend on the audience?

3. Like Bass, several other writers in this collection can be considered "nature writers"—Scott Russell Sanders, Annie Dillard, and Barry Lopez, for instance. Looking back through essays by these other authors, do you see any characteristics in the writing, other than subjects that can be considered "natural," that are similar and might be considered part of what makes writing "nature writing"? That is, other than subject matter, do the essays of these authors have similar rhetorical characteristics?

Looking Beyond

ESSAYS

The Book of Yaak. Boston: Houghton Mifflin, 1996.

Brown Dog of the Yaak: Essays on Art and Activism. Minneapolis: Milkweed Editions, 1999.

The Deer Pasture. 1985. New York: Norton, 1996.
Wild to the Heart. New York: Norton, 1987.

NONFICTION

The Lost Grizzlies: A Search for Survivors in the Wilderness of Colorado. Boston: Houghton Mifflin, 1995.
The Ninemile Wolves: An Essay. Livingston, Montana: Clark City Press, 1992.
Oil Notes. Boston: Seymour Lawrence—Houghton Mifflin, 1989.
Winter: Notes from Montana. Boston: Seymour Lawrence—Houghton Mifflin, 1991.

FICTION

In the Loyal Mountains. Boston: Houghton Mifflin, 1995.
The Watch: Stories. New York: Norton, 1989.
Where the Sea Used to Be. Boston: Houghton Mifflin, 1998.

Joan Didion

Joan Didion has been recognized for her writing since her days as an undergraduate at the University of California, Berkeley. Though she writes in a variety of genres, including fiction and nonfiction, her reputation as an author of importance grows primarily from her success as a writer of essays. When she attended UC, Berkeley as an English major, she entered and won a contest sponsored by *Vogue* magazine for essay writing in 1956. *Vogue* hired the young writer, and Didion worked for the magazine from 1956 until 1963, primarily as an essay writer. Eventually she rose to the position of associate features editor. While working at *Vogue,* Didion met author John Gregory Dunne, and after years of friendship the two married. They have collaborated on several writing projects including several screenplays. According to Didion, Dunne reads everything she writes and she reads everything he writes. Didion's first novel, *Run River,* was published in 1963. In addition to the 1956 *Vogue* Prix de Paris prize, Didion's work has earned her a range of awards including the National Book Award nomination in fiction in 1971 for her book *Play It as It Lays,* the National Book Critics Circle Prize nomination in nonfiction in 1981 for her book *The White Album,* and the Edward McDowell Medal in 1996.

Raised in Sacramento, California, Didion often writes of her life with her family and the tensions of family life. While Didion's writing has earned a good deal of acclaim, she has not produced a large body of work since she began publishing in 1963. Many critics note that Didion's lower rate of production might be due to her extensive concentration on and attention to her craft. In an interview printed in the *Los Angeles Times,* Didion explained that she is "not interested in spontaneity," but rather she is concerned with "total control." She noted that she spends a good deal of time revising her writing in order to get the details just right. It is specifically this kind of attention to detail that has earned her the highest acclaims from critics. John Leonard, writing in the *New York Times,* said that "nobody writes better English prose than Joan Didion. Try to rearrange one of her sentences, and you've realized that the sentence was inevitable, a hologram." In a 1999 interview with Lewis Burke Frumkes, Didion noted that her early influences included Hemingway "because of his clear sentences. It was exciting to me when I discovered them." Didion has also recounted that by the time she was thirteen she would type pages from Hemingway and Joseph Conrad books in order to see "how the sentences worked." Her writing exhibits her intense study of sentences.

During the late 1960s, Didion spent time in the Haight-Asbury area in San Francisco, the center of the counterculture (hippie) movement. During this period, Didion wrote a good deal about the condition of America. When some of her work was questioned as not offering any insight into "the American condition" as it had been characterized, but rather was a simple report about a specific cultural phenomenon in a small region, Didion began to question the relevance of the act of writing. Politically, *Contemporary Authors* lists Didion as a Republican, and she has commented to Sara Davidson in the *New York Times Book Review* that not only does she not vote often, but that "the politics I personally want are anarchic." She goes on to say, "Throw out the laws. Tear it down. Start all over." She is vocally opposed to modern feminism and has been critiqued for writing about "passive losers for heroines."

When Frumkes asked Didion "what advice would you give to beginning writers," Didion responded:

> The most important and hardest thing for any writer to learn is the discipline of sitting down and writing even when you have to spend three days writing bad stuff before the fourth day, when you write something better. If you've been away from what you've been working on even for a day and a half, you have to put in those three days of bad writing to get to the fourth, or you lose the thread, you lose the rhythm. When you are a young writer, those three days are so unpleasant that you tend to think, "I'll go away until the mood strikes me." Well, you're out of the mood because you're not sitting there, because you haven't had that period of trying to push through till the fourth day when the rhythm comes.

Ms. magazine once asked Didion to draw a self-portrait of herself for the magazine, and Didion submitted a thumbprint and a short piece of writing that said: "This is Joan Didion Dunne, five feet two inches, ninety-five pounds, hair red, eyes hazel. Must wear corrective lenses. Too thin. Astigmatic. Has no visual sense of herself."

As you read the selected essays of Didion, pay attention to her construction of sentences, and to the attention she pays to sentences. Think about the choices of words Didion uses to provide remarkable detail in her writing. Note the effect such details have on your engagement with the writing.

Didion on Writing

At First Glance

This essay is a revised version of a Regents' Lecture that Didion gave at her alma mater, the University of California, Berkeley. In the essay "Why I Write," Didion wrote, "in many ways writing is the act of saying I, *of imposing oneself upon other people, of saying* listen to me, see it my way, change your mind." *While you are reading this essay, pay attention to what Didion means by this, and ask yourself how your own writing might be an act of imposing yourself on the lives of your readers.*

Why I Write

Of course I stole the title for this talk from George Orwell. One reason I stole it was that I like the sound of the words: Why I Write. There you have three short unambiguous words that share a sound; and the sound they share is this:

I

I

I

In many ways writing is the act of saying *I,* of imposing oneself upon other people, of saying *listen to me, see it my way, change your mind.* It's an aggressive, even a hostile act. You can disguise its aggressiveness all you want with veils of subordinate clauses and qualifiers and tentative subjunctives, with ellipses and evasions—with the whole manner of intimating rather than claiming, of alluding rather than stating—but there's no getting around the fact that setting words on paper is the tactic of a secret bully, an invasion, an imposition of the writer's sensibility on the reader's most private space.

I stole the title not only because the words sounded right but because they seemed to sum up, in a no-nonsense way, all I have to tell you. Like many writers I have only this one "subject," this one "area": the act of writing. I can bring you no reports from any other front. I may have other interests: I am "interested," for example, in marine biology, but I don't flatter myself that you would come out to hear me talk about it. I am not a scholar. I am not in the least an intellectual, which is not to say that when I hear the word "intellectual" I reach for my gun, but only to say that I do not think in abstracts. During the years when I was an undergraduate at Berkeley I tried, with a kind of hopeless late-adolescent energy, to buy some temporary visa into the world of ideas, to forge for myself a mind that could deal with the abstract.

In short I tried to think. I failed. My attention veered inexorably back to the specific, to the tangible, to what was generally considered, by everyone I knew then

79

and for that matter have known since, the peripheral. I would try to contemplate the Hegelian dialectic and would find myself concentrating instead on a flowering pear tree outside my window and the particular way the petals fell on my floor. I would try to read linguistic theory and would find myself wondering instead if the lights were on in the bevatron up the hill. When I say that I was wondering if the lights were on in the bevatron you might immediately suspect, if you deal in ideas at all, that I was registering the bevatron as a political symbol, thinking in shorthand about the military-industrial complex and its role in the university community, but you would be wrong. I was only wondering if the lights were on in the bevatron, and how they looked. A physical fact.

I had trouble graduating from Berkeley, not because of this inability to deal with ideas—I was majoring in English, and I could locate the house-and-garden imagery in *The Portrait of a Lady* as well as the next person, "imagery" being by definition the kind of specific that got my attention—but simply because I had neglected to take a course in Milton. For reasons which now sound baroque I needed a degree by the end of that summer, and the English department finally agreed, if I would come down from Sacramento every Friday and talk about the cosmology of *Paradise Lost,* to certify me proficient in Milton. I did this. Some Fridays I took the Greyhound bus, other Fridays I caught the Southern Pacific's *City of San Francisco* on the last leg of its transcontinental trip. I can no longer tell you whether Milton put the sun or the earth at the center of his universe in *Paradise Lost,* the central question of at least one century and a topic about which I wrote ten thousand words that summer, but I can still recall the exact rancidity of the butter in the *City of San Francisco*'s dining car, and the way the tinted windows on the Greyhound bus cast the oil refineries around Carquinez Straits into a grayed and obscurely sinister light. In short my attention was always on the periphery, on what I could see and taste and touch, on the butter, and the Greyhound bus. During those years I was traveling on what I knew to be a very shaky passport, forged papers; I knew that I was no legitimate resident in any world of ideas. I knew I couldn't think. All I knew then was what I couldn't do. All I knew then was what I wasn't, and it took me some years to discover what I was.

Which was a writer.

By which I mean not a "good" writer or a "bad" writer but simply a writer, a person whose most absorbed and passionate hours are spent arranging words on pieces of paper. Had my credentials been in order I would never have become a writer. Had I been blessed with even limited access to my own mind there would have been no reason to write. I write entirely to find out what I'm thinking, what I'm looking at, what I see and what it means. What I want and what I fear. Why did the oil refineries around Carquinez Straits seem sinister to me in the summer of 1956? Why have the night lights in the bevatron burned in my mind for twenty years? *What is going on in these pictures in my mind?*

When I talk about pictures in my mind I am talking, quite specifically, about images that shimmer around the edges. There used to be an illustration in every elementary psychology book showing a cat drawn by a patient in varying stages of schizophrenia. This cat had a shimmer around it. You could see the molecular structure breaking down at the very edges of the cat: the cat became the background and the background the cat, everything interacting, exchanging ions. People on hallucinogens describe the same perception of objects. I'm not a schizophrenic, nor do I take hallucinogens, but certain images do shimmer for me. Look hard enough, and you can't miss the shimmer. It's there. You can't think too much about these pictures that shimmer. You just lie low and let them develop. You stay quiet. You don't talk to many people and you keep your nervous system from shorting out and you try to locate the cat in the shimmer, the grammar in the picture.

Just as I meant "shimmer" literally I mean "grammar" literally. Grammar is a piano I play by ear, since I seem to have been out of school the year the rules were mentioned. All I know about grammar is its infinite power. To shift the structure of a sentence alters the meaning of that sentence, as definitely and inflexibly as the position of a camera alters the meaning of the object photographed. Many people know about camera angles now, but not so many know about sentences. The arrangement of the words matters, and the arrangement you want can be found in the picture in your mind. The picture dictates the arrangement. The picture dictates whether this will be a sentence with or without clauses, a sentence that ends hard or a dying-fall sentence, long or short, active or passive. The picture tells you how to arrange the words and the arrangement of the words tells you, or tells me, what's going on in the picture. *Nota bene:*

It tells you.

You don't tell it.

Let me show you what I mean by pictures in the mind. I began *Play It As It Lays* just as I have begun each of my novels, with no notion of "character" or "plot" or even "incident." I had only two pictures in my mind, more about which later, and a technical intention, which was to write a novel so elliptical and fast that it would be over before you noticed it, a novel so fast that it would scarcely exist on the page at all. About the pictures: the first was of white space. Empty space. This was clearly the picture that dictated the narrative intention of the book—a book in which anything that happened would happen off the page, a "white" book to which the reader would have to bring his or her own bad dreams—and yet this picture told me no "story," suggested no situation. The second picture did. This second picture was of something actually witnessed. A young woman with long hair and a short white halter dress walks through the casino at the Riviera in Las Vegas at one in the morning. She crosses the casino alone and picks up a house telephone. I watch her because I have heard her paged, and recognize her name: she is a minor actress I see around Los Angeles from time to time, in places like Jax and once in a gynecologist's office in the Beverly Hills Clinic, but have never met. I know nothing about her. Who is paging her? Why is she here to be paged? How exactly did she come to this? It was precisely this moment in Las Vegas that made *Play It As It Lays* begin to tell itself to me, but the moment appears in the novel only obliquely, in a chapter which begins: "Maria made a list of things she would never do. She would never: walk through the Sands or Caesar's alone after midnight. She would never: ball at a party, do S-M unless she wanted to, borrow furs from Abe Lipsey, deal. She would never: carry a Yorkshire in Beverly Hills."

That is the beginning of the chapter and that is also the end of the chapter, which may suggest what I meant by "white space."

I recall having a number of pictures in my mind when I began the novel I just finished, *A Book of Common Prayer.* As a matter of fact one of these pictures was of that bevatron I mentioned, although I would be hard put to tell you a story in which nuclear energy figures. Another was a newspaper photograph of a hijacked 707 burning on the desert in the Middle East. Another was the night view from a room in which I once spent a week with paratyphoid, a hotel room on the Colombian coast. My husband and I seemed to be on the Colombian coast representing the United States of America at a film festival (I recall invoking the name "Jack Valenti" a lot, as if its reiteration could make me well), and it was a bad place to have fever, not only because my indisposition offended our hosts but because every night in this hotel the generator failed. The lights went out. The elevator stopped. My husband would go to the event of the evening and make excuses for me and I would stay alone in this hotel room, in the dark. I remember standing at the window trying to call Bogotá (the telephone seemed to work on the same principle as the generator) and watching the night wind come up and wondering what I was doing eleven degrees off the equator with a fever of 103. The view from that window definitely figures in *A Book of Common Prayer,* as does the burning 707, and yet none of these pictures told me the story I needed.

The picture that did, the picture that shimmered and made these other images coalesce, was the Panama airport at 6 A.M. I was in this airport only once, on a plane to Bogotá that stopped for an hour to refuel, but the way it looked that morning remained superimposed on everything I saw until the day I finished *A Book of Common Prayer.* I lived in that airport for several years. I can still feel the hot air when I step off the plane, can see the heat already rising off the tarmac at 6 A.M. I can feel my skirt damp and wrinkled on my legs. I can feel the asphalt stick to my sandals. I remember the big tail of a Pan American plane floating motionless down at the end of the tarmac. I remember the sound of a slot machine in the waiting room. I could tell you that I remember a particular woman in the airport, an American woman, a *norteamericana,* a thin *norteamericana* about forty who wore a big square emerald in lieu of a wedding ring, but there was no such woman there.

I put this woman in the airport later. I made this woman up, just as I later made up a country to put the airport in, and a family to run the country. This woman in the airport is neither catching a plane nor meeting one. She is ordering tea in the airport coffee shop. In fact she is not simply "ordering" tea but insisting that the water be boiled, in front of her, for twenty minutes. Why is this woman in this airport? Why is she going nowhere, where has she been? Where did she get that big emerald? What derangement, or disassociation, makes her believe that her will to see the water boiled can possibly prevail?

> She had been going to one airport or another for four months, one could see it, looking at the visas on her passport. All those airports where Charlotte Douglas's passport had been stamped would have looked alike. Sometimes the sign on the tower would say "Bienvenidos" and sometimes the sign on the

tower would say "Bienvenue," some places were wet and hot and others dry and hot, but at each of these airports the pastel concrete walls would rust and stain and the swamp off the runway would be littered with the fuselages of cannibalized Fairchild F-227's and the water would need boiling.

    I knew why Charlotte went to the airport even if Victor did not.

    I knew about airports.

These lines appear about halfway through *A Book of Common Prayer,* but I wrote them during the second week I worked on the book, long before I had any idea where Charlotte Douglas had been or why she went to airports. Until I wrote these lines I had no character called "Victor" in mind: the necessity for mentioning a name, and the name "Victor," occurred to me as I wrote the sentence: *I knew why Charlotte went to the airport* sounded incomplete. *I knew why Charlotte went to the airport even if Victor did not* carried a little more narrative drive. Most important of all, until I wrote these lines I did not know who "I" was, who was telling the story. I had intended until that that the "I" be no more than the voice of the author, a nineteenth-century omniscient narrator. But there it was:

    I knew why Charlotte went to the airport even if Victor did not.

    I knew about airports.

This "I" was the voice of no author in my house. This "I" was someone who not only knew why Charlotte went to the airport but also knew someone called "Victor." Who was Victor? Who was this narrator? Why was this narrator telling me this story? Let me tell you one thing about why writers write: had I known the answer to any of these questions I would never have needed to write a novel.

Double Take

1. Why do you suppose Didion uses the metaphor of photography, of pictures, as representative of writing? Are there similarities between writing and photography? Do we "read" photographs the same way we read writing? Do photographs and writing transmit knowledge in similar ways?

2. In this essay, Didion writes, "It's an aggressive, even a hostile act. You can disguise its aggressiveness all you want with veils and subordinate clauses and qualifiers and tentative subjunctives, with ellipses and evasions—with the whole manner of intimating rather than claiming, of alluding rather than stating—but there's no getting around the fact that setting words on paper is the tactic of a secret bully, an invasion, an imposition of the writer's sensibility on the reader's private space." What does Didion mean by this? Do you think of your own writing as aggressive or hostile? As an imposition into readers' private spaces? How do you decide the ways you will allow your writing to impose or not impose?

3. Didion makes specific comments in this essay about how choices in sentences influence the effect of her writing. For instance, she claims, "All I know about grammar is its infinite power. To shift the structure of a sentence alters the meaning of

that sentence, as definitely and inflexibly as the position of a camera alters the meaning of the object photographed. Many people know about camera angles now, but not so many know about sentences." In looking at Didion's own sentences, can you identify choices she makes in order to convey particular meanings? Do Didion's choices about sentences offer you suggestions about choices you might make in constructing sentences?

4. Ultimately, Didion claims she writes to answer questions. She claims that had she known the answers before writing, she would not have the need to write. That is, writing is often part of a larger process of discovery, learning, knowledge making. Think about things that you have written. Have they led you to learn about different subjects, about your own writing, or about how others read your writing? Did those writing projects change how you approached other writing projects? Do you agree with Didion's ultimate assessment about why we write?

At First Glance

"The Women's Movement" was first published in 1972. In this essay, Didion considers "our national life." In doing so she critiques the ways that the women's movement has proceeded in the United States. As you read this essay, it is important to consider the historical context in which it was written. We should probably say this of any essay or any text we read. Yet, the historical setting in which Didion writes this essay is of particular interest. As you read this essay, consider not only how Didion's argument fit into larger conversations of that time, but think about what rhetorical choices Didion would have had to make specifically because of the historical and political situation in which she was writing. That is, do you think Didion would have written this essay differently if she were writing it today? If so, how might she have approached the subject today? Also, consider how our current political positions affect how we read this essay. Do we criticize it for being out of line with current thinking? Do we read it as a historical document? Ultimately, we need to be conscious of our historical and political contexts not only when we critique other writing, but when we think about the choices we want to make in our own writing.

The Women's Movement

To make an omelette you need not only those broken eggs but someone "oppressed" to break them: every revolutionist is presumed to understand that, and also every woman, which either does or does not make fifty-one percent of the population of the United States a potentially revolutionary class. The creation of this revolutionary "class" was from the virtual beginning the "idea" of the women's movement, and the tendency for popular discussion of the movement to center for so long around daycare centers is yet another instance of that studied resistance to political ideas which characterizes our national life.

"The new feminism is not just the revival of a serious political movement for social equality," the feminist theorist Shulamith Firestone announced flatly in 1970. "It is the second wave of the most important revolution in history." This was scarcely a statement of purpose anyone could find cryptic, and it was scarcely the only statement of its kind in the literature of the movement. Nonetheless, in 1972, in a "special issue" on women, *Time* was still musing genially that the movement might well succeed in bringing about "fewer diapers and more Dante."

That was a very pretty image, the idle ladies sitting in the gazebo and murmuring *lasciate ogni speranza,* but it depended entirely upon the popular view of the movement as some kind of collective inchoate yearning for "fulfillment," or "self-expression," a yearning absolutely devoid of ideas and capable of engendering only the most *pro forma* benevolent interest. In fact there was an idea, and the idea was Marxist, and it was precisely to the extent that there was this Marxist idea that the curious historical anomaly known as the women's movement would have seemed to have any interest at all. Marxism in this country had ever been an eccentric and quixotic passion. One oppressed class after another had seemed finally to miss the point. The have-nots, it turned out, aspired mainly to having. The minorities seemed to promise more, but finally disappointed: it developed that they actually cared about the issues, that they tended to see the integration of the luncheonette and the seat in the front of the bus as real goals, and only rarely as ploys, counters in a larger game. They resisted that essential inductive leap from the immediate reform to the social ideal, and, just as disappointingly, they failed to perceive their common cause with other minorities, continued to exhibit a self-interest disconcerting in the extreme to organizers steeped in the rhetoric of "brotherhood."

And then, at that exact dispirited moment when there seemed no one at all willing to play the proletariat, along came the women's movement, and the invention of women as a "class." One could not help admiring the radical simplicity of this instant transfiguration. The notion that, in the absence of a cooperative proletariat, a revolutionary class might simply be invented, made up, "named" and so brought into existence, seemed at once so pragmatic and so visionary, so precisely Emersonian, that it took the breath away, exactly confirmed one's idea of where nineteenth-century transcendental instincts, crossed with a late reading of Engels and Marx, might lead. To read the theorists of the women's movement was to think not of Mary Wollstonecraft but of Margaret Fuller at her most high-minded, of rushing position papers off to mimeo and drinking tea from paper cups in lieu of eating lunch; of thin raincoats on bitter nights. If the family was the last fortress of capitalism, then let us abolish the family. If the necessity for conventional reproduction of the species seemed unfair to women, then let us transcend, via technology, "the very organization of nature," the oppression, as Shulamith Firestone saw it, "that goes back through recorded history to the animal kingdom itself." *I accept the universe,* Margaret Fuller had finally allowed: Shulamith Firestone did not.

It seemed very New England, this febrile and cerebral passion. The solemn *a priori* idealism in the guise of radical materialism somehow bespoke old-fashioned self-reliance and prudent sacrifice. The clumsy torrent of words became a principle, a renunciation of style as unserious. The rhetorical willingness to break eggs became, in practice, only a thrifty capacity for finding the sermon in every stone. Burn the literature, Ti-Grace Atkinson said in effect when it was suggested that, even come the revolution, there would still remain the whole body of "sexist" Western literature. But of course no books would be burned: the women of this movement were perfectly capable of crafting didactic revisions of whatever apparently intractable material came to hand. "As a parent you should become an interpreter of myths," advised Letty Cottin Pogrebin in the preview issue of *Ms.* "Portions of any fairy tale or children's story can be salvaged during a critique session with your child." Other literary analysts devised ways to salvage other books: Isabel Archer in *The Portrait of a Lady* need no longer be the victim of her own idealism. She could be, instead, the victim of a sexist society, a woman who had "internalized the conventional definition of wife." The narrator of Mary McCarthy's *The Company She Keeps* could be seen as "enslaved because she persists in looking for her identity in a man." Similarly, Miss McCarthy's *The Group* could serve to illustrate "what happens to women who have been educated at first-rate women's colleges—taught philosophy and history—and then are consigned to breast-feeding and gourmet cooking."

The idea that fiction has certain irreducible ambiguities seemed never to occur to these women, nor should it have, for fiction is in most ways hostile to ideology. They had invented a class; now they had only to make that class conscious. They seized as a political technique a kind of shared testimony at first called a "rap session," then called "consciousness-raising," and in any case a therapeutically oriented American reinterpretation, according to the British feminist Juliet Mitchell, of a Chinese revolutionary practice known as "speaking bitterness." They purged and regrouped and purged again, worried out one another's errors and deviations, the "elitism" here, the "careerism" there. It would have been merely sententious to call some of their thinking Stalinist: of course it was. It would have been pointless even to speak of whether one considered these women "right" or "wrong," meaningless to dwell upon the obvious, upon the coarsening of moral imagination to which such social idealism so often leads. To believe in "the greater good" is to operate, necessarily, in a certain ethical suspension. Ask anyone committed to Marxist analysis how many angels on the head of a pin, and you will be asked in return to never mind the angels, tell me who controls the production of pins.

To those of us who remain committed mainly to the exploration of moral distinctions and ambiguities, the feminist analysis may have seemed a particularly narrow and cracked determinism. Nonetheless it was serious, and for these high-strung idealists to find themselves out of the mimeo room and onto the Cavett show must have been in certain ways more unsettling to them than it ever was to the viewers. They were being heard, and yet not really. Attention was finally being paid, and yet that attention was mired in the trivial. Even the brightest movement women found themselves engaged in sullen public colloquies about the inequities of dishwashing and the intolerable humiliations of being observed by construction workers on

Sixth Avenue. (This grievance was not atypic in that discussion of it seemed always to take on unexplored Ms. Scarlett overtones, suggestions of fragile cultivated flowers being "spoken to," and therefore violated, by uppity proles.) They totted up the pans scoured, the towels picked off the bathroom floor, the loads of laundry done in a lifetime. Cooking a meal could only be "dogwork," and to claim any pleasure from it was evidence of craven acquiescence in one's own forced labor. Small children could only be odious mechanisms for the spilling and digesting of food, for robbing women of their "freedom." It was a long way from Simone de Beauvoir's grave and awesome recognition of woman's role as "the Other" to the notion that the first step in changing that role was Alix Kates Shulman's marriage contract ("wife strips beds, husband remakes them"), a document reproduced in *Ms.,* but it was toward just such trivialization that the women's movement seemed to be heading.

Of course this litany of trivia was crucial to the movement in the beginning, a key technique in the politicizing of women who had perhaps been conditioned to obscure their resentments even from themselves. Mrs. Shulman's discovery that she had less time than her husband seemed to have was precisely the kind of chord the movement had hoped to strike in all women (the "click! of recognition," as Jane O'Reilly described it), but such discoveries could be of no use at all if one refused to perceive the larger point, failed to make that inductive leap from the personal to the political. Splitting up the week into hours during which the children were directed to address their "personal questions" to either one parent or another might or might not have improved the quality of Mr. and Mrs. Shulman's marriage, but the improvement of marriages would not a revolution make. It could be very useful to call housework, as Lenin did, "the most unproductive, the most barbarous and the most arduous work a woman can do," but it could be useful only as the first step in a political process, only in the "awakening" of a class to its position, useful only as a metaphor: to believe, during the late sixties and early seventies in the United States of America, that the words had literal meaning was not only to stall the movement in the personal but to seriously delude oneself.

More and more, as the literature of the movement began to reflect the thinking of women who did not really understand the movement's ideological base, one had the sense of this stall, this delusion, the sense that the drilling of the theorists had struck only some psychic hardpan dense with superstitions and little sophistries, wish fulfillment, self-loathing and bitter fancies. To read even desultorily in this literature was to recognize instantly a certain dolorous phantasm, an imagined Everywoman with whom the authors seemed to identify all too entirely. This ubiquitous construct was everyone's victim but her own. She was persecuted even by her gynecologist, who made her beg in vain for contraceptives. She particularly needed contraceptives because she was raped on every date, raped by her husband, and raped finally on the abortionist's table. During the fashion for shoes with pointed toes, she, like "many women," had her toes amputated. She was so intimidated by cosmetics advertising that she would sleep "huge portions" of her day in order to forestall wrinkling, and when awake she was enslaved by detergent commercials on television. She sent her child to a nursery school where the little girls huddled in a "doll corner," and were forcibly restrained from playing with building blocks. Should she work she was paid "three to ten times less" than an (always) unqualified man holding the same job, was prevented from attending business lunches because she would be "embarrassed" to appear in public with a man not her husband, and, when she traveled alone, faced a choice between humiliation in a restaurant and "eating a doughnut" in her hotel room.

The half-truths, repeated, authenticated themselves. The bitter fancies assumed their own logic. To ask the obvious—why she did not get herself another gynecologist, another job, why she did not get out of bed and turn off the television set, or why, the most eccentric detail, she stayed in hotels where only doughnuts could be obtained from room service—was to join this argument at its own spooky level, a level which had only the most tenuous and unfortunate relationship to the actual condition of being a woman. That many women are victims of condescension and exploitation and sex-role stereotyping was scarcely news, but neither was it news that other women are not: nobody forces women to buy the package.

But of course something other than an objection to being "discriminated against" was at work here, something other than an aversion to being "stereotyped" in one's sex role. Increasingly it seemed that the aversion was to adult sexual life itself: how much cleaner to stay forever children. One is constantly struck, in the accounts of lesbian relationships which appear from time to time in movement literature, by the emphasis on the superior "tenderness" of the relationship, the "gentleness" of the sexual connection, as if the participants were wounded birds. The derogation of assertiveness as "machismo" has achieved such currency that one imagines several million women too delicate to deal at any level with an overtly heterosexual man. Just as one had gotten the unintended but inescapable suggestion, when told about the "terror and revulsion" experienced by women in the vicinity of construction sites, of creatures too "tender" for the abrasiveness of daily life, too fragile for the streets, so now one was getting, in the later literature of the movement, the impression of women too "sensitive" for the difficulties of adult life, women unequipped for reality and grasping at the movement as a rationale for denying that reality. The transient stab of dread and loss which accompanies menstruation simply never happens: we only thought it happened, because a male-chauvinist psychiatrist told us so. No woman need have bad dreams after an abortion: she has only been told she should. The power of sex is just an oppressive myth, no longer to be feared, because what the sexual connection really amounts to, we learn in one woman's account of a postmarital affair presented as liberated and liberating, is "wisecracking and laughing" and "lying together and then leaping up to play and sing the entire *Sesame Street Songbook*." All one's actual apprehension of what it is like to be a woman, the irreconcilable difference of it—that sense of living one's deepest life underwater, that dark involvement with blood and birth and death—could now be declared invalid, unnecessary, *one never felt it at all*.

One was only told it, and now one is to be reprogrammed, fixed up, rendered again as inviolate and unstained as the "modern" little girls in the Tampax advertisements. More and more we have been hearing the wishful voices of just such perpetual adolescents, the voices of women scarred not by their class position as women but by the failure of their childhood expectations and misapprehensions. "Nobody ever so much as mentioned" to Susan Edmiston "that when you say 'I do,' what you are doing is not, as you thought, vowing your eternal love, but rather subscribing to a whole system of rights, obligations and responsibilities that may well be anathema to your most cherished beliefs." To Ellen Peck "the birth of children too often means the dissolution of romance, the loss of freedom, the abandonment of ideals to economics." A young woman described on the cover of *New York* as "The Suburban Housewife Who Bought the Promises of Women's Lib and Came to the City to Live Them" tells us what promises she bought: "The chance to respond to the bright lights and civilization of the Big Apple, yes. The chance to compete, yes. But most of all, the chance to have some fun. Fun is what's been missing."

Eternal love, romance, fun. The Big Apple. These are relatively rare expectations in the arrangements of consenting adults, although not in those of children, and it wrenches the heart to read about these women in their brave new lives. An ex-wife and mother of three speaks of her plan to "play out my college girl's dream. I am going to New York to become this famous writer. Or this working writer. Failing that, I will get a job in publishing." She mentions a friend, another young woman who "had never had any other life than as a daughter or wife or mother" but who is "just discovering herself to be a gifted potter." The childlike resourcefulness—to get a job in publishing, to become a gifted potter!—bewilders the imagination. The astral discontent with actual lives, actual men, the denial of the real generative possibilities of adult sexual life, somehow touches beyond words. "It is the right of the oppressed to organize around their oppression *as they see and define it,*" the movement theorists insist doggedly in an effort to solve the question of these women, to convince themselves that what is going on is still a political process, but the handwriting is already on the wall. These are converts who want not a revolution but "romance," who believe not in the oppression of women but in their own chances for a new life in exactly the mold of their old life. In certain ways they tell us sadder things about what the culture has done to them than the theorists ever did, and they also tell us, I suspect, that the movement is no longer a cause but a symptom.

Double Take

1. Didion takes on some fairly large, and difficult to talk about, subjects in this essay: "our national life," oppression, minority rights, women's rights, to name a few. How does she manage to focus these grand topics into a coherent essay? That is, how does Didion rein in what can be wieldy topics to fit her argumentative needs here?

2. When Didion claims that "fiction is in most ways hostile to ideology," she is placing writing—or at least a particular kind of writing—in an interesting dialogue with ideology. More often ideology is described as affecting writing and writing affecting ideology in a reciprocal dialogue. Granted, ideology can *change* writing and writing can *change* ideology (think about revolutionary writing like Einstein's theory of relativity), but placing some kinds of writing as hostile to ideology is an

interesting maneuver. In what ways might fiction writing or other writings resist ideology? Can writing be free of ideology? How might ideology affect our choices as writers, even if what we write is hostile to ideology?

3. Didion takes a rather large step in her critique of feminism by writing "To those of us who remain committed mainly to the exploration of moral distinctions and ambiguities, the feminist analysis may have seemed a particularly narrow and cracked determinism." This statement is fairly obviously an argument against feminism of the 1970s. What does Didion gain by making such a direct attack on feminism?

At First Glance

Joan Didion's essay "In Bogotá" makes some interesting observations about being "American" in a foreign country. For instance, she writes that when in the company of another American, "He seemed very concerned that no breach of American manners be inferred, and so, absurdly, did I. We had nothing in common except the eagles on our passports, but those eagles made us, in some way I did not entirely understand, co-conspirators, two strangers heavy with responsibility for seeing that the eagle should not offend. We would prefer the sweet local Roman-Cola to the Coca-Cola the Colombians liked. We would think of Standard Oil as Esso Colombiano." In essence, Didion is making social commentary about Americans in South American countries and the ways in which other cultures adopt (by force or choice) American and European customs. While reading about Didion's time in Bogotá, identify the numbers of ways she addresses these commentaries to her audience, both in the anecdotes she offers and the descriptions of what she observes.

In Bogotá

On the Colombian coast it was hot, fevered, eleven degrees off the equator with evening trades that did not relieve but blew hot and dusty. The sky was white, the casino idle. I had never meant to leave the coast but after a week of it I began to think exclusively of Bogotá, floating on the Andes an hour away by air. In Bogotá it would be cool. In Bogotá one could get *The New York Times* only two days late and the *Miami Herald* only one day late and also emeralds, and bottled water. In Bogotá there would be fresh roses in the bathrooms at the Hotel Tequendama and hot water twenty-four hours a day and numbers to be dialed for chicken sandwiches from room service and Xerox *rápido* and long-distance operators who could get Los Angeles in ten minutes. In my room in Cartagena I would wake to the bleached coastal morning and find myself repeating certain words and phrases under my breath, an incantation: *Bogotá, Bacatá*. El Dorado. Emeralds. Hot water. Madeira consommé in cool dining rooms. *Santa Fé de Bogotá del Nuevo Reino de Granada de las Indias del Mar Océano.* The Avianca flight to Bogotá left Cartagena every morning at ten-forty, but such was the slowed motion of the coast that it took me another four days to get on it.

Maybe that is the one true way to see Bogotá, to have it float in the mind until the need for it is visceral, for the whole history of the place has been to seem a mirage, a delusion on the high savannah, its gold and its emeralds unattainable, inaccessible, its isolation so splendid and unthinkable that the very existence of a city astonishes. There on the very spine of the Andes gardeners espalier roses on embassy walls. Swarms of little girls in proper navy-blue school blazers line up to enter the faded tent of a tatty traveling circus: the elephant, the strong man, the tattooed man from Maracaibo. I arrived in Bogotá on a day in 1973 when the streets seemed bathed in mist and thin brilliant light and in the amplified pop voice of Nelson Ned, a Brazilian dwarf whose records played in every *disco* storefront. Outside the sixteenth-century Church of San Francisco, where the Spanish viceroys took office when the country was Nueva Granada and where Simón Bolívar assumed the presidency of the doomed republic called Gran Colombia, small children and old women hawked Cuban cigars and cartons of American cigarettes and newspapers with the headline "JACKIE Y ARI." I lit a candle for my daughter and bought a paper to read about Jackie and Ari, how the princess *de los norteamericanos* ruled the king of the Greek sea by demanding of him pink champagne every night and *medialunas* every morning, a story a child might invent. Later, in the Gold Museum of the Banco de la República, I looked at the gold the Spaniards opened the Americas to get, the vision of El Dorado which was to animate a century and is believed to have begun here, outside Bogotá, at Lake Guatavita. "Many golden offerings were cast into the lake," wrote the anthropologist Olivia Vlahos of the nights when the Chibcha Indians lit bonfires on the Andes and confirmed their rulers at Guatavita.

> Many more were heaped on a raft. . . . Then into the firelight stepped the ruler-to-be, his nakedness coated with a sticky resin. Onto the resin his priests applied gold dust and more gold dust until he gleamed like a golden statue. He stepped onto the raft, which was cut loose to drift into the middle of the lake. Suddenly he dived into the black water. When he emerged, the gold was gone, washed clean from his body. And he was king.

Until the Spaniards heard the story, and came to find El Dorado for themselves. "One thing you must understand," a young Colombian said to me at dinner that night. We were at Eduardo's out in the Chico district and the piano player was playing "Love Is Blue" and we were drinking an indifferent bottle of Château Léoville-Poyferré which cost $20 American. "Spain sent all its highest aristocracy to South America." In fact I had heard variations on this hallucination before, on the coast: when Colombians spoke about the past I often had the sense of being in a place where history tended to sink, even as it happened, into the traceless solitude of autosuggestion. The princess was drinking pink champagne. High in the mountains the men were made of gold. Spain sent its highest aristocracy to South America. They were all stories a child might invent.

Many years later, as he faced the firing squad, Colonel Aureliano Buendía was to remember that distant afternoon when his father took him to discover ice.

—The opening line of ONE HUNDRED
YEARS OF SOLITUDE, by the
Colombian novelist Gabriel García
Márquez.

At the big movie theaters in Bogotá in the spring of 1973 *The Professionals* was playing, and *It's a Mad Mad Mad Mad World,* two American pictures released in, respectively, 1967 and 1964. The English-language racks of paperback stands were packed with Edmund Wilson's *The Cold War and the Income Tax,* the 1964 Signet edition. This slight but definite dislocation of time fixed on the mind the awesome isolation of the place, as did dislocations of other kinds. On the fourth floor of the glossy new Bogotá Hilton one could lunch in an orchid-filled gallery that overlooked the indoor swimming pool, and also overlooked a shantytown of packing-crate and tin-can shacks where a small boy, his body hideously scarred and his face obscured by a knitted mask, played listlessly with a yo-yo. In the lobby of the Hotel Tequendama two Braniff stewardesses in turquoise-blue Pucci pantsuits flirted desultorily with a German waiting for the airport limousine; a third ignored the German and stood before a relief map on which buttons could be pressed to light up the major cities of Colombia. Santa Marta, on the coast; Barranquilla, Cartagena. Medellín, on the Central Cordillera. Cali, on the Cauca River, San Agustín on the Magdalena. Leticia, on the Amazon.

I watched her press the buttons one by one, transfixed by the vast darkness each tiny bulb illumined. The light for Bogotá blinked twice and went out. The girl in the Pucci pantsuit traced the Andes with her index finger. *Alto arrecife de la aurora humana,* the Chilean poet Pablo Neruda called the Andes. *High reef of the human dawn.* It cost the *conquistador* Gonzalo Jiménez de Quesada two years and the health of most of his men to reach Bogotá from the coast. It cost me $26.

"I knew they were your bags," the man at the airport said, producing them triumphantly from a moraine of baggage and cartons and rubble from the construction that seemed all over Bogotá a chronic condition. "They smelled American." *Parece una turista norteamericana,* I read about myself in *El Espectador* a few mornings later. She resembles an American tourist. In fact I was aware of being an American in Colombia in a way I had not been in other places. I kept running into Americans, compatriots for whom the emotional center of Bogotá was the massive concrete embassy on Carrera 10, members of a phantom colony called "the American presence" which politesse prevented them from naming out loud. Several times I met a young American who ran an "information" office, which he urged me to visit; he had extremely formal manners, appeared for the most desultory evening in black tie, and was, according to the Colombian I asked, CIA. I recall talking at a party to a USIS man who spoke in a low mellifluous voice of fevers he had known, fevers in Sierra Leone, fevers in Monrovia, fevers on the Colombian coast. Our host interrupted this litany, demanded to know why the ambassador had not come to the party. "Little situation in Cali," the USIS man said, and smiled professionally. He seemed very concerned that no breach of American manners be inferred, and so, absurdly, did I. We had nothing in common except the eagles on our passports, but those eagles made us, in some way I did not entirely understand, co-conspirators, two strangers heavy with responsibility for seeing that the eagle should not offend. We would prefer the sweet local Roman-Cola to the Coca-Cola the Colombians liked. We would think of Standard Oil as Esso Colombiano. We would not speak of fever except to one another. Later I met an American actor who had spent two weeks taking cold showers in Bogotá before he discovered that the hot and cold taps in the room assigned him were simply reversed: he had never asked, he said, because he did not want to be considered an arrogant *gringo.*

In *El Tiempo* that morning I had read that General Gustavo Rojas Pinilla, who took over Colombia in a military coup in 1953 and closed down the press before he was overthrown in 1957, was launching a new bid for power on a Peronist platform, and I had thought that perhaps people at the party would be talking about that, but they were not. Why had the American film industry not made films about the Vietnam War, was what the Colombian stringer for the Caribbean newspaper wanted to talk about. The young Colombian filmmakers looked at him incredulously. "What would be the point," one finally shrugged. "They run that war on television."

The filmmakers had lived in New York, spoke of Rip Torn, Norman Mailer, Ricky Leacock, Super 8. One had come to the party in a stovepipe preacher's hat; another in a violet macramé shawl to the knees. The girl with them, a famous beauty from the coast, wore a flamingo-pink sequinned midriff, and her pale red hair was fluffed around her head in an electric halo. She watched the *cumbia* dancers and fondled a baby ocelot and remained impassive both to the possibility of General Gustavo Rojas Pinilla's comeback and to the question of why the American film industry had not made films about the Vietnam War. Later, outside the gate, the filmmakers lit thick marijuana cigarettes in view of the uniformed *policia* and asked if I knew Paul Morrissey's and Andy Warhol's address in Rome. The girl from the coast cradled her ocelot against the wind.

Of the time I spent in Bogotá I remember mainly images, indelible but difficult to connect. I remember the walls on the second floor of the Museo Nacional, white and cool and lined with portraits of the presidents of Colombia, a great many presidents. I remember the emeralds in shop windows, lying casually in trays, all of them oddly pale at the center, somehow watered, cold at the very heart where one expects the fire. I asked the price of one: "Twenty-thousand American," the woman said. She was reading a booklet called *Horóscopo: Sagitario* and did not look up. I remember walking across Plaza Bolívar, the great square from which all Colombian power emanates, at mid-afternoon when men in dark European suits stood talking on the steps of the Capitol and the mountains floated all around, their perspective made fluid by sun and shadow; I remember the way the mountains dwarfed a deserted Ferris wheel in the Parque Nacional in late afternoon.

In fact the mountains loom behind every image I remember, and perhaps are themselves the connection. Some afternoons I would drive out along their talus slopes through the Chico district, out Carrera 7 where the grounds of the great houses were immaculately clipped and the gates bore brass plaques with the names of European embassies and American foundations and Argentinian neurologists. I recall stopping in El Chico to make a telephone call one day, from a small shopping center off Carrera 7; the shopping center adjoined a church where a funeral mass had just taken place. The mourners were leaving the church, talking on the street, the women, most of them, in black pantsuits and violet-tinted glasses and pleated silk dresses and Givenchy coats that had not been bought in Bogotá. In El Chico it did not seem so far to Paris or New York, but there remained the mountains, and beyond the mountains that dense world described by Gabriel García Márquez as so recent that many things lacked names.

And even just a little farther, out where Carrera 7 became the Carretera Central del Norte, the rutted road that plunged through the mountains to Tunja and eventually to Caracas, it was in many ways a perpetual frontier, vertiginous in its extremes. Rickety buses hurtled dizzyingly down the center of the road, swerving now and then to pick up a laborer, to avoid a pothole or a pack of children. Back from the road stretched large *haciendas,* their immense main houses barely visible in the folds of the slopes, their stone walls splashed occasionally with red paint, crude representations of the hammer and sickle and admonitions to vote *comunista.* One day when I was out there a cloud burst, and because my rented car with 110,000 miles on it had no windshield wipers, I stopped by the side of the road. Rain streamed over the MESA ARIZONA WESTWOOD WARRIORS and GO TIDE decals on the car windows. Gullies formed on the road. Up in the high gravel quarries men worked on, picking with shovels at the Andes for twelve and a half pesos a load.

> *Through another of our cities without a center, as hideous*
> *as Los Angeles, and with as many cars*
> *per head, and past the 20-foot neon sign*
> *for* Coppertone *on a church, past the population*
> *earning $700 per capita*
> *in jerry skyscraper living-slabs, and on to the White House*
> *of El Presidente Leoni, his small men with 18-*
> *inch repeating pistols, firing 45 bullets a minute,*
> *the two armed guards petrified beside us, while we had champagne,*
> *and someone bugging the President: "Where are the girls?"*
> *And the enclosed leader, quite a fellow, saying,*
> *"I don't know where yours are, but I know where to find mine.". . .*
> *This house, this pioneer democracy, built*
> *on foundations, not of rock, but blood as hard as rock.*
>
> —ROBERT LOWELL, "Caracas"

There is one more image I remember, and it comes in two parts. First there was the mine. Tunneled into a mountain in Zipaquirá, fifty kilometers north of Bogotá, is a salt mine. This single mine produces, each year, enough salt for all of South America, and has done so since before Europeans knew the continent existed: salt, not gold, was the economic basis of the Chibcha Empire, and Zipaquirá one of its capitals. The mine is vast, its air oppressive. I happened to be inside the mine because inside the mine there is, carved into the mountain 450 feet below the surface, a cathedral in which 10,000 people can hear mass at the same time. Fourteen massive stone pilasters support the vault. Recessed fluorescent tubes illuminate the Stations of the Cross, the dense air absorbing and dimming the light unsteadily. One could think of Chibcha sacrifices here, of the *conquistador* priests struggling to superimpose the European mass on the screams of the slaughtered children.

But one would be wrong. The building of this enigmatic excavation in the salt mountain was undertaken not by the Chibcha but by the Banco de la República, in 1954. In 1954 General Gustavo Rojas Pinilla and his colonels were running Colombia, and the country was wrenched by *La Violencia,* the fifteen years of anarchy that followed the assassination of Jorge Gaitán in Bogotá in 1948. In 1954 people were fleeing the terrorized countryside to squat in shacks in the comparative safety of Bogotá. In 1954 Colombia still had few public works projects, no transportation to speak of: Bogotá would not be connected by rail with the Caribbean until 1961. As I stood in the dim mountain reading the Banco de la República's dedicatory plaque, 1954 seemed to me an extraordinary year to have hit on the notion of building a cathedral of salt, but the Colombians to whom I mentioned it only shrugged.

The second part of the image. I had come up from the mine and was having lunch on the side of the salt mountain, in the chilly dining room of the Hostería del Libertador. There were heavy draperies that gave off a faint muskiness when touched. There were white brocade tablecloths, carefully darned. For every stalk of blanched asparagus served, there appeared another battery of silverplated flatware and platters and *vinaigrette* sauceboats, and also another battery of "waiters": little boys, twelve or thirteen years old, dressed in tailcoats and white gloves and taught to serve as if this small inn on an Andean precipice were Vienna under the Hapsburgs.

I sat there for a long time. All around us the wind was sweeping the clouds off the Andes and across the savannah. Four hundred and fifty feet beneath us was the cathedral built of salt in the year 1954. *This house, this pioneer democracy, built on foundations, not of rock, but blood as hard as rock.* One of the little boys in white gloves picked up an empty wine bottle from a table, fitted it precisely into a wine holder, and marched toward the kitchen holding it stiffly before him, glancing covertly at the *maître d'hôtel* for approval. It seemed to me later that I had never before seen and would perhaps never again see the residuum of European custom so movingly and pointlessly observed.

Double Take

1. In the final sentence of this essay, Didion writes, "It seemed to me later that I had never before seen and would perhaps never again see the residuum of European custom so movingly and pointlessly observed." Pairing the words "movingly" and "pointlessly"—words we would often see as opposites—seems to be an interesting, and very deliberate, strategy. What do you suppose Didion is trying to

convey about what she witnessed by pairing these words together? Do you think this wording is effective?

2. "In Bogotá" blends a good number of vivid descriptions of different events and stories to compile a single essay. As you think about the many images depicted in this piece, ask yourself which one stands out as the best? Why do you suppose that one image stands out above the others? What are some ways Didion links the many images in this essay to create cohesion between them?

3. In a couple of instances, Didion turns to the words of other writers, such as Colombian writer Gabriel García Márquez and Chilean poet Pablo Neruda, as well as anthropologist Olivia Vlahos. What does Didion accomplish by citing these authors? Why do you think she selected these authors in particular?

Seeing for Yourself

At First Glance

In 1975 Patricia Campbell Hearst, granddaughter of William Randolph Hearst, one of the country's most famous newspaper moguls, was kidnapped from her home by the Symbionese Liberation Army (SLA), a radical terrorist group. She was arrested after aiding the SLA in a series of bank robberies and after opening fire on a San Francisco street with a machine gun. Hearst's trial was one of the most widely covered news stories of the 1970s. In "Girl of the Golden West" Joan Didion recounts the events that led to Hearst's trial and the events of the trial. Her essay is a commentary not only on the fascinating events themselves, but on the ways that the media covered these events. For many of us, reading Didion's essay may evoke images of other famous media events: the O.J. Simpson trial, the Menendez brothers' trial, the Bill Clinton impeachment trials, and so on. As you read this essay, think about how Didion's commentary on media coverage of such events as the Hearst case might be read today. That is, could a similar essay be written now about more contemporary events? How might such an essay be written?

Girl of the Golden West

The domestic details spring to memory. Early on the evening of February 4, 1974, in her duplex apartment at 2603 Benvenue in Berkeley, Patricia Campbell Hearst, age nineteen, a student of art history at the University of California at Berkeley and a granddaughter of the late William Randolph Hearst, put on a blue terrycloth bathrobe, heated a can of chicken-noodle soup and made tuna fish sandwiches for herself and her fiancé, Steven Weed; watched "Mission Impossible" and "The Magician" on television; cleaned up the dishes; sat down to study just as the doorbell rang; was abducted at gunpoint and held blindfolded, by three men and five women who called themselves the Symbionese Liberation Army, for the next fifty-seven days.

From the fifty-eighth day, on which she agreed to join her captors and was photographed in front of the SLA's cobra flag carrying a sawed-off M-1 carbine, until September 18, 1975, when she was arrested in San Francisco, Patricia Campbell Hearst participated actively in the robberies of the Hibernia Bank in San Francisco and the Crocker National Bank outside Sacramento; sprayed Crenshaw Boulevard in Los Angeles with a submachine gun to cover a comrade apprehended for shoplifting; and was party or witness to a number of less publicized thefts and several bombings, to which she would later refer as "actions," or "operations."

On trial in San Francisco for the Hibernia Bank operation she appeared in court wearing frosted-white nail polish, and demonstrated for the jury the bolt action necessary to chamber an M-1. On a psychiatric test administered while she was in custody she completed the sentence "Most men . . ." with the words ". . . are assholes." Seven years later she was living with the bodyguard she had married, their infant daughter, and two German shepherds "behind locked doors in a Spanish-style house equipped with the best electronic security system available," describing herself as "older and wiser," and dedicating her account of these events, *Every Secret Thing,* to "Mom and Dad."

It was a special kind of sentimental education, a public coming-of-age with an insistently literary cast to it, and it seemed at the time to offer a parable for the period. Certain of its images entered the national memory. We had Patricia Campbell Hearst in her first-communion dress, smiling, and we had Patricia Campbell Hearst in the Hibernia Bank surveillance stills, not smiling. We again had her smiling in the engagement picture, an unremarkably pretty girl in a simple dress on a sunny lawn, and we again had her not smiling in the "Tania" snapshot, the famous Polaroid with the M-1. We had her with her father and her sister Anne in a photograph taken at the Burlingame Country Club some months before the kidnapping: all three Hearsts smiling there, not only smiling but wearing leis, the father in maile and orchid leis, the daughters in pikake, that rarest and most expensive of lei, strand after strand of tiny Arabian jasmine buds strung like ivory beads.

We had the bank of microphones in front of the Hillsborough house whenever Randolph and Catherine Hearst ("Dad" and "Mom" in the first spectral messages from the absent daughter, "pig Hearsts" as the spring progressed) met the press, the potted flowers on the steps changing with the seasons, domestic upkeep intact in the face of crisis: azaleas, fuchsias, then cymbidium orchids massed for Easter. We had, early on, the ugly images of looting and smashed cameras and frozen turkey legs hurled through windows in West Oakland, the violent result of the Hearsts' first attempt to meet the SLA ransom demand, and we had, on television the same night, the news that William Knowland, the former United States senator from California and the most prominent member of the family that had run Oakland for half a century, had taken the pistol he was said to carry as protection against terrorists, positioned himself on a bank of the Russian River, and blown off the top of his head.

All of these pictures told a story, taught a dramatic lesson, carrying as they did the *frisson* of one another, the invitation to compare and contrast. The image of Patricia Campbell Hearst on the FBI "wanted" fliers was for example cropped from the image of the unremarkably pretty girl in the simple dress on the sunny lawn, schematic evidence that even a golden girl could be pinned in the beam of history. There was no actual connection between turkey legs thrown through windows in West Oakland and William Knowland lying facedown in the Russian River, but the paradigm was manifest, one California busy being born and another busy dying. Those cymbidiums on the Hearsts' doorstep in Hillsborough dissolved before our eyes into the image of a flaming palm tree in south-central Los Angeles (the model again was two Californias), the palm tree above the stucco bungalow in which Patricia Campbell Hearst was believed for a time to be burning to death on live television. (Actually Patricia Campbell Hearst was in yet a third California, a motel room at Disneyland, watching the palm tree burn as we all were, on television, and it was Donald DeFreeze, Nancy Ling Perry, Angela Atwood, Patricia Soltysik, Camilla Hall, and William Wolfe, one black escaped convict and five children of the white middle class, who were dying in the stucco bungalow.)

Not only the images but the voice told a story, the voice on the tapes, the depressed voice with the California inflection, the voice that trailed off, now almost inaudible, then a hint of whine, a schoolgirl's sarcasm, a voice every parent recognized: *Mom, Dad. I'm OK. I had a few scrapes and stuff, but they washed them up. . . . I just hope you'll do what they say, Dad. . . . If you can get the food thing organized before the nineteenth then that's OK. . . . Whatever you come up with is basically OK, it was never intended that you feed the whole state. . . . I am here because I am a member of a ruling-class family and I think you can begin to see the analogy. . . . People should stop acting like I'm dead, Mom should get out of her black dress, that doesn't help at all. . . . Mom, Dad . . . I don't believe you're doing all you can . . . Mom, Dad . . . I'm starting to think that no one is concerned about me anymore. . . .* And then: *Greetings to the people. This is Tania.*

Patricia Campbell Hearst's great-grandfather had arrived in California by foot in 1850, unschooled, unmarried, thirty years old with few graces and no prospects, a Missouri farmer's son who would spend his thirties scratching around El Dorado and Nevada and Sacramento counties looking for a stake. In 1859 he found one, and at his death in 1891 George Hearst could leave the schoolteacher he had married in 1862 a fortune taken from the ground, the continuing proceeds from the most productive mines of the period, the Ophir in Nevada, the Homestake in South Dakota, the Ontario in Utah, the Anaconda in Montana, the San Luis in Mexico. The widow, Phoebe Apperson Hearst, a tiny, strong-minded woman then only forty-eight years old, took this apparently artesian income and financed her only child in the publishing empire he wanted, underwrote a surprising amount of the campus where her great-granddaughter would be enrolled at the time she was kidnapped, and built for herself, on sixty-seven thousand acres on the McCloud River in Siskiyou County, the original Wyntoon, a quarried-lava castle of which its architect, Bernard Maybeck, said simply: "Here you can reach all that is within you."

The extent to which certain places dominate the California imagination is apprehended, even by Californians, only dimly. Deriving not only from the landscape but from the claiming of it, from the romance of emigration, the radical abandonment of established attachments, this imagination remains obdurately symbolic, tending to locate lessons in what the rest of the country perceives only as scenery. Yosemite, for example, remains what Kevin Starr has called "one of the primary California symbols, a fixed factor of identity for all those who sought a primarily California aesthetic." Both the community of and the coastline at Carmel have a symbolic meaning lost to the contemporary visitor, a lingering allusion to art as freedom, freedom as craft, the "bohemian" pantheism of the early twentieth century. The Golden Gate Bridge, referring as it does to both the infinite and technology, suggests, to the Californian, a quite complex representation of land's end, and also of its beginning.

Patricia Campbell Hearst told us in *Every Secret Thing* that the place the Hearsts called Wyntoon was "a mystical land," "fantastic, otherworldly," "even more than San Simeon," which was in turn "so emotionally moving that it is still beyond my powers of description." That first Maybeck castle on the McCloud River was seen by most Californians only in photographs, and yet, before it burned in 1933, to be replaced by a compound of rather more playful Julia Morgan chalets ("Cinderella House," "Angel House," "Brown Bear House"), Phoebe Hearst's gothic Wyntoon and her son's baroque San Simeon seemed between them to embody certain opposing impulses in the local consciousness: northern and southern, wilderness sanctified and wilderness banished, the aggrandizement of nature and the aggrandizement of self. Wyntoon had mists, and allusions to the infinite, great trunks of trees left to rot where they fell, a wild river, barbaric fireplaces. San Simeon, swimming in sunlight and the here and now, had two swimming pools, and a zoo.

It was a family in which the romantic impulse would seem to have dimmed. Patricia Campbell Hearst told us that she "grew up in an atmosphere of clear blue skies, bright sunshine, rambling open spaces, long green lawns, large comfortable houses, country clubs with swimming pools and tennis courts and riding horses." At the Convent of the Sacred Heart in Menlo Park she told a nun to "go to hell," and thought herself "quite courageous, although very stupid." At Santa Catalina in Monterey she and Patricia Tobin, whose family founded one of the banks the SLA would later rob, skipped Benediction, and received "a load of demerits." Her father taught her to shoot, duck hunting. Her mother did not allow her to wear jeans into San Francisco. These were inheritors who tended to keep their names out of the paper, to exhibit not much interest in the world at large ("Who the hell is this guy again?" Randolph Hearst asked Steven Weed when the latter suggested trying to approach the SLA through Regis Debray, and then, when told, said, "We need a goddamn South American revolutionary mixed up in this thing like a hole in the head"), and to regard most forms of distinction with the reflexive distrust of the country club.

Yet if the Hearsts were no longer a particularly arresting California family, they remained embedded in the symbolic content of the place, and for a Hearst to be kidnapped from Berkeley, the very citadel of Phoebe Hearst's aspiration, was California as opera. "My thoughts at this time were focused on the single issue of survival," the heiress to Wyntoon and San Simeon told us about the fifty-seven days she spent in the closet. "Concerns over love and marriage, family life, friends, human relationships, my whole previous life, had really become, in SLA terms, bourgeois luxuries."

This abrupt sloughing of the past has, to the California ear, a distant echo, and the echo is of emigrant diaries. "Don't let this letter dishearten anybody, never take no cutoffs and hurry along as fast as you can", one of the surviving children of the Donner Party concluded her account of that crossing. "Don't worry about it", the author of *Every Secret Thing* reported having told herself in the closet after her first sexual encounter with a member of the SLA. "Don't examine your feelings. Never examine your feelings—they're no help at all." At the time Patricia Campbell Hearst was on trial in San Francisco, a number of psychiatrists were brought in to try to plumb what seemed to some an unsoundable depth in the narrative, that moment at which the victim binds over her fate to her captors. "She experienced what I call the death anxiety and the breaking point," Robert Jay Lifton, who was one of these psychiatrists, said. "Her external points of reference for maintenance of her personality had disappeared," Louis Jolyon West, another of the psychiatrists, said. Those were two ways of looking at it, and another was that Patricia Campbell Hearst had cut her losses and headed west, as her great-grandfather had before her.

The story she told in 1982 in *Every Secret Thing* was received, in the main, querulously, just as it had been when she told it during *The United States of America v. Patricia Campbell Hearst,* the 1976 proceeding during which she was tried for and convicted of the armed robbery of the Hibernia Bank (one count) and (the second count), the use of a weapon during the commission of a felony. Laconic, slightly ironic, resistant not only to the prosecution but to her own defense, Patricia Hearst was not, on trial in San Francisco, a conventionally ingratiating personality. "I don't know," I recall her saying over and over again during the few days I attended the trial. "I don't remember." "I suppose so." Had there not been, the prosecutor asked one day, telephones in the motels in which she had stayed when she drove across the country with Jack Scott? I recall Patricia Hearst looking at him as if she thought him deranged. I recall Randolph Hearst looking at the floor. I recall Catherine Hearst arranging a Galanos jacket over the back of her seat.

"Yes, I'm sure," their daughter said.

Where, the prosecutor asked, were these motels?

"One was . . . I think . . ." Patricia Hearst paused, and then: "Cheyenne? Wyoming?" She pronounced the names as if they were foreign, exotic, information registered and jettisoned. One of these motels had been in Nevada, the place from which the Hearst money originally came: the heiress pronounced the name *Nevahda,* like a foreigner.

In *Every Secret Thing* as at her trial, she seemed to project an emotional distance, a peculiar combination of passivity and pragmatic recklessness ("I had crossed over. And I would have to make the best of it . . . to live from day to day, to do whatever they said, to play my part, and to pray that I would survive") that many people found inexplicable and irritating. In 1982 as in 1976, she spoke only abstractly about *why,* but quite specifically about *how.* "I could not believe that I had actually fired that submachine gun," she said of the incident in which she shot up Crenshaw Boulevard, but here was how she did it: "I kept my finger pressed on the trigger until the entire clip of thirty shots had been fired . . . I then reached for my own weapon, the semi-automatic carbine. I got off three more shots . . ."

And, after her book as after her trial, the questions raised were not exactly about her veracity but about her authenticity, her general intention, about whether she was, as the assistant prosecutor put it during the trial, "for real." This was necessarily a vain line of inquiry (whether or not she "loved" William Wolfe was the actual point on which the trial came to turn), and one that encouraged a curious rhetorical regression among the inquisitors. "Why did she choose to write this book?" Mark

Starr asked about *Every Secret Thing* in *Newsweek,* and then answered himself: "Possibly she has inherited her family's journalistic sense of what will sell." "The rich get richer," Jane Alpert concluded in *New York* magazine. "Patty," Ted Morgan observed in the *New York Times Book Review,* "is now, thanks to the proceeds of her book, reverting to a more traditional family pursuit, capital formation."

These were dreamy notions of what a Hearst might do to turn a dollar, but they reflected a larger dissatisfaction, a conviction that the Hearst in question was telling less than the whole story, "leaving something out," although what the something might have been, given the doggedly detailed account offered in *Every Secret Thing,* would be hard to define. If "questions still linger," as they did for *Newsweek,* those questions were not about how to lace a bullet with cyanide: the way the SLA did it was to drill into the lead tip to a point just short of the gunpowder, dip the tiny hole in a mound of cyanide crystals, and seal it with paraffin. If *Every Secret Thing* "creates more puzzles than it solves," as it did for Jane Alpert, those questions were not about how to make a pipe bomb: the trick here was to pack enough gunpowder into the pipe for a big bang and still leave sufficient oxygen for ignition, a problem, as Patricia Hearst saw it, of "devising the proper proportions of gunpowder, length of pipe and toaster wire, minus Teko's precious toilet paper." "Teko," or Bill Harris, insisted on packing his bombs with toilet paper, and, when one of them failed to explode under a police car in the Mission District, reacted with "one of his worst temper tantrums." Many reporters later found Bill and Emily Harris the appealing defendants that Patricia Hearst never was, but *Every Secret Thing* presented a convincing case for their being, as the author put it, not only "unattractive" but, her most pejorative adjective, "incompetent."

As notes from the underground go, Patricia Hearst's were eccentric in detail. She told us that Bill Harris's favorite television program was "S.W.A.T." (one could, he said, "learn a lot about the pigs' tactics by watching these programs"); that Donald DeFreeze, or "Cinque," drank plum wine from half-gallon jugs and listened to the radio for allusions to the revolution in song lyrics; and that Nancy Ling Perry, who was usually cast by the press in the rather glamorous role of "former cheerleader and Goldwater Girl," was four feet eleven inches tall, and affected a black accent. Emily Harris trained herself to "live with deprivation" by chewing only half sticks of gum. Bill Harris bought a yarmulke, under the impression that this was the way, during the sojourn in the Catskills after the Los Angeles shoot-out, to visit Grossinger's unnoticed.

Life with these people had the distorted logic of dreams, and Patricia Hearst seems to have accepted it with the wary acquiescence of the dreamer. Any face could turn against her. Any move could prove lethal. "My sisters and I had been brought up to believe that we were responsible for what we did and could not blame our transgressions on something being wrong inside our heads. I had joined the SLA because if I didn't they would have killed me. And I remained with them because I truly believed that the FBI would kill me if they could, and if not, the SLA would." She had, as she put it, crossed over. She would, as she put it, make the best of it, and not "reach back to family or friends."

This was the point on which most people foundered, doubted her, found her least explicable, and it was also the point at which she was most specifically the child of a certain culture. Here is the single personal note in an emigrant diary kept by a relative of mine, William Kilgore, the journal of an overland crossing to Sacramento in 1850: "This is one of the trying mornings for me, as I now have to leave my family, or back out. Suffice it to say, we started." Suffice it to say. Don't examine your feelings, they're no help at all. Never take no cutoffs and hurry along as fast as you can. We need a goddamn South American revolutionary mixed up in this thing like a hole in the head. This was a California girl, and she was raised on a history that placed not much emphasis on *why*.

She was never an idealist, and this pleased no one. She was tainted by survival. She came back from the other side with a story no one wanted to hear, a dispiriting account of a situation in which delusion and incompetence were pitted against delusion and incompetence of another kind, and in the febrile rhythms of San Francisco in the midseventies it seemed a story devoid of high notes. The week her trial ended in 1976, the *San Francisco Bay Guardian* published an interview in which members of a collective called New Dawn expressed regret at her defection. "It's a question of your self-respect or your ass," one of them said. "If you choose your ass, you live with nothing." This idea that the SLA represented an idea worth defending (if only on the grounds that any idea must be better than none) was common enough at the time, although most people granted that the idea had gone awry. By March of 1977 another writer in the *Bay Guardian* was making a distinction between the "unbridled adventurism" of the SLA and the "discipline and skill" of the New World Liberation Front, whose "fifty-odd bombings without a casualty" made them a "definitely preferable alternative" to the SLA.

As it happened I had kept this issue of the *Bay Guardian,* dated March 31, 1977 (the *Bay Guardian* was not at the time a notably radical paper, by the way, but one that provided a fair guide to local tofu cookery and the mood of the community), and when I got it out to look at the piece on the SLA I noticed for the first time another piece: a long and favorable report on a San Francisco minister whose practice it was to "confront people and challenge their basic assumptions . . . as if he can't let the evil of the world pass him by, a characteristic he shares with other moral leaders." The minister, who was compared at one point to Cesar Chavez, was responsible, according to the writer, for a "mind-boggling" range of social service programs— food distribution, legal aid, drug rehabilitation, nursing homes, free Pap smears—as well as for a "twenty-seven-thousand-acre agricultural station." The agricultural station was in Guyana, and the minister of course was the Reverend Jim Jones, who eventually chose self-respect over his own and nine hundred other asses. This was another local opera, and one never spoiled by a protagonist who insisted on telling it her way.

A CLOSER LOOK AT JOAN DIDION

1. In looking at these four essays as representative of Joan Didion's work as an essayist, you may begin to notice certain traits in her writing that carry through from essay to essay, such as the delicate attention she pays to writing her sentences, as we mentioned earlier. But you may also want to consider what is different about these essays. That is, where, if at all, does Didion vary her writing—not necessarily the subjects about which she writes—but the ways in which she writes about those subjects? Does she write about issues like feminism in different ways than she writes about writing, about people? Do the subjects we write about affect the ways that we write? Select two of Didion's essays, and in an essay of your own, compare and contrast her writing in each.

2. In each of these essays, Didion approaches some fairly controversial and debatable subjects: feminism, American and European influence on other countries, the media's role in America, and the power of writing. Why do you suppose she chooses the essay as the form in which to address these issues? That is, does the essay as a genre lend itself to discussing and debating contested issues? Make an argument that either defends the essay as a useful form for addressing these topics or argue against the essay as an effective medium in these discussions. Be sure to clarify what you mean both by *essay* and the kinds of subjects Didion uses.

3. In each of these essays, Didion conveys a good deal of information about the subjects on which she writes. For instance, in "The Women's Movement" she provides background about the feminisms she argues against. In "In Bogotá" she tells us about how Bogotá is perceived by Americans traveling in that part of the world. In "Girl of the Golden West," Didion gives us both a history lesson about the Patricia Hearst case and a review of how the media covered that and similar events. Why do you suppose Didion spends so much time providing so much detail? What effect does the information she provides readers have on the structure of her essays? Does the information have any impact on you as a reader? In an essay of your own, respond to these questions, making sure to establish and support your response as an argument.

Looking from Writer to Writer

1. In the introductory information we provide here about Joan Didion, we note that Didion is exceptionally self-conscious of her sentences and how she constructs them. Similarly, Joseph Epstein articulates a very self-conscious attention to the language level of his writing. Looking back over the careful sentence construction of these two authors, do you recognize any characteristics about their sentences

that make their writing enjoyable (or even unpleasant) to you? Does their writing seem more exact than any of the other authors' work found in this collection? Can you find anything about their sentences that you might want to model in your own writing?

2. The first essay in this writer-chapter is Joan Didion's "Why I Write," which is a revised version of a Regents' Lecture that she delivered at the University of California, Berkeley. Similarly, the first essay in the Ursula Le Guin writer-chapter, "Prospects for Women in Writing," was also first delivered as a talk and revised as a published essay. John Updike's essay "Why Write?" was originally given as a speech at the Festival of Arts in Adelaide, South Australia. Reread all three of these essays and consider whether they share any similar traits that might have resulted from their having been written first as speeches.

3. Joan Didion addresses issues of feminism in several of her essays, including those printed here. Likewise, bell hooks, Ursula Le Guin, Barbara Ehrenreich, and Alice Walker all address feminist issues in their essays in this anthology. How do each of these authors take on such an important subject like feminist issues? Do you find similarities in their writing? Differences?

Looking Beyond

NONFICTION
Miami. 1987. New York: Vintage Books, 1998.
Salvador. 1983. New York: Vintage Books, 1994.
Sentimental Journeys. New York: HarperCollins, 1993.
Slouching Towards Bethlehem. 1968. New York: Modern Library, 2000.
The White Album. 1979. New York: Noonday Press, 1990.

FICTION
A Book of Common Prayer. 1977. New York: Vintage Books, 1995.
Democracy: A Novel. 1984. New York: Vintage Books, 1995.
The Last Thing He Wanted. 1996. New York: Vintage Books, 1997.
Play It As It Lays: A Novel. 1970. New York: Noonday Press, 1990.
Run River. 1963. New York: Vintage Books, 1994.

Annie Dillard

Annie Dillard has had an extensive and influential career as a writer and educator. She has written for numerous magazines, including *Atlantic Monthly, American Scholar, Poetry, New York Times Magazine, New York Times Book Review, Chicago Review,* and as a columnist for *The Living Wilderness,* to name but a few. She served as editor of *Harper's* magazine from 1973 until 1985. Dillard has taught at several colleges and universities, and in 1982 served on the United States Cultural Delegation to China. But mostly, Annie Dillard is known for her writing, for which she has been honored with an array of awards. Most significant of these awards was the 1975 Pulitzer Prize for general nonfiction for her collection of essays, *Pilgrim at Tinker Creek.* For her contributions to the study of Catholic traditions and literature, she won the 1994 Milton Prize and the 1994 Campion Medal. There is little question that since she was awarded the Pulitzer Prize, Annie Dillard has been one of the most influential writers of the late 20th century and the early 21st century.

Annie Doak was born on April 30, 1945, in Pittsburgh to Frank and Pam Doak. She attended a private girls' school and began writing fiction and poetry while in high school. She received her bachelor's degree from Hollins College in Roanoke, Virginia, in 1967 where she majored in writing and was elected to Phi Beta Kappa. She went on to earn a master's degree from Hollins in 1968. While enrolled at Hollins, Annie Doak married her teacher R. H. W. Dillard, also a writer. In 1988 Dillard converted to Catholicism, a conversion of devotion that is often reflected in her writing.

In 1974 Dillard's first book, *Tickets for a Prayer Wheel,* was published. This book of poetry contained several previously published poems and many never before published poems. As would become true of most of her writing, the poems in *Tickets for a Prayer Wheel* reflected her devotion to nature and her deep devotion to and curiosity about God. Dillard is often thought of as a "nature writer," but her writing also ponders the significance of God and religious faith. For Dillard, the question of the existence of God is crucial, for she is able to see the wonders and beauty of a world created by God, but she also questions God's existence because the world is full of pain and suffering. Only when Dillard's writing specifically addresses writing, as it does in books like *Living by Fiction* and *The Writing Life,* does she temporarily abandon her quest for answers about God.

In many ways, Dillard is a difficult writer to label. She writes in several genres, including fiction, nonfiction, and poetry. She addresses a range of subject matter, and can best be described as a "wanderer." Dillard says of herself, "I am a wanderer with a background in theology and a penchant for quirky facts." Not only does her writing describe her travels around the world, but her rhetorical strategies and writing styles also wander, as though she were exploring the world through her writing as one might wander across a country. Dillard's writing has often been compared to that of Henry David Thoreau, and *Pilgrim at Tinker Creek,* in particular, seems reminiscent of Thoreau's *Walden.* In a book review of *Tickets for a Prayer Wheel,* Loren Eiseley proclaimed that Dillard "loves the country below. Like Emerson, she sees the virulence in nature as well as the beauty that entrances her."

While reading the essays gathered here, pay attention to the choices Dillard makes in her writing. She is known as a meticulous writer who "strives for excellence in her writing." Note specifically her voice in each essay and the way she addresses the reader. Consider how her carefully detailed descriptions emphasize points she makes and how those descriptions affect her credibility as a writer. That is, think about how the inclusion of details makes an author seem knowledgeable about a particular subject or place. And, while seeing the details she presents, notice how she asks readers to ponder deeply philosophical and sophisticated questions through writing that is both comfortable and considerate of the reader.

Dillard on Writing

At First Glance

As you read the selection here from The Writing Life, *you will probably notice that Annie Dillard compares the activity of writing to a variety of activities: wood carving, surgery, carpentry, painting, opening gifts, photography, and so on. In addition, she uses a good number of images to illuminate her notions of the activity of writing: an inchworm, a shoe salesman, an X ray, among others. While reading this essay, think about how Dillard uses these allusions, images, similes, and metaphors to assist in achieving her goals. What choices might she have made in each instance to turn to the examples she does?*

From *The Writing Life,* "Chapter One" A Line of Words

When you write, you lay out a line of words. The line of words is a miner's pick, a wood-carver's gouge, a surgeon's probe. You wield it, and it digs a path you follow. Soon you find yourself deep in new territory. It is a dead end, or have you located the real subject? You will know tomorrow, or this time next year.

You make the path boldly and follow it fearfully. You go where the path leads. At the end of the path, you find a box canyon. You hammer out reports, dispatch bulletins.

The writing has changed, in your hands, and in a twinkling, from an expression of your notions to an epistemological tool. The new place interests you because it is not clear. You attend. In your humility, you lay down the words carefully, watching all the angles. Now the earlier writing looks soft and careless. Process is nothing; erase your tracks. The path is not the work. I hope your tracks have grown over; I hope birds ate the crumbs; I hope you will toss it all and not look back.

The line of words is a hammer. You hammer against the walls of your house. You tap the walls, lightly, everywhere. After giving many years' attention to these things, you know what to listen for. Some of the walls are bearing walls; they have to stay, or everything will fall down. Other walls can go with impunity; you can hear the difference. Unfortunately, it is often a bearing wall that has to go. It cannot be helped. There is only one solution, which appalls you, but there it is. Knock it out. Duck.

Courage utterly opposes the bold hope that this is such fine stuff the work needs it, or the world. Courage, exhausted, stands on bare reality: this writing weakens the work. You must demolish the work and start over. You can save some of the sentences, like bricks. It will be a miracle if you can save some of the paragraphs, no matter how excellent in themselves or hard–won. You can waste a year worrying about it, or you can get it over with now. (Are you a woman, or a mouse?)

The part you must jettison is not only the best-written part; it is also, oddly, that part which was to have been the very point. It is the original key passage, the passage on which the rest was to hang, and from which you yourself drew the courage to begin. Henry James knew it well, and said it best. In his preface to *The Spoils of Poynton,* he pities the writer, in a comical pair of sentences that rises to a howl: "Which is the work in which he hasn't surrendered, under dire difficulty, the best thing he meant to have kept? In which indeed, before the dreadful *done,* doesn't he ask himself what has become of the thing all for the sweet sake of which it was to proceed to that extremity?"

So it is that a writer writes many books. In each book, he intended several urgent and vivid points, many of which he sacrificed as the book's form hardened. "The youth gets together his materials to build a bridge to the moon," Thoreau noted mournfully, "or perchance a palace or temple on the earth, and at length the middle–aged man concludes to build a wood-shed with them." The writer returns to these materials, these passionate subjects, as to unfinished business, for they are his life's work.

It is the beginning of a work that the writer throws away.

A painting covers its tracks. Painters work from the ground up. The latest version of a painting overlays earlier versions, and obliterates them. Writers, on the other hand, work from left to right. The discardable chapters are on the left. The latest version of a literary work begins somewhere in the work's middle, and hardens toward the end. The earlier version remains lumpishly on the left; the work's beginning greets the reader with the wrong hand. In those early pages and chapters anyone may find bold leaps to nowhere, read the brave beginnings of dropped themes, hear a tone since abandoned, discover blind alleys, track red herrings, and laboriously learn a setting now false.

Several delusions weaken the writer's resolve to throw away work. If he has read his pages too often, those pages will have a necessary quality, the ring of the inevitable, like poetry known by heart; they will perfectly answer their own familiar rhythms. He will retain them. He may retain those pages if they possess some virtues, such as power in themselves, though they lack the cardinal virtue, which is pertinence to, and unity with, the book's thrust. Sometimes the writer leaves his early chapters in place from gratitude; he cannot contemplate them or read them without feeling again the blessed relief that exalted him when the words first appeared—relief that he was writing anything at all. That beginning served to get him where he was going, after all; surely the reader needs it, too, as groundwork. But no.

Every year the aspiring photographer brought a stack of his best prints to an old, honored photographer, seeking his judgment. Every year the old man studied the prints and painstakingly ordered them into two piles, bad and good. Every year the old man moved a certain landscape print into the bad stack. At length he turned ˄ the young man: "You submit this same landscape every year, and every year I ˅n the bad stack. Why do you like it so much?" The young photographer said, ˅ I had to climb a mountain to get it."

A cabdriver sang his songs to me, in New York. Some we sang together. He had turned the meter off; he drove around midtown, singing. One long song he sang twice; it was the only dull one. I said, You already sang that one; let's sing something else. And he said, "You don't know how long it took me to get that one together."

How many books do we read from which the writer lacked courage to tie off the umbilical cord? How many gifts do we open from which the writer neglected to remove the price tag? Is it pertinent, is it courteous, for us to learn what it cost the writer personally?

You write it all, discovering it at the end of the line of words. The line of words is a fiber optic, flexible as wire; it illuminates the path just before its fragile tip. You probe with it, delicate as a worm.

Few sights are so absurd as that of an inchworm leading its dimwit life. Inchworms are the caterpillar larvae of several moths or butterflies. The cabbage looper, for example, is an inchworm. I often see an inchworm: it is a skinny bright green thing, pale and thin as a vein, an inch long, and apparently totally unfit for life in this world. It wears out its days in constant panic.

Every inchworm I have seen was stuck in long grasses. The wretched inchworm hangs from the side of a grassblade and throws its head around from side to side, seeming to wail. What! No further? Its back pair of nubby feet clasps the grass stem; its front three pairs of nubs rear back and flail in the air, apparently in search of a footing. What! No further? What? Is searches everywhere in the wide world for the rest of the grass, which is right under its nose. By dumb luck it touches the grass. Its front legs hang on; it lifts and buckles its green inch, and places its hind legs just behind its front legs. Its body makes a loop, a bight. All it has to do now is slide its front legs up the grass stem. Instead it gets lost. It throws up its head and front legs, flings its upper body out into the void, and panics again. What! No further? End of world? And so forth, until it actually reaches the grasshead's tip. By then its wee weight may be bending the grass toward some other grass plant. Its davening, apocalyptic prayers sway the grasshead and bump it into something. I have seen it many times. The blind and frantic numbskull makes it off one grassblade and onto another one, which it will climb in virtual hysteria for several hours. Every step brings it to the universe's rim. And now— What! No further? End of world? Ah, here's ground. What! No further? Yike!

"Why don't you just jump?" I tell it, disgusted. "Put yourself out of your misery."

I admire those eighteenth-century Hasids who understood the risk of prayer. Rabbi Uri of Strelisk took sorrowful leave of his household every morning because he was setting off to his prayers. He told his family how to dispose of his manuscripts if praying should kill him. A ritual slaughterer, similarly, every morning bade goodbye to his wife and children and wept as if he would never see them again. His friend asked him why. Because, he answered, when I begin I call out to the Lord. Then I pray, "Have mercy on us." Who knows what the Lord's power will do to me in that moment after I have invoked it and before I beg for mercy?

When you are stuck in a book; when you are well into writing it, and know what comes next, and yet cannot go on; when every morning for a week or a month you enter its room and turn your back on it; then the trouble is either of two things. Either the structure has forked, so the narrative, or the logic, has developed a hairline fracture that will shortly split it up the middle—or you are approaching a fatal mistake. What you had planned will not do. If you pursue your present course, the book will explode or collapse, and you do not know about it yet, quite.

In Bridgeport, Connecticut, one morning in April 1987, a six-story concrete-slab building under construction collapsed, and killed twenty-eight men. Just before it collapsed, a woman across the street leaned from her window and said to a passerby, "That building is starting to shake." "Lady," he said, according to the Hartford *Courant*, "you got rocks in your head."

You notice only this: your worker—your one and only, your prized, coddled, and driven worker—is not going out on that job. Will not budge, not even for you, boss. Has been at it long enough to know when the air smells wrong; can sense a tremor through boot soles. Nonsense, you say; it is perfectly safe. But the worker will not go. Will not even look at the site. Just developed heart trouble. Would rather starve. Sorry.

What do you do? Acknowledge, first, that you cannot do nothing. Lay out the structure you already have, x-ray it for a hairline fracture, find it, and think about it for a week or a year; solve the insoluble problem. Or subject the next part, the part at which the worker balks, to harsh tests. It harbors an unexamined and wrong premise. Something completely necessary is false or fatal. Once you find it, and if you can accept the finding, of course it will mean starting again. This is why many experienced writers urge young men and women to learn a useful trade.

Every morning you climb several flights of stairs, enter your study, open the French doors, and slide your desk and chair out into the middle of the air. The desk and chair float thirty feet from the ground, between the crowns of maple trees. The furniture is in place; you go back for your thermos of coffee. Then, wincing, you step out again through the French doors and sit down on the chair and look over the desktop. You can see clear to the river from here in winter. You pour yourself a cup of coffee.

Birds fly under your chair. In spring, when the leaves open in the maples' crowns, you view stops in the treetops just beyond the desk; yellow warblers hiss and whisper on the high twigs, and catch flies. Get to work. Your work is to keep cranking the flywheel that turns the gears that spin the belt in the engine of belief that keeps you and your desk in midair.

Putting a book together is interesting and exhilarating. It is sufficiently difficult and complex that it engages all your intelligence. It is life at its most free. Your freedom as a writer is not freedom of expression in the sense of wild blurting; you may not let rip. It is life at its most free, if you are fortunate enough to be able to try it, because you select your materials, invent your task, and pace yourself. In the democ-
 ⸱s, you may even write and publish anything you please about any governments
  ⸱ions, even if what you write is demonstrably false.

The obverse of this freedom, of course, is that your work is so meaningless, so fully for yourself alone, and so worthless to the world, that no one except you cares whether you do it well, or ever. You are free to make several thousand close judgment calls a day. Your freedom is a by-product of your days' triviality. A shoe salesman—who is doing others' tasks, who must answer to two or three bosses, who must do his job their way, and must put himself in their hands, at their place, during their hours—is nevertheless working usefully. Further, if the shoe salesman fails to appear one morning, someone will notice and miss him. Your manuscript, on which you lavish such care, has no needs or wishes; it knows you not. Nor does anyone need your manuscript; everyone needs shoes more. There are many manuscripts already—worthy ones, most edifying and moving ones, intelligent and powerful ones. If you believed *Paradise Lost* to be excellent, would you buy it? Why not shoot yourself, actually, rather than finish one more excellent manuscript on which to gag the world?

To find a honey tree, first catch a bee. Catch a bee when its legs are heavy with pollen; then it is ready for home. It is simple enough to catch a bee on a flower; hold a cup or glass above the bee, and when it flies up, cap the cup with a piece of cardboard. Carry the bee to a nearby open spot—best an elevated one—release it, and watch where it goes. Keep your eyes on it as long as you can see it, and hie you to that last known place. Wait there until you see another bee; catch it, release it, and watch. Bee after bee will lead toward the honey tree, until you see the final bee enter the tree. Thoreau describes this process in his journals. So a book leads its writer.

You may wonder how you start, how you catch the first one. What do you use for bait?

You have no choice. One bad winter in the Arctic, and not too long ago, an Algonquin woman and her baby were left alone after everyone else in their winter camp had starved. Ernest Thompson Seton tells it. The woman walked from the camp where everyone had died, and found at a lake a cache. The cache contained one small fishhook. It was simple to rig a line, but she had no bait, and no hope of bait. The baby cried. She took a knife and cut a strip from her own thigh. She fished with the worm of her own flesh and caught a jackfish; she fed the child and herself. Of course she saved the fish gut for bait. She lived alone at the lake, on fish, until spring, when she walked out again and found people. Seton's informant had seen the scar on her thigh.

To comfort friends discouraged by their writing pace, you could offer them this: It takes years to write a book—between two and ten years. Less is so rare as to be statistically insignificant. One American writer has written a dozen major books over six decades. He wrote one of those books, a perfect novel, in three months. He speaks of it, still, with awe, almost whispering. Who wants to offend the spirit that hands out such books?

Faulkner wrote *As I Lay Dying* in six weeks; he claimed he knocked it off in his spare time from a twelve-hour-a-day job performing manual labor. There are other examples from other continents and centuries, just as albinos, assassins, saints, big people, and little people show up from time to time in large populations. Out of a human population on earth of four and a half billion, perhaps twenty people can write a serious book in a year. Some people lift cars, too. Some people enter week-long sled-dog races, go over Niagara Falls in barrels, fly planes through the Arc de Triomphe. Some people feel no pain in childbirth. Some people eat cars. There is no call to take human extremes as norms.

Graham Greene noticed that since a novel "takes perhaps years to write, the author is not the same man at the end of the book as he was at the beginning . . . as though [the novel] were something he had begun in childhood and was finishing now in old age." The long poem, John Berryman said, takes between five and ten years. Thomas Mann was a prodigy of production. Working full time, he wrote a page a day. That is 365 pages a year, for he did write every day—a good-sized book a year. At a page a day, he was one of the most prolific literary writers who ever lived. Flaubert wrote steadily, with only the usual, appalling, strains. For twenty-five years he finished a big book every five to seven years. If a full-time writer averages a book every five years, that makes seventy-three usable pages a year, or a usable fifth of a page a day. The years that biographers and other nonfiction writers spend amassing and mastering materials match the years novelists and short story writers spend fabricating solid worlds that answer to immaterial truths. On plenty of days the writer can write three or four pages, and on plenty of other days he concludes he must throw them away. These truths comfort the anguished. They do not mean, by any means, that faster-written books are worse books. They just mean that most writers might well stop berating themselves for writing at a normal, slow pace.

Octavio Paz cites the example of "Saint-Pol Roux, who used to hang the inspiration 'The poet is working' from his door while he slept."

The notion that one can write better during one season of the year than another Samuel Johnson labeled, "Imagination operating upon luxury." Another luxury for an idle imagination is the writer's own feeling about the work. There is neither a proportional relationship, nor an inverse one, between a writer's estimation of a work in progress and its actual quality. The feeling that the work is magnificent, and the feeling that it is abominable, are both mosquitoes to be repelled, ignored, or killed, but not indulged.

The reason to perfect a piece of prose as it progresses—to secure each sentence before building on it—is that original writing fashions a form. It unrolls out into nothingness. It grows cell to cell, bole to bough to twig to leaf; any careful word may suggest a route, may begin a strand of metaphor or event out of which much, or all, will develop. Perfecting the work inch by inch, writing from the first word toward the last, displays the courage and fear this method induces. The strain, like Giacometti's penciled search for precision and honesty, enlivens the work and impels it toward its truest end. A pile of decent work behind him, no matter how small, fuels the writer's ~ne, too; his pride emboldens and impels him. One Washington writer—Charlie ~so prizes momentum, and so fears self-consciousness, that he writes fiction ⸢his own devising. He leaves his house on distracting errands, hurries in without taking off his coat, sits at a typewriter and retypes in a blur of speed all of the story he has written to date. Impetus propels him to add another sentence or two before he notices he is writing and seizes up. Then he leaves the house and repeats the process; he runs in the door and retypes the entire story, hoping to squeeze out another sentence the way some car engines turn over after the ignition is off, or the way Warner Bros.' Wile E. Coyote continues running for several yards beyond the edge of a cliff, until he notices.

The reason not to perfect a work as it progresses is that, concomitantly, original work fashions a form the true shape of which it discovers only as it proceeds, so the early strokes are useless, however fine their sheen. Only when a paragraph's role in the context of the whole work is clear can the envisioning writer direct its complexity of detail to strengthen the work's ends.

Fiction writers who toss up their arms helplessly because their characters "take over"—powerful rascals, what is a god to do?—refer, I think, to these structural mysteries that seize any serious work, whether or not it possesses fifth-column characters who wreak havoc from within. Sometimes part of a book simply gets up and walks away. The writer cannot force it back in place. It wanders off to die. It is like the astonishing—and common—starfish called the sea star. A sea star is a starfish with many arms; each arm is called a ray. From time to time a sea star breaks itself, and no one knows why. One of the rays twists itself off and walks away. Dr. S. P. Monks describes one species, which lives on rocky Pacific shores:

"I am inclined to think that *Phataria* . . . always breaks itself, no matter what may be the impulse. They make breaks when conditions are changed, sometimes within a few hours after being placed in jars. . . . Whatever may be the stimulus, the animal can and does break of itself. . . . The ordinary method is for the main portion of the starfish to remain fixed and passive with the tube feet set on the side of the departing ray, and for this ray to walk slowly away at right angles to the body, to change position, twist, and do all the active labor necessary to the breakage." Marine biologist Ed Ricketts comments on this: "It would seem that in an animal that deliberately pulls itself apart we have the very acme of something or other."

The written word is weak. Many people prefer life to it. Life gets your blood going, and it smells good. Writing is mere writing, literature is mere. It appeals only to the subtlest senses—the imagination's vision, and the imagination's hearing—and the moral sense, and the intellect. This writing that you do, that so thrills you, that so rocks and exhilarates you, as if you were dancing next to the band, is barely audible to anyone else. The reader's ear must adjust down from loud life to the subtle, imaginary sounds of the written word. An ordinary reader picking up a book can't yet hear a thing; it will take half an hour to pick up the writing's modulations, its ups and downs and louds and softs.

An intriguing entomological experiment shows that a male butterfly will ignore a living female butterfly of his own species in favor of a painted cardboard one, if the cardboard one is big. If the cardboard one is bigger than he is, bigger than any female butterfly ever could be. He jumps the piece of cardboard over and over again, he jumps the piece of cardboard. Nearby, the real, living female butterfly opens and closes her wings in vain.

Films and television stimulate the body's senses too, in big ways. A nine-foot handsome face, and its three-foot-wide smile, are irresistible. Look at the long legs on that man, as high as a wall, and coming straight toward you. The music builds. The moving, lighted screen fills your brain. You do not like filmed car chases? See if you can turn away. Try not to watch. Even knowing you are manipulated, you are still as helpless as the male butterfly drawn to painted cardboard.

That is the movies. That is their ground. The printed word cannot compete with the movies on their ground, and should not. You can describe beautiful faces, car chases, or valleys full of Indians on horseback until you run out of words, and you will not approach the movies' spectacle. Novels written with film contracts in mind have a faint but unmistakable, and ruinous, odor. I cannot name what, in the text, alerts the reader to suspect the writer of mixed motives; I cannot specify which sentences, in several books, have caused me to read on with increasing dismay, and finally close the books because I smelled a rat. Such books seem uneasy being books; they seem eager to fling off their disguises and jump onto screens.

Why would anyone read a book instead of watching big people move on a screen? Because a book can be literature. It is a subtle thing—a poor thing, but our own. In my view, the more literary the book—the more purely verbal, crafted sentence by sentence, the more imaginative, reasoned, and deep—the more likely people are to read it. The people who read are the people who like literature, after all, whatever that might be. They like, or require, what books alone have. If they want to see films that evening, they will find films. If they do not like to read, they will not. People who read are not too lazy to flip on the television; they prefer books. I cannot imagine a sorrier pursuit that struggling for years to write a book that attempts to appeal to people who do not read in the first place.

You climb a long ladder until you can see over the roof, or over the clouds. You are writing a book. You watch your shod feet step on each round rung, one at a time; you do not hurry and do not rest. Your feet feel the steep ladder's balance; the long muscles in your thighs check its sway. You climb steadily, doing your job in the dark. When you reach the end, there is nothing more to climb. The sun hits you. The bright wideness surprises you; you had forgotten there was an end. You look back at the ladder's two feet on the distant grass, astonished.

The line of words fingers your own heart. It invades arteries, and enters the heart on a flood of breath; it presses the moving rims of thick valves; it palpates the dark muscle strong as horses, feeling for something, it knows not what. A queer picture beds in the muscle like a worm encysted—some film of feeling, some song forgotten, a scene in a dark bedroom, a corner of the woodlot, a terrible dining room, that exalting sidewalk; these fragments are heavy with meaning. The line of words peels them back, dissects them out. Will the bared tissue burn? Do you want to expose these ᵔnes to the light? You may locate them and leave them, or poke the spot hard till ᵔ bleeds on your finger, and write with that blood. If the sore spot is not fatal, ᵔt grow and block something, you can use its power for many years, until ᵔbs it.

The line of words feels for cracks in the firmament.

The line of words is heading out past Jupiter this morning. Traveling 150 kilometers a second, it make no sound. The big yellow planet and its white moons spin. The line of words speeds past Jupiter and its cumbrous, dizzying orbit; it looks neither to the right nor to the left. It will be leaving the solar system soon, single-minded, rapt, rushing heaven like a soul. You are in Houston, Texas, watching the monitor. You saw a simulation: the line of words waited still, hushed, pointed with longing. The big yellow planet spun toward it like a pitched ball and passed beside it, low and outside. Jupiter was so large, the arc of its edge at the screen's bottom looked flat. The probe twined on; its wild path passed between white suns small as dots; these stars fell away on either side, like the lights on a tunnel's walls.

Now you watch symbols move on your monitor; you stare at the signals the probe sends back, transmits in your own tongue, numbers. Maybe later you can guess at what they mean—what they might mean about space at the edge of the solar system, or about your instruments. Right now, you are flying. Right now, your job is to hold your breath.

Double Take

1. Many writers and writing teachers often talk about the "writing process." In *The Writing Life,* Annie Dillard writes that "process is nothing" in regard to how a writer writes. She says, "the path is not the work." Do you agree with Dillard? How do you think about your own writing process—is it an important part of the writing? What choices do you make in your own writing that affect its outcome? What choices do you suspect Dillard has made in this essay?
2. Dillard writes: "Some of the walls are bearing walls; they have to stay, or everything will fall down. Other walls can go with impunity; you can hear the difference. Unfortunately, it is often a bearing wall that has to go. It cannot be helped. There is only one solution, which appalls you, but there it is. Knock it out. Duck." Dillard is, of course, writing about revision, a subject that is crucial to this essay. How do you revise? How have other essayists talked about revision?
3. Dillard uses a series of dramatic anecdotes and metaphors to clarify her vision of the task of writing. As a reader, how do you react to the anecdotes? What do they teach you about writing? What is Dillard's strategy for using them in this piece?

At First Glance

One of the structural things that makes "Total Eclipse" interesting is its division into numbered "chapters" or sections. As you read this essay, ask why Dillard has decided to divide the essay into smaller sections, like the chapters of a book. Can an essay have chapters? What effect does such a division have on you as you read the essay?

Total Eclipse

I

It had been like dying, that sliding down the mountain pass. It had been like the death of someone, irrational, that sliding down the mountain pass and into the region of dread. It was like slipping into fever, or falling down that hole in sleep from which you wake yourself whimpering. We had crossed the mountains that day, and now we were in a strange place—a hotel in central Washington, in a town near Yakima. The eclipse we had traveled here to see would occur early the next morning.

I lay in bed. My husband, Gary, was reading beside me. I lay in bed and looked at the painting on the hotel room wall. It was a print of a detailed and lifelike painting of a smiling clown's head, made out of vegetables. It was a painting of the sort which you do not intend to look at, and which, alas, you never forget. Some tasteless fate presses it upon you; it becomes part of the complex interior junk you carry with you wherever you go. Two years have passed since the total eclipse of which I write. During those years I have forgotten, I assume, a great many things I wanted to remember—but I have not forgotten that clown painting or its lunatic setting in the old hotel.

The clown was bald. Actually, he wore a clown's tight rubber wig, painted white; this stretched over the top of his skull, which was a cabbage. His hair was bunches of baby carrots. Inset in his white clown makeup, and in his cabbage skull, were his small and laughing human eyes. The clown's glance was like the glance of Rembrandt in some of the self-portraits: lively, knowing, deep, and loving. The crinkled shadows around his eyes were string beans. His eyebrows were parsley. Each of his ears was a broad bean. His thin, joyful lips were red chili peppers; between his lips were wet rows of human teeth and a suggestion of a real tongue. The clown print was framed in gilt and glassed.

To put ourselves in the path of the total eclipse, that day we had driven five hours inland from the Washington coast, where we lived. When we tried to cross the Cascades range, an avalanche had blocked the pass.

A slope's worth of snow blocked the road; traffic backed up. Had the avalanche buried any cars that morning? We could not learn. This highway was the only winter road over the mountains. We waited as highway crews bulldozed a passage through the avalanche. With two-by-fours and walls of plyboard, they erected a one-way, roofed tunnel through the avalanche. We drove through the avalanche tunnel, crossed the pass, and descended several thousand feet into central Washington and the broad Yakima valley, about which we knew only that it was orchard country. As we lost altitude, the snows disappeared; our ears popped; the trees changed, and in the trees ~ strange birds. I watched the landscape innocently, like a fool, like a diver in the ˑf the deep who plays on the bottom while his air runs out.

lobby was a dark, derelict room, narrow as a corridor, and seemingly ⁄e waited on a couch while the manager vanished upstairs to do something unknown to our room. Beside us on an overstuffed chair, absolutely motionless, was a platinum-blond woman in her forties wearing a black silk dress and a strand of pearls. Her long legs were crossed; she supported her head on her fist. At the dim far end of the room, their backs toward us, sat six bald old men in their shirtsleeves, around a loud television. Two of them seemed asleep. They were drunks. "Number six!" cried the man on television, "Number six!"

On the broad lobby desk, lighted and bubbling, was a ten-gallon aquarium containing one large fish; the fish tilted up and down in its water. Against the long opposite wall sang a live canary in its cage. Beneath the cage, among spilled millet seeds on the carpet, were a decorated child's sand bucket and matching sand shovel.

Now the alarm was set for six. I lay awake remembering an article I had read downstairs in the lobby, in an engineering magazine. The article was about gold mining.

In South Africa, in India, and in South Dakota, the gold mines extend so deeply into the earth's crust that they are hot. The rock walls burn the miners' hands. The companies have to air-condition the mines; if the air conditioners break, the miners die. The elevators in the mine shafts run very slowly, down, and up, so the miners' ears will not pop in their skulls. When the miners return to the surface, their faces are deathly pale.

Early the next morning we checked out. It was February 26, 1979, a Monday morning. We would drive out of town, find a hilltop, watch the eclipse, and then drive back over the mountains and home to the coast. How familiar things are here; how adept we are; how smoothly and professionally we check out! I had forgotten the clown's smiling head and the hotel lobby as if they had never existed. Gary put the car in gear and off we went, as off we have gone to a hundred other adventures.

It was before dawn when we found a highway out of town and drove into the unfamiliar countryside. By the growing light we could see a band of cirrostratus clouds in the sky. Later the rising sun would clear these clouds before the eclipse began. We drove at random until we came to a range of unfenced hills. We pulled off the highway, bundled up, and climbed one of these hills.

II

The hill was five hundred feet high. Long winter-killed grass covered it, as high as our knees. We climbed and rested, sweating in the cold; we passed clumps of bundled people on the hillside who were setting up telescopes and fiddling with cameras. The top of the hill stuck up in the middle of the sky. We tightened our scarves and looked around.

East of us rose another hill like ours. Between the hills, far below, was the highway which threaded south into the valley. This was the Yakima valley; I had never seen it before. It is justly famous for its beauty, like every planted valley. It extended south into the horizon, a distant dream of a valley, a Shangri-la. All its hundreds of low, golden slopes bore orchards. Among the orchards were towns, and roads, and plowed and fallow fields. Through the valley wandered a thin, shining river; from the river extended fine, frozen irrigation ditches. Distance blurred and blued the sight so that the whole valley looked like a thickness or sediment at the bottom of the sky. Directly behind us was more sky, and empty lowlands blued by distance, and Mount Adams. Mount Adams was an enormous, snow-covered volcanic cone rising flat, like so much scenery.

Now the sun was up. We could not see it; but the sky behind the band of clouds was yellow, and, far down the valley, some hillside orchards had lighted up. More people were parking near the highway and climbing the hills. It was the West. All of us rugged individualists were wearing knit caps and blue nylon parkas. People were climbing the nearby hills and setting up shop in clumps among the dead grasses. It looked as though we had all gathered on hilltops to pray for the world on its last day. It looked as though we had all crawled out of spaceships and were preparing to assault the valley below. It looked at though we were scattered on hilltops at dawn to sacrifice virgins, make rain, set stone stelae in a ring. There was no place out of the wind. The straw grasses banged our legs.

Up in the sky where we stood the air was lusterless yellow. To the west the sky was blue. Now the sun cleared the clouds. We cast rough shadows on the blowing grass; freezing, we waved our arms. Near the sun, the sky was bright and colorless. There was nothing to see.

It began with no ado. It was odd that such a well-advertised public event should have no starting gun, no overture, no introductory speaker. I should have known right then that I was out of my depth. Without pause or preamble, silent as orbits, a piece of the sun went away. We looked at it through welders' goggles. A piece of the sun was missing; in its place we saw empty sky.

I had seen a partial eclipse in 1970. A partial eclipse is very interesting. It bears almost no relation to a total eclipse. Seeing a partial eclipse bears the same relation to seeing a total eclipse as kissing a man does to marrying him, or as flying in an airplane does to falling out of an airplane. Although the one experience precedes the other, it in no way prepares you for it. During a partial eclipse the sky does not darken—not even when 94 percent of the sun is hidden. Nor does the sun, seen colorless through protective devices, seem terribly strange. We have all seen a sliver of light in the sky; we have all seen the crescent moon by day. However, during a partial eclipse the air does indeed get cold, precisely as if someone were standing between you and the fire. And blackbirds do fly back to their roosts. I had seen a partial eclipse before, and here was another.

What you see in an eclipse is entirely different from what you know. It is especially different for those of us whose grasp of astronomy is so frail, that, given a flashlight, a grapefruit, two oranges, and fifteen years, we still could not figure out which way to set the clocks for Daylight Saving Time. Usually it is a bit of a trick to keep your knowledge from blinding you. But during an eclipse it is easy. What you see is much more convincing than any wild-eyed theory you may know.

You may read that the moon has something to do with eclipses. I have never seen ⌐ yet. You do not see the moon. So near the sun, it is as completely invisible ⌐ by day. What you see before your eyes is the sun going through phases. ⌐r and narrower, as the waning moon does, and, like the ordinary moon, ⌐e in the simple sky. The sky is of course background. It does not appear to eat the sun; it is far behind the sun. The sun simply shaves away; gradually, you see less sun and more sky.

The sky's blue was deepening, but there was no darkness. The sun was a wide crescent, like a segment of tangerine. The wind freshened and blew steadily over the hill. The eastern hill across the highway grew dusky and sharp. The towns and orchards in the valley to the south were dissolving into the blue light. Only the thin river held a trickle of sun.

Now the sky to the west deepened to indigo, a color never seen. A dark sky usually loses color. This was a saturated, deep indigo, up in the air. Stuck up into that unworldly sky was the cone of Mount Adams, and the alpenglow was upon it. The alpenglow is that red light of sunset which holds out on snowy mountaintops long after the valleys and tablelands are dimmed. "Look at Mount Adams," I said, and that was the last sane moment I remember.

I turned back to the sun. It was going. The sun was going, and the world was wrong. The grasses were wrong; they were platinum. Their every detail of stem, head, and blade shone lightless and artificially distinct as an art photographer's platinum print. This color has never been seen on earth. The hues were metallic; their finish was matte. The hillside was a nineteenth-century tinted photograph from which the tints had faded. All the people you see in the photograph, distinct and detailed as their faces look, are now dead. The sky was navy blue. My hands were silver. All the distant hills' grasses were finespun metal which the wind laid down. I was watching a faded color print of a movie filmed in the Middle Ages; I was standing in it, by some mistake. I was standing in a movie of hillside grasses filmed in the Middle Ages. I missed my own century, the people I knew, and the real light of day.

I looked at Gary. He was in the film. Everything was lost. He was a platinum print, a dead artist's version of life. I saw on his skull the darkness of night mixed with the colors of day. My mind was going out; my eyes were receding the way galaxies recede to the rim of space. Gary was light-years away, gesturing inside a circle of darkness, down the wrong end of a telescope. He smiled as if he saw me; the stringy crinkles around his eyes moved. The sight of him, familiar and wrong, was something I was remembering from centuries hence, from the other side of death: yes, *that* is the way he used to look, when we were living. When it was our generation's turn to be alive. I could not hear him; the wind was too loud. Behind him the sun was going. We had all started down a chute of time. At first it was pleasant; now there was no stopping it. Gary was chuting away across space, moving and talking and catching my eye, chuting down the long corridor of separation. The skin on his face moved like thin bronze plating that would peel.

The grass at our feet was wild barely. It was the wild einkorn wheat which grew on the hilly flanks of the Zagros Mountains, above the Euphrates valley, above the valley of the river we called *River*. We harvested the grass with stone sickles, I remember. We found the grasses on the hillsides; we built our shelter beside them and cut them down. That is how he used to look then, that one, moving and living and catching my eye, with the sky so dark behind him, and the wind blowing. God save our life.

From all the hills came screams. A piece of the sky beside the crescent sun was detaching. It was a loosened circle of evening sky, suddenly lighted from the back. It was an abrupt black body out of nowhere; it was a flat disk; it was almost over the sun. That is when there were screams. At once this disk of sky slid over the sun like a lid. The sky snapped over the sun like a lens cover. The hatch in the brain slammed. Abruptly it was dark night, on the land and in the sky. In the night sky was a tiny ring of light. The hole where the sun belongs is very small. A thin ring of light marked its place. There was no sound. The eyes dried, the arteries drained, the lungs hushed. There was no world. We were the world's dead people rotating and orbiting around and around, embedded in the planet's crust, while the earth rolled down. Our minds were light-years distant, forgetful of almost everything. Only an extraordinary act of will could recall to us our former, living selves and our contexts in matter and time. We had, it seems, loved the planet and loved our lives, but could no longer remember the way of them. We got the light wrong. In the sky was something that should not be there. In the black sky was a ring of light. It was a thin ring, an old, thin silver wedding band, an old, worn ring. It was an old wedding band in the sky, or a morsel of bone. There were stars. It was all over.

III

It is now that the temptation is strongest to leave these regions. We have seen enough; let's go. Why burn our hands any more than we have to? But two years have passed; the price of gold has risen. I return to the same buried alluvial beds and pick through the strata again.

I saw, early in the morning, the sun diminish against a backdrop of sky. I saw a circular piece of that sky appear, suddenly detached, blackened, and backlighted; from nowhere it came and overlapped the sun. It did not look like the moon. It was enormous and black. If I had not read that it was the moon, I could have seen the sight a hundred times and never thought of the moon once. (If, however, I had not read that it was the moon—if, like most of the world's people throughout time, I had simply glanced up and seen this thing—then I doubtless would not have speculated much, but would have, like Emperor Louis of Bavaria in 840, simple died of fright on the spot.) It did not look like a dragon, although it looked more like a dragon than the moon. It looked like a lens cover, or the lid of a pot. It materialized out of thin air— black, and flat, and sliding, outlined in flame.

Seeing this black body was like seeing a mushroom cloud. The heart screeched. The meaning of the sight overwhelmed its fascination. It obliterated meaning itself. If you were to glance out one day and see a row of mushroom clouds rising on the horizon, you would know at once that what you were seeing, remarkable as it was, was intrinsically not worth remarking. No use running to tell anyone. Significant as it was, it did not matter a whit. For what is significance? It is significance for people. No people, no significance. This is all I have to tell you.

In the deeps are the violence and terror of which psychology has warned us. But if you ride these monsters deeper down, if you drop with them farther over the world's rim, you find what our sciences cannot locate or name, the substrate, the ocean or matrix or ether which buoys the rest, which gives goodness its power for good, and evil its power for evil, the unified field: our complex and inexplicable caring for each other, and for our life together here. This is given. It is not learned.

The world which lay under darkness and stillness following the closing of the lid was not the world we know. The event was over. Its devastation lay round about us. The clamoring mind and heart stilled, almost indifferent, certainly disembodied, frail, and exhausted. The hills were hushed, obliterated. Up in the sky, like a crater from some distant cataclysm, was a hollow ring.

You have seen photographs of the sun taken during a total eclipse. The corona fills the print. All of those photographs were taken through telescopes. The lenses of telescopes and cameras can no more cover the breadth and scale of the visual array than language can cover the breadth and simultaneity of internal experience. Lenses enlarge the sight, omit its context, and make of it a pretty and sensible picture, like something on a Christmas card. I assure you, if you send any shepherds a Christmas card on which is printed a three-by-three photograph of the angel of the Lord, the glory of the Lord, and a multitude of the heavenly host, they will not be sore afraid. More fearsome things can come in envelopes. More moving photographs than those of the sun's corona can appear in magazines. But I pray you will never see anything more awful in the sky.

You see the wide world swaddled in darkness; you see a vast breadth of hilly land, and an enormous, distant, blackened valley; you see towns' lights, a river's path, and blurred portions of your hat and scarf; you see your husband's face looking like an early black-and-white film; and you see a sprawl of black sky and blue sky together, with unfamiliar stars in it, some barely visible bands of cloud, and over there, a small white ring. The ring is as small as one goose in a flock of migrating geese—if you happen to notice a flock of migrating geese. It is one 360th part of the visible sky. The sun we see is less than half the diameter of a dime held at arm's length.

The Crab Nebula, in the constellation Taurus, looks, through binoculars, like a smoke ring. It is a star in the process of exploding. Light from its explosion first reached the earth in 1054; it was a supernova then, and so bright it shone in the daytime. Now it is not so bright, but it is still exploding. It expands at the rate of seventy million miles a day. It is interesting to look through binoculars at something expanding seventy million miles a day. It does not budge. Its apparent size does not increase. Photographs of the Crab Nebula taken fifteen years ago seem identical to photographs of it taken yesterday. Some lichens are similar. Botanists have measured some ordinary lichens twice, at fifty-year intervals, without detecting any growth at all. And yet their cells divide; they live.

The small ring of light was like these things—like a ridiculous lichen up in the sky, like a perfectly still explosion 4,200 light-years away: it was interesting, and lovely, and in witless motion, and it had nothing to do with anything.

It had nothing to do with anything. The sun was too small, and too cold, and too far away, to keep the world alive. The white ring was not enough. It was feeble and worthless. It was as useless as a memory; it was as off kilter and hollow and wretched as a memory.

When you try your hardest to recall someone's face, or the look of a place, you see in your mind's eye some vague and terrible sight such as this. It is dark; it is insubstantial; it is all wrong.

The white ring and the saturated darkness made the earth and the sky look as they must look in the memories of the careless dead. What I saw, what I seemed to be standing in, was all the wrecked light that the memories of the dead could shed upon the living world. We had all died in our boots on the hilltops of Yakima, and were alone in eternity. Empty space stoppered our eyes and mouths; we cared for nothing. We remembered our living days wrong. With great effort we had remembered some sort of circular light in the sky—but only the outline. Oh, and then the orchard trees withered, the ground froze, the glaciers slid down the valleys and overlapped the towns. If there had ever been people on earth, nobody knew it. The dead had forgotten those they had loved. The dead were parted one from the other and could no longer remember the faces and lands they had loved in the light. They seemed to stand on darkened hilltops, looking down.

IV

We teach our children one thing only, as we were taught: to wake up. We teach our children to look alive there, to join by words and activities the life of human culture on the planet's crust. As adults we are almost all adept at waking up. We have so mastered the transition we have forgotten we ever learned it. Yet it is a transition we make a hundred times a day, as, like so many will-less dolphins, we plunge and surface, lapse and emerge. We live half our waking lives and all of our sleeping lives in some private, useless, and insensible waters we never mention or recall. Useless, I say. Valueless, I might add—until someone hauls their wealth up to the surface and into the wide-awake city, in a form that people can use.

I do not know how we got to the restaurant. Like Roethke, "I take my waking slow." Gradually I seemed more or less alive, and already forgetful. It was now almost nine in the morning. It was the day of a solar eclipse in central Washington, and a fine adventure for everyone. The sky was clear; there was a fresh breeze out of the north.

The restaurant was a roadside place with tables and booths. The other eclipse-watchers were there. From our booth we could see their cars' California license plates, their University of Washington parking stickers. Inside the restaurant we were all eating eggs or waffles; people were fairly shouting and exchanging enthusiasms, like fans after a World Series game. Did you see. . . ? Did you see . . . ? Then somebody said something which knocked me for a loop.

A college student, boy in a blue parka who carried a Hasselblad, said to us, "Did you see that little white ring? It looked like a Life Saver. It looked like a Life Saver up in the sky."

And so it did. The boy spoke well. He was a walking alarm clock. I myself had at that time no access to such a word. He could write a sentence, and I could not. I grabbed that Life Saver and rode it to the surface. And I had to laugh. I had been dumbstruck on the Euphrates River, I had been dead and gone and grieving, all over the sight of something which, if you could claw your way up to that level, you would grant looked very much like a Life Saver. It was good to be back among people so clever; it was good to have all the world's words at the mind's disposal, so the mind could begin its task. All those things for which we have no words are lost. The mind— the culture—has two little tools, grammar and lexicon: a decorated sand bucket and a matching shovel. With these we bluster about the continents and do all the world's work. With these we try to save our very lives.

There are a few more things to tell from this level, the level of the restaurant. One is the old joke about breakfast. "It can never be satisfied, the mind, never." Wallace Stevens wrote that, and in the long run he was right. The mind wants to live forever, or to learn a very good reason why not. The mind wants to know all the world, and all eternity, and God. The mind's sidekick, however, will settle for two eggs over easy.

The dear, stupid body is as easily satisfied as a spaniel. And, incredibly, the simple spaniel can lure the brawling mind to its dish. It is everlastingly funny that the proud, metaphysically ambitious, clamoring mind will hush if you give it an egg.

Further: while the mind reels in deep space, while the mind grieves or fears or exults, the workaday senses, in ignorance or idiocy, like so many computer terminals printing out market prices while the world blows up, still transcribe their little data and transmit them to the warehouse in the skull. Later, under the tranquilizing influence of fried eggs, the mind can sort through this data. The restaurant was a halfway house, a decompression chamber. There I remembered a few things more.

The deepest, and most terrifying, was this: I have said that I heard screams. (I have since read that screaming, with hysteria, is a common reaction even to expected total eclipses.) People on all the hillsides, including, I think, myself, screamed when the black body of the moon detached from the sky and rolled over the sun. But something else was happening at that same instant, and it was this, I believe, which made us scream.

The second before the sun went out we saw a wall of dark shadow come speeding at us. We no sooner saw it than it was upon us, like thunder. It roared up the valley. It slammed our hill and knocked us out. It was the monstrous swift shadow cone of the moon. I have since read that this wave of shadow moves 1,800 miles an hour. Language can give no sense of this sort of speed—1,800 miles an hour. It was 195 miles wide. No end was in sight—you saw only the edge. It rolled at you across the land at 1,800 miles an hour, hauling darkness like plague behind it. Seeing it, and knowing it was coming straight for you, was like feeling a slug of anesthetic shoot up your arm. If you think very fast, you may have time to think, "Soon it will hit my brain." You can feel the deadness race up your arm; you can feel the appalling, inhuman speed of your own blood. We saw the wall of shadow coming, and screamed before it hit.

This was the universe about which we have read so much and never before felt: the universe as a clockwork of loose spheres flung at stupefying, unauthorized speeds. How could anything moving so fast not crash, not veer form its orbit amok like a car out of control on a turn?

Less than two minutes later, when the sun emerged, the trailing edge of the shadow cone sped away. It coursed down our hill and raced eastward over the plain, faster than the eye could believe; it swept over the plain and dropped over the planet's rim in a twinkling. It had clobbered us, and now it roared away. We blinked in the light. It was as though an enormous, loping god in the sky had reached down and slapped the earth's face.

Something else, something more ordinary, came back to me along about the third cup of coffee. During the moments of totality, it was so dark that drivers on the highway below turned on their car's headlights. We could see the highway's route as a strand of lights. It was bumper-to-bumper down there. It was eight-fifteen in the morning, Monday morning, and people were driving into Yakima to work. That it was as dark as night, and eerie as hell, an hour after dawn, apparently meant that in order to *see* to drive to work, people had to use their headlights. Four or five cars pulled off the road. The rest, in a line at least five miles long, drove to town. The highway ran between hills; the people could not have seen any of the eclipsed sun at all. Yakima will have another total eclipse in 2019. Perhaps, in 2019, businesses will give their employees an hour off.

From the restaurant we drove back to the coast. The highway crossing the Cascades range was open. We drove over the mountain like old pros. We joined our places on the planet's thin crust; it held. For the time being, we were home free.

Early that morning at six, when we had checked out, the six bald men were sitting on folding chairs in the dim hotel lobby. The television was on. Most of them were awake. You might drown in your own spittle, God knows, at any time; you might wake up dead in a small hotel, a cabbage head watching TV while snows pile up in the passes, watching TV while the chili peppers smile and the moon passes over the sun and nothing changes and nothing is learned because you have lost your bucket and shovel and no longer care. What if you regain the surface and open your sack and find, instead of treasure, a beast which jumps at you? Or you may not come back at all. The winches may jam, the scaffolding buckle, the air conditioning collapse. You may glance up one day and see by your headlamp the canary keeled over in its cage. You may reach into a cranny for pearls and touch a moray eel. You yank on your rope; it is too late.

Apparently people share a sense of these hazards, for when the total eclipse ended, an odd thing happened.

When the sun appeared as a blinding bead on the ring's side, the eclipse was over. The black lens cover appeared again, backlighted, and slid away. At once the yellow light made the sky blue again; the black lid dissolved and vanished. The real world began there. I remember now: we all hurried away. We were born and bored at a stroke. We rushed down the hill. We found our car; we saw the other people streaming down the hillsides; we joined the highway traffic and drove away.

We never looked back. It was a general vamoose, and an odd one, for when we left the hill, the sun was still partially eclipsed—a sight rare enough, and one which, in itself, we would probably have driven five hours to see. But enough is enough. One turns at last even from glory itself with a sigh of relief. From the depths of mystery, and even from the heights of splendor, we bounce back and hurry for the latitudes of home.

Double Take

1. Why does Annie Dillard describe the clown painting in such detail at the beginning of "Total Eclipse"? What effect does this description have on the rest of the essay? Why would an author begin with such a description rather than getting right to the core of the narrative?
2. Dillard switches between present tense verbs and past tense verbs throughout this essay. At one moment she may tell us that "We teach our children one thing only, as we were taught: to wake up." And then, "It was the day of the solar eclipse." Only moments later she tells us that "the sky was clear; there was a fresh breeze out of the north." Throughout this essay, Dillard makes these moves between present and past. What might be the reason for such a maneuver?
3. Dillard uses a good deal of color in her descriptions in this essay. Locate four places where Dillard's use of color captures and conveys a particular mood. Would these passages convey the same description had she not used colors in the way she has? Think about how you might revise the four passages to eliminate the colors and why Dillard might not have chosen to engage in similar revision.

At First Glance

Dillard's essay "Teaching a Stone to Talk" is the first essay in her collection by the same title. In this essay Dillard makes connections between the ways that humanity has stopped listening to the natural and spiritual world and the ways that her neighbor is trying to teach a stone to talk. Because this essay deals with subjects that can be deeply personal—God and Nature, for instance—Dillard reveals a good deal of the personal for the audience. Note, for instance, as you read this essay, the number of sentences that make use of the simple personal subject and verb construction, such as "I know," "I wish," "I think," or "I'm sorry." Think about how these sentences fit with the subjects presented in the essay.

Teaching a Stone to Talk

I

The island where I live is peopled with cranks like myself. In a cedar-shake shack on a cliff—but we all live like this—is a man in his thirties who lives alone with a stone he is trying to teach to talk.

Wisecracks on this topic abound, as you might expect, but they are made as it were perfunctorily, and mostly by the young. For in fact, almost everyone here respects what Larry is doing, as do I, which is why I am protecting his (or her) privacy, and confusing for you the details. It could be, for instance, a pinch of sand he is teaching to talk, or a prolonged northerly, or any one of a number of waves. But it is, in fact, I assure you, a stone. It is—for I have seen it—a palm-sized oval beach cobble whose dark gray is cut by a band of white which runs around and, presumably, through it; such stones we call "wishing stones," for reasons obscure but not, I think, unimaginable.

He keeps it on a shelf. Usually the stone lies protected by a square of untanned leather, like a canary asleep under its cloth. Larry removes the cover for the stone's lessons, or more accurately, I should say, for the ritual or rituals which they perform together several times a day.

No one knows what goes on at these sessions, least of all myself, for I know Larry but slightly, and that owing only to a mix-up in our mail. I assume that like any other meaningful effort, the ritual involves sacrifice, the suppression of self-consciousness, and a certain precise tilt of the will, so that the will becomes transparent and hollow, a channel for the work. I wish him well. It is a noble work, and beats, from any angle, selling shoes.

Reports differ on precisely what he expects or wants the stone to say. I do not think he expects the stone to speak as we do, and describe for us its long life and many, or few, sensations. I think instead that he is trying to teach it to say a single word, such as "cup," or "uncle." For this purpose he has not, as some have seriously suggested, carved the stone a little mouth, or furnished it in any way with a pocket of air which it might then expel. Rather—and I think he is wise in this—he plans to initiate his son, who is now an infant living with Larry's estranged wife, into the work, so that it may continue and bear fruit after his death.

II

Nature's silence is its one remark, and every flake of world is a chip off that old mute and immutable block. The Chinese say that we live in the world of the ten thousand things. Each of the ten thousand things cries out to us precisely nothing.

God used to rage at the Israelites for frequenting sacred groves. I wish I could find one. Martin Buber says: "The crisis of all primitive mankind comes with the discovery of that which is fundamentally not-holy, the a-sacramental, which withstands the methods, and which has no 'hour,' a province which steadily enlarges itself." Now we are no longer primitive; now the whole world seems not-holy. We have drained the light from the boughs in the sacred grove and snuffed it in the high places and along the banks of sacred streams. We as a people have moved from pantheism to pan-atheism. Silence is not our heritage but our destiny; we live where we want to live.

The soul may ask God for anything, and never fail. You may ask God for his presence, or for wisdom, and receive each at his hands. Or you may ask God, in the words of the shopkeeper's little gag sign, that he not go away mad, but just go away. Once, in Israel, an extended family of nomads did just that. They heard God's speech and found it too loud. The wilderness generation was at Sinai; it witnessed there the thick darkness where God was: "and all the people saw the thunderings, and the lightnings, and the noise of the trumpet, and the mountain smoking." It scared them witless.

Then they asked Moses to beg God, please, never speak to them directly again. "Let not God speak with us, lest we die." Moses took the message. And God, pitying their self-consciousness, agreed. He agreed not to speak to the people anymore. And he added to Moses, "Go say to them, Get into your tents again."

III

It is difficult to undo our own damage, and to recall to our presence that which we have asked to leave. It is hard to desecrate a grove and change your mind. The very holy mountains are keeping mum. We doused the burning bush and cannot rekindle it; we are lighting matches in vain under every green tree. Did the wind use to cry, and the hills shout forth praise? Now speech has perished from among the lifeless things of earth, and living things say very little to very few. Birds may crank out sweet gibberish and monkeys howl; horses neigh and pigs say, as you recall, oink oink. But so do cobbles rumble when a wave recedes, and thunders break the air in lightning storms. I call these noises silence. It could be that wherever there is motion there is noise, as when a whale breaches and smacks the water—and wherever there is stillness there is the still small voice, God's speaking from the whirlwind, nature's old song and dance, the show we drove from town. At any rate, now it is all we can do, and among our best efforts, to try to teach a given human language, English, to chimpanzees.

In the forties an American psychologist and his wife tried to teach a chimp actually to speak. At the end of three years the creature could pronounce, in a hoarse whisper, the words "mama," "papa," and "cup." After another three years of training she could whisper, with difficulty, still only "mama," "papa," and "cup." The more recent successes at teaching chimpanzees American Sign Language are well known. Just the other day a chimp told us, if we can believe that we truly share a vocabulary, that she had been sad in the morning. I'm sorry we asked.

What have we been doing all these centuries but trying to call God back to the mountain, or, failing that, raise a peep out of anything that isn't us? What is the difference between a cathedral and a physics lab? Are not they both saying: Hello? We spy on whales and on interstellar radio objects; we starve ourselves and pray till we're blue.

IV

I have been reading comparative cosmology. At this time most cosmologists favor the picture of the evolving universe described by Lemaître and Gamow. But I prefer a suggestion made years ago by Valéry—Paul Valéry. He set forth the notion that the universe might be "head-shaped."

The mountains are great stone bells; they clang together like nuns. Who shushed the stars? There are a thousand million galaxies easily seen in the Palomar reflector; collisions between and among them do, of course, occur. But these collisions are very long and silent slides. Billions of stars sift among each other untouched, too distant even to be moved, heedless as always, hushed. The sea pronounces something, over and over, in a hoarse whisper; I cannot quite make it out. But God knows I have tried.

At a certain point you say to the woods, to the sea, to the mountains, the world, Now I am ready. Now I will stop and be wholly attentive. You empty yourself and wait, listening. After a time you hear it: there is nothing there. There is nothing but those things only, those created objects, discrete, growing or holding, or swaying, being rained on or raining, held, flooding or ebbing, standing, or spread. You feel the world's word as a tension, a hum, a single chorused note everywhere the same. This is it: this hum is the silence. Nature does utter a peep—just this one. The birds and insects, the meadows and swamps and rivers and stones and mountains and clouds: they all do it; they all don't do it. There is a vibrancy to the silence, a suppression, as if someone were gagging the world. But you wait, you give your life's length to listening, and nothing happens. The ice rolls up, the ice rolls back, and still that single note obtains. The tension, or lack of it, is intolerable. The silence is not actually suppression; instead, it is all there is.

V

We are here to witness. There is nothing else to do with those mute materials we do not need. Until Larry teaches his stone to talk, until God changes his mind, or until the pagan gods slip back to their hilltop groves, all we can do with the whole inhuman array is watch it. We can stage our own act on the planet—build our cities on its plains, dam its rivers, plant its topsoils—but our meaningful activity scarcely covers the terrain. We do not use the songbirds, for instance. We do not eat many of them; we cannot befriend them; we cannot persuade them to eat more mosquitoes or plant fewer weed seeds. We can only witness them—whoever they are. If we were not here, they would be songbirds falling in the forest. If we were not here, material events like the passage of seasons would lack even the meager meanings we are able to muster for them. The show would play to an empty house, as do all those falling stars which fall in the daytime. That is why I take walks: to keep an eye on things. And that is why I went to the Galápagos islands.

All this becomes especially clear on the Galápagos islands. The Galápagos islands are just plain here—and little else. They blew up out of the ocean, some plants blew in on them, some animals drifted aboard and evolved weird forms—and there they all are, whoever they are, in full swing. You can go there and watch it happen, and try to figure it out. The Galápagos are a kind of metaphysics laboratory, almost wholly uncluttered by human culture or history. Whatever happens on those bare volcanic rocks happens in full view, whether anyone is watching or not.

What happens there is this, and precious little it is: clouds come and go, and the round of similar seasons; a pig eats a tortoise or doesn't eat a tortoise; Pacific waves fall up and slide back; a lichen expands; night follows day; an albatross dies and dries on a cliff; a cool current upwells from the ocean floor; fishes multiply, flies swarm, stars rise and fall, and diving birds dive. The news, in other words, breaks on the beaches. And taking it all in are the trees. The *palo santo* trees crowd the hillsides like any outdoor audience; they face the lagoons, the lava lowlands, and the shores.

I have some experience of these *palo santo* trees. They interest me as emblems of the muteness of the human stance in relation to all that is not human. I see us all as *palo santo* trees, holy sticks, together watching all that we watch, and growing in silence.

In the Galápagos, it took me a long time to notice the *palo santo* trees. Like everyone else, I specialized in sea lions. My shipmates and I liked the sea lions, and envied their lives. Their joy seemed conscious. They were engaged in full-time play. They were all either fat or dead; there was no halfway. By day they played in the shadows, alone or together, greeting each other and us with great noises of joy, or they took a turn offshore and body-surfed in the breakers, exultant. By night on the sand they lay in each other's flippers and slept. Everyone joked, often, that when he "came back," he would just as soon do it all over again as a sea lion. I concurred. The sea lion game looked unbeatable.

But a year and a half later, I returned to those unpeopled islands. In the interval my attachment to them had shifted, and my memories of them had altered, the way memories do, like particolored pebbles rolled back and forth over a grating, so that after a time those hard bright ones, the ones you thought you would never lose, have vanished, passed through the grating, and only a few big, unexpected ones remain, no longer unnoticed but now selected out for some meaning, large and unknown.

Such were the *palo santo* trees. Before, I had never given them a thought. They were just miles of half-dead trees on the red lava sea cliffs of some deserted islands. They were only a name in a notebook: *"Palo santo*—those strange white trees." Look at the sea lions! Look at the flightless cormorants, the penguins, the iguanas, the sunset! But after eighteen months the wonderful cormorants, penguins, iguanas, sunsets, and even the sea lions, had dropped from my holey heart. I returned to the Galápagos to see the *palo santo* trees.

They are thin, pale, wispy trees. You walk among them on the lowland deserts, where they grow beside the prickly pear. You see them from the water on the steeps that face the sea, hundreds together, small and thin and spread, and so much more pale than their red soils that any black-and-white photograph of them looks like a negative. Their stands look like blasted orchards. At every season they all look newly dead, pale and bare as birches drowned in a beaver pond—for at every season they look leafless, paralyzed, and mute. But in fact, if you look closely, you can see during the rainy months a few meager deciduous leaves here and there on their brittle twigs. And hundreds of lichens always grow on their bark in the mute, overlapping explosions which barely enlarge in the course of the decade, lichens pink and orange, lavender, yellow, and green. The *palo santo* trees bear the lichens effortlessly, unconsciously, the way they bear everything. Their multitudes, transparent as line drawings, crowd the cliffsides like whirling dancers, like empty groves, and look out over cliff-wrecked breakers toward more unpeopled islands, with their freakish lizards and birds, toward the grieving lagoons and the bays where the sea lions wander, and beyond to the clamoring seas.

Now I no longer concurred with my shipmates' joke; I no longer wanted to "come back" as a sea lion. For I thought, and I still think, that if I came back to life in the sunlight where everything changes, I would like to come back as a *palo santo* tree, one of thousands on a cliffside on those godforsaken islands, where a million events occur among the witless, where a splash of rain may drop on a yellow iguana the size of a dachshund, and ten minutes later the iguana may blink. I would like to come back as a *palo santo* tree on the weather side of an island, so that I could be, myself, a perfect witness, and look, mute, and wave my arms.

VI

The silence is all there is. It is the alpha and the omega. It is God's brooding over the face of the waters; it is the blended note of the ten thousand things, the whine of wings. You take a step in the right direction to pray to this silence, and even to address the prayer to "World." Distinctions blur. Quit your tents. Pray without ceasing.

Double Take

1. What do you think Annie Dillard means when she writes, "Silence is not our heritage but our destiny"?
2. In "Teaching a Stone to Talk," Dillard writes, "Now speech has perished from among the lifeless things of earth, and living things say very little to very few." Considering this claim, how might Dillard characterize writing as a kind of speech of the living things?
3. Why would someone want to teach a stone to talk? That is, what is Dillard suggesting about speech, about listening, and about the world in which we live?

Seeing for Yourself

At First Glance

"Spring" is one of several essay chapters found in Dillard's book Pilgrim at Tinker Creek, *for which she was awarded the Pulitzer Prize. This essay covers a range of time, from February until May. During this time, Dillard relates her observations of the change of seasons as spring evolves from winter to summer. This essay is filled with wonderful descriptions of her observations. As you read this essay, make note of the details Dillard uses to depict her observations. How, for instance, does she describe animals, people, events?*

Spring

I

When I was quite young I fondly imagined that all foreign languages were codes for English. I thought that "hat," say, was the real and actual name of the thing, but that people in other countries, who obstinately persisted in speaking the code of their forefathers, might use the word "ibu," say, to designate not merely the concept hat, but the English *word* "hat." I knew only one foreign word, "oui," and since it had three letters as did the word for which it was a code, it seemed, touchingly enough, to confirm my theory. Each foreign language was a different code, I figured, and at school I would eventually be given the keys to unlock some of the most important codes' systems. Of course I knew that it might take years before I became so fluent in another language that I could code and decode easily in my head, and make of gibberish a nimble sense. On the first day of my first French course, however, things rapidly took on an entirely unexpected shape. I realized that I was going to have to learn speech all over again, word by word, one word at a time—and my dismay knew no bounds.

The birds have started singing in the valley. Their February squawks and naked chirps are fully fledged now, and long lyrics fly in the air. Birdsong catches in the mountains' rim and pools in the valley; it threads through forests, it slides down creeks. At the house a wonderful thing happens. The mockingbird that nests each year in the front-yard spruce strikes up his chant in high places, and one of those high places is my chimney. When he sings there, the hollow chimney acts as a sound box, like the careful emptiness inside a cello or violin, and the notes of the song gather fullness and reverberate through the house. He sings a phrase and repeats it

133

exactly; then he sings another and repeats that, then another. The mockingbird's invention is limitless; he strews newness about as casually as a god. He is tireless, too; towards June he will begin his daily marathon at two in the morning and scarcely pause for breath until eleven at night. I don't know when he sleeps.

When I lose interest in a given bird, I try to renew it by looking at the bird in either of two ways. I imagine neutrinos passing through its feathers and into its heart and lungs, or I reverse its evolution and imagine it as a lizard. I see its scaled legs and that naked ring around a shiny eye; I shrink and deplume its feathers to lizard scales, unhorn its lipless mouth, and set it stalking dragonflies, cool-eyed, under a palmetto. Then I reverse the process once again, quickly; its forelegs unfurl, its scales hatch feathers and soften. It takes to the air seeking cool forests; it sings songs. This is what I have on my chimney; it might as well keep me awake out of wonder as rage.

Some reputable scientists, even today, are not wholly satisfied with the notion that the song of birds is strictly and solely a territorial claim. It's an important point. We've been on earth all these years and we still don't know for certain why birds sing. We need someone to unlock the code to this foreign language and give us the key; we need a new Rosetta stone. Or should we learn, as I had to, each new word one by one? It could be that a bird sings I am sparrow, sparrow, sparrow, as Gerard Manley Hopkins suggests: "myself it speaks and spells, Crying *What I do is me: for that I came.*" Sometimes birdsong seems just like the garbled speech of infants. There is a certain age at which a child looks at you in all earnestness and delivers a long, pleased speech in all the true inflections of spoken English, but with not one recognizable syllable. There is no way you can tell the child that if language had been a melody, he had mastered it and done well, but that since it was in fact a sense, he had botched it utterly.

Today I watched and heard a wren, a sparrow, and the mocking-bird singing. My brain started to trill why why why, what is the meaning meaning meaning? It's not that they know something we don't; we know much more than they do, and surely they don't even know why they sing. No; we have been as usual asking the wrong question. It does not matter a hoot what the mockingbird on the chimney is singing. If the mockingbird were chirping to give us the long-sought formulae for a unified field theory, the point would be only slightly less irrelevant. The real and proper question is: Why is it beautiful? I hesitate to use the word so baldly, but the question is there. The question is there since I take it as given, as I have said, that beauty is something objectively performed—the tree that falls in the forest—having being externally, stumbled across or missed, as real and present as both sides of the moon. This modified lizard's song welling out of the fireplace has a wild, utterly foreign music; it becomes more and more beautiful as it becomes more and more familiar. If the lyric is simply "mine mine mine," then why the extravagance of the score? It has the liquid, intricate sound of every creek's tumble over every configuration of rock creek-bottom in the country. Who, telegraphing a message, would trouble to transmit a five-act play, or Coleridge's "Kubla Khan," and who, receiving the message, could understand it? Beauty itself is the language to which we have no key; it is the mute cipher, the cryptogram, the uncracked, unbroken code. And it could be that for beauty, as it turned out to be for French, that there is no key, that "oui" will never make sense in our language but only in its own, and that we need to start all over again, on a new continent, learning the strange syllables one by one.

It is spring. I plan to try to control myself this year, to watch the progress of the season in a calm and orderly fashion. In spring I am prone to wretched excess. I abandon myself to flights and compulsions; I veer into various states of physical disarray. For the duration of one entire spring I played pinochle; another spring I played second base. One spring I missed because I had lobar pneumonia; one softball season I missed with bursitis; and every spring at just about the time the leaves first blur on the willows, I stop eating and pale, like a silver eel about to migrate. My mind wanders. Second base is a Broadway, a Hollywood and Vine; but oh, if I'm out in right field they can kiss me goodbye. As the sun sets, sundogs, which are mock suns—chunks of rainbow on either side of the sun but often very distant from it—appear over the pasture by Carvin's Creek. Wes Hillman is up in his biplane; the little Waco lords it over the stillness, cutting a fine silhouette. It might rain tomorrow, if those ice crystals find business. I have no idea how many outs there are; I luck through the left-handers, staring at rainbows. The field looks to me as it must look to Wes Hillman up in the biplane: everyone is running, and I can't hear a sound. The players look so thin on the green, and the shadows so long, and the ball a mystic thing, pale to invisibility. . . . I'm better off in the infield.

In April I walked to the Adams' woods. The grass had greened one morning when I blinked; I missed it again. As I left the house I checked the praying mantis egg case. I had given all but one of the cases to friends for their gardens; now I saw that small black ants had discovered the one that was left, the one tied to the mock-orange hedge by my study window. One side of the case was chewed away, either by the ants or by something else, revealing a rigid froth slit by narrow cells. Over this protective layer the ants scrambled in a frenzy, unable to eat; the actual mantis eggs lay secure and unseen, waiting, deeper in.

The morning woods were utterly new. A strong yellow light pooled between the trees; my shadow appeared and vanished on the path, since a third of the trees I walked under were still bare, a third spread a luminous haze wherever they grew, and another third blocked the sun with new, whole leaves. The snakes were out—I saw a bright, smashed one on the path—and the butterflies were vaulting and furling about; the phlox was at its peak, and even the evergreens looked greener, newly created and washed.

Long racemes of white flowers hung from the locust trees. Last summer I heard a Cherokee legend about the locust tree and the moon. The moon goddess starts out with a big ball, the full moon, and she hurls it across the sky. She spends all day retrieving it; then she shaves a slice from it and hurls it again, retrieving, shaving, hurling, and so on. She uses up a moon a month, all year. Then, the way Park Service geologist Bill Wellman tells it, "'long about spring of course she's knee-deep in moon-shavings," so she finds her favorite tree, the locust, and hangs the slender shavings from its boughs. And there they were, the locust flowers, pale and clustered in crescents.

The newts were back. In the small forest pond they swam bright and quivering, or hung alertly near the water's surface. I discovered that if I poked my finger into the water and wagged it slowly, a newt would investigate; then if I held my finger still, it would nibble at my skin, softly, the way my goldfish does—and, also like my goldfish, it would swim off as if in disgust at a bad job. This is salamander metropolis. If you want to find a species wholly new to science and have your name inscribed Latinly in some secular version of an eternal rollbook, then your best bet is to come to the southern Appalachians, climb some obscure and snakey mountain where, as the saying goes, "the hand of man has never set foot," and start turning over rocks. The mountains act as islands; evolution does the rest, and there are scores of different salamanders all around. The Peaks of Otter on the Blue Ridge Parkway produce their own unique species, black and spotted in dark gold; the rangers there keep a live one handy by sticking it in a Baggie and stowing it in the refrigerator, like a piece of cheese.

Newts are the most common of salamanders. Their skin is a lighted green, like water in a sunlit pond, and rows of very bright red dots line their backs. They have gills as larvae; as they grow they turn a luminescent red, lose their gills, and walk out of the water to spend a few years padding around in damp places on the forest floor. Their feet look like fingered baby hands, and they walk in the same leg patterns as all four-footed creatures—dogs, mules, and, for that matter, lesser pandas. When they mature fully, they turn green again and stream to the water in droves. A newt can scent its way home from as far as eight miles away. They are altogether excellent creatures, if somewhat moist, but no one pays the least attention to them, except children.

Once I was camped "alone" at Douthat State Park in the Allegheny Mountains near here, and spent the greater part of one afternoon watching children and newts. There were many times more red-spotted newts at the edge of the lake than there were children; the supply exceeded even that very heavy demand. One child was collecting them in a Thermos mug to take home to Lancaster, Pennsylvania, to feed an ailing cayman. Other children ran to their mothers with squirming fistfuls. One boy was mistreating the newts spectacularly: he squeezed them by their tails and threw them at a shoreline stone, one by one. I tried to reason with him, but nothing worked. Finally he asked me, "Is this one a male?" and in a fit of inspiration I said, "No, it's a baby." He cried, "Oh, isn't he *cute!*" and cradled the newt carefully back into the water.

No one but me disturbed the newts here in the Adams' woods. They hung in the water as if suspended from strings. Their specific gravity put them just a jot below the water's surface, and they could apparently relax just as well with lowered heads as lowered tails; their tiny limbs hung limp in the water. One newt was sunning on a stick in such an extravagant posture I thought she was dead. She was half out of the water, her front legs grasping the stick, her nose tilted back to the zenith and then some. The concave arch of her spine stretched her neck past believing; the thin ventral skin was a bright taut yellow. I should not have nudged her—it made her relax the angle of repose—but I had to see if she was dead. Medieval Europeans believed that salamanders were so cold they could put out fires and not be burned themselves; ancient Romans thought that the poison of salamanders was so cold that if anyone ate the fruit of a tree that a salamander had merely touched, that person would die of a terrible coldness. But I survived these mild encounters—my being nibbled and my poking the salamander's neck—and stood up.

The woods were flush with flowers. The redbud trees were in flower, and the sassafras, dully; so also were the tulip trees, catawbas, and the weird pawpaw. On the floor of the little woods, hepatica and dogtooth violet had come and gone; now I saw the pink spring beauty here and there, and Solomon's seal with its pendant flowers, bloodroot, violets, trillium, and May apple in luxuriant stands. The mountains would be brilliant in mountain laurel, rhododendron, and flame azalea, and the Appalachian Trail was probably packed with picnickers. I had seen in the steers' pasture daisies, henbits, and yellow-flowering oxalis; sow thistle and sneeze weed shot up by the barbed-wire fence. Does anything eat flowers? I couldn't recall ever having seen anything actually eat a flower—are they nature's privileged pets?

But I was much more interested in the leafing of trees. By the path I discovered a wonderful tulip-tree sapling three feet tall. From its tip grew two thin slips of green tissue shaped like two tears; they enclosed, like cupped palms sheltering a flame, a tiny tulip leaf that was curled upon itself and bowed neatly at the middle. The leaf was so thin and etiolated it was translucent, but at the same time it was lambent, minutely, with a kind of pale and sufficient light. It was not wet, nor even damp, but it was clearly moist inside; the wrinkle where it folded in half looked less like a crease than a dimple, like the liquid dip a skater's leg makes on the surface film of still water. A barely concealed, powerful juice swelled its cells, and the leaf was uncurling and rising between the green slips of tissue. I looked around for more leaves like it—that part of the Adams' woods seems to be almost solely tulip trees—but all the other leaves had just lately unfurled, and were waving on pale stalks like new small hands.

The tulip-tree leaf reminded me of a newborn mammal I'd seen the other day, one of the neighborhood children's gerbils. It was less than an inch long, with a piggish snout, clenched eyes, and swollen white knobs where its ears would grow. Its skin was hairless except for an infinitesimal set of whiskers; the skin seemed as thin as the membrane on an onion, tightly packed as a sausage casing, and bulging roundly with wet, bloody meat. It seemed near to bursting with possibilities, like the taut gum over a coming tooth. This three-foot sapling was going somewhere, too; it meant business.

There's a real power here. It is amazing that trees can turn gravel and bitter salts into these soft-lipped lobes, as if I were to bite down on a granite slab and start to swell, bud, and flower. Trees seem to do their feats so effortlessly. Every year a given tree creates absolutely from scratch ninety-nine percent of its living parts. Water lifting up tree trunks can climb one hundred and fifty feet an hour; in full summer a tree can, and does, heave a ton of water every day. A big elm in a single season might make as many as *six million* leaves, wholly intricate, without budging an inch; I couldn't make one. A tree stands there, accumulating deadwood, mute and rigid as an obelisk, but secretly it seethes; it splits, sucks, and stretches; it heaves up tons and hurls them out in a green, fringed fling. No person taps this free power; the dynamo in the tulip tree pumps out ever more tulip tree, and it runs on rain and air.

John Cowper Powys said, "We have no reason for denying to the world of plants a certain slow, dim, vague, large, leisurely semi-consciousness." He may not be right, but I like his adjectives. The patch of bluets in the grass may not be long on brains, but it might be, at least in a very small way, awake. The trees especially seem to bespeak a generosity of spirit. I suspect that the real moral thinkers end up, wherever they may start, in botany. We know nothing for certain, but we seem to see that the world turns upon growing, grows towards growing, and growing green and clean.

I looked away from the tulip leaf at the tip of the sapling, and I looked back. I was trying to determine if I could actually see the bent leaf tip rise and shove against the enclosing flaps. I couldn't tell whether I was seeing or merely imagining progress, but I knew the leaf would be fully erect within the hour. I couldn't wait.

I left the woods, spreading silence before me in a wave, as though I'd stepped not through the forest, but on it. I left the wood silent, but I myself was stirred and quickened. I'll go to the Northwest Territories, I thought, Finland.

"Why leap ye, ye high hills?" The earth was an egg, freshened and splitting; a new pulse struck, and I resounded. Pliny, who, you remember, came up with the Portuguese wind-foals, must have kept his daughters in on windy days, for he also believed that plants conceive in the spring of the western wind Flavonius. In February the plants go into rut; the wind impregnates them, and their buds swell and burst in their time, bringing forth flowers and leaves and fruit. I could smell the loamy force in the wind. I'll go to Alaska, Greenland. I saw hundred of holes in the ground everywhere I looked; all kinds of creatures were popping out of the dim earth, some for the first time, to be lighted and warmed directly by the sun. It is a fact that the men and women all over the northern hemisphere who dream up new plans for a perpetual motion machine conceive their best ideas in the spring. If I swallowed a seed and some soil, could I grow grapes in my mouth? Once I dug a hole to plant a pine, and found an old gold coin on a stone. Little America, the Yukon. . . . "Why leap ye, ye high hills?"

On my way home, every bird I saw had something in its mouth. A male English sparrow, his mouth stuffed, was hopping in and out of an old nest in a bare tree, and sloshing around in its bottom. A robin on red alert in the grass, trailing half a worm from its bill, bobbed three steps and straightened up, performing unawares the universal robin trick. A mockingbird flew by with a red berry in its beak; the berry flashed in the sun and glowed like a coal from some forge or cauldron of the gods.

Finally I saw some very small children playing with a striped orange kitten, and overheard their mysterious conversation, which has since been ringing in my brain like a gong. The kitten ran into a garden, and the girl called after it, "Sweet Dreams! Sweet Dreams! Where are you?" And the boy said to her crossly, "Don't call Sweet Dreams *'you'!*"

II

Now it is May. The walrus are migrating; Diomede Island Eskimos follow them in boats through the Bering Strait. The Netsilik Eskimos hunt seal. According to Asen Balikci, a seal basks in the sun all day and slips into the water at midnight, to return at dawn to emerge from the same hole. In spring the sun, too, slips below the horizon for only a brief period, and the sky still glows. All the Netsilik hunter has to do in spring is go out at midnight, watch a seal disappear into a given hole, and wait there quietly in the brief twilight, on a spread piece of bearskin. The seal will be up soon, with the sun. The glaciers are calving; brash ice and grease ice clog the bays. From land you can see the widening of open leads on the distant pack ice by watching the "water sky"—the dark patches and streaks on the glaring cloud cover that are breaks in the light reflected from the pack.

You might think the Eskimos would welcome the spring and the coming of summer; they did, but they looked forward more to the coming of winter. I'm talking as usual about the various Eskimo cultures as they were before modernization. Some Eskimos used to greet the sun on its first appearance at the horizon in stunned silence, and with raised arms. But in summer, they well knew, they would have to eat lean fish and birds. Winter's snow would melt to water and soak the thin thawed ground down to the permafrost; the water couldn't drain away, and it would turn the earth into a sop of puddles. Then the mosquitoes would come, the mosquitoes that could easily drive migrating caribou to a mad frenzy so that they trampled their newborn calves, the famous arctic mosquitoes of which it is said, "If there were any more of them, they'd have to be smaller."

In winter the Eskimos could travel with dog sleds and visit; with the coming of warm weather, their pathways, like mine in Virginia, closed. In interior Alaska and northern Canada, breakup is the big event. Old-timers and cheechakos alike lay wagers on the exact day and hour it will occur. For the ice on rivers there does not just simply melt; it rips out in a general holocaust. Upstream, thin ice breaks from its banks and races down river. Where it rams solid ice it punches it free and shoots it downstream, buckling and shearing: ice adds to ice, exploding a Juggernaut into motion. A grate and roar blast the air, the ice machine razes bridges and fences and trees, and the whole year's ice rushes out like a train in an hour. Breakup: I'd give anything to see it. Now for the people in the bush the waterways are open to navigation but closed to snowmobile and snowshoe, and it's harder for them, too, to get around.

Here in the May valley, fullness is at a peak. All the plants are fully leafed, but intensive insect damage hasn't begun. The leaves are fresh, whole, and perfect. Light in the sky is clear, unfiltered by haze, and the sun hasn't yet withered the grass.

Now the plants are closing in on me. The neighborhood children are growing up; they aren't keeping all the paths open. I feel like buying them all motorbikes. The woods are a clog of green, and I have to follow the manner of the North, or of the past, and take to the waterways to get around. But maybe I think things are more difficult than they are, because once, after I had waded and slogged in tennis shoes a quarter of a mile upstream in Tinker Creek, a boy hailed me from the tangled bank. He had followed me just to pass the time of day, and he was barefoot.

When I'm up to my knees in honeysuckle, I beat a retreat, and visit the duck pond. The duck pond is a small eutrophic pond on cleared land near Carvin's Creek. It is choked with algae and seething with frogs; when I see it, I always remember Jean White's horse.

Several years ago, Jean White's old mare, Nancy, died. It died on private property where it was pastured, and Jean couldn't get permission to bury the horse there. It was just as well, because we were in the middle of a July drought, and the clay ground was fired hard as rock. Anyway, the problem remained: What do you do with a dead horse? Another friend once tried to burn a dead horse, an experiment he never repeated. Jean White made phone calls and enlisted friends who made more phone calls. All experts offered the same suggestion: try the fox farm. The fox farm is south of here; it raises various animals to make into coats, It turned out that the fox farm readily accepts dead horses from far and wide to use a "fresh" meat for the foxes. But it also turned out, oddly enough, that the fox farm was up to its hem in dead horses already, and had room for no more.

It was, as I say, July, and the problem of the dead mare's final resting place was gathering urgency. Finally someone suggested that Jean try the landfill down where the new interstate highway was being built. Certain key phone calls were made, and, to everybody's amazement, government officials accepted the dead horse. They even welcomed the dead horse, needed the dead horse, for its bulk, which, incidentally, was becoming greater each passing hour. A local dairy farmer donated his time; a crane hauled the dead horse into the farmer's truck, and he drove south. With precious little ceremony he dumped the mare into the landfill on which the new highway would rest—and that was the end of Jean White's horse. If you ever drive through Virginia on the new interstate highway between Christiansburg and Salem, and you feel a slight dip in the paving under your wheels, then loose thy shoe from off thy foot, for the place whereon thou drivest is Jean White's horse.

All this comes to mind at the duck pond, because the duck pond is rapidly turning into a landfill of its own, a landfill paved in frogs. There are a million frogs here, bullfrogs hopping all over each other on tangled mats of algae. And the pond is filling up. Small ponds don't live very long, especially in the South. Decaying matter piles up on the bottom, depleting oxygen, and the shore plants march to the middle. In another couple of centuries, if no one interferes, the duck pond will be a hickory forest.

On an evening in late May, a moist wind from Carvin's Cove shoots down the gap between Tinker and Brushy mountains, tears along Carvin's Creek valley, and buffets my face as I stand by the duck pond. The surface of the duck pond doesn't budge. The algal layer is a rigid plating; if the wind blew hard enough, I imagine it might audibly creak. On warm days in February the primitive plants start creeping over the pond, filamentous green and blue-green algae in sopping strands. From a sunlit shallow edge they green and spread, thickening throughout the water like bright gelatin. When they smother the whole pond they block sunlight, strangle respiration, and snarl creatures in hopeless tangles. Dragonfly nymphs, for instance, are easily able to shed a leg or two to escape a tight spot, but even dragonfly nymphs get stuck in the algae strands and starve.

Several times I've seen a frog trapped under the algae. I would be staring at the pond when the green muck by my feet would suddenly leap into the air and then subside. It looked as though it had been jabbed from underneath by a broom handle. Then it would leap again, somewhere else, a jumping green flare, absolutely silently— this is a very disconcerting way to spend an evening. The frog would always find an open place at last, and break successfully onto the top of the heap, trailing long green slime from its back, and emitting a hollow sound like a pipe thrown into a cavern. Tonight I walked around the pond scaring frogs; a couple of them jumped off, going, in effect, eek, and most grunted, and the pond was still. But one big frog, bright green like a poster-paint frog, didn't jump, so I waved my arm and stamped to scare it, and it jumped suddenly, and I jumped, and then everything in the pond jumped, and I laughed and laughed.

There is a muscular energy in sunlight corresponding to the spiritual energy of wind. On a sunny day, sun's energy on a square acre of land or pond can equal 4500 horsepower. These "horses" heave in every direction, like slaves building pyramids, and fashion, from the bottom up, a new and sturdy world.

The pond is popping with life. Midges are swarming over the center, and the edges are clotted with the jellied egg masses of snails. One spring I saw a snapping turtle lumber from the pond to lay her eggs. Now a green heron picks around in the pond weed and bladderwort; two muskrats at the shallow end are stockpiling cattails. Diatoms, which are algae that look under a microscope like crystals, multiply so fast you can practically watch a submersed green leaf transform into a brown fuzz. In the plankton, single-cell algae, screw fungi, bacteria, and water mold abound. Insect larvae and nymphs carry on their eating business everywhere in the pond. Stillwater caddisses, alderfly larvae, and damselfly and dragonfly nymphs stalk on the bottom debris; mayfly nymphs hide in the weeds, mosquito larvae wriggle near the surface, and red-tailed maggots stick their breathing tubes up from between decayed leaves along the shore. Also at the pond's muddy edges it is easy to see the tiny red tubifex worms and bloodworms; the convulsive jerking of hundreds and hundreds together catches my eye.

Once, when the pond was younger and the algae had not yet taken over, I saw an amazing creature. At first all I saw was a slender motion. Then I saw that it was a wormlike creature swimming in the water with a strong, whiplike thrust, and it was two feet long. It was also slender as a thread. It looked like an inked line someone was nervously drawing over and over. Later I learned that it was a horsehair worm. The larvae of horsehair worms live as parasites in land insects; the aquatic adults can get to be a yard long. I don't know how it gets from the insect to the pond, or from the pond to the insect, for that matter, or why on earth it needs such an extreme shape. If the one I saw had been so much as an inch longer or a shave thinner, I doubt if I would ever have come back.

The plankton bloom is what interests me. The plankton animals are all those microscopic drifting animals that so staggeringly outnumber us. In the spring they are said to "bloom," like so many poppies. There may be five times as many of these teeming creatures in spring as in summer. Among them are the protozoans—amoebae and other rhizopods, and millions of various flagellates and ciliates; gelatinous moss animalcules or byrozoans; rotifers—which wheel around either free or in colonies; and all the diverse crustacean minutiae—copepods, ostracods, and cladocerans like the abundant daphnias. All these drifting animals multiply in sundry bizarre fashions, eat tiny plants or each other, die, and drop to the pond's bottom. Many of them have quite refined means of locomotion—they whirl, paddle, swim, slog, whip, and sinuate—but since they are so small, they are no match against even the least current in the water. Even such a sober limnologist as Robert E. Coker characterizes the movement of plankton as "milling around."

A cup of duck-pond water looks like a seething broth. If I carry the cup home and let the sludge settle, the animalcules sort themselves out, and I can concentrate them further by dividing them into two clear glass bowls. One bowl I paint all black except for a single circle where the light shines through; I leave the other bowl clear except for a single black circle against the light. Given a few hours, the light-loving creatures make their feeble way to the clear circle, and the shade-loving creatures to the black. Then, if I want to, I can harvest them with a pipette and examine them under a microscope.

There they loom and disappear as I fiddle with the focus. I run the eyepiece around until I am seeing the drop magnified three hundred times, and I squint at the little rotifer called monostyla. It zooms around excitedly, crashing into strands of spirogyra alga or zipping around the frayed edge of a clump of debris. The creature is a flattened oval; at its "head" is a circular fringe of whirling cilia, and at its "tail" a single long spike, so that it is shaped roughly like a horseshoe crab. But it is so incredibly small, as multicelled animals go, that it is translucent, even transparent, and I have a hard time telling if it is above or beneath a similarly transparent alga. Two monostyla drive into view from opposite directions; they meet, bump, reverse, part. I keep thinking that if I listen closely I will hear the high whine of tiny engines. As their drop heats from the light on the mirror, the rotifers skitter more and more frantically; as it dries, they pale and begin to stagger, and at last can muster only a halting twitch. Then I either wash the whole batch down the sink's drain, or in a rush of sentiment walk out to the road by starlight and dump them in a puddle. Tinker Creek where I live is too fast and rough for most of them.

I don't really look forward to these microscopic forays: I have been almost knocked off my kitchen chair on several occasions when, as I was following with strained eyes the tiny career of a monostyla rotifer, an enormous red roundworm whipped into the scene, blocking everything, and writhing in huge, flapping convulsions that seemed to sweep my face and fill the kitchen. I do it as a moral exercise; the microscope at my forehead is a kind of phylactery, a constant reminder of the facts of creation that I would just as soon forget. You can buy your child a microscope and say grandly, "Look, child, at the Jungle in a Little Drop." The boy looks, plays around with pond water and bread mold and onion sprouts for a month or two, and then starts shooting baskets or racing cars, leaving the microscope on the basement table staring fixedly at its own mirror forever—and you say he's growing up. But in the puddle or pond, in the city reservoir, ditch, or Atlantic Ocean, the rotifers still spin and munch, the daphnia still filter and are filtered, and the copepods still swarm hanging with clusters of eggs. These are real creatures with real organs leading real lives, one by one. I can't pretend they're not there. If I have life, sense, energy, will, so does a rotifer. The monostyla goes to the dark spot on the bowl: To which circle am I heading? I can move around right smartly in a calm; but in a real wind, in a change of weather, in a riptide, am I really moving, or am I "milling around"?

I was created from a clot and set in proud, free motion: so were they. So was this rotifer created, this monostyla with its body like a lightbulb in which pale organs hang in loops; so was this paramecium created, with a thousand propulsive hairs jerking in unison, whipping it from here to there across a drop and back. *Ad majorem Dei gloriam?*

Somewhere, and I can't find where, I read about an Eskimo hunter who asked the local missionary priest, "If I did not know about God and sin, would I go to hell?" "No," said the priest, "not if you did not know." "Then why," asked the Eskimo earnestly, "did you tell me?" If I did not know about the rotifers and paramecia, and all the bloom of plankton clogging the dying pond, fine; but since I've seen it I must somehow deal with it, take it into account. "Never lose a holy curiosity," Einstein said; and so I lift my microscope down from the shelf, spread a drop of duck pond on a glass slide, and try to look spring in the eye.

A CLOSER LOOK AT ANNIE DILLARD

1. In the introduction to this section about Annie Dillard, we suggest that Dillard is a "wanderer." Her essays wander over a lot of territory—Alaska, Virginia, Canada—and a lot of the writing, too, wanders among descriptions of different places and observations. Consider what such a rhetorical wandering does for the reader. What kind of trip does Dillard's rhetoric take us on as readers? Write a description of Dillard's rhetorical wandering and address the effect such wandering has on her writing.

2. Dillard uses a great many names—both scientific and common—that are potentially unfamiliar to readers in her descriptions of places and things she sees: diatoms, screw fungi, horsehair worm, rhizopods, byrozoans, copepods, and cladocerans, to name but a few. Consider what effect Dillard achieves by attaching specific names to the things she describes. What effect does the act of naming something have for a reader? Does it affect how you envision the writer? Does it affect how you read the essay? Does it affect ethos or credibility? Argue in favor of or against Dillard's use of names. Be sure to offer examples not only of the names she uses, but explanations of how those names affect the agendas of her essays.

3. Dillard's writing often contains an intimacy of details. She is attentive to how she presents places and organisms. Part of her ability to offer such magnificent descriptions—descriptions that often give the reader a kind of experience in the place described—is her willingness to observe and become familiar with the details of a place. Select a place with which you feel you are

deeply familiar. In an essay, describe that place to an audience of your peers and suggest what the casual observer might not notice about the place in a casual observation.

4. Many of Annie Dillard's essays are divided into untitled or numbered subsections. Consider the organizational patterns and strategies for subdividing an essay. Do these subdivisions affect transition? Do they affect meaning? Select either an essay that you have previously written or select an essay from one of the other authors in this book and revise it to take on a new organizational pattern, one in which you can subdivide distinct sections for emphasis and effect.

5. Without question, Annie Dillard's works are rhetorically designed to elicit particular emotional responses from her audience. Think about the essays you have written in the past and the strategies you have employed to evoke emotional response from your audience. In a new essay, address a subject about which you have written before, but concentrate now in your writing specifically on coercing your audience into an emotive response.

Looking from Writer to Writer

1. Often, Annie Dillard turns to a kind of scientific language to describe the plants and animals she writes about. Some of the other authors in this collection also rely heavily on languages of the sciences. Edward O. Wilson and Stephen Jay Gould, for example, rely heavily on a scientific kind of writing, primarily because they are scientists. Dillard, however, is not a scientist. Look back at the essays of both Gould and Wilson and consider how their writing might be considered "scientific," and then consider whether or not Dillard's writing reflects any characteristics of scientific writing.

2. Annie Dillard's writing is often characterized by her attention to detail, her careful and articulate descriptions of places and animals she observes. Edward Hoagland's writing also manifests a careful attention to detail and careful descriptions of those details. Compare the ways that both Dillard and Hoagland make use of detail and description in their writing. Does their attention to description affect how you read their work?

3. Annie Dillard's "Total Eclipse" contains a good deal of detail about images. That is, the essay is rather dependent upon the visual (the clown painting and the shadow of the eclipse, for instance). Similarly, John Updike's essay "Cemeteries" offers a rather pictorial quality, with a good deal of description of visual images. Look carefully at how these authors incorporate the visual or pictorial into their writing. How do they describe images? What effect do those images have on the essay in which they appear?

Looking Beyond

NONFICTION

An American Childhood. 1987. New York: HarperCollins, 1998.

The Annie Dillard Library. New York: HarperCollins, 1989.

The Annie Dillard Reader. New York: HarperCollins, 1994.

Encounters with Chinese Writers. Middletown, CT: Wesleyan University Press, 1984.

Holy the Firm. 1977. New York: HarperCollins, 1998.

Living by Fiction. 1982. New York: HarperCollins, 1998.

Pilgrim at Tinker Creek. 1974. New York: Harper Perennial, 1998.

Teaching a Stone to Talk: Expeditions and Encounters. 1982. New York: HarperCollins, 1999.

Three by Annie Dillard. New York: HarperCollins, 1990.

The Writing Life. New York: HarperCollins, 1999.

FICTION

The Living. New York: HarperCollins, 1992.

POETRY

Mornings Like This: Found Poems. New York: HarperCollins, 1995.

Tickets for a Prayer Wheel. Columbia, MO: University of Missouri Press, 1974.

Barbara Ehrenreich

A prolific writer and political activist, Barbara Ehrenreich is one of America's most vocal and insightful social critics, speaking and writing on such subjects as feminism, class, the family, health care, poverty, the labor movement, and sex. In addition to her essays, which have appeared in *Time, The Nation, Harper's, Z Magazine, Ms., Mother Jones,* the *New Republic,* and the *New York Times Magazine,* Ehrenreich is also the author of numerous books, including *Fear of Falling: The Inner Life of the Middle Class* (nominated for a National Book Critics Award in 1989). In 1980 she shared the National Magazine Award for Excellence in Reporting, and in 1987–88 she was awarded a Guggenheim Fellowship. In addition to her writing, Ehrenreich is well known as a public speaker and radio and television talk-show guest. She has also lectured in various countries around the world. In 1983 she cochaired the Democratic Socialists of America. As Pulitzer Prize–winning columnist Ellen Goodman has noted, "Ehrenreich's scorn withers, her humor stings, and her radical light shines on."

Ehrenreich was born August 26, 1941, in Butte, Montana, where her father worked as a copper miner. Her parents came from a blue-collar, working-class background and were strongly pro-union. "There were two rules in our family," Ehrenreich explained in a 1989 interview: "One was you never cross a union picket line and the other was you never vote Republican." As her parents moved up in terms of social class and income, and as they moved around the country, they remained connected to their working-class roots, her father maintaining a "scorn of class pretensions" reflected in his blue-collar class prejudice against the professional middle class. (To this day, she proclaims, "I'm a little more comfortable with the Budweiser crowd.") Ehrenreich's family and community left her with an abiding class-conscious view of American society, which she carried with her as she went on to receive a BA in chemistry and physics and then a PhD in biology from Rockefeller University in 1968. She decided not to become a research scientist, however, and instead became involved in social activism during the Vietnam War, writing leaflets and investigative articles. From involvement in social and political activism, her interest in writing emerged. She explains, "I think I started writing things because I felt they ought to be written."

Ehrenreich's writing, and her essays in particular, are deeply connected to contemporary issues. As she wrote in the introduction to her second essay collection, *The Snarling Citizen,* essay writing is akin to social commentating. An essay writer, she explains, is a "zeitgeist-watcher," someone who critically observes the habits and customs and spirit of her culture. Indeed, Ehrenreich's writing has an analytical strength ("looking for ways things fit together," as she expresses it) that owes something to her science background, but she explains her writing is also driven by anger and curiosity. She writes about issues that she is passionate about, issues that affect women, the working class, the poor. In her books especially, she seeks to uncover social phenomena such as the origin of war, the construction of women in our culture, and the fears of the middle class. Ehrenreich explains, "I'm sort of a myth buster by trade. I like to say I specialize in ideas—bad ideas." A characteristic of Ehrenreich's writing is its humor. She exposes "bad ideas" and other social injustices, but she very often does it satirically. She states: "humor actually can be a way of expressing a lot of aggression. I mean, satirical humor . . . Nobody wants to hear a rant."

As you read the essays that follow, pay attention to how Ehrenreich uses satire to express aggression and make arguments, and think about why this strategy is effective. Consider, that is, what makes the humor work in her writing—how it conveys her point, helps make her argument more powerful, and makes her writing seem less like a "rant." Also, pay attention to what she writes about, her subject matter. Her writing seems to be less meticulously stylized than, say, Cynthia Ozick's, and her arguments are more explicit, but her subject matter is just as significant. She explains how she keeps her readers' interest: "You have to have lots of things that are concrete. It can't be all generalizations. You have to be able to sort of see, feel, hear, touch, smell what's going on." Think about what effect her more confrontational, more concrete style has on you as a reader. As you consider this question, also think about what makes her writing perhaps particularly suited to social activism. In particular, think about what makes the essay itself as a genre suited for social commentary and activism.

Ehrenreich on Writing

At First Glance

The following essay serves as the introduction to Ehrenreich's second essay collection, The Snarling Citizen. *In it, she describes how she gets her inspiration to write, and in so doing, indirectly describes how she defines the role of the writer and what it means to write essays. She portrays the essay writer as a "zeitgeist watcher," someone who is in touch with trends and cultural characteristics. The zeitgeist means "the spirit of the age." As you read the essay, think about what it specifically means to be a zeitgeist watcher. And consider whether you agree that a writer should be in touch with the zeitgeist or if, as a writer, you define your role differently. Also, think about whether or not you agree with Ehrenreich's characterization of our contemporary zeitgeist.*

Introduction to *The Snarling Citizen*

In the old days journalists vied for the zeitgeist watch. To be assigned to the zeitgeist meant that you could be trusted with an expense account and allowed out of the office during work hours. Veteran geist-watchers used the money to finance a cab ride to some arbitrary destination, interviewed the cab driver, and had their story written by late afternoon. Today, however, journalists fear to leave their desks lest their health insurance be canceled while they are out, and few cabbies can communicate outside their native Russian or Arabic. Geist-watching has sedimented to the lowest ranks of the journalism profession—freelancers, like myself; guest essayists; and illegal immigrants who lack the skills that are required in the restaurant industry.

The problem is that zeitgeist-watching is no longer considered an outdoor activity, worthy of Pulitzers and five-figure pay. Every home now has geist-gauging equipment, generally located in the bedrooms and den, and even children are capable of turning it on and operating it by remote. Hence the expectation that geist-watchers and social commentators will generally pursue their professions while performing some other small but remunerative task, such as babysitting for the neighbors' children or knitting ski caps for sale.

This is, in fact, how most of the insights in the following essays were obtained. First comes the phone call or, most likely, just a message on the answering machine from the editor of one of our major media outlets. "Barbara," the voice says, or at least some similar-sounding name, "I hope I have the right number because we need the Mood in America (or the Future of Life on Earth, or Whatever Happened to Our

149

Way of Life?) by Thursday at the latest. And if I've got the wrong number, I'd appreciate knowing if there's someone else there who could do it instead." Then, flattered and brimming with investigative zeal, I rush to the den, wrestle the remote out of a loved one's hand, and settle down to work.

It's not as easy as you may be imagining, this geist-gazing, insight-garnering line of work. There are the difficulties attendant on any form of home work, as opposed to that performed in factories or offices. Children screaming underfoot, for example, when you happen to step on them or remark that most other twenty-two-year-olds are out in the workforce by now. Neighbors fleeing homicidal family members, oily-toned telemarketers arriving by phone, elderly dependents who must be shooed away from the six-pack in the fridge lest they exhaust their supply of Attends.

But I persist, hour after hour, clicking doggedly away at the remote. Sometimes days go by with no palpable product, only a swirl of numbing patter enlivened by jokes about body functions and tips on the cleaning of dentures. The neighbors admire my attention span, the ability to remain glued to my work no matter how painful or exhausting. The take-out containers mount up; phone calls go unanswered; pets sicken and die; family members pack up and move to distant states, leaving only their house keys behind.

Then, sometimes when you least expect it, the zeitgeist begins to emerge from the screen. If you were hoping maybe for a winged and helmeted figure of noble visage, then you have been reading too much Hegel and not watching enough CNN. Our contemporary zeitgeist is a low, snarly creature that oozes out from the TV and settles lumplike in the middle of the den, where it pulses lethargically and makes an occasional lunge for the dog. And here is another reason why well-paid celebrity journalists will have nothing to do with the zeitgeist anymore: it is not the kind of thing you would like to find on your family-room floor.

The modern zeitgeist feeds on images, though historians tell us that in the distant past it ate rougher stuff, like raw experience and epic poems. Now it wants images night and day, and it hardly matters to the zeitgeist whether the scenes it consumes are the result of actual real-world events or artful cinematic deception. The bloated corpses on the screen may be the product of painful human deaths or of extras working for hourly wages. They can be the victims of genocidal clashes in Bosnia or Rwanda, of some deranged celebrity killer in Brentwood, California, or of Arnold Schwarzenegger on a fictional rampage—the zeitgeist finds them almost equally tasty.

There are times, I will admit, when the zeitgeist can be an amusing companion and a refreshing break from the so-called real world of traffic jams, collection agencies, and malls. When it's been snacking on a delicious presidential sex scandal, for example, or an outbreak of mayhem on the Olympic figure-skating team—at such moments the whole family troops merrily into the den, nachos and bean dip in hand. For who cannot be charmed by the zeitgeist as it pounces playfully on some topic or personality, chews it to shreds, and then rolls over, sated, to wait for the next?

But, as we know all too well, it can turn nasty overnight. After feeding long enough on stories of crime and the transgressions of foreign rulers, or when it has been whipped into a frenzy by foam-mouthed right-wing preachers and talk-show hosts, the zeitgeist can assume a form that is menacing to human life. It swells until it fills the entire room and spills out onto the lawn, screaming with infantile rage, clawing at the sky, howling for blood.

At such moments it is wise to remain huddled together indoors, preferably under the bed. When the geist craves blood, no one is entirely safe. Wars are declared, often against populations that have no clear idea what transgressions their rulers may have committed. New prisons are slapped together, young people are paddled and caned. Human sacrifices may even be required, preferably of criminals who have exhausted their right to appeal. For the zeitgeist, fully aroused, resembles nothing so much as a toddler in a tantrum or a full-grown Republican in a characteristic outbreak of punitive rage.

It was not supposed to be this way, of course. Important pundits and dreamers had announced that the zeitgeist of the 1990s would be distinctively different from its 1980s incarnation. Greed and violence would give way to "acts of random kindness and senseless beauty"; the military would wither away, leaving a lavish peace dividend in its place; "government" would come to mean something other than the IRS. And for ten seconds of historical time, it almost looked as if these predictions would come true. We put a cuddly new president in the White House, a man with a feisty wife and mistresses and an unshakable commitment to a program defined boldly by the content-free word *change*. There was even some wild talk about a return of sex (long banned as a source of disease and offense to the Christian right), of domestic spending, of dancing in the street.

Within months though, the new president had himself been mauled by the geist. Oh, he did everything possible to appease it, with the help of his able wife. No president had ever studied it so carefully, monitored it with so many polls, and attempted so earnestly to charm it with smiles and beguile it with charts and graphs. He darted to the right, and then to the right, and yet again further to the right. The Haitians were abandoned for years to tread water with the sharks; the Iraqis were bombed and rebombed; workers continued to be mocked with an hourly minimum wage that barely exceeds a skycap's tip; little kids on welfare were threatened with starvation if their mothers didn't go out and cook burgers for strangers. Yet somehow the zeitgeist was not appeased, and began instead to see in Bill Clinton a cruel caricature of its own unloveliest traits—fickleness, mendacity, and a craving for high-fat foods. The ferocity with which it turned on our poor head of state was terrible to watch.

No one had expected the zeitgeist to evolve into a living thing, capable of destroying grown men. It was supposed to be a mere emanation, a kind of mist rising from the general mind. But something happened, probably in the mid-1980s, that still baffles the psychosociological experts. Perhaps we had to reach some critical mass in terms of the number of people watching TV at any one time. This may have occurred when the airports installed CNN, or perhaps at the point when college students abandoned their books for *Melrose Place*. Then, for the first time in human history, hundreds of millions of individual minds were wired together in a single teleneurological system, inhabiting a self-contained universe of image and jingle and slogan.

Still, the zeitgeist might not have sprung to life if it had not been for the media's increasing reliance on ratings and polls. With these new computerized, high-tech mood-gauging instruments, the media folk can instantly tell how an image or idea is faring in the collective mind, and withdraw or reinforce that image at will, as required to keep the viewers transfixed. Thus the writing that connects us all together goes not simply from "real world" to media to human mind but in the other direction as well. If you don't like "the news," if it drags or annoys, you can be sure it will be replaced soon by something better. Infotainment flows in one direction, polls and ratings in the other, to produce a simulated macrobrain. What has emerged, in layperson's terms, is a closed loop in which bizarre feedback phenomena readily develop, along with something eerily resembling biological life.

Who could have imagined such an outcome? Telecommunications, combined with computers and polls, were supposed to make us smarter, more connected, better able to right wrongs as we found them. But the collective mind that emerges from our vast media circuitry turns out to be cruder and more credulous than the sum of its parts. Individually we may hate injustice and love logic and reason. Wired together and resonating with infotainment, we become something terrifyingly different—a franken-geist.

Hence the hasty decline of what was once proudly known as the "political process." Not so long ago, the person seeking "change" of some sort, as our president terms it—the abolition of slavery, for example, or the preservation of one of our few remaining freestanding trees—would go from door to door, engaging the neighbors in earnest discussion. Arguments would be waged, pots of coffee consumed, doors slammed or petitions signed. The "process" would inch along. But today, that same change-oriented person would be an object of suspicion just for appearing out of doors and on foot. He or she would be labeled an "activist," a term suggesting some unfortunate tendency to fidget and twitch. And if a door ever opened to him or her, it would reveal a room full of citizens deeply engrossed in the plight of some homicidal car-rental spokesman or penisless former Marine. Slavery and trees would have to wait.

And what if our activist succeeded in calling attention to some awful injustice or omen of environmental doom? Suppose people even began to picket and protest. Would the zeitgeist pay any attention—or would these small signs of human initiative be swallowed up in the onrush of unrelated imagery, self-righteous talk-show talk, new and improved products, celebrity trials, cop shows, and televised psychics?

So you can see there are hazards to this line of work. Perhaps no one can monitor the zeitgeist without being drawn ineluctably into it. After hours at my work, a certain fretfulness sets in, a sense of emptiness and total futility that can be relieved only by ever more vivid images and sensations—bigger and better wars, crimes involving torture and cannibalism!

At such times I am grateful for the small distractions that are part of a home worker's life. A sweet-faced child enters the den, clambers onto my shoulder or knee, and asks why we always have to have this gross-looking zeitgeist prowling around on the floor. Then, although the child is well into his or her twenties and is in danger of crushing my shoulder or knee, I am reminded that there are precious aspects of existence that cannot be accessed by clicking a remote.

It comes to me, in a surge of revolutionary insight, that our lives—meaning whatever it is that continues to happen when the TV is off and even when the power has failed—are richer and vastly more curious than anything we will find in the flickering realm of image and spectacle. That even those of us who will never be subjects for docudramas, who will never invent ingenious new ways of killing our family members and getting rid of the bodies—yes, even we who can never hope to enter the realm of image but who remain day after day in the nonvirtual world of tactile sensation—we also matter. We are, or are entitled to be, the heroes of at least our own lives. And that may be the most empowering and subversive insight available in this premillennial, postmodern era.

Act on it.

Double Take

1. Having read the essay, what do you think Ehrenreich means by the zeitgeist? Why do you think the zeitgeist is so important for her as a writer, especially as an essay writer? Do you agree that the essayist must be in touch with it?
2. What does it mean for a writer to be in touch with the zeitgeist? How can a writer, according to Ehrenreich, get in touch with it? Do you agree? How do you as a writer get in touch with the subject you are writing about?
3. Toward the end of the essay, Ehrenreich describes zeitgeist-watching as hazardous work. What do you think she means by that? In what ways do you think essay writing might also be hazardous work?
4. As a writer, what motivates you to write? Where do you turn for your material?

At First Glance

"Stamping Out a Dread Scourge" was first published in the essay section of Time *magazine, so the fact that it deals with a contemporary news topic, breast implants, is appropriate to readers who are interested in current news and events. Rather than choosing to confront her topic directly, though, Barbara Ehrenreich confronts it satirically. Satire is a risky rhetorical strategy and can backfire. If a reader does not recognize the satire, then he or she might think Ehrenreich is actually endorsing breast implants. As you read it, think about what makes Ehrenreich's essay successful as a satirical piece. Also, think about why the satire makes her argument more powerful, and how you might be able to use satire in your own writing.*

Stamping Out a Dread Scourge

In the spirit of a public-health campaign, the American Society for Plastic and Reconstructive Surgery (ASPRS) has launched a PR drive to "tell the other side of the [breast-implant] story." Public health? Slicing women's chests open so that they can be stuffed with a close chemical relative of Silly Putty? Yes, indeed, because the plastic surgeons understand what the Food and Drug Administration is so reluctant to acknowledge: that small breasts are not just a harmless challenge to the bikini wearer or would-be topless entertainer. They are a disease, a disfiguring illness for which the technical term is *micromastia.*

As the ASPRS tried to explain to the FDA ten years ago, "there is a substantial and enlarging body of medical information and opinion to the effect that these deformities [small breasts] are really a disease." Not a fatal disease perhaps, to judge from the number of sufferers who are still hobbling around untreated, but a disease nonetheless, like flu or TB. And anyone tempted to fault the medical establishment for inaction on breast cancer or AIDS should consider its quiet, but no less heroic progress against the scourge of micromastia: in the last thirty years, 1.6 million victims have been identified, diagnosed, and cured. Who says our health system doesn't work?

Once we understand that small breasts are a "disease," it's easier to see why Dow Corning and others rushed so breathlessly to get their implants onto the market. Why diddle around with slow, costly tests while an epidemic is raging out there? And everyone's life is touched by the tragedy of micromastia because everyone has a friend, sister, co-worker, or wife who falls pitifully short in the mammary department. In the past, small groups of health-conscious males, typically gathered at construction sites, would offer free diagnoses to women passersby, but there was little that could be done until the advent of the insertable Silly Putty breast.

Admittedly, micromastia is in some ways an atypical disease. It is painless, which is why many victims put off treatment for years, and it in no way diminishes breast function, if that is still defined in the old-fashioned way as lactation. The implants, on the other hand, can interfere with lactation, and they make mammograms tricky to read (not to mention the occasional disfiguring or life-threatening side effect like lupus or scleroderma). But so what if micromastia has no functional impact? Why can't a disease be manifested solely by size?

Consider the rigorously scientific methods employed by the medical profession in its efforts to curb the epidemic. Not just anyone could get breast implants. No, the doctor had to study the afflicted area first to decide whether they were truly needed. A friend of mine, an inquiring journalist of average proportions, called a New York–area plastic surgeon to inquire about implants and was told to come in for an exam. One quick, searching look and he told her that, yes, she needed them, badly.

In fact, according to the tabloids, Jessica Hahn needed them too, as may have Melanie Griffith, Jane Fonda, Brigitte Nielsen, and even, gasp, Dolly Parton. Why take chances? The doctors know there are not only obvious forms of micromastia, discernable to the man on the street, but insidious, hidden forms—very well hidden indeed.

So we can see why the plastic surgeons were willing to cough up hundreds of dollars each to finance the ASPRS's campaign to show the bright side of the breast-implant story. Though nearly two million micromastia victims have been cured, millions more remain untreated, as shown by the continued existence of the plague's dread symbol—the A-cup bra. There have been many earnest attempts to reach the untreated: public-health-oriented magazines like *Playboy* repeatedly print photos illustrating normal breast size for the woman in doubt. Tragically though, many women still live in denial, concealing their condition under mannish blazers and suit jackets, forgoing the many topless forms of employment.

And we can see too why there was nothing sexist about American Medical Association spokesman Dr. Mitchell Karlin's warning that the recent moratorium on implants would cause "absolute hysteria among women." Look at those unruly AIDS and breast-cancer activists—why not a mass movement of micromastia victims, marching and chanting for immediate help?

Now, a cynic might see the silicone-implant business as another scam on the scale of the Dalkon Shield (which had a tendency to cause devastating infections), DES (which could cause cancer in the user's offspring), or the high-estrogen birth-control pill (which was also rushed to market after hasty and dubious testing). A cynic might point to the medical profession's long habit of exploting the female body for profit—from the nineteenth-century custom of removing the ovaries as a cure for "hysteria," to our more recent traditions of unnecessary hysterectomies and cesareans. A cynic might conclude that the real purpose of the $500-million-a-year implant business is the implantation of fat in the bellies and rumps of underemployed plastic surgeons.

But our cynic would be missing the point of modern medical science. We may not have a cure for every disease, alas, but there's no reason we can't have a disease for every cure. With silicone implants, small breasts became micromastia. With injectable growth hormone, short kids become treatable dwarves. Plastic surgeons can now cure sagging jowls and chins, droopy eyelids and insufficiently imposing male chests and calves. So we can expect to hear soon about the menace of new diseases like saggy jowlitis, prolapsed eyelid, and hypopectoralis.

It will be hard, though, to come up with anything quite so convincing as micromastia. As the plastic surgeons must have realized, American culture is almost uniquely obsessed with large, nurturing bosoms. And with the silicone scandal upon us, we can begin to see why: in a society so unnurturing that even health care can be sadistically perverted for profit, people are bound to have a desperate, almost pathological need for the breast.

Double Take

1. How do we know that this essay is a satire? What clues in the text reveal the satire?
2. Ehrenreich creates a very satirical persona in this essay. Why do you think she chose to do this? What does such a rhetorical move do for the essay and its argument? Is it effective? Explain why or why not.
3. What audience do you think this essay was intended for? That is, who is Ehrenreich trying to convince? Is it more for men or women—or both? Is it for women with breast implants or women without—or both? Explain what hints Ehrenreich gives in the essay to suggest that she might have had a particular audience in mind.
4. Who is the "cynic" Ehrenreich refers to at the end of the essay?

At First Glance

Ehrenreich wrote "Premature Pragmatism" for Ms. *magazine. Before you read the essay, think about what Ehrenreich would have known about her audience before she started writing, and then consider if that knowledge of audience is reflected in her writing. Who reads* Ms.*? What shared values and assumptions might these readers hold? Then, as you read, consider how Ehrenreich's readers might have responded to her essay—in particular, if they would have found her argument compelling. Also, consider the different strategies Ehrenreich uses to convey her argument; for example, she includes statistics. What else does she use?*

Premature Pragmatism

The setting was one of those bucolic Ivy League campuses where the tuition exceeds the average American annual income and the favorite sport is white-water rafting—as far, in other words, as one might hope to get from the banal economic worries that plague the grown-up world. The subject, among the roomful of young women who had come to meet with me, turned to "life after college"—"if there is one" (nervous giggles). "My dream was to go into psychiatric social work," offered a serious young woman in overalls and a "Divest Now" button, "but I don't think I could live on that, so I'm going into banking instead." When I protested that she should hold on to her ideals and try to get by on the $30,000 or so a year psychiatric social workers earn, she looked baffled, as if I were recommending an internship with Mother Teresa.

"Ideals are all right when you're young," declared another woman, a campus activist who certainly seemed to fit the age group for which she found idealism appropriate, "but you do have to think of earning a living." Well, yes, I thought to myself, we older feminists have been saying for some time that the goal of higher education for women is not the "MRS" degree, but when did we ever say that it was *banking*?

Not that a little respect for the dollar isn't a fine thing in the young, and a useful antidote, in my day anyway, for the effects of too much Hesse or Kahlil Gibran. But no one in the room had gone so far as to suggest a career in almsgiving, washing lepers' feet, or doing literacy training among the Bushmen. "Idealism," to these undergraduates, was defined as an ordinary, respectable profession in the human services. "Realism" meant plunging almost straight from pubescence into the stone-hearted world of finance capitalism.

I call this mind-set, which you will find on almost any campus today, "premature pragmatism," and I am qualified to comment because I, too, was once a victim of it. I had gone to college with an intellectual agenda that included solving the mind-body problem, discovering the sources of human evil, and getting a tentative reading on the purpose of life. But within a few months I had dropped all that and become a chemistry major—partly because I had figured out that there were only meager rewards, in this world, for those who know the purpose of life and the source of all evil.

The result, twenty-odd years later, is more or less what you'd expect: I'm an ex-science major with no definite occupation (unless you count "writing," that universal cover for those who avoid wage slavery at all costs), and I am still obsessed by the Ultimate Questions, such as What It's All About and Whether the Universe Will Expand Forever. I could have turned out much worse; I could have stayed in chemistry and gone into something distinctly unidealistic like nerve gas or plastics, in which case I might have become rich and would almost certainly also have become an embittered alcoholic or a middle-aged dropout. The point is that premature pragmatism didn't work for me, and I doubt that it will work for any young person intending to set aside a "Divest Now" button for one reading "You Have a Friend at Chase Manhattan."

Yet premature pragmatism has become as popular on campuses as, in past eras, swallowing goldfish to impress one's friends or taking over the administration building to demand a better world. There has been a precipitous decline, just since the seventies, in the number of students majoring in mind-expanding but only incidentally remunerative fields like history and mathematics. Meanwhile, business—as an academic pursuit—is booming: almost one-fourth of all college graduates were business majors in 1983, compared to about one-seventh in 1973, while the proportions who major in philosophy or literature have vanished beyond the decimal point to less than 1 percent.

Even more alarming, to anyone whose own life has been scarred by premature pragmatism, is the decline in "idealism" as expressed by undergraduates and measured by pollsters. In 1968, 85 percent of college students said that they hoped their education would help them "develop a philosophy of life," etc., etc. In 1985, only 44 percent adhered to such lofty goals, while the majority expected that education would help them "earn a lot of money." There has been, in other words, almost a 50 percent decline in idealism and a 100 percent increase in venality, or to put it less judgmentally, premature pragmatism.

I concede, though, that there are good reasons for the hard-nosed pragmatism of today's college students. They face rougher times, economically, than did my generation or the generation before mine. As economists Frank Levy and Richard Michel have recently shown, today's baby boomers (and especially the younger ones) are far less likely than their own parents to be able to buy a home, maintain a family on one income, or to watch their standard of living improve as they grow older.

So the best comeback for the young woman in overalls would have been for her to snap at me, "You think I should live on thirty thousand dollars a year! Well, perhaps you hadn't noticed that the National Association of Homebuilders now estimates that it takes an income of thirty-seven thousand dollars a year to be able to afford a modest, median-priced home. Or that if I want to send my own eventual children to a college like this I will need well over fifty thousand dollars a year. Or are you suggesting that I rely on a rich husband?" And she would have been dead on the mark: in today's economy, idealism is a luxury that most of us are likely to enjoy only at the price of simple comforts like housing and education. The mood on campus isn't so much venality as it is *fear.*

But still, premature pragmatism isn't necessarily a winning strategy. In the first place, what looks like "realism" at age eighteen may become sheer folly by age thirty-eight. Occupations go in and out of corporate favor, so that chemistry, for example—which seemed to be a safe bet two decades ago—has become one of those disciplines that prepare people for a life in the retail end of the newspaper business. The same may eventually happen to today's campus favorites—like law, management, and finance. At least it seems to me that there must be an ecological limit to the number of paper pushers the earth can sustain, and that human civilization will collapse when the number of, say, tax lawyers exceeds the world's total population of farmers, weavers, fisherpersons, and pediatric nurses.

Furthermore, with any luck at all, one becomes a rather different person at age thirty-eight than one was at eighteen. The list of famous people who ended up in a different line of work than the one they first embarked on includes Clark Gable (former lumberjack), artist Henri Rousseau (postal clerk), Elvis Presley (truck driver), St. Augustine (playboy), Walt Disney (ambulance driver), and Che Guevara (physician). Heads of state are notoriously ill prepared for their mature careers; think of Adolf Hitler (landscape painter), Ho Chi Minh (seaman), and our own Ronald Reagan. Women's careers are if anything even more unpredictable, to judge from my own friends: Barbara (a biochemist turned novelist), Sara (French literature professor, now a book editor), cousin Barb (anthropology to medicine).

But the saddest thing about today's premature pragmatists is not that they will almost certainly be unprepared for their mid-life career destinations, but that they will be unprepared for Life, in the grand sense, at all. The years between eighteen and twenty-two were not given to us to be frittered away in contemplation of future tax shelters and mortgage payments. In fact, it is almost a requirement of developmental biology that these years be spent in erotic reverie, metaphysical speculation, and schemes for universal peace and justice. Sometimes, of course, we lose sight of the heroic dreams of youth later on, as overdue bills and carburetor problems take their toll. But those who never dream at all start to lose much more—their wit, empathy, perspective, and, for lack of a more secular term, their immortal souls.

Then what about the fact that it takes nearly a six-figure income to achieve what used to be known as a "middle-class" lifestyle? What about my young Ivy League friend, forced to choose between a career in human service and what she believes, perhaps realistically, to be an adequate income? All I can say is that there is something grievously wrong with a culture that values Wall Street sharks above social workers, armament manufacturers above artists, or, for that matter, corporate lawyers above homemakers. Somehow, we're going to have to make the world a little more habitable for idealists, whether they are eighteen or thirty-eight. In fact, I suspect that more and more young people, forced to choose between their ideals and their economic security, will start opting instead for a career in social change. "The pay is lousy," as veteran writer-historian-social-change-activist Irving Howe likes to say, "but it's steady work."

Double Take

1. Does the essay "Premature Pragmatism," in its subject matter, style, and argument, reflect an awareness of its readers? If so, where in the essay is that awareness most evident? Where, perhaps, is it least evident? What place does Ehrenreich seem to connect more to her readers than others?
2. At one point in the essay, Ehrenreich sympathizes with her readers, showing that she understands their point of view. What effect do you think this rhetorical move has on her readers? Why as a writer would you want to make such a move? How can you do it without sacrificing the integrity of your argument?
3. What do you think are Ehrenreich's most effective, compelling arguments in this essay? Explain what makes them so.
4. Although funny in places, "Premature Pragmatism" is not as satirical as "Stamping Out a Dread Scourge." Why do you think Ehrenreich chose a more direct, perhaps even a little more serious, writing style in this essay? What do you think would have happened, given her readers and her context, had she chosen a more satirical approach?

Seeing for Yourself

At First Glance

"Oh, Those Family Values" reveals many of the characteristics that can be found in other essays by Barbara Ehrenreich. As you read it, try to identify what these characteristics are, looking for those conventions in style, subject matter, and structure that you noticed in the previous essays. This essay, like "Stamping Out a Dread Scourge," also appeared in Time *magazine; compare the two to see if they reveal a similar awareness of the audience. In addition, try to evaluate those qualities in this essay that make it particularly "activist"—that make it push a certain agenda.*

Oh, *Those* Family Values

A disturbing subtext runs through our recent media fixations. Parents abuse sons—allegedly, at least, in the Menendez case—who in turn rise up and kill them. A husband torments a wife, who retaliates, in the best-known case, with a kitchen knife. Love turns into obsession, between the Simpsons anyway, and then perhaps into murderous rage. The family, in other words, as personal hell.

This accounts for at least part of our fascination with the Bobbitts and the Simpsons and the rest of them. We live in a culture that fetishizes the family as the ideal unit of human community, the perfect container for our lusts and loves. Politicians of both parties are aggressively "profamily"; even abortion-rights bumper stickers proudly link "profamily" and "prochoice." Only with the occasional celebrity crime do we allow ourselves to think the nearly unthinkable: that the family may not be the ideal and perfect living arrangement after all—that it can also be a nest of pathology and a cradle of gruesome violence.

It's a scary thought, since the family is at the same time our "haven in a heartless world." Theoretically, and sometimes actually, the family nurtures warm, loving feelings, uncontaminated by greed or power hunger. Within the family, and often only within the family, individuals are loved "for themselves," and whether or not they are infirm, incontinent, infantile, or eccentric. The strong (adults and, especially, males) lie down peaceably with the small and the weak.

But consider the matter of wife battery. We managed to dodge it in the Bobbitt case and downplay it as a force in Tonya Harding's life. Thanks to O.J., though, we're caught up now in a mass consciousness-raising session, grimly absorbing the fact that in some areas domestic violence sends more women to emergency rooms than any other form of illness, injury, or assault.

160

Still, we shrink from the obvious inference: for a woman, home is, statistically speaking, the most dangerous place to be. Her worst enemies and potential killers are not strangers but lovers, husbands, and those who claimed to love her once. Similarly, for every Polly Klaas who is killed by a deranged criminal on parole, dozens of children are abused and murdered by their own parents, uncles, or stepfathers. Home is all too often where the small and the weak fear to lie down and shut their eyes.

At some deep, queasy Freudian level we all know this. Even in the ostensibly "functional," nonviolent family, where no one is killed or maimed, feelings are routinely bruised and even twisted out of shape. There is the slap or put-down that violates a child's shaky sense of self; the cold, distracted stare that drives a spouse to tears; the little digs and rivalries. At best, the family teaches the finest things human beings can learn from one another—generosity and love. But it is also, all too often, where we learn nasty things like hate and rage and shame.

Americans act out their ambivalence about the family without ever owning up to it. Millions adhere to creeds—religious and political—that are militantly "profamily." But at the same time, millions flock to therapists and self-help groups that offer to heal the "inner child" from damage inflicted by family life. Legions of women band together to revive the self-esteem they lost in supposedly loving relationships and to learn to love a little less. We are all, it is often said, "in recovery." And from what? Our families, in most cases.

There is a long and honorable tradition of what might be called "antifamily" thought. The early-nineteenth-century French philosopher Charles Fourier taught that the family was a barrier to human progress and encouraged the formation of family-free alternative communities. Early feminists saw a degrading parallel between marriage and prostitution, and challenged the patriarchal authority of the husband/father. In the 1960s, radical psychiatrists denounced the family as a hotbed of neurosis, and the renowned British anthropologist Edmund Leach stated that "far from being the basis of the good society, the family, with its narrow privacy and tawdry secrets, is the source of all our discontents."

But communes proved harder to sustain than plain old couples, and the conservatism of the 1980s crushed the last vestiges of "lifestyle experimentation." Today, even gays and lesbians are eager to get married and take up family life. Feminists have learned to couch their concerns as "family issues," and public figures would sooner advocate crack-cocaine as a cure for stress than propose the family as a target for reform. Hence our unseemly interest in O.J, Erik, Lyle, and Lorena: they allow us, however gingerly, to break the silence on the hellish side of family life.

But the discussion needs to become a lot more open and forthright. We may be stuck with the family—at least until someone invents a sustainable alternative—but the family, with its deep, impacted tensions and longings, can hardly be expected to be the moral foundation of everything else. In fact, many families could use a lot more outside interference in the form of counseling and policing, and some are so dangerously dysfunctional that they ought to be encouraged to disband right away. Even healthy families need outside sources of moral guidance to keep those tensions from imploding—and this means, among other things, a public philosophy of gender equality and concern for child welfare. When, instead, the larger culture aggrandizes wife beaters, degrades women, or nods approvingly at child slappers, the family gets a little more dangerous for everyone, and so, inevitably, does the larger world.

A CLOSER LOOK AT BARBARA EHRENREICH

1. Of the four essays collected above, which one do you think makes the most effective argument? As you develop your case, try to include as many concrete examples as possible, showing why certain elements in the essay work for you and explaining your reasons. Write an essay in which you present your argument.

2. Several of the essayists in this book, like Barbara Ehrenreich, use the essay to render social commentary and to raise social awareness. What do you think makes the essay as a genre especially useful as a way to observe the world? What about the genre makes it effective as a way to observe? Write an essay in which you address the relationship between the essay as a genre and its potential as a medium for discussing social issues.

3. In the essays reprinted above, Ehrenreich argues against breast implants, questions the value of the family, and urges young women to shun pragmatism in favor of idealism. These are controversial topics, and can be argued for and against in several ways. Writing for the same audience that Ehrenreich was writing to, choose one of these topics and write a counterargument, one that, for example, defends the value of the family despite the problems with it that Ehrenreich raises.

4. Using Ehrenreich's "Stamping Out a Dread Scourge" as your model, write an essay that takes a satirical look at a contemporary topic. Then, after you have completed it, try to explain how you created this satirical effect.

Looking from Writer to Writer

1. Compare Barbara Ehrenreich's activism with that of Rick Bass. What rhetorical qualities do both essayists use as they attempt to convince readers of their agenda? In what ways do they differ in their approaches? Which approach do you think works more effectively?
2. Barbara Ehrenreich, Henry Louis Gates, Jr., and bell hooks can all be described as "public intellectuals," intellectuals who address the larger public rather than the academic community alone. In doing so, they take issues such as gender, race, and class, and address them in popular forums such as magazines and talk shows. What rhetorical strategies do they use in their essays to make these complex issues accessible to the larger public?
3. Both Scott Russell Sanders and Edward Hoagland can be described as revealing the personal in their writing and, hence, writing what Sanders refers to as "personal essays." Ehrenreich also often reveals the personal in her essays. Does that, however, make her essays "personal essays" as defined by Sanders? Why or why not?

Looking Beyond

ESSAYS

The Snarling Citizen: Essays. New York: Farrar, Straus and Giroux, 1995.
The Worst Years of Our Lives: Irreverent Notes from a Decade of Greed. New York: Pantheon Books, 1990.

NONFICTION

Blood Rites: Origins and History of the Passions of War. New York: Metropolitan Books, 1997.
Fear of Falling: The Inner Life of the Middle Class. New York: Pantheon Books, 1989.
For Her Own Good: One Hundred Fifty Years of the Experts' Advice to Women. Garden City, NY: Anchor Books, 1978.
The Hearts of Men: American Dreams and the Flight from Commitment. Garden City, NY: Anchor Press–Doubleday, 1983.
Nickel and Dimed: On (Not) Getting By in America. New York: Henry Holt, 2002.
Women. Garden City, NY: Anchor Press, 1978.

FICTION

Kipper's Game. New York: Farrar, Straus, and Giroux, 1993.

Joseph Epstein

Though he is resistant to being called "prolific," Joseph Epstein is a productive writer of essays who has earned a reputation as one of the country's most outspoken essayists, particularly as one who writes about writing. Epstein was born in Chicago in January 1939; he is the son of Maurice and Belle (Abrams) Epstein. He attended the University of Chicago and earned his AB in 1959. From 1975 to 1997, Epstein served as editor of *The American Scholar,* the quarterly journal of Phi Beta Kappa, the national honor society. During his time as editor, he wrote more than 90 essays for *The American Scholar.* Since 1974 Epstein has also served as visiting lecturer at Northwestern University. In 1989, the *Chicago Tribune* awarded Epstein the Heartland Prize for his collection *Partial Payments: Essays on Writers and Their Lives.* Without question, Epstein is a connoisseur of the essay.

In addition to writing for *The American Scholar,* Epstein has written for *Commentary, Harper's, New York Times Magazine, New York Times Book Review, New Criterion, Hudson Review, New Republic, Current History,* and *The New Yorker,* often under the pen name "Aristides"—a name associated with five important figures: Aristides the Just, who commanded Greek forces at Marathon, insisted that Athens focus on becoming a military rather than a naval power, and became an important statesman in Athens; Aristedes, the author of the *Apology of Aristides,* a defense of the Christian faith which was written in the second century A.D. and found on Mt. Sinai in 1889; Theodorus Aristides, the Greek rhetorician who persuaded the Roman emperor Marcus Aurelius to rebuild Smyrna after an earthquake destroyed it in 178 A.D.; Quintillianus Aristides, the first-century A.D. Greek writer who wrote what is considered the most important ancient book on music; and Aristides of Thebes, a Greek painter of the fourth century B.C. In his final essay printed in *The American Scholar,* Epstein wrote, "No writing, I have to report, has come as easily to me. I never wanted for a subject, and—capacious gasbag that I am—I always had the 6,500 words needed to cover that subject. By rough count, I have written nearly 600,000 words for this space. I have produced five books of essays from the Aristides column and am preparing a sixth. Aristides the Just? A lot closer to Aristides the Loquacious, I'd say."

Throughout his career, Epstein became known as a guardian of language, calling himself a "language snob." He claims that "the duty of everyone who considers himself educated is to keep language alive by using it with respect and precision." Much of his writing targets those whom he sees as misusing and disrespectful of language, often those Epstein describes as "well-scrubbed college-educated." Many of Epstein's essays reflect a running theme that suggests that standards of language have been allowed to be breached when standards of excellence, correctness, and clarity are given up in favor of "political and popular trends." Epstein often argues that much of contemporary American writing falls "short of the mark." He notes particularly writers like John Updike, John Irving, Joan Didion, and Norman Mailer as completely "missing the mark" despite the wide popularity of their books. His writing is often deeply critical of the work of other writers. He often contends that part of what has weakened American writing is that many writers learn and practice their craft in American universities, sheltered from real experiences. Epstein has argued that prior to World War II many writers were not affiliated with universities, but that after that war writers began to write from within the walls of college campuses—what he calls being "locked away." In an essay that appeared in *Harper's*, he writes that this has led to "two full generations of American novelists who, through their college education, have been brought up on a bitter diet of literary modernism and the tradition of alienation from their country." He has also commented that "American writing has never seemed less important, and more lost, than it does now."

As you read Epstein's essays, think not only about how he levels criticism against other writers and the act of contemporary writing, but also how writing becomes a subject about which he writes. Think, for instance, about how self-conscious of his own writing Epstein must be in order to comment so extensively about writing and writers. Think also about how Epstein makes use of humor in his writing. Consider how humor affects the rest of his writing and how readers might react to more light-hearted approaches to subjects.

Epstein on Writing

At First Glance

As Joseph Epstein writes in this essay about his own thoughts on writing, one strategy he uses is to turn to the words of other authors and their thoughts about essays. Notice the great ease with which Epstein moves from his thoughts to the words of other writers; his smooth transitions between each writer seem to suggest a deep familiarity with the words of those he quotes. As you read this piece, think about the effect this shift between citation and narrator's voice has on the reader.

Compose Yourself

As more and more of my illusions about myself continue to fall away—to name just a few among them: that I was a fine little athlete, not a bad dancer, a pretty serious lover, an elegant dresser, a nice-looking fella—the one that I can't shake is that I am a fast worker. This illusion is reinforced by various people telling me that I am very productive, though they usually stop short of using the term, vaguely insulting to writers of our day, "prolific." Odd, but somehow I don't feel in the least productive; I feel, in fact, rather slothful. I feel slothful, first, because I know how much of my working day is given over to empty diversions; and, second, owing to my illusion that I am a fast worker, I am always inclined to feel that I could—and should—be doing so much more.

It's far from clear that the world requires any more from me than I now provide. Some might prefer rather less. Philip Larkin, whose poetry I much admire, when reviewing a collection of my essays in the London *Times Literary Supplement* a number of years ago, remarked upon how queer it was that essays such as mine were written in the United States at all. He ended by saying that "the situation would seem to be one of supply rather than demand." Something to it, I fear. I fear, too, that one's writing resembles one's children, if only in the sense that, however much writing one does (or however many children one has), it seems all that one can possibly do (or have). And yet the nagging feeling persists that one should have done—should be doing—more.

The inky-fingered Balzac, whom no one is ever likely to have faulted for paucity of production, writing with debtors at his back and visions of glory before him, used to talk about smoking enchanted cigarettes, by which he meant conversation about books he wished to, but knew he never would, write. I have puffed upon a few of those cigarettes myself, going so far as actually to take publishers' advances for a biography

167

of John Dos Passos and for a book on snobbery. (Returning a publisher's advance, which I had to do on both occasions, is not easy; one has to imagine setting a money-stuffed wallet with no identification in it back onto the street where one found it; not only does one feel bereft of the cash, but one feels that it will only fall into worse hands than one's own.) I have no great regret about not having written either of these books: I have discovered that I have too bulky an ego to devote years of my own life to writing a lengthy book about someone else's life; and, as for the snobbery book, well, I still puff on that enchanted cigarette from time to time, telling myself I may do it yet.

But the book I really regret not having written is the trilogy that I could have written on the job when, as a young man, I worked as a senior editor at a large Midwestern publishing firm. True, I am not a novelist; true, even if I had been, when I worked there, in my late twenties and early thirties, I probably would not have had the material or the maturity to write a trilogy. But it was also true that, in nearly five years on this job, I had enough time to write three trilogies, a Finnish epic, and a study of net games in Patagonia. Viewed in retrospect, it was like being on some very generous grant, though not realizing it until afterwards.

On that job, for which I was quite well paid, there were long periods during which I was asked to do very little. A meeting might be called for Friday, and the Thursday before a secretary would appear to announce that the man who had called the meeting had to go out of town and wouldn't return until the following Wednesday. No further assignment was given; there was no backlog of work to catch up on. Five days lay before me, on each of which I put on a suit and tie, took a train into the city, and did nothing, *nada,* absolutely zilch. This happened fairly regularly. Much of this free time was spent in general grousing with fellow editors; some in audacious but quite useless philosophical speculation; a good bit more in office gossip. The years whirred by. I wrote twenty or thirty book reviews on the job and a few essays. But I have always regretted that I never did anything more substantial. A poet, the Russian proverb has it, always cheats his boss, which, I assume, means that his mind is on his poems when it should be on the job. Why should any other kind of writer do less?

From the beginning of my interest in becoming a writer, I found myself fascinated by the conditions under and methods by which famous writers worked. For a short while I was taken in by the false drama of the supposedly excruciating difficulty of writing. This drama was probably most economically set out by the excellent sportswriter Red Smith, who said, apropos of the difficulty he found in composition, that he merely sat at his typewriter until little drops of blood appeared on his forehead. It was not uncommon to find others comparing the act of writing to that ultimate act of creation, childbirth, drawing out an elaborate analogy between the stages of writing and those of pregnancy, from insemination (with an idea) through post-partum depression (after delivering a book). Thus the music critic and composer Cecil Gray, in his autobiography *Musical Chairs,* writes:

> Like everything I have written, words or music, or both, it was the outcome
> of a long period of gestation followed by a rapid parturition. The short score
> sketch of all three acts was completed in as many months, but the conception

had been in my mind for ten years. (Oh, my elephantine pregnancies! How I envy and yet despise the quick, slick rabbit litters of the facile mediocrities!)

Speaking as (evidently) a rabbit-litter man, I have never had a baby, surprising as this news may be, but my view is that, not even nearly all things considered, if it is delivery we are talking about, I should much prefer delivering a piece of writing every time.

Another part of the drama of writing speaks to the deep loneliness of writers. Even my beloved Henry James could not resist sounding this note. "We work in the dark," are the words he put into the mouth of the novelist Dencombe in his story "The Middle Years," "—we do what we can—we give what we have. Our doubt is our passion and our passion is our task. The rest is the madness of art." Mencken, reacting to the general plaint of the loneliness of writers, suggested that any writer who felt overwhelmed by the loneliness of his task ought, as a cure, to spend a few days in a factory on an assembly line, where he would find plenty of opportunities to talk with his mates. If the drama of writers is even minimally true, why, one wonders, would anyone take up such a hard calling? I have myself always thought that it had something to do with the notion that writing, whatever its complications and difficulties, still beats working, though I could be wrong.

To continue with the *Iliad* of writers' woes, let us not forget the perpetual wrestle with language. Among the famous wrestlers, the great Hulk Hogan of modern literature, Gustave Flaubert, reported regularly to his mistress Louise Colet on this endless tussle. "I spent *five days on one page* last week, and I gave up everything for it," he characteristically complains while at work on *Madame Bovary.* Joseph Conrad was another famous groaner about the excruciation of composition, likening himself to a criminal dragging "the ball and chain of one's selfhood to the end," but Conrad at least had the excuse that he was working in English, which was his third language. Valéry used to say that he never finished but only abandoned his poems. But with the great writers, in the end, pain dissolves into love, and even so incessant a complainer as Flaubert has to allow that, when it is going well, the world offers no keener pleasure than that provided by writing:

> . . . it is grand to write [he reports to Louise Colet], to cease to be *oneself,* and to move among creatures one is describing. Today, for instance, I have been a man and woman at the same time, lover and mistress together, riding in the forest on an autumn afternoon under the yellowing leaves; and I have been the horses, too, and the leaves, and the wind, and the words they spoke and the red sun that made them blink their eyes that swam with love. It may be out of pride or of reverence, from a foolish gush of excessive self-conceit or a vague but lofty religious sense, but when I reflect, after experiencing these joys, I feel tempted to offer up a prayer of thanksgiving to God, if only I knew he could hear me. But praise be His Name that I was not born a cotton merchant, a music hall artist, or a wit, etc.

Which brings me to a topic I approach with the apprehension that only serious superstition makes possible. I speak—fingers crossed, a string of garlic round my neck, and in supplication on my knees—of writer's block, that psychological condition that stanches a writer's flow of words. Baudelaire spoke of this condition of "'*stéril-ités des écrivains nerveux'* . . . that anguished suspension of all power of thought that comes to one in the midst of a very revel of production, like the slave with his *memento mori* at a feast." I have—touch wood, *kayn aynboreb,* Lordy be—never undergone writer's block, but I have known people who have and have some inkling of what a horrendous psychological affliction it can be. Hard to know what causes this afflic-tion that leaves writers stranded like ruptured ducks, and we are not talking here about *mallards imaginaires.* A psychiatrist named Edmund Bergler, in New York in the 1950s and 1960s, used to claim a high record of cure for writer's block. His modus operandi, I gather, was to inform writers that this block business was all a lot of non-sense, a sign of immaturity, and that they ought to knock it off and get the hell back to the typewriter. (Bergler was apparently a man who yelled in a German accent, which can be effective.)

My own guess is that a writer can be blocked because he is, in some fundamen-tal way, unclear about what it is he wants to write; or he can be fearful, knowing that what he must write will expose him in a way that he senses could be ruinous to him, or at least to his sense of himself; or he may not have been able to recognize and work through some deep flaw in the composition before him; or, perhaps gravest danger of all, he is stung by tyrannous perfectionism, a perfectionism leading on to literary constipation. In his novel *To an Early Grave,* Wallace Markfield has a charac-ter, a minor critic named Holly Levine, who suffers from the latter variant of writer's block. "Certainly, Professor Gombitz's essays, gathered together for the first time, yield pleasure of a kind," Levine begins a book review. Then he alters the sentence to read: "An essay by Gombitz will clearly yield . . ." Then he decides that perhaps it is better formulated as "An essay by Gombitz will surely yield . . ." Which is sup-planted by "Surely, essays such as these are bound to yield . . ." The possibilities being nearly endless, the review remains beginningless. The whole project is hopelessly blocked.

Out of fear of such blockage, every writer senses that he must manipulate things so that his flow of words not only begins but continues. The first trick is begin-ning. In a useful little essay, "A Writer's Discipline," Jacques Barzun, writing out of his own ample experience, states the problem and puts the point with precision: "There is only one way: to study one's needs and quirks, and circumvent one's tricks for escape." Barzun's excellent advice is to give in to those needs and quirks, but only as a reward against escape. "Suit thyself," he writes, "but pay for it, i.e., *work!*"

The needs and quirks, since I have quite a few of my own, especially interest me. I have always loved to read about the idiosyncrasies connected with the composition of other, chiefly famous, writers. Thornton Wilder must have had a similar interest, for he reports that "many writers have told me that they have built up mnemonic devices to start them off on each day's writing task. Hemingway once told me he sharpened twenty pencils; Willa Cather that she read a passage from the Bible—not from piety, she was quick to add, but to get in touch with fine prose. . . . My spring-board has always been long walks."

My fascination with all this made me a natural reader—if "groupie" isn't the more precise word—of the interviews in the *Paris Review.* My interest was invariably most enlivened when the interviewer would get around to asking, What are some of your writing habits? Do you use a desk? Do you write on a machine? Here I always hoped for the most exotic responses. "I prefer to sumo-wrestle an alligator, eat two pounds of pastrami and a large, thinly sliced Bermuda onion on a baguette with strong horse-radish, and listen to all six Brandenburg Concertos before getting down to work. For the actual writing, I like to wear my black velour FILA jogging suit, tie my hair into a short ponytail, slip into my Air-Faulkner writing shoes, and, hey, baby, like the Nike commercial says, 'Just do it!'" I hyperbolize but I do not entirely exaggerate. Here is how the then-young Truman Capote answered the same questions:

> I am a completely horizontal author. I can't think unless I'm lying down, either in bed or stretched on a couch and with a cigarette and coffee handy. I've got to be puffing and sipping. As the afternoon wears on, I shift from coffee to mint tea to sherry to martinis. No, I don't use a typewriter. Not in the begin-ning. I write my first version in longhand (pencil). Then I do a complete revi-sion, also in longhand.

If Capote was a horizontal author, Ernest Hemingway was a vertical one. He wrote standing up, usually in his bedroom in his house in Cuba, using the top of a bookcase, on which room was cleared, to quote the *Paris Review*, "for a typewriter, a wooden reading board, five or six pencils, and a chunk of copper ore to weight down papers when the wind blows in from the east windows." It gets better. Hemingway "stands in a pair of his oversized loafers on the worn skin of a Lesser Kudu—the typewriter and the reading board chest-high opposite him." He told his interviewer, George Plimpton, that he began in pencil, then shifted to his typewriter when his writing was going extremely well or when he wrote dialogue. Each day he kept count of the words he produced: "from 450, 575, 462, 1,250, back to 512, the higher figures on days Hemingway puts in extra work so he won't feel guilty spending the following day fishing on the Gulf Stream." Hemingway was a strange old man, as he himself might have put it, but, when it came to writing, no stranger than most.

Hemingway wrote in the mornings, as the majority of writers tend to do, though I seem to remember reading that John O'Hara used to do his writing only after the completion of the last movie on television—"The Late Show" as it was called before the advent of cable and twenty-four-hour television—ending his work only after sunrise. T. S. Eliot, whether writing prose or poetry, felt himself good for roughly three hours of work at a sitting. Evelyn Waugh, a more concentrated worker than most, thought two thousand words a good day's work and tended to write best in provincial hotels, generally finishing his earlier novels, revisions and all, in roughly six weeks. Georges Simenon seldom took more than eleven days to write his Mai-gret novels, and usually had a physical before beginning a new one, so intensely absorbed was he in the work before him. Thomas Mann, another morning worker, used to consider the production of a single good page sufficient unto any day, and most days he produced that page. A page a day, if you don't knock off for too many weekends, would give you approximately a book a year. Nothing to sneeze at.

Except by Anthony Trollope, who would doubtless have used up several boxes of Kleenex sneezing at what he would have considered such paltry production. Trol-lope, in his autobiography, recounts that he always kept a precise record of his liter-ary production, and that it tended to average forty pages (at 250 words to the page) a week, sometimes falling as low as twenty pages but once having risen to 112 pages. Trollope, who may have been the most completely professional writer ever to have lived, took great pride in delivering all his manuscripts exactly on time and as close as possible to the agreed-upon length. He accomplished all this, what is more, while holding a full-time job with the English postal system. This achievement is a rebuke to every writer awaiting grants, inspiration, encouragement, or mother love. Trollope's view was that one ought to regard one's work as the normal condition of one's life. "I therefore venture to advise young men who look forward to authorship as the business of their lives, even when they propose that that authorship be of the highest class known, to avoid enthusiastic rushes with their pens, and to seat themselves at their desks day by day as though they were lawyers' clerks;—and so let them sit till their allotted tasks shall be accomplished."

Trollope tells of finishing his novel *Doctor Thorne* one day and beginning another, *The Bertrams,* the next. With a talent I have developed of improving upon already extraordinary stories, I artfully misremembered and retold this story so that Trollope had finished a novel in the middle of a morning's work and, rather than let the rest of his morning working session go to waste, took out a fresh piece of paper and began another novel that same morning. Not impossible, after all, for behind Trollope's impressive work habits was a strong conscience, a conscience quite properly fueled by fear of future remorse. "It was not on my conscience," he writes, "that I have ever scamped my work. My novels, whether good or bad, have been as good as I could make them." He then adds that had he put three months of idleness between these two novels, the second would probably not have been any better.

Conscience, remorse, heavy and even self-invented guilt—ah, now we are coming into my country—the country, to misappropriate Sarah Orne Jewett's famous title, of the pointed fingers. I am not sure I could function without fear of incurring guilt in letting down editors, publishers, and now even myself. I am a writer who writhes and therefore writes best under deadline (a phrase whose etymology derives from the Confederate prisoner-of-war camp at Andersonville; any prisoner who crossed the line drawn around the perimeter of the camp was to be shot on sight). As a writer, I am eager to please and anxious lest I disappoint; and here I am talking about pleasing and not disappointing readers and editors. But the critic toughest to get by is myself: not, let me make plain, only the critic of quality—though I hope he is on the job, too—but of quantity.

On any day that I do not turn out a reasonable number of words I feel poorly about myself. Let three or four such days go by and I am able to make myself quite miserable. Deep loathing sets in somewhere between five days and a week of less-than-decent work. Longer than this and it becomes extremely difficult for me to justify my existence. A decent day's work is somewhere between eight hundred and twelve hundred not entirely awkward, imprecise, or ignoble words. On those rare days when I have been able to write two thousand or so such words, I am so deliriously smug that I am really quite unfit to speak even to myself.

Because my own self-regard is at stake—and for so self-regarding a fellow, no stakes could be higher—it is important that I work well. And since I spend a fair amount of my waking life selecting and arranging words, I am intensely interested in anything that will make the job more efficient. Hence my interest in other people's ways of going about it. I am ever on the lookout for new methods, tricks, secrets to improve the flow of my own words onto the page. For years I thought there might be a magic fountain pen that would make me a better writer. I still think there may be stationery of a kind that will make my words, when written out upon it, stronger, clearer, longer-lived.

Is there some method of composition I have not yet tried that could make the difference? Lionel Trilling many years ago reported that the writer Robert Warshow "composed by a method which is unusual; he formed each sentence slowly in his mind, and, when it was satisfactory, wrote it down as irrevocable." Trilling thought it a method beyond his own practical comprehension. How astounded he would have been by the performance of Edward Gibbon, who, after remarking that, as his great history progressed, he found less reason to revise his prose and went on to state that "it has always been my practise to cast a long paragraph in a single mould, to try it by my ear, to deposit it in my memory; but to suspend the action of the pen, till I had given the last polish to my work." In other words—though why one should want words other than Gibbon's I am not sure—Gibbon formed entire paragraphs in his mind before writing them out, and he wrote, as everyone knows, wondrously intricate periodic sentences embedded in impressively lengthy, neatly pointed paragraphs.

My own mind runs only to remembering phrases, never more. I generally have no idea of what any sentence is going to look like until I write the damn thing out, and then I usually rework it a time or two. Because of this, I have never—not as a student, not now—been able to avail myself of outlines. Until I write that first sentence down, I can have no idea of what my second sentence is going to say or look like, let alone what my fifth paragraph will contain.

My method of composition, then, resembles on-the-job training, only at the verbal level. I have grown used to this loose, slightly riff-like method, which often brings with it pleasant surprises. "How can I tell what I think till I see what I say," E. M. Forster once remarked. I believe I may do him one better in not being sure what I write even while I am writing it.

Just because there is no order in my compositional life doesn't mean that I don't crave at least the appearance of order. I am extremely partial to having plenty of folders about, also lots of colored paper clips, and fine-leaded mechanical pencils. (I am quite nuts generally about office supplies.) But especially do I long for order, elegant order, in my manuscripts. "My Essay," wrote Gibbon, referring to his *L'Essai sur l'étude de la littérature,* "was finished in about six weeks, and as soon as a fair copy had been transcribed by one of the French prisoners at Petersfield I looked round for a critic and a judge of my first performance." I have always loved the phrase "fair copy," and seem to recall a photograph of the family of Count Tolstoy writing out a "fair copy" of *War and Peace.* Fair copy—implying as it does a fine tidiness, a beautiful intelligibility of outward form to fit what one hopes is a genuine clarity of inward thought—fair copy has long been the name of my desire.

Attempting to produce it without the aid of French prisoners or a large aristocratic Russian family has not proven easy for me. But, somehow, without a reasonable tidiness in my manuscripts, I generally feel a vague but quite real discomfort.

Freudians used to term this condition anality. ("Anality, my ass," replies a character in an English novel when faced with this charge.) My method of attempting to achieve this tidiness was formerly a most complicated one. I wrote the paragraphs of my first draft in longhand; then typed out each of these paragraphs, usually making changes as I went; and, when this second, typed draft seemed fairly decent, I would then retype it, making still other, usually smaller changes, onto a final, or what I thought of as a fair, copy. Truth to tell, I should have preferred to make fair copies in a perfect handwriting, and would have done so, but for the fact that my handwriting could never produce anything considered anywhere near fair.

I took great pleasure in watching my typed fair-copy versions grow larger. But I also felt this fair copy, once created, inviolable. Making changes upon it, which, given my penchant for tidiness, would entail vast amounts of time in retyping, was not something I looked forward to; I would, in fact, only agree to do so in emergency situations: when I discovered something on my fair copy that was simply wrong or when I felt I had found something so pleasing to add that the additional pain of retyping was less than the pleasure of having it in my manuscript.

And yet, unlike Peter De Vries, who once said that he liked everything about writing except the paperwork, I tend to like the paperwork above all. Writing, I hope it does not depress others to learn, has not only grown easier for me, but I find I enjoy it even more as I grow older. One of the nicest compliments I have ever had was that my writing seemed to show an obvious pleasure in the making; I took this to mean that the author (me) seemed to have a good time setting down the words. I fear it's true. Such cheerfulness about the act of writing, which is supposed to be so exasperating and hideously painful an activity, cannot do my small reputation much good, but there it is.

I remember, as a much younger man, walking down the street shaping sentences in my mind for a composition on which I was then at work, trying out and rejecting phrases and words, when it occurred to me that mine was a funny kind of life. I produced nothing but words about my observations and reformulated the words and observations of others who had written in the past. I also made up stories. For this I was paid, not handsomely but sufficiently. It's a living. Sometimes I have not been altogether certain whether it was also a life. But since I haven't another in mind, I ought, I decided then and there, to calm down and stay on the job, as Harry Truman once told the servants at the White House whom he found weeping upon learning of his decision not to run again for the presidency in 1952. Besides, by then I had been at it long enough to feel, with Montaigne, that "no pleasure for me has any savor without communication."

"The prospect of fame, wealth, and daily amusement encourage me to persist," wrote Gibbon somewhere in the middle of the composition of *The Decline and Fall of the Roman Empire*. When I first came across that sentence, I typed it out and taped it to the side of the black standard Royal typewriter I had used for some twenty years. I acquired that machine, which was probably already twenty-five years old, in trade for twenty-five dollars and a then-new Olivetti portable with an italic typeface that I couldn't abide. I adored—I use the word with forethought—that old machine. I liked the action of its keys, which I sometimes pounded as if I were playing the ending of one of the more dramatic of Beethoven's piano sonatas. I wrote everything but sonnets and suicide notes on it. I had it cleaned fairly regularly, frequently changed its ribbon—Dorothy Parker, a two-fingered typist, allowed that she knew so little about typewriters that she once bought a new one because she couldn't figure out how to change the ribbon on the one she had—and finally I wore it out. The key for the letter *d* refused to work. I hadn't been aware that over the years I had written so many words with the letter *d* in them. Damn.

This noble machine was replaced by a sleeker item, as it then seemed, a used IBM Correcting Selectric III. I am apparently someone who needs to be dragged into the future, even on small items. With the exception of indoor plumbing, I remain skeptical about most modern inventions. Gadgetry, in itself, does not much interest me. I was late to have a colored television set; and, though I now own a machine that plays compact discs instead of records, I continue to like the look and feel of my old albums. I am a sentimental, entirely passive, and in the end inevitably defeated Luddite. What sold me on the IBM was its correcting device, which, allowing one to dispense with Wite-Out for erasures, appealed to my instinct for tidiness. It gave—and continues to give—excellent service. On its beige metal side I have taped the motto, this one from Henry James, written after his disastrous adventure in writing for the London stage: "Produce again—produce; produce better than ever, and all will be well."

Perceptive readers will already have sensed that this essay is going to get around to its hero's arrival, round-shouldered and squint-eyed, before a computer. Some among them, who count upon me as a stalwart rearguard man and a permanent back number, may be a little disappointed to find me there. I do not seem to myself the very model of a computer man. For years I have made fun of computerese, both in my own mind and in the margins of the papers of students, for whom such language is not jargon at all but of the air they breathe. In place of such words as *user-friendly, hands-on,* and *interface,* I continue to say, at least to myself, *usure-friendly* (which you might call a genial loan shark), *pants-on,* and *in your face.*

Writing friends who have gone over to the computer worked at my conversion. All marveled to me about how using the word-processing portion of a computer improved both the quantity and quality of their writing. I listened to them, outwardly polite, inwardly haughty and disdainful. I think I should never have attempted to use a computer had not the university where I teach offered me the loan of a computer for nothing. I took a bite of the Apple (a Macintosh Plus, as it turns out) that many had promised would lead me into the new Garden of Eden, from where I am writing this essay.

I have, for more than a year now, been writing everything but my personal correspondence on a computer. I have not typed out and pasted to the side of this computer "Man rides machine." (Was it Emerson or some other hyperventilating nineteenth-century author who said that?) After what I am told was the standard two- or three-week terror of "losing" everything one has written and infuriation at one's own initial ineptitude, I came to grow enamored of the computer as a writing instrument. I shall not go on to report, à la the subtitle of *Dr. Strangelove,* how I learned to stop worrying and love my machine, but candor compels me to report that I have grown fond of the little bugger. Sometimes, at the end of a decent day's work, I have been known to rise from my desk, pat it gently in gratitude, and mutter, "Thanks, pal."

I am chiefly grateful to the computer for the splendid possibilities it presents for revision. Working with it, I find myself reworking things, I won't say endlessly and I won't say effortlessly, but with a freedom and ease that I never felt working on a typewriter. This seems to me an uncomplicated and clear gain. The computer also gives me a keen sense of false organization. On what is known as my primary screen— what a friend calls his "primary scream"—I have such handsome categories, or folders, as Essays and Pieces, Lectures and Letters, Snobbery (the butt from that not-yet smoked-out enchanted cigarette), and Stories and Tales (let it pass that I have never written a tale, and seem unlikely ever to do so). I find that I turn on my computer more readily than I used to go to my typewriter, and that I do so at different hours— in the late afternoon, for example—than formerly. I believe I spend more time word processing, if that is what I am doing here, than I used to spend writing.

Yet some of the pleasures are less. I used to enjoy watching my manuscripts grow larger, as their pages mounted up. I rather enjoyed the sound of the typewriter, with its sharp staccato as opposed to the muted clackety-clack of the computer keyboard. (Leroy Anderson, the composer, it may be recalled, wrote a composition titled *The Typewriter,* which was an orchestral arrangement that featured the sound of someone typing at high speed and which will one day be perfectly incomprehensible to people.) I prefer the noble look of an older typewriter to the portable-television-set appearance of a personal computer.

Then, too, the puritan in me sometimes thinks that writing is made *too* easy on the computer. I guess I believe that writing ought not to be too smoothly turned out. In ways I am not quite clear about, the computer, like statistics, doesn't care who uses it, and seems somehow to have made it possible for bad writers to write even worse. Alastair Forbes, writing in the London *Spectator,* refers to a recent biography of Anastasia as coming "from the ill-tuned, unmistakably American wordprocessor" of a writer who, though he may not be shameless, shall here be nameless. One rather knows what Mr. Forbes means. I cannot say exactly why, but a book ill written on a typewriter figures, somehow, to be a bit better than a book ill written on a word processor.

For one thing, the latter is likely to be longer, wordier, more garrulous generally—this owing to the ease with which words flow from the computer. As the television with its many carefully spaced commercials has decreased the national attention span, so has writing on a computer increased the national garrulity. I now often get four-, five-, even six-page single-spaced letters from people who once would have said all they had to say in a letter of a page or two. The great value of the computer lies in its editing and revising function. But the same machine also makes it so simple to add material; it is the great friend of second, third, and even fourth thoughts on any subject. Press a few keys, manipulate the cursor, clack in a few more sentences, then watch as the paragraphs nicely reshape themselves and the composition you are working on lengthens correspondingly. Imagine Balzac, Trollope, Dickens armed with computers! If Proust, who had a penchant for adding things to his already vast manuscript, had written *Remembrance of Things Past* on a computer, he would have had to retitle it "Remembrance of Things Past, Present, and Future, Including Many Things Not Remembered at All."

In its editing function—the ease with which nearly endless revisions can be made—lies both the joy and the horror of writing on the computer. One of the most dismaying things about writing is the knowledge that nearly anything one writes can be cut fairly drastically—and then cut again. "You never cut anything out of a book you regret later," F. Scott Fitzgerald told Thomas Wolfe, who had a ferocious cut man—to use the word in a very different sense—in his corner in his editor Maxwell Perkins. The Gettysburg Address has 272 words; my guess is that an aggressive editor could pare it down to two hundred and not many people would notice. An editor in New York used to boast that he could cut the Lord's Prayer in half and improve it in doing so. The computer, of course, lures one to go the other way: not to cut but to add.

So seductive is the computer as a writing instrument that I find myself less and less ready to write without it. I still type my letters. I still write in my journal in longhand. I still travel with two fountain pens and a thick pad of graph paper, in the hope of adding to compositions I am currently working on. But I notice I now turn out less writing when traveling and away from my machine, so accustomed have I become to the ease it affords. (I think of my own laziness here with shame when I consider Aleksandr Solzhenitsyn, who wrote out his lengthy manuscripts in a minuscule handwriting, the better to hide them from the authorities and make them available in samizdat.) Dragged yet further into the future, I shall doubtless one day before long have to acquire a laptop computer. But I intend to defer it as long as possible. *Laptop* sounds awfully like *lapdog* to me. Not altogether clear here, either, who is the dog and who the master. There goes machine, it seems pretty clear to me, riding man again.

The fear in the heart of every writer is the arrival of the time when he must recognize that such magic as he has had has left him and he now writes not only differently but worse. A change in the methods with which a writer works is likely to turn the mind to this possibility. Henry James seemed to undergo no such worry when, in his late fifties, after suffering pain in his right wrist, he started to dictate his books to a series of typists. Some critics have contended that, with this new method of composing, James cut it too fine and began badly to garrulate. Others refer to his new period as Henry James's Major Phase. Who is correct remains in the flux of controversy.

What isn't in the flux of controversy is that the act of writing, even after one drains it of the often false drama some of its practitioners like to give it, retains a strong element of mystery. "Read 'em and weep," say poker players, confidently setting down what they are sure is a winning hand. But you can write 'em and weep, too, or write 'em and laugh, or write 'em and wonder, reverently, from where 'em derive. Whence derives that lilting phrase, that prettily precise formulation, that obliquely subtle observation, that perfectly paced paragraph? Are there more where those came from? Best, perhaps, to shut up and just keep writing.

Double Take

1. To discuss his approaches to writing and thoughts about writing, Joseph Epstein provides a large number of anecdotes about other writers in "Compose Yourself." How do these long strings of anecdotes succeed or fail in helping you as a reader gain a better sense of how Epstein thinks about writing? Could Epstein have written the same kind of essay with fewer anecdotes? Longer, more detailed ones?

2. This essay considers at length both Epstein's vision of writing and how other authors approach writing. To whom do you suppose Epstein is writing and under what circumstances? That is, what might be the situation in which an author would write an essay about his or her writing? How might Epstein envision his audience? Why might that audience be interested in reading about Epstein's vision of writing? Where might an essay like this be published? How would Epstein, or any author, have to shape an essay for that forum?

3. In "Compose Yourself" Epstein writes, "One of the nicest compliments I have ever had was that my writing seemed to show an obvious pleasure in the making; I took this to mean that the author (me) seemed to have a good time setting down the words. I fear it's true. Such cheerfulness about the act of writing, which is supposed to be so exasperating and hideously painful an activity, cannot do my small reputation much good, but there it is." Other than this statement, do you see clues in the writing that the author is enjoying himself in "setting down the words"? If so, what choices has Epstein made in this essay that convey to readers a sense of what he is feeling?

4. Late in this essay, Epstein reveals that he is writing the essay on an Apple computer. As he discusses his move to writing on a computer, he writes, "I have not typed out and pasted on the side of this computer 'Man rides machine.' (Was it Emerson or some other hyperventilating nineteenth-century author who said that?)" Why do you suppose Epstein adds this parenthetical statement? What does he gain (or lose) by doing so?

At First Glance

Although the title of Joseph Epstein's essay "A Mere Journalist" might suggest an essay about journalism, this essay is about the activity of keeping a journal, a diary. It recounts why and how Epstein began to keep a journal and, as one might expect of Epstein, the opinions of other writers on keeping a journal. One of the unique things about this essay is that as Epstein chronicles his experiences with writing journals, the essay itself takes on some characteristics of journal keeping: It begins early in his life and chronicles important events in his writing of journals up to the present moment—the writing of this essay. Though the essay does not take on the form of a journal, including things such as date headers, and though the essay was most likely written with the intent of appearing in print as a singular work rather than as a series of dated entries, it nonetheless teaches us quite a bit about journals. As you read this essay, think about the differences between writing an essay and keeping a journal. What sorts of characteristics differentiate the two? Think about whether or not readers might be interested in reading someone's journal and what characteristics might be needed for a journal to be of interest to a reader other than the author.

A Mere Journalist

I began keeping a journal not long after it became clear to me that I wished to be famous. Perhaps that is not quite accurate, for, as I think back on it now, it occurs to me that I always wished to be famous. As other people have an imagination for disaster, I have had an imagination for fame. I can remember as a boy of nine or ten returning home alone from the playground in the early evening after dinner, dodging, cutting, stiff-arming imaginary tacklers on my way to scoring imaginary touchdowns before enormous imaginary throngs who chanted my name. Practicing free throws alone in my backyard I would pretend that I was shooting them at a crucial moment in a big game at Madison Square Garden. Later, as a boy tennis player, before falling off to sleep, I imagined the Duchess of Kent presenting me with the winner's trophy on the center court at Wimbledon. I wrote none of this down, because I had not yet become a scribbling man. Fame was still a general, not a particular, desire. Once I determined to become a writer the desire became quite particular. As for the extent of my fame today, it is best measured by way of analogy through an anecdote a friend told me about having once asked a historian of medicine at what point in history physicians began saving more patients than they killed. "I regret to report," the historian replied, "that we haven't achieved it yet." I can say roughly the same thing about my fame.

But should fame ever arrive, I shall be prepared for it. Off and on for more than twenty years I have been keeping a journal. One expects a famous writer to keep a journal. In my case, jumping the gun somewhat, I began keeping a journal well before I had done much writing. Yet one has to start somewhere, and why not with a journal or diary or notebooks? "I have never understood why people write diaries," Max Beerbohm said. "I never had the slightest desire to do so—one has to be so very self-conscious." No argument about the need for the journalist to be self-conscious, since the journal is the personal house organ for self-consciousness. But it is hard to believe that so subtle a writer as Max Beerbohm hadn't the requisite self-consciousness. My own guess is that Beerbohm didn't keep a journal or diary because he didn't need one; fame came to him early—while he was still at Oxford, in fact—and thus he was quite without need of what is the first function of a young writer's journal: a place to grouse, a place to dramatize one's condition in prose, and a place to bemoan the fact that, once again, this time in the instance of oneself, the world in its ignorance is failing to recognize another genius.

It may be, too, that, along with so many other arts and games, keeping a journal is an activity that one must begin while still fairly young. By thirty it may be too late to begin. For the journalist, habit is nearly everything. Mordecai Richler once remarked that, for a writer, all experience is divided between the time before he decides to write and the time after. After the decision has been made, life becomes in large part copy, all experience grist for a mill that closes down only at death. For the keeper of a journal, experience is turned into words before the sun sets twice; sometimes, like dry cleaners, he gives same-day service. When something of interest occurs in the life of a journal keeper, he not only notes it mentally but also notes that he must note it in his journal. A short while ago, for example, I was at dinner with a number of academic historians. The group among contemporary historians known as the cliometricians came up for discussion. "Whatever happened to the cliometricians?" someone asked. I thought immediately of the radical feminist historians, and I leaned toward a historian seated on my right, a woman of a certain age and the sophistication to go with it, and whispered. "They were replaced in academic fashion, I believe, by the clitoromeretricians." Not bad, I thought to myself; must note it down. You will find the remark in my journal under October 2, 1985.

You will find a great deal else besides such mots in my journals, but one thing you will not find is anything approximating a record of contemporary history of the kind available in the diaries of Harold Nicolson or Chips Channon or Richard Crossman. This for the simple reason that I have had no serious or intimate connection with contemporary history, and perhaps an insufficient interest in it. The only large public event noted in my journals is the assassination of John F. Kennedy and the dreary events surrounding his funeral. Even here, though, I noted his death, in the wholly egotistical manner of the journalist, less for its effect on the country than for its effect on the hero of my journals, me. What I thought of John F. Kennedy—which, at the time, wasn't very much—cannot be of any great interest to the world; nor, I have reasoned since, can what I think of other public events and political tendencies of our time be of any staggering significance. Who really cares what I think of, say, the Sino-Soviet dispute? (For the record, I happen to be rather partial to this particular dispute, which I hope will continue all of my days.)

Along with an absence of political content, neither will you find much in the way of spirituality in my journals. Unlike *The Intimate Journal of Henri Fréderic Amiel,* from whose pen flowed an abundance of such sentences as "Love that is sublime, single, invincible leads straight to the brink of the great abyss, for it speaks at once of infinity and eternity," my journal seldom strikes the religious note. In it my arguments with God go unrecorded. The closest I get to spirituality is self-pity, which, I recognize, is not quite the same thing. Especially when young, I could be very strong in the line of self-pity; I whined exceedingly well. Here, for example, is our hero on December 29, 1962, at the age of twenty-five, living in New York and working as an editor on a political magazine in a job he rightly realized was a dead end:

> Well, I have worked one year at this job. What have I learned? What have I lost? What have I missed?
> Learned: (1) A few writing tricks, though mostly tricks with other people's writing; (2) a trade, or—perhaps more accurately—a wide but not altogether firm knowledge of how to go about a trade; (3) a few pieces of extraneous information; (4) how to talk about politics—quite different from learning how politics truly work; and (5) how to read and judge a composition somewhat more surely than before.

Lost: (1) A good deal of, sadly, enthusiasm; (2) youthful intransigence on many subjects and issues where intransigence is the only proper attitude; (3) sympathy; and (4) some hair.

Missed: (1) Sitting down to do some writing that I might take pride in; (2) friendship.

As I grew older, this self-pity swelled and expanded nicely into a fine case of melancholia, so that, on October 28, 1970, after a falling-out with a dear friend, I discover our boy, now thirty-three, noting that "at such moments you know how tenuous are the strongest of human bonds—and you rediscover what you at this instant feel yourself a fool for ever forgetting: that you are absolutely alone in the world." Returning to the subject some seven months later, he says of human loneliness and vulnerability, "Perhaps for the best, most of us are unable to keep this devastating fact in mind for much of the time. I am currently reading Conrad *(Victory),* who never for a moment forgot it." Our jolly melancholic's notion of a good time is insomnia, that is if you believe an entry of February 16, 1971, which in part reads: "It is now nearly two in the morning, and unless I get extremely tired, I think I shall try to stay up to see the dawn in. I have ample provisions: cigarettes, tea, an all-night classical music station, the *Letters of Thomas Mann,* a new (to me) book of William Hazlitt essays, some writing to do, and (for now) this notebook." Our hero had just gone through a divorce, of which, mercifully, his journal says little directly; but, not to worry, there is sufficient dolorosity to go round. Thus on July 20, 1971, we find him inditing, "Five years ago I found much about life absurd; nowadays I find many of the same things merely sad. It would be good to be able to regress a little in this sphere." As a Borscht Belt comedian might say, "Hey, c'mon folks, these are the jokes—yuk it up!" The comedian's name in this case might be young Jackie Werther.

Self-pity, melancholia, depression—best of course to do without all these; but if suffer from them one must, next best is not to impose them on others, or so I was brought up to believe. A journal, though, is not a bad place to deposit them. For people who do not slide easily into the public therapeutic mode, a journal can function as a book of consolation. For many among us, writing things out appears to be therapy enough; it is also a solution that cuts out the middleman, the therapist, thereby in one stroke eluding both the problem of transference and the transference of funds. There is, though, a middleman named Dr. Ira Progoff who wishes to cut himself back in. Dr. Progoff runs something called a "journal workshop," in which he holds out the promise, through the use of journals in something he calls the "Intensive Journal" process, of "a potential for growth in a human being . . . as infinite as the universe." (Beware doctors bearing botanical metaphors, and especially doctors bearing them into workshops.) But in any case Doc Progoff has come too late for me. In my journal, and as much as possible in my life, I have done my best to cease complaining and have taken as my motto the line from the beer commercials that runs, "I guess it doesn't get much better than this."

Not that I am committed to the cheerful view, or that I decided that complaint is always a mistake. But I do note, in my journal for April 17, 1975, the following shift in emphasis openly declared: "The time has come to turn this journal away from being a chronicle of complaint—an Iliad of woe—and into a name-dropping affair. Through my ersatz eminence as editor of a respected, if still less than dazzling, magazine, I find myself more frequently in touch with writers and intellectuals of some—how to say it?—standing. Might as well note down these meetings, for the practice they provide in portraiture and for a 20-watt light bulb on the age."

Here I have to report, with regret, that my journals are not, as the English say, as "namey" as a lively literary journal ought to be. Saul Bellow appears from time to time, Lillian Hellman is there, and so are John Sparrow and Martha Graham. I. F. Stone shows up when I am in Greece, and Henry Kissinger puts in a cameo appearance. But my journals contain no Mitford sisters, no Cyril Connolly, no Evelyn Waugh (insulting me as a boorish American, doubtless), no Diaghilev, no Virginia and Leonard Woolf, no André, Willie, or Morgan, no Prince of Wales and Mrs. Simpson, no royalty whatsoever, I regret to say. In his diary the snobbish Chips Channon reports once having two queens dine at his home on the same evening, but in his utter elation, he became too drunk to recall anything about the evening. Unlike Chips Channon, or Harold Nicolson, or other keepers of namey journals and diaries, I do not leave my apartment often enough to compile a really interesting index—one of the kind that, under the letter *R,* for example, lists Walther Rathenau, Maurice Ravel, Max Reinhardt, Sir John Reith, Rilke, Rodin, and Ida Rubinstein.

"This afternoon Cocteau and Picasso suddenly entered my room and were just as suddenly gone again." That sentence, written by Count Harry Kessler, strikes me as precisely a sentence of the kind the keeper of a namey journal requires. In a single stroke it shows its author to be a man of the great world, as the German-born Harry Kessler, a cosmopolitan at home in art and politics and publishing, indubitably was. Kessler provides many such sentences: "In the afternoon visited Baby Goldschmidt-Rothschild. She received me in bed, between pink damask sheets and in blue pyjamas, the Chinese bed upholstered in yellow satin." "Maillol and Mlle Passavant lunch with me." "Luncheon at the Princess Bassiano's in Versailles with André Gide and others." "Sammy Fischer and his wife invited me to lunch with Gerhart Hauptmann." "Lunch with Albert Einstein, Nicolai, Rubakin, Sytin (the Russian publisher), and Hugo Simon to discuss Rubakin's people's library project." "Dinner at Martin du Gard's with Helen, Paul Valéry, and Edmond Jaloux." One might think one could not hope to run so namey a journal on a low-calorie diet, yet Count Kessler was stiletto thin, thus rendering his diary, along with its being a splendid literary work, a simultaneous tribute to his energy and powers of abstinence.

If one cannot run a journal on meetings with famous people, for simple want of such meetings, then another possibility is to feature introspection and self-analysis. Introspection, even in a journal, has its limits. The diaries of Anaïs Nin, in which I have never been able to make much headway, seem to me subject to this criticism. She is too intent on "the quest for the self," as she more than once puts it, but after a page or two I invariably find myself giving her quest a rest. Even the higher introspection of Amiel soon loses it edge. Better, perhaps, to keep introspection where it belongs—to oneself.

In my own journal I tend to serve up introspection with a La Rochefoucauldian twist. "Vanity without foundation in either physical beauty or true talent is one of the most pathetic of human spectacles," I wrote on July 22, 1971, quite obviously referring to myself. "New bookcases," I wrote years later, "give one the splendid illusion that one can bring order to one's life." A week or so afterward I wrote: "I suppose I believe that art, like sex, is better for being made a bit difficult." And yet again, "Writing well is the best revenge," though what I had to revenge myself against is far from clear. This is La Rochefoucauld all right, but La Rochefoucauld, as I read it now, living well below what the old Department of Health, Education, and Welfare used to call the poverty level.

Sometimes my journal entries are little more than doodling in prose. In one such entry I describe what I call "a purist's dream," which is to write an entire essay in which no sentence begins with *it* or *there* and in which the words *but, yet, still,* and *however* never appear. Sometimes a single phrase will prompt me to repair to my journal, as when I describe a restaurant I had dined in the day before as the haunt "not merely of the old but of the militantly old," or when I refer to a greatly neurotic novelist of small talents I know as yet another case of "big wound, small bow." Like a precocious and rather spoiled child who runs off to his mother to report his smallest achievement, I run off to my journal to report my most fugitive thoughts. Five years into my career as a teacher, for example, I remark: "How, in its way, like courtship teaching can be, with the teacher as the male, the class a dumb but nonetheless desirable female who needs to be won each time afresh." Scraps of literary criticism go into my journal as well, so that, after finding myself disappointed with the closing chapters of *The Confessions of Saint Augustine,* I wrote, "As secular autobiography tends to grow dull once success has been achieved, so in religious autobiography dullness sets in once the autobiographer has found God." I also mark my own birthdays: "I am 41 today. Apart from this flu, I have no strenuous complaints. I am required to do nothing ignominious to earn my living; everything ignominious I do, I do of my own volition."

I have by now filled nearly nine hundred pages with such matter. "Who," Igor Stravinsky used to remark when presented with a new work, "needs this?" I suppose I alone do. Something in me impels me to record what I have thought, or experienced, or read, or heard. "Most of life is so dull that there is nothing to be said about it," E.M. Forster wrote in *A Passage to India.* I could not disagree more. I find keeping a journal quickens life; it provides the double pleasure of first living life and then savoring it through the formation of sentences about it. Here I recall the cliché philosophical problem about whether a tree makes any noise falling in the forest if no one is there to hear it. As someone who keeps a journal, I prefer to keep a record of all the trees I hear fall, and by now I seem to have piled up, in my various notebooks, a great deal of lumber.

A journal can also function as the intellectual equivalent of a photo album or home movies. Reading through my journal, as I have been doing while writing this essay, I feel like a man watching a slide show that features himself. Why, there I am being turned down, at the age of twenty-six, for a job I then much wanted at a New York magazine. Here I am, in his office at the City University of New York, chatting intimately with Irving Howe, who was so kind to me when I was a young writer. Here I am again, pleased to receive a pleasant letter from Anthony Powell, a novelist I much admire, saying kind things about an essay of mine in the *TLS* and noting, in my journal, that such pleasure as my essay may have given him is "small quid for large quo." There I am marking the onset of boorishness in myself, at age thirty-nine, after a lunch with a young academic, about which I note that I have done most of the talking and said nothing that I have not said many times before. Here, there, everywhere, I am making firm resolutions I shall not come close to keeping—learning ancient Greek among them. And yet is this slide show any less boring that one given by a middle-aged suburban couple of their recent trip to Europe? I don't know, but I do know that, in my case, the host is having a swell time.

How is it that so many otherwise highly productive writers, in the midst of turning out novels, poems, essays, and criticism, have also found time to keep extensive journals or diaries? Ralph Waldo Emerson, Samuel Butler, Arnold Bennett, Theodore Dreiser, André Gide, Virginia Woolf, Evelyn Waugh, H. L. Mencken, and Edmund Wilson are but a handful of prominent names among such writers. One might have thought their already copious literary production would have been sufficient, but, no, they all needed to spill still more ink in notebooks, journals, and diaries. Having already used gallons of ink on their public thoughts, they poured out quarts more on their private ones. Enough, one would have thought, was enough—and yet for these writers it wasn't.

Are we talking here about the writer's disease known as graphomania? This is a disease that can take many forms. For some, graphomania takes the form of simply being unable to put the pen down—the authorly equivalent of logorrhea. For others—those, I should say, who have the disease in its advanced stage—it takes the form of needing to write everything down because anything that hasn't been written down isn't quite real. My guess is that Edmund Wilson had an advanced case. I know of no other explanation for the fact that Wilson felt the need, and acted upon it in his journals, to record his sexual congress with his own wife, which I find at once astonishing and repulsive (quotations on request—send self-addressed plain brown wrapper).

Were he alive today, Anthony Comstock, organizer and special agent for the New York Society for the Suppression of Vice, could read my journal without missing a pulse beat. No future biographer, in the unlikely event that there is to be one, figures to find evidence in my journal for establishing the thesis that I am, say, a suppressed lesbian. And yet unsympathetic as I am to Edmund Wilson's chronicling of his conjugal sex life, as a journalist and something of a graphomaniac myself, I half understand his impulse to do so. It is the impulse to make one's days a matter of record—"no ink, no life," is the graphomaniac's slogan. Reading through my own journals I am sometimes amazed at how little in the way of stimulus I require to journalize:

5-2-78 a.m.
Yesterday: wrote a few pages of my [Maxwell] Perkins essay. Translated my Yourcenar passage. Graded some student papers. Had a call from Caedmon records to write 750 words of album jacket copy for a record of Saul Bellow reading from *Herzog;* fee: $100 and some records. I chose not to do so.

Not exactly a day in the life of Ivan Denisovich, I grant you, but still I felt the need to record it.

On the other, larger hand, many are the private thoughts that a journalist can confide only to his journal. In *Samuel Butler's Notebooks,* which are mostly given over to general thoughts about art and life, there is an odd entry entitled "Myself at the William Rossettis." In it Butler records his ill feelings about Mrs. Rossetti's family, the Madox Browns, whom he used to visit but "who wanted me to climb my pole too much and too often before they would let me have [a bun], and it was not a good bun when it came. . . ." Nevertheless, when he is invited to visit, Butler pays his call and it is all rather a botch, even though he is on his good behavior. Before he leaves, though, Butler notes: "I had a few words with William Rossetti. I said how beautiful his pictures were; in reality I hated them, but I did all as I should, and it was accepted as about what I ought to have said." Here we have a fine example of the use of a journal as a personal corrective to what is deemed to be the world's necessary hypocrisy. Butler has gone through his paces, paid his false obeisances, but reports his true feelings in his notebook. Let the record show, then, that Samuel Butler found the Rossetti and Brown families a great pain in a soft place.

What record? you might ask. In Samuel Butler's case, of course, the record is the printed record, since his notebooks have been judged worthy of publication, in both complete and abridged form. Yet I believe that not only do few people keep a diary or journal for themselves alone, but most people who do keep a journal, even if they are not professional writers, at least half hope that theirs, too, will one day be published. Stranger things have happened. The great diarist Samuel Pepys, who earned his living as a naval administrator, wrote a diary that lay unpublished for some hundred and fifty-six years after he ceased keeping it; first published in abbreviated form in 1825, it has since been republished in various incomplete, bowdlerized, and complete forms time and again. A very rich and rather unpleasant man named Arthur Inman made the maintenance of his diary his life's work and left enough money to Harvard University to make certain that it was published, as it was in 1986. William Saroyan, a relentless diarist, left a good portion of his estate to the William Saroyan Foundation, which maintains his diaries and other papers. "In effect, he left his estate to himself," his son Aram Saroyan wrote. "He took it with him." The rest of us journalists and diarists have to trust to luck for posthumous publication of our journals and diaries; but my guess is that most of us are ready to do so.

While patiently awaiting the condition of posthumy, to be followed at a decent interval by posthumous publication, those of us who keep journals and diaries keep scribbling away. I note that in my own journal I once copied out an apposite line from Chamfort: *"Quand M. de R—a passé une journée sans écrire, il repéte le mot de Titus: 'J'ai perdu un jour.'"* Although I know exactly what M. de R—and Titus meant, I must confess that I do not write in my journal every day. On many days the world is too much with me and my life is too crowded even for a brief entry. I generally write in my journal in the early morning, before setting out to earn my livelihood. Sometimes I write down a paragraph or two after lunch, but I scarcely ever write in it at night, by which time, as an early rising man, I am usually drained of such mental powers as I possess. But when I do write something in my journal, I feel rather more complete, in the way I suspect an observant Moslem might feel for having done his ablutions. Not that journal writing elevates me—it doesn't, usually—but I do feel upon having made an entry in my journal as if I have done my duty, completed, in effect, an act of intellectual hygiene.

"I can no more recover one of my days in memory," wrote Amiel, "than a glass of water poured into a lake; it is not so much lost as melted away." I do not often look into my journals, yet whenever I do I am impressed by how much experience has slipped through the net of my memory. I note the name of a student in one of my classes whom I describe as "easily the most intelligent" I have come across during the then current academic year, whom, I go on to describe physically, yet whom today, a mere seven years later, I cannot call to mind. I had quite forgotten having read a life of Voltaire by Jean Orieux, "a life that," as I recorded it in my journal, "in Orieux's telling, seems to have been made up of carefree fornication and witticisms, with a moment out here and there for writing." I completely forgot once describing a review I had to write of the book of a touchy acquaintance, an exercise I described as resembling "eating spaghetti while on a tightrope—and with chopsticks." At table on a Greek-owned ship on the Mediterranean, my journal reminds me, a companion at dinner, a tall blonde, rather raffish woman, a producer for the BBC, announced "I then began to understand that the real interest in Yoga was the hope that one would develop body control enough to reverse one's ejaculations and levitate oneself"—an unforgettable bit of table talk, one might have thought, except that I seem to have forgotten it. I seem to have forgotten, too, that when a young intellectual, rather baldly on the make, stopped to visit me on a trip to the Middle West, I wrote in my journal: "I am for him an item (rather a minor one) on what I gather has been an extended tour of intellectual sight-seeing—on this tour I am the intellectual equivalent, perhaps, of Siena." That was in 1978; I was smarter then.

I suspect that anyone who keeps a journal must believe that the world revolves around himself. All autobiographers are liars, Orwell once said; quite possibly all those who keep journals or diaries are convinced of their own importance. When a figure from the world of letters dies, for example, I feel it essential that I record it in my journal and offer my opinion of his worth. On August 8, 1980, I wrote:

> Kenneth Tynan died last week, at 53, of emphysema, in Los Angeles. He was not a writer I admired, but I generally read him with interest. He was the bright young man come down from Oxford, all marked out for success; but like so many such young men—beginning at least with Cyril Connolly—he did not quite come up to expectations. He was apparently a leftist of the decadent kind—for the people and for pornography, too. He had a pretty good roll of the dice, I suppose, as theatre critic for *The Observer* and *The New Yorker* and Literary Manager of the National Theatre. . . . [Here I cite a piece of exotic gossip about him.] His, Tynan's, seems an agitated life; he is still now.

"Excuse me, buddy," I hear a voice with a strong Yiddish inflection inquire, "but who asked you should put in your two cents?" An interesting question, except that the person asking it clearly understands nothing about the impulse felt by the keeper of a journal, who is a man with a bottomless pocket of pennies and who, in his heart, feels that his, and not *The Times* of either New York or London, is the true journal of record. The phrase "a modest journalist," referring to anyone who keeps a journal, is an oxymoron. It may well be that no man is a hero to his valet, but neither is any man a pip-squeak to himself, and especially not the man—or woman—who keeps a journal.

As the journal of record—the record, specifically, of my own opinions and impressions—my own journal is not without a certain edge. Reading some of the things about contemporaries that I have written in it, I seem rather stronger in the line of cutting comment than I had thought. I am not so strong as the Brothers Goncourt are in their journal, but then I hadn't their opportunities. Paging through my journals I cannot miss a certain enthusiasm on my part for a well-turned insult. I see that I have described an English writer as "almost always wrong and frequently original"; a certain American intellectual as someone about whom I can never be certain if he is a man of principle or an opportunist, since his principles seem generally to run along the same track as his opportunities; another English writer, a man now in his seventies but still very much on the sexual attack, I have described as "a bent rake"; after attending a lecture by a famous but disappointingly dull scholar, I wrote that "I did not have to shield my eyes from the dazzle." And these comments, you understand, are all about people who have never done me the least harm; they are the result of sheer verbal exuberance, the rising thoughts of a journalist after a good night's sleep. Imagine, then, my journal entries about people whom I feel are my enemies. Vengeance, the Italians say, is a dish best served cold. My plan is to serve mine posthumously, which is to say, when I, the cook, am cold.

But who is to eat from this dish? The longer I live, the more I write in my journals and the lengthier they become, the less I can expect them ever to be published. My only hope is that standards continue to fall at the same splendidly alarming rate as they have been for some years now, so that I become a fit subject for a doctoral dissertation or a candidate for a book in an author series that has already exhausted such authors for the ages as Kurt Vonnegut and Philip Roth. Vengeance, then, I fear, will first be served not to my enemies but to some hapless graduate student or junior professor who will have to repair to bed bleary-eyed after reading the hundreds and hundreds of pages that I rose, dewey-eyed in the morning, to write in my journal. Perhaps an advance apology is in order. Sorry, fella, I had quantities of ink and a sturdy fountain pen and not all that much else to do but fill up all these notebooks. Nothing personal, which, if you will permit me to say so, is the way I hope (against hope, I realize) that you will write about my life.

After reading through my journals, what sort of man is this graduate student or professor likely to discover? Forgive me for saying so, but the man he finds there will not quite be me. He will find my literary opinions, many views on writing and writers, portraits, antipathies, criticism, invective, even sadness. He will, I believe, find a writer but not a man. I quote an entry from my journal on March 18, 1978, that reads: "Insofar as a journal is supposed to be the true record of a person's days, this one fails, for the main event of my life over the past five months or so has been the disintegration. . . ." and I then go on to mention, briefly, the breakdown of an important relationship in my life. Again, my journal touches scarcely at all on my family life. Although she is often mentioned as being with me at this dinner or on that trip, my wife, who is the central figure in my life, is never talked about at any length in my journals, nor is my love for her discussed or analyzed, but then neither do I write about my appetite for oxygen. Lengthy though these journals of mine are, the most important truths of my life do not have much place in them.

At the same time, I would maintain that everything I have written in these journals is true—or at least as true as I could make it at the time I wrote it. Lying as such is not, I believe, a question in my journal: I do not claim to have met famous people I have not met; I do not deliberately falsify emotion to show what a bighearted fellow I am. Yet the truth of a journal of the kind I keep is truth of a proximate kind. Sometimes I discover, upon rereading, that I have simply not been smart enough, and thus have made judgments about other people that are inaccurate, or inept, or oddly askew. Sometimes I am too hard on people; sometimes I am not hard enough. Then there is the problem of self-deception. I do not think I brag in my journal, but neither do I specialize in modesty. I hope that the habit of self-mockery has helped me to elude the trap of self-inflation. I try, when writing in my journal, to keep in mind the twin truths that I am someone of the greatest importance to myself and that I am also ultimately insignificant. This is not always easily accomplished.

One of the reasons I think my journal is not too greatly marred by falsity is that in writing it I have had very little at stake. Unlike other journals, especially those of politicians, mine has almost nothing in it of the tone of self-exculpation. No reason it should have, since I have not been accused of anything more serious than having strong opinions with which some people have disagreed. As a writer, I do not feel in the least unappreciated; I feel very nicely appreciated—and quite lucky in this as in many other regards. I haven't, in sum, a case to make, but am instead a rather happy graphomaniac, a mere journalist with inky fingers and many blank notebooks and taste for endlessly making distinctions and discriminations.

Harold Nicolson once remarked that a man should keep a diary or journal for the amusement of his great-grandson. I find that fellow rather difficult to imagine, let alone to write for. Although like every other man or woman who has kept a journal or diary I wish some portion of my journal will one day be published, just now it is being written for a good-natured and highly appreciative audience of one—me. Highly appreciative is quite accurate, for I tend to be partial to the younger man who wrote in my journal. (Will I like as much the middle-aged one who is writing in it now?) He could be gloomy, this young man, but he also understood that there was no point in letting his gloom get him down. He was forever imploring himself to work harder, and at one point he quotes a culture hero of his, Henry James, who, on the subjects of depression and work, wrote: "If only I can concentrate myself: this is the great lesson of life. . . . When I am really at work, I am happy, I feel strong, I see many opportunities ahead. It is the only thing that makes life endurable." After entering this quotation, my young journalist wrote: "Ah, those James boys!"

Sometimes I am astonished at the items that find their way into this journal of mine. On Tuesday morning, June 12, 1979, after noting that I had finished the first volume of a biography of Bernard Berenson, I also note the death of John Wayne. After remarking that, though I had no special reverence for him as an actor, as one of the larger-than-life movie stars of my youth, he had become, I wrote, "part of the furniture of one's life. The first half of one's life, it strikes me, one fills up one's rooms with such furniture; the second half one watches this furniture, piece by piece, being removed." My journal, in this connection, has served as a running inventory of my days, and I am pleased to have kept it. It has made life seem rather less the dream that I sometimes fear it may be.

"Life can only be understood backward," wrote Søren Kierkegaard, himself a journal-keeping man, "but we must live it forward." Too true—and a little sad. Yet a journal does provide backward understanding. Like the rewind button on a video-cassette recorder, it is a great aid in replaying segments of past experience, in running over important and even trivial events, in recollecting moods and moments otherwise lost to memory. A journal is a simple device for blowing off steam, privately settling scores, clarifying thoughts, giving way to vanities, rectifying (if only to oneself) hypocrisies, and generally leaving an impression and record of your days. And when you are through with it, when the time has come to leave this mud pie, as my journal recently reminded me that Mencken used to call the earth, you can even pass the damn thing along to your as yet unborn great-grandchildren. It is an extraordinary invention, better even than an American Express card, and I don't go anywhere without mine.

Double Take

1. In the essay "A Mere Journalist," Joseph Epstein recounts his history as a writer of journals, a form that is often rather personal and not intended for a public audience (though as Epstein explains, journals are sometimes made public). As he writes about his journaling experiences, he refers to himself in the first person—I—as this is an essay about him. A few times, however, Epstein refers to the figure writing his journal as "our hero." For instance, before giving the example from his journal in which he recounts what he learned as a young editor, he writes, "here, for example, is our hero on December 29, 1969." Why does Epstein discuss himself as he appears in journal entries as "our hero," a third person representation of himself, while he maintains calling himself "I" in the rest of the essay? Has he adopted a particular strategy in doing this? What might this do for how we read this essay?

2. Perhaps it might be accurate to say that this essay is about two different subjects: journals and Epstein himself. We learn quite a bit about the author from this essay. The title of this piece, "A Mere Journalist," suggests an essay not about journals per se, but about a particular writer of journals. This being the case, what situation might call for Epstein to write an essay about Epstein? If, as Epstein claims at the beginning of the essay, he is not famous enough to warrant us reading his journals, why might he write an essay about himself and his journals? Where might one publish such an essay (other than in a textbook about essays)?

3. Throughout "A Mere Journalist" Epstein uses a strategy of asking questions as transition into his next area of discussion. Often, the questions seem to be anticipatory of what his audience might ask about his previous point; more often they seem to be his own questions about what he has just written. He then responds to his own question as a means of answering himself or his audience without ever really hearing from them. For instance, after discussing the writing of a few other

authors, Epstein writes, "How is it that so many otherwise highly productive writ-ers, in the midst of turning out novels, poems, essays, and criticism, have also found time to keep extensive journals or diaries?" What effect does Epstein gain by using these kinds of questions?

At First Glance

This essay is about taking naps. Think about that for a second. Naps. Short periods of sleep taken generally during the day. Are naps a subject about which you would expect someone to write an essay? As you read this essay, think about the thought Joseph Epstein has put into a subject that many might consider mundane, without depth, and not worthy of a full-length essay. Also, consider the breadth of discussion here about naps and how Epstein manages to keep his readers' interest. What strategies does he use for keeping you interested as a reader? What do you like or dislike about this essay? Does it leave you more aware of the intricacies of naps? Are naps something that you would have considered "artful"? Do you wish you could take a nap right now?

The Art of the Nap

Intellectual serenity in the United States, I have heard it said, consists in not giving a damn about Harvard. Having been in Cambridge recently, I sensed—no, actually, I knew—I had achieved it. Bopping about Harvard Square, peeping into the Yard, popping into a building or two, I felt not the least yearning. I did not wish to be the Seymour Boylston Professor at Harvard or even to give the Charles Eliot Skolnik Lectures—not now, not ever. I have no children whom I wished to be admitted to Harvard. Yes, Harvard could continue to get along nicely without me, as it seems to have done over the past 350-odd years, and I, in the time remaining to me, can get along nicely without it.

With such serene thoughts, I set myself on my back on my comfortable bed at The Inn at Harvard, the hotel where I was staying. I had on gray wool trousers, a blue shirt, and a four-in-hand knit tie, which I didn't bother to unloosen. My hands were folded together on my chest in the corpse-in-the-casket position, and I hadn't both-ered to turn back the bedspread. It was three-thirty on a cold and gray February after-noon. My next appointment was at five o'clock. There was nothing, at that moment, that I was eager to read. Into the arms of Morpheus I slipped, and for the next half hour I slept, I won't say like a baby, or like a log, or like a turtle, but like what I now prefer to think myself—a man who has mastered, in all its delicate intricacy, the art of the nap.

I did not move, I did not stir. I woke, as planned, without a wrinkle in my shirt, trousers, or cheek, not a hair out of place. A most impressive, if I do say so myself—

and at that moment I did say so to myself—performance. Really quite brilliant. The term "control freak" is almost never used approvingly, I know, but I felt myself at that moment a control freak entirely happy in his work—that is to say, in perfect control. I carefully slipped off the bed and walked into the bathroom, where I gazed at my clear eyes in the large mirror. Another fine nap successfully brought off. I was rested, perhaps a touch less than radiant, and ready to continue not giving a damn about Harvard.

I don't ordinarily nap on a bed or on my back. As a nap-master, I fear too much comfort and the consequent difficulty of pulling myself out of the pleasures of too deep sleep to go back into the world. I also wish to avoid rumpledness, the toll that a nap on one's back on a couch often takes. Most of my napping therefore is done sitting up, on a couch, shoes off, with my feet resting on a low footstool. Having one's feet up is important.

Most of my naps—and I usually get on the average of three or four a week—take place late in the afternoon, around five or five-thirty, with the television news playing softly in the background. As the reports of earthquakes, plagues, arson, pillaging, and general corruption hum on, I snooze away, a perfect symbol of the indifference of man in the modern age. These naps last from twenty to thirty-five minutes. ("A nap after dinner was silver," said old Prince Bolkonsky in *War and Peace,* "a nap before dinner golden.") Should the telephone ring while I am in mid-nap, I answer it in an especially clear and wide-awake voice that I don't usually bother evoking when I am in fact wide awake. Some of these naps leave me a touch groggy, though this soon enough disappears. Usually, they all do the job, which is to help get me through the evening.

Taste in naps differs. I not long ago asked a friend, an Englishman, if he naps. "Whenever possible," he replied. Prone or sitting up? "Prone." On a bed or couch? "Bed." Trousers on or off? "Generally off." And for how long? "That depends," he said, "on when the cats choose to depart." Joseph Conrad wrote that his task was "by the power of the written word, to make you hear, to make you feel—it is, before all, to make you *see.*" The picture of my friend with his cats napping atop him is almost too easily seen.

I nap well on airplanes, trains, buses, and cars and with a special proficiency at concerts and lectures. I am, when pressed, able to nap standing up. In certain select company, I wish I could nap while being spoken to. I have not yet learned to nap while I myself am speaking, though I have felt the urge to do so. I had a friend named Walter B. Scott who, in his late sixties, used to nap at parties of ten or twelve people that he and his wife gave. One would look over and there Walter would be, chin on his chest, lights out, nicely zonked; he might as well have hung a Gone Fishing sign on his chest. Then, half an hour or so later, without remarking upon his recent departure, he would smoothly pick up the current of the talk, not missing a stroke, and get finely back into the flow. I saw him do this perhaps four or five times, always with immense admiration.

Certain jobs seem to carry (unspoken) napping privileges. Writing in 1931, H. L. Mencken noted that one of the tests of a good cop was the talent of "stealing three naps a night in a garage without getting caught by the rounds-man." Surely, movie projectionists get to nap to their heart's content. Cab and limousine drivers must nap. Napping on the job can scarcely be unknown to psychoanalysts and other workers in the head trades. ("Uh-huh," mumbles the dozing psychiatrist in the caption of a cartoon that shows the feet of his patient who has just jumped out the window.) The only job in which I ardently longed to nap was guard duty in army motor pools on cold nights in Missouri, Texas, and Arkansas. Ah, to have slipped into the back of a deuce and a half (as the big trucks in the army were called) and zzz'd-out for a quick half hour! But fear, that first goad to conscience, won out and, difficult though it was, I stayed awake.

At a job I held one summer in college at a phonograph needle factory, one of the maintenance men, a dwarfish man of Italian ancestry, regularly slipped up to the fourth floor for a forty-minute shot of sleep. I have seen lots of people nod off at corporate meetings and at conferences. One steamy summer day in Washington, at a meeting of the national council of the National Endowment for the Arts, held at the Old Post Office Building on Pennsylvania Avenue, I noted an entire half table of council members, heads nodding, necks jerking, eyelids drooping, effectively sedated by a slide show on city planning. I envied them, and doubtless should have joined them but for the fact that I had myself only recently awoken from a delightfully soporific lecture on the meaning of the avant-garde.

I have always slept reasonably well during lectures and never better than when a lecturer is foolhardy enough to darken the room for slides. Lecture and classroom naps tend to be of the variety I call whiplash naps—the ones where your head seems always to be snapping to. At the University of Chicago, I slept through the better part of the Italian Renaissance, or at any rate through a course in the history of its art. As a teacher myself, I am now being justly repaid by having students fall asleep in my own classes. I don't say that they drift off in droves, but I have—how to put it?—relaxed a respectable number of students in my time. At first, I found myself resenting a student falling asleep in one of my classes. But I long ago ceased taking it personally. I have come to look upon it avuncularly: poor dears, they may have been up all the previous night doing I prefer not to think what. My view of students sleeping in my classes is that, what the hell, if they cannot arise from my teaching inspired, let them at least awake refreshed.

My own youthful naps were owing, as I hope are those of my students, to happy excess. My current napping, I regret to report, is all too much part of the machinery beginning to break down. Not that I long for a nap each afternoon; if I am out in the world, I do not think about napping. My condition certainly does not yet begin to approximate the eponymous hero of Goncharov's novel Oblomov: "Lying down was not for Oblomov a necessity as it is for a sick man or for a man who is sleepy; or a matter of chance, as it is for a man who is tired; or a pleasure, as it is for a lazy man; it was his normal condition." Still, if an opportunity for a nap presents itself, I find I take it.

I live in an early morning household. I generally rise by 4:45 A.M. I like the early morning; it is, for me, the best part of the day. I used to joke that one met a better class of person (namely, oneself) at that hour, but, in fact, what I enjoy about it is the stillness, the absence of interruption it provides, the gradual awakening of life around me. I make coffee, I begin reading; sometimes, if what I am reading is not all-demanding, I turn on a classical music station. And life seems under control, flush with possibility, hope-filled.

I have become, no doubt about it, a morning person. I was not always thus. As a young man, I used to come in around the time I now wake up. Weekends I slept till two or three in the afternoon, resting up to return to the sweet fray. So much was I a night person—a player in all-night card games, a dropper-off of dates at three or four in the morning—so congenial did I find the night that, one quarter at university, when all my classes met in the morning, I decided to sleep days and stay up nights.

Time has never again seemed so expansive as it did during that quarter. I would return from my classes, eat a light lunch, and sleep till six-thirty or seven. After arising, watering and feeding myself, I searched for distractions: movies, television, ball or card games. Not the least pressed for time, I schmoozed with all and sundry. Generally, I socialized till eleven or twelve and then I returned to my room with its hot plate, box of tea, small record collection, and books.

I might study for two or three hours. Then I found myself alone, no one else up in the student quarters in which I lived, at three in the morning, with nothing to do but read or listen to music, or both, till roughly eight in the morning. I went to a school where only great books were taught, so these free hours allowed me time to read some merely good books, for which I was hungry. I read, as I recall, chiefly novels: Christopher Isherwood and John O'Hara and Truman Capote and Evelyn Waugh; also lots of Edmund Wilson's literary criticism, which I had just discovered. I drank dark tea till my nerves achieved a fine jangle; I greeted the rising sun with a slight palsy of the hands: wired, happy, ready for class.

After my classes, I returned to bed and began the entire cycle again. This period of time lasted ten weeks and, from my present perspective, is something of a blur, but it was, it seems to me, time deliciously well spent. It also gave me the first evidence of my taste, and even minor talent, for solitude.

Something there is about being awake for sunrise that gives pleasure. The only exception to this that I can recall are those times, also at college, when I decided to stay up all night to cram for an examination. My junior year at school I discovered, through a friend, the stimulating effects of the pill known as Dexamyl (or was it Dexedrine?). These little pellets allowed me to stay up round the clock while mastering narratives of English history. They also, toward sunrise, set my heart pounding at a furious clip. I can recall my heart clanging away in my chest as I sat in a classroom giving three significant effects of enclosure on British politics and five reasons for the bloodlessness of the 1688 revolution. By the time I got back to my room, my heart was playing a very up-tempo version of "Take the A Train." I used to think of it as studying English history with only a slight threat of death behind it. Nothing, though, that twelve or fourteen hours of sleep couldn't cure, and always did.

I have been fortunate in my sleep life. For one thing, the night, from as far back as I can recall, never held any terror for me. Not even as a small child did I imagine monsters in the corner, snakes under the bed, spiders on the spread, or anything else that might go bump in the night. The chief reason for this, I suspect, was that when I was a child my family lived in fairly small urban apartments and my parents were always nearby, so the element of fear was largely removed, as it wasn't for children who lived in large two- and three-story houses. I have no memories of nightmares. I had the reverse of nightmares—sweetmares, night-delights? I remember often dreaming of being in possession of marvelous things—elaborate electric trains, entirely realistic metal cap pistols, vast quantities of bubble gum—that weren't available to children during World War II. Toward morning, I regretted having to wake and, alas, give them up.

So well do I generally sleep that, when I roll round in bed for more than fifteen minutes or so before falling off, I consider it a troublous night. Occasionally, and at no set intervals I can make out, I will hit a dread night of insomnia. Usually, this comes about less from anxiety than from the condition I think of as a racing mind. Too much is flying loose in my skull: words and phrases for things I am writing, obligations, trivial yet nagging memories, and (the last step, the nail in the mattress) fear that, owing to not being able to sleep, I shall be tired and blow the next day. I roll, I turn, I mutter, finally I surrender and get up. Less than an hour's bleary reading or listening to the idiot chatter of a late-night television talk show generally does the trick, and I slog back to my bed, where Somnus almost always agrees to treat me more hospitably.

True insomnia of the relentless night-after-night kind must be absolute hell. Such a torture is it that I don't for a moment believe Bertrand Russell, who said: "Men who are unhappy, like men who sleep badly, are always proud of the fact." I have a number of friends who have suffered from insomnia. One walked about with the dark-rimmed eyes of a raccoon to prove it. Another friend suffered insomnia and (nonclinical) paranoia, which allowed him to stay up most of the night and think about his enemies. Once, in Florence, I suffered an extended—that is, roughly two-week—bout of insomnia, not at all helped by a too soft bed and an almost continuous flow of motor-scooter traffic vrooming past my hotel window. I tried to concentrate on pleasant things: small animals I have loved, tennis courts in the rain, giraffes cantering off into the distance. None of it worked. All I was finally left to think about was the longing for sleep itself—a topic always guaranteed to keep one awake.

Insomnia has its own small place in literature. Ernest Hemingway deals with the subject in his story "Now I Lay Me," which is about a wounded soldier in World War I who is recovering in a military hospital but unable to sleep. He is afraid that, should he fall asleep, "my soul would go out of my body." The soldier, who tells the story—and it seems a very autobiographical story—remembers every trout stream he fished as a boy and invents others, he says prayers for all the people he has known, he imagines what kind of wives the various girls he has met would make. He allows that some nights he must have "slept without knowing it—but I never slept knowing it," which is exactly what the sleep of insomnia often feels like.

F. Scott Fitzgerald cites Hemingway's story at the outset of "Sleeping and Waking," his essay of 1934. Fitzgerald himself suffered insomnia, beginning in his late thirties, and became something of a connoisseur of the illness, if that is what it is. He tells of a friend, awakened one night by a mouse nibbling on his finger, who never slept peacefully again without a dog or cat in the room. Fitzgerald's own insomnia began with a battle with a mosquito, which he won, though only in a Pyrrhic sense, for ever afterward he was haunted by what he called "sleep-consciousness," which meant he worried in advance whether he would be able to fall asleep. With an imagination for disaster, he prepared for sleeplessness, setting by his bedside "the books, the glass of water, the extra pyjamas lest I wake in rivulets of sweat, the luminol pills in the little round tube, the notebook and pencil in case of a night thought worth recording."

Fitzgerald's insomnia took the not uncommon form of dividing his sleep into two parts. He slept, that is, until roughly two-thirty, then woke for a cruel ninety-minute or so intermission during which pleasant fantasies (of playing football at Princeton, of wartime heroics) availed him nothing. He was left, awake against his own desires, to think of the horror and waste of his life: "what I might have been and done that is lost, spent, gone, dissipated, unrecapturable. I could have acted thus, refrained from this, been bold where I was timid, cautious where I was rash." And so he tortured himself, until, like a reverse mugger, sleep beautifully snuck up on him, and his dreams, "after the catharsis of the dark hours, are of young and lovely people doing young and lovely things, the girls I knew once, with big brown eyes, real yellow hair."

Vladimir Nabokov was another insomniac, though he referred to himself instead as "a poor go-to-sleeper." (That *iac* suffix has something sad or reprehensible about it: hemophiliac, hypochondriac, paranoiac, kleptomaniac, none of them jolly conditions.) Easy sleep was a matter of amazement to him, so much so that he found something vulgar about people who slept easily: "People in trains, who lay their newspapers aside, fold their silly arms, and immediately, with an offensive familiarity of demeanor, start snoring, amaze me as much as the uninhibited chap who cozily defecates in the presence of a chatty tubber, or participates in huge demonstrations, or joins some union in order to dissolve in it." The fact is, Nabokov not only didn't like but rather resented sleep, which put his endlessly inventive mind temporarily out of commission. He calls sleepers, in *Speak, Memory,* "the most moronic fraternity in the world, with the heaviest dues and crudest rituals."

Perhaps if one had a mind as richly stocked, as assailed by perception, as happily imaginative as Vladimir Nabokov's, one wouldn't wish to turn it off either. But enough writers have suffered from insomnia to make it seem almost an occupational disease. De Quincey, Nietzsche, Jorge Luis Borges, who once referred to the "atrocious lucidity of insomnia," all knew its horrors. Borges is the only one to write his way to a cure—specifically, through "Funes the Memorious," his wonderful story about a young man who dies from what one can only call a memory overload.

Does insomnia inflame the imagination? Or is an inflamed imagination the cause of insomnia? But then, too, life can deal out punishment of a kind that allows no easing even in sleep. After his wife's death, Raymond Chandler reported: "I sit up half the night playing records when I have the blues and can't get drunk enough to get sleepy. My nights are pretty awful." Sufficiently awful, it turned out, for Chandler, during this period, to attempt suicide.

Even as a middle-aged adult I have known the condition of not wishing to turn off my mental machinery and retire to sleep; and I have also known the pleasure of awakening eager to turn it back on. Most nights, though, I am ready to close up shop, pack it in, send up the white flag, not of surrender, but of cease-fire. Sleep on such occasions seems a marvelously sensible arrangement. But on other nights sleep seems an inconvenience, a drag, even something of a bore.

What removes some of the boredom is that one can never be sure what awaits one in sleep. "But she slept lightly and impatiently," writes Robert Musil in his story "The Temptation of Quiet Veronica," "as someone for whom the next day there is something extraordinary in store." Sometimes it seems there are quite as many states of sleep as of wakefulness: light sleep, troubled sleep, restless sleep, wakeful sleep, deep sleep, well-earned sleep. People talk, walk, snore, and emit semen in their sleep. They may be more receptive of the truth when asleep than when awake. "To sleep:" as the man with the notably receding hairline said, "perchance to dream. . . ." Not much perchance about it.

Envy has long ago begun to desert me, but I admit to feeling it for people who seem not to require much sleep. Those who can get by, indefinitely, on four or five hours of sleep a night have a small jump on the rest of us. I myself require six or seven hours of sleep, which beats by a bit the line from the old song that runs: "I work eight hours, I sleep eight hours, that leaves eight hours for fun." Still, the prospect of sleeping roughly a third of one's life away is more than a little dismaying.

But then who among us would like to be presented with a careful accounting of how he has spent his time on earth? My own might look something like this: sleep—slightly less than one third of total; watching men hit, chase, kick, and throw various-sized balls—eleven years, seven months; reading—thirteen years, four months; following the news—three years, six months; eating and activities connected with digestion—four years, eleven months; daydreaming and hopeless fantasizing—five years and seven months; gossiping, sulking, talking on the telephone, and miscellaneous time wasting—undeterminable but substantial . . .

As a fellow mindful of time, I tremendously dislike the notion of losing any of this valuable substance. Worry about the loss of time must kick in at a certain age. I know that it has been more than two decades since I have been able to stay abed later than seven in the morning with a good conscience. When I have, I feel as if the day has quite escaped me. Yet I recall reading with admiration, in *Howards End,* about the character Mrs. Wilcox, who spends entire days in bed, paying bills, answering letters, taking care of the small but necessary details in her life as well as recharging her batteries. I have also heard, as doubtless we all have, about people who in defeat, or more often in depression, repair to their beds and do not emerge for days, sometimes weeks. Not getting out of bed for weeks at a time—there's something, I find, rather enticing about that. My guess, though, is that I could not last more than an eight-hour stretch, and then I would lose to guilt whatever I gained in rest.

Sleeping in some beds, of course, is more pleasurable than sleeping in others. From childhood memories, doubtless by now nicely coated with nostalgia, I recall the comfort of sleeping on trains, with the clickety-clack of the tracks beneath, the stars above, the occasional lights from towns passing by. I have only read about sleepers on airplanes, which were in service, I gather, during World War II; or at least I recall A. J. Liebling remarking that, trying to sleep in a bed on a military transport, he heard his watch and pen, in a bedside table, rattling around "like dice in a crapshooter's hand." It would have been nice, I imagine, to have watched the sky pass as one awaited sleep. As a boy, I would have been delighted to have slept in a bunk bed; I only did so later in the army. I have never slept in a hammock. The idea of camping out-of-doors, which I also had a taste of in the army, could only be made tolerable to me today if I could find a campsite where room service was included. Sleeping in the cramped quarters of a submarine wouldn't be easy for me. Sleeping alone in a hotel in a king-size bed, on the other hand, gives me the willies.

I often go to sleep with music playing. My bedside clock radio has a sleeper function, which allows the radio to play for a specified amount of time before it clicks off automatically. Usually I go to sleep listening to classical music. Cello music is perhaps most soporific. Opera music, with only rare exceptions, doesn't work: too much blatant emotion. Most modern music is hopeless for sleeping. (Glenn Gould also slept with his radio on and said that sometimes the news got into his dreams.) But nothing puts me out faster than Chicago Cub games broadcast from the West Coast. When heard late at night from a prone position, the droning of the announcers, who with their impressive assemblage of clichés are describing a game in which there is nothing whatsoever at stake—a Mickey Finn could not be more effective.

It is 4:15 in the afternoon, and, owing to my having had less sleep than usual the night before, I am beginning to grow a bit tired. So I walk out to mail a few letters, and on the way back I stop at the public library a block or so away to pick up a copy of Freud's *Interpretation of Dreams.* The brief walk in the fresh air has put me in the perfect mood for a little nap.

I betake myself to the couch on which I do my serious napping. I remove my glasses, loosen the belt on my trousers, slip out of my shoes, rest my feet on a small black leather-covered footstool, and set my head against the back of the couch. I call out to my cat, who chooses not to join me (she is napping elsewhere in the apartment). I am, for the next thirty minutes, history—sleeping with my head back and, I believe, my mouth open. I am now nicely fortified for the longish drive I have to make out to the western suburbs to meet with cousins for dinner. A bit of water over the eyes, a rinse of mouthwash, and, yo! I'm on my way.

I do not recall having had any dreams, but if I did they must not have been worth remembering. I tend not to dream, at any rate not very vividly, when napping. My dreaming during the night seems to me, if I may say so, rather commonplace, even a little drab. By setting us to the task of interpreting our dreams, Sigmund Freud put us all on the road to being both novelist and critic of our own sleep life. Beginning well before Freud, though, there exists a lengthy literature on the meaning and function of dreams. To what extent one's dreams provide the key to one's unconscious and subconscious still seems to me very much, after all these years, in the flux of controversy. From time to time—less often than I would like—people I love who are dead show up in my dreams; I long for them not to leave, but, like the electric trains, cap pistols, and bubble gum of my childhood, they, too, inevitably depart. Many of my own dreams are sheer whimsy. The other night, for example, I dreamt about a bespoke suit that cost only $150. When I asked the woman in whose shop I saw it how she was able to produce such a suit at so low a price, she authoritatively answered: "Simple—low-quality material and poor workmanship."

When I have nightmares, I find I am able, after only a brief spell, to turn them off, rather as if I am changing television channels. In fact, sometimes I will gain semiconsciousness during such nightmares and quite lucidly announce to myself, Who needs this? and then turn over and await another dream. In sleep, if not in actual life, I seem to have something akin to a satellite dish with almost endless channels available to me.

Along with the whimsy channel, I seem fairly often to find myself on the anxiety channel. My dentist informs me that I am a man who grinds his teeth at night, a sufferer from the dental problem known as bruxism, which these anxiety dreams must help along. One of these dreams, in fact, which comes up perhaps once a year, is about losing my teeth, or at least a few key teeth. Occasionally, I have a mugging dream, in which I find myself in a hallway or on a deserted street confronting two or three young guys, one of whom has a knife, who want my money. Usually I am able to change channels, or I simply awake, before any violence is done.

My more common anxiety dreams, though, have to do with my making a great fool of myself in public. The setting here is invariably pedagogic. I have agreed to give a lecture or to teach a course on a subject about which I know absolutely nothing: Persian literature, say, or astrophysics. Screwup follows hard upon screwup. I cannot find the room; I have lost my notes; I need frightfully to make water. "Persian literature," I begin, before a large crowd well stocked with Iranian faces, "is extremely rich." And then I realize that I do not know the names of any Persian writers apart from Omar Khayyám. I hem. I haw. I wonder what extraordinary hubris propelled me into agreeing to deliver this lecture in the first place. "Persian literature," I continue, "is more than extremely rich—it is highly varied. Take the case of Omar Khayyám . . ."

When young, I had a student variant of these anxiety dreams in which I walk into a final exam of a course I have not attended all quarter long. The course is inevitably on a subject that is abstract yet also specific—Boolean algebra, say, or eighteenth-century musicology—something, in other words, that I cannot bluff my way through with stylish writing. Particular knowledge is needed, and, in these dreams, particular knowledge is exactly what I never have. Now, thirty years later, as a teacher rather than a student, in my dreams I still don't have it.

I occasionally have more ordinary nightmares: squirrels or possums or other animals with sharp claws are crowding in on me. A thief is at the window, but I cannot muster the energy to shut it as he begins to crawl in. I am traveling to Europe by plane, and I cannot locate my luggage, my tickets, my wife. Time is running out. I am never going to make it. As I say, all these seem to me fairly commonplace dreams. I have had only a single dream in which the Nazis figured, and it was connected, as I remember noting, to no recent book or movie or discussion of the subject I had encountered. It just came up arbitrarily—out of the dark, one might say. I am just not much of a world-historical dreamer.

Unlike Graham Greene, who kept a dream diary that has recently been published under the title *A World of My Own,* and whose dreams had a richness that make my own scarcely worth changing into pajamas for. Greene regularly dreamed of popes and heads of state and dictators. He dreamed of spying; in one dream, he helped capture Hitler. His dreams have a political line—they are reliably anti-American. Living and dead writers drop in with some frequency. Kim Philby recruits Ernest Hemingway to work for the Communists in Hong Kong. Evelyn Waugh, in another dream, shoots W. H. Auden. Henry James joins Greene on a river trip to Bogotá. T. S. Eliot queries a line of a poem he has written and turns out to be wearing a mustache.

Greene's nightmares have to do with birds and spiders and urinating *crevettes* and *langoustines*. But in a darker, a true writer's, nightmare, his publisher cannot be talked out of praising the novels of C. P. Snow.

Graham Greene refers, in this book, to his dreamworld as "My Own World," in contradistinction to "the world I share," which is his designation for the real world. Impressively rich though the world Greene shared was—filled with mistresses, politics, intrigue, literary success, religious crises, and the rest of it—his Own World is even richer. With dreams of the kind he records, I should imagine he could hardly wait to get to sleep at night.

But then artists have always been dreamers. Maurice Ravel felt that because they do spend so much time dreaming, even when awake, it wasn't fair for artists to marry. In my own case, though much of the material of my youthful fantasies—world fame, sexual conquest, appalling riches, enemies nicely discouraged—has lost its allure, I still manage to spend a goodly portion of my waking hours in a semi–dream state. I wish I could tell you more precisely than I can what it is I daydream about, but so vague, not to say misty, are these little sallies on which I float off that they are quite unmemorable and insubstantial. I am in a gentle clime; I drive along a blue coast in a convertible with a grandchild seated next to me; I have written something immemorially beautiful.

Many years ago, I read in a biography of Hannah Arendt that Miss Arendt set aside an hour every afternoon during which she lay on a couch in her Manhattan apartment and did nothing but think. I kitchen- or rather couch-tested this procedure and found I was unable to concentrate that long when on my back; in fact, engaged in concentrated thinking, I soon dozed off. Most of my thinking, if thinking it really is, comes in inconvenient spurts while daydreaming: in the shower, at the wheel of my car, with a book in my hand, while napping, just before falling off to sleep at night. For me, stray—and occasionally useful—thoughts, if not responsibilities, begin in dreams.

I was of that generation of children who said their prayers before going to sleep. I cannot recall whether doing so was my parents' or my own idea. But the prologue to the prayer I said was the standard one that ran:

> *Now I lay me down to sleep;*
> *I pray the Lord my soul to keep.*
> *If I should die before I wake,*
> *I pray the Lord my soul to take.*
> *God bless my mother, my father . . .*

Looking at these words in cold type, this little prayer seems quite terrifying—at least for a small child—holding out as it does the distinct prospect of imminent death coming in one's sleep. Beyond a certain age—nowadays I suppose it is eighty—it is thought extremely good luck to be allowed to die in one's sleep. She just slept, and slipped, away, one reports of some deaths, usually with a suggestion in one's voice of the mercifulness of the arrangement. Departing thus does deprive one of the drama of possibly uttering profound last words—"More light!" "What is the question?" "Trade Kingman!" "Is it a little hot in here, or do I imagine it?"—but most people, I suspect, would be willing to forgo those last words for a calmer because unconscious departure.

Shelley refers, in the opening lines of *Queen Mab,* to "Death and his brother Sleep!" Sleep itself has been called "little death." It's not a bad description of the phenomenon of sleep. To fall asleep, after all, entails a letting go, a giving up of consciousness, a journey to one knows not where. As with death, so with sleep, no one knows with certainty what awaits on the other side: nightmares, sweetmares, brief (one hopes) oblivion.

I have described my prowess at napping, or the art of napping in action. What I have not gone into is the secret behind the attainment of this prowess. In no small part, it has to do with wanting a time-out—with wanting out of life, not deeply, not permanently, but at least for a while. The English writer A. Alvarez, in a book titled *Night,* allows that he has become addicted to sleep—that he finds it no less than, in his own word, "sensual." He remarks that in his adolescence and twenties he chiefly thought about sex; once he married and that department of his life was in order, in his thirties "the obsession with sex was replaced by an obsession with food"; and now, in his sixties, this has been "usurped by a new obsession: sleep."

I wonder if the larger meaning of the obsession with sleep isn't a slow, albeit unconscious, preparation for closing up shop. I wonder, too, if this is such a bad thing. I know many people will despise this notion, arguing that one must never give in, give out, give up. They will claim, with much right on their side, that life is too precious a gift for one to permit it to slip away of one's own volition—in effect, for one to welcome death. Stay in the game, turn up the music, keep fighting, they will argue, plenty of time for napping in the grave. And they are, again, right.

Yet there is something marvelously seductive about sleep, and especially about a nap, which might best be viewed as a lovely and harmless touch of cheating, comparable, if one wishes to talk about sleep in terms usually reserved for sex instead of for death, to an afternoon tryst. As an artful napper, a nap remains, in my mind, one of life's fine things just so long as, when napping, one doesn't dream that one has been made some fantastic, some really quite impossible to refuse, offer by Harvard.

Double Take

1. Why does Epstein begin and end "The Art of the Nap" with an account of his apathy (or perhaps even dislike) toward Harvard? What does this brief segment of the essay have to do with the primary point of the essay? Could the essay be written without the first paragraph? What effect does this first paragraph have on your reading of the essay?
2. Is this a funny essay? Why or why not? What elements are required to make an essay funny (this or any essay)?
3. Think about the structure of this essay. How does it flow? That is, what characteristics of this essay make it cohesive? How is the essay organized? Are there distinct parts to this essay? What effect does the organization have on the overall presentation of the essay?

Seeing for Yourself

At First Glance

"Penography" was originally published in The American Scholar, *the quarterly journal for members of Phi Beta Kappa, the national honor society. As you read this essay, consider how Joseph Epstein must envision his audience and what rhetorical choices he might have made to address them. For instance, what assumptions might Epstein have made in choosing a subject such as penmanship and pens for this audience? What assumptions do you make about the piece now that you know it was written for* The American Scholar? *Why? What assumptions do you make about that audience? Why?*

Penography

A fetish—finally. Ah, sweet mystery of life at last I've found you. And just in time. I have for so long liked a lot of things a little that it is exhilarating to like a little thing a lot. I speak of fetish neither in the primitive nor the sexual meaning, but rather in the sense of fetish as an object for which one has an obsessive devotion, a slightly irrational reverence. My fetish speaks for me and I through it. It is for pens, fountain pens specifically, and I tell you straight out, Doctor, I have this thing for fountain pens—I am nuts about them, Doctor, do you hear me, absolutely bonkers!

Evidently I am not alone in this madness. I am told that fountain pens are currently making a small comeback in popularity. Magazines carry advertisements for them; department stores and office-supply and stationery stores display them prominently. Not that fountain pens are exactly sweeping the country. Few drugstores any longer carry ink, though once they all did. I doubt if many schoolchildren at present use fountain pens. Whole generations have by now grown up inkless, learning to write with ball-point pens and felt-tipped markers. Some members of those generations are discovering the pleasures of the fountain pen for the first time. For me, it's the second time.

I returned to using fountain pens roughly five years ago. But I am old enough to have used wooden penholders and steel nibs in grade school, and to recall teachers coming round to fill our inkwells from gallon jugs of board-of-education ink. I spoke above of pleasures, but what a spectacular mess those ancient instruments could make! Blotting paper was in the pencil box of every child. The rigid metal of the nibs combined with the drippings from the ink could make writing a wretched business. Only a few years later—around fifth grade—did I come to use my first fountain pen, an Esterbrook, a rather blunt-looking instrument, which came in an orange-brown color over something akin to a herringbone pattern. The Esterbrook was a sturdy pen, a Model A among pens; it did not leak—much—and I believe it then cost $1.49.

By this time, age eleven or so, my handwriting was already quite ruined. At least I myself never cared for it. Nor did any of my grade-school teachers. The slant of my letters was erratic; letters that should have been closed (*s*'s, *p*'s, *d*'s) were often left open; neither my ascenders nor my descenders were of a uniform height or depth; my capitals were pretentious in the extreme; even my periods lacked authority. Graphologically speaking, I was a disaster.

This was no minor disaster, either; for penmanship, as instruction in handwriting was called, was one of the important grade-school subjects. Every child had a penmanship manual offering instruction in something called the Palmer Method, and daily we practiced the loops and slants of what was felt to be classical cursive handwriting. One day an instructor from the company that published the manuals visited our school. A tall slender woman with a southwestern accent, she did capital *O*'s and *S*'s at the blackboard. "Swat, swat, swat that skeeter!" she called out as she made the long slanted line of the *S,* then looped it at its top for the trip down and back. Her aim, and that of the manuals, was to give us clear, regular, and quite uniform handwriting.

This was, of course, an enterprise destined for failure. A person's handwriting is one of the distinctive things about him, and no two handwritings, like no two sets of fingerprints, are the same. There is something about handwriting that seems to cry out for the expression of idosyncrasy. Circles for dotting *i*'s, Gothic touches on capitals, swooping flourishes at a word's end—there is no graphic stunt people won't try in the effort to be elegant and individual. Handwriting is tied up with what people nowadays are pleased to call their "identity." It is a most intimate matter, and richly complicated.

If a graphologist were to have examined my youthful handwriting, he might well have diagnosed an identity crisis. (Family therapy, he might even have concluded, was indicated.) Perhaps it is in one's handwriting that one first sets out to create a style for oneself. The handwriting of my childhood was part Palmer Method, part imitation of my father's handwriting, part Declaration of Independence signature—and what was left was me. It didn't, if I may say so, come off. I secretly thought that my poor handwriting was a sign of poor character. Had I been a girl, I should have been in serious trouble. Some boys did have nice handwriting, but boys were not really expected to have nice handwriting. Girls, though, were under an *obligation* to write beautifully. To fail in that regard was tantamount to failing hygienically. A girl with poor handwriting seemed nearly a slut. I don't recall any girls in our class with poor handwriting. It wasn't allowed.

I brought an additional difficulty to the job of handwriting. I was precocious in one thing only: I learned to print letters before I went to school. In doing so I taught myself to hold a pencil—and, later, a pen—in a manner I can only describe as highly individual. It involved an odd bunching of fingers around the writing instrument, a bunching that resembled nothing so much as the bout-ending hold of a wrestler named Cyclone Anaya, which he called the Cobra Twist. Added to this was an odd turning inward of my wrist, which led most people to think I wrote left-handed. Naturally I hid this unorthodox grip from my grade-school teachers, though I refused to give it up for my serious writing (and have only finally done so a few years ago).

Wicked friends were always amused by this grip; kind strangers, when first seeing it, assumed I had a debilitating muscular disease.

Holding a pen as I did, no pen was my friend. Fountain pens were, though, a very big item when I was young. A comedy record, spinning a joke off the fact that fountain pens were so frequently given as bar mitzvah gifts, had a young Jewish boy announce in his bar mitzvah speech, "Today I am a fountain pen!" Many were the manufacturers of fountain pens: Eversharp, Sheaffer, Parker, Waterman, Wearever. Owning an expensive pen-and-pencil set seemed a mark of very great distinction. Such a set was part of an elegant man's accoutrement, which in those days might include cuff links, a key chain, a money clip, a small gold pen-knife, perhaps a signet ring. But the expensive fountain pen was knocked out of the box—or, rather, pocket—by the ball-point pen. The first ball-point pen was invented by a Hungarian named Laszlo Jozsef Biro and patented in 1939. But it rose to prominence when it was marketed in this country by a man named Milton Reynolds, who produced a pen called the Reynolds Rocket. The Reynolds Rocket sold for $12.50—a big figure in 1945—and the claim made for it was that it could write underwater, which it could. Above water, though, it was scarcely any good at all. Nonetheless, on October 29, 1945, the first day it was marketed at Gimbels in New York, ten thousand were sold.

Ball-point pens rose even higher in popularity as they fell in price. They had much in the way of convenience to recommend them: they didn't blot, they didn't require refilling, they were eminently disposable, rather like toothpicks. Being for the most part made of plastic, ball-point pens became part of that body of items one used and threw away. Or if one didn't exactly throw them away, it was no great heartbreak if they became lost, because, first they were not very expensive, and second one had developed no attachment to them. It is difficult to imagine anyone, even a child, feeling saddened because he has lost his favorite ball-point pen.

To the degree that ball-point pens rose in popularity did the general interest in handwriting seem to fall off. The early ball-points tended to skip, and even the more expensive ones seemed to run away with one's handwriting. A fit analogy here might be that of driving a car with a gearshift or driving one with an automatic transmission. The automatic transmission (the ball-point) had much to recommend it, but the gearshift (the fountain pen) gave you a great feeling of control. My own handwriting, poor with fountain pens, became fully hideous with ball-point pens.

"What is handwriting but silent speech?" Erasmus wrote. "How warmly we respond whenever we receive from friends or scholars letters written in their own hands." And he continued: "An elegant script is like a fine picture; it has a pleasure of its own which engages the author of a letter while he is composing it no less than the recipient when he is studying it." Thus, thank-you notes, letters of condolence, and other missives of a personal kind seem to call for handwriting, as if handwriting is the most personal, and hence most sincere, form of communication. When Henry James began to dictate his novels and letters to a series of typists, he mounted elaborate Jamesian apologies to his correspondents for "this cold-blooded process," also referring to it as this "fierce legibility" and "the only epistolary tongue of my declining years."

Of course, there is something talismanic about handwriting. How else can one account for the attraction of autographs and the passion of autograph hunters, be they either children or hardened professionals? Writing that comes from the hand of an admired or famous person is perhaps as close as one can get to touching that hand. The apostle Paul was supposed to have written to the Galatians in his own hand. Imagine what the autograph of Jesus of Nazareth would bring on the open market! One way of calibrating contemporary fame might be to find out whose signature among contemporaries fetches the highest price among autograph collectors.

An author's signature is felt to enhance the value of a book. On a few occasions I have been asked to sign a hundred or so copies of books I have written. It sounds a charming thing to do, one of the triumphant rites of authorly achievement. In fact, after signing the first half-dozen copies, it becomes inexpressibly boring. In a used-book store I once came across the book of a well-known critic, affectionately inscribed to a famous novelist; the affection was evidently less than reciprocal, else what would the book be doing in a used-book bin? At first, I found this highly amusing; then I thought that perhaps I had seen something I oughtn't to have seen. The novelist would probably have done better to rip out the signature page before he sold the book. Selling the book with the inscription seemed, somehow, slightly sacrilegious, almost as if the recipient were selling a part of the author's spirit, or the man himself.

Few novelists still consider a person's handwriting part of his or her character—something, in any case, to be noted, like the color of a person's eyes or his smile. Thackeray, though, was a novelist who did, whenever the chance permitted, note his characters' handwriting. In *Vanity Fair,* one of his characters writes "a fine mercantile hand," another writes a "schoolboy hand"; of yet another character Thackeray remarks that he had "the best of characters and handwritings." As for their own handwriting, many writers surprise. Proust, for example, wrote a loose and inelegant hand, where one would have expected quite the reverse. Max Beerbohm's handwriting is just as one would have expected: compact, clear, with very little slant. Wordsworth wrote in a small, cramped hand. But the smallest handwriting is that of Aleksandr Solzhenitsyn, who trained himself to write as small as possible so that his books would come to fewer manuscript pages and thus would be easier to hide and smuggle out of the Soviet Union. Evelyn Waugh wrote a clear hand with many an interesting idiosyncrasy—in an otherwise cursive handwriting he wrote his *r*'s as if they were printed capitals—and, with his penchant for marching backward, ever backward, he wrote with a wooden penholder and steel nib.

As some people imagine what a writer looks like, I think of what his or her handwriting looks like. William Plomer, the English man of letters, has filled in some of these blanks for me. In his memoirs he not infrequently describes a person's handwriting. Christopher Isherwood's handwriting he calls "imperturbable." Lady Ottoline Morrell's proclaimed her "not a type but an individual." Virginia Woolf's handwriting, "sharp, delicate, and rhythmical as her prose, was pleasing in itself." Of the blanks that remain blanks, I could be quite wrong, but I imagine writers of voluminous works—Balzac, Dickens, Tolstoy—to have had scrawling, untidy handwriting, with little or no interest in crossing *t*'s and dotting *i*'s. In this connection I recall a charming scene in Henri Troyat's biography of Tolstoy. Troyat pictures the great writer in his upstairs study at Yasnaya Polyana, turning out page after page of *War and Peace,* while downstairs his wife and older children are reworking each page into "fair copy." It is a scene worthy of a Russian Jane Austen. As for Jane Austen, I imagine her handwriting to have been very neatly formed indeed—exquisite crewelwork, like her novels. But then I tend to think—quite without any knowledge to back it up—of eighteenth-century handwriting as small and elegant, of nineteenth-century handwriting as strong and sprawling.

As for twentieth-century handwriting, allow me, solipsistically, to put forth my own. It is a hodgepodge, a cacophony on the page. Erasmus had it that elegance of handwriting is primarily based on four things: the shape of letters, the way they are joined, their linear arrangement, and their proportion. Of these four, I should say that I do only one, joining letters, passably well. Of the remainder, I make a frightful botch. Inconsistency is the chief difficulty. In the same word I will loop the descender of the letter *p* and then bring the same descender down a few letters later without a loop. I may end one word with a flourish tantamount to a deep bow from the waist, then end the next without so much as a by-your-leave. What is more, I am not even consistently inconsistent: every so often I will turn out two or three beautifully formed words in a row. At forty-six I continue to fool around with my signature. If I hold up two of my own signatures, they sometimes seem to me as if written by two different people. I am surprised that by now my bank hasn't reported me for forgery of my own name.

I am what people schooled in the rude jargon of Vienna call an anal type—or, more precisely, I aspire to anality, insofar as that Freudian term means a love of tidiness, a rage for order. I say aspire, for this love, this rage, has remained an aspiration only. Still, applied to handwriting, it is for neatness that I yearn. What I desire is endless elegant notebooks filled with penetrating observations, all written in a fine script. As it happens, I do keep a journal, but not in elegant notebooks. I fear that the reason for this is that my handwriting is not up to expensive paper. My handwriting on costly stationery would be like chili on Limoges china.

What, I wonder, would graphologists make of my handwriting? What, I further wonder, do I make of graphology? The purpose of graphology is to relate elements of a person's handwriting to traits of his personality. Sometimes this is done in a most general, and therefore most unhelpful, way, as when large handwriting is said to characterize a large-spirited, ambitious person and small handwriting to characterize a mean-spirited, pedantic person. But when graphologists get more specific they do not necessarily get more persuasive. Here, for example, is Huntington Hartford, an ardent graphologist and author of a book entitled *You Are What You Write,* on the significations of dotting the *i:*

> An "i" dot before the letter means procrastination, for example, and beyond
> it, impatience; a club-shaped "i" dot, temper, brutality. There are three or four
> meanings peculiar to the "i" dot, however, about which most graphologists
> agree. For some reason they often link the dot precisely placed above the
> "i" with a good memory and a wavy dot with a sense of humor. (I am not
> 100 percent convinced!) They ascribe a critical faculty to those who, in supe-
> rior scripts like those of Einstein, Lessing, and Pasteur, connect the dot with

either the preceding or the following letter. Finally, there is the "i" dotted with a complete little circle. Before the days of Walt Disney, with the circular dot over the "i" in his famous signature, Louise Rice informed us . . . that the users of this sign are "the adapters of art."

Important if true; if not true, then amusing. I at any rate find it amusing, but many eminent intellectuals and artists have found graphology more than amusing; among its adherents have been Madame de Staël, Goethe, Poe, Leibniz, and, in our day, Randall Jarrell. Foolish though graphology may seem in its particulars, most of us, I suspect, believe in it a little, if only in an ex post facto way. A book review editor, speaking of a writer who had failed to meet a deadline, not long ago said to me, "From his creepy handwriting I should have known not to trust him." Similarly, if I show you a handwriting filled with energy and obvious confidence, then tell you that this is the handwriting of Sigmund Freud—whose handwriting, very rhythmic, does so seem—you are likely to say, "How appropriate!"

Can madness be revealed in a person's handwriting? Graphologists tend to think so, and so did the late John Cheever, who, in his story "The Five-Forty-Eight," uses handwriting as a clue to mental breakdown. The chief character in this story notes of his secretary, with whom he is to enter into a love affair, that "he had found only one thing in her that he could object to—her handwriting." Cheever continues:

> He could not associate the crudeness of her handwriting with her appearance. He would have expected her to write a rounded backhand, and in her writing there were intermittent traces of this, mixed with clumsy printing. Her writing gave him the feeling that she had been the victim of some inner— some emotional—conflict that had in its violence broken the continuity of the lines she was able to make on the paper.

On the other hand, judgment by handwriting must clearly be guarded against. In his novel *Lament for the Death of an Upper Class,* Henri de Montherlan puts the case for the anti-graphology point of view very neatly, when of a meek and terrified character he notes: "It is amusing to observe that M. de Coantré's writing, very upright, well formed and weighty, the signature, heavily underlined and the lines rising, would, according to the rules of graphology, have made one attribute to the writer all the qualities of character in which he was most certainly and most completely deficient."

Yet, within very strict limits, handwriting can reveal traits, if not of character, then of personality. In a person's handwriting, one can often read his aspirations— toward orderliness, elegance, grandeur. Handwriting can also reveal pretentiousness, affectation, exhibitionism, and many another minor excess. Or take illegible handwriting. What does it say about a person that his handwriting is illegible? I should say that it speaks to a sense of self-importance. American physicians are famously illegible. Horace Greeley wrote in a hand so illegible that letters of dismissal from him were often used by fired employees as recommendations for new jobs, for all that new employers could usually make out was Greeley's signature.

Illegibility has never been my problem; legibility has been. My clear dissatisfaction with my clear handwriting has brought about my fairly recent interest in fountain pens. My hope here is for a technological solution: a better writing instrument will make for a better handwriting—or so I reason. Thus far, though, I have been forced to conclude, in the fashion of the public-relations wing of the National Rifle Association, that pens don't kill handwriting, people do.

Meanwhile I am building up quite a nice arsenal of fountain pens. I have the little dears on my desk before me. Let me take inventory: two rather dud Sheaffers, one maroon with gold trim, one black with silver cap; two Parkers, one a 1932 model in black and gray horizontal stripes with a dull silver clip, the other sleek black, with a cap in two different shades of gold and a beige stone at its tip; a dark red Waterman, silver trim, a slender litle jobby with a stainless steel point; a Pelikan, black with gold trim and a removable point; and, finally, in my hand at the moment, the fine Swiss pen, a Mont Blanc, No. 24, black with gold trim and Mont Blanc's traditional six-point star at both top and bottom. Owning so many pens may seem extravagant, but I myself think this is a quite modest collection. My family, I know, is grateful that I do not go in for skywriting.

Different strokes for different folks, and different pens for different yens. Sometimes I have a yen for the streamlined feel of my gold-capped Parker; sometimes I have a yen for my Pelikan, which is feathery light; sometimes I have a yen for my 1932 Parker, which, along with its being half a century old, gives off a delicious smell of ink (I warned you we were talking here of a fetish). My Mont Blanc is most serviceable for writing lengthy things. Sheaffers are often my choice for writing checks. I tend to travel with my Waterman, which is the only one of my pens with a cartridge ink supply. I am not, I should say here, one of those gents who walks about with nine pens, a six-inch ruler, and an air gauge in his shirt pocket, all tucked into a plastic shield that has Fergusson's Hardware & Supply printed on it. No, I prefer to pick out and wear a single pen to fit the mood of the day, rather like picking out and wearing a necktie.

I continue to look for the perfect pen—the pen, you might say, ultimate. I read catalogues from pen companies with an intensity similar to that with which men, long at sea, read *Playboy*. I check stationery shops; at antique stores I inquire whether they have any old pens in stock. Who knows, I may come across a Waterman Patrician, first manufactured in 1928, or the splendid plastic and rolled gold Mont Blanc of the mid-1960s, or the costly French-made S. T. Dupont at a vastly cut-rate price. What I am looking for, of course, is a pen that feels exactly right, that will flow along in exact cadence with my thoughts—indeed, whose even flow will cause ideas to flow in me. Choice of a fountain pen, after all, entails the same meticulous attention to individual preference as does, say, choice of a tennis racquet: weight, grip, balance— each can affect performance crucially. As for ink, I find myself regularly buying new brands, trying out new colors, mixing like a mad chemist one with another . . . but I had better not get started on the subject of ink.

Since we are talking here about a fetish, allow me to report a recent dream. In this dream a friend of mine produced from his suit-coat pocket a pen—a somewhat battered Mont Blanc with a partially translucent green top—which, he announced with a smile, had once belonged to Rudyard Kipling. Even in my sleep I was ill with envy for his ownership of that pen. But I arose the next morning with what I feel is a winning marketing idea. Why not autograph model fountain pens, on the order of Chris Evert tennis racquets, Jack Nicklaus golf clubs, Pete Rose baseball gloves? Why not, in other words, Dante, Shakespeare, Jane Austen pens? True, fountain pens did not come into use until 1884, when the firm of L. E. Waterman produced the first usable ones, but this is a mere technical difficulty that can be surmounted. Patent, meanwhile, pending.

The market for this particular item might be severely limited to one—me. I have always been inordinately interested in the conditions of composition. Whenever I read a literary biography I linger lovingly over the descriptions of the rooms in which writers work, of their oddities and idiosyncrasies in the actual act of writing. Hemingway, for example, wrote standing up at a high desk; W. H. Auden amidst a clutter of paper and cigarette ash; William Faulkner in a shed behind his house in Oxford, Mississippi. (Faulkner, incidentally, had a most deceptive handwriting; it was straight up and down, small, fine, and extremely tidy, when, given his flights of rhetoric, one would have expected thick strokes, slashes really, strewn messily about the page.) Theodora Bosanquet, Henry James's secretary-typist, wrote a charming little book on James's work methods; in it she compared taking dictation from James to accompanying a fine singer on the piano.

Nothing so facilitates writing as actually having something to say, yet the conditions under which, and the tools with which, writing is done can contribute to facility—or to difficulty. From my own experience, the one time I can recall having a truly wretched time getting writing done—the one time, that is, when the problem was neither knowing what I wanted to say nor knowing how to say it—was after I had recently bought an Olivetti portable typewriter with italic type. No sooner had I brought that machine home than I realized I had made a mistake. How I loathed the look of that type on my pages! Everything I wrote seemed, in that type, arrhythmic, dull, stupid. I put the typewriter to the test by typing out a paragraph from E. M. Forster, a few sentences from Orwell, and four or five lines from a poem by T. S. Eliot—all of which seemed to me, in that type, arrhythmic, dull, stupid. This machine, I concluded, must go. And go presently it did. I traded it in—traded down, as they say on the used-car lot—for a Royal standard twenty years older than the Olivetti. We, the Royal standard and I, have lived happily ever after.

As for pens, the search goes on. I note those among my acquaintances who use fountain pens and those who do not. In movies my interest peaks whenever someone writes a letter. In a film about the life of Gustav Mahler, Mahler, when composing, used a long and elegant black pen of a kind I have never seen before or since. Do composers and choreographers, I wonder, use special pens? In a television series made from the memoirs of Albert Speer, whenever the actor who plays Hitler signs a document he uses the large Mont Blanc Diplomat (current U.S. price $250). This is a pen I have long admired yet do not quite covet. The pen is almost a bit too grand, a bit too pretentious. I myself would be embarrassed to take it out in public, for it seems unsuitable for anything less momentous than, say, signing a declaration of war—something I do not often do. Putting such a pen into the hand of Hitler, however, seemed an altogether appropriate touch. Give that propman an Emmy.

Some people wish to live surrounded by art, others require high-powered and finely mechanized automobiles. All I ask for is a pen. True, I am looking for a perfect pen, a Bucephalus, a Joe DiMaggio, a Sarah Vaughan of a pen. This would be a pen that would make my handwriting worthy of the approbation of the sniffiest Jane Austen heroine. From it ideas would flow in orderly profusion. It would blot when breaches of good sense, self-deceptions, and lies were written with it. Held loosely, it would toss off charmingly witty sentences; pressed down upon, it would touch the profound. It would permit no dull patches; only brilliance would issue from it: penetrating insights, fantastic formulations. Writing with such a pen would be like cantering along the Pacific Ocean on a palomino, instead of what writing really is— stopping and starting in a junk wagon down a thousand broken-up alleys. What a glory it would be to own such a pen! I keep searching, ever hopeful, even as I am confident that, were I to find such a pen, no ink for it would be available.

A CLOSER LOOK AT JOSEPH EPSTEIN

1. In "A Mere Journalist" Joseph Epstein provides readers with a history of his writing journals. From this history we learn a good deal about both Epstein and his history with writing. This concept of writing about one's history with writing holds some interesting possibilities. For instance, ask yourself what kind of writing you have produced most in your own life: do you write in a journal? Do you write letters? E-mails? Do you mostly write papers for school? Once you have considered what kinds of writing have dominated your writing history, think about how you would write about your writing history. Who would be interested in reading your writing history? What would you want to convey about your experiences with writing? What kinds of examples would you include, if any? In short, what choices would you make in writing about your own writing? Then, once you have made these considerations, write a writing history.

2. In Joseph Epstein's essays that are gathered here, Epstein often turns to the words of other authors and figures in support of his own positions. He also frequently provides anecdotes to clarify his positions. It seems that in most of Epstein's work, he writes about subjects about which he is deeply familiar, subjects about which he is capable of providing anecdotes and the words of others without much research; Epstein's citations and anecdotes often seem to be part of his general knowledge of a subject. Think about this ability for

a moment. If Epstein's references are part of his general knowledge about a subject, what does this suggest about his ability to write about an array of subjects? If these citations and anecdotes require vast research on Epstein's behalf for each essay, what does this suggest about his ability to integrate research into a text? Now, consider your own ability to speak or write at length about a particular subject—a subject about which you can provide numerous examples without researching the subject. Write an essay about that subject, weaving as many examples and anecdotes into the essay as possible.

3. Throughout the four essays found here, we learn a little bit about Joseph Epstein. We also become familiar with his voice as he writes in the first person in each essay. In many ways, these four essays are stylistically similar. How would you describe Epstein's writing in these four essays? What similar traits do you see in the four essays? Are those traits reflective of what you have learned about Epstein as a writer? How or how not? In an essay, describe Epstein as you have come to know him from these readings. What specifically gives you the clues to make the assumptions you do about Epstein and the decisions to describe him as you do?

Looking from Writer to Writer

1. In the introduction to this section about Joseph Epstein, we noted that Epstein has been critical of writers such as Joan Didion and John Updike, writers who are also featured in this book. After reading Epstein's essays gathered here, turn to the essays of Didion and Updike and consider how they differ from those of Epstein and why he might be critical of their writing. Do you prefer Epstein's writing to that of Didion or Updike? Why or why not?

2. Joseph Epstein writes quite a bit about writing, as do Scott Russell Sanders and bell hooks. Unlike many of the authors included in this anthology, for whom we have included only a single essay about writing, these three write about writing frequently enough that including several essays about writing is more representative of their bodies of work. Compare the ways that hooks, Epstein, and Sanders write about writing. Do you notice similarities or differences in their writing strategies when they write about writing? Do they hold similar or diverse views on writing? Which pieces about writing of these authors is most in line with your own thoughts on writing?

3. In his essay "A Mere Journalist," Joseph Epstein makes use of a series of questions asked of his audience. Jamaica Kincaid, in her essay "In History," also asks a lot of questions. How do each of these authors make use of the question in their essays? Do you find asking questions to be an effective rhetorical strategy? In what ways

is it or is it not effective? Are there other ways these two authors could have elicited the same effect in their essays without asking questions?

Looking Beyond

ESSAYS
A Line Out for a Walk: Familiar Essays. New York: Norton, 1991.
Ambition: The Secret Passion. New York: E. P. Dutton, 1980.
Divorced in America: Marriage in an Age of Possibility. New York: Dutton, 1974.
Familiar Territory: Observations on American Life (addresses, essays, lectures). New York: Oxford University Press, 1979.
Life Sentences: Literary Essays. New York: Norton, 1997.
The Middle of My Tether: Familiar Essays. New York: Norton, 1983.
Once More around the Block: Familiar Essays. New York: Norton, 1987.
Partial Payments: Essays on Writers and Their Lives. New York: Norton, 1989.
Pertinent Players: Essays on the Literary Life. New York: Norton, 1993.
Plausible Prejudices: Essays on American Writing. New York: Norton, 1985.
Snobbery: The American Version. Boston: Houghton Mifflin, 2002.
With My Trousers Rolled: Familiar Essays. New York: Norton, 1997.

FICTION
The Goldin Boys: Stories. New York: Norton, 1991.

EDITED COLLECTIONS
(Editor and author of introduction) *Masters: Portraits of Great Teachers.* New York: Basic Books, 1981.
(Editor) *The Norton Book of Personal Essays.* New York: Norton, 1997.

Henry Louis Gates, Jr.

Henry Louis Gates, Jr. was born in Keyser, West Virginia, on September 16, 1950, and has lived a deeply exciting and intellectually stimulating life. He graduated summa cum laude from Yale in 1973 and earned a master's degree (1974) and a PhD (1979) from Cambridge. In the years since, Gates has become one of the most important—and often one of the most controversial—scholars of African-American studies. Part of Gates's success as a writer and scholar came from experiences while in school. During his undergraduate years at Yale, Gates traveled to Africa, where he studied different African cultures in 15 countries. He traveled extensively in that continent, mainly by hitchhiking and by boat. He spent part of his time in Africa working at the Anglican Mission Hospital in the village of Kilimatinde in Tanzania. He was also able to study with African writer Wole Soyinka while in school at Cambridge. Gates has been awarded several student fellowships, Mellon Foundation and Ford Foundation fellowships, and a "genius grant" from the MacArthur foundation in 1981. While at Cambridge, Gates shifted his area of study from history to literature.

Without question, Gates was a successful student, even working as director of student affairs for John D. Rockefeller IV when Rockefeller ran for governor of West Virginia in 1971, and as Rockefeller's director of research while a senior at Yale. The campaign provided Gates with the background for writing his honor's thesis at Yale. Gates's success as a student carried him into an extremely successful academic career, first as an instructor in English at Yale and, after earning his doctoral degree, as assistant professor and director of the undergraduate Afro-American Studies Program at Yale. Gates has since taught at a variety of schools, including Cornell University, Duke University, Harvard University, and Virginia Commonwealth University.

Most impressive, too, has been Gates's career as a writer. He has written and edited (sometimes collaboratively) more than 40 books. His writing and teaching have helped him to become one of the most recognized scholars in African-American Studies and a "public intellectual" for his work to bring his knowledge to larger communities beyond the university and his frequent public appearances on documentaries and talk shows. But with his fame has also come a rash of criticism, which reached a height when Gates testified on behalf of the rap group 2 Live Crew at their obscenity trial.

Gates writes in many genres and on an array of subjects, though his general focus is usually present on issues of importance to African-American culture. His books cover a range of subjects but often focus on scholarly examinations of race and culture. In *The Signifying Monkey,* one of his more famous books, Gates turns to jazz, a true passion in his life, to help explain how African Americans have developed traditions of expression in a variety of texts, including literature and music. As one biographer of Gates expressed it, "The practice of signifying . . . is a common one not only in Afro-American literature and music but in the texture and the rituals of black American life in general, and Gates traces a line of direct transmission from Yoruba land to the black world of the Caribbean and the United States."

Gates's writing is both intellectually stimulating and deeply personal. Because of his intent to address large audiences beyond the academic community, his writing often turns away from traditional academic discourse in favor of more widely readable language. As you read the essays gathered here, think about how language choices give Gates the ability to move between academic audiences and larger public audiences. Notice, for instance, in the first essay how Gates not only turns to a good deal of research and citations as opposed to the second and third essays, but also how his voice takes on a more personal relationship with you as the reader. That is, notice how adept Gates is at moving from one kind of rhetoric in one essay to another kind in a different essay. Consider how he must think about such moves and how you might think about the demand for different strategies in the various writing projects in which you engage.

Gates on Writing

At First Glance

The essay "Writing, 'Race,' and the Difference It Makes" by Henry Louis Gates, Jr., was first published in the journal Critical Inquiry *in 1985. It is a sophisticated study of the relationship between writing and race, but it is also vastly readable. The essay was likely intended for an academic audience as Gates takes a more scholarly approach to making his argument than he does in many of his other essays. Gates is an intellectual, and thus participates in conversations with other intellectuals, but this essay is nonetheless accessible to a variety of readers. As you read this interesting piece, you should note several things: first, and most obviously, is the connection Gates makes between the activity of writing and the construction of race. Second, think about what makes this essay "academic." It might be simple to answer this by saying that the vocabulary is not what one might choose if writing to an audience of nonacademics, but as you read think about how Gates formulates his argument, how he uses examples, how he organizes the essay, and what other structural and stylistic choices he makes. Do these assist in making the essay academic? What do we mean by "academic essay"? By "academic"?*

Writing, "Race," and the Difference It Makes

The truth is that, with the fading of the Renaissance ideal through progressive stages of specialism, leading to intellectual emptiness, we are left with a potentially suicidal movement among "leaders of the profession," while, at the same time, the profession sprawls, without its old center, in helpless disarray.

One quickly cited example is the professional organization, the Modern Language Association.... A glance at its thick program for its last meeting shows a massive increase and fragmentation into more than 500 categories! I cite a few examples:... "The Trickster figure in Chicano and Black Literature."... Naturally, the progressive trivialization of topics has made these meetings a laughingstock in the national press.

—W. JACKSON BATE

... language, for the individual consciousness, lies on the borderline between oneself and the other. The word in language is half someone else's. It becomes "one's own" only when the speaker populates it with his own intention, his own accent, when he appropriates the word, adapting it to his own semantic and expressive intention. Prior to this moment of appropriation, the word does not exist in a neutral and impersonal language (it is not, after all, out of a dictionary that the speaker gets his words!), but rather it exists in other people's mouths, in other people's contexts, serving other people's intentions: it is from there that one must take the word, and make it "one's own."

—MIKHAIL BAKHTIN

They cannot represent themselves; they must be represented.

—MARX

I

Of what import is "race" as a meaningful category in the study of literature and the shaping of critical theory? If we attempt to answer this question by examining the history of Western literature and its criticism, our initial response would ostensibly be "nothing," or at the very least, "nothing explicitly." Indeed, until the past decade or so, even the most subtle and sensitive literary critics would most probably have argued that, except for aberrant moments in the history of criticism, "race" has been brought to bear upon the study of literature in no apparent way. The Western literary tradition, after all, and the canonical texts that comprise this splendid tradition, has been defined since Eliot as a more-or-less closed set of works that somehow speak to, or respond to, the "human condition" and to each other in formal patterns of repetition and revision. And while judgment is subject to the moment and indeed does reflect temporal-specific presuppositions, certain works seem to transcend value judgments of the moment, speaking irresistibly to the "human condition." The question of the place of texts written by "the Other" (be that odd metaphor defined as African, Arabic, Chinese, Latin American, female, or Yiddish authors) in the proper study of "literature," "Western literature," or "comparative literature" has, until recently, remained an unasked question, suspended or silenced by a discourse in which the "canonical" and the "noncanonical" stand as the ultimate opposition. "Race," in much of the thinking about the proper study of literature in this century, has been an invisible quality, present implicitly at best.

This was not always the case, of course. By the middle of the nineteenth century, "national spirit" and "historical period" had become widely accepted metaphors within theories of the nature and function of literature which argued that the principal value in a "great" work of literary art resided in the extent to which these categories were *reflected* in that work of art. Montesquieu's *Esprit des lois* had made a culture's formal social institution the repository of its "guiding spirit," while Vico's *Principii d'una scienza nuova* had read literature against a complex pattern of historical cycles. The two Schlegels managed rather deftly to bring to bear upon the interpretation of literature "both national spirit and historical period," as Walter Jackson Bate has shown. But it was Taine who made the implicit explicit by postulating "race, moment, and *milieu*" as positivistic criteria through which any work could be read, and which, by definition, any work reflected. Taine's *History of English Literature* is the great foundation upon which subsequent nineteenth-century notions of "national literatures" would be constructed.

What Taine called "race" was the source of all structures of feeling. To "track the root of man," he wrote, "is to consider the race itself, . . . the structure of his character and mind, his general processes of thought and feeling. . . . the irregularity and revolutions of his conception, which arrest in him the birth of fair dispositions and harmonious forms, the disdain of appearances, the desire for truth, the attachment for bare and abstract ideas, which develop in him conscience, at the expense of all else." In "race," Taine concluded, was predetermined "a particularity inseparable from all the motions of his intellect and his heart. Here lie the grand causes, for they are the universal and permanent causes, . . . indestructible, and finally infallibly supreme." "Poetries," as Taine put it, and all other forms of social expression, "are in fact only the imprints stamped by their seal."

"Race," for Taine was "the first and richest source of these master faculties from which historical events take their rise"; it was a "community of blood and intellect which to this day binds its off-shoots together." Lest we misunderstand the *naturally* determining role of "race," Taine concluded that it "is no simple spring but a kind of lake, a deep reservoir wherein other springs have, for a multitude of centuries, discharged their several streams."

Taine's originality lay not in these ideas about the nature and role of race, but in their almost "scientific" application to the history of literature. These ideas about race were received from the Enlightenment, if not from the Renaissance. By midpoint in the nineteenth century, ideas of irresistible racial differences were commonly held: when Abraham Lincoln invited a small group of black leaders to the White House in 1862 to share with them his ideas about returning all blacks in America to Africa, his argument turned upon these "natural" differences. "You and we are different races," he said. "We have between us a broader difference than exists between any other two races." Since this sense of difference was never to be bridged, Lincoln concluded, the slaves and the ex-slaves should be returned to their own. The growth of canonical "national" literatures was coterminous with the shared assumption among intellectuals that "race" was a "thing," an ineffaceable quantity, which irresistibly determined the shape and contour of thought and feelings as surely as it did the shape and contour of human anatomy.

How did the great movement away from "race, moment, and *milieu*" and toward the language of the text in the 1920s and 1930s in the Practical Criticism movement at Cambridge and the New Criticism movement at Yale affect this category of "race" in the reading of literature? Race, along with all sorts of other unseemly or untoward notions about the composition of the literary work of art, was bracketed or suspended. Race, within these theories of literature to which we are all heir, was rendered *implicit* in the elevation of ideas of canonical *cultural* texts that comprise the Western tradition in Eliot's simultaneous order, with a simultaneous existence. History, *milieu,* and even moment were brought to bear upon the interpretation of literature through philology and etymology: the dictionary—in the Anglo-American tradition, the *Oxford English Dictionary*—was the castle in which Taine's criteria took refuge. Once the concept of value became encased in the belief in a canon of texts whose authors purportedly shared a "common culture" inherited from *both* the Greco-Roman and the Judeo-Christian traditions, no one need speak of matters of "race" since "the race" of these authors was "the same." One not heir to these traditions was, by definition, of another "race." This logic was impenetrable.

Despite their beliefs in the unassailable primacy of language in the estimation of a work of literature, however, both I. A. Richards and Allen Tate, in separate prefaces to books of poems by black authors, paused to wonder aloud about the black faces of the authors, and the import this had upon the reading of their texts. The often claimed "racism" of the Southern Agrarians, while an easily identifiable target, was only an explicit manifestation of presuppositions that formed a large segment of the foundation upon which formalism was built. The citizens of the republic of literature, in other words, were all white, and mostly male. Difference, if difference obtained at all, was a difference obliterated by the "simultaneity" of Eliot's "tradition." Eliot's fiction of tradition, for the writer of a culture of color, was the literary equivalent of the "grandfather clause." So, in response to Robert Penn Warren's statement in "Pondy Woods"—"Nigger, your breed ain't metaphysical"—Sterling A. Brown wrote "Cracker, your breed ain't exegetical." The Signifyin(g) pun deconstructed the "racialism" inherent in these claims of tradition.

II

"Race" as a meaningful criterion within the biological sciences has long been recognized to be a fiction. When we speak of the "white race" or the "black race," the "Jewish race" or the "Aryan race," we speak in misnomers, biologically, and in metaphors, more generally. Nevertheless, our conversations are replete with usages of *race* which have their sources in the dubious pseudoscience of the eighteenth and nineteenth centuries. One need only flip through the pages of the *New York Times* to find headlines such as "Brown University President Sees School Racial Problems" or "Sensing Racism, Thousands March in Paris." In a lead editorial of its March 29, 1985, number, "The Lost White Tribe," the *Times* notes that while "racism is not unique to South Africa," we must condemn that society because "Betraying the religious tenets underlying Western culture, it has made race the touchstone of political rights." Eliot's "dissociation of sensibility," caused in large part by the "fraternal" atrocities of the World War I, and then by the inexplicable and insane member of European Jews two decades later, the *Times* editorial echoes. (For millions of people who originated outside Europe, however, this dissociation of sensibility had its origins in colonialism and human slavery.) *Race,* in these usages, pretends to be an objective term of classification, when in fact it is a trope.

The sense of difference defined in popular usages of the term *race* has been used both to describe and *inscribe* differences of language, belief system, artistic tradition, "gene pool," and all sorts of supposedly "natural" attributes such as rhythm, athletic ability, cerebration, usury, and fidelity. The relation between "racial character" and these sorts of "characteristics" has been inscribed through tropes of race, lending to even supposedly "innocent" descriptions of cultural tendencies and differences the sanction of God, biology, or the natural order. "Race consciousness," Zora Neale Hurston wrote, "is a deadly explosive on the tongues of men." I even heard a member of the House of Lords in 1973 describe the differences between Irish Protestants and Catholics in terms of their "distinct and clearly definable differences of race."

"You mean to say that you can tell them apart?" I asked incredulously.

"Of course," responded the lord. "Any Englishman can."

Race has become a trope of ultimate, irreducible difference between cultures, linguistic groups, or practitioners of specific belief systems, who more often than not have fundamentally opposed economic interests. Race is the ultimate trope of difference because it is so very arbitrary in its application. The sanction of biology contained in sexual difference, simply put, does not and can never obtain when one is speaking of "racial difference." Yet, we carelessly use language in such a way as to *will* this sense of *natural* difference into our formulations. To do so is to engage in a pernicious act of language, one which exacerbates the complex problem of cultural or "ethnic" difference, rather than assuages or redresses it. This is especially the case at a time when racism has become fashionable, once again. That, literally every day, scores of people are killed in the name of differences ascribed to "race" only makes even more imperative this gesture to "deconstruct," if you will, the ideas of differences inscribed in the trope of race, to take discourse itself as our common subject to be explicated to reveal the latent relations of power and knowledge inherent in popular and academic usages of "race." When twenty-five thousand people feel compelled to gather on the Rue de Rivoli in support of the antiracist "Ne touche pas à mon pote" movement, when thousands of people willingly accept arrest to protest apartheid, when Iran and Iraq feel justified in murdering the other's citizens because of their "race," when Beirut stands as a museum of shards and pieces reflecting degrees of horror impossible to comprehend, the gesture that we make here seems local and tiny.

There is a curious dialectic between formal language use and the inscription of metaphorical "racial" differences. At times, as Nancy Stepan expertly shows in *The Idea of Race in Science,* these metaphors have sought a universal and transcendent sanction in biological science. Western writers in French, Spanish, German, Portuguese, and English have sought to make literal these rhetorical figures of "race," to make them natural, absolute, essential. In doing so, they have *inscribed* these differences as fixed and finite categories which they merely report or draw upon for authority. But it takes little reflection to recognize that these pseudoscientific categories are themselves figures of thought. Who has seen a black or red person, a white, yellow, or brown? These terms are arbitrary constructs, not reports of reality. But language is not only the medium of this often pernicious tendency, it is its *sign.* Language use signifies the difference between cultures and their possession of power, spelling the difference between subordinate and superordinate, between bondsman and lord. Its call into use is simultaneous with the shaping of an economic order in which the cultures of color have been dominated in several important senses by Western Judeo-Christian, Greco-Hellenic cultures and their traditions. To use contemporary theories of criticism to explicate these modes of inscription is to demystify large and obscure ideological relations and indeed theory itself. It would be useful here to consider a signal example of the black tradition's confinement and delimitation by the commodity of writing. For literacy, as I hope to demonstrate, could be the most pervasive emblem of capitalist commodity functions.

III

Where better to test this thesis than in the example of the black tradition's first poet in English, the African slave girl Phillis Wheatley. Let us imagine a scene:

One bright morning in the spring of 1772, a young African girl walked demurely into the courthouse at Boston, to undergo an oral examination, the results of which would determine the direction of her life and work. Perhaps she was shocked upon entering the appointed room. For there, gathered in a semicircle, sat eighteen of Boston's most notable citizens. Among them was John Erving, a prominent Boston merchant; the Reverend Charles Chauncey, pastor of the Tenth Congregational Church and a son of Cotton Mather; and John Hancock, who would later gain fame for his signature on the Declaration of Independence. At the center of this group would have sat His Excellency, Thomas Hutchinson, governor of the colony, with Andrew Oliver, his lieutenant governor, close by his side.

Why had this august group been assembled? Why had it seen fit to summon this young African girl, scarcely eighteen years old, before it? This group of "the most respectable characters in *Boston*," as it would later define itself, had assembled to question the African adolescent closely on the slender sheaf of poems that the young woman claimed to have written by herself. We can only speculate on the nature of the questions posed to the fledgling poet. Perhaps they asked her to explain for all to hear exactly who were the Greek and Latin gods and poets alluded to so frequently in her work. Or perhaps they asked her to conjugate a verb in Latin, or even to translate randomly selected passages from the Latin, which she and her master, John Wheatley, claimed that she "had made some progress in." Or perhaps they asked her to recite from memory key passages from the texts of Milton and Pope, the two poets by whom the African claimed to be most directly influenced. We do not know.

We do know, however, that the African poet's responses were more than sufficient to prompt the eighteen august gentlemen to compose, sign, and publish a two-paragraph "Attestation," an open letter "To the Publick" that prefaces Phillis Wheatley's book, and which reads in part:

> We whose Names are underwritten, do assure the World, that the poems specified in the following Page, were (as we veribly believe) written by Phillis, a young Negro Girl, who was but a few Years since, brought an uncultivated Barbarian from *Africa,* and has ever since been, and now is, under the Disadvantage of serving as a Slave in a Family in this Town. She has been examined by some of the best judges, and is thought qualified to write them.

So important was this document in securing a publisher for Phillis's poems that it forms the signal element in the prefatory matter printed in the opening pages of her *Poems on Various Subjects, Religious and Moral,* published at London in 1773.

Without the published "Attestation," Wheatley's publisher claimed, few would believe that an African could possibly have written poetry all by herself. As the eighteen put the matter clearly in their letter, "Numbers would be ready to suspect they were not really the Writings of Phillis." Phillis's master, John Wheatley, and Phillis had attempted to publish a similar volume in 1770 at Boston, but Boston publishers had been incredulous. Three years later, "Attestation" in hand, Phillis and her mistress's son, Nathaniel Wheatley, sailed for England, where they completed arrangements for the publication of a volume of her poems, with the aid of the Countess of Huntington and the Earl of Dartmouth.

This curious anecdote, surely one of the oddest oral examinations on record, is only a tiny part of a larger, and even more curious, episode in the eighteenth century's Enlightenment. At least since 1600, Europeans had wondered aloud whether or not the African "species of men," as they most commonly put it, *could* ever create formal literature, could ever master the "arts and sciences." If they could, the argument ran, then the African variety of humanity and the European variety were fundamentally related. If not, then it seemed clear that the African was destined by nature to be a slave.

Determined to discover the answer to this crucial quandary, several Europeans and Americans undertook experiments in which young African slaves were tutored and trained along with white children. Phillis Wheatley was merely one result of such an experiment. Francis Williams, a Jamaican who took the B.A. at the University of Cambridge before 1730; Jacobus Capitein, who earned several degrees in Holland; Wilheim Amo, who took the doctorate degree in philosophy at Halle; and Ignatius Sancho, who became a friend of Sterne's and who published a volume of letters in 1782—these were just a few of the black subjects of such "experiments." The published writings of these black men and one woman, who wrote in Latin, Dutch, German, and English, were seized upon both by pro- and antislavery proponents as proof that their arguments were sound.

So widespread was the debate over "the nature of the African" between 1730 and 1830 that not until the Harlem Renaissance would the work of black writers be as extensively reviewed as it was in the eighteenth century. Phillis Wheatley's list of reviewers includes Votaire, Thomas Jefferson, George Washington, Samuel Rush, and James Beatty, to name only a few. Francis Williams's work was analyzed by no less than David Hume and Immanuel Kant. Hegel, writing in the *Philosophy of History* in 1813, used the writings of these Africans as the sign of their innate inferiority. The list of commentators is extensive, amounting to a "Who's Who" of the French, English, and American Enlightenment.

Why was the *creative writing* of the African of such importance to the eighteenth century's debate over slavery? I can briefly outline one thesis: After Descartes, *reason* was privileged, or valorized, among all other human characteristics. Writing, especially after the printing press became so widespread, was taken to be the *visible* sign of reason. Blacks were "reasonable," and hence "men," if—and only if—they demonstrated mastery of the "arts and sciences," the eighteenth century's formula for writing. So, while the Enlightenment is famous for establishing its existence upon the human ability to reason, it simultaneously used the absence and presence of "reason" to delimit and circumscribe the very humanity of the cultures and people of color which Europeans had been "discovering" since the Renaissance. The urge toward the systematization of all human knowledge, by which we characterize the Enlightenment, led directly to the relegation of black people to a lower rung on the Great Chain of Being, an eighteenth-century construct that arranged all of creation on a vertical scale from animals and plants and insects through humans to the angels and God himself.

By 1750, the chain had become individualized; the human scale slid from "the lowliest Hottentot" (black south Africans) to "glorious Milton and Newton." If blacks could write and publish imaginative literature, then they could, in effect, take a few Giant Steps up the Chain of Being, in a pernicious game of "Mother, May I?" As the Reverend James W. C. Pennington, an ex-slave who wrote a slave narrative and who was a prominent black abolitionist, summarized this curious idea in his prefatory note "To the Reader" that authorized Ann Plato's 1841 book of essays, biographies, and poems: "The history of the arts and sciences is the history of individuals, of individual nations." Only by publishing books such as Plato's, he argued, could blacks demonstrate "the fallacy of that stupid theory, *that nature has done nothing but fit us for slaves, and that art cannot unfit us for slavery!*"

IV

The relation between what, for lack of a better term, I shall call the "nonwhite" writer and the French, Portuguese, Spanish, and English languages and literatures manifests itself in at least two ways of interest to theorists of literature and literary history. I am thinking here of what in psychoanalytic criticism is sometimes called "the other," and more especially of this "other" as the subject and object in literature. What I mean by citing these two overworked terms is precisely this: how blacks are figures in literature, and also how blacks *figure*, as it were, literature of their own making.

These two poles of a received opposition have been formed, at least since the early seventeenth century, by an extraordinary *subdiscourse* of the European philosophies of aesthetic theory and language. The two subjects, often in marginal ways, have addressed directly the supposed relation among "race," defined variously as language use and "place in nature." Human beings wrote books. Beautiful books were reflections of sublime genius. Sublime genius was the province of the European.

Blacks, and other people of color, could not "write." "Writing," these writers argued, stood alone among the fine arts as the most salient repository of "genius," the visible sign of reason itself. In this subordinate role, however, "writing," although secondary to "reason," was nevertheless the *medium* of reason's expression. They *knew* reason by its writing, by its representations. This representation could assume the spoken or the written form. And while several superb scholars gave priority to the *spoken* as the privileged of the pair, in their writings about blacks, at least, Europeans privileged *writing* as the principal measure of Africans' "humanity," their "capacity for progress," their very place in "the great chain of being."

This system of signs is arbitrary. Key words, such as *capacity*, which became a metaphor for cranial size, reflect the predominance of "scientific" discourse in metaphysics. That "reason," moreover, could be seen to be "natural" was the key third term of a homology which, in practice, was put to pernicious uses. The transformation of writing from an activity of mind into a commodity not only reflects larger mercantile relations between Africa and Europe but is also the subject I wish to explore here. Let me retrace, in brief, the history of this idea, of the relationship of the absence of "writing" and the absence of "humanity" in European letters of 1600.

We must understand this correlation of use and *presence* in language if we are to begin to learn how to read, for example, the slave's narrative within what Geoffrey H. Hartman calls its "text-milieu." The slave narratives, taken together, represent the attempt of blacks to *write themselves into being*. What a curious idea: Through the mastery of formal Western languages, the presupposition went, a black person could posit a full and sufficient self, as an act of self-creation through the medium of language. Accused of having no collective history by Hegel, blacks effectively responded by publishing hundreds of individual histories which functioned as the part standing for the whole. As Ralph Ellison defined this relation, "We tell ourselves our individual stories so as to become aware of our *general* story.

Writing as the visible sign of Reason, at least since the Renaissance in Europe, had been consistently invoked in Western aesthetic theory in the discussion of the enslavement and status of the black. The origin of this received association of political salvation and artistic genius can be traced at least to the seventeenth century. What we arrive at by extracting a rather black and slender thread from among the philosophical discourses of the Enlightenment is a reading of another side of the philosophy of enlightenment, indeed its nether side. Writing in *The New Organon* in 1620, Sir Francis Bacon, confronted with the problem of classifying the people of color which a seafaring Renaissance Europe had "discovered," turned to the arts as the ultimate measure of a race's place in nature. "Again," he wrote, "let a man only consider what a difference there is between the life of men in the most civilized province of Europe, and in the wildest and most barbarous districts of New India; he will feel it be great enough to justify the saying that 'man is a god to man,' not only in regard to aid and benefit, but also by comparison of condition. And this difference comes not from soil, not from climate, not from race, but from the arts." Eleven years later, Peter Heylyn, in his *Little Description of the Great World,* used Bacon's formulation to relegate the blacks to a subhuman status: Black Africans, he wrote, lacked completely "the use of Reason which is peculiar unto man; [they are] of little Wit; and destitute of all arts and sciences; prone to luxury, and for the greatest part Idolators." All subsequent commentaries on the matter were elaborations upon Heylyn's position.

By 1680, Heylyn's key words, *reason* and *wit,* had been reduced to "reading and writing," as Morgan Godwyn's summary of received opinion attests:

> [A] disingenuous and unmanly *Position* had been formed; and privately (and as it were *in the dark*) handed to and again, which is this, That the Negro's though in their figure they carry some resemblances of manhood, yet are indeed *no* men. . . . the consideration of the shape and figure of our Negro's Bodies, their Limbs and members; their Voice and Countenance, in all things according with other mens; together with their *Risibility* and *Discourse* (man's Peculiar Faculties) should be sufficient Conviction. How should they otherwise be capable of *Trades,* and other no less manly imployments; as also of *Reading* and *Writing,* or show so much Discretion in management of Business; . . .

but wherein (we know) that many of our own People are *deficient,* were they not truly Men?

Such a direct correlation of political rights and literacy helps us to understand both the transformation of writing into a commodity and the sheer burden of received opinion that motivated the black slave to seek his or her text. As well, it defined the "frame" against which each black text would be read. The following 1740 South Carolina Statute was concerned to make it impossible for black literacy mastery even to occur:

> *And whereas* the having of slaves taught to write, or suffering them to be employed in writing, may be attending with great inconveniences;

> *Be it enacted,* that all and every person and persons whatsoever, who shall hereafter teach, or cause any slave or slaves to be taught to write, or shall use or employ any slave as a scribe in any manner of writing whatsoever, hereafter taught to write; every such person or persons shall, for every offense, forfeith the sum of one hundred pounds current money.

Learning to read and to write, then, was not only difficult, it was a violation of a law. That Frederick Douglass, Thomas Smallwood, William Wells Brown, Moses Grandy, James Pennington, and John Thompson, among numerous others, all rendered statements about the direct relation between freedom and discourse not only as central scenes of instruction but also as repeated fundamental structures of their very rhetorical strategies only emphasizes the dialectical relation of black texts to a "context," defined here as "*other,*" racist texts, against which the slave's narrative, by definition, was forced to react.

By 1705, a Dutch explorer, William Bosman, had encased Peter Heylyn's bias into a myth which the Africans he had "discovered" had purportedly related to him. It is curious insofar as it justifies human slavery. According to Bosman, the blacks "tell us that in the beginning God created Black as well as White men; thereby giving the Blacks the first Election, who chose Gold, and left the Knowledge of Letters to the White. God granted their request, but being incensed at their Avarice, resolved that the Whites should ever be their masters, and they obliged to wait on them as their slaves." Bosman's fabrication, of course, was a myth of origins designed to sanction through mythology a political order created by Europeans. It was David Hume, writing at midpoint in the eighteenth century, who gave to Bosman's myth the sanction of Enlightenment philosophical reasoning.

In a major essay, "Of National Characters" (1748), Hume discussed the "characteristics" of the world's major division of human beings. In a footnote added to his original text in 1753 (the margins of his discourse), Hume posited with all of the authority of philosophy the fundamental identity of complexion, character, and intellectual capacity. "I am apt to suspect the negroes," he wrote,

> and in general all the other species of men (for there are four or five different kinds) to be naturally inferior to the whites. There never was a civilized nation of any other complexion than white, nor even any individual eminent either

in action or speculation. No ingenious manufacturers amongst them, *no arts, no sciences.* . . . Such a uniform and constant difference could not happen, in so many countries and ages, if *nature* had not made our original distinction betwixt these breeds of men. Not to mention our colonies, there are Negroe slaves dispersed all over Europe, of which none ever discovered any symptoms of ingenuity; . . . In Jamaica, indeed they talk of one negroe as a man of parts and learning [Francis Williams, the Cambridge-educated poet who wrote verse in Latin]; but 'tis likely he is admired for very slender accomplishments, like a parrot who speaks a few words plainly.

Hume's opinion on the subject, as we might expect, became prescriptive.

Writing in 1764, in his *Observations on the Feelings of the Beautiful and the Sublime,* Immanuel Kant elaborated upon Hume's essay in a fourth section entitled "Of National Characteristics, as far as They Depend upon the Distinct Feeling of the Beautiful and the Sublime." Kant first claimed that "So fundamental is the difference between [the black and white] races of man, and it appears to be as great in regard to mental capacities as in color." Kant, moreover, was one of the earliest major European philosophers to conflate "color" with "intelligence," a determining relation he posited with dictatorial surety. The excerpt bears citation:

> . . . Father Labat reports that a Negro carpenter, whom he reproached for haughty treatment toward his wives, answered: "You whites are indeed fools, for first you make great concessions to your wives, and afterward you complain when they drive you mad." And it might be that there were something in this which perhaps deserved to be considered; but in short, this fellow was *quite black* from head to foot, a clear proof that what he said was stupid. (emphasis added)

The correlation of "blackness" and "stupidity" Kant posited as if self-evident.

Writing in "Query XIV" of *Notes on the State of Virginia,* Thomas Jefferson maintained that "Never yet could I find that a black had uttered a thought above the level of plain narration, never see even an elementary trait of painting or sculpture." Of Wheatley, the first black person to publish a book of poetry in England, Jefferson the critic wrote, "Misery is often the parent of the most affecting touches in poetry. Among the blacks is misery enough, God knows, but not poetry. . . . The compositions published under her name are below the dignity of criticism."

In that same year (1785), Kant, basing his observations on the absence of published writing among blacks, noted as if simply obvious that "Americans [Indians] and blacks are lower in their mental capacities than all other races." Again, Hegel, echoing Hume and Kant, noted the absence of history among black people and derided them for failing to develop indigenous African scripts, or even to master the art of writing in modern languages.

Hegel's strictures on the African about the absence of "history" presume a crucial role of *memory*—a collective, cultural memory—in the estimation of civilization. Metaphors of the "childlike" nature of the slaves, of the masked, puppetlike "personality" of the black, all share this assumption about the absence of memory. Mary

Langdon, in her 1855 novel *Ida May: A Story of Things Actual and Possible,* wrote that "but then they *are* mere children. . . . You seldom hear them say much about anything that's past, if they only get enough to eat and drink at the present moment." Without writing, there could exist no *repeatable* sign of the workings of reason, of mind. Without memory or mind, there could exist no history. Without history, there could exist no "humanity," as defined consistently from Vico to Hegel. As William Gilmore Simms argued at the middle of the nineteenth century:

> [If one can establish] that the negro intellect is fully equal to that of the white race . . . you not only take away the best argument for keeping him in subjection, but you take away the possibility of doing so. *Prima facie,* however, the fact that he *is* a slave, is conclusive against the argument for his freedom, as it is against his equality of claim in respect of intellect. . . . Whenever the negro shall be fully fit for freedom, he will make himself free, and no power on earth can prevent him.

V

Ironically, Anglo-African writing arose as a response to allegations of its absence. Black people responded to these profoundly serious allegations about their "nature" as directly as they could: they wrote books, poetry, autobiographical narratives. Political and philosophical discourse were the predominant forms of writing. Among these, autobiographical "deliverance" narratives were the most common, and the most accomplished. Accused of lacking a formal and collective history, blacks published individual histories which, taken together, were intended to narrate, in segments, the larger yet fragmented history of blacks in Africa, now dispersed throughout a cold New World. The narrated, descriptive "eye" was put into service as a literary form to posit both the individual "I" of the black author and the collective "I" of the race. Text created author, and black authors, it was hoped, would create, or re-create, the image of the race in European discourse. The very *face* of the race, representations of the features of which are common in all sorts of writings about blacks at this time, was contingent upon the recording of the black *voice.* Voice presupposes a face but also seems to have been thought to determine the contours of the black face.

The recording of an "authentic" black voice, a voice of deliverance from the deafening discursive silence which an enlightened Europe cited as proof of the absence of the African's humanity, was the millennial instrument of transformation through which the African would become the European, the slave become the ex-slave, the brute animal become the human being. So central was this idea to the birth of the black literary tradition in the eighteenth century that five of the earliest slave narratives draw upon the figure of the voice in the text as crucial "scenes of instruction" in the development of the slave on the road to freedom. James Gronniosaw in 1770, John Marrant in 1785, Ottobah Cugoano in 1787, Olaudah Equiano in 1789, and John Jea in 1815—all drew upon "the trope of the talking book." Gronniosaw's usage bears citing here especially because it repeats Kant's correlation of physical—and, as it were, metaphysical—characteristics:

My master used to read prayers in public to the ship's crew every Sabbath day; and when I first saw him read, I was never so surprised in my life, as when I saw the book talk to my master, for I thought it did, as I observed him to look upon it, and move his lips. I wished it would do so with me. As soon as my master had done reading, I followed him to the place where he put the book, being mightily delighted with it, and when nobody saw me, I opened it, and put my ear down close upon it, in great hope that it would say something to me; but I was very sorry, and greatly disappointed, when I found that it would not speak. This thought immediately presented itself to me, that every body and every thing despised me because I was black.

Even for this black author, his own mask of black humanity was a negation, a sign of absence. Gronniosaw accepted his role as a nonspeaking would-be subject and the absence of his common humanity with the European.

That the figure of the talking book recurs in these five black eighteenth-century texts says much about the degree of presupposition and intertextuality in early black letters, more than we heretofore thought. Equally important, however, this figure itself underscores the received correlation between silence and blackness which we have been tracing, as well as the urgent need to make the text speak, the process by which the slave marked his distance from the master. The voice in the text was truly a millennial voice for the African person of letters in the eighteenth century, for it was that very voice of deliverance and of redemption which would signify a new order for the black.

These narrators, linked by revision of a trope into the very first black chain of signifiers, implicitly signify upon another "chain," the metaphorical Great Chain of Being. Blacks were most commonly represented on the chain either as the "lowest" of the human races, or as first cousin to the ape. Since writing, according to Hume, was the ultimate sign of difference between animal and human, these writers implicitly were Signifyin(g) upon the figure of the chain itself, simply by publishing autobiographies that were indictments of the received order of Western culture, of which slavery, to them, by definition stood as the most salient sign. The writings of Gronniosaw, Marrant, Equiano, Cugoano, and Jea served as a critique of the sign of the Chain of Being and the black person's figurative "place" on the chain. This chain of black signifiers, regardless of their intent or desire, made the first political gesture in the Anglo-African literary tradition "simply" by the act of writing, a collective act that gave birth to the black literary tradition and defined it as the "other's chain," the chain of black being as black people themselves would have it. Making the book speak, then, constituted a motivated, and political, engagement with the condemnation of Europe's fundamental figure of domination, the Great Chain of Being.

The trope of the talking book is not a trope of the presence of voice at all, but of its absence. To speak of a "silent voice" is to speak in an oxymoron. There is no such thing as a silent voice. Furthermore, as Juliet Mitchell has put the matter, there is something untenable about the attempt to represent what is not there, to represent that which is *missing* or absent. Given that this is what these five black authors sought to do, we are justified in wondering aloud if the sort of subjectivity that they sought could be realized through a process that was so very ironic from the outset. Indeed, how can the black subject posit a full and sufficient self in a language in which blackness is a sign of absence? Can writing, the very "difference" it makes and marks, mask the blackness of the black face that addresses the text of Western letters, in a voice that "speaks English" in an idiom that contains the irreducible element of cultural difference that shall always separate the white voice from the black? Black people, we know, have not been "liberated" from racism by their writings, and they accepted a false premise by assuming that racism would be destroyed once white racists became convinced that we were human, too. Writing stood as a complex "certificate of humanity," as Paulin J. Hountondji put it. Black writing, and especially the literature of the slave, served not to obliterate the difference of "race," as a would-be white man such as Gronniosaw so ardently desired; rather, the inscription of the black voice in Western literatures has preserved those very cultural differences to be imitated and revised in a separate Western literary tradition, a tradition of black difference.

Blacks, as we have seen, tried to write themselves out of slavery, a slavery even more profound than mere physical bondage. Accepting the challenge of the great white Western tradition, black writers wrote as if their lives depended upon it—and, in a curious sense, their lives did, the "life" of "the race" in Western discourse. But if blacks accepted this challenge, we also accepted its premises, premises in which perhaps lay concealed a trap. What trap might this be? Let us recall the curious case of M. Edmond Laforest.

In 1915, Edmund Laforest, a prominent member of the Haitian literary movement called La Ronde, made of his death a symbolic, if ironic, statement of the curious relation of the "non-Western" writer to the act of writing in a modern language. M. Laforest, with an inimitable, if fatal, flair for the grand gesture, stood upon a bridge, calmly tied a Larousse dictionary around his neck, then proceeded to leap to his death by drowning. While other black writers, before and after M. Laforest, have suffocated as artists beneath the weight of various modern languages, Laforest chose to make his death an emblem of this relation of indenture.

It is the challenge of the black tradition to critique this relation of indenture, an indenture that obtains for our writers and for our critics. We must master, as Derrida wrote, "how to speak the other's language without renouncing (our) own." When we attempt to appropriate, by inversion, *race* as a term for an essence, as did the Negritude movement, for example ("We feel, therefore we are," as Senghor argued of the African), we yield too much, such as the basis of a shared humanity. Such gestures, as Anthony Appiah has observed, are futile, and dangerous because of their further inscription of new and bizarre stereotypes. Who do we meet Derrida's challenge in the discourse of criticism? The Western critical tradition has a canon, just as does the Western literary tradition. Whereas I once thought it our most important gesture to *master* the canon of criticism, to *imitate* and *apply* it, I now believe that we must turn to the black tradition itself to arrive at theories of criticism indigenous to our literatures. Alice Walker's revision of a parable of white interpretation written in 1836 by Rebecca Cox Jackson, a Shaker eldress and black visionary, makes this point most tellingly. Jackson, who like John Jea claimed to have been taught to read by the Lord, wrote in her autobiography that she dreamed that a "white man" came to her house to teach her how to *interpret* and "understand" the word of God, now that God had taught her to read:

> A white man took me by my right hand and led me on the north side of the room, where sat a square table. On it lay a book open. And he said to me, "Thou shall be instructed in this book, from Genesis to Revelations." And then he took me on the west side, where stood a table. And it looked like the first. And said, "Yea, thou shall be instructed from the beginning of creation to the end of time." And then he took me on the east side of the room also, where stood a table and book like the two first, and said, "I will instruct thee— yea, thou shall be instructed from the beginning of all things to the end of all things. Yea, thou shall be well instructed. I will instruct."

★ ★ ★

> And then I awoke, and I saw him as plain as I did in my dream. And after that he taught me daily. And when I would be reading and come to a hard word, I would see him standing by my side and he would teach me the word right. And often, when I would be in meditation and looking into things which was hard to understand, I would find him by me, teaching and giving me understanding. And oh, his labor and care which he had with me often caused me to weep bitterly, when I would see my great ignorance and the great trouble he had to make me understand eternal things. For I was so buried in the depth of the tradition of my forefathers, that it did seem as if I never could be dug up.

In response to Jackson's relation of interpretive indenture to a "white man," Alice Walker, writing in *The Color Purple,* records an exchange between Celie and Shug about turning away from "the old white man," which soon turns into a conversation about the elimination of "man" as a mediator between a woman and "everything":

> . . . You have to git man off your eyeball, before you can see anything a'tall.
> Man corrupt everything, say Shug. He on your box of grits, in your head, and all over the radio. He try to make you think he everywhere. Soon as you think he everywhere, you think he God. But he ain't. Whenever you trying to pray, and man plot himself on the other end of it, tell him to git lost, say Shug.

Celie and Shug's omnipresent "man," of course, echoes the black tradition's epithet for the white power structure, "the man."

For non-Western, so-called noncanonical critics, getting the "man off your eyeball" means using the most sophisticated critical theories and methods generated by the Western tradition to reappropriate and to define our own "colonial" discourses. We must use these theories and methods insofar as these are relevant and applicable to the study of our own literatures. The danger in doing so, however, is best put, again by Anthony Appiah in his definition of what he calls the "Naipaul fallacy": "It is not necessary to show that African literature is fundamentally the same as European literature in order to show that it can be treated with the same tools. . . . Nor should we endorse a more sinister line . . . : the post-colonial legacy which requires us to show that African literature is worthy of study precisely (but only) because it is fundamentally the same as European literature." We *must* not, Appiah concludes, "ask the reader to understand Africa by embedding it in European culture."

We must, of course, analyze the ways in which writing relates to "race," how attitudes toward racial differences generate and structure literary texts by us *and* about us; we must determine how critical methods can effectively disclose the traces of racial difference in literature; but we must also understand how certain forms of difference and the *languages* we employ to define those supposed "differences" not only reinforce each other but tend to create and maintain each other. Similarly, and as importantly, we must analyze the language of contemporary criticism itself, recognizing that hermeneutical systems, especially, are not "universal," "color blind," or "apolitical," or "neutral." Whereas some critics wonder aloud, as Appiah notes, about such matters as whether or not "a structuralist poetics is inapplicable in Africa because structuralism is European," the concern of the "Third World" critic should properly be to understand the ideology subtext which any critical theory reflects and embodies, and what relation this subtext bears to the production of meaning. No critical theory—be that Marxism, feminism, poststructuralism, Nkrumah's consciencism, or whatever—escapes the specificity of value and ideology, no matter how mediated these may be. To attempt to appropriate our own discourses using Western critical theory "uncritically" is to substitute one mode of neocolonialism for another. To begin to do this in my own tradition, theorists have turned to the black vernacular tradition—to paraphrase Rebecca Cox Jackson, to dig into the depths of the tradition of our foreparents—to isolate the signifying black difference through which to theorize about the so-called Discourse of the Other.

Double Take

1. Gates begins this essay with three epigraphs—the quotes at the beginning of the essay. Many authors use epigraphs in writing essays and other kinds of texts. What role do the epigraphs play in this essay? That is, what function do these quotes have in the rest of the essay? In what circumstances and for what occasions would you envision using an epigraph in your own writing?
2. Notice in Part II of "Writing, 'Race,' and the Difference It Makes" that Gates uses the plural pronoun "we" when discussing the kinds of language used in relation to the word "race." What does Gates gain (or even lose) by inviting the audience to be part of this "we"? Why might Gates have aligned himself with his audience in this way while talking about race?
3. Because this essay was likely intended for an academic audience, Gates also selected certain words to address that audience. Frequently we refer to the kinds of words intended for a particular audience as "jargon"—words that convey a disciplinary familiarity. Simply put, because they have special meanings within a particular group. For instance, doctors have their own jargon, as do auto mechanics. Jargon is not intended so much to exclude nonmembers of a community, but to make communication for members more efficient. Turn back to the pages of this essay

and identify 10 words that might be considered jargon. Then rewrite the sentences in which those words appear so that they are accessible to an audience not familiar with the jargon. What kinds of changes did you have to make in the sentences so that they make sense and do not lose any of their meaning? What can you discern from such an exercise about the kinds of choices Gates must have made when writing the original sentences?

4. In this essay Gates addresses the often "controversial" subject of race. Conversations about race can frequently take on heated argumentative rhetoric. Certainly Gates is making an argument here, yet he doesn't yield to the assumptions many might make about an essay on race. What strategies does Gates use to make such an important argument as he does?

At First Glance

The first thing you may notice about "Sunday" is the essay's length, particularly in light of the first essay by Gates reprinted here. While this essay is certainly shorter than many in this collection, it is important to note how cleverly, succinctly, and gracefully Gates is still able to convey a completeness to this essay without leaving readers wanting for more. This essay, despite its brevity, is unquestionably whole. Many writers consider the ability to convey complete narratives within short pieces to be the mark of the most accomplished writers. Think about the defining characteristics of this essay: What makes it complete? Why didn't Gates go into greater detail and explication? Could he have? Should he have? How well do we get to know the narrator in such a short piece? What do we know about the narrator? Do we want to know more?

Sunday

White people couldn't cook; everybody knew that. Which made it a puzzle why such an important part of the civil rights movement had to do with integrating restaurants and lunch counters. The food wasn't any good anyway. Principle of the thing, Daddy's buddy Mr. Ozzie Washington would assert. They don't know nothin' about seasoning, my aunt Marguerite would say. I like my food seasoned, she'd add.

If there is a key to unlocking the culinary secrets of the Coleman family, it is that a slab of fatback or a cupful of bacon drippings or a couple of ham hocks and a long simmering time are absolutely essential to a well-cooked vegetable. Cook it till it's *done*, Mama would say. Cook it till it's dead, we'd learn to say much later. When I first tasted a steamed vegetable, I thought it was raw. The Colemans were serious about their cooking and their eating. There was none of this eating on the run; meals lasted for hours, with lots of good conversation thrown in. The happiest I ever saw my aunts and uncles in the Coleman family was when they'd slowly eat their savory meals, washing everything down with several glasses of iced tea. Especially at the Family Reunion, or on Christmas Day up at Big Mom's house. "Eating good"—with plenty of fat and cholesterol—was held to be essential to proper health and peace of mind.

There were plenty of Colemans: nine brothers—known as "the boys"—and four sisters, the youngest of whom had died when she was a day or two old. (There's enough niggers in your mother's family, Daddy would remark, to cast a Tarzan movie.)

Sunday in Piedmont was everybody's favorite day, because you could eat yourself silly, starting just after church. Mama didn't go to church on Sundays, except to read out her obituaries. She'd cook while we were at Sunday school. Rarely did the menu vary: fried chicken, mashed potatoes, baked corn (corn pudding), green beans and potatoes (with lots of onions and bacon drippings and a hunk of ham), gravy, rolls, and a salad of iceberg lettuce, fresh tomatoes (grown in Uncle Jim's garden), a sliced boiled egg, scallions, and Wishbone's Italian dressing. We'd eat Mama's Sunday dinners in the middle of the day and keep nibbling for the rest of the afternoon and evening. White people just can't cook good, Aunt Marguerite used to say; that's why they need to hire us.

Double Take

1. As we have seen, Gates is deeply interested in issues of race. Even in this short essay, he keys on important issues of race and civil rights. How successful is this as a political essay? Does Gates make a political argument here? How?
2. There are many characters in this essay: Daddy, Daddy's buddy Mr. Ozzie Washington, Aunt Marguerite, Mama, the Colemans (13 of them), aunts and uncles, Big Mom, Uncle Jim, and the narrator. That's at least 21 people appearing in a mere four paragraphs. How is Gates able to create a sense of familiarity with each of these characters in such a short piece? Is it important that he does?
3. What effect does Gates gain by including Daddy's joke in the third paragraph and Aunt Marguerite's joke at the end of the essay? Why do you suppose he's positioned Daddy's joke as a parenthetical and Aunt Marguerite's as the final line in the essay?

At First Glance

Like many of his essays, "In The Kitchen" reflects Gates's close attention to issues of race. Even though this essay is wonderfully personal and a comforting insight to Gates's family life, Gates also uses the opportunity to make strong commentary and critique about issues of race and culture. Notice, for instance, early in the essay the family joke of adding the phrase "a white man told me" to sentences. As you read, note the numbers of times that Gates offers commentary on issues of race as he writes about his family. Take special note of the importance of the title in his commentary and what exactly he means to demarcate with the word "kitchen."

In the Kitchen

We always had a gas stove in the kitchen, though electric cooking became fashionable in Piedmont, like using Crest toothpaste rather than Colgate, or watching Huntley and Brinkley rather than Walter Cronkite. But for us it was gas, Colgate, and good ole Walter Cronkite, come what may. We used gas partly out of loyalty to Big Mom, Mama's mama, because she was mostly blind and still loved to cook, and she could feel her way better with gas than with electric.

But the most important thing about our gas-equipped kitchen was that Mama used to do hair there. She had a "hot comb,"—a fine-toothed iron instrument with a long wooden handle—and a pair of iron curlers that opened and closed like scissors: Mama would put them into the gas fire until they glowed. You could smell those prongs heating up.

I liked what that smell meant for the shape of my day. There was an intimate warmth in the women's tones as they talked with my mama while she did their hair. I knew what the women had been through to get their hair ready to be "done," because I would watch Mama do it to herself. How that scorched kink could be transformed through grease and fire into a magnificent head of wavy hair was a miracle to me. Still is.

Mama would wash her hair over the sink, a towel wrapped round her shoulders, wearing just her half-slip and her white bra. (We had no shower until we moved down Rat Tail Road into Doc Wolverton's house, in 1954.) After she had dried it, she would grease her scalp thoroughly with blue Bergamot hair grease, which came in a short, fat jar with a picture of a beautiful colored lady on it. It's important to grease your scalp real good, my mama would explain, to keep from burning yourself.

Of course, her hair would return to its natural kink almost as soon as the hot water and shampoo hit it. To me, it was another miracle how hair so "straight" would so quickly become kinky again once it even approached some water.

My mama had only a few "clients" whose heads she "did"—and did, I think, because she enjoyed it, rather than for the few dollars it brought in. They would sit on one of our red plastic kitchen chairs, the kind with the shiny metal legs, and brace themselves for the process. Mama would stroke that red-hot iron, which by this time had been in the gas fire for half an hour or more, slowly but firmly through their hair, from scalp to strand's end. It made a scorching, crinkly sound, the hot iron did, as it burned its way through damp kink, leaving in its wake the straightest of hair strands, each of them standing up long and tall but drooping at the end, like the top of a heavy willow tree. Slowly, steadily, with deftness and grace, Mama's hands would transform a round mound of Odetta kink into a darkened swamp of everglades. The Bergamot made the hair shiny; the heat of the hot iron gave it a brownish-red cast. Once all the hair was as straight as God allows kink to get, Mama would take the well-heated curling iron and twirl the straightened strands into more or less loosely wrapped curls. She claimed that she owed her strength and skill as a hairdresser to her wrists, and her little finger would poke out the way it did when she sipped tea. Mama was a southpaw, who wrote upside down and backwards to produce the cleanest, roundest letters you've ever seen.

The "kitchen" she would all but remove from sight with a pair of shears bought for this purpose. Now, the *kitchen* was the room in which we were sitting, the room where Mama did hair and washed clothes, and where each of us bathed in a galvanized tub. But the word has another meaning, and the "kitchen" I'm speaking of now is the very kinky bit of hair at the back of the head, where the neck meets the shirt collar. If there ever was one part of our African past that resisted assimilation, it was the kitchen. No matter how hot the iron, no matter how powerful the chemical, no matter how stringent the mashed-potatoes-and-lye formula of a man's "process," neither God nor woman nor Sammy Davis, Jr., could straighten the kitchen. The kitchen was permanent, irredeemable, invincible kink. Unassimilably African. No matter what you did, no matter how hard you tried, nothing could dekink a person's kitchen. So you trimmed it off as best you could.

When hair had begun to "turn," as they'd say, or return to its natural kinky glory, it was the kitchen that turned first. When the kitchen started creeping up the back of the neck, it was time to get your hair done again. The kitchen around the back, and nappy edges at the temples.

Sometimes, after dark, Mr. Charlie Carroll would come to have his hair done. Mr. Charlie Carroll was very light-complected and had a ruddy nose, the kind of nose that made me think of Edmund Gwenn playing Kris Kringle in *Miracle on 34th Street*. At the beginning, they did it after Rocky and I had gone to sleep. It was only later that we found out he had come to our house so Mama could iron his hair—not with a hot comb and curling iron but with our very own Proctor-Silex steam iron. For some reason, Mr. Charlie would conceal his Frederick Douglass mane under a big white Stetson hat, which I never saw him take off. Except when he came to our house, late at night, to have his hair pressed.

(Later, Daddy would tell us about Mr. Charlie's most prized piece of knowledge, which the man would confide only after his hair had been pressed, as a token of intimacy. "Not many people know this," he'd say in a tone of circumspection, "but George Washington was Abraham Lincoln's daddy." Nodding solemnly, he'd add the clincher: "A white man told me." Though he was in dead earnest, this became a humorous refrain around the house—"a white man told me"—used to punctuate especially preposterous assertions.)

My mother furtively examined my daughters' kitchens whenever we went home for a visit in the early eighties. It became a game between us. I had told her not to do it, because I didn't like the politics it suggested of "good" and "bad" hair. "Good" hair was straight. "Bad" hair was kinky. Even in the late sixties, at the height of Black

Power, most people could not bring themselves to say "bad" for "good" and "good" for "bad." They still said that hair like white hair was "good," even if they encapsulated it in a disclaimer like "what we used to call 'good.'"

Maggie would be seated in her high chair, throwing food this way and that, and Mama would be cooing about how cute it all was, remembering how I used to do the same thing, and wondering whether Maggie's flinging her food with her left hand meant that she was going to be a southpaw too. When my daughter was just about covered with Franco-American SpaghettiOs, Mama would seize the opportunity and wipe her clean, dipping her head, tilted to one side, down under the back of Maggie's neck. Sometimes, if she could get away with it, she'd even rub a curl between her fingers, just to make sure that her bifocals had not deceived her. Then she'd sigh with satisfaction and relief, thankful that her prayers had been answered. No kink . . . yet. "Mama!" I'd shout, pretending to be angry. (Every once in a while, if no one was looking, I'd peek too.)

I say "yet" because most black babies are born with soft, silken hair. Then, sooner or later, it begins to "turn," as inevitably as do the seasons or the leaves on a tree. And if it's meant to turn, it *turns,* no matter how hard you try to stop it. People once thought baby oil would stop it. They were wrong.

Everybody I knew as a child wanted to have good hair. You could be as ugly as homemade sin dipped in misery and still be thought attractive if you had good hair. Jesus Moss was what the girls at Camp Lee, Virginia, had called Daddy's hair during World War II. I know he played that thick head of hair for all it was worth, too. Still would, if he could.

My own hair was "not a bad grade," as barbers would tell me when they cut my head for the first time. It's like a doctor reporting the overall results of the first full physical that he has given you. "You're in good shape" or "Blood pressure's kind of high; better cut down on salt."

I spent much of my childhood and adolescence messing with my hair. I definitely wanted straight hair. Like Pop's.

When I was about three, I tried to stick a wad of Bazooka bubble gum to that straight hair of his. I suppose what fixed that memory for me is the spanking I got for doing so: he turned me upside down, holding me by my feet, the better to paddle my behind. Little *nigger,* he shouted, walloping away. I started to laugh about it two days later, when my behind stopped hurting.

When black people say "straight," of course, they don't usually mean "straight," literally, like, say, the hair of Peggy Lipton (the white girl on *The Mod Squad*) or Mary of Peter, Paul and Mary fame; black people call that "stringy" hair. No, "straight" just means not kinky, no matter what contours the curl might take. Because Daddy had straight hair, I would have done *anything* to have straight hair—and I used to try everything to make it straight, short of getting a process, which only riffraff were dumb enough to do.

Of the wide variety of techniques and methods I came to master in the great and challenging follicle prestidigitation, almost all had two things in common: a heavy, oil-based grease and evenly applied pressure. It's no accident that many of the biggest black companies in the fifties and sixties made hair products. Indeed, we do have a vast array of hair grease. And I have tried it all, in search of that certain silky touch, one that leaves neither the hand nor the pillow sullied by grease.

I always wondered what Frederick Douglass put on *his* hair, or Phillis Wheatley. Or why Wheatley has that rag on her head in the little engraving in the frontispiece of her book. One thing is for sure: you can bet that when Wheatley went to England to see the Countess of Huntington, she did not stop by the Queen's Coiffeur on the way. So many black people still get their hair straightened that it's a wonder we don't have a national holiday for Madame C. J. Walker, who invented the process for straightening kinky hair, rather than for Dr. King. Jheri-curled or "relaxed"—it's still fried hair.

I used all the greases, from sea-blue Bergamot, to creamy vanilla Duke (in its orange-and-white jar), to the godfather of grease, the formidable Murray's. Now, Murray's was some *serious* grease. Whereas Bergamot was like oily Jell-O and Duke was viscous and sickly sweet, Murray's was light brown and *hard*. Hard as lard and twice as greasy, Daddy used to say whenever the subject of Murray's came up. Murray's came in an orange can with a screw-on top. It was so hard that some people would put a match to the can just to soften it and make it more manageable. In the late sixties, when Afros came into style, I'd use Afro-Sheen. From Murray's to Duke to Afro-Sheen: that was my progression in black consciousness.

We started putting hot towels or washrags over our greased-down Murray's-coated heads, in order to melt the wax into the scalp and follicles. Unfortunately, the wax had a curious habit of running down your neck, ears, and forehead. Not to mention your pillowcase.

Another problem was that if you put two palmfuls of Murray's on your head, your hair turned white. Duke did the same thing. It was a challenge: if you got rid of the white stuff, you had a magnificent head of wavy hair. Murray's turned kink into waves. Lots of waves. Frozen waves. A hurricane couldn't have blown those waves around.

That was the beauty of it. Murray's was so hard that it froze your hair into the wavy style you brushed it into. It looked really good if you wore a part. A lot of guys had parts *cut* into their hair by a barber, with clippers or a straight-edge razor. Especially if you had kinky hair—in which case you'd generally wear a short razor cut, or what we called a Quo Vadis.

Being obsessed with our hair, we tried to be as innovative as possible. Everyone knew about using a stocking cap, because your father or your uncle or the older guys wore them whenever something really big was about to happen, secular or sacred, a funeral or a dance, a wedding or a trip in which you confronted official white people, or when you were trying to look really sharp. When it was time to be clean, you wore a stocking cap. If the event was really a big one, you made a new cap for the occasion.

A stocking cap was made by asking your mother for one of her hose, and cutting it with a pair of scissors about six inches or so from the open end, where the elastic goes up to the top of the thigh. Then you'd knot the cut end, and behold—a conical-shaped hat or cap, with an elastic band that you pulled down low on your forehead and down around your neck in the back. A good stocking cap, to work well, had to fit tight and snug, like a press. And it had to fit that tightly because it *was* a press: it pressed your hair with the force of the hose's elastic. If you greased your hair down real good and left the stocking cap on long enough—*violà:* you got a head of pressed-against-the-scalp waves. If you used Murray's, and if you wore a stocking cap to sleep, you got a *whole lot* of waves. (You also got a ring around your forehead when you woke up, but eventually that disappeared.)

And then you could enjoy your concrete 'do. Swore we were bad, too, with all that grease and those flat heads. My brother and I would brush it out a bit in the morning, so it would look—ahem—"natural."

Grown men still wear stocking caps, especially older men, who generally keep their caps in their top drawer, along with their cuff links and their see-through silk socks, their Maverick tie, their silk handkerchief, and whatever else they prize most.

A Murrayed-down stocking cap was the respectable version of the process, which, by contrast, was most definitely not a cool thing to have, at least if you weren't an entertainer by trade.

Zeke and Keith and Poochie and a few other stars of the basketball team all used to get a process once or twice a year. It was expensive, and to get one you had to go to Pittsburgh or D.C. or Uniontown, someplace where there were enough colored people to support a business. They'd disappear, then reappear a day or two later, strutting like peacocks, their hair burned slightly red from the chemical lye base. They'd also wear "rags" or cloths or handkerchiefs around it when they slept or played basketball. Do-rags, they were called. But the result was *straight* hair, with a hint of wave. No curl. Do-it-yourselfers took their chances at home with a concoction of mashed potatoes and lye.

The most famous process, outside of what Malcolm X describes in his *Autobiography* and maybe that of Sammy Davis, Jr., was Nat King Cole's. Nat King Cole had patent-leather hair.

"That man's got the finest process money can buy." That's what Daddy said the night Cole's TV show aired on NBC, November 5, 1956. I remember the date because everyone came to our house to watch it and to celebrate one of Daddy's buddies' birthdays. Yeah, Uncle Joe chimed in, they can do shit to his hair that the average Negro can't even *think* about—secret shit.

Nat King Cole was *clean*. I've had an ongoing argument with a Nigerian friend about Nat King Cole for twenty years now. Not whether or not he could sing, any fool knows that he could sing. But whether or not he was a handkerchief-head for wearing that patent-leather process.

Sammy Davis's process I detested. It didn't look good on him. Worse still, he liked to have a fried strand dangling down the middle of his forehead, shaking it out from the crown when he sang. But Nat King Cole's hair was a thing unto itself, a beautifully sculpted work of art that he and he alone should have had the right to wear.

The only difference between a process and a stocking cap, really, was taste; yet Nat King Cole—unlike, say, Michael Jackson—looked *good* in his process. His head looked like Rudolph Valentino's in the twenties, and some say it was Valentino that the process imitated. But Nat King Cole wore a process because it suited his face, his demeanor, his name, his style. He was as clean as he wanted to be.

I had forgotten all about Nat King Cole and that patent-leather look until the day in 1971 when I was sitting in an Arab restaurant on the island of Zanzibar, surrounded by men in fezzes and white caftans, trying to learn how to eat curried goat and rice with the fingers of my right hand, feeling two million miles from home, when all of a sudden the old transistor radio sitting on top of a china cupboard stopped blaring out its Swahili music to play "Fly Me to the Moon" by Nat King Cole. The restaurant's din was not affected at all, not even by half a decibel. But in my mind's eye, I saw it: the King's sleek black magnificent tiara. I managed, barely, to blink back the tears.

Double Take

1. In his essay "In the Kitchen," Henry Louis Gates, Jr. relates his history of trying to make his hair straight. While this is an interesting and sometimes amusing auto-biographical account, Gates uses this story to make larger political points about why African Americans like him wanted straight hair. What effect does Gates gain by couching his ideas about race in such a memorable narrative? Could he have made the same point without the discussion of hair straightening? And what effect would that have had?

2. After Gates has discussed his own hair-straightening processes and some of the other processes that were popular, he writes about the processes used by two famous African-American entertainers: Nat King Cole and Sammy Davis, Jr. Why do you suppose Gates writes about these two men? That is, what point is he trying to make by identifying that famous entertainers engaged in the same quest for straight hair as did Gates and his friends and family? Why did Gates wait until the end of this essay to make this point?

3. Within "In the Kitchen," Gates makes several references to the kinds of language used to describe hair and the processes of straightening it. By recounting these terms, what might Gates be suggesting about the role of language in daily life? By labeling some kinds of hair as "good" and others as "bad," is Gates perhaps suggesting that more than hair is being assigned value? What might be his reason for making such references in this essay?

Seeing for Yourself

At First Glance

Like the other essays by Gates gathered here, "Prime Time" also addresses issues of race and does so through a nostalgic autobiographical narrative. In this essay, however, Gates addresses integration and the relationships between African Americans and white Americans. He addresses these relationships in terms of personal experience, the politics of desegregation, and television entertainment. As you read this essay, consider not only how important the media have been in shaping contemporary views of race and politics, but how Gates writes about television and radio. Note, for instance, the nostalgia conveyed about old TV and radio shows, but also note how he positions this nostalgia in a larger political statement.

Prime Time

I guess some chafed more than others against the mundane impediments of the color line. "It's no disgrace to be colored," the black entertainer Bert Williams famously observed early in this century, "but it is awfully inconvenient." For most of my childhood, we couldn't eat in restaurants or sleep in hotels, we couldn't use certain bathrooms or try on clothes in stores. Mama insisted that we dress up when we went to shop. She was a fashion plate when she went to clothing stores, and wore white pads called shields under her arms so her dress or blouse would show no sweat. We'd like to try this on, she'd say carefully, articulating her words precisely and properly. We don't buy clothes we can't try on, she'd say when they declined, as we'd walk, in Mama's dignified manner, out of the store. She preferred to shop where we had an account and where everyone knew who she was.

As for me, I hated the fact that we couldn't sit down in the Cut-Rate. No one colored was allowed to, with one exception: my father. It was as if there were a permanent TAKE-AWAY ONLY sign for colored people. You were supposed to stand at the counter, get your food to go, and leave. I don't know for certain why Carl Dadisman, the proprietor, wouldn't stop Daddy from sitting down. But I believe it was in part because Daddy was so light-complected, and in part because, during his shift at the phone company, he picked up orders for food and coffee for the operators, and Dadisman relied on that business. At the time, I never wondered if it occurred to Daddy not to sit down at the Cut-Rate when neither his wife nor his two children were allowed to, although now that I am a parent myself, the strangeness of it crosses my mind on occasion.

239

Even when we were with Daddy, you see, we had to stand at the counter and order takeout, then eat on white paper plates using plastic spoons, sipping our vanilla rickeys from green-and-white paper cups through plastic flexible-end straws. Even after basketball games, when Young Doc Bess would set up the team with free Cokes after one of the team's many victories, the colored players had to stand around and drink out of paper cups while the white players and cheerleaders sat down in the red Naugahyde booths and drank out of glasses. Integrate? I'll shut it down first, Carl Dadisman had vowed. He was an odd-looking man, with a Humpty-Dumpty sort of head and bottom, and weighing four or five hundred pounds. He ran the taxi service, too, and was just as nice as he could be, even to colored people. But he did not want us sitting in his booths, eating off his plates and silverware, putting our thick greasy lips all over his glasses. He'd retire first, or die.

He had a heart attack one day while sitting in the tiny toilet at his place of business. Daddy and some other men tried to lift him up, while he was screaming and gasping and clutching his chest, but he was stuck in that cramped space. They called the rescue squad at the Fire Department. Lowell Taylor and Pat Amoroso came. Lowell was black and was the star of the soccer team at the high school across the river in Westernport. He looked like Pele, down to the shape of his head.

They sawed and sawed and sawed, while the ambulance and the rescue squad sat outside on Third Street, blocking the driveway to the town's parking lot. After a while, Carl Dadisman's cries and moans became quieter and quieter. Finally, they wedged in a couple of two-by-fours and dragged out his lifeless body. By then it made little difference to Carl that Lowell was black.

Maybe Carl never understood that the racial dispensation he took for granted was coming to an end. As a child, I must once have assumed that this dispensation could no more be contested than the laws of gravity, or traffic lights. And I'm not sure when I realized otherwise.

I know that I had rich acquaintance early on with the inconveniences to which Bert Williams alluded. But segregation had some advantages, like the picnic lunch Mama would make for the five-hour train ride on the National Limited to Parkersburg, where you had to catch the bus down to the state capital, Charleston, to visit her sister Loretta. So what if we didn't feel comfortable eating in the dining car? Our food was better. Fried chicken, baked beans, and potato salad . . . a book and two decks of cards . . . and I didn't care if the train ever got there. We'd sing or read in our own section, munching that food and feeling sorry for the people who couldn't get any, and play 500 or Tonk or Fish with Mama and Daddy, until we fell asleep.

The simple truth is that the civil rights era came late to Piedmont, even though it came early to our television set. We could watch what was going on Elsewhere on television, but the marches and sit-ins were as remote to us as, in other ways, was the all-colored world of *Amos and Andy*—a world full of black lawyers, black judges, black nurses, black doctors.

Politics aside, though, we were starved for images of ourselves and searched TV to find them. Everybody, of course, watched sports, because Piedmont was a big sports town. Making the big leagues was like getting to Heaven, and everybody had hopes that they could, or a relative could. We'd watch the games day and night, and listen on radio to what we couldn't see. Everybody knew the latest scores, batting averages, rbi's, and stolen bases. Everybody knew the standings in the leagues, who could still win the pennant and how. Everybody liked the Dodgers because of Jackie Robinson, the same way everybody still voted Republican because of Abraham Lincoln. Sports on the mind, sports in the mind. The only thing to rival the Valley in fascination was the big-league baseball diamond.

I once hear Mr. James Helms say, "You got to give the white man his due when it comes to technology. One on one, though, and it's even-steven. Joe Louis showed 'em that." We were obsessed with sports in part because it was the only time we could compete with white people even-steven. And the white people, it often seemed, were just as obsessed with this primal confrontation between the races as we were. I think they integrated professional sports, after all those years of segregation, just to capitalize on this voyeuristic thrill of the forbidden contact. What interracial sex was to the seventies, interracial sports were to the fifties. Except for sports, we rarely saw a colored person on TV.

Actually, I first got to know white people as "people" through their flickering images on television shows. It was the television set that brought us together at night, and the television set that brought in the world outside the Valley. We were close enough to Washington to receive its twelve channels on cable. Piedmont was transformed from a radio culture to one with the fullest range of television, literally overnight. During my first-grade year, we'd watch *Superman, Lassie,* Jack Benny, Danny Thomas, *Robin Hood, I Love Lucy, December Bride,* Nat King Cole (of course), *Wyatt Earp, Broken Arrow,* Phil Silvers, Red Skelton, *The $64,000 Question, Ozzie and Harriet, The Millionaire, Father Knows Best, The Lone Ranger,* Bob Cummings, *Dragnet, The People's Choice, Rin Tin Tin, Jim Bowie, Gunsmoke, My Friend Flicka, The Life of Riley, Topper, Dick Powell's Zane Grey Theater, Circus Boy,* and Loretta Young—all in prime time. My favorites were *The Life of Riley,* in part because he worked in a factory like Daddy did, and *Ozzie and Harriet,* in part because Ozzie never seemed to work at all. A year later, however, *Leave It to Beaver* swept most of the others away.

With a show like *Topper,* I felt as if I was getting a glimpse, at last, of the life that Mrs. Hudson, and Mrs. Thomas, and Mrs. Campbell, must be leading in their big mansions on East Hampshire Street. Smoking jackets and cravats, spats and canes, elegant garden parties and martinis. People who wore suits to eat dinner! This was a world so elegantly distant from ours, it was like a voyage to another galaxy, light-years away.

Leave It to Beaver, on the other hand, was a world much closer, but just out of reach nonetheless. Beaver's street was where we wanted to live, Beaver's house where we wanted to eat and sleep, Beaver's father's firm where we'd have liked Daddy to work. These shows for us were about property, the property that white people could own and that we couldn't. About a level of comfort and ease at which we could only wonder. It was the world that the integrated school was going to prepare us to enter and that, for Mama, would be the prize.

If prime time consisted of images of middle-class white people who looked nothing at all like us, late night was about the radio, listening to *Randy's Record Shop* from Gallatin, Tennessee. My brother, Rocky, kept a transistor radio by his bed, and he'd listen to it all night, for all I knew, long after I'd fallen asleep. In 1956, black music hadn't yet broken down into its many subgenres, except for large divisions such as jazz, blues, gospel, rhythm and blues. On *Randy's*, you were as likely to hear The Platters doing "The Great Pretender" and Clyde McPhatter doing "Treasure of Love" as you were to hear Howlin' Wolf do "Smokestack Lightning" or Joe Turner do "Corrine, Corrine." My own favorite that year was the slow, deliberate sound of Jesse Belvin's "Goodnight, My Love." I used to fall asleep singing it in my mind to my Uncle Earkie's girlfriend, Ula, who was a sweet caffè latté brown, with the blackest, shiniest straight hair and the fullest, most rounded red lips. Not even in your dreams, he had said to me one day, as I watched her red dress slink down our front stairs. It was my first brush with the sublime.

We use to laugh at the way the disc jockey sang "Black Strap Lax-a-teeves" during the commercials. I sometimes would wonder if the kids we'd seen on TV in Little Rock or Birmingham earlier in the evening were singing themselves to sleep with *their* Ulas.

Lord knows, we weren't going to learn how to be colored by watching television. Seeing somebody colored on TV was an event.

"Colored, colored, on Channel Two," you'd hear someone shout. Somebody else would run to the phone, while yet another hit the front porch, telling all the neighbors where to see it. And *everybody* loved *Amos and Andy*—I don't care what people say today. For the colored people, the day they took *Amos and Andy* off the air was one of the saddest days in Piedmont, about as sad as the day of the last mill pic-a-nic.

What was special to us about *Amos and Andy* was that their world was *all* colored, just like ours. Of course, *they* had their colored judges and lawyers and doctors and nurses, which we could only dream about having, or becoming—and we *did* dream about those things. Kingfish ate his soft-boiled eggs delicately, out of an egg cup. He even owned an acre of land in Westchester County, which he sold to Andy, using the facade of a movie set to fake a mansion. As far as we were concerned, the foibles of Kingfish or Calhoun the lawyer were the foibles of individuals who happened to be funny. Nobody was likely to confuse them with the colored people we knew, no more than we'd confuse ourselves with the entertainers and athletes we saw on TV or in *Ebony* or *Jet,* the magazines we devoured to keep up with what was happening with the race. And people took special relish in Kingfish's malapropisms. "I denies the allegation, Your Honor, and I resents the alligator."

In one of my favorite episodes of *Amos and Andy*, "The Punjab of Java-Pour," Andy Brown is hired to advertise a brand of coffee and is required to dress up as a turbaned Oriental potentate. Kingfish gets the bright idea that if he dresses up as a potentate's servant, the two of them can enjoy a vacation at a luxury hotel for free. So attired, the two promenade around the lobby, running up an enormous tab and generously dispensing "rubies" and "diamonds" as tips. The plan goes awry when people try to redeem the gems and discover them to be colored glass. It was widely suspected that this episode was what prompted two Negroes in Baltimore to dress like African princes and demand service in a segregated four-star restaurant. Once it was clear to the management that these were not American Negroes, the two were treated royally. When the two left the restaurant, they took off their African headdresses and robes and enjoyed a hearty laugh at the restaurant's expense. "They weren't like our Negroes," the maître d' told the press in explaining why he had agreed to seat the two "African princes."

Whenever the movies *Imitation of Life* and *The Green Pastures* would be shown on TV, we watched with similar hunger—especially *Imitation of Life*. It was never on early; only the late *late* show, like the performances of Cab Calloway and Duke Ellington at the Crystal Palace. And we'd stay up. Everybody colored. The men coming home on second shift from the paper mill would stay up. Those who had to go out on the day shift and who normally would have been in bed hours earlier (because they had to be at work at 6:30) would stay up. As would we, the kids, wired for the ritual at hand. And we'd all sit in silence, fighting back the tears, watching as Delilah invents the world's greatest pancakes and a down-and-out Ned Sparks takes one taste and says, flatly, "We'll box it." Cut to a big white house, plenty of money, and Delilah saying that she doesn't want her share of the money (which should have been *all* the money); she just wants to continue to cook, clean, wash, iron, and serve her good white lady and her daughter. (Nobody in our living room was going for *that*.) And then Deliliah shows up at her light-complected daughter's school one day, unexpectedly, to pick her up, and there's the daughter, Peola, ducking down behind her books, and the white teacher saying, "I'm sorry, ma'am, there must be some mistake. We have no little colored children here." And then Delilah, spying her baby, says, "Oh, yes you do. Peola! Peola! Come here to your mammy, honey chile." And then Peola runs out of the room, breaking her poor, sweet mother's heart. And Peola continues to break her mother's heart, by passing, leaving the race, and marrying white. Yet her mama understands, always understands, and, dying, makes detailed plans for her own big, beautiful funeral, complete with six white horses and a carriage and a jazz band, New Orleans style. And she dies and is about to be buried, when, out of nowhere, comes grown-up Peola, saying, "Don't die, Mama, don't die, Mama, I'm sorry, Mama, I'm sorry," and throws her light-and-bright-and-damn-near-white self onto her mama's casket. By this time, we have stopped trying to fight back the tears and are boo-hooing all over the place. Then we turn to our *own* mama and tell her how much we love her and swear that we will *never, ever* pass for white. I promise, Mama. I promise.

Peola had sold her soul to the Devil. This was the first popular Faust in the black tradition, the bargain with the Devil over the cultural soul. Talk about a cautionary tale.

The Green Pastures was an altogether more uplifting view of things, our Afro Paradiso. Make way for the Lawd! Make way for the Lawd! And Rex Ingram, dressed in a long black frock coat and a long white beard, comes walking down the Streets Paved with Gold, past the Pearly Gates, while Negroes with the whitest wings of fluffy cotton fly around Heaven, playing harps, singing spirituals, having fish fries, and eating watermelon. Hard as I try, I can't stop seeing God as that black man who played Him in *The Green Pastures* and seeing Noah as Rochester from the Jack Benny show, trying to bargain with God to let him take along an extra keg of wine or two.

Civil rights took us all by surprise. Every night we'd wait until the news to see what "Dr. King and dem" were doing. It was like watching the Olympics or the World Series when somebody colored was on. The murder of Emmett Till was one of my first memories. He whistled at some white girl, they said; that's all he did. He was beat so bad they didn't even want to open the casket, but his mama made them. She wanted the world to see what they had done to her baby.

In 1957, when I was in second grade, black children integrated Central High School in Little Rock, Arkansas. We watched it on TV. All of us watched it. I don't mean Mama and Daddy and Rocky. I mean *all* the colored people in America watched it, together, with one set of eyes. We'd watch it in the morning, on the *Today* show on NBC, before we'd go to school; we'd watch it in the evening, on the news, with Edward R. Murrow on CBS. We'd watch the Special Bulletins at night, interrupting our TV shows.

The children were all well scrubbed and greased down, as we'd say. Hair short and closely cropped, parted, and oiled (the boys); "done" in a "permanent" and straightened, with turned-up bangs and curls (the girls). Starched shirts, white, and creased pants, shoes shining like a buck private's spit shine. Those Negroes were *clean*. The fact was, those children trying to get the right to enter that school in Little Rock looked like black versions of models out of *Jack & Jill* magazine, to which my mama had subscribed for me so that I could see what children outside the Valley were up to. "They hand-picked those children," Daddy would say. "No dummies, no nappy hair, heads not too kinky, lips not too thick, no disses and no dats." At seven, I was dismayed by his cynicism. It bothered me somehow that those children would have been chosen, rather than just having shown up or volunteered or been nearby in the neighborhood.

Daddy was jaundiced about the civil rights movement, and especially about the Reverend Dr. Martin Luther King, Jr. He'd say all of his names, to drag out his scorn. By the mid-sixties, we'd argue about King from sunup to sundown. Sometimes he'd just mention King to get a rise from me, to make a sagging evening more interesting, to see if I had *learned* anything real yet, to see how long I could think up counter arguments before getting so mad that my face would turn purple. I think he just liked the color purple on my face, liked producing it there. But he was not of two minds about those children in Little Rock.

The children would get off their school bus surrounded by soldiers from the National Guard and by a field of state police. They would stop at the steps of the bus and seem to take a very deep breath. Then the phalanx would start to move slowly along this gulley of sidewalk and rednecks that connected the steps of the school bus with the white wooden double doors of the school. All kinds of crackers would be lining that gulley, separated from the phalanx of children by rows of state police, who formed a barrier arm in arm. Cheerleaders from the all-white high school that was desperately trying to stay that way were dressed in those funny little pleated skirts, with a big red *C* for "Central" on their chests, and they'd wave their pom-poms and start to cheer: "Two, four, six, eight—We don't want to integrate!" And all those crackers and all those rednecks would join in that chant as if their lives depended on it. Deafening, it was: even on our twelve-inch TV, a three-inch speaker buried along the back of its left side.

The TV was the ritual arena for the drama of race. In our family, it was located in the living room, where it functioned like a fireplace in the proverbial New England winter. I'd sit in the water in the galvanized tub in the middle of our kitchen, watching the TV in the next room while Mama did the laundry or some other chore as she waited for Daddy to come home from his second job. We watched people getting hosed and cracked over their heads, people being spat upon and arrested, rednecks siccing fierce dogs on women and children, our people responding by singing and marching and staying strong. Eyes on the prize. Eyes on the prize. George Wallace at the gate of the University of Alabama, blocking Autherine Lucy's way. Charlayne Hunter at the University of Georgia. President Kennedy interrupting our scheduled program with a special address, saying that James Meredith will *definitely* enter the University of Mississippi; and saying it like he believed it (unlike Ike), saying it like the big kids said "It's our turn to play" on the basketball court and walking all through us as if we weren't there.

Whatever tumult our small screen revealed, though, the dawn of the civil rights era could be no more than a spectator sport in Piedmont. It was almost like a war being fought overseas. And all things considered, white and colored Piedmont got along pretty well in those years, the fifties and early sixties. At least as long as colored people didn't try to sit down in the Cut-Rate or at the Rendezvous Bar, or eat pizza at Eddie's, or buy property, or move into the white neighborhoods, or dance with, date, or dilate upon white people. Not to mention try to get a job in the craft unions at the paper mill. Or have a drink at the white VFW, or join the white American Legion, or get loans at the bank, or just generally get out of line. Other than that, colored and white got on pretty well.

A CLOSER LOOK AT HENRY LOUIS GATES, JR.

1. As we mentioned in the introduction to this writer-chapter, the writing of Henry Louis Gates, Jr., often addresses issues of race and African-American culture. In many ways Gates makes use of the essay form to convey important political critique, as do many essay authors in this collection and others. Why do you suppose the essay is such a popular contemporary form for discussing issues like race or other political subjects? How does the essay help readers better situate and work through their own thinking about such issues? In an essay of your own, address how and why the contemporary essay is a

useful genre for addressing political topics. Consider specifically what an essay must do to be effective as a conveyor of political thought.

2. In three of the essays, Gates provides autobiographical anecdotes as bases for his essays. Consider what role the personal anecdote has in these essays. Do you find these moments of the essays to be effective? Why or why not? Would you consider the last three essays to be "personal essays" because they contain personal moments from Gates's life? Or are they intended to be read, not as personal essays, but as political essays instead? What differences can you identify between personal and political essays, or are they the same thing? Write an essay that describes how Gates uses references to his personal life in his writing. Cite examples from the essays found here, and also discuss why Gates might have decided to include personal anecdotes in the way he has.

3. While Gates has a reputation as an important and accomplished essay writer— critics do not often comment on his ability as a storyteller—yet his essays contain elements of stories that often bind the essays together. What effect is gained in blending storytelling and essay writing? Is there a difference? How might you make use of telling a story within the structure of an essay you are writing? Write an essay that explains the role of storytelling in essay writing. Turn to Gates's own work to support your argument.

Looking from Writer to Writer

1. Many of the essays in this collection deal with political or sometimes "controversial" issues, such as Gates's frequent address of issues of race. For instance, André Aciman writes about how Jewish identity is defined within Alexandria, Egypt. Compare the ways that Aciman remembers issues about his cultural identity as a boy in Egypt with the ways that Gates writes about his childhood.

2. In "Writing, 'Race,' and the Difference It Makes," Henry Louis Gates, Jr. seems to be addressing a more academic audience than a larger public audience. Edward O. Wilson's essay "Ethics and Religion" also seems to address a more academic audience. Consider both essays and think, first, about what makes them more "academic." Then consider the subject matter of each essay. Are there ways that Wilson and Gates could have written about race and writing or ethics and religion that would be more accessible to a wider audience? How might these essays be reconfigured to make the same points and arguments but be directed toward a nonacademic audience?

3. Like Gates, Jamaica Kincaid's work relies heavily on personal anecdotes. Turn to Kincaid's essays collected here and compare the ways that she uses personal anecdotes to those of Gates. What do you notice about how each uses anecdotes in his or her writing? Do you like how one uses anecdotes better than the other? Why?

Looking Beyond

SELECTED ESSAYS

"Being, the Will, and the Semantics of Death: Wole Soyinka's Death and the King's Horseman." *Harvard Educational Review* 51 (February 1981): 163–173.

"James Gronniosaw and the Trope of the Talking Book." *Southern Review* 22 (April 1986): 252–272.

"On 'The Blackness of Blackness': A Critique of the Sign and the Signifying Monkey." *Critical Inquiry* 9 (June 1983): 685–723.

"Wole Soyinka: Writing, Africa and Politics." *New York Times Book Review,* June 23, 1985, 1, 28–29.

ESSAYS

Loose Canons: Notes on the Culture Wars. New York: Oxford University Press, 1992.

NONFICTION

Colored People: A Memoir. New York: Knopf, 1994.

Figures in Black: Words, Signs, and the "Racial Self." New York: Oxford University Press, 1987.

The Future of the Race (with Cornell West). New York: Vintage Books, 1996.

The Signifying Monkey: Towards a Theory of Afro-American Literary Criticism. New York: Oxford University Press, 1988.

Speaking of Race: Hate Speech, Civil Rights, and Civil Liberties. New York: New York University Press, 1994.

Thirteen Ways of Looking at a Black Man. New York: Random House, 1997.

Stephen Jay Gould

Stephen Jay Gould, a professor of geology and zoology at Harvard University and curator for invertebrate paleontology at Harvard's Museum of Comparative Zoology, grew up in New York City, where he was born in 1941. He completed his undergraduate work at Antioch College, a liberal arts college, and received his PhD at Columbia University. Although he taught courses in geology and the history of science, Gould's specializations were paleontology (a branch of geology that studies fossils) and evolutionary biology. In 1972, in his early thirties, Gould, along with Niles Eldredge, published his theory of punctuated equilibrium, a theory that revised Charles Darwin's theory of evolution by reinterpreting the fossil record to show that evolution is not a gradual process, but rather occurs through bursts of change interspersed between periods of stability. Until his untimely death in 2002, Gould was one of the world's leading evolutionary biologists.

It is as a writer, especially an essayist, however, that Gould achieved his greatest popularity. He was one of only a handful of scientists who were able to achieve fame both in their profession and in the public. This made him a true "public intellectual" able to articulate and make accessible the specialized work in the sciences to nonscientists without compromising its complexity—without, as Gould put it, any "dumbing down of ideas." As a result, Gould used his scientific knowledge, accessibility, and public presence to challenge cultural (and often racist) assumptions and to promote social awareness about such issues as IQ testing. In the battles between creation and evolution, Gould also fought against teaching creationism in schools and identified himself as "a card-carrying member of the guild of evolutionists." Indeed, Gould's work sought to debunk a great many creation myths, attempts on the part of human beings to explain the origin of things through myths about their beginnings. As he wrote about various subjects, from baseball to the evolution of horses and land snails, he shed scientific light on them while at the same time treating them humanistically—that is, by paying attention to how these subjects affect and are affected by culture and human activities and relations. This is why he often referred to himself as a "humanistic naturalist," someone who is "enthused by nature's constitution, but even more fascinated by trying to grasp how an odd and excessively fragile instrument—the human mind—comes to know this world outside, and how the contingent history of the human body, personality, and society impact the pathways to this knowledge."

This combination of humanism and naturalism, of art and nature, defines Gould's essays. Gould stumbled into essay writing unexpectedly. In 1973 the editor of *Natural History* magazine asked Gould if he would write monthly columns, and Gould agreed to write 3 or 4. These 3 or 4 columns turned into 300 as Gould continued to write for *Natural History* an essay every month (not missing a single deadline) for the next 27 years, culminating in the millennial issue, January 2001. (Gould likened this feat to that of his personal hero, Joe DiMaggio who had a record-setting 56-game hitting streak.) Gould began his essay-writing career with two precepts: to treat his subject matter in all its conceptual richness and to use what he termed a "humanistic bridge" to connect readers to the world of science. And indeed, these precepts are evident in his body of work. In his essay about baseball, "The Creation Myths of Cooperstown," for example, Gould showed how the evolution of baseball parallels in interesting ways the evolution of biological species, thereby demonstrating how science and culture inform each other. Many of Gould's essays, like essays in general, use details as a springboard to discuss issues and subjects of much larger scope. In his essay on Columbus, for example, Gould described how the small land snail, *Cerion,* enables us to shed light on the cycle of human history. Gould explained that his essays often begin "with something small and curious and then [work] outward and onward by a network of lateral connections." As you read the essays that follow, pay attention to how Gould performs these connections in his writing.

Gould is the author of over 15 books, the most recent of which was *The Lying Stones of Marrakech,* a collection of essays. He also published books on theories of evolution, IQ testing, cultural ideas about progress, geology, and paleontology. For his work, Gould received numerous awards, among them the National Book Critics Circle Award, the National Magazine Award, the American Book Award for Science, and the Science Book Prize. He also was named Scientist of the Year by *Discover* magazine and was voted Humanist Laureate for his contribution to the humanities. What made Gould's writing so popular is not only its insight into the nature of things, but its accessibility. His essays in particular allowed countless readers (whom he called "perceptive and intelligent laypersons") "to graph nature's richness and add to a lifetime of understanding." While reading his essays, consider whether or not you are the reader Gould had in mind. Also, reflect on how Gould made his essays accessible—what strategies he used to take complex ideas from science and make them intelligible to nonscientists. All the while, think about how you can use some of these strategies to make your own writing more intelligible.

Gould on Writing

At First Glance

"Pieces of Eight" serves as the introduction to Gould's 1998 essay collection, Leonardo's Mountain of Clams and the Diet of Worms. *In it, Gould explains how he began writing essays and describes some of the essays that appear in the collection. As you read, pay specific attention to how Gould defines essay writing and what he means when he describes himself as a "Humanistic Naturalist." Most of all, look carefully at the list of four research and writing strategies Gould describes and consider how you might be able to utilize some of these strategies in your own writing.*

Pieces of Eight: Confession of a Humanistic Naturalist

I can easily understand why, for most naturalists, the highest form of beauty, inspiration, and moral value might be imputed to increasingly rare patches of true wilderness—that is, to parcels of nature devoid of any human presence, either in current person or by previous incursion. When we recognize that all but the last geological eyeblink of life's history evolved in competence and fascination (but to whose notice?) before humans intruded upon the scene—and when we acknowledge that most of our substantial incursions cannot be viewed as fortunate either for local organisms or environments—why should we not glory in bits of space that have perpetuated a 4.5-billion-year tradition of noninterference by any self-conscious agency? (As I do not wish to engage the theological dimensions of the last sentence, I will restrict my meaning to overt "footprints" of undeniable physical presence.)

I do have a confession to make in this context. My odd attitude may arise only from the happenstance of my birth and happy childhood in New York City, when safe subways cost a nickel, museums were free, and the Yankees, led by Joe DiMaggio, ruled the world. Wordsworth's wisdom cannot be gainsaid. Childhood's sense of wonder cannot be sustained in the same manner through life, but the child is father to the man. So childhood's "splendor in the grass" and "glory in the flower" must set a lifelong prototype for aesthetic wonder. And my early epiphanic moments included the view of Lower Manhattan's buildings at sunset, seen from the magnificent walkway in the center of the Brooklyn Bridge; the growing tip of Manhattan as the Staten Island Ferry (also only a nickel) passes the Statue of Liberty and heads for the Battery; the lobbies of the Woolworth and Chrysler buildings (each, in turn and temporarily, the tallest skyscraper in the world); and the building line of the surrounding city, seen in winter from the middle of Central Park through bare tree branches.

I am not speaking here, by absurd dichotomy, of city versus wilderness, with a personal preference for the former based on accidents of upbringing. Rather, the dichotomy itself has no meaning, if only because "pure" examples of either extreme scarcely exist when plastic flotsam pervades the seas, and twisted jetsam washes up on the beaches of every isolated and uninhabited Pacific island; and when almost every spot perceived with rapture as "virgin" wilderness (at least here in northeastern America) really represents old farmland reclaimed by new forest. No satanic "purity" marks the other end either, except in science fiction scenarios. We do not build cities without parks, streets without trees, homes without gardens. At a bare minimum, bits of nature's diversity still burst through, if only as rats by the garbage piles, cockroaches in the kitchen, mushrooms through the pavement, weeds galore in the lot, and bacteria everywhere—to cite all major kingdoms of life in the big city.

For whatever reasons of childhood's happenstances and gifts of temperament, I am a humanist at heart, and I love, best of all, the sensitive and intelligent conjunction of art and nature—not the domination of one by the other. We want, in our wondrously diverse world, a full spectrum of interactions from near wilderness to near artificiality, but I will seek my own aesthetic optimum right in the middle, where human activity has tweaked or shaped a landscape, but with such respect and integration that a first glance may detect no fault line, no obvious partitioning: the wooded hillslope adjoining Kiyomizudera in Kyoto, where the gorgeous scene looks so perfectly "rustic" and untouched until you realize that every tree has been selected, pruned, and trained; the genius of Olmsted's big city parks, with their sculpted diversity of "natural" landscapes crisscrossed by a respectful system of constructed pathways, built of local stones artificially rusticated if necessary; the smooth transition between a Chinese "scholar's rock" (selected for calming contemplation based on the fortune of naturally formed beauty, but usually sculpted a bit to enhance the appearance), and the wooden stand expressly carved to accommodate every random bump and crevice of the stone above; and the Hopi pueblo towns, built of local rocks as a layer on the tops of mesas made of horizontal strata, so that the town, from a distance, can hardly be distinguished from the natural layers below, a village marked as a human construction only by vertical ladders protruding from the tops of kivas.

I even believe—though I would not push the point, for the concept can too easily cede to human arrogance and a discounting of natural forms—that intelligent reconstruction can "improve" upon natural design (though only by the criterion of human aesthetic preference, the most parochial of all possible judgments). I do ally myself with the most famous quatrain of Omar Khayyám's *Rubáiyát* (in FitzGerald's Victorian version), a passage usually misinterpreted today because the subjunctive mood has virtually disappeared from modern English:

A Book of Verses underneath the Bough,
A Jug of Wine, a Loaf of Bread—and Thou
Beside me singing in the Wilderness—
Oh, Wilderness were Paradise enow!

That is, if you would join me in the wilderness, and we could share good reading, food, drink (and perhaps more), then even the ugly, scary, untamed forest would become a paradise, literally a lovely *enclosed and cultivated garden.* (The old subjunctive of the last line must be read: "Even wilderness *would be* close enough to paradise" if you and all the accoutrements would join me there.) After all, in many cultures, wilderness (with an etymology of "wild beast") denotes fear and foreignness, while human cultivation tames a landscape to beauty and peace of soul. (I also love the old legend—maybe it's even true—that Eugene O'Neill changed Omar's last line to "Ah, Wilderness!" so that the title for his marvelous coming-of-age play would appear first in *The New York Times*'s alphabetical list of Broadway shows.)

I make this humanistic confession (or profession, really) because I have tried, in the prefaces to each of my essay volumes (this is the eighth in a series that will reach ten before the millennium calls a halt), to figure out how the present effort differs from (and, I hope, builds upon) the varying themes of preceding books. I began with emphasis on evolutionary basics, proceeded to evolutionary implications, social and philosophical usages, the interaction of predictive rules with contingent history to form the unique and surprising patterns of life's history, and the interaction of human history with natural environments.

This eighth volume, as usual, includes all these themes, but differs in emphasis primarily in my own increasing comfort with my unconventional approach to "natural history" writing, as outlined above. If any overarching theme pervades this body of writing (now standing at 270 successive monthly essays), I suppose that a groping effort toward the formulation of a humanistic natural history must unite the disparity. I think that I have been reluctant to recognize, address, or even admit this feature, either to myself or to my readers, because such an approach does contravene a deep (and usually unstated) convention in writing about nature. We are supposed to love nature for itself, and we are, therefore, presumably charged with the task of characterizing and interpreting nature (as she is) so that interested people with less expertise can learn new information and draw appropriate messages, both factual and ethical. Well, I do love nature—as fiercely as anyone who has ever taken up a pen in her service. But I am even more fascinated by the complex level of analysis just above and beyond (and I do mean "abstracted from," not "better than")—that is, the history of how humans have learned to study and understand nature. I am primarily a "humanistic naturalist" in this crucial sense.

Of course I yearn for answers to all the puzzles, great and small, that build the order (and wondrous disorder) of nature "out there"—an order that our intellectual ancestors could only read (understandably) as a proof of God's existence and benevolent intent. And I am convinced that such answers exist, if only to be seen "through a glass darkly," given the necessary interposition of human history, sociology, and psychology between the "real" world, and any abstractions of disembodied logic that might manipulate and order our observations. (In this sense, no practicing scientist can be a pure "relativist," although I trust the more sophisticated and self-analytical among us know that "pure" observation, "unsullied" by human foibles and preferences, can only rank as idealized legend.)

But I prefer to emphasize the interaction of this outside world with something unique in the history of life on Earth—the struggle of a conscious and questioning agent to understand the whys and wherefores, and to integrate this knowledge with the meaning of its own existence. That is, I am enthused by nature's constitution, but even more fascinated by trying to grasp how an odd and excessively fragile instrument—the human mind—comes to know this world outside, and how the contingent history of the human body, personality, and society impacts the pathways to this knowledge.

A map of the roadblocks—imposed by the evolutionary limitations of an instrument clearly not designed for this style of inquiry, and then joined with the improbable and unrepeatable contingencies that built our modern technological society—holds just as much interest as an accurate map of nature's geography. Moreover, a humanistic focus on how we know about nature—rather than an "objective" account, unattainable in any case, of how nature "is"—gives an essayist a "whole 'nother" level of juicy material, for we lose nothing of the primary topic, the world as we find it, and gain all the foibles and fascination of *how* we find it so.

As another benefit of this humanistic focus, we acquire a surprising source of rich and apparently limitless novelty from the primary documents of great thinkers throughout our history. But why should any nuggets, or even flakes, be left for intellectual miners in such terrain? Hasn't the *Origin of Species* been read untold millions of times? Hasn't every paragraph been subjected to overt scholarly scrutiny and exegesis?

Let me share a secret rooted in general human foibles, and in the faint tinge of anti-intellectualism that has always pervaded American culture. Very few people, including authors willing to commit to paper, ever really read primary sources—certainly not in necessary depth and completion, and often not at all. Nothing new here, but this shortcutting propensity of the ages has been abetted in our "journalistic" era by a lamentable tendency to call experts, rather than to read and ponder—yet another guarantee of authorial passivity before secondary sources, rather than active dialogue, or communion by study, with the great thinkers of our past.

I stress this point primarily for a practical, even an ethical, reason, and not merely to vent my spleen. When writers close themselves off to the documents of scholarship, and rely only on seeing or asking, they become conduits and sieves rather than thinkers. When, on the other hand, you study the great works of predecessors engaged in the same struggle, you enter a dialogue with human history and the rich variety of our intellectual traditions. You insert yourself, and your own organizing powers, into this history—and you become an active agent, not merely a "reporter." Then, and only then, can you become an original contributor, even a discoverer, and not only a mouthpiece.

What could be more democratic than the principle that nuggets of real discovery abound in primary sources, located in such accessible places as major university and city libraries, for those willing to do the work and develop the skills. (And there's the rub. I do, of course, acknowledge the impediment for most Americans that many of these works, representing the ecumenical range of international scholarship, have never been translated into English—a fact that should be a spur to study, and not a barrier.) Good anatomists have told me that novel and important observations can still be made by dissecting a common frog, despite millions of prior efforts spanning several centuries. I can attest that all major documents of science remain chock-full of distinctive and illuminating novelty, if only people will study them—in full and in the original editions. Why would anyone *not* yearn to read these works; not hunger for the opportunity? What a thrill, whatever the outcome in personal enlightenment, to thus engage the greatest thinkers and doers of our past, to thumb the pages of their own printings, to speculate about past readers who pondered the same copies with the differing presuppositions of other centuries, as the candle of nighttime illuminated their silent labor.

Of the six parts in this humanist's natural history of evolutionary essays, the first four—on art and science, mini-biographies, human prehistory with emphasis on paleolithic cave art, and human history from a naturalist's standpoint—emphasize our side, though several focus on particular organisms, as in chapter 9 on giant deer ("Irish elks") painted on cave walls, chapter 11 on Bahamian land snails for a fable about Columbus, and chapter 12 on the dodo's fate, made even sadder by human insult added to the ultimate injury of extirpation. The essays of the last two sections— on evolutionary theory, and on perspectives of other organisms—focus on the non-human side (again with such exceptions, as chapter 14 on papal statements about evolution, chapter 15 on the contrast of Robert Boyle and Charles Darwin on natural design, and chapter 18 on Percival Lowell versus Alfred Russel Wallace on Martian canals and the true domination of earthly life by bacteria.)

All these essays are grounded in a precious paradox that has defined the best of the genre ever since Montaigne: intimate and accurate detail—the foundation of most good essays—serves as a source of delight in itself and also as a springboard to discourse about generalities of broadest scope. I would never dare to take on "the nature of truth" by frontal assault and abstract generalization—for fear of becoming an empty, tendentious buffoon, pontificating about the unanswerable and undefinable. But the subject must rivet us, and we can legitimately "sneak up on" (and even genuinely illuminate) this great issue by discussing how Darwin and his creationist American soulmate Dana constructed alternative taxonomies for toothed birds that should not have existed under previous concepts of reality, but had just been discovered as fossils (chapter 5). Similarly, if I tackled "the nature of tolerance" head-on, naked of intriguing and specific illustration, I would sound like a vain preacher crying in the wilderness (negative definition!). But if I confess some childhood humor in juxtaposing, for alliteration as well as content, the Diet of Worms with the Defenestration of Prague (chapter 13), then a seemingly superficial, even ridiculous, union wins legitimacy for joint illustration, and provides fair access to factual and moral dimensions of the general topic.

These essays probe, arrange, join, and parry the details within a diverse forest of data, located both in nature and in the documents of human struggle—all to access an inherently confusing but infinitely compelling world. As I survey the contents of this eighth volume, I find that I have followed four primary strategies to promote these details into coherent frameworks with sufficient generality to incite an essay.

1. In some cases, an intense study of original sources yields genuine discovery, despite the paradox that materials for a solution have always been patent. The story of non-use for the giraffe's neck by early evolutionists had not been documented before (chapter 16), and surprising absences often reveal as much as unrecognized presences.

I located a new dimension, largely in favor of the "vanquished" Owen and not the "victor" Huxley, in the great hippocampus debate that animated evolutionary discussion in the 1860s (chapter 6). Dana's important theory of cephalization, and its link with his natural theology (in interesting contrast with Darwin's developing alternative), has never been elucidated, in part because Dana scattered his views through so many short and technical papers (chapter 5).

But I am, I confess, most proud of the opening title essay on Leonardo's paleontology. The excellence and prominence of his observations on fossils have been recognized—and dutifully honored in all accounts, popular, textbook, and technical—for more than a century, since the full publication of his private notebooks in the 1880s. But no one had identified the special reasons (based on his own, and largely medieval, views of the earth as analogous to a living body) for his intense focus on fossils, and for the placement of his statements in a codex largely devoted to the nature of water. So these wonderful observations had stood out, disembodied from context, and misinterpreted as the weird anachronisms of a transcendent and largely unfathomable genius. But the full document of the Leicester Codex sets the proper context, when read in its entirety and understood by the physics of Leonardo's own time.

2. In most cases, I do not report observations never made before, but try to place unfamiliar (or even well-known) items into a novel context by juxtaposition with other subjects not previously viewed as related—invariably in the service of illuminating a general point about the practice of science, the structure of nature, or the construction of knowledge. In reviewing the essays for this volume (not planned as an ensemble when first written, but collected from my monthly series for *Natural History* magazine), I noticed that I had most often made such a juxtaposition by the minimal method of pairing, or contrast between two—perhaps a general mode of operation for the human mind, at least according to several prominent schools of research (discussed here in the context of paleolithic cave art in chapter 8). For example, all the essays in part 2 on mini-biographies, although focusing on one previously unappreciated or misunderstood character, interpret their subject by his contrast with a standard figure—Linnaeus and the eighteenth-century English Jewish naturalist Mendes da Costa (chapter 4), James D. Dana and his British soulmate Darwin (chapter 5), Richard Owen versus T. H. Huxley (chapter 6), and the tragic Russian genius Vladimir Kovalevsky (and his equally tragic and more brilliant wife, Sophia, one of the greatest mathematicians of the nineteenth century) with Darwin on the potential of error to illuminate scientific truth (chapter 7).

Many other essays also pursue this strategy of illumination by paired contrast, with novelty in the joining: Boyle and Darwin on natural theology and evolution (chapter 15); Percival Lowell versus Alfred Russel Wallace on the canals of Mars and the uniqueness of life (chapter 18); sloths and vultures as prototypes for traits that we, in our parochial and irrelevant way, judge as negative but yearn to understand (chapter 20); the Diet of Worms and the Defenestration of Prague as events of European history, related by more than their shared initial *D* and funny names (chapter 13); the Abbé Breuil and André Leroi-Gourhan for two sequential and maximally contrasting (but strangely similar) theories about the genesis of cave art (chapter 8); the great artist Turner and the prime engineer Brunel on the similarity of art and science (chapter 2); a forgotten theory about the origin of vertebrates with stunning new data to validate an even older view, all as an entrée to the subject of major evolutionary transitions and the prejudices that impede our understanding of this topic (chapter 17); the dodo of Mauritius and the first New World victims of Western genocide (chapter 12); and the striking difference between two popes in their common willingness to support the factual truth of evolution (chapter 14).

3. If my second category works by joining disparate details, a third strategy operates by careful excavation—elucidation by digging rather than elucidation by joining. As the mineshaft widens and deepens, one may reach a richness of detail justifying promotion to an essay because the requisite generality has been attained by one of two routes: (1) By casting a truly novel, or at least sufficiently different, light on an old subject, so that readers become willing to devote renewed interest, and may even obtain some provocative insight (Darwin always wrote to his creationist friends that he dared not expect to change their minds, but did hope to "stagger" them a bit)—as when intricate details of the life cycle of the maximally "degenerate" parasite *Sacculina* suggest new attention to the fallacies of evolutionary progress (chapter 19), and when the subtle (and almost entirely unreported) distinctions in the affirmation of evolution by two very different popes (Pius XII and John Paul II) illuminate the old and overly discussed issue of proper relationships between science and religion (chapter 14). (2) By gaining the "right" to address a large and general issue through the new perspective of previously unapplied detail (as in the examples of chapters 5 and 13, previously discussed, and chapter 10 on the relevance of new data about the multiplicity of human species until 30,000–40,000 years ago and the consequent oddity of our current status as a single species spread throughout the globe) for a discussion of predictability versus historical contingency in the evolution of self-conscious life on Earth.

4. "Promotion" to an essay may depend upon the coalescence of details into a general theme worthy of report, but sometimes those details, all by themselves, become arresting enough to merit treatment entirely for their own value (and then I will confess to using the emerging generality as an excuse for almost baroque attention to the details). I do value the theme eventually addressed, but don't you adore, entirely for their own sake as stories, the four tales of conventional prey that devour their predators (chapter 21), or the excruciatingly intricate and beautiful details of the bizarrely complex life cycle of the barnacle parasite, the "root-head" *Sacculina* (chapter 19)? And, as my personal favorite (and here I do rest my case), how could anyone but a dolt not be moved by the fact that we know about the giant deer's hump only because paleolithic cave painters left us a record—and that no other even potential source of evidence exists (chapter 9). I tell this story within a perfectly valid and sufficiently interesting context of discourse on biological adaptation as a general evolutionary principle, but don't you thrill to the notion of this kind of gift provided by such distant forebears; and aren't you riveted by the details of these rare images, and the story of their discovery and recognition?

    The foregoing discussion accounts for all individual bits in this eighth piece of my series. But just as the "two bits" of legend represented a cut from a totality called a "piece of eight,"[1] my bits have no coherence or valid generality without an over-arching rationale or coordinating theme to make them whole. I pay my homage to evolution in the preface to every volume of this series, and will now do so again. Of all general themes in science, no other could be so rich, so deep, so fascinating in extension, or so troubling (to our deepest hopes and prejudices) in implication. Therefore, for an essayist in need of a ligature for disparate thoughts and subjects, no binder could possibly be more appropriate—in fascination and legitimacy—than evolution, the concept that inspired the great biologist Theodosius Dobzhansky to remark, in one of the most widely quoted statements of twentieth-century science, that "nothing in biology makes sense except in the light of evolution."

Moreover, and finally, with this series' emphasis on a humanistic natural history—an account of evolution that focuses as much on how we come to know and understand this great principle as on how such a process shapes the history of life—we encounter an endless recursion that provides even greater scope and interest to the subject. The wondrously peculiar human brain arose as a product of evolution, replete with odd (and often misleading) modes of reasoning originally developed for other purposes, or for no explicit purpose at all. This brain then discovers the central truth of evolution, but also constructs human cultures and societies, replete with hopes and prejudices that predispose us toward rejecting many modes and implications of the very process that created us. And thus, in a kind of almost cosmically wicked recursion, evolution builds the brain, and the brain invents both the culture that must face evolution and the modes of reasoning that might elucidate the process of its own creation. Round and round we go—into a whorl that may be endless and eternal, yet seems to feature some form of increasing understanding in all the gyrations that, at the very least, give us topics for essays and, at best, provide some insight into the nature of our being.

Double Take

1 What does Stephen Jay Gould mean when he defines himself as a "humanistic naturalist"? In what ways do his views on essay writing reflect that definition?
2. Summarize and describe in your own words the four writing and research strategies Gould lists in the essay "Pieces of Eight." What strategies stand out the most to you?
3. Which of the strategies strike you as being most useful for the writing you are or will be doing in this class or in college? Explain your reasons.
4. As a writer, list your own set of strategies for writing and research that you have accumulated in your writing experiences.

---

1. The etymology is much disputed, but I will follow John Ciardi's *Browser's Dictionary* (Harper & Row, 1980) for the conventional story that American colonials (in the absence of an official mint before we became a nation) used the coins of several countries for change. The Spanish silver "piece of eight" (so called because the coin bore a large number 8 to signify its value as eight *reals*) was often cut into pieces, called "bits." Since the *real* was worth about 12½ cents, two bits became an American quarter, four bits a half-dollar, and so on—in terminology still used today.

At First Glance

"The Creation Myths of Cooperstown," like most of Stephen Jay Gould's essays, was first published in Natural History *magazine. And, like so many of Gould's essays, it deals with the subject of evolution in a circular, interconnected way by taking bits of detail and connecting them to make a larger point, in this case evolution versus creationism. While reading it, pay close attention to how Gould connects the parts: the Cardiff Giant, baseball, and evolution. Look at the strategies he uses, especially the transitions that connect one part to another. Consider how and why these transitions work. Think how you might use them in your own writing.*

The Creation Myths of Cooperstown

You may either look upon the bright side and say that hope springs eternal or, taking the cynic's part, you may mark P. T. Barnum as an astute psychologist for his proclamation that suckers are born every minute. The end result is the same: You can, Honest Abe notwithstanding, fool most of the people all of the time. How else to explain the long and continuing compendium of hoaxes—from the medieval shroud of Turin to Edwardian Piltdown Man to an ultramodern array of flying saucers and astral powers—eagerly embraced for their consonance with our hopes or their resonance with our fears.

Some hoaxes make a sufficient mark upon history that their products acquire the very status initially claimed by fakery—legitimacy (although as an object of human or folkloric, rather than natural, history; I once held the bones of Piltdown Man and felt that I was handling an important item of Western culture).

The Cardiff Giant, the best American entry for the title of paleontological hoax turned into cultural history, now lies on display in a shed behind a barn at the Farmer's Museum in Cooperstown, New York. This gypsum man, more than ten feet tall, was "discovered" by workmen digging a well on a farm near Cardiff, New York, in October 1869. Eagerly embraced by a gullible public, and ardently displayed by its creators at fifty cents a pop, the Cardiff Giant caused quite a brouhaha around Syracuse, and then nationally, for the few months of its active life between exhumation and exposure.

The Cardiff Giant was the brainchild of George Hull, a cigar manufacturer (and general rogue) from Binghamton, New York. He quarried a large block of gypsum from Fort Dodge, Iowa, and shipped it to Chicago, where two marble cutters fashioned the rough likeness of a naked man. Hull made some crude and minimal attempts to give his statue an aged appearance. He chipped off the carved hair and beard because experts told him that such items would not petrify. He drove darning needles into a wooden block and hammered the statue, hoping to simulate skin pores. Finally, he dumped a gallon of sulfuric acid all over his creation to simulate extended erosion. Hull then shipped his giant in a large box back to Cardiff.

Hull, as an accomplished rogue, sensed that his story could not hold for long and, in that venerable and alliterative motto, got out while the getting was good. He sold a three-quarter interest in the Cardiff Giant to a consortium of highly respectable businessmen, including two former mayors of Syracuse. These men raised the statue from its original pit on November 5 and carted it off to Syracuse for display.

The hoax held on for a few more weeks, and Cardiff Giant fever swept the land. Debate raged in newspapers and broadsheets between those who viewed the giant as a petrified fossil and those who regarded it as a statue wrought by an unknown and wondrous prehistoric race. But Hull had left too many tracks—at the gypsum quarries in Fort Dodge, at the carver's studio in Chicago, along the roadways to Cardiff (several people remembered seeing an awfully large box passing by on a cart). By December, Hull was ready to recant, but held his tongue a while longer. Three months later, the two Chicago sculptors came forward, and the Cardiff Giant's brief rendezvous with fame and fortune ended.

The common analogy of the Cardiff Giant with Piltdown Man works only to a point (both were frauds passed off as human fossils) and fails in one crucial respect. Piltdown was cleverly wrought and fooled professionals for forty years, while the Cardiff Giant was preposterous from the start. How could a man turn to solid gypsum, while preserving all his soft anatomy, from cheeks to toes to penis? Geologists and paleontologists never accepted Hull's statue. O. C. Marsh, later to achieve great fame as a discoverer of dinosaurs, echoed a professional consensus in his unambiguous pronouncement: "It is of very recent origin and a decided humbug."

Why, then, was the Cardiff Giant so popular, inspiring a wave of interest and discussion as high as any tide in the affairs of men during its short time in the sun? If the fraud had been well executed, we might attribute this great concern to the dexterity of the hoaxers (just as we grant grudging attention to a few of the most accomplished art fakers for their skills as copyists). But since the Cardiff Giant was so crudely done, we can only attribute its fame to the deep issue, the raw nerve, touched by the subject of its fakery—human origins. Link an absurd concoction to a noble and mysterious subject and you may prevail, at least for a while. My opening reference to P. T. Barnum was not meant sarcastically; he was one of the great practical psychologists of the nineteenth century—and his motto applies with special force to the Cardiff Giant: "No humbug is great without truth at bottom." (Barnum made a copy of the Cardiff Giant and exhibited it in New York City. His mastery of hype and publicity assured that his model far outdrew the "real" fake when the original went on display at a rival establishment in the same city.)

For some reason (to be explored, but not resolved, in this essay), we are powerfully drawn to the subject of beginnings. We yearn to know about origins, and we readily construct myths when we do not have data (or we suppress data in favor of legend when a truth strikes us as too commonplace). The hankering after an origin myth has always been especially strong for the closest subject of all—the human race. But we extend the same psychic need to our accomplishments and institutions— and we have origin myths and stories for the beginning of hunting, of language, of art, of kindness, of war, of boxing, bow ties, and brassieres. Most of us know that the Great Seal of the United States pictures an eagle holding a ribbon reading *e pluribus unum*. Fewer would recognize the motto on the other side (check it out on the back of a dollar bill): *annuit coeptis*—"he smiles on our beginnings."

Cooperstown may house the Cardiff Giant, but the fame of this small village in central New York does not rest upon its celebrated namesake, author James Fenimore, or its lovely Lake Otsego or the Farmer's Museum. Cooperstown is "on the map" by virtue of a different origin myth—one more parochial but no less powerful for many Americans than the tales of human beginnings that gave life to the Cardiff Giant. Cooperstown is the sacred founding place in the official myth about the origin of baseball.

Origin myths, since they are so powerful, can engender enormous practical problems. Abner Doubleday, as we shall soon see, most emphatically did not invent baseball at Cooperstown in 1839 as the official tale proclaims; in fact, no one invented baseball at any moment or in any spot. Nonetheless, this creation myth made Cooperstown the official home of baseball, and the Hall of Fame, with its associated museum and library, set its roots in this small village, inconveniently located near nothing in the way of airports or accommodations. We all revel in bucolic imagery on the field of dreams, but what a hassle when tens of thousands line the roads, restaurants, and Port-a-potties during the annual Hall of Fame weekend, when new members are enshrined and two major league teams arrive to play an exhibition game at Abner Doubleday Field, a sweet little 10,000-seater in the middle of town. Put your compass point at Cooperstown, make your radius at Albany—and you'd better reserve a year in advance if you want any accommodation within the enormous resulting circle.

After a lifetime of curiosity, I finally got the opportunity to witness this annual version of forty students in a telephone booth or twenty circus clowns in a Volkswagen. Since Yaz (former Boston star Carl Yastrzemski to the uninitiated) was slated to receive baseball's Nobel in 1989, and his old team was playing in the Hall of Fame game, and since I'm a transplanted Bostonian (although still a New Yorker and not-so-secret Yankee fan at heart), Tom Heitz, chief of the wonderful baseball library at the Hall of Fame, kindly invited me to join the sardines in this most lovely of all cans.

The silliest and most tendentious of baseball writing tries to wrest profundity from the spectacle of grown men hitting a ball with a stick by suggesting linkages between the sport and deep issues of morality, parenthood, history, lost innocence, gentleness, and so on, seemingly *ad infinitum*. (The effort reeks of silliness because baseball is profound all by itself and needs no excuses; people who don't know this are not fans and are therefore unreachable anyway.) When people ask me how baseball imitates life, I can only respond with what the more genteel newspapers used to call a "barnyard epithet," but now, with growing bravery, usually render as "bullbleep." Nonetheless, baseball is a major item of our culture, and the sport does have a long and interesting history. Any item or institution with these two properties must generate a set of myths and stories (perhaps even some truths) about beginnings. And the subject of beginnings is the bread and butter of these essays on evolution in the broadest sense. I shall make no woolly analogies between baseball and life; this is an essay on the origins of baseball, with some musings on why beginnings of all sorts hold such fascination for us. (I thank Tom Heitz not only for the invitation to Cooperstown at its yearly acme but also for drawing the contrast between creation and evolution stories of baseball, and for supplying much useful information from his unparalleled storehouse.)

Stories about beginnings come in only two basic modes. An entity either has an explicit point of origin, a specific time and place of creation, or else it evolves and has no definable moment of entry into the world. Baseball provides an interesting example of this contrast because we know the answer and can judge received wisdom by the two chief criteria, often opposed, of external fact and internal hope. Baseball evolved from a plethora of previous stick-and-ball games. It has no true Coopers-town and no Doubleday. Yet we seem to prefer the alternative model of origin by a moment of creation—for then we can have heroes and sacred places. By contrasting the myth of Cooperstown with the fact of evolution, we can learn something about our cultural practices and their frequent disrespect for truth.

The official story about the beginning of baseball is a creation myth, and a review of the reasons and circumstances of its fabrication may give us insight into the cultural appeal of stories in this mode. A. G. Spalding, baseball's first great pitcher during his early career, later founded the sporting goods company that still bears his name and became one of the great commercial moguls of America's gilded age. As publisher of the annual *Spalding's Official Base Ball Guide,* he held maximal power in shaping both public and institutional opinion on all facets of baseball and its history. As the sport grew in popularity, and the pattern of two stable major leagues coalesced early in our century, Spalding and others felt the need for clarification (or merely for codification) of opinion on the hitherto unrecorded origin of an activity that truly merited its common designation as America's "national pastime."

In 1907, Spalding set up a blue ribbon committee to investigate and resolve the origin of baseball. The committee, chaired by A. G. Mills and including several prominent businessmen and two senators who had also served as presidents of the National League, took much testimony but found no smoking gun. Then, in July 1907, Spalding himself transmitted to the committee a letter from an Abner Graves, then a mining engineer in Denver, who reported that Abner Doubleday had, in 1839, interrupted a marbles game behind the tailor's shop in Cooperstown, New York, to draw a diagram of a baseball field, explain the rules of the game, and designate the activity by its modern name of "base ball" (then spelled as two words).

Such "evidence" scarcely inspired universal confidence, but the commission came up with nothing better—and the Doubleday myth, as we shall soon see, was eminently functional. Therefore, in 1908, the Mills Commission reported its two chief findings: first, "that base ball had its origins in the United States"; and second, "that the first scheme for playing it, according to the best evidence available to date, was devised by Abner Doubleday, at Cooperstown, New York, in 1839." This "best evidence" consisted only of "a circumstantial statement by a reputable gentleman"— namely Graves's testimony as reported by Spalding himself.

When cited evidence is so laughably insufficient, one must seek motivations other than concern for truth. The key to underlying reasons stands in the first conclusion of Mills's committee: Hoopla and patriotism (cardboard version) decreed that a national pastime must have an indigenous origin. The idea that baseball had evolved from a wide variety of English stick-and-ball games—although true— did not suit the mythology of a phenomenon that had become so quintessentially

American. In fact, Spalding had long been arguing, in an amiable fashion, with Henry Chadwick, another pioneer and entrepreneur of baseball's early years. Chadwick, born in England, had insisted for years that baseball had developed from the British stick-and-ball game called rounders; Spalding had vociferously advocated a purely American origin, citing the colonial game of "one old cat" as a distant precursor, but holding that baseball itself represented something so new and advanced that a pinpoint of origin—a creation myth—must be sought.

Chadwick considered the matter of no particular importance, arguing (with eminent justice) that an English origin did not "detract one iota from the merit of its now being unquestionably a thoroughly American field sport, and a game too, which is fully adapted to the American character." (I must say that I have grown quite fond of Mr. Chadwick, who certainly understood evolutionary change and its chief principle that historical origin need not match contemporary function.) Chadwick also viewed the committee's whitewash as a victory for his side. He labeled the Mills report as "a masterful piece of special pleading which lets my dear old friend Albert [Spalding] escape a bad defeat. The whole matter was a joke between Albert and myself."

We may accept the psychic need for an indigenous creation myth, but why Abner Doubleday, a man with no recorded tie to the game and who, in the words of Donald Honig, probably "didn't know a baseball from a kumquat"? I had wondered about this for years, but only ran into the answer serendipitously during a visit to Fort Sumter in the harbor of Charleston, South Carolina. There, an exhibit on the first skirmish of the Civil War points out that Abner Doubleday, as captain of the Union artillery, had personally sighted and given orders for firing the first responsive volley following the initial Confederate attack on the fort. Doubleday later commanded divisions at Antietam and Fredericksburg, became at least a minor hero at Gettysburg, and retired as a brevet major general. In fact, A. G. Mills, head of the commission, had served as part of an honor guard when Doubleday's body lay in state in New York City, following his death in 1893.

If you have to have an American hero, could anyone be better than the man who fired the first shot (in defense) of the Civil War? Needless to say, this point was not lost on the members of Mills's committee. Spalding, never one to mince words, wrote to the committee when submitting Graves's dubious testimony: "It certainly appeals to an American pride to have had the great national game of base ball created and named by a Major General in the United States Army." Mills then concluded in his report: "Perhaps in the years to come, in view of the hundreds of thousands of people who are devoted to baseball, and the millions who will be, Abner Doubleday's fame will rest evenly, if not quite as much, upon the fact that he was its inventor . . . as upon his brilliant and distinguished career as an officer in the Federal Army."

And so, spurred by a patently false creation myth, the Hall of Fame stands in the most incongruous and inappropriate locale of a charming little town in central New York. Incongruous and inappropriate, but somehow wonderful. Who needs another museum in the cultural maelstroms (and summer doldrums) of New York, Boston, or Washington? Why not a major museum in a beautiful and bucolic setting? And what could be more fitting than the spatial conjunction of two great American origin myths—The Cardiff Giant and the Doubleday Fable? Thus, I too am quite content to treat the myth gently, while honesty requires 'fessing up. The exhibit on

Doubleday in the Hall of Fame Museum sets just the right tone in its caption: "In the hearts of those who love baseball, he is remembered as the lad in the pasture where the game was invented. Only cynics would need to know more." Only in the hearts; not in the minds.

Baseball evolved. Since the evidence is so clear (as epitomized below), we must ask why these facts have been so little appreciated for so long, and why a creation myth like the Doubleday story ever gained a foothold. Two major reasons have conspired: first, the positive block of our attraction to creation stories; second, the negative impediment of unfamiliar sources outside the usual purview of historians. English stick-and-ball games of the nineteenth century can be roughly classified into two categories along social lines. The upper and educated classes played cricket, and the history of this sport is copiously documented because literati write about their own interests and because the activities of men in power are well recorded (and constitute virtually all of history, in the schoolboy version). But the ordinary pastimes of rural and urban working people can be well nigh invisible in conventional sources of explicit commentary. Working people played a different kind of stick-and-ball game, existing in various forms and designated by many names, including "rounders" in western England, "feeder" in London, and "base ball" in southern England. For a large number of reasons, forming the essential difference between cricket and baseball, cricket matches can last up to several days (a batsman, for example, need not run after he hits the ball and need not expose himself to the possibility of being put out every time he makes contact). The leisure time of working people does not come in such generous gobs, and the lower-class stick-and-ball games could not run more than a few hours.

Several years ago, at the Victoria and Albert Museum in London, I learned an important lesson from an excellent exhibit on late nineteenth century history of the British music hall. This is my favorite period (Darwin's century, after all), and I consider myself tolerably well informed on cultural trends of the time. I can sing any line from any of the Gilbert and Sullivan operas (a largely middle-class entertainment), and I know the general drift of high cultural interests in literature and music. But the music hall provided a whole world of entertainment for millions, a realm with its heroes, its stars, its top-forty songs, its gaudy theaters—and I knew nothing, absolutely nothing, about this world. I felt chagrined, but my ignorance had an explanation beyond personal insensitivity (and the exhibit had been mounted explicitly to counteract the selective invisibility of certain important trends in history). The music hall was a chief entertainment of Victorian working classes, and the history of working people is often invisible in conventional written sources. This history must be rescued and reconstituted from different sorts of data; in this case, from posters, playbills, theater accounts, persistence of some songs in the oral tradition (most were never published as sheet music), recollections of old-timers who knew the person who knew the person. . . .

The early history of baseball—the stick-and-ball game of working people—presents the same problem of conventional invisibility, and the same promise of rescue by exploration of unusual sources. Work continues and intensifies as the history of sport becomes more and more academically respectable, but the broad outlines (and much fascinating detail) are now well established. As the upper classes played a codified and well-documented cricket, working people played a largely unrecorded and much more diversified set of stick-and-ball games ancestral to baseball. Many sources, including primers and boys' manuals, depict games recognizable as precursors to base-ball well into the eighteenth century. Occasional references even spill over into high culture. In *Northanger Abbey,* written in 1798 or 1799, Jane Austen remarks: "It was not very wonderful that Catherine . . . should prefer cricket, base ball, riding on horse-back, and running about the country, at the age of fourteen, to books." As this quo-tation illustrates, the name of the game is no more Doubleday's than the form of play.

These ancestral styles of baseball came to America with early settlers and were clearly well established by colonial times. But they were driven ever further under-ground by Puritan proscriptions of sport for adults. They survived largely as chil-dren's games and suffered the double invisibility of location among the poor and the young. But two major reasons brought these games into wider repute and led to a codification of standard forms quite close to modern baseball between the 1820s and the 1850s. First, a set of social reasons, from the decline of Puritanism to increased concern about health and hygiene in crowded cities, made sport an acceptable activ-ity for adults. Second, middle-class and professional people began to take up these early forms of baseball, and this upward social drift inspired teams, leagues, written rules, uniforms, stadiums, guidebooks: in short, all the paraphernalia of conventional history.

I am not arguing that these early games could be called baseball with a few trivial differences (evolution means substantial change, after all), but only that they stand in a complex lineage, better designated a nexus, from which modern baseball emerged, eventually in a codified and canonical form. In those days before instant communi-cation, every region had its own version, just as every set of outdoor steps in New York City generated a different form of stoopball in my youth, without threatening the basic identity of the game. These games, most commonly called town ball, dif-fered from modern baseball in substantial ways. In the Massachusetts Game, a codi-fication of the late 1850s drawn up by ball players in New England towns, four bases and three strikes identify the genus, but many specifics are strange by modern stan-dards. The bases were made of wooden stakes projecting four feet from the ground. The batter (called the striker) stood between first and fourth base. Sides changed after a single out. One hundred runs (called tallies), not higher score after a specified num-ber of innings, spelled victory. The field contained no foul lines, and balls hit in any direction were in play. Most important, runners were not tagged out, but rather dis-missed by "plugging," that is, being hit with a thrown ball while running between bases. Consequently, since baseball has never been a game for masochists, balls were soft—little more than rags stuffed into leather covers—and could not be hit far. (Tom Heitz has put together a team of Cooperstown worthies to re-create town ball for interested parties and prospective opponents. Since few other groups are well schooled in this lost art, Tom's team hasn't been defeated in ages, if ever. "We are the New York Yankees of town ball," he told me. His team is called, quite appro-priately in general but especially for this essay, the Cardiff Giants.)

Evolution is continual change, but not insensibly gradual transition; in any con-tinuum, some points are always more interesting than others. The conventional nom-ination for most salient point in this particular continuum goes to Alexander Joy

Cartwright, leader of a New York team that started to play in Lower Manhattan, eventually rented some changing rooms and a field in Hoboken (just a quick ferry ride across the Hudson), and finally drew up a set of rules in 1845, later known as the New York Game. Cartwright's version of town ball is much closer to modern baseball, and many clubs followed his rules—for standardization became ever more vital as the popularity of early baseball grew and opportunity for play between regions increased. In particular, Cartwright introduced two key innovations that shaped the disparate forms of town ball into a semblance of modern baseball. First, he eliminated plugging and introduced tagging in the modern sense; the ball could now be made harder, and hitting for distance became an option. Second, he introduced foul lines, again in the modern sense, as his batter stood at a home plate and had to hit the ball within lines defined from home through first and third bases. The game could now become a spectator sport because areas close to the field but out of action could, for the first time, be set aside for onlookers.

The New York Game may be the highlight of a continuum, but it provides no origin myth for baseball. Cartwright's rules were followed in various forms of town ball. His New York Game still included many curiosities by modern standards (twenty-one runs, called aces, won the game, and balls caught on one bounce were outs). Moreover, our modern version is an amalgam of the New York Game plus other town-ball traditions, not Cartwright's baby grown up by itself. Several features of the Massachusetts Game entered the modern version in preference to Cartwright's rules. Balls had to be caught on the fly in Boston, and pitchers threw overhand, not underhand as in the New York Game (and in professional baseball until the 1880s).

Scientists often lament that so few people understand Darwin and the principles of biological evolution. But the problem goes deeper. Too few people are comfortable with evolutionary modes of explanation in any form. I do not know why we tend to think so fuzzily in this area, but one reason must reside in our social and psychic attraction to creation myths in preference to evolutionary stories—for creation myths, as noted before, identify heroes and sacred places, while evolutionary stories provide no palpable, particular object as a symbol for reverence, worship, or patriotism. Still, we must remember—and an intellectual's most persistent and nagging responsibility lies in making this simple point over and over again, however noxious and bothersome we render ourselves thereby—that truth and desire, fact and comfort, have no necessary, or even preferred, correlation (so rejoice when they do coincide).

To state the most obvious example in our current political turmoil: Human growth is a continuum, and no creation myth can define an instant for the origin of an individual life. Attempts by anti-abortionists to designate the moment of fertilization as the beginning of personhood make no sense in scientific terms (and also violate a long history of social definitions that traditionally focused on the quickening, or detected movement, of the fetus in the womb). I will admit—indeed, I emphasized as a key argument of this essay—that not all points on a continuum are equal. Fertilization is a more interesting moment than most, but it no more provides a clean definition of origin than the most intriguing moment of baseball's continuum—Cartwright's codification of the New York Game—defines the beginning of our national pastime. Baseball evolved and people grow; both are continua without definable points of origin. Probe too far back and you reach absurdity, for you will see Nolan Ryan on the hill when the first ape hit a bird with a stone, or you will define both masturbation and menstruation as murder—and who will then cast the first stone? Look for something in the middle, and you find nothing but continuity—always a meaningful "before," and always a more modern "after." (Please note that I am not stating an opinion on the vexatious question of abortion—an ethical issue that can only be decided in ethical terms. I only point out that one side has rooted its case in an argument from science that is not only entirely irrelevant to the proper realm of resolution but also happens to be flat-out false in trying to devise a creation myth within a continuum.)

And besides, why do we prefer creation myths to evolutionary stories? I find all the usual reasons hollow. Yes, heroes and shrines are all very well, but is there not grandeur in the sweep of continuity? Shall we revel in a story for all humanity that may include the sacred ball courts of the Aztecs, and perhaps, for all we know, a group of *Home erectus* hitting rocks or skulls with a stick or a femur? Or shall we halt beside the mythical Abner Doubleday, standing behind the tailor's shop in Cooperstown, and say "behold the man"—thereby violating truth and, perhaps even worse, extinguishing both thought and wonder?

Double Take

1. Why does Stephen Jay Gould begin the essay about baseball, "The Creation Myths of Cooperstown," with the story of the Cardiff Giant? Do you think it is an effective way to begin?
2. How does Gould connect the various parts of this essay? In responding to this question, look for specific places in the essay that you think work to connect one part, one idea, to another, and explain why you think they work.
3. This essay is an argument on behalf of evolution. Do you think it is an effective argument? What makes it so? Does the connection with baseball help the argument? Why or why not?
4. What would Gould have to change about this essay, if anything, if it was to be published in *Sports Illustrated* instead of *Natural History* magazine? Cite specific changes you think Gould might have to make in order to have the essay work effectively for that new readership. If you think no changes are necessary, explain why.

At First Glance

Stephen Jay Gould wrote "A Cerion *for Christopher" late in his career; the essay was published in his 1998 collection,* Leonardo's Mountain of Clams and the Diet of Worms. *It, too, was originally published in* Natural History *magazine. Before you read the essay, think about what Gould could assume about his audience before he started writing, and then consider if that knowledge of the audience is reflected in his writing. This essay also provides an excellent example of Gould's technique of building an essay using bits of data that, woven together, form a larger meaning. As you read it, pay attention to how Gould leads his readers through the data, especially how he generates their interest in the subject. Pay special attention to how Gould introduces the* Cerion, *the land snail, into the essay and how the snail then becomes a way for him to connect the different parts into a larger whole.*

A *Cerion* for Christopher

If China had promoted, rather than intentionally suppressed, the technology of oceanic transport and navigation, the cardinal theme for the second half of the millennium might well have been eastward, rather than westward, expansion into the New World. We can only speculate about the enormously different consequences of such an alternative but unrealized history. Would Asian mariners have followed a path of conquest in the Western sense? Would their closer ethnic tie to Native Americans (who had migrated from Asia) have made any difference in treatment and relationship? At the very least, I suppose, any modern author of a book printed on the American East Coast would be writing this chapter either in a Native American tongue or in some derivative of Mandarin.

But China did not move east, so Christopher Columbus sailed west, greedy to find the gold of Cathay and the courts of the grand Khan as described by his countryman Marco Polo, who had traveled by different means and from the other direction. And Columbus encountered an entire world in between, blocking his way.

I can think of no other historical episode more portentous, or more replete with both glory and horror, than the Western conquest of America. Since we can neither undo an event of such magnitude nor hope for any simple explanation as an ineluctable consequence of nature's laws, we can only chronicle the events as they occurred, search for patterns, and seek understanding. When dense narrative of this sort becomes a primary method of analysis, detail assumes unusual importance. The symbolic beginning must therefore elicit special attention and fascination. Let us therefore take up an old and unresolved issue: Where did Columbus unite the hemispheres on October 12, 1492?

Surrounded by hints of nearby land, yet faced with a crew on the verge of rebellion, Columbus knew that he must soon succeed or turn back. Then, at 2:00 A.M. on the morning of October 12, the *Pinta's* lookout, Rodrigo de Triana, saw a white cliff in the moonlight and shouted the transforming words of human history: *"Tierra! Tierra!"*—land, land. But what land did Columbus first see and explore?

Why should such a question pose any great difficulty? Why not just examine Columbus's log, trace his route, look for artifacts, or consult the records of people first encountered? For a set of reasons, both particular and general, none of these evident paths yields an unambiguous answer. We know that Columbus landed somewhere in the Bahama Islands, or in the neighboring Turks and Caicos. We also know that the local Taino people called this first landfall Guanahaní—and that Columbus, kneeling in thanks and staking his claim for the monarchs of Spain, renamed the island San Salvador, or Holy Savior. But the Bahamas include more than seven hundred islands, and several offer suitable harbors for Columbus's vessels. Where did he first land?

Navigation, in Columbus's time, was far too imprecise an art to provide much help (and Columbus had vastly underestimated the earth's diameter, thereby permitting himself to believe that he had sailed all the way to Asia). Mariners of the fifteenth century could not determine longitude, and therefore could not locate themselves at sea with pinpoint accuracy. Columbus used the two primary methods then available. Latitude could be determined (though only with difficulty on a moving ship) by sighting the altitude of Polaris (the North Star), or of the sun at midday. A ship could therefore sail to a determined latitude and then proceed either due east or west, as desired. (Columbus, in fact, was a poor celestial navigator, and made little use of latitudes. In one famous incident, he misidentified his position by nearly twenty degrees because he mistook another star for Polaris.)

In the other time-tested method, called dead reckoning, one simply takes a compass bearing, keeps track of time, judges the ship's speed, and then plots the distance and direction covered. Needless to say, dead reckoning cannot be very precise—especially when winds and currents complicate any determination of speed, and when (as on Columbus's ships) sailors measure time by turning a sandglass every half hour! Columbus, by all accounts, was an unusually skilled and spectacularly successful dead reckoner, but the method still doesn't allow any precise reconstruction of his routing.

We are further hindered by a paucity of documents. Columbus's original log, presented to Queen Isabella, has been lost. A copy, given to Columbus before his second voyage, has also disappeared. Bartolomé de Las Casas, the Dominican priest who spoke so eloquently for the lost cause of kindness, made a copy of Columbus's second version—and our modern knowledge derives from this document. Thus, we are using a copy of a copy as our "primary" text, and uncertainties therefore prevail on all crucial points.

The best possible source of evidence—artifacts and recorded histories kept by an unbroken line of original inhabitants—does not exist for another reason that motivated this essay. In the first case of New World genocide perpetrated by the Old, Spanish conquerors completely wiped out the native Bahamians within twenty years of contact, despite (or rather, one must sadly say, enabled by) the warm and trusting hospitality shown to Columbus by the peaceful Tainos.

With so little data to constrain speculation, virtually all major Bahamian islands have been proposed as San Salvador, the site of Columbus's first landfall. (The Turks and Caicos Islands, just to the southeast of the Bahamas, form a politically separate entity. They are, however, geographically and ecologically continuous with the Bahamas, and therefore figure in this discussion as well.) The major contenders include Watling Island, Cat Island, Mayaguana, Samana Cay, Grand Turk, and several of the Caicos. Cat Island held an early advantage, and once even bore the name San Salvador in acknowledgment. But, in 1926, the Bahamian government, persuaded by a growing consensus, transferred Columbus's designation to Watling Island—the favored site, and Columbus's name bearer ever since.

Two traditional sources of evidence favor Watling as San Salvador: correspondence of size and topography with the fairly detailed descriptions of Columbus's log (as known by the Las Casas copy), and nautical tracing of Columbus's route for the rest of his first voyage, from San Salvador to other Bahamian islands, and finally to Cuba and Hispaniola. Samuel Eliot Morison's "semiofficial" case, made in his 1942 classic, *Admiral of the Ocean Sea,* remains the standard expression of this favored hypothesis.

During the past twenty years, archaeology has provided a third source of evidence from excavations made by Charles A. Hoffman and others at Long Bay, within sight of the favored location for Columbus's landfall. (A good account of this work, and of virtually all else connected with the discussion of Columbus's initial landing, may be found in the *Proceedings of the 1986 San Salvador Conference on Columbus and His World,* edited by Donald T. Gerace and published by the Bahamian Field Station on San Salvador.) Along with native pottery and other Taino artifacts, several European objects were found, all consistent with Spanish manufacture at the right time, and all eminently plausible as items for trade—glass beads, metal buckles, hooks, and nails. One discovery exceeded all others in importance: a single Spanish coin of low value, known as a *blanca*—the standard "small change" of the times, and surely the most common coin in circulation among Columbus's men. Moreover, this particular *blanca* was only issued between 1471 and 1474, and no comparable, copper-based coin was minted again until 1497.

Of course, these finds do not positively identify San Salvador as the first landfall for two reasons: Columbus visited several other Bahamian islands on this voyage, and the local Tainos moved freely among adjacent islands. In fact, three days after his first landing, and again on open waters, Columbus encountered a Taino in a canoe, carrying some beads and *blancas* received in trade on San Salvador.

Nonetheless, and all other things considered, the archaeological evidence supports the usual view that San Salvador has now been correctly identified. Still, everything cited so far relies upon European impressions or artifacts. Wouldn't we welcome some hard data from the other side for corroboration? How about one distinctive item of local history, either natural or cultural?

I do not mean to exaggerate the current uncertainty in this debate. Most experts seem satisfied that Columbus first landed on the island now called San Salvador by the Bahamian government. Nonetheless, several dogged and knowledgeable opponents still advocate their alternatives with gusto, and the issue remains vigorously open. I recently spent a week on San Salvador, where I sifted through all the evidence and visited all the sites. I found no reason for dissatisfaction with the conventional view. Nonetheless, if only because we prefer near certainty to high probability, I write this essay to announce that I could truly resolve any remaining doubt about Columbus's first landfall if only the good admiral had added one little activity to the usual drill of kissing the ground, praising God, raising the flag, claiming sovereignty, and trading with the locals. If Christopher Columbus had only picked up (and properly labeled, of course) a single shell of my favorite animal, the land snail *Cerion*—and they are so common that he was probably kneeling on one anyway!—I would know for sure where he had landed.

No one can be objective about his own children, but *Cerion* truly ranks as a natural marvel, and an exemplar of evolution for a particular reason well illustrated by its potential utility for identifying San Salvador. In shell form, *Cerion* may be the most protean land snail in the world—and evolutionists thrive on variation, the result and raw material of biological change. *Cerion* ranges in size from dwarfs of 5 millimeters to giants more than 70 millimeters in length (for folks wedded to good old ways, 25.4 millimeters make an inch)—and in shape from pencil-thin cylinders to golf balls.

Naturalists have named more than six hundred species from *Cerion's* two major geographic centers in Cuba and the Bahama Islands. Most of these names are technically invalid because members of the respective populations can interbreed, but the designations do record a striking biological reality—that so many local populations of *Cerion* have evolved unique and clearly recognizable shell forms. In particular, nearly every Bahamian island can be identified by a distinctive kind of *Cerion*. Thus, bring me a single shell, and I can usually tell you where you spent your last vacation.

Marine species, by contrast, generally maintain much larger and more continuous populations. Broader patterns of variation preclude any pinpoint definition of island coastlines (at Bahamian scale) by distinctive shapes or sizes of clams, snails, corals, or other oceanic forms. Terrestrial species, therefore, offer our only real hope for distinguishing islands by unique biological inhabitants. Individual Bahamian islands might house an endemic insect, or perhaps a plant, but *Cerion* surely provides the best biological marker for specifying particular locales. Insects and plants are less distinctive and harder to preserve; but if Columbus had just slipped a nearly indestructible *Cerion* shell into his vest pocket, his trusty scabbard, or his old kit bag, then we would know. Moreover, *Cerion* must have been the first terrestrial zoological object to enter Columbus's field of vision in the New World (unless a lizard darted across his path, or a mosquito drew first Caucasian blood)—though I cannot guarantee that the Admiral of the Ocean Sea had eyes to see at this scale. For *Cerion* lives right at the coastline in large populations. As they say, you can't miss 'em. And all putative landing sites on San Salvador sport large and obvious populations of my favorite snail.

While I was on San Salvador attending a biennial conference on Caribbean geology at the Bahamian Field Station, I played extensive hooky to do a survey of the local *Cerion*. San Salvador houses two major species of *Cerion*—a large, robust, whitish shell, pointed at the top, and found on promontories on the windward east coast; and a smaller, ribbier, brownish shell, barrel-shaped at the top, and found all along the leeward west coast (and most of the island interior). A single shell of either form can easily be distinguished from the characteristic *Cerion* of all other favored sites for Columbus's initial landfall.

Cerion piratarum, Mayaguana's species, belongs to the same basic group as the east-coast *Cerion* of San Salvador, but is bigger, whiter, entirely different in shape, and quite distinct from the San Salvadorian form. Similarly, *Cerion regina* of the Turks and Caicos belongs to the same general division within *Cerion,* but could not be confused with the species on San Salvador. Samana Cay, perhaps the leading alternative landing site of recent years, also houses a large and distinctive *Cerion,* easily separated from anything living on San Salvador. As a single possible exception, I confess that I could not, from one specimen, unambiguously separate the east-coast windward species of San Salvador from *Cerion fordii,* a species restricted to a few small regions of Cat Island. Columbus almost surely landed on the leeward west coast of San Salvador, however, and the *Cerion* at this site cannot be confused with the local species of any other proposed landing place. (*Cerion eximium,* the leeward, west-coast species of Cat Island, is longer, smoother, thinner-shelled, and more mottled in color than the leeward form of San Salvador.)

Erection of monuments at putative landing sites has been something of a cottage industry on San Salvador for more than a century. Three major markers now adorn the island, each located amid a large population of *Cerion*. The *Chicago Herald* built the first monument in 1891, in preparation for the four-hundredth-anniversary celebrations of Columbus's landing and the great Chicago Columbian exposition, held a year late, in 1893. This monument, constructed largely of exotic stones and featuring a limestone globe set within the base of an obelisk, is now eroding away on the largely inaccessible promontory of Crab Cay (a two-mile walk from the nearest path, along a beautiful beach, but then up a narrow and treacherous slope). The monument sits amid one of the densest *Cerion* populations on San Salvador. I don't think that anyone would now advocate this reefy, windward site as a conceivable landing place (though the cliff might have reflected moonlight for Rodrigo's first sight of land)—yet the monument reads: "On this spot Christopher Columbus first set foot upon the soil of the New World. Erected by The Chicago Herald. June, 1891."

The other two monuments are located a mile or two apart on more plausible landing sites of the leeward west coast—both among the extensive and distinctive *Cerion* populations of this region. The second monument, placed beside an earlier obelisk erected by a yachtsman in 1951, anticipates the quincentenary of 1992 and celebrates a Japanese voyage of hope and rediscovery:

> In October 1991, a replica of *Santa Maria*—built by the Não Santa Maria foundation of Japan—made landfall here on its journey from Barcelona, Spain, to Kobe, Japan. We came to pay homage to Columbus and his crew and to carry our message of hope for a grand harmony in the future: harmony between men and nations, between man and the environment, and between the earth and the universe.
>
> —Haruo Yamamoto
> Captain, *Não Santa Maria*

The plaque on the "official" monument, a cross erected in 1954 on Long Bay, within site of the excavation that yielded the late-fifteenth-century coin, simply reads: "On or near this spot, Christopher Columbus landed on the 12th of October, 1492. Admiral Samuel Eliot Morison, USNR." The base contains yet another message of reconciliation:

> Dedication and Christmas services shared by all churches 25 December, 1956. Americans and natives worshipped together as [a] symbol of faith, love, and unity between all nations for peace on earth.

And so we reach the crux of all the tension, all the triumph and tragedy, all the drama of this great historical tale—however illuminated or alleviated by a little side story about a distinctive land snail. We must not carp. Columbus opened a new world, and began a process that altered human history in a permanent and fundamental way. He was a brilliant and courageous sailor, and his accomplishments merit all the messages of hope and fortitude proclaimed in unison by the monuments of San Salvador. The messages are therefore "true" in this narrow sense—but ever so partial, and therefore misleading as well.

As I read Columbus's log, I could thrill to his accomplishments, but I also felt waves of revulsion at two persistent themes that never find expression on ceremonial tablets, but also set the pathways of later history. First, his lust for gold, his almost single-minded search for the currency that would justify his endeavor and all future exploitation. On San Salvador, he noticed small gold rings in the noses of some Taino natives, and he persistently inquired about the source. He went from island to island, looking for mines, and thinking that he would soon encounter either the fabled golden isle of Cipangu (Japan), or the rich courts of the grand Khan in Cathay (China). As he visited progressively more powerful caciques (local chiefs), he found more and more gold, but never a source area—and (obviously) never the rich and fabled civilizations of eastern Asia. Finally, and tragically for the local people, he did discover a source of gold on Hispaniola—and his kinsmen built the mines that precipitated the enslavement and genocide of the Tainos, and the total depopulation of the Bahamas.

On October 13, 1492, his second day in the New World, Columbus had already begun his inquiries, writing in his log: "And by signs I was able to understand that, going to the south or rounding the islands to the south, there was a king who had large vessels of it and had very much gold." In a classic passage, Samuel Eliot Morison writes:

> All the rest of his First Voyage was, in fact, a search for gold and Cipangu, Cathay and the Grand Khan; but gold in any event. In all else he might fail, but gold he must bring home in order to prove *la empresa* [the undertaking] a success.

In the Bahamas, his Taino guides spoke of a large nearby island called Colba (Cuba)—but Columbus heard "China" and went off in search of gold. On Cuba, he heard a rumor of gold in the island's interior at Cubanacan (meaning mid-Cuba)—but he heard *El Gran Can,* and thought that he would soon reach the imperial court. On the shore of Hispaniola, two days before Christmas, Columbus learned about gold in Cibao (the local name for central Hispaniola)—and he heard Cipangu, or Japan. But this time his countrymen would find their reward.

Second, Columbus praised the kindness and hospitality of the native Tainos. He could not have proceeded nearly so well without their enthusiastic help. Yet, his commentary speaks only about ease of domination and compulsion to service, not of gratitude or appreciation. In his very first entry for October 12, following his initial meeting and trading session with the Tainos of San Salvador, Columbus noted:

> I gave to some of them red caps and to some glass beads, which they hung on their necks, and many other things of slight value, in which they took much pleasure; they remained so much our friends that it was a marvel; and later they came swimming to the ships' boats . . . and brought us parrots and cotton

thread in skeins and darts and many other things . . . everything they had, with good will.

Columbus then made an observation with practical import:

They bear no arms, nor know thereof; for I showed them swords and they grasped them by the blade and cut themselves through ignorance; they have no iron.

And he drew a conclusion about domination, not brotherhood:

They ought to be good servants and of good skill, for I see that they repeat very quickly all that is said to them; and I believe that they would easily be made Christians, because it seemed to me that they belonged to no religion. I, praise Our Lord, will carry off six of them at my departure to Your Highnesses, so that they may learn to speak.

Two days later, he wrote more openly about servitude: "These people are very unskilled in arms . . . With fifty men they could all be subjected and made to do all that one wished." And, from Hispaniola, near the end of the voyage, Columbus stated a plan for enslavement more explicitly: "They bear no arms, and are all unprotected and so very cowardly that a thousand would not face three; so they are fit to be ordered about and made to work, to sow and do aught else that may be needed."

And history then unfolded according to the Admiral's suggestion. The mines and estates of New Spain needed labor, and the local people, whom Columbus had called "Indians" in a mistaken belief that he had reached eastern Asia, became serfs and slaves because they could not stand against the Spanish technology of swords and gunpowder. As the natives of Hispaniola died from disease, overwork, cruelty, and (no doubt) inner distress, the Spanish governors authorized a "harvesting" of new bodies from neighboring places. And they turned to Columbus's first landfall—the Bahama islands, small bits of land with good anchorages, and unarmed people with no place to hide. In his classic book *The Early Spanish Main,* C. O. Sauer writes:

Jamaica was known to be populous . . . Its size and tracts of difficult terrain, however, would have demanded well-organized expeditions to round up natives in number. Cuba, large and less well known, would have required even more effort. The Lucayas [Bahamas] on the other hand were a great lot of small islands, lacking refuges except by flight to another island and their people were known to be without guile; these would be the easiest to seize.

Starting in 1509, and largely under the command of Ponce de León, the lieutenant governor of Puerto Rico, Spanish ships began to capture the Bahamian Tainos to work as slaves in Hispaniola and neighboring islands. The conquerors were thorough and rapid in their grisly work. Estimates vary, but several tens of thousands may have been thus enslaved. As the Bahamian population dwindled, the price per head rose from five to 150 gold pesos. By 1512, only twenty years after the first Columbian contact, not one Taino remained in the Bahamas. (They did not long survive in the mines of New Spain, either—and Africans were soon imported as "replacements," thus beginning another major chapter of shame in the history of the New World.) We all learned in school that Ponce de León discovered Florida in 1513 as part of a heroic and romantic quest for the Fountain of Youth. Perhaps, in part. But Ponce de León, the chief agent of Taino destruction, had sailed primarily to find a new source of slaves beyond the thoroughly depopulated Bahamian islands.

Bartolomé de Las Casas (1474–1566) began his manhood as a soldier, and sailed for Hispaniola in 1502. He participated in the conquest of Cuba and received an *encomienda* (a royal grant of land with Indian slaves). But Las Casas had a change of heart and became a priest. He preached a sermon against slavery and ill treatment of native peoples in 1514, and returned his Indian serfs to the governor. In 1515, he sailed for Spain to plead before the court for better treatment of Native Americans. He later joined the Dominican order and, in the course of a long and active life spent writing treatises and shuttling between Spain and the New World, he became a passionate and effective advocate for humane treatment of the New World's first inhabitants.

The same Las Casas copied Columbus's log to use as a source for his historical writings. As he considered Columbus's role in the story of Indian conquest and servitude, Las Casas noted the tragic beginning that might have unfolded otherwise, had only decency been able to conquer greed. Las Casas explicitly discusses the passages from Columbus's log cited earlier in this essay:

> Note here, that the natural, simple and kind gentleness and humble condition of the Indians, and want of arms or protection, gave the Spaniards the insolence to hold them of little account, and to impose upon them the harshest tasks that they could, and become glutted with oppression and destruction. And sure it is that here the Admiral [Columbus] enlarged himself in speech more than he should and that what he here conceived and set forth from his lips, was the beginning of the ill usage he afterwards inflicted upon them.

As a final result, and in one of history's greatest and cruelest ironies, the first people that Europeans encountered in the New World also became the first victims of Western genocide. As one tiny consequence, no historical continuity could be maintained to preserve a human record or legend of Columbus's first landfall—and we must therefore resort to a fable about a land snail as a hypothetical way (though guaranteed for success if only Columbus had collected a single shell) to resolve this initial puzzle in the modern history of a hemisphere.

San Salvador remained uninhabited for nearly three hundred years (legends about transient pirate landings notwithstanding)—until British loyalists, fleeing the American Revolution, built plantations and imported slaves of African origin. The descendants of these slaves built the second culture of San Salvador, now vigorously in force.

We may soften the old observation that a second historical cycle often replays an initial tragedy as a derived farce. Let us only note that repeat performances tend to be more gentle. The wake of Columbus destroyed the first culture of San Salvador in the most cruelly literal way. The long arm of Columbus now threatens the second— not with death this time, but with assimilation to international corporate blandness. Most islands of the outer Bahamas remain largely "undeveloped" by modern tourism and resort culture, but the idea of Columbus's landfall provides a hook for luring people to San Salvador. After a century of small hostelries that fit well with local culture, Club Med has just built a major establishment that may change this small island into a playground of tinsel.

But many forces resist homogenization, and we should take heart. Of two examples, consider first the humor of *Homo sapiens.* A small establishment on the main road of San Salvador calls itself "Ed's First and Last Bar"—because people tend to stop by both before and after their visit to a much larger and more popular watering hole up the road a piece. But a new sign now graces the First and Last—"Club Ed," of course!

As a second example, and if only for symbolic value, consider the tenacity of *Cerion.* Club Med and its clones may one day envelop the island, sweeping up the vestiges of local culture into a modern, rootless fairyland of more gentle (and literally profitable) modern exploitation. But *Cerion* will hang tough as a marker of San Salvador's uniqueness. Unless the entire island becomes paved and manicured, *Cerion* will survive. *Cerion,* hearty and indestructible, poses no threat to agriculture or urban existence, and therefore passes largely beyond (and beneath) human notice; *Cerion* also inhabits the scrubby shoreline environments least attractive for human utility.

Cerion will survive to provide an unbroken continuity with Columbus and the original Taino inhabitants. Any snail among thousands crowded around the first Columbian monument on Crab Cay may be the great-great-great-great grandchild of a forebear that looked back at the *Pinta*—and wondered about the future in its aimless, snail-like way—when Rodrigo de Triana first raised his cry of *"Tierra!"* and altered human history forever.

Double Take

1. How does Stephen Jay Gould generate the reader's interest in "A *Cerion* for Christopher," especially in the beginning? What techniques does he use to get readers engaged? Do you think they are effective? Explain.
2. Look at how Gould introduces the *Cerion,* the land snail, into his discussion of Columbus and the Western conquest of America. How does he do it? What makes it work as a connecting device? How does Gould use the snail to achieve his overall meaning?
3. What do you think Gould is trying to accomplish in this essay? What do you think are Gould's most effective, compelling arguments? Explain what makes them so.
4. In what ways does the essay, in its subject matter, style, and argument, reflect an awareness of its readers? Where in the essay is that awareness most evident? Where, perhaps, is it least evident?

Seeing for Yourself

At First Glance

"The Great Western *and the Fighting* Temeraire*" reveals many of the characteristics that can be found in other essays by Stephen Jay Gould, but it is probably an extreme version of these characteristics. In it, Gould is much more directive, explicitly guiding the reader from detail to detail using phrases such as "now let us return . . ." As you read the essay, consider the effect of these directions and why you might want to use (or not use) them in your own writing. Also, think about how this essay reflects a major theme in Gould's essays, the relationship between the humanities and sciences. Examine, for example, how this essay might capture what Gould means when he describes himself as a "humanistic naturalist."*

The *Great Western* and the Fighting *Temeraire*

Science progresses; art changes. Scientists are interchangeable and anonymous before their universal achievements; artists are idiosyncratic and necessary creators of their unique masterpieces. If Copernicus and Galileo had never lived, the earth would still revolve around the sun, and earthlings would have learned this natural truth in due time. If Michelangelo had never lived, the Sistine Chapel might still have a painted vault, but the history of art would be different and humanity would be a good deal poorer. This "standard" account of the differences between art and science belongs to our distressing but prevalent genre of grossly oversimplified dichotomies—stark contrasts that both enlighten in their boldness and distort in their formulaic divisions of complexly intertwined entities into two strictly separated piles—"and never the twain shall meet,/Till Earth and Sky stand presently at God's great Judgment Seat."

The supposed inexorability of technological progress, under this distorting dichotomy, leads to the myth of science as virtually disembodied—a machine endowed with its own momentum, and therefore striding forward almost independently of any human driver. Scientists, under this model, become anonymous and virtually invisible. A few names survive as icons and heroes—Edison and Bell as doers, Darwin and Einstein as thinkers. But, if we accept the premise that technological innovation (in manufacturing, warfare, transportation, and communication) has powered social change far beyond all other consequences of human emotion and ingenuity, how can we resolve the paradox that the people most responsible for propelling human history remain so invisible? Who can name anyone connected with the invention of the crossbow, the zipper, the typewriter, the Xerox machine, or the computer?

Artists, politicians, and soldiers win plaudits and notoriety, though so many impose themselves only lightly and transiently upon the motors of social change. Scientists, engineers, and technologists forge history and gain oblivion as a reward—in large part as a consequence of the false belief that individuality has little relevance when a progressive chain of discoveries proceeds in logical and inexorable order. Let me illustrate our different treatment of scientists versus statesmen and artists with two pairings.

Colonel Calverly, head of a company of dragoon guards in Gilbert and Sullivan's *Patience,* introduces his troops by giving the audience a formula for their construction:

> *If you want a receipt for that popular mystery,*
> *Known to the world as a heavy dragoon,*
> *Take all the remarkable people in history,*
> *Rattle them off to a popular tune . . .*

The Colonel then rips off (at patter-song speed) two hilarious doggerel verses, listing thirty-eight historical figures, including a few fictional and general characters. Only one is a scientist. (The notoriously sexist Gilbert listed three times as many women— Queen Anne, the generic and demeaning "Odalisque on a divan," and Madame Tussaud, founder of the great London wax museum.) The scientist appears in the first quatrain:

> *The pluck of Lord Nelson on board of the* Victory—
> *Genius of Bismarck devising a plan—*
> *The humor of Fielding (which sounds contradictory)—*
> *Coolness of Paget about to trepan.*

Most of us will have no trouble with the first three—Admiral Horatio Nelson dying at the battle of Trafalgar, the great German statesman, and the author of *Tom Jones.* But scientists gain little recognition in their own times and quickly fade from later memory. So who is Mr. Paget, about to open his patient's skull? Sir James Paget, surgeon to the queen and a founder of the science of pathology, may have been a household name to his Victorian contemporaries, but few of us know him today (and I couldn't have made the identification without my trusty encyclopedia). So scientists and engineers create history, but Gilbert chooses only one to participate in the construction of English fiber, and even this man has since sunk to oblivion in the general culture of educated people.

For the second paring, let us return to Admiral Nelson and the story of Trafalgar. On October 21, 1805, Nelson's fleet of twenty-seven ships met and destroyed a combined French and Spanish force of thirty-three vessels off Cape Trafalgar, near the Strait of Gibraltar. Nelson's forces captured twenty ships and put 14,000 of the enemy out of commission (about half killed or wounded, and half captured), while suffering only 1,500 casualties and losing no ships. This victory ended Napoleon's threat to invade England and established a supremacy of British naval power that would endure for more than a century.

Nelson, "on board of the *Victory*," engaged his flagship with the French *Redoutable*. The opposing ship fired at such close range that a French sniper, shooting from the mizzentop of the *Redoutable*, easily picked off Nelson from a distance of only fifteen yards. Nelson died of this wound a few hours later, but with secure knowledge of his triumph.

Nelson's ship, and much of the battle, was saved by the second man-of-war on the line, the *Temeraire*. This vessel rescued the *Victory* by firing a port broadside into the *Redoutable* and disabling the French ship (The mainmast of the *Redoutable* fell right across the *Temeraire;* the French ship then surrendered, and the *Temeraire's* crew boarded her and lashed the defeated vessel to her port side.) Another French ship, the *Fougueux,* then attacked the *Temeraire,* but the British man-of-war fired her starboard broadside, to equally good effect, and secured her second prize, lashed this time to her starboard side. The *Temeraire,* now disabled herself, but with her two prizes lashed to her sides, had to be towed into port by a frigate.

Enter J. M. W. Turner (1775–1851), Britain's greatest nineteenth-century artist and the first subject of my second pairing. Early in his career, in 1806, Turner painted a conventionally heroic scene of the conflict: *The Battle of Trafalgar, as Seen from the Mizen Starboard Shrouds of the* Victory. We see Nelson, surrounded by his officers and dying on deck. The *Temeraire* stands in the background, firing away at the *Fougueux*.

Late in his career, in 1839, Turner returned to the ships of Trafalgar and depicted a very different scene, magnificent in philosophical and emotional meaning, and one of the world's most popular paintings ever since: *The Fighting* Temeraire, *Tugged to Her Last Berth to Be Broken Up, 1838.* The large men-of-war, with their three major tiers of guns, were beautiful, terrible (in the old sense of inspiring terror), and awesome fighting machines. The *Temeraire,* constructed of oak, was built at Chatham and launched in 1798. The ship carried a crew of 750, far more than needed to sail the ship (with a gundeck 185 feet in length), but required to operate the ninety-eight guns—for each gun employed several men in elaborate procedures of loading, aiming, firing, and controlling the recoil. But these "hearts of oak" (the favored patriotic name for the great men-of-war) fell victim to their own success. Their supremacy removed the threat of future war, while advancing technologies of steam and iron soon outpaced their wood and sails. These ships never fought again after the Napoleonic wars, and most were reduced to various workaday and unsentimental duties in or near port. The *Temeraire,* for example, was decommissioned in 1812 and then served as a floating prison and a victualing station.

Eventually, as timbers rotted and obsolescence advanced, these great vessels were stripped and sold to ship breakers to be dismantled for timber, plank by plank. John Beatson, a ship breaker at the yards of Rotherhithe, bought the *Temeraire* at auction for 5,530 pounds. Two steam tugs towed the bulk of the *Temeraire* fifty-five miles from Sheerness to Rotherhithe in September 1838.

Turner's painting presents a wrenchingly dramatic view, quite inaccurate in an entirely studied way, of the *Temeraire's* last sad trip. The great man-of-war, ghostly white, still bears its three masts proudly, with light rigging in place, and sails furled on the yards. The small steam tug, painted dark red to black, stands in front, smoke belching from its tall stack to obscure part of the *Temeraire*'s mast behind. One of Turner's most brilliant sunsets—with clear metaphorical meaning—occupies the right half of the painting. The most majestic and heart-stopping product of the old order sails passively to her death, towed by a relatively diminutive object of the new technology. John Ruskin wrote: "Of all pictures not visibly involving human pain, this is the most pathetic that ever was painted."

Turner clearly set his scene for romance and meaning, not for accuracy. Ships sold for timber were always demasted, so the *Temeraire* sailed to her doom as a hulk without masts, sails, or rigging of any sort—a most uninspiring, if truthful, image. Moreover, Rotherhithe lies due west of Sheerness, so the sun never could have set *behind* the *Temeraire*!

A simplistic and evidently false interpretation has often been presented for Turner's painting—one that, if true, would establish bitter hostility between art and science, thus subverting the aim of this essay: to argue that the two fields, while legitimately separate in some crucial ways, remain bound in ties of potentially friendly and reinforcing interaction. In this adversarial interpretation, recalling Blake's contrast of "dark Satanic mills" with "England's green and pleasant land," the little steam tug is a malicious enemy—a symbol of technology's power to debase and destroy all that previous art had created in nobility. In a famous, if misguided, assessment, William Makepeace Thackeray (one of the thirty-eight in Gilbert's recipe for a heavy dragoon), wrote in 1839, when Turner first displayed his painting:

> "The Fighting Temeraire"—as grand a picture as ever figured on the walls of any academy, or came from the easel of any painter. The old Temeraire is dragged to her last home by a little, spiteful, diabolical steamer . . . The little demon of a steamer is belching out a volume . . . of foul, lurid, red-hot malignant smoke, paddling furiously, and lashing up the water around it; while behind it . . . slow, sad and majestic, follows the brave old ship, with death, as it were, written on her.

This reading makes little sense because Turner, like so many artists of the nineteenth century, was captivated by new technologies, and purposefully sought to include them in his paintings. In fact, Turner had a special fascination for steam, and he clearly delighted in mixing the dark smoke of the new technology with nature's lighter daytime colors.

In *Turner: The Fighting* Temeraire, art historian Judy Egerton documents Turner's numerous, and clearly loving, paintings of steam vessels—starting with a paddle-steamer shown prominently in a painting of Dover Castle in 1822 (passenger steamboats only started to operate between Calais and Dover in 1821), and culminating in a long series of paintings and drawings featuring steamboats on the Seine, and done during the 1830s. A perceptive commentator, writing anonymously in the *Quarterly Review* in 1836, praised Turner for creating "a new object of admiration—a new instance of the beautiful—the upright and indomitable march of the self-impelling steamboat." He then specifically lauded "the admirable manner in which Turner, the most ideal of our landscape painters, has introduced the steamboat in some views taken from the Seine."

This reviewer then credits Turner for his fruitful and reinforcing union of nature and technology:

The tall black chimney, the black hull, and the long wreath of smoke left lying on the air, present, on this river, an image of life, and of majestic life, which appears only to have assumed its rightful position when seen amongst the simple and grand productions of nature.

The steam tug in *The Fighting* Temeraire is not spiteful or demonic. She does not mock her passive burden on the way to destruction. She is a little workaday boat doing her appointed job. If Turner's painting implies any villain, we must surely look to the bureaucrats of the British Admiralty who let the great men-of-war decay, and then sold them for scrap.

Which brings me to Isambard Kingdom Brunel, the engineer who goes with Turner in my second pairing. How many of you know his name? How many even recognized the words as identifying a person, rather than a tiny principality somehow never noticed in our atlas or stamp album? Yet one can make a good argument—certainly in symbolic terms for the enterprise he represented, if not in actuality for his personal influence—that Isambard Kingdom Brunel was the most important figure in the entire nineteenth-century history of Britain.

Brunel was the great practical builder and engineer in British industrial history—and industry powered the Victorian world, often setting the course of politics as firmly as the routes of transportation. Brunel (1806–1859) built bridges, docks, and tunnels. He constructed a floating armored barge, and designed the large guns as well, for the attack on Kronstadt during the Crimean War. He built a complete prefabricated hospital, shipped in sections to the Crimea in 1855.

But Brunel achieved his greatest impact in the world of steam, both on land and at sea—and now we begin to grasp the tie to Turner. He constructed more than one thousand miles of railroad in Great Britain and Ireland. He also built two railways in Italy and served as adviser for other lines in Australia and India. In the culmination of his career, Brunel constructed the three greatest steam vessels of his age, each of the world's largest at launching. His first, the *Great Western,* establishes the symbolic connection with Turner and *The Fighting* Temeraire. The *Great Western,* a wooden paddle-wheel vessel 236 feet in length and weighing 1,340 tons, was the first steamship to provide regular transatlantic service. She began her crossings in 1838, the year of the *Temeraire*'s last tow and demise. In fact, on August 17, 1838, the day after the sale of the *Temeraire,* the *Great Western* arrived in New York and the *Shipping and Mercantile Gazette* declared that "the whole of the mercantile world . . . will from this moment adopt the new conveyance." The little tug in Turner's painting did not doom or threaten the great sailing ships. Brunel's massive steam vessels signaled the inevitable end of sail as a principal and practical method of oceanic transport.

Brunel went on, building bigger and better steamships. He launched the *Great Britain* in 1844, an iron-hulled ship 322 feet long, and the first large steam vessel powered by a screw propeller rather than side paddles. Finally, in 1859, Brunel launched the *Great Eastern,* with a double iron hull and propulsion by both screws and paddles. The *Great Eastern* remained the world's largest steamship for forty years. She never worked well as a passenger vessel, but garnered her greatest fame in laying the first successful transatlantic cable. Brunel, unfortunately, did not live to see the *Great Eastern* depart on her first transoceanic voyage. He suffered a serious stroke on board the ship, and died just a few days before the voyage.

Turner and Brunel are bound by tighter connections than the fortuitous link of the *Temeraire*'s demise with the inauguration of regular transoceanic service by the *Great Western* in the same year of 1838. Turner also loved steam in its major manifestation on land—railroads. In 1844, his seventieth year, Turner painted a canvas that many critics regard as his last great work: *Rain, Steam, and Speed—The Great Western Railway.* Brunel built this two-hundred-mile line between London and Birmingham between 1834 and 1838 (and then used the same name for his first great steamship). Turner's painting shows a train, running on Brunel's wide seven-foot gauge, as the engine passes over the Maidenhead Railway Bridge, another famous construction, featuring the world's flattest brick arch, as designed and built by Isambard Kingdom Brunel. The trains could achieve speeds in excess of fifty miles per hour, but Turner had painted a hare running in front of the engine—and, though one can't be sure, the hare seems poised to outrun the train, not to be crushed under "the ringing grooves of change," to cite Tennyson's famous metaphor about progress, inspired by the poet's first view of a railroad.

We revere Turner, and rightly so. But why has the name Isambard Kingdom Brunel, as inspired in engineering as Turner in painting, as influential in nineteenth-century history as any person in the arts, slipped so far from public memory? I do not know the full answer to this conundrum, but the myth of inexorability in discovery, ironically fostered by science as a source of putative prestige, has surely contributed by depicting scientists as interchangeable cogs in the wheel of technological progress— as people whose idiosyncrasy and individual genius must be viewed as irrelevant to an inevitable sequence of advances.

Art and science are different enterprises, but the boundaries between them remain far more fluid and interdigitating, and the interactions far richer and more varied, than the usual stereotypes proclaim. As a reminder of both overlaps and differences, I recently read the first issue of *Scientific American*—for August 28, 1845, and republished by the magazine to celebrate its 150th anniversary.

Scientific American was founded by Rufus Porter, a true American original in eccentric genius and entrepreneurial skill. Porter had spent most of his time as an itinerant mural painter, responsible for hundreds of charming and primitively painted landscape scenes on the interior walls of houses throughout New England. Yet he chose to start a journal devoted primarily to the practical side of science in engineering and manufacturing. In fact, the initiating issue features, as the main article, a story about the first landing in New York of "the greatest maritime [sic] curiosity ever seen in our harbour"—none other than Brunel's second ship, the *Great Britain*. "This mammoth of the ocean," Porter writes, "has created much excitement here as well as in Europe . . . During the first few days since her arrival at New York, she has been visited by about 12,000 people, who have paid 25 cents for the gratification."

If an artist could initiate a leading journal in science, if Turner could greatly enhance his painted sunsets by using a new pigment, iodine scarlet, just invented by

Humphrey Davy of the Royal Institution, a leading scientific laboratory founded by Count Rumford in 1799, then why do we so consistently stress the differences and underplay the similarities between these two greatest expressions of human genius? Why do we pay primary attention to the artist's individuality, while constantly emphasizing the disembodied logic of science? Aren't these differences of focus mostly a matter of choice and convention, not only of evident necessity? The individuality of scientists bears respect and holds importance as well. I do accept that we would now know about evolution even if Darwin had never been born. But the discovery would then have been made by other people, perhaps in different lands, and surely with dissimilar interests and concerns—and these potential variations in style may be no less profound or portentous than the disparity between such artistic contemporaries as Verdi and Wagner.

I do not deny that the accumulative character of scientific change—the best justification for a notion of progress in human history—establishes the major difference between art and science. I found a poignant reminder within a small item in the first issue of *Scientific American*. An advertisement for daguerreotypes on the last page includes the following come-on: "Likenesses of deceased persons taken in any part of the city and vicinity." I then remembered a book published a few years ago on daguerreotypes of dead children—often the only likeness that parents would retain of a lost son or daughter. (Daguerreotypes required long exposures, and young children could rarely be enticed to sit still for the requisite time—but the dead do not move, and daguerreotypists therefore maintained a thriving business, however ghoulish by modern standards, in images of the deceased, particularly of children.)

No example of scientific progress can be less subject to denial or more emotionally immediate than our ever-increasing ability to prevent the death of young people. Even the most wealthy and privileged parents of Turner and Brunel's time expected to lose a high percentage of their children. As Brunel built his railways and Turner painted, Darwin's geology teacher, Adam Sedgwick, wrote to a friend about the achievements of his young protégé, then sailing around the world on the *Beagle,* and therefore in constant medical danger, far from treatment in lands with unknown diseases. "[He] is doing admirable work in South America, and had already sent home a collection above all price . . . There was some risk of his turning out an idle man, but his character will now be fixed, and if God spares his life he will have a great name among the naturalists of Europe." A concerned mentor would not need to fret so intensely today—a blessing from science to all of us.

I previously quoted the beginning of Colonel Calverly's recipe for a heavy dragoon, and will now close with the end:

Beadle of Burlington—Richardson's show—
Mr. Micawber and Madame Tussaud!

We know Mr. Micawber from *David Copperfield,* and Mme. Tussaud for her wax statues. "Richardson's show" puzzled me until I found the following entry in my 1897 edition of *Chambers's Biographical Dictionary:* John Richardson, 1767–1837, "the

'penny showman' from Marlow work house who rose to become a well-to-do trav-
elling manager." But who, or what, is the Beadle of Burlington?

I fell in love with Gilbert and Sullivan at age twelve, and have therefore been
wondering about that Beadle for forty years (not always actively, to be sure!). Then,
six months ago and to my utter delight, I ran right into the Beadle of Burlington
when no subject could have been farther from my mind. I was walking down an
early-nineteenth-century shopping arcade, just off Piccadilly in London, on my way
to a meeting at the Royal Institution, where Humphrey Davy had invented Turner's
new pigment. Lord George Cavendish founded the Burlington Arcade in 1819 "for
the gratification of the public" and "to give employment to industrious females" in
the shops. Lord George established firm rules of conduct for people moving through
the arcade—"no whistling, singing, hurrying, humming, or making merry." Such
decent standards have to be enforced—and so they have been, ever since 1819, by a
two-man private security force, the Beadles of Burlington. Traditions must be maintained, of course, and the Beadles still wear their ancient garb of top hat, gloves, and
coat with tails.

I looked at one of the Beadles in all his antiquated splendor, and I saw that he
held both hands clasped behind his back. So I moseyed around to his other side (no
hurrying) to find out what he might be holding—and I noted a cellular phone in
his gloved hands. Technology and tradition. The old and elegant; the new and functional. The Fighting *Temeraire* and the steam tug. Art and science. The prophet Amos
said, "Can two walk together, except they be agreed?"

A CLOSER LOOK AT STEPHEN JAY GOULD

1. In what ways do the essays collected above demonstrate what Stephen Jay
   Gould calls humanistic naturalism? What is humanistic about them? How
   would you define humanism? Humanistic naturalism? Write an essay in which
   you define these terms and then explain how Gould's writing might be identified as exhibiting humanistic naturalism. Use examples from the essays found
   here to support your arguments.
2. In the preface to his essay collection *The Lying Stones of Marrakech,* Gould
   explains that he uses his "humanistic and historical interests as a 'user friendly'
   bridge to bring readers into the accessible world of science." Turning to his

essays as a reference, write your own essay in which you describe how Gould uses such a bridge, and then argue whether or not you find his use of such a bridge effective. Does the bridge make the world of science more accessible to you as a reader?

3. Write an essay using Gould's rhetorical strategy of connecting a series of details and facts and then making from them a larger, more general observation. "The *Great Western* and the Fighting *Temeraire*" provides a good example of this strategy.

4. Throughout Gould's work runs a strong iconoclastic streak that seeks to debunk various creation myths such as the biblical origins of life and the Cooperstown origin of baseball. Write an essay in which you argue for or against such myths. For many, such myths are very comforting, even when they might know they are just that, myths. What is to be gained or lost by debunking such myths? If you argue on behalf of these myths, imagine Gould as your audience.

Looking from Writer to Writer

1. Both Stephen Jay Gould and Edward O. Wilson are scientists who write essays. Both can be described as "popularizers" of science. And both argue that the sciences and humanities need not be incompatible. Comparing their essays, examine how each makes science accessible in his essays. Does one, in your estimation, make better use of the essay in writing about his subject than the other? If so, how? If not, then how do both effectively make science accessible through their writing?

2. Several of the essayists we have read, like Barbara Ehrenreich and Rick Bass, use the essay to render social commentary and to raise social awareness. In what ways can we group Gould with these essayists? What makes Gould's, Ehrenreich's, and Bass's essays activist?

3. Both Gould and Henry Louis Gates, Jr. are academics who write essays. Comparing their rhetorical strategies and styles, which of the two in your opinion is more effective at reaching a wider, more popular audience? Explain your reasoning with examples from the essays.

Looking Beyond

ESSAYS

An Urchin in the Storm. New York: Norton, 1987.

Bully for Brontosaurus: Reflections in Natural History. New York: Norton, 1991.

Eight Little Piggies: Reflections in Natural History. New York: Norton, 1993.
Ever Since Darwin: Reflections in Natural History. New York: Norton, 1977.
The Flamingo's Smile: Reflections in Natural History. New York: Norton, 1985.
Hen's Teeth and Horse's Toes. New York: Norton, 1983.
Leondardo's Mountain of Clams and the Diet of Worms: Essays on Natural History. New York: Harmony Books, 1998.
The Lying Stones of Marrakech: Penultimate Reflections in Natural History. New York: Harmony Books, 2000.
The Panda's Thumb: More Reflections in Natural History. New York: Norton, 1980.

NONFICTION

Full House: The Spread of Excellence from Plato to Darwin. New York: Harmony Books, 1996.
The Mismeasure of Man. New York: Norton, 1981.
Ontogeny and Phylogeny. Cambridge, MA: Belknap Press–Harvard University Press, 1977.
Rocks of Ages: Science and Religion in the Fullness of Life. New York: Ballantine, 1999.
Time's Arrow, Time's Cycle: Myth and Metaphor in the Discovery of Geological Time. Cambridge, MA: Harvard University Press, 1987.
Wonderful Life: The Burgess Shale and the Nature of History. New York: Norton, 1989.

Edward Hoagland

Described by John Updike as the best living American essayist, Edward Hoagland was born in 1932 in New York City, and grew up "rebelliously disillusioned," as he puts it, amid yacht club life in Greenwich, Connecticut. (His father, a Wall Street lawyer, tried to block the publication of Hoagland's first novel as well as his career as a writer for fear that his writing would endanger the family's social status.) After graduating from Harvard, Hoagland turned to writing stories and novels, completing four books at four-year intervals. In 1968, while writing a travel journal about frontier life in northern British Columbia, *Notes from the Century Before: A Journal from British Columbia* (1969), Hoagland discovered essay writing as an avocation that allowed him not so much to invent life (what he describes as the work of novels) but to record it. This recording impulse, a prominent characteristic of essays in general, runs deep in Hoagland's essays and is particularly well-suited to someone who is perhaps best known as a nature writer. Hoagland writes that an essayist "should be a man for all seasons . . . loafing attentively, seizing risks, mastering data, summarizing what we'd nearly thought to say ourselves. He should know everything that two eyes can be expected to take in, yet make a virtue out of being a freelance observer, operating solo, not as a committee." As a freelance observer, Hoagland has traveled, among other places, to Antarctica, Africa, India, Egypt, Israel, and Cyprus.

Whether it is novels, essays, or travel books, Edward Hoagland's writing is rooted in and grows out of his and others' lived experiences. In preparing *Cat Man* (1956), a novel of life in a circus, Hoagland spent five months working in a Ringling Brothers circus, attending to the big cats. Later, while living in New York's Lower East Side, he wrote his second book, *The Circle Home*, a novel about New York boxing. For his travel book, *Notes from the Century Before*, Hoagland lived with and chronicled the lives of frontiersmen living along the Stikine River, 800 miles north of Vancouver,

British Columbia. And in his many essays, comprising seven book collections over 30 years, Hoagland is at times agonizingly honest in disclosing and recording his personal, even intimate experiences, ranging from sexual performance, severe stuttering, strained relationship with his father, infidelities, and failed marriages to his maturity as a writer, overcoming blindness, and love of nature.

For the most part, Hoagland's essays can best be described as personal essays, different from the more academic essays of Stephen Jay Gould and bell hooks, the more political essays of Barbara Ehrenreich and Salman Rushdie, and the more literary essays of Cynthia Ozick and John Updike. Hoagland's essays, like essays in general, are recordings of the world, but his essays tend to record the world introspectively, as it is filtered through the lens of his own personal perspective—that is, his essays do not so much record the world as they record his impressions of the world and the world's impressions on him. This is not the same, however, as saying that his essays are egotistical, pour-out-your-heart effusions. Rather, it is more akin to saying that Hoagland's essays give us glimpses of the world as it pivots around his personal perspective. As such, his essays admit that we cannot know the world objectively; we can only know it as we experience it subjectively. It is perhaps for this reason that in his essay about writing ("To the Point: Truths only Essays Can Tell"), Hoagland maintains that essayists do not need exceptional memories like novelists do; they mainly record impressions "written mostly in the present tense."

Sight and insight play off of one another in Hoagland's essays. As he maintains, he became an observer at an early age chiefly because he suffered from a severe stutter that left him often unable to communicate. So he observed instead. Writing essays thus became a way for him to "speak." In a well-known statement, Hoagland explains, "essays are how we speak to one another in print—carooming thoughts not merely in order to convey a certain packet of information, but with a special edge or bounce of personal character in a kind of public letter." When he lost his eyesight in his mid-50s due to cataracts (becoming legally blind), Hoagland's writing stalled. Ironically, it was then that his stuttering stopped. A series of eye operations in the early 1990s restored his eyesight after three years of blindness, the experiences of which he captured in *Compass Points: How I Lived* (2001).

The tension and balance between speaking and writing is a recurring theme in Hoagland's life and essays. He describes his essays as the result of "mind speaking to mind." As you read the essays that follow, pay attention to this dialogue between minds that Hoagland describes. In what ways does what we are reading constitute a sort of mental dialogue between our minds and Hoagland's mind? How does Hoagland achieve this effect rhetorically? In addition, think about the balance of sight and insight that emerges from his writing, especially the ways that Hoagland manages to record external observations through internal introspection. And most of all, think about what makes his essays "personal" rather than more academic, political, or literary. What demands does such personal writing put on the writer, the reader, and the subject matter?

Hoagland on Writing

At First Glance

"To the point: Truths only Essays Can Tell," published in Harper's Magazine, *is both a statement about essay writing and an example of essay writing. It enacts what it describes. As you read, see if Hoagland's essay does what he claims essays should do. For example, Hoagland claims that essayists do not need exceptional memories, but he proceeds to write about memories of his father, grandfather, and great-grandfather. Pay attention to what having an essayistic memory might mean to Hoagland. In the essay, Hoagland also contrasts essays with novels. Think about what such a contrast reveals about his attitudes toward essays, especially the role of the essayist and the social function of essays.*

To the Point: Truths only Essays Can Tell

In my late thirties I hit my stride as a writer (as many do), and caught my second wind. Earlier, I had published three novels, but I was stalled on the fourth and in the meantime had discovered essay writing through the vehicle of a long travel journal, *Notes From the Century Before,* which I had published in 1969, about the old men of Telegraph Creek, a frontier hamlet on the Stikine River eight hundred miles north of Vancouver, British Columbia.

Wilds had intrigued me since my teens, when I had ridden horseback in the Wind River Range in Wyoming, then fought forest fires in the Santa Ana Mountains in California another summer, and joined the Ringling Bros. and Barnum & Bailey Circus for two spells of caring for the menagerie cats. I'd written a successful novel about that latter experience; another, less vivid, about New York boxing; and a third, about a Pied Piper in a welfare hotel. Fiction was my first love—I had wanted to be the great American novelist—but I lacked the exceptional memory novelists need. (Montaigne, in his essay "On Liars," says he found "scarcely a trace of it" in himself: "I do not believe there is another man in the world so hideously lacking.") Perhaps as a result, I had focused upon honing a poetic style, which is an inadequate substitute. Still (as Montaigne adds), a weak memory makes you think for yourself—you can't remember what other people have written or said.

Essays, though sprinkled with subordinated memories, are written mostly in the present tense and aren't primarily narratives. The point the essayist is trying to illustrate takes precedence over his "story." The other obvious handicap I'd been laboring under in trying to become a great novelist was my disbelief that life *has* many narratives. I think life seldom works in blocks of related events. Rather, you can break your fingernails trying to undo the knots and they will stay knots. My sister and her last husband lived next to each other in isolated farmhouses without speaking for years, she with the children and the fields they'd worked, he as a hired man on other people's land. Like any rural residents, they both owned guns, and so if this were fiction their rancid feelings would finally have erupted into gunfire, arson, flight, or nervous collapse. But life is usually stasis, not a narrative; sadness, not a story. Like a car that won't start, it just won't start.

Yet my main reason for turning into an essayist had less to do with mnemonic deficiencies or any theory of life as connected to fiction than with the painful fact that I stuttered so badly that writing essays was my best chance to talk. Is *this,* therefore, maybe a story? Well, because it afflicted me so soon—and because it seems to stem from a gene passed down from an uncle of mine who also stuttered, until he died under the wheels of a Kansas City trolley car before my father's eyes at the age of nine—the idea hasn't too much novelistic interest, unless you count the wringing-out effect of the sight on my father, who later made me suffer: which to me is an essay. Just as I didn't know the great-grandmother on my mother's side, from whom I probably inherited my bad eyesight, I never knew that stuttering uncle. I have only seen his photo, standing next to my father, both of them in Indian headdresses and buckskin suits.

Their sister had died of blackwater fever at the age of three in a cypress swamp where my grandfather, out of medical school, had taken a job as a contract doctor. Those deep-forest, Spanish-moss swamps of Louisiana, where I've since paddled and camped with Cajun trappers, are spellbinding, larger than life, with gators, panthers, spoonbills, and storks, plus legends African, French, Atakapas. But after the death of two of his three children, my grandfather forswore further adventures and remained an obstetrician back in Missouri till the First World War. He did not see action (his own father and father-in-law had fought on opposite sides of the Civil War) but enjoyed the comradeship of army life so much that he stayed in the reserves for the next twenty years, rising to lieutenant colonel in the medical corps. After his wife's death from cancer at fifty-nine, he retired from active practice in Kansas City and quietly managed a rental property he'd invested in. He was a member of the Ivanhoe Masonic Lodge, the Modern Woodmen of American, and the Sanford Brown post of the American Legion. He sang in the choir of St. Paul's Reformed Church, took a flier in a few West Texas dry-hole oil leases, and died suddenly of meningitis at sixty-seven in 1940 with an estate of $5,000, which is all the Depression had left him.

My father, though a blue-chip lawyer (in the semi-military phase of his own career, when he worked as a negotiator for the Defense Department in Europe, his rank was the civilian equivalent of major general), shared with my grandfather that ambiguity about their chosen professions, likewise retiring early, in his case to try to become a business-school professor and memoir writer. But my father's overly methodical cast of mind did not fit either vocation, and cancer meanly overwhelmed him at sixty-three. His adventuresomeness, instead of heading him from Kansas City to Louisiana, Texas, and a military uniform, had led him east to Yale, Wall Street, and Europe to explore the museums, restaurants, splendid scenery, the history and social complexity, Berlin, London, the Parthenon, the Grand Canal. We once crossed paths at the Trevi Fountain in Rome and had supper together, and to the pretty music of its plash he told me that "an enemy" of his had lived in this square during his period as a U.S. negotiator ten years before. But, with characteristic discretion, he refused to specify who had won or whether his adversary had been a personal rival or an outside foe of the United States.

Both he and my grandfather were genially clubby, easing their hearts among groups of men more easily than I, though perhaps not as inclined to close confidences. Nerdy, squirrelly, yet bold enough within the sphere of a loner, I was leery of the extended compromises membership entails, and maybe too odd to make them. But the professed purpose of my solitude was to speak to loads of people.

My great-grandfather Martin Hoagland, 1843–1926, of "Holland Dutch" descent, as it used to be said, to distinguish Dutch from Germans, who were called "Pennsylvania Dutch," was born on a farm in Bardolph, Illinois, and enlisted as a private in the 57th Illinois Infantry regiment in 1861, mustering out as a lieutenant in 1865 after service at Shiloh under Grant and the battles for Atlanta and Savannah and up through both Carolinas under Sherman. At eighteen he had been shipped from Chicago almost straight to Shiloh. Soon after his discharge he married Emma Jane McPhey, she being an orphan from Yellow Creek, Ohio, raised by a Bardolph uncle and aunt, and they bought a farm in Bardolph. But in 1871, with three of what would wind up being seven children, they set out by Conestoga wagon for central Kansas, settling on a soldier's homestead claim on Brandy Lake in the Arkansas River valley, digging a sod house, the westernmost then, said his front-page banner-headline obituary in the *Hutchinson Herald* fifty-five years later.

There were buffalo and Indians about, and he picked up some cash by hauling supplies for the Atchison, Topeka & Santa Fe Railway construction crews as they crossed Kansas for the second cross-continental linkup in 1881. But his major enthusiasm was in becoming a Johnny Appleseed to this dry region, bringing in apples and peaches, the first to be grown in central Kansas, and carrying the fruiting branches to other farms to show it could be done. He shipped some to the U.S. Centennial Exposition in Philadelphia in 1876 and became a crop reporter for the Department of Agriculture, remaining so for half a century. He learned irrigation techniques with windmill wells, grew the first local sorghum, timothy, and "rice wheat" (the "Turkey Red" wheat that made Kansas famous was introduced by Russian Mennonites at about the same time), and brought in Berkshire hogs and Cherokee milk cows. In the 1880s he entered the meat-and-grain business in the new city of Hutchinson, opened a clothing store, and later served as town councilman, street commissioner, police judge. But my grandfather was born in that sod house, and in my travels over a couple of decades to the Yukon, British Columbia, and Alaska I may have been in search of just this patriarch.

Ah, you might say, a multi-generational novel—but I don't think so. My father went east to become an attorney for an international oil company, others of his generation ended up with cog jobs in the white suburbs of Los Angeles, and I know of no gunfire, epiphanies, or deathbed conversions among them. To me they illustrate the flattening of the earth more than a story line; the Atchison, Topeka & Santa Fe as a bureaucracy, agribusiness monoculture replacing individual Johnny Appleseeds. I've written about John Chapman of the Ohio frontier, the ascetic saint who was the real Johnny Appleseed, and he is, in fact, an exemplar of the benign, pacific nature of a majority of the early pioneers.

I've sought frontiersmen in the river drainages of the taiga country—the least accessible country on the continent and thus last to be settled—and these people were growing parsnips and potatoes, keeping bees and chickens, coaxing peas and lettuce, storing carrots and turnips. Their pride was in their carpentry, not gunsmithing, in getting half a dozen Herefords or packhorses through the winter on the resources of a beaver meadow, not in reaming their neighbor out of five hundred bucks. I've stood at so many trail ends and hollered greetings to a log cabin set in a rough, stumpy clearing a hundred yards away, lest the person living there be startled by me, that I feel confident I know what pioneers on the frontier elsewhere were like.

These weren't gunslingers or deal hustlers; they were generally peaceable, fairly balanced souls who liked the sound of a stream outdoors, planted flower beds in front and a rhubarb patch. If they were placer miners and had found a pocket of gold grains in an old creek bed, instead of going out for a whoopee spree and never coming back, they just worked the spot and bought new stuff for the cabin (a zinc sink, an iron stove that didn't have holes in it, a mattress that hadn't yet become a hive for mice) or more hydraulic equipment and a truck, a boat, a snowmobile to haul and float and sled it in. They, of course, were throwbacks, not ordinary people, having chosen to leave the loop of suburban malls for a riverbank. But ordinary folk did not leave the loop in Europe and come to America in the first place—or then leave the seaboard for Sioux country, living off the land, not in a money economy. Their guns were like our wallets, having the purpose of procuring food, and were not a penis or fetish.

These people whom I'd sit with for an evening were content to watch the fire flicker in the stove and the flame of a kerosene lamp or a miner's candle for enter-tainment, though they might have a bit of corn whiskey too, or birch syrup, apple champagne or plum brandy, huckleberry muffins or home-pulled taffy for a treat. Water diverted from a brook ran forever through a food cooler into the sink, and a fire burned continually no matter what the weather was—these were the constants during the summer, when they dressed more warmly, and in the winter, when they dressed more lightly, than I. Their fires of regret were banked, their eyes lacked my squint under the open sky, and they didn't wish for sharp divergences from day to day, as I tend to. They were subjects for an essay, in other words, more than for fiction.

My grandmother on my mother's side collected bowlfuls of used tinfoil and balls of broken string, wrote letters to her friends on scraps of paper, and, whenever she trav-eled by ship or train, organized her suitcase so tightly, with her socks and foot med-ications at one end and her face cream and hair net at the other, that she could unpack in the dark. She would carry a dozen magazines on a trip, with the advertisements already torn out to save on weight, but, because she thought that only natural light was good for the eyes, would put her reading material away as night fell. Though she was an enthusiastic walker, the foot medications were necessary to ease her discom-fort because her toes had been crushed out of shape by wearing borrowed shoes when she was a child. Her parents were pauperized by the panic of 1873, when the small-town bank they owned in Homer, New York, failed. Her uncle had been handsomely painted by Abraham Lincoln's principal portraitist, but under the weight of this disgraceful calamity her father wasted away, and after his death she and her sister and brother and mother were forced to creep to Flint, Michigan, and move in with cousins, whose shoes she wore.

So *here's* a story, you may say. Elizabeth limps on crushed toes in hand-me-down footwear as a poor relation after her father's business failure. Then she becomes a schoolteacher and marries a businessman, A. J. Morley, after his first wife—one of her prosperous cousins, and also a teacher—dies in childbirth. They move first to Chicago, where he manages his family's wholesale saddlery store, and then to Grays Harbor in Washington State, where, around 1905, he buys with Morley family money (the family was so conservative that they declined, right there in Flint, to invest in the start-up of General Motors, and later, in Washington State, were to refuse to bet on Boeing) seven thousand acres of old-growth forestland on Delezene Creek and launches a logging and shingle-mill operation in Douglas fir country. For saddlery people from Michigan who were expanding into the general hardware business, to participate also in the last hurrah of pioneering in the American Northwest was gambling of an appealingly conservative variety; and besides, they were chasing bad money with good, because A.J.'s scampish older brother Walter (later to be dragooned into the ministry as penance) had already gone west to Grays Harbor and fouled up among the con men on F Street and the brothels on Hume Street and Heron Street in Aberdeen.

A.J. was successful; yet my grandmother continued to save slivers of soap and yesterday's bread. You could cast this as a story, but I wouldn't. To me what's interesting about my grandmother is how, for example, after those virgin hemlocks, firs, and spruces had paid for her to sail to Europe with a grown granddaughter who was honeymooning, and the couple were in Rome and she was in Florence and she wished to rejoin them before the plan called for it, she simply entrained for Rome, took a taxi to the Forum, and sat down on a ruin, figuring any tourist, even honeymooners, would soon go there. Sure enough, within an hour they showed up. My mother, whose childhood was sunnier, enjoyed this commanding sort of confidence, too.

But Grandfather, as his four children grew up and went east to school (he believed, quite sensibly, that eastern children should come west for summer jobs and western children should travel east for social skills and book learning), took a mistress or two, in the fashion of a logging baron in a salmon-canning and raw, tall-timber town of four thousand people on the wild Pacific in the 1920s—though for this role, as well, he preferred the local schoolteachers to the bar girls who'd gotten Walter into trouble. Grandmother's response was to travel extensively, with or without younger companions, on cruise ships and museum tours, or else, less happily, to check into the Aberdeen General Hospital for a week's rest. One time, returning from abroad, she discovered a red nightgown hanging in her closet and thought up a better solution. Instead of fleeing to the hospital, she washed it and wore it every night until it was threadbare, never mentioning why to her husband or telling her sons about the incident until they were driving her home from their father's funeral, twenty years later.

Flamboyance, poignancy, oddity; drama, and cause and effect are all present in some modest measure, but not, I think, *plot,* in her "story." I do have another ancestor, Reuben Hitchcock Morley, a "writer/traveler," who was murdered by a traveling companion in Mongolia en route to the Russo-Japanese War in 1905. Two years before that, Benjamin Franklin Morley had lost his life in his own gold mine in Buena Vista, Colorado, and in 1942 a cousin of my mother's named John Morley died on the Bataan death march. Reuben had fought in the Spanish-American War, and lived among the Yaqui Indians of Mexico and the Igorot tribespeople in the Philippines. But much more often I see life as being slower, flatter, more draggy and anticlimactic, repetitive and yet random, perhaps briefly staccato but then limpid, than all but a handful of novels, and these not the best.

I love great fiction. More than the essays of Montaigne, fiction rivets, inspires, sticks in the mind, makes life seem worth living if ever it doesn't. Novels when upliftingly tragic or vivid with verisimilitude can be unforgettably gripping. But I don't find my own life in many of them. That is, for instance, I wouldn't have married Madame Bovary or shipped out with Ahab. My life has not been Joseph Andrews's, David Copperfield's, or Raskolnikov's. I will always remember such characters, but my own marital blunders, childhood collisions, career nicks and scrapes, and even my chthonic exaltation on certain radiant days when stretching my legs out-of-doors are not synchronous with those that are plumbed in what we call masterpieces. Like Prince Andrey after the battle of Austerlitz in *War and Peace,* I've lain on my back gazing into the sky—but not so near death or to quite the same end. I'm convinced by his feelings and have known their like fitfully after quick bouts with blindness, suicidal impulses, and so on. But if mine were really the same, I'd have ceased, with Buddhist resignation, to write books.

Instead of the breakneck conundrums and rapturous gambits of some of the novels I love, it is the business of essays to be more familiar, unassuming, humdrum. The Declaration of Independence was also an essay, but there aren't many of these; and when I am miffed with my sister, at sixes and sevens with my mother, groping for an intelligent (as distinct from blind) empathy with my daughter, or tangling with the woman I presently share my life with, I'd as soon read a first-rate collection of essays for guidance as *Anna Karenina.* The personal essay is meant to be like a household implement, a frying pan hanging from a punchboard, or a chat at the kitchen table, though it need not remain domestic; it can become anguished, confessional, iconoclastic, or veer from comfortable wit to mastectomy, chemotherapy, and visions of death, just as the talk in a parlor does. Essayists are ambidextrous, not glamorous; switch-hitters going for the single, not the home run. They're character actors, not superstars. They plug along in a modest manner (if any writer can be called modest), piling up masonry incrementally, not trying for the Taj Mahal like an ambitious novelist.

"Trifles make the sum of life," said David Copperfield; and novelists and essayists share that principle. A book is chambered like a beehive, and prose is like comb honey—honey sweeter (to its devotees) because it has its wax still on. Going the other way, from fifteen years of essay writing to doing a novel again, can be exhilarating, as I later found, because one is inventing, not simply recording, the world. I could myth-make a little, draw things a bit differently from how they were, grab for the brass ring, go larger than life, escape the nitty-gritty of reality for a while. Novelists want the site of their drama to be ground zero, but most of us do not live at ground zero. Most of us live like stand-up comedians on a vaudeville stage—the way an essayist does—by our humble wits, messing up, swallowing an aspirin, knowing Hollywood won't call, thinking no one we love will die today, just another day of sunshine and rain.

Double Take

1. What are the "truths" that only essays can tell?
2. In the essay "To the Point," Edward Hoagland writes, "the point the essayist is trying to illustrate takes precedence over his 'story.'" What does Hoagland mean by this, and how does his own essay about the essay reflect this point?
3. Toward the end of the essay, Hoagland describes metaphorically the qualities of the personal essay and the personal essayist. In your own words, what does it mean to describe a personal essay as a "household implement" and the essayist as a "character actor" and a "switch-hitter going for the single"? If these are the qualities that define personal essays, what does that say about their social function, especially when contrasted with novels?
4. Why do you think Hoagland spends so much time chronicling his family history in this essay that is supposed to be about the essay?

At First Glance

"The Courage of Turtles" is one of Edward Hoagland's early essays, having first appeared in the Village Voice. *Yet it is characteristic of many of Hoagland's later essays, especially in its detailed observation and description, its focus on the observer as much as the thing observed, and its concern for animals. While reading it, think about what Hoagland is trying to argue. His point is not made explicit, yet, as he explains in "To the Point: Truths only Essays Can Tell," the point an essay is trying to make is more important than the story it tells. Think also about the "I" that is speaking in the essay, and why Hoagland inserts so many of them, especially into an essay that is supposed to be about turtles. Finally, given Hoagland's reputation as a nature conservationist, consider whether you think this essay is an effective plea on behalf of nature, paying special attention to its tone.*

The Courage of Turtles

TURTLES ARE A KIND of bird with the governor turned low. With the same attitude of removal, they cock a glance at what is going on, as if they need only to fly away.

Until recently they were also a case of virtue rewarded, at least in the town where I grew up, because, being humble creatures, there were plenty of them. Even when we still had a few bobcats in the woods the local snapping turtles, growing up to forty pounds, were the largest carnivores. You would see them through the amber water, as big as greeny wash basins at the bottom of the pond, until they faded into the inscrutable mud as if they hadn't existed at all.

When I was ten I went to Dr. Green's Pond, a two-acre pond across the road. When I was twelve I walked a mile or so to Taggart's Pond, which was lusher, had big water snakes and a waterfall; and shortly after that I was bicycling way up to the adventuresome vastness of Mud Pond, a lake-sized body of water in the reservoir system of a Connecticut city, possessed of cat-backed little islands and empty shacks and a forest of pines and hardwoods along the shore. Otters, foxes and mink left their prints on the bank; there were pike and perch. As I got older, the estates and forgotten back lots in town were parceled out and sold for nice prices, yet, though the woods had shrunk, it seemed that fewer people walked in the woods. The new residents didn't know how to find them. Eventually, exploring, they did find them, and it required some ingenuity and doubling around on my part to go for eight miles without meeting someone. I was grown by now, I lived in New York, and that's what I wanted on the occasional weekends when I came out.

Since Mud Pond contained drinking water I had felt confident nothing untoward would happen there. For a long while the developers stayed away, until the drought of the mid-1960s. This event, squeezing the edges in, convinced the local water company that the pond really wasn't a necessity as a catch basin, however; so they bulldozed a hole in the earthen dam, bulldozed the banks to fill in the bottom, and landscaped the flow of water that remained to wind like an English brook and provide a domestic view for the houses which were planned. Most of the painted turtles of Mud Pond, who had been inaccessible as they sunned on their rocks, wound up in boxes in boys' closets within a matter of days. Their footsteps in the dry leaves gave them away as they wandered forlornly. The snappers and the little musk turtles, neither of whom leave the water except once a year to lay their eggs, dug into the drying mud for another siege of hot weather, which they were accustomed to doing whenever the pond got low. But this time it was low for good; the mud baked over them and slowly entombed them. As for the ducks, I couldn't stroll in the woods and not feel guilty, because they were crouched beside every stagnant pothole, or were slinking between the bushes with their heads tucked into their shoulders so that I wouldn't see them. If they decided I had, they beat their way up through the screen of trees, striking their wings dangerously, and wheeled about with that headlong, magnificent velocity to locate another poor puddle.

I used to catch possums and black snakes as well as turtles, and I kept dogs and goats. Some summers I worked in a menagerie with the big personalities of the animal kingdom, like elephants and rhinoceroses. I was twenty before these enthusiasms began to wane, and it was then that I picked turtles as the particular animal I wanted to keep in touch with. I was allergic to fur, for one thing, and turtles need minimal care and not much in the way of quarters. They're personable beasts. They see the same colors we do and they seem to see just as well, as one discovers in trying to sneak up on them. In the laboratory they unravel the twists of a maze with the hot-blooded rapidity of a mammal. Though they can't run as fast as a rat, they improve on their errors just as quickly, pausing at each crossroads to look left and right. And they rock rhythmically in place, as we often do, although they are hatched from eggs, not the womb. (A common explanation psychologists give for our pleasure in rocking quietly is that it recapitulates our mother's heartbeat *in utero.*)

Snakes, by contrast, are dryly silent and priapic. They are smooth movers, legalistic, unblinking, and they afford the humor which the humorless do. But they make challenging captives; sometimes they don't eat for months on a point of order—if the light isn't right, for instance. Alligators are sticklers too. They're like war-horses, or German shepherds, and with their bar-shaped, vertical pupils adding emphasis, they have the *idée fixe* of eating, eating, even when they choose to refuse all food and stubbornly die. They delight in tossing a salamander up towards the sky and grabbing him in their long mouths as he comes down. They're so eager that they get the jitters, and they're too much of a proposition for a casual aquarium like mine. Frogs are depressingly defenseless: that moist, extensive back, with the bones almost sticking through. Hold a frog and you're holding its skeleton. Frogs' tasty legs are the staff of life to many animals—herons, raccoons, ribbon snakes—though they themselves are hard to feed. It's not an enviable role to be the staff of life, and after frogs you descend down the evolutionary ladder a big step to fish.

Turtles cough, burp, whistle, grunt and hiss, and produce social judgments. They put their heads together amicably enough, but then one drives the other back with the suddenness of two dogs who have been conversing in tones too low for an onlooker to hear. They pee in fear when they're first caught, but exercise both pluck and optimism in trying to escape, walking for hundreds of yards within the confines of their pen, carrying the weight of that cumbersome box on legs which are cruelly positioned for walking. They don't feel that the contest is unfair; they keep plugging, rolling like sailorly souls—a bobbing, infirm gait, a brave, sea-legged momentum—stopping occasionally to study the lay of the land. For me, anyway, they manage to contain the rest of the animal world. They can stretch out their necks like a giraffe, or loom underwater like an apocryphal hippo. They browse on lettuce thrown on the water like a cow moose which is partly submerged. They have a penguin's alertness, combined with a build like a Brontosaurus when they rise up on tiptoe. Then they hunch and ponderously lunge like a grizzly going forward.

Baby turtles in a turtle bowl are a puzzle in geometrics. They're as decorative as pansy petals, but they are also self-directed building blocks, propping themselves on one another in different arrangements, before upending the tower. The timid individuals turn fearless, or vice versa. If one gets a bit arrogant he will push the others off the rock and afterwards climb down into the water and cling to the back of one of those he has bullied, tickling him with his hind feet until he bucks like a bronco. On the other hand, when this same milder-mannered fellow isn't exerting himself, he will stare right into the face of the sun for hours. What could be more lionlike? And he's at home in or out of the water and does lots of metaphysical tilting. He sinks and rises, with an infinity of levels to choose from; or, elongating himself, he climbs out on the land again to perambulate, sits boxed in his box, and finally slides back in the water, submerging into dreams.

I have five of these babies in a kidney-shaped bowl. The hatchling, who is a painted turtle, is not as large as the top joint of my thumb. He eats chicken gladly. Other foods he will attempt to eat but not with sufficient perseverance to succeed because he's so little. The yellow-bellied terrapin is probably a yearling, and he eats salad voraciously, but no meat, fish or fowl. The Cumberland terrapin won't touch salad or chicken but eats fish and all of the meats except for bacon. The little snapper, with a black crenelated shell, feasts on any kind of meat, but rejects greens and fish. The fifth of the turtles is African. I acquired him only recently and don't known him well. A mottled brown, he unnerves the green turtles, dragging their food off to his lairs. He doesn't seem to want to be green—he bites the algae off his shell, hanging meanwhile at daring, steep, head-first angles.

The snapper was a Ferdinand until I provided him with deeper water. Now he snaps at my pencil with his downturned and fearsome mouth, his swollen face like a napalm victim's. The Cumberland has an elliptical red mark on the side of his green-and-yellow head. He is benign by nature and ought to be as elegant as his scientific name (*Pseudemys scripta elegans*), except he has contracted a disease of the air bladder which has permanently inflated it; he floats high in the water at an undignified slant and can't go under. There may have been internal bleeding, too, because his carapace is stained along its ridge. Unfortunately, like flowers, baby turtles often die. Their mouths fill up with a white fungus and their lungs with pneumonia. Their organs clog up from the rust in the water, or diet troubles, and, like a dying man's, their eyes and heads become too prominent. Toward the end, the edge of the shell becomes flabby as felt and folds around them like a shroud.

While they live they're like puppies. Although they're vivacious, they would be a bore to be with all the time, so I also have an adult wood turtle about six inches long. Her shell is the equal of any seashell for sculpturing, even a Cellini shell; it's like an old, dusty, richly engraved medallion dug out of a hillside. Her legs are salmon-orange bordered with black and protected by canted, heroic scales. Her plastron—the bottom shell—is splotched like a margay cat's coat, with black ocelli on a yellow background. It is convex to make room for the female organs inside, whereas a male's would be concave to help him fit tightly on top of her. Altogether, she exhibits every camouflage color on her limbs and shells. She has a turtleneck neck, a tail like an elephant's, wise old pachydermous hind legs and the face of a turkey—except that when I carry her she gazes at the passing ground with a hawk's eyes and mouth. Her feet fit to the fingers of my hand, one to each one, and she rides looking down. She can walk on the floor in perfect silence, but usually she lets her shell knock portentously, like a footstep, so that she resembles some grand, concise, slow-moving id. But if an earthworm is presented, she jerks swiftly ahead, poises above it and strikes like a mongoose, consuming it with wild vigor. Yet she will climb on my lap to eat bread or boiled eggs.

If put into a creek, she swims like a cutter, nosing forward to intercept a strange turtle and smell him. She drifts with the current to go downstream, maneuvering behind a rock when she wants to take stock, or sinking to the nether levels, while bubbles float up. Getting out, choosing her path, she will proceed a distance and dig into a pile of humus, thrusting herself to the coolest layer at the bottom. The hole closes over her until it's as small as a mouse's hole. She's not as aquatic as a musk turtle, not quite as terrestrial as the box turtles in the same woods, but because of her versatility she's marvelous, she's everywhere. And though she breathes the way we breathe, with scarcely perceptible movements of her chest, sometimes instead she pumps her throat ruminatively, like a pipe smoker sucking and puffing. She waits and blinks, pumping her throat, turning her head, then sets off like a loping tiger in slow motion, hurdling the jungly lumber, the pea vine and twigs. She estimates angles so well that when she rides over the rocks, sliding down a drop-off with her rugged front legs extended, she has the grace of a rodeo mare.

But she's well off to be with me rather than at Mud Pond. The other turtles have fled—those that aren't baked into the bottom. Creeping up the brooks to sad, constricted marshes, burdened as they are with that box on their backs, they're walking into a setup where all their enemies move thirty times faster than they. It's like the nightmare most of us have whimpered through, where we are weighted down disastrously while trying to flee; fleeing our home ground, we try to run.

I've seen turtles in still worse straits. On Broadway, in New York, there is a penny arcade which used to sell baby terrapins that were scrawled with bon mots in enamel paint, such as KISS ME BABY. The manager turned out to be a wholesaler as well, and once I asked him whether he had any larger turtles to sell. He took me upstairs to a loft room devoted to the turtle business. There were desks for the paper work and a series of rocks that held shallow tin bins atop one another, each with several hundred babies crawling around in it. He was a smudgy-complexioned, serious fellow and he did have a few adult terrapins, but I was going to school and wasn't actually planning to buy; I'd only wanted to see them. They were aquatic turtles, but here they went without water, presumably for weeks, lurching about in those dry bins like handicapped citizens, living on gumption. An easel where the artist worked stood in the middle of the floor. She had a palette and a clip attachment for fastening the babies in place. She wore a smock and a beret, and was homely, short and eccentric-looking, with funny black hair, like some of the ladies who show their paintings in Washington Square in May. She had a cold, she was smoking, and her hand wasn't very steady, although she worked quickly enough. The smile that she produced for me would have looked giddy if she had been happier, or drunk. Of course the turtles' doom was sealed when she painted them, because their bodies inside would continue to grow but their shells would not. Gradually, invisibly, they would be crushed. Around us their bellies—two thousand belly shells—rubbed on the bins with a mournful, momentous hiss.

Somehow there were so many of them I didn't rescue one. Years later, however, I was walking on First Avenue when I noticed a basket of living turtles in front of a fish store. They were as dry as a heap of old bones in the sun; nevertheless, they were creeping over one another gimpily, doing their best to escape. I looked and was touched to discover that they appeared to be wood turtles, my favorites, so I bought one. In my apartment I looked closer and realized that in fact this was a diamond-back terrapin, which was bad news. Diamondbacks are tidewater turtles from brackish estuaries, and I had no sea water to keep him in. He spent his days thumping inter-minably against the baseboards, pushing for an opening through the wall. He drank thirstily but would not eat and had none of the hearty, accepting qualities of wood turtles. He was morose, paler in color, sleeker and more Oriental in the carved ridges and rings that formed his shell. Though I felt sorry for him, finally I found his unre-lenting presence exasperating. I carried him, struggling in a paper bag, across town to the Morton Street Pier on the Hudson. It was August but gray and windy. He was very surprised when I tossed him in; for the first time in our association, I think, he was afraid. He looked afraid as he bobbed about on top of the water, looking up at me from ten feet below. Though we were both accustomed to his resistance and rigid-ity, seeing him still pitiful, I recognized that I must have done the wrong thing. At least the river was salty, but it was also bottomless; the waves were too rough for him, and the tide was coming in, bumping him against the pilings underneath the pier. Too late, I realized that he wouldn't be able to swim to a peaceful inlet in New Jersey, even if he could figure out which way to swim. But since, short of diving in after him, there was nothing I could do, I walked away.

Double Take

1. How would you characterize the tone of "The Courage of Turtles"? How does Hoagland achieve this tone? What effect does the tone have on you as a reader?
2. Given that Hoagland says (in his essay about writing) that only certain subjects are proper subjects for essays, in what way are turtles a proper subject for this essay?
3. Why are there so many occurrences of the pronoun "I" in an essay purportedly about turtles? Does the "I" detract from or add to the observations of turtles? Does the presence of the "I" make this a personal essay? How so?
4. What is Hoagland trying to accomplish in this essay? What sort of point does the essay make? What sort of "truth" is it telling?
5. What do you make of the ending of the essay? Could the ending be connected in some way to the larger meaning of the essay?

At First Glance

In many ways "Learning to Eat Soup" challenges our conceptions of what makes an essay an essay. It reads like a series of sometimes unrelated, mostly fragmented thoughts and recol-lections. Imagine that you are a reader of Harper's Magazine, where this essay was first published; what would be your reaction upon reading it, especially since it appeared in the "essay" section of the magazine? As you read it, draw in general upon what you have been reading about essays in this book, and in particular, draw upon what Hoagland says about essays in "To the Point," his essay about writing. Consider the extent to which this essay, far from pushing the boundaries of what an essay is, might actually be the purest form of an essay.

Learning to Eat Soup

Learning to eat soup: Like little boats that go out to sea, I push my spoon ahead of me.

At my parents' wedding in Michigan, one of Mother's uncles leaned over before the cake cutting and whispered to her, "Feed the brute and flatter the ass." The uncles threw rice at them as they jumped into their car, and Dad, after going a mile down the road, stopped and silently swept it out. That night, before deflowering each other (both over thirty), they knelt by the bed to consecrate the experience.

To strike a balance is everything. If a person sings quietly to himself on the street, people smile with approval; but if he talks, it's not all right; they think he's crazy. The singer is presumed to be happy and the talker unhappy, which counts heavily against him. . . . To strike a balance: If, for example, walking in the woods, we flake off a bit of hangnail skin and an ant drags this bonanza away, we might say that the ants were feasting on human flesh, but probably wouldn't. On the other hand, if a man suffers a heart attack there and festers undiscovered, then we would.

•

Baby inside M.'s stomach feels like the popping and simmering of oatmeal cooking, as I lay my hand across. Pain, "a revelation to me like fireworks, those comets that whirl," she says in the labor room. She lies like a boy under stress in the canoe-shaped cot, the nurses gathering gravely, listening to the baby's heartbeat through the stethoscope between contractions—heart like a drumbeat sounded a block away. Baby, with bent monkey feet, is born still in its sac. Doctor is unlocatable. The interns gather. A nurse picks up both phones simultaneously and calls him with urgency. The crowd, the rooting and cheering in the delivery room—as if the whole world were gathered there—after the solitary labor room.

Very old people age somewhat as bananas do.

Two Vietcong prisoners: An American drew crosses on their foreheads, one guy's cross red, other guy's green, to distinguish which was the target and which the decoy to be thrown out of the helicopter to make the target talk.

Winter travel: Snowbanks on river ice means thin ice because snow layers shield the ice from the cold. And water is always wearing it away from underneath; therefore keep on the *inside* of curves and away from all cutbanks, where the current is fast. Travel on barest ice and avoid obstacles like rocks and drift piles sticking through, which also result in a thinning of the cover. Gravel bars may dam the river, causing overflows, which "smoke" in cold weather like a fire, giving some warning before you sink through the slush on top and into the overflow itself. Overflows also can occur in slow sections of the river where the ice is thick and grinds against itself. A special danger area is the junction of incoming creeks whose whirlpools have kept the water open under a concealment of snow. If the water level falls abruptly, sometimes you can walk on the dry edges of the riverbed under solid ice which remains on top as though you were in a tunnel, but that can be dangerous because bears enjoy following such a route too.

You butter a cat's paws when moving it to a new home, so it can find its way back after going out exploring the first time.

•

My friend Danny Chapman, the Ringling Bros. clown, had a sliding, circus sort of face, like the eternal survivor, marked by the sun, wind, pain, bad luck, and bad dealings, the standard lusts and equivocations, like a stone that the water had slid over for sixty years. Face was much squarer when not in august-clown blackface, its seams smudged by reacting to all he'd seen, and holding so many expressions in readiness that none could be recognized as characteristic of him.

Success in writing, versus painting, means that your work becomes *cheaper,* purchasable by anybody.

The New York Times is a vast democratic souk in which every essayist can find a place to publish his or her voice. But otherwise, for a native New Yorker with proud and lengthy ties to the city, it's not so easy. The *New York Review of Books* is published by a group of sensibilities that give the impression of having been born in this metropolis but of wishing they were Londoners instead. And *The New Yorker* traditionally has been the home of writers and editors born in Columbus, Ohio—who yearned so much to seem like real New Yorkers that their city personalities in print had an artificial, overeager sophistication and snobbery.

I ride my stutter, posting over its jolts, swerving with it, guiding it, if never "mastering" it.

At the annual sports show at the New York Coloseum: "Stay straight with sports," says a poster, a picture of a girl wearing a T-shirt with that slogan over her breasts. An exhibitor tells me he just saw two men fondling each other in the men's room— "It just turns your stomach." A woman wearing a huge odd-looking hat made of dried pheasants' heads is cooing affectionately at a cageful of pheasants. A skinning contest is held in which three taxidermists go to work on the carcasses of three Russian boars.

"If two people are in love they can sleep on the blade of a knife."

•

Karl Wheeler used a baby bottle until he was five years old, whereupon his mother said to him, "That's your last bottle, Karl. When you break that one you'll never get another one!" and he began to toss it idly in the air to catch it, but missed.

First white men in British Columbia sold some of the Indians their names: $10 for a fine name like O'Shaughnessy, $5 for the more modest Harris.

At 6:00 A.M. I shoot a porcupine in the garage (knew about it from seeing Bimbo vomit from a fear reaction after his many tangles with porcupines). It goes under the building to die but not too far for a rake to reach. I take it to Paul Brooks's house. In his freezer he has woodchucks, beaver, bear, deer, bobcat, and porcupine meat (he is a man living only on Social Security), and he cleans it for me. We see it's a mama with milk in her breasts. His mouth fills with saliva as he works; he's also preparing a venison roast for lunch, with garlic salt, Worcestershire sauce, pepper, onions, etc. Says this time of year, first of June, the woodchucks are light as your hat, the winter has been so long for them; you can feel their thin legs. Porcupine liver is a delicacy, the rest not so much. The porcupine had been chewing at my garage for the salts; I eat the porcupine; therefore I'm eating my garage—dark drumsticks that night by kerosene lamp. Game tastes herby even without herbs—best is bobcat and muskrat, in my experience, not counting big meats like moose. One countryman we know had his ashes scattered on his muskrat pond. The porcupine had chattered its teeth and rattled its poor quiver of quills as I approached with my gun. Was so waddly it could not even limp properly when badly wounded. Lay on its side gurgling, choking, and sighing like a man dying.

At the Freifields' one-room cabin, with snowshoes hung under steep roof, I read Larry's father's hectic journal, written in Austro-English, of desperate orphanhood on the Austrian-Russian front in WWI. He, adopted by the rival armies as they overran the town, living in the trenches with them, living off stolen crusts otherwise, surviving the bombardments, dodging the peasants who hated Jews, but cherished by Austrian soldiers, who then were killed—saw one's legs blown off just after he'd changed places with him. That night peed in his pants in the trench and froze himself to the ground.

"Old Bet," the first circus elephant in America, was bought by Hachaliah Bailey from an English ship captain in 1815 but was shot eventually by religious fanatics in Connecticut as resembling the biblical Behemoth of the Book of Job (as indeed she did).

My first overtly sexual memory is of me on my knees in the hallways outside our fifth-grade classroom cleaning the floor, and Lucy Smith in a white blouse and black skirt standing above me, watching me.

My first memory is of being on a train which derailed in a rainstorm in Dakota one night when I was two—and of hearing, as we rode in a hay wagon toward the distant weak lights of a little station, that a boy my age had just choked to death from breathing mud. But maybe my first real memory emerged when my father was dying. I was thirty-five and I dreamed so incredibly vividly of being dandled and rocked and hugged by him, being only a few months old, giggling helplessly and happily.

Had supper at a local commune where they have a fast turnover and have made life hard. They buy $20 used cars instead of spending $200, use kerosene instead of the electricity they have, and a team of horses to plow. They got 180 gallons of maple syrup out of their trees, but they washed 1,400 sugaring pails in the bathtub in cold water, never having put in a hot-water heater. Much husky embracing, like wrestlers; and before they eat their supper they have Grace, where twenty-some people clasp hands around the table, meditating and squeezing fingers. Bread bakes on a puffy wood stove. Rose hips and chili peppers hang from the ceiling on strings, other herbs everywhere and pomegranates and jars of basic grains. The toilet is a car on blocks up the hill. Supper is a soup bowl full of rice and chard and potato pancakes with two sour sauces and apple butter, yogurt for dessert; and we drink from mason jars of water passed around. And the final "course" is dental floss, which everybody solemnly uses. A dulcimer is played with the quill of a feather, accompanied by bongo drums. The women ended the public festivities by each announcing where she was going to sleep that night, which bedroom or which hayloft, in case anyone wished to join her. Clothing is heaped in a feed bin near the bottom of the stairs, and everybody is supposed to reach in in the morning and remove the first items that fit them and come to hand, without regard for which particular sex the clothes were originally made for. The saddest moment of the evening for me was when a little girl came around to her mother carrying a hairbrush in her hand and asking to be put to bed. The mother lost her temper. "Why run to me? she said. "Everybody in this room is your parent. Anybody can brush your hair and tell you a story and put you to bed."

Manhattan, now 14,310 acres, was 9,800.

Bernard Malamud speaks of writing as a battle: "go to paper" with a novel. At age sixty-one is trying to "write wise," a new aim, and hard. Being between books, I say I'm in a period of withdrawal and inaction like that of a snake that is shedding its skin.

On the crest of Moose Mountain is an old birch growing low and twisty out of the ruins of a still older, bigger bole, surrounded by ferns, and it's there that the deer that feed in my field bed down during the day.

There is a whole literary genre that consists, first, of foolish writing and then later capitalizing upon the foolishness by beating one's breast and crying *mea culpa.* Why *was* I a white Black Panther, a drug swallower, a jackbooted feminist, a jet-set-climbing novelist, a 1940s Communist? How interesting and archetypal of me to have shared my generation's extremes.

Busybodies are called in Yiddish *kochleffl,* "cooking spoon," because they stir people up.

•

The hollow in the center of the upper lip is where "the angel touched you and told you to forget what you had seen in heaven."

Wife of F.'s uncle, to prevent him from going to work one morning when she preferred he stay home, set the alarm so that it seemed it was too late for him to make the train when he woke. But he did rush so terribly he got to the station, and there collapsed and died, and she, only twenty-seven, never remarried.

Joyce consulted Jung, who diagnosed his poor daughter as incurably schizophrenic partly on the evidence of her brilliant, obsessive punning. Joyce remarked that he, too, was a punner. "You are a deep-sea diver," said Jung. "She is drowning."

The cure for stuttering of holding stones in one's mouth works because of the discomfort of them rattling against one's teeth. Stones from a crocodile's stomach were thought to be best.

Amerigo Vespucci said that Indian women enlarged their lovers' sexual parts by applying venomous insects to them.

After losing her virginity at seventeen, she felt unstopped on the street, like a hollow tube, as though the wind could blow right through her.

The sea, at the village of Soya on Hokkaido island in 1792, was so fertile that twelve quarts of dry rice could be bartered for 1,200 herring, 100 salmon, 300 trout, or 3 sealskins.

How Davy Crockett kept warm when lost in the woods one night: climbing thirty feet up a smooth tree trunk and sliding down.

•

Am drunk from a soft-shell-crab lunch with Random House's Joe Fox, but stutter so vigorously with William Shawn as to obscure both from him and myself my drunkenness—stutter through it and give myself time to recall names like Numeiry and Assad, necessary to win Shawn's backing for the trip to Africa. He, as reported, is excessively solicitous of my comfort and state of mind; insulated and jittery; heated by electric heater (in August), yet fanned by electric fan; in his shirtsleeves, and immediately suggests I remove my coat. He has an agonized, bulging baby's head with swallowed-up eyes, like that of the tormented child in Francis Bacon's painting *The Scream*. Questions me effectively, however, on my knowledge of the Sudan and the prospects for a salable article there. Says O.K. I go to 42nd St. and watch screwing to relax—crazily enough, less is charged to see live souls (25 cents) than for a porno flick—then walk home. Lunch the next day with Alfred Kazin, my old teacher (and the day after that with Barthelme, who has just broken through a writing block, he says, and is therefore more cheerful and sober than I have seen him in a considerable while; says women's movement will produce changes as profound as the abolition of slavery). Kazin as always is a veritable tumult of impressions, like H. S. Commager and other busy intellectuals I have liked, but in Kazin's case it is enormously in earnest and felt. Expresses hurt at Bellow's recent inexplicable anger. Otherwise an outpouring of talk about his new book on the forties, when he published his first book and met the literary figures of the day. Played violin with drunken Alan Tate. Advances the idea that William James, a hero of his, is a better direct heir of Emerson than Thoreau; also the view that students now resent the fact that a professor knows more than they do, want him to learn along with them in class, as in group therapy, and when caught out on homework facts, get offended instead of trying to fake through, as in the old days. On Ph.D. orals, the candidates seem to have no favorite poem, no poem they can quote from, when he asks them for one at the end.

I like Easterners more than Westerners but Western geography more than Eastern geography; and I like the country more than the city, but I like city people more than country people.

•

Essays, the most conversational form, have naturally drawn me, who have a hard time speaking with my actual mouth.

Tail end of hurricane rains buckets, flooding Barton River. Then the sky clears with nearly full moon, and I hear the deer whickering and whanging to one another gleefully, the mountain behind them gigantic and white.

Bellow says in Jerusalem journal that "light may be the outer garment of God."

Oil spills seem to attract aquatic birds; the sheen may resemble schooling fish. Also, oil slicks calm the surface, look like a landing area.

Roth speaks of his debt to both Jean Genet and the Fugs for *Portnoy*. Roth a man who wears his heart on his sleeve, thus rather vulnerable to insult and injury; part of his exceptional generosity. Tells story of man bleeding in front of God but trying to hide blood from His sight apologetically.

William Gaddis: jockeylike, narrow-boned, fastidious Irishman, clever and civilized, with none of the usual hang-dog bitterness of the neglected writer.

Warhol: keen, Pan face with tight manipulated skin that makes it ageless except for his eyes. Bleached hair hanging to his leather collar. Fame based upon being immobile.

Pete Hamill, bursting personality, does columns in half an hour, movie script in three weeks, discipline based upon not drinking till day's stint is through. Fewer bar brawls now, more empathetic, though still lives from a suitcase. "Irish Ben Hecht," he laughs.

Malamud: not at all the "Jewish businessman's face" I'd heard about, but a sensitive, gentle face, often silent or dreamy at Podhoretz's, disagreeing with the host and Midge, but holds his tongue and hugs him at the end with professional gratitude to an editor who once published him. When he speaks, his voice is young, light, and quick, an enthusiast's, idealist's. Hurt by attacks on him in *Jerusalem Post,* for dovishness. Extremely solicitous of me, as kind in his way as Bellow, though style of it is modulated lower. Both of us distressed by Israeli's grinning description of Arab prisoners being beaten up. William Phillips says he thinks the Palestinians probably have a point but that he's not interested in hearing what it is. Podhoretz mentions Israel's "Samson option," pulling everything down, and makes fun of Malamud's "ego" when he's left.

Grace Paley: short, stocky woman who at first sight on the Sarah Lawrence campus I mistook for the cleaning woman; asked her where the men's room was. We rode rubbing knees throughout that semester in the back seat of a car pool. She'd been marching in protests since high school (Ethiopia and Spanish civil war), but her exhilaration at being arrested in Washington peace march in midterm reminded me of my own exuberance at completing the hard spells of army basic training. Yes, we were good enough!

Heard MacLeish at YMHA. Afterward unrecovered yet from defeat of his play *Scratch* on B'way. Sweetness and bounce of his voice, however, is unchanged in twenty years; sounds forty, a matinee tenor, and the old lilt to his rhetoric. Face like a sachem's, too wise, too heroic, with a public man's nose. Talks of friendships with Joyce and Hemingway and imitates Sandburg's O very well. Talks of Saturday Club in Boston where monthly Harlow Shapley debated Robert Frost. Reminisces of artillery lieutenant days in World War I, "making the world safe for democracy," where his brother was killed. Five years later he and other nondead *did* die a bit when they realized it had been a "commercial" war and they had been lied to. He is a man of Hector-type heroes. Says Andrew Marvell poem was written while going home from Persia after his father's death.

Berryman given $5,000 prize at the Guggenheim reading, wearing a graybeard's beard which hides tieless collar. Reads best "Dream Songs," plus two sonnets and Rilke, Ralph Hodgson, and eighteenth-century Japanese poet. Emphatically, spouting drunk, reads with frail man's grotesqueries, contortions, and his own memorable concoction of earnestness, coyness, staginess, name dropping, and absolutely forceful, rock-bottom directness. Becomes louder and louder at the end of this floodlighted moment after long years of obscurity and hardship. Here was the current Wild Man, people thought, successor to Pound, there being one to a generation, though many others may have been reminded of Dylan Thomas as he fell into the arms of Robert Lowell, punching him affectionately, when he finished. His whole life was thereupon paraded before him, when old mistresses and chums and students like me came up, expecting recognition, and one of his old wives, presenting him with a son whom obviously he hadn't laid eyes on for a long while. He boomed with love and guilt, with repeated thanks for letters informing him that So-and-so had had a child or remarried, till one was wearied of watching. One felt guilty too, as though competing for his attention with the neglected son. I felt Berryman had not long to live and I ought to be content with my memories of him and lessons learned and not join in the hounding of him. Nevertheless, I did go next afternoon to the Chelsea Hotel, with bronze plaques outside memorializing other tragic figures, like Thomas and Brendan Behan. He'd said the son would be there, so I was afraid that, like my last visit with Bellow, I would be taking time away from a son who needed to see him much more. But the son had left—all that remained was a note in Ann B.'s handwriting. Instead a *Life* photographer and reporter were talking with him, plying him with drinks, though he was holding back dignifiedly, talking of fame, of Frost, and his own dog Rufus. Frost was a shit who tried to hurt him, but he quoted the wonderful couplet about God forgiving our little faux pas if we forgive Him His great big joke on us. Is bombastic in his total commitment to words. Legs look very small, but chest inflates with importance of uttering snatches of poems, till he collapses in coughs. Rubs beard and hair exhaustedly, recklessly spendthrift with his strength, and begins harder drinking; leads me to bar, where waiter, thinking from his red face and thin clothing that he is a bum, won't serve him till he lays a ten-dollar bill on the table. I soon leave, but he was hospitalized within a couple of days. "Twinkle" was his favorite word at this time. He used it for commentary, by itself, and irony, or expostulation, quoting an enemy like Oscar Williams, then merely adding a somber "Twinkle."

Turgenev's brain was the heaviest ever recorded, 4.7 pounds; three is average.

Child's tale about a man who suffered from shortness of breath. Afraid he would run out, he blew up a bunch of balloons as an extra supply for emergencies. Blew up so many that he floated away holding on to them.

Updike comes to U. of Iowa for first workshop session in three years (hasn't really taught for sixteen years) but handles himself in a classy manner nevertheless, and very well prepared with students' manuscripts beforehand, and in the exhilaration of reading his own work in front of 1,000 people in McBride Hall (which we call Mammal Hall because it's part of Nat'l Hist. Museum), freely sheds his private-person role that had made him a bit stiff before, when he'd refused even a newspaper interview. Signs autograph cards for eleven-year-old boys and physics texts for Japanese students and mimeo forms for students with nothing better to offer him. Wife is ample, attractive woman with large, intense face, obviously both loving and sexy, a relaxed, close companion—he is wearing a wedding ring and ignoring the ambitious students who show up for his morning class wearing cocktail dresses. We talk of Africa—both finishing Africa books—and classmates and lit. hierarchies. He mentions Cheever's drunkenness—once he had to dress him after a party like dressing a father. Our mothers are same age. "Poor Johnny," his said, watching a TV program about senility with him recently.

Updike says he quit teaching years ago because he "felt stupid," seeing only one way to write a given story properly, not the endless alternatives students proposed in discussions.

Indians used to scratch small children with mouse teeth fastened to a stick as a punishment for crying in front of white men. (White man, of course, a "skinned" man.)

•

Short stories tend to be boat-shaped, with a lift at each end, to float.

Richard Yates says art is a result of a quarrel with oneself, not others.

Five toes to a track means it's wild, four toes means cat or dog.

Writers customarily write in the morning and try to make news, make love, or make friends in the afternoon. But alas, I write all day.

Bellow says he spent the first third of his life absorbing material, the second third trying to make himself famous, and the last third trying to evade fame.

"A woman without a man is like a fish without a bicycle": T-shirt.

People say they'll take a dip in the sea as if it were like dipping into a book, but I nearly drowned in surf's riptide off Martha's Vineyard's South Beach. Repeatedly changed swimming strokes to rest myself as I struggled in the water, surf too loud to shout over, and I'm too nearsighted to see where to shout to. Reaching beach, I sprawled for an hour before moving further. Spent next day in bed, next week aching.

New England is "pot-bound," says Charlton Ogburn; thus superfertile.

Petrarch, climbing Mount Ventoux in 1336, began the Renaissance by being the first learned man ever to climb a mountain only for the view.

Rahv told Roth, "You can't be both Scott Fitzgerald and Franz Kafka."

•

People who marry their great loves sometimes wish they'd married their best friends; and vice versa.

Trapeze artists some days complain "there's too much gravity," when a change of the weather or the magnetic field affects their bodies. Elvin Bale bought his heel-hook act from Geraldine Soules, who after a fall started doing a dog act instead. Soules had, in turn, bought it from Vander Barbette, who, walking funny after *his* fall, had become a female impersonator and trainer of circus showgirls.

In old-time Georgia you ate mockingbird eggs for a stutter; boiled an egg for jaundice and went and sat beside a red-ant anthill and ate the white and fed the yolk to the ants. For warts, you bled them, put the blood on grains of corn, and fed that to a chicken. Fiddlers liked to put a rattlesnake rattle inside their fiddles.

The fifties are an interim decade of life, like the thirties. In the thirties one still has the energy of one's twenties, combined with the judgment (sometimes) of the forties. In the fifties one still has the energy of one's forties, combined with the composure of the sixties.

The forties are the old age of youth and the fifties the youth of old age.

Adage: "God sends meat, the Devil sends cooks."

Carnival stuntman whom Byron Burford banged the drum for used to swallow live rats and Ping-Pong balls, up-chucking whichever ones the crowd asked for first. Stunned the rats with cigar smoke before he swallowed them.

> *The intellect of man is forced to choose*
> *Perfection of the life, or of the work,*
> *And if it take the second must refuse*
> *A heavenly mansion, raging in the dark.*
>
> —YEATS, "Choice"

Lying to my lieutenant as a private at Fort Sam Houston as to whether I'd shaved that morning before inspection, or only the night before—he reaching out and rubbing his hand down my face.

Glenn Gould liked to practice with the vacuum cleaner on, to hear "the skeleton of the music."

Nature writers, I sometimes think, are second only to cookbook writers in being screwed up.

Deer follow moose in these woods, says Toad. I say maybe they look like father (mother) figures to them.

At Academy-Institute ceremonial, the big scandal is Ellison's lengthy introduction of Malamud for a prize and Barbara Tuchman's brutal interruption of it. Stegner very youthful, as befits an outdoorsman. Cowley very food-hungry as always, as befits a 1930s survivor. Commager tells my wife that his daughter loved me and so he loved me. Lots of cold-faced ambitious poets cluster around each other and Northrop Frye; Galway seems likably unaffected and truthful next to them. Ditto Raymond Carver. Ellison had tried to speak of blacks and Jews.

Joe Flaherty's line for the Brooklyn Bridge: "the Irish gangplank."

Whale mother's milk would stain the sea after she was harpooned, and the calf would circle the ship forlornly. "I do not say that John or Jonathan will realize all this," said Thoreau, in finishing *Walden*; and that's the central and tragic dilemma as the environmental movement fights its rearguard battles.

In starving midwinter, foxes catch cats by rolling on their backs like a kitten ready to play.

Warblers average 8,000 or 10,000 songs a day in spring; vireo 20,000. Woodchucks wag their tails like a dog. Blue jays like to scare other birds by imitating a red-shouldered hawk.

My bifocals are like a horse's halter, binding the lower half of my eyes to the day's work.

•

At my frog pond a blue heron circles low overhead while a brown-muzzled black bear clasps chokecherry bushes and eats off them thirty yards away from me.

Only six hours old, a red calf stumbles toward the barn, as mother is herded in by Hugh Stevens on ATV vehicle, and is eventually tied to its mother's stanchion with hay twine, while a six-inch red tab of its previous cord hangs from its belly. It's as shiny as a new pair of shoes, its deerlike hooves perfectly formed, including the dew claws. Mother and calf had had a brief wild idyll under the summer sky before they were discovered by Hugh—the last sky this vealer will ever see.

Crocodiles yawn to cool themselves in hot weather, but coyotes yawn as an agonistic device. Mice yawn from sleepiness, as people do, but we also yawn from boredom, which is to say contempt—agonistic again.

Old people seem wise because they have grown resigned and because they remember the axioms, even if they've forgotten the data.

"When you come to the end of your life, make sure you're used up."

I trust love more than friendship, which is why I trust women more than men.

"All hat and no cows." Or, "Big hat, no cattle": Texas saying.

"Eat with the rich, laugh with the poor."

Buying a new car after thirteen years, I discover why country people like to keep the old one about the yard. First, it makes the house look occupied. Second, it's a nesting site for ducks and geese and a shelter for chickens during the day. Third, it reminds you of *you*.

Double Take

1. How do you think Edward Hoagland wants us to read "Learning to Eat Soup"? After all, he surely had to imagine people reading it when he wrote. What sort of role do you think he imagines for the reader? What role do you find yourself in while reading the essay?
2. What do you think holds this essay—full of quotes, vignettes, facts, and memories—together? Is there an order, a logic, to the groupings and fragments? If so, what is it? If not, then what is the point to writing and reading it?
3. What is the meaning of the title—and the first sentence, for that matter—of this essay?
4. Think about observational and conversational qualities Hoagland attributes to essays—how essays reflect a process of mind speaking to mind. To what extent do these qualities appear in this essay? To what extent can this essay be considered a hyper example of an essay—an essay in its most extreme, purest form?

Seeing for Yourself

At First Glance

The following essay, "In Okefenokee," first appeared in the National Geographic Traveler. *The essay demonstrates Hoagland's skills as a travel writer, especially his ability to describe the experience of the journey through the Okefenokee Swamp in such richness of detail that readers feel as if they had experienced the journey as well. As you read the essay, notice how Hoagland creates this effect. Look for specific places in the essay where you feel most drawn into the experience and try to articulate why and how the writing works on you. In particular, look at how Hoagland's descriptions mirror in their density the thickness of the swamp; what writing techniques does he use to create this density? Also look not only at how he describes the swamp and his fellow travelers, but also at what he chooses to describe; is there something significant about what he chooses to describe and what he neglects?*

In Okefenokee

Okefenokee Swamp in southeastern Georgia comprises about six hundred square miles. It's home to perhaps twelve thousand alligators, a hundred fifty black bears, six hundred otters, eighteen thousand white ibises at the peak of the summer, nine hundred great blue herons, a hundred fifty sandhill cranes, twenty-five ospreys, forty-five hundred egrets of three species, four thousand wood ducks, and assorted populations of pileated woodpeckers, wood storks, barred owls, red-shouldered hawks, parula and prothonotary warblers, and numerous more commonplace songbirds. All told, there are forty kinds of mammals and forty of fish, thirty-five species of snakes, fourteen of turtles, eleven of lizards, twenty-two of frogs or toads, within the national wildlife refuge, which is by far the largest in the eastern U.S. And yet it's not really such a swatch of swamp—thirty-five by twenty-seven miles at its longest and widest—considering the ecological and even mythological freight that it must carry for all of the uncountable wild wetlands that have been drained, plowed, and subdivided.

Okefenokee is much smaller than Florida's Everglades (which is a national park), but because of its isolated location it has been less injured by the pressure of development at its boundaries. The soil at surrounding drier elevations is the color of a supermarket shopping bag, and indeed the principal industry roundabout is raising and cutting twenty-year-old slash pines for pulpwood that goes to manufacture paper bags. The swamp lies in the shallow dish of an old seabed, forty-five miles west of Georgia's present lush coastline and about the same distance east of the rich pecan-, peanut-, tobacco-, and cotton-growing country that begins near the prosperous city of Valdosta. It forms the headwaters of the Suwanee and Saint Marys rivers, and for the local Indian tribes, too, it was a region of mystery and legend, a hunting ground more than a home, until the Seminoles, the last of the tribes in the area, hid there as white settlers spread across the South after the War of 1812, raided the whites who were encircling them, then finally were driven out by army troops in 1838, escaping toward the deeper fastnesses of the Everglades.

Okefenokee was the last haunt of the panther and wolf in Georgia. They and its mosquitoes and reptiles—as well as the raffish reputation of its "swampers," the families who lived on its islands and hunted and trapped its hammocks and watery "prairies" by poling themselves in dugouts or trudging knee-deep through the peat bogs—kept most other people out. Some swampers were said to be descended from Civil War draft dodgers. At dawn and dusk they would let out ululating two-mile "hollers" that went on for a minute or two from their feeling of pride and primacy, and they were serious moonshiners, distilling corn whiskey from the sugarcane and white corn that they grew in locations no federal agent was likely to reach on his own or alive. In towns like Fargo, at the southwest corner of the swamp, a bootlegger could park his high-springed truck loaded with jugs in front of the post office and chat for an hour and nobody thought twice about it.

However, the whole swamp was logged for its cypresses and crisscrossed by a network of tramways in the first quarter of this century. Earlier, during the 1890s, a brief but concerted attempt had been made to drain it to create agricultural land with a canal, which remains to this day the principal pathway inside. Because wildlife refuges differ from national parks in that their first purpose is supposed to be the preservation of habitat, off this canal one travels into Okefenokee only by canoe and only by precut water trails through the sea of floating lilies and other vegetation to wooden camping platforms set out on the prairies five or ten miles apart, each trail and platform being reserved for a single party of canoers by arrangements made with the refuge manager beforehand.

In my capacity as a chronicler of other people's vacations, I paddled about forty miles on a four-day trip last spring that wound through the more familiar passages of the swamp from refuge headquarters near the town of Folkston, on the east side, to the Suwanee River at Fargo on the western edge, as part of a group of eighteen people, including two guides provided by an outfitting company called Wilderness Southeast. Except for our guides, who were women of thirty-four and twenty-two, and two teenagers on spring vacation, we were mostly in our fifties—a marine engineer from California, a career IBM man, an army defoliant chemist, a closemouthed, wise-looking country lawyer from Kentucky, a folksy, rawboned radiologist from Valdosta, a hospital head-of-pharmacy, a Cincinnati schoolteacher, and the wives of the IBM man, the defoliant chemist, the lawyer, and the radiologist. Although, except for the teacher, these women were housewives, our guides were enthusiastically liberated women who immediately asked us men whether we were wondering where the real, *male* guides were. To distinguish us and help us remember each other, they had us attach animal names to ourselves, such as Art Aardvark, Beetle Bob, Betty Bee, Bear Bill, Betsy Beaver, Bobcat Bob, Evelyn Eagle, Polly Parrot, Jackass Jason, Ouzel

Ottway, Possum Pollard, Ted Turtle, Lynn Lynx, Mary Mouse, and so on. I thought it a vaguely humiliating procedure, but it did furnish us food for thought about each other. Jason, the radiologist, was anything but a jackass, for instance, and his wife, "Polly Parrot," besides being a regent of the Daughters of the American Revolution, whose grandfather had been toted about in his infancy on the back of a male slave, had recently gone through an Outward Bound program, rappeling down cliffsides, and had soloed in an airplane. "Mary Mouse," the teacher, wore a sweatshirt saying "It's sporty to be forty" and said she made a habit of spending summer vacations in places like New Guinea or Newfoundland, when she wasn't picking up pocket money delivering vans nationwide from a factory in South Bend. "Bobcat Bob," on the other hand, did look like a likely hunter, and "Evelyn Eagle" gave the impression of being an outdoorswoman who probably did truly aspire to wings. "Possum Pollard" looked as if he could play dead in court and then wake up and surprise the opposition, and "Ouzel Ottway," a bachelor pharmacist, was a passionate Sierra Club devotee and was signaling as much, because John Muir, the founder of the Sierra Club a century ago, often wrote of the water ouzel as his favorite bird.

We had compulsory campfire gatherings for group-think purposes in the evening, our leader Viva!—she spelled it with an exclamation point—having worked previously as a counselor in juvenile-delinquent prerelease programs. She encouraged us to explore our behavior patterns and do things differently from what we were used to (indeed, on the application forms, the fee for the trip had been labeled "Tuition"), but this was a rather unnecessary suggestion, because although the self-employed people—lawyer, doctor, marine engineer—didn't much change their personalities, which at home and on the job were approximately the same, the men who worked as cogs in large organizations had turned zany by the second day. The IBM man became bombastic and mock lecherous and the army chemist "fuzzy," eccentric, bewildered, "unstrung." Viva!—who paddled with me for most of the trip—spoke of her "listening skills" and "confrontation skills" in Reality therapy and Gestalt therapy, but I got quite fond of her even as she tried to tinker with my motivations, because she was so sympathetic, affectionate, vulnerable, and earnest, and her own personality seemed so contradictory. She had a skinny straight nose, a string-bean frame, and a frenetic metabolism that grew desperately hungry at frequent intervals, so that she would stop paddling in the midst of a downpour to gobble nuts and dried fruits almost in sight of our tent frames. She confessed that she had been disillusioned by the "fail rate" among her contingents of delinquents but that she believed everyone had control of his own destiny; and for all the intensity with which she tried to mold us into a unique, "bonded" group, permanently enriched by the experience of crossing this swamp, she said she herself "burned out" quickly in groups. Ours was the only one she had scheduled herself to guide that spring. She usually preferred to stay in the office or else went out for extended sojourns alone in a cabin in the woods.

It's a phenomenon nowadays that youngish retired people, or prosperous couples on the verge of retirement, venture in increasing numbers into outdoor group adventures led by young ideologues from what is left of the counterculture, who pay themselves almost nothing (Wilderness Southeast's partners got $8,500 a year) but who believe in a special agenda of education, activism, and behavior modification, often incongruously at odds with the beliefs and careers of their customers. What they all do have in common is the modern conviction that life is lived in modest niches— whether one occupies a slot at a huge corporation or mildly does one's own thing, protectively colored by a graduate degree—that our aspirations are complexly and dauntingly circumscribed, and that life must be selective and specialized.

We had spent the first night in a small piney graveyard in Folkston and next morning left solid land at the entrance to the Suwanee Canal near Chesser Island, paddling ten miles on this twenty-yard-wide relic of Harry Jackson's 1889–95 attempt to drain Okefenokee, while listening to cricket frogs gick-gicking, carpenter frogs calling with a sound like a hammer tapping, pig frogs grunting like impatient hogs. These species are not musically the prettiest of amphibians—not like toads or spring peepers—but here in their confident legions they reminded us that their race probably fathered all of the vertebrate music on earth. We stopped to watch two warblers weaving a nest of Spanish moss and several fishing spiders poised to grab insect larvae on the rims of the lily pads. Viva said she was "heavily into snakes and spiders. It's like a secret, looking for spiders, because nobody else is."

Fish crows flew about uttering *uh-uh,* and *uh-uh* again, for which reason they are known as virgin birds, our younger guide, Nancy, told us, while paddling in her black bathing suit in the stern of the *National Geographic* photographer's canoe. He, "Bear Bill," was a former quarterback and "monster back" for Arizona State, and she was a sharp, smart naturalist, just out of the University of Vermont, who, with her chipmunk cheeks and sorority hairdo, looked collegiate when paired with him, though neither in fact was unduly so. Viva and I raced ineffectually with them, when we had a chance, though mostly our job was to harry poor Pollard, the Kentucky lawyer, who was casting for bass at the rear of our procession of nine canoes, quite competent with his rod and possessed of an eye that loved currents. But he was supposed to keep up.

Under the warm sun, the alligators lying on both banks seemed more assured in the presence of humans than they would have been in chilly weather, when they have to make allowances for the sluggishness of their own bodies by sliding into hiding underwater much sooner. Their heads were flat-looking and grimacey because of the long mask of their mouths—a grin that is two hundred million years old. Swimming alligators have horsey heads, however; the eyes and high nostrils are emphasized, instead of their fixed somber smiles. They look more like a sea horse than a sea horse does (though the inches between their nostrils and eyes denote their total length as measured in feet).

When they bellowed, the gators sounded like motors starting up, not like horses whinnying, and, besides answering each other, felt obligated to answer the airplanes that crossed the swamp. Such an outlandish challenge from high above may sometimes conceal from them the triumph of their position at the top of the food chain here (since people in a wildlife refuge don't kill them for their skins or to eat their tasty tails). A baby alligator's first meal is likely to be a crayfish, but the adults eat an occasional bear cub whose mother was forced to cross deep water between islands; and they will camp under the nursery trees where colonies of ibises, herons, and egrets

nest, to devour not only the nestlings that have the misfortune to fall but also the raccoons that otherwise would decimate the baby birds ensconced in the branches above.
Alligators create new water trails through the matted plant life during their nocturnal wanderings and dig essential water holes used by many other creatures during a
drought.

One twelve-footer we met, after we had left Suwanee Canal and entered the narrow passageways of Chase Prairie, hissed and blew itself up formidably when it felt
surrounded, but then let us slide by in a gingerly file, without flailing its muscular
tail. The tail is both a chief weapon and the alligator's main means of travel; but they
have a variety of sounds, including the primeval roar of conquest that a great one will
utter when it charges and seizes a deer mired in mud and lifts it bodily out and swaggers back to its pool with the deer gripped crosswise in its jaws—a roar that sounds
more Triassic than contemporary, more like a titanic burp than a lion's intellectual
roar, and therefore more nightmarish and terrifying, which surely helps to stun and
immobilize deer. On the other hand, a male in courtship hums *umphs* underwater in
such a way that the water vibrates deliciously around the female, until she closes her
eyes, puts her chin on his head, and twists her body around his. And this is the sound
the alligator hunters of Okefenokee used to imitate, groaning softly while mouthing
the end of a punting pole thrust into the water near where they knew a gator was
lurking.

On Chase Prairie we heard an osprey mewing as it hovered above a fishing stretch,
and two hawks crying to each other connubially, two owls barking back and forth
informatively, two cranes garrooing as they beat by in uxorious, coordinated majesty,
a woodpecker cukcukking loudly from a line of cypress trees, and a bellowing alligator in full rut—all at once. Chase Prairie is named for the chases the swampers used
to conduct, one man driving game animals off the hammocks and islands, another
poling fast after them in his dugout or jonboat as they waded and swam to escape.

We were in the midst of pond lilies and bonnet lilies, bladderworts and pipeworts, neverwet and maiden cane, pitcher plants and pickerelweed, wampee and hard-
head grass—all that mob of plant life that defines the swamp. The leaves and stalks,
dying off in the winter, settle on the decomposing layers of peat on the bottom, ten
or fifteen feet thick from the centuries of vegetation that have rioted on the surface
in the sultry sun and died and rained down on the impermeable clay understrata.
Their constant decomposition produces gases that now and again push up whole mats
of this peat, called "blow-ups," which, if they float for long, catch seeds of sedges and
grasses and, as they get larger and larger, twenty yards across and more, are called
"batteries," so solidly bound together that they can support a person, though often
swaying under his feet because they may be floating on six feet of water. ("Okefenokee" comes from an Indian name meaning "land of the trembling earth.") Then
cypresses, buttonbush, titi and gallberry shrubs and bay tree seedlings grow and send
down roots that eventually stabilize the battery, until, when enough of a patch of dry
soil has formed that finally the old swampers could have camped there on their alligator hunts, the battery is called a "house." "Hammocks" are large "houses" where
hardwood trees like water oaks, laurel oaks, swamp maples, black gum and sweet
gum trees have gotten a foothold. Also, there are as many as seventy regular islands

in Okefenokee Swamp, most of them former sandbars left from half a million years ago, when, probably, this area was part of the sea. On the islands are forests of loblolly and slash pine, as well as large cypresses, magnolias, and other glories. But the swamp is gradually, over the millennia, filling in; the actual open prairies that are most "swampy" constitute only fifteen percent of it today.

At lunch we'd talked of trips down the Snake River and the Grand Canyon, into the Smokies, the Sierras, and the Wind River Range, all taken under the tutelage of America's drifting populace of "wilderness guides"; and as we paddled along in wildlife-refuge-type silence, I doubt that many of us failed to think intermittently of retirement strategies and financial stratagems, of midlife crises, romantic tangles, children-at-a-standstill, or whatever middle-age hex happened to be enlivening our existence at the time, while my austere, frenetic friend Viva—who would certainly have risked her own life in a flash to rescue a stranger—sat ready to help us or save us.

Nancy was as enthusiastic a naturalist as Viva was an educator. At her urging we stopped to look at larval dragonflies preying on other larvae under the lily pads. After a year or two of doing that, the nymphs metamorphose and crawl onto a stalk, to dry in the sun and pump blood into their wings for some still more dramatic hunting activities performed in the air. We stopped to watch this occurring too. And there were predatory diving beetles, known as "water tigers" in their larval stage, and hunting-diving grasshoppers, as well as the fishing spiders waiting on the water lilies. Cormorants flew over, black, agile diving birds, which old fishermen across the South still like to call "nigger geese" because they're dark and fly like geese, although they live on fish, not plants, as geese mostly do. The many turkey vultures soared with a dihedral cock to their wings; and the few ospreys with a flat, boomerang-type crook to theirs. In this cost-effective era, no spectacular bird such as an osprey can expect to be allotted enough space to nest and feed its brood unless it pays for its acreage by being ogled by hundreds of human beings. The pair nesting along our route were magnificently wild-looking, nevertheless, with their brown capes and backs, white heads and underbodies, their handsome straight postures when they clasped a branch, and utter mastery of the air, oddly combined with a repertoire of chirps, cheeps, kiweeks, and kyews.

We used yellow fiberglass Mohawk canoes and green Eureka tents, and when we reached our camping platform, which measured twenty by twenty-eight feet in the midst of a mile-square parcel of water, Viva had us stand in a circle and massage one another's shoulders. The sunset was only a rip in the clouds, but ruby, carmine, and puce all the same, and ibises, egrets, herons, and storks flew home in discrete flocks to their several roosts and rookeries after the long day's frogging and fishing. Being bird buffs, we didn't mind feeling caged in their garden spot, but, after a supper of salami and cheese, went out again in our canoes to see more alligators by shining our flashlights into their eyes, which reflect like coal embers. Nighttime is when alligators come alive and hunt, so we located a number of them, their eyes that prodigally passionate color. The raccoons' shone bright white, by contrast, as they foraged the house and hammock margins; and the spiders on the lily pads had eyes that glittered emerald green. Frogs had white eyes, and besides the cricket, carpenter, and pig frogs, bullfrogs were croaking, and pickerel frogs that sounded like two balloons being rubbed together. Bear Bill, Violet Viva, and I (Ted Turtle) slid close to a raccoon that was feeling for frogs in the shallows under the silhouettes of tall trees. He was silvery and ghostly in our flashlight beams, displaying a stand-up, tiptoe curiosity elaborately tempered with fear. Up on his hind legs and down he went, ears pricked, fluid with tremulous life, until, still undecided about us, he finally fled.

The white-eyed frogs would gobble the emerald-eyed spiders, and the white-eyed raccoons ate the frogs when they could, but the coal-eyed alligators would devour the raccoons eventually. For each, it was a case of waiting and traveling, waiting and traveling, and by quiet paddling toward a coal-colored pair of eyes we got close enough to a middling gator to have killed it as the old gator hunters would have done, with a .22 bullet shot into one of the red coals, for twenty cents a foot for its belly skin.

Sunrise next morning was another blaze of reds glimpsed through the clouds. A ten-foot alligator cruised close to our platform, belatedly waiting for the couple of coons who had swum over during the night to climb the posts and scavenge our leftovers. So much of nature's picturesqueness is really a series of relentless tests of stamina. This Jurassic beast, like hundreds of its toothy fellows in the Okefenokee that are just as big, floated unobtrusively or lounged on the bank night and day, waiting for hunger to operate irresistibly on the possums, coons, rabbits, deer, and bobcats living on various dabs of land surrounding this wet prairie so that they'd enter the water to swim from one to another to feed. (Overpopulation alone would force most of the year's crop of young to do this, but wise veteran animals wait for autumn, when temperatures fall, to relocate or range about much.) And the herons, watchfully statuesque in shallow water, waited by the minute or hour for some frantic frog, hidden in the mud but smothering for air, to make a desperate dash for breath.

Large birds, with the freedom of the skies, swept toward their hunting grounds to the west—the egrets flapping and sailing, the herons with a rocking slow downbeating flight—while we sat and gazed at their grandeur over our Sierra Club cups of scrambled eggs. The Sierra Club, like any other significant institution, combines bits of the sublime with the ridiculous. What's ridiculous are these smallish metal cups from which its wilderness votaries are supposed to eat all manner of meals, from steaks to soup, with a single spoon, which our particular outfitter provided on a red cord to be worn around the neck betweentimes, along with a hand lens for looking at plants and a whistle for emergencies. All good fun, perhaps—like our leaders' "teachable moments" and "solo time" or "private space"—except that my tentmate, Bill, from *National Geographic,* and I were out of temper because, in order to discipline us for what they claimed was his snoring, they had made us take our tent down that morning, although after canoeing a circuit we would be coming back to the same platform in the afternoon. And sure enough, three miles out, the clouds burst with the first of what would add up to five inches of rain. The wind ribbed the water; everybody was drenched and chilled, though the tree swallows swooped down festively to grab disoriented insects, and wading birds rushed in hasty uncharacteristic glee to grab subsurface creatures that the wild water forced out. Viva and I in the last canoe watched the black paddles of the eight craft ahead of us rising and falling, like fish crows descending to feed and rising swiftly to descend again. She teased me, but then assuaged Bill's and my chagrin by installing him with Nancy and her in her own tent and me in Mary Mouse's, to shiver, be comforted, and sleep.

It was a rough storm, testing everybody's cheeriness. Our IBM man performed a comedy routine that had worked well, he said, during bad thunderstorms on dude-ranch rides in the Rockies. He seemed to be the most Thoreauvian of us all and most objected to the regimented parts of the trip, but everyone who signs up for wilderness trips has a soft spot somewhere, a feeling for wild things—which is to say for the underdog, nowadays—underneath a frequently quirky, abrasive, or camouflaged exterior. We all had in common a respect for privacy, individualism, and self-sufficiency, a love of birds, plants, and animals, and because we were, in the manner of the eighties, a "single-issue constituency," we had no political arguments, being content to ignore everything else. Gone with the 1970s was the unanimity of the old alliance on civil rights, a dovish foreign policy, and the "ecology movement." When one of our number said she believed in shooting any robber you caught in your gunsights, somehow none of the rest of us objected, because she'd also said that she believed in "protecting God's creatures."

Next day the sun smiled, and the flocks of ibises arrived again, with their splendid red bills. We paddled to Floyd's Island, past blooming iris, pipewort flowers like upright hatpins, and the flowers that the bladderworts send up like innocuous buttercups while the voracious bulk of the plant beneath the surface consumes minute crustaceans and water larvae. Everywhere there was neverwet, its spadix shaped like a thick pencil, white with a golden tip. And when the bottom lifted under us and scraped our canoes, we entered into effusions of greenbrier, wild grape, pepperbush ("poor man's soap"), yaupon, holly, titi and gallberry (both favorites of the honey-bees), and, especially, thickets of the "hurrah bush" (a relative of fetterbush and stagger-bush), as the swampers called it because it is so dense that anyone struggling through might wish to yell "Hurrah!" at the end.

We saw and heard an otter chirping to its mate; saw the personable kind of lizard known as a skink on a loblolly bay tree; heard yellow-throated and prothonotary warblers—the latter golden orange—and mockingbirds, catbirds, red-winged blackbirds, and one painted bunting, which was blue, green, red, and brown. On the island were some magnificent live oak trees that the loggers had spared, one with resurrection ferns spreading high from a crotch and another with a beehive inside. Floyd's Island was the site of the Seminoles' last encampment in Okefenokee. Under their resident chief, Bolek, called "Billy Bowlegs" by the whites, they raided a settler family on Cowhouse Island, on the northeastern edge of the swamp, killed seven people, and then retreated most of its width and much of its length to Billy's Island, pursued by troops under General Floyd, who chased them on here, whence they escaped unscathed.

On Billy's Island, a little later, we encountered a diamondback rattlesnake and saw where the "Good Black" and "Bad Black" cypress loggers had been quartered (the latter were prisoners who'd been bailed out of jail), as well as the site of the "juke" where Good Blacks danced, or "juked," on Saturday nights.

The sun seethed on the currents in myriad popping points of light or lay like a platter of gold where the water was still. Because of the peat's tannic acid, Okefenokee's water itself is the color of dark tea and a perfect reflecting medium, so that on the narrower waterways, lined with gum and bay trees and cypresses festooned with Spanish moss, a photograph not only is arrestingly beautiful but may look the same upside down. When a wind blows, however, the resplendent image of the trees on the water is broken into zebra zigzags.

We finished crossing the swamp at Stephen Foster State Park, on the Fargo side, where the Suwanee River starts flowing in earnest, and paddled six miles downstream past many Ogeechee lime trees, whose fruit makes good pies and preserves, and water tupelo and black tupelo gum trees, whose blossoms are a nearly peerless honey-making source for the bees, and then camped at the fishing camp of a famous old-time bootlegger and guide named Lem Griffis, now an apiary and campground run by Arden, his gentler, law-abiding son. The river was at its highest level in ten years—the people on Wilderness Southeast's previous trip had eaten a canebrake rattle-snake that had been flooded out of its usual holes—and we built big bonfires for our final two evening confabs, with mosquitoes whining near us of a size that swampers say "will dress out at a pound."

We had white stubble beards and white-and-black beards, and the women were as sturdy as those with the beards. Our lawyer said that when the bull alligators in rut were bellowing, it was just what he'd heard the hippos in Kenya say: *I want some!* Our doctor repeated to us several times that he'd "promised my wife's daddy thirty-seven years ago that I was going to take care of her, and he would kill me now if he saw her in this swamp." But she was the one who had rappeled down cliffs and soloed in an airplane. Our Thoreauvian IBM man—whom my heart went out to because he kept trying to pretend that there weren't eighteen people on this trip—grew quickly impatient when the sociable moments veered at Viva's urging toward a conventional group-grope session. He would grab his wife's hand and say this was their wedding anniversary, for God's sake, and they had to get to their tent—which really did have the desired effect the first night.

By the time we quit paddling, my shoulders were getting stronger and my back felt delightfully limber, as though I could push on to California if only some of the populace between Fargo and there would clear out of the way. Both Viva and I were heading for solitary spells in isolated portions of the Appalachians. Bill, the photographer, on the other hand, was returning to Miami, the base from which he often goes to crisis assignments in Central America. Nancy, equally a modernist—her mother a socialite, her father an airline pilot, and she a Miamian who had chosen to go to the University of Vermont—was on her way to a career in wildlife management. More and more women are entering the environmental fields and gradually transforming the predatory bent of those vocations. The wardens used to be hunters who preyed on lesser hunters—who poached the poachers—but now the swing will be to a more protective, even "maternal" approach, which will be necessary if wildlife is to survive at all. And this is going to be how the wilderness will be experienced in the next century: in groups of twenty people, by prearrangement, led by specialists in group dynamics to preselected birding or bear-viewing sites, and efficiently out. Otherwise there won't be any wilderness.

I poked around Fargo a little and looked up Barney Cone, aged sixty-six, who has retired after many years as the refuge's patrol officer and has the likably boiled look of W. C. Fields. As we talked, riding around in his pickup truck, he would raise two fingers from the wheel every time that we met another vehicle. Before his day, he said with a lawman's aplomb, plume hunters had combed the swam after egrets, and when plume sales had been outlawed, the swampers went after gators. When the refuge was established, in 1937, that had to be stopped. He'd paddled its water trails with a partner by night for thirty-five dollars a week, watching for the gas lamps that the poachers mesmerized the animals with. "At first, if you made a case against a poacher, the judge would just about run you out of court. But gradually it got to where they were sending them off for a year and a day," he said.

The local sheriffs wouldn't help him, but the state game wardens sometimes did, and the sheriffs at least didn't interfere with him the way they warned the moonshiners about the revenuers' raids. Not until "nineteen and thirty-eight" had a paved road reached Fargo, so before then the moonshiners had pretty much run everything during the rainy season, when the roads were mud, and the dry season, when the sand was a trap. "Shine" sold for $4.50 for a five-gallon jug. A hundred-pound sack of sugar cost that (if you didn't raise your own), but you made two jugs of shine with that hundred pounds, soaking it for three days with a mash consisting of fifty pounds of cornmeal and fifty pounds of whole-grained rye that had already soaked together for three days to get good and sour, then "running it off" (distilling it).

"How else did people make money?" I asked him.

"Oh, dipping turpentine, or at the sawmills," he said. "They cut cypress for crossties for the railroad, they cut black gum trees and water oaks for plywood and boxes. Sold peat moss. Raised those backwoods cows that you didn't have to feed, or the hogs too. Ate wild meat and huckleberries," he added with a laugh, though he'd stopped eating bear meat after a plague of screwworms reached Georgia in the 1930s and bored into the bears—burrowed into the cattle too, till the cattle got so sick the bears started catching up with them, and of course that sent the swampers out after the bears with their dogs. "That hurt the bears a whole hell of a lot. The beekeepers were already after them."

The price for alligator skins had risen from twenty cents a foot at the turn of the century to fifteen dollars a foot in the 1960s, but in 1955, during a drought, the swamp suffered four major fires, the gators each time going into their holes underwater to try to survive. Even so, he found many of them whose tails had been scorched because they hadn't been able to get all of themselves inside. Without law enforcement the population would have plunged. The hunters used a "pig pole" with a barbed spear on hook on the end for fishing up the animals that sank after they had "shined" them with the lamp and shot them from real close. "They'd fill the boat and pile them out, kill some more and pile them out, four or five at once, and go on ahead and next day come back to all of the piles and skin them out. Or in a dry spell, they walked the swamp looking for holes in the mat where a gator was and haul him out and ax him in the head.

"You know what a redneck was?" Barney continued with a chuckle. "A redneck didn't just mean somebody who got himself sunburned out in the fields. It meant a man who only buttoned his shirt collar to go to church, so his neck looked chafed on Monday morning."

I went back to Folkston, on the east side of Okefenokee, and talked with Ralph Davis, who's seventy-three and mostly Irish but one-eighth Cherokee. He says he helped survey the refuge's boundaries. Claims jokingly that, after that, the government men chased him for forty years in airboats and motorboats because of his poaching, until finally they had sense enough to save themselves some money by hiring him. He says by then he knew the swamp so well at night he could hardly find his way around in it during the day. He'd killed maybe a thousand gators, though tried to limit his kill to bulls by leaving the pools alone where he saw babies. He got a dollar a foot for skins in the Depression, and since he could kill twenty-five or thirty in a four- or five-day excursion, it was very good money.

Mr. Davis seems quite "Cherokee" in his sentiments, bad-mouthing the Seminoles, saying that the seven-footers of an unknown tribe buried in mounds before history began were probably "a better class of Indian" and joking about "hundred-and-fifty-pound coons" coming as tourists to the swamp "to look at the coons." In a kinder tone, he speaks of how he loves the smell of "spirits of turpentine," which is best from a green young tree—you can put either crude pine gum or its spirits directly onto a cut or pour the liquid on the dressing after bandaging it. And a few drops on a lump of sugar will defeat a cold. From March to October was the gathering season. The pine trees were precisely scarred, about chest-high, and a two-quart can was hung on a nail underneath to catch the drippings, emptied once a month. They got paid from thirty to fifty dollars for a fifty-gallon barrel, and the resin left after the spirits were boiled off was used to caulk their boats with. (More famously, by pitchers in baseball.)

Davis, a chair-loving fellow but vociferously folksy, claims his father named Bugaboo Island—the wildest island left in the swamp—once when the wind caused two trees to rub together all night, moaning above his campsite. Honey Island had bee trees, and Blackjack Island blackjack oaks. John's Negro Island was where a slave stolen from a man named John was secreted. The Chesser family arrived in "eighteen and fifty-eight," and their homestead on Chesser Island, now watched over by him, has been restored by the refuge management, with its cane-boiling syrup equipment, its "hog gallows" and toothed otter traps, its gourds hanging up for purple martins to nest in and clear the air of mosquitoes and flies, the whole yard scraped bare so wandering snakes or scorpions would have no place to hide. While he was growing up, the Chessers cultivated melons, corn, peas, beans, and sweet potatoes, and ran loose livestock in the swamp, and grew about thirty acres of sugarcane, which made a clear, sweet syrup of renown. A bobcat skin was worth only fifty cents and a fox three dollars, but in the winter he and his friends would go out after fur for a week or so in a twelve-foot dugout, carrying their traps, their bacon and sweet potatoes, pushing themselves with an eight-foot pole with a Civil War bayonet strapped to the top end to fight off alligators, planning to meet other kids who were trapping at a certain "house" in the middle of the swamp and camp there, drink and swap stories, butchering a deer or a "piney-woods rooter"—one of the bristly, gray, big-headed, big-tusked, wild-running hogs. At dawn they'd let out a couple of old-time Okefenokee two-mile, one-minute hollers to wake up the sun and wake up the swamp.

Okefenokee is sometimes called the Yellowstone among wildlife refuges, it's so important. Yet as I drove around its perimeter it seemed awfully small and fragile, like a drop in a dynamo, when I knew what encircled it. In the town of Waycross

I met Johnny Hickox, a round-faced, mellow-looking gentleman of fifty-nine in gold-rimmed glasses, with a straight short smile, a farmer's sloping shoulders, and bib overalls. Though neither a retired lawman nor a reformed outlaw, he grew up on Cowhouse Island, "dipping turpentine" from the collection pails for sixty-five cents a day in his first job, then hunting alligator belly skins, until, after World War II, you could make fifty cents an hour at the sawmill. The steers his father raised in the swamp grass sold for only ten dollars, and bearskins had no better use than being cut into wads to stuff in the holes the pigs dug under the fences, to scare them back inside. ("Most pitiful thing, to hear them holler for mercy if a bear caught them!") His grandfather at the turn of the century had earned only ten cents a day, logging cypresses, including the services of his horse. But in that era you could buy swamp-land for eleven cents an acre.

A guy and he would spend two weeks "pushing a pole," wandering a whimsical course from Waycross to Fargo with a load of traps, and sell whatever furs they'd caught, then enjoy another two weeks poling back, with many stops. No swamper ever starved in the swamp. There were so many fish to catch that "you had to hide from them to put your bait on," Johnny says. Four-pound pickerel, two-pound "mud-cats," and the smaller "buttercats," which are catfish with yellow on their bellies. Twelve-pound bass, swarms of perch, and delicious soft-shell turtles. His great-great-grandfather had fathered twenty-one children, by only one wife—which is one rea-son nearly everybody around this patch of swamp seems to be related to him—but nobody went hungry.

There is no lawman-outlaw edge to Johnny Hickox; and from the tourist park where he works, he took me out along the "Wagon Road," a water trail that logs used to be floated over, to "Sapling Prairie" for a picnic in a jonboat with a light motor on it—though he paused to demonstrate his push-poling for fun, telling me it was a skill that, like riding a bike, you never lose the hang of. He said these old water trails "tuckered out" if not cleared by a government cutter boat or a big alligator swim-ming through occasionally, and he pointed out a few other trails leading off through the wet maze of sedges, lilies, swamp grass, and bushes to former haunts where he had camped and earned a living with his ax and fish lines and traps. A gator was eat-ing bonnet lily roots, while a "Florida cooter" turtle steered well clear of it. He pointed out swamp iris, and wampee, with an arrow-shaped leaf and hot roots that the Indians seasoned meat with, and Virginia chain fern, and "soap bush," whose leaves make suds when scrubbed, and "hen-and-biddies" pitcher plants, named for the lineup of their bloom and leaves, and pipeworts, also called "ladies' hatpins."

"I was married to this swamp," he said happily, though he has four grandchil-dren already and his wife still pampers him. He showed me what bears like to eat—black gum berries, greenbrier berries, highbush blueberries, live oak acorns, wild-hive honey, and palmetto fruit—as if to indicate how much abundance they also found here.

We ate our sandwiches on a "house" on Dinner Pond, ten miles out, facing one of only two virgin stands of cypress trees left in Okefenokee, and listened to a Car-olina wren sing *tea-kettle, tea-kettle, TEA-kettle*. Two paired cranes flew overhead as if they were married. The trees' strange "knees" sticking out of the water and the hang-ing Spanish moss (which old-timers burned in smudge fires to keep the mosquitoes off) gave us the pleasure of their company, not to be encountered widely in the South anymore because cypress fetches so much as a log and air pollution kills the moss. Eight or nine days' traveling in the jonboat would bring us to the Gulf of Mexico, a happy trip, he said.

Southerners, like New Englanders, whom I know better, are survivors by temperament. But they use talk instead of taciturnity, zaniness instead of stoicism, as their method of getting by, and that's more fun. We agreed, over our tea at Dinner Pond, that neither of us would ever see a wilderness that was as pristine as what we had loved before. But wildernesses have a special value, apart from sheltering so many primeval creatures that elsewhere are nearly gone. The South is becoming homogenized into the rest of America because so many Northerners are moving there. And it may be that regionalism will survive best in wild places such as Okefenokee, where the South is not the "Sunbelt" but remains the South to eye and ear. Cypresses and ibises, wood storks, snowy egrets, timeless turtles, hordes of frogs, hurrah bushes, and Ogeechee lime trees can preserve alive our sense of human as well as natural history.

A CLOSER LOOK AT EDWARD HOAGLAND

1. Describing frontiersmen in "To the Point: Truths only Essays Can Tell," Hoagland writes, "their fires of regret were banked, their eyes lacked my squint under the open sky, and they didn't wish for sharp divergences from day to day, as I tend to do. They were subjects for an essay, in other words, more than for fiction." Reflecting on this statement as well as the essay in which it appears, think about why Hoagland considers these frontiersmen's lives an appropriate subject for essays. Then choose one or more of Hoagland's essays and examine what makes their subject essayistic. What is essayistic about the subjects he deals with? In an essay about Hoagland's essays, explain why Hoagland might write about the subjects he likes in essay form.

2. On a number of occasions, Hoagland has described how essay writing for him began as a way to overcome his severe stutter, thus giving him a means of talking to others when his own physical voice failed him. In rereading his essays, pay attention to their "spoken" quality. To what extent do his essays

allow him to speak to others in print? To what extent do his essays constitute a kind of "public letter" as he puts it? In what ways, that is, do his essays reflect a process of "mind speaking to mind"? Write about how Hoagland's essays reflect (or do not reflect) the spoken word. Be sure to give examples from the essays, and steer clear of the overly simple claim that certain parts of Hoagland's work just "sounds like it's spoken."

3. Reread "In Okefenokee," paying close attention to elements of its style, especially to Hoagland's use of detailed description. Then, using that same style, write your own essay describing a journey you have recently taken or are about to take. This can be any kind of journey, from a hike in the woods to a bus ride to a walk through a supermarket. Try to use the same observation techniques Hoagland uses. When you have completed your essay, reflect on how the style you used shaped the way you observed.

Looking from Writer to Writer

1. Hoagland is not the only essayist in this collection who defines essays in part by contrasting them with works of fiction such as novels and stories. Cynthia Ozick and Rick Bass do the same, setting up distinctions that help them account for what essays can and cannot do. Read the essays on writing by Ozick and Bass, paying special attention to their statements about the differences between essay writing and fiction writing. Are the distinctions each writer makes similar? Does a pattern emerge from their distinctions? If so, what is that pattern? If not, what does that reveal about the essay as a genre? Finally, why make such distinctions in the first place?

2. Hoagland has been described by John Updike as the best living American essayist. As much as this speaks to Hoagland's accomplishments as a writer, it speaks just as much to Updike's own taste in essays. Why do you think Updike feels this way? What does that praise reveal about Updike's attitudes toward essay writing? Read what Updike has to say about essays and read Updike's own essays to see if you can deduce the reasons for his appreciation of Hoagland's work.

3. Edward Hoagland, Barry Lopez, Scott Russell Sanders, Annie Dillard, and Rick Bass can all be described as nature writers. Their essays exhibit in some way or another a deep connection with and a reverence for nature. In each essayist, however, that connection manifests itself in different ways—for example, in different attitudes about conservations, wilderness, hunting, the place of human beings in nature, and so on. Comparing their rhetorical strategies and styles, which of these essayists presents the most compelling case for natural conservation? That is, whose essays speak most profoundly on behalf of the need to protect and revere nature? Explain your reasoning with examples from the essays.

Looking Beyond

ESSAYS

Balancing Acts. New York: Simon & Schuster, 1992.

Compass Points: How I Lived. New York: Pantheon Books, 2001.

The Courage of Turtles: Fifteen Essays about Compassion, Pain, and Love. New York: Random House, 1970.

Heart's Desire: The Best of Edward Hoagland: Essays from Twenty Years. New York: Summit Books, 1988.

Red Wolves and Black Bears. New York: Random House, 1976.

Tigers & Ice: Reflections on Nature and Life. New York: Lyons Press, 1999.

The Tugman's Passage. New York: Random House, 1982.

Walking the Dead Diamond River. New York: Random House, 1973.

FICTION

Cat Man. New York: Arbor House, 1984.

The Final Fate of the Alligators: Stories from the City. Santa Barbara: Capra Press, 1992.

Seven Rivers West. New York: Summit Books, 1986.

TRAVEL WRITING

African Calliope: A Journey to the Sudan. New York: Random House, 1979.

Notes from the Century Before: A Journal from British Columbia. New York: Random House, 1969.

bell hooks

bell hooks, photographed by Jill Krementz, in New York

Gloria Jean Watkins was born on September 25, 1952, in Hopkinsville, Kentucky, to Veodis Watkins, a custodian, and Rosa Bell, a homemaker. Watkins writes under the name "bell hooks," which was the name of her grandmother. As she has explained many times, she chose this name not only as a tribute to her grandmother but to "honor the unlettered wisdom of her foremothers"—that is to say, the name is reflective of the voices of women who were not allowed to share their wisdom through publication but who nonetheless influenced hooks's life, and as a remembrance of all of the women who have been denied the right to speak and write publicly. hooks also adopted writing her name with all lowercase letters as a sign that writing, language, and discourse need not always comply with traditional, male doctrines of correctness. The name bell hooks then serves to remind readers of the often unheard voices of black women, and hooks uses the name to disrupt the traditional conventions that have enforced that silence. As one biographer of hooks has noted, "it is the unheard voice of black women which drives her overall work."

hooks earned her BA from Stanford University in 1973, her master's degree from the University of Wisconsin, Madison, in 1976, and her PhD from the University of California, Santa Cruz, in 1983. While hooks has taught at the University of Southern California, San Francisco State University, Yale University, Oberlin College, and City College of New York, she is known primarily as a social critic and author. In 1991 she was awarded the American Book Award for *Yearning: Race, Gender, and Cultural Politics,* and in 1994 she received the Writer's Award, Lila Wallace–Reader's Digest Fund. She has written more than 20 books since 1981. hooks explains, "for a vast majority of my life I have longed to write."

bell hooks is also known as a public intellectual—one who works to bring intellectual work to larger audiences than just the university community. For hooks, writing has to reach more than an audience of college professors and students; it has to reach the people it will affect. Hence, a good deal of hooks's writing appears in popular magazines and journals, and her books address issues that are important to many people: race, feminism, culture. She writes about films, music, books and authors, and public figures. She writes about sex and love. She writes of nature and the environment. In *Wounds of Passion: A Writing Life* and *Remembered Rapture,* she writes about writing—a subject that is deeply important to hooks. Writing in the *Women's Review of Books,* P. Gabrielle Foreman noted that readers of hooks's writing "will cheer through one essay and scowl through another." Her writing teaches and affects a large audience. As you read the essays by hooks, think about what it means to be a "public intellectual" and how hooks writes to large public audiences. Consider how hooks's writing might be read by a wide range of audiences; think about how those audiences might react to her. Also, consider the ways in which hooks addresses large, often intellectual, issues with this wide audience. What factors of her writing allow her to reach such a large public? Is there some particular characteristic about her writing that makes it particularly accessible? Are there things about her writing that limit it to certain audiences?

hooks on Writing

At First Glance

In "Women Who Write Too Much," bell hooks addresses her philosophies about writing and writes not only about why she writes, but also how she writes. She claims that "ideas are the tools I search out and work with to create different and alternative epistemologies (ways of knowing)." As you read this essay, think about the kinds of ideas hooks addresses and how her discussions of those ideas help direct audiences to thinking differently or alternatively to how they might have approached those ideas. Finally, as you read about hooks's own writing process, consider how you write and how your own writing process affects the kinds of writing you produce.

Women Who Write Too Much

There are writers who write for fame. And there are writers who write because we need to make sense of the world we live in; writing is a way to clarify, to interpret, to reinvent. We may want our work to be recognized, but that is not the reason we write. We do not write because we must; we always have choice. We write because language is the way we keep a hold on life. With words we experience our deepest understandings of what it means to be intimate. We communicate to connect, to know community. Even though writing is a solitary act, when I sit with words that I trust will be read by someone, I know that I can never be truly alone. There is always someone who waits for words, eager to embrace them and hold them close.

For the vast majority of my life I have longed to write. In my girlhood writing was the place where I could express ideas, opinions, beliefs that could not be spoken. Writing has then always been where I have turned to work through difficulties. In some ways writing has always functioned in a therapeutic manner for me. In *The Dancing Mind,* Toni Morrison suggests that the therapeutic ways writing can function are at odds with, or at least inferior to, a commitment to writing that is purely about the desire to engage language imaginatively. She contends: "I have always doubted and disliked the therapeutic claims made on behalf of writing and writers . . . I know now, more than I ever did (and I always on some level knew it), that I need that intimate, sustained surrender to the company of my own mind while it touches another. . . ." Morrison's description of the urge that leads to writing resonates with me. Still, I believe that one can have a complete imaginative engagement with writing as craft and still experience it in a manner that is therapeutic; one urge does not diminish the other. However, writing is not therapy. Unlike therapy, where anything

331

may be spoken in any manner, the very notion of craft suggests that the writer must necessarily edit, shape, and play with words in a manner that is always subordinated to desired intent and effect. I call attention to the way writing has functioned therapeutically for me as a location where I may articulate that which may be difficult, if not impossible to speak in other locations because this need leads me to turn and turn again to the written words and partially explains the sheer volume of my written work.

As long as I had only written and published one or two books no one ever inquired or commented on my writing process, on how long it took me to complete the writing of a book. Once I began to write books regularly, sometimes publishing two at the same time, more and more comments were made to me about how much I was writing. Many of these comments conveyed the sense that I was either doing something wrong by writing so much, or at least engaged in writing acts that needed to be viewed with suspicion. When I first took creative-writing classes from women professors who taught from a feminist perspective, we were encouraged to examine the way that sexism had always interfered with women's creativity, staging disruptions that not only limited the breadth and range of women's writing but the quantity as well. In a feminist studies course taught by writer Tillie Olsen I learned reading her essays on writing that prior to the 1960s it was rare if a white female writer, or a black female or male writer, published more than one book. We talked in class both about the material conditions that "silence" writers as well as the psychological barriers (i.e., believing that work will not be received or that what one has to say is either not important or had already been said). Knowing that black writers had faced difficulties that inhibited their capacity to write or complete works that had been started did serve as a catalyst challenging me to write against barriers—to complete work, to not be afraid of the writing process.

To overcome fears about writing, I began to write every day. My process was not to write a lot but to work in small increments, writing and rewriting. Of course I found early on that if I did this diligently these small increments would ultimately become a book. In *The Writing Life,* Annie Dillard reminds readers: "It takes years to write a book—between two and ten years. Less is so rare as to be statistically insignificant. One American writer has written a dozen major books over six decades. . . . Out of a human population on earth of four and a half billion perhaps twenty people can write a book in a year." Dillard's numbers may no longer be accurate as writers today not only have more time to write but have more writing aids (like the computer). Certainly as a writer who has handwritten, then typed or keyed into computer, all my books, I know how the computer and printer speed up the process. Typing and retyping a book takes much more time than keying in rewrites on a computer. I never approach writing thinking about quantity. I think about what it is I want to say. These days when I see the small yet ample stack of books I have written (usually seen at book signings), I know that this body of work emerged because I am again and again overwhelmed by ideas I want to put in writing. Since my interests are broad and wide-ranging, I am not surprised that there is an endless flow of ideas in my mind.

I write as one committed simultaneously to intellectual life, which means that ideas are the tools I search out and work with to create different and alternative epistemologies (ways of knowing). That I am continuously moved to share these ideas, to share thought processes in writing is sometimes as much a mystery to me as it is to readers. For I have writing comrades who work with ideas in the mind as much as I do but who are not as driven as I am to articulate those ideas in writing. A driving force behind my writing passion is political activism. Contrary to popular assumption writing can function as a form of political resistance without in any way being propagandistic or lacking literary merit. Concurrently, writing may galvanize readers to be more politically aware without that being the writer's sole intent.

A covert form of censorship is always at work when writing that is overtly espousing political beliefs and assumptions is deemed less serious or artistically lacking compared to work that does not overtly address political concerns. In our culture practically every aspiring writer realizes that work that is not addressing the status quo, the mainstream, that addresses unpopular political standpoints will rarely be given attention. It certainly will not make the best-seller list. Since I began my writing career utterly uninterested in writing anything other than poetry and fiction, work that I did not see as political, I was more acutely aware than most writers might be that by writing critical essays on unpopular political issues, I might never be seen by the mainstream world of critics and readers as an artistically "serious" writer. It has been challenging to maintain a commitment to dissident writing while also writing work that is not overtly political, that aspires to be more purely imaginative.

Successful writing in one genre often means that any work done in another genre is already marked as less valuable. While I have been castigated for writing critical essays that are too radical or simplistic, just "wrong-minded," the poetry I write along with other work that does not overtly address political concerns is often either ignored or castigated for not being political enough. Until we no longer invest in the conventional assumption that a dichotomy exists between imaginative writing and nonfiction work, writers will always feel torn. Writers will always censor their work to push it in the direction that will ensure it will receive acclaim. Everyone knows that dissident writing is less likely to bring literary recognition and reward.

Dissident voices are rarely published by mainstream presses. Many writers from marginal groups and/or with unpopular perspectives have relied on small presses to publish their work. Indeed, my writing would not have achieved public acclaim were it not for the alternative small presses publishing my work at a time when large publishing houses simply held to the conviction that writing about race and gender would not sell. Mainstream publishers showed interest in my writing only after sales of work published with small presses documented that an established book-buying audience existed. Significantly, the publication of my work by a mainstream press was also possible because many young college-educated workers in the industry were familiar with the work because they had studied it in school or knew that other students were excited about it and they could affirm the existence of an established readership.

My zeal for writing has intensified over the years and the incredible affirming feedback from readers is one catalyst. In my early writing years I thought this zeal was purely a function of will. However I found that rejection by the publishing world really affected my capacity to write. It left me feeling blocked, as though no one wanted to hear my ideas. No writer writes often or well if they despair of ever having an audience for their work. Knowing that readers want to hear my ideas stimulates my writing. While it does not lead me to write if I am uninspired, it does enhance my capacity to work when inspired. Long solitary hours spent writing feel more worthwhile when a writer knows there are eager readers waiting for new work. Oftentimes I write about issues readers have repeatedly asked me questions about at public lectures. My professional work, which includes both classroom settings and public lectures, keeps me in closer touch with reader response to my work than I might be were I creating work in a more isolated manner. It is equally true that engaged dialogue about ideas is also a stimulant for writing. Sometimes I feel an urgent need to write ideas down on paper to make room for new ideas to arrive, keep my mind from becoming too crowded.

Historically the writers in our culture who were the most prolific were white males. Now this is changing. However, as more writers from marginal groups break silences or barriers that led to the creation of only one work, producing a body of work is often viewed with disdain or disparagement. While it is true that market forces lead the publishing industry to encourage writers to produce books that may simply be repetitive, poorly written, and uninspired simply because anything specific successful writers write will sell, it does not follow from this that every writer who has an ample body of work is merely responding to market-driven demands. Since I have never tried to make a living as a writer, I have had the extreme good fortune to be able to write only what I want to write when I want to write it. Not being at the mercy of the publishing industry to pay the rent or put food on the table has meant that I have had enormous freedom to resist attempts by the industry to "package" my work in ways that would be at odds with my artistic vision. Reflecting on the interplay between writing and the marketplace in *Art {Objects}*, Jeanette Winterson comments: "Integrity is the true writer's determination not to buckle under market forces, not to strangle her own voice for the sake of a public who prefers its words in whispers. The pressures on young writers to produce to order and to produce more of the same, if they have had a success, is now at overload, and the media act viciously in either ignoring or pillorying any voice that is not their kind of journalese." When I choose to write an essay book that includes work that may have been published first in magazines, reviewers will often write about the work as though it is stale, nothing new. A book of mine might include ten new essays (which alone could be a book) and four or five pieces that were published elsewhere and a reviewer might insist that there is no new work in the collection. Men can produce collections in which every piece has been published elsewhere and this will not even be mentioned in reviews. This critical generosity cuts across race. Two books that come to mind are Cornel West's collection *Race Matters* and Henry Louis Gates Jr.'s book *Thirteen Ways of Looking at a Black Man*. While feminist intervention altered the nature of contemporary women's writing, it has had little impact on critical evaluations of that work in the mainstream press.

Dissident writing is always more likely to be trashed in mainstream reviews. Rarely do mainstream critiques of my work talk about the content of the writing— the ideas. It took years of writing books that were published by alternative presses for this work to be acknowledged by the mainstream publishing world. Had I stopped writing early on it is unlikely that my books would ever have received any notice in mainstream culture. Ironically, producing a body of work has been one of the reasons it has not been easy for critics to overlook my writing even as they often imply in written critique and conversation that I should write less. Usually these critics are other women. While contemporary feminism highlighted difficulties women writers face by challenging and intervening on institutionalized barriers, it also opened up new possibilities (i.e., women's presses, more women entering the field of publishing). The incredible success of feminist and/or women's writing in the marketplace certainly compelled mainstream publishers to reconsider old approaches to writing by and about women. It is simply easier for women writers to write and sell work than ever before. As a consequence it has become more difficult for women to attribute failure to write or sustain creativity solely to sexist biases. These changes have led to conflict and competition between women who write a lot and those who do not, especially when the latter attribute nonproduction to sexist barriers. The harshest critics of my work have been less well-known black women writers and/or individuals who have had difficulty producing new work.

Like other women writers, who face barriers but surmount them to do the work they feel called to do, I find it disheartening when our literary triumphs however grand or small are not seen as part of a significant advance for all women writers. Until the prolific female writer, and more specifically the black female writer, is no longer seen as an anomaly we cannot rest assured that the degree of gender equity that exists currently in the writing and publishing world is here to stay. And while women writers should not be in any way fixated on the notion of quantity, we all should feel utterly free to write as much as time, grace, and the imagination allow.

Time remains a central concern for all women writers. It is not simply a question of finding time to write—one also writes against time, knowing that life is short. Like the poet Donald Hall I was enchanted by the Scripture that admonishes us to "work while it is day for the night cometh when no man can work." Even as a child these words made an impression. They haunted my own search for discipline as a writer. In his memoir *Life Work* Hall contemplates the relation between writing and dying, stating that "if work is no antidote to death, nor a denial of it, death is a powerful stimulus to work. Get done what you can." Annie Dillard urges us to "write as if you were dying." A large number of black women writers both past and present have gone to early graves. To know their life stories is to be made aware of how death hovers. When I was a young girl I studied the lives of writers I admired hoping to find guidance for my work. One of my favorite literary mentors was the playwright and critical thinker Lorraine Hansberry, who died in her mid-thirties. Her essay "The Negro Writer and His Roots" posed challenging questions for a young writer and intellectual. Hansberry declared: "The foremost enemy of the Negro intelligentsia of the past has been and remains—isolation. No more than can the Negro people afford to imagine themselves removed from the most pressing world issues of our time—war and peace, colonialism, capitalism vs. socialism—can I believe that the Negro writer imagines that he will be exempt from artistic examination of questions which plague the intellect and spirit of man." Of course, I often pondered the paths Hansberry might have taken had she lived longer. Her death and the early deaths of Pat Parker, Audre Lorde, Toni Cade Bambara, to name only a few, stand as constant reminders that life is not promised—that it is crucial for a writer to respect time. Without urgency or panic, a writer can use this recognition to both make the necessary time for writing and make much of that time.

Like many writers, I am protective of the time I spend writing. Even though women write more today than ever before, most women writers still grapple with the issue of time. Often writing is the task saved for the end of the day. Not just because it is hard to value writing time, to place it above other demands, but because writing is hard. Oftentimes the writer seeks to avoid the difficulties that must be faced when we work with words. Although I have written many books, writing is still not easy. Writing so much has changed me. I no longer stand in awe of the difficulties faced when working with words, overwhelmed by the feeling of being lost in a strange place unable to find my way or crushed into silence. Now I accept that facing the difficult is part of the heroic journey of writing, a preparation, a ritual of sanctification—that it is through this arduous process of grappling with words that writing becomes my true home, a place of solace and comfort.

Double Take

1. Why does hooks call this essay "Women Who Write Too Much"? What does the title suggest? Why might hooks have selected such a title for this piece? When you read the title before reading the essay, what did you expect to read about? After you read the essay, what meaning did you attribute to the title?

2. This essay was taken from a book by bell hooks called *Remembered Rapture,* which is a collection of linked essays about writing. Why might an author like hooks—someone whose very name resounds with the history of silenced women—write not only an essay about writing, but a book about writing? That is, under what circumstances might hooks have been writing? What is the political climate that would encourage such a book? What choices might hooks have had to make to write such a book in such a climate? Who might be interested in reading that kind of book and how does hooks address them in this essay? In other words, for whom is hooks writing and in what ways does she address the audience?

3. In this essay, hooks writes, "I never approach writing thinking about quantity. I think about what I want to say." Think about the many essays and other kinds of writing that you have produced for your work in school. Think about how often those assignments have been guided by the requirements of page length or word length. How often have you written a paper for school guided primarily by the number of pages you were required to write? How often have you had to write for quantity rather than being guided by what you have to say? How might thinking and writing about what you have to say affect the way an essay turns out as opposed to an essay written to fulfill a page requirement? Why do you suppose hooks identifies a difference in these two kinds of motivation? Would the choices you (or hooks) make differ in a paper written for quantity from one written about what one has to say? In what ways?

4. Throughout this essay, hooks writes not only about her own writing, but about some of the writing that has affected her thinking about writing. Why does hooks turn to the work of other writers? Does the inclusion of these authors affect how you read, understand, or interpret hooks's own writing or how she talks about writing? That is, a good portion of this essay focuses on hooks as the first-person singular "I"; how does the inclusion of the other authors affect how you get to know that "I"?

At First Glance

In many ways, "Black Women Writing" is not only about writing, but about the political climate that does not always (or rarely) supports black women authors. As you read this essay, consider how hooks addresses both issues of writing and the political atmosphere in which black women authors write. Think about the ways that hooks is able not only to make political commentary, but also to teach her audience about the struggle of black women authors and about writing. Pay close attention to how she weaves together these two seemingly different subjects to present a remarkably provocative argument. As you look at hooks's argument, consider also her position as a well-known black woman author and what authority that position grants her in making this argument. How does hooks establish that authority here? What rights does it afford her? Would this argument sound different if another author had made it?

▌ Black Women Writing: Creating More Space

To many people, black women writers are everywhere—on the cover of *Newsweek,* the *New York Times Magazine,* on talk shows, on speaking circuits. Just the other day I was in a bookstore and the clerk who took my money for Paule Marshall's novel *Praisesong for the Widow* told me if I intend to write a novel, this is the time—that "they" are looking for black women writers. "They" are the publishers and they are supposedly looking for us because our work is a new commodity. The invisible "they" who control publishing may have only recently fully realized that there is a market for fiction written by black women, but it does not necessarily follow that they are actively seeking to find more material by black women; that black women are writing more than ever before; or that it is any easier for unknown black women writers to find ways to publish their work. It is more likely that those black women writers who have been writing unnoticed for some time, who have already found a way to get their foot in the door or have managed to open it wider have managed to enter and can now find publishers for their work. Publication of their work reminds me and many black women writers/readers that our voices can be heard, that if we create, there is "hope" that our work will one day be published. I am always excited when I hear that another black woman writer has published (fiction or any other genre), especially if she is new and unknown. The more of us there are entering the publishing world the more likely we will continue writing. Yet we are not entering the publishing world in large numbers. Every time someone comments on the "tremendous" attention black women writers are receiving, how easy it is for us to find publishers, how many of us there are, I stop and count, make lists, sit in groups of black women and try to come up with new names. What we've noticed is that the number of visible, published black women writers of fiction is not large. Anyone who teaches courses on black women's fiction knows how difficult it is to find the works of black women (they go out of print rapidly, do not get reprinted, or if reprinted come out in editions that are so expensive that students can rarely afford to buy them for their personal libraries and certainly cannot teach them in classes where many books must be purchased). The reprinted edition of Gwendolyn Brooks's *Maud Martha* (first published in 1953) is one example. It is however better to have expensive reprints rather than no reprints. Books like Ann Petry's *The Street,* Jessie Fauset's *Plum Bun,* Frances Harper's *Iola Leroy,* Kristin Hunter's *The Survivors* and *The Lakestown Rebellion* are often not available. Yet all of these black women writers were or are well known and their works were or are widely read.

I assume that publishing quotas exist that determine the number of black women who will publish books of fiction yearly. Such quotas are not consciously negotiated and decided upon but are the outcomes of institutionalized racism, sexism, and classism. These systems of domination operate in such a way as to ensure that only a very few fiction books by black women will be published at any given time. This has many negative implications for black women writers, those who are published and those who have yet to be published. Published black women writers, even those who are famous, are well aware that their successes do not ensure that their books will be on bookstore shelves years from now. They know that the spirit of new commodity faddism that stimulates much of the current interest in black women's writing can dissipate. It is likely that these writers know that they must "strike while the iron is hot" and this knowledge produces the sense that they cannot always wait for inspiration, cannot linger too long between the publication of one book and the writing of another. They are often compelled to spread themselves thin—teaching, writing, giving talks in the interest of making a living but also in the interest of promoting awareness of the existence and significance of their work. These pressures, whether imposed or chosen, will necessarily affect the writer's work.

Black women writers who are not published, who are still nurturing and developing their skills often find it difficult to maintain the sense that what they have to say is important, especially if they are not in an environment where their commitment to writing is encouraged and affirmed. They must also struggle with the demands of surviving economically while writing. The difficulty of this process for black women has changed little through the years. For every one black woman writer that managed to be published, hundreds if not thousands cease writing because they cannot withstand the pressures, cannot sustain the effort without affirmation, or because they fear that to risk everything in pursuit of one's creative work seems foolish because so few will make it in the end.

Often new writers find that college creative-writing courses provide a positive atmosphere wherein one's work will be read, critiqued, affirmed. Black women attending universities could and do find in such courses a place to strengthen creative writing skills. However, black students are rarely present in these courses at campuses where students are predominantly white. At some campuses where students are predominantly black there is often little or no interest in creative writing. Young black women recognize the precariousness of our collective economic lot (increased unemployment, poverty, etc.) and tend to look for those courses that strengthen their ability to succeed in careers. The promising young black woman writer who must work to provide or help provide for herself and family often cannot find the energy or time to concentrate on and develop her writing. Often black women in professions (teachers, doctors, lawyers, etc.) who are also writers find that the demands of their jobs often leave little room for the cultivation of creative work.

Few black women have imagined that they can make a living writing. I was thirteen when I decided that I wanted to be a writer. At that time I was primarily writing poetry and I realized that I would not be able to make a living with writing. I chose to study literature because I thought it would lead to a profession compatible with writing. When poetry was my primary concern I was fascinated by the work lives of poets who had professions but wrote extensively. Many of these poets were men— Langston Hughes, Wallace Stevens, William Carlos Williams. When I read about their lives I did not reflect on the supportive role women played in the lives of heterosexual male writers, who were probably not coping with domestic chores or raising children while working in professional jobs and writing (their female companions probably attended to these matters). Rare is the woman writer of any race who is free (from domestic chores or caring for others—children, parents, companions) to focus solely on her writing. I know of few black women writers who have been able to concentrate solely on their development as writers without working other jobs at the same time.

In retrospect I can see that I was always trying to attend college, hold part-time jobs, and make a space for writing, as well as taking care of domestic matters. It has become clear to me that I was most free to develop as a writer/poet when I was home with my parents and they were providing economic support, with mama doing the majority of domestic chores and all the cooking. This was the time in my life when I had time to read, study, and write. They and my siblings were also continually affirming my creativity, urging me to develop my talent (after I did my small number of assigned chores). I often heard from them and other folk in the community that talent was a gift from God, and was not to be taken lightly but nourished, developed, or it would be taken away. While I no longer hear this message literally—that the ability to write will be taken away—I do see that the more I write the easier and more joyous a labor it becomes. The less I write the harder it is for me to write and the more it appears to be so arduous a task that I seek to avoid it. I think if any would-be writer avoids writing long enough then they are likely to "lose" the desire, the ability, the power to create.

One must write and one must have time to write. Having time to write, time to wait through silences, time to go to the pen and paper or typewriter when the breakthrough finally comes, affects the type of work that is written. When I read contemporary black women's fiction I see much similarity in choices of subject matter, geographical location, use of language, character formation, and style. There could be many reasons for such similarities. On the one hand, there is the reality of the social status black women share, which has been shaped by the impact of sexism and racism on our lives and shared cultural and ethnic experiences. On the other hand, there is the possibility that many of us pattern work after the fiction of those writers who have been published and are able to earn a living as writers. There is also the possibility that a certain type of writing (the linear narrative story) may be easier to write because it is more acceptable to the reading public than experimental works, especially those that would not focus on themes of black experience or tell a story in a more conventional way. These restrictions apply to many groups of writers in our society. It is important that there be diversity in the types of fiction black women produce and that varied types of writing by black women receive attention and be published. There should not be a stereotyped image of a black woman writer or a preconceived assumption about the type of fiction she will produce.

It must not be assumed that the successes of contemporary black women writers like Toni Morrison, Alice Walker, Paule Marshall, Toni Cade Bambara, Ntozake Shange, and others indicate that a new day has arrived for a majority or even a substantial minority of black women writers. Their individual successes and continued creative development are crucial components of what should be an overall artistic movement to encourage and support writing by black women. Such a movement could take many forms. On a very basic level it can begin with communities stressing the importance of young black children acquiring reading and writing skills and developing along with those skills a positive attitude toward writing. Many of us learned reading and writing but disliked or hated writing. Throughout my twenty years of teaching at a number of universities I have witnessed the terror and anguish many students feel about writing. Many acknowledge that their hatred and fear of writing surfaced in grade school and gathered momentum through high school, reaching a paralyzing peak in the college years.

An intense effort to create and sustain interest in writing must take place in schools and communities. Entering writing competitions should be encouraged by parents, teachers, and friends for young writers. Black women and other people who are interested in the future development of black writers should establish more writing competitions where prizes could be as low as twenty-five dollars to stimulate interest in writing. There should be grant programs for newly published but not yet successful black women writers so that we can have a summer or a year to concentrate solely on our work. Though programs exist that fund writers (like the National Endowment for the Humanities), only the occasional lucky black woman writer receives one of these grants. Often the same few writers receive a number of grants from different sources. While this is good for the individual, it does not increase the number of black women writers receiving aid. Money could be given to a number of universities to sponsor individual black women as part of creative-writing programs.

It seems easier for black women writers to receive monetary support of one kind or another, grants, teaching positions, and talks after they have struggled in isolation and achieved success. Yet only a few black women writers make it in this way. It took me seven years to finish the writing of *Ain't I a Woman: Black Women and Feminism* in part because I did extensive research before writing but also because every avenue I turned toward seeking monetary support failed. I would write after working my eight hours a day at the phone company or after other jobs. When the book was completed almost six years before it was published I sent it off to a number of publishers who rejected it. Without the support of my companion, who helped both financially and emotionally (affirming me as a writer), it would have been impossible to continue. I hear this same story from other black women who know firsthand, as I do, how devastating working in isolation can be. On several occasions I contacted established black women writers seeking acceptance, advice, and critiques but got little response. However, Alice Walker was one person who told me that she was very busy but would take time to read the manuscript if she could. I did not send it to her because I felt that I was imposing, perhaps taking her attention away from her work. Also I think the other black women writers I approached were constantly asked to respond, to give support and advice to younger writers and there is a point when one must say no if you are overextended.

Black women need not be the only group who give support and affirmation to aspiring black female writers. A teacher, friend, or colleague can provide the encouragement and affirmation that fosters and promotes work. When I first met Gloria Naylor, author of the novel *Women of Brewster Place,* I asked her how she had found a publisher. Gloria was a student at Yale working on an M.A. focusing on creative writing. She found support and affirmation for her work in this academic environment. It was with the help of a friend that she was able to find an editor to read her novel and consider it for publication. Having people around who affirm one during the writing process is as vital to the aspiring writer as finding someone to publish one's work.

When I was an undergraduate taking creative-writing courses, I remember a black male poet advising me not to worry about publication but to focus on writing, then when I had produced a body of work to worry about finding a publisher. This bit of advice has been very useful over the years, reminding me that the primary emphasis for the aspiring writer has to be initially on the production of work. I find in teaching creative-writing classes that aspiring writers are often so desperate for the affirmation that comes with publication that they are not interested in rewriting, or putting away a piece for a time and coming back to it. After *Ain't I a Woman* was rejected I spent almost nine months away from the work before I took the box down from its hiding place in the closet and began massive rewriting. Like Gloria Naylor, I learned from a friend who had seen their ad in a Bay Area women's newspaper that South End Press was seeking books on feminism and race. In retrospect, despite the pain I suffered when the manuscript was continually rejected, I can see now that it was not ready for publication at that time. I now consider it fortunate that no one accepted it then. I have completed many books that focus on feminist and cultural issues, one poetry manuscript, one dissertation, two novels in manuscript, and yet I still confront daily the difficulty of providing for myself economically while seeking to grow and develop as a writer.

When I told Chinosole, a black woman friend and fellow writer-scholar, about this essay, she commented that it is amazing how much writing we black women can produce even when we are worried sick about finances and job pressures. It is my hope that the current interest in works of a few black women writers will lead to the recognition of the need to encourage and promote such writing—not just the work of famous black women but the work of unknown, struggling, aspiring writers who need to know that their creative work is important, that it deserves their concentrated attention, and that it need not be abandoned.

Double Take

1. In "Black Women Writing: Creating More Space," hooks writes about the climate of writing classes in American universities for black students, and she writes about some of her own experiences in college atmospheres as a student writer and a teacher of writing. In some ways, it seems as though hooks is establishing the college or university environment as a location where writing can be best taught and learned, or practiced. Why do you suppose she chooses the college or university setting as a place for the discussion of writing? Is this the only place where one might learn about writing or practice the act of writing?

2. In "Black Women Writing," hooks notes, "there is also the possibility that a certain type of writing (the linear narrative story) may be easier to write because it is more acceptable to the reading public than experimental works, especially those that would not focus on themes of black experience or tell a story in a more conventional way." First, what are some of the characteristics of a linear narrative story? Could this essay be considered a linear narrative? If so, why might hooks have decided to use a linear narrative to write about the lack of experimental writing from black women who write and publish? What might experimental writing look like?

3. hooks writes, "Throughout my twenty years of teaching at a number of universities, I have witnessed the terror and anguish many students feel about writing. Many acknowledge that their hatred and fear of writing surfaced in grade school and gathered momentum through high school, reaching a paralyzing peak in the college years." As a college student, do you hate and fear writing? Where do you think that fear stems from? Have you tried to express that fear in your writing? What does hooks accomplish by addressing student fears of writing in a piece of writing? To whom might hooks be speaking when she makes this statement? Students? Teachers?

At First Glance

In her essay "Touching the Earth," bell hooks writes about the importance of the connection to nature for African Americans. She begins this essay by writing, "When we love the earth, we are able to love ourselves more fully." She further explains that "Native American and African people shared with one another a respect for the life-giving forces of nature." She argues that such a respect for and connection to nature is crucial for black self-recovery: "Collective black self-recovery takes place when we begin to renew our relationship to the earth."

Part of this recovery, hooks argues, was derailed when black culture began to move from the agrarian lifestyle of the South to the more industrialized society of the North. As you read this wonderfully rich essay, consider how hooks's notion of place, particularly the place of the South, affects her writing, its sound and organization. Also, consider the ways that she expertly weaves in a range of other voices to clarify her argument.

Touching the Earth

When we love the earth, we are able to love ourselves more fully. I believe this. The ancestors taught me it was so. As a child I loved playing in dirt, in that rich Kentucky soil, that was a source of life. Before I understood anything about the pain and exploitation of the southern system of sharecropping, I understood that grown-up black folks loved the land. I could stand with my grandfather Daddy Jerry and look out at fields of growing vegetables, tomatoes, corn, collards, and know that this was his handiwork. I could see the look of pride on his face as I expressed wonder and awe at the magic of growing things. I knew that my grandmother Baba's backyard garden would yield beans, sweet potatoes, cabbage, and yellow squash, that she too would walk with pride among the rows and rows of growing vegetables showing us what the earth will give when tended lovingly.

From the moment of their first meeting, Native American and African people shared with one another a respect for the life-giving forces of nature, of the earth. African settlers in Florida taught the Creek Nation runaways, the "Seminoles," methods for rice cultivation. Native peoples taught recently arrived black folks all about the many uses of corn. (The hotwater cornbread we grew up eating came to our black southern diet from the world of the Indian.) Sharing the reverence for the earth, black and red people helped one another remember that, despite the white man's ways, the land belonged to everyone. Listen to these words attributed to Chief Seattle in 1854:

> How can you buy or sell the sky, the warmth of the land? The idea is strange to us. If we do not own the freshness of the air and the sparkle of the water, how can you buy them? Every part of this earth is sacred to my people. Every shining pine needle, every sandy shore, every mist in the dark woods, every clearing and humming insect is holy in the memory and experience of my people. We are part of the earth and it is part of us. The perfumed flowers are our sisters; the deer, the horse, the great eagle, these are our brothers. The rocky crests, the juices in the meadows, the body heat of the pony, and man all belong to the same family.

The sense of union and harmony with nature expressed here is echoed in testimony by black people who found that even though life in the new world was "harsh, harsh," in relationship to the earth one could be at peace. In the oral autobiography of granny midwife Onnie Lee Logan, who lived all her life in Alabama, she talks about the richness of farm life growing vegetables, raising chickens, and smoking meat. She reports:

> We lived a happy, comfortable life to be right outa slavery times. I didn't know nothing else but the farm so it was happy and we was happy. We couldn't do anything else but be happy. We accept the days as they come and as they were. Day by day until you couldn't say there was any great hard time. We overlooked it. We didn't think nothin about it. We just went along. We had what it takes to make a good livin and go about it.

Living in modern society, without a sense of history, it has been easy for folks to forget that black people were first and foremost a people of the land, farmers. It is easy for folks to forget that at the first part of the 20th century, the vast majority of black folks in the United States lived in the agrarian south.

Living close to nature, black folks were able to cultivate a spirit of wonder and reverence for life. Growing food to sustain life and flowers to please the soul, they were able to make a connection with the earth that was ongoing and life-affirming. They were witnesses to beauty. In Wendell Berry's important discussion of the relationship between agriculture and human spiritual well-being, *The Unsettling of America,* he reminds us that working the land provides a location where folks can experience a sense of personal power and well-being:

> We are working well when we use ourselves as the fellow creature of the plants, animals, material, and other people we are working with. Such work is unifying, healing. It brings us home from pride and despair, and places us responsibly within the human estate. It defines us as we are: not too good to work without our bodies, but too good to work poorly or joylessly or selfishly or alone.

There has been little or no work done on the psychological impact of the "great migration" of black people from the agrarian south to the industrialized north. Toni Morrison's novel *The Bluest Eye* attempts to fictively document the way moving from the agrarian south to the industrialized north wounded the psyches of black folk. Estranged from a natural world, where there was time for silence and contemplation, one of the "displaced" black folks in Morrison's novel, Miss Pauline, loses her capacity to experience the sensual world around her when she leaves southern soil to live in a northern city. The south is associated in her mind with a world of sensual beauty most deeply expressed in the world of nature. Indeed, when she falls in love for the first time she can name that experience only by evoking images from nature, from an agrarian world and near wilderness of natural splendor:

> When I first seed Cholly, I want you to know it was like all the bits of color from that time down home when all us chil'ren went berry picking after a funeral and I put some in the pocket of my Sunday dress, and they mashed up and stained my hips. My whole dress was messed with purple, and it never did wash out. Not the dress nor me. I could feel that purple deep inside me. And that lemonade Mama used to make when Pap came in out of the fields. It be cool and yellowish, with seeds floating near the bottom. And that streak of

green them june bugs made on the trees that night we left from down home. All of them colors was in me. Just sitting there.

Certainly, it must have been a profound blow to the collective psyche of black people to find themselves struggling to make a living in the industrial north away from the land. Industrial capitalism was not simply changing the nature of black work life, it altered the communal practices that were so central to survival in the agrarian south. And it fundamentally altered black people's relationship to the body. It is the loss of any capacity to appreciate her body, despite its flaws, Miss Pauline suffers when she moves north.

The motivation for black folks to leave the south and move north was both material and psychological. Black folks wanted to be free of the overt racial harassment that was a constant in southern life and they wanted access to material goods, to a level of material well-being that was not available in the agrarian south where white folks limited access to the spheres of economic power. Of course, they found that life in the north had its own perverse hardships, that racism was just as virulent there, that it was much harder for black people to become landowners. Without the space to grow food, to commune with nature, or to mediate the starkness of poverty with the splendor of nature, black people experienced profound depression. Working in conditions where the body was regarded solely as a tool (as in slavery), a profound estrangement occurred between mind and body. The way the body was represented became more important than the body itself. It did not matter if the body was well, only that it appeared well.

Estrangement from nature and engagement in mind/body splits made it all the more possible for black people to internalize white-supremacist assumptions about black identity. Learning contempt for blackness, southerners transplanted in the north suffered both culture shock and soul loss. Contrasting the harshness of city life with an agrarian world, the poet Waring Cuney wrote this popular poem in the 1920s, testifying to lost connection:

> *She does not know her beauty*
> *She thinks her brown body*
> *has no glory.*
> *If she could dance naked,*
> *Under palm trees*
> *And see her image in the river*
> *She would know.*
> *But there are no palm trees on the street,*
> *And dishwater gives back no images.*

For many years, and even now, generations of black folks who migrated north to escape life in the south, returned down home in search of a spiritual nourishment, a healing, that was fundamentally connected to reaffirming one's connection to nature, to a contemplative life where one could take time, sit on the porch, walk, fish, and catch lightning bugs. If we think of urban life as a location where black folks learned to accept a mind/body split that made it possible to abuse the body, we can better understand the growth of nihilism and despair in the black psyche. And we can know that when we talk about healing that psyche we must also speak about restoring our connection to the natural world.

Wherever black folks live we can restore our relationship to the natural world by taking the time to commune with nature, to appreciate the other creatures who share this planet with humans. Even in my small New York City apartment I can pause to listen to birds sing, find a tree and watch it. We can grow plants—herbs, flowers, vegetables. Those novels by African-American writers (women and men) that talk about black migration from the agrarian south to the industrialized north describe in detail the way folks created space to grow flowers and vegetables. Although I come from country people with serious green thumbs, I have always felt that I could not garden. In the past few years, I have found that I can do it—that many gardens will grow, that I feel connected to my ancestors when I can put a meal on the table of food I grew. I especially love to plant collard greens. They are hardy, and easy to grow.

In modern society, there is also a tendency to see no correlation between the struggle for collective black self-recovery and ecological movements that seek to restore balance to the planet by changing our relationship to nature and to natural resources. Unmindful of our history of living harmoniously on the land, many contemporary black folks see no value in supporting ecological movements, or see ecology and the struggle to end racism as competing concerns. Recalling the legacy of our ancestors who knew that the way we regard land and nature will determine the level of our self-regard, black people must reclaim a spiritual legacy where we connect our well-being to the well-being of the earth. This is a necessary dimension of healing. As Berry reminds us:

> Only by restoring the broken connections can we be healed. Connection is health. And what our society does its best to disguise from us is how ordinary, how commonly attainable, health is. We lose our health and create profitable diseases and dependencies by failing to see the direct connections between living and eating, eating and working, working and loving. In gardening, for instance, one works with the body to feed the body. The work, if it is knowledgeable, makes for excellent food. And it makes one hungry. The work thus makes eating both nourishing and joyful, not consumptive, and keeps the eater from getting fat and weak. This health, wholeness, is a source of delight.

Collective black self-recovery takes place when we begin to renew our relationship to the earth, when we remember the way of our ancestors. When the earth is sacred to us, our bodies can also be sacred to us.

Double Take

1. hooks devotes a good portion of "Touching the Earth" to the words of others in order to support her own position. Why do you suppose she has chosen to rely so heavily on citations? Are there any characteristics of the citations she uses that seem most effective? Could this essay have been written without the citations? Consider reading the essay without the quotes or the references to their authors. Certainly the essay would be considerably shorter, but would the argument be as effective? Would the essay be as powerful?

2. Toward the middle of this essay (p. 345), hooks has included a break between sections. What might she be conveying with this break? What effect does this break have on the structure of the essay? Does the section before the break have any marked differences from the section following it?

3. Though hooks discusses the relationships between African-American culture, self-recovery, identity, and nature, she also seems to be articulating a consideration for the relationship between writing and nature. Notice, for instance, that she addresses much of what she has to say about nature and the black experience through the words of authors who address issues of nature, place, and African-American experience. Do you suppose that hooks might also be making links between nature and writing, and how black experience and attitudes toward nature are bound up with writing? What evidence do you find for such a claim about hooks's argument? Why might hooks have decided to address this issue in such an understated way? Could she have rewritten this essay to address the role of writing here more deliberately? How might she have approached such a revision?

Seeing for Yourself

At First Glance

In "Justice: Childhood Love Lessons," bell hooks writes about how children conceive of love and how punishment and abuse can often confuse a child's understanding of love. This essay, a powerful examination of how adults teach children to understand, or often misunderstand love, incorporates a good number of short anecdotes linked within the larger narrative. As you read this essay, consider not only how these anecdotes affect the larger narrative, but how hooks has linked them together, the choices she has made in order to best use the examples she provides.

Justice: Childhood Love Lessons

> Severe separations in early life leave emotional scars on the brain because they assault the essential human connection: The [parent-child] bond which teaches us that we are lovable. The [parent-child] bond which teaches us how to love. We cannot be whole human beings—indeed, we may find it hard to be human—without the sustenance of this first attachment.
>
> —JUDITH VIORST

We learn about love in childhood. Whether our homes are happy or troubled, our families functional or dysfunctional, it's the original school of love. I cannot remember ever wanting to ask my parents to define love. To my child's mind love was the good feeling you got when family treated you like you mattered and you treated them like they mattered. Love was always and only about good feeling. In early adolescence when we were whipped and told that these punishments were "for our own good" or "I'm doing this because I love you," my siblings and I were confused. Why was harsh punishment a gesture of love? As children do, we pretended to accept this grown-up logic; but we knew in our hearts it was not right. We knew it was a lie. Just like the lie grown-ups told when they explained after harsh punishment, "It hurts me more than it hurts you." There is nothing that creates more confusion about love in the minds and hearts of children than unkind and/or cruel punishment meted out by the grown-ups they have been taught they should love and respect. Such children learn early on to question the meaning of love, to yearn for love even as they doubt it exists.

On the flip side there are masses of children who grow up confident love is a good feeling who are never punished, who are allowed to believe that love is only

348

about getting your needs met, your desires satisfied. In their child's minds love is not about what they have to give, love is mostly something given to them. When children like these are overindulged either materially or by being allowed to act out, this is a form of neglect. These children, though not in any way abused or uncared for, are usually as unclear about love's meaning as their neglected and emotionally abandoned counterparts. Both groups have learned to think about love primarily in relation to good feelings, in the context of reward and punishment. From early childhood on, most of us remember being told we were loved when we did things pleasing to our parents. And we learned to give them affirmations of love when they pleased us. As children grow they associate love more with acts of attention, affection, and caring. They still see parents who attempt to satisfy their desires as giving love.

Children from all classes tell me that they love their parents and are loved by them, even those who are being hurt or abused. When asked to define love, small children pretty much agree that it's a good feeling, "like when you have something to eat that you really like" especially if it's your f-a-v-o-r-i-t-e. They will say, "My mommy loves me 'cause she takes care of me and helps me do everything right." When asked how to love someone, they talk about giving hugs and kisses, being sweet and cuddly. The notion that love is about getting what one wants, whether it's a hug or a new sweater or a trip to Disneyland, is a way of thinking about love that makes it difficult for children to acquire a deeper emotional understanding.

We like to imagine that most children will be born into homes where they will be loved. But love will not be present if the grown-ups who parent do not know how to love. Although lots of children are raised in homes where they are given some degree of care, love may not be sustained or even present. Adults across lines of class, race, and gender indict the family. Their testimony conveys worlds of childhood where love was lacking—where chaos, neglect, abuse, and coercion reigned supreme. In her recent book *Raised in Captivity: Why Does America Fail Its Children?,* Lucia Hodgson documents the reality of lovelessness in the lives of a huge majority of children in the United States. Every day thousands of children in our culture are verbally and physically abused, starved, tortured, and murdered. They are the true victims of intimate terrorism in that they have no collective voice and no rights. They remain the property of parenting adults to do with as they will.

There can be no love without justice. Until we live in a culture that not only respects but also upholds basic civil rights for children, most children will not know love. In our culture the private family dwelling is the one institutionalized sphere of power that can easily be autocratic and fascistic. As absolute rulers, parents can usually decide without any intervention what is best for their children. If children's rights are taken away in any domestic household, they have no legal recourse. Unlike women who can organize to protest sexist domination, demanding both equal rights and justice, children can only rely on well-meaning adults to assist them if they are being exploited and oppressed in the home.

We all know that, irrespective of class or race, other adults rarely intervene to question or challenge what their peers are doing with "their" children.

At a fun party, mostly of educated, well-paid professionals, a multiracial, multigenerational evening, the subject of disciplining kids by hitting was raised. Almost all the guests over thirty spoke about the necessity of using physical punishment. Many of us in the room had been smacked, whipped, or beaten as children. Men spoke the loudest in defense of physical punishment. Women, mostly mothers, talked about hitting as a last resort, but one that they deployed when necessary.

As one man bragged about the aggressive beatings he had received from his mother, sharing that "they had been good for him," I interrupted and suggested that he might not be the misogynist woman-hater he is today if he had not been brutally beaten by a woman as a child. Although it is too simplistic to assume that just because we are hit as kids we will grow up to be people who hit, I wanted the group to acknowledge that being physically hurt or abused by grown-ups when we are children has harmful consequences in our adult life.

A young professional, the mother of a small boy, bragged about the fact that she did not hit, that when her son misbehaved she clamped down on his flesh, pinching him until he got the message. But this, too, is a form of coercive abuse. The other guests supported this young mother and her husband in their methods. I was astounded. I was a lone voice speaking out for the rights of children.

Later, with other people, I suggested that had we all been listening to a man tell us that every time his wife or girlfriend does something he does not like he just clamps down on her flesh, pinching her as hard as he can, everyone would have been appalled. They would have seen the action as both coercive and abusive. Yet they could not acknowledge that it was wrong for an adult to hurt a child in this way. All the parents in that room claim that they are loving. All the people in that room were college educated. Most call themselves good liberals, supportive of civil rights and feminism. But when it came to the rights of children they had a different standard.

One of the most important social myths we must debunk if we are to become a more loving culture is the one that teaches parents that abuse and neglect can coexist with love. Abuse and neglect negate love. Care and affirmation, the opposite of abuse and humiliation, are the foundation of love. No one can rightfully claim to be loving when behaving abusively. Yet parents do this all the time in our culture. Children are told they are loved even though they are being abused.

It is a testimony to the failure of loving practice that abuse is happening in the first place.

Many of the men who offer their personal testimony in *Boyhood, Growing Up Male* tell stories of random violent abuse by parents that inflicted trauma. In his essay "When My Father Hit Me," Bob Shelby describes the pain of repeated beatings by his dad, stating: "From these experiences with my father, I learned about the abuse of power. By physically hitting my mother and me, he effectively stopped us from reacting to his humiliation of us. We ceased to protest his violations of our boundaries and his ignoring our sense of being individuals with needs, demands and rights of our own." Throughout his essay Shelby expresses contradictory understandings about the meaning of love. On the one hand, he says: "I have no doubt that my father loved me, but his love became misdirected. He said he wanted to give me what he didn't have as a child." On the other hand, Shelby confesses: "What he most showed me, however, was his difficulty in being loved. All his life he had struggled with feelings of being unloved." When Shelby describes his childhood it is clear that his dad had affection for him and also gave him care some of the time. However, his dad did not know how to give and receive love. The affection he gave was undermined by the abuse.

Writing from the space of adult recollection, Shelby talks about the impact of physical abuse on his boyhood psyche: "As the intensity of the pain of his hits increased, I felt the hurt in my heart. I realized what hurt me the most were my feelings of love for this man who was hitting me. I covered my love with a dark cloth of hate." A similar story is told by other men in autobiographical narrative—men of all classes and races. One of the myths about lovelessness is that it exists only among the poor and deprived. Yet lovelessness is not a function of poverty or material lack. In homes where material privileges abound, children suffer emotional neglect and abuse. In order to cope with the pain of wounds inflicted in childhood, most of the men in *Boyhood* sought some form of therapeutic care. To find their way back to love they had to heal.

Many men in our culture never recover from childhood unkindnesses. Studies show that males and females who are violently humiliated and abused repeatedly, with no caring intervention, are likely to be dysfunctional and will be predisposed to abuse others violently. In Jarvis Jay Masters's book *Finding Freedom: Writings from Death Row,* a chapter called "Scars" recounts his recognition that a vast majority of the scars covering the bodies of fellow inmates (not all of whom were on death row) were not, as one might think, the result of violent adult interactions. These men were covered with scars from childhood beatings inflicted by parenting adults. Yet, he reports, none of them saw themselves as the victims of abuse: "Throughout my many years of institutionalization, I, like so many of these men, unconsciously took refuge behind prison walls. Not until I read a series of books for adults who had been abused as children did I become committed to the process of examining my own childhood." Organizing the men for group discussion, Masters writes: "I spoke to them of the pain I had carried through more than a dozen institutions. And I explained how all these events ultimately trapped me in a pattern of lashing out against everything. Like many abused children, male and female, these men were beaten by mothers, fathers, and other parental caregivers."

When Masters's mother dies he feels grief that he cannot be with her. The other inmates do not understand this longing, since she neglected and abused him. He responds: "She had neglected me, but am I to neglect myself as well by denying that I wished I'd been with her when she died, that I still love her?" Even on death row, Masters's heart remains open. And he can honestly confess to longing to give and receive love. Being hurt by parenting adults rarely alters a child's desire to love and be loved by them. Among grown-ups who were wounded in childhood, the desire to be loved by uncaring parents persists, even when there is a clear acceptance of the reality that this love will never be forthcoming.

Often, children will want to remain with parental caregivers who have hurt them because of their cathected feelings for those adults. They will cling to the misguided assumption that their parents love them even in the face of remembered abuse, usually by denying the abuse and focusing on random acts of care.

In the prologue to *Creating Love,* John Bradshaw calls this confusion about love "mystification." He shares: "I was brought up to believe that love is rooted in blood relationships. You naturally loved anyone in your family. Love was not a choice. The love I learned about was bound by duty and obligation. . . . My family taught me our culture's rules and beliefs above love . . . even with the best intentions our parents often confused love with what we would now call abuse." To demystify the meaning of love, the art and practice of loving, we need to use sound definitions of love when talking with children, and we also need to ensure that loving action is never tainted with abuse.

In a society like ours, where children are denied full civil rights, it is absolutely crucial that parenting adults learn how to offer loving discipline. Setting boundaries and teaching children how to set boundaries for themselves prior to misbehavior is an essential part of loving parenting. When parents start out disciplining children by using punishment, this becomes the pattern children respond to. Loving parents work hard to discipline without punishment. This does not mean that they never punish, only that when they do punish, they choose punishments like time-outs or the taking away of privileges. They focus on teaching children how to be self-disciplining and how to take responsibility for their actions. Since the vast majority of us were raised in households where punishment was deemed the primary, if not the only, way to teach discipline, the fact that discipline can be taught without punishment surprises many people. One of the simplest ways children learn discipline is by learning how to be orderly in daily life, to clean up any messes they make. Just teaching a child to take responsibility for placing toys in the appropriate place after playtime is one way to teach responsibility and self-discipline. Learning to clean up the mess made during playtime helps a child learn to be responsible. And they can learn from this practical act how to cope with emotional mess.

Were there current television shows that actually modeled loving parenting, parents could learn these skills. Television shows oriented toward families often favorably represent children when they are overindulged, are disrespectful, or are acting out. Often they behave in a more adult manner than the parents. What we see on television today actually, at best, models for us inappropriate behavior, and in worst-case scenarios, unloving behaviors. A great example of this is a movie like *Home Alone,* which celebrates disobedience and violence. But television can portray caring, loving family interaction. There are whole generations of adults who talk nostalgically about how they wanted their families to be like the fictive portraits of family life portrayed on *Leave It to Beaver* or *My Three Sons.* We desired our families to be like those we saw on the screen because we were witnessing loving parenting, loving households. Expressing to parents our desire to have families like the ones we saw on the screen, we were often told that the families were not realistic. The reality was, however, that parents who come from unloving homes have never learned how to love and cannot create loving home environments or see them as realistic when watching them on television. The reality they are most familiar with and trust is the one they knew intimately.

There was nothing utopian about the way problems were resolved on these shows. Parent and child discussion, critical reflection, and finding a way to make amends was usually the process by which misbehavior was addressed. On both shows there was never just one parenting figure. Even though the mother was absent on *My Three*

Sons, the lovable Uncle Charlie was a second parent. In a loving household where there are several parental caregivers, when a child feels one parent is being unjust, that child can appeal to another adult for mediation, understanding, or support. We live in a society where there are a growing number of single parents, female and male. But the individual parent can always choose a friend to be another parenting figure, however limited their interaction. This is why the categories of godmother and godfather are so crucial. When my best girlhood friend chose to have a child without a father in the household, I became the godmother, a second parenting figure.

My friend's daughter turns to me to intervene if there is a misunderstanding or miscommunication between her and her mom. Here's one small example. My adult friend had never received an allowance as a child and did not feel she had the available extra money to offer an allowance to her daughter. She also believed her daughter would use all the money to buy sweets. Telling me that her daughter was angry with her over this issue, she opened up the space for us to have a dialogue. I shared my belief that allowances are important ways to teach children discipline, boundaries, and working through desires versus needs. I knew enough about my friend's finances to challenge her insistence that she could not afford to pay a small allowance, while simultaneously encouraging her not to project the wrongs of her childhood onto the present. As to whether the daughter would buy candy, I suggested she give the allowance with a statement of hope that it would not be used for overindulgence and see what happened.

It all worked out just fine. Happy to have an allowance, the daughter chose to save her money to buy things she thought were really important. And candy was not on this list. Had there not been another adult parenting figure involved, it might have taken these two a longer time to resolve their conflict, and unnecessary estrangement and wounding might have occurred. Significantly, love and respectful interaction between two adults exemplified for the daughter (who was told about the discussion) ways of problem solving. By revealing her willingness to accept criticism and her capacity to reflect on her behavior and change, the mother modeled for her daughter, without losing dignity and authority, the recognition that parents are not always right.

Until we begin to see loving parenting in all walks of life in our culture, many people will continue to believe we can only teach discipline through punishment, and that harsh punishment is an acceptable way to relate to children. Because children can innately offer affection or respond to affectionate care by returning it, it is often assumed that they know how to love and therefore do not need to learn the art of loving. While the will to love is present in very young children, they still need guidance in the ways of love. Grown-ups provide that guidance.

Love is as love does, and it is our responsibility to give children love. When we love children we acknowledge by our every action that they are not property, that they have rights—that we respect and uphold their rights.

Without justice there can be no love.

A CLOSER LOOK AT BELL HOOKS

1. Now that you have read the essays by bell hooks, you may start to notice some writing characteristics that appear consistently throughout her writing, no matter what subject she addresses. For instance, in each of the four essays included here, hooks conveys a strong sense of the narrator, of her voice, of the presence of the "I." Also, in each of these essays, there is frequently a strong link to the notion of writing or to texts, whether she is specifically addressing writing (as she does in the first two essays) or not. Considering these and any other consistent characteristics or rhetorical choices you may notice about hooks's writing, first ask yourself how such rhetorical consistencies affect your response to her body of work. Second, if you identify any of these characteristics as particularly effective, consider how and in what ways you might learn from those strategies in developing your own writing. Then, in an essay of your own, explain how hooks's consistencies affect how you read her essays. Be sure to cite several examples from each of her essays included here to support your argument.

2. In the brief introduction to this section, we noted that bell hooks is often described as a "public intellectual," one who tries to make her work accessible to a wider, more public audience. Now that you have read four examples of hooks's writing, what rhetorical choices does hooks make in order to specifically reach larger audiences? What effects do those choices have on how you read her work? Write an essay in which you analyze what makes her writing work for a larger audience.

3. In the first two essays, hooks writes about writing. Taking your cue from hooks, write an essay that details your own approach to and understanding of writing. What does writing mean to you? How important is it to you? How do you use writing in your life? Use these questions to begin reflecting on writing.

Looking from Writer to Writer

1. In her essay "Women Who Write Too Much," bell hooks cites Annie Dillard's comments about writers in *The Writing Life*. In many ways, hooks and Dillard take similar approaches and views toward their writing. Look at Dillard's four essays included in this collection—particularly those from *The Writing Life*—and compare her work with that of hooks. Are there recognizable similarities? Differences?

2. Much like Henry Louis Gates, Jr., hooks often makes use of anecdotal experiences to qualify and clarify her arguments. Compare hooks's writing to that of Gates, and consider how each uses anecdotes to enhance their essays.

3. Both bell hooks and Ursula Le Guin write specifically about writing and women writers. Compare the ways that hooks and Le Guin talk about women writers and their future as writers.

Looking Beyond

ESSAYS

Art on My Mind: Visual Politics. New York: New Press, 1995.
Outlaw Culture: Resisting Representations. New York: Routledge, 1994.

NONFICTION

Ain't I a Woman: Black Women and Feminism. Boston: South End Press, 1981.
All about Love: New Visions. New York: William Morrow, 2000.
Black Looks: Race and Representation. Boston: South End Press, 1992.
Bone Black: Memories of Girlhood. New York: Henry Holt, 1996.
Breaking Bread: Insurgent Black Intellectual Life (written with Cornell West). Boston: South End Press, 1991.
Feminist Theory: From Margin to Center. Boston: South End Press, 1984.
Killing Rage: Ending Racism. New York: Henry Holt, 1995.
Reel to Real: Race, Sex, and Class at the Movies. New York: Routledge, 1996.
Remembered Rapture: The Writer at Work. New York: Henry Holt, 1999.
Sisters of the Yam: Black Women and Self Recovery. Boston: South End Press, 1993.
Talking Back: Thinking Feminist, Thinking Black. Boston: South End Press, 1988.
Teaching to Transgress: Education as the Practice of Freedom. New York: Routledge, 1994.
Wounds of Passion: A Writing Life. New York: Owl Books, 1997.
Yearning: Race, Gender, and Cultural Politics. Boston: South End Press, 1990.

POETRY

A Woman's Mourning Song. New York: Writers and Readers, 1992.

CHILDREN'S BOOKS

Happy to Be Nappy (illustrated by Chris Raschka). New York: Jump at the Sun—Disney Books, 1999.
Homemade Love. New York: Jump at the Sun—Disney Books, 2001.

Jamaica Kincaid

Jamaica Kincaid says, "For me, writing isn't a way of being public or private; it's just a way of being. The process is always full of pain, but I like that. It's a reality, and I just accept it as something not to be avoided. This is the life I have. This is the life I write about." She also says, "I think in many ways the problem that my writing would have with an American reviewer is that Americans find difficulty very hard to take. They are inevitably looking for a happy ending. Perversely, I will not give the happy ending. I think life is difficult and that's that. I am not at all—absolutely not at all—interested in the pursuit of happiness. I am not interested in the pursuit of positivity. I am interested in pursuing a truth, and the truth often seems to be not happiness but its opposite." Kincaid's subjects are often difficult subjects to address: colonialism, race, slavery and servitude, the death of her brother from AIDS. Her writing often reflects the events of her own life, autobiographical in many ways, as the title of some of her books suggests: *The Autobiography of My Mother* and *My Brother.* Her book *Lucy* is also autobiographical in form.

Jamaica Kincaid is the pen name of Elaine Potter Richardson. She was born in 1949 on the island of Antigua in the West Indies. She lived with her mother, whom Kincaid often describes as abusive, and her stepfather, a carpenter. Their home had no bathroom, no plumbing, and no electricity. As a child, her chores around the house included registering their outhouse with the Public Works Department every Wednesday so that the "night soil men" would take away their filled basin and replace it with a clean one as well as going every morning and afternoon to get water from a public pipe. In 1966 her mother shipped her off to New York to work as an au pair, a position Kincaid describes as that of a servant. When she left Antigua, she was 17 years old and penniless. She did not return to her home on the island until she was 36. In the interim, *New Yorker* columnist George Trow printed one of Kincaid's articles in the "Talk of the Town" section of the magazine, and the reading public thereby discovered the writer Jamaica Kincaid. Her book *Lucy* tells the story of a poor island girl who travels to New York to become an au pair. Kincaid served as a staff writer for *The New Yorker* from 1976 until 1995.

Kincaid studied photography at the New York School for Social Research and attended Franconia College in New Hampshire. She has earned a good number of awards for her writing, including the Morton Dauwen Zabel Award by the American Academy and Institute of Arts and Letters for her book of short stories *At the Bottom of the River,* and the Lila Wallace–Reader's Digest Fund annual writers award in 1992. Kincaid's *The Autobiography of My Mother* was a finalist for both the PEN Faulkner Award and the National Book Critics Circle Award for fiction. Kincaid's writing is often referred to as stark, brutally honest, yet lyrical. As you read these essays consider those accolades and note how stark her writing can be, but at the same time how lyrical and easy to read it is. Consider why a flow, rhythm, and tone that are described as "lyrical" might be (or might not be) suitable for the subjects about which she writes.

Kincaid on Writing

At First Glance

In addressing each of the other writers in this collection, we have begun by including an essay about writing by each writer. Unlike other chapters, we begin here with a less traditional essay (if we can call it that) form: an interview with Jamaica Kincaid about her writing. While Kincaid is very outspoken about her views on writing, she does not often put those views into writing. The interview included here, conducted by Brad Goldfarb in October 1997, provides insight into Kincaid's views on writing, not as an example of an essay per se. However, as you read this interview, consider the ways it might be considered an essay—that is, does it contain any characteristics of an essay?

Writing = Life
Interview with Writer Jamaica Kincaid

Jamaica Kincaid's extraordinary new book is called *My Brother*. It is about all of us.

Were one to do an analysis of every review, feature story, commentary, and press release written about Jamaica Kincaid over the years, chances are one would find that the single word most frequently used to describe her work is honesty. Certainly this word, this characteristic, is what comes to mind when thinking about *My Brother* (Farrar, Straus, and Giroux), Kincaid's first memoir. It is a breathtakingly deep account of the story of her family in Antigua, written after the AIDS-related death of her youngest brother, Devon. Devon, we learn through the words of his sister, was beautiful and gifted: a talented musician who shared her love for books, a promising athlete, a charmer of both men and women, a Rastafarian. But there were secrets in his past—not least of which was his role in a murder at the age of fourteen. Kincaid does not shy away from painting as complete a picture as possible of her family and her brother. In fact she's committed to it: She'll show us her mother's cruelty, as well as her brother's pain, his suffering, his loneliness—but also his selfishness, his destructiveness, his inclination towards self-pity. As with any memoir, *My Brother* is as much about the person doing the writing as it is about "the subject," and the author is equally ruthless in her determination to give us a true account of herself and her own feelings. This is the source of her book's great power.

When you read *My Brother*, you understand the profound implications of the now-famous phrase Silence = Death. As Kincaid herself told me, more than any other

359

project she has ever undertaken, this was a book that demanded to be written—the words flowed out of her fingertips so quickly she sometimes couldn't type fast enough to keep up. The process, she recalls, was agonizing and could only happen in the dead of night, after "the dishes were cleared away and everybody was in bed."

> BRAD GOLDFARB: One of the big themes of *My Brother* is that to gain our own lives we sometimes have to separate ourselves from our families. For instance, there's a line in your book in which you acknowledge that you could not have become a writer among the people who knew you best.

> JAMAICA KINCAID: Yes, this is true, in the same way that I see that my brother couldn't be a homosexual among the people whom he knew best. He couldn't live his life without fear. He couldn't live his life openly. It wasn't that people would have hurt him physically; it's that he would have been scorned. The mental pain was more than he could have accepted. And so, too, for me as a writer I think the mental, the verbal, the spiritual scorn from my community would have been more painful, in a way, than being stoned to death. There is something so deeply cruel about the place I am from.

> BG: When you say "place," you mean Antigua?

> JK: Yes, the place, and my family in it.

> BG: Do you think your mother was typical in her sensibility and in the way she treated you and your brothers, or was it a uniquely cruel situation?

> JK: We had an extraordinarily intelligent and unusual person in our mother. Her way of humiliating us was just astonishing and harsh—very cruel and very painful. And in that way, coupled with the narrow-mindedness of Antigua—it's a narrow place with narrow people—in that way it was unique.
>
> Someone was saying something to me recently about my mother and domesticity, and I said, "Oh, my mother was a domestic god, not a goddess." And she was. Within a place that's very domestic—as poor people in poor places usually are—even within that, we lived with someone who ruled the home like a kingdom.

> BG: At one point in the book, you describe her as a force of nature, like a tornado or a wildfire.

> JK: It sounds almost like bragging, but yes, she's quite remarkable, it must be said. It would have been just fine with me to come from someone less remarkable. An ordinary mother would have served me better, one that didn't require great distance to escape from.

> BG: Silence seems to have been a requirement too. For the subjects you're writing about here, silence is a universal way of coping—and not coping. There seems to be a long tradition of not speaking to one another in your family.

JK: Right! But while conducting these enormous conversations with the person you're not speaking to in your head. In my case, of course, I carry on these conversations in books.

BG: I am struck by the fact that the same protective mechanisms—for instance, the long silences between you and your mother—seem to have contributed to the tragedy around your brother. In his case, silence had another outcome. His inability to speak openly, to express who he was, perhaps cost him his life.

JK: *[sighs]* That will always be really painful. That's why the feeling of being able to speak freely is so important. And it's not just to speak freely, but to act in a way that is consistent with something you know to be true inside of you. I think it's almost a divine right, this right to self-realization. I think, had I not had writing, that would have been me. Assuming we really are made in the image of God, to know oneself must be, could be, a way of knowing God. It always feels so tragic that Devon never knew who he might have been, or who he was. But it's fair to say he didn't.

BG: Only enough to act on his sexual impulses.

JK: Yes, and after he died it all made sense. Before, there were all these men who would visit him but whose connection to him I didn't understand. I'd say, "Who is that? Is that a friend?" I remember some man wanted to take Devon to Trinidad, and I asked him, "But why would a man want to take you to Trinidad? Who is this?" And he said, "Oh, just someone." And then it didn't work out, because I think the questions I asked scared Devon away [from his plans]. There was always all this talk about women; and then of course I began to realize, after things became clear, that my brother had never really been interested in women at all, that this stuff about women was just some sort of elaborate facade.

BG: It's certainly one of the great agonies of AIDS that in losing our friends or loved ones or co-workers, we often learn who they are for the first time.

JK: I know! It's just heartbreaking, because so much of the time what they are hiding just isn't that important. It isn't worth keeping secret. It isn't worth dying for. It's just not worth dying because you can't say you're gay. But what Devon would have had heaped on him had he come out, and what that would have deprived him of spiritually, was more than he could take.

BG: Indeed, your description of how gays and HIV-infected people are treated in Antigua is wrenching.

JK: I'll never forget visiting that man named Freeston [mentioned in *My Brother* as one of the few openly gay, HIV-positive men in Antigua]. He was so interesting, because he acted as if he thought he could out-run the disease—he was going to stay one step ahead. He looked so haunted, as if there was somebody creeping up on him. He just fought and fought. At one point he was always on the airwaves warning people about unsafe sex and AIDS, and he was talked about and laughed at and teased. But he just sort of persevered. And then he died and no one ever mentioned him again. It was as if he was the only person for whom AIDS meant anything or posed any danger, and when he died, the voice for those with this disease went with him. It all just went away.

In the book, I wrote about how another man who died from AIDS was buried on the same day as my brother, within waving distance, and the fact that the two families never said anything to each other. Their bodies were even in the same funeral parlor. It's just strange. And it's strange to witness all this beneath a brightly lit sky.

BG: This happy-looking place where people go for holidays.

JK: It's like watching a play with the wrong backdrop. You want to say to the director, "You know, I like this play, but the set is quite wrong. It needs to be set somewhere very dark, with a lot of bad weather."

BG: It's astounding how little progress there's been in Antigua. Your brother died in 1996, yet in terms of people's consciousness about the disease, your descriptions make it seem more like 1985.

JK: 1985, plus the Middle Ages. But you know, Antigua is a very superstitious place. One of the reasons no one would talk about Freeston after he died is that we still have these very old-world—and by that I mean African-world—feelings about the dead and about disease and about ill fortune. You like to look at people's ill fortune because it's interesting and entertaining, but you don't like to get too close, because you might catch it.

BG: Did you ever have the desire or the temptation to try to bring your brother back to the States, where he might have been able to get better medical care?

JK: Dr. Ramsey [Devon's doctor, and one of the few people in Antigua with a sound understanding of AIDS] was always really up on the latest information, and the climate Devon was in was most kind for him: The temperature never changes in Antigua. So no, it wasn't even a consideration. I suppose I could have investigated whether it was possible to get him a visa, but really, even if it had been an option I don't think I would have done it. I wouldn't have made that kind of demand on my family; I wouldn't have made that kind of demand on myself. I don't know what it would have done to the little happiness that I have managed to put together for myself. And I am not a martyr. I am interested in doing the right thing, but I'm not unusually kind or interested in looking spiritually wonderful.

You have to understand that helping my brother was the most thankless thing in the world. At the end of his life, he was a monster. If he could have brought us all with him, he would have.

BG: You imply that when you reveal how he continued to have unprotected sex even after he knew he had full-blown AIDS.

JK: Oh, he was monstrous! But he was also troubled. He hurt a lot and had suffered a lot—that was also true. But bringing Devon to the States would only have caused other people misery. I learned long ago to be ruthless about the people I grew up with—my family—the people I've been forced to know in this world. I went into great debt buying my brother his medicines, flying down to see him, Federal Expressing him things from the health-food store, the paying for doctors, the telephone calls. There were times when I tried very hard to convince myself that emotional connection wasn't there. I would say, I'm not going to call, I'm not going to call—and then I would call. I'd be thinking, I can't believe I've called. But I couldn't stand not to know how he was doing. I was quite helpless in my response.

BG: There are a number of moments in *My Brother* when you share your own surprise at discovering that you in fact love this person.

JK: *[laughs]* Well, all these tugs that people have on you that you don't choose—it seems very unfair.

BG: Your writing is marked by an almost ruthless desire to get at the truth.

JK: I grew up in a place where the truth is in the shadows—which is to say there is none, and one makes it up. I grew up with so many things that were, well, not quite true; but when people said them enough, they became true, or were accepted as true. When I was a child, I was much praised for my memory because it was very precocious. I could remember everything I saw and heard, and I would complete people's stories—everyone thought it was so charming. And then when I kept it up and told people things they didn't want to remember, everyone grew annoyed with me. I have often overheard my mother describing some incident that I was directly involved in as a child, and it just enrages me, because her telling of it is always so different from how I remember it. But you know, she plays with memory. It's not a lie. She will just deeply remember something quite the way it did not happen. So for my own sake, I like to say, Well, this is what it is. And of course a lot of what's happening in situations like these is that people are trying to protect themselves from all sorts of humiliations. You know, there are a lot of things about oneself that one doesn't want people to know, but if something really happened, it really happened. I want to try to live with my humiliations. It's just life. I wet my bed until I was thirteen, and before I stopped wetting my bed, I was having my period and wetting my bed, and in the morning my sheets used to be just filled with my bloody pee. That was very embarrassing. But there it is. It did happen.

BG: In the book, you recount what was, for you, one of your greatest humiliations at the hands of your mother: the burning of your books.

JK: Yeah. It's a brutal scene, isn't it? You know, I'd completely forgotten that incident, and then something she said around the time of my brother's death made me remember it. But it must have been a source of enormous shame that made me suppress it, and when I remembered it and began to write about it, I found it very painful. But I wanted to write it. I almost feel that one's sources of humiliation should be immediately put on public display so they lose their power. Yes, it's a humiliating thing to admit, for me to acknowledge. And it's not that I care about people knowing it or not knowing it, but more for me to acknowledge this thing in my life: that the person who brought me into the world had at one point almost extinguished my life. Those books were my life. I don't mean to overdramatize it, but it really did feel like an attempt at murder. My books were the only thing that connected me to a world apart from the cesspool I was in, and then they were just ashes. It felt murderous.

BG: It's understandable that the issue of autonomy would be so important to you, both in your writing and in your life.

JK: *[laughs]* Oh dear, it's sad to be so transparent, but you're absolutely right. Yes, I feel suffocated very easily. I'm always very quick to think that I'd rather die freeing myself than to live under any kind of tyranny. I like to free myself of bullies.

BG: One of the hard realities of writing, particularly the kind you're doing here, is that it can make for sticky relations with the people you're writing about.

JK: Well, I've only ever written about my family, and I've never written about them so frankly as I have in this book. But I feel with these people that I paid a price for being a part of them. I got stuck with them, they got stuck with me, and the only way I can make sense of it is through words and through memory—two things they hate, really. Nobody in my family reads anymore. The one who read, died.

BG: I got a sense from this book that not only were you struggling to make sense of your brother's death and your feelings about him and your family, but to replace for yourself your sense of who your readers are.

JK: This is so true. I realized that I had always written for Mr. Shawn [William Shawn, former editor of *The New Yorker*], and even after he was dead I continued writing for him, especially since I still wrote for *The New Yorker.* It was only when I didn't write for *The New Yorker* anymore that I realized Mr. Shawn was dead and that he would never read anything I wrote again. It's a loss for me as a writer to know that I don't have this reader anymore, and that there will never be a reader like this for me again. It's part of the things I've had and the things I've lost.

Double Take

1. Early in this interview, Jamaica Kincaid claims that "for me as a writer, I think the mental, the verbal, the spiritual scorn from my community would have been more painful, in a way, than being stoned to death." She also talks about the danger in writing about her own family. Why might writers be concerned about, even afraid of, having a certain audience reading their work? What effects might such a fear or audience awareness have on a writer's choices?
2. Why might Brad Goldfarb (who conducted the interview) have decided to call this interview "Writing = Life" rather than something like "Kincaid Writes from Life Experience"?
3. Kincaid makes the claim in this interview that just as silence might have led to the death of her brother, "had I not had writing, that would have been me." What kind of power is Kincaid associating with writing? What kind of power does your own writing have?
4. At the end of the interview, Kincaid talks about losing an important reader of her works, Mr. Shawn, the longtime editor of *The New Yorker* magazine. She notes that it was a "loss for me as a writer to know that I don't have this reader anymore." Why might a single reader be so important to a writer, even a writer like Kincaid who reaches so many readers? When you write, who do you envision as your reader(s)?

At First Glance

Jamaica Kincaid's "In History" addresses the issues of history as narrative. Kincaid suggests that history, or the history that we know, is the story we tell about that history. Her account of the history of how we have come to know both her island of Antigua and Kincaid and her people is critical to the story we tell of that history. As you read this intriguing essay, ask yourself several questions: What narrative is Kincaid creating here? That is, what history is she offering us as readers? Could we critique our own histories in ways similar to those that Kincaid offers? How is Kincaid writing history here?

In History

What to call the thing that happened to me and all who look like me?

Should I call it history?

If so, what should history mean to someone like me?

Should it be an idea, should it be an open wound and each breath I take in and expel healing and opening the wound again and again, over and over, or is it a moment that began in 1492 and has come to no end yet? Is it a collection of facts, all true and precise details, and, if so, when I come across these true and precise details, what should I do, how should I feel, where should I place myself?

Why should I be obsessed with all these questions?

My history began like this: in 1492, Christopher Columbus discovered the New World. Since this is only a beginning and I am not yet in the picture, I have not yet made an appearance, the word "discover" does not set off an alarm, and I am not yet confused by this interpretation. I accept it. I am only taken by the personality of this quarrelsome, restless man. His origins are sometimes obscure; sometimes no one knows just where he really comes from, who he really was. His origins are sometimes quite vivid: his father was a tailor, he came from Genoa, he as a boy wandered up and down the Genoese wharf, fascinated by sailors and their tales of lands far away; these lands would be filled with treasures, as all things far away are treasures. I am far away, but I am not yet a treasure: I am not a part of this man's consciousness, he does not know of me, I do not yet have a name. And so the word "discover," as it is applied to this New World, remains uninteresting to me.

He, Christopher Columbus, discovers this New World. That it is new only to him, that it had a substantial existence, physical and spiritual, before he became aware of it, does not occur to him. To cast blame on him now for this childlike immaturity has all the moral substance of a certificate given to a schoolgirl for good behavior. To be a well-behaved schoolgirl is not hard. When he sees this New World, it is really new to him: he has never seen anything like it before, it was not what he had expected, he had images of China and Japan, and, though he thought he was in China and Japan, it was not the China or Japan that he had fixed in his mind. He couldn't find enough words to describe what he saw before him: the people were new, the flora and fauna were new, the way the water met the sky was new, this world itself was new, it was the New World.

"If one does not know the names, one's knowledge of things is useless." This is attributed to Isidorus, and I do not know if this is the Greek Isidorus or the other Isidorus, the bishop of Seville; but now put it another way: to have knowledge of things, one must first give them a name. This, in any case, seems to me to have been Christopher Columbus's principle, for he named and he named: he named places, he named people, he named things. This world he saw before him had a blankness to it, the blankness of the newly made, the newly born. It had no before—I could say that it had no history, but I would have to begin again, I would have to ask those questions again: What is history? This blankness, the one Columbus met, was more like the blankness of paradise; paradise emerges from chaos, and this chaos is not history; it is not a legitimate order of things. Paradise, then, is the arrangement of the ordinary and the extraordinary. But in such a way as to make it, paradise, seem as if it had fallen out of the clear air. Nothing about it suggests the messy life of the builder, the carpenter, the quarrels with the contractor, the people who are late with the delivery of materials, their defense which, when it is not accepted, is met with their back chat. This is an unpleasant arrangement; this is not paradise. Paradise is the thing just met when all the troublesome details have been vanquished, overcome.

Christopher Columbus met paradise. It would not have been paradise for the people living there; they would have had the ordinary dreariness of living anywhere day after day, the ordinary dreariness of just being alive. But someone else's ordinary dreariness is another person's epiphany.

The way in which he wanted to know these things was not in the way of satisfying curiosity, or in the way of correcting an ignorance; he wanted to know them, to possess them, and he wanted to possess them in a way that must have been a surprise to him. His ideas kept not so much changing as evolving: he wanted to prove the world was round, and even that, to know with certainty that the world was round, that it did not come to an abrupt end at a sharp cliff from which one could fall into nothing; to know that is to establish a claim also. And then after the world was round, this round world should belong to his patrons, the king and queen of Spain; and then finding himself at the other side of the circumference and far away from his patrons, human and other kind, he loses himself, for it becomes clear: the person who really can name the thing gives it a life, a reality, that it did not have before. His patrons are in Spain, looking at the balance sheet: if they invest so much, will his journey yield a return to make the investment worthwhile? But he—I am still speaking of Columbus—is in the presence of something else.

His task is easier than he thought it would be; his task is harder than he could have imagined. If he had only really reached Japan or China, places like that already had an established narrative. It was not a narrative that these places had established themselves; it was a narrative that someone like him had invented, Marco Polo, for instance; but this world, China or Japan, in the same area of the world to him (even as this familiarity with each other—between China and Japan—would surprise and even offend the inhabitants of these places), had an order, and the order offered a comfort (the recognizable is always so comforting). But this new place, what was it? Sometimes it was just like Seville; sometimes it was like Seville but only more so; sometimes it was more beautiful than Seville. Mostly it was "marvelous," and this word "marvelous" is the word he uses again and again, and when he uses it, what the reader (and this is what I have been, a reader of this account of the journey, and the account is by Columbus himself) can feel, can hear, can see, is a great person whose small soul has been sundered by something unexpected. And yet the unexpected turned out to be the most ordinary things: people, the sky, the sun, the land, the water surrounding the land, the things growing on the land.

What were the things growing on the land? I pause for this. What were the things growing on that land, and why do I pause for this?

I come from a place called Antigua. I shall speak of it as if no one has ever heard of it before; I shall speak of it as if it is just new. In the writings, in anything representing a record of the imagination of Christopher Columbus, I cannot find any expectation for a place like this. It is a small lump of insignificance, green, green, green, and green again. Let me describe this landscape again: it is green, and unmistakably so; another person, who would have a more specific interest, a painter, might say it is a green that often verges on blue, a green that often is modified by reds and yellows and even other more intense or other shades of green. To me, it is green and green and green again. I have no interest other than this immediate and urgent one: the landscape is green. For it is on this green landscape that, suddenly, I and the people who look like me made an appearance.

I, me. The person standing in front of you started to think of all this while really focused on something and someone else altogether. I was standing in my garden; my garden is in a place called Vermont; it is in a village situated in a place called Vermont. From the point of view of growing things, that is the gardener's, Vermont is not in the same atmosphere as that other place I am from, Antigua. But while standing in that place, Vermont, I think about the place I am from, Antigua. Christopher Columbus never saw Vermont at all; it never entered his imagination. He saw Antigua, I believe on a weekday, but if not, then it would have been a Sunday, for in this life there would have been only weekdays or Sundays, but he never set foot on it, he only came across it while passing by. My world then—the only world I might have known if circumstances had not changed, intervened, would have entered the human imagination, the human imagination that I am familiar with, the only one that dominates the world in which I live—came into being as a footnote to someone just passing by. By the time Christopher Columbus got to the place where I am from, the place that forms the foundation of the person you see before you, he was exhausted, he was sick of the whole thing, he longed for his old home, or he longed just to sit still and enjoy the first few things that he had come upon. The first few things that he came on were named after things that were prominent in his thinking, his sponsors especially; when he came to the place I am from, he (it) had been reduced to a place of worship; the place I am from is named after a church. This church might have been an important church to Christopher Columbus, but churches are not important, originally, to people who look like me. And if people who look like me have an inheritance, among this inheritance will be this confusion of intent; nowhere in his intent when he set out from his point of embarkation (for him, too, there is not origin: he originates from Italy, he sails from Spain, and this is the beginning of another new traditional American narrative, point of origin and point of embarkation): "here is something I have never seen before, I especially like it because it has no precedent, but it is frightening because it has no precedent, and so to make it less frightening I will frame it in the thing I know; I know a church, I know the name of the church, even if I do not like or know the people connected to this church, it is more familiar to me, this church, than the very ground I am standing on; the ground has changed, the church, which is in my mind, remains the same."

I, the person standing before you, close the quotation marks. Up to this point, I and they that look like me am not yet a part of this narrative. I can look at all these events: a man setting sail with three ships, and after many, many days on the ocean, finding new lands whose existence he had never even heard of before, and then finding in these new lands people and their things and these people and their things, he had never heard of them before, and he empties the land of these people, and then he empties the people, he just empties the people. It is when this land is completely empty that I and the people who look like me begin to make an appearance, the food I eat begins to make an appearance, the trees I will see each day come from far away and begin to make an appearance, the sky is as it always was, the sun is as it always was, the water surrounding the land on which I am just making an appearance is as it always was; but these are the only things left from before that man, sailing with his three ships, reached the land on which I eventually make an appearance.

When did I begin to ask all this? When did I begin to think of all this and in just this way? What is history? Is it a theory? I no longer live in the place where I and those who look like me first made an appearance. I live in another place. It has another narrative. Its narrative, too, can start with that man sailing on his ships for days and days, for that man sailing on his ships for days and days is the source of many narratives, for he was like a deity in the simplicity of his beliefs, in the simplicity of his actions; just listen to the straightforward way many volumes featuring this man sailing on his ships begin: "In fourteen hundred and ninety-two . . ." But it was while standing in this other place, which has a narrative mostly different from the place in which I make an appearance, that I began to think of this.

One day, while looking at the things that lay before me at my feet, I was having an argument with myself over the names I should use when referring to the things that lay before me at my feet. These things were plants. The plants, all of them and they were hundreds, had two names: they had a common name—that is, the name assigned to them by people for whom these plants have value—and then they have a proper name, or a Latin name, and that is a name assigned to them by an agreed-on group of botanists. For a long time I resisted using the proper names of the things that lay before me. I believed that it was an affectation to say "eupatorium" when you could say "joe-pye weed." I then would only say "joe-pye weed." The botanists are from the same part of the world as the man who sailed on the three ships, that same man who started the narrative from which I trace my beginning. And in a way, too, the botanists are like that man who sailed on the ships: they emptied the worlds of things animal, mineral, and vegetable of their names, and replaced these names with names pleasing to them; the recognized names are now reasonable, as reason is a pleasure to them.

Carl Linnaeus was born on May 23, 1707, somewhere in Sweden. (I know where, but I like the highhandedness of not saying so.) His father's name was Nils Ingemarsson; the Ingemarssons were farmers. Apparently, in Sweden then, surnames were uncommon among ordinary people, and so the farmer would add "son" to his name or he was called after the farm on which he lived. Nils Ingemarsson became a Lutheran minister, and on doing so he wanted to have a proper surname, not just a name with "son" attached to it. On his family's farm grew a linden tree. It had grown there for generations and had come to be regarded with reverence among neighboring farmers; people believed that misfortune would fall on you if you harmed this tree in any way. This linden tree was so well regarded that people passing by used to pick up twigs that had dropped from it and carefully place them at the base of the tree. Nils Ingemarsson took his surname from this tree: Linnaeus is the Latinized form of the Swedish word *lind,* which means linden. Other branches of this family who also needed a surname drew inspiration from this tree; some took the name Tiliander—the Latin word for linden is *tilia*—and some others who also needed a surname took the name Lindelius, from the same Swedish word *lind.*

Carl Linnaeus's father had a garden. I do not know what his mother had. His father loved growing things in this garden and would point them out to the young

Carl, but when the young Carl could not remember the names of the plants, his father gave him a scolding and told him he would not tell him the names of any more plants. (Is this story true? But how could it not be?) He grew up not far from a forest filled with beech, a forest with pine, a grove filled with oaks, meadows. His father had a collection of rare plants in his garden (but what would be rare to him and in that place, I do not know). At the time Linnaeus was born, Sweden—this small country that I now think of as filled with well-meaning and benign people interested mainly in the well-being of children, the well-being of the unfortunate no matter their age—was the ruler of an empire, but the remains of it are visible only in the architecture of the main square of the capital of places like Estonia. And so what to make of all this, this small detail that is the linden tree, this large volume of the Swedish empire, and a small boy whose father was a Lutheran pastor? At the beginning of this narrative, the narrative that is Linnaeus, I have not made an appearance yet; the Swedes are not overly implicated in the Atlantic slave trade, not because they did not want to have a part in it, only because they weren't allowed to do so; other people were better at it than they.

He was called "the little botanist" because he would neglect his studies and go out looking for flowers; if even then he had already showed an interest in or the ability to name and classify plants, this fact is not in any account of his life that I have come across. He went to university at Uppsala; he studied there with Olof Rudbeck. I can pause at this name, Rudbeck, and say rudbeckia, and say, I do not like rudbeckia. I never have it in my garden, but then I remember a particularly stately, beautiful yellow flower in a corner of my field garden, *Rudbeckia nitida,* growing there. He met Anders Celsius (the Celsius scale of temperature measurement), who was so taken with Linnaeus's familiarity and knowledge of botany that he gave Linnaeus free lodging in his house. Linnaeus became one of the youngest lecturers at the university. He went to Lapland and collected plants and insects native to that region of the world; he wrote and published an account of it called *Flora Lapponica.* In Lapland, he acquired a set of clothing that people native to that region of the world wore on festive occasions; I have seen a picture of him dressed in these clothes, and the caption under the picture says that he is wearing his Lapland costume. Suddenly I am made a little uneasy, for just when is it that other people's clothes become your costume? But I am not too uneasy, I haven't really entered this narrative yet, I shall soon. In any case, I do not know the Laplanders, they live far away, I don't believe they look like me.

I enter the picture only when Linnaeus takes a boat to Holland. He becomes a doctor to an obviously neurotic man (obvious only to me, I arbitrarily deem him so; no account of him I have ever come across has described him so) named George Clifford. George Clifford is often described as a rich merchant banker; just like that, a rich merchant banker, and this description often seems to say that to be a rich merchant banker is just a type of person one could be, an ordinary type of person, anyone could be that. And now how to go on, for on hearing that George Clifford was a rich merchant in the eighteenth century, I am now sure I have become a part of the binomial-system-of-plant-nomenclature narrative.

George Clifford had glass houses full of vegetable material from all over the world. This is what Linnaeus writes of it:

I was greatly amazed when I entered the greenhouses, full as they were of so many plants that a son of the North must feel bewitched, and wonder to what strange quarter of the globe he had been transported. In the first house were cultivated an abundance of flowers from southern Europe, plants from Spain, the South of France, Italy, Sicily and the isles of Greece. In the second were treasures from Asia, such as Poincianas, coconut and other palms, etc.; in the third, Africa's strangely shaped, not to say misshapen plants, such as the numerous forms of Aloe and Mesembryanthemum families, carnivorous flowers, Euphorbias, Crassula and Proteas species, and so on. And finally in the fourth greenhouse were grown the charming inhabitants of America and the rest of the New World; large masses of Cactus varieties, orchids, cruciferea, yams, magnolias, tulip-trees, calabash trees, arrow, cassias, acacias, tamarinds, pepper-plants, Anona, manicinilla, cucurbitaceous trees and many others, and surrounded by these, plantains, the most stately of all the world's plants, the most beauteous Hernandia, silver-gleaming species of Protea and camphor trees. When I then entered the positively royal residence and the extremely instructive museum, whose collections no less spoke in their owner's praise, I, a stranger, felt completely enraptured, as I had never before seen its like. My heartfelt wish was that I might lend a helping hand with its management.

In almost every account of an event that has taken place sometime in the last five hundred years, there is always a moment when I feel like placing an asterisk somewhere in its text, and at the end of this official story place my own addition. This chapter in the history of botany is such a moment. But where shall I begin? George Clifford is interesting—shall I look at him? He has long ago entered my narrative; I now feel I must enter his. What could it possibly mean to be a merchant banker in the eighteenth century? He is sometimes described as making his fortune in spices. Only once have I come across an account of him that says he was a director of the Dutch East India Company. The Dutch East India Company would not have been involved in the Atlantic trade in human cargo from Africa, but human cargo from Africa was a part of world trade. To read a brief account of the Dutch East India trading company in my very old encyclopedia is not unlike reading the label on an old can of paint. The entry mentions dates, the names of Dutch governors or people acting in Dutch interest; it mentions trade routes, places, commodities, incidents of war between the Dutch and other European people; it never mentions the people who lived in the area of the Dutch trading factories. Places like Ceylon, Java, the Cape of Good Hope, are emptied of their people as the landscape itself was emptied of the things they were familiar with, the things that Linnaeus found in George Clifford's greenhouse.

"If one does not know the names, one's knowledge of things is useless." It was in George Clifford's greenhouse that Linnaeus gave some things names. The Adam-like quality of this effort was lost on him. "We revere the Creator's omnipotence," he says, meaning, I think, that he understood he had not made the things he was describing, he was only going to give them names. And even as a relationship exists between George Clifford's activity in the world, the world as it starts out on ships leaving the seaports of the Netherlands, traversing the earth's seas, touching on the world's peoples and the places they are in, the things that have meant something to them being renamed and a whole new set of narratives imposed on them, narratives that place them at a disadvantage in relationship to George Clifford and his fellow Dutch, even as I can say all this on one breath or in one large volume, so too then does an invisible thread, a thread that no deep breath or large volume can contain, hang between Carolus Linnaeus, his father's desire to give himself a distinguished name, the name then coming from a tree, the linden tree, a tree whose existence was regarded as not ordinary, and his invention of a system of naming that even I am forced to use?

The invention of this system has been a good thing. Its narrative would begin this way: in the beginning, the vegetable kingdom was chaos; people everywhere called the same things by a name that made sense to them, not by a name that they arrived at by an objective standard. But who has an interest in an objective standard? Who would need one? It makes me ask again what to call the thing that happened to me and all who look like me? Should I call it history? And if so, what should history mean to someone who looks like me? Should it be an idea, should it be an open wound and each breath I take in and expel healing and opening the wound again and again, over and over, or is it a long moment that begins anew each day since 1492?

Double Take

1. The "I" in Jamaica Kincaid's "In History" often refers to more than just an individual person. Looking back at this essay, consider how Kincaid uses that "I." Does she use it effectively? In what ways? Do you read the "I" any differently than you have in other essays, other texts? Does Kincaid use the "I" in different ways in this essay? Can you distinguish between her meanings of the "I"?

2. The issue of naming is important in this essay. Kincaid discusses the power of naming things. Why does she concentrate so much on the issue of naming in an essay about history? How does she connect the history of naming with the discussion of her history? Could she have done so in another way? Are the examples she uses powerful, effective, provocative? Could she have used other kinds of examples, other ways to talk about naming? If so, what might have been an alternative and effective way to discuss naming?

3. In many ways, this essay asks a lot more questions than it provides answers. Notice, for instance, that both the beginning and ending of this essay contain a series of questions rather than statements. What is the strategy of these interrogative sections of the essay? Why might Kincaid have decided to ask so many questions rather than make statements? To whom is she directing these questions? That is, who should answer these questions?

At First Glance

In "Alien Soil," published in The New Yorker *in 1993, Jamaica Kincaid is rather critical of the ways that colonizing groups reshape landscapes and introduce flora to a region to make that place more familiar to the colonizers. She offers a good number of examples of how such ecocolonial conquests befell her native Antigua. In this context, she also makes some intriguing connections between gardening and wealth. Yet she also identifies that she too has become a gardener, one who moves plants around to suit her aesthetic desires. As you read this essay, think about not only how Kincaid addresses issues of colonialism, but how the structure of her essay moves from a larger critique of colonialism and gardening to a personal identification with the desire to garden. In other words, consider how Kincaid has organized this essay to level a large political critique and to situate herself within that critique. Think about how carefully she has paid attention to the organization and construction of this essay.*

Alien Soil

Whatever it is in the character of the English people that leads them to obsessively order and shape their landscape to such a degree that it looks like a painting (tamed, framed, captured, kind, decent, good, pretty), while a painting never looks like the English landscape, unless it is a bad painting—this quality of character is blissfully lacking in the Antiguan people. I make this unfair comparison (unfair to the Antiguan people? unfair to the English people? I cannot tell, but there is an unfairness here somewhere) only because so much of the character of the Antiguan people is influenced by and inherited, through conquest, from the English people. The tendency to shower pity and cruelty on the weak is among the traits the Antiguans inherited, and so is a love of gossip. (The latter, I think, is responsible for the fact that England has produced such great novelists, but it has not yet worked to the literary advantage of the Antiguan people.) When the English were a presence in Antigua—they first came to the island as slaveowners, when a man named Thomas Warner established a settlement there in 1632—the places where they lived were surrounded by severely trimmed hedges of plumbago, topiaries of willow (casuarina), and frangipani and hibiscus; their grass was green (odd, because water was scarce; the proper word for the climate is not "sunny" but "drought-ridden") and freshly cut; they kept trellises covered with roses, and beds of marigolds and cannas and chrysanthemums.

Ordinary Antiguans (and by "ordinary Antiguans" I mean the Antiguan people, who are descended from the African slaves brought to this island by Europeans; this turns out to be a not uncommon way to become ordinary), the ones who had some money and could live in houses of more than one room, had gardens in which only flowers were grown. This made it even more apparent that they had some money, in that all their outside space was devoted not to feeding their families but to the sheer beauty of things. I can remember in particular one such family, who lived in a house with many rooms (four, to be exact). They had an indoor kitchen and a place for bathing (no indoor toilet, though); they had a lawn, always neatly cut, and they had beds of flowers, but I can now remember only roses and marigolds. I can remember those because once I was sent there to get a bouquet of roses for my godmother on her birthday. The family also had, in the middle of their small lawn, a willow tree, pruned so that it had the shape of a pine tree—a conical shape—and at Christmastime this tree was decorated with colored lights (which was so unusual and seemed so luxurious to me that when I passed by this house I would beg to be allowed to stop and stare at it for a while). At Christmas, all willow trees would suddenly be called Christmas trees, and for a time, when my family must have had a small amount of money, I, too, had a Christmas tree—a lonely, spindly branch of willow sitting in a bucket of water in our very small house. No one in my family and, I am almost certain, no one in the family of the people with the lighted-up willow tree had any idea of the origins of the Christmas tree and the traditions associated with it. When these people (the Antiguans) lived under the influence of these other people (the English), there was naturally an attempt among some of them to imitate their rulers in this particular way—by rearranging the landscape—and they did it without question. They can't be faulted for not asking what it was they were doing; that is the way these things work. The English left, and most of their landscaping influence went with them. The Americans came, but Americans (I am one now) are not interested in influencing people directly; we instinctively understand the childish principle of monkey see, monkey do. And at the same time we are divided about how we ought to behave in the world. Half of us believe in and support strongly a bad thing our government is doing, while the other half do not believe in and protest strongly against the bad thing. The bad thing succeeds, and everyone, protester and supporter alike, enjoys immensely the results of the bad thing. This ambiguous approach in the many is always startling to observe in the individual. Just look at Thomas Jefferson, a great American gardener and our country's third president, who owned slaves and strongly supported the idea of an expanded American border, which meant the extinction of the people who already lived on the land to be taken, while at the same time he was passionately devoted to ideas about freedom—ideas that the descendants of the slaves and the people who were defeated and robbed of their land would have to use in defense of themselves. Jefferson, as president, commissioned the formidable trek his former secretary, the adventurer and botany thief Meriwether Lewis, made through the West, sending plant specimens back to the president along the way. The *Lewisia rediviva,* state flower of Montana, which Lewis found in the Bitterroot River valley, is named after him; the clarkia, not a flower of any state as far as I can tell, is named for his co-adventurer and botany thief, William Clark.

What did the botanical life of Antigua consist of at the time another famous adventurer—Christopher Columbus—first saw it? To see a garden in Antigua now will not supply a clue. I made a visit to Antigua this spring, and most of the plants I saw there came from somewhere else. The bougainvillea (named for another restless European, the sea adventurer Louis-Antoine de Bougainville, first Frenchman to cross the Pacific) is native to tropical South America; the plumbago is from southern Africa; the croton (genus *Codiaeum*) is from Malay Peninsula; the *Hibiscus rosa-sinensis* is from Asia and the *Hibiscus schizopetalus* is from East Africa; the allamanda is from Brazil; the poinsettia (named for an American ambassador, Joel Poinsett) is from Mexico; the bird of paradise flower is from southern Africa; the Bermuda lily is from Japan; the flamboyant tree is from Madagascar; the casuarina is from Australia; the Norfolk pine is from Norfolk Island; the tamarind tree is from Africa; the mango is from Asia. The breadfruit, the most Antiguan (to me) and starchy food, the bane of every Antiguan child's palate, is from the East Indies. This food has been the cause of more disagreement between parents and their children than anything else I can think of. No child has ever liked it. It was sent to the West Indies by Joseph Banks, the English naturalist and world traveler and the head of Kew Gardens, which was then a clearinghouse for all the plants stolen from the various parts of the world where the English had been. (One of the climbing roses, *Rosa banksiae,* from China, was named for Banks's wife.) Banks sent tea to India; to the West Indies he sent the breadfruit. It was meant to be a cheap food for feeding slaves. It was the cargo that Captain Bligh was carrying to the West Indies on the ship *Bounty* when his crew so rightly mutinied. It's as though the Antiguan child senses intuitively the part this food has played in the history of injustice and so will not eat it. But, unfortunately for her, it grows readily, bears fruit abundantly, and is impervious to drought. Soon after the English settled in Antigua, they cleared the land of its hardwood forests to make room for the growing of tobacco, sugar, and cotton, and it is this that makes the island drought-ridden to this day. Antigua is also empty of much wildlife natural to it. When snakes proved a problem for the planters, they imported the mongoose from India. As a result there are no snakes at all on the island—nor other reptiles, other than lizards—though I don't know what damage the absence of snakes causes, if any.

What herb of beauty grew in this place then? What tree? And did the people who lived there grow anything beautiful for its own sake? I do not know; I can only make a straightforward deduction: the frangipani, the mahogany tree, and the cedar tree are all native to the West Indies, so these trees are probably indigenous. And some of the botany of Antigua can be learned from medicinal folklore. My mother and I were sitting on the steps in front of her house one day during my recent visit, and I suddenly focused on a beautiful bush (beautiful to me now; when I was a child I thought it ugly) whose fruit I remembered playing with when I was little. It is an herbaceous plant that has a red stem covered with red thorns, and emerald-green, simple leaves, with the same red thorns running down the leaf from the leafstalk. I cannot remember what its flowers looked like, and it was not in flower when I saw it while I was there with my mother, but its fruit is a small, almost transparent red berry, and it is this I used to play with. We children sometimes called it "china berry," because of its transparent, glassy look—it reminded us of china dinnerware, though we were only vaguely familiar with such a thing as china, having seen it no more than once or twice—and sometimes "baby tomato," because of its size, and to signify that it was not real; a baby thing was not a real thing. When I pointed the bush out to my mother, she called it something else; she called it cancanberry bush, and said that in the old days, when people could not afford to see doctors, if a child had thrush they would make a paste of this fruit and rub it inside the child's mouth, and this would make the thrush go away. But, she said, people rarely bother with this remedy anymore. The day before, a friend of hers had come to pay a visit, and when my mother offered her something to eat and drink the friend declined, because, she said, she had some six-sixty-six and maidenblush tea waiting at home for her. This tea is taken on an empty stomach, and it is used for all sorts of ailments, including to help bring on abortions. I have never seen six-sixty-six in flower, but its leaves are a beautiful ovoid shape and a deep green—qualities that are of value in a garden devoted to shape and color of leaf.

People who do not like the idea that there is a relationship between gardening and wealth are quick to remind me of the cottage gardener, that grim-faced English person. Living on land that is not his own, he has put bits and pieces of things together, things from here and there, and it is a beautiful jumble—but just try duplicating it; it isn't cheap to do. And I have never read a book praising the cottage garden written by a cottage gardener. This person—the cottage gardener—does not exist in a place like Antigua. Nor do casual botanical conversation, knowledge of the Latin names for plants, and discussions of the binomial system. If an atmosphere where these things could flourish exists in this place, I am not aware of it. I can remember very well the cruel Englishwoman who was my botany teacher, and that, in spite of her cruelty, botany was one of my two favorite subjects in school. (History was the other.) With this in mind I visited a bookstore (the only bookstore I know of in Antigua) to see what texts are now being used in the schools and to see how their content compares with what was taught to me back then; the botany I had studied was a catalogue of the plants of the British Empire, the very same plants that are now widely cultivated in Antigua and are probably assumed by ordinary Antiguans to be native to their landscape—the mango, for example. But it turns out that botany as a subject is no longer taught in Antiguan schools; the study of plants is now called agriculture. Perhaps that is more realistic, since the awe and poetry of botany cannot be eaten, and the mystery and pleasure in the knowledge of botany cannot be taken to market and sold.

And yet the people of Antigua have a relationship to agriculture that does not please them at all. Their very arrival on this island had to do with the forces of agriculture. When they (we) were brought to this island from Africa a few hundred years ago, it was not for their pottery-making skills or for their way with a loom; it was for the free labor they could provide in the fields. Mary Prince, a nineteenth-century African woman who was born in Bermuda and spent part of her life as a slave in Antigua, writes about this in an autobiographical account, which I found in *The Classic Slave Narratives,* edited by Henry Louis Gates, Jr. She says:

> My master and mistress went on one occasion into the country, to Date Hill, for change of air, and carried me with them to take charge of the children, and to do the work of the house. While I was in the country, I saw how the field negroes are worked in Antigua. They are worked very hard and fed but scantily. They are called out to work before daybreak, and come home

after dark; and then each has to heave his bundle of grass for the cattle in the pen. Then, on Sunday morning, each slave has to go out and gather a large bundle of grass; and, when they bring it home, they have all to sit at the manager's door and wait till he come out: often they have to wait there till past eleven o'clock, without any breakfast. After that, those that have yams or potatoes, or fire-wood to sell, hasten to market to buy . . . salt fish, or pork, which is a great treat for them.

Perhaps it makes sense that a group of people with such a wretched historical relationship to growing things would need to describe their current relationship to it as dignified and masterly (agriculture), and would not find it poetic (botany) or pleasurable (gardening).

In a book I am looking at (to read it is to look at it: the type is as tall as a doll's teacup), *The Tropical Garden,* by William Warren, with photographs by Luca Invernizzi Tettoni, I find statements like "the concept of a private garden planted purely for aesthetic purposes was generally alien to tropical countries" and "there was no such tradition of ornamental horticulture among the inhabitants of most hot-weather places. Around the average home there might be a few specimens chosen especially because of their scented flowers or because they were believed to bring good fortune. . . . Nor would much, if any, attention be paid to attractive landscape design in such gardens: early accounts by travellers in the tropics abound in enthusiastic descriptions of jungle scenery, but a reader will search in vain for one praising the tasteful arrangement of massed ornamental beds and contrasting lawns of well-trimmed grass around the homes of natives." What can I say to that? No doubt it is true. And no doubt contrasting lawns and massed ornamental beds are a sign of something, and that is that someone—someone other than the owner of the lawns—has been humbled. To give just one example: on page 62 of this book is a photograph of eight men, natives of India, pulling a heavy piece of machinery used in the upkeep of lawns. They are without shoes. They are wearing the clothing of schoolboys—khaki shorts and khaki short-sleeved shirts. There is no look of bliss on their faces. The caption for the photograph read, "Shortage of labour was never a problem in the maintenance of European features in large colonial gardens; here a team of workers is shown rolling a lawn at the Gymkhana Club in Bombay."

And here are a few questions that occur to me: what if the people living in the tropics, the ones whose history isn't tied up with and contaminated by slavery and indenturedness, are contented with their surroundings, are happy to observe an invisible hand at work and from time to time laugh at some of the ugly choices this hand makes; what if they have more important things to do than make a small tree large, a large tree small, or a tree whose blooms are usually yellow bear black blooms; what if these people are not spiritually feverish, restless, and full of envy?

When I was looking at the book of tropical gardens, I realized that the flowers and the trees so familiar to me from my childhood do not now have a hold on me. I do not long to plant and be surrounded by the bougainvillea; I do not like the tropical hibiscus; the corallita (from Mexico), so beautiful when tended, so ugly when left to itself, which makes everything around it look rusty and shabby, is not a plant I like at all. I returned from my visit to Antigua, the place where I was born, to a small village in Vermont, the place where I choose to live. Spring had arrived. The tulips I had planted last autumn were in bloom, and I liked to sit and caress their petals, which felt disgustingly delicious, like scraps of peau de soie. The dizzy-making yellow of dandelions and cowslips was in the fields and riverbanks and marshes. I like these things. (I do not like daffodils, but that's a legacy of the English approach: I was forced to memorize the poem by William Wordsworth when I was a child.) I transplanted to the edge of a grove of pine trees some foxgloves that I grew from seed in late winter. I found some Virginia bluebells in a spot in the woods where I had not expected to find them, and some larches growing grouped together, also in a place I had not expected. On my calendar I marked the day I would go and dig up all the mulleins I could find and replant them in a very sunny spot across from the grove of pine trees. This is to be my forest of mulleins, though in truth it will appear a forest only to an ant. I marked the day I would plant the nasturtiums under the fruit trees. I discovered a clump of Dutchman's-breeches in the wildflower bed that I inherited from the man who built and used to own the house in which I now live, Robert Woodworth, the botanist who invented time-lapse photography. I waited for the things I had ordered in the deep cold of winter to come. They started to come. Mr. Pembroke, who represents our village in the Vermont legislature, came and helped me dig some of the holes where some of the things I wanted to put in were to be planted. Mr. Pembroke is a very nice man. He is never dressed in the clothing of schoolboys. There is not a look of misery on his face; on his face is the complicated look of an ordinary human being. When he works in my garden, we agree on a price; he sends me a bill, and I pay it. The days are growing longer and longer, and then they'll get shorter again. I am now used to that ordered progression, and I love it. But there is no order in my garden. I live in America now. Americans are impatient with memory, which is one of the things order thrives on.

Double Take

1. Why does Jamaica Kincaid make a connection between gardening and wealth in "Alien Soil"? What is she conveying about the control of, molding of, and mapping of plant life? Is this a useful or powerful way to talk about issues of wealth? Is the connection effective for you as a reader?
2. What might Kincaid mean by the final statement of this essay?—"Americans are impatient with memory, which is one of the things order thrives on." Why might she have decided to end the essay with this statement?
3. To what does Kincaid refer in the title of this essay: "Alien Soil"? Does the title evoke a particular meaning for the essay? That is, does the title affect how you read the essay? Why might a well-selected title be important to an essay? How do you select titles for your own writing?

Seeing for Yourself

At First Glance

Like other essays gathered here by Jamaica Kincaid, "Garden of Envy" uses gardening not only as a subject about which she writes but as a metaphor for larger issues. As you read this essay, think about not only how Kincaid writes about gardening, but how writers in general often write about familiar subjects in order to address larger issues. Are there ways that you might be able to write about something important and familiar to you as a metaphor for a larger issue? What makes this strategy effective?

Garden of Envy

I know gardeners well (or at least I think I do, for I am a gardener, too, but I experience gardening as an act of utter futility). I know their fickleness, I know their weakness for wanting in their own gardens the thing they have never seen before, or never possessed before, or saw in a garden (their friend's), something which they do not have and would like to have (though what they really like and envy—and especially that, envy—is the entire garden they are seeing, but as a disguise they focus on just one thing: the Mexican poppies, the giant butter burr, the extremely plump blooms of white, purple, black, pink, green, or the hellebores emerging from the cold, damp, and brown earth).

I would not be surprised if every gardener I asked had something definite that they liked or envied. Gardeners always have something they like intensely and in particular, right at the moment you engage them in the reality of the borders they cultivate, the space in the garden they occupy; at any moment, they like in particular this, or they like in particular that, nothing in front of them (that is, in the borders they cultivate, the space in the garden they occupy) is repulsive and fills them with hatred, or this thing would not be in front of them. They only love, and they only love in the moment; when the moment has passed, they love the memory of the moment, they love the memory of that particular plant or that particular bloom, but the plant of the bloom itself they have moved on from, they have left it behind for something else, something new, especially something from far away, and from so far away, a place where they will never live (occupy, cultivate; the Himalayas, just for example).

Of all the benefits that come from having endured childhood (for it is something to which we must submit, no matter how beautiful we find it, no matter how enjoyable it has been), certainly among them will be the garden and the desire to be involved with gardening. A gardener's grandmother will have grown such and such a rose, and the smell of that rose at dusk (for flowers always seem to be most fragrant at the end of the day, as if that, smelling, was the last thing to do before going to sleep), when the gardener was a child and walking in the grandmother's footsteps as she went about her business in her garden—the memory of that smell of the rose combined with the memory of that smell of the grandmother's skirt will forever inform and influence the life of the gardener, inside or outside the garden itself. And so in a conversation with such a person (a gardener), a sentence, a thought that goes something like this—"You know when I was such and such an age, I went to the market for a reason that is no longer of any particular interest to me, but it was there I saw for the first time something that I have never and can never forget"—floats out into the clear air, and the person from whom these words or this thought emanates is standing in front of you all bare and trembly, full of feeling, full of memory. Memory is a gardener's real palette; memory as it summons up the past, memory as it shapes the present, memory as it dictates the future.

I have never been able to grow *Meconopsis benticifolia* with success (it sits there, a green rosette of leaves looking at me, with no bloom. I look back at it myself, without a pleasing countenance), but the picture of it that I have in my mind, a picture made up of memory (I saw it some time ago), a picture made of "to come" (the future, which is the opposite of remembering), is so intense that whatever happens between me and this plant will never satisfy the picture I have of it (the past remembered, the past to come). I first saw it (*Meconopsis benticifolia*) in Wayne Winterrowd's garden (a garden he shares with that other garden eminence Joe Eck), and I shall never see this plant (in flower or not, in the wild or cultivated) again without thinking of him (of them, really—he and Joe Eck) and saying to myself, it shall never look quite like this (the way I saw it in their garden), for in their garden it was itself and beyond comparison (whatever that should amount to right now, whatever that might ultimately turn out to be), and I will always want it to look that way, growing comfortably in the mountains of Vermont, so far away from the place to which it is endemic, so far away from the place in which it was natural, unnoticed, and so going about its own peculiar ways of perpetuating itself (perennial, biannual, monocarpic or not).

I first came to the garden with practicality in mind, a real beginning that would lead to a real end: where to get this, how to grow that. Where to get this was always nearby, a nursery was never too far away: how to grow that led me to acquire volume upon volume, books all with the same advice (likes shade, does not tolerate lime, needs staking), but in the end I came to know how to grow the things I like to grow through looking—at other people's gardens. I imagine they acquired knowledge of such things in much the same way—looking and looking at somebody else's garden.

But we who covet our neighbor's garden must finally return to our own with all its ups and downs, its disappointments, its rewards. We come to it with a blindness, plus a jumble of feelings that mere language (as far as I can see) seems inadequate to express, to define an attachment that is so ordinary: a plant, loved especially for something endemic to it (it cannot help its situation: it loves the wet, it loves the dry, it reminds the person seeing it of a wave or a waterfall or some event that contains so personal an experience such as, when my mother would not allow me to do something I particularly wanted to do, and in my misery I noticed that the frangipani tree was in bloom).

I shall never have the garden I have in my mind, but that for me is the joy of it; certain things can never be realized and so all the more reason to attempt them. A garden, no matter how good it is, must never completely satisfy. The world as we know it, after all, began in a very good garden, a completely satisfying garden—Paradise—but after a while the owner and the occupants wanted more.

A CLOSER LOOK AT JAMAICA KINCAID

1. Now that you have read the essays by Jamaica Kincaid gathered here, think about some of the themes that run through her work: gardening, colonialism, Antigua, history, writing, and narrative. Why might a writer like Kincaid write about similar subjects in more than one essay? For example, why does Kincaid return to gardening in her writing? What is gained or lost by using familiar and often similar subjects in your writing over and over? Do you find yourself returning to the same subject, telling the same story, using the same example in your different writing projects? Write an essay about the ramifications—both positive and negative—of writing about similar subjects in multiple essays.

2. In the introduction to this section on Jamaica Kincaid, we noted that Kincaid has claimed to seek truth in her writing and that sometimes that truth can be uncomfortable, even unpleasant. What moments in these essays, if any, exemplify that claim for Kincaid? What effect do those moments have (or not have) on you as a reader? Write an essay about why moments you have identified as uncomfortable might be considered so, not only for you, but for others who also have read Kincaid's work.

Looking from Writer to Writer

1. Like many of the other writers whose works are found in this collection, Jamaica Kincaid writes quite a lot about concepts of place. However, unlike many writers who write about place, Kincaid often depicts her home place—Antigua—and

the people of that place—particularly her family—in a negative light. Look at the essays by Rick Bass, Annie Dillard, and Scott Russell Sanders and consider how and why Kincaid differs from those authors when addressing issues of place.

2. Both André Aciman and Jamaica Kincaid write about places where they were born and then were forced to leave. Each also ended up living in New York City after they left the homes of their birth. Compare the ways that these two authors think about the memory of their birthplaces. Notice, for instance, that each writes about returning to their childhood homes after being away. How do they differ or share in their experiences?

3. In the interview with Jamaica Kincaid by Brad Goldfarb, Kincaid talks about the influence of her family on her writing and how difficult her childhood was. In her two essays on writing, bell hooks addresses how powerful writing can be for women who have not traditionally had the opportunity to voice themselves in their writing. Take a look at hooks's essays on writing and consider whether or not Kincaid's writing reflects hooks's claim. Do hooks and Kincaid share similar views on writing?

Looking Beyond

ESSAYS

A Small Place. New York: Farrar, Straus, and Giroux, 1988.

FICTION

Annie, Gwen, Lilly, Pam and Tulip (illustrated by Eric Fischl). New York: Knopf, 1989.

Annie John. New York: Farrar, Straus, and Giroux, 1985.

At the Bottom of the River. 1983. New York: Vintage Books, 1985.

The Autobiography of My Mother. New York: Farrar, Straus, and Giroux, 1996.

Lucy. New York: Plume–Penguin, 1991.

My Brother. New York: Farrar, Straus, and Giroux, 1997.

Ursula K. Le Guin

Ursula Kroeber was born in 1953 in Berkeley, California. Her father Alfred Kroeber was an anthropologist and her mother Theodora Kroeber was a writer. Ursula Kroeber earned a bachelor's degree from Radcliffe College. When she finished her graduate work at Columbia University in Renaissance history, she married history professor Charles Le Guin. In 1961 she published her first short story "An die Musik" in *Western Humanities Review*. In an interview with the *Boston Globe*, Le Guin explained that she had "always wanted to write, and I always knew it would be hard to make a living at it." She also explained that it took a lot of work and time before she could write and publish the way she wanted to. Now she is known as one of the first women to successfully develop a career in traditionally male genres: science fiction and fantasy. However, Le Guin is also clear that we cannot be sure if male and female perspectives differ. "I don't think you can really tell whether a man or woman wrote something," she says, only that male and female differences have been "culturally constructed to be different from an early age." Like many of the essayists found in this collection, Ursula Le Guin is known not only for her essays, but for a wide range of writing, including magic realism and poetry, in addition to science fiction and fantasy. Le Guin herself prefers not to be categorized as "essayist" or "science fiction writer" or any other label that limits her writing. "I'm one of those lucky writers," Le Guin says, "who enjoys writing in all forms. I make no deliberate choice about which form I'm going to use." While reading the essays gathered here, consider what implications Le Guin's lack of choice about form might have on the meaning she conveys.

In 1964 *Amazing Science Fiction Stories* published Le Guin's short story "The Dowry of Angyar" that would serve as a basis for her first novel *Rocannon's World*. In 1973 Le Guin was both awarded the Hugo Award and nominated for the Nebula

Award for best novella and short work for *The Word for World Is Forest* and "The Ones Who Walk Away from Omelas." In each of these short works, Le Guin began to experiment with themes that have recurred throughout her career as a writer. *The Word for World Is Forest* examines attitudes and aggressions imposed against foreign or alien populations; many believed that this was also a commentary on American involvement in the Vietnam conflict. "The Ones Who Walk Away from Omelas" also introduced readers to Le Guin's themes of utopian societies and the role of individual morality within those societies. Le Guin's writing, no matter the genre or subject, is often political, often feminist, environmentalist, and always engaging. She comments about her political edge: "There comes a point when you've got to stand up and be counted on issues on which relentless pressure is exerted from the other side. It's not always that I've wanted to do it, but sometimes I've had to if I wanted to keep my own conscience healthy." Certainly, many of Le Guin's essays convey this desire to stand up. Le Guin says, "The one thing a writer has to have is a pencil and some paper. That's enough, so long as she knows that she and she alone is in charge of that pencil, and responsible, she and she alone, for what it writes on that paper."

Le Guin on Writing

At First Glance

One form of essay that Le Guin often uses is the short address, or talk. Two of the three essays gathered here were first delivered as talks and then revised into print forms, including the first selection, "Prospects for Women in Writing." Le Guin first delivered "Prospects for Women in Writing" as a brief talk given in Portland, Oregon, at the 1986 Conference on Women in the Year 2000. Her presentation was part of a larger panel titled "Women in the Arts." Each member of the panel presented a brief talk about the prospects for women in her chosen discipline. Le Guin discussed women in writing. The essay form of the talk was later reprinted in Le Guin's collection Dancing at the Edge of the World: Thoughts on Words, Women, Places. *As you read this short piece, consider not only what Le Guin has to say about the roles of women as writers, but also what rhetorical choices Le Guin must make to present her position in a talk—a piece of writing that the audience does not necessarily "read," but rather hears—and the manner in which those choices affect a reading audience when the piece is published. As you read, think about the differences between a spoken address and an essay meant to be read.*

Prospects for Women in Writing

It's only been about two hundred years since women gained access to literacy and began to empower themselves with that great power, the written word. And they have written. The works of women acknowledged as "great"—Austen, the Brontës, Dickinson, Eliot, Woolf—make a high road for other women writers to follow, so wide and clear that even the conscious or unconscious misogyny of most critics and teachers of literature hasn't been able to hide or close it.

There is less sexism in book and magazine publishing than in any field I know about. Of course most publishers are men, but most publishers now aren't even human: they're corporations. Many editors and other human beings in publishing are women or unmacho men. And thirty to fifty percent of living authors are women. With talent and obstinacy, then, a woman can and will get her writing published; with talent, obstinacy, and luck, her writing will be widely read and taken notice of. But.

As Tillie Olsen has demonstrated in *Silences,* although thirty to fifty percent of books are written by women, what is called "literature" remains eighty-eight to ninety percent male, decade after decade. No matter how successful, beloved, influential her work was, when a woman author dies, nine times out of ten she gets dropped

385

from the lists, the courses, the anthologies, while the men get kept. If she had the nerve to have children, her chances of getting dropped are higher still. So we get Anthony Trollope coming out of the ears while Elizabeth Gaskell is ignored, or endless studies of Nathaniel Hawthorne while Harriet Beecher Stowe is taught as a footnote to history. Most women's writing—like most work by women in any field—is called unimportant, secondary, by masculinist teachers and critics of both sexes; and literary styles and genres are constantly redefined to keep women's writing in second place. So if you want your writing to be taken seriously, don't marry and have kids, and above all, don't die. But if you have to die, commit suicide. They approve of that.

To find out what women writers are up against, if you want the useful blues, read Tillie Olsen, and if you want to get cheerfully enraged, read Joanna Russ's *How to Suppress Women's Writing* or Dale Spender's wonderful *Man Made Language*.

To try to summarize my own experience: The more truly your work comes from your own being, body and soul, rather than fitting itself into male conventions and expectations of what to write about and how to write it, the less it will suit most editors, reviewers, grant givers, and prize committees. But among all those are women and men to whom the real thing, the art, comes first; and you have to trust them. You have to trust yourself. And you have to trust your readers.

The writer only does half the job. It takes two to make a book. Many more women buy and read books than men. And in the last fifteen years there has been an increasing sense of strength and mutual validation among women writers and readers, a resistance to the male control over reading, a refusal to join men in sneering at what women want to write and read. Get hold of *The Norton Anthology of Literature by Women* and read it and then tell me women can't show men how to write and what to write about! The English profs keep sweeping our work under the rug, but that rug is about three feet off the floor by now, and things are coming out from under it and eating the English profs. Housework is woman's work, right? Well, it's time to shake the rugs.

Who's afraid of Virginia Woolf? Every little macho dodo, from Hemingway to Mailer. There is no more subversive act than the act of writing from a woman's experience of life using a woman's judgment. Woolf knew that and said it in 1930. Most of us forgot it and had to rediscover it all over again in the sixties. But for a whole generation now, women have been writing, publishing, and reading one another, in artistic and scholarly and feminist fellowship. If we go on doing that, by the year 2000 we will—*for the first time ever*—have kept the perceptions, ideas, and judgments of women alive in consciousness as an active, creative force in society for more than one generation. And our daughters and granddaughters won't have to start from zero the way we did. To keep women's words, women's works, alive and powerful—that's what I see as our job as writers and readers for the next fifteen years, and the next fifty.

Double Take

1. In writing "It takes two to make a book," Ursula Le Guin alludes to the role a reader plays in "making" a piece of text. When writers write, they must always

have some sense of whom they are writing to. What sorts of things might writers imagine about their audiences that might affect how they write? How do you suppose Le Guin imagined the audience of "Prospects for Women in Writing"?

2. Consider Le Guin's statement that "There is no more subversive act than the act of writing from a woman's experience of life using a woman's judgment." What do you suppose she means by "subversive"? How can writers be subversive? What writers come to mind when you think about subversive writers? What characteristics do the works of those writers exhibit that make them subversive?

3. In this essay Le Guin situates herself—the narrator, the writer—in the essay. First consider who the "I" is in this essay. Then describe what effect is achieved for the audience by introducing the "I."

4. Le Guin makes some claims about what will happen to and for women writers by the year 2000. Keeping in mind that Le Guin wrote these words in 1986 and that we are reading them well after the year 2000, assess Le Guin's predictions and consider the role of women writers now. What are the prospects for women writers now?

At First Glance

Like "Prospects for Women in Writing," "The Fisherwoman's Daughter" is an essay that was first delivered as a talk to an audience. When writing about the evolution of this piece, Ursula Le Guin explains that she revised this essay a number of times before publishing it. She first delivered the paper at Brown University and Miami University in Ohio, and then revised it for a talk at Wesleyan College in Georgia. She then rewrote the entire piece before delivering it again at Portland State University, and once more before addressing an audience at Tulane University in New Orleans. She then revised that version for Tulane's series of Mellon Papers where it was published under the title "A Woman Writing." She then gave the talk one more time in San Francisco, a version that incorporated more information about her own mother who had been a writer in the San Francisco area. Le Guin next revised, one final time and with the assistance of an editor, the version of the essay found here. As you read this essay, consider why an author might revise a single piece of writing as many times as Le Guin revised "The Fisherwoman's Daughter."

The Fisherwoman's Daughter

"'So of course,' wrote Betty Flanders, pressing her heels rather deeper in the sand, 'there was nothing for it but to leave.'"

That is the first sentence of Virginia Woolf's *Jacob's Room*.[1] It is a woman writing. Sitting on the sand by the sea, writing. It's only Betty Flanders, and she's only writing a letter. But first sentences are doors to worlds. This world of Jacob's room, so strangely empty at the end of the book when the mother stands in it holding out a pair of her son's old shoes and saying, "What am I to do with these?"—this is a world in which the first thing one sees is a woman, a mother of children, writing.

On the shore, by the sea, outdoors, is that where women write? Not at a desk, in a writing room? Where does a woman write, what does she look like writing, what is my image, your image of a woman writing? I asked my friends: "A woman writing: what do you see?" There would be a pause, then the eyes would light up, seeing. Some sent me to paintings, Fragonard, Cassatt, but mostly these turned out to be paintings of a woman reading or with a letter, not actually writing or reading the letter but looking up from it with unfocused eyes: Will he never never return? Did I remember to turn off the pot roast? . . . Another friend responded crisply, "A woman writing is taking dictation." And another said, "She's sitting at the kitchen table, and the kids are yelling."

And that last is the image I shall pursue. But first let me tell you my own first answer to my question: Jo March. From the immediacy, the authority, with which Frank Merrill's familiar illustrations of *Little Women*[2] came to my mind as soon as I asked myself what a woman writing looks like, I know that Jo March must have had real influence upon me when I was a young scribbler. I am sure she has influenced many girls, for she is not, like most "real" authors, either dead or inaccessibly famous; nor, like so many artists in books, is she set apart by sensitivity or suffering or general superlativity; nor is she, like most authors in novels, male. She is close as a sister and common as grass. As a model, what does she tell scribbling girls? I think it worthwhile to follow the biography of Jo March the Writer until we come to that person of whom, as a child and until quite recently, I knew almost nothing: Louisa May Alcott.

We first meet Jo as a writer when sister Amy vengefully burns her manuscript, "the loving work of several years. It seemed a small loss to others, but to Jo it was a dreadful calamity." How could a book, several years' work, be "a small loss" to anyone? That horrified me. How could they ask Jo to forgive Amy? At least she nearly drowns her in a frozen lake before forgiving her. At any rate, some chapters later Jo is

> very busy in the garret . . . seated on the old sofa, writing busily, with her papers spread out on a trunk before her. . . . Jo's desk up here was an old tin kitchen . . .

—the *OED* says, "New England: a roasting pan." So Jo's room of her own at this stage is a garret furnished with a sofa, a roasting pan, and a rat. To any twelve-year-old, heaven.

> Jo scribbled away till the last page was filled, when she signed her name with a flourish. . . . Lying back on the sofa she read the manuscript carefully through, making dashes here and there, and putting in many exclamation points, which looked like little balloons; then she tied it up with a smart red ribbon and sat a minute looking at it with a sober, wistful expression, which plainly showed how earnest her work had been.

I am interested here by the counterplay of a deflating irony—the scribbling, the dashes, the balloons, the ribbon—and that wistful earnestness.

Jo sends her story to a paper, it is printed, and she reads it aloud to her sisters, who cry at the right places. Beth asks, "Who wrote it?"

> The reader suddenly sat up, cast away the paper, displaying a flushed countenance, and with a funny mixture of solemnity and excitement, replied, in a loud voice, "Your sister."

The March family makes a great fuss, "for these foolish, affectionate people made a jubilee of every little household joy"—and there again is deflation, a writer's first publication reduced to a "little household joy." Does it not debase art? And yet does it not also, by refusing the heroic tone, refuse to inflate art into something beyond the reach of any "mere girl"?

So Jo goes on writing; here she is some years later, and I quote at length, for this is the central image.

> Every few weeks she would shut herself up in her room, put on her scribbling suit, and "fall into a vortex," as she expressed it, writing away at her novel with all her heart and soul, for till that was finished she could find no peace. Her "scribbling suit" consisted of a black woollen pinafore on which she could wipe her pen at will, and a cap of the same material, adorned with a cheerful red bow. . . . This cap was a beacon to the inquiring eyes of her family, who during these periods kept their distance, merely popping in their heads semi-occasionally to ask, with interest, "Does genius burn, Jo?" They did not always venture even to ask this question, but took an observation of the cap, and judged accordingly. If this expressive article of dress was drawn low upon the forehead, it was a sign that hard work was going on; in exciting moments it was pushed rakishly askew; and when despair seized the author it was plucked wholly off and cast upon the floor. At such times the intruder silently withdrew; and not until the red bow was seen gayly erect upon the gifted brow, did anyone dare address Jo.
>
> She did not think herself a genius by any means; but when the writing fit came on, she gave herself up to it with entire abandon, and led a blissful life, unconscious of want, care, or bad weather, while she sat safe and happy in an imaginary world, full of friends almost as real and dear to her as any in the flesh. Sleep forsook her eyes, meals stood untasted, day and night were all too short to enjoy the happiness which blessed her only at such times, and made these hours worth living, even if they bore no other fruit. The divine afflatus usually lasted a week or two, and then she emerged from her vortex, hungry, sleepy, cross, or despondent.

This is a good description of the condition in which the work of art is done. This is the real thing—domesticated. The cap and bow, the facetious turns and the disclaimers, deflate without degrading, and allow Alcott to make a rather extraordinary statement: that Jo is doing something very important and doing it entirely seriously and that there is nothing unusual about a young woman's doing it. This passion of work and this happiness which blessed her in doing it are fitted without fuss into a girl's commonplace life at home. It may not seem much; but I don't know where else I or many other girls like me, in my generation or my mother's or my daughters', were to find this model, this validation.

Jo writes romantic thrillers and they sell; her father shakes his head and says, "Aim at the highest and never mind the money," but Amy remarks, "The money is the best part of it." Working in Boston as a governess-seamstress, Jo sees that "money conferred power: money and power, therefore, she resolved to have; not to be used for herself alone," our author's author hastily adds, "but for those whom she loved more than self. . . . She took to writing sensation stories." Her first visit to the editorial office of the *Weekly Volcano* is handled lightly, but the three men treat her as a woman who has come to sell herself—true Lévi-Straussians, to whom what a woman does is entirely subsumed in woman as commodity. Refusing shame, Jo writes on, and makes money by her writing; admitting shame, she does not "tell them at home."

> Jo soon found that her innocent experience had given her but few glimpses of the tragic world which underlies society; so, regarding it in a business light, she set about supplying her deficiencies with characteristic energy. . . . She searched newspapers for accidents, incidents, and crimes; she excited the suspicions of public librarians by asking for works on poisons; she studied faces in the street, and characters good, bad, and indifferent all about her. . . . Much describing of other people's passions and feelings set her to studying and speculating about her own—a morbid amusement, in which healthy young minds do not voluntarily indulge—

but which one might think appropriate, even needful, to the young novelist? However, "wrongdoing always brings its own punishment, and when Jo most needed hers, she got it."

Her punishment is administered by the Angel in the House, in the form of Professor Bhaer. Knowing that she is soiling her pure soul, he attacks the papers she writes for: "I do not like to think that good young girls should see such things." Jo weakly defends them, but when he leaves she rereads her stories, three months' work, and burns them. Amy doesn't have to do it for her any more; she can destroy herself. Then she sits and wonders: "I almost wish I hadn't any conscience, it's so inconvenient!" A cry from the heart of Bronson Alcott's daughter. She tries a pious tale and a children's story, which don't sell, and gives up: she "corked up her inkstand."

Beth dies, and trying to replace her, Jo tries "to live for others"—finally driving her mother to say, "Why don't you write? That always used to make you happy." So she does, and she writes both well and successfully—until Professor Bhaer returns and marries her, evidently the only way to make her stop writing. She has his two boys to bring up, and then her two boys, and then all those Little Men in the next volume; at the end of *Little Women,* in the chapter called "Harvest Time," she says, "I haven't given up the hope that I may write a good book yet, but I can wait."

The harvest seems indefinitely deferred. But, in Rachel Blau Du Plessis' phrase,[3] Jo writes beyond the ending. In the third volume, *Jo's Boys,* she has gone back in middle age to writing, and is rich and famous. There is realism, toughness, and comedy in the descriptions of her managing the household, mothering the teenagers, writing her chapters, and trying to avoid the celebrity hunters. In fact this, like the whole story of Jo the Writer, is quite close to Louisa Alcott's own story, with one large difference. Jo marries and has children. Lu did not.

And yet she undertook the responsibility for a family, some of whom were as improvident and self-centered as any baby. There is a heartbreaking note in her journal[4] for April 1869, when she was suffering a "bad spell" of mercury poisoning (the calomel given her to cure fever when she was a nurse in the Civil War made her sick the rest of her life):

> Very poorly. Feel quite used up. Don't care much for myself, as rest is heavenly, even with pain; but the family seems so panic stricken and helpless when I break down, that I try to keep the mill going. Two short tales for L., $50; two for Ford, $20; and did my editorial work, though two months are unpaid for. Roberts wants a new book, but am afraid to get into a vortex lest I fall ill.

Alcott used the same word Jo used for her passions for writing; here are a couple of journal passages comparable to the "vortex" passage in *Little Women*.

> August 1860—"Moods" [a novel]. Genius burned so fiercely that for four weeks I wrote all day and planned nearly all night, being quite possessed by my work. I was perfectly happy, and seemed to have no wants.

> February 1861—Another turn at "Moods," which I remodelled. From the 2d to the 25th I sat writing, with a run at dusk; could not sleep, and for three days was so full of it I could not stop to get up. Mother made me a green silk cap with a red bow, to match the old red and green party wrap, which I wore as a "glory cloak." Thus arrayed sat in a grove of manuscripts, "living for immortality" as May said. Mother wandered in and out with cordial cups of tea, worried because I couldn't eat. Father thought it fine, and brought his reddest apples and hardest cider for my Pegasus to feed upon. . . . It was very pleasant and queer while it lasted. . . .

And it is pleasant to see how the family whose debts she slaved to pay off, and which she strove so to protect and keep in comfort, tried to protect and help her in return.

Like so many women of her century, then, Lu Alcott had a family, though she did not marry. "Liberty is a better husband than love to many of us," she wrote, but in fact she had very little liberty, in the sense of freedom from immediate, personal responsibilities. She even had a baby—her sister May's. Dying from complications of childbirth, May asked the beloved older sister, then forty-eight, to bring up little Lu; which she did until her death eight years later.

All this is complex, more complex, I think, than one tends to imagine; for the Victorian script calls for a clear choice—either books or babies for a woman, not both. And Jo *seems* to make that choice. I was annoyed at myself when I realized that I had forgotten Jo's survival as a writer—that my memory, except for one nagging scrap that led me to look up *Jo's Boys* at last, had followed the script. That, of course, is the power of the script: you play the part without knowing it.

Here is a classic—a scriptural—description of a writing woman, the mother of children, one of whom is just now in the process of falling down the stairs.

> Mrs Jellyby was a pretty, very diminutive, plump woman, of from forty to fifty, with handsome eyes, though they had a curious habit of seeming to look a long way off. . . . [She] had very good hair, but was too much occupied with her African duties to brush it. . . . We could not help noticing that her dress didn't nearly meet up the back, and that the open space was railed across with a latticework of stay-laces—like a summer-house.
>
> The room, which was strewn with papers and nearly filled by a great writing-table covered with similar litter, was, I must say, not only very untidy, but very dirty. We were obliged to take notice of that with our sense of sight, even while, with our sense of hearing, we followed the poor child who had tumbled downstairs: I think into the back kitchen, where somebody seemed to stifle him. But what principally struck us was a jaded and unhealthy-looking, though by no means plain girl, at the writing-table, who sat biting the feather of her pen, and staring at us. I suppose nobody ever was in such a state of ink.[5]

I will, with difficulty, restrain myself from reading you the rest of *Bleak House.* I love Dickens and will defend his Mrs. Jellyby and her correspondence with Borrioboola-Gha as an eternal send-up of those who meddle with foreign morals while remaining oblivious to the misery under their nose. But I observe also that he uses a woman to make this point, probably because it was, and is, safe: few readers would question the assumption that a woman should put family before public responsibility, or that if she does work outside the "private sphere" she will be neglectful of her house, indifferent to the necks of her children, and incompetent to fasten her clothing. Mrs. Jellyby's daughter is saved from her enforced "state of ink" by marriage, but Mrs. Jellyby will get no help from her husband, a man so inert that their marriage is described as the union of mind and matter. Mrs. Jellyby is a joy to me, she is drawn with so much humor and good nature; and yet she troubles me, because behind her lurks the double standard. Nowhere among Dickens' many responsible, intelligent women is there one who does real artistic or intellectual work, to balance Mrs. Jellyby and reassure us that it isn't what she does but how she does it that is deplorable. And yet the passage just quoted is supposed to have been written by a woman—the character Esther Summerson. Esther herself is a problem. How does she write half Dickens' novel for him while managing Bleak House and getting smallpox and everything else? We never catch her at it. As a woman writing, Esther is invisible. She is not in the script.

There may be a sympathetic portrait of a woman writer with children in a novel written by a man. I have read versions of this paper in Rhode Island, Ohio, Georgia, Louisiana, Oregon, and California, and asked each audience please to tell me if they knew of any such. I wait in hope. Indeed, the only sympathetic picture of a woman novelist in a man's novel that I know is the protagonist of *Diana of the Crossways.* Meredith shows her writing novels for her living, doing it brilliantly, and finding her freedom in her professionalism. But, self-alienated by a disastrous infatuation, she begins to force her talent and can't work—the script apparently being that love is incidental for a man, everything for a woman. At the end, well off and happily married, she is expecting a baby, but not, it appears, a book. All the same, Diana still stands, nearly a century later, quite alone at her crossways.

Invisibility as a writer is a condition that affects not only characters but authors, and even the children of authors. Take Elizabeth Barrett Browning, whom we have consistently put to bed with a spaniel, ignoring the fact that when she wrote *Aurora Leigh* she was the healthy mother of a healthy four-year-old—ignoring, in fact, the fact that she wrote *Aurora Leigh,* a book about being a woman writer, and how difficult one's own true love can make it for one.

Here is a woman who had several children and was a successful novelist, writing a letter to her husband about a hundred and fifty years ago, or maybe last night:

> If I *am* to write, I must have a room to myself, which shall be *my* room. All last winter I felt the need of some place where I could go and be quiet. I could not [write in the dining room] for there was all the setting of tables and clearing up of tables and dressing and washing of children, and everything else going on, and . . . I never felt comfortable there, though I tried hard. Then if I came into the parlor where you were, I felt as if I were interrupting you, and you know you sometimes thought so too.[6]

What do you mean? Not at all! Silly notion! Just like a woman!

Fourteen years and several more children later, that woman wrote *Uncle Tom's Cabin*—most of it at the kitchen table.

A room of one's own—yes. One may ask why Mr. Harriet Beecher Stowe got a room to himself to write in, while the woman who wrote the morally effective American novel of the nineteenth century got the kitchen table. But then one may also ask why she accepted the kitchen table. Any self-respecting man would have sat there for five minutes and then stalked out shouting, "Nobody can work in this madhouse, call me when dinner's ready!" But Harriet, a self-respecting woman, went on getting dinner with the kids all underfoot *and* writing her novels. The first question, to be asked with awe, is surely, How? But then, Why? *Why* are women such patsies?

The quick-feminist-fix answer is that they are victims of and/or accomplices with the patriarchy, which is true but doesn't really get us anywhere new. Let us go to another woman novelist for help. I stole the Stowe quotation (and others) from Tillie Olsen's *Silences,* a book to which this paper stands in the relation of a loving but undutiful daughter—Hey, Ma, that's a neat quotation, can I wear it? This next one I found for myself, in the *Autobiography* of Margaret Oliphant, a fascinating book, from the generation just after Stowe. Oliphant was a successful writer very young, married, had three kids, went on writing, was left a widow with heavy debts and the three kids plus her brother's three kids to bring up, did so, went on writing. . . . When her second book came out, she was still, like Jo March, a girl at home.

> I had a great pleasure in writing, but the success and the three editions had no particular effect upon my mind. . . . I had nobody to praise me except my

mother and [brother] Frank, and their applause—well, it was delightful, it was everything in the world—it was life—but it did not count. They were part of me, and I of them, and we were all in it.[7]

I find that extraordinary. I cannot imagine any male author saying anything like that at all. There is a key here—something real that has been neglected, been hidden, been denied.

... The writing ran through everything. But then it was also subordinate to everything, to be pushed aside for any little necessity. I had no table even to myself, much less a room to work in, but sat at the corner of the family table with my writing-book, with everything going on as if I had been making a shirt instead of writing a book.... My mother sat always at needlework of some kind, and talked to whoever might be present, and I took my share in the conversation, going on all the same with my story, the little groups of imaginary persons, these other talks evolving themselves quite undisturbed.

How's that for an image, the group of imaginary people talking in the imaginary room in the real room among the real people talking, and all of it going on perfectly quiet and unconfused.... But it's shocking. She can't be a real writer. Real writers writhe on solitary sofas in cork-lined rooms, agonizing after *le mot juste*—don't they?

My study, all the study I have ever attained to, is the little second drawing-room where all the life of the house goes on ...

—you recall that she was bringing up six children?—

... and I don't think I have ever had two hours undisturbed (except at night when everybody is in bed) during my whole literary life. Miss Austen, I believe, wrote in the same way, and very much for the same reason; but at her period the natural flow of life took another form. The family were half ashamed to have it known that she was not just a young lady like the others, doing her embroidery. Mine were quite pleased to magnify me and to be proud of my work, but always with a hidden sense that it was an admirable joke ...

—perhaps artists cast off their families and go to the South Sea Islands because they want to be perceived as heroes and their families think they are funny?—

... a hidden sense that it was an admirable joke, and no idea that any special facilities or retirement was necessary. My mother would have felt her pride much checked, almost humiliated, if she had conceived that I stood in need of any artificial aids of that description. That would at once have made the work unnatural to her eyes, and also to mine.

Oliphant was a proud Scotswoman, proud of her work and her strength; yet she wrote nonfiction potboilers rather than fight her male editors and publishers for better pay for her novels. So, as she says bitterly, "Trollope's worst book was better paid than my best." Her best is said to be *Miss Marjoribanks,* but I have never yet been able to get a copy of it; it has disappeared, along with all her other books.

Thanks to publishers such as Virago we can now get Oliphant's *Hester,* a stunning novel, and *Kirsteen* and a few others, but they are still taught, so far as I know, only in women's studies courses; they are not part of the Canon of English Literature, though Trollope's potboilers are. No book by a woman who had children has ever been included in that august list.

I think Oliphant gives us a glimpse of why a novelist might not merely endure writing in the kitchen or the parlor amidst the children and the housework, but might endure it willingly. She seems to feel that she profited, that her writing profited, from the difficult, obscure, chancy connection between the art work and the emotional/manual/managerial complex of skills and tasks called "housework," and that to sever that connection would put the writing itself at risk, would make it, in her word, unnatural.

The received wisdom of course is just the opposite: that any attempt to combine art work with housework and family responsibility is impossible, unnatural. And the punishment for unnatural acts, among the critics and the Canoneers, is death.

What is the ethical basis of this judgment and sentence upon the housewife-artist? It is a very noble and austere one, with religion at its foundation: it is the idea that the artist must sacrifice himself to his art. (I use the pronoun advisedly.) His responsibility is to his work alone. It is a motivating idea of the Romantics, it guides the careers of poets from Rimbaud to Dylan Thomas to Richard Hugo, it has given us hundreds of hero figures, typical of whom is James Joyce himself and his Stephen Dedalus. Stephen sacrifices all "lesser" obligations and affections to a "higher" cause, embracing the moral irresponsibility of the soldier or the saint. This heroic stance, the Gauguin Pose, has been taken as the norm—as natural to the artist—and artists, both men and women, who do not assume it have tended to feel a little shabby and second-rate.

Not, however, Virginia Woolf. She observed factually that the artist needs a small income and a room to work in, but did not speak of heroism. Indeed, she said, "I doubt that a writer can be a hero. I doubt that a hero can be a writer." And when I see a writer assume the full heroic posture, I incline to agree. Here, for example, is Joseph Conrad:

> For twenty months I wrestled with the Lord for my creation . . . mind and will and conscience engaged to the full, hour after hour, day after day . . . a lonely struggle in a great isolation from the world. I suppose I slept and ate the food put before me and talked connectedly on suitable occasions, but I was never aware of the even flow of daily life, made easy and noiseless for me by a silent, watchful, tireless affection.[8]

A woman who boasted that her conscience had been engaged to the full in such a wrestling match would be called to account by both women and men; and women are now calling men to account. What "put food" before him? What made daily life so noiseless? What in fact was this "tireless affection," which sounds to me like an old Ford in a junkyard but is apparently intended as a delicate gesture towards a woman whose conscience was engaged to the full, hour after hour, day after day, for twenty months, in seeing to it that Joseph Conrad could wrestle with the Lord in a very relatively great isolation, well housed, clothed, bathed, and fed?

Conrad's "struggle" and Jo March/Lu Alcott's "vortex" are descriptions of the same kind of all-out artistic work; and in both cases the artist is looked after by the family. But I feel an important difference in their perceptions. Where Alcott receives a gift, Conrad asserts a right; where she is taken into the vortex, the creative whirl-wind, becoming part of it, he wrestles, struggles, seeking mastery. She is a partici-pant; he is a hero. And her family remain individuals, with cups of tea and timid inquiries, while his is depersonalized to "an affection."

Looking for a woman writer who might have imitated this heroic infantilism, I thought of Gertrude Stein, under the impression that she had used Alice Toklas as a "wife" in this utilitarian sense; but that, as I should have guessed, is an anti-lesbian canard. Stein certainly took hero-artist poses and indulged an enormous ego, but she played fair; and the difference between her domestic partnership and that of Joyce or Conrad is illuminating. And indeed, lesbianism has given many artists the network of support they need—for there *is* a heroic aspect to the practice of art; it is lonely, risky, merciless work, and every artist needs some kind of moral support or sense of solidarity and validation.

The artist with the least access to social or aesthetic solidarity or approbation has been the artist-housewife. A person who undertakes responsibility both to her art and to her dependent children, with no "tireless affection" or even tired affection to call on, has undertaken a full-time double job that can be simply, practically, destroy-ingly impossible. But that isn't how the problem is posed—as a recognition of immense practical difficulty. If it were, practical solutions would be proposed, begin-ning with childcare. Instead the issue is stated, even now, as a moral one, a matter of ought and ought not. The poet Alicia Ostriker puts it neatly: "That women should have babies rather than books is the considered opinion of Western civilization. That women should have books rather than babies is a variation on that theme."9

Freud's contribution to this doctrine was to invest it with such a weight of the-ory and mythology as to make it appear a primordial, unquestionable fact. It was of course Freud who, after telling his fiancée what it is a woman wants, said that what we shall never know is what a woman wants. Lacan is perfectly consistent in fol-lowing him, if I as a person without discourse may venture to say so. A culture or a psychology predicated upon man as human and woman as other cannot accept a woman as artist. An artist is an autonomous, choice-making self: to be such a self a woman must unwoman herself. Barren, she must imitate the man—imperfectly, it goes without saying.★

★A particularly exhilarating discussion of this issue is the essay "Writing and Motherhood" by Susan Rubin Suleiman, in *The (M)other Tongue: Essays in Feminist Psychoanalytic Interpretation,* edited by Gar-ner, Kahane, and Springnether (Ithaca: Cornell University Press, 1985). Suleiman gives a short history of the nineteenth-century books-or-babies theory and its refinement in the twentieth century by such psychologists as Helene Deutsch, remarking that "it took psychoanalysis to transform moral obligation into a psychological 'law,' equating the creative impulse with the procreative one and decreeing that she who has a child feels no need to write books." Suleiman presents a critique of the feminist rever-sal of this theory (she who has a book feels no need to have children) and analyzes current French feminist thinking on the relationship between writing and femininity/motherhood.

Hence the approbation accorded Austen, the Brontës, Dickinson, and Plath, who though she made the mistake of having two children compensated for it by killing herself. The misogynist Canon of Literature can include these women because they can be perceived as incomplete women, as female men.

Still, I have to grit my teeth to criticize the either-books-or-babies doctrine, because it has given real, true comfort to women who could not or chose not to marry and have children, and saw themselves as "having" books instead. But though the comfort may be real, I think the doctrine false. And I hear that falseness when a Dorothy Richardson tells us that other women can have children but nobody else can write *her* books. As if "other women" could have had *her* children—as if books came from the uterus! That's just the flip side of the theory that books come from the scrotum. This final reduction of the notion of sublimation is endorsed by our chief macho dodo writer, who has announced that "the one thing a writer needs to have is balls." But he doesn't carry the theory of penile authorship to the extent of saying that if you "get" a kid you can't "get" a book and so fathers can't write. The analogy collapsed into identity, the you-can't-create-if-you-procreate myth, is applied to women only.

I've found I have to stop now and say clearly what I'm not saying. I'm not saying a writer ought to have children, I'm not saying a parent ought to be a writer, I'm not saying any woman *ought* to write books *or* have kids. Being a mother is one of the things a woman can do—like being a writer. It's a privilege. It's not an obligation, or a destiny. I'm talking about mothers who write because it is almost a taboo topic—because women have been told that they *ought not* to try to be both a mother and a writer because both the kids and the books will *pay*—because it can't be done—because it is unnatural.

This refusal to allow both creation and procreation to women is cruelly wasteful: not only has it impoverished our literature by banning the housewives, but it has caused unbearable personal pain and self-mutilation: Woolf obeying the wise doctors who said she must not bear a child; Plath who put glasses of milk by her kids' beds and then put her head in the oven.

A sacrifice, not of somebody else but of oneself, is demanded of women artists (while the Gauguin Pose demands of men artists only that they sacrifice others). I am proposing that this ban on a woman artist's full sexuality is harmful not only to the woman but to the art.

There is less censure now, and more support, for a woman who wants both to bring up a family and work as an artist. But it's a small degree of improvement. The difficulty of trying to be responsible, hour after hour day after day for maybe twenty *years,* for the well-being of children and the excellence of books, is immense: it involves an endless expense of energy and an impossible weighing of competing priorities. And we don't know much about the process, because writers who are mothers haven't talked much about their motherhood—for fear of boasting? for fear of being trapped in the Mom trap, discounted?—nor have they talked much about their writing as in any way connected with their parenting, since the heroic myth demands that the two jobs be considered utterly opposed and mutually destructive.

But we heard a hint of something else from Oliphant; and here (thanks, Tillie) is the painter Käthe Kollwitz:

> I am gradually approaching the period in my life when work comes first. When both the boys were away for Easter, I hardly did anything but work. Worked, slept, ate, and went for short walks. But above all I worked.
>
> And yet I wonder whether the "blessing" isn't missing from such work. No longer diverted by other emotions, I work the way a cow grazes.

That is marvelous—"I work the way a cow grazes." That is the best description of the "professional" at work I know.

> Perhaps in reality I accomplish a little more. The hands work and work, and the head imagines it's producing God knows what, and yet, formerly, when my working time was so wretchedly limited, I was more productive, because I was more sensual; I lived as a hman being must live, passionately interested in everything. . . . Potency, potency is diminishing.[10]

This *potency* felt by a woman is a potency from which the Hero-Artist has (and I choose my words carefully) cut himself off, in an egoism that is ultimately sterile. But it is a potency that has been denied by women as well as men, and not just women eager to collude with misogyny.

Back in the seventies Nina Auerbach wrote that Jane Austen was able to write because she had created around her "a child-free space." Germ-free I knew, odor-free I knew, but child-free? And Austen? who wrote in the parlor, and was a central figure to a lot of nieces and nephews? But I tried to accept what Auerbach said, because although my experience didn't fit it, I was, like many women, used to feeling that my experience was faulty, not right—that it was *wrong*. So I was probably wrong to keep on writing in what was then a fully child-filled space. However, feminist thinking evolved rapidly to a far more complex and realistic position, and I, stumbling along behind, have been enabled by it to think a little for myself.

The greatest enabler for me was always, is always, Virginia Woolf. And I quote now from the first draft of her paper "Professions for Women,"[11] where she gives her great image of a woman writing.

> I figure her really in an attitude of contemplation, like a fisherwoman, sitting on the bank of a lake with her fishing rod held over its water. Yes that is how I see her. She was not thinking; she was not reasoning; she was not constructing a plot; she was letting her imagination down into the depths of her consciousness while she sat above holding on by a thin but quite necessary thread of reason.

Now I interrupt to ask you to add one small element to this scene. Let us imagine that a bit farther up the bank of the lake sits a child, the fisherwoman's daughter. She's about five, and she's making people out of sticks and mud and telling stories with them. She's been told to be very quiet please while Mama fishes, and she really is very quiet except when she forgets and sings or asks questions; and she watches in fascinated silence when the following dramatic events take place. There sits our woman writing, our fisherwoman, when—

suddenly there is a violent jerk; she feels the line race through her fingers.

The imagination has rushed away; it has taken to the depths; it has sunk heaven knows where—into the dark pool of extraordinary experience. The reason has to cry "Stop!" the novelist has to pull on the line and haul the imagination to the surface. The imagination comes to the top in a state of fury.

Good heavens she cries—how dare you interfere with me—how dare you pull me out with your wretched little fishing line? And I—that is, the reason—have to reply, "My dear you were going altogether too far. Men would be shocked." Calm yourself I say, as she sits panting on the bank— panting with rage and disappointment. We have only got to wait fifty years or so. In fifty years I shall be able to use all this very queer knowledge that you are ready to bring me. But not now. You see I go on, trying to calm her, I cannot make use of what you tell me—about women's bodies for instance— their passions—and so on, because the conventions are still very strong. If I were to overcome the conventions I should need the courage of a hero, and I am not a hero.

I doubt that a writer can be a hero. I doubt that a hero can be a writer.

. . . Very well, says the imagination, dressing herself up again in her petti-coat and skirts, we will wait. We will wait another fifty years. But it seems to me a pity.

It seems to me a pity. It seems to me a pity that more than fifty years have passed and the conventions, though utterly different, still exist to protect men from being shocked, still admit only male experience of women's bodies, passions, and exis-tence. It seems to me a pity that so many women, including myself, have accepted this denial of their own experience and narrowed their perception to fit it, writing as if their sexuality were limited to copulation, as if they knew nothing about preg-nancy, birth, nursing, mothering, puberty, menstruation, menopause, except what men are willing to hear, nothing except what men are willing to hear about house-work, childwork, lifework, war, peace, living, and dying as experienced in the female body and mind and imagination. "Writing the body," as Woolf asked and Hélène Cixous asks, is only the beginning. We have to rewrite the world.

White writing, Cixous calls it, writing in milk, in mother's milk. I like that image, because even among feminists, the woman writer has been more often con-sidered in her sexuality as a lover than in her sexuality as pregnant-bearing-nursing-childcaring. Mother still tends to get disappeared. And in losing the artist-mother we lose where there's a lot to gain. Alicia Ostriker thinks so. "The advantage of motherhood for a woman artist," she says—have you ever heard anybody say that before? the *advantage* of motherhood for an artist?—

The advantage of motherhood for a woman artist is that it puts her in imme-diate and inescapable contact with the sources of life, death, beauty, growth, corruption. . . . If the woman artist has been trained to believe that the activi-ties of motherhood are trivial, tangential to the main issues of life, irrelevant to the great themes of literature, she should untrain herself. The training is misogynist, it protects and perpetuates systems of thought and feeling which prefer violence and death to love and birth, and it is a lie.

. . . "We think back through our mothers, if we are women," declares Woolf, but through whom can those who are themselves mothers . . . do their thinking? . . . we all need data, we need information, . . . the sort provided by poets, novelists, artists, from within. As our knowledge begins to accumulate, we can imagine what it would signify to all women, and men, to live in a culture where childbirth and mothering occupied the kind of position that sex and romantic love have occupied in literature and art for the last five hundred years, or . . . that warfare has occupied since literature began.[12]

My book *Always Coming Home* was a rash attempt to imagine such a world, where the Hero and the Warrior are a stage adolescents go through on their way to becoming responsible human beings, where the parent-child relationship is not forever viewed through the child's eyes but includes the reality of the mother's experience. The imagining was difficult, and rewarding.

Here is a passage from a novel where what Woolf, Cixous, and Ostriker ask for is happening, however casually and unpretentiously. In Margaret Drabble's *The Millstone*,[13] Rosamund, a young scholar and freelance writer, has a baby about eight months old, Octavia. They share a flat with a friend, Lydia, who's writing a novel. Rosamund is working away on a book review:

> I had just written and counted my first hundred words when I remembered Octavia; I could hear her making small happy noises. . . .
>
> I was rather dismayed when I realized she was in Lydia's room and that I must have left the door open, for Lydia's room was always full of nasty objects like aspirins, safety razors and bottles of ink; I rushed along to rescue her and the sight that met my eyes when I opened the door was enough to make anyone quake. She had her back to the door and was sitting in the middle of the floor surrounded by a sea of torn, strewed, chewed paper. I stood there transfixed, watching the neat small back of her head and her thin stalk-like neck and flowery curls: suddenly she gave a great screech of delight and ripped another sheet of paper. "Octavia," I said in horror, and she started guiltily, and looked round at me with a charming deprecating smile: her mouth, I could see, was wedged full of wads of Lydia's new novel.
>
> I picked her up and fished the bits out and laid them carefully on the bedside table with what was left of the typescript; pages 70 to 123 seemed to have survived. The rest was in varying stages of dissolution: some pages were entire but badly crumpled, some were in large pieces, some in small pieces, and some, as I have said, were chewed up. The damage was not, in fact, as great as it appeared at first sight to be, for babies, though persistent, are not thorough: but at first sight it was frightful. . . . In a way it was clearly the most awful thing for which I had ever been responsible, but as I watched Octavia crawl around the sitting room looking for more work to do, I almost wanted to laugh. It seemed so absurd, to have this small living extension of myself, so dangerous, so vulnerable, for whose injuries and crimes I alone had to suffer. . . .

It really was a terrible thing . . . and yet in comparison with Octavia being so sweet and so alive it did not seem so very terrible. . . .

Confronted with the wreckage, Lydia is startled, but not deeply distressed:

. . . and that was it, except for the fact that Lydia really did have to rewrite two whole chapters as well as doing a lot of boring sellotaping, and when it came out it got bad reviews anyway. This did succeed in making Lydia angry.

I have seen Drabble's work dismissed with the usual list of patronizing adjectives reserved for women who write as women, not imitation men. Let us not let her be disappeared. Her work is deeper than its bright surface. What is she talking about in this funny passage? Why does the girl-baby eat not her mother's manuscript but another woman's manuscript? Couldn't she at least have eaten a manuscript by a man?—no, no, that's not the point. The point, or part of it, is that babies eat manuscripts. They really do. The poem not written because the baby cried, the novel put aside because of a pregnancy, and so on. Babies eat books. But they spit out wads of them that can be taped back together; and they are only babies for a couple of years, while writers live for decades; and it is terrible, but not very terrible. The manuscript that got eaten *was* terrible; if you know Lydia you know the reviewers were right. And that's part of the point too—that the supreme value of art depends on other equally supreme values. But that subverts the hierarchy of values; "men would be shocked. . . ."

In Drabble's comedy of morals the absence of the Hero-Artist is a strong ethical statement. Nobody lives in a great isolation, nobody sacrifices human claims, nobody even scolds the baby. Nobody is going to put their head, or anybody else's head, into an oven: not the mother, not the writer, not the daughter—these three and one who, being women, do not separate creation and destruction into *I create / You are destroyed,* or vice versa. Who are responsible, take responsibility, for both the baby and the book.★

But I want now to turn from fiction to biography and from general to personal; I want to talk a bit about my mother, the writer.

Her maiden name was Theodora Kracaw; her first married name was Brown; her second married name, Kroeber, was the one she used on her books; her third

---

★My understanding of this issue has been much aided by Carol Gilligan's *In a Different Voice* (Cambridge: Harvard University Press, 1982), as well as by Jean Baker Miller's modestly revolutionary *Toward a New Psychology of Women* (Boston: Beacon Press, 1976). Gilligan's thesis, stated very roughly, is that our society brings up males to think and speak in terms of their rights, females in terms of their responsibilities, and that conventional psychologies have implicitly evaluated the "male" image of a hierarchy of rights as "superior" (hierarchically, of course) to the "female" image of a network of mutual responsibilities. Hence a man finds it (relatively) easy to assert his "right" to be free of relationships and dependents, à la Gauguin, while women are not granted and do not grant one another any such right, preferring to live as part of an intense and complex network in which freedom is arrived at, if at all, mutually. Coming at the matter from this angle, one can see why there are no or very few "Great Artists" among women, when the "Great Artist" is defined as inherently superior to and not responsible towards others.

married name was Quinn. This sort of many-namedness doesn't happen to men; it's inconvenient, and yet its very cumbersomeness reveals, perhaps, the being of a woman writer as not one simple thing—the author—but a multiple, complex process of being, with various responsibilities, one of which is to her writing.

Theodora put her personal responsibilities first—chronologically. She brought up and married off her four children before she started to write. She took up the pen, as they used to say—she had the most amazing left-handed scrawl—in her mid-fifties. I asked her once, years later, "Did you want to write, and put it off intentionally, till you'd got rid of us?" And she laughed and said, "Oh, no, I just wasn't *ready.*" Not an evasion or a dishonest answer, but not, I think, the whole answer.

She was born in 1897 in a wild Colorado mining town, and her mother boasted of having been *born* with the vote—in Wyoming, which ratified woman suffrage along with statehood—and rode a stallion men couldn't ride; but still, the Angel in the House was very active in those days, the one whose message is that a woman's needs come after everybody else's. And my mother really came pretty close to incarnating that Angel, whom Woolf called "the woman men wish women to be." Men fell in love with her—all men. Doctors, garage mechanics, professors, roach exterminators. Butchers saved sweetbreads for her. She was also, to her daughter, a demanding, approving, nurturing, good-natured, loving, lively mother—a first-rate mother. And then, getting on to sixty, she became a first-rate writer.

She started out, as women so often do, by writing some books for children—not competing with men, you know, staying in the "domestic sphere." One of these, *A Green Christmas,* is a lovely book that ought to be in every six-year-old's stocking. Then she wrote a charming and romantic autobiographical novel—still on safe, "womanly" ground. Next she ventured into Native American territory with *The Inland Whale*; and then she was asked to write the story of an Indian called Ishi, the only survivor of a people massacred by the North American pioneers, a serious and risky subject requiring a great deal of research, moral sensitivity, and organizational and narrative skill.

So she wrote it, the first best seller, I believe, that University of California Press ever published. *Ishi* is still in print in many languages, still used, I think, in California schools, still deservedly beloved. It is a book entirely worthy of its subject, a book of very great honesty and power.

So, if she could write that in her sixties, what might she have written in her thirties? Maybe she really "wasn't ready." But maybe she listened to the wrong angel, and we might have had many more books from her. Would my brothers and I have suffered, have been cheated of anything, if she had been writing them? I think my aunt Betsy and the household help we had back then would have kept things going just fine. As for my father, I don't see how her writing could have hurt him or how her success could have threatened him. But I don't know. All I do know is that once she started writing (and it was while my father was alive, and they collaborated on a couple of things), she never stopped; she had found the work she loved.

Once, not long after my father's death, when *Ishi* was bringing her the validation of praise and success she very much needed, and while I was still getting every story I sent out rejected with monotonous regularity, she burst into tears over my latest rejection slip and tried to console me, saying that she wanted rewards and success for me, not for herself. And that was lovely, and I treasured her saying it then as I do now. That she didn't really mean it and I didn't really believe it made no difference. Of course she didn't want to sacrifice her achievement, her work, to me—why on earth should she? She shared what she could of it with me by sharing the pleasures and anguishes of writing, the intellectual excitement, the shoptalk—and that's all. No angelic altruism. When I began to publish, we shared that. And she wrote on; in her eighties she told me, without bitterness, "I wish I had started sooner. Now there isn't time." She was at work on a third novel when she died.

As for myself: I have flagrantly disobeyed the either-books-or-babies rule, having had three kids and written about twenty books, and thank God it wasn't the other way around. By the luck of race, class, money, and health, I could manage the double-tightrope trick—and especially by the support of my partner. He is not my wife; but he brought to marriage an assumption of mutual aid as its daily basis, and on that basis you can get a lot of work done. Our division of labor was fairly conventional; I was in charge of house, cooking, the kids, and novels, because I wanted to be, and he was in charge of being a professor, the car, the bills, and the garden, because he wanted to be. When the kids were babies I wrote at night; when they started school I wrote while they were at school; these days I write as a cow grazes. If I needed help he gave it without making it into a big favor, and—this is the central fact—he did not ever begrudge me the time I spent writing, or the blessing of my work.

That is the killer: the killing grudge, the envy, the jealousy, the spite that so often a man is allowed to hold, trained to hold, against anything a woman does that's not done in his service, for him, to feed his body, his comfort, his kids. A woman who tries to work against that grudge finds the blessing turned into a curse; she must rebel and go it alone, or fall silent in despair. Any artist must expect to work amid the total, rational indifference of everybody else to their work, for years, perhaps for life: but no artist can work well against daily, personal, vengeful resistance. And that's exactly what many women artists get from the people they love and live with.

I was spared all that. I was free—born free, lived free. And for years that personal freedom allowed me to ignore the degree to which my writing was controlled and constrained by judgments and assumptions which I thought were my own, but which were the internalized ideology of a male supremacist society. Even when subverting the conventions, I disguised my subversions from myself. It took me years to realize that I chose to work in such despised, marginal genres as science fiction, fantasy, young adult, precisely because they were excluded from critical, academic, canonical supervision, leaving the artist free; it took ten more years before I had the wits and guts to see and say that the exclusion of genres from "literature" is unjustified, unjustifiable, and a matter not of quality but of politics. So too in my choice of subjects: until the mid-seventies I wrote my fiction about heroic adventures, high-tech futures, men in the halls of power, men—men were the central characters, the women were peripheral, secondary. Why don't you write about women? my mother asked me. I don't know how, I said. A stupid answer, but an honest one. I did not know how to write about women—very few of us did—because I thought that what men had written about women was the truth, was the true way to write about women. And I couldn't.

My mother could not give me what I needed. When feminism began to reawaken, she hated it, called it "those women's libbers"; but it was she who had steered me years and years before to what I would and did need, to Virginia Woolf. "We think back through our mothers," and we have many mothers, those of the body and those of the soul. What I needed was what feminism, feminist literary theory and criticism and practice, had to give me. And I can hold it in my hands—not only *Three Guineas,* my treasure in the days of poverty, but now all the wealth of *The Norton Anthology of Literature by Women* and the reprint houses and the women's presses. Our mothers have been returned to us. This time, let's hang on to them.

And it is feminism that has empowered me to criticize not only my society and myself but—for a moment now—feminism itself. The books-or-babies myth is not only a misogynist hang-up, it can be a feminist one. Some of the women I respect most, writing for publications that I depend on for my sense of women's solidarity and hope, continue to declare that it is "virtually impossible for a heterosexual woman to be a feminist," as if heterosexuality were heterosexism; and that social marginality, such as that of lesbian, childless, Black, or Native American women, "appears to be necessary" to form the feminist. Applying these judgments to myself, and believing that as a woman writing at this point I have to be a feminist to be worth beans, I find myself, once again, excluded—disappeared.

The rationale of the exclusionists, as I understand it, is that the material privilege and social approbation our society grants the heterosexual wife, and particularly the mother, prevent her solidarity with less privileged women and insulate her from the kind of anger and the kind of ideas that lead to feminist action. There is truth in this; maybe it's true for a lot of women; I can oppose it only with my experience, which is that feminism has been a life-saving *necessity* to women trapped in the wife/mother "role." What do the privilege and approbation accorded the housewife-mother by our society in fact consist of? Being the object of infinite advertising? Being charged by psychologists with total answerability for children's mental well-being, and by the government with total answerability for children's welfare, while being regularly equated with apple pie by sentimental warmongers? As a social "role," motherhood, for any woman I know, simply means that she does everything everybody else does plus bringing up the kids.

To push mothers back into "private life," a mythological space invented by the patriarchy, on the theory that their acceptance of the "role" of mother invalidates them for public, political, artistic responsibility, is to play Old Nobodaddy's game, by his rules, on his side.

In *Writing Beyond the Ending,* Du Plessis shows how women novelists write about the woman artist: they make her an ethical force, an activist trying "to change the life in which she is also immersed."[14] To have and bring up kids is to be about as immersed in life as one can be, but it does not always follow that one drowns. A lot of us can swim.

Again, whenever I give a version of this paper, somebody will pick up on this point and tell me that I'm supporting the Superwoman syndrome, saying that a woman *should* have kids write books be politically active and make perfect sushi. I am not saying that. We're all asked to be Superwoman; I'm not asking it, our society does that. All I can tell you is that I believe it's a lot easier to write books while bringing up kids than to bring up kids while working nine to five plus housekeeping. But that is what our society, while sentimentalizing over Mom and the Family, demands of most women—unless it refuses them any work at all and dumps them onto welfare and says, Bring up your kids on food stamps, Mom, we might want them for the army. Talk about superwomen, those are the superwomen. Those are the mothers up against the wall. Those are the marginal women, without either privacy or publicity; and it's because of them more than anyone else that the woman artist has a responsibility to "try to change the life in which she is also immersed."

And now I come back round to the bank of that lake, where the fisherwoman sits, our woman writer, who had to bring her imagination up short because it was getting too deeply immersed. . . . The imagination dries herself off, still swearing under her breath, and buttons up her blouse, and comes to sit beside the little girl, the fisherwoman's daughter. "Do you like books?" she says, and the child says, "Oh, yes. When I was a baby I used to eat them, but now I can read. I can read all of Beatrix Potter by myself, and when I grow up I'm going to write books, like Mama."

"Are you going to wait till your children grow up, like Jo March and Theodora?"

"Oh, I don't think so," says the child. "I'll just go ahead and do it."

"Then will you do as Harriet and Margaret and so many Harriets and Margarets have done and are still doing, and hassle through the prime of your life trying to do two full-time jobs that are incompatible with each other in practice, however enriching their interplay may be both to the life and art?"

"I don't know," says the little girl. "Do I have to?"

"Yes," says the imagination, "if you aren't rich and you want kids."

"I might want one or two," says reason's child. "But why do women have two jobs where men only have one? It isn't reasonable, is it?"

"Don't ask me!" snaps the imagination. "I could think up a dozen better arrangements before breakfast! But who listens to me?"

The child sighs and watches her mother fishing. The fisherwoman, having forgotten that her line is no longer baited with the imagination, isn't catching anything, but she's enjoying the peaceful hour; and when the child speaks again she speaks softly. "Tell me, Auntie. What is the one thing a writer has to have?"

"I'll tell you," says the imagination. "The one thing a writer has to have is not balls. Nor is it a child-free space. Nor is it even, speaking strictly on the evidence, a room of her own, though that is an amazing help, as is the goodwill and cooperation of the opposite sex, or at least the local, in-house representative of it. But she doesn't have to have that. The one thing a writer has to have is a pencil and some paper. That's enough, so long as she knows that she and she alone is in charge of that pencil, and responsible, she and she alone, for what it writes on the paper. In other words, that she's free. Not wholly free. Never wholly free. Maybe very partially. Maybe only in this one act, this sitting for a snatched moment being a woman writing, fishing the mind's lake. But in this, responsible; in this, autonomous; in this, free."

"Auntie," says the little girl, "can I go fishing with you now?"

NOTES

1. Virginia Woolf, *Jacob's Room* (New York: Harcourt Brace Jovanovich, n.d.), p. 7.
2. The edition of *Little Women* I used was my mother's and is now my daughter's. It was published in Boston by Little, Brown, undated, around the turn of the century, and Merrill's fine drawings have also been reproduced in other editions.
3. Rachel Blau Du Plessis, *Writing Beyond the Ending: Narrative Strategies of Twentieth-Century Women Writers* (Bloomington, Indiana University Press, 1985).
4. Louisa May Alcott, *Life, Letters, and Journals* (Boston: Roberts Brothers, 1890). The passages quoted are on pp. 203, 122, and 125.
5. Charles Dickens, *Bleak House* (New York: Thomas Y. Crowell, n.d.), p. 41.
6. Harriet Beecher Stowe, 1841, quoted in Tillie Olsen, *Silences* (New York: Dell, Laurel Editions, 1983), p. 227.
7. This and the subsequent connected passages are from the *Autobiography and Letters of Mrs. Margaret Oliphant,* edited by Mrs. Harry Coghill (Leicester, England: Leicester University Press, The Victorian Library, 1974), pp. 23–24.
8. Joseph Conrad, quoted in Olsen, p. 30.
9. Alicia Ostriker, *Writing Like a Woman,* Michigan Poets on Poetry Series (Ann Arbor: University of Michigan Press, 1983), p. 126.
10. Käthe Kollwitz, *Diaries and Letters,* quoted in Olsen, pp. 235–236.
11. The talk, known in its revised form as "Professions for Women" and so titled in the Essays, was given on January 21, 1931, to the London National Society for Women's Service, and can be found complete with all deletions and alternate readings in Mitchell Leaska's editing of Woolf's *The Pargiters* (New York: Harcourt Brace Jovanovich, 1978).
12. Ostriker, p. 131.
13. Margaret Drabble, *The Millstone* (New York: NAL, Plume Books, 1984), pp. 122–23. Also published under the title *Thank You All Very Much.*
14. Du Plessis, p. 101.

Double Take

1. Ursula Le Guin writes, "Invisibility as a writer is a condition that affects not only characters but authors, and even the children of authors." Consider this statement in light of Le Guin's encompassing conversation about women writers and discuss the "invisibility" of women writers.
2. What does Le Guin see as the flaw to the "babies-or-books" argument? Why should such an argument evolve in the first place? That is, why does Le Guin need to make the point about the "babies-or-books" argument in support of her own position?

3. Explain, according to Le Guin, Hélène Cixous's notion of "writing the body." What does such writing provide for women writers? Why is it different from other forms of writing?

At First Glance

Ursula Le Guin's third essay "The Carrier Bag Theory of Fiction" first appeared in the 1986 collection Women of Vision, *edited by Denise M. Du Pont. As she often does, Le Guin critiques the ways that we have come to know and accept certain ideas as given. In this essay she questions whether weapons designed for killing or vessels designed for carrying were the first tools and what effect those origins had on the evolution of storytelling. Throughout the essay, Le Guin uses moments of clever humor to exemplify her points. As you read, ask yourself whether these moments are effective and what they contribute to the essay.*

The Carrier Bag Theory of Fiction

In the temperate and tropical regions where it appears that hominids evolved into human beings, the principal food of the species was vegetable. Sixty-five to eighty percent of what human beings ate in those regions in Paleolithic, Neolithic, and prehistoric times was gathered; only in the extreme Arctic was meat the staple food. The mammoth hunters spectacularly occupy the cave wall and the mind, but what we actually did to stay alive and fat was gather seeds, roots, sprouts, shoots, leaves, nuts, berries, fruits, and grains, adding bugs and mollusks and netting or snaring birds, fish, rats, rabbits, and other tuskless small fry to up the protein. And we didn't even work hard at it—much less hard than peasants slaving in somebody else's field after agriculture was invented, much less hard than paid workers since civilization was invented. The average prehistoric person could make a nice living in about a fifteen-hour work week.

Fifteen hours a week for subsistence leaves a lot of time for other things. So much time that maybe the restless ones who didn't have a baby around to enliven their life, or skill in making or cooking or singing, or very interesting thoughts to think, decided to slope off and hunt mammoths. The skillful hunters then would come staggering back with a load of meat, a lot of ivory, and a story. It wasn't the meat that made the difference. It was the story.

It is hard to tell a really gripping tale of how I wrested a wild-oat seed from its husk, and then another, and then another, and then another, and then another, and then I scratched my gnat bites, and Ool said something funny, and we went to the creek and got a drink and watched newts for a while, and then I found another patch of oats. . . . No, it does not compare, it cannot compete with how I thrust my spear deep into the titanic hairy flank while Oob, impaled on one huge sweeping tusk, writhed screaming, and blood spouted everywhere in crimson torrents, and Boob was crushed to jelly when the mammoth fell on him as I shot my unerring arrow straight through eye to brain.

That story not only has Action, it has a Hero. Heroes are powerful. Before you know it, the men and women in the wild-oat patch and their kids and the skills of the makers and the thoughts of the thoughtful and the songs of the singers are all part of it, have all been pressed into service in the tale of the Hero. But it isn't their story. It's his.

When she was planning the book that ended up as *Three Guineas,* Virginia Woolf wrote a heading in her notebook, "Glossary"; she had thought of reinventing English according to a new plan, in order to tell a different story. One of the entries in this glossary is *heroism,* defined as "botulism." And *hero,* in Woolf's dictionary, is "bottle." The hero as bottle, a stringent reevaluation. I now propose the bottle as hero.

Not just the bottle of gin or wine, but bottle in its older sense of container in general, a thing that holds something else.

If you haven't got something to put it in, food will escape you—even something as uncombative and unresourceful as an oat. You put as many as you can into your stomach while they are handy, that being the primary container; but what about tomorrow morning when you wake up and it's cold and raining and wouldn't it be good to have just a few handfuls of oats to chew on and give little Oom to make her shut up, but how do you get more than one stomachful and one handful home? So you get up and go to the damned soggy oat patch in the rain, and wouldn't it be a good thing if you had something to put Baby Oo Oo in so that you could pick the oats with both hands? A leaf a gourd a shell a net a bag a sling a sack a bottle a pot a box a container. A holder. A recipient.

> The first cultural device was probably a recipient. . . . Many theorizers feel that the earliest cultural inventions must have been a container to hold gathered products and some kind of sling or net carrier.

So says Elizabeth Fisher in *Women's Creation* (McGraw-Hill, 1975). But no, this cannot be. Where is that wonderful, big, long, hard thing, a bone, I believe, that the Ape Man first bashed somebody with in the movie and then, grunting with ecstasy at having achieved the first proper murder, flung up into the sky, and whirling there it became a space ship thrusting its way into the cosmos to fertilize it and produce at the end of the movie a lovely fetus, a boy of course, drifting around the Milky Way without (oddly enough) any womb, any matrix at all? I don't know. I don't even care. I'm not telling that story. We've heard it, we've all heard all about all the sticks and spears and swords, the things to bash and poke and hit with, the long, hard things, but we have not heard about the thing to put things in, the container for the thing contained. That is a new story. That is news.

And yet old. Before—once you think about it, surely long before—the weapon, a late, luxurious, superfluous tool; long before the useful knife and ax; right along with the indispensable whacker, grinder, and digger—for what's the use of digging up a lot of potatoes if you have nothing to lug the ones you can't eat home in—with or before the tool that forces energy outward, we made the tool that brings energy home. It makes sense to me. I am an adherent of what Fisher calls the Carrier Bag Theory of human evolution.

This theory not only explains large areas of theoretical obscurity and avoids large areas of theoretical nonsense (inhabited largely by tigers, foxes, and other highly territorial mammals); it also grounds me, personally, in human culture in a way I never felt grounded before. So long as culture was explained as originating from and elaborating upon the use of long, hard objects for sticking, bashing, and killing, I never thought that I had, or wanted, any particular share in it. ("What Freud mistook for her lack of civilization is woman's lack of *loyalty* to civilization," Lillian Smith observed.) The society, the civilization they were talking about, these theoreticians, was evidently theirs; they owned it, they liked it; they were human, fully human, bashing, sticking, thrusting, killing. Wanting to be human too, I sought for evidence that I was; but if that's what it took, to make a weapon and kill with it, then evidently I was either extremely defective as a human being, or not human at all.

That's right, they said. What you are is a woman. Possibly not human at all, certainly defective. Now be quiet while we go on telling the Story of the Ascent of Man the Hero.

Go on, say I, wandering off towards the wild oats, with Oo Oo in the sling and little Oom carrying the basket. You just go on telling how the mammoth fell on Boob and how Cain fell on Abel and how the bomb fell on Nagasaki and how the burning jelly fell on the villagers and how the missiles will fall on the Evil Empire, and all the other steps in the Ascent of Man.

If it is a human thing to do to put something you want, because it's useful, edible, or beautiful, into a bag, or a basket, or a bit of rolled bark or leaf, or a net woven of your own hair, or what have you, and then take it home with you, home being another, larger kind of pouch or bag, a container for people, and then later on you take it out and eat it or share it or store it up for winter in a solider container or put it in the medicine bundle or the shrine or the museum, the holy place, the area that contains what is sacred, and then next day you probably do much the same again—if to do that is human, if that's what it takes, then I am a human being after all. Fully, freely, gladly, for the first time.

Not, let it be said at once, an unaggressive or uncombative human being. I am an aging, angry woman laying mightily about me with my handbag, fighting hoodlums off. However I don't, nor does anybody else, consider myself heroic for doing so. It's just one of those damned things you have to do in order to be able to go on gathering wild oats and telling stories.

It is the story that makes the difference. It is the story that hid my humanity from me, the story the mammoth hunters told about bashing, thrusting, raping, killing, about the Hero. The wonderful, poisonous story of Botulism. The killer story.

It sometimes seems that that story is approaching its end. Lest there be no more telling of stories at all, some of us out here in the wild oats, amid the alien corn, think we'd better start telling another one, which maybe people can go on with when the old one's finished. Maybe. The trouble is, we've all let ourselves become part of the killer story, and so we may get finished along with it. Hence it is with a certain feeling of urgency that I seek the nature, subject, words of the other story, the untold one, the life story.

It's unfamiliar, it doesn't come easily, thoughtlessly to the lips as the killer story does; but still, "untold" was an exaggeration. People have been telling the life story for ages, in all sorts of words and ways. Myths of creation and transformation, trickster stories, folktales, jokes, novels . . .

The novel is a fundamentally unheroic kind of story. Of course the Hero has frequently taken it over, that being his imperial nature and uncontrollable impulse, to take everything over and run it while making stern decrees and laws to control his uncontrollable impulse to kill it. So the Hero has decreed through his mouthpieces the Lawgivers, first, that the proper shape of the narrative is that of the arrow or spear, starting *here* and going straight *there* and THOK! hitting its mark (which drops dead); second, that the central concern of narrative, including the novel, is conflict; and third, that the story isn't any good if he isn't in it.

I differ with all of this. I would go so far as to say that the natural, proper, fitting shape of the novel might be that of a sack, a bag. A book holds words. Words hold things. They bear meanings. A novel is a medicine bundle, holding things in a particular, powerful relation to one another and to us.

One relationship among elements in the novel may well be that of conflict, but the reduction of narrative to conflict is absurd. (I have read a how-to-write manual that said, "A story should be seen as a battle," and went on about strategies, attacks, victory, etc.) Conflict, competition, stress, struggle, etc., within the narrative conceived as carrier bag / belly / box / house / medicine bundle, may be seen as necessary elements of a whole which itself cannot be characterized either as conflict or as harmony, since its purpose is neither resolution nor stasis but continuing process.

Finally, it's clear that the Hero does not look well in this bag. He needs a stage or a pedestal or a pinnacle. You put him in a bag and he looks like a rabbit, like a potato.

That is why I like novels: instead of heroes they have people in them.

So, when I came to write science-fiction novels, I came lugging this great heavy sack of stuff, my carrier bag full of wimps and klutzes, and tiny grains of things smaller than a mustard seed, and intricately woven nets which when laboriously unknotted are seen to contain one blue pebble, an imperturbably functioning chronometer telling the time on another world, and a mouse's skull; full of beginnings without ends, of initiations, of losses, of transformations and translations, and far more tricks than conflicts, far fewer triumphs than snares and delusions; full of space ships that get stuck, missions that fail, and people who don't understand. I said it was hard to make a gripping tale of how we wrested the wild oats from their husks, I didn't say it was impossible. Who ever said writing a novel was easy?

If science fiction is the mythology of modern technology, then its myth is tragic. "Technology," or "modern science" (using the words as they are usually used, in an unexamined shorthand standing for the "hard" sciences and high technology founded upon continuous economic growth), is a heroic undertaking, Herculean, Promethean, conceived as triumph, hence ultimately as tragedy. The fiction embodying this myth will be, and has been, triumphant (Man conquers earth, space, aliens, death, the future, etc.) and tragic (apocalypse, holocaust, then or now).

If, however, one avoids the linear, progressive, Time's-(killing)-arrow mode of the Techno-Heroic, and redefines technology and science as primarily cultural carrier bag rather than weapon of domination, one pleasant side effect is that science fiction can be seen as a far less rigid, narrow field, not necessarily Promethean or apocalyptic at all, and in fact less a mythological genre than a realistic one.

It is a strange realism, but it is a strange reality.

Science fiction properly conceived, like all serious fiction, however funny, is a way of trying to describe what is in fact going on, what people actually do and feel, how people relate to everything else in this vast sack, this belly of the universe, this womb of things to be and tomb of things that were, this unending story. In it, as in all fiction, there is room enough to keep even Man where he belongs, in his place in the scheme of things; there is time enough to gather plenty of wild oats and sow them too, and sing to little Oom, and listen to Ool's joke, and watch newts, and still the story isn't over. Still there are seeds to be gathered, and room in the bag of stars.

Double Take

1. In describing the Carrier Bag Theory of human evolution, Ursula Le Guin twice comments that "It is the story that makes the difference." It seems that Le Guin is alluding to the notion that events do not matter as much as how those events are relayed to others—that is, Le Guin seems to be making a statement about the power of creating history, of telling the stories of events, of creating truth and knowledge. She even says that she thinks "we'd better start telling another one." Why do you suppose Le Guin emphasizes this point in "The Carrier Bag Theory of Fiction"? What other stories can be told?
2. According to Le Guin, what has been the traditional structure of a novel? How does she envision novels differently? How does the structure of a novel differ from how Le Guin writes essays? What different rhetorical choices do writers make in essays and novels?
3. Le Guin compares words to carrier bags, claiming "words hold things." What does Le Guin mean by this? When you write, what do you think words do for you?

At First Glance

Ursula Le Guin's "Along the Platte" was first published in The Oregonian *in August 1983. Unlike many essays that we read, this essay is written primarily in the present tense because it is derived mostly from a series of journal notes recounting a trip. As you read, notice when the verb tense shifts and what happens to your reading of the essay when the events described are recounted as happening at the same time you read them.*

Along the Platte

Some people fly to Tierra del Fuego and Katmandu; some people drive across Nebraska in a VW bus.

Living in Oregon, with family in Georgia, we drive the United States corner to corner every now and then. It takes a while. On the fifth day out of Macon, just crossing the Missouri, we look up to see a jet trail in the big sky. That plane going west will do two thousand miles while we do two hundred. A strange thought. But the strangeness works both ways. We'll drive about four hundred miles today. On foot with an ox-drawn wagon, that distance would take up to a month.

These are some notes from a day and a half on the Oregon Trail.

About ten in the morning we cross the wide Missouri into the West. Nebraska City looks comfortable and self-reliant, with its railyards and grain elevators over the big brown river. From it we drive out into rolling, spacious farmlands, dark green corn, pale yellow hay stubble, darkening gold wheat. The farmhouses, with big barns and a lot of outbuildings, come pretty close together: prosperous land. The signs say: Polled Shorthorns . . . Hampshire Swine . . . Charolais . . . Yorkshire and Spotted Swine.

We cross the North Fork of the Little Nemaha. The rivers of American have beautiful names. What was the language this river was named in? Nemaha— Omaha—Nebraska . . . Eastern Siouan, I guess. But it's a guess. We don't speak the language of this country.

Down in the deep shade of trees in high thick grass stand three horses, heads together, tails swishing, two black and one white with black tail and mane. Summertime . . .

Around eleven we're freewaying through Lincoln, a handsome city, the gold dome on its skyscraper capitol shining way up in the pale blue sky, and on our left the biggest grain elevator I ever saw, blocks long, a cathedral of high and mighty cylinders of white. On KECK, Shelley and Dave are singing, "Santa Monica free-way, sometimes makes a country girl blue . . ." After a while the DJ does the announcements. There will be a State Guernsey Picnic on Saturday, if I heard right.

Now we're humming along beside the Platte—there's a language I know. Platte means Flat. It's pretty flat along the Platte, all right, but there are long swells in this prairie, like on the quietest sea, and the horizon isn't forever: it's a blue line of trees way off there, under the farthest line of puffball fair-weather clouds.

We cross some channels of the braided Platte at Grand Island and stop for lunch at a State Wayside Park called Mormon Island, where it costs two bucks to eat your picnic. A bit steep. But it's a pretty place, sloughs or channels of the river on all sides, and huge black dragonflies with silver wingtips darting over the shallows, and blue darning-needles in the grass. The biggest mosquito I ever saw came to eat my husband's shoulder. I got it with my bare hand, but a wrecking ball would have been more appropriate. There used to be buffalo here. They were replaced by the mosquitoes.

On along the Platte, which we're going to cross and recross eleven times in Nebraska and one last time in Wyoming. The river is in flood, running hard between its grey willows and green willows, aspens and big cottonwoods. Some places the trees are up to their necks in water, and west of Cozad the hayfields are flooded, hayrolls rotting in the water, grey-white water pouring through fields where it doesn't belong.

The cattle are in pure herds of Black Angus, Aberdeen, Santa Gertrudis, and some beautiful mixed herds, all shades of cream, dun, brown, roan. There's a Hereford bull in with his harem and descendants, big, frowning, curly-headed, like an angry Irishman.

In 1976 Nebraska commissionied ten sculptures for the roadside rest areas along Interstate 80, and going west you see five of them; we stop at each one to see and photograph it, as does the grey-haired man with two daughters who pose with the sculpture for his photograph. The pieces are all big, imaginative, bold. The one we like best resides in a pond a couple miles west of Kearny. It's aluminum in planes and curves and discs; parts of it are balanced to move softly, without sound; all of it floats on the flickering, reflecting water. It's called *The Nebraska Wind Sculpture.* "What is it?" says a grinning man. I say, "Well, the AAA tourbook says it looks like H.G. Wells's Time Machine." He says, "O.K., but what *is* it?"—and I realize he thinks it may be "something," not "just" a work of art; and so he's looking at it and grinning, enjoying the damfool thing. If he knew it was Art, especially Modern Art, would he be afraid of it and refuse to see it at all? A fearless little boy, meanwhile, haunts the pool and shouts, "Look! A lobster!" pointing at a crayfish, and nearly falls into the scummy shallows reflecting the silver Nebraska Wind.

Down the road a town called Lexington advertises itself:

ALL-AMERICAN CITY
ALL-NEBRASKA COMMUNITY

Those are some kind of national and state awards for something, I suppose, but how disagreeable, how unfriendly and exclusive they sound. But then, what other state of the union thought of celebrating the Bicentennial with big crazy sculptures right out for every stranger driving I-80 to see? Right on, Nebraska!

We pull in for the night at a motel in North Platte, a town that has a rodeo every night of every summer every year, and we sure aren't going to miss that. After dinner we drive out Rodeo Road to Buffalo Bill Avenue to the Cody Arena (by now we have the idea that that old fraud came from around here), and the nice cowgirl selling tickets says, trying to give us a senior citizen savings, "Would you be over sixty at all?" No, we can't manage that yet, so she gives us full-price tickets and a beautiful smile. All the seats are good. It's a warm dry prairie evening, the light getting dusty and long. Young riders on young horses mill around the arena enjoying the attention till the announcer starts the show the way all rodeos start, asking us to salute "the most beautiful flag in the world," a pleasure, while the horses fidget and the flag bearer sits stern, but the announcer goes on about how this flag has been "spat and trampled and mocked and burned on campuses," boy, does he have it in for campuses, what decade is he living in? The poison in his voice is pure Agent Orange. More of this "patriotism" that really means hating somebody. Shut up, please, and let's get on with what all us Americans are here to see—and here to do, for ten bucks prize money.

The first cowboy out of the chute, bareback bronc-riding, gets thrown against the fence, and another gets his leg broken right under the stands. Rodeos are hard on horses, hard on cattle, hard on men. A lousy way to earn ten bucks. Ladies, don't let your sons grow up to be cowboys, as the song says. But the calf-roping is done for the joy of skill, of teamwork, horse and man, and the barrel-riding girls are terrific, whipping around those barrels like the spinning cars on a fairground octopus, and then the quirt flicks and the snorting pony lays out blurry-legged and belly to the ground on the home stretch with the audience yipping and yahooing all the way. By now the lady from Longview, Washington, with the six-pack on the next bench is feeling no pain. A bull is trying to destroy the chutes before the rider even gets onto him. The rodeo is one of the few places where people and animals still fully interact. How vain and gallant horses are, not intelligent, but in their own way wise; how fine the scared, wily vigor of the calves and the power of the big Brahma bulls—the terrific vitality of cattle, which we raise to kill. People who want matadors mincing around can have them, there's enough moments of truth for me in a two-bit rodeo.

Driving back after the show over the viaduct across Bayley Yard, a huge Union Pacific switching center, we see high floodlights far down the line make gold rivers of a hundred intertwining tracks curving off into the glare and dazzling dark. Trains are one of the really good things the Industrial Revolution did—totally practical and totally romantic. But on all those tracks, one train.

Next morning we stop at Ogallala for breakfast at the Pioneer Trails Mall. I like that name. Two eggs up, hashbrowns, and biscuits. The restaurant radio loudspeaker plays full blast over the South Platte River roaring past full of logs and junk and way over the speed limit for rivers.

We leave that river at last near where the Denver road splits off, and come into the low, bare hills across it. As the water dries out of the ground and air, going west, the blur of humidity is gone; colors become clear and pale, distance vivid. Long, light-gold curves of wheat and brown plowed land stripe the hills. At a field's edge the stiff wheat sticks up like a horse's mane cropped short. The wind blows in the tall yellow clover on the roadsides. Sweet air, bright wind. Radio Ogallala says that now is the time to be concerned about the European corn borer.

Between the wheat and corn fields scarped table-lands begin to rise, and dry washes score the pastures. The bones of the land show through, yellowish-white rocks. There's a big stockyard away off the road, the cattle, dark red-brown, crowded together, looking like stacked wood in a lumberyard. Yucca grows wild on the hills here; this is range land. Horses roam and graze far off in the soft-colored distances. We're coming to the Wyoming border, leaving this big, long, wide, bright Nebraska; a day and a half, or forty minutes, or a month in the crossing. From a plane I would remember nothing of Nebraska. From driving I will remember the willows by the river, the sweet wind. Maybe that's what they remembered when they came across afoot and horseback, and camped each night a few miles farther west, by the willows and the cottonwoods down by the Platte.

A CLOSER LOOK AT URSULA K. LE GUIN

1. Considering that Ursula Le Guin is known for writing about a range of subjects in a variety of genres, think about what genres might be most appropriate for addressing different kinds of issues. How does the treatment of the same subject in a different genre affect the meaning of the subject? In an essay, address the relationships between genres and subjects; consider specifically how an essay affects the subject it addresses.
2. In "Prospects for Women in Writing," Le Guin writes that "Many more women buy and read books than men. And in the last fifteen years there has been an increasing sense of strength and mutual validation among women writers and readers, a resistance to the male control over reading, a refusal to join men in sneering at what women want to write and read." Le Guin's statement points out that women and men writers and readers may read and write differently. Are there any qualities of Le Guin's writing that make it uniquely female gendered? Would you describe her writing as "female"?

Write an essay that describes what kinds of characteristics might make a piece of writing particularly male or female.

3. As a class activity, write a short essay that you construct to be delivered first as a talk to the class, then revise the talk into a version of the essay that can be read by an audience. Discuss the different rhetorical choices involved and how they can affect meaning. Consider the rhetorical choices that make spoken essays different from written essays.

Looking from Writer to Writer

1. Like Ursula LeGuin, bell hooks writes about women and writing. Turn to the essays in this collection by hooks that address women and writing—"Women Who Write Too Much" and "Black Women Writing"—and compare the ways that hooks and LeGuin write about women and writing.

2. In her essay "Stamping Out a Dread Scourge," Barbara Ehrenreich writes a satirical essay about breast implants for women. In many ways, Ehrenreich's essay is also a commentary on the relationships between technology and women's bodies. Similarly, Le Guin's "The Carrier Bag Theory of Fiction" also makes some interesting claims regarding the relationships between women's bodies and male technology. Compare these two essays and consider how each writer might respond to the claims of the other. How, for instance, might LeGuin respond to and write about Ehrenreich's position regarding breast implants?

3. Le Guin's essay "The Carrier Bag Theory of Fiction" addresses the importance of storytelling. Barry Lopez's essay "We Are Shaped by the Sound of the Wind, the Slant of Sunlight" also addresses the importance of storytelling; Lopez writes, "We keep each other alive with stories." Read these two essays together and consider their similarities and differences.

Looking Beyond

ESSAYS

Dancing at the Edge of the World: Thoughts on Words, Women, Places. New York: Grove Press, 1989.

Dreams Must Explain Themselves (Critical Essays). New York: ALGOL Press, 1975.

The Language of the Night: Essays on Fantasy and Science Fiction (Critical Essays). New York: Putnam, 1979.

FICTION

The Compass Rose: Short Stories. New York: Harper and Row, 1982.

The Dispossessed: An Ambiguous Utopia. New York: Harper and Row, 1974.

The Left Hand of Darkness. New York: Ace, 1969.

The Lathe of Heaven. New York: Scribner, 1971.

Planet of Exile. New York: Garland Publishing, 1975.

Rocannon's World. New York: Garland Publishing, 1975.

Unlocking the Air and Other Stories. New York: HarperCollins, 1996.

The Wind's Twelve Quarters: Short Stories. New York: Harper and Row, 1975.

A Wizard of Earthsea. 1968. New York: Atheneum-Macmillan International, 1991.

The Word for World Is Forest (Novella). 1972. New York: Ace Books, 1989.

Worlds of Exile and Illusion. New York: Orb, 1996.

POETRY

Going Out With Peacocks and Other Poems. New York: Harper Perennial, 1994.

Hard Words, and Other Poems. New York: Harper and Row, 1981.

Wild Oats and Fireweed. New York: Harper Perennial, 1988.

CHILDREN'S BOOKS

Buffalo Gals, Won't You Come Out Tonight. 1987. Rohnert Park, CA: Pomegranate, 1994.

Catwings. New York: Orchard, 1988.

Catwings Return. New York: Scholastic, 1991.

A Visit from Dr. Katz. New York: Atheneum, 1988.

Barry Lopez

Barry Holstun Lopez was born January 6, 1945, to Adrian Bernard and Mary Holstun Lopez in Port Chester, New York. He earned his AB in 1966 and his MAT in 1968 from Notre Dame University, and attended graduate school at the University of Oregon from 1969 until 1970. In 1970 Barry Lopez became a full-time writer. His career as a writer has earned Lopez a host of awards, including in 1979 both the John Burroughs Medal for distinguished natural history writing and the Christopher Medal for humanitarian writing. In 1980 he was nominated for an American Book Award for *Of Wolves and Men,* and in 1981 he received the National Book Award for nonfiction. He has earned many other awards for his writing.

Lopez is perhaps best known as a "nature writer" and his writing often addresses the natural histories and environmental concerns of places. As he explains, "this area of writing will not only one day produce a major and lasting body of American literature, but . . . it might also provide the foundation for a reorganization of American political thought." His more recent work takes on a philosophical edge, and his writing now is known to use environmentalism and natural history as a way of writing about larger moral and ethical issues. Lopez's attention to natural places and environmental concerns can be seen clearly through the titles of many of his best-known books: *Desert Notes: Reflections in the Eye of a Raven* (1976), *Giving Birth to Thunder, Sleeping with His Daughter: Coyote Builds North America* (1978), *Of Wolves and Men* (1978), *River Notes: The Dance of Herons* (1979), *Winter Count* (1981), *Arctic Dreams: Imagination and Desire in a Northern Landscape* (1986), and *Crossing Open Ground* (1988). These titles also suggest that Lopez has a connection with the West Coast and his writing reflects that connection. Lopez's family moved to Southern California soon after he was born where they lived for 10 years before returning to New York. These 10 years had a great impact on Lopez, so when he was 23 he returned to the West Coast to attend graduate school. However, Lopez decided that he preferred the life of a writer to that of a student, so in 1970 he and his wife Sandra Landers moved to western Oregon, settled on the McKenzie River, and Lopez began a career as a writer.

Much of Lopez's writing questions the role of humans in nature. For instance, *Arctic Dreams* is noted as an important discussion of how humans have interacted with nature. In a *Los Angeles Times* book review, Richard Eder writes, "It is a lyrical geography and natural history, an account of Eskimo life, and a history of northern exploration." Eder goes on to say that "mainly it is a . . . reflection about the meaning of mankind's encounter with the planet." He continues, "Its question, starting as ecology and working into metaphysics, is whether civilization can find a way of adapting itself to the natural world, before its predilection for adapting the natural world to itself destroys self and world both." This theme can be seen in a good deal of Lopez's work.

Lopez also identifies a "stillness" in his own writing. In an interview in *Contemporary Writers,* Lopez acknowledges, "I'm often trying to act as intermediary in my work between particular situations and the reader. I find clarity in stillness—which is probably why I'm more attracted to deserts and places like the Arctic than to the woods where there's more visual chaos." As you read Lopez's essays, consider this statement and look for the ways that Lopez negotiates between the situations he describes and his readers. That is, think about how Lopez brings his readers in contact with particular situations about which he is concerned. At the same time, consider the stillness of his writing, of the places about which he writes. For instance, in the essay "The Stone Horse" (perhaps Lopez's most famous essay) consider the stillness not only of the artifact Lopez describes, but the ways in which his writing is itself still.

Also, as you read the four essays by Lopez, pay attention to his concepts of place, to how he describes and often protects places. In "The Stone Horse" notice his ability to describe in such detail the place of the stone horse without ever identifying where that place is. Consider also how Lopez protects the stone horse by not revealing its location and think about what effect revealing the place might have on the place.

Finally, as you read Lopez's essays, think about how his concern and care for places and animals is conveyed to you as reader without Lopez ever saying directly to you: "You must care about this." Think about the strategies Lopez uses to connect with his readers without beating them about the head with morals and ethics.

Lopez on Writing

At First Glance

Barry Lopez's essay "We Are Shaped by the Sound of Wind, the Slant of Sunlight" first appeared in Portland *magazine and then in* High Country News: A Paper for People Who Care about the West *(1998). In this essay Lopez writes about the tradition of nature writing and makes some important and emphatic claims about its role. He writes, "The real topic of nature writing, I think, is not nature, but the evolving structure of communities from which nature has been removed." In other words, though Lopez is writing about nature writing, he is also addressing larger issues of ethics and morality. As you read this essay, consider how Lopez navigates between large questions of human ethics toward nature and the idea of nature writing.*

We Are Shaped by the Sound of the Wind, the Slant of Sunlight

In the United States in recent years, a kind of writing variously called "nature writing" or "landscape writing" has begun to receive critical attention, leading some to assume that this is a relatively new kind of work.

In fact, writing that takes into account the impact nature and place have on culture is one of the oldest—and perhaps most singular—threads in American writing.

Melville in *Moby-Dick,* Thoreau, of course, and novelists such as Willa Cather, John Steinbeck and William Faulkner come quickly to mind here, and more recently Peter Matthiessen, Wendell Berry, Wallace Stegner, and the poets W. S. Merwin, Amy Clampitt and Gary Snyder.

If there is anything different in this area of North American writing—and I believe there is—it is the hopeful tone it frequently strikes in an era of cynical detachment, and its explicitly dubious view of technological progress, even of capitalism.

The real topic of nature writing, I think, is not nature but the evolving structure of communities from which nature has been removed, often as a consequence of modern economic development. It is writing concerned, further, with the biological and spiritual fate of those communities. It also assumes that the fate of humanity and nature are inseparable. Nature writing in the United States merges here, I believe, with other sorts of post-colonial writing, particularly in Commonwealth countries.

In numerous essays it addresses the problem of spiritual collapse in the West and, like those literatures, it is in search of a modern human identity that lies beyond nationalism and material wealth.

This is a huge—not to say unwieldy—topic, and different writers approach it in vastly different ways. The classic struggle of writers to separate truth from illusion, to distinguish between roads to heaven and detours to hell, knows only continuance, not ending or solution.

But I sense collectively now in writing in America the emergence of a concern for the world outside the self. It is as if someone had opened the door to a stuffy and too-much-studied room and shown us a great horizon where once there had been only walls.

I want to concentrate on a single aspect of this phenomenon—geography—but in doing so I hope to hew to a larger line of truth. I want to talk about geography as a shaping force, not a subject.

Another way critics have of describing nature writing is to call it "the literature of place." A specific and particular setting for human experience and endeavor is, indeed, central to the work of many nature writers. I would say, further, that it is also critical to the development of a sense of morality and human identity.

No writer may presume to speak for his colleagues in defining these matters, but as someone who is identified with "nature writing" I'd like to try to explain the importance of place to me. I am someone who returns again and again to geography, as the writers of another generation once returned repeatedly to Freud and psychoanalysis.

I believe that a human imagination is shaped by the architecture it encounters at an early age. The visual landscape, of course, or the depth, elevation, and hues of a cityscape play a part here, as does the way sunlight everywhere etches lines to accentuate forms. But the way we imagine is also affected by streams of scent flowing faint or sharp in the larger ocean of air; by what the North American composer John Luther Adams calls the sonic landscape; and, say, by an awareness of how temperature and humidity rise and fall in a place over a year.

A SLOW, SILENT DETONATION

My imagination was shaped by the exotic nature of water in a dry Southern California valley; by the sound of wind in the crowns of eucalyptus trees; by the tactile sensation of sheened earth, turned in furrows by a gang plow; by banks of saffron, mahogany and scarlet cloud piled above a field of alfalfa at dusk; by encountering the musk from orange blossoms at the edge of an orchard; by the aftermath of a Pacific storm crashing a hot, flat beach.

Added to the nudge of these sensations were an awareness of the height and breadth of the sky, and of the geometry and force of the wind. Both perceptions grew directly out of my efforts to raise pigeons and from the awe I felt before them as they maneuvered in the air. They gave me permanently a sense of the vertical component of life.

I became intimate with the elements of that particular universe. They fashioned me. I return to them regularly in essays and stories in order to clarify or explain abstractions or to strike contrasts. I find the myriad relationships in that universe comforting. They form a "coherence" of which I once was a part.

If I were to try to explain the process of becoming a writer, I could begin by saying that the comforting intimacy I knew in that California valley erected in me a kind of story I wanted to tell, a pattern I wanted to evoke in countless ways. And I would add to this two things that were profoundly magical to me as a boy: animals and language.

It's relatively easy to say why animals might seem magical. Spiders and birds are bound differently than we are by gravity. Many wild creatures travel unerringly through the dark. And animals regularly respond to what we, even at our most attentive, cannot discern.

It is harder to say why language seemed magical, but I can be precise about this. The first book I read was *The Adventures of Tom Sawyer.* I still have the book. Underlined in it in pen are the first words I could recognize: the, a, stop, to go, to see. I pick up the book today and recall the expansion of my first feelings, a slow, silent detonation: Words I heard people speak I could now perceive as marks on a page. I myself was learning to make these same marks on ruled paper. It seemed as glorious and mysterious as a swift flock of tumbler pigeons exploiting the invisible wind.

I can understand my life as prefigured in those two kinds of magic, the uncanny lives of creatures different from me (and, later of cultures different from my own); and the twinned desires—to go, to see. I became a writer who travels and one who focuses, to be succinct, mostly on what logical positivists sweep aside.

A DEFENSE AGAINST LONELINESS

My travel is often to remote places—Antarctica, the Tanami Desert in central Australia, northern Kenya. In these places I depend on my own wits and resources, but heavily and more often on the knowledge of interpreters—archaeologists, field scientists, anthropologists.

Eminent among such helpers are indigenous people; and I can quickly give you three reasons for my dependence on their insights. As a rule, indigenous people pay much closer attention to nuance in the physical world. They see more. And from only a handful of evidence, thoroughly observed, they can deduce more.

Second, their history in a place, a combination of tribal and personal history, is typically deep. This history creates a temporal dimension in what is otherwise only a spatial landscape.

Third, indigenous people tend to occupy the same moral universe as the land they sense. Their bonds with the earth are as much moral as biological.

Over time I have come to think of these three qualities—paying intimate attention; a storied relationship to a place rather than a solely sensory awareness of it; and living in some sort of ethical unity with a place—as a fundamental human defense against loneliness.

If you're intimate with a place, a place with whose history you're familiar, and you establish an ethical conversation with it, the implication that follows is this: The place knows you're there. It feels you. You will not be forgotten, cut off; abandoned.

As a writer I want to ask on behalf of the reader: How can a person obtain this? How can you occupy a place and also have it occupy you? How can you find such a reciprocity?

The key, I think, is to become vulnerable to a place. If you open yourself up, you can build intimacy. Out of such intimacy may come a sense of belonging, a sense of not being isolated in the universe.

My question—how to secure this—is not meant to be idle. How does one actually enter a local geography? (Many of us daydream, I think, about re-entering childhood landscapes that might dispel a current anxiety. We often court such feelings for a few moments in a park or sometimes during an afternoon in the woods.) To respond explicitly and practicably, my first suggestion would be to be silent. Put aside the bird book, the analytic state of mind, any compulsion to identify, and sit still.

Concentrate instead on feeling a place, on deliberately using the sense of proprioception. Where in this volume of space are you situated? The space behind you is as important as what you see before you. What lies beneath you is as relevant as what stands on the far horizon. Actively use your ears to imagine the acoustical hemisphere you occupy. How does birdsong ramify here? Through what kind of air is it moving? Concentrate on smells in the belief you *can* smell water and stone. Use your hands to get the heft and texture of a place—the tensile strength in a willow branch, the moisture in a pinch of soil, the different nap of leaves.

Open a vertical line to the place by joining the color and form of the sky to what you see out across the ground. Look away from what you want to scrutinize in order to gain a sense of its scale and proportion. Be wary of any obvious explanation for the existence of color, a movement. Cultivate a sense of complexity, the sense that another landscape exists beyond the one you can subject to analysis.

The purpose of such attentiveness is to gain intimacy, to rid yourself of assumption. It should be like a conversation with someone you're attracted to, a person you don't want to send away by having made too much of yourself. Such conversations, of course, can take place simultaneously on several levels. And they may easily be driven by more than simple curiosity. The compelling desire, as in human conversation, might be to institute a sustaining or informing relationship.

A succinct way to describe the frame of mind one should bring to a landscape is to say it rests on the distinction between imposing and proposing one's views. With a sincere proposal you hope to achieve an intimate, reciprocal relationship that will feed you in some way. To impose your views from the start is to truncate such a possibility, to preclude understanding.

Many of us, I think, long to become the companion of a place, not its authority, not its owner. And this brings me to a final point. I think many wonder, as I do, why over the last few decades people in Western countries have become so anxious about the fate of undeveloped land, and so concerned about losing the intelligence of people who've kept up intimate relations with those places.

I don't know where the thinking of others has led them, but I believe curiosity about good relations with a particular stretch of land now is directly related to speculation that it may be more important to human survival to be in love than to be in a position of power. It may be more important now to enter into an ethical and reciprocal relationship with everything around us than to continue to work toward the sort of control of the physical world that, until recently, we aspired to.

The simple issue of our biological plausibility, our chance for biological survival, has become so basic a question, that finding a way out of the predicament—if one is to be had—is imperative. It calls on our collective imaginations with an urgency we've never known before. We are in need not just of another kind of logic, another way of knowing. We need a radically different philosophical sensibility.

When I was a boy, running through orange groves in Southern California, watching wind swirl in a grove of blue gum, and swimming ecstatically in the foam of Pacific breakers, I had no such imperative thoughts. I was content to watch a brace of pigeons fly across an azure sky, rotating on an axis that to this day I don't think I could draw.

My comfort, my sense of inclusion in the small universe I inhabited, came from an appreciation of, a participation in, all that I saw, smelled, tasted, and heard. That sense of inclusion not only assuaged my sense of loneliness as a child, it confirmed my imagination. And it is that single thing, the power of the human imagination to extrapolate from an odd handful of things—faint movement in a copse of trees, a wing-beat, the damp cold of field stones at night—the human ability to make from all this a pattern, to compose a story out of it, that fixed in me a sense of hope.

We keep each other alive with stories.

We need to share these patterns, as much as we need to share food. We also require good companions to ensure our spiritual, mental and physical health. Remarkably, one of the extraordinary things about the land is that it knows both these things. It compels language from some of us—writers—so that as a community we may converse about this or that place, and so that we can speak of our need to be in good relations with the world.

To include nature in our stories is to return to an older form of human awareness in which nature is not scenery, not a warehouse of natural resources, not real estate, not a possession, but a continuation of community.

Double Take

1. What, if anything, does Lopez gain by listing at the beginning of the essay the names of the authors he considers important nature writers? What is he trying to achieve? What is its effect?
2. About midway through this essay, Lopez asks a series of questions regarding the interaction of humans with nature. He then offers a few suggestions on how to enhance that interaction. For instance, he writes: "Open a vertical line to the place by joining the color and form of the sky to what you see out across the ground." In this brief set of directions—part of a series of suggestions directed at his readers—how does Lopez bring his readers into his writing? That is, how does Lopez speak to his audience in this portion of the essay?

3. Toward the end of the essay, Lopez includes a short paragraph that reads simply, "We keep each other alive with stories." Why might Lopez have decided to include this statement as a paragraph unto itself? That is, what does the essay gain from the emphasis on this statement by setting it apart from other paragraphs?

At First Glance

"The Stone Horse" is one of Barry Lopez's best-known essays and is published in his collection Crossing Open Ground *(1988). It chronicles his finding of an ancient carving of a stone horse in Southern California. Lopez uses the opportunity to describe not only the horse itself, but a wide range of histories that played a role in the horse's existence and in the place where he finds the horse. As you read "The Stone Horse," think about the ways that Lopez details not only the visual description of the horse, but all of the information he provides regarding the horse's possible history. Consider what these details offer the reader beyond mere description of the horse.*

The Stone Horse

The deserts of southern California, the high, relatively cooler and wetter Mojave and the hotter, dryer Sonoran to the south of it, carry the signatures of many cultures. Prehistoric rock drawings in the Mojave's Coso Range, probably the greatest concentration of petroglyphs in North America, are at least three thousand years old. Big game hunting cultures that flourished six or seven thousand years before that are known from broken spear tips, choppers, and burins left scattered along the shores of great Pleistocene lakes, long since evaporated. Weapons and tools discovered at China Lake may be thirty thousand years old; and worked stone from a quarry in the Calico Mountains is, some argue, evidence that human beings were here more than two hundred thousand years ago.

Because of the long-term stability of such arid environments, much of this prehistoric stone evidence still lies exposed on the ground, accessible to anyone who passes by—the studious, the acquisitive, the indifferent, the merely curious. Archaeologists do not agree on the sequence of cultural history beyond about twelve thousand years ago, but it is clear that these broken bits of chalcedony, chert, and obsidian, like the animal drawings and geometric designs etched on walls of basalt throughout the desert, anchor the earliest threads of human history, the first record of human endeavor here.

Western man did not enter the California desert until the end of the eighteenth century, 250 years after Coronado brought his soldiers into the Zuni pueblos in a bewildered search for the cities of Cibola. The earliest appraisals of the land were cursory, hurried. People traveled *through* it, en route to Santa Fe or the California coastal settlements. Only miners tarried. In 1823 what had been Spain's became Mexico's and in 1848 what had been Mexico's became America's; but the bare, jagged mountains and dry lake beds, the vast and uniform plains of creosote bush and yucca plants, remained as obscure as the northern Sudan until the end of the nineteenth century.

Before 1940 the tangible evidence of twentieth-century man's passage here consisted of very little—the hard tracery of travel corridors; the widely scattered, relatively insignificant evidence of mining operations; and the fair expanse of irrigated fields at the desert's periphery. In the space of a hundred years or so the wagon roads were paved, railroads were laid down, and canals and high-tension lines were built to bring water and electricity across the desert to Los Angeles from the Colorado River. The dark mouths of gold, talc, and tin mines yawned from the bony flanks of desert ranges. Dust-encrusted chemical plants stood at work on the lonely edges of dry lake beds. And crops of grapes, lettuce, dates, alfalfa, and cotton covered the Coachella and Imperial valleys, north and south of the Salton Sea, and the Palo Verde Valley along the Colorado.

These developments proceeded with little or no awareness of earlier human occupations by cultures that preceded those of the historic Indians—the Mohave, the Chemehuevi, the Quechan. (Extensive irrigation began to actually change the climate of the Sonoran Desert, and human settlements, the railroads, and farming introduced many new, successful plants and animals into the region.)

During World War II, the American military moved into the desert in great force, to train troops and to test equipment. They found the clear weather conducive to year-round flying, the dry air, and isolation very attractive. After the war, a complex of training grounds, storage facilities, and gunnery and test ranges was permanently settled on more than three million acres of military reservations. Few perceived the extent or significance of the destruction of aboriginal sites that took place during tank maneuvers and bombing runs or in the laying out of highways, railroads, mining districts, and irrigated fields. The few who intuited that something like an American Dordogne Valley lay exposed here were (only) amateur archaeologists; even they reasoned that the desert was too vast for any of this to matter.

After World War II, people began moving out of the crowded Los Angeles basin into homes in Lucerne, Apple, and Antelope valleys in the western Mojave. They emigrated as well to a stretch of resort land at the foot of the San Jacinto Mountains that included Palm Springs, and farther out to old railroad and military towns like Twentynine Palms and Barstow. People also began exploring the desert, at first in military-surplus jeeps and then with a variety of all-terrain and off-road vehicles that became available in the 1960s. By the mid-1970s, the number of people using such vehicles for desert recreation had increased exponentially. Most came and went in innocent curiosity; the few who didn't wreaked a havoc all out of proportion to their numbers. The disturbance of previously isolated archaeological sites increased by an order of magnitude. Many sites were vandalized before archaeologists, themselves late to the desert, had any firm grasp of the bounds of human history in the desert. It was as though in the same moment an Aztec library had been discovered intact various lacunae had begun to appear.

The vandalism was of three sorts: the general disturbance usually caused by souvenir hunters and by the curious and the oblivious; the wholesale stripping of a place by professional thieves for black-market sale and trade; and outright destruction, in which vehicles were actually used to ram and trench an area. By 1980, the Bureau of Land Management estimated that probably thirty-five percent of the archaeological sites in the desert had been vandalized. The destruction at some places by rifles and shotguns, or by power winches mounted on vehicles, was, if one cared for history, demoralizing to behold.

In spite of public education, land closures, and stricter law enforcement in recent years, the BLM estimates that, annually, about one percent of the archaeological record in the desert continues to be destroyed or stolen.

2

A BLM archaeologist told me, with understandable reluctance, where to find the intaglio. I spread my Automobile Club of Southern California map of Imperial County out on his desk, and he traced the route with a pink felt-tip pen. The line crossed Interstate 8 and then turned west along the Mexican border.

"You can't drive any farther than about here," he said, marking a small *x*. "There's boulders in the wash. You walk up past them."

On a separate piece of paper he drew a route in a smaller scale that would take me up the arroyo to a certain point where I was to cross back east, to another arroyo. At its head, on higher ground just to the north, I would find the horse.

"It's tough to spot unless you know it's there. Once you pick it up . . ." He shook his head slowly, in a gesture of wonder at its existence.

I waited until I held his eye. I assured him I would not tell anyone else how to get there. He looked at me with stoical despair, like a man who had been robbed twice, whose belief in human beings was offered without conviction.

I did not go until the following day because I wanted to see it at dawn. I ate breakfast at 4 A.M. in El Centro and then drove south. The route was easy to follow, though the last section of road proved difficult, broken and drifted over with sand in some spots. I came to the barricade of boulders and parked. It was light enough by then to find my way over the ground with little trouble. The contours of the landscape were stark, without any masking vegetation. I worried only about rattlesnakes.

I traversed the stone plain as directed, but, in spite of the frankness of the land, I came on the horse unawares. In the first moment of recognition I was without feeling. I recalled later being startled, and that I held my breath. It was laid out on the ground with its head to the east, three times life size. As I took in its outline I felt a growing concentration of all my senses, as though my attentiveness to the pale rose color of the morning sky and other peripheral images had now ceased to be important. I was aware that I was straining for sound in the windless air and I felt the uneven pressure of the earth hard against my feet. The horse, outlined in a standing profile on the dark ground, was as vivid before me as a bed of tulips.

I've come upon animals suddenly before, and felt a similar tension, a precipitate heightening of the senses. And I have felt the inexplicable but sharply boosted intensity of a wild moment in the bush, where it is not until some minutes later that you discover the source of electricity—the warm remains of a grizzly bear kill, or the still moist tracks of a wolverine.

But this was slightly different. I felt I had stepped into an unoccupied corridor. I had no familiar sense of history, the temporal structure in which to think: This horse was made by Quechan people three hundred years ago. I felt instead a head-long rush of images: people hunting wild horses with spears on the Pleistocene veld of southern California; Cortés riding across the causeway into Montezuma's Tenochtitlán; a short-legged Comanche, astride his horse like some sort of ferret, slashing through cavalry lines of young men who rode like farmers. A hoof explod-ing past my face one morning in a corral in Wyoming. These images had the weight and silence of stone.

When I released my breath, the images softened. My initial feeling, of facing a wild animal in a remote region, was replaced with a calm sense of antiquity. It was then that I became conscious, like an ordinary tourist, of what was before me, and thought: This horse was probably laid out by Quechan people. But when, I won-dered? The first horses they saw, I knew, might have been those that came north from Mexico in 1692 with Father Eusebio Kino. But Cocopa people, I recalled, also came this far north on occasion, to fight with their neighbors, the Quechan. And *they* could have seen horses with Melchior Díaz, at the mouth of the Colorado River in the fall of 1540. So, it could be four hundred years old. (No one in fact knows.)

I still had not moved. I took my eyes off the horse for a moment to look south over the desert plain into Mexico, to look east past its head at the brightening sun-rise, to situate myself. Then, finally, I brought my trailing foot slowly forward and stood erect. Sunlight was running like a thin sheet of water over the stony ground and it threw the horse into relief. It looked as though no hand had ever disturbed the stones that gave it its form.

The horse had been brought to life on ground called desert pavement, a tight, flat matrix of small cobbles blasted smooth by sand-laden winds. The uniform, monochromatic blackness of the stones, a patina of iron and magnesium oxides called desert varnish, is caused by long-term exposure to the sun. To make this type of low-relief ground glyph, or intaglio, the artist either selectively turns individual stones over to their lighter side or removes areas of stone to expose the lighter soil underneath, creating a negative image. This horse, about eighteen feet from brow to rump and eight feet from withers to hoof, had been made in the latter way, and its outline was bermed at certain points with low ridges of stone a few inches high to enhance its three-dimensional qualities. (The left side of the horse was in full pro-file; each leg was extended at 90 degrees to the body and fully visible, as though seen in three-quarter profile.)

I was not eager to move. The moment I did I would be back in the flow of time, the horse no longer quivering in the same way before me. I did not want to feel again the sequence of quotidian events—to be drawn off into deliberation and analysis. A human being, a four-footed animal, the open land. That was all that was present—and a "thoughtless" understanding of the very old desires bearing on this particular animal: to hunt it, to render it, to fathom it, to subjugate it, to honor it, to take it as a companion.

What finally made me move was the light. The sun now filled the shallow basin of the horse's body. The weighted line of the stone berm created the illusion of a mane and the distinctive roundness of an equine belly. The change in definition impelled me. I moved to the left, circling past its rump, to see how the light might flesh the horse out from various points of view. I circled it completely before squatting on my haunches. Ten or fifteen minutes later I chose another view. The third time I moved, to a point near the rear hooves, I spotted a stone tool at my feet. I stared at it a long while, more in awe than disbelief, before reaching out to pick it up. I turned it over in my left palm and took it between my fingers to feel its cutting edge. It is always difficult, especially with something so portable, to rechannel the desire to steal.

I spent several hours with the horse. As I changed positions and as the angle of the light continued to change I noticed a number of things. The angle at which the pastern carried the hoof away from the ankle was perfect. Also, stones had been placed within the image to suggest, at precisely the right spot, the left shoulder above the foreleg. The line that joined thigh and hock was similarly accurate. The muzzle alone seemed distorted—but perhaps these stones had been moved by a later hand. It was an admirably accurate representation, but not what a breeder would call perfect conformation. There was the suggestion of a bowed neck and an undershot jaw, and the tail, as full as a winter coyote's, did not appear to be precisely to scale.

The more I thought about it, the more I felt I was looking at an individual horse, a unique combination of generic and specific detail. It was easy to imagine one of Kino's horses as a model, or a horse that ran off from one of Coronado's columns. What kind of horses would these have been, I wondered? In the sixteenth century the most sought-after horses in Europe were Spanish, the offspring of Arabian stock and Barbary horses that the Moors brought to Iberia and bred to the older, eastern European strains brought in by the Romans. The model for this horse, I speculated, could easily have been a palomino, or a descendant of horses trained for lion-hunting in North Africa.

A few generations ago, cowboys, cavalry quartermasters, and draymen would have taken this horse before me under consideration and not let up their scrutiny until they had its heritage fixed to their satisfaction. Today, the distinction between draft and harness horses is arcane knowledge, and no image may come to mind for a blue roan or a claybank horse. The loss of such refinement in everyday conversation leaves me unsettled. People praise the Eskimo's ability to distinguish among forty types of snow but forget the skill of others who routinely differentiate between overo and tobiano pintos. Such distinctions are made for the same reason. You have to do it to be able to talk clearly about the world.

For parts of two years I worked as a horse wrangler and packer in Wyoming. It is dim knowledge now; I would have to think to remember if a buckskin was a kind of dun horse. And I couldn't throw a double-diamond hitch over a set of panniers—the packer's basic tie-down—without guidance. As I squatted there in the desert, however, these more personal memories seemed tenuous in comparison with the sweep of this animal in human time. My memories had no depth. I thought of the Hittite cavalry riding against the Syrians 3,500 years ago. And the first of the Chinese emperors, Ch'in Shih Huang, buried in Shensi Province in 210 B.C. with thousands of life-size horses and soldiers, a terra-cotta guardian army. What could I know of what was in the mind of whoever made this horse? Was there some racial memory of it as an animal that had once fed the artist's ancestors and then disappeared from North America? And then returned in this strange alliance with another race of men?

Certainly, whoever it was, the artist had observed the animal very closely. Certainly the animal's speed had impressed him. Among the first things the Quechan would have learned from an encounter with Kino's horses was that their own long-distance runners—men who could run down mule deer—were no match for this animal.

From where I squatted I could look far out over the Mexican plain. Juan Bautista de Anza passed this way in 1774, extending El Camino Real into Alta California from Sinaloa. He was followed by others, all of them astride the magical horse; *gente de razón,* the people of reason, coming into the country of *los primitivos.* The horse, like the stone animals of Egypt, urged these memories upon me. And as I drew them up from some forgotten corner of my mind—huge horses carved in the white chalk downs of southern England by an Iron Age people; Spanish horses rearing and wheeling in fear before alligators in Florida—the images seemed tethered before me. With this sense of proportion, a memory of my own—the morning I almost lost my face to a horse's hoof—now had somewhere to fit.

I rose up and began to walk slowly around the horse again. I had taken the first long measure of it and was looking now for a way to depart, a new angle of light, a fading of the image itself before the rising sun, that would break its hold on me. As I circled, feeling both heady and serene at the encounter, I realized again how strangely vivid it was. It had been created on a barren bajada between two arroyos, as nondescript a place as one could imagine. The only plant life here was a few wands of ocotillo cactus. The ground beneath my shoes was so hard it wouldn't take the print of a heavy animal even after a rain. The only sounds I had heard here were the voices of quail.

The archaeologist had been correct. For all its forcefulness, the horse is inconspicuous. If you don't care to see it you can walk right past it. That pleases him, I think. Unmarked on this bleak shoulder of the plain, the site signals to no one; so he wants no protective fences here, no informative plaque, to act as beacons. He would rather take a chance that no motorcyclist, no aimless wanderer with a flair for violence and a depth of ignorance, will ever find his way here.

The archaeologist had given me something before I left his office that now seemed peculiar—an aerial photograph of the horse. It is widely believed that an aerial view of an intaglio provides a fair and accurate description. It does not. In the photograph the horse looks somewhat crudely constructed; from the ground it appears far more deftly rendered. The photograph is of a single moment, and in that split second the horse seems vaguely impotent. I watched light pool in the intaglio at dawn; I imagine you could watch it withdraw at dusk and sense the same animation I did. In those prolonged moments its shape and so, too, its general character changed—noticeably. The living quality of the image, its immediacy to the eye, was brought out by the light-in-time, not, at least here, in the camera's frozen instant.

Intaglios, I thought, were never meant to be seen by gods in the sky above. They were meant to be seen by people on the ground, over a long period of shifting light.

This could even be true of the huge figures on the Plain of Nazca in Peru, where people could walk for the length of a day beside them. It is our own impatience that leads us to think otherwise.

This process of abstraction, almost unintentional, drew me gradually away from the horse. I came to a position of attention at the edge of the sphere of its influence. With a slight bow I paid my respects to the horse, its maker, and the history of us all, and departed.

3

A short distance away I stopped the car in the middle of the road to make a few notes. I had not been able to write down what I was thinking when I was with the horse. It would have seemed disrespectful, and it would have required another kind of attention. So now I patiently drained my memory of the details it had fastened itself upon. The road I'd stopped on was adjacent to the All American Canal, the major source of water for the Imperial and Coachella valleys. The water flowed west placidly. A disjointed flock of coots, small, dark birds with white bills, was paddling against the current, foraging in the rushes.

I was peripherally aware of the birds as I wrote, the only movement in the desert; and of a series of sounds from a village a half-mile away. The first sounds from this collection of ramshackle houses in a grove of cottonwoods were the distracted dawn voices of dogs. I heard them intermingled with the cries of a rooster. Later, the high-pitched voices of children calling out to each other came disembodied through the dry desert air. Now, a little after seven, I could hear someone practicing on the trumpet, the same rough phrases played over and over. I suddenly remembered how as children we had tried to get the rhythm of a galloping horse with hands against our thighs, or by fluttering our tongues against the roofs of our mouths.

After the trumpet, the impatient calls of adults, summoning children. Sunday morning. Wood smoke hung like a lens in the trees. The first car starts—a cold, eight-cylinder engine, of Chrysler extraction perhaps, goosed to life, then throttled back to murmur through dual mufflers, the obbligato music of a shade-tree mechanic. The rote bark of mongrel dogs at dawn, the jagged outcries of men and women, an engine coming to life. Like a thousand villages from West Virginia to Guadalajara.

I finished my notes—where was I going to find a description of the horses that came north with the conquistadors? Did their manes come forward prominently over the brow, like this one's, like the forelocks of Blackfeet and Assiniboine men in nineteenth-century paintings? I set the notes on the seat beside me.

The road followed the canal for a while and then arced north, toward Interstate 8. It was slow driving and I fell to thinking how the desert had changed since Anza had come through. New plants and animals—the MacDougall cottonwood, the English house sparrow, the chukar from India—have about them now the air of the native-born. Of the native species, some—no one knows how many—are extinct. The populations of many others, especially the animals, have been sharply reduced. The idea of a desert impoverished by agricultural poisons and varmint hunters, by off-road vehicles and military operations, did not seem as disturbing to me, however, as this other horror, now that I had been those hours with the horse. The vandals, the few who crowbar rock art off the desert's walls, who dig up graves, who punish the ground that holds intaglios, are people who devour history. Their self-centered scorn, their disrespect for ideas and images beyond their ken, create the awful atmosphere of loose ends in which totalitarianism thrives, in which the past is merely curious or wrong.

I thought about the horse sitting out there on the unprotected plain. I enumerated its qualities in my mind until a sense of its vulnerability receded and it became an anchor for something else. I remembered that history, a history like this one, which ran deeper than Mexico, deeper than the Spanish, was a kind of medicine. It permitted the great breadth of human expression to reverberate, and it did not urge you to locate its apotheosis in the present.

Each of us, individuals and civilizations, has been held upside down like Achilles in the River Styx. The artist mixing his colors in the dim light of Altamira; an Egyptian ruler lying still now, wrapped in his byssus, stored against time in a pyramid; the faded Dorset culture of the Arctic; the Hmong and Samburu and Walbiri of historic time; the modern nations. This great, imperfect stretch of human expression is the clarification and encouragement, the urging and the reminder, we call history. And it is inscribed everywhere in the face of the land, from the mountain passes of the Himalayas to a nameless bajada in the California desert.

Small birds rose up in the road ahead, startled, and flew off. I prayed no infidel would ever find that horse.

Double Take

1. "The Stone Horse" is divided into three sections. The first and third sections are shorter and serve as introduction and conclusion to the essay. Yet, nowhere in the first section does Lopez mention anything about the stone horse. Considering what you know and assume about introductions, is this an effective introduction? Why or why not? What do you imagine Lopez is trying to accomplish in this introduction?

2. Think about the vocabulary Lopez chooses to describe such an ancient relic and his feelings when encountering it. Whom do you suppose he is writing to? That is, what assumptions can we make about the audience that Lopez is addressing? What do sentences such as "I did not want to feel again the sequence of quotidian events—to be drawn off into deliberation and analysis" reveal about Lopez's intended audience?

3. This essay is filled with descriptions of various historical events that Lopez recalls after discovering and being in awe of the stone horse. Consider why Lopez might describe the stone horse in conjunction with so many historical references. What effect is gained? Could he convey the historical significance of the horse, or even its beauty, with other kinds of references besides the historical? How else might Lopez have presented the stone horse in an essay?

At First Glance

Barry Lopez's "A Passage of the Hands" was first published in the December 1996/January 1997 issue of Men's Journal. *Before you read the essay, think about what Lopez could have assumed about his audience before and as he wrote, and how those assumptions might have informed his writing choices. Then, as you read the essay, try to identify some of the choices in subject matter, style, perspective, and so on that strike you as appropriate for that audience. In addition, consider Lopez's purpose in writing the essay and why he would have wanted to publish it in* Men's Journal. *Like many of Lopez's essays, "A Passage of the Hands" links together a series of events and memories. As you move through these memories as readers, examine how Lopez links them together through a series of transitions and how you might be able to use similar transitions in your own writing.*

A Passage of the Hands

My hands were born breech in the winter of 1945, two hours before sunrise. Sitting with them today, two thousand miles and more from that spot, turning each one slowly in bright sunshine, watching the incisive light raise short, pale lines from old cuts, and seeing the odd cant of the left ring finger, I know they have a history, though I cannot remember where it starts. As they began, they gripped whatever might hold me upright, surely caressed and kneaded my mother's breasts, yanked at the restrictions of pajamas. And then they learned to work buttons, to tie shoelaces and lift the milk glass, to work together.

The pressure and friction of a pencil as I labored down the spelling of words right-handed raised the oldest permanent mark, a callus on the third joint of the middle finger. I remember no trying accident to either hand in these early years, though there must have been glass cuts, thorn punctures, spider bites, nails torn to the cuticle, scrapes from bicycle falls, pin blisters from kitchen grease, splinters, nails blackened from door pinches, pain lingering from having all four fingers forced backward at once, and the first true weariness, coming from work with lumber and stones, with tools made for larger hands.

It is from these first years, five and six and seven, that I am able to remember so well, or perhaps the hands themselves remember, a great range of texture—the subtle corrugation of cardboard boxes, the slickness of the oilcloth on the kitchen table, the shuddering bend of a horse's short-haired belly, the even give in warm wax, the raised oak grain in my school-desk top, the fuzziness of dead bumble-bees, the coarseness of sheaves immediate to the polished silk of unhusked corn, the burnish of rake handles and bucket bails, the rigidness of the bony crest rising beneath the skin of a dog's head, the tackiness of flypaper, the sharpness of saws and ice picks.

It is impossible to determine where in any such specific memory, of course, texture gives way to heft, to shape, to temperature. The coolness of a camellia petal seems inseparable from that texture, warmth from the velvet rub of a horse's nose, heft from a brick's dry burr. And what can be said, as the hand recalls the earliest touch and exploration, of how texture changes with depth? Not alone the press of the palm on a dog's head or fingers boring to the roots of wool on a sheep's flank, but of, say, what happens with an orange: the hands work in concert to disassemble the fruit, running a thumb over the beaded surface of the skin, plying the soft white flay of the interior, the string net of fiber clinging to the translucent skin cases, dividing the yielding grain of the flesh beneath, with its hard, wrinkled seeds. And, further, how is one to separate these textures from a memory of the burst of fragrance as the skin is torn, or from the sound of the sections being parted—to say nothing of the taste, juice dripping from the chin, or the urge to devour, then, even the astringent skin, all initiated by the curiosity of the hands?

Looking back, it's easy to see that the education of the hands (and so the person) begins like a language: a gathering of simple words, the assembly of simple sentences, all this leading eventually to the forging of instructive metaphors. Afterward nothing can truly be separated, to stand alone in the hands' tactile memory. Taking the lay of the dog's fur, the slow petting of the loved dog is the increasingly complicated heart speaking with the hand.

Still, because of an occasional, surprising flair of the hands, the insistence of their scarred surfaces, it is possible for me to sustain the illusion that they have a history independent of the mind's perception, the heart's passion; a history of gathering what appeals, of expressing exasperation with their own stupidity, of faith in the accrual of brute work. If my hands began to explore complex knowledge by seeking and sorting texture—I am compelled to believe this—then the first names my memory truly embraced came from the hands' differentiating among fruits and woven fabrics.

Growing on farms and in orchards and truck gardens around our home in rural California was a chaos of fruit: naval and Valencia oranges, tangerines, red and yellow grapefruit, pomegranates, lemons, pomelos, greengage and damson plums, freestone and cling peaches, apricots, figs, tangelos, Concord and muscadine grapes. Nectarines, Crenshaw, casaba, and honeydew melons, watermelons, and cantaloupes. My boyish hands knew the planting, the pruning, the picking, and the packing of some of these fruits, the force and the touch required. I sought them all out for the resilience of their ripeness and knew the different sensation of each—pips, radius, cleavage. I ate even tart pomegranates with ardor, from melons I dug gobs of succulent meat with mouth and fingers. Slicing open a cantaloupe or a melon with a knife, I would hesitate always at the sight of the cleft fistula of seeds. It unsettled me, as if it were the fruit's knowing brain.

The fabrics were my mother's. They were stacked in bolts catawampus on open shelves and in a closet in a room in our small house where she both slept and sewed, where she laid out skirts, suits, and dresses for her customers. Lawn, organdy, batiste, and other fine cottons; cambric and gingham; silks—moiré, crepe de chine, taffeta; handkerchief and other weights of linen; light wools like gabardine; silk and cotton damasks; silk and rayon satins; cotton and wool twills; velvet; netted cloths like tulle.

These fabrics differed not only in their texture and weave, in the fineness of their threads, but in the way they passed or reflected light, in their drape, and, most obviously from a distance, in their color and pattern.

I handled these fabrics as though they were animal skins, opening out bolts on the couch when Mother was working, holding them against the window light, raking them with my nails, crumpling them in my fist, then furling them as neatly as I could. Decades later, reading "samite of Ethnise" and "uncut rolls of brocade of Tabronit" in a paperback translation of Wolfram von Eschenbach's *Parzival,* I watched my free hand rise up to welcome the touch of these cloths.

It embarrassed and confounded me that other boys knew so little of cloth, and mocked the knowledge; but growing up with orchards and groves and vine fields, we shared a conventional, peculiar intimacy with fruit. We pelted one another with rotten plums and the green husks of walnuts. We flipped gourds and rolled melons into the paths of oncoming, unsuspecting cars. This prank of the hand—throwing, rolling, flipping—meant nothing without the close companionship of the eye. The eye measured the distance, the crossing or closing speed of the object, and then the hand—the wrist snapping, the fingers' tips guiding to the last—decided upon a single trajectory, measured force, and then a rotten plum hit someone square in the back or sailed wide, or the melon exploded beneath a tire or rolled cleanly to the far side of the road. And we clapped in glee and wiped our hands on our pants.

In these early years—eight and nine and ten—the hands became attuned to each other. They began to slide the hafts of pitchforks and pry bars smoothly, to be more aware of each other's placement for leverage and of the slight difference in strength. It would be three or four more years before, playing the infield in baseball, I would sense the spatial and temporal depth of awareness my hands had of each other, would feel, short-hopping a sharp grounder blind in front of third base, flicking the ball from gloved-left to bare-right hand, making the cross-body throw, that balletic poise of the still fingers after the release, would sense how mindless the beauty of it was.

I do not remember the ascendancy of the right hand. It was the one I was forced to write with, though by that time the right hand could already have asserted itself, reaching always first for a hammer or a peach. A I began to be judged according to the performance of my right hand alone—how well it imitated the Palmer cursive, how legibly it totaled mathematical figures—perhaps here is where the hands first realized how complicated their relationship would become. I remember a furious nun grabbing my six-year-old hands in prayer and wrenching the right thumb from under the left. Right over left, she insisted. *Right over left.* Right over left in prayer to God.

In these early years my hands were frequently folded in prayer. They, too, collected chickens' eggs, contended with the neat assembly of plastic fighter planes, picked knots from bale twine, clapped chalkboard erasers, took trout off baited hooks, and trenched flower beds. They harbored and applauded homing pigeons. When I was eleven, my mother married again and we moved east to New York. The same hands took on new city tasks, struggled more often with coins and with tying the full Windsor knot. Also, now, they pursued a more diligent and precise combing of my hair. And were in anxious anticipation of touching a girl. And that caress having been given, one hand confirmed the memory later with the other in exuberant disbelief. They overhauled and pulled at each other like puppies.

I remember from these years—fourteen and fifteen and sixteen—marveling at the dexterity of my hands. In games of catch, one hand tipped the falling ball to the other, to be seized firmly in the same instant the body crashed to the ground. Or the hands changed effortlessly on the dribble at the start of a fast break in basketball. I remember disassembling, cleaning, and reassembling a two-barrel carburetor, knowing the memory of where all the parts fit was within my hands. I can recall the baton reversal of a pencil as I wrote then erased, wrote then erased, composing sentences on a sheet of paper. And I remember how the hands, so clever with a ball, so deft with a pair of needle-nose pliers, fumbled attaching a cymbidium orchid so close to a girl's body, so near the mysterious breast.

By now, sixteen or so, my hands were as accustomed to books, to magazines, newspapers, and typing paper, as they were to mechanic's tools and baseballs. A blade in my pocketknife was a shape my fingers had experienced years earlier as an oleander leaf. The shape of my fountain pen I knew first as a eucalyptus twig, drawing make-believe roads in wet ground. As my hands had once strained to bring small bluegills to shore, now they reeled striped bass from the Atlantic's surf. As they had once entwined horses' manes, now they twirled girls' ponytails. I had stripped them in those years of manure, paint, axle grease, animal gore, plaster, soap suds, and machine oil; I had cleaned them of sap and tar and putty, of pond scum and potting soil, of fish scales and grass stains. The gashes and cuts had healed smoothly. They were lithe, strenuous. The unimpeded reach of the fingers away from one another in three planes, their extreme effective span, was a subtle source of confidence and wonder. They showed succinctly the physical intelligence of the body. They expressed so unmistakably the vulnerability in sexual desire. They drew so deliberately the curtains of my privacy.

One July afternoon I stood at an ocean breakwater with a friend, firing stones one after another in long, beautiful arcs a hundred feet to the edge of the water. We threw for accuracy, aiming to hit small breaking waves with cutting *thwips*. My friend tired of the game and lay down on his towel. A few moments later I turned and threw in a single motion just as he leaped to his feet. The stone caught him full in the side of the head. He was in the hospital a month with a fractured skull, unable to speak clearly until he was operated on. The following summer we were playing baseball together again, but I could not throw hard or accurately for months after the accident, and I shied away completely from a growing desire to be a pitcher.

My hands lost innocence or gained humanity that day, as they had another day when I was pulled off my first dog, screaming, my hands grasping feebly in the air, after he'd been run over and killed in the road. Lying awake at night I sometimes remember throwing the near deadly stone, or punching a neighbor's horse with my adolescent fist, or heedlessly swinging a 16-gauge shotgun, leading quail—if I hadn't forgotten to switch off the trigger safety, I would have shot an uncle in the head. My hands lay silent at my sides those nights. No memory of their grace or benediction could change their melancholy stillness.

While I was in college I worked two summers at a ranch in Wyoming. My hands got the feel of new tools—foot nips, frog pick, fence pliers, skiving knife. I began to see that the invention, dexterity, and quickness of the hands could take many directions in a man's life; and that a man should be attentive to what his hands loved to do, and so learn not only what he might be good at for a long time but what would make him happy. It pleased me to smooth every wrinkle from a saddle blanket before I settled a saddle squarely on a horse's back. And I liked, too, to turn the thin pages of a Latin edition of the *Aeneid* as I slowly accomplished them that first summer, feeling the impression of the type. It was strengthening to work with my hands, with ropes and bridles and hay bales, with double-bitted axes and bow saws, currying horses, scooping grain, adding my hands' oil to wooden door latches in the barn, calming horses at the foot of a loading ramp, adjusting my hat against the sun, buckling my chaps on a frosty morning. I'd watch the same hand lay a book lovingly on a night table and reach for the lamp's pull cord.

I had never learned to type, but by that second summer, at nineteen, I was writing out the first few stories longhand in pencil. I liked the sound and the sight of the writing going on, the back pressure through my hand. When I had erased and crossed out and rewritten a story all the way through, I would type it out slowly with two or sometimes four fingers, my right thumb on the space bar, as I do to this day. Certain keys and a spot on the space bar are worn through to metal on my typewriters from the oblique angles at which my fingernails strike them.

Had I been able to grasp it during those summers in Wyoming, I might have seen that I couldn't get far from writing stories and physical work, either activity, and remain happy. It proved true that in these two movements my hands found their chief joy, aside from the touching of other human beings. But I could not see it then. My hands only sought out and gave in to the pleasures.

I began to travel extensively while I was in college. Eventually I visited many places, staying with different sorts of people. Most worked some substantial part of the day with their hands. I gravitated toward the company of cowboys and farmers both, to the work of loggers and orchardists, but mostly toward the company of field biologists, college-educated men and women who worked long days open to the weather, studying the lives of wild animals. In their presence, sometimes for weeks at a time, occasionally in stupefying cold or under significant physical strain, I helped wherever I could and wrote in my journal what had happened and, sometimes, what I thought of what had happened. In this way my hands came to know the prick and compression of syringes, the wiring and soldering of radio collars, the arming of anesthetizing guns, the setting of traps and snares, the deployment of otter trawls and plankton tows, the operation of calipers and tripod scales, and the manipulation of various kinds of sieves and packages used to sort and store parts of dead animals, parts created with the use of skinning and butchering knives, with bone saws, teasing needles, tweezers, poultry shears, and hemostatic clamps. My hands were in a dozen kinds of blood, including my own.

Everywhere I journeyed I marveled at the hands of other creatures, at how their palms and digits revealed history, at how well they performed tasks, at the elegant and incontrovertible beauty of their design. I cradled the paws of wolves and polar bears, the hooves of caribou, the forefeet of marine iguanas, the foreflippers of ringed seals and sperm whales, the hands of wallabies, of deer mice. Palpating the tendons, muscles, and bones beneath the skin or fur, I gained a rough understanding of the range of ability, of expression. I could feel where a broken bone had healed and see from superficial scars something of what a life must have been like. Deeper down, with mammals during a necropsy, I could see how blood vessels and layers of fat in a paw or in a flipper were arranged to either rid the creature of its metabolic heat or hoard it. I could see the evidence of arthritis in its phalanges, how that could come to me.

I have never touched a dead human, nor do I wish to. The living hands of another person, however, draw me, as strongly as the eyes. What is their history? What are their emotions? What longing is there? I can follow a cabinetmaker's hands for hours as they verify and detect, shave, fit, and rub; or a chef's hands adroitly dicing vegetables or shaping pastry. And who has not known faintness at the sight of a lover's hand? What man has not wished to take up the hands of the woman he loves and pore over them with reverence and curiosity? Who has not in reverie wished to love the lover's hands?

Years after my mother died I visited her oldest living friend. We were doing dishes together and she said, "You have your mother's hands." Was that likeness a shade of love? And if now I say out of respect for my hands I would buy only the finest tools, is that, too, not love?

The hands evolve, of course. The creases deepen and the fingers begin to move two or three together at a time. If the hands of a man are put to hard use, the fingers grow blunt. They lose dexterity and the skin calluses over like hide. Hardly a pair of man's hands known to me comes to mind without a broken or dislocated finger, a lost fingertip, a permanently crushed nail. Most women my age carry scars from kitchen and housework, drawer pinches, scalds, knife and glass cuts. We hardly notice them. Sunlight, wind, and weather obscure many of these scars, but I believe the memory of their occurrence never leaves the hands. When I awaken in the night and sense my hands cupped together under the pillow, or when I sit somewhere on a porch, idly watching wind crossing a ripening field and look down to see my hands nested in my lap as if asleep like two old dogs, it is not hard for me to believe they know. They remember all they have done, all that has happened to them, the ways in which they have been surprised or worked themselves free of desperate trouble, or lost their grip and so caused harm. It's not hard to believe they remember the heads patted, the hands shaken, the apples peeled, the hair braided, the wood split, the gears shifted, the flesh gripped and stroked, and that they convey their feelings to each other.

In recent years my hands have sometimes been very cold for long stretches. It takes little cold now to entirely numb thumbs and forefingers. They cease to speak what they know. When I was thirty-one, I accidentally cut the base of my left thumb, severing nerves, leaving the thumb confused about what was cold, what was hot, and whether or not it was touching something or only thought so. When I was thirty-six, I was helping a friend butcher a whale. We'd been up for many hours under twenty-four-hour arctic daylight and were tired. He glanced away and without thinking drove the knife into my wrist. It was a clean wound, easy to close, but with it I lost the nerves to the right thumb. Over the years each thumb has regained some sensitivity, and I believe the hands are more sympathetic to each other because of their similar wounds. The only obvious difference lies with the left hand. A broken metacarpal forced a rerouting of tendons to the middle and ring fingers as it healed and raised a boss of carpal bone tissue on the back of the hand.

At the base of the right thumb is a scar from a climbing accident. On the other thumb, a scar the same length from the jagged edge of a fuel-barrel pump. In strong sunlight, when there is a certain tension in the skin, as I have said, I can stare at my hands for a while, turning them slowly, and remember with them the days, the weather, the people present when some things happened that left scars behind. It brings forth affection for my hands. I recall how, long ago, they learned to differentiate between cotton and raw silk, between husks of the casaba and the honeydew melon, and how they thrilled to the wire bristle of a hog's back, how they clipped the water's surface in swimming-pool fights, how they painstakingly arranged bouquets, how they swung and lifted children. I have begun to wish they would speak to me, tell me stories I have forgotten.

I sit in a chair and look at the scars, the uneven cut of the nails, and reminisce. With them before me I grin as though we held something secret, remembering bad times that left no trace. I cut firewood for my parents once, winter in Alabama, swamping out dry, leafless vines to do so. Not until the next day did I realize the vines were poison ivy. The blisters grew so close and tight my hands straightened like paddles. I had to have them lanced to continue a cross-country trip, to dress and feed myself. And there have been days when my hands stiffened with cold so that I had to quit the work being done, sit it out and whimper with pain as they came slowly back to life. But these moments are inconsequential. I have looked at the pale, wrinkled hands of a drowned boy, and I have seen handless wrists.

If there were a way to speak directly to the hands, to allow them a language of their own, what I would most wish to hear is what they recall of human touch, of the first exploration of the body of another, the caresses, the cradling of breast, of head, of buttock. Does it seem to them as to me that we keep learning, even when the caressed body has been known for years? How do daydreams of an idealized body, one's own or another's, affect the hands' first tentative inquiry? Is the hand purely empirical? Does it apply an imagination? Does it retain a man's shyness, a boy's clumsiness? Do the hands anguish if there is no one to touch?

Tomorrow I shall pull blackberry vines and load a trailer with rotten timber. I will call on my hands to help me dress, to turn the spigot for water for coffee, to pull the newspaper from its tube. I will put my hands in the river and lift water where the sunlight is brightest, a playing with fractured light I never tire of. I will turn the pages of a book about the history of fire in Australia. I will sit at the typewriter, working through a story about a trip to Matagorda Island in Texas. I will ask my hands to undress me. Before I turn out the light, I will fold and set my reading glasses aside. Then I will cup my hands, the left in the right, and slide them under the pillow beneath my head, where they will speculate, as will I, about what we shall handle the next day, and dream, a spooling of their time we might later remember together and I, so slightly separated from them, might recognize.

Double Take

1. What about this essay makes it appropriate—in subject matter, style, examples, perspective, and so on—to its audience, readers of *Men's Journal*? Of the rhetorical choices Lopez makes in writing this essay, which seem most well-suited to his readers?

2. What is Lopez trying to communicate to his readers in "A Passage of the Hands"? Is there something that resembles an argument in the essay? If so, what is it? If it is not making an argument, then what is the essay doing?

3. The hands, of course, are the point of reference in this essay, but in it Lopez ranges across time, events, and memories. Describe and examine some of the transitions Lopez uses to move his readers through time, events, and memories. What makes these transitions work?

4. What different choices would Lopez have to make if he chose to revise and publish this essay, with the same title, in *Ms.* magazine?

Seeing for Yourself

At First Glance

"A Presentation of Whales" is a rather moving essay about the beaching of 41 whales in Oregon in 1979. Unlike many accounts of beached whales that we might read or see on television, "A Presentation of Whales" examines the various groups of people who showed up to witness, to help, and to study the whales that beached themselves. In this essay Barry Lopez considers large ethical and moral actions of scientists, police, community leaders, members of the general public, and the press during the event. As you read this essay, think not only about how Lopez represents each of these groups, but also how he positions himself as writer in relation to the different people. Also, think about how you might have positioned yourself in this event.

A Presentation of Whales

On that section of the central Oregon coast on the evening of June 16, 1979, gentle winds were blowing onshore from the southwest. It was fifty-eight degrees. Under partly cloudy skies the sea was running with four-foot swells at eight-second intervals. Moderately rough. State police cadets Jim Clark and Steve Bennett stood at the precipitous edge of a foredune a few miles south of the town of Florence, peering skeptically into the dimness over a flat, gently sloping beach. Near the water's edge they could make out a line of dark shapes, and what they had taken for a practical joke, the exaggeration a few moments before of a man and a woman in a brown Dodge van with a broken headlight, now sank in for the truth.

Clark made a hasty, inaccurate count and plunged with Bennett down the back of the dune to their four-wheel-drive. Minutes before, they had heard the voice of Corporal Terry Crawford over the radio; they knew he was patrolling in Florence. Rather than call him, they drove the six miles into town and parked across the street from where he was issuing a citation to someone for excessive noise. When Crawford had finished, Clark went over and told him what they had seen. Crawford drove straight to the Florence State Police office and phoned his superiors in Newport, forty-eight miles up the coast. At that point the news went out over police radios: thirty-six large whales, stranded and apparently still alive, were on the beach a mile south of the mouth of the Siuslaw River.

There were, in fact, forty-one whales—twenty-eight females and thirteen males, at least of one of them dying or already dead. There had never been a stranding quite like it. It was first assumed that they were gray whales, common along the

442

coast, but they were sperm whales: *Physeter catodon.* Deep-ocean dwellers. They ranged in age from ten to fifty-six and in length from thirty to thirty-eight feet. They were apparently headed north when they beached around 7:30 P.M. on an ebbing high tide.

The information shot inland by phone, crossing the Coast Range to radio and television stations in the more-populous interior of Oregon, in a highly charged form: giant whales stranded on a public beach accessible by paved road on a Saturday night, still alive. Radio announcers urged listeners to head for the coast to "save the whales." In Eugene and Portland, Greenpeace volunteers, already alerted by the police, were busy throwing sheets and blankets into their cars. They would soak them in the ocean, to cool the whales.

The news moved as quickly through private homes and taverns on the central Oregon coast, passed by people monitoring the police bands. In addition to phoning Greenpeace—an international organization with a special interest in protecting marine mammals—the police contacted the Oregon State University Marine Science Center in South Beach near Newport, and the Oregon Institute of Marine Biology in Charleston, fifty-eight miles south of Florence. Bruce Mate, a marine mammalogist at the OSU Center, phoned members of the Northwest Regional [Stranding] Alert Network and people in Washington, D.C.

By midnight, the curious and the awed were crowded on the beach, cutting the night with flashlights. Drunks, ignoring the whales' sudden thrashing, were trying to walk up and down on their backs. A collie barked incessantly; flash cubes burst at the huge, dark forms. Two men inquired about reserving some of the teeth, for scrimshaw. A federal agent asked police to move people back, and the first mention of disease was in the air. Scientists arrived with specimen bags and rubber gloves and fishing knives. Greenpeace members, one dressed in a bright orange flight suit, came with a large banner. A man burdened with a television camera labored over the foredune after them. They wished to tie a rope to one whale's flukes, to drag it back into the ocean. The police began to congregate with the scientists, looking for a rationale to control the incident.

In the intensifying confusion, as troopers motioned onlookers back (to "restrain the common herd of unqualified mankind," wrote one man later in an angry letter-to-the-editor), the thinking was that, somehow, the whales might be saved. Neal Langbehn, a federal protection officer with the National Marine Fisheries Service, denied permission to one scientist to begin removing teeth and taking blood samples. In his report later he would write: "It was my feeling that the whales should be given their best chance to survive."

This hope was soon deemed futile, as it had appeared to most of the scientists from the beginning—the animals were hemorrhaging under the crushing weight of their own flesh and were beginning to suffer irreversible damage from heat exhaustion. The scientific task became one of securing as much data as possible.

As dawn bloomed along the eastern sky, people who had driven recreational vehicles illegally over the dunes and onto the beach were issued citations and turned back. Troopers continued to warn people over bullhorns to please stand away from the whales. The Oregon Parks Department, whose responsibility the beach was, wanted no part of the growing confusion. The U.S. Forest Service, with jurisdiction over land in the Oregon Dunes National Recreation Area down to the foredune, was willing to help, but among all the agencies there was concern over limited budgets; there were questions, gently essayed, about the conflict of state and federal enforcement powers over the body parts of an endangered species. A belligerent few in the crowd shouted objections as the first syringes appeared, and yelled to scientists to produce permits that allowed them to interfere in the death of an endangered species.

Amid this chaos, the whales, sealed in their slick black neoprene skins, mewed and clicked. They slammed glistening flukes on the beach, jarring the muscles of human thighs like Jell-O at a distance of a hundred yards. They rolled their dark, purple-brown eyes at the scene and blinked.

They lay on the western shore of North America like forty-one derailed boxcars at dawn on a Sunday morning, and in the days that followed, the worst and the best of human behavior was shown among them.

The sperm whale, for many, is the most awesome creature of the open seas. Imagine a forty-five-year-old male fifty feet long, a slim, shiny black animal with a white jaw and marbled belly cutting the surface of green ocean water at twenty knots. Its flat forehead protects a sealed chamber of exceedingly fine oil; sunlight sparkles in rivulets running off folds in its corrugated back. At fifty tons it is the largest carnivore on earth. Its massive head, a third of its body length, is scarred with the beak, sucker, and claw marks of giant squid, snatched out of subterranean canyons a mile below, in a region without light, and brought writhing to the surface. Imagine a four-hundred-pound heart the size of a chest of drawers driving five gallons of blood at a stroke through its aorta: a meal of forty salmon moving slowly down twelve-hundred feet of intestine; the blinding, acrid fragrance of a two-hundred-pound wad of gray ambergris lodged somewhere along the way; producing sounds more shrill than we can hear—like children shouting on a distant playground—and able to sort a cacophony of noise: electric crackling of shrimp, groaning of undersea quakes, roar of upwellings, whining of porpoise, hum of oceanic cables. With skin as sensitive as the inside of your wrist.

What makes them awesome is not so much these things, which are discoverable, but the mysteries that shroud them. They live at a remarkable distance from us and we have no *Pioneer II* to penetrate their world. Virtually all we know of sperm whales we have learned on the slaughter decks of oceangoing whalers and on the ways at shore stations. We do not even know how many there are; in December 1978, the Scientific Committee of the International Whaling Commission said it could not set a quota for a worldwide sperm whale kill—so little was known that any number written down would be ridiculous.★

★A quota of 5000 was nevertheless set. In June 1979, within days of the Florence stranding but apparently unrelated to it, the IWC dropped the 1980 world sperm whale quota to 2203 and set aside the Indian Ocean as a sanctuary. (By 1987 the quota was 0, though special exemptions permit some 200 sperm whales still to be taken worldwide.)

The sperm whale, in all its range of behaviors—from the enraged white bull called Mocha Dick that stove whaling ships off the coast of Peru in 1810, to a nameless female giving birth to a fourteen-foot, one-ton calf in equatorial waters in the Pacific—remains distant. The general mystery is enhanced by specific mysteries: the sperm whale's brain is larger than the brain of any other creature that ever lived. Beyond the storage of incomprehensible amounts of information, we do not know what purpose such size serves. And we do not know what to make of its most distinctive anatomical feature, the spermaceti organ. An article in *Scientific American,* published several months before the stranding, suggests that the whale can control the density of its spermaceti oil, thereby altering its specific gravity to assist it in diving. It is argued also that the huge organ, located in the head, serves as a means of generating and focusing sound, but there is not yet any agreement on these speculations.

Of the many sperm whale strandings in recorded history, only three have been larger than the one in Oregon. The most recent was of fifty-six on the eastern Baja coast near Playa San Rafael on January 6, 1979. But the Florence stranding is perhaps the most remarkable. Trained scientists arrived almost immediately; the site was easily accessible, with even an airstrip close by. It was within an hour's drive of two major West Coast marine-science centers. And the stranding seemed to be of a whole social unit. That the animals were still alive meant live blood specimens could be taken. And by an uncanny coincidence, a convention of the American Society of Mammalogists was scheduled to convene June 18 at Oregon State University in Corvallis, less than a two-hour drive away. Marine experts from all over the country would be there. (As it turned out, some of them would not bother to come over; others would secure access to the beach only to take photographs; still others would show up in sports clothes—all they had—and plunge into the gore that by the afternoon of June 18 littered the beach.)

The state police calls to Greenpeace on the night of June 16 were attempts to reach informed people to direct a rescue. Michael Piper of Greenpeace, in Eugene, was the first to arrive with a small group at about 1:30 A.M., just after a low tide at 12:59 A.M.

"I ran right out of my shoes," Piper says. The thought that they would still be alive—clicking and murmuring, their eyes tracking human movement, lifting their flukes, whooshing warm air from their blowholes—had not penetrated. But as he ran into the surf to fill a bucket to splash water over their heads, the proportions of the stranding and the impending tragedy overwhelmed him.

"I knew, almost from the beginning, that we were not going to get them out of there, and that even if we did, their chances of survival were a million to one," Piper said.

Just before dawn, a second contingent of Greenpeace volunteers arrived from Portland. A Canadian, Michael Bailey, took charge and announced there was a chance with the incoming tide that one of the smaller animals could be floated off the beach and towed to sea (weights ranged from an estimated three and a half to twenty-five tons). Bruce Mate, who would become both scientific and press coordinator on the beach (the latter to his regret), phoned the Port of Coos Bay to see if an ocean-going tug or fishing vessel would be available to anchor offshore and help—Bailey's crew would ferry lines through the surf with a Zodiac boat. No one in Coos Bay was interested. A commercial helicopter service with a Skycrane capable of lifting nine tons also begged off. A call to the Coast Guard produced a helicopter, but people there pronounced any attempt to sky-tow a whale too dangerous.

The refusal of help combined with the apparent futility of the effort precipitated a genuinely compassionate gesture: Bailey strode resolutely into the freezing water and, with twenty-five or thirty others, amid flailing flukes, got a rope around the tail of an animal that weighed perhaps three or four tons. The waves knocked them down and the whale yanked them over, but they came up sputtering, to pull again. With the buoyancy provided by the incoming tide they moved the animal about thirty feet. The effort was heroic and ludicrous. As the rope began to cut into the whale's flesh, as television cameramen and press photographers crowded in, Michael Piper gave up his place on the rope in frustration and waded ashore. Later he would remark that, for some, the whale was only the means to a political end—a dramatization of the plight of whales as a species. The distinction between the suffering individual, its internal organs hemorrhaging, its flukes sliced by the rope, and the larger issue, to save the species, confounded Piper.

A photograph of the Greenpeace volunteers pulling the whale showed up nationally in newspapers the next day. A week later, a marine mammalogist wondered if any more damaging picture could have been circulated. It would convince people something could have been done, when in fact, he said, the whales were doomed as soon as they came ashore.

For many, transfixed on the beach by their own helplessness, the value of the gesture transcended the fact.

By midmorning Piper was so disturbed, so embarrassed by the drunks and by people wrangling to get up on the whales or in front of photographers, that he left. As he drove off through the crowds (arriving now by the hundreds, many in campers and motor homes), gray whales were seen offshore, with several circling sperm whales. "The best thing we could have done," Piper said, alluding to this, "was offer our presence, to be with them while they were alive, to show some compassion."

Irritated by a callous (to him) press that seemed to have only one question—Why did they come ashore?—Piper had blurted out that the whales may have come ashore "because they were tired of running" from commercial whalers. Scientists scoffed at the remark, but Piper, recalling it a week later, would not take it back. He said it was as logical as any other explanation offered in those first few hours.

Uneasy philosophical disagreement divided people on the beach from the beginning. Those for whom the stranding was a numinous event were estranged by the clowning of those who regarded it as principally entertainment. A few scientists irritated everyone with their preemptive, self-important air. When they put chain saws to the lower jaws of dead sperm whales lying only a few feet from whales not yet dead, there were angry shouts of condemnation. When townspeople kept at bay—"This is history, dammit," one man screamed at a state trooper, "and I want my kids to see it!"—saw twenty reporters, each claiming an affiliation with the same weekly newspaper, gain the closeness to the whales denied them, there were shouts of cynical derision.

"The effect of all this," said Michael Gannon, director of a national group called Oregonians Cooperating to Protect Whales, of the undercurrent of elitism and outrage, "was that it interfered with the spiritual and emotional ability of people to deal with the phenomenon. It was like being at a funeral where you were not allowed to mourn."

Bob Warren, a patrolman with the U.S. Forest Service, said he was nearly brought to tears by what faced him Sunday morning. "I had no conception of what a whale beaching would be like. I was apprehensive about it, about all the tourists and the law-enforcement atmosphere. When I drove up, the whole thing hit me in the stomach: I saw these *numbers,* these damn orange numbers—41, 40, 39—spray-painted on these dying animals. The media were coming on like the marines, in taxicabs, helicopters, low-flying aircraft. Biologists were saying, 'We've got to *euthanize* them.' It made me sick."

By this time Sunday morning, perhaps five hundred people had gathered; the crowd would swell to more than two thousand before evening, in spite of a drizzling rain. The state trooper who briefed Warren outlined the major problems: traffic was backing up on the South Jetty Road almost five miles to U.S. 101; the whales' teeth were "as valuable as gold" and individuals with hammers and saws had been warned away already; people were sticking their hands in the whales' mouths and were in danger of being killed by the pounding flukes; and there was a public-health problem—the whales might have come ashore with a communicable disease. (According to several experts, the danger to public health was minor, but in the early confusion it served as an excuse to keep the crowd back so scientists could work. Ironically, the threat would assume a life of its own two days later and scientists would find themselves working frantically ahead of single-minded state burial crews.)

One of the first things Warren and others did was to rope off the whales with orange ribbon and lath stakes, establishing a line beyond which the public was no longer permitted. Someone thoughtful among them ran the ribbon close enough to one whale to allow people to peer into the dark eyes, to see scars left by struggling squid, lamprey eels, and sharp boulders on the ocean floor, the patches of diatoms growing on the skin, the marbling streaking back symmetrically from the genital slit, the startlingly gentle white mouth ("What a really beautiful and chaste-looking mouth!" Melville wrote. "From floor to ceiling lined, or rather papered with a glistening white membrane, glossy as bridal satins"), to see the teeth, gleaming in the long, almost absurdly narrow jaw. In *The Year of the Whale,* Victor Scheffer describes the tooth as "creamy white, a cylinder lightly curved, a thing of art which fits delightfully in the palm of my hand."

The temptation to possess—a Polaroid of oneself standing over a whale, a plug of flesh removed with a penknife, a souvenir squid beak plucked deftly from an exposed intestine by a scientist—was almost palpable in the air.

"From the beginning," Warren continued, "I was operating on two levels: as a law-enforcement officer with a job, and as a person." He escorted people away from the whales, explaining as well as he could the threat of disease, wishing himself to reach out with them, to touch the animals. He recalls his rage watching people poke at a sensitive area under the whale's eyes to make them react, and calmly directing people to step back, to let the animals die in peace. Nothing could be done, he would say. How do you know? They would ask. He didn't.

Warren was awed by the sudden, whooshing breath that broke the silence around an animal perhaps once every fifteen minutes, and saddened by the pitiable way some of them were mired with their asymmetrical blow-hole sanded in, dead. Near those still breathing he drove in lath stakes with the word LIVE written on them. The hopelessness of it, he said, and the rarity of the event were rendered absurd by his having to yell into a bullhorn, by the blood on the beach, the whales' blinking, the taunters hoisting beer cans to the police.

One of the things about being human, Warren reflected, is learning to see beyond the vulgar. Along with the jocose in the crowd, he said, there were hundreds who whispered to each other, as if in a grove of enormous trees. And faces that looked as though they were awaiting word of relatives presumed dead in an air crash. He remembers in particular a man in his forties, "dressed in polyesters," who stood with his daughter in a tidal pool inside the barrier, splashing cool water on a whale. Warren asked them to please step back. "Why?" the man asked. Someone in the crowd yelled an obscenity at Warren. Warren thought to himself: Why is there no room for the decency of this gesture?

The least understood and perhaps most disruptive incident on the beach on that first day was the attempt of veterinarians to kill the whales, first by injecting M–99, a morphine-base drug, then by ramming pipes into their pleural cavities to collapse their lungs, and finally by severing major arteries and letting them bleed to death. The techniques were crude, but no one knew enough sperm whale anatomy or physiology to make a clean job of it, and no one wanted to try some of the alternatives—from curare to dynamite—that would have made the job quicker. The ineptitude of the veterinarians caused them a private embarrassment to which they gave little public expression. Their frustration at their own inability to do anything to "help" the whales was exacerbated by nonscientists demanding from the sidelines that the animals be "put out of their misery." (The reasons for attempting euthanasia were poorly understood, philosophically and medically, and the issue nagged people long after the beach bore not a trace of the incident itself.)

As events unfolded on the beach, the first whale died shortly after the stranding, the last almost thirty-six hours later; suffocation and overheating were the primary causes. By waiting as long as they did to try to kill some of the animals and by allowing others to die in their own time, pathologists, toxicologists, parasitologists, geneticists, and others got tissues of poor quality to work with.* The disappointment was all the deeper because never had so many scientists been in a position to

---

*A subsequent report, presented at a marine-mammals conference in Seattle in October 1979, made it clear that the whales began to suffer the effects of heat stress almost immediately. The breakdown of protein structures in their tissues made discovery of a cause of death difficult; from the beginning, edema, capillary dilation, and hemorrhaging made their recovery unlikely. Ice, seawater pumps, and tents for shade rather than Zodiac boats and towlines were suggested if useful tissue was to be salvaged in the future from large whales.

gather so much information. (Even with this loss and an initial lack of suitable equipment—chemicals to preserve tissues, blood-analysis kits, bone saws, flensing knives—the small core of twenty or so scientists "increased human knowledge about sperm whales several hundred percent," according to Mate.)

The fact that almost anything learned was likely to be valuable was meager consolidation to scientists hurt by charges that they were cold and brutal people, irreverently jerking fetuses from the dead. Among these scientists were people who sat alone in silence, who departed in anger, and who broke down and cried.

No one knows why whales strand. It is almost always toothed whales that do, rather than baleen whales, most commonly pilot whales, Atlantic white-sided dolphins, false killer whales, and sperm whales—none of which are ordinarily found close to shore. Frequently they strand on gently sloping beaches. Among the more tenable explanations: 1) extreme social cohesion, where one sick animal is relentlessly followed ashore by many healthy animals; 2) disease or parasitic infection that affects the animals' ability to navigate; 3) harassment, by predators and, deliberate or inadvertent, by humans; 4) a reversion to phylogenetically primitive escape behavior—get out of the water—precipitated by stress.

At a public meeting in Florence—arranged by the local librarian to explain to a public kept off the beach what had happened, and to which invited scientists did not come—other explanations were offered. Someone had noticed whales splashing in apparent confusion near a river dredge and thought the sound of its engines might have driven the whales crazy. Local fishermen said there had been an unusual, near-shore warm current on June 16, with a concentration of plankton so thick they had trouble penetrating it with their depth finders. Another suggestion was that the whales might have been temporarily deranged by poisons in diatoms concentrated in fish they were eating.

The seventy-five or so people at the meeting seemed irritated that there was no answer, as did local reporters looking for an end to the story. Had scientists been there it is unlikely they could have suggested one. The beach was a gently sloping one, but the Florence whales showed no evidence of parasitism or disease, and modern research makes it clear that no single explanation will suffice. For those who would blame the machinations of modern man, scientists would have pointed out that strandings have been recorded since the time of Aristotle's *Historia animalium.*

The first marine biologist to arrive on the beach, at 3:30 A.M. Sunday, was Michael Graybill, a young instructor from the Oregon Institute of Marine Biology. He was not as perplexed as other scientists would be; a few months before he had dismantled the rotting carcass of a fifty-six-foot sperm whale that had washed ashore thirty miles south of Florence.

Graybill counted the animals, identified them as sperm whales, noted that, oddly, there were no nursing calves or obviously young animals, and that they all seemed "undersized." He examined their skin and eyes, smelled their breath, looked for signs of oral and anal discharge, and began the task of sexing and measuring the animals.

Driving to the site, Graybill worried most about someone "bashing their teeth out" before he got there. He wasn't worried about communicable disease; he was "willing to gamble" on that. He regarded efforts to save the whales, however, as unnatural interference in their death. Later, he cynically observed "how much 'science' took place at the heads of sperm whales" where people were removing teeth; and he complained that if they really cared about the worldwide fate of whales, Greenpeace volunteers would have stayed to help scientists with postmortems. (Some did. Others left because they could not stand to watch the animals die.)

Beginning Sunday morning, scientists had their first chance to draw blood from live, unwounded sperm whales (they used comparatively tiny one-and-a-half-inch, 18-gauge hypodermic needles stuck in vessels near the surface of the skin on the flukes). With the help of a blue, organic tracer they estimated blood volume at five hundred gallons. In subsequent stages, blubber, eyes, teeth, testicles, ovaries, stomach contents, and specific tissues were removed—the teeth for aging, the eyes for corneal cells to discover genetic relationships within the group. Postmortems were performed on ten females; three near-term fetuses were removed. An attempt was made to photograph the animals systematically.

The atmosphere on the beach shifted perceptibly over the next six days. On Sunday, a cool, cloudy day during which it rained, as many as three thousand people may have been on the beach. Police finally closed the access road to the area to discourage more from coming. Attempts to euthanize the animals continued, the jaws of the dead were being sawed off, and, in the words of one observer, "there was a television crew with a backdrop of stranded whales every twenty feet on the foredune."

By Monday the crowds were larger, but, in the estimation of a Forest Service employee, "of a higher quality. The type of people who show up at an automobile accident were gone; these were people who really wanted to see the whales. It was a four-and-a-half-mile walk in from the highway, and I talked with a woman who was seven months pregnant who made it and a man in a business suit and dress shoes who drove all the way down from Seattle."

Monday afternoon the crowds thinned. The beach had become a scene of postmortem gore sufficient to turn most people away. The outgoing tide had carried off gallons of blood and offal, drawing spiny dogfish sharks and smoothhound sharks into the breakers. As the animals died, scientists cut into them to relieve gaseous pressure—the resultant explosions could be heard half a mile away. A forty-pound chunk of liver whizzed by someone's back-turned shoulders; sixty feet of pearly-gray intestine unfurled with a snap against the sky. By evening the beach was covered with more than a hundred tons of intestines. Having to open the abdominal cavities so precipitately precluded, to the scientists' dismay, any chance of an uncontaminated examination.

By Tuesday the beach was closed to the public. The whale carcasses were being prepared for burning and burial, a task that would take four days, and reporters had given up asking why the stranding had happened, to comment on the stench.

The man responsible for coordinating scientific work at the stranding, thirty-three-year-old Bruce Mate, is well regarded by his colleagues. Deborah Duffield, a geneticist from Portland State University, reiterated the feelings of several when she said of him: "The most unusual thing was that he got all of us with our different, sometimes competing, interests to work together. You can't comprehend what an extraordinary achievement that is in a situation like this."

On the beach Mate was also the principal source of information for the press. Though he was courteous to interviewers and careful not to criticize a sometimes impatient approach, one suspected he was disturbed by the role and uncertain what, if anything, he owed the nonscientific community.

In his small, cramped office at the Marine Science Center in South Beach, Mate agreed that everyone involved—scientists, environmentalists, the police, the state agencies, the public—took views that were occasionally in opposition and that these views were often proprietary. He thought it was the business of science to obtain data and physical specimens on the beach, thereby acquiring rights of "ownership," and yet he acknowledged misgivings about this because he and others involved are to some extent publicly funded scientists.

The task that faced him was deceptively simple: get as much information as possible off the beach before the burning crews, nervous about a public-health hazard and eager to end the incident, destroyed the animals. But what about the way science dominated the scene, getting the police, for example, to keep the crowd away so science could exercise its proprietary interest? "I don't know how to cope with the public's desire to come and see. Letting those few people onto the beach would have precluded our getting that much more information to give to a much larger, national audience."

What about charges that science operated in a cold-blooded and, in the case of trying to collapse the whales' lungs, ignorant way? "Coming among these whales, watching them die and in some cases helping them to die—needless suffering is almost incomprehensible to me . . ." Mate paused, studied the papers on his desk, unsatisfied, it seemed, with his tack; ". . . there are moral and ethical questions here. It's like dealing with terminal cancer."

No one, he seemed to suggest, liked how fast it had all happened.

Had he been worried about anything on the beach? "Yes! I was appalled at the way professional people were going about [postmortems] without gloves. I was afraid for the Greenpeace people in a potentially life-threatening situation in the surf." He was also afraid that it would all get away from him because of the unknowns. What, in fact, *did* one save when faced with such an enormous amount of bone and tissue? But he came away happy. "This was the greatest scientific shot anyone ever had with large whales." After a moment he added, " If it happened tomorrow, we would be four times better."

Sitting at his desk, nursing a pinched nerve in his back, surrounded by phone messages from the press, he seemed seasoned.

Mate's twenty-seven-year-old graduate assistant, Jim Harvey, arrived on the beach at dawn on Sunday. At the first sight of the whales from the top of the dunes, strung out nose to flukes in a line five or six hundred yards long, the waves of a high tide breaking over them, Harvey simply sat down, awestruck at their size and number. He felt deeply sad, too, but as he drew near he felt "a rush of exhilaration, because there was so much information to be gathered." He could not get over the feeling, as he worked, of the size of them. (One afternoon a scientist stood confounded in a whale's abdomen, asking a colleague next to him, "Where's the liver?")

Deborah Duffield said of her experience on the beach: "It hurt me more than watching human beings die. I couldn't cope with the pain, the futility. . . . I just turned into myself. It brought out the scientist in me." Another scientist spoke of his hostility toward the sullen crowd, of directing that anger at himself, of becoming cold and going to work.

For Harvey and others, there was one incident that broke scientific concentration and brought with it a feeling of impropriety. Several scientists had started to strip blubber from a dead whale. Suddenly the whale next to it began pounding the beach with its flukes. The pounding continued for fifteen minutes—lifting and slamming the flukes to the left, lifting and slamming the flukes to the right.

When the animal quieted, they resumed work.

"Scientists rarely get a chance to express their feelings," Harvey said. "I was interested in other people's views, and I wanted to share mine, which are biological. I noticed some people who sat quietly for a long time behind the barriers in religious stances. I very much wanted to know their views. So many of the people who came down here were so sympathetic and full of concern—I wished I had the time to talk to them all." Harvey remembered something vividly. On the first day he put his face near the blowhole of one of the whales: a cylinder of clean, warm, humid air almost a foot in diameter blew back his hair.

★ ★ ★

"My view on it," said Joe Davis of the Oregon Parks Department, "wasn't the scientific part. My thought on it now is how nice it would have been to have been somewhere else." His smile falls between wryness and regret.

When something remarkable happens and bureaucrats take it for only a nuisance, it is often stripped of whatever mystery it may hold. The awesome becomes common. Joe Davis, park manager at Honeyman Dunes State Park, adjacent to the stranding, was charged by the state with getting rid of the whales. He said he didn't take a moment to wonder at the mystery of it.

If ethical problems beset scientists, and mystical considerations occupied other onlookers, a set of concerns more prosaic confronted the police and the Oregon Parks Department. On Sunday night, June 17, police arrested a man in a camouflage suit caught breaking teeth out of a whale's jaw with a hammer and chisel. That night (and the next, and the next) people continued to play games with the police. The Parks Department, for its part, was faced with the disposal of five hundred tons of whale flesh that county environmental and health authorities said they couldn't burn—the solution to the problem at Playa San Rafael—and scientists said couldn't be buried. If buried, the carcasses would become hard envelopes of rotting flesh, the internal organs would liquefy and leach out onto the beach, and winter storms would uncover the whole mess.

This controversy, the public-health question, what to do about excessive numbers of press people, and concern over who was going to pay the bill (the Forest

Service had donated tools, vehicles, and labor, but two bulldozers had had to be hired, at a hundred dollars and sixty dollars an hour) precipitated a meeting in Florence on Tuesday morning, June 19. A Forest Service employee, who asked not to be identified, thought the pressures that led to the meeting marked a difference between those who came to the beach out of compassion and genuine interest and those for whom it was "only a headache."

The principal issue, after an agreement was reached to burn the whales, then bury them, was who was going to pay. The state was reluctant; the scientists were impoverished. (It would be months before Mate would begin to recover $5,000 of his own money advanced to pay for equipment, transportation, and bulldozer time. "No one wants to fund work that's finished," Mate observed sardonically.) Commercial firms were averse to donating burning materials, or even transportation for them; G.P. Excavating of Florence did reduce rental fees on its bulldozers by about one-third and "broke even" after paying its operators.

The state finally took responsibility for the disposal and assumed the $25,000 cleanup bill, but it wanted to hear nothing about science's wish to salvage skeletons—it wanted the job finished.★ Arrangements were made to bring in a crew of boys from the Young Adult Conservation Corps, and the Forest Service, always, it seemed, amenable, agreed to donate several barrels of Alumagel, a napalmlike substance.

It was further decided to ban the public from the beach during the burning, for health and safety reasons. Only the disposal crews, scientists, police, and selected press would be admitted. The criterion for press admittance was possession of "a legitimate press card."

The role of the press at such events is somewhat predictable. They will repeatedly ask the same, obvious questions; they will often know little of the science involved; occasionally they will intimidate and harass in order to ascertain (or assign) blame. An upper-level Forest Service employee accused the press of asking "the most uninteresting and intimidating kinds of questions." A State Parks employee felt the press fostered dissension over who was going to pay for the disposal. He was also angry with newspaper people for ignoring "the human side," the fact that many state police troopers worked long hours of overtime, and that Forest Service employees performed a number of menial tasks in an emotionally charged environment of rotting flesh. "After a week of sixteen-hour days, your nerves are raw, you stink, you just want to get away from these continual questions."

In the press's defense, the people who objected most were those worried about criticism of their own performance and those deeply frustrated by the trivialization of the event. The press—probing, perhaps inexpertly—made people feel no more than their own misgivings.

★Three months later on September 6, 1979, an eighty-five-foot female blue whale washed ashore in Northern California. Ensuing argument over responsibility for disposal prevented scientists from going near the whale until September 13, by which time it had been severely battered on the rocks and vandalized.

The publisher of the local *Siuslaw News,* Paul Holman, said before it was over that the whale stranding had become a nuisance. When police closed the road to the beach a man in a stateside truck began ferrying people the four and a half miles to the whales for a dollar each. And a dollar back. The local airport, as well as tourist centers offering seaplane rides, were doing a "land-office business" in flyovers. Gas station operators got tired of telling tourists how to get to the beach. The Florence City Hall was swamped with calls about the burning, one from a man who was afraid his horses would be killed by the fallout on his pasture. Dune-buggy enthusiasts were angry at whale people who for two days blocked access to their hill-climbing area.

Whatever its interest, the press was largely gone by Monday afternoon. As the burning and burying commenced, the number of interested scientists also thinned. By Wednesday there were only about thirty people left on the beach. Bob Adams, acting director of the Lane Regional Air Pollution Authority, was monitoring the smoke. Neal Langbehn of the National Marine Fisheries Service stood guard over a pile of plastic-wrapped sperm whale jaws. Michael Graybill led a team flensing out skulls. The state fretted over a way to keep the carcasses burning. (It would finally be done with thousands of automobile and truck tires, cordwood, diesel fuel, and Alumagel.) As Mate watched he considered the threshold of boredom in people, and mourned the loss, among other things, of forty-one sperm whale skeletons.

A journalist, one of the last two or three, asked somebody to take her picture while she stood with a small poodle in her arms in front of the burning pits.

As is often the case with such events, what is salvaged is as much due to goodwill as it is to expertise. The Forest Service was widely complimented for helping, and Stafford Owen, the acting area ranger at the agency's Oregon Dunes National Recreation Area during the incident, tried to say why: "Most of us aren't highly educated people. We have had to work at a variety of things all our lives—operating a chain saw, repairing a truck engine, running a farm. We had the skills these doctors and scientists needed."

A soft-spoken colleague, Gene Large, trying to elaborate but not to make too much of himself, said, "I don't think the scientists had as much knowledge [of large mammalian anatomy] as I did. When it came to it, I had to show some of them where the ribs were." After a moment, Large said, "Trying to cut those whales open with a chain saw was like trying to slaughter a beef with a pen knife." "I didn't enjoy any part of it," Large said of the dismembering with chain saws and winches. "I think the older you get, the more sensitive you get." He mentioned an older friend who walked away from a dead, fifteen-foot, near-term fetus being lifted out of a gutted whale, and for a time wouldn't speak.

On Wednesday afternoon the whales were ignited in pits at the foot of the fore-dune. As they burned they were rendered, and when their oil caught fire they began to boil in it. The seething roar was muffled by a steady onshore breeze; the oily black smoke drifted southeast over the dunes, over English beach grass and pearly everlasting, sand verbena, and the purple flowers of beach pea, green leaves of sweet clover, and the bright yellow blooms of the monkey flower. It thinned until it disappeared against a weak-blue sky.

While fire cracked the blubber of one-eyed, jawless carcasses, a bulldozer the size of a two-car garage grunted in a trench being dug to the north for the last of them. These were still sprawled at the water's edge. Up close, the black, blistered skin, bearing scars of knives and gouging fingernails, looked like the shriveled surface of a pond evaporated beneath a summer sun. Their gray-blue innards lay about on the sand like bags of discarded laundry. Their purple tongues were wedged in retreat in their throats. Spermaceti oil dripped from holes in their heads, solidifying in the wind to stand in translucent stalagmites twenty inches high. Around them were tidal pools opaque with coagulated blood and, beyond, a pink surf.

As far as I know, no novelist, no historian, no moral philosopher, no scholar of Melville, no rabbi, no painter, no theologian had been on the beach. No one had thought to call them or to fly them in. At the end they would not have been allowed past the barricades.

The whales made a sound, someone had said, like the sound a big fir makes breaking off the stump just as the saw is pulled away. A thin screech.

A CLOSER LOOK AT BARRY LOPEZ

1. Now that you have read the four essays by Barry Lopez, think about the "stillness" that he claims is characteristic of his writing. What might Lopez mean by saying that his writing has a stillness to it? How does he accomplish this stillness? That is, how does Lopez write "stillness"? Can you point out moments of stillness in his writing? Write an essay that defines "stillness" and provides examples of stillness from Lopez's work to support your definition.
2. Consider who might read the kinds of essays that Barry Lopez writes. How does Lopez address his audience in each essay? That is, how does Lopez involve his audience when he discusses not only issues of environmentalism and conservation, but also larger moral issues such as the place of humans in nature or the human approach to death? Discuss in an essay how Lopez is attuned to his audience and how that attention affects his writing in any one of these essays. Be sure to identify examples from the essay to support your claim.

3. After having read the four essays by Lopez, how would you take what you have learned from his writing to write your own essay? Are there strategies that Lopez uses to address writing about nature that you find particularly interesting and that you might incorporate into your next essay—whether or not you write about nature? Rather than writing an essay, make a list of the things you like (or dislike) about Lopez's writing and explain how you might incorporate each of those things into your own writing. Be specific; move beyond simple ideas ("I like how he did that: I think I'll do that") to more sophisticated explanations of why you like something, how Lopez did it, and how you might do a similar thing.

Looking from Writer to Writer

1. Like Barry Lopez, several other writers in this collection can be considered "nature writers"—Scott Russell Sanders, Annie Dillard, and Rick Bass, for instance. Looking back through the essays by these writers, do you see any characteristics in the writing—other than subjects that can be considered "natural"—that are similar and might be considered part of what makes writing "nature writing"? Other than subject matter, are there similar rhetorical characteristics in the essays of these authors?

2. In his essay, "The Capital of Memory," André Aciman remembers his home in Alexandria, Egypt, from which he and his family were exiled. In this essay Aciman returns to Alexandria and writes of his memories and his experiences in the city upon his return. In many ways, Lopez's "The Stone Horse" can be seen as a similar kind of essay, one that both describes a place and the memory of a place. Compare these two essays and examine how each writer approaches the descriptions and memories of place.

3. In "We Are Shaped by the Sound of the Wind, the Slant of Sunlight," Barry Lopez writes about a kind of writing called "nature writing." He claims that he writes because "I want to talk about geography as a shaping force, not a subject." Likewise, he explains throughout this essay why he writes about "nature." In her essay "Why I Write," Joan Didion takes a very different approach to why she writes. And while the subjects of each of these two essays (writing) is similar, the essays themselves are quite different. Other than the writers' approaches to writing as a subject, how do these two essays differ? What differences do you see in the way Lopez and Didion write?

Looking Beyond

NONFICTION

About This Life: Journeys on the Threshold of Memory. New York: Knopf, 1998.

Arctic Dreams: Imagination and Desire in a Northern Landscape. New York: Scribner, 1986.

Crossing Open Ground. New York: Scribner, 1988.

Of Wolves and Men. New York: Scribner, 1978.

FICTION

Desert Notes: Reflections in the Eye of a Raven. Kansas City, KS: Sheed, Andrews, & McMeel, 1976.

Giving Birth to Thunder, Sleeping with His Daughter: Coyote Builds North America. Kansas City, KS: Sheed, Andrews, & McMeel 1978.

River Notes: The Dance of Herons. Kansas City, KS: Sheed, Andrews, & McMeel, 1979.

Winter Count. New York: Scribner, 1981.

OTHER WORKS

Apologia. Athens, GA: University of Georgia Press, 1998.

Cynthia Ozick

In an essay titled "Pear Tree and Polar Bear: A Word on Life and Art," Cynthia Ozick writes, "As for life, I don't like it. I notice no 'interplay of life and art.' Life is that which—pressingly, persistently, unfailingly, imperially—interrupts." Yet it is this very interplay of life and art that seems continuously to engage Ozick in many of her essays. Life or art, nonfiction or fiction; these are some of the tensions that reoccur in Ozick's work, tensions that are played out most powerfully in her essays and her views about essay-writing.

Cynthia Ozick was born in New York City in 1928. She grew up in the Pelham Bay section of the Bronx, the daughter of Russian Jews in a predominantly Irish Catholic neighborhood. Growing up during the Depression, Ozick watched her father, a pharmacist, and her mother struggle economically while she found solace and escape in books. In "A Drugstore in Winter" (reprinted here), Ozick describes how her mother, "not yet forty, wears bandages on her ankles, covering oozing varicose veins" from long days of standing: "Like my father, she is on her feet until one in the morning, the Park View [Pharmacy's] closing hour. My mother and father are in trouble, and I don't know it. I am too happy. I feel the secret center of eternity, nothing will ever alter, no one will ever die." Here again, we notice the interplay of life and art.

Isolated at school because she was Jewish, Ozick turned to books, everything she could find at the Traveling Library. Years later she would recall in her essays the influence of Henry James on her early aspirations, describing how, at the age of 17, after reading "The Beast in the Jungle," she had fallen "into the jaws of James." Ozick writes, "I became Henry James." "I was not a genius" and "I was not prolific," she explains, "But I carried the Jamesian idea, I was of his cult, I was a worshipper of literature, literature was my single altar." A self-proclaimed worshipper of literature, Ozick earned her BA in English literature in 1949 at New York University, and then completed an MA in literature at Ohio State University in 1951, where she wrote her master's thesis on parables in the novels of Henry James.

After a year as a copywriter in a Boston department store, Ozick married and returned to New York where she began writing novels, the first of which, *Trust,* was published in 1966.

However, Ozick's acclaim has not come from writing novels but from her short stories and essays. Her short stories appear in three collections, *The Pagan Rabbi and Other Stories* (1971), *Bloodshed and Three Novellas* (1976), and *Levitation: Five Fictions* (1982). For these, she has been awarded the O. Henry First Prize Award three times. Ozick's essays are collected in *Art and Arbor* (1983), *Metaphor and Memory* (1989), and *Fame and Folly* (1996).

For Ozick, the essay as a genre seems to produce a recurring tension, a tension that results from the essay's refusal to ignore the interplay between life and art. "I never meant to write essays," she explains in the foreword to *Art and Arbor.* Rather, her essays are "mainly written as spurs pressed hard in the dark, in response to an occasional summons from a chance voice." The source for many of her essays is indeed external, most often a book she has read, a writer she has met, a place she has visited. Ozick's essays are mainly responses to persons, objects, and events in the world. They deal— "pressingly, persistently, unfailingly"—with life. Yet this is the very thing that made Ozick suspicious of the essay as a form of art—"essays know too much."

"Essays summarize. They do not invent," writes Ozick. "In undertaking the writing of an essay . . . , I know beforehand what I think. I see the end, it is all the while uncompromisingly, inflexibly there, in sight, and my task is to traverse the space between. The risks are small. The way is predictable." Ozick says that "an essayist is generally assumed to be a reliable witness, sermonizer, lecturer, polemicist, persuader, historian, advocate: a committed intelligence, a single-minded truth-speaker." Life tugs closely at the identity of the essay. Fiction is different. "In beginning a story," Ozick explains, "I know nothing at all: surely not where I am going, and hardly at all how to get there . . . Fiction is all discovery . . . It deals with art, essays with life."

Nevertheless, Ozick seems to have reconciled the interplay of art and life. These are the essays that to her are worth writing. She explains, "a story is a hypothesis, a tryout of human nature under the impingement of certain given materials; so is an essay." Indeed, for Ozick, the best essays should be adventures the way that stories are: the best kind of essay "lacks the summarizing gift, is heir to nothing, and sets out with empty pockets from scratch."

Rhetorically, her essays achieve this fictional quality by giving the impression that they are working through something. She begins "Truman Capote Reconsidered" like this: "Truth at length becomes justice. A useful if obscure-sounding literary aphorism just this moment invented. What it signifies is merely this: if a writer lives long enough, he may himself eventually put behind him the work that brought him early fame, and which the world ought to have put aside in the first place." The effect here creates the impression of immediacy—that Ozick has just now lighted on this idea and will proceed to work through it. Similarly, even though many of her essays are ostensibly reviews of authors and their work, they do not merely summarize. Hers is not the objective style of one who looks at a subject as if it were an ornament to be admired. Rather, she uses the subject as an occasion to contemplate her own experience and those of others. In this way her essays do not "know too much"; instead, they give the impression of knowing as they go.

Ozick on Writing

At First Glance

"On Permission to Write" captures the life versus art tension that runs through many of Cynthia Ozick's essays. In this essay about writing, she distinguishes between the writer as artist and the writer as citizen. As you read it, think about what it means for Ozick to be a writer and compare her view with what you think it means to be a writer. Are some writers given greater permission to write than others? Think about how you would define and describe the best writing conditions, those that you have found give you the most permission to write.

On Permission to Write

> I hate everything that does not relate to literature, conversations bore me (even when they relate to literature), to visit people bores me, the joys and sorrows of my relatives bore me to my soul. Conversation takes the importance, the seriousness, the truth, out of everything I think.
>
> —FRANZ KAFKA, from his diary, 1918

In a small and depressing city in a nearby state there lives a young man (I will call him David) whom I have never met and with whom I sometimes correspond. David's letters are voluminous, vehemently bookish, and—in obedience to literary modernism—without capitals. When David says "I," he writes "i." This does not mean that he is insecure in his identity or that he suffers from a weakness of confidence—David cannot be characterized by thumbnail psychologizing. He is like no one else (except maybe Jane Austen). He describes himself mostly as poor and provincial, as in Balzac, and occasionally as poor and black. He lives alone with his forbearing and bewildered mother in a flat "with imaginary paintings on the walls in barren rooms," writes stories and novels, has not yet published, and appears to spend his days hauling heaps of books back and forth from the public library.

He has read, it seems, everything. His pages are masses of flashy literary allusions—nevertheless entirely lucid, witty, learned and sane. David is not *exactly* a crank who writes to writers, although he is probably a bit of that too. I don't know how he gets his living, or whether his letters romanticize either his poverty (he reports only a hunger for books) or his passion (ditto); still, David is a free intellect, a free imagination. It is possible that he hides his manuscripts under a blotter, Jane-Austenly, when his mother creeps mutely in to collect his discarded socks. (A week's worth, perhaps, curled on the floor next to Faulkner and Updike and Cummings and *Tristram Shandy*. Of the latter he remarks: "a worthy book. dare any man get off-spring on less?")

On the other hand, David wants to be noticed. He wants to be paid attention to. Otherwise, why would he address charming letters to writers (I am not the only one) he has never met? Like Joyce in "dirty provincial Dublin," he says, he means to announce his "inevitable arrival on the mainland." A stranger's eye, even for a letter, is a kind of publication. David, far from insisting on privacy, is a would-be public man. It may be that he pants after fame. And yet in his immediate position—his secret literary life, whether or not he intends it to remain secret—there is something delectable. He thirsts to read, so he reads; he thirsts to write, so he writes. He is in the private cave of his freedom, an eremite, a solitary; he orders his mind as he pleases. In this condition he is prolific. He writes and writes. Ah, he is poor and provincial, in a dim lost corner of the world. But his lonely place (a bare cubicle joyfully tumbling with library books) and his lonely situation (the liberty to be zealous) have given him the permission to write. To be, in fact, prolific.

I am not David. I am not poor, or provincial (except in the New York way), or unpublished, or black. (David, the sovereign of his life, invents an aloofness from social disabilities, at least in his letters, and I have not heard him mythologize "negritude"; he admires poets for their words and cadences.) But all this is not the essential reason I am not like David. I am not like him because I do not own his permission to write freely, and zealously, and at will, and however I damn please; and abundantly; and always.

There is this difference between the prolific and the non-prolific: the prolific have arrogated to themselves the permission to write.

By permission I suppose I ought to mean *inner* permission. Now "inner permission" is a phrase requiring high caution: it was handed to me by a Freudian dogmatist, a writer whose energy and confidence depend on regular visits to his psychoanalyst. In a useful essay called "Art and Neurosis," Lionel Trilling warns against the misapplication of Freud's dictum that "we are all ill, i.e., neurotic," and insists that a writer's productivity derives from "the one part of him that is healthy, by any conceivable definition of health . . . that which gives him the power to conceive, to plan, to work, and to bring his work to a conclusion." The capacity to write, in short, comes from an uncharted space over which even all-prevailing neurosis can have no jurisdiction or dominion. "The use to which [the artist] puts his power . . . may be discussed with reference to his particular neurosis," Trilling concedes; yet Trilling's verdict is finally steel: "But its essence is irreducible. It is, as we say, a gift."

If permission to write (and for a writer this is exactly equal to the power to write) is a gift, then what of the lack of permission? Does the missing "Go ahead" mean neurosis? I am at heart one of those hapless pre-moderns who believe that the light bulb is the head of a demon called forth by the light switch, and that Freud is a German word for pleasure; so I am not equipped to speak about principles of electricity or psychoanalysis. All the same, it seems to me that the electrifying idea of inward obstacle—neurosis— is not nearly so often responsible for low productivity as we are told. Writer's permission is not something that is switched off by helpless forces inside the writer, but by social currents—human beings and their ordinary predilections and prejudices—outside. If David writes freely and others don't, the reason might be that, at least for a while, David has kidnapped himself beyond the pinch of society. He is Jane Austen with her hidden manuscript momentarily slipped out from under the blotter; he is Thoreau in his cabin. He is a free man alone in a room with imaginary pictures on the walls, reading and writing in a private rapture.

There are some writers who think of themselves as shamans, dervishes of inspiration, divinely possessed ecstatics—writers who believe with Emerson that the artist "has cast off the common motives of humanity and has ventured to trust himself for a taskmaster": himself above everyone. Emerson it is who advises writers to aspire, through isolation, to "a simple purpose . . . as strong as iron necessity is to others," and who—in reply to every contingency—exhorts, "O father, O mother, O wife, O brother, O friend, I have lived with you after appearances hitherto. Henceforward I am the truth's." These shaman-writers, with their cult of individual genius and romantic egoism, may be self-glamorizing holy madmen, but they are not maniacs; they know what is good for them, and what is good for them is fences. You cannot get near them, whatever your need or demand. O father, O mother, O wife, O brother, O friend, they will tell you—*beat it*. They call themselves caviar, and for the general their caviar is a caveat.

Most writers are more modest than this, and more reasonable, and don't style themselves as unbridled creatures celestially privileged and driven. They know that they are citizens like other citizens, and have simply chosen a profession, as others have. These are the writers who go docilely to gatherings where they are required to marvel at every baby; who yield slavishly to the ukase that sends them out for days at a time to scout a samovar for the birthday of an elderly great-uncle; who pretend to overnight guests that they are capable of sitting at the breakfast table without being consumed by print; who craftily let on to in-laws that they are diligent cooks and sheltering wives, though they would sacrifice a husband to a hurricane to fetch them a typewriter ribbon; and so on. In short, they work at appearances, trust others for taskmasters, and do not insist too rigorously on whose truth they will live after. And they are honorable enough. In Company, they do their best to dress like everyone else: if they are women they will tolerate panty hose and high-heeled shoes, if they are men they will show up in a three-piece suit; but in either case they will be concealing the fact that during any ordinary row of days they sleep in their clothes. In the same company they lend themselves, decade after decade, to the expectation that they will not lay claim to unusual passions, that they will believe the average belief, that they will take pleasure in the average pleasure. Dickens, foreseeing the pain of relinquishing his pen at a time not of his choosing, reportedly would not accept an invitation. "Thank God for books," Auden said, "as an alternative to conversation." Good-citizen writers, by contrast, year after year decline no summons, refuse no banquet, turn away from no tedium, willingly enter into every anecdote and brook the assault of any amplified band. They will put down their pens for a noodle pudding.

And with all this sterling obedience, this strenuous courtliness and congeniality, this anxious flattery of unspoken coercion down to the third generation, something goes wrong. One dinner in twenty years is missed. Or no dinner at all is missed, but an "attitude" is somehow detected. No one is fooled; the cordiality is pronounced insincere, the smile a fake, the goodwill a dud, the talk a fib, the cosseting a cozening. These sweating citizen-writers are in the end always found out and accused. They are accused of elitism. They are accused of snobbery. They are accused of loving books and bookishness more feelingly than flesh and blood.

Edith Wharton, in her cool and bitter way, remarked of the literary life that "in my own family it created a kind of restraint that grew with the years. None of my relations ever spoke to me of my books, either to praise or to blame—they simply ignored them; . . . the subject was avoided as if it were a kind of family disgrace, which might be condoned but could not be forgotten."

Good-citizen writers are not read by their accusers; perhaps they cannot be. "If I succeed," said Conrad, "you shall find there according to your deserts: encouragement, consolation, fear, charm—all you demand—and, perhaps, also that glimpse of truth for which you have forgotten to ask." But some never demand, or demand less. "If you simplified your style," a strict but kindly aunt will advise, "you might come up to par," and her standard does not exempt Conrad.

The muse-inspired shaman-writers are never called snobs, for the plain reason that no strict but kindly aunt will ever get within a foot of any of them. But the good-citizen writers—by virtue of their very try at citizenship—are suspect and resented. Their work will not be taken for work. They will always be condemned for not being interchangeable with nurses or salesmen or schoolteachers or accountants or brokers. They will always be found out. They will always be seen to turn longingly after a torn peacock's tail left over from a fugitive sighting of paradise. They will always have hanging from a back pocket a telltale shred of idealism, or a cache of a few grains of noble importuning, or, if nothing so grandly quizzical, then a single beautiful word, in Latin or Hebrew; or else they will tip their hand at the wedding feast by complaining meekly of the raging horn that obliterates the human voice; or else they will forget not to fall into Montaigne over the morning toast, or else they will embarrass everyone by oafishly banging on the kettle of history; or else, while the room fills up with small talk, they will glaze over and inwardly chant "This Lime-Tree Bower My Prison"; or else—but never mind. What is not understood is not allowed. These citizens-pretenders will never be respectable. They will never come up to par. They will always be blamed for their airs. They will always be charged with superiority, disloyalty, coldness, want of family feeling. They will always be charged with estranging their wives, husbands, children. They will always be called snob.

They will never be granted the permission to write as serious writers are obliged to write: fanatically, obsessively, consumingly, torrentially, above all comically—and for life.

And therefore: enviable blissful provincial prolific lonesome David!

Double Take

1. What can we learn from this essay about Cynthia Ozick's views of writing? Given that the essay first appeared in *The New York Times Book Review,* which likely means it was read by people who are committed to a life of reading and to writers, do you think Ozick's readers would find her view of writing and writers appealing? Why or why not?
2. Do you think it is possible for a writer to write if she or he is isolated from citizenship (family relations, politics, human interaction, and so on)? Explain your response, drawing from your own experiences with writing.
3. Are there times when you find you have less permission to write than others? What are the conditions that you find most productive? What are the least productive? As a writer, what can you do to give yourself the most "permission" to write?

At First Glance

The "Hole/Birth Catalogue" was first published in Ms. *magazine. As you read the essay, think about who Cynthia Ozick's audience would likely have been and how Ozick's subject matter and style reflect the concerns and interests of that audience. In what ways are her descriptions of gender and her arguments about women effective given her audience? As you read, notice also the shift in tone from part 1 to part 2 of the essay. What is the rhetorical effect of this shift on you as a reader? Think about how this shift might be an early attempt on Ozick's part to combine features of the essay with features of the story—life and art.*

The Hole/Birth Catalogue

1. THE LOGIC OF THE HOLE

It may be that almost everything that separates women from men is a social fabrication—clothing, occupations, thinking habits, temperament. It may be that when we say "woman" we are invoking a heritage of thought, a myth, a learned construct: an *idea.* But childbirth is not any of these. "Woman" can be an imagining, a convenient dream of law or economics or religion. But childbirth is an event, *the* event of the race, and only half the race undergoes it. Is it, for that half, an illimitable experience, endlessly influencing, both before and afterward, an event that dominates until death?

Everyone is born, everyone dies, and though styles of death are subject to invention and misfortune—getting a bullet through your skull feels different, presumably, from the slow drugged death of the terminal cancer victim—we all struggle out of the birth canal with the same gestures and responses. What happens immediately afterward—who cares for the infant, and how, and where—is all at once the expression of the culture. If anatomy is destiny, technology is also a kind of destiny, and the baby bottle, no less than the jet plane, can alter a civilization. Beds, stirrups, hospitals, doctors, nurses, stitches, bandages, pills, pillows, all the debris of folklore that flies out after every birth with the certainty of the expulsion of the placenta—these are the social impedimenta that clutter the event. They seem almost to be the event itself.

But the person in childbirth can be alone in a forest, and still the baby's head will be driven through the hole at the bottom of her torso. It is sensible for the hole not to be covered. The baby is born entirely exposed, either with a hole of its own or with an inseminatory rod. It is attached by a string of flesh. When the string is cut, that is the end of the event.

Is it the end of the event?

How long is the event of childbirth? Several hours; it varies with the individual. How long is human life? Here the variation is greater. It is possible to die at birth, to be run over by a truck at thirty, to be bombed at forty, to live to be old. But "woman" is concretely—not mythologically—woman only for the sake of the few hours of childbirth. All the rest of the time her life and body are subject to more ordinary interruptions, by which she is distinguished very little from anyone else. Childbirth is an appointment (menstruation is the appointment calendar, listing only cancellations; like any negative calendar it requires small attention)—an appointment undertaken nine months before: which, unless nullified by abortion, must inevitably be kept.

But imagine a lucky and healthful land where a human being is likely to live peaceably until eighty. Imagine one who has experienced childbirth only twice, with the event lasting each time about six hours. For the sake of twelve hours out of a life seven hundred and one thousand two hundred and eighty hours long, this person is called "woman." For the sake of twelve hours out of a life seven hundred and one thousand two hundred and eighty hours long, this person is thrust into an ethos that enjoins rigid duties on her, almost none of them rationally related to the two six-hour events of childbirth.

Or imagine, in this lucky and healthful land, a person sixty years old. She is widowed and lives alone in a dark little flat. Consider her. Thirty years ago she spent six hours expelling an infant out of her hole via powerful involuntary muscular contractions. She did it in a special room in a big building. It was a rod-bearing infant, which afterward grew to be somewhat under six feet in height, dressed itself in two cloth tubes cut off at the ankles, and by now has spurted semen up a number of human holes; having settled down in a house in California, it has inseminated one hole three times. The person in the dark little flat thinks of herself as the grandmother of Linda, Michael, and Karen. Which is to say: she thinks of herself as a hole; the Ur-hole, so to speak; and that is very interesting.

It is also very interesting to look closely at this person who thinks of herself as a hole. She is covered up by a cloth tube cut off at the knees. Why is she covered up by one cloth tube cut off at the knees, instead of two cloth tubes cut off at the ankles? Thirty years ago she expelled an infant out of her hole; that is the reason.

Anatomy is destiny, and it is her destiny, because of her hole, to wear one cloth tube cut off at the knees instead of two cloth tubes cut off at the ankles.

Now look at the hair that grows on her head. Do not look for the hair in her armpits; she has clipped that. The reason she has clipped the hair in her armpits is that thirty years ago she expelled an infant out of her hole. But her head hair: look at that. It is of a certain length and is artificially curled. The reason her head hair is of that length, artificially curled, is that thirty years ago she expelled an infant out of her hole.

Watch her. She is sitting at the kitchen table sewing another cloth tube. Once in a while she rises and stirs something in a pot. The reason she is sitting at the kitchen table sewing a cloth tube (the kind cut off at the knees), the reason she gets up now and then to stir her pot, is not that she is hungry or is in need of another cloth tube. No: the reason is that thirty years ago she expelled an infant out of her hole, and ever since then she has conscientiously performed the duties that do not flow from the event.

And if the event had not taken place? She would still conscientiously perform those duties that do not flow from the event that did not happen. The hole in her body dictates her tasks, preoccupations, proprieties, tastes, character. Wondrous hole! Magical hole! Dazzlingly influential hole! Noble and effulgent hole! From this hole everything follows logically; first the baby, then the placenta, then, for years and years and years until death, a way of life. It is all logic, and she who lives by the hole will live also by its logic.

It is, appropriately, logic with a hole in it.

2. DESTINY, BIRTH, LIFE, DEATH

"Anatomy is destiny." These are Freud's words, and they have become almost as famous as his name itself. But, ah, fame is not truth; and destiny is precisely what anatomy is *not*. A hole is not destiny. A protuberance is not destiny. Even two protuberances—a pair of legs, nearly half the human body—are not destiny. If anatomy were destiny, the wheel could not have been invented; we would have been limited by legs.

Destiny is what is implicit in the very area we cannot speak of because it is not known—the sense of things beyond and apart from shape or dimension or hole or protuberance. There is an armless painter who holds the brush between his toes. Cut off two more limbs and he will use his teeth. The engineering is secondary to the vision. Anatomy is only a form of technology—nature's engineering. Destiny means, at the lowest, a modification of anatomy, and, at the highest, a soaring beyond anatomy. A person—and "person" is above all an idea—escapes anatomy. To reduce the person altogether to her anatomy is to wish the person into a nullity.

There is, first of all, the nullity of the servant.

In *Civilization and Its Discontents,* Freud posits a remarkable anatomical theory for the secondary and dependent condition of woman. The argument begins with the assertion that since fire represents the power of civilization, whoever can control fire can be dominant over civilization. By the "control" of fire, Freud explains, he means the ability to put it out at will. A man can pee on a fire from a little distance. Prevented by her anatomy, a woman cannot. Therefore man is in charge of civilization and woman cannot be.

Later in the same essay Freud identifies woman as having a "retarding and restraining influence" on civilization. This is because the tasks of civilization require "instinctual sublimations of which women are little capable."

But all this is the later Freud. *Civilization and Its Discontents* was composed after cancer had already begun to ravage Freud's face, and when Hitlerism had already begun to corrode German civilization. If he was writing, under such circumstances, with a kind of melancholy truculence, it might be instructive to see what Freud's views were at an earlier and happier time. Consider, then, Freud in love.

In love with Martha Bernays, Freud translated John Stuart Mill's essay "On the Subjection of Woman" into German. He did not notice its relevance to his fiancée's position—she had committed herself to a long and chaste engagement, during which she was to idle away years in waiting for the marriage. As for the essay itself, he did not like it. For one thing, he complained of its "lifeless style." (In a footnote Freud's biographer, Ernest Jones, a Freudian disciple, explains: "In exculpation of Mill one should mention that his wife is supposed to have been the main author of the book in question." It is axiomatic that a "wife's" style is inferior.) Freud's letter about Mill, written to his fiancée, is long; but worth, one supposes, the attention due genius:

> He [Mill] was perhaps the man of the century who best managed to free himself from the domination of customary prejudices. On the other hand—and that always goes together with it—he lacked in many matters the sense of the absurd; for example, in that of female emancipation and in the woman's question altogether. I recollect that in the essay I translated a prominent argument was that a married woman could earn as much as her husband. We surely agree that the management of a house, the care and bringing up of children, demand the whole of a human being and almost exclude any earning, even if a simplified household relieve her of dusting, cleaning, cooking, etc. He had simply forgotten all that, like everything else concerning the relationship between the sexes. That is altogether a point with Mill where one simply cannot find him human. His autobiography is so prudish or so ethereal that one could never gather from it that human beings consist of men and women and that this distinction is the most significant one that exists. In his whole presentation it never emerges that women are different beings—we will not say lesser, rather the opposite—from men. He finds the suppression of women an analogy to that of Negroes. Any girl, even without a suffrage or legal competence, whose hand a man kisses and for whose love he is prepared to dare all, could have set him right. It is really a stillborn thought to send women into the struggle for existence exactly as men. If, for instance, I imagined my sweet gentle girl as a competitor it would only end in my telling her . . . that I am fond of her and that I implore her to withdraw from the strife into the calm uncompetitive activity of my home. It is possible that changes in upbringing may suppress all a woman's tender attributes, needful of protection and yet so

victorious, and that she can then earn a livelihood like men. It is also possible that in such an event one would not be justified in mourning the passing away of the most delightful thing the world can offer us—our ideal of womanhood. I believe that all reforming action in law and education would break down in front of the fact that, long before the age at which a man can earn a position in society, Nature has determined woman's destiny through beauty, charm, and sweetness. Law and custom have much to give women that has been withheld from them, but the position of women will surely be what it is: in youth an adored darling and in mature years a loved wife.

"Nature has determined woman's destiny." It is, to borrow from Jones, no exculpation of Freud to note that he was a man of his class and era, and that this letter was written before 1890. Mill's essay is dated 1869; if Freud was, at his own valuation, a judge of human affairs, he was a retrogressive judge. And if he is, at the valuation of his posterity, a genius, his is the genius of retrogression.

But also of something worse. We come now to the nullity of death.

Mill, all lucidity and sanity, is called "prudish" and "ethereal"—words meaning precisely the opposite of what Mill's essay exhibits to everyone who has ever read it attentively, with the exception of its German translator. Who is the prude—the man who sees the distinction between men and women as "the most significant one that exists," significant chiefly for reducing women to petlike dependency in "my home," or the man who refuses to turn distinctions into liabilities? Who is the ethereal thinker—the man who poetizes about tender attributes and adored darlings and miracle-working kisses, or the man who draws up a solid catalogue of palpable discriminations against women? In inventing anatomy-is-destiny, Freud justified his having a household servant all the days of his life. The letter to his fiancée (who appears to have swallowed it all) is not only prudish and ethereal, but also bleatingly sentimental—because that is what sentimentality *is:* justification, exculpation, a covering-over, a retreat from clarity, prudishness and etherealism concealing real conditions.

Still, running a household, after all, is not tantamount to death, anguish, or even waste. Decent and fulfilling lives have gone down that road, if fulfillment is counted in pies and sock-washings. And why not? Bureaucrats and dentists are equal drudges and fiddlers, jobs are cells of domesticated emotion, offices are repetitious and restrictive boxes. Both men and women practice housewifery, wherever they are. Hemingway's early stories are cookbooks. If only "the management of a house" were the whole story! But no: once invoke Nature and Destiny and you are inviting an intensified preoccupation with death. Death becomes the whole story.

This is simply because all the truth any philosophy can really tell us about human life is that each new birth supplies another corpse. Philosophy tells only that; it is true; and if the woman is seen only as childbearer, she is seen only as disgorger of corpses. What is a baby-machine if not also a corpse-maker? Philosophy—Freud is a philosopher—leads only to the inexorable cadaver, and never to the glorious So What: the life-cry.

To say anatomy-is-destiny is to misunderstand the So What, that insatiable in-between which separates the fresh birth from the cadaver it turns out to be. To say anatomy-is-destiny is to reverse the life instinct—to reverse not only the findings of Darwin, but civilization in general. If the fish had stuck to its gills there would have been no movement up to the land. Lungs came because a creature of the sea wanted to take a walk, not vice versa. When a previous abundance of water began to evaporate during the breakup of the Ice Age, the unlucky fish had either to adapt to its destiny—air—or die. Air preceded lungs. In the history of evolution, destiny always precedes anatomy, and anatomy conforms by thinking up a convenient modification. In the history of civilization, dream precedes engineering. Imagine walking on the moon, and the artifact to take you there will follow the conception.

Freud, a retrograde thinker, had it backward. Celebrated for theorizing on evanescent and gossamer dream-life, he nevertheless limited humanity to the grossest designs of the flesh. In postulating anatomy-is-destiny, he stopped at the flesh; and the flesh dies. It is no surprise that Freud came finally to "discover" what he called the "death instinct." He divided the mind between Eros and destructiveness, making death as central to his scheme as sexuality. And in choosing the centrality of death, he reinvented as instinct what the priests of the Pharaohs took to be ontology. By putting birth first, he put death before life.

This is no paradox. The life instinct, insofar as we can define it (and we cannot), is the struggle to dare higher and higher, beyond the overtly possible, and in spite of knowing we will die. "The force that through the green fuse drives the flower/Drives my green age."

In the light of Freud's assertion of the death instinct, it is absolutely no wonder that he distorted, misunderstood, and hated religion—which is to say holiness: which is to say the struggle to dare higher and higher, beyond the overtly possible. Freud's *Selbsthass* was of a piece with his hatred for his inherited faith.★ He despised Judaism because it had in the earliest moment of history rejected the Egyptian preoccupation with a literal anatomy of death and instead hallowed, for its own sake, the time between birth and dying. Judaism has no dying god, no embalming of dead bodies, above all no slightest version of death instinct—"Choose life." In revenge against Judaism's declared life principle, and to satisfy the urgencies and priorities of the death instinct, Freud—this was the theme of *Moses and Monotheism*—turned Moses into an Egyptian. It meant he was turning himself into an Egyptian. It is no joke to notice that for mummies anatomy is all the destiny they will ever own.

3. DEATH (CONTINUED), A LETTER FROM A MADMAN, AND A PRUDISH AND ETHEREAL CONCLUSION

The being-born belongs to all of us, yet we remember nothing. In the forgetting itself lies the life principle, the glorious So What—you are here, get started, live, see, do, dream, figure a destiny, and make its mold for your little time. This is the meaning of the forgetting. And just as the being-born belongs to all of us, so the giving-

---

★He was joyous when Jung became a disciple—until then, he wrote Karl Abraham, psychoanalysis had seemed like a "Jewish national affair," but now, with a Gentile attached to it, it would gain in value.

birth belongs to no one. It is not a property or a lasting act. The making of the child gets done, and thereafter the child is a person, not a consequence or an ornament, and must be seen to with the diligence and generosity due all persons.

To make of the giving-birth a lifelong progression of consequences is to make a shrine of an act. It is a species of idolatry. A moment is mummified and consecrated—that very moment which the whole human race cannot remember. We are told that the capacity for childbirth makes a "woman." Woman, then, becomes the amnesia of the race. She is nullified into an absence.

But now there is a contradiction. She is not an absence; she represents, above all, the protoplasmic *thereness* of the human animal. She represents precisely what decays. She stands for dust, being dust-bringer. I took note earlier of that stupendously simple point: whoever creates the babies creates the corpses. Whoever signifies Birth signifies Death. Anatomy—in the case of woman, parturition—is destiny, the uterus is a grave, the childbearer carries death.

Freud saw woman wholly as childbearer. Seemingly apart from this perception, he came upon the notion of the death instinct. This he related to the killing of the "primal father" by the sons banded together (a curious unprovable fiction on which a great part of Freud's work rests). He, the great connector, did not connect his perception of the destructiveness and aggressiveness in human nature with the act of parturition. Logic makes the connection. Whoever destroys, whoever is aggressive, has first to be born; the childbearer becomes Shiva the Destroyer. It is the logical product of anatomy-is-destiny. The uterus destines the woman to spew destruction.

How can this terrible logic, this ultimate *reductio* which places the whole burden of humankind's failings on the woman's uterus, be contravened?

With great simplicity. Do not define woman solely by the act of parturition, and the demonic structure dissolves. Then the woman bears the baby, but her entry into parenthood—parenthood, that brevity—does not tie off the world. Parenthood becomes a rich episode in a life struck full with diverse and multiform episodes. She is a mother, a worker, a reader, a sailor. She is a judge, a peddler, a druggist, a polisher of shoes, a pilot, a publisher, an engineer. She is any combination of anything. She chooses life. She is not mythologized by a definition: one-who-gives-birth-and-therefore-spreads-destruction-and-creates-graveyards.

Now it is time to tell about my letter. It is from a madman. The usefulness of madmen is famous: they demonstrate society's logic carried out flagrantly down to its last scrimshaw scrap.

My madman's letter is typed on four long sheets of legal-sized paper, and all in carbon. Many copies of this letter have been broadcast by the diligent fellow, typing day and night on his machine. Here and there, at some especially passionate point, he has underlined with a heavy pencil. I pity him so much labor.

The reason he has sent the letter to me is clear. I have published some pieces on woman and society. He must somehow have worked up a list (he is a master of lists, as we shall see)—a list of writers on the Woman Question, and we are his targets.

"Friend," he begins, "women will soon be the hated and despised of all living things. It is your fanaticism for fecundity that is overpopulating the earth and ruining our ecology."

Good: my madman is not so crazy after all. He wants to save the environment. And he calls me friend. Already I like him a little.

But already I notice the Freudian turn in him. He too thinks of woman solely as childbearer.

"Years ago," he continues, "the fist was man's weapon to slay other men. Then the rock and the club were used. Spears and swords followed, with long lances. The bow and arrow preceded the rifle and six-shooter. The machine guns, artillery pieces, tanks, and aerial bombs follow. Finally, the A-bomb." Another Freudian turn. My madman has discovered the death instinct. But, though mad, he is logical (and here he underlined with a furious blackness): *"The progress of weaponry corresponds with the output of women's wombs.* That sums it up!"

But apparently the summing-up is insufficient. There is more, much more: "anyone who has a money-interest in population growth is apt to be against birth control and abortion." He means us to understand that it is women who are preeminently against birth control and abortions. It follows that women represent the money-interests. But now begin my madman's lists, and here is a little lapse: his catalogue of money-interests is curiously devoid of women. He lists doctors, diaper manufacturers, morticians, sellers of graveyard space, tombstones, funeral flowers, caskets, chauffeurs who drive hearses and funeral limousines, publishers of schoolbooks, auto firms that sell cars, trucks, and school buses, oil firms, tire manufacturers, road builders, realtors, contractors. "Lawyers, judges, cops, and jailers get their cut too."

"I don't mean to be harsh," he finishes kindly. "But you women will have to assess your priorities a bit better!" You women, with your mania to procreate to keep the Pentagons of the world up all through the small hours night after night scheming ways to kill and maim the product of your overworked wombs. Great will be the animosity toward your overwhelming womb-output! Toward your selfish spawning! *Soon"*—now he begins to underline again, and this makes his saliva flow nastily— *"soon pregnant women will be spat on, assaulted, and even killed!"*

So much for Freud's adored darlings. The death instinct, having given up on the primal father, is ganging up on pregnant women, who always used to be sure of at least a seat on the bus.

Reductio ad absurdum. My madman is after all a madman. But he is also, observe, a *practical* logician. Further, he owns the courage of connection which Freud lacked. He celebrates the Logic of the Hole measurelessly extended. Reduce woman to her anatomy—to Womb—and it is death, death, death, all the way; death and death and death, always, endlessly, gluttonously death. The destiny of anatomy is death.

Double Take

1. Comparing parts 1 and 2 of Cynthia Ozick's "The Hole/Birth Catalogue," what do you notice as different about them? In what ways is the difference between them accompanied by a shift in rhetoric (sentence structure, tone, use of evidence, argument, and so forth)? Describe these rhetorical differences with exam-

ples and then speculate how they affect the way readers might read and interpret this essay. That is, what effect does this shift in rhetoric have?

2. Based on your assumptions about essays as a genre, which of the two parts is more "essayistic"? Why?

3. What makes this essay especially appropriate and effective given its audience— readers of *Ms.* magazine? Be specific in your response, looking at Ozick's examples, her claims, her style, and so on.

4. What does Ozick mean by "The destiny of anatomy is death"? Why is this simple sentence such a powerful way to end this essay?

At First Glance

Like "On Permission to Write," "A Drugstore in Winter" was also first published in The New York Times Book Review, *where many of Ozick's essays first appeared. Yet this essay is not specifically a book review. As you read it, think not only about how it differs from your sense of what a book review should be, but also about why the editors of* The New York Times Book Review *deemed it appropriate for their book review section. How do you imagine readers would have reacted to the essay and why? Why do you think readers of* The New York Times Book Review *would have found this essay interesting? Also, as you read this essay, notice the interplay of life and art at work in it. Notice how Ozick draws her subject matter (her father's drugstore) from life, but then makes of it an occasion to explore ideas and experiences. Look at how Ozick creates the effect of working through the ideas. Think about how these rhetorical conventions, in storylike fashion, create the effect of taking readers on a journey.*

A Drugstore in Winter

This is about reading; a drugstore in winter; the gold leaf on the dome of the Boston State House; also loss, panic, and dread.

First, the gold leaf. (This part is a little like a turn-of-the-century pulp tale, though only a little. The ending is a surprise, but there is no plot.) Thirty years ago I burrowed in the Boston Public Library one whole afternoon, to find out—not out of curiosity—how the State House got its gold roof. The answer, like the answer to most Bostonian questions, was Paul Revere. So I put Paul Revere's gold dome into an "article" and took it (though I was just as scared by recklessness then as I am now) to the *Boston Globe,* on Washington Street. The Features Editor had a bare severe head, a closed parenthesis mouth, and silver Dickensian spectacles. He made me wait, standing, at the side of his desk while he read; there was no bone in me that did not rattle. Then he opened a drawer and handed me fifteen dollars. Ah, joy of Homer, joy of Milton! Grub Street bliss!

The very next Sunday, Paul Revere's gold dome saw print. Appetite for more led me to a top-floor chamber in Filene's department store: Window Dressing. But no one was in the least bit dressed—it was a dumbstruck nudist colony up there, a mob of naked frozen enigmatic manikins, tall enameled skinny ladies with bald breasts and skulls, and legs and wrists and necks that horribly unscrewed. Paul Revere's dome paled beside this gold mine! A sight—mute numb Walpurgis-nacht—easily worth another fifteen dollars. I had a Master's degree (thesis topic: "Parable in the Later Novels of Henry James") and a job as an advertising copy-writer (9 A.M. to 6 P.M. six days a week, forty dollars per week; if you were male and had no degree at all, sixty dollars). Filene's Sale Days—Crib Bolsters! Lulla-Buys! Jonnie-Mops! Maternity Skirts with Expanding Invisible Trick Waist! And a company show; gold watches to mark the retirement of elderly Irish salesladies; for me the chance to write song lyrics (to the tune of "On Top of Old Smoky") hon-oring our Store. But "Mute Numb Walpurgisnacht in Secret Downtown Chamber" never reached the *Globe.* Melancholy and meaning business, the Advertising Direc-tor forbade it. Grub Street was bad form, and I had to promise never again to sink to another article. Thus ended my life in journalism.

Next: reading, and certain drugstore winter dusks. These come together. It is an aeon before Filene's, years and years before the Later Novels of Henry James. I am scrunched on my knees at a round glass table near a plate glass door on which is inscribed, in gold leaf Paul Revere never put there, letters that must be read back-ward: ⟨PARK VIEW PHARMACY⟩ There is an evening smell of late coffee from the fountain, and all the librarians are lined up in a row on the tall stools, sipping and chattering. They have just stepped in from the cold of the Traveling Library, and so have I. The Traveling Library is a big green truck that stops, once every two weeks, on the corner of Continental Avenue, just a little way in from Westchester Avenue, not far from a house that keeps a pig. Other houses fly pigeons from their roofs, other yards have chickens, and down on Mayflower there is even a goat. This is Pel-ham Bay, the Bronx, in the middle of the Depression, all cattails and weeds, such a lovely place and tender hour! Even though my mother takes me on the subway far, far downtown to buy my winter coat in the frenzy of Klein's on Fourteenth Street, and even though I can recognize the heavy power of a quarter, I don't know it's the Depression. On the trolley on the way to Westchester Square I see the children who live in the boxcar strangely set down in an empty lot some distance from Spy Oak (where a Revolutionary traitor was hanged—served him right for siding with red-coats); the lucky boxcar children dangle their stick-legs from their train-house maw and wave; how I envy them! I envy the orphans of the Gould Foundation, who have their own private swings and seesaws. Sometimes I imagine I am an orphan, and my father is an imposter pretending to be my father.

My father writes in his prescription book: *#59330 Dr. O'Flaherty Pow .60/ #59331 Dr. Mulligan Gtt .65/ #59332 Dr. Tbron Tab .90.* Ninety cents! A terrifi-cally expensive medicine; someone is really sick. When I deliver a prescription around the corner or down the block, I am offered a nickel tip. I always refuse, out of conscience; I am, after all, the Park View Pharmacy's own daughter, and it wouldn't be seemly. My father grinds and mixes powders, weighs them out in tiny snowy heaps on an apothecary scale, folds them into delicate translucent papers or meticulously drops them into gelatin capsules.

In the big front window of the Park View Pharmacy there is a startling display—goldfish bowls, balanced one on the other in amazing pyramids. A German lady enters, one of my father's cronies—his cronies are both women and men. My quiet father's eyes are water-color blue, he wears his small skeptical quiet smile and receives the neighborhood's life-secrets. My father is discreet and inscrutable. The German lady pokes a punchboard with a pin, pushes up a bit of rolled paper, and cries out—she has just won a goldfish bowl, with two swimming goldfish in it! Mr. Jaffe, the salesman from McKesson & Robbins, arrives, trailing two mists: winter steaminess and the animal fog of his cigar,★ which melts into the coffee smell, the tarpaper smell, the eerie honeyed tangled drugstore smell. Mr. Jaffe and my mother and father are intimates by now, but because it is the 1930s, so long ago, and the old manners still survive, they address one another gravely as Mr. Jaffe, Mrs. Ozick, Mr. Ozick. My mother calls my father Mr. O, even at home, as in a Victorian novel. In the street my father tips his hat to ladies. In the winter his hat is a regular fedora; in the summer it is a straw boater with a black ribbon and a jot of blue feather.

What am I doing at this round glass table, both listening and not listening to my mother and father tell Mr. Jaffe about their struggle with "Tessie," the lion-eyed landlady who has just raised, threefold, in the middle of that Depression I have never heard of, the Park View Pharmacy's devouring rent? My mother, not yet forty, wears bandages on her ankles, covering oozing varicose veins; back and forth she strides, dashes, runs, climbing cellar stairs or ladder; she unpacks cartons, she toils behind drug counters and fountain counters. Like my father, she is on her feet until one in the morning, the Park View's closing hour. My mother and father are in trouble, and I don't know it. I am too happy. I feel the secret center of eternity, nothing will ever alter, no one will ever die. Through the window, past the lit goldfish, the gray oval sky deepens over our neighborhood wood, where all the dirt paths lead down to seagull-specked water. I am familiar with every frog-haunted monument: Pelham Bay Park is thronged with WPA art—statuary, fountains, immense rococo staircases cascading down a hillside, Bacchus-faced stelae—stone Roman glories afterward mysteriously razed by an avenging Robert Moses. One year—how distant it seems now, as if even the climate is past returning—the bay froze so hard that whole families, mine among them, crossed back and forth to City Island, strangers saluting and calling out in the ecstasy of the bright trudge over such a sudden wilderness of ice.

In the Park View Pharmacy, in the winter dusk, the heart in my body is revolving like the goldfish fleet-finned in their clear bowls. The librarians are still warming up over their coffee. They do not recognize me, though only half an hour ago I was scrabbling in the mud around the two heavy boxes from the Traveling Library— oafish crates tossed with a thump to the ground. One box contains magazines— *Boy's Life, The American Girl, Popular Mechanix.* But the other, the other! The other

---

★Mr. Matthew Bruccoli, another Bronx drugstore child, has written to say that he remembers with certainty that Mr. Jaffe did not smoke. In my memory the cigar is somehow there, so I leave it.

transforms me. It is tumbled with storybooks, with clandestine intimations and transfigurations. In school I am a luckless goosegirl, friendless and forlorn. In P.S. 71 I carry, weighty as a cloak, the ineradicable knowledge of my scandal—I am cross-eyed, dumb, an imbecile at arithmetic; in P.S. 71 I am publicly shamed in Assembly because I am caught not singing Christmas carols; in P.S. 71 I am repeatedly accused of deicide. But in the Park View Pharmacy, in the winter dusk, branches blackening in the park across the road, I am driving in rapture through the Violet Fairy Book and the Yellow Fairy Book, insubstantial chariots snatched from the box in the mud. I have never been *inside* the Traveling Library; only grownups are allowed. The boxes are for the children. No more than two books may be borrowed, so I have picked the fattest ones, to last. All the same, the Violet and the Yellow are melting away. Their pages dwindle. I sit at the round glass table, dreaming, dreaming. Mr. Jaffe is murmuring advice. He tells a joke about Wrong-Way Corrigan. The librarians are buttoning up their coats. A princess, captive of an ogre, receives a letter from her swain and hides it in her bosom. I can visualize her bosom exactly—she clutches it against her chest. It is a tall and shapely vase, with a hand-painted flower on it, like the vase on the secondhand piano at home.

I am incognito. No one knows who I truly am. The teachers in P.S. 71 don't know. Rabbi Meskin, my *cheder* teacher, doesn't know. Tessie the lion-eyed landlady doesn't know. Even Hymie the fountain clerk can't know—though he understands other things better than anyone: how to tighten roller skates with a skatekey, for instance, and how to ride a horse. On Friday afternoons, when the new issue is out, Hymie and my brother fight hard over who gets to see *Life* magazine first. My brother is older than I am, and doesn't like me; he builds radios in his bedroom, he is already W2LOM, and operates his transmitter *(da-di-da-dit, da-da -di-da)* so penetratingly on Sunday mornings that Mrs. Eva Brady, across the way, complains. Mrs. Eva Brady has a subscription to *The Writer;* I fill a closet with her old copies. How to Find a Plot. Narrative and Character, the Writer's Tools. Because my brother has a ham license, I say "I have a license too." "What kind of license?" my brother asks, falling into the trap. "Poetic license," I reply; my brother hates me, but anyhow his birthday presents are transporting: one year *Alice in Wonderland, Pinocchio* the next, then *Tom Sawyer.* I go after Mark Twain, and find *Joan of Arc* and my first satire, *Christian Science.* My mother surprises me with *Pollyanna,* the admiration of her Lower East Side childhood, along with *The Lady of the Lake.* Mrs. Eva Brady's daughter Jeannie has outgrown her Nancy Drews and Judy Boltons, so on rainy afternoons I cross the street and borrow them trying not to march away with too many—the child of immigrants, I worry that the Brady's, true and virtuous Americans, will judge me greedy or careless. I wrap the Nancy Drews in paper covers to protect them. Old Mrs. Brady, Jeannie's grandmother, invites me back for more. I am so timid I can hardly speak a word, but I love her dark parlor; I love its black bookcases. Old Mrs. Brady sees me off, embracing books under an umbrella; perhaps she divines who I truly am. My brother doesn't care. My father doesn't notice. I think my mother knows. My mother reads the *Saturday Evening Post* and the *Woman's Home Companion;* sometimes the *Ladies' Home Journal,* but never *Good Housekeeping.* I read all my mother's magazines. My father reads *Drug Topics* and *Der*

Tog, the Yiddish daily. In Louie Davidowitz's house (waiting our turn for the rabbi's lesson, he teaches me chess in *cheder*) there is a piece of furniture I am in awe of: a shining circular table that is also a revolving bookshelf holding a complete set of Charles Dickens. I borrow *Oliver Twist.* My cousins turn up with *Gulliver's Travels, Just So Stories, Don Quixote,* Oscar Wilde's *Fairy Tales,* uncannily different from the usual kind. Blindfolded, I reach into a Thanksgiving grabbag and pull out *Mrs. Leicester's School,* Mary Lamb's desolate stories of rejected children. Books spill out of rumor, exchange, miracle. In the Park View Pharmacy's lending library I discover, among the nurse romances, a browning, brittle miracle: *Jane Eyre.* Uncle Morris comes to visit (*his* drugstore is on the other side of the Bronx) and leaves behind, just like that, a three-volume Shakespeare. Peggy and Betty Provan, Scottish sisters around the corner, lend me their *Swiss Family Robinson.* Norma Foti, a whole year older, transmits a rumor about Louisa May Alcott; afterward I read *Little Women* a thousand times. Ten thousand! I am no longer incognito, not even to myself. I am Jo in her "vortex"; not Jo exactly, but some Jo-of-the-future. I am under an enchantment: who I truly am must be deferred, waited for and waited for. My father, silently filling capsules, is grieving over his mother in Moscow. I write letters in Yiddish to my Moscow grandmother, whom I will never know. I will never know my Russian aunts, uncles, cousins. In Moscow there is suffering, deprivation, poverty. My mother, threadbare, goes without a new winter coat so that packages can be sent to Moscow. Her fiery justice-eyes are semaphores I cannot decipher.

Some day, when I am free of P.S. 71, I will write stories; meanwhile, in winter dusk, in the Park View, in the secret bliss of the Violet Fairy Book, I both see and not see how these grains of life will stay forever, papa and mama will live forever, Hymie will always turn my skatekey.

Hymie, after Italy, after the Battle of the Bulge, comes back from the war with a present: *From Here to Eternity.* Then he dies, young. Mama reads *Pride and Prejudice* and every single word of Willa Cather. Papa reads, in Yiddish, all of Sholem Aleichem and Peretz. He reads Malamud's *The Assistant* when I ask him to.

Papa and mama, in Staten Island, are under the ground. Some other family sits transfixed in the sun parlor where I read *Jane Eyre* and *Little Women* and, long afterward, *Middlemarch.* The Park View Pharmacy is dismantled, turned into a Hallmark card shop. It doesn't matter! I close my eyes, or else only stare, and everything is in its place again, and everyone.

A writer is dreamed and transfigured into being by spells, wishes, goldfish, silhouettes of trees, boxes of fairy tales dropped in the mud, uncles' and cousins' books, tablets and capsules and powders, papa's Moscow ache, his drugstore jacket with his special fountain pen in the pocket, his beautiful Hebrew paragraphs, his Talmudist's rationalism, his Russian-Gymnasium Latin and German, mama's furnace-heart, her masses of memoirs, her paintings of autumn walks down to the sunny water, her braveries, her reveries, her old, old school hurts.

A writer is buffeted into being by school hurts—Orwell, Forster, Mann!—but after a while other ambushes begin: sorrows, deaths, disappointments, subtle diseases, delays, guilts, the spite of the private haters of the poetry side of life, the snubs of the glamorous, the bitterness of those for whom resentment is a daily gruel, and so on and so on; and then one day you find yourself leaning here, writing at that selfsame round glass table salvaged from the Park View Pharmacy—writing this, an impossibility, a summary of how you came to be where you are now, and where, God knows, is that? Your hair is whitening, you are a well of tears, what you meant to do (beauty and justice) you have not done, papa and mama are under the earth, you live in panic and dread, the future shrinks and darkens, stories are only vapor, your inmost craving is for nothing but an old scarred pen, and what, God knows, is that?

Double Take

1. How is this essay about reading, as Cynthia Ozick says it is in the first sentence? What does "A Drugstore in Winter" teach us about reading?
2. In what ways does this essay support or open to debate Ozick's view that there is no "interplay of life and art"? Is such an interplay at work in this essay? How so, and what is its effect?
3. "A Drugstore in Winter" is full of details—her father's prescriptions (#59330 Dr. O'Flaherty Pow .60), names of businesses (McKesson & Robbins), titles of magazines *(Boy's Life)*. In what ways does this detailed information contribute to the meaning of the essay? Do you find this detail helpful? What does such detail allow writers to do?
4. Ozick uses a great deal of embedded clauses within her writing, as in the following sentence from "A Drugstore in Winter": "What am I doing at this round glass table, both listening and not listening to my mother and father tell Mr. Jaffe about their struggle with 'Tessie,' the lion-eyed landlady who has raised, threefold, in the middle of the Depression I have never heard of, the Park View Pharmacy's devouring rent?" Ozick could have divided this complex sentence into several more simple sentences. What does she gain by not doing so? As a writer, how do you make such decisions about style?

Seeing for Yourself

At First Glance

"Rushdie in the Louvre" is one of Cynthia Ozick's more recent essays. Since you have just read some of Ozick's earlier essays, think about how her writing has evolved as you read this essay. Look for recurring and new stylistic and thematic patterns. Also, pay attention to how Ozick infuses her political views into the essay and consider whether these views detract from or strengthen her writing.

Rushdie in the Louvre

A while ago—it was in Paris, in the Louvre—I saw Salman Rushdie plain. He was sitting in a high-backed chair at the foot of an incalculably long banquet table fitted out with two rows of skinny microphones, each poking upward like a knuckly finger. His hands lays docile, contained, disciplined, on a dark-red leather portfolio stamped with his name in gilt. A gargantuan crystal chandelier, intricately designed, with multiple glinting pendants, hung from a ceiling painted all over with rosy royal nymphs—a ceiling so remote that the climate up there seemed veiled in haze. Who could measure that princely chamber, whether in meters or in history? And all around, gold, gold, gold.

The day before, in a flood of other visitors, I had penetrated an even more resplendent hall of the Louvre, the *Galerie d'Apollon*—a long, spooky corridor encrusted with kingly treasures: ewers and reliquaries of jasper and crystal, porphyry vases, scepters of coronations anciently repudiated, and, forlorn in their powerlessness, the Crown Jewels. All these hide in the gloom of their glass cases, repelling whatever gray granules of light drizzle down from above, throwing a perpetual dusk over the march of regal portraits that once commanded awe, and now, in the half-dark, give out a bitter look of faint inner rot. Here, among its glorious leavings, one can feel the death of absolutism. "I can stand a great deal of gold," Henry James once said; and so could the kings of France, and the Napoleons who succeeded them, all devoted to the caressings and lustings of gold—Midaslike objects of gold, soup bowls and spoons, fretwork and garnishings and pilasters of gold, gold as a kind of contagion or irresistible eruption.

James was enchanted; for him that rash of gold hinted at no disease, whether of self-assertion or force of terror. He equated the artist's sovereign power with what he had "inhaled little by little" in the Gallery of Apollo—"an endless golden riot and relief, figured and flourished in perpetual revolution, breaking into great high-hung circles and symmetries of squandered picture, opening into deep outward embrasures," a glory that signified for him "not only beauty and art and supreme design but history and fame and power." On his deathbed, confused by a stroke, he imagined himself to be Napoleon in the midst of a project of renovating the Louvre: "I call your attention," he dictated to his secretary, "to the precious enclosed transcripts of plans and designs for the decoration of certain apartments of the palaces here, of the Louvre and the Tuileries, which you will find addressed in detail to artists and workmen who are to take them in hand."

James's Napoleonic hallucination of 1916 has been realized seven decades later. Artists and workmen *have* taken the Louvre and the Tuileries in hand. There are cranes and sandy excavations—a broad tract of these at the end of the gardens of the Tuileries abutting the Louvre—and then, suddenly, there is the great living anti-Ozymandian I. M. Pei Pyramid, swarming with visitors, a peaked postmodernist outcropping of glass and steel in the wide square courtyard of this brilliant old palace: a purposeful visual outrage conceived in amazing wit and admirable utility, flanked by a triplet of smaller pyramids like three echoing laughters. The apartments of the Louvre's Richelieu wing, where Rushdie sat—balding, bearded, in sober coat and tie—was undergoing reconstruction: visitors' shoes left plaster-powder footprints on the red-carpeted grand stair. But visitors were few, anyhow, during the renovation, when the Richelieu was closed to the public. On the day Rushdie came, the entire Louvre was closed, and the Richelieu wing was effectively sealed off by a formidable phalanx of security men in black outfits, with black guns at their hips. Rushdie's arrival was muted, unnoticed; out of the blue he was there, unobtrusive yet somehow enthroned—ennobled—by the ongoing crisis of terror that is his visible nimbus.

He was attending a seminar of the Académie Universelle des Cultures, the brainchild of then President François Mitterand. The Academy's president, appointed by Mitterrand, is Elie Wiesel, recipient of the Nobel Peace Prize, and there are nine other Nobel-winning members, among them Wole Soyinka of Nigeria (in Literature), and the Americans Joshua Lederberg (in Medicine and Physiology) and Toni Morrison (the 1993 laureate in Literature). The official meeting place of this newborn organization—it is still in the process of formulating its by-laws and refining its overall aims—is in the Richelieu apartments. Unlike the twilight majesties of the Gallery of Apollo, the Academy's space is brightly warmed in sun from immense windows. Peering out, one sees a bit of courtyard, but mainly the long line of an encircling balcony, ranged with mammoth stone figures in plumed Monte Cristo headgear and bucked eighteenth-century pumps, the very soles of which seem mountainously tall. It is as if hallucinations can inhabit even daylight. A low door—low in relation to the ceiling—opens into what might pass for a giantess's pantry, a series of closets white with plaster dust and smelling of an unfinished moistness, and then a sort of gangway leading to just-installed toilets. On the day Rushdie came, it was up to an armed guard to decide whether or not to let one through to the plumbing.

The other end of this vast sanctum is the threshold to salon after palatial salon, magnificence serving as vestibule to still more magnificence, everything freshly gilded everywhere: the Napoleonic dream re-imagined for the close of a century that has given new and sinister vitality to the meaning of absolutism. The gas chambers and the ovens: the gulag; and finally the terror that invents car bombs, airplane hijackings, ideological stabbings of civilians at bus stops, the murder of ambassadors and Olympic athletes and babies in their cribs, the blowing up of an embassy in Buenos Aires, the World Trade Center in New York, the financial district of London, a restaurant in Paris, a synagogue in Istanbul. Under the shadow of this decades-long record, the setting of a price on a novelist's head is hardly a culmination, though it is surely, in an era of imaginative atrocity, a new wrinkle, a kind of hallucination in itself. Hallucination, after all, is make-believe taken literally; dream assessed as fact.

Long before he dreamt himself the imperial Napoleon ordering the rehabilitation of the Louvre, Henry James had a dream of limitless terror. The dream was of the Gallery of Apollo—but now those inhalations of absolutism were wholly altered: what had been seen as the potency of fame and the absolute rule of beauty and art turned away its sublime face to reveal absolutism's underside, a thing uncompromisingly deadly, brutal, irrational. Artist and dreamer, James in his nightmare is being pursued down the length of the Galerie d'Apollon by an "appalling" shape intent on murdering him. (Note the dreamer's pun: Apollo, appalling. Supremacy transmogrified into horror.) A door is shut against the powerful assassin; the assassin— "the awful agent, creature, or presence, whatever he was"—presses back. And then, all at once, in a burst of opposing power, the dreamer defends himself: "Routed, dismayed, the tables turned upon him by my so surpassing him for straight aggression and dire intention, my visitant was already but a diminished spot in the long perspective, the tremendous, glorious hall, . . . over the far-gleaming floor of which, cleared for the occasion of its great line of priceless *vitrines* down the middle, he sped for *his* life, while a great storm of thunder and lightning played through the deep embrasures of high windows on the right."

Not far from the Gallery of Apollo, the Richelieu apartments of the Louvre do not quake with the storm of nightmare, but the members of the Academy (men and women from the four corners of our slightly ovoid planet), discreet, courtly, inhale the appalling breath of the pursuer. The image of routing is dim: what weapon is there against a hidden assassin who may strike a moment from now, or tomorrow, or the day after? The arsenal of intellect—what we mean by the principles or intuitions of culture—is helpless before such willed, wild atrocity: anybody here might overnight become Rushdie. The Academy's President, a survivor of Auschwitz, has already *been* Rushdie: a human being pitilessly hunted as prey. No one cranes down the endless table, with its line of microphones, to gape at this newest human prey; yet Rushdie's quiet reality is electrifying, a prodigy in itself. It is his first appearance at a meeting since his unanimous election to the Academy. His arrival was hinted at—discreetly, elusively—by President Wiesel the evening before, but would the man who is hunted and stalked actually show up? His plain humanity is a marvel— a fellow sitting in a chair, loosening his tie, taking off his jacket as the afternoon warms. He is no metaphor, no legend, no symbol. His fame, once merely novelist's fame, is now the fame of terror. A writer has been transmuted into a pharaoh, wrapped in hiddenness, mummified in life. It happens that Rushdie nowadays looks more scribbler than pharaoh: a certain scruffiness of falling-out hair and indecisive beard, the telltale fleshiness of the sedentary penman; the redundant mien of someone who hates wearing a tie. How different from that slender princeling who, at the Forty-eighth International PEN Conference in New York in 1986, stood up to speechify in the aisle! What we saw then was a singularly beautiful young man got up in bright Indian (or perhaps pseudo-Indian) tunic, black-haired, black-eyed, as ravishing in outline as some gilt Persian miniature. I no longer recollect what he said on that occasion, though I retain something of his point of view: rigidly "Third World," loyally "progressive." A document protesting Middle Eastern terrorism was circulating through that body for some days; Rushdie did not append his name to it.

The bristling protection that surrounds him now is an offense, an enormity: professional, determined, watchful, admitting no breach; above all, conducted on a kingly scale. There is a twist of corruption—civilization undone—in Rushdie's necessary retinue, a retinue that shocks: all these sentries, these waiting police cars in the courtyard, dedicated to the preservation of a single human life. Or one could easily, and more justly, claim the opposite: that it is civilization's high humane standard, a society's concrete and routine glory, that so much sheltering force should be dedicated to the protection of one man under threat. But the first response is the sharper one: the sensation of recoil from the stealthily meandering armed men in black, the armed men lurking on the way to the toilet, the squad of armed men churning in this or that passageway or bunched oddly against a wall. When, at the beginning of the year, President Mitterrand came for the official inauguration of the Académie Unverselle des Cultures, the crush of television cameras, reporters, ambassadors, distinguished oglers, assorted intellectuals, and the charmed hoopla of fervent French *gloire* brought in the wake of the President's footsteps a troop of security men drumming over the Louvre's burnished floors—but there was nothing grim in that train. It signified honor and festivity. Monarchs and presidents may have to live like targets in danger of being detonated; for their guests at a celebration, though, that busy retinue, however fearsomely occupied, registers as innocently as a march of bridesmaids. Rushdie, by contrast, is tailed by a reminder of death. Whoever is in a room with him, no matter how secured against intruders, remembers that the would-be assassin is on the alert for opportunity, whether for greed or for God.

Rushdie's so-called blasphemy is the fabrication of literalists whose piety can be respected but whose literalism assumes what may not be assumed: that the Creator of the Universe can be diminished by any human agency, that the sacred is susceptible of human soiling. How can a novel blaspheme? How can a work of art (which can also mean a work of dream, play, and irony) blaspheme? Islam, like Judaism, is not an iconic creed (both are famously the opposite), but the philosophers of even iconic religious expressions like medieval Christianity and classical Hinduism do not locate the divine literally in paint or carving, and know that art, while it may, for some, kindle reverence, cannot be a medium for the soiling of the sacred. Art cannot blaspheme because it is not in the power of humankind to demean or besmirch the divine. Can a man's book tarnish God? "Where wast thou when I laid the foundations of the earth?" the Lord rebukes Job. "Knowest thou the ordinances of heaven? canst thou set the dominion thereof in the earth? . . . Who hath put wisdom in the inward parts? or who hath given understanding to the heart?" After which, Job is chastened enough to "lay mine hand upon my mouth."

Men who were not there when the foundations of the earth were laid neverthe-less lay their hands on a novelist's mouth. One of Rushdie's translators, the Japanese Hitoshi Igarashi, has been murdered; another, the Italian Ettore Capriolo, was seri-ously wounded. The American publishers of the paperback *Satanic Verses* hide behind an anonymous "consortium." And meanwhile Rushdie walks or rides nowhere without his train of guards. After lunching in a dining room of the Pyra-mid, the other members of the Academy stroll the few yards across the Louvre's inner court to return to the Richelieu for the afternoon plenary; but Rushdie, emerging alone from the Pyramid like the pharaonic figure he has been made into, is invisibly placed, alone, in a limousine that moves with glacial languor from one part of the courtyard to the other, accompanied by security men slowly pacing beside it and all around it. Rushdie is the prisoner both of his protectors and of his accusers.

In the eyes of his accusers, his very existence is a blasphemy to be undone and a blemish to be annihilated. Barricaded day and night against fanatic absolutists who look for a chance to kill, who despise reason and discourse, repudiate compromise, and reject amelioration, he has become, in his own person, a little Israel—or, rather, Israel as it felt its circumstances until just recently, before the Rabin-Arafat peace accord (and as it continues to feel them vis-à-vis Hamas and other rejectionists). This is something that, in all logic, has cried out to be said aloud ever since the *fatwa* was first promulgated; but Rushdie's defenders, by and large, have not said it—some because they feared to exacerbate his situation (but how could it have been wors-ened?), some because they have themselves been among Israel's fiercest ideological opponents. But one fact is incontrovertible: for the mullahs of Iran, who oppose both recognition and peace, Rushdie and the Jews of Israel are to be granted the same doom. What can be deduced from this ugly confluence is, it seems to me, also incontrovertible: morally and practically, there is no way to distinguish between the terrorist whose "cause" is pronounced "just" (and whose assaults on civilians are euphemized as political or religious resistance) and the terrorist who seeks to carry out the mullahs' *fatwa* against Rushdie (a call to assassination euphemized as reli-gious duty). One cannot have exculpated Arafat's Fatah for its long-standing pro-gram of bloodshed—not yet wholly suppressed—directed against both Jews and Arabs (the latter for what is termed "collaboration"), while at the same time defend-ing Rushdie and deploring his plight. And in one way, after all, Rushdie is better off than women knifed on street corners or bus passengers blown up: he is at every moment under the surveillance of his security team. On the other hand, individual civilians on their errands, exposed to the brutal lottery of ambush, have their lucky and unlucky days; Rushdie, no longer a civilian, drafted into the unwilling army of victimhood, has drawn the targeted ticket. All his days are unlucky.

But like James in the Gallery of Apollo, today in the Louvre he means to turn the tables.

Why link Henry James and Salman Rushdie? They are separated by a century. They were born continents apart. One is a vast and completed library; the other, unfathomable as to his ultimate stature, is in the middle of the way. Moreover (as for the issue of terror), what threatens Rushdie had a name, *fatwa,* and a habitation—Iran, and all those other places and men and women driven by the mullahs' imaginings of God's imperatives. Whereas what threatened James was no more than his own imagination, an extrusion of the psyche's secrets, nothing enacted in the world of real and ferocious event. What threatened James was a fable of his own making. But a dream, gossamer and ephemeral though it may be, is like a *genius loci,* the spirit of a site, which can send out exhalations with the force of ciphers or glyphs. Ciphers can be decoded; glyphs can be read across centuries. (Is it the Louvre itself that will speak up for Rushdie? Wait and see.) There is, besides, an arresting nexus of situation and temperament. Like James, Rushdie left the country of his birth for England: each sought, and won, a literary London life. Each kept a backward-glancing eye on his native society. As James never abandoned interest, inquisitiveness, sympathy, and the sometimes adversarial passions of kinship with regard to America, so Rushdie retains a familial, historical and scholarly connection to Islam, warmed by kinship, interest, sympathy. Both men were charged with apostasy—James because near the end of his life, out of gratitude to Britain, he gave up his American citizenship; Rushdie more savagely, on account of having written a fable. Both are in thrall to fable; both have an instinct for the intercultural tale of migration, what James called "the international theme." Both are beguiled by notions of assimilation and strangeness, of native and newcomer.

There is more. Rushdie, like James, is secular, history-minded, skeptical, impatient with zealotry. James's father, though harmless enough, was a man metaphysically besotted, a true believer, dogmatically sunk in Swedenborgian fogs. Having been reared in an atmosphere of private fanaticism, James repudiated its public expression wherever he encountered it. He had nothing but contempt for the accusers of Dreyfus, the French Jewish army officer condemned for treason. He followed the case day by day. "I sit . . . and read L'Affaire Dreyfus. What a bottomless and sinister *affaire* and in what a strange mill it is grinding. . . . I eat and drink, I sleep and dream Dreyfus." He did better than that. He wrote to Zola to congratulate him on the publication of *J'Accuse,* a defense of Dreyfus—"one of the most courageous things ever done"—for which Zola was brought to trial and convicted. In James's view, if Zola had not fled from his sentencing, "he would have been torn *limb from limb* by the howling mob in the street."

Bottomless and sinister; apostasy and treason; the howling mob in the street. It is all familiar and instantly contemporary. The determination of the anti-Dreyfusards in France, and their fellow travelers all over Europe, to destroy an innocent and consummately patriotic Frenchman by conspiracy and forgery, and especially by the incitement of mobs, reminds one that the concept of *fatwa* is not held exclusively by mullahs. And Rushdie too had been conspired against by a kind of forgery: having written a fable, he is represented as having issued a curse: he is charged with betraying Islam. Dreyfus was charged with betraying France. Millions were avid to believe it, until his champion Zola turned the tables on the persecutors.

It is now clearer than ever that Rushdie is resolved to become, however obliquely, his own champion. Though ringed always by his ferocious security apparatus, he ventures more and more into the hot zone of political sausion. His meeting with President Clinton at the White House in November of 1993 may have constituted, for Rushdie, the hottest—the most influential—zone of all. The mullahs, whose denunciations followed immediately, hardly disagreed, and the White House visit triggered instant State Department warnings to Americans overseas about possible retaliation. No one forgets the murder of that translator; as the anonymity of Rushdie's paperback publishers shows, it is not easy for others to speak up for him. Even among writers' organizations, Rushdie's cause is sometimes reduced to a half-yawning obligatory gesture; after a while even a celebrated crisis grows humdrum and loses the glamor that writers notoriously enjoy. Wole Soyinka (himself in difficulties with an undemocratic regime in Nigeria) points out that standing up for Rushdie is currently out of fashion and looked down on among certain "multicultural" academics: it is considered an intellectual offense to the mores and sensibilities of another culture—very much in the spirit of the Congress on Human Rights in Vienna not long ago, where the idea of the universalism of human rights was initially resisted either as prejudicial to national sovereignty, or else as an objectionable parochial contrivance being foisted on societies that are satisfied with their own standards and values. The danger in defending Rushdie's right to exist is no longer the simple business of turning oneself into one more lightning rod to attract the assassins. Nowadays, standing up for Rushdie brings another sort of risk: it places one among the stereotypers and the "Orientalists," as they are often called, who are accused of denigrating whole peoples. To stand up for Rushdie is to display a colonialist mentality. A man's right to exist is mired in the politics of anti-colonialism—and never mind the irony of this, given Rushdie's origins as a Muslim born in India.

Though Iran responded to Rushdie's White House appearance by labeling the President "the most hated man before all the Muslims of the world," and though the majority of other Muslim governments have shown official indifference to Rushdie's situation, not all Muslims have been silent, even in the face of personal endangerment. One hundred Muslim and Arab writers and intellectuals have contributed to *For Rushdie,* a volume of poems and essays protesting the *fatwa*—among them the Egyptian Nobel winner Naguib Mahfouz, later attacked and seriously injured by a Muslim extremist in Cairo, and for the same reasons cited by the mullahs of Iran. "Without freedom," one of the essayists in *For Rushdie* wrote, "there is no creation, no life, no beauty."

In the Academy's afternoon plenary session, André Miquel, the president of the Collège de France and a distinguished specialist in Arabic literature, proposes a resolution condemning the systematic assassination of Algerian intellectuals by fundamentalist extremists. The language of the resolution is plain: "A terrible thing is happening in Algeria— people are being killed simply because they think." This action comes under the heading of Intervention, the Academy's chosen topic for its first year of life—a philosophic theme, but spurred on by the urgencies of Bosnia and Somalia. (Marc Kravetz, editor-in-chief of the French newspaper *Libération,* a visiting lecturer at this session, counts forty separate conflicts ongoing in the world. How many are cause for intervention, and by whom, and for whom?) Rushdie, who had earlier quietly remarked that he "hoped to speak of something besides myself," keeps to his word. Without directly offering himself in illustration, he argues against "the specific thrust of the motion," and suggests that the particular case of Algeria is "typical, part of a larger phenomenon, not just an isolated thing"—that "there is a concentrated program to oppress intellectuals in many countries." Yashar Kemal, of Turkey (currently in trouble with his own government), mentions the killings in southern Turkey by Hezbollah, the Party of God, and the murder of Turkish intellectuals "fighting for lay principles." The resolution is altered. "In many countries, and recently in Algeria," it now begins, "a terrible thing is happening." Someone raises a question of credibility: is it appropriate for an Academy as newly formed as this one to be sending out resolutions? Don't we first have to settle down a little, and acquire a recognizable character? To which Rushdie replies: "We should issue motions even if the Academy is newborn. *We* are not newborn."

Luc Ferry, a professor of philosophy at the University of Caen, and another visitor to the plenary, had described Muslim societies, insofar as they fail to separate religion from matters like human rights, as "premodern." Rushdie, scribbling away as Ferry develops this idea, disputes the term. Moral fundamentalism, Rushdie argues, is not premodern but postmodern—in short, decidedly contemporary. Secular ideals, though they may be taken for granted in Europe, are very seriously under threat elsewhere. In Saudi Arabia, for instance, modernity has been declared to be against religion, and its practitioners denounced as heretical. The concept of human rights is regarded by fundamentalists as an expression of modernity, and is rejected and despised. Moreover, not only are there conflicts between opposing cultures—between, say fundamentalism and the secularizing West— but the same kind of conflict can occur *within* a culture, and on its own ground. Finally, if intervention means that you set out from home to supply assistance to another people, then what of terror, which leaves its place of origin to seek you out and destroy you in your own country? "Terror," Rushdie finishes, "is a reverse form of intervention."

He had, as he had promised, not spoken of himself or of his condition. Though composed and eloquent, he had not spoken much at all. When he was neither speaking nor writing, he sat very still, as immobile as a Buddha statue. One got the impression (but impressions can violate) that he had learned to be still; that he had taught himself to be *that* still. He was, in fact, a magnet of stillness—it was as if that great splendid room were shrinking to a single point of awareness: Rushdie sitting there in his shirtsleeves.

Come back now to Henry James, and the glyphs he has left behind. In another part of the Louvre on this day, past turnings of corridors, is the darkened Gallery of Apollo, empty but for its portraits and carvings and accretions of gold—as deserted as it was in James's hot imagining, when the appalling pursuer scrabbled after him over those polished floors. The ghosts of the Louvre are many—kings, cardinals, emperors. Add to these the generations of museum-goers; remember also that Emerson walked here when America itself was almost new—Emerson, whose mind James once described as a "ripe unconsciousness of evil." In this fanciful place it is today not possible to escape the fullest, ripest consciousness of evil; Rushdie's hunted presence draws it out. He is poet, fabulist, ironist; he is the one they want to kill because his intelligence is at play. But these ancient galleries, these tremendous, glorious halls, reverberate with a memory of the tables being turned, the pursuer diminished and in flight. Dream? Hallucination? Rushdie in Paris calls up that old nightmare of panic in the Louvre, and how the stalker was driven to retreat. And Paris itself calls up Dreyfus, who was no dream, and the heroic Zola, who routed evil with reason. Still, there is a difference. The terror of our time is stone deaf to reason, and it is not enough for the Dreyfus of our time to suffer being Dreyfus. Against all the odds, he must take on being Zola too.

A CLOSER LOOK AT CYNTHIA OZICK

1. Which of Cynthia Ozick's essays reprinted here, in your opinion, is the most essayistic? In an essay, explain and support your opinion with examples and analysis. Be sure to include examples of content and language use to support your argument.
2. In a number of places, Ozick explains that she wants her essays to be more like stories—adventurous, inventive, exploratory. Do her essays have this effect? Do they exhibit elements of fiction? In what ways? And if so, what keeps them essays? Using Ozick's writing as a point of departure, write an essay in which you explain how essays might be storylike.
3. In both "The Hole/Birth Catalogue" and "Rushdie in the Louvre," Ozick politicizes her subjects, bringing social and political issues such as gender, religion, and terrorism into her essays. Does the presence of such political issues undermine Ozick's desire to separate life and art? Respond to this question in an essay. In developing your argument, comment on what you think the role of politics should play in essay writing.
4. Ozick has written, "Nothing is so awesomely unfamiliar as the familiar that discloses itself at the end of a journey . . . Traveling is seeing; it is the implicit that we travel by. Travelers are fantasists, conjurers, seers—and what they finally discover is that every round object everywhere is a crystal ball: stone, teapot, the marvelous globe of the human eye." In what way are Ozick's essays about making the familiar unfamiliar? In what way do essays represent a kind of traveling for Ozick? Write an essay of your own that addresses how Ozick makes the familiar unfamiliar.

Looking from Writer to Writer

1. Cynthia Ozick's writing is often referred to as meticulously stylized, almost to the point, as some critics claim, of being extravagant. As she herself admits, "nothing matters more to me so much as a comely and muscular sentence . . . I miter every pair of abutting sentences as scrupulously as Uncle Jake fitted one strip of rosewood against another." The writing of Joan Didion and Joseph Epstein has likewise been described as meticulous, known for its craftsmanship. Read again the essays by Didion, Epstein, and Ozick, and examine the way they achieve this meticulousness. What makes their sentences so well crafted? What is the effect of this meticulousness on the reader? How does it affect the subject matter of the essays?

2. Like Rick Bass, Edward Hoagland, and Alice Walker, Cynthia Ozick defines the essay as a genre by comparing and contrasting it in part, to another genre, either the short story or the novel, hence setting up a distinction between fiction and nonfiction. In reading the distinctions these essayists make between the essay and other genres, what definition of the essay emerges? Does a pattern of definition emerge from their distinctions? If so, what is that pattern? If not, how do these essayists define the essay differently?

3. As we mentioned in the introduction, Cynthia Ozick is interested in the interplay of art and life, and often notes a tension between the two. For example, she distinguishes between the role of the writer as muse-inspired shaman and the writer as citizen. Barbara Ehrenreich seems to fall more clearly on the side of the writer as citizen; the title of one her essay collections is *The Snarling Citizen.* Comparing the essays of Ozick and Ehrenreich paying attention to the role of the writer in each. Then make an argument as to which role you think is more effective. Explain your reasons and assumptions.

Looking Beyond

ESSAYS

Art and Ardor: Essays. New York: Knopf, 1983.
Fame and Folly: Essays. New York: Knopf, 1996.
Metaphor and Memory: Essays. New York: Knopf, 1988.

FICTION

Bloodshed and Three Novellas. 1976. Syracuse, NY: Syracuse University Press, 1995.
The Cannibal Galaxy. New York: Knopf, 1983.
Levitation: Five Fictions. New York: Knopf, 1982.
The Messiah of Stockholm: A Novel. New York: Knopf, 1987.
The Pagan Rabbi and Other Stories. 1971. New York: Dutton, 1983.
The Shawl. New York: Knopf, 1989.

Salman Rushdie

More than any other author in this book, Salman Rushdie reveals to us the power and the politics of writing. Many of the essayists here write about the connections between writing and place and between writing and identity. Others produce essays about writing and memory, about the power of writing to connect the past and the present. Still others discuss the power writing has to create change in the world and, conversely, the ways writing can be used to dominate others. But no other essayist in this collection has experienced at such a deeply personal level the politics of writing and the power writing has to affect one's life as Rushdie has. Rushdie's work reminds us that writing makes things happen, both good and bad. Writing affects readers and the world they inhabit. And in so doing, writing has an effect on the world. Rushdie's work, in other words, reminds us that writing makes a difference.

Salman Rushdie is best known for his extremely controversial novel *The Satanic Verses,* which was published in 1988. Although it was critically well received, winning the Whitebread Award in 1988, the novel offended many Muslims, including Muslim religious leaders and Islamic scholars, who felt that the novel violated religious taboos by making irreverent references to people, places, and objects sacred to Islam. Deemed blasphemous (a charge Rushdie carefully refutes in his essay "In Good Faith" reprinted in this book), the novel was banned in most of the Islamic world as well as in India and South Africa. In many countries, including England, the book was burned in public, and bookstores carrying the book were vandalized and their owners threatened. Most powerful of all, though, was the call in 1989 by the Iranian leader Ayatollah Khomeini for the death of Rushdie, for which he offered a million dollars. As a result of the death order, Rushdie went into hiding for the next 10 years, only beginning to make public appearances in 1999, a year after the Iranian government rescinded the death order. To this day, Rushdie travels surrounded by bodyguards and keeps his schedule a secret.

Even before the publication of *The Satanic Verses,* however, Rushdie's writing was embroiled in politics, provoking readers to think about questions of racial prejudice, the politics of India and Pakistan, migration, and religion. Indeed, it could be said that from the beginning of his life Rushdie's identity was political. He was born in Bombay, India, in 1947, the same year India won its independence from British rule. (Rushdie's second novel, *Midnight's Children,* chronicles the experiences of Indian children, like himself, born on the eve of independence.) He grew up in a middle-class Muslim family at a time when tensions between Hindus and Muslims had reached the point that his family, in 1964, migrated to Pakistan. At age 14, Rushdie was sent to a boys' school in Great Britain, where once again he experienced the politics of identity that accompany being in a minority. Rushdie says, "I've been in a minority group all my life—a member of an Indian Muslim family in Bombay, then of a 'mahajir'—migrant—family in Pakistan, and now as a British Asian." In 1968 he graduated from King's College, Cambridge University, and spent time working as an actor and a freelance advertising copy editor before writing his first novel, *Grimus,* in 1975. This multiplicity of identities has shaped the perspective of the world Rushdie brings to his writing.

Rushdie's many identities have also driven him to embrace and defend secularism while rejecting communalism, the strong identification with one's religious and ethnic group that according to Rushdie leads to religious hatred. As Susan Sontag has noted, "what Salman Rushdie stands for is the right to secularism, pluralism, freedom of expression, tolerance—values that I hope we are all united in supporting."

In his essay "Imaginary Homelands," Rushdie writes, "the real risks of any artist are taken in the work, in pushing the work to the limits of what is possible, in the attempt to increase the sum of what it is possible to think. Books become good when they go to this edge and risk falling over it—when they endanger the artist by reason of what he has, or has not, *artistically* dared." These words, written before the controversy surrounding *The Satanic Verses,* have proven prophetic. Rushdie's writing is daring and it has literally endangered him. But his writing also pushes the limits of what it is possible to think. His novels are often difficult to define, much like the political and religious secularism he advocates. He draws from various genres to create what has been described as "magic realism," bringing together fantasy, mythology, and religion. While his essays are less "fantastic," they too push the limits of what is possible, challenging readers to become aware of different perspectives, beliefs, and versions of reality.

As you read the essays that follow, pay attention to how Rushdie challenges his readers. Look at the arguments his essays are making and think about the stakes involved. In particular, examine how he structures and supports his arguments, paying attention to his use of examples. There is always something at stake in Rushdie's essays, whether he is arguing about what it means to write, how prejudice occurs in Britain, or why his novel *The Satanic Verses* is not what it has been made out to be. In each case, there is a great deal at stake in how effectively Rushdie makes his arguments—indeed, in the essay "In Good Faith," his life depends on it.

Rushdie on Writing

At First Glance

Salman Rushdie wrote the essay "Imaginary Homelands" as his contribution to a seminar about Indian writing in English held in London during the Festival of India in 1982. At the time, he was a young writer, having just published his second novel Midnight's Children, *which had won him the Booker Prize and brought him international fame. Almost all the important Indo-British writers attended the seminar. As you read, think about the rhetorical choices Rushdie had to make when writing this essay to this audience. The essay itself is a forceful, at times even controversial, articulation of his views about writing. Consider how Rushdie manages to relate to and engage his readers. Consider also how he establishes credibility so that his readers will respect what he is claiming. Finally, pay attention to what he has to say about the role of the writer and writing, especially the politics involved, and relate that to your own views about what it means to write.*

Imaginary Homelands

An old photograph in a cheap frame hangs on a wall of the room where I work. It's a picture dating from 1946 of a house into which, at the time of its taking, I had not yet been born. The house is rather peculiar—a three-storeyed gabled affair with tiled roofs and round towers in two corners, each wearing a pointy tiled hat. "The past is a foreign country," goes the famous opening sentence of L. P. Hartley's novel *The Go-Between,* "they do things differently there." But the photograph tells me to invert this idea; it reminds me that it's my present that is foreign, and that the past is home, albeit a lost home in a lost city in the mists of lost time.

A few years ago I revisited Bombay, which is my lost city, after an absence of something like half my life. Shortly after arriving, acting on an impulse, I opened the telephone directory and looked for my father's name. And, amazingly, there it was; his name, our old address, the unchanged telephone number, as if we had never gone away to the unmentionable country across the border. It was an eerie discovery. I felt as if I were being claimed, or informed that the facts of my faraway life were illusions, and that this continuity was the reality. Then I went to visit the house in the photograph and stood outside it, neither daring nor wishing to announce myself to its new owners. (I didn't want to see how they'd ruined the interior.) I was overwhelmed. The photograph had naturally been taken in black and white; and my memory, feeding on such images as this, had begun to see my childhood in the same way, monochromatically. The colours of my history had seeped out of my mind's

491

eye; now my other two eyes were assaulted by colours, by the vividness of the red tiles, the yellow-edged green of cactus-leaves, the brilliance of bougainvillaea creeper. It is probably not too romantic to say that that was when my novel *Midnight's Children* was really born; when I realized how much I wanted to restore the past to myself, not in the faded greys of old family-album snapshots, but whole, in CinemaScope and glorious Technicolor.

Bombay is a city built by foreigners upon reclaimed land; I, who had been away so long that I almost qualified for the title, was gripped by the conviction that I, too, had a city and a history to reclaim.

It may be that writers in my position, exiles or emigrants or expatriates, are haunted by some sense of loss, some urge to reclaim, to look back, even at the risk of being mutated into pillars of salt. But if we do look back, we must also do so in the knowledge—which gives rise to profound uncertainties—that our physical alienation from India almost inevitably means that we will not be capable of reclaiming precisely the thing that was lost; that we will, in short, create fictions, not actual cities or villages, but invisible ones, imaginary homelands, Indias of the mind.

Writing my book in North London, looking out through my window on to a city scene totally unlike the ones I was imagining on to paper, I was constantly plagued by this problem, until I felt obliged to face it in the text, to make clear that (in spite of my original and I suppose somewhat Proustian ambition to unlock the gates of lost time so that the past reappeared as it actually had been, unaffected by the distortions of memory) what I was actually doing was a novel of memory and about memory, so that my India was just that: "my" India, a version and no more than one version of all the hundreds of millions of possible versions. I tried to make it as imaginatively true as I could, but imaginative truth is simultaneously honourable and suspect, and I knew that my India may only have been one to which I (who am no longer what I was, and who by quitting Bombay never became what perhaps I was meant to be) was, let us say, willing to admit I belonged.

This is why I made my narrator, Saleem, suspect in his narration; his mistakes are the mistakes of a fallible memory compounded by quirks of character and of circumstance, and his vision is fragmentary. It may be that when the Indian writer who writes from outside India tries to reflect that world, he is obliged to deal in broken mirrors, some of whose fragments have been irretrievably lost.

But there is a paradox here. The broken mirror may actually be as valuable as the one which is supposedly unflawed. Let me again try and explain this from my own experience. Before beginning *Midnight's Children,* I spent many months trying simply to recall as much of the Bombay of the 1950s and 1960s as I could; and not only Bombay—Kashmir, too, and Delhi and Aligarh, which, in my book, I've moved to Agra to heighten a certain joke about the Taj Mahal. I was genuinely amazed by how much came back to me. I found myself remembering what clothes people had worn on certain days, and school scenes, and whole passages of Bombay dialogue verbatim, or so it seemed; I even remembered advertisements, film-posters, the neon Jeep sign on Marine Drive, toothpaste ads for Binaca and for Kolynos, and a foot-bridge over the local railway line which bore, on one side, the legend "Esso puts a tiger in your tank" and, on the other, the curiously contradictory admonition: "Drive like Hell and you will get there." Old songs came back to me from nowhere: a street entertainer's version of "Good Night, Ladies," and, from the film *Mr 420* (a very appropriate source for my narrator to have used), the hit number "Mera Joota Hai Japan,"★ which could almost be Saleem's theme song.

I knew that I had tapped a rich seam; but the point I want to make is that of course I'm not gifted with total recall, and it was precisely the partial nature of these memories, their fragmentation, that made them so evocative for me. The shards of memory acquired greater status, greater resonance, because they were *remains;* fragmentation made trivial things seem like symbols, and the mundane acquired numinous qualities. There is an obvious parallel here with archaeology. The broken pots of antiquity, from which the past can sometimes, but always provisionally, be reconstructed, are exciting to discover, even if they are pieces of the most quotidian objects.

It may be argued that the past is a country from which we have all emigrated, that its loss is part of our common humanity. Which seems to me self-evidently true; but I suggest that the writer who is out-of-country and even out-of-language may experience this loss in an intensified form. It is made more concrete for him by the physical fact of discontinuity, of his present being in a different place from his past, of his being "elsewhere." This may enable him to speak properly and concretely on a subject of universal significance and appeal.

But let me go further. The broken glass is not merely a mirror of nostalgia. It is also, I believe, a useful tool with which to work in the present.

John Fowles begins *Daniel Martin* with the words: "Whole sight: or all the rest is desolation." But human beings do not perceive things whole; we are not gods but wounded creatures, cracked lenses, capable only of fractured perceptions. Partial beings, in all the senses of that phrase. Meaning is a shaky edifice we build out of scraps, dogmas, childhood injuries, newspaper articles, chance remarks, old films, small victories, people hated, people loved; perhaps it is because our sense of what is the case is constructed from such inadequate materials that we defend it so fiercely, even to the death. The Fowles position seems to me a way of succumbing to the guru-illusion. Writers are no longer sages, dispensing the wisdom of the centuries. And those of us who have been forced by cultural displacement to accept the provisional nature of all truths, all certainties, have perhaps had modernism forced upon

---

★*Mera joota hai Japani*
Yé patloon Inglistani
Sar pé lal topi Rusi—
Phir bhi dil hai Hindustani
—which translates roughly as:
O, my shoes are Japanese
These trousers English, if you please
On my head, red Russian hat—
My heart's Indian for all that.
[This is also the song sung by Gibreel Farishta as he tumbles from the heavens at the beginning of *The Satanic Verses.*]

us. We can't lay claim to Olympus, and are thus released to describe our worlds in the way in which all of us, whether writers or not, perceive it from day to day.

In *Midnight's Children,* my narrator Saleem uses, at one point, the metaphor of a cinema screen to discuss this business of perception: "Suppose yourself in a large cinema, sitting at first in the back row, and gradually moving up, . . . until your nose is almost pressed against the screen. Gradually the stars' faces dissolve into dancing grain; tiny details assume grotesque proportions; . . . it becomes clear that the illusion itself is reality." The movement towards the cinema screen is a metaphor for the narrative's movement through time towards the present, and the book itself, as it nears contemporary events, quite deliberately loses deep perspective, becomes more "partial." I wasn't trying to write about (for instance) the Emergency in the same way as I wrote about events half a century earlier. I felt it would be dishonest to pretend, when writing about the day before yesterday, that it was possible to see the whole picture. I showed certain blobs and slabs of the scene.

I once took part in a conference on modern writing at New College, Oxford. Various novelists, myself included, were talking earnestly of such matters as the need for new ways of describing the world. Then the playwright Howard Brenton suggested that this might be a somewhat limited aim: does literature seek to do no more than to describe? Flustered, all the novelists at once began talking about politics.

Let me apply Brenton's question to the specific case of Indian writers, in England, writing about India. Can they do no more than describe, from a distance, the world that they have left? Or does the distance open any other doors?

These are of course political questions, and must be answered at least partly in political terms. I must say first of all that description is itself a political act. The black American writer Richard Wright once wrote that black and white Americans were engaged in a war over the nature of reality. Their descriptions were incompatible. So it is clear that redescribing a world is the necessary first step towards changing it. And particularly at times when the State takes reality into its own hands, and sets about distorting it, altering the past to fit its present needs, then the making of the alternative realities of art, including the novel of memory, becomes politicized. "The struggle of man against power," Milan Kundera has written, "is the struggle of memory against forgetting." Writers and politicians are natural rivals. Both groups try to make the world in their own images; they fight for the same territory. And the novel is one way of denying the official, politicians' version of truth.

The "State truth" about the war in Bangladesh, for instance, is that no atrocities were committed by the Pakistani army in what was then the East Wing. This version is sanctified by many persons who would describe themselves as intellectuals. And the official version of the Emergency in India was well expressed by Mrs Gandhi in a recent BBC interview. She said that there were some people around who claimed that bad things had happened during the Emergency, forced sterilizations, things like that; but, she stated, this was all false. Nothing of this type had ever occurred. The interviewer, Mr Robert Kee, did not probe this statement at all. Instead he told Mrs Gandhi and the *Panorama* audience that she had proved, many times over, her right to be called a democrat.

So literature can, and perhaps must, give the lie to official facts. But is this a proper function of those of us who write from outside India? Or are we just dilettantes in such affairs, because we are not involved in their day-to-day unfolding, because by speaking out we take no risks, because our personal safety is not threatened? What right do we have to speak at all?

My answer is very simple. Literature is self-validating. That is to say, a book is not justified by its author's worthiness to write it, but by the quality of what has been written. There are terrible books that arise directly out of experience, and extraordinary imaginative feats dealing with themes which the author has been obliged to approach from the outside.

Literature is not in the business of copywriting certain themes for certain groups. And as for risk: the real risks of any artist are taken in the work, in pushing the work to the limits of what is possible, in the attempt to increase the sum of what it is possible to think. Books become good when they go to this edge and risk falling over it—when they endanger the artist by reason of what he has, or has not, *artistically* dared.

So if I am to speak for Indian writers in England I would say this, paraphrasing G. V. Desani's H. Hatterr: The migrations of the fifties and sixties happened. "We are. We are here." And we are not willing to be excluded from any part of our heritage; which heritage includes both a Bradford-born Indian kid's right to be treated as a full member of British society, and also the right of any member of this post-diaspora community to draw on its roots for its art, just as all the world's community of displaced writers has always done. (I'm thinking, for instance, of Grass's Danzig-become-Gdansk, of Joyce's abandoned Dublin, of Isaac Bashevis Singer and Maxine Hong Kingston and Milan Kundera and many others. It's a long list.)

Let me override at once the faintly defensive note that has crept into these last few remarks. The Indian writer, looking back at India, does so through guilt-tinted spectacles. (I am of course, once more, talking about myself.) I am speaking now of those of us who emigrated . . . and I suspect that there are times when the move seems wrong to us all, when we seem, to ourselves, post-lapsarian men and women. We are Hindus who have crossed the black water; we are Muslims who eat pork. And as a result—as my use of the Christian notion of the Fall indicates—we are now partly of the West. Our identity is at once plural and partial. Sometimes we feel that we straddle two cultures; at other times, that we fall between two stools. But however ambiguous and shifting this ground may be, it is not an infertile territory for a writer to occupy. If literature is in part the business of finding new angles at which to enter reality, then once again our distance, our long geographical perspective, may provide us with such angles. Or it may be that that is simply what we must think in order to do our work.

Midnight's Children enters its subject from the point of view of a secular man. I am a member of that generation of Indians who were sold the secular ideal. One of the things I liked, and still like, about India is that it is based on a non-sectarian philosophy. I was not raised in a narrowly Muslim environment; I do not consider Hindu culture to be either alien from me or more important than the Islamic heritage. I believe this has something to do with the nature of Bombay, a metropolis in which the multiplicity of commingled faiths and cultures curiously creates a remarkably secular ambience. Saleem Sinai makes use, eclectically, of whatever elements from whatever sources he chooses. It may have been easier for his author to do this from outside modern India than inside it.

I want to make one last point about the description of India that *Midnight's Children* attempts. It is a point about pessimism. The book has been criticised in India for its allegedly despairing tone. And the despair of the writer-from-outside may indeed look a little easy, a little pat. But I do not see the book as despairing or nihilistic. The point of view of the narrator is not entirely that of the author. What I tried to do was to set up a tension in the text, a paradoxical opposition between the form and content of the narrative. The story of Saleem does indeed lead him to despair. But the story is told in a manner designed to echo, as closely as my abilities allowed, the Indian talent for non-stop self-regeneration. This is why the narrative constantly throws up new stories, why it "teems." The form—multitudinous, hinting at the infinite possibilities of the country—is the optimistic counterweight to Saleem's personal tragedy. I do not think that a book written in such a manner can really be called a despairing work.

England's Indian writers are by no means all the same type of animal. Some of us, for instance, are Pakistani. Others Bangladeshi. Others West, or East, or even South African. And V. S. Naipaul, by now, is something else entirely. This word "Indian" is getting to be a pretty scattered concept. Indian writers in England include political exiles, first-generation migrants, affluent expatriates whose residence here is frequently temporary, naturalized Britons, and people born here who may never have laid eyes on the subcontinent. Clearly, nothing that I say can apply across all these categories. But one of the interesting things about this diverse community is that, as far as Indo-British fiction is concerned, its existence changes the ball game, because that fiction is in future going to come as much from addresses in London, Birmingham and Yorkshire as from Delhi or Bombay.

One of the changes has to do with attitudes towards the use of English. Many have referred to the argument about the appropriateness of this language to Indian themes. And I hope all of us share the view that we can't simply use the language in the way the British did; that it needs remaking for our own purposes. Those of us who do use English do so in spite of our ambiguity towards it, or perhaps because of that, perhaps because we can find in that linguistic struggle a reflection of other struggles taking place in the real world, struggles between the cultures within ourselves and the influences at work upon our societies. To conquer English may be to complete the process of making ourselves free.

But the British Indian writer simply does not have the option of rejecting English, anyway. His children, her children, will grow up speaking it, probably as a first language; and in the forging of a British Indian identity the English language is of central importance. It must, in spite of everything, be embraced. (The word "translation" comes, etymologically, from the Latin for "bearing across." Having been borne across the world, we are translated men. It is normally supposed that something always gets lost in the translation; I cling, obstinately, to the notion that something can also be gained.)

To be an Indian writer in this society is to face, every day, problems of definition. What does it mean to be "Indian" outside India? How can culture be preserved without becoming ossified? How should we discuss the need for change within ourselves and our community without seeming to play into the hands of our racial enemies? What are the consequences, both spiritual and practical, of refusing to make any concessions to Western ideas and practices? What are the consequences of embracing those ideas and practices and turning away from the ones that came here with us? These questions are all a single, existential question: How are we to live in the world?

I do not propose to offer, prescriptively, any answers to these questions; only to state that these are some of the issues with which each of us will have to come to terms.

To turn my eyes outwards now, and to say a little about the relationship between the Indian writer and the majority white culture in whose midst he lives, and with which his work will sooner or later have to deal:

In common with many Bombay-raised middle-class children of my generation, I grew up with an intimate knowledge of, and even sense of friendship with, a certain kind of England: a dream-England composed of Test Matches at Lord's presided over by the voice of John Arlott, at which Freddie Trueman bowled unceasingly and without success at Polly Umrigar; of Enid Blyton and Billy Bunter, in which we were even prepared to smile indulgently at portraits such as "Hurree Jamset Ram Singh," "the dusky nabob of Bhanipur." I wanted to come to England. I couldn't wait. And to be fair, England has done all right by me; but I find it a little difficult to be properly grateful. I can't escape the view that my relatively easy ride is not the result of the dream-England's famous sense of tolerance and fair play, but of my social class, my freak fair skin and my "English" English accent. Take away any of these, and the story would have been very different. Because of course the dream-England is no more than a dream.

Sadly, it's a dream from which too many white Britons refuse to awake. Recently, on a live radio programme, a professional humorist asked me, in all seriousness, why I objected to being called a wog. He said he had always thought it a rather charming word, a term of endearment. "I was at the zoo the other day," he revealed, "and a zoo keeper told me that the wogs were best with the animals; they stuck their fingers in their ears and wiggled them about and the animals felt at home." The ghost of Hurree Jamset Ram Singh walks among us still.

As Richard Wright found long ago in America, black and white descriptions of society are no longer compatible. Fantasy, or the mingling of fantasy and naturalism, is one way of dealing with these problems. It offers a way of echoing in the form of our work the issues faced by all of us: how to build a new, "modern" world out of an old, legend-haunted civilization, an old culture which we have brought into the heart of a newer one. But whatever technical solutions we may find, Indian writers in these islands, like others who have migrated into the north from the south, are capable of writing from a kind of double perspective: because they, we, are at one and the same time insiders and outsiders in this society. This stereoscopic vision is perhaps what we can offer in place of "whole sight."

There is one last idea that I should like to explore, even though it may, on first hearing, seem to contradict much of what I've so far said. It is this: of all the many elephant traps lying ahead of us, the largest and most dangerous pitfall would be the adoption of a ghetto mentality. To forget that there is a world beyond the community to which we belong, to confine ourselves within narrowly defined cultural frontiers, would be, I believe, to go voluntarily into that form of internal exile which in South Africa is called the "homeland." We must guard against creating, for the most virtuous of reasons, British-Indian literary equivalents of Bophuthatswana or the Transkei.

This raises immediately the question of whom one is writing "for." My own, short, answer is that I have never had a reader in mind. I have ideas, people, events, shapes, and I write "for" those things, and hope that the completed work will be of interest to others. But which others? In the case of *Midnight's Children* I certainly felt that if its subcontinental readers had rejected the work, I should have thought it a failure, no matter what the reaction in the West. So I would say that I write "for" people who feel part of the things I write "about," but also for everyone else whom I can reach. In this I am of the same opinion as the black American writer Ralph Ellison, who, in his collection of essays *Shadow and Act,* says that he finds something precious in being black in America at this time; but that he is also reaching for more than that. "I was taken very early" he writes, "with a passion to link together all I loved within the Negro community and all those things I felt in the world which lay beyond."

Art is a passion of the mind. And the imagination works best when it is most free. Western writers have always felt free to be eclectic in their selection of theme, setting, form; Western visual artists have, in this century, been happily raiding the visual storehouses of Africa, Asia, the Philippines. I am sure that we must grant ourselves an equal freedom.

Let me suggest that Indian writers in England have access to a second tradition, quite apart from their own racial history. It is the culture and political history of the phenomenon of migration, displacement, life in a minority group. We can quite legitimately claim as our ancestors the Huguenots, the Irish, the Jews; the past to which we belong is an English past, the history of immigrant Britain. Swift, Conrad, Marx are as much our literary forebears as Tagore or Ram Mohan Roy. America, a nation of immigrants, has created great literature out of the phenomenon of cultural transplantation, out of examining the ways in which people cope with a new world; it may be that by discovering what we have in common with those who preceded us into this country, we can begin to do the same.

I stress this is only one of many possible strategies. But we are inescapably international writers at a time when the novel has never been a more international form (a writer like Borges speaks of the influence of Robert Louis Stevenson on his work; Heinrich Böll acknowledges the influence of Irish literature; cross-pollination is everywhere); and it is perhaps one of the more pleasant freedoms of the literary migrant to be able to choose his parents. My own—selected half consciously, half not—include Gogol, Cervantes, Kafka, Melville, Machado de Assis; a polyglot family tree, against which I measure myself, and to which I would be honoured to belong.

There's a beautiful image in Saul Bellow's latest novel, *The Dean's December.* The central character, the Dean, Corde, hears a dog barking wildly somewhere. He imagines that the barking is the dog's protest against the limit of dog experience. "For God's sake," the dog is saying, "open the universe a little more!" And because Bellow is, of course, not really talking about dogs, or not only about dogs, I have the feeling that the dog's rage, and its desire, is also mine, ours, everyone's. "For God's sake, open the universe a little more!"

Double Take

1. Why are the homelands Salman Rushdie refers to in the title of this essay "imaginary"? What makes them imaginary?
2. Describe Rushdie's method of addressing his readers. What strategies does he use to connect to his readers? To what extent are these strategies effective?
3. How does Rushdie define his role as writer in this essay? What does it mean for him to write? Do Rushdie's views of the writer and writing relate in any way to your views of the writer and writing? How so? If they don't relate, what do you think might account for the differences?
4. At the end of the essay, Rushdie cites Saul Bellow's image of the barking dog protesting the limits of dog experience. He writes, "I have the feeling that the dog's rage, and its desire, is also mine, ours, everyone's. 'For God's sake, open the universe a little more!'" What is Rushdie pleading for here?

At First Glance

Salman Rushdie originally wrote "The New Empire within Britain" in 1982 as a lecture about racial prejudice for the Opinions *television program in Great Britain. Although the lecture received a favorable response from many British blacks and Asians as well as whites, it received a hostile response from some members of the white community, who accused Rushdie of equating Britain with Nazi Germany and of betraying his adopted country. Rushdie admits that what he wrote was meant to provoke the white majority to think about "how life in Britain all too often felt to members of racial minority groups." As he claims, "I make no apology for being angry about racial prejudice." But he denies that he was equating Britain with Nazi Germany. In republishing the lecture as an essay in his book* Imaginary Homelands, *Rushdie asks readers "to decide for themselves whether [the Britain as Nazi Germany critique] was justified or not." As you read the essay, decide for yourself if the critique is justified. Try to see why some readers would be offended by the essay and some would react favorably. Pay specific attention to how Rushdie makes his argument for the existence of racial prejudice in Britain, looking especially at the rhetorical choices he makes regarding tone, structure, and examples to support his claims.*

The New Empire within Britain

Britain isn't South Africa. I am reliably informed of this. Nor is it Nazi Germany. I've got that on the best authority as well. You may feel that these two statements are not exactly the most dramatic of revelations. But it's remarkable how often they, or similar statements, are used to counter the arguments of anti-racist campaigners. "Things aren't as bad as all that," we are told, "you exaggerate, you're indulging in special pleading, you must be paranoid." So let me concede at once that, as far as I know, there are no pass laws here. Inter-racial marriages are permitted. And Auschwitz hasn't been rebuilt in the Home Counties. I find it odd, however, that those who use such absences as defences rarely perceive that their own statements indicate how serious things have become. Because if the defence for Britain is that mass extermination of racially impure persons hasn't yet begun, or that the principle of white supremacy hasn't actually been enshrined in the constitution, then something must have gone very wrong indeed.

I want to suggest that racism is not a side-issue in contemporary Britain; that it's not a peripheral minority affair. I believe that Britain is undergoing a critical phase of its postcolonial period, and this crisis is not simply economic or political. It's a crisis of the whole culture, of the society's entire sense of itself. And racism is only the most clearly visible part of this crisis, the tip of the kind of iceberg that sinks ships.

Now I don't suppose many of you think of the British Empire as a subject worth losing much sleep over. After all, surely the one thing one can confidently say about that roseate age of England's precedence, when the map of half the world blushed with pleasure as it squirmed beneath the Pax Britannica, is that it's over, isn't it? Give or take a Falkland Island, the imperial sun has set. And how fine was the manner of its setting; in what good order the British withdrew. Union Jacks fluttered down their poles all round the world, to be replaced by other flags, in all manner of outlandish colours. The pink conquerors crept home, the boxwallahs and memsahibs and bwanas, leaving behind them parliaments, schools, Grand Trunk Roads and the rules of cricket. How gracefully they shrank back into their cold island, abandoning their lives as the dashing people of their dreams, diminishing from the endless steaming landscapes of India and Africa into the narrow horizons of the pallid, drizzled streets. The British have got other things to worry about now; no point, you may say, in exhuming this particular dead horse in order to flog the poor, decomposed creature all over again.

But the connection I want to make is this: that those same attitudes are in operation right here as well, here in what E. P. Thompson has described as the last colony of the British Empire. It sometimes seems that the British authorities, no longer capable of exporting governments, have chosen instead to import a new Empire, a new community of subject peoples of whom they think, and with whom they can deal, in very much the same way as their predecessors thought of and dealt with "the fluttered folk and wild," the "new-caught, sullen peoples, half-devil and half-child," who made up, for Rudyard Kipling, the White Man's Burden. In short, if we want to understand British racism—and without understanding no improvement is possible—it's impossible even to begin to grasp the nature of the beast unless we accept its historical roots. Four hundred years of conquest and looting, four centuries of being told that you are superior to the Fuzzy-Wuzzies and the wogs, leave their stain. This stain has seeped into every part of the culture, the language and the daily life; and nothing much has been done to wash it out.

For proof of the existence of this stain, we can look, for instance, at the huge, undiminished appetite of white Britons for television series, films, plays and books all filled with nostalgia for the Great Pink Age. Or think about the ease with which the English language allows the terms of racial abuse to be coined: wog, frog, kraut, dago, spic, yid, coon, nigger, Argie. Can there be another language with so wide-ranging a vocabulary of racist denigration? And, since I've mentioned Argies, let me quote from Margaret Thatcher's speech at Cheltenham on the third of July, her famous victory address: "We have learned something about ourselves," she said then, "a lesson which we desperately need to learn. When we started out, there were the waverers and the fainthearts . . . The people who thought we could no longer do the great things which we once did . . . that we could never again be what we were. There were those who would not admit it . . . but—in their heart of hearts—they too had their secret fears that it was true: that Britain was no longer the nation that had built an Empire and ruled a quarter of the world. Well, they were wrong."

There are several interesting aspects to this speech. Remember that it was made by a triumphant Prime Minister at the peak of her popularity; a Prime Minister who could claim with complete credibility to be speaking for an overwhelming majority of the electorate, and who, as even her detractors must admit, has a considerable gift for assessing the national mood. Now if such a leader at such a time felt able to invoke the spirit of imperialism, it was because she knew how central that spirit is to the self-image of white Britons of all classes. I say white Britons because it's clear that Mrs Thatcher wasn't addressing the two million or so blacks, who don't feel quite like that about the Empire. So even her use of the word "we" was an act of racial exclusion, like her other well-known speech about the fear of being "swamped" by immigrants. With such leaders, it's not surprising that the British are slow to learn the real lessons of their past.

Let me repeat what I said at the beginning: Britain isn't Nazi Germany. The British Empire isn't the Third Reich. But in Germany, after the fall of Hitler, heroic attempts were made by many people to purify German thought and the German language of the pollution of Nazism. Such acts of cleansing are occasionally necessary in every society. But British thought, British society, has never been cleansed of the filth of imperialism. It's still there, breeding lice and vermin, waiting for unscrupulous people to exploit it for their own ends. One of the key concepts of imperialism was that military superiority implied cultural superiority, and this enabled the British to condescend to and repress cultures far older than their own; and it still does. For the citizens of the new, imported Empire, for the colonized Asians and blacks of Britain, the police force represents that colonizing army, those regiments of occupation and control.

Now the peoples whom I've characterized as members of a new colony would probably be described by most of you as "immigrants." (You'll notice, by the way, that I've pinched one of Mrs Thatcher's strategies and the You to whom I'm talking is a white You.) So now I'd like to ask you to think about this word "immigrant," because it seems to me to demonstrate the extent to which racist concepts have been allowed to seize the central ground, and to shape the whole nature of the debate. The facts are that for many years now there has been a sizeable amount of white immigration as well as black, that the annual number of emigrants leaving these shores is now larger than the number of immigrants coming in; and that, of the black communities, over forty per cent are not immigrants, but black Britons, born and bred, speaking in many voices and accents of Britain, and with no homeland but this one. And still the word "immigrant" means "black immigrant," the myth of "swamping" lingers on; and even British-born blacks and Asians are thought of as people whose real "home" is elsewhere. Immigration is only a problem if you are worried about blacks; that is, if your whole approach to the question is one of racial prejudice.

But perhaps the worst thing about the so-called "numbers game" is its assumption that less black immigration is self-evidently desirable. The effect of this assumption is that governments of both parties have eagerly passed off gross injustice as success. Let me explain. The immigration laws of this country have established a quota system for migration of UK passport holders from various countries. But after Idi Amin drove out the Ugandan Asians, and Britain did her best to prevent those British citizens from entering this country, that African quota was never increased; and, as a result, the total number of black immigrants to Britain has fallen. Now you might think that natural justice would demand that the already lamentably low quotas for British citizens from Africa would be made available to those same citizens, many of whom are now living as refugees in India, a desperately poor country which can ill-afford to care for them. But natural justice has never been much in evidence in this field. In fact, the British tax system now intends to withhold tax relief from wage-earners here whose dependents are trapped abroad. So first you keep people's families away from them and then you alter your laws to make it twice as hard for those people to keep their families fed. They're only "immigrants," after all.

A couple of years ago the British press made a huge stink about a family of African Asians who arrived at Heathrow airport and were housed by the very reluctant local authority. It became a classic media witch hunt: "They come over here, sponge off the State and jump the housing queue." But that same week, another family also landed at Heathrow, also needing, and getting, housing from the same local authority. This second family barely made the papers. It was a family of white Rhodesians running away from the prospect of a free Zimbabwe. One of the more curious aspects of British immigration law is that many Rhodesians, South Africans and other white non-Britons have automatic right of entry and residence here, by virtue of having one British-born grandparent; whereas many British citizens are denied these rights, because they happen to be black.

One last point about the "immigrants." It's a pretty obvious point, but it keeps getting forgotten. It's this: they came because they were invited. The Macmillan government embarked on a large-scale advertising campaign to attract them. They were extraordinary advertisements, full of hope and optimism, which made Britain out to be a land of plenty, a golden opportunity not to be missed. And they worked. People travelled here in good faith, believing themselves wanted. This is how the new Empire was imported. This country was named "perfidious Albion" long ago; and that shaming nickname is now being earned all over again.

So what's it like, this country to which the immigrants came and in which their children are growing up? You wouldn't recognize it. Because this isn't the England of fair play, tolerance, decency and equality—maybe that place never existed anyway, except in fairy-tales. In the streets of the new Empire, black women are abused and black children are beaten up on their way home from school. In the run-down housing estates of the new Empire, black families have their windows broken, they are afraid to go out after dark, and human and animal excrement arrives through their letter-boxes. The police offer threats instead of protection, and the courts offer small hope of redress. Britain is now two entirely different worlds, and the one you inhabit is determined by the colour of your skin. Now in my experience, very few white people, except for those active in fighting racism, are willing to believe the descriptions of contemporary reality offered by blacks. And black people, faced with what Professor Michael Dummett has called "the will not to know—a chosen ignorance, not the ignorance of innocence," grow increasingly suspicious and angry.

A gulf in reality has been created. White and black perceptions of everyday life have moved so far apart as to be incompatible. And the rift isn't narrowing; it's getting wider. We stand on opposite sides of the abyss, yelling at each other and sometimes hurling stones, while the ground crumbles beneath our feet. I make no apology for taking an uncompromising view of the reasons for the existence of this chasm. The will to ignorance of which Professor Dummett speaks arises out of the desire not to face the consequences of what is going on.

The fact remains that every major institution in this country is permeated by racial prejudice to some degree, and the unwillingness of the white majority to recognize this is the main reason why it can remain the case. Let's take the Law. We have, in Britain today, judges like McKinnon who can say in court that the word "nigger" cannot be considered an epithet of racial abuse because he was nicknamed "Nigger" at his public school; or like the great Lord Denning, who can publish a book claiming that black people aren't as fit as whites to serve on juries, because they come from cultures with less stringent moral codes. We've got a police force that harasses blacks every day of their lives. There was a policeman who sat in an unmarked car on Railton Road in Brixton last year, shouting abuse at passing black kids and arresting the first youngsters who made the mistake of answering back. There were policemen at a Southall demonstration who sat in their vans, writing letters NF in the steam of their breath on the windows. The British police have even refused to make racial discrimination an offence in their code of conduct, in spite of Lord Scarman's recommendations. Now it is precisely because the law courts and the police are not doing their jobs that these activities of racist hooligans are on the increase. It's just not good enough to deplore the existence of neo-Fascists in the society. They exist because they are permitted to exist. (I said every major institution, so let's consider the government itself. When the Race Relations Act was passed, the government of Britain specifically exempted itself and all its actions from the jurisdiction of the Act.)

A friend of mine, an Indian, was deported recently for the technical offence known as "overstaying." This means that after a dozen or so years of living here, he was found to be a couple of days late sending in the forms applying for an extension to his stay. Now neither he nor his family had ever claimed a penny in welfare, or, I suppose I should say, been in trouble with the police. He and his wife financed themselves by running a clothes stall, and gave all their spare time and effort to voluntary work helping their community. My friend was chairman of his local traders' association. So when the deportation order was made, this association, all three of his borough MPs and about fifty other MPs of all parties pleaded with the Home Office for clemency. None was forthcoming. My friend's son had a rare disease, and a doctor's report was produced stating that the child's health would be endangered if he was sent to India. The Home Office replied that it considered there were no compassionate grounds for reversing its decision. In the end, my friend offered to leave voluntarily—he had been offered sanctuary in Germany—and he asked to be allowed to go freely, to avoid the stigma of having a deportation order stamped into his passport. The Home Office refused him this last scrap of his self-respect, and threw him out. As the Fascist John Kingsley Read once said, one down, a million to go.

The combination of this sort of institutional racism and the willed ignorance of the public was clearly in evidence during the passage through Parliament of the Nationality Act of 1981. This already notorious piece of legislation, expressly designed to deprive black and Asian Britons of their citizenship rights, went through in spite of some, mainly non-white, protests. And because it didn't really affect the position of whites, you probably didn't even realize that one of your most ancient rights, a right you had possessed for nine hundred years, was being stolen from you. This was the right to citizenship by virtue of birth, the *ius soli,* or right of the soil. For nine centuries any child born on British soil was British. Automatically. By right. Not by permission of the State. The Nationality Act abolished the *ius soli.* From now on citizenship is the gift of government. You were blind, because you believed the Act was aimed at the blacks; and so you sat back and did nothing as Mrs Thatcher stole the birthright of every one of us, black and white, and of our children and grandchildren for ever.

Now it's possible that this blindness is incurable. One of the SDP's better-known candidates told me recently that while he found the idea of working-class racism easy to accept, the parallel notion of widespread prejudice in the middle classes was unconvincing to him. Yet, after many years of voluntary work in this field, I know that the management levels of British industry and business are just as shot through by the threads of prejudice as are many unions. It is believed for instance, that as many as fifty per cent of all telephone calls made by employers to employment agencies specify no blacks. Black unemployment is much, much higher than white; and such anomalies don't arise by accident.

Let me illustrate my point by talking about television. I once earned my living by writing commercials, and I found the prejudice of senior executives in British industry quite appalling. I could tell you the name of the chairman of a leading building society who rejected a jingle on the grounds that the off-screen singer sounded as if he had a black voice. The irony was that the singer was actually white, but the previous year's jingle *had* been sung by a black man who obviously had the good fortune not to sound like one. I know the marketing director of a leading confectionery firm who turned down all requests to cast a black child—as one of an otherwise white group of children—in his commercial. He said his research showed such casting would be counter-productive. I know an airline advertising manager who refused to permit the use, in his TV ads, of a genuine air stewardess employed by his own airline, because she was black. She was good enough to serve his customers their drinks, but not good enough to be shown doing so on television.

A language reveals the attitudes of the people who use and shape it. And a whole declension of patronizing terminology can be found in the language in which inter-racial relations have been described inside Britain. At first, we were told, the goal was "integration." Now this word rapidly came to mean "assimilation": a black man could only become integrated when he started behaving like a white one. After "integration" came the concept of "racial harmony." Now once again, this sounded virtuous and desirable, but what it meant in practice was that blacks should be persuaded to live peaceably with whites, in spite of all the injustices done to them every day. The call for "racial harmony" was simply an invitation to shut up and smile while nothing was done about our grievances. And now there's a new catchword: "multiculturalism." In our schools this means little more that teaching the kids a few bongo rhythms, how to tie a sari and so forth. In the police training programme, it means telling cadets that black people are so "culturally different" that they can't help making trouble. Multiculturalism is the latest token gesture towards Britain's blacks, and it ought to be exposed, like "integration" and "racial harmony," for the sham it is.

Meanwhile, the stereotyping goes on. Blacks have rhythm, Asians work hard. I've been told by Tory politicians that the Conservative Party seriously discusses the idea of wooing the Asians and leaving the Afro-Caribbeans to the Labour Party, because Asians are such good capitalists. In the new Empire, as in the old one, it seems our masters are willing to use the tried and trusted strategies of divide-and-rule.

But I've saved the worst and most insidious stereotype for last. It is the characterization of black people as a Problem. You talk about the Race Problem, the Immigration Problem, all sorts of problems. If you are liberal, you say that black people have problems. If you aren't, you say they are the problem. But the members of the new colony have only one real problem, and that problem is white people. British racism, of course, is not our problem. It's yours. We simply suffer from the effects of your problem.

And until you, the whites, see that the issue is not integration, or harmony, or multiculturalism, or immigration, but simply the business of facing up to and eradicating the prejudices within almost all of you, the citizens of your new, and last, Empire will be obliged to struggle against you. You could say that we are required to embark on a new freedom movement.

And so it's interesting to remember that when Mahatma Gandhi, the father of an earlier freedom movement, came to England and was asked what he thought of English civilization, he replied: "I think it would be a good idea."

Double Take

1. Who is Salman Rushdie's audience in "The New Empire within Britain"? In the essay, where does he address that audience most directly? How does he address that audience? In formulating your response, draw upon specific examples from the essay.
2. Given the subject matter, do you think Rushdie's choice to address his readers directly is an effective one? Why or why not? As a writer, what do you think you would gain by addressing the reader in this way? What would you lose?
3. This essay is essentially an argument: Rushdie is trying to prove the prevalence of racial prejudice in Britain. In making this argument, what sorts of examples does Rushdie use as supporting evidence? Given the audience, to what extent do you think these examples are effective? What makes them work?
4. In the introduction to this essay, we described the hostile response Rushdie received from some white Britons. Looking carefully at its tone, do you think this hostile response was warranted? Why or why not? Was Rushdie justified in using the tone that he did? If so, why? If not, then what would you recommend he do to revise the essay? That is, how would you tone down the aggressive tone while keeping the argument intact? Is that possible to do here?

At First Glance

The essay "In Good Faith" addresses the crisis that arose following the publication of Salman Rushdie's novel The Satanic Verses. *In the essay, Rushdie defends himself and the novel against charges of blasphemy. As you can imagine, there is a great deal riding on this defense. His life has been threatened; his novel has been banned and burned. So this is a very delicate balance he must strike: On the one hand, he has to defend himself and his work; on the other hand, he has to present himself as reasonable and credible. Rhetorically, then, Rushdie needs to be careful. As you read the essay, look at how Rushdie achieves this balance, if indeed he does. Look also at how he addresses his target audience, whom he terms "fair-minded Muslims." Finally, trace and analyze the structure of his argument, looking for ways he builds his defense.*

In Good Faith

It has been a year since I last spoke in defence of my novel *The Satanic Verses*. I have remained silent, though silence is against my nature, because I felt that my voice was simply not loud enough to be heard above the clamour of the voices raised against me.

I hoped that others would speak for me, and many have done so eloquently, among them an admittedly small but growing number of Muslim readers, writers and scholars. Others, including bigots and racists, have tried to exploit my case (using my name to taunt Muslim and non-Muslim Asian children and adults, for example) in a manner I have found repulsive, defiling and humiliating.

At the centre of the storm stands a novel, a work of fiction, one that aspires to the condition of literature. It has often seemed to me that people on both sides of the argument have lost sight of this simple fact. *The Satanic Verses* has been described, and treated, as a work of bad history, as an anti-religious pamphlet, as the product of an international capitalist-Jewish conspiracy, as an act of murder ("he has murdered our hearts"), as the product of a person comparable to Hitler and Attila the Hun. It felt impossible, amid such a hubbub, to insist on the fictionality of fiction.

Let me be clear: I am not trying to say that *The Satanic Verses* is "only a novel" and thus need not be taken seriously, even disputed with the utmost passion. I do not believe that novels are trivial matters. The ones I care most about are those which attempt radical reformulations of language, form and ideas, those that attempt to do what the word *novel* seems to insist upon: to see the world anew. I am well aware that this can be a hackle-raising, infuriating attempt.

What I have wished to say, however, is that the point of view from which I have, all my life, attempted this process of literary renewal is the result not of the self-hating, deracinated Uncle-Tomism of which some have accused me, but precisely of my determination to create a literary language and literary forms in which the experience of formerly colonized, still-disadvantaged peoples might find full expression. If *The Satanic Verses* is anything, it is a migrant's-eye view of the world. It is written from the very experience of uprooting, disjuncture and metamorphosis (slow or rapid, painful or pleasurable) that is the migrant condition, and from which, I believe, can be derived a metaphor for all humanity.

Standing at the centre of the novel is a group of characters most of whom are British Muslims, or not particularly religious persons of Muslim background, struggling with just the sort of great problems that have arisen to surround the book, problems of hybridization and ghettoization, of reconciling the old and the new. Those who oppose the novel most vociferously today are of the opinion that intermingling with a different culture will inevitably weaken and ruin their own. I am of the opposite opinion. *The Satanic Verses* celebrates hybridity, impurity, intermingling, the transformation that comes of new and unexpected combinations of human beings, cultures, ideas, politics, movies, songs. It rejoices in mongrelization and fears the absolutism of the Pure. *Mélange,* hotchpotch, a bit of this and a bit of that is *how newness enters the world.* It is the great possibility that mass migration gives the world, and I have tried to embrace it. *The Satanic Verses* is for change-by-fusion, change-by-conjoining. It is a love-song to our mongrel selves.

Throughout human history, the apostles of purity, those who have claimed to possess a total explanation, have wrought havoc among mere mixed-up human beings. Like many millions of people, I am a bastard child of history. Perhaps we all are, black and brown and white, leaking into one another, as a character of mine once said, *like flavours when you cook.*

The argument between purity and impurity, which is also the argument between Robespierre and Danton, the argument between the monk and the roaring boy, between primness and impropriety, between the stultifications of excessive respect and the scandals of impropriety, is an old one; I say, let it continue. Human beings understand themselves and shape their futures by arguing and challenging and questioning and saying the unsayable; not by bowing the knee, whether to gods or to men.

The Satanic Verses is, I profoundly hope, a work of radical dissent and questioning and reimagining. It is not, however, the book it has been made out to be, that book containing "nothing but filth and insults and abuse" that has brought people out on to the streets across the world.

That book simply does not exist.

This is what I want to say to the great mass of ordinary, decent, fair-minded Muslims, of the sort I have known all my life, and who have provided much of the inspiration for my work: to be rejected and reviled by, so to speak, one's own characters is a shocking and painful experience for any writer. I recognize that many Muslims have felt shocked and pained, too. Perhaps a way forward might be found through the mutual recognition of that mutual pain. Let us attempt to believe in each other's good faith.

I am aware that this is asking a good deal. There has been too much name-calling. Muslims have been called savages and barbarians and worse. I, too, have received my share of invective. Yet I still believe—perhaps I must—that understanding remains possible, and can be achieved without the suppression of the principle of free speech.

What it requires is a moment of good will; a moment in which we may all accept that the other parties are acting, have acted, in good faith.

You see, it's my opinion that if we could only dispose of the "insults and abuse" accusation, which prevents those who believe it from accepting that *The Satanic Verses* is a work of any serious intent or merit whatsoever, then we might be able, at the very least, to agree to differ about the book's real themes, about the relative value of the sacred and the profane, about the merits of purity and those of hotch-potch, and about how human beings really become whole: through the love of God or through the love of their fellow men and women.

And to dispose of the argument, we must return for a moment to the actually existing book, not the book described in the various pamphlets that have been circulated to the faithful, not the "unreadable" text of legend, not two chapters dragged out of the whole; not a piece of blubber, but the whole wretched whale.

Let me say this first: I have never seen this controversy as a struggle between Western freedoms and Eastern unfreedom. The freedoms of the West are rightly vaunted, but many minorities—racial, sexual, political—just as rightly feel excluded from full possession of these liberties; while, in my lifelong experience of the East, from Turkey and Iran to India and Pakistan, I have found people to be every bit as passionate for freedom as any Czech, Romanian, German, Hungarian or Pole.

How is freedom gained? It is taken: never given. To be free, you must first assume your right to freedom. In writing *The Satanic Verses,* I wrote from the assumption that I was, and am, a free man.

What is freedom of expression? Without the freedom to offend, it ceases to exist. Without the freedom to challenge, even to satirize all orthodoxies, including religious orthodoxies, it ceases to exist. Language and the imagination cannot be imprisoned, or art will die, and with it, a little of what makes us human. *The Satanic Verses* is, in part, a secular man's reckoning with the religious spirit. It is by no means always hostile to faith. "If we write in such a way as to pre-judge such belief as in some way deluded or false, then are we not guilty of élitism, of imposing our world-view on the masses?" asks one of its Indian characters. Yet the novel does contain doubts, uncertainties, even shocks that may well not be to the liking of the devout. Such methods have, however, long been a legitimate part even of Islamic literature.

What does the novel dissent from? Certainly not from people's right to faith, though I have none. It dissents most clearly from imposed orthodoxies *of all types,* from the view that the world is quite clearly This and not That. It dissents from the end of debate, of dispute, of dissent. Hindu communalist sectarianism, the kind of Sikh terrorism that blows up planes, the fatuousnesses of Christian creationism are dissented from as well as the narrower definitions of Islam. But such dissent is a long way from "insults and abuse." I do not believe that most of the Muslims I know would have any trouble with it.

What they have trouble with are statements like these: "Rushdie calls the Prophet Muhammad a homosexual." "Rushdie says the Prophet Muhammad asked God for permission to fornicate with every woman in the world." "Rushdie says the Prophet's wives are whores." "Rushdie calls the Prophet by a devil's name." "Rushdie calls the Companions of the Prophet *scum and bums.*" "Rushdie says that the whole Qur'an was the Devil's work." And so forth.

It has been bewildering to watch the proliferation of such statements, and to watch them acquire the authority of truth by virtue of the power of repetition. It has been bewildering to learn that people, millions upon millions of people, have been willing to judge *The Satanic Verses* and its author, without reading it, without finding out what manner of man this fellow might be, on the basis of such allegations as these. It has been bewildering to learn that people *do not care about art.* Yet the only way I can explain matters, the only way I can try and replace the non-existent novel with the one I actually wrote, is to tell you a story.

The Satanic Verses is the story of two painfully divided selves. In the case of one, Saladin Chamcha, the division is secular and societal: he is torn, to put it plainly, between Bombay and London, between East and West. For the other, Gibreel

Farishta, the division is spiritual, a rift in the soul. He has lost his faith and is strung out between his immense need to believe and his new inability to do so. The novel is "about" their quest for wholeness.

Why "Gibreel Farishta" (*Gabriel Angel*)? Not to "insult and abuse" the "real" Archangel Gabriel. Gibreel is a movie star, and movie stars hang above us in the darkness, larger than life, halfway to the divine. To give Gibreel an angel's name was to give him a secular equivalent of angelic half-divinity. When he loses his faith, however, this name becomes the source of all his torments.

Chamcha survives. He makes himself whole by returning to his roots and, more importantly, by facing up to, and learning to deal with, the great verities of love and death. Gibreel does not survive. He can neither return to the love of God, nor succeed in replacing it by earthly love. In the end he kills himself, unable to bear his torment any longer.

His greatest torments have come to him in the form of dreams. In these dreams he is cast in the role of his namesake, the Archangel, and witnesses and participates in the unfolding of various epic and tragic narratives dealing with the nature and consequences of revelation and belief. These dreams are not uniformly sceptical. In one, a non-believing landowner who has seen his entire village, and his own wife, drown in the Arabian Sea at the behest of a girl-seer who claimed the waters would open so that the pilgrims might undertake a journey to Mecca, experiences the truth of a miracle at the moment of his own death, when he opens his heart to God, and "sees" the waters part. All the dreams do, however, dramatize the struggle between faith and doubt.

Gibreel's most painful dreams, the ones at the centre of the controversy, depict the birth and growth of a religion something like Islam, in a magical city of sand named Jahilia (that is "ignorance," the name given by Arabs to the period before Islam). Almost all the alleged "insults and abuse" are taken from these dream sequences.

The first thing to be said about these dreams is that they are *agonizingly painful to the dreamer.* They are a "nocturnal retribution, a punishment" for his loss of faith. This man, desperate to regain belief, is haunted, possessed, by visions of doubt, visions of scepticism and questions and faith-shaking allegations that grow more and more extreme as they go on. He tries in vain to escape them, fighting against sleep; but then the visions cross over the boundary between his waking and sleeping self, they infect his daytimes: that is, they drive him mad. The dream-city is called "Jahilia" not to "insult and abuse" Mecca Sharif, but because the dreamer, Gibreel, has been plunged by his broken faith back into the condition the word describes. The first purpose of these sequences is not to vilify or "disprove" Islam, but to portray a soul in crisis, to show how the loss of God can destroy a man's life.

See the "offensive" chapters through this lens, and many things may seem clearer. The use of the so-called "incident of the satanic verses," the quasi-historical tale of how Muhammad's revelation seemed briefly to flirt with the possibility of admitting three pagan and female deities into the pantheon, at the semi-divine, intercessory level of the archangels, and of how he then repudiated these verses as being

satanically inspired—is, first of all, a key moment of doubt in dreams which perse-
cute a dreamer by making vivid the doubts he loathes but can no longer escape.

The most extreme passage of doubting in the novel is when the character
"Salman the Persian"—named not to "insult and abuse" Muhammad's companion
Salman al-Farisi, but more as an ironic reference to the novel's author—voices his
many scepticisms. It is quite true that the language here is forceful, satirical, and
strong meat for some tastes, but it must be remembered that the waking Gibreel is a
coarse-mouthed fellow, and it would be surprising if the dream-figures he conjures
up did not sometimes speak as rough and even obscene a language as their dreamer.
It must also be remembered that this sequence happens late in the dream, when the
dreamer's mind is crumbling along with his certainties, and when his derangement,
to which these violently expressed doubts contribute, is well advanced.

Let me not be disingenuous, however. The rejection of the three goddesses in
the novel's dream-version of the "satanic verses" story is also intended to make other
points, for example about the religion's attitude to women. "Shall He [God] have
daughters while you have sons? That would be an unjust division," read the verses
still to be found in the Qur'an. I thought it was at least worth pointing out that one
of the reasons for rejecting these goddesses was that *they were female.* The rejection
has implications that are worth thinking about. I suggest that such highlighting is a
proper function of literature.

Or again, when Salman the Persian, Gibreel's dream-figment, fulminates against
the dream-religion's aim of providing "rules for every damn thing," he is not only
tormenting the dreamer, but asking the reader to think about the validity of religion's rules. To those participants in the controversy who have felt able to justify the
most extreme Muslim threats towards me and others by saying that I have broken an
Islamic rule, I would ask the following question: are all the rules laid down at a religion's origin immutable for ever? How about the penalties for prostitution (stoning
to death) or thieving (mutilation)? How about the prohibition of homosexuality?
How about the Islamic law of inheritance, which allows a widow to inherit only an
eighth share, and which gives to sons twice as much as it does to daughters? What
of the Islamic law of evidence, which makes a woman's testimony worth only half
that of a man? Are these, too, to be given unquestioning respect: or may writers and
intellectuals ask the awkward questions that are a part of their reason for being what
they are?

Let no one suppose that such disputes about rules do not take place daily
throughout the Muslim world. Muslim religious leaders may wish female children
of Muslim households to be educated in segregated schools, but the girls, as they say
every time anybody asks them, do not wish to go. (The Labour Party doesn't ask
them, and plans to deliver them into the hands of the mullahs.) Likewise, Muslim
divines may insist that women dress "modestly," according to the Hijab code, covering more of their bodies than men because they possess what one Muslim recently
and absurdly described on television as "more adorable parts"; but the Muslim
world is full of women who reject such strictures. Islam may teach that women
should be confined to the home and to child-rearing, but Muslim women everywhere insist on leaving the home to work. If Muslim society questions its own rules

daily—and make no mistake, Muslims are as accustomed to satire as anyone else—why must a novel be proscribed for doing the same?

But to return to the text. Certain supposed "insults" need specific rebuttals. For example, the scene in which the Prophet's companions are called "scum" and "bums" is a depiction of the early persecution of the believers, and the insults quoted are clearly not mine but those hurled at the faithful by the ungodly. How, one wonders, could a book portray persecution without allowing the persecutors to be seen persecuting? (Or again: how could a book portray doubt without allowing the uncertain to articulate their uncertainties?)

As to the matter of the Prophet's wives: what happens in Gibreel's dreams is that the whores of a brothel *take the names* of the wives of the Prophet Mahound in order to arouse their customers. The "real" wives are clearly stated to be "living chastely" in their harem. But why introduce so shocking an image? For this reason: throughout the novel, I sought images that crystallized the opposition between the sacred and profane worlds. The harem and the brothel provide such an opposition. Both are places where women are sequestered, in the harem to keep them from all men except their husband and close family members, in the brothel for the use of strange males. Harem and brothel are antithetical worlds, and the presence in the harem of the Prophet, the receiver of a sacred text, is likewise contrasted with the presence in the brothel of the clapped-out poet, Baal, the creator of profane texts. The two struggling worlds, pure and impure, chaste and coarse, are juxtaposed by making them echoes of one another; and, finally, the pure eradicates the impure. Whores and writer ("I see no difference here," remarks Mahound) are executed. Whether one finds this a happy or sad conclusion depends on one's point of view.

The purpose of the "brothel sequence," then, was not to "insult and abuse" the Prophet's wives, but to dramatize certain ideas about morality; and sexuality, too, because what happens in the brothel—called *Hijab* after the name for "modest" dress as an ironic means of further highlighting the inverted echo between the two worlds—is that the men of "Jahilia" are enabled to act out an ancient dream of power and possession, the dream of possessing the queen. That men should be so aroused by the great ladies' whorish counterfeits says something about *them,* not the great ladies, and about the extent to which sexual relations have to do with possession.

I must have known, my accusers say, that my use of the old devil-name "Mahound," a medieval European demonization of "Muhammad," would cause offence. In fact, this is an instance in which de-contextualization has created a complete reversal of meaning. A part of the relevant context is on page ninety-three of the novel. "To turn insults into strengths, whigs, tories, Blacks all chose to wear with pride the names they were given in scorn; likewise, our mountain-climbing prophet-motivated solitary is to be the medieval baby-frightener, the Devil's synonym: Mahound." Central to the purposes of *The Satanic Verses* is the process of reclaiming language from one's opponents. (Elsewhere in the novel we find the poet Jumpy Joshi trying to reclaim Enoch Powell's notorious "rivers of blood" simile. Humanity itself can be thought of as a river of blood, he argues; the river flows in our bodies, and we, as a collectivity, are a river of blood flowing down the ages. Why abandon so potent and evocative an image to the racists?) "Trotsky" was Trotsky's jailer's name. By taking it for his own, he symbolically conquered his captor and set himself free. Something of the same spirit lay behind my use of the name "Mahound."

The attempt at reclamation goes even further than this. When Saladin Chamcha finds himself transformed into a goatish, horned and hoofy demon, in a bizarre sanatorium full of other monstrous beings, he's told that they are all, like him, aliens and migrants, demonized by the "host culture's" attitude to them. "They have the power of description, and we succumb to the pictures they construct." If migrant groups are called devils by others, that does not really make them demonic. And if devils are not necessarily devilish, angels may not necessarily be angelic. . . . From this premise, the novel's exploration of morality as internal and shifting (rather than external, divinely sanctioned, absolute) may be said to emerge.

The very title, *The Satanic Verses,* is an aspect of this attempt at reclamation. You call us devils? it seems to ask. Very well, then, here is the devil's version of the world, of "your" world, the version written *from the experience* of those who have been demonized by virtue of their otherness. Just as the Asian kids in the novel wear toy devil-horns proudly, as an assertion of pride in identity, so the novel proudly wears its demonic title. The purpose is not to suggest that the Qur'an is written by the devil; it is to attempt the sort of act of affirmation that, in the United States, transformed the word *black* for the standard term of racist abuse into a "beautiful" expression of cultural pride.

And so on. There are times when I feel that the original intentions of *The Satanic Verses* have been so thoroughly scrambled by events as to be lost for ever. There are times when I feel frustrated that the terms in which the novel is discussed seem to have been set exclusively by Muslim leaders (including those, like Sher Azam of the Bradford Council of Mosques, who can blithely say on television, "Books are not my thing"). After all, the process of hybridization which is the novel's most crucial dynamic means that its ideas derive from many sources other than Islamic ones.

There is, for example, the pre-Christian belief, expressed in the Books of Amos and Deutero-Isaiah and quoted in *The Satanic Verses,* that God and the Devil were one and the same: "It isn't until the Book of Chronicles, merely fourth century B.C., that the word *Satan* is used to mean a being, and not only an attribute of God." It should also be said that the two books that were most influential on the shape this novel took do not include the Qur'an. One was William Blake's *Marriage of Heaven and Hell,* the classic meditation on the interpenetration of good and evil; the other *The Master and Margarita* by Mikhail Bulgakov, the great Russian lyrical and comical novel in which the Devil descends upon Moscow and wreaks havoc upon the corrupt, materialist, decadent inhabitants and turns out, by the end, not to be such a bad chap after all. *The Master and Margarita* and its author were persecuted by Soviet totalitarianism. It is extraordinary to find my novel's life echoing that of one of its greatest models.

Nor are these the only non-Muslim influences at work. I was born an Indian, and not only an Indian, but a Bombayite—Bombay, the most cosmopolitan, most hybrid, most hotchpotch of Indian cities. My writing and thought have therefore been as deeply influenced by Hindu myths and attitudes as Muslim ones (and my movie star Gibreel is also a figure of inter-religious tolerance, playing Hindu gods without causing offence, in spite of his Muslim origins). Nor is the West absent from Bombay. I was already a mongrel self, history's bastard, before London aggravated the condition.

To be an Indian of my generation was also to be convinced of the vital importance of Jawaharlal Nehru's vision of a secular India. Secularism, for India, is not simply a point of view; it is a question of survival. If what Indians call "communalism," sectarian religious politics, were to be allowed to take control of the polity, the results would be too horrifying to imagine. Many Indians fear that that moment may now be very near. I have fought against communal politics all my adult life. The Labour Party in Britain would do well to look at the consequences of Indian politicians' willingness to play the communalist card, and consider whether some Labour politicians' apparent willingness to do the same in Britain, for the same reason (votes), is entirely wise.

To be a Bombayite (and afterwards a Londoner) was also to fall in love with the metropolis. The city as reality and as a metaphor is at the heart of all my work. "The modern city," says a character in *The Satanic Verses,* "is the *locus classicus* of incompatible realities." Well, that turned out to be true. "As long as they pass in the night, it's not so bad. But if they meet! It's uranium and plutonium, each makes the other decompose, boom." It is hard to express how it feels to have attempted to portray an objective reality and then to have become its subject . . .

The point is this: Muslim culture has been very important to me, but it is not by any means the only shaping factor. I am a modern, and modern*ist,* urban man, accepting uncertainty as the only constant, changes as the only sure thing. I believe in no god, and have done so since I was a young adolescent. I have spiritual needs, and my work has, I hope, a moral and spiritual dimension, but I am content to try and satisfy those needs without recourse to any idea of a Prime Mover or ultimate arbiter.

To put it as simply as possible: *I am not a Muslim.* It feels bizarre, and wholly inappropriate, to be described as some sort of heretic after having lived my life as a secular, pluralist, eclectic man. I am being enveloped in, and described by, a language that does not fit me. I do not accept the charge of blasphemy, because, as somebody says in *The Satanic Verses,* "where there is no belief, there is no blasphemy." I do not accept the charge of apostasy, because I have never in my adult life affirmed any belief, and what one has not affirmed one cannot be said to have apostasized from. The Islam I know states clearly that "there can be no coercion in matters of religion." The many Muslims I respect would be horrified by the idea that they belong to their faith *purely by virtue of birth,* and that any person so born who freely chose not to be a Muslim could therefore be put to death.

When I am described as an apostate Muslim, I feel as if I have been concealed behind a *false self,* as if a shadow has become substance while I have been relegated to the shadows. Sections of the non-Muslim British media have helped in the creation of other aspects of this false self, portraying me as egomaniacal, insolent, greedy, hypocritical and disloyal. It has been suggested that I prefer to be known by an Anglicization of my name ("Simon Rushton"). And, to perfect the double bind, this Salman Rushdie is also "thin-skinned" and "paranoid," so that any attempt by him to protest against falsifications will be seen as further proof of the reality of the false self, the golem.

The Muslim attack against me has been greatly assisted by the creation of this false self. "Simon Rushton" has featured in several Muslim portrayals of my debased, deracinated personality. My "greed" fits well into the conspiracy theory, that I sold my soul to the West and wrote a carefully planned attack on Islam in return for pots of money. "Disloyalty" is useful in this context, too. Jorge Luis Borges, Graham Greene and other writers have written about their sense of an Other who goes about the world bearing their name. There are moments when I worry that my Other may succeed in obliterating me.

On 14 February 1989, within hours of the dread news from Iran, I received a telephone call from Keith Vaz, MP, during which he vehemently expressed his full support for me and my work, and his horror at the threat against my life. A few weeks later, this same gentleman was to be found addressing a demonstration full of men demanding my death, and of children festooned with murderous placards. By now Mr Vaz wanted my work banned, and threats against my life seemed not to trouble him any longer.

It has been that sort of year. Twelve months ago, the *Guardian*'s esteemed columnist, Hugo Young, teetered on the edge of racism when he told all British Muslims that if they didn't like the way things were in Britain, they could always leave ("if not Dagenham, why not Tehran?"); now this same Mr Young prefers to lay the blame for the controversy at my door. (I have, after all, fewer battalions at my disposal.) No doubt, Mr Young would now be relieved if I went back where I came from.

And, and, and. Lord Dacre thought it might be a good idea if I were beaten up in a dark alley. Rana Kabbani announced with perfect Stalinist fervour that writers should be "accountable" to the community. Brian Clark (the author, ironically enough, of *Whose Life Is It Anyway?*), claiming to be on my side, wrote an execrable play which, mercifully, nobody has yet agreed to produce, entitled *Who Killed Salman Rushdie?*, and sent it along in case I needed something to read.

And Britain witnessed a brutalization of public debate that seemed hard to believe. Incitement to murder was tolerated on the nation's streets. (In Europe and the United States, swift government action prevented such incitement at a very early stage.) On TV shows, studio audiences were asked for a show of hands on the question of whether I should live or die. A man's murder (mine) became a legitimate subject for a national opinion poll. And slowly, slowly, a point of view grew up, and was given voice by mountebanks and bishops, fundamentalists and Mr John le Carré, which held that *I knew exactly what I was doing*. I must have known what would happen; therefore, did it on purpose, to profit by the notoriety that would result. This accusation is, today, in fairly wide circulation, and so I must defend myself against it, too.

I find myself wanting to ask questions: when Osip Mandelstam wrote his poem against Stalin, did he "know what he was doing" and so deserve his death? When the students filled Tiananmen Square to ask for freedom, were they not also, and knowingly, asking for the murderous repression that resulted? When Terry Waite was taken hostage, hadn't he been "asking for it"? I find myself thinking of Jodie Foster in her Oscar-winning role in *The Accused*. Even if I were to concede (and I do not concede it) that what I did in *The Satanic Verses* was the literary equivalent of flaunting oneself shamelessly before the eyes of aroused men, is that really a justification for being, so to speak, gang-banged? Is any provocation a justification for rape?

Threats of violence ought not to coerce us into believing the victims of intimidation to be responsible for the violence threatened. I am aware, however, that rhetoric is an insufficient response. Nor is it enough to point out that nothing on the scale of this controversy has, to my knowledge, ever happened in the history of literature. If I had told anyone before publication that such events would occur as a result of my book, I would instantly have proved the truth of the accusations of egomania . . .

It's true that some passages in *The Satanic Verses* have now acquired a prophetic quality that alarms even me. "Your blasphemy, Salman, can't be forgiven . . . To set your words against the Word of God." Et cetera. But to write a dream based around events that took place in the seventh century of the Christian era, and to create metaphors of the conflict between different sorts of "author" and different types of "text"—to say that literature and religion, like literature and politics, fight for the same territory—is very different from somehow knowing, in advance, that your dream is about to come true, that the metaphor is about to be made flesh, that the conflict your work seeks to explore is about to engulf it, and its publishers and booksellers; and you.

At least (small comfort) I wasn't wrong.

Books choose their authors; the act of creation is not entirely a rational and conscious one. But this, as honestly as I can set it down, is, in respect of the novel's treatment of religion, what "I knew I was doing."

I set out to explore, through the process of fiction, the nature of revelation and the power of faith. The mystical, revelatory experience is quite clearly a genuine one. This statement poses a problem to the non-believer: if we accept that the mystic, the prophet, is sincerely undergoing some sort of transcendent experience, but we cannot believe in a supernatural world, then *what is going on?* To answer this question, among others, I began work on the story of "Mahound." I was aware that the "satanic verses" incident is much disputed by Muslim theologians; that the life of Muhammad has become the object of a kind of veneration that some would consider un-Islamic, since Muhammad himself always insisted that he was merely a messenger, an ordinary man; and that, therefore, great sensitivities were involved. I genuinely believed that my overt use of fabulation would make it clear to any reader that I was not attempting to falsify history, but to allow a fiction to take off from history. The use of dreams, fantasy, et cetera was intended to say: the point is not whether this is "really" supposed to be Muhammad, or whether the satanic verses incident "really" happened; the point is to examine what such an incident might reveal about what revelation is, about the extent to which the mystic's conscious personality informs and interacts with the mystical event; the point is to try and understand the human event of revelation. The use of fiction was a way of creating the sort of distance from actuality that I felt would prevent offence from being taken. I was wrong.

Jahilia, to use once again the ancient Arab story-tellers' formula I used often in *The Satanic Verses,* both "is and is not" Mecca. Many of the details of its social life are drawn from historical research; but it is also a dream of an Indian city (its concentric street-plan deliberately recalls New Delhi), and, as Gibreel spends time in England, it becomes a dream of London, too. Likewise, the religion of "Submission" both is and is not Islam. Fiction uses facts as a starting-place and then spirals away to explore its real concerns, which are only tangentially historical. Not to see this, to treat fiction as if it were fact, is to make a serious mistake of categories. The case of *The Satanic Verses* may be one of the biggest category mistakes in literary history.

Here is more of what I knew: I knew that stories of Muhammad's doubts, uncertainties, errors, fondness for women abound in and around Muslim tradition. To me, they seemed to make him more vivid, more human, and therefore more interesting, even more worthy of admiration. The greatest human beings must struggle against themselves as well as the world. I never doubted Muhammad's greatness, nor, I believe, is the "Mahound" of my novel belittled by being portrayed as human.

I knew that Islam is by no means homogeneous, or as absolutist as some of its champions make it out to be. Islam contains the doubts of Iqbal, Ghazali, Khayyám as well as the narrow certainties of Shabbir Akhtar of the Bradford Council of Mosques and Kalim Siddiqui, director of the pro-Iranian Muslim Institute. Islam contains ribaldry as well as solemnity, irreverence as well as absolutism. I knew much about Islam that I admired, and still admire, immensely; I also knew that Islam, like all the world's great religions, had seen terrible things done in its name.

The original incident on which the dream of the villagers who drown in the Arabian Sea is based is also a part of that I "knew." The story awed me, because of what it told me about the huge power of faith. I wrote this part of the novel to see if I could understand, by getting inside their skins, people for whom devotion was as great as this.

He did it on purpose is one of the strangest accusations ever levelled at a writer. Of course I did it on purpose. The question is, and it is what I have tried to answer: what is the "it" that I did?

What I did not do was conspire against Islam; or write—after years and years of anti-racist work and writing—a text of incitement to racial hatred; or anything of the sort. My golem, my false Other, may be capable of such deeds, but I am not.

Would I have written differently if I had known what would happen? Truthfully, I don't know. Would I change any of the text now? I would not. It's too late. As Friedrich Dürrenmatt wrote in *The Physicists*: "What has once been thought cannot be unthought."

The controversy over *The Satanic Verses* needs to be looked at as a political event, not purely a theological one. In India, where the trouble started, the Muslim fundamentalist MP Syed Shahabuddin used my novel as a stick with which to threaten the wobbling Rajiv Gandhi government. The demand for the book's banning was a power-play to demonstrate the strength of the Muslim vote, on which Congress has traditionally relied and which it could ill afford to lose. (In spite of the ban, Congress lost the Muslims and the election anyway. Put not your trust in Shahabuddins.)

In South Africa, the row over the book served the purpose of the regime by driving a wedge between the Muslim and non-Muslim members of the UDF. In Pakistan, it was a way for the fundamentalists to try and regain the political initiative after their trouncing in the general election. In Iran, too, the incident could only be properly understood when seen in the context of the country's internal political struggles. And in Britain, where secular and religious leaders had been vying for power in the community for over a decade, and where, for a long time, largely secular organizations such as the Indian Workers Association (IWA) had been in the ascendant, the "affair" swung the balance of power back towards the mosques. Small wonder, then, that the various councils of mosques are reluctant to bring the protest to an end, even though many Muslims up and down the country find it embarrassing, even shameful, to be associated with such illiberalism and violence.

The responsibility for violence lies with those who perpetrate it. In the past twelve months, bookshop workers have been manhandled, spat upon, verbally abused, bookshop premises have been threatened and, on several occasions, actually firebombed. Publishing staff have had to face a campaign of hate mail, menacing phone calls, death threats and bomb scares. Demonstrations have, on occasion, turned violent, too. During the big march in London last summer, peaceful counter-demonstrations on behalf of humanism and secularism were knocked to the ground by marchers, and a counter-demo by the courageous (and largely Muslim) Women Against Fundamentalism group was threatened and abused.

There is no conceivable reason why such behaviour should be privileged because it is done in the name of an affronted religion. If we are to talk about "insults," "abuse," "offence," then the campaign against *The Satanic Verses* has been, very often, as insulting, abusive and offensive as it's possible to be.

As a result, racist attitudes have hardened. I did not invent British racism, nor did *The Satanic Verses.* The Commission for Racial Equality (CRE), which now accuses me of harming race relations, knows that for years it lent out my videotaped anti-racist Channel 4 broadcast to all sorts of black and white groups and seminars. Readers of *The Satanic Verses* will not be able to help noticing its extremely strong anti-racist line. I have never given the least comfort or encouragement to racists; but the leaders of the campaign against me certainly have, by reinforcing the worst racist stereotypes of Muslims as repressive, anti-liberal, censoring zealots. If Norman Tebbit has taken up the old Powellite refrains and if his laments about the multi-cultural society find favour in the land, then a part of the responsibility at least must be laid at the door of those who burn, and would ban, books.

I am not the first writer to be persecuted by Islamic fundamentalism in the modern period; among the greatest names so victimized are the Iranian writer Ahmad Kasravi, stabbed to death by fanatics, and the Egyptian Nobel laureate Nagiub Mahfouz, often threatened but still, happily, with us. I am not the first artist to be accused of blasphemy and apostasy; these are, in fact, probably the most common weapons with which fundamentalism has sought to shackle creativity in the modern age. It is sad, then, that so little attention has been paid to this crucial literary context; and that Western critics like John Berger, who once spoke messianically of the need for new ways of seeing, should now express their willingness to privilege one such way over another, to protect a religion boasting one billion believers from the solitary figure of a single writer brandishing an "unreadable" book.

As for the British Muslim "leaders," they cannot have it both ways. Sometimes they say I am entirely unimportant, and only the book matters; on other days they hold meetings at mosques across the nation and endorse the call for my killing. They say they hold to the laws of this country, but they also say that Islamic law has moral primacy for them. They say they do not wish to break British laws, but only a very few are willing openly to repudiate the threat against me. They should make their position clear; are they democratic citizens of a free society or are they not? Do they reject violence or do they not?

After a year, it is time for a little clarity.

To the Muslim community at large, in Britain and India and Pakistan and everywhere else, I would like to say: do not ask your writers to create *typical* or *representative* fictions. Such books are almost invariably dead books. The liveliness of literature lies in its exceptionality, in being the individual, idiosyncratic vision of one human being, in which, to our delight and great surprise, we may find our own image reflected. A book is a version of the world. If you do not like it, ignore it; or offer your own version in return.

And I would like to say this: life without God seems to believers to be an idiocy, pointless, beneath contempt. It does not seem so to non-believers. To accept that the world, here, is all there is; to go through it, towards and into death, without the consolations of religion seems, well, at least as courageous and rigorous to us as the espousal of faith seems to you. Secularism and its work deserve your respect, not your contempt.

A great wave of freedom has been washing over the world. Those who resist— in China, in Romania—find themselves bathed in blood. I should like to ask Muslims—that great mass of ordinary, decent, fair-minded Muslims to whom I have imagined myself to be speaking for most of this piece—to choose to ride the wave; to renounce blood; not to let Muslim leaders make Muslims seem less tolerant than they are. *The Satanic Verses* is a serious work, written from a non-believer's point of view. Let believers accept that, and let it be.

In the meantime, I am asked, how do I feel? I feel grateful to the British government for defending me. I hope that such a defence would be made available to any citizen so threatened, but that doesn't lessen my gratitude. I needed it, and it was provided. (I'm still no Tory, but that's democracy.)

I feel grateful, too, to my protectors, who have done such a magnificent job, and who have become my friends.

I feel grateful to everyone who has offered me support. The one real gain for me in this bad time has been the discovery of being cared for by so many people. The only antidote to hatred is love.

Above all, I feel gratitude towards, solidarity with and pride in all the publishing people and bookstore workers around the world who have held the line against intimidation, and who will, I am sure, continue to do so as long as it remains necessary.

I feel as if I have been plunged, like Alice, into the world beyond the looking-glass, where nonsense is the only available sense. And I wonder if I'll ever be able to climb back through the mirror.

Do I feel regret? Of course I do: regret that such offence has been taken against my work when it was not intended—when dispute was intended, and dissent, and even, at times, satire, and criticism of intolerance, and the like, but not the thing of which I'm most often accused, not "filth," not "insult," not "abuse." I regret that so many people who might have taken pleasure in finding their reality given pride of place in a novel will now not read it because of what they believe it to be, or will come to it with their minds already made up.

And I feel sad to be so grievously separated from my community, from India, from everyday life, from the world.

Please understand, however: I make no complaint. I am a writer. I do not accept my condition. I will strive to change it; but I inhabit it, I am trying to learn from it.

Our lives teach us who we are.

Double Take

1. What are some of the main arguments Salman Rushdie makes in defense of his novel *The Satanic Verses*? Do you find these arguments persuasive? Do you think his intended readers would find his arguments persuasive? Why or why not?
2. In addition to defending his novel, Rushdie also has to gain credibility as a writer, presenting himself as someone his readers will be inclined to trust and perhaps even sympathize with. To what extend does Rushdie achieve this credibility? How does he do it? What rhetorical strategies does he use to achieve it?
3. As a student writer who will be asked to write numerous argument-based papers during your college career, what strikes you as most impressive about Rushdie's style and strategy of argumentation in this essay? What can you learn about writing arguments from reading "In Good Faith"?
4. If a reader was predisposed to disagree with Rushdie before reading his essay "In Good Faith," what might be that reader's reaction to this essay? What aspects of the essay would he or she react to most negatively? Why? Are there any places in the essay where such a reader might be moved or convinced to see Rushdie's point of view? Why or why not?

Seeing for Yourself

At First Glance

One thing that stands out about Salman Rushdie's short essay "Censorship" is its subtle humor, something we do not really see in his other essays reprinted here. It is also perhaps a little more conversational than the other essays, although those too exhibit a conversational tone. Look for these qualities as you read the essay and think about what function they play. In addition, Rushdie refers in the essay to places and names that may be unfamiliar to Western readers. As you read the essay, consider the effect of this unfamiliarity on you as a reader. Think about what you as a writer could do to minimize and/or utilize unfamiliarity in your own writing.

Censorship

My first memories of censorship are cinematic: screen kisses brutalized by prudish scissors which chopped out the moments of actual contact. (Briefly, before comprehension dawned, I wondered if that were all there was to kissing, the languorous approach and then the sudden turkey-jerk away.) The effect was usually somewhat comic, and censorship still retains, in contemporary Pakistan, a strong element of comedy. When the Pakistani censors found that the movie *El Cid* ended with a dead Charlton Heston leading the Christians to victory over live Muslims, they nearly banned it, until they had the idea of simply cutting out the entire climax, so that the film as screened showed El Cid mortally wounded, El Cid dying nobly, and then ended. Muslims 1 Christians 0.

The comedy is sometimes black. The burning of the film *Kissa Kursi Ka* (*Tale of a Chair*) during Mrs Gandhi's Emergency rule in India is notorious; and, in Pakistan, a reader's letter to the *Pakistan Times,* in support of the decision to ban the film *Gandhi* because of its unflattering portrayal of M. A. Jinnah, criticized certain "liberal elements" for having dared to suggest that the film should be released so that Pakistanis could make up their own minds about it. If they were less broad-minded, the letter-writer suggested, these persons would be better citizens of Pakistan.

My first direct encounter with censorship took place in 1968, when I was twenty-one, fresh out of Cambridge and full of the radical fervour of that famous year. I returned to Karachi, where a small magazine commissioned me to write a piece about my impressions on returning home. I remember very little about this piece (mercifully, memory is a censor, too), except that it was not at all political. It tended, I think, to linger melodramatically, on images of dying horses with flies settling on their eyeballs. You can imagine the sort of thing. Anyway, I submitted my piece, and a couple weeks later was told by the magazine's editor that the Press Council, the national censors, had banned it completely. Now it so happened that I had an uncle on the Press Council, and in a very unradical, string-pulling mood I thought I'd just go and see him and everything would be sorted out. He looked tired when I confronted him. "Publication," he said immovably, "would not be in your best interest." I never found out why.

Next I persuaded Karachi TV to let me produce an act in Edward Albee's *The Zoo Story*, which they liked because it was forty-five minutes long, had a cast of two and required only a park bench for a set. I then had to go through a series of astonishing censorship conferences. The character I played had a long monologue in which he described his landlady's dog's repeated attacks on him. In an attempt to befriend the dog, he bought it half a dozen hamburgers. The dog refused the hamburgers and attacked him again. "I was offended," I was supposed to say. "It was six perfectly good hamburgers with not enough pork in them to make it disgusting." "Pork," a TV executive told me solemnly, "is a four-letter word." He had said the same thing about "sex," and "homosexual," but this time I argued back. The text, I pleaded, was saying the right thing about pork. Pork, in Albee's view, made hamburgers so disgusting that even dogs refused them. This was superb anti-pork propaganda. It must stay. "You don't see," the executive told me, wearing the same tired expression as my uncle had, "the word pork may not be spoken on Pakistan television." And that was that. I also had to cut the line about God being a coloured queen who wears a kimono and plucks his eyebrows.

The point I'm making is not that censorship is a source of amusement, which it usually isn't, but that—in Pakistan, at any rate—it is everywhere, inescapable, permitting no appeal. In India the authorities control the media that matter—radio and television—and allow some leeway to the press, comforted by their knowledge of the country's low literacy level. In Pakistan they go further. Not only do they control the press, but the journalists, too. At the recent conference of the Non-Aligned Movement in New Delhi, the Pakistan press corps was notable for its fearfulness. Each member was worried one of the other guys might inform on him when they returned—for drinking, or consorting too closely with Hindus, or performing other unpatriotic acts. Indian journalists were deeply depressed by the sight of their opposite numbers behaving like scared rabbits one moment and quislings the next.

What are the effects of total censorship? Obviously, the absence of information and the presence of lies. During Mr Bhutto's campaign of genocide in Baluchistan, the news media remained silent. Officially, Baluchistan was at peace. Those who died, died unofficial deaths. It must have comforted them to know that the State's truth declared them all to be alive. Another example: you will not find the involvement of Pakistan's military rulers with the booming heroin industry much discussed in the country's news media. Yet this is what underlies General Zia's concern for the lot of the Afghan refugees. Afghan entrepreneurs help to run the Pakistan heroin business, and they have had the good sense to make sure that they make the army rich as well as themselves. How fortunate that the Qur'an does not mention anything about the ethics of heroin pushing.

But the worst, most insidious effect of censorship is that, in the end, it can deaden the imagination of the people. Where there is no debate, it is hard to go on remembering, every day, that there is a suppressed side to every argument. It becomes almost impossible to conceive of what the suppressed things might be. It becomes easy to think that what has been suppressed was valueless, anyway, or so dangerous that it needed to be suppressed. And then the victory of the censor is total. The anti-*Gandhi* letter-writer who recommended narrow-mindedness as a national virtue is one such casualty of censorship; he loves Big Brother—or *Burra Bhai,* perhaps.

It seems, now, that General Zia's days are numbered. I do not believe that the present disturbances are the end, but they are the beginning of the end, because they show that the people have lost their fear of his brutal regime, and if the people cease to be afraid, he is done for. But Pakistan's big test will come after the end of dictatorship, after the restoration of civilian rule and free elections, whenever that is, in one year or two or five; because if leaders do not then emerge who are willing to lift censorship, to permit dissent, to believe and to demonstrate that opposition is the bedrock of democracy, then, I am afraid, the last chance will have been lost. For the moment, however, one can hope.

A CLOSER LOOK AT SALMAN RUSHDIE

1. In "Imaginary Homelands" Salman Rushdie writes, "description is itself a political act . . . So it is clear that redescribing a world is the necessary first step towards changing it." What does he mean by this? In what way is description political, and how does redescription change the world? Address these questions in an essay of your own, and turn to Rushdie's own essays for examples. How are his own descriptions political?

2. In an interview, Rushdie reflects on the connections between language and identity. He explains, "every family has stories about itself. You could argue, in fact, that the collection of stories a family has about itself is actually the definition of the family. When someone joins a family—a child is born,

somebody marries into it—they are gradually told all the secret family stories. And when you finally know all the stories, you belong to the family."
Reflecting on your own experiences, write an essay about the stories that
define your own family, the stories that signal a sense of belonging in the
family.

3. In his essay "The New Empire within Britain," Rushdie addresses the issue
of multiculturalism. He writes, "in our schools, this means little more than
teaching the kids a few bongo rhythms, how to tie a sari and so forth. In the
police training programme, it means telling cadets that black people are so
'culturally different' that they can't help making trouble. Multiculturalism is
the latest token gesture towards Britain's blacks, and it ought to be exposed,
like 'integration' and 'racial harmony,' for the sham it is." Why do you think
Rushdie presents multiculturalism as a sham? Given that multiculturalism
has been promoted by many teachers and scholars as a recognition and validation of different cultures in school and society, do you think Rushdie's
assessment of multiculturalism is fair? To what extent is multiculturalism a
positive step toward a more pluralistic society? To what extent is it a token
gesture? Considering your experiences in college and Rushdie's claims,
write an essay that addresses how multiculturalism is presented on your campus.

4. Each of the four essays by Salman Rushdie can be seen as making a fairly
explicit argument. As you read the essays pay attention to the ways that
Rushdie structures his arguments, looking at his use of examples, transitions,
word choices, tone, and style. What patterns can you trace in the ways he
structures his arguments? What rhetorical strategies does he use most often?
Then write an essay that answers these questions and compares these strategies to your own strategies for argument. In what ways are they similar and
in what ways do they differ?

Looking from Writer to Writer

1. In her essay "Rushdie at the Louvre," Cynthia Ozick writes about her experience of seeing Salman Rushdie at a writers' conference in Paris in 1996, a time
during which he was still in hiding from the death sentence imposed on him.
Read Ozick's essay, which treats Rushdie both sympathetically and critically,
and compare it to Rushdie's own representation of himself in his essay "In Good
Faith." To what extent does Ozick's representation reflect Rushdie's representation of himself? In what ways do the representations differ? What do these similarities and differences tell us about the nature of perspective?

2. Reflecting on language and identity, Rushdie notes, "it's interesting to me how much of what it is to be a family is governed by language use." Think about what Rushdie means in this statement, and then apply it to Amy Tan's ideas concerning family and language. In what ways does Rushdie's statement support Tan's argument about the various "Englishes" she grew up using?

3. In their essays collected in this book, André Aciman and Edward Said both write about exile and the longing for home, but from different perspectives. Aciman writes from a Jewish perspective and Said from a Palestinian perspective. Writing from an Indo-British perspective, Rushdie also reflects on what it means to feel out of place. In "Imaginary Homelands" particularly, Rushdie examines what is lost and gained by living between cultures. In comparing their views on life as an exile, how do the three essayists characterize the loss and gain that comes from being displaced? Do you find agreement among them? If so, in what ways do they agree? If not, how do their views on exile differ? Does one of them offer a more helpful vision than the others? How and why?

Looking Beyond

ESSAYS

Imaginary Homelands: Essays and Criticism, 1981–1991. London: Granta Books, 1991.

NONFICTION

The Jaguar Smile: A Nicaraguan Journey. New York: Viking, 1987.

FICTION

Grimus. 1975. New York: Overlook Press, 1979.
The Ground Beneath Her Feet: A Novel. New York: Henry Holt, 1999.
Haroun and the Sea of Stories. London: Granta Books, 1990.
Midnight's Children: A Novel. 1980. New York: Knopf, 1981.
The Moor's Last Sigh. New York: Pantheon Books, 1995.
The Satanic Verses. 1988. New York: Viking, 1989.
Shame. New York: Knopf, 1983.

Edward W. Said

Even when he is not writing directly about the fate of the Palestinian people, it is difficult to separate Edward Said's writing from the politics of his experience as an Arab, and particularly as a Palestinian. Said's work as a literary scholar—he is University Professor of English and Comparative Literature at Columbia University—is also shaped by what he calls "the experience of dislocation, exile, migration, and empire," all of which predispose him to identify and articulate moments of alienation in writers such as Joseph Conrad, whose writing represents "the fate of lostness and disorientation." Indeed, nowhere perhaps is Said's writing more powerful than in its attempt to chronicle the experience of exile—"the unhealable rift forced between a human being and a native place"—and the feeling of perpetual loss that attends it. In the face of such loss, Said's work (e.g., *The Question of Palestine, After the Late Sky, The Politics of Dispossession,* and *Out of Place*) can be read as a kind of partial reclamation, an attempt to make sense of what it means to be "out of place." Just as significantly, Said's work (e.g., *Orientalism, Culture and Imperialism,* and *Covering Islam*) can also be read as a critique of Eurocentrism and empire, examining as it does how Western representations of the Middle and Near East have served to render such places and people both different as well as inferior.

Edward Said was born in Talbiya, Palestine, in 1935. At the time Talbiya was a prosperous part of West Jerusalem inhabited mainly by Christian Palestinians. Both his parents were Palestinian, although his father lived and studied in the United States for a few years, acquiring U.S. citizenship during World War I. Since his father's family business had expanded from Jerusalem to Cairo, Said spent his childhood living both in Palestine and Egypt until 1948 when, after the establishment of Israel, his family was driven out of Palestine and became refugees in Egypt. Growing up, Said explains that "the overriding sensation I had was of always being out of place." He writes: "with an unexceptionally Arab family name like Said connected to an improbably British first name . . . I was an uncomfortably anomalous student all through my early years: a Palestinian going to school in Egypt, with an English first name, an American passport, and no certain identity at all." This experience of hybridity was compounded by Said's attendance at elite British colonial schools in Palestine and Cairo before his expulsion in 1951 for unruly behavior. That same year, Said's parents sent him to a boarding school in the United States where, except for vacations to the Middle East, he has continued to live to this day, completing undergraduate work at Princeton University and then a PhD at Harvard University before accepting a teaching position at Columbia University in New York in 1963.

Today, Said is internationally renowned as a scholar and a political figure. In his scholarship, he recognizes that literary texts are "worldly," meaning that they are "part of the social world, human life, and of course the historical moments in which they are located and interpreted." Similarly, Said's political writing also recognizes that the way one culture defines and dominates another is located and interpreted within historical moments. In response, Said's work can be described in part as an attempt to make these historical moments visible, to show how people's interpretations of themselves and others are shaped by their historical conditions. Said refers to this awareness as "critical consciousness," a kind of heightened perspective that allows people to "be in the world and self-aware simultaneously." It is this "knowing and unafraid attitude toward exploring the world we live in" that best defines Said's work and life as an intellectual.

Said achieves this critical vision in part by writing from his own multiple and tenuous identity as an Arab and an American. As he expresses in "The Mind of Winter" (printed in this collection), "Most people are principally aware of one culture, one setting, one home; exiles are aware of at least two, and this plurality of vision gives rise to an awareness of simultaneous dimensions." Such critical consciousness has at once made Said a passionate supporter of the Palestinian people (a support that resulted in numerous death threats and acts of violence targeted toward him) as well as at times a critic of Palestinian leadership (criticism that made him the object of left-wing nationalist hostility).

In 1991 Said was diagnosed with leukemia, a diagnosis that prompted him to turn his critical attention inward, toward his own life. Since then his writing has become much more personal, resulting in the publication of his memoir *Out of Place* in 1999. As you read the essays collected here, think about the difference between Said's personal, political, and academic essays. Each in its own way deals with the recurring themes of colonialism, exile, language, and identity. Yet each also arrives at these themes from different vantages. Think about how these vantages shape the subject matter.

Said on Writing

At First Glance

This essay appeared in an essay collection titled Letters of Transit: Reflections on Exile, Identity, Language, and Loss, *edited by André Aciman (see the chapter on Aciman in this book). It may not be immediately apparent that this essay is about writing. Indeed, it seems to be more about questions of language, loss, and identity felt at a personal level. Yet the essay is very much about writing. As you read it, think about the role that writing plays in relation to language, loss, and identity. Said, for example, begins the essay with a discussion of Joseph Conrad's writing and ends it with a discussion about writing his own memoir. Why do you think Said frames the essay in this way? As you read, also try to make sense of the connection between writing and loss, between writing and finding a place to live, and between writing and identity.*

No Reconciliation Allowed

In the first book I wrote, *Joseph Conrad and the Fiction of Autobiography,* published more than thirty years ago, and then in an essay called "Reflections on Exile" that appeared in 1984, I used Conrad as an example of someone whose life and work seemed to typify the fate of the wanderer who becomes an accomplished writer in an acquired language, but can never shake off his sense of alienation from his new— that is, acquired—and, in Conrad's rather special case, admired home.[1] His friends all said of Conrad that he was very contented with the idea of being English, even though he never lost his heavy Polish accent and his quite peculiar moodiness, which was thought to be very un-English. Yet the moment one enters his writing, the aura of dislocation, instability, and strangeness is unmistakable. No one could represent the fate of lostness and disorientation better than he did, and no one was more ironic about the effort of trying to replace that condition with new arrangements and accommodations—which invariably lured one into further traps, such as those Lord Jim encounters when he starts life again on his little island. Marlow enters the heart of darkness to discover that Kurtz was not only there before him but is also incapable of telling him the whole truth; so that, in narrating his own experiences, Marlow cannot be as exact as he would have liked, and ends up

---

1. *Joseph Conrad and the Fiction of Autobiography* (Cambridge: Harvard University Press, 1966); and "Reflections on Exile," *Granta* 13 (Autumn 1984), pp. 159–72.

producing approximations and even falsehoods of which both he and his listeners seem quite aware.

Only well after his death did Conrad's critics try to reconstruct what has been called his Polish background, very little of which had found its way directly into his fiction. But the rather elusive meaning of his writing is not so easily supplied, for even if we find out a lot about his Polish experiences, friends, and relatives, that information will not of itself settle the core of restlessness and unease that his work relentlessly circles. Eventually we realize that the work is actually constituted by the experience of exile or alienation, which cannot ever be rectified. No matter how perfectly he is able to express something, the result always seems to him an approximation of what he had wanted to say, and to have been said too late, past the point where the saying of it might have been helpful. "Amy Foster," the most desolate of his stories, is about a young man from Eastern Europe, shipwrecked off the English coast on his way to America, who ends up as the husband of the affectionate but inarticulate Amy Foster. The man remains a foreigner, never learns the language, and even after he and Amy have a child cannot become a part of the very family he has created with her. When he is near death and babbling deliriously in a strange language, Amy snatches their child from him, abandoning him to his final sorrow. Like so many of Conrad's fictions, the story is narrated by a sympathetic figure, a doctor who is acquainted with the pair, but even he cannot redeem the young man's isolation, although Conrad teasingly makes the reader feel that he might have been able to. It is difficult to read "Amy Foster" without thinking that Conrad must have feared dying a similar death, inconsolable, alone, talking away in a language no one could understand.

The first thing to acknowledge is the loss of home and language in the new setting, a loss that Conrad has the severity to portray as irredeemable, relentlessly anguished, raw, untreatable, always acute—which is why I have found myself over the years reading and writing about Conrad like a *cantus firmus*, a steady groundbass to much that I have experienced. For years I seemed to be going over the same kind of thing in the work I did, but always through the writings of other people. It wasn't until the early fall of 1991 when an ugly medical diagnosis suddenly revealed to me the mortality I should have known about before that I found myself trying to make sense of my own life as its end seemed alarmingly nearer. A few months later, still trying to assimilate my new condition, I found myself composing a long explanatory letter to my mother, who had already been dead for almost two years, a letter that inaugurated a belated attempt to impose a narrative on a life that I had left more or less to itself, disorganized, scattered, uncentered. I had had a decent enough career in the university, I had written a fair amount, I had acquired an unenviable reputation (as the "professor of terror") for my writing and speaking and being active on Palestinian and generally Middle Eastern or Islamic and anti-imperialist issues, but I had rarely paused to put the whole jumble together. I was a compulsive worker, I disliked and hardly ever took vacations, and I did what I did without worrying too much (if at all) about such matters as writer's block, depression, or running dry.

All of a sudden, then, I found myself brought up short with some though not a great deal of time available to survey a life whose eccentricities I had accepted like so many facts of nature. Once again I recognized that Conrad had been there before me—except that Conrad was a European who left his native Poland and became an Englishman, so the move for him was more or less within the same world. I was born in Jerusalem and had spent most of my formative years there and, after 1948, when my entire family became refugees, in Egypt. All my early education had, however, been in elite colonial schools, English public schools designed by the British to bring up a generation of Arabs with natural ties to Britain. The last one I went to before I left the Middle East to go to the United States was Victoria College in Cairo, a school in effect created to educate those ruling-class Arabs and Levantines who were going to take over after the British left. My contemporaries and classmates included King Hussein of Jordan, several Jordanian, Egyptian, Syrian, and Saudi boys who were to become ministers, prime ministers, and leading businessmen, as well as such glamorous figures as Michel Shalhoub, head prefect of the school and chief tormentor when I was a relatively junior boy, whom everyone has seen on screen as Omar Sharif.

The moment one became a student at Victoria College one was given the school handbook, a series of regulations governing every aspect of school life—the kind of uniform we were to wear, what equipment was needed for sports, the dates of school holidays, bus schedules, and so on. But the school's first rule, emblazoned on the opening page of the handbook, read: "English is the language of the school; students caught speaking any other language will be punished." Yet there were no native English-speakers among the students. Whereas the masters were all British, we were a motley crew of Arabs of various kinds, Armenians, Greeks, Italians, Jews, and Turks, each of whom had a native language that the school had explicitly outlawed. Yet all, or nearly all, of us spoke Arabic—many spoke Arabic and French—and so we were able to take refuge in a common language in defiance of what we perceived as an unjust colonial stricture. British imperial power was nearing its end immediately after World War II, and this fact was not lost on us, although I cannot recall any student of my generation who would have been able to put anything as definite as that into words.

For me, there was an added complication, in that although both my parents were Palestinian—my mother from Nazareth, my father from Jerusalem—my father had acquired U.S. citizenship during World War I, when he served in the American Expeditionary Force under Pershing in France. He had originally left Palestine, then an Ottoman province, in 1911, at the age of sixteen, to escape being drafted to fight in Bulgaria. Instead, he went to the United States, studied and worked there for a few years, then returned to Palestine in 1919 to go into business with his cousin. Besides, with an unexceptionally Arab family name like Said connected to an improbably British first name (my mother very much admired the Prince of Wales in 1935, the year of my birth), I was an uncomfortably anomalous student all through my early years: a Palestinian going to school in Egypt, with an English first name, an American passport, and no certain identity at all. To make matters worse,

Arabic, my native language, and English, my school language, were inextricably mixed: I have never known which was my first language, and have felt fully at home in neither, although I dream in both. Every time I speak an English sentence, I find myself echoing it in Arabic, and vice versa.

All this went through my head in those months after my diagnosis revealed to me the necessity of thinking about final things. But I did so in what for me was a characteristic way. As the author of a book called *Beginnings*,[2] I found myself drawn to my early days as a boy in Jerusalem, Cairo, and Dhour el Shweir, the Lebanese mountain village which I loathed but where for years and years my father took us to spend our summers. I found myself reliving the narrative quandaries of my early years, my sense of doubt and of being out of place, of always feeling myself standing on the wrong corner, in a place that seemed to be slipping away from me just as I tried to define or describe it. Why, I remember asking myself, could I not have had a simple background, been all Egyptian, or all something else, and not have had to face the daily rigors of questions that led back to words that seemed to lack a stable origin? The worst part of my situation, which time has only exacerbated, has been the warring relationship between English and Arabic, something that Conrad had not had to deal with since his passage from Polish to English via French was effected entirely within Europe. My whole education was Anglocentric, so much so that I knew a great deal more about British and even Indian history and geography (required subjects) than I did about the history and geography of the Arab world. But although taught to believe and think like an English schoolboy, I was also trained to understand that I was an alien, a Non-European Other, educated by my betters to know my station and not to aspire to being British. The line separating Us from Them was linguistic, cultural, racial, and ethnic. It did not make matters easier for me to have been born, baptized, and confirmed in the Anglican Church, where the singing of bellicose hymns like "Onward Christian Soldiers" and "From Greenland's Icy Mountains" had me in effect playing the role at once of aggressor and aggressed against. To be at the same time a Wog and an Anglican was to be in a state of standing civil war.

In the spring of 1951 I was expelled from Victoria College, thrown out for being a troublemaker, which meant that I was more visible and more easily caught than the other boys in the daily skirmishes between Mr. Griffith, Mr. Hill, Mr. Lowe, Mr. Brown, Mr. Maundrell, Mr. Gatley, and all the other British teachers, on the one hand, and us, the boys of the school, on the other. We were all subliminally aware, too, that the old Arab order was crumbling: Palestine had fallen, Egypt was tottering under the massive corruption of King Farouk and his court (the revolution that brought Gamal Abdel Nasser and his Free Officers to power was to occur in July 1952), Syria was undergoing a dizzying series of military coups, Iran, whose Shah was at the time married to Farouk's sister, had its first big crisis in 1951, and so on. The prospects for deracinated people like us were so uncertain that my father decided it would be best to send me as far away as possible—in effect, to an austere, puritanical school in the northwestern corner of Massachusetts.

---

2. *Beginnings: Intention and Method* (New York: Basic Books, 1975).

The day in early September 1951 when my mother and father deposited me at the gates of that school and then immediately left for the Middle East was probably the most miserable of my life. Not only was the atmosphere of the school rigid and explicitly moralistic, but I seemed to be the only boy there who was not a native-born American, who did not speak with the required accent, and who had not grown up with baseball, basketball, and football. For the first time ever, I was deprived of the linguistic environment I had depended on as an alternative to the hostile attentions of Anglo-Saxons whose language was not mine, and who made no bones about my belonging to an inferior, or somehow disapproved, race. Anyone who has lived through the quotidian obstacles of colonial routine will know what I am talking about. One of the first things I did was to look up a teacher of Egyptian origin whose name had been given to me by a family friend in Cairo. "Talk to Ned," our friend said, "and he'll instantly make you feel at home." On a bright Saturday afternoon I trudged over to Ned's house, introduced myself to the wiry, dark man who was also the tennis coach, and told him that Freddie Maalouf in Cairo had asked me to look him up. "Oh yes," the tennis coach said rather frostily, "Freddie." I immediately switched to Arabic, but Ned put up his hand to interrupt me. "No, brother, no Arabic here. I left all that behind when I came to America." And that was the end of that.

Because I had been well trained at Victoria College, I did well enough in my Massachusetts boarding school, achieving the rank of either first or second in a class of about a hundred and sixty. But I was also found to be morally wanting, as if there was something mysteriously not-quite-right about me. When I graduated, for instance, the rank of valedictorian or salutatorian was withheld from me on the grounds that I was not fit for the honor—a moral judgment which I have ever since found difficult either to understand or to forgive. Although I went back to the Middle East on vacations (my family continued to live there, moving from Egypt to Lebanon in 1963), I found myself becoming an entirely Western person; both at college and in graduate school I studied literature, music, and philosophy, but none of it had anything to do with my own tradition. During the 1950s and early 60s, students from the Arab world were almost invariably scientists, doctors, and engineers, or specialists in the Middle East, getting degrees at places like Princeton and Harvard and then, for the most part, returning to their countries to become teachers in universities there. I had very little to do with them, for one reason or another, and this naturally increased my isolation from my own language and background. By the time I came to New York to teach at Columbia in the fall of 1963, I was considered to have an exotic, but somewhat irrelevant Arabic background—in fact I recall that it was easier for most of my friends and colleagues not to use the word "Arab," and certainly not "Palestinian," preferring the much easier and vaguer "Middle Eastern," a term that offended no one. A friend who was already teaching at Columbia later told me that when I was hired I had been described to the department as an Alexandrian Jew! I remember a sense of being accepted, even courted, by older colleagues at Columbia, who with one or two exceptions saw me as a promising, even very promising, young scholar of "our" culture. Since there was no political activity then that was centered on the Arab world, I found that my concerns in my teaching and research, which were canonical though slightly unorthodox, kept me within the pale.

The big change came with the Arab-Israeli war of 1967, which coincided with a period of intense political activism on campus over civil rights and the Vietnam war. I found myself naturally involved on both fronts, but, for me, there was the further difficulty of trying to draw attention to the Palestinian cause. After the Arab defeat there was a vigorous reemergence of Palestinian nationalism, embodied in the resistance movement located mainly in Jordan and the newly occupied territories. Several friends and members of my family had joined the movement, and when I visited Jordan in 1968, 69, and 70, I found myself among a number of like-minded contemporaries. In the United States, however, my politics were rejected—with a few notable exceptions—both by anti-war activists and by supporters of Martin Luther King, Jr. For the first time I felt genuinely divided between the newly assertive pressures of my background and language and the complicated demands of a situation in the United States that scanted, in fact despised, what I had to say about the quest for Palestinian justice—which was considered anti-Semitic and Nazi-like.

In 1972 I had a sabbatical and took the opportunity to spend a year in Beirut, where most of my time was taken up with the study of Arabic philology and literature, something I had never done before, at least not at that level, out of a feeling that I had allowed the disparity between my acquired identity and the culture into which I was born, and from which I had been removed, to become too great. In other words, there was an existential as well as a felt political need to bring one self into harmony with the other, for as the debate about what had once been called "the Middle East" metamorphosed into a debate between Israelis and Palestinians, I was drawn in, ironically enough, as much because of my capacity to speak as an American academic and intellectual as by the accident of my birth. By the mid-70s I was in the rich but unenviable position of speaking for two diametrically opposed constituencies, one Western, the other Arab.

For as long as I can remember, I had allowed myself to stand outside the umbrella that shielded or accommodated my contemporaries. Whether this was because I was genuinely different, objectively an outsider, or because I was temperamentally a loner I cannot say, but the fact is that although I went along with all sorts of institutional routines because I felt I had to, something private in me resisted them. I don't know what it was that caused me to hold back, but even when I was most miserably solitary or out of synch with everyone else, I held onto this private aloofness very fiercely. I may have envied friends whose language was one or the other, or who had lived in the same place all their lives, or who had done well in accepted ways, or who truly belonged, but I do not recall ever thinking that any of that was possible for me. It wasn't that I considered myself special, but rather that I didn't fit the situations I found myself in and wasn't too displeased to accept this state of affairs. I have, besides, always been drawn to stubborn autodidacts, to various sorts of intellectual misfit. In part it was the heedlessness of their own peculiar angle of vision that attracted me to writers and artists like Conrad, Vico, Adorno, Swift, Adonis, Hopkins, Auerbach, Glenn Gould, whose style, or way of thinking, was highly individualistic and impossible to imitate, for whom the medium of expression, whether music or words, was eccentrically charged, very worked-over, self-conscious in the highest degree. What impressed me about them was not the mere fact of their self-invention but that the enterprise was deliberately and fastidiously located within a general history which they had excavated *ab origine.*

Having allowed myself gradually to assume the professional voice of an American academic as a way of submerging my difficult and unassimilable past, I began to think and write contrapuntally, using the disparate halves of my experience, as an Arab and as an American, to work with and also against each other. This tendency began to take shape after 1967, and though it was difficult, it was also exciting. What prompted the initial change in my sense of self, and in the language I was using, was the realization that in accommodating to the exigencies of life in the U.S. melting pot, I had willy-nilly to accept the principle of annulment of which Adorno speaks so perceptively in *Minima Moralia:*

> The past life of émigrés is, as we know, annulled. Earlier it was the warrant of arrest, today it is intellectual experience, that is declared non-transferable and unnaturalizable. Anything that is not reified, cannot be counted and measured, ceases to exist. Not satisfied with this, however, reification spreads to its own opposite, the life that cannot be directly actualized; anything that lives on merely as thought and recollection. For this a special rubric has been invented. It is called "background" and appears on the questionnaire as an appendix, after sex, age and profession. To complete its violation, life is dragged along on the triumphal automobile of the united statisticians, and even the past is no longer safe from the present, whose remembrance of it consigns it a second time to oblivion.[3]

For my family and for myself, the catastrophe of 1948 (I was then twelve) was lived unpolitically. For twenty years after their dispossession and expulsion from their homes and territory, most Palestinians had to live as refugees, coming to terms not with their past, which was lost, annulled, but with their present. I do not want to suggest that my life as a schoolboy, learning to speak and coin a language that let me live as a citizen of the United States, entailed anything like the suffering of that first generation of Palestinian refugees, scattered throughout the Arab world, where invidious laws made it impossible for them to become naturalized, unable to work, unable to travel, obliged to register and reregister each month with the police, many of them forced to live in appalling camps like Beirut's Sabra and Shatila, which were the sites of massacres thirty-four years later. What I experienced, however, was the suppression of a history as everyone around me celebrated Israel's victory, its terrible swift sword, as Barbara Tuchman grandly put it, at the expense of the original inhabitants of Palestine, who now found themselves forced over and over again to prove that they had once existed. "There are no Palestinians," said Golda Meir in 1969, and that set me, and many others, the slightly preposterous challenge of disproving her, of beginning to articulate a history of loss and dispossession that had to be extricated, minute by minute, word by word, inch by inch, from the very real

---

3. Theodor Adorno, *Minima Moralia: Reflections from Damaged Life,* trans. By E.F.N. Jephcott (London: New Left Books, 1974), pp. 46–47.

history of Israel's establishment, existence, and achievements. I was working in an almost entirely negative element, the non-existence, the non-history which I had somehow to make visible despite occlusions, misrepresentations, and denials.

Inevitably, this led me to reconsider the notions of writing and language, which I had until then treated as animated by a given text or subject—the history of the novel, for instance, or the idea of narrative as a theme in prose fiction. What concerned me now was how a subject was constituted, how a language could be formed—writing as a construction of realities that served one or another purpose instrumentally. This was the world of power and representations, a world that came into being as a series of decisions made by writers, politicians, philosophers to suggest or adumbrate one reality and at the same time efface others. The first attempt I made at this kind of work was a short essay I wrote in 1968 entitled "The Arab Portrayed,"[4] in which I described the image of the Arab that had been manipulated in journalism and some scholarly writing in such a way as to evade any discussion of history and experience as I and many other Arabs had lived them. I also wrote a longish study of Arabic prose fiction after 1948 in which I reported on the fragmentary, embattled quality of the narrative line.

During the 1970s I taught my courses in European and American literature at Columbia and elsewhere, and bit by bit entered the political and discursive worlds of Middle Eastern and international politics. It is worth mentioning here that for the forty years that I have been teaching I have never taught anything other than the Western canon, and certainly nothing about the Middle East. I've long had the ambition of giving a course on modern Arabic literature, but I haven't gotten around to it, and for at least thirty years I've been planning a seminar on Vico and Ibn Khaldun, the great fourteenth-century historiographer and philosopher of history. But my sense of identity as a teacher of Western literature has excluded this other aspect of my activity so far as the classroom is concerned. Ironically, the fact that I continued to write and teach my subject gave sponsors and hosts at university functions at which I had been invited to lecture an excuse to ignore my embarrassing political activity by specifically asking me to lecture on a literary topic. And there were those who spoke of my efforts on behalf of "my people," without ever mentioning the name of that people. "Palestine" was still a word to be avoided.

Even in the Arab world Palestine earned me a great deal of opprobrium. When the Jewish Defense League called me a Nazi in 1985, my office at the university was set fire to and my family and I received innumerable death threats, but when Anwar Sadat and Yasser Arafat appointed me Palestinian representative to the peace talks (without ever consulting me) and I found it impossible to step outside my apartment, so great was the media rush around me, I became the object of extreme left-wing nationalist hostility because I was considered too liberal on the question of Palestine and the idea of coexistence between Israeli Jews and Palestinian Arabs. I've been consistent in my belief that no military option exists for either side, that only

---

4. "The Arab Portrayed," pp. 1–9 in Ibrahim Abu-Lughod, ed., *The Arab-Israeli Confrontation of June 1967: An Arab Perspective* (Evanston, IL: Northwestern University Press, 1970).

a process of peaceful reconciliation, and justice for what the Palestinians have had to endure by way of dispossession and military occupation, would work. I was also very critical of the use of slogan-clichés like "armed struggle" and of the revolutionary adventurism that caused innocent deaths and did nothing to advance the Palestinian case politically. "The predicament of private life today is shown by its arena," Adorno wrote. "Dwelling, in the proper sense, is now impossible. The traditional residences we grew up in have grown intolerable: each trait of comfort in them is paid for with a betrayal of knowledge, each vestige of shelter with the musty pact of family interests." Even more unyieldingly, he continued:

> The house is past. . . . The best mode of conduct, in the face of all this, still seems an uncommitted, suspended one: to lead a private life, as far as the social order and one's own needs will tolerate nothing else, but not to attach weight to it as something still socially substantial and individually appropriate. "It is even part of my good fortune not to be a house-owner," Nietzsche already wrote in *The Gay Science*. Today we should have to add: it is part of morality not to be at home in one's home.[5]

For myself, I have been unable to live an uncommitted or suspended life: I have not hesitated to declare my affiliation with an extremely unpopular cause. On the other hand, I have always reserved the right to be critical, even when criticism conflicted with solidarity or with what others expected in the name of national loyalty. There is a definite, almost palpable discomfort to such a position, especially given the irreconcilability of the two constituencies, and the two lives they have required.

The net result in terms of my writing has been to attempt a greater transparency, to free myself from academic jargon, and not to hide behind euphemism and circumlocution where difficult issues have been concerned. I have given the name "worldliness" to this voice, by which I do not mean the jaded savoir-faire of the man about town, but rather a knowing and unafraid attitude toward exploring the world we live in. Cognate words, derived from Vico and Auerbach, have been "secular" and "secularism" as applied to "earthly" matters; in these words, which derive from the Italian materialist tradition that runs from Lucretius through to Gramschi and Lampedusa, I have found an important corrective to the German Idealist tradition of synthesizing the antithetical, as we find it in Hegel, Marx, Lukács, and Habermas. For not only did "earthly" connote this historical world made by men and women rather than by God or "the nation's genius," as Herder termed it, but it suggested a territorial grounding for my argument and language, which proceeded from an attempt to understand the imaginative geographies fashioned and then imposed by power on distant lands and people. In *Orientalism and Culture and Imperialism,*[6] and then again in the five or six explicitly political books concerning Palestine and the Islamic world that I wrote around the same time, I felt

---

5. Adorno, pp. 38–39.

6. *Orientalism* (New York: Pantheon Books, 1978; reissued, with new Afterword, New York: Vintage Books, 1994); and *Culture and Imperialism* (New York: Knopf, 1993).

that I had been fashioning a self who revealed for a Western audience things that had so far either been hidden or not discussed at all. Thus, in talking about the Orient, hitherto believed to be a simple fact of nature, I tried to uncover the long-standing, very varied geographical obsession with a distant, often inaccessible world that helped Europe to define itself by being its opposite. Similarly, I believed that Palestine, a territory effaced in the process of building another society, could be restored as an act of political resistance to injustice and oblivion.

Occasionally, I'd notice that I had become a peculiar creature to many people, and even a few friends, who had assumed that being Palestinian was the equivalent of being something mythological like a unicorn or a hopelessly odd variation of a human being. A Boston psychologist who specialized in conflict resolution, and whom I had met at several seminars involving Palestinians and Israelis, once rang me from Greenwich Village and asked if she could come uptown to pay me a visit. When she arrived, she walked in, looked incredulously at my piano—"Ah, you actually play the piano," she said, with a trace of disbelief in her voice—and then turned around and began to walk out. When I asked her whether she would have a cup of tea before leaving (after all, I said, you have come a long way for such a short visit), she said she didn't have time. "I only came to see how you lived," she said without a hint of irony. Another time, a publisher in another city refused to sign my contract until I had lunch with him. When I asked his assistant what was so important about having a meal with me, I was told that the great man wanted to see how I handled myself at the table. Fortunately, none of these experiences affected or detained me for very long: I was always in too much of a rush to meet a class or a deadline, and I quite deliberately avoided the self-questioning that would have landed me in a terminal depression. In any case, the Palestinian intifada that erupted in December 1987 confirmed our people-hood in as dramatic and compelling a way as anything I might have said. Before long, however, I found myself becoming a token figure, hauled in for a few hundred written words or a ten-second soundbite testifying to "what the Palestinians are saying," and I determined to escape that role, especially given my disagreements with the PLO leadership from the late 1980s on.

I am not sure whether to call this a kind of perpetual self-invention or a constant restlessness. Either way, I've long since learned to cherish it. Identity as such is about as boring a subject as one can imagine. Nothing seems less interesting than the narcissistic self-study that today passes in many places for identity politics, or ethnic studies, or affirmations of roots, cultural pride, drum-beating nationalism, and so on. We have to defend peoples and identities threatened with extinction or subordinated because they are considered inferior, but that is very different from aggrandizing a past invented for present reasons. Those of us who are American intellectuals owe it to our country to fight the coarse anti-intellectualism, bullying, injustice, and provincialism that disfigure its career as the last superpower. It is far more challenging to try to transform oneself into something different than it is to keep insisting on the virtues of being American in the ideological sense. Having myself lost a country with no immediate hope of regaining it, I don't find much comfort in cultivating a new garden, or looking for some other association to join. I learned from Adorno that reconciliation under duress is both cowardly and inauthentic: better a lost cause than a triumphant one, more satisfying a sense of the provisional and contingent—a rented house, for example—than the proprietary solidity of permanent ownership. This is why strolling dandies like Oscar Wilde or Baudelaire seem to me intrinsically more interesting than extollers of settled virtue like Wordsworth or Carlyle.

For the past five years I have been writing two columns a month for the Arabic press; and despite my extremely anti-religious politics, I am often glowingly described in the Islamic world as a defender of Islam, and considered by some of the Islamic parties to be one of their supporters. Nothing could be further from the truth, any more than it is true that I have been an apologist for terrorism. The prismatic quality of one's writing when one isn't entirely of any camp, or a total partisan of any cause, is difficult to handle, but there, too, I have accepted the irreconcilability of the various conflicting, or at least incompletely harmonized, aspects of what, cumulatively, I appear to have stood for. A phrase by Günter Grass describes the predicament well: that of the "intellectual without mandate." A complicated situation arose in late 1993 when, after seeming to be the approved voice of the Palestinian struggle, I wrote increasingly sharply of my disagreements with Arafat and his bunch. I was immediately branded "anti-peace" because I had the lack of tact to describe the Oslo treaty as deeply flawed. Now that everything has ground to a halt, I am regularly asked what it is like to be proved right, but I was more surprised by that than anyone: prophecy is not part of my arsenal.

For the past three or four years, I have also been trying to write a memoir of my early—that is, pre-political—life, largely because I think it's a story worthy of rescue and commemoration, given that the three places I grew up in have ceased to exist. Palestine is now Israel, Lebanon, after twenty years of civil war, is hardly the stiflingly boring place it was when we spent our summers locked up in Dhour el Shweir, and colonial, monarchical Egypt disappeared in 1952. My memories of those days and places remain extremely vivid, full of little details that I seem to have preserved as if between the covers of a book, full also of unexpressed feelings generated out of situations and events that occurred decades ago but seem to have been waiting to be articulated now. Conrad says in *Nostromo* that a desire lurks in every heart to write down once and for all a true account of what happened, and this certainly is what moved me to write my memoir, just as I had found myself writing a letter to my dead mother out of a desire once again to communicate something terribly important to a primordial presence in my life. "In his text," Adorno says,

> the writer sets up house. . . . For a man who no longer has a homeland, writing becomes a place to live. . . . [Yet] the demand that one harden oneself against self-pity implies the technical necessity to counter any slackening of intellectual tension with the utmost alertness, and to eliminate anything that has begun to encrust the work or to drift along idly, which may at an earlier stage have served, as gossip, to generate the warm atmosphere conducive to growth, but is now left behind, flat and stale. In the end, the writer is not even allowed to live in his writing.[7]

7. Adorno, p. 87.

One achieves at most a provisional satisfaction, which is quickly ambushed by doubt, and a need to rewrite and redo that renders the text uninhabitable. Better that, however, than the sleep of self-satisfaction and the finality of death.

Double Take

1. Language and home are connected for Edward Said in his essay "No Reconciliation Allowed." In what way are they connected? Why do you think they are connected?
2. Why do you think Said titled this essay "No Reconciliation Allowed"? What reconciliation is he referring to? Why is such reconciliation not allowed?
3. In what ways does Said describe language and writing as political instruments? What, for example, does Said mean when he defines writing "as a construction of realities"?
4. At the end of the essay, Said cites Theodor Adorno, who writes, "the writer sets up house . . . For a man who no longer has a homeland, writing becomes a place to live." What does Adorno mean? Why do you think this statement appeals to Said? What does it reveal about Said's view of writing?

At First Glance

"The Mind of Winter: Reflections on Life in Exile" originally appeared in the essay section of Harper's Magazine *in 1984. Like "No Reconciliation Allowed," this essay by Edward Said also deals with the pain that accompanies the loss of one's home, identity, and past. Yet "The Mind of Winter" is a much more "academic" essay in its perspective, tone, and examples. As you read, think specifically about what makes this essay more academic. Consider also how the academic nature of this essay affects how readers relate to it. Finally, after you have finished reading the essay, reflect on what you think Said's purpose was in writing it and how the rhetorical choices he makes support that purpose.*

The Mind of Winter: Reflections on Life in Exile

There is no sense of ease like the ease we felt in those scenes where we were born, where objects became dear to us before we had known the labour of choice, and where the outer world seemed only an extension of our personality.

—GEORGE ELIOT, *The Mill on the Floss*

Exile is the unhealable rift forced between a human being and a native place, between the self and its true home. The essential sadness of the break can never be surmounted. It is true that there are stories portraying exile as a condition that produces heroic, romantic, glorious, even triumphant episodes in a person's life. But these are no more than stories, efforts to overcome the crippling sorrow of estrangement. The achievements of any exile are permanently undermined by his or her sense of loss.

If true exile is a condition of terminal loss, why has that loss so easily been transformed into a potent, even enriching, motif of modern culture? One reason is that we have become accustomed to thinking of the modern period itself as spiritually orphaned and alienated. This is supposedly the age of anxiety and of the lonely crowd. Nietzsche taught us to feel uncomfortable with tradition, and Freud to regard domestic intimacy as the polite face painted on patricidal and incestuous rage.

The canon of modern Western culture is in large part the work of exiles, émigrés, refugees. American academic, intellectual, and aesthetic thought is what it is today because of refugees from fascism, communism, and other regimes given over to the oppression and expulsion of dissidents. One thinks of Einstein, and his impact on his century. There have been political thinkers, such as Herbert Marcuse. The critic George Steiner once proposed that a whole genre of twentieth-century Western literature, a literature by and about exiles—among them Beckett, Nabokov, Pound— reflects "the age of the refugee." In the introduction to his book *Extraterritorial,* Steiner wrote:

> It seems proper that those who create art in a civilization of quasi-barbarism, which has made so many homeless, should themselves be poets unhoused and wanderers across language. Eccentric, aloof, nostalgic, deliberately untimely . . .

In other places and times, exiles had similar cross-cultural and transnational visions, suffered the same frustrations and miseries, performed the same elucidating and critical tasks. The difference, of course, between earlier exiles and those of our own time is scale. Modern warfare, imperialism, and the quasi-theological ambitions of totalitarian rulers have seen to that. Ours is indeed the age of the refugee, the displaced person, mass immigration.

Against this larger and more impersonal setting exile cannot function as a tonic. To think of exile as beneficial, as a spur to humanism or to creativity, is to belittle its mutilations. Modern exile is irremediably secular and unbearably historical. It is produced by human beings for other human beings; it has torn millions of people from the nourishment of tradition, family, and geography.

To see a poet in exile—as opposed to reading the poetry of exile— is to see exile's antinomies embodied and endured. Several years ago I spent some time with Faiz Ahmad Faiz, the greatest of contemporary Urdu poets. He had been exiled from his native Pakistan by Zia ul-Haq's military regime and had found a welcome of sorts in the ruins of Beirut. His closest friends were Palestinian, but I sensed that although there was an affinity of spirit between them, nothing quite matched— language, poetic convention, life history. Only once, when Eqbal Ahmad, a Pakistani friend and fellow exile, came to Beirut, did Faiz seem to overcome the estrangement written all over his face. The three of us sat in a dingy restaurant late one night, and Faiz recited poems to us. After a time he and Eqbal stopped translating his verses for my benefit, but it did not matter. For what I watched required no translation: an enactment of homecoming steeped in defiance and loss, as if to say exultantly to Zia, "We are here." Of course, Zia was the one who was at home.

Exiled poets objectify and lend dignity to a condition designed to deny dignity. To understand exile as a contemporary political punishment it is necessary to map territories of experience beyond those mapped by literature. It is necessary to set aside Joyce and Nabokov and even Conrad, who wrote of exile with such pathos, but of exile without cause or rationale. Think instead of the uncountable masses for whom UN agencies have been created, of refugees without urbanity, with only ration cards and agency numbers. Paris is famous for attracting cosmopolitan exiles, but it is also a place where men and women we have never heard of have spent years of miserable loneliness: Vietnamese, Algerians, Cambodians, Lebanese, Senegalese, Peruvians. Think also of Cairo, Beirut, Bangkok, Mexico City. As the distance from the Atlantic world increases, so too do the hopelessly large numbers, the forlorn waste, the compounded misery of "undocumented" people without a tellable history. To reflect on exiled Haitians in America, Bikinians in Oceania, or Palestinians throughout the Arab world we must leave the modest refuge provided by subjectivity, by art, and resort to the arithmetic abstractions of mass politics. Negotiations, wars of national liberation, people bundled out of their homes and prodded, bused or walked to camps in other states: What do these experiences add up to? Are they not designed by the forces that brought them about to be denied, avoided, forgotten?

We come to nationalism and its essential association with exile. Nationalism is an assertion of belonging to a place, a people, a heritage. It affirms the home created by a community of language, culture, and customs; and by so doing, it fends off the ravages of exile. Indeed, it is not too much to say that the interplay between nationalism and exile is like Hegel's dialectic of servant and master, opposites informing and constituting each other. All nationalisms in their early stages posit as their goal the overcoming of some estrangement—from soil, from roots, from unity, from destiny. The struggles to win American independence, to unify Germany, to liberate Algeria were those of national groups separated—exiled—from what was construed to be their rightful way of life. Triumphant nationalism can be used retrospectively as well as prospectively to justify a heroic narrative. Thus all nationalisms have their founding fathers, their basic, quasi-religious texts, their rhetoric of belonging, their historical and geographical landmarks, their official enemies and heroes. This collective ethos forms what Pierre Bourdieu, the French sociologist, calls the *habitus,* the coherent amalgam of practices linking habit with inhabitance. In time, successful nationalisms arrogate truth exclusively to themselves and assign falsehood and inferiority to outsiders.

Just beyond the perimeter of what nationalism constructs as the nation, at the frontier separating "us" from what is alien, is the perilous territory of not-belonging. This is where, in primitive times, people were banished, and where, in the modern era, immense aggregates of humanity loiter as refugees and displaced persons.

One enormous difficulty in describing this no man's land is that nationalisms are about groups, whereas exile is about the absence of an organic group situated in a native place. How does one surmount the loneliness of exile without falling into the encompassing and thumping language of national pride, collective sentiments, group passions? What is there worth saving and holding on to between the extremes of exile on the one hand and the often bloody-minded affirmations of nationalism on the other? Are nationalism and exile reactive phenomena? Do they have any intrinsic attributes? Are they simply two conflicting expressions of paranoia?

These questions cannot be fully answered because each of them assumes that exile and nationalism can be discussed neutrally, without reference to each other. Because both terms include everything from the most collective of collective sentiments to the most private of private emotions, there is no language adequate for both, and certainly there is nothing about nationalism's public and all-inclusive ambitions that touches the truth of the exile's predicament.

For exile is fundamentally a discontinuous state of being. Exiles are cut off from their roots, their land, their past. They generally do not have armies, or states, though they are often in search of these institutions. This search can lead exiles to reconstitute their broken lives in narrative form, usually by choosing to see themselves as part of a triumphant ideology or a restored people. Such a story is designed to reassemble an exile's broken history into a new whole.

At bottom, exile is a jealous state. With very little to possess, you hold on to what you have with aggressive defensiveness. What you achieve in exile is precisely what you have no wish to share, and it is in the drawing of lines around you and your compatriots that the least attractive aspects of being an exile emerge: an exaggerated sense of group solidarity as well as a passionate hostility toward outsiders, even those who may in fact be in the same predicament as you. What could be more intransigent than the conflict between Zionist Jews and Arab Palestinians? The Palestinians feel that they have been turned into exiles by the proverbial people of exile, the Jews. But the Palestinians also know that their sense of national identity has been nourished in the exile milieu, where everyone not a blood brother or sister is an enemy, where every sympathizer is really an agent of some unfriendly power, and where the slightest deviation from the accepted line is an act of rankest treachery.

Perhaps this is the only way to comprehend the most poignant of exile's fates, which is to be exiled by exiles, and to be condemned, seemingly without respite, to continue to be exiled by exiles. All Palestinians during the summer of 1982 asked themselves what inarticulate urge drove Israel, which had displaced them in 1948, to expel them from the refugee camps in Lebanon. It was as if the reconstructed Jewish collective experience, as represented by Israel and modern Zionism, could not tolerate the existence of another experience of dispossession and loss alongside it and so had to dispossess again—avoiding, denying, repressing this other story, in strange concert with some of its neighboring Arab countries. Exile begets exile.

Since 1948, however, Palestinian nationalism has been painfully reassembling itself in exile into a national identity. A sense of the Palestinians' need to reconstruct the self out of the refractions and discontinuities of exile is found in the earlier poems of Mahmud Darwish, whose considerable work amounts to an epic effort to transform the lyrics of loss into the indefinitely postponed drama of return. In the following lines he describes concretely his sense of homelessness:

> *But I am the exile.*
> *Seal me with your eyes.*
> *Take me wherever you are—*
> *Take me wherever you are.*
> *Restore to me the color of face*
> *And the warmth of body,*
> *The light of heart and eye,*
> *The salt of bread and rhythm,*
> *The taste of earth . . . the Motherland.*
> *Shield me with your eyes.*
> *Take me as a relic from the mansion of sorrow.*
> *Take me as a verse from my tragedy;*
> *Take me as toy, a brick from the house,*
> *So that our children will remember to return.*

The pathos of exile resides in the loss of contact with the solidity and satisfactions of earth. That is why exiles look at non-exiles with a certain resentment: *What is it like to be born in a place and to live there more or less forever, to know that you are of it?*

Although it is true that anyone prevented from returning home is an exile, some distinctions can be made between exiles, refugees, expatriates, and émigrés. Exile originated in the age-old practice of banishment. Once banished, the exile lives an anomalous and miserable life, with the stigma of being an outsider. Ovid's exile in Tomi is an example from classical antiquity, Hugo's banishment to Jersey by Napoleon III an example from the modern era. Refugees, on the other hand, are a creation of the twentieth-century state. The word "refugee" has become a political one, suggesting large herds of innocent and bewildered people requiring urgent international assistance, whereas "exile" carries with it, I think, a touch of solitude and spirituality.

Expatriates voluntarily live in an alien country, usually for personal or social reasons. Hemingway and Fitzgerald were not forced to live in France. Expatriates may share in the solitude and estrangement of exile, but they do not suffer under its rigid proscriptions. Emigrés enjoy an ambiguous status. Technically, an émigré is anyone who emigrates to a new country. Choice in the matter is certainly a possibility. Colonial officials, missionaries, technical experts, mercenaries, and military advisors on loan may in a sense live in exile, but they have not been banished. White settlers in Africa, parts of Asia, and Australia may once have been exiles, but as pioneers and nation-builders the label "exile" dropped away from them.

Much of the exile's life is taken up with compensating for disorienting loss by creating a new world to rule, which is why many exiles are novelists, chess players, political activists, and intellectuals. Each of these occupations requires a minimal investment in objects and places a great premium on mobility and skill. The exile's new world, logically enough, is unnatural, and its unreality resembles fiction. Georg Lukács, in *Theory of the Novel*, argued with compelling force that the novel, a literary form created out of the unreality of ambition and fantasy, is *the* form of "transcendental homelessness." Classical epics, Lukács wrote, emanate from settled cultures in which values are clear, identities stable, life unchanging. The European novel is grounded in precisely the opposite experience, that of a changing society in which an itinerant and disinherited middle-class hero or heroine seeks to construct a new world that somewhat resembles an old one left behind forever. In the epic there is no *other* world, only the finality of *this* one. Odysseus returns to Ithaca after years of wandering; Achilles will die because he cannot escape his fate. The novel, however, exists because other worlds *may* exist, alternatives for bourgeois speculators, wanderers, exiles.

No matter how well they may do, exiles are always eccentrics who *feel* their difference (even as they frequently exploit it) as a kind of orphan-hood. Anyone who is really homeless regards the habit of seeing estrangement in everything modern as an affectation, a display of modish attitudes. Clutching difference like a weapon to be used with stiffened will, the exile jealously insists on his right to refuse to belong.

This usually translates into an intransigence that is not easily ignored. Willfulness, exaggeration, overstatement: these are characteristic styles of being an exile, methods for compelling the world to accept your vision—which you make more unacceptable because you are in fact unwilling to have it accepted. It is yours, after all. Composure and serenity are the last things associated with the work of exiles. Artists in exile are decidedly unpleasant, and their stubbornness insinuates itself into even their exalted works. Dante's vision in *The Divine Comedy* is tremendously powerful in its universality and detail, but even the beatific peace achieved in the *Paradiso* bears traces of the vindictiveness and severity of judgment embodied in the *Inferno*. Who but an exile like Dante, banished from Florence, would use eternity as a place for settling old scores?

The literature of exile has taken its place alongside the literature of adventure, education, and discovery as a *topos* of human experience. How did this come about? Is this the *same* exile that dehumanizes and often quite literally kills? Or is it some more benign variety?

The answer is the latter, I believe. As an element in the Christian and humanistic tradition of redemption through loss and suffering—and Western literature is part of this tradition—exile has played a consistent role. Not for nothing was Virgil Dante's guide, or the *Aeneid's* vision of a burning Troy succeeded by the founding of Rome. Even if we do not doubt the pangs of Petrarch's exile or the sadness of Aeneas's distance from his native Troy, we know that they are a prelude to something bigger, more important. Exile, then, is an experience to be endured so as to restore identity, or even life itself, to fuller, more meaningful status. This redemptive view of exile is primarily religious, although it has been claimed by many cultures, political ideologies, mythologies, and traditions. Exile becomes the necessary pre-condition to a better state. We see this in stories about a nation's exile before statehood, a prophet's exile from home prior to a triumphant return. Moses, Mohammed, Jesus.

Much of the contemporary interest in exile can be traced to the somewhat pal-lid notion that non-exiles can share in the benefits of exile as a redemptive motif. There is no point in trying to dismiss this idea, because it has a certain plausibility and truth to it. Like medieval itinerant scholars or learned Greek slaves in the Roman Empire, exiles—the exceptional ones among them—do leaven their envi-ronments. And naturally "we" concentrate on that enlightening aspect of "their" presence among us, not on their misery or their demands. But looked at from the bleak political perspective of modern mass dislocations, individual exiles force us to recognize the tragic fate of homelessness in a necessarily heartless world.

A generation ago, Simone Weil posed the dilemma of exile as concisely as it has ever been posed. Even if one disagrees, as I do, with her essentially religious program for "growing roots," her acknowledgement of exile has lost little of its force. "To be rooted," she said, "is perhaps the most important and least recognized need of the human soul." Yet Weil also saw that most remedies for uprootedness in this era of world wars, deportations, and mass exterminations are almost as danger-ous as what they purportedly remedy. Of these, the state—or, more accurately, sta-tism—is one of the most insidious, since worship of the state tends to supplant all other human bonds.

Weil exposes us anew to that whole complex of pressures and constraints that lie at the center of the exile's predicament. There is the immense fact of isolation and displacement, which produces the kind of narcissistic masochism that resists all efforts at amelioration, acculturation, and community. As this extreme the exile can make a fetish of exile, a practice that distances him or her from all connections and commitments. To live as if everything around you were temporary and perhaps triv-ial is to fall prey to petulant cynicism as well as to querulous lovelessness. More common is the pressure on the exile to join—parties, national movements, the state. The exile is offered a new set of affiliations and develops new loyalties. But there is also a loss—of critical perspective, of intellectual reserve, of moral courage.

Is there some middle ground between these two alternatives? Before this can be answered, it must be recognized that the defensive nationalism of exiles often fosters self-awareness as much as it does the less attractive forms of self-assertion. By that I mean that such reconstitutive projects as assembling a nation out of exile (and this is true in this century for Jews and Palestinians) involve constructing a national his-tory, reviving an ancient language, founding national institutions like libraries and universities. And these, while they sometimes promote strident ethnocentrism, also give rise to investigations of self that inevitably go far beyond such simple and pos-itive facts as "ethnicity." For example, there is the self-consciousness of an individual trying to understand why the histories of the Palestinians and the Jews have certain patterns to them, why in spite of oppression and the threat of extinction a particu-lar ethos remains alive in exile.

Necessarily, then, I am speaking of exile not as a privileged site for individual self-reflection but as an *alternative* to the mass institutions looming over much of modern life. If the exile is neither going to rush into an uncritical gregariousness nor sit on the sidelines nursing a wound, he or she must cultivate a scrupulous (not indulgent or sulky) subjectivity.

Perhaps the most rigorous example of such subjectivity is to be found in the writing of Theodor Adorno, the German-Jewish philosopher and critic. Adorno's masterwork, *Minima Moralia,* is an autobiography written while in exile; it is subtitled *Reflexionen aus dem beschadigten Leben* (Reflections from a Mutilated Life). Ruthlessly opposed to what he called the "administered" world, Adorno saw all life as pressed into ready-made forms, prefabricated "homes." He argued that everything that one says or thinks, as well as every object one possesses, is ultimately a mere commodity. Language is jargon, objects are for sale. To refuse this state of affairs is the exile's intellectual mission. Adorno wrote with grave irony, "It is part of morality not to be at home in one's home."

To follow Adorno is to stand away from "home" in order to look at it with the exile's detachment. For there is considerable merit to the practice of noting the discrepancies between various concepts and ideas and what they actually produce. We take home and language for granted; they become nature, and their underlying assumptions recede into dogma and orthodoxy.

The exile knows that in a secular and contingent world, homes are always provisional. Borders and barriers, which enclose us within the safety of familiar territory, can also become prisons, and are often defended beyond reason or necessity. Exiles cross borders, break barriers of thought and experience.

Hugo of St. Victor, a twelfth-century monk from Saxony, wrote these hauntingly beautiful lines:

> It is, therefore, a source of great virtue for the practised mind to learn, bit by bit, first to change about invisible and transitory things, so that afterwards it may be able to leave them behind altogether. The man who finds his homeland sweet is still a tender beginner; he to whom every soil is as his native one is already strong; but he is perfect to whom the entire world is as a foreign land. The tender soul has fixed his love on one spot in the world; the strong man has extended his love to all places; the perfect man has extinguished his.

Erich Auerbach, the great twentieth-century literary scholar who spent the war years as an exile in Turkey, has cited this passage as a model for anyone wishing to transcend national or provincial limits. Only by embracing this attitude can a historian begin to grasp human experience and its written records in their diversity and particularity; otherwise he or she will remain committed more to the exclusions and reactions of prejudice than to the freedom that accompanies knowledge. But note that Hugo twice makes it clear that the "strong" or "perfect" man achieves independence and detachment by *working though* attachments, not by rejecting them. Exile is predicated on the existence of, love for, and bond with one's native place; what is true of all exile is not that home and love of home are lost, but that loss is inherent in the very existence of both.

Regard experiences *as if* they were about to disappear. What is it that anchors them in reality? What would you save of them? What would you give up? Only someone who has achieved independence and detachment, someone whose homeland is "sweet" but whose circumstances make it impossible to recapture that sweetness, can answer those questions. (Such a person would also find it impossible to derive satisfaction from substitutes furnished by illusion or dogma.)

This may seem like a prescription for an unrelieved grimness of outlook and, with it, a permanently sullen disapproval of all enthusiasm or buoyancy of spirit. Not necessarily. While it perhaps seems peculiar to speak of the pleasures of exile, there are some positive things to be said for a few of its conditions. Seeing "the entire world as a foreign land" makes possible originality of vision. Most people are principally aware of one culture, one setting, one home; exiles are aware of at least two, and this plurality of vision gives rise to an awareness of simultaneous dimensions, an awareness that—to borrow a phrase from music—is *contrapuntal*.

For an exile, habits of life, expression, or activity in the new environment inevitably occur against the memory of these things in another environment. Thus both the new and the old environments are vivid, actual, occurring together contrapuntally. There is a unique pleasure in this sort of apprehension, especially if the exile is conscious of other contrapuntal juxtapositions that diminish orthodox judgment and elevate appreciative sympathy. There is also a particular sense of achievement in acting as if one were at home wherever one happens to be.

This remains risky, however: the habit of dissimulation is both wearying and nerve-racking. Exile is never the state of being satisfied, placid, or secure. Exile, in the words of Wallace Stevens, is "a mind of winter" in which the pathos of summer and autumn as much as the potential of spring are nearby but unobtainable. Perhaps this is another way of saying that a life of exile moves according to a different calendar, and is less seasonal and settled than life at home. Exile is life led outside habitual order. It is nomadic, decentered, contrapuntal; but no sooner does one get accustomed to it than its unsettling force erupts anew.

Double Take

1. Why do you think Edward Said wrote "The Mind of Winter"? What is the essay's rhetorical purpose? What do you suspect Said is responding to? What is he trying to accomplish? Do you think he succeeds in creating exigency (a timeliness and significance) for his subject matter? Why or why not?

2. On a number of occasions in this essay, Said addresses the reader directly, as when he writes, "Think about," "We come to nationalism," and "Ours is indeed." Who, specifically, is implied in these statements? What is Said trying to communicate to his readers? What do you think Said achieves when he addresses his readers directly in this way?

3. In the introduction, we describe Said's tone in this essay as more "academic" than in "No Reconciliation Allowed." Do you agree with this characterization? If so,

explain what makes the essay academic. If not, explain why it is not academic. In either case, find examples from the essay—tone, structure, and content—to support your claim.

4. There are places in the essay where Said shifts from writing about exile in the abstract to describing the struggles of Palestinians in exile. In terms of rhetorical effect, do these more current "political" moments add to or detract from Said's argument about exile? How so?

At First Glance

"Palestine, Then and Now," like the previous essay, was published in Harper's *Magazine. Rather than appearing in the "essay" section of the magazine, however, this essay appeared in the "travelogue" section. This makes sense—after all, the essay is an account of Edward Said and his family's journey through Israel and the Occupied Territories in June 1992. It begins at the airport in Tel Aviv, Israel, and ends at the Jordanian border. In between, the essay chronicles Said's experiences as he visits the places of his birth and youth after 45 years of exile. Reading the essay, however, one gets the feeling that it is somehow more—or maybe less—than a travelogue. As you read the essay, think about what readers of* Harper's *would expect from a travelogue and try to predict how they might have reacted to the essay, especially to its more political moments. Think also about how and why these moments strengthen or weaken the essay.*

Palestine, Then and Now: An Exile's Journey through Israel and the Occupied Territories

I. THE ROAD TO JERUSALEM

On Friday, June 12, 1992, at about 7:45 P.M., my Air France flight touched down at Tel Aviv's Ben-Gurion Airport. It was now, with the plane safely on the ground, that I grew more nervous. I was born, in November 1935, in Talbiya, then a mostly new and prosperous Arab quarter of Jerusalem. By the end of 1947, just months before Talbiya fell to Jewish forces, I'd left with my family for Cairo; and although I did spend a few days on the West Bank and in East Jerusalem twenty-five years ago, I had never, in any meaningful way, attempted a journey back. Forty-five years of my life had elapsed, and at last I was returning.

The Palestine I left as a twelve-year-old and the Israel I had just set down in are very different places. Arab Palestine was destroyed in 1948, its people, all but about 120,000 of them, having fled or been driven out in a terrifying exodus. A new Jewish state, Israel, came into existence, and in the decades that followed, political upheaval, war, technological and social developments, and majors shifts in population transformed the entire Middle East. I had come to the United States as a schoolboy in 1951, but in the years that followed I would remain close to the Arab world, becoming actively involved in the struggle for Palestinian rights. Most of my extended family, all of whom left Palestine in early 1948, had found refuge in Beirut, Amman, and Cairo, and I had visited them many times. Now I was returning with my own family.

My wife, Mariam, who was born in Lebanon, had visited Arab East Jerusalem a few times in the early fifties and sixties, when the city had been a part of Jordan. But my son, Wadie, twenty, and my daughter, Najla, eighteen, had never before been to any part of the Holy Land. Some months earlier I had received a shocking medical diagnosis: I was suffering from a chronically insidious blood disease. This news had convinced me for the first time of a mortality I had ignored, and which I now needed to come to terms with, with my own family, at the source, so to speak—in Palestine.

"Just a minute, please," said the young immigration officer, taking my American passport with her to a nearby office, leaving the three others on her desk. Would they send us back? Would they grill us—me especially—and go through our bags? Or—this was my private nightmare—would they march me off to prison? Between 1977 and 1991 I had been a member of the Palestine National Council, the parliament-in-exile of the Palestinians, proscribed as an enemy organization by Israel. I knew Yasir Arafat, was (crudely) referred to as "his man," and at times had even been described, by the scurrilous propagandists of the pro-Israel lobby in the United States, as an accomplice of terrorists.

The immigration officer came back ten minutes later. "Okay," she said. "You can go now." No questions at all. We proceeded to a security barrier, where another young woman stood guard. Exactly the same thing happened with my passport, except that this time we were also greeted by a familiar face—that of Mohammed Miari, an Israeli Knesset member, who, when I'd informed him of my planned trip, had agreed to meet us at the airport. (His parliamentary immunity allowed him access to the arrivals area.) What immediately struck me about Mohammed was how easily, unaffectedly, he spoke with the uniformed personnel, all of whom were Israeli Jews. I had assumed that there would be a manifest uneasiness or even fear, as between members of subaltern and dominant groups. I was already learning the reality of things.

Mine was the generation raised in an Arab world that accorded the Jewish state no recognition at all; even the idea of Israel was anathema. This odd proposition, that Israel did not exist, made possible a policy of non-knowledge, a void that erected a wall around itself, allowing both Israeli and Arab leaders to get away with literally everything in the name of security. Until 1967 the Arab world, including the millions of Palestinians floundering in exile, nearly forgot about their compatriots who remained in Israel after 1948. Until 1967 it was nearly impossible to use the word "Israel" in Arabic writing. All this was supposed to cost Israel in legitimacy and resolve, so that if we didn't acknowledge its presence it would go away. Of course it didn't, although even those many of us whose passports and safe jobs made it feasible to return needed a long time to make the trip, cross the barrier, and confront the difficult reality.

It took only a few moments and we were out of the airport, minus my suitcases, which were apparently "lost." (Not to worry, said the lost-and-found official, with a smile. "They'll turn up in forty-eight hours," which they did, a little untidy inside.) Miari had brought along his wife and daughter and also my American-Palestinian friend Rashid Khalidi, who teaches at the University of Chicago, is an advisor to the Palestinian delegation participating in the ongoing Middle East peace talks, and was in Jerusalem for the summer. In Miari's car my family and I were driven up to Jerusalem, that extraordinary city, in the quickly darkening twilight. When we arrived a brilliant star-dotted sky swept by cold winds vaulted the city's heights, and as we crossed the handsome stone threshold of the American Colony Hotel, I was already conscious of trying to stem the torrent of memories, expectations, and disoriented impressions that assaulted me.

Tentatively at first, boldly later, I found myself repeating to myself that I did have a right to be here, that I was a native, and that nearly everything in my life could be traced to the city of my birth. I was baptized in the Anglican St. George's Cathedral (built in 1898), a couple of hundred yards from the hotel; along with most of the male members of my family, I had attended the cathedral school, St. George's; my family had owned property in Jerusalem barely a mile from where I now stood, was connected to a whole network of other families—was, in fact, as Palestinian as one could be. What remained now? I asked myself. What could be reconstituted through memory and then experienced in a ten-day visit, despite the politics of extreme antagonism that I had lived for forty-five years?

II. INTO THE OLD CITY

The Church of the Holy Sepulcher, that center of centers, was exactly as I recalled it—a rundown place full of frumpy, middle-aged tourists milling about in the decrepit and ill-lit area where Coptic, Greek Orthodox, and other Christian churches nurtured their unattractive ecclesiastical gardens in sometimes open combat with one another. I remembered being carried around here on my father's shoulders, wondering: Who were those bearded foreigners? Could *this* be the actual site of Christ's last hours? Both Najla and Wadie seemed perplexed and upset by the incongruities: Najla was particularly disturbed by the third-rate commercialization—"like a market," she said—and Wadie by the rambunctious, seemingly hostile priests.

The four of us wormed our way into a Greek Orthodox service that was in progress, and the chanting and jostling did little, alas, to compose our irritated souls. All of the tour groups are now led by Israeli guides, even at the splendid Dome of the Rock, one of Islam's holiest shrines. A friend later told me that no Palestinian guides now work, since the Israeli army occupying East Jerusalem, in which the Old City lies, holds the sites and the Israeli government trains the guides; after all, it is through Israel that most visitors today enter East Jerusalem or go on to the West Bank. My paternal grandfather had for a time worked as a tour guide, and when he was a boy my father sold crowns of thorns to tourists near the Sepulcher. That particular association was now ended.

Still, a few yards away from the Sepulcher, underneath a declivity in the city wall, we stumbled upon Zalatimo's, the renowned pastry shop whose specialty, *mtabaqa,* a flat pancake folding in hazelnuts and sugar, was a great family favorite. A wizened old baker was in there stoking the oven, but he looked as though he was only barely surviving.

Rashid Khalidi's cousin, Haifa, resides in the Old City, and she invited us to lunch. She lives with her elderly parents and uncle, in a house her family has owned for generations. Its main problem is that one of its sides gives out on the Wailing Wall and it is therefore a coveted site for Jewish settlers as they try to change Arab East Jerusalem into a new Jewish city. Routinely she finds these zealots peering over into her house from adjoining properties they've already taken, taunting her, provoking her with jeers, threatening to take the house from her. Earlier that day in the Old City, which has been Arab for hundreds of years, I saw such settlers walking through crowds of Palestinians, completely oblivious to them, usually armed with handguns or Uzis (sometimes both), always—it seemed to me—flaunting their power to be there, in the heart of the Arab Kasbah.

After lunch I visited a nearby home, where I was introduced to an elderly widow whose house had been summarily seized by a group of settlers. She now lived in the basement of the house, whose dark, airless interior was damp and unimaginably crowded, although it did miraculously accommodate six or seven people. One of her daughters was laboriously blowing a hair dryer on some wet clothes. "They won't let us hang our washing outside," she said, pointing to her former home above. "When we try to they pour garbage and dirty water on it."

The man who took me to the poor widow's house, Hayel Sandouqa, was in late middle age. A longtime teacher, he is also the head of a local defense committee working against settler incursions into Jerusalem. A man of quiet, if sad, authority, he showed me a modest house around which settlers had taken rooms and various bits of the courtyard, thus making entry to the Arab house impossible except by walking through their gauntlet. The committee's first priority is to organize links among Palestinian inhabitants of the Old City, quarter by quarter, house by house. As Sandouqa told me, the committee then pinpoints the houses that are immediately threatened, either because the settlers are trying to literally force people out or because they are trying to buy them out using supposed—or, alas, authentic—Arab realtors. He told us of another widow (widows are prime settler targets) who had taken her case against Jewish squatters to court, had won the case, but was now trying rather fruitlessly to get the court order implemented. Another family I was introduced to told me of how they had come home one evening to find a lone settler wandering about inside their house. When asked what he thought he was doing he responded that he was there to look over "my house."

These episodes are at the core of the Palestinian predicament today, which is essentially territorial and geographical. Little about the peace talks has had much effect on the slow and relentless advance of the Israelis into more and more Palestinian space. Aside from the constant military presence everywhere—in Jerusalem, on the West Bank, and along the Gaza Strip—there is the equally constant settler presence. On most of the hills surrounding Jerusalem, one sees the dreaded settlements. To look at them all day, as I did, is to glimpse an important clue to the yearlong wrangle between the Bush Administration and the Palestinians on the one hand, and both the old Shamir and the new Rabin governments of Israel on the other.

All of the settlements appear to be made up of two parts. First is the group of prefab houses that are finished and inhabited. Usually behind them, standing row upon row, is the second part—houses that are unfinished, empty, and awaiting money for completion. (Sometimes the "houses" are simply trailer homes.) Their number is undetermined, but not their reason for being. The empty houses are there to "thicken" the settlements, make a show of Israeli presence in Arab territory so as to maintain pressure for irreversible Israeli sovereignty. So when George Bush agreed to provide Israel with the $10 billion loan guarantees in return for a "freeze" on Israeli settlements, these unfinished houses were accepted as already "existing," with a further loss in Palestinian territory. The West Bank and Gaza, seized by Israel in 1967 and militarily under the control of Israeli soldiers and settlers, together comprise only 22 percent of the whole of the Palestine I left forty-five years ago. Of that 22 percent, it is estimated that more than 50 percent has since been expropriated and settled by Israelis.

As we were leaving the Old City, nearing the Damascus Gate, we came upon a group of soldiers sitting at the entrance of an imposing house, at the top of which there is an incongruously large menorah. This is where General Ariel Sharon has planted his banner, enlisting a small battalion of soldiers to maintain a place for his right-wing zealotry.

III. A SEARCH FOR FAMILY LANDMARKS

There were four thriving Arab quarters in the West Jerusalem of my childhood: Upper and Lower Baqa'a, Qatamon, and Talbiya. I recalled that during my last weeks in Palestine, in the fall of 1947, I had to traverse three of the security zones instituted by the British to get to St. George's School in East Jerusalem from my home in Talbiya. And by February 1948 Talbiya was in the hands of the Haganah, the Jewish underground. Now, as we drove around looking for my family's house, I saw no Arabs, although the handsome old stone houses still bear their Arab identity.

I remembered the house itself quite clearly: two stories, a terraced entrance, a balcony at the front, a palm tree and a large conifer as you climbed toward the front door, a spacious and (at the time) empty square, designated to be a park, that lay before the room in which I was born, which faced the King David Hotel. I could not recall street names from that time (there was no name to our street when I lived there, it turns out), but my cousin Yousef, now in Canada, had drawn me a map from memory that he sent along with a copy of the title deed. Years before, I had heard that Martin Buber lived in the house for a time after 1948 but had died elsewhere. No one seemed to know what became of the house after the middle 1960s.

Our guide this day was George Khodr, who had been a friend of my father's and an accountant for the family business, the Palestine Educational Company. I could vividly recall the company's main premises, with its wonderful bookshop at which Abba Eban had been a regular customer, built against the stretch of city wall running between the Jaffa and New gates. All gone now, I saw, as we drove past the wall and up Mamilla Road. What in my childhood had been a bustling Arab commercial block was, last summer, a construction site.

Khodr's family had also lived in Talbiya, in a house he took us to so as to orient himself. Save for the Mediterranean flora, one might have been in an elegant Zurich suburb, so strongly did Talbiya bespeak its new European personality. As we walked around, Khodr called off the names of the villas and their original Palestinian owners—Kitaneh, Sununu, Tannous, Haramy, Salameh— a sad roll call of the vanished past, for Mariam a reminder of the Palestinian refugees with the very same names who fetched up in Beirut during the fifties and sixties.

It took almost two hours to find the old family house, and it is a tribute to my cousin's memory that only by sticking very carefully to his map did we finally locate it. Today the street is called Nahum Sokolow; the sandy little square now an elegant, even manicured park. My daughter later told me that, using her camera with manic excitement, I reeled off twenty-six photos of the house.

It bore the nameplate "International Christian Embassy" at the gate. To have found my family's house now occupied not by an Israeli Jewish family but by a right-wing fundamentalist Christian and militantly pro-Zionist group, run by a South African Boer no less! Anger and melancholy overtook me, so that when an American woman came out of the house holding an armful of laundry and asked if she could help, I could not bring myself to ask to go inside.

More than anything else, perhaps, it was the house I did not, could not, enter that symbolized the eerie finality of a history. It seemed to stare down at me from behind its shaded windows. Palestine as I had known it was over, and I found myself thinking of my last view of my father a few days before he died in Beirut. I was about to return to my work in New York; he lay in a bed, already slipping in and out of a cancer-caused coma, and then after I hugged him good-bye he turned his face to the wall and seemed quickly to fall asleep. That was January 1971.

Four days after finding the house I took my family to St. George's to visit the old "Bishop's School," as it is known among Jerusalem's Arabs. There I showed my son, Wadie, his grandfather Wadie's name on the cricket and soccer First Eleven boards for the years 1906 through 1911. In the assembly room, where morning prayers used to be held, a seventy-year-old caretaker asked us shyly whether we'd like to see old school pictures. He went to the cellar and brought up a number of them—a class picture from 1942, the staff in 1927—one of which riveted my attention. It was signed "Kh. Raad," for Khalil Raad, Palestine's most famous photographer, a nervous but gifted man whom I remember would fussily arrange and rearrange us for group pictures during weddings, confirmations, and the like. There, seated on the floor next to a young man carrying a soccer ball with "1906" written across it, was my father, age thirteen.

So many histories, starting and ending in Jerusalem. A fitting accompaniment to the ebbing of my life on the one hand, and, on the other, a concrete reminder that just as *they* had started and ended, I did and would too, and so also would my children, who could now see for the first time the linked narrative of our family's generations, where that story belonged but from which it had been banished.

IV. DRIVING NORTH

The distances I remembered from my childhood never corresponded to the actual distances I traveled during our visit. Jericho and Jerusalem, for example, were much closer than I had supposed. My saintly maternal grandmother used to spend her winters in Jericho, and it had seemed to me back then that it must have been another country as I watched her prepare her bags meticulously and laboriously several days before she went. Jericho, in fact, is less than twenty miles from Jerusalem, a half-hour drive to reach a dusty and unprepossessing place. Early memories of regions such as the Galilee were overlain in my mind with more recent visual impressions—photographs, movie scenes, commercials promoting Israeli tourism, and pictures conjured up by reams of prose. Among the things this visit was doing was clearing away years of neglect and weedlike growth.

My mother's family was originally from Safad, north of Lake Tiberias, and then moved to Nazareth. Over the years I came to feel that Safad was some sort of counterbalance—in its less middle-class tone, its more eccentric and inspired waywardness—to the dour formality of my father's Jerusalem. (Until her dying day, my father's sister, Nabiha, referred to her closest friend as "Mrs. Marmura," who in turn always referred to "Mrs. Said," and this after more than fifty years of friendship!) I was heading north in search of this past.

As we drove, I could not help but be struck by the disparity between the gentle and rather dry rolling hills, with their moderate-sized evergreens, gray rocks, and brownish sands, and the unyieldingly uniform buildings put up by the Israelis everywhere, buildings that suggest not so much incompatibility as a kind of unfriendliness, as if the land they took had to be disciplined, compelled into submission.

Then, as we made our way east toward Lake Tiberias, I noticed again something I had seen all along the coast, up from Jerusalem to the ports of Haifa and then Acre: how practically every open space, whether soccer field, orchard, or park, seemed surrounded with barbed wire. This fixation on enclosure blended in tidily with the numerous prisons I saw along the Haifa road, prisons holding mostly Palestinian prisoners behind fence inside fence (two-, three-, four-deep) of wire. And then another contrast, in the resort town of Tiberias: the sudden, overblown assertiveness of luxury hotels, high-rise condos, and the like, blaring out a message of expensive holidays.

After Tiberias we stopped at Tabgha, a tiny village at the north end of Lake Tiberias. I had in mind this picture from years ago: a beach of singular calm and modest beauty that I also associated with roast corn, sold at the water's edge by itinerant peddlers. Tabgha is where the biblical miracle of the loaves and fishes took place. We used to go down to Tabgha from Safad, which is where my maternal uncle Munir lived and where as a unique treat we would spend time in the summer.

A renowned doctor, he and his wife wound up refugees in Jordan. They have been dead for fifteen years. There is now an ostentatious German chapel that spoils the view, and we left Tabgha quickly for Safad.

Clinging to the side of a steep mountain, Safad has been entirely purged of its Arab inhabitants. A combination religious and artistic colony, it so sprawls in different clusters and directions that I had the hardest time remembering where Uncle Munir's house actually was. Eventually I did spot its oddly high balcony and saw that the house retained its decorative Ottoman arches and steep stairs flanking a side wall. But how changed was old Safad. Across the street from the house were a group of Lubavitcher Hasidim doing exactly what they do in New York: selling their literature, looking for converts.

The same gloomy feeling I had in Talbiya soon came over me here, a melancholy brought on by the sense of a history finished, packed up, taking place elsewhere. Uncle Munir's house was identified by a plaque as being the "Municipal Building," but to look through one of its less soiled windows was to ascertain immediately that not only was it unused but its interior, chairs and tables scattered desultorily about, seemed frozen in time like Miss Havisham's Satis House.

South, to Nazareth. Of all the Palestinian sites out of my past it is among the richest in significance and the dimmest in memory. My maternal grandfather, Shukry Musa-Bishouty, is buried here. He had founded and built the local Baptist church early in this century and brought up a gifted, perhaps even remarkable, brood of children: my mother, Hilda, and four boys—a doctor, a lawyer, a physicist, and a banker—all charming, all musical; all very different (despite, or perhaps because of, their father's unrelenting Baptist fundamentalism) from the gray Victorian Anglicanism I associate with my father's Jerusalem family. What also courses through the Musa-Bishouty family is a Lebanese current that connects us to the Levantine archness and hedonistic dash of that quixotic land, with its perplexing combination of wit and bloody-mindedness.

Nazareth today is really two towns: one, the bustling Arab *madina* where the Musas once flourished; and upper, Jewish new Nazareth, set ostentatiously on hills that command the Arab, or lower, city. For Mariam and myself, Arab Nazareth was the only place we visited where we could quickly feel at home; it was like a small-scale Amman or Beirut—a Palestinian town not totally interrupted and violated by subsequent history. We were welcomed by close family friends, the Abbouds, whose sumptuous table gathered in other friends, including the celebrated Palestinian author Emile Habiby. Later, we explored the town a little. As we entered the main square, I almost instinctively made out St. Mary's Well, very close to where my mother was born. The essential topography has remained unchanged. It felt like a Palestinian town. Unlike Jerusalem, Nazareth is, in effect, the same place it was in 1948. Perhaps this explains why, although the Musa house had been demolished and the Baptist Church rebuilt, I felt more life in Nazareth, and considerably less sorrow, than in Jerusalem.

The new Baptist church, incidentally, has an unbecoming honeycomb-like facade, and, as a friendly American voice told me over the phone, my grandfather's tomb had been moved from the old church to a nearby cemetery. "We did it very well," he assured me, with Israeli health inspectors to ratify the proceedings, and then added, as if apologetically, "All we found inside were some old bones and a Bible!" I prevented myself from asking what else he had expected after seventy years.

V. THE PALESTINIAN INSIDE

The 850,000 Palestinians of Israel—I am not speaking here of the 2 million Palestinians on the Israeli-occupied West Bank and in Gaza, where as a people we claim sovereignty and the right to establish a state—are clearly designated second-class citizens. One need only glance at the figures supplied by Israel's Central Bureau of Statistics to see how Jews and "non-Jews" (the designation for the Arabs in Israel, who constitute 18.2 percent of the population) are separated into two classes, one of which is *always* considerably lower in status. This is reflected in levels of health care, education, unemployment, quality of life—right across the board.

Yet what impressed me on this visit is that inside Israel Palestinians do, in fact, survive as a community—survive first of all by a fantastic, even maddening, and almost inadvertent stubbornness; and second, by here and there undertaking imaginative and courageous schemes for self-development and improvement.

One instance of the latter is to be found in the north, in Acre, very sad place today. We walked at the water's edge through what had been a medieval Arab port and were depressed by the sense of life being slowly and systematically choked off, buildings (including the el-Jazzar Mosque) left unrepaired or empty, desolate people walking about in poor circumstances. And still, as if in defiance of all this, one can find the Acre Pedagogical Center, headed by Mariam Marei. Marei has set up a modest program whose purpose is to train young people to teach poor Palestinian children. Her methods are improvisatory, refreshingly unbureaucratic: puppet shows, cardboard models, folk poetry, incredibly colorful displays, invigorating talk. The center is located in a nice old Arab house and exudes a sense of discovery and optimism, totally undeterred by the lack of funds or the obstacles put in its way. The point she made to me was that by training teachers, who in turn taught young children, "we" would have better alternatives than those offered by Israel.

The "we" Marei spoke of stuck with me. Traveling, there were times I didn't feel like an outsider—which in many ways I was—but rather like a partner, one of the "we," in the problems and hopes encountered by people in daily life. I'd be sitting at breakfast at the hotel and a young man or woman would come up to me with great politeness and ask if he or she could have a minute of time. I would then hear of plans, notions, dreams, and schemes, and be asked for my ideas on the matter; no one I met asked me for direct help, for money or contacts, only for sources, books, ideas. At such times I felt most connected, and hopeful.

VI. DESCENDING INTO GAZA

It was when we went down to the Gaza Strip that my recent memories of a trip to South Africa kicked in with considerable force. In 1991 I had been invited to give the T.B. Davie Academic Freedom Lecture at the University of Cape Town; this required clearance from the cultural boycott committee, which I got, as well as additional sponsorship from the African National Congress and two other universities. One of the first things I did in Johannesburg was to visit Soweto, as well as other black townships in the vicinity and in Cape Town. Nothing I saw in South Africa can compare with Gaza in misery, in confinement and racial discrimination, in sheer oppression. In Gaza both Mariam and I quickly noticed the proliferation of military observation posts, the incongruously high street lights (so that they can't be hit by stones), the acres of barbed wire, and the large number of patrolling "white" soldiers. Israel has been spared universal criticism, as South Africa has not. Somehow Israel is viewed as unconnected to its practices in Gaza.

The day we drove down from Jerusalem began ominously with an unusual hail-and thunder-storm. By the time we got to Gaza two hours later, vast pools of mud and stagnant water made passage extremely messy, especially in the Jabalya camp, which has the highest population density in the world, housing more than 65,000 refugees displaced from as far north as Acre. You enter the Gaza Strip through a military checkpoint, which is closed at night; this gives the area the appearance of an enormous concentration camp. Numerous Israeli soldiers man barriers that stop each car, empty out passengers, check the magnetized pass cards.

Since the car I was in had West Bank license plates that prohibited us from entering without a permit, we were met at the gate by a close friend, Raji Sourani, a young Gazan lawyer who last year won the Robert F. Kennedy Human Rights Award for his heroic efforts on behalf of Palestinian prisoners—although, as he always tells visitors with a wry smile, he's never won a case. What he mostly does, therefore, is visit his clients, making them feel that someone is looking out for them, keeping contact between them and their unusually forlorn and often quite helpless families. This gives him additional prestige among Palestinians in the Occupied Territories and elsewhere, but this prestige, in turn, has not at all protected him from the Israelis. He has served five jail sentences, varying from a few months to a couple of years.

Jabalya camp is the most appalling place I have ever seen. Children crowd its unpaved streets. There is no sewage system, the stench tears at your gut, and everywhere you look you see people falling all over one another, poorly dressed, glumly making their way from one seemingly hopeless task to another. The statistics are nightmarish: terrible infant-mortality rates, high unemployment, the lowest per capita income in the Occupied Territories, the most days of curfew, the least medical services, and on and on.

Raji had gathered about twenty men, leaders in such fields as health, education, and employment, for me to talk with in Jabalya. The house we met in was spotlessly clean on the inside but surrounded by tiny little houses made of wood, mud, and tin, jammed together like so many boxes heaped up on one another. No zoning, no landscaping here. Any change in the physical layout of the place, any attempt to drain the putrid stagnating water, for instance, or to improve a house, is forbidden, or requires a permit that is next to impossible to get.

I didn't hear a single hopeful thing in the two hours I was with the men. One of them spoke of having spent seventeen years in jail, of his children sick, of relatives destitute. There was a lot of anger. The phrase I kept hearing was *"mawt batiq,"* slow death. There seemed to be considerable animus against West Bankers, who were variously characterized by Gazans as spoiled, or privileged, or insensitive. We are forgotten, they all said, and because of the unimaginably difficult job of dramatically (or even slightly) improving the general lot of Gazans, I was repeatedly enjoined *at least* not to forget.

Even as I write about it now I cringe at the memory of the place, despite (or perhaps because of) the unfailing generosity and gentleness of the people we met. Raji arranged for us to see Dr. Haidar Abdel Shafi, an eminent physician and the official head of the Palestinian delegation to the peace talks, in his home a few miles from Jabalya. The strip itself is made up of several towns (Rafah, Khan Younis, Gaza City), of refugee camps, and most offensive, of a number of posh-looking Israeli settlements, with spacious lawns and swimming pools. Abdel Shafi immediately communicated the sense of calm decency that has elevated him to universal admiration in Gaza and throughout the Palestinian world in part because, unlike, say, Arafat, he is not principally a political man. Speaking to him and his wife, I suddenly felt the whole fragmented picture of Palestinian society making some collective sense, because in people like the Shafis and Raji and so many others that I met during that fateful trip to Gaza, the idea of an actual society that bound us all together somehow *did* survive the ravages of our history, its tragic mistakes, misfortunes, and the destructive course of Israel's policies.

An affecting reinforcement to what I had experienced earlier in Gaza took place as we came to leave, and more pieces fell into place. Raji wanted me to meet the mother of one of his clients, again a widow, whose imprisoned son was slated for deportation: there were some legal points to be discussed, and since the daily curfew time was approaching, the visit had to be a brief one. This was in Rafah, only a few yards away from the Egyptian border. The house was nondescript, but the woman herself, Um Mohammed, was surprisingly self-possessed and politicized. We had been told that her oldest son, a PLO cadre, had been killed in Lebanon; we met his young daughter, whose name was Beirut. In a matter of minutes I discovered that Um Mohammed's brother was Yussef Najjar, one of the three PLO leaders assassinated in Beirut by the Israelis in 1973. (Kamal Nasser, another of the three, was a poet and a close friend of mine with whom I had had dinner the night before he was killed.)

So there on a dusty side street, as Raji Sourani explained to the family how their son was to be deported (the sentence has since been rescinded by the Rabin government), several additional strands of the Palestinian experience came together and were illuminated for me as rarely before: the gifted young lawyer, a native of Gaza; the refugee woman, a camp dweller who had one son killed in battle, another in jail, and a brother, an early guerilla leader, who had also been killed; an American Palestinian, an exile still tied to this strange and tormented land after forty-five years.

My children, too, tied their own strands. My daughter's way of being connected was her delight in the children, who surrounded her wherever we went and whose spritely vitality affected her more than their difficulties; Wadie, on the other hand, has been studying Arabic and Palestinian history passionately, so for him the visit was a goad to renewed effort, fortified commitment.

VII. TOWARD A FUTURE

The very last thing I did before leaving for Jordan was to spend half a day at Bir Zeit University, on the West Bank near Ramallah. I can barely recall the Bir Zeit I knew as a child, which was then only a junior college. Its new campus today stands on land given to it by the Nasir family, connected to mine through marriage and a long history of associations. Earlier during my trip, I had been scheduled to give a seminar and lecture at Bir Zeit, both of which had to be canceled because Hamas, the Islamic party active in the Occupied Territories, had called a strike. (I must say that these periodic shutdowns of the West Bank seem to me colossally stupid and wasteful. With shops and schools closed, and an immense amount of time lost in posturing, no one is hurt by them except Palestinians.)

Bir Zeit had only recently been permitted to reopen after a four-year shutdown. I am particularly bitter about this facet of the Israeli occupation, which appears to have targeted Palestinian education as a vulnerable enemy. The criminalization of teaching and learning has been made worse by the incredible silence of Western academics and intellectuals who regularly waltz in and out of Israeli universities without protest and without making any significant noise about the outrage. Miraculously, however, Bir Zeit battles on. We saw a rich exhibition of architectural models and drawings set up by the students, as well as various laboratories where solid work on Palestinian agriculture and nutrition is being carried out.

A heavily politicized faculty and student body exist at Bir Zeit; many of the former are either involved in the ongoing peace process or are in opposition to it, so the informal talk I was to give in place of the canceled seminar and lecture— making comments, answering questions—was bound to be rousing. I was a little hesitant to go in for oratory in the classical Arabic style (which is always expected) because, living for years in an environment where my public speaking is based on an essentially conversational mode, I find it difficult to transform myself into a (for me) stiff public rhetorician. I ended up using a slightly refined variant on the spoken language, without the requisite eloquence but also without obfuscation.

A very large crowd filled the hall. I suspected that many had heard of me, some had read me, but most were there to find out what I thought about the current peace process, the U.S. role, and prospects for the future. I was warmly introduced by George Giacaman, who teaches philosophy, and then gave (by request) a short precis in English of my forthcoming book on culture and imperialism. Thereafter discussion switched back into Arabic, and was moderated by Giacaman and Ali Jerbawi, a professor of political science. The first questions sought clarifications of what I had just said, most of them having to do with the role of the United States as a sort of new imperial power, which, I kept reiterating, is scarcely understood in the Arab world, despite the ceaseless verbiage spewed out about it. Then came the first challenge, a simple question that asked me to spell out my "real" position on the Gulf

War. I denounced Saddam Hussein as a dictator and a fool, and his occupation of Kuwait as an unacceptable aggression. But I was unsparing in my criticism of the American-led war, as well as the Arab members of the coalition.

In no time we were heavily into Salman Rushdie, whom I defended categorically, and political Islam, which I also criticized, somewhat impetuously. I made, I think, one rather far-out analogy between the Israeli penchant for barbed-wire fences and the now current separation of "us")Palestinians, Arabs, Muslims) from the West, saying that all cultures were in fact hybrid and any attempt to push a homogenizing line was not only false but demagogic.

As we left Bir Zeit, Albert Aghazarian, the genial man who runs the university's public programs, introduced me to two young men who were campus Islamic leaders. Expecting the worst, I confronted them. I was thunderstruck when they told me that although "there were points of disagreement," they appreciated my honesty. Would I please come back? I was honored to be asked and resolved to make frequent returns to Bir Zeit, doing something I had imagined for years, translating my type of cultural criticism into the language and concerns of Palestinian students. And that, more even than the fact of residence, could become my contribution to a Palestine that would be neither insular nor ruled by orthodoxy.

Crossing into Jordan at the Allenby Bridge, we were greeted by a sign announcing YOU ARE IN JORDAN. SMILE. This brought unexpected relief, especially since the omnipresent barbed wire had disappeared once we got across the river. We hadn't been questioned by the Israeli border people at all, even though we were kept waiting for ninety minutes.

The first thought that came to me after leaving the West Bank was how small a role pleasure now seems to play not only in Israel but in the Occupied Territories. A harsh, driven quality rules life, by necessity for Palestinians, by some other logic, which I can barely understand, for Israelis. After so many years of thinking about it, I now feel that the two peoples are locked together without much real sympathy, but locked together they are, and very slowly perhaps they will improve the relationship.

I would find it very hard to live there, I think: exile seems to me a more liberated state, but, I have to admit, I am privileged and can afford to experience the pleasures, rather than the burdens, of exile. Yet I also feel that, as a family, the four of us need the connection, need the assurances that Palestine and Palestinians have really survived, and this we now have. I think I needed the chance metaphorically to bury the dead, and, what with the large number of funerary associations for me, what had been Palestine was indeed a mournful place. But I can feel and sometimes actually see a different future as I couldn't before.

Double Take

1. Based on your own expectations of what a travelogue should be and do, in what ways is Edward Said's essay "Palestine, Then and Now" more than just a travelogue?

2. In this essay, Said shifts in key moments from the pronoun "I" to "we." Locate where he does this and think about what effect this shift in pronouns has on the way the reader relates to the writer as well as the way the writer relates to his own experiences.

3. If a reader of *Harper's* was predisposed to agree with Said regarding the struggle of the Palestinians, what aspects of this essay do you think he or she would find most compelling? Why? How might you use some of these strategies in your own writing?

4. If a reader of *Harper's* was predisposed to disagree with Said about the Palestinian situation, what might be his or her reaction to this essay? What aspects of the essay would this reader react to most negatively? Why? Are there any places in the essay where such a reader might be moved to see Said's point of view? Why or why not?

Seeing for Yourself

At First Glance

Of the four essays by Edward Said collected here, "Jungle Calling," first published in Interview *magazine in 1989, is the most lighthearted and playful. While it too addresses questions of exile and colonialism, the essay turns its attention to the Tarzan films of the 1930s and 1940s. As you read it, look for rhetorical patterns this essay shares with Said's other essays. In what way is this essay similar to the others? In what ways is it different? In addition, try to identify and articulate Said's argument in the essay. The argument is never stated directly, but something unmistakably holds the essay together. What is that something? As you read, think about strategies Said uses to construct his essay which you might be able to use in your own writing.*

Jungle Calling

Unlike Harpo Marx, Tarzan as played by Johnny Weissmuller was not completely mute, but what he had to say ("Tarzan-Jane") in the twelve films he made between 1932 and 1948 was rather minimal. And even that, on one occasion, was considered too much. The following story appears in Gabe Essoe's *Tarzan of the Movies:*

> Johnny's passion for a straight part can best be illustrated by a story he was especially fond of telling: "I remember once (as Tarzan) I was supposed to point somewhere and say, "You go." I must've felt talkative that day because I pointed and said, 'You go quick.' 'Cut,' the director yelled. 'What's the matter, Johnny? We don't want to load this scene with any long speeches. Just do it like it's written.'"

Compare this bit of elegant compression with a speech by Tarzan (whose real identity is John Clayton, Lord Greystoke) in *Tarzan of the Apes* (1912) the first of the Edgar Rice Burroughs novels on the jungle hero:

> "You are free now, Jane," he ([Tarzan] said, "and I have come across the ages out of the dim and distant past from the lair of the primeval man to claim you—for your sake I have become a civilized man—for your sake I have crossed oceans and continents—for your sake I will be whatever you will me to be. I can make you happy, Jane, in the life you know and love best. Will you marry me?"

The surprise is that the original Tarzan—Burrough's fantasy—is so cultivated, whereas the movie Tarzan is a barely human creature, monosyllabic, primitive, simple. Perhaps for that reason the Weissmuller creation, one of the only serial-film characters of the 1930s not to be rehabilitated and seriously studied by critics, is so little appreciated or remembered. It is as if he, Weissmuller and the Tarzan he played, happened without too much fuss and then disappeared into a well-deserved oblivion. The fact, however, is that anyone who saw Weissmuller in his prime can associate Tarzan only with his portrayal. The stream of comic-book, television, and other movie Tarzans, from Lex Barker and Gordon Scott to Ron Ely and Jock Mahoney, end up being trite variations on a noble theme. Weissmuller's apeman was a genuinely mythic figure, a pure Hollywood product that was built out of Burrough's Anglophilic and racist fantasy as well as a number of other almost whimsical elements (for example, Tarzan's phenomenal swimming powers, which are nowhere mentioned by Burroughs) that came together in a surprisingly effective way. No one was Tarzan for as long as Weissmuller, and no one since his time could do much more than ring some generally uninteresting changes on the routines he established, grunts, tree swinging, Methodist-like rectitude, and all.

Weissmuller's Tarzan had several Janes, of whom only Maureen O'Sullivan really counted in my opinion. An Irishwoman, O'Sullivan had a British accent, unlike her literary prototype, who was Jane Porter from Wisconsin. As Johnny's first lady she acted with a fresh abandon never equaled since. In the days when films were ruled by an iron law concerning nudity (even belly buttons were not supposed to be seen), O'Sullivan appeared almost naked: there was a notorious scene in *Tarzan and His Mate,* the second Weissmuller film, in which as she dives into the water she sheds her nightgown and quickly reveals a breast. This scene was removed or pared down in subsequent releases, but I am certain that I saw the original version, since the recollection of that astonishing sight on the screen seems definitively imprinted on my memory (or imagination, as the case may be). Between them, Weissmuller and O'Sullivan seem to have had a sexual paradise: he worshiped her; she fretted, scolded, and smiled demurely, but without all the encumbrances of suburban domesticity around them—no lawns to mow, no car pools, no plumbing problems—and in between adventures, they seemed to spend a lot of time making out. What scenes there were of "jungle life," whether those were of swimming or swinging through the trees, or just lying around in their tree house, were shot through with sexual suggestion. After all, they rarely wore any clothes to speak of.

One of the saddest things, therefore, was how their basic loincloth costumes grew progressively from tiny fig leaves to grotesquely large and flappy dowager beach costumes. With that change the sexual motif diminished and the tree house grew larger and more elaborate (the change is obvious in *Tarzan Escapes,* 1936): one could watch the embourgeoisement of the Tarzan family taking place before one's eyes. Three films into the series, Tarzan and Jane "found" a baby son (1939), who was thereafter known as "Boy." (The child, incidentally, was adopted so as not to clutter their sexual paradise with the digressive rituals of childbearing; besides, Jane could not wear her costume or go swimming if she was pregnant.) Then again, over time, we could observe Boy growing into adolescence and subsequently into manhood. After ten years of being Tarzan's son, the actor Johnny Sheffield finally left the family, mainly, it seems, because he had grown too large. He reappeared in another series at another studio as Bomba the jungle boy.

The most interesting thing about Weissmuller was how his portrayal of Tarzan paralleled, but did not really match, the ape-man imagined by Chicago-born Edgar Rice Burroughs (1875–1950), a resolutely minor but prolific talent whose creation was an unimaginable, totally unlikely hodgepodge of polymorphous perversity. Burroughs was obviously influenced by *Robinson Crusoe,* Kipling's Mowgli, and Jack London. For the most part, the heroes of his Tarzan novels are always "grey eyed," tall Anglo-Saxons; their heroines less emphatically WASP ladies with sinewy, clinging bodies, "feminine" to a fault. The villains are unfailingly males—East European Jews, Arabs, blacks—women being almost completely exempted from evil or sin.

Tarzan is the son of an English aristocrat, Lord Greystoke, and Lady Alice, his wife. They are shipwrecked off the coast of Africa and then killed by a band of apes, one of whom, Kala, has recently lost her child. Kala takes the puling infant from the cabin's debris and turns Tarzan into her surrogate son: as he grows older he is always at a disadvantage, as much because he is hairless and relatively small compared with the other young apes as because he is the butt of the tribe's jokes and abuse. During one of his solitary forays, Tarzan discovers his parents' cabin and laboriously teaches himself to read and write from the books and papers left there. This growing capacity for self-consciousness and knowledge, however, does not relieve him of the ape tribe's unpleasant attentions, until as a young man he is forced to challenge the biggest male, Kerchak, to a fight unto death. Tarzan wins the fight, achieves leadership over the apes, but also realizes that he is not after all an ape. Through clumsily engineered plot coincidences Tarzan meets up with a cousin of his and Jane Porter, as well as with Paul D'Arnot, a French lieutenant who is rescued by Tarzan and gives him a private education to rival John Stuart Mill's. Some of this material appears in the film *Greystoke,* a recent but unsuccessful attempt to revive the Tarzan story.

Over the years Burroughs turned out twenty-eight Tarzan novels, in which the aristocratic ape-man (who marries Jane in novel two, *The Return of Tarzan*) sires a splendid son—John, whose jungle name is Korak—and has every conceivable kind of adventure, each of which concludes with a triumphant reassertion of Tarzan's power, moral force, authority. The interesting thing about Burroughs's creation is that his novels have a system from which he never deviates. Thus Tarzan is always both the savage ape-man (whose forehead scar, the result of his battle with an insubordinate ape in volume one, always turns red when he gets angry) as well as the voluble and learned John Clayton, Lord Greystoke. In the jungle world the anthropoids, men included, are divided into several related species: the Tarmangani, or white men; the Mangani, or great apes; the Bolgani, or gorillas; and Gomangani, or local blacks. Tarzan is often accompanied by a little monkey (not a chimpanzee), Nkima; in one novel he rescues and becomes the friend of a magnificent black-maned lion, Jad-Bal-Ja, who often goes on adventures with him. Most of the jungle animals have names (Tantor the elephant, Histah the snake, etc.) in the ape language that Tarzan learned first; these names are repeated from novel to novel. (An "ape-English" dictionary is provided in Robert Fenton's book *The Big Swingers*.) Tarzan's wealth as an English lord is ensured by the treasures he finds in the lost city of Opar, to which he returns periodically for the replenishment of his coffers and the renewal of his amorous contacts with the tawny La, the high priestess. He has invincible strength, brilliant intelligence, faithful friends and relatives (he is the honorary king of an entire tribe of natives, thus giving himself the black vote in darkest Africa), and seems absolutely ageless. We discover in a late novel that he has had a fountain of youth available to him in one of his Africa domains, so that although he has turned ninety he never appears to be more than thirty-five.

The fascinating thing, however, is that Johnny Weissmuller has nothing at all like the complexity of all this, which aside from being almost unimaginable in visual terms is also intended to be incongruous and antithetical intellectually, like Jekyll and Hyde. Weissmuller is far more mysterious that the novelistic Tarzan, who by comparison is a walking genealogical table. Burroughs was a relentless Darwinian who believed that the white man would come out on top no matter how handicapped he was by nature or by the far superior strengths of lower forms of anthropoid life. Indeed, Tarzan's life and adventures are heavily plotted proof of this dictum, that the white man must triumph because, as Burroughs never tires of telling us, he has Reason. On the other hand, Weissmuller's power and origins are almost totally obscure. We are never told where he comes from, or how he got the way he did: of his wonderful strength and authority over the jungle there is no doubt. He has a special affinity for elephants, who frequently come to his aid en masse, something that does not occur in the novels. Only once in the entire film series (*Tarzan and His Mate,* 1934) is Tarzan shown to be the special friend of apes.

An Olympic champion many times over, Weissmuller was considered the greatest swimmer in the first half of the twentieth century. Unlike any of the other movie Tarzans who followed him, however, he was not at all muscle-bound; until he got older and fatter his swimmer's physique blended perfectly with the general mystery of his origins and the source of his power. Everything about Weissmuller was flowing, harmonious, and natural. There were no unsightly bulges on his biceps or across his abdomen, just as his unself-conscious presence in the jungle was undisturbed by residues of a narrative that might have explained his history. Weissmuller's Tarzan was pure existence, a sort of degree zero transmuted into the figure and motions of an Adonis-like man. Moreover, his monosyllabic utterances resonated with no background, no symbolic system, no special significance. In the twelve films he made Weissmuller pronounced only one non-English word—"umgawa"—which was an order barked rather briskly at animals who would then obey his command to do something specific, like push a tree trunk out of the way. On a few occasions "umgawa" was an angry expostulation used for telling Cheetah, Weissmuller's semi-delinquent chimpanzee companion (for whom there is no exact equivalent in the novels), to go away or to behave. Les frequently "umgawa" was a shout directed at the recalcitrant blacks who people the series, either as threatening savages or as cowering and incompetently subservient porters, servants, coolies.

Whereas Burroughs clearly had a worked-out theory about the hierarchy of races, the film Tarzan as represented by Weissmuller was actually *more* complex in his racial attitudes. Everyone who has seen the films remembers that the treatment of blacks is in the main very hostile. Tarzan spends considerable time fighting native tribes who worship strange gods, kidnap, torture, and cannibalize other human beings, and who generally do not observe the assumed norms of human behavior. Several of these groups, such as the Leopard men (*Tarzan and the Leopard Woman,* 1946), are animal worshipers and deviants; others, like the Ganelonis in *Tarzan Escapes* (1936), are emanations of an almost gratuitous evil. Yet Tarzan's relationships with whites, especially those who visit Africa, are uniformly poor. Most often Tarzan suspects them on sight. He regularly confiscates and destroys their cameras and guns, totally distrusts their schemes (even when Jane intercedes on their behalf), and is routinely the victim of their nefarious designs. White men are hunters, they are slave dealers, they traffic in contraband, and, by the time World War II has rolled around, they are Nazi agents. Weissmuller signifies his disapproval of them most basically when he immediately refuses to help them capture wild animals, not only for exhibition but for scientific purposes. In the one film whose main action is set in the Western (and white) world, *Tarzan's New York Adventure,* Tarzan is shown to be completely at odds with the "normal" world: he cannot wear a suit; he is upset by civilized justice and creates mayhem in a courtroom. He finally eludes the police by diving off the Brooklyn Bridge.

Weissmuller's taciturn opposition to any white outsider does not exactly balance his savagery when dealing with blacks, but at least it is consistent with his general attitude toward the jungle. Although I cannot absolutely vouch for it, I feel practically certain in saying that Tarzan does not actively provoke even the most menacing and appalling of his black antagonists. He encounters them only when for one reason or another he must stray into their territory, and I can recall him saying on one occasion that he would prefer not to do even that. In other words, Weissmuller's position is that of the jungle inhabitant who understands and accepts the system, even when it conflicts with his values or threatens his life. Any intruders or over-reachers are to be opposed and fought because they destroy the finely tuned ecological zero state from which Tarzan himself springs, and which he defends earnestly. So that while Burroughs and the various directors and writers who made the films expressed essentially racist views about "inferior" people, there is an unresolved contradiction between those views and Weissmuller's behavior, which is irreducibly hostile not just to unfriendly (but unjustifiably provoked) blacks but to anything that might introduce change into the ensemble of jungle balance.

One of the strangest and most unlikely partial confirmations of my theory comes from Frantz Fanon, the brilliant anti-imperialist author who was born in Martinique, became a psychiatrist, and then joined the Algerian FLN as one of its leading theoreticians of struggle against French colonialism. He died of leukemia in 1961, one year before Algerian independence was achieved, at just about the time his last book, *The Wretched of the Earth* (with a famous preface by Jean-Paul Sartre), was published. In an earlier book, *Black Skins, White Masks* (1952), Fanon spoke about Tarzan in a footnote, noting that when one of the films was seen in

Martinique everyone in the audience tended to side with Tarzan against the blacks; the same people seeing the film in France feel their black identity much more acutely and are consequently upset by the sight of a white abusing a lot of natives. Tarzan appears as the racial enemy in one setting, whereas in another he is interpreted as a hero who fights to preserve a natural order against those who disturb it.

This is not to deny that Tarzan's world—or rather the world of Weissmuller—is uncomplicated and dangerous, but to say that Tarzan's powers are always adequate to it. It comes as a small surprise to recall that Weissmuller was preceded by a few other screen competitors, none of whom lasted as long as he did or are remembered with anything like his aura. He was the natural hero in an age of heroes with supernatural or extra-human powers, men like Captain Marvel, Superman, Spiderman, whose relatively boring attraction was that they could do things only dreamed of by ordinary men and woman. Weissmuller embodied the man whose entirely human powers allowed him to exist in the jungle with dignity and prestige. This was a matter not just of killing lions and giant snakes (he did that brilliantly) but also of flying through trees like a wonderfully resourceful trapeze artist, or swimming in beautiful lakes (constructed on a back lot in Hollywood) faster than the fastest crocodile, or climbing tremendous heights in bare feet and a loincloth. Surrounded by danger and challenge, Weissmuller was never armed with anything more than a large hunting knife and, on occasion, a lariat plus bow and arrows. In one of the rare ecstatic moments of my early adolescence—I must have been about ten—I recall saying to an older male relative that once in the trees or on his escarpment Weissmuller-Tarzan could hold off twenty or thirty, or maybe even fifty, men on the ground.

Juxtaposed with the wall-to-wall elaborate tackiness of the contemporary world there is an irrelevant beauty to the whole idea of Weissmuller's self-sufficiency and relative silence. Yet I still find it attractively compelling. Remember that Weissmuller seemed to have no life *except* in the Tarzan films. This was before the days of talk shows, of massive television hype, of academic analyses of popular culture. When I saw him in the late 1940s and early 1950s as Jungle Jim—an older, chubbier, and fully clothed man who actually spoke, and seemed to reason, like everyone else— Weissmuller in a sense had already happened and was over. He belonged to the world of Hollywood's fantasy lands: the Orient that was peopled with Jon Hall, Maria Montez, and Sabu (in which Genghis Khan was referred to as "Genghiz Kaahan"); Betty Grable's Hawaii; the roads that led Bob Hope and Bing Crosby to places like Morocco; and Carmen Miranda's Latin America. Weissmuller's African jungle was never filmed on location, but it had a modest integrity, unlike the primitive and mischievous hyperrealism of Schwarzenegger's Conan films, whose relationship (and debt) to Tarzan is similar to the way plastic toys resemble, but are somehow inferior to, wooden toys.

Weissmuller's life after his career as Tarzan was like a grotesque parody of his jungle life—Tarzan lost in civilization, or Tarzan from riches to rags. Four of his five marriages ended in divorce. Most of the money he made was squandered on high living (his drinking problems were notorious), and until his death he was plagued by the IRS. For a time he worked at Caesar's Palace in Las Vegas, but he moved to Fort Lauderdale, where he was honorary curator of the International Swimming Hall of

Fame until a series of strokes in the 1970s left him an invalid. In 1984 he died in Acapulco, a short distance from the beach where his last Tarzan movie, the only one shot outside Hollywood, *Tarzan and the Mermaids* (1948), was filmed.

Certainly the Tarzan films and novels readily lend themselves to the disenchantments of Freudian and Marxist analysis. Tarzan is an infantilized "lord of the jungle," a man whose apparent adult authority is actually undermined by his activities as an overgrown child running around in a bathing suit, escaping grown-up responsibility more or less forever. Tarzan is the embodiment of an unresolved (avoided?) Oedipal tension; this is especially true in the films, where Weissmuller's parentage is not even referred to, leading one to suspect that he did away with both father and mother. Nor does Tarzan's jungle world, with its superficially utopian atmosphere of what Marx called "primitive communism," bear up under scrutiny. He exploits everyone—blacks, animals, women—and does precious little besides. Lolling about in the trees is not the same thing as productive work.

Yet before we throw Tarzan completely away as a useless degenerate without either social or aesthetic value, he ought to be given a chance as what in fact he is, an immigrant. Yes, he belongs to the same epoch that produced traveling imperialists like Lawrence of Arabia, Kurtz in Conrad's *Heart of Darkness* and of course Cecil Rhodes, but despite Hollywood and Burroughs himself, Tarzan is much *less* of a dominant figure than any of those white men. He is vulnerable, disadvantaged, and, because of his lonely silence in the movies, pathetic. Weissmuller's face tells a story of stoic deprivation. In a world full of danger this orphan without upward mobility or social advancement as alternatives is, I've always felt, a forlorn survivor. Quite clearly that is not what Hollywood intended to convey. But it is what still comes through: Tarzan the hero diverted from worldly success and with no hope of rehabilitation, in permanent exile. More unusual still is the fact that Weissmuller's performances as Tarzan are both better and more uncompromising than the novelistic original. Time for a Weissmuller revival.

A CLOSER LOOK AT EDWARD W. SAID

1. In his later writing especially, Edward Said turns to his own personal experiences and memories in order to reflect on larger social and political issues, such as Palestinian struggle and identity. Given that his later work is so often

personal in nature, write an essay in which you explain how Said achieves this social awareness through personal reflection. How does he arrive at the collective while focusing on the personal? In what ways does this strategy strengthen or weaken his purpose?

2. Said writes: "Everyone lives life in a given language; everyone's experiences therefore are had, absorbed, and recalled in that language." Write an essay in which you reflect on the power of language in your own life. In particular, think about the way language has been used to define you and your experiences, and how you have used language to define yourself and others.

3. In the essays collected here, we see Edward Said's range as an essayist. "No Reconciliation Allowed" is more of a personal essay; "The Mind of Winter" and "Jungle Calling" are more academic essays; and "Palestine, Then and Now" is more of a political essay. And yet, as we have noted above, these essays share many thematic patterns. Write an essay in which you analyze how these different essay perspectives (academic, personal, and political) shape the way Said treats his subject and the way you as a reader relate to it. Which of Said's essays, in your opinion, renders most powerfully and convincingly his theme of exile, identity, and loss? Explain your reasoning with examples from the essay.

4. At the end of his essay on writing, "No Reconciliation Allowed," Said cites Theodor Adorno, who writes, "the writer sets up house . . . For a man who no longer has a homeland, writing becomes a place to live." Write an essay that explains what Adorno means in this statement. Then show how this statement is at work in Said's essays. How can writing become a place to live? In what way does Said's writing become a place for him to live? Is such a "place" enough?

Looking from Writer to Writer

1. Like Edward Said, Alice Walker reflects on the power of language. She writes, "it is language more than anything else that reveals and validates one's existence, and if the language we actually speak is denied us, then it is inevitable that the form we are permitted to assume historically will be one of caricature, reflecting someone else's literary or social fantasy." Keeping in mind what Said has to say about language and identity in "No Reconciliation Allowed," compare the views on language of Walker and Said. In what ways are their views similar? How do they differ? What do you think accounts for the similarities and differences in their views?

2. Joseph Epstein, whose essays in this collection you may have read earlier, is known as a guardian of language, calling himself a "language snob." He claims that "the duty of everyone who considers himself educated is to keep language alive by using it with respect and precision." Many of Epstein's essays reflect a running theme that suggests that standards of language have been allowed to be breached when standards of excellence, correctness, and clarity are given up in favor of "political and popular trends." Compare Epstein's views on language with those of Amy Tan, Edward Said, and Alice Walker. How would Tan, Walker, and Said respond to Epstein's claims about the "correctness" of language? What sorts of arguments would they make against such a prescriptive view of language?

3. André Aciman and Edward Said both write about place, identity, and exile, but from different perspectives—Aciman from a Jewish perspective and Said from a Palestinian perspective. In Aciman's case, his exile and subsequent return as a visitor to Alexandria, Egypt, have been the subject of most of his work. He explains, "I write about place, or the memory of place. I write about a city called Alexandria, which I'm supposed to have loved, and about other cities that remind me of a vanished world to which I allegedly wish to return. I write about exile, remembrance and the passage of time." Write an essay in which you compare the notions of exile of Aciman and Said. What do their notions have in common? How and why do they differ? How much of this similarity and difference can be accounted for by their cultural experiences?

Looking Beyond

ESSAYS

Reflections on Exile and other Essays. Cambridge, MA: Harvard University Press, 2000.

NONFICTION

After the Late Sky: Palestinian Lives. 1986. New York: Columbia University Press, 1999.

Beginnings: Intention and Method. New York: Basic Books, 1975.

Covering Islam: How the Media and Experts Determine How We See the Rest of the World. 1981. New York: Vintage Books, 1997.

Culture and Imperialism. New York: Knopf, 1993.

The End of the Peace Process: Oslo and After. New York: Pantheon Books, 2000.

Joseph Conrad and the Fiction of Autobiography. Cambridge, MA: Harvard University Press, 1966.

Musical Elaborations. New York: Columbia University Press, 1991.

Orientalism. 1978. New York: Vintage Books, 1994.

Out of Place: A Memoir. New York: Knopf, 1999.

Peace and Its Discontents: Essay on Palestine in the Middle East Peace Process.
  New York: Vintage Books, 1996.
*The Politics of Dispossession: The Struggle for Palestinian Self-Determination,
  1969–1994.* New York: Pantheon Books, 1994
The Question of Palestine. 1979. New York: Vintage Books, 1992.
Representations of the Intellectual: The 1993 Reith Lectures. 1994. New York:
  Vintage Books, 1996.
The World, the Text, and the Critic. Cambridge, MA: Harvard University
  Press, 1983.

Scott Russell Sanders

Scott Russell Sanders is both a writer and a teacher, and his writing reflects both of those roles. Frequently, Sanders's essays are about the activity of writing; that is, Sanders is conscious of his role as writer, and his role of teacher makes him question what responsibilities writers have and what the act of writing entails. Though Sanders is best known as a "nature writer," we have included here three essays that address the act of writing and specifically the notion of the essay. At the same time, these essays expose readers to Sanders's focus on nature, environment, and bioregionalism. Sanders also carries these same themes to his works in fiction and children's literature. He has written more than 20 books, several of which are collections of his essays.

Sanders was born near Memphis, Tennessee, and the Mississippi River in October 1945—"two months after the bombing of Hiroshima," he writes. He attended Brown University in Rhode Island and claims that he always felt out of place at Brown—a Tennessee/Ohio "hick among sophisticates." Despite his uncomfortableness, or perhaps because of it, Sanders worked hard to fit in and graduated first in his class at Brown. In the fall of 1967, Sanders went to Cambridge University to further his studies. Accompanying him was Ruth Ann McClure, a woman he had known since high school and college. Sanders says that their relationship, founded in the letters they shared, "revealed to me the power in writing." While at Cambridge, Sanders completed his dissertation, a manuscript that would later become his first book, *D.H. Lawrence: The World of the Major Novel,* which Sanders says, reveals as much about him as it does about Lawrence. The same can be said about most of Sanders's writing, which is often grounded in the personal. He often writes about his own life and feelings. While reading the selections here by Sanders, notice how much he reveals of himself while addressing a range of subjects.

After Cambridge, Sanders and his wife returned to the United States to live in the Midwest, the region that they most considered home—and with which they had the deepest connection. Indeed, Sanders is probably best known for promoting the importance of knowing one's home region. This theme is evidenced in the selections by Sanders found here, but it becomes more evident as one moves beyond this short sampling to the wide range of his other writing. He often writes about the history of the Midwest, the plants and animals of that region, and the people who inhabit those places. His book *Wilderness Plots: Tales about the Settlement of the American Land,* for instance, is a collection of short fictional pieces about individuals and the history of settlement in Ohio. In addition to his many books, Sanders's short stories and essays have been published in a variety of publications: *Cambridge Review, Transatlantic Review, Stand, The Ohio Review, Georgia Review, ADE Bulletin, Harper's,* and *Kenyon Review,* to name but a few.

Sanders on Writing

At First Glance

Because Scott Russell Sanders is both a writer and a teacher of writing, his own work often considers the role of writing, particularly the role of the essay, in contemporary America. In the first selection, "The Singular First Person," Sanders discusses the personal essay and the rise of its popularity among contemporary American writers. As you read this essay and the other three essays by Sanders, consider specifically what the genre of the personal essay entails. Consider Sanders's claim that the personal essay is a risky thing to write, a form that exposes the author. Think about the investments that writers place in writing essays, particularly personal essays like those Sanders writes. And think about the investment you place in your writing.

The Singular First Person

The first soapbox orator I ever saw was haranguing a crowd beside the Greyhound Station in Providence, Rhode Island, about the evils of fluoridated water. What the man stood on was actually an upturned milk crate, all the genuine soapboxes presumably having been snapped up by antique dealers. He wore an orange plaid sports coat and matching bow tie and held aloft a bottle filled with mossy green liquid. I don't remember the details of his spiel, except his warning that fluoride was an invention of the Communists designed to weaken our bones and thereby make us pushovers for a Red invasion. What amazed me, as a tongue-tied kid of seventeen newly arrived in the city from the boondocks, was not his message but his courage in delivering it to a mob of strangers. I figured it would have been easier for me to jump straight over the Greyhound Station than to stand there on that milk crate and utter my thoughts.

To this day, when I read or when I compose one of those curious monologues we call the personal essay, I often think of that soapbox orator. Nobody had asked him for his two cents' worth, but there he was declaring it with all the eloquence he could muster. The essay, although enacted in private, is no less arrogant a performance. Unlike novelists and playwrights, who lurk behind the scenes while distracting our attention with the puppet show of imaginary characters, unlike scholars and journalists, who quote the opinions of others and shelter behind the hedges of neutrality, the essayist has nowhere to hide. While the poet can lean back on a several-thousand-year-old legacy of ecstatic speech, the essayist inherits a much briefer and skimpier tradition. The poet is allowed to quit after a few lines, but the essayist must

575

hold our attention over pages and pages. It is a brash and foolhardy form, this one-man or one-woman circus, which relies on the tricks of anecdote, conjecture, memory, and wit to enthrall us.

Addressing a monologue to the world seems all the more brazen or preposterous an act when you consider what a tiny fraction of the human chorus any single voice is. At the Boston Museum of Science an electronic meter records with flashing lights the population of the United States. Figuring in the rate of births, deaths, emigrants leaving the country and immigrants arriving, the meter calculates that we add one fellow citizen every twenty-one seconds. When I looked at it recently, the count stood at 249,958,483. As I wrote that figure in my notebook, the final number jumped from three to four. Another mouth, another set of ears and eyes, another brain. A counter for the earth's population would stand somewhere past five billion at the moment, and would be rising in a blur of digits. Amid this avalanche of selves, it is a wonder that anyone finds the gumption to sit down and write one of those naked, lonely, quixotic letters-to-the-world.

A surprising number do find the gumption. In fact, I have the impression there are more essayists at work in America today, and more gifted ones, than at any time in recent decades. Whom do I have in mind? Here is a sampler: Wendell Berry, Carol Bly, Joan Didion, Annie Dillard, Stephen Jay Gould, Elizabeth Hardwick, Edward Hoagland, Phillip Lopate, Barry Lopez, Peter Matthiessen, John McPhee, Cynthia Ozick, Paul Theroux, Lewis Thomas, Tom Wolfe. No doubt you could make up a list of your own— with a greater ethnic range, perhaps, or fewer nature enthusiasts—a list that would provide equally convincing support for the view that we are blessed right now with an abundance of essayists. We do not have anyone to rival Emerson or Thoreau, but in sheer quantity of first-rate work our time stands comparison with any period since the heyday of the form in the mid-nineteenth century.

Why are so many writers taking up this risky form, and why are so many readers—to judge by the statistics of book and magazine publication—seeking it out? In this era of prepackaged thought, the essay is the closet thing we have, on paper, to a record of the individual mind at work and play. It is an amateur's raid in a world of specialists. Feeling overwhelmed by data, random information, the flotsam and jetsam of mass culture, we relish the spectacle of a single consciousness making sense of a portion of the chaos. We are grateful to Lewis Thomas for shining his light into the dark corners of biology, to John McPhee for laying bare the geology beneath our landscape, to Annie Dillard for showing us the universal fire blazing in the branches of a cedar, to Peter Matthiessen for chasing after snow leopards and mystical insights in the Himalayas. No matter if they are sketchy, these maps of meaning are still welcome. As Joan Didion observes in her own collection of essays, *The White Album,* "We live entirely, especially if we are writers, by the imposition of a narrative line upon disparate images, by the 'ideas' with which we have learned to freeze the shifting phantasmagoria which is our actual experience." Dizzy from a dance that seems to accelerate hour by hour, we cling to the narrative line, even though it may be as pure an invention as the shapes drawn by Greeks to identify the constellations.

The essay is a haven for the private, idiosyncratic voice in an era of anonymous babble. Like the blandburgers served in their millions along our highways, most language served up in public these days is textureless, tasteless mush. On television, over the phone, in the newspaper, wherever humans bandy words about, we encounter more and more abstractions, more empty formulas. Think of the pablum ladled out by politicians. Think of the fluffy white bread of advertising. Think, lord help us, of committee reports. By contrast, the essay remains stubbornly concrete and particular: it confronts you with an oil-smeared toilet at the Sunoco station, a red vinyl purse shaped like a valentine heart, a bow-legged dentist hunting deer with an elephant gun. As Orwell forcefully argued, and as dictators seem to agree, such a bypassing of abstractions, such an insistence on the concrete, is a politically subversive act. Clinging to this door, that child, this grief, following the zigzag motions of an inquisitive mind, the essay renews language and clears trash from the springs of thought. A century and a half ago, in the rousing manifesto entitled *Nature,* Emerson called on a new generation of writers to cast off the hand-me-down rhetoric of the day, to "pierce this rotten diction and fasten words again to visible things." The essayist aspires to do just that.

As if all these virtues were not enough to account for a renaissance of this protean genre, the essay has also taken over some of the territory abdicated by contemporary fiction. Whittled down to the bare bones of plot, camouflaged with irony, muttering in brief sentences and grade-school vocabulary, peopled with characters who stumble like sleepwalkers through numb lives, today's fashionable fiction avoids disclosing where the author stands on anything. In the essay, you had better speak from a region pretty close to the heart or the reader will detect the wind of phoniness whistling through your hollow phrases. In the essay you may be caught with your pants down, your ignorance and sentimentality showing, while you trot recklessly about on one of your hobbyhorses. You cannot stand back from the action, as Joyce instructed us to do, and pare your fingernails. You cannot palm off your cockamamie notions on some hapless character.

To our list of the essay's contemporary attractions we should add the perennial ones of verbal play, mental adventure, and sheer anarchic high spirits. To see how the capricious mind can be led astray, consider the foregoing paragraph, which drags in metaphors from the realms of toys, clothing, weather, and biology, among others. That is bad enough; but it could have been worse. For example, I began to draft a sentence in that paragraph with the following words: "More than once, in sitting down to beaver away at a narrative, felling trees of memory and hauling brush to build a dam that might slow down the waters of time. . . ." I had set out to make some innocent remark, and here I was gnawing down trees and building dams, all because I had let that *beaver* slip in. On this occasion I had the good sense to throw out the unruly word. I don't always, as no doubt you will have noticed. Whatever its more visible subject, an essay is also about the way a mind moves, the links and leaps and jigs of thought. I might as well drag in another metaphor—and another unoffending animal—by saying that each doggy sentence, as it noses forward into the underbrush of thought, scatters a bunch of rabbits that go bounding off in all directions. The essayist can afford to chase more of those rabbits than the fiction writer can, but fewer than the poet. If you refuse to chase any of them, and keep plodding along in a straight line, you and your reader will have a dull outing. If you chase too many, you will soon wind up lost in a thicket of confusion with your tongue hanging out.

The pursuit of mental rabbits was strictly forbidden by the teachers who instructed me in English composition. For that matter, nearly all the qualities of the personal essay, as I have been sketching them, violate the rules that many of us were taught in school. You recall we were supposed to begin with an outline and stick by it faithfully, like a train riding its rails, avoiding sidetracks. Each paragraph was to have a topic sentence pasted near the front, and these orderly paragraphs were to be coupled end-to-end like so many boxcars. Every item in those boxcars was to bear the stamp of some external authority, preferably a footnote referring to a thick book, although appeals to magazines and newspapers would do in a pinch. Our diction was to be formal, dignified, shunning the vernacular. Polysyllabic words derived from Latin were preferable to the blunt lingo of the streets. Metaphors were to be used only in emergencies, and no two of them were to be mixed. And even in emergencies we could not speak in the first person singular.

Already as a schoolboy, I chafed against those rules. Now I break them shamelessly, in particular the taboo against using the lonely capital *I*. Just look at what I'm doing right now. My speculations about the state of the essay arise, needless to say, from my own practice as reader and writer, and they reflect my own tastes, no matter how I may pretend to gaze dispassionately down on the question from a hot-air balloon. As Thoreau declares in his cocky manner on the opening page of *Walden*: "In most books the *I*, or first person, is omitted; in this it will be retained; that, in respect to egotism, is the main difference. We commonly do not remember that it is, after all, always the first person that is speaking. I should not talk so much about myself if there were anybody else whom I knew as well." True for the personal essay, it is doubly true for an essay about the essay: one speaks always and inescapably in the first person singular.

We could sort out essays along a spectrum according to the degree to which the writer's ego is on display—with John McPhee, perhaps, at the extreme of self-effacement, and Norman Mailer at the opposite extreme of self-dramatization. Brassy or shy, center stage or hanging back in the wings, the author's persona commands our attention. For the length of an essay, or a book of essays, we respond to that persona as we would to a friend caught up in a rapturous monologue. When the monologue is finished, we may not be able to say precisely what it was about, any more than we can draw conclusions from a piece of music. "Essays don't usually boil down to a summary, as articles do," notes Edward Hoagland, one of the least summarizable of companions, "and the style of the writer has a 'nap' to it, a combination of personality and originality and energetic loose ends that stand up like the nap of a piece of wool and can't be brushed flat" ("What I Think, What I Am"). We make assumptions about that speaking voice, assumptions we cannot validly make about the narrators in fiction. Only a sophomore is permitted to ask if Huckleberry

Finn ever had any children; but even literary sophisticates wonder in print about Thoreau's love life, Montaigne's domestic arrangements, De Quincey's opium habit, Virginia Woolf's depression.

Montaigne, who not only invented the form but nearly perfected it as well, announced from the start that his true subject was himself. In his note "To the Reader" at the beginning of the *Essays,* he slyly proclaimed:

> I want to be seen here in my simple, natural, ordinary fashion, without strain-ing or artifice; for it is myself that I portray. My defects will here be read to the life, and also my natural form, as far as respect for the public has allowed. Had I been placed among those nations which are said to live still in the sweet free-dom of nature's first laws, I assure you I should very gladly have portrayed myself here entirely and wholly naked.

A few pages after this disarming introduction, we are told of the Emperor Maxim-ilian, who was so prudish about exposing his private parts that he would not let a servant dress him or see him in the bath. The Emperor went so far as to give orders that he be buried in his underdrawers. Having let us in on this intimacy about Max-imilian, Montaigne then confessed that he himself, although "bold-mouthed," was equally prudish, and that "except under great stress of necessity or voluptuousness," he never allowed anyone to see him naked. Such modesty, he feared, was unbecom-ing in a soldier. But such honesty is quite becoming in an essayist. The very confes-sion of his prudery is a far more revealing gesture than any doffing of clothes.

A curious reader will soon find out that the word *essay,* as adapted by Montaigne, means a trial or attempt. The Latin root carries the more vivid sense of a weighing out. In the days when that root was alive and green, merchants discovered the value of goods and alchemists discovered the composition of unknown metals by the use of scales. Just so the essay, as Montaigne was the first to show, is a weighing out, an inquiry into the value, meaning, and true nature of experience; it is a private exper-iment carried out in public. In each of three successive editions, Montaigne inserted new material into his essays without revising the old material. Often the new state-ments contradicted the original ones, but Montaigne let them stand, since he believed that the only consistent fact about human beings is their inconsistency. In a celebration called "Why Montaigne Is Not a Bore," Lewis Thomas has remarked of him that "He [was] fond of his mind, and affectionately entertained by everything in his head." Whatever Montaigne wrote about—and he wrote about everything under the sun: fears, smells, growing old, the pleasures of scratching—he weighed on the scales of his own character.

It is the *singularity* of the first person—its warts and crotchets and turn of voice—that lures many of us into reading essays, and that lingers with us after we finish. Consider the lonely, melancholy persona of Loren Eiseley, forever wandering, for-ever brooding on our dim and bestial past, his lips frosty with the chill of the Ice Age. Consider the volatile, Dionysian persona of D. H. Lawrence, with his incandes-cent gaze, his habit of turning peasants into gods and trees into flames, his quick hatred and quicker love. Consider that philosophical farmer, Wendell Berry, who speaks with a countryman's knowledge and a deacon's severity. Consider E. B. White, with his cheery affection for brown eggs and dachshunds, his unflappable way of herding geese while the radio warns of an approaching hurricane.

E. B. White, that engaging master of the genre, a champion of idiosyncrasy, introduced his own volume of *Essays* by admitting the danger of narcissism:

> I think some people find the essay the last resort of the egoist, a much too self-conscious and self-serving form for their taste; they feel that it is presumptuous of a writer to assume that his little excursions or his small observations will interest the reader. There is some justice in their complaint. I have always been aware that I am by nature self-absorbed and egoistical; to write of myself to the extent I have done indicates a too great attention to my own life, not enough to the lives of others.

Yet the self-absorbed Mr. White was in fact a delighted observer of the world and shared that delight with us. Thus, after describing memorably how a circus girl practiced her bareback riding in the leisure moments between shows ("The Ring of Time"), he confessed: "As a writing man, or secretary, I have always felt charged with the safekeeping of all unexpected items of worldly or unworldly enchantment, as though I might be held personally responsible if even a small one were to be lost." That may still be presumptuous, but it is a presumption turned outward on the creation.

This looking outward helps distinguish the essay from pure autobiography, which dwells more complacently on the self. Mass murderers, movie stars, sports heroes, Wall Street crooks, and defrocked politicians may blather on about whatever high jinks or low jinks made them temporarily famous, may chronicle their exploits, their diets, their hobbies, in perfect confidence that the public is eager to gobble up every least gossipy scrap. And the public, according to sales figures, generally is. On the other hand, I assume the public does not give a hoot about my private life. If I write of hiking up a mountain with my one-year-old boy riding like a papoose on my back, and of what he babbled to me while we gazed down from the summit onto the scudding clouds, it is not because I am deluded into believing that my baby, like the offspring of Prince Charles, matters to the great world. It is because I know the great world produces babies of its own and watches them change cloudfast before its doting eyes. To make that climb up the mountain vividly present for readers is harder work than the climb itself. I choose to write about my experience not because it is mine, but because it seems to me a door through which others might pass.

On that cocky first page of *Walden,* Thoreau justified his own seeming self-absorption by saying that he wrote the book for the sake of his fellow citizens, who kept asking him to account for his peculiar experiment by the pond. There is at least a sliver of truth to this, since Thoreau, a town character, had been invited more than once to speak his mind at the public lectern. Most of us, however, cannot honestly say the townspeople have been clamoring for our words. I suspect that all writers of the essay, even Norman Mailer and Gore Vidal, must occasionally wonder if they are egomaniacs. For the essayist, in other words, the problem of authority is inescapable. By what right does one speak? Why should anyone listen? The traditional sources of authority no longer serve. You cannot justify your words by appealing to the Bible or some other holy text, you cannot merely stitch together a patchwork of quotations from classical authors, you cannot lean on a podium at the Atheneum and deliver your wisdom to a rapt audience.

In searching for your own soapbox, a sturdy platform from which to deliver your opinionated monologues, it helps if you have already distinguished yourself at some other, less fishy form. When Yeats describes his longing for Maud Gonne or muses on Ireland's misty lore, everything he says is charged with the prior strength of his poetry. When Virginia Woolf, in *A Room of One's Own,* reflects on the status of women and the conditions necessary for making art, she speaks as the author of *Mrs. Dalloway* and *To the Lighthouse.* The essayist may also lay claim to our attention by having lived through events or traveled through terrains that already bear a richness of meaning. When James Baldwin writes his *Notes of a Native Son,* he does not have to convince us that racism is a troubling reality. When Barry Lopez takes us on a meditative tour of the far north in *Arctic Dreams,* he can rely on our curiosity about that fabled and forbidding place. When Paul Theroux climbs aboard a train and invites us on a journey to some exotic destination, he can count on the romance of railroads and the allure of remote cities to bear us along.

Most essayists, however, cannot draw on any source of authority from beyond the page to lend force to the page itself. They can only use language to put themselves on display and to gesture at the world. When Annie Dillard tells us in the opening lines of *Pilgrim at Tinker Creek* about the tomcat with bloody paws who jumps through the window onto her chest, why should we listen? Well, because of the voice that goes on to say: "And some mornings I'd wake in daylight to find my body covered with paw prints in blood; I looked as though I'd been painted with roses." Listen to her explaining a few pages later what she is up to in this book, this broody, zestful record of her stay in the Roanoke Valley: "I propose to keep here what Thoreau called 'a meteorological journal of the mind,' telling some tales and describing some of the sights of this rather tamed valley, and exploring, in fear and trembling, some of the unmapped dim reaches and unholy fastness to which those tales and sights so dizzyingly lead." The sentence not only describes the method of her literary search, but also exhibits the breathless, often giddy, always eloquent and spiritually hungry soul who will do the searching. If you enjoy her company, you will relish Annie Dillard's essays; if you don't, you won't.

Listen to another voice which readers tend to find either captivating or insufferable:

> That summer I began to see, however dimly, that one of my ambitions, perhaps my governing ambition, was to belong fully to this place, to belong as the thrushes and the herons and the muskrats belonged, to be altogether at home here. That is still my ambition. But now I have come to see that it proposes an enormous labor. It is a spiritual ambition, like goodness. The wild creatures

belong to the place by nature, but as a man I can belong to it only by understanding and by virtue. It is an ambition I cannot hope to succeed in wholly, but I have come to believe that it is the most worthy of all.

That is Wendell Berry in "The Long-Legged House" writing about his patch of Kentucky. Once you have heard that stately, moralizing, cherishing voice, laced through with references to the land, you will not mistake it for anyone else's. Berry's themes are profound and arresting ones. But it is his voice, more than anything he speaks about, that either seizes us or drives us away.

Even so distinct a persona as Wendell Berry's or Annie Dillard's is still only a literary fabrication, of course. The first person singular is too narrow a gate for the whole writer to squeeze through. What we meet on the page is not the flesh-and-blood author, but a simulacrum, a character who wears the label *I*. Introducing the lectures that became *A Room of One's Own,* Virginia Woolf reminded her listeners that "'I' is only a convenient term for somebody who has no real being. Lies will flow from my lips, but there may perhaps be some truth mixed up with them; it is for you to seek out this truth and to decide whether any part of it is worth keeping." Here is a part I consider worth keeping: "Women have served all these centuries as looking-glasses possessing the magic and delicious power of reflecting the figure of man at twice its natural size." It is from such elegant, revelatory sentences that we build up our notion of the "I" who speaks to us under the name of Virginia Woolf.

What the essay tells us may not be true in any sense that would satisfy a court of law. As an example, think of Orwell's brief narrative, "A Hanging," which describes an execution in Burma. Anyone who has read it remembers how the condemned man as he walked to the gallows stepped aside to avoid a puddle. That is the sort of haunting detail only an eyewitness should be able to report. Alas, biographers, those zealous debunkers, have recently claimed that Orwell never saw such a hanging, that he reconstructed it from hearsay. What then do we make of his essay? Or has it become the sort of barefaced lie we prefer to call a story?

Frankly, I don't much care what label we put on "A Hanging"—fiction or nonfiction, it is a powerful statement either way—but Orwell might have cared a great deal. I say this because not long ago I was bemused and then vexed to find one of my own essays treated in a scholarly article as a work of fiction. Here was my earnest report about growing up on a military base, my heartfelt rendering of indelible memories, being confused with the airy figments of novelists! To be sure, in writing the piece I had used dialogue, scenes, settings, character descriptions, the whole fictional bag of tricks; sure, I picked and chose among a thousand beckoning details; sure, I downplayed some facts and highlighted others; but I was writing about the actual, not the invented. I shaped the matter, but I did not make it up.

To explain my vexation, I must break another taboo, which is to speak of the author's intent. My teachers warned me strenuously to avoid the intentional fallacy. They told me to regard poems and plays and stories as objects washed up on the page from some unknown and unknowable shoes. Now that I am on the other side of the page, so to speak, I think quite recklessly of intention all the time. I believe that if we allow the question of intent in the case of murder, we should allow it in literature. The essay is distinguished from the short story, not by the presence or absence of literary devices, not by tone or theme or subject, but by the writer's stance toward the material. In composing an essay about what it was like to grow up on that military base, I *meant* something quite different from what I mean when concocting a story. I meant to preserve and record and help give voice to a reality that existed independently of me. I meant to pay my respects to a minor passage of history in an out-of-the-way place. I felt responsible to the truth as known by other people. I wanted to speak directly out of my own life into the lives of others.

You can see I am teetering on the brink of metaphysics. One step farther and I will plunge into the void, wondering as I fall how to prove there is any external truth for the essayist to pay homage to. I draw back from the brink and simply declare that I believe one writes, in essays, with a regard for the actual world, with a respect for the shared substance of history, the autonomy of other lives, the being of nature, the mystery and majesty of a creation we have not made.

When it comes to speculating about the creation, I feel more at ease with physics than with metaphysics. According to certain bold and lyrical cosmologists, there is at the center of black holes a geometrical point, the tiniest conceivable speck, where all the matter of a collapsed star has been concentrated, and where everyday notions of time, space, and force break down. That point is called a singularity. The boldest and most poetic theories suggest that anything sucked into a singularity might be flung back out again, utterly changed, somewhere else in the universe. The lonely first person, the essayist's microcosmic "I," may be thought of as a verbal singularity at the center of the mind's black hole. The raw matter of experience, torn away from the axes of time and space, falls in constantly from all sides, undergoes the mind's inscrutable alchemy, and reemerges in the quirky, unprecedented shape of an essay.

Now it is time for me to step down, before another metaphor seizes hold of me, before you notice that I am standing, not on a soapbox, but on the purest air.

Double Take

1. In "The Singular First Person," Scott Russell Sanders claims that "the essayist has nowhere to hide" and that the essay is "a brash and foolhardy form, this one-man or one-woman circus, which relies on the tricks of anecdote, conjecture, memory, and wit to enthrall us." Given this claim, why do you think Sanders writes in the essay form? Since the essayist has nowhere to hide and the essay is a rhetorical site constructed by the author, how does the essay structurally prevent the essayist from being able to hide?

2. Why does Sanders think so many writers in America today write in the essay form? Does Sanders's assessment seem to apply to other writers you have read?

3. If, as Scott Russell Sanders writes, "whatever its more visible subject, an essay is also about the way a mind moves, the links and leaps and jigs of thought," what

might "The Singular First Person" suggest about Sanders's own thinking? How are these links and leaps and jigs rhetorically negotiated—that is, how are these maneuvers actually made in this essay?

4. To what extent does Sanders's definition of "essay" fit with the definition you are beginning to develop for yourself?

At First Glance

In "Writing from the Center," Scott Russell Sanders writes, "let me say as plainly as I can what I am seeking. I would like to know where authentic writing comes from." To search out the answer to this question, Sanders turns to the metaphor of guide and follower and asks where a writer fits. Consider not only how Sanders addresses issues of home and regionalism while discussing where writers fit, but how his writing itself is an exercise in regionalism. While you read "Writing from the Center," ask yourself what strategies Sanders uses in the piece to "center" and "locate" his writing within larger conversations and explorations of the questions he seeks to answer.

Writing from the Center

In Kenya, a man hungry for sweetness walks into a clearing and blows a few notes on a whistle. Soon a bird flutters at the edge of the clearing, chatters loudly, then flies a short distance into the woods. The man follows, carrying an ax. When the man draws near to where the bird has perched, it flies again, and the man follows. And so they move into the forest, on wing and foot, until they come to a tree the bird has chosen. If the man walks too far, the bird circles back, circles back, until at last the man discovers the right tree. He chops a hole in the hollow trunk and lifts out the dripping combs, gathering honey for tongues back home. The bird eats what the man leaves behind, honey and bee larvae and wax. So bird and man serve each other, one pointing the way and one uncovering the sweetness.

The bird belongs to a cluster of species called honey guides. The man belongs to a tribe that has known for generations how to summon, how to follow, and how to honor these helpers. No one can say how the cooperation came about, whether birds taught humans or humans taught birds, but it has lasted as long as the tribe's memory. Seek in a proper manner, these people know, and you will be reliably led.

For a writer, the search is more chancy. You cannot be sure what clearing to enter, what notes to whistle. Moved by nameless hungers, armed with words instead of an ax, you slip into the forest, avoiding the trails because so many others have trampled them, following a bird that refuses to show itself, a bird that may be leading you astray, a wild goose instead of a honey guide. You may never find the hollow tree, may wander lost for weeks or years, forgetting why you set out. And even if you do find the tree, it may be filled with bitterness rather than sweetness, and the bees may rush out and sting you. Still you wander the woods. What lures you? How do you know when you have found the hidden food that will satisfy your hunger? And if in a rare hour you find the source, how do you speak of it, how by mere words can you drag the slippery essence into light?

Setting aside metaphor briefly—only briefly, because metaphors are the elusive birds that lead me on—let me say as plainly as I can what I am seeking. I would like to know where authentic writing comes from; I would like to know the source of those lines that are worth keeping, the writing that brings some clarity and beauty into the confusion of our lives. I know all too well the sources of phony, forgettable writing—mimicry, trickery, exhibitionism, habit, reflex, fashion, whimsy, conceit.

But already in my plain statement there is a wrinkle, for who is to judge which lines are phony and which are authentic? The writer, to begin with, and then the reader. If you hope to write well, and not merely transcribe whatever drifts through your head, you must distinguish the honest from the dishonest, the deep from the shallow, by testing each line against all that you have read or thought, all that you have lived through. The reader never sees more than a tiny portion of what the writer could have passed along—and a good thing, too. Of the sentences that come to me, I throw away a hundred for every one I keep, and perhaps I should throw away a thousand; I wait for a sentence that utterly convinces me, then I wait for another and another, each one building upon all that went before and preparing for all that follow, until, if I am patient and fervent and lucky enough, the lines add up to something durable and whole. My business here is to say what I have come to understand, through my own practice, about the source and conditions for such writing.

In America, during the past century or so, we have expected worthy writing to come from the margins—of the psyche, of the community, of the continent. We have expected the writer to be a misfit, an outsider, a stranger in strange lands, uprooted, lonely and lorn. We have often taken moodiness, madness, or suicide to be evidence of genius. We have celebrated the avant-garde, as though writers were soldiers. We have praised the cutting edge, the experimental, the new, as though literature were a kind of technology. We have assumed that talent would either be born on the coasts or be drawn to them, toward the shining Atlantic or Pacific, away from the dark interior.

Literature may come from the edge, of course; but to believe that it comes *only* from the edge is a damaging myth, an especially beguiling one for young writers who are insecure about their background and eager for sophistication. In my own first attempts at writing I blundered far enough toward the edge to lose my way. I was born in the Mississippi Valley and reared in the Ohio Valley, deep in that dark interior from which writers are supposed to emigrate. In the 1960s I left the Midwest to attend graduate school in New England, then left America to attend graduate school in Old England. When I began writing earnestly I was living in Cambridge, and I had the impression that true art could only be made far from the numbing influence of one's home ground, in exile and rebellion. Didn't Eliot, Pound, Hemingway, Fitzgerald, Stein, and Baldwin leave the United States for

Europe? Didn't Joyce and Beckett leave Ireland? Didn't Conrad leave Poland and Nabokov leave Russia? Didn't Lawrence shake the dust of England from his heels and roam the world?

Reasons for quitting America were not hard to find: the Vietnam War, the nuclear arms race, riots in the cities, squalor in the countryside, the cult of money and power, the blight of advertising, the idiocy of television, the assault on air and water and soil. England and Europe were just as tainted, I soon realized, but their ills were not my responsibility. I could live abroad without feeling called upon to join in the work of healing. And wasn't that the ideal writer's stance, as Joyce taught by word and example, to stand aloof from the human fray, paring one's fingernails, disentangled, free?

During my four years at Cambridge I wrote steadily and badly, in tortured sentences, about expatriates and drifters. In bleak times I thought of suicide—who hasn't?—and in genial times I struck poses. I learned the poses from biographies of writers who had scorned their home places, had leapt from bridges or boats, had breathed gas in rented kitchens, had taken to drink or drugs or dalliance, abandoning spouses and children, betraying friends, consuming self and others for the sake of the work, as though the poems or novels or plays were so many precious lumps of charcoal left from the burning of a forest. My posing never gave way to serious action, because I had no stomach for alcohol or betrayal. I knew that writers are supposed to be eccentric, but I could not force myself to go very far off-center. I could not persuade myself that anyone else should suffer for the sake of my writing. As it turned out, I could not even bear exile.

When I finished my degree I applied for a teaching position at a university in the south of England, and to my surprise I was offered the job. Teaching jobs were so scarce, the officials expected me to say yes on the spot, as I had every intention of doing; but when, at the end of a wearisome day of interviews, the chancellor smiled behind his rimless spectacles and put the choice before me, to stay there and make a career in England, I trembled and said no. For all my dismay over America, for all my infatuation with literary exile, I could not become an expatriate. The gravity of home was too strong.

On the train ride back to Cambridge, shaken by my decision, I began remembering the neighbors from my country childhood who had lost jobs, the discouraged men, the bruised women, the hungry kids begging food at school, patches on their clothes, rain leaking through the roofs of their shacks, hurt leaking from their voices. Instead of fretting over my own future, I sat on the train making notes about those faces, recovering those voices, recalling stories from the Ohio Valley, describing people and places I thought I had left forever, and in that way, ambushed by memory, I finally wrote a few lines worth keeping.

Those four years in England were also the opening years of a marriage that seemed a wonder and blessing to me, as filled with trials and revelations as any trek to the Pole. Ruth and I had known one another since before we were old enough to drive. We had courted chiefly through the mail, exchanging hundreds of letters. The desire to impress her on the page with my flair and affection had given me the first powerful incentive to write well. It seemed miraculous that she had become my wife, my companion in daily discoveries, my fellow traveler. We looked forward to having children, buying a small house with a bit of garden out back, sharing work and neighbors, settling down. The country of marriage, as Wendell Berry calls it, was more vivid to me in those years than any country defined by maps.

So I was troubled when I came across Flaubert's advice to a friend: "Stay always as you are, don't get married, don't have children, get as little emotionally involved as possible, give the least hold to the enemy. I've seen what they call happiness at close quarters and I looked at its underside; to wish to possess it is a dangerous mania." I could not imagine being more deeply involved with another person, waking and sleeping, than I was with Ruth, nor could I believe that made her the enemy of my art. And yet Flaubert's warning was echoed by Turgenev: "It is not a good thing for an artist to marry. As the ancients used to say, if you serve a Muse, you must serve her and no one else. An unhappy marriage may perhaps contribute to the development of talent, but a happy one is no good at all."

If those two crusty old bachelors were the only ones who thought that writers should be loners, I could simply have ignored what they had to say. But Flaubert and Turgenev were voicing the dogma of a sizable denomination in the Church of Literature, a sect whose members are mostly but not exclusively male. The dogma holds that if you are to be a serious writer, a writer for the ages, a writer to be reckoned with in the hall of fame, then you must sacrifice everyone and everything else to your work. Resist all other claims on your mind, your emotions, your loyalties. Love art with all your heart. Stand apart.

A writer need not be single in order to believe in the virtues of detachment. Emerson, for example, though very much the paterfamilias, confided to his journal that "the writer ought not to be married, ought not to have a family. I think the Roman Church with its celibate clergy & its monastic cells was right. If he must marry, perhaps he should be regarded happiest who has a shrew for a wife, a sharp-tongued notable dame who can & will assume the total economy of the house."

Here the terms of the choice are clearly masculine: the writer should become either a monk, entirely devoted to the word, or else a literary prince, waited on hand and foot by the sort of helpmate whom Conrad, alluding to his own wife, called "a silent, watchful, tireless affection." The writer's wife need not be silent, Emerson suggests, so long as she not be lovable. Let her be a shrew, but a good manager. Then while the uncaptivating mistress runs the house, the master may compose in solitude, emerging only to deliver manuscripts or to pat the children on the head.

For all the masculine tinge of those pronouncements on marriage, there is more than male arrogance behind the yearning for detachment. Some female writers have imagined themselves as nuns, in the manner of Emily Dickinson; many have remained single, as did Jane Austen, Willa Cather, and Flannery O'Connor; others, including Kate Chopin and Isak Dinesen, have come into their own as writers only after the end of marriage; and a few at least of the married ones have turned husbands and children into acolytes. Women have had to tug harder and longer to open doors into rooms of their own; but the desire for such a room, for the uncluttered space of mind, for the freedom to pursue one's imaginings without restraint from any other soul, is neither male nor female.

In "Silences," a much-quoted statement about the conditions for writing, Tillie Olsen argues that "substantial creative work" can be produced only when "writing is one's profession, practiced habitually, in freed, protected, undistracted time as needed, when it is needed. Where the claims of creation cannot be primary, the results are atrophy; unfinished work; minor effort and accomplishment; silences." It would be hard for any writer who has tried juggling job and marriage and art to disagree with Olsen; and yet her argument begins to sound ominous when she sums it up by quoting Kafka: "Evil is whatever distracts." The patients of Chekhov or William Carlos Williams must have been distracting, and likewise the death-camp mates of Primo Levi, the friends of Nadine Gordimer suffering from apartheid, the students of Theodore Roethke and Denise Levertov, the war comrades of Tim O'Brien, the enslaved ancestors of Toni Morrison, the husbands or wives of other writers, the grandparents, the daily news, the hummingbird at the feeder, the violet in the grass, the rising moon, the great worrisome world with its needs and splendors. If whatever distracts is evil, then we are back to Flaubert's advice, that the writer should flee as from an enemy anyone or anything that makes an emotional claim.

Marriage means—in the usual course of things—children, in-laws, neighbors, mortgages, insurance, furniture, quarrels: it means being snarled in the world, being *answerable*. What writer, embroiled in family and household and job, has never dreamed of stealing away into seclusion? What writer of either sex has not sometimes yearned, as Emerson phrased it, "to be released from every species of public or private responsibility"? No bills to pay, dishes to wash, deadlines to meet, no oil or diapers to change, no ringing phones or barking dogs, no letters to answer or drains to unclog, no one and nothing to contend with except the work at hand. Arts colonies thrive because they offer just such a release, however temporarily. If anyone out there has labored at writing without ever craving such freedom, please will your brain to science, so that we might discover the secret of your serenity.

Of course it is easier to make books if you are single, childless, and looked after by servants, especially if you also enjoy a private income. Yet Flaubert, Turgenev, Emerson, Olsen, and other advocates of the unencumbered life argue not merely that such a life will be easier but also that the fruits will be finer. They are saying that books made in splendid isolation will be superior to those made in the midst of family. If the family is afflicted with happiness, so much the worse, for joy will lull you to dullness. Do not go gentle into that delight, the champions of detachment warn us. Do not become entangled. Love nothing except your work, lest you confuse the Muse. Be single-minded, ruthless, aloof.

There is a seductive purity in that vision of the writing life, as there is in any life consecrated to a single labor. Yet for anyone who, in spite of Flaubert's caveat, cannot help being "emotionally involved," for anyone who relishes the moil of marriage, it is also a limiting vision. Thoroughly wedded to Ruth, I have never desired to become Ruth-less, neither during those Cambridge years nor at any time since. Nor would I, having become a father, choose to be childless, even though my mind and mood sway in the most distracting sympathy with the movements of my children.

Instead of regarding marriage as a hindrance, I have come to see it as the arena where I wrestle with concerns that are as old as our species. That is what Gary Snyder means, I believe, when he speaks in *The Real Work* of family as "the Practice Hall." From his time in Zen monasteries and fire towers, Snyder understands the virtues of solitude; but he also understands the virtues of companionship. "I have a certain resistance," he explains, "to artificially created territories to do practice in, when we don't realize how much territory for practice we have right at hand always." The goal of the writer's practice is the same as anyone else's: to seek understanding of who and where and what we are, to come fully awake. If you are well married, sharing a life and not merely a bed or a bank account, then family may become your territory for doing the real work—spiritual as well as practical—of being human.

When I said no to the offer of a teaching post in England, it was a married man's decision, for Ruth had even less of a desire than I did to become an expatriate. As a scientist, she had never succumbed to the Romantic notion that creativity flourishes only on the margins, in wandering and exile. Nor did she see any reason why a person could not make discoveries in the middle of the country as well as on the coasts. So when I was offered jobs back in America beside the shining Atlantic and Pacific, Ruth persuaded me to turn them down in favor of one in her home state of Indiana, in Bloomington, where she had studied chemistry. Southern Indiana was in the Ohio Valley, she pointed out, so the people and houses and churches and landscape would remind me of the places where I had first paid attention to the world.

As soon as we unpacked our bags in Bloomington, I set out to explore the neighborhood, to learn its ways and wildflowers, to hike the trails, drive the back roads, listen and watch. I bought Geological Survey maps and traced the contour lines. I sat in on trials at the courthouse. At the farmer's market I found out what to plant in our yard. On street corners, park benches, and parlor sofas I heard local tales and songs. I read graffiti in the alleyways, gravestones in the cemeteries, gravels in the creekbeds. In dirt and rocks, in museums and books, I studied the history of my region, beginning with the ancient oceans, on through periods of mountain-building and glaciation, through ten thousand years of civilization by native people, centuries of European exploration and settlement, the clearing of forests, homesteading, farming, manufacturing, the spread of canals and railroads and highways, the rise of cities, right up to my own tumultuous time. In all these explorations, I was not following a literary strategy, I was following my nose—or, to invoke a more elegant organ, my heart. Weary of travel, I was glad to give up being a visitor and ready to become an inhabitant. I wished to make my new home ground the ground of my imagination.

The impulse to marry a place, like the impulse to marry a person, runs against the grain of much writerly advice. In *The Triggering Town,* to choose an influential example, Richard Hugo urges us to avoid writing about our own neighborhoods, and to write instead about strange towns, where we feel no "emotional investment," where we are constrained by "no trivial concerns such as loyalty to truth, a nagging consideration had [we] stayed home." As an outsider a sort of literary tourist, you need be faithful only to your words. "You owe reality nothing," Hugo insists, "and the truth about your feelings everything." Surely that is an odd disjunction, to set feelings against reality, as if the writer's imagination were sealed inside a floating bubble. Hugo does acknowledge that "after a long time and a lot of writing you may be able to go back armed to places of real personal significance." But by that time you may well have been confirmed in the role of literary tourist, one who wanders in search of material, as the strip miner hunts for coal or the timber cruiser hunts for board feet.

Whitman envisioned the American land as a patchwork of neighborhoods, but also as an expanse to be overcome. In our view of the continent, there has always been this tension between an attachment to place and a yearning to conquer distances. Our frenzied building of roads, our restless mobility, our taste for the standardized fare of franchises are all expressions of this anxiety about wide open spaces. The net effect of Whitman's rhetoric, if not his biography, was to glamorize the mover at the expense of the settler. Much of our literature is the work of earnest pilgrims, idle drifters, travelers who write from a distance about places they have abandoned, or nomads who write about no place at all.

I am more attracted by the examples of American writers who, sometimes after periods of wandering, have settled down and rooted their art in a chosen place: most famously Thoreau, of course, in Concord; Faulkner in his patch of Mississippi, Eudora Welty in hers; William Carlos Williams in Rutherford, New Jersey; Flannery O'Connor in Milledgeville, Georgia; Grace Paley in New York City; Wendell Berry on his farm beside the Kentucky River; Ursula Le Guin amidst the rain and rhododendrons of western Oregon; Gary Snyder in the Sierra foothills of northern California; Mary Oliver on Cape Cod. Each of these writers possesses a "locus of the imagination"—to borrow a phrase from the Dakota poet Thomas McGrath—and each one has engaged in a lover's quarrel with his or her place, seeing it critically in light of knowledge about other places and other possibilities.

Even though her white skin has at times made her feel unwelcome as well as guilty in her homeland, Nadine Gordimer has chosen to stay in South Africa to use her intelligence and imagination in the struggle for a free society. "One thing is clear," Gordimer insists, "ours is a period when few can claim the absolute value of a writer without reference to a context of responsibilities." It is striking, how directly she contradicts Emerson's desire "to be released from every species of public or private responsibility." In an age of totalitarian politics and coercive mass media, those responsibilities include giving voice to the silent, upholding the integrity and precision of language, speaking truth to power.

By chance and necessity, Pablo Neruda lived in a good many countries, and yet, according to his *Memoirs*, he never let go of his native land, and the land never let go of him. When his period of foreign service and political exile was over, he returned to Chile:

> I believe a man should live in his own country and I think the deracination of human beings leads to frustration, in one way or another obstructing the light of the soul. I can live only in my own country. I cannot live without having my feet and my hands on it and my ear against it, without feeling the move-

ment of its waters and its shadows, without feeling my roots reach down into its soil for maternal nourishment.

For writers who are firmly in place, the metaphor of roots is inescapable. "Nothing can grow unless it taps into the soil," William Carlos Williams tells us in his *Autobiography*. To put down roots does not mean, however, that one can no longer budge. Our legs were made for walking, as the heartbreak songs proclaim. But instead of walking away from our messes and confusions, as Americans have traditionally done, instead of rambling forever toward pay dirt or sunset, aimless as tumbleweed, we need to move in loops, out and back again, exploring our home ground, as owls or foxes or indigenous people explore the territory they use for hunting, gathering, mating, and play.

The writer who is steadfast rather than footloose risks being dismissed as regional or quaint. What could be more backward than staying put in a culture that rushes about? How can you see the big picture from a small place? I find the beginnings of an answer in the word *stead* itself, which derives from an Indo-European word meaning to stand. To be steadfast is to stand by someone or something, out of a conviction that what you are committed to is worth loving and defending. A homestead is a place where one makes a stand. A farmstead in the Midwest is typically a huddle of sheds and barns and silos around a house, with trees for shade in summer and for windbreak in winter, surrounded by hundreds of acres of pastures or cultivated fields, like a tiny human island in a fertile sea. Whenever I see those farmsteads, I sense the smothering isolation, but I also sense the gathered purpose.

Knowledge of how one's region fits into larger patterns is the surest defense against parochialism. "Being regional, being in place, has its own sort of bias," Gary Snyder concedes, "but it cannot be too inflated because it is rooted in the inviolable processes of the natural world." We need to recover the ancient sense of homeland as an area defined not by armies and flags, not by religion or race, but by nature and geography and by the history of human dwelling there, a habitat shared with other creatures, known intimately, carried in mind as a living presence.

The effort to know and care for and speak from your home ground is a choice about living as well as writing. In that effort you are collaborating with everyone else who keeps track, everyone who works for the good of the community and the land. None of us is likely to fulfill the grand ambition of Joyce's young artist, Stephen Dedalus, to forge in the smithy of our souls the conscience of our race; but we might help form the conscience of a *place,* and that seems to me ambition enough for a lifetime's labor. Trees tap into the soil, drawing nourishment and returning fertility. Capturing sunlight, breaking down stone, dropping a mulch of leaves, replenishing the air, trees improve the conditions for other species and for the saplings that will replace them. So might writers, through works of imagination, give back to the places that feed them a more abundant life.

By choosing to settle in the Midwest, far from the mythical cutting edge and the actual publishing houses, I made another unfashionable decision. Every young writer I knew in my wandering years wished to live in London or Paris, New York or Boston, San Francisco or Los Angeles. My friends asked me what on earth I would do way out there in Indiana. Whom would I talk with? How would I keep my mind alive? Did Hoosiers give a hoot about literature? Booth Tarkington had left Indiana to seek fame and fortune elsewhere, and so had Theodore Dreiser, Kenneth Rexroth, and Kurt Vonnegut. But what writer of consequence had ever *moved* there? At age twenty-five, a writer of no consequence whatsoever, I could not answer those questions.

I found little support for my decision in books. The most celebrated literature about the Midwest has been written by those who left—Mark Twain, Willa Cather, Sherwood Anderson, Sinclair Lewis, Ernest Hemingway, Wright Morris, Toni Morrison—and who made a case for their leaving. You can read variations on the case in *Adventures of Huckleberry Finn, Main Street* or *Winesburg, Ohio,* in *My Ántonia* or *Sula;* the Midwest is a realm of rich soils and pinch-penny souls, a country of raw farms and small towns and grubby industrial cities, populated by gossips and boosters and Bible-thumpers who are hostile to ideas, conformist, moralistic, utilitarian, and perpetually behind the times.

There is enough truth in this portrait for it to be commonly mistaken for the whole truth. Midwesterners themselves often accept the grim account, apologizing for living where they do, expecting culture to arrive from far away, like tropical fruit, and looking askance at anyone who makes art in their own neighborhood. If you were any good, they say to the writers in their midst, wouldn't you be somewhere else? Wouldn't you be living within a taxi-ride of the talk show studios? Wouldn't you be rubbing elbows with literary movers and shakers in those glitzy settings where folks move and shake? No offense, now, but if you were serious, wouldn't you abandon this homely country for someplace more inspiring?

Midwesterners buy the same environmental calendars that other Americans buy, we browse through the same books of landscape photographs, watch the same dazzling wilderness expeditions on film, and from all of those images we learn that real nature, like real culture, is somewhere else. Real nature means the sort of thing you see on posters—mountains and old growth forests, painted deserts, buttes, hot springs, volcanoes, glaciers, rocky coasts and white-water streams—and for scenery like that you have to drive a long, long way. The Midwest does not often show up on posters. It is a modest, subtle, working landscape. Yet even in this country of prairies and glacial plains and wooded hills, wilderness wells up everywhere, in the midst of towns, inside closed rooms, within our own bodies. No matter where we live, the energy of creation flows in each of us, every second. We can feel it in heartbeat and dream and desire; we can sense it in everything that grows, from bacteria to beech trees, from babies to butterflies.

Since well before the Civil War—when Audubon began sketching birds along the Ohio River and Sam Clemens opened his eyes and ears to life on the Mississippi—the Midwest has been feeding the imaginations of writers. It has begun feeding their bellies in a more dependable way during the past few decades, as universities and arts councils have become patrons of the arts. Only recently, however, in fits and starts, here and there, has the Midwest begun to nourish its writers with a sense of purpose, a sense of doing work that matters in a region that matters.

Many readers still welcome reports from the interior of other continents—the secret depths of the Himalayas, the heart of Africa, the Australian outback, the Amazon jungle, the Russian steppes—while neglecting reports from the interior of our own continent. The pundits who define literary fashion may continue to think of the Midwest, if they think of it at all, as the blank space over which one must tediously fly on the way to somewhere important. The blank spaces are not on the land, however, they are in our minds. Life struggles and blossoms and mutates here as it does everywhere. We will never know the whole truth, about this region or any other, but we could use a much fuller account of the Midwest than we have yet received.

If we imagine North America as Turtle Island, to borrow a metaphor from the old people, then out in the Midwest we are on the hump of the shell. Every bit of the shell deserves our attention. Some parts have been intricately carved and painted, filmed and photographed, rendered in prose and poetry, while many other parts have scarcely been noticed. The writer's work is to notice, record, and remember, to inscribe the shell with stories. The surest way of convincing your neighbors that they, too, live in a place that matters is to give them honest and skillful writing about your mutual home.

To be sure, worthy books have been written in exile, in isolation, on the margins of continents, in the precincts of madness. There is much to be said for writing from the edge, and it has been said over and over. In our infatuation with edges, we have scorned the center, a word that carries for me spiritual and psychological as well as geographical meanings. I am suspicious of theories about the writing life that urge us to abandon the common in favor of the exotic, the local in favor of the distant. The truth about our existence is to be found not in some remote place or extreme condition but right-here and right-now; we already dwell in the place worth seeking. I write from within a family, a community, and a landscape, concentric rings of duty and possibility. I refuse to separate my search for a way of writing from my search for a way of living.

Whatever the orthodoxy may be in the larger society, among artists there is a widespread belief that fidelity to anything besides art is foolish. Listen long enough to writers, and you will hear many of them chant, along with Yeats,

> *The intellect of man is forced to choose*
> *Perfection of the life, or of the work,*
> *And if it take the second must refuse*
> *A heavenly mansion, raging in the dark.*

But the choice seems false to me. One's work grows out of one's entire life, including—if those are the choices you have made—the pleasures and struggles of marriage, of fatherhood or motherhood, of householding and citizenship. Yes, in order to work you must withdraw, if only into the room of imagination. But you carry into that private space every scrap of your experience, however acquired.

The Romantic image of the writer as an isolated genius, inventing worlds from scratch, legislating for humankind—an image that seems to rule over much of what passes for "creative writing" in universities—also seems to me a dangerous illusion. We are the servants, not the masters, of words. Language arises from the long human effort to make sense of things, and therefore even the simplest sentence binds us to our fellows, to history, and, by what it designates and celebrates, to the earth.

Early in my explorations of Bloomington I came across a limestone marker half buried in the lawn of the courthouse square and bearing the words, CENTER OF POPULATION USA 1910 CENSUS. When I read the inscription, I visualized a slab in the shape of the United States, with all the citizens of 1910 represented by stick figures, each figure in its appropriate spot, the whole array balancing on a point beneath my town. With the migration of Americans toward the setting sun, the imaginary point has kept moving westward. For a brief spell, however, the citizens of Bloomington could imagine they were living at the center of something, if only of a census map. The limestone marker was a pitch for importance, akin to all those claims one sees on license plates and billboards, naming this village a gateway, naming that state the heart of it all.

According to the historian of religion, Mircea Eliade, humans have always and everywhere imagined their town, their tribe, their temple, their sacred mountain as the center of the world, "the point at which the Creation began." So we have Mecca, Golgotha, Mount Olympus, the holy centers where profane and sacred meet. The very name of Babylon means "gate of the gods." The Lakota people can show you their sacred mountain in the Black Hills. The Hopi believe their ancestors emerged from an earlier, fallen world into the present one through a hole in their homeland, and that hole remains the source of all things. Depending on the gods we worship, those of us who descend from more recent immigrants to America locate our holy centers in Hollywood or Times Square, on Wall Street, Bourbon Street, or Pennsylvania Avenue, on the peak of Mt. Katahdin or the bottom of the Grand Canyon, on the front stoop or in the backyard.

The more geographers reveal about the earth and the more astronomers reveal about the universe, the harder it is for us to believe in the cosmic importance of any particular spot. Viewed from the moon, the grandest metropolis is only a molehill. The earth itself is no more than a speck of grit in a run-of-the-mill galaxy. And our entire galaxy, viewed from a few light years away, dwindles to the size of a struck match. If we fancy that our address gives us unique access to the source of things, we are only flattering ourselves.

None of us lives at the point where the Creation began. But every one of us lives at a point where the Creation *continues.* We ride on a powerful current, and so does everything else we can touch or taste or see. If the current were to falter, the world would cease to be. Because it is steady, because the order of the universe is so dependable, we forget it is there, as we forget the air we breathe. Spiritual practices are ways of recollecting and experiencing this orderly power. Zen sitting, Navajo chanting, Quaker silence, Hopi kachina dancing, the whirling of Sufi dervishes, the postures of yogis, the prayers of Muslims and Christians and Jews, countless varieties of meditation and song, are all techniques for reaching toward the ground of being.

Quakers describe what they experience in the prayerful silence as a "centering down" to spiritual depths, below the chatter and buzz of our normal preoccupations, and they speak of the insights that come to them, the words that rise out of the silence, as "openings." Both of these terms have helped me to understand writing itself as a spiritual practice. Ordinarily the mind is bottled up inside the ego like a firefly in a jar. The jar is cluttered with frets and desires, with calculations and calendars, with the day's doings and the night's fears. Our task is to open the jar, or let it be opened, so that a greater reality may come streaming in.

According to the materialistic philosophy that prevails in literary circles, the universe is an accidental collision of atoms, and the only reality beyond the self is the muddle of rival selves we call society, and art is an ingenious game played with empty tokens. But if there is a transcendent source, as I believe there is, then a literature of slick surfaces, private angst and social manners, of sexual capers and money-chasing and political intrigue, seems not only tedious but deceitful; it wastes our time; it scatters our attention; it fattens us on lies. Art that insistently refers to itself, to its own cleverness and importance, its own materials and procedures, seems petty beside art that points beyond itself to the great sustaining order. The ego is too small an enclosure and too feeble a source for enduring art; the social scene is too shallow. Unless you draw from deeper springs, the work will be thin and vaporous. "Why, thirty or forty skins or hides, just like an ox's or a bear's, so thick and hard, cover the soul," says Meister Eckhart. "Go into your own ground and learn to know yourself there." When we say that a person or a song, a story or a poem has soul, we are acknowledging the presence of more-than-personal meaning and power.

For one who senses depths beyond the self, writing becomes a centering down, an inward listening for openings in the stillness, through which authentic words may come. "I know no advice for you save this," Rilke tells the young poet, "to go into yourself and test the deeps in which your life takes rise; at its source you will find the answer to the question whether you *must* create." If the answer is yes, Rilke says, then "only be attentive to that which rises up in you and set it above everything that you observe about you. What goes on in your innermost being is worthy of your whole love." This may not sound all that different from Richard Hugo's motto: "You owe reality nothing and the truth about your feelings everything." But Rilke is talking about a level deeper than feelings. The depths to which he invites us, the depths from which the individual's life takes rise, are also the source and pattern for everything else. Find your way to that ultimate ground, root your work there, and you will have something worth saying.

Mystics report that every bit of the world radiates from one center—every cricket, every grain of dust, every dream, every image, everything under the sun or beyond the sun, all art and myth and wildness. If they are right, then we can have no more important task than to seek that center. Here is the honey, here is the slippery essence that eludes all language. We dwell midway between two infinities, of the unimaginably large and the infinitesimally small, and between the twin mysteries of birth and death. For better or worse, here we are, in a flickering, fleeting patch of light surrounded by darkness. We have no reliable device for pointing the way to the center of being, as the carpenter's plumb bob points to the center of gravity. We have no maps or birds to guide us there. We have only consciousness, patience, craft.

Double Take

1. Where does Scott Russell Sanders say we have to expect worthy writing to come from in America? Do you agree with him?
2. According to Sanders in "Writing from the Center," why might a writer want to consider not getting married? What can you infer from this suggestion about Sanders's perception of the life of a writer? Does the life of a writer affect how a writer writes? To what extent does your life affect how you write?
3. According to Sanders, what is the goal of the writerly practice? What do you see as the goal of the writerly practice? How has Sanders achieved that writing goal in "Writing from the Center"?

At First Glance

This essay by Scott Russell Sanders is constructed, as the title suggests, in the style of a letter. While the essay does not take on the form of a letter with salutations, greetings, and inside addresses, it does assume the tone of a letter addressed to a specific audience; that is, this essay is written with the audience specifically and consciously in mind. Sanders is speaking to us—the readers. His address is to each of us, not some amorphous idea of audience. While reading this essay, consider how Sanders's language addresses us as readers rather than how we as readers enter his essay as distant gazers upon the work. How does this form shape our relationship with the text?

Letter to a Reader

Since you ask for an account of my writing, I will give you one. But I do so warily, because when writers speak about their work they often puff up like blowfish. Writing *is* work, and it can leave you gray with exhaustion, can devour your days, can break your heart. But the same is true of all the real work that humans do, the planting of crops and nursing of babies, the building of houses and baking of bread. Writing is neither holy nor mysterious, except insofar as everything we do with our gathered powers is holy and mysterious. Without trumpets, therefore, let me tell you how I began and how I have pursued this art. Along the way I must also tell you something of my life, for writing is to living as grass is to soil.

I did not set out to become a writer. I set out to become a scientist, for I wished to understand the universe, this vast and exquisite order that runs from the depths of our bodies to the depths of space. In studying biology, chemistry, and above all physics, I drew unwittingly on the passions of my parents. Although neither of them had graduated from college, my father was a wizard with tools, my mother with plants. My father could gaze at any structure—a barn or a music box—and see how it fit together. He could make from scratch a house or a hat, could mend a stalled watch or a silent radio. He possessed the tinkerer's genius that has flourished in the stables and cellars and shops of our nation for three hundred years. My mother's passion is for nature, the whole dazzling creation, from stones to birds, from cockleburs to constellations. Under her care, vegetables bear abundantly and flowers bloom. The Depression forced her to give up the dream of becoming a doctor, but not before she had acquired a lifelong yen for science. When I think of them, I see my father in his workshop sawing a piece of wood, my mother in her garden planting seeds. Their intelligence speaks through their hands. I learned from them to think of writing as manual labor, akin to farming and carpentry.

I was born to these parents in October, 1945, two months after the bombing of Hiroshima and Nagasaki, so I have lived all my days under the sign of the mushroom cloud. My first home was a farm near Memphis, close enough to the Mississippi to give me an abiding love for rivers, far enough south to give me an abiding guilt over racism. Across the road from our house was a prison farm, where I helped the black inmates pick cotton under the shotgun eyes of guards. My sister Sandra, three years older than I, taught me to read on the screened back porch of that house as we listened to the locusts and the billy goat and the cow. By the age of four I could turn the ink marks on paper into stories in my head, an alchemy I still find more marvelous than the turning of lead into gold.

My birth along the Mississippi, those forlorn black faces in the prison fields, and the country turn of my father's speech all prepared me to be spellbound when, at the age of eight, I climbed aboard the raft with Huckleberry Finn and Jim. That novel was the first big book I read from cover to cover. After finishing the last page, I returned immediately to page one and started over. From that day onward, I have known that the speech of back roads and fields and small towns—*my* speech—is a language worthy of literature. Nor have I forgotten how close laughter is to pain. Nor have I doubted that stories can bear us along on their current as powerfully as any river.

The summer before I started school, my family moved from Tennessee to Ohio, where we lived for the next few years on a military reservation surrounded by soldiers and the machinery of war. This place, the Ravenna Arsenal, would later provide me with the title and central themes for my book of essays, *The Paradise of Bombs.* The move from South to North, from red dirt to concrete, from fields planted in cotton to fields planted in bombs, opened a fissure in me that I have tried to bridge, time and again, with words.

An Army bus, olive drab to hide it from enemy planes, carried us children to a tiny school just outside the chain-link fence. There were thirteen in my class, the sons and daughters of truck drivers, mechanics, farmers, electricians. At recess I learned whose father had been laid off, whose mother had taken sick, whose brother had joined the Marines. From our desks we could see armed guards cruising the Arsenal's perimeter, the long antennas on their camouflaged Chevrolets whipping the air. And in the opposite direction, beyond the playground, we could see horses grazing in a pasture and trees pushing against the sky.

Before I finished the eight grades of that school, my family moved from the Arsenal to a patch of land nearby, and there I resumed my country ways, raising ponies and hoeing beans and chasing dogs through the woods. On local farms I helped bale hay and boil maple syrup. Sputnik was launched in the month I turned twelve, adding to my adolescence the romance of space to go along with the romance of girls. I mixed black powder in the basement and fired model rockets from the pigpen, brooding on the curves of orbits and lips. Our neighbors were mostly poor, living in trailers or tar paper shacks, often out of work, forever on the shady side of luck. Several of those aching people, their lives twisted by fanaticism or loss, would show up in my first book of stories, *Fetching the Dead*.

Many of the adults and some of the children in those trailers and shacks were alcoholic, as was my own good father. Throughout my childhood, but especially in my high school years, he drank with a fearful thirst. Instead of putting out the fire in his gut, the alcohol made it burn more fiercely. This man who was so gentle and jovial when sober would give in to sulks and rages when drunk. The house trembled. I feared that the windows would shatter, the floors buckle, the beds collapse. Above all I feared that neighbors or friends would learn our bitter secret. The pressure of that secret, always disguised, shows up in my early books, especially in *Fetching the Dead* and the novel *Bad Man Ballad*.

I was not able to write openly about my father's drinking until well after his death, in "Under the Influence," the lead essay in *Secrets of the Universe*. As a boy, I felt only bewilderment and shame. Craving order, I hurled myself into one lucid zone after another—the chessboard, the baseball diamond and basketball court, the periodic table, the wiring diagrams of electronics, the graphs of calculus, the formulas of physics. I pitched the baseball so hard I tore up my elbow; I rushed down the basketball court so recklessly I broke my foot against the gymnasium wall; I scrambled so far into mathematics that I could scarcely find my way back; I searched the teeming pool under the microscope for clues that would bind together the tatters of the world.

A scholarship to study physics paid my way to Brown University in Providence, where I spent four years feeling like a country duckling among swans. My classmates arrived with luggage bearing flight tags from the world's airports, wallets bulging with credit cards, voices buzzing with the voltage of cities. These polished men and women seemed to know already more than I could ever learn. My own pockets were empty. My voice betrayed the hills of Tennessee and the woods of Ohio. My devotion to the abstruse games of science marked me as odd. Fear of failing kept me so steadily at my books that I graduated first in my class. I mention the achievement because I am proud of it, but also because I have still not overcome that dread of failure, that sense of being an outsider, a hick among sophisticates.

Standing on the margin, I formed the habit of looking and listening. On the margin, I was free to envision a way of life more desirable and durable than this one that excluded me.

The public turmoil of the 1960s and early 1970s deepened my private confusion. Even though I am the least political of animals, during those college years I was gripped by one cause after another—securing full rights for women and blacks and Native Americans, saving the environment, ending the Vietnam War. All these causes seemed utterly removed from the bloodless abstractions of physics. I began to gasp for air among the crystalline formulas. I longed for the smell of dirt, the sound of voices, the weight of tools in my hands. I grew dizzy with the desire to heal—to heal my father and myself, to comfort the poor and despised, to speak for the mute, to care for the earth.

In this time of great confusion I began keeping a journal. I strung out sentences like guy wires to hold myself upright in the winds of uncertainty. In those creamy pages, I wrote as though my life depended on it—and in a sense it did. Gradually I found words to address the inescapable questions: Who am I? What sense can I make of this inner tumult? How should I live? Does the universe have a purpose? Do we? What finally and deeply matters? What is true, and how can we know? I was too naive to realize that worldly men and women do not brood on such imponderable matters. I brooded. I pondered. I haunted the library, cross-examined the stars, walked the grimy streets of Providence looking for answers. Here science failed me. These mysteries lay in shadow outside the bright circle of scientific method, beyond the reach of gauges or graphs. There were no diagrams for meaning, and I desired meaning with an unappeasable hunger.

Pushed by spiritual hungers and pulled by social concerns, I decided in my junior year at Brown that I could not become a physicist. Then what new path should I follow? I considered history, philosophy, religion, and psychology; but at length I settled on literature, which had been calling to me ever since my sister taught me to read on that porch in Tennessee. All those years I had been living within the curved space of books. I read as I breathed, incessantly. Books lined the walls of my room, they rested on the table beside my pillow as I slept, they rode with me everywhere in pockets or pack, they poured through me constantly their murmur of words. At the age of twenty I still did not imagine that I would make any books of my own, but I knew that I would live in their company.

Another scholarship enabled me to continue my study of literature at Cambridge University. I sailed to England in the fall of 1967 along with my new bride, Ruth Ann McClure. I had met her at a summer science camp when she was fifteen and I was sixteen, the fruity smells of organic chemistry lab in our hair, and for five years we had carried on an epistolary romance. At first we exchanged letters monthly, then weekly, and at last daily, through the rest of high school and all through college. Page by page, this girl turned into a woman before my eyes, and page by page I stumbled on from boy to man.

During those five years, Ruth and I saw one another in the flesh no more than a dozen times. And yet, after exchanging sheaves of letters, I knew this woman more thoroughly, understood more about her beliefs and desires, and loved her more deeply than I would have if I had been living next door to her all that while. Even more than the keeping of a journal, that epistolary courtship revealed to me the power in writing. It convinced me that language can be a showing forth rather than a hiding, a joining rather than a sundering. It persuaded me that we can discover who we are through the search for words. In composing those letters, I was moved by affection for my reader and my subject, as I am still moved by affection in all that I write.

Marriage to Ruth is the air I have breathed now for over half my life. From the richness of marriage, its depths and delights, I have learned the meaning of commitment—to a person, to a place, to a chosen work. Outside of this union I would have written quite different books, or perhaps none at all. To speak adequately of our shared life would require a much longer story; I have made a beginning, but only a beginning, in my fourth book of personal narratives, *Staying Put.*

At Cambridge, once more I was a duck among swans. Once more I felt raw and rough, like a backwoodsman trying to move in the parlors of the gentry without upsetting the tea cart or the vicar. Despite my good marriage, despite my success at Brown, despite the scholarship that had brought me to England, I still needed to prove myself. It seemed to me that all the other students were entering upon their rightful inheritance, while I had to earn, day by day, the privilege of being there.

For the subject of my dissertation I chose D. H. Lawrence. He was another outsider, another scholarship boy, with a father given to drink, a mother given to worry, a childhood divided between ugly industry and beautiful countryside. I was troubled by much of what Lawrence wrote about women, and I despised his authoritarian politics. I grew impatient when he played the shaman or crowed about blood. Yet he knew how it feels to emerge from the hinterland and fight to join the great conversation of culture. He honored the work of hands, whether of colliers or gamekeepers or cooks. He wrote about the earth, about flowers and birds and beasts, with something close to the shimmer of life itself. He knew that we are bound through our flesh to the whole of nature, and that nature may be all we can glimpse of the sacred. The dissertation, much revised, became my first book, *D. H. Lawrence: The World of the Major Novels.* Whatever it may reveal about Lawrence, it says a great deal about me.

On the sly, while pursuing graduate studies, I began writing stories. The earliest of them were clumsy and gaudy efforts to speak of what I found troubling in my own life—the Arsenal, the bombs, the black prisoners on that Tennessee farm, the pinched lives of poor whites in Ohio, my father's drinking, my mother's discontent, the war that was devouring my generation. The stories were clumsy because I was a beginner. They were gaudy because I felt I had to dress up my scrawny experience in costumes borrowed from the great modernists—from Lawrence, of course, but also from Joyce, Woolf, Gide, Proust, Yeats, and Eliot. I fancied that the point of writing was to dazzle your readers, keep them off balance, show them what intricate knots you could tie with strings of words. I suspected that real life occurred only on foreign soil, usually in cities, and among bored expatriates.

I was saved from the worst of these illusions through reading another modernist, a Mississippian like my father, a man haunted by the legacy of racism and by

the sound of American speech. Faulkner inspired me for a spell to even flashier verbal hot-dogging, but, along with Lawrence and Mark Twain, he cured me of thinking that the life I knew on back roads was too obscure or too shabby for literature.
Eventually I stopped showing off, accepted the material that my life had given me,
and began learning to say as directly as I could what I had to say.

During those years in England I formed the habit of rising at five or six, to
write for a couple of hours before breakfast, before looking at the calendar, before
yielding to the demands of the day. The world's hush, broken only by bird song or
passing cars, the pool of light on the table encircled by darkness, the peck of the
keyboard, the trail of ink on paper—these became the elements in a morning ritual
that I have practiced ever since. I wake early in order to write, and I write in order
to come more fully awake.

A few of those stories, written dawn after dawn, found their way into British
magazines, the very first in *Cambridge Review* in 1968, when I was twenty-two, then
others in *Transatlantic Review* and *Stand* the following year. I suspect that the editors
overlooked my feverish style for the sake of my characters—the Mississippi sharecroppers and Ohio prophets and Greyhound bus riders—whom they would never
have met before through Her Majesty's mails. When I received my first check, I was
amazed that a magazine would not only do me the honor of printing my work but
would actually pay me for it. To celebrate, Ruth and I took these unexpected few
pounds and went to see an exhibit of Van Gogh's paintings in London. By 1969 I
was reviewing fiction for *Cambridge Review,* and over the next two years I served as
that magazine's literary editor. My association with this old, illustrious journal, and
my friendship with the young, industrious editors, Eric Homberger and Iain
Wright, were crucial in helping me see my way toward becoming a writer.

With the change left over from my scholarship and with money Ruth earned as
a teacher's aide, we traveled during vacations all over Europe and the British Isles.
For me, these were literary pilgrimages, so that in Ireland I was looking for Joyce
and Yeats, in Wales for Dylan Thomas, in Scotland for Burns. Inevitably, I saw the
Lake District through the lines of Wordsworth and Coleridge, London through
Dickens and Orwell and Woolf, the industrial Midlands through Lawrence, the
southern counties through Wells and James, the western counties through Austen
and Hardy, all of England through Shakespeare. I read Balzac, Hugo, and Sartre in
Paris, Cervantes in Madrid, Kafka in Prague, Günter Grass in Berlin, Thomas Mann
in Venice, Calvino in Rome. Traveling with books, I came to understand that all
enduring literature is local, rooted in place, in landscape or cityscape, in particular
ways of speech and climates of mind.

In 1971, I brought back with me from England a fresh Ph.D. and a suitcase of manuscripts. The degree had earned me several offers of teaching jobs. (I never considered trying to write without holding a job. The unemployed men I had known
while growing up were miserable, humiliated, broken.) I chose to come to Indiana
University because it is in my home region, the Midwest, because it attracts students
with backgrounds similar to my own, and because the people who interviewed me
for the job had gone to the trouble of reading my fiction as well as my criticism.

They wanted me to come, they assured me, even if I turned out to be a writer instead of a scholar. Here I came, and here I have stayed. Of course I travel; I spend months and even occasional years living elsewhere. I hear the call of cities and oceans, mountains and museums. But I keep returning to this terrain, this town, this house, this work. The why and how of that commitment became the subject of *Staying Put*.

Fidelity to place, not common for writers in any part of the United States, may be least common of all in the Midwest. This region is more famous for the writers who have left than for those who have stayed. Samuel Clemens, William Dean Howells, Willa Cather, Ernest Hemingway, F. Scott Fitzgerald, Theodore Dreiser, T. S. Eliot, Sherwood Anderson, Hart Crane, Langston Hughes, Kurt Vonnegut, Robert Coover, Toni Morrison: the list of departed Midwesterners is long and luminous. You don't have to look hard for reasons to leave. The region has not been very hospitable to writers. Vachel Lindsay, who chose to stay and make his poems in Springfield, Illinois, complained of "the usual Middle West crucifixion of the artist." I think he had in mind the grudging, grinding legacy of puritanical religion and agrarian politics: art may shock Grandmother or corrupt the children; you cannot raise art in the fields or mass-produce it in factories, cannot sell it by the pound. Publishers and reviewers, most of whom live on the coasts, often regard the heart of the country as an emptiness one must fly over on the way between New York and California.

The message of all those departures from the Midwest is that life happens elsewhere, in Boston or Paris, in the suburbs of London or San Francisco. Some editors and fellow writers have asked me, directly or indirectly, how I can bear to live in a backwater. I tell them there are no backwaters. There is only one river, and we are all in it. Wave your arm, and the ripples will eventually reach me. For the writer, for anyone, where you live is less important than how devotedly and perceptively you inhabit that place. I stay here in the Midwest out of affection for the land, the people, the accents and foods, the look of towns and lay of farms, for the trees and flowers and beasts. I also stay from a sense of responsibility. Every acre of the planet could use some steady attention. I open my eyes on a place that has scarcely been written about. However great or small my talents, here is where they will do the most good.

Those talents did not bear much fruit during my first years in Indiana. I revised the Lawrence book, which appeared from a London publisher in 1973 and from Viking Press in 1974. On the strength of my few, feverish stories, two senior Viking editors, Marshall Best and Malcolm Cowley, secured for me a modest advance on a first novel. I had been laboring on a novel called *Warchild* since returning from England, but I was at last able to complete it thanks to the generosity of Phillips Exeter Academy, in New Hampshire, where I spent the school year of 1974–75 as writer-in-residence. The hero was a young man suspiciously like myself: born under the sign of the mushroom cloud, reared on an arsenal, conscientious objector during the Vietnam War. In passing, the novel also chronicled the decline of industrial civilization and the death of nature. Thomas Mann in his late years or Tolstoy in his prime might have done justice to my scheme; I could not. In all of its innumerable drafts,

Warchild remained a sprawling, operatic, rambunctious book. Just before I mailed it to Cowley and Best, Viking had been purchased by Penguin, and as a result the lesser contracts, including mine, had become scrap paper., After the gloom cleared, I realized that the world was better off with *Warchild* in a box on my shelf.

While at Exeter, in mourning for my botched first novel, I chanced to read the account of a murder that had occurred in 1813 in the northeastern Ohio county of Portage, where I grew up. A roving peddler was killed in the woods near the county seat. Suspicion immediately fell on the muscular back of a gigantic foundryman who had been carrying the peddler's goods. Two local men volunteered to pursue the giant through the woods. They caught up with him, led him back for trial, and assisted at his hanging. After the burial, three separate groups tried to steal the huge corpse. All this transpired against the bloody backdrop of the War of 1812, amid skirmishes with the English and the Indians. The conjunction of war and wilderness, a fearful village and a mysterious fugitive, set me thinking. The fruit of that thinking, begun in Exeter and carried on intermittently for eight years, was *Bad Man Ballad,* a novel that opens with bird song and closes with human song, veering from history toward myth. The concerns of the book are not so different for those of *Warchild,* for I was still trying to figure out how we had become so violent— toward strangers and neighbors, toward animals and trees and the land itself.

Reading in my haphazard way about the frontier period in the Ohio Valley, hoping to get the feel of history into *Bad Man Ballad,* I kept turning up curious anecdotes about the settlers. An escaped slave, a philosophical cobbler, a savvy farmer, a lovestruck carpenter would be preserved in the dusty chronicles on the strength of a single flamboyant gesture. A few of these worthies made their way into *Bad Man Ballad* as minor characters; but most of them would not fit. Unwilling to abandon them once more to the archives, yet unwilling to interrupt work on my novel long enough to write full stories, I began composing two-page summaries of what I found memorable in these frontier lives.

At first, I thought I would return to elaborate these compressed narratives later on; but I soon found them to be satisfying in all their brevity, with a flavor of ballads and folk tales, forms that have always appealed to me because they cut to the heart of experience. Over the next few years I kept writing these miniature tales in batches, until I had accumulated fifty, spanning the period of settlement in the Ohio Valley, from the Revolution to the Civil War. These were gathered into *Wilderness Plots,* a slim volume for which I feel an ample fondness, in part because it came to me like an unexpected child, in part because, although it was the fourth book of fiction I wrote, it was the first one published.

By now you may have noticed, if you pay attention to dates, that long periods elapsed between the writing of my early books and their publication. This is a fate so common for young writers, and so discouraging, as to deserve a few words here. The latest of the stories in *Fetching the Dead* was completed seven years before that book appeared. *Bad Man Ballad* took five years to reach print and *Terrarium,* my next novel, took four. By the time William Morrow gave me a contract for *Wilderness Plots* in 1982, I had been writing seriously for a dozen years, with only a single book of criticism to show for it. Dawn after dawn I forced myself from bed, hid away in my cramped study, bent over the keyboard, and hammered lines across the blank pages, all the while struggling to ignore the voices of my young children, first Eva and then Jesse, who clamored at the door, struggling to forget the well-meaning questions of friends who asked me whatever had become of this book or that, fighting against my own doubts. Every writer must pass through such seasons of despondency, some for shorter periods, some for longer. Each of us must find reasons to keep on.

What kept me writing? Stubbornness, for one thing—a refusal to give up certain stories, questions, images, and characters. The pleasure of living among words, for another thing. When I was in the flow of work, I felt free and whole. I played the eighty-eight keys of language as a musician improvises on piano, my fingers and ears captured by it, my body swaying. Although it is unfashionable to say so, a good marriage also helped me keep writing. I hid my gloom from everyone except Ruth, who stood by me in the dark, and who urged me to follow my talent, no matter how crooked it was, no matter if the world never took any notice.

In the late 1970s, even while my books languished, my short fiction continued to appear in magazines, mostly quarterlies and reviews. For me, as for many writers of my generation, the magazines—with their underpaid editors working on shoestring budgets—have provided a training ground and a community of readers. In the years when I could but dimly see my way forward, I was greatly encouraged by a handful of editors—Roger Mitchell at *Minnesota Review*, Wayne Dodd at *Ohio Review*, Stanley Lindberg at *Georgia Review*, Robley Wilson at *North American Review*, and Ellen Datlow at *Omni*.

The final item in that list may strike you as out of place. Unlike the others, *Omni* is a glossy production, pays handsomely, and publishes science fiction. After exploring the past in *Bad Man Ballad* and *Wilderness Plots*, I began pushing my questions into the future. Where might our fear of wildness and our infatuation with technology lead us? How far could we carry our divorce from nature? What might keep us from ravaging the earth? According to the arbitrary divisions imposed by critics and publishers, to speculate about the future is to enter the realm of science fiction. And yet, whether set in past or future, all my fiction interrogates the present, which is where we live.

Beginning with a visit to Oregon in 1978–79, and continuing for the next ten years, I wrote a series of stories that appeared in *Omni, The Magazine of Fantasy and Science Fiction, Isaac Asimov's Science Fiction Magazine, New Dimensions,* and several anthologies; and I wrote three speculative novels. The first of these, *Terrarium,* arose from a nightmare image of domed cities afloat on the oceans, all bound into a global network by translucent tubes. Citizens of this Enclosure would pass their whole lives without going outside, without meeting anything except what humans had made. Set over against this claustrophobic image were the green mountains and rocky coast of Oregon, where *Terrarium* was conceived, and where my fictional renegades would try to make a new life. I returned to this Enclosure world in *The Engineer of Beasts,* a novel whose central figure builds robot animals for disneys, the successors to zoos in those denatured cities. The central figure in *The Invisible Com-*

pany, third of my future histories, is a physicist who must come to terms with the lethal consequences of his own early discoveries, while caught in a technological masquerade inspired by Thomas Mann's *Death in Venice.*

As though I had not already violated enough boundaries by writing science fiction, historical fiction, criticism, fables, and short stories, during the 1980s I added personal essays, documentary, biographical fiction, and children's books to my profusion of forms. And why not a profusion? The world is various. Nature itself is endlessly inventive. How dull, if birds had stopped with sparrows and not gone on to ospreys and owls. How dull, if plants had not spun on from ferns to lilacs and oaks. Why squeeze everything you have to say into one or two literary molds for the convenience of booksellers and critics? Anyone persistent enough to read my work from beginning to end will find, beneath the surface play of form, the same few themes: our place in nature, our murderous and ingenious technology, the possibilities of community, love and strife within families, the search for a spiritual ground.

The subject of my biographical fiction is John James Audubon, a virtuoso who combined a number of classic American roles: immigrant, entrepreneur, real estate speculator, salesman, artist, naturalist, frontiersman, and man of letters. He was also a neighbor of mine, in geography and spirit, because he lived for a dozen years in the Ohio Valley and he formed his vision of wilderness in contact with the birds, beasts, rivers, and woods of my region. Although I have sketched a novel about his entire life, from the illegitimate birth in Haiti to senile retirement on the Hudson River, I have thus far been able to imagine freely only his childhood and youth, about which the scholars know few facts. *Wonders Hidden* follows Audubon up to the age of eighteen, when he escaped from France to avoid Napoleon's draft and set out for America, where his name would eventually become a talisman for the protection of wildlife.

I began writing for children in response to an invitation from Richard Jackson, founder and longtime director of Bradbury Press. He liked the narrative flair of *Wilderness Plots* and wanted to know if I had considered telling stories for children. Yes, indeed, I replied, for in those days I was making up stories nightly for my young son and daughter. Then propose something, he said. I offered to write my own versions of the tales that lay behind twenty American folk songs, like "Yankee Doodle" and "John Henry" and "Blue-Tailed Fly," songs my father had sung to me when I was a boy and that I now sang to Jesse and Eva. The result was *Hear the Wind Blow,* a book that runs the gamut from tragedy to farce, rejoicing all the while in our mongrel speech. Also for Bradbury Press, I adapted a pair of stories from *Wilderness Plots* to make two picture books, *Aurora Means Dawn* and *Warm as Wool;* and for Macmillan I have composed a series of tales about the settlement of the Midwest, including, thus far, *Here Comes the Mystery Man, The Floating House,* and *A Place Called Freedom.* Children are a tough audience, refusing to feign an interest they do not feel, and they are also an inspiring one, for they have not lost their delight in the play of words and the shapes of stories, nor their capacity for wonder.

I was lured into writing a documentary narrative by the quirks of my childhood and the accidents of geology. My home in southern Indiana happens to be surrounded by the largest outcropping of premium limestone in North America.

Wherever you see gritty stone buildings the color of biscuits or gravy, from New York's Empire State skyscraper to San Francisco's City Hall, from the Pentagon to the Dallas Museum of Art and Chicago's Tribune Tower, you are probably looking at rock that was quarried and milled in my neighborhood. After a boyhood on farms and construction sites, in munitions loadlines and factories and workshops, I am drawn to men and women who labor with their bodies, using heavy tools to wrestle with raw, stubborn matter. So how could I resist the quarries, with their bristling derricks, or the humpbacked mills with their perpetual grinding, or the stone cutters with their shrewd eyes and skilled hands? In its original version, my portrait of these people and their landscape appeared with photographs by Jeffrey Wolin in a volume entitled *Stone Country,* and then my revised text later appeared as *In Limestone Country.*

Some years earlier, baffled in my work on a novel, I had begun writing another kind of nonfiction, the personal essays that would be collected in *The Paradise of Bombs, Secrets of the Universe, Staying Put,* and *Writing from the Center.* The earliest of these were straightforward accounts of experiences that had moved me—carrying my infant son up a mountain in Oregon, listening to owls beside an Indiana lake. Gradually I enlarged the scope of the essays until they began to disclose patterns in my life that I had never before seen, such as the confrontation between wilderness and technology in "At Play in the Paradise of Bombs," or the legacy of a rural child-hood in "Coming from the Country," or the impact of my father's drinking in "Under the Influence," or the quest for the holy in "Wayland." Although grounded in the personal, all my essays push toward the impersonal; I reflect on my own experience in hopes of illuminating the experience of others.

The challenge for any writer is to be faithful at once to your vision and your place, to the truth you have laboriously found and the people whom this truth might serve. In order to work, I must withdraw into solitude, must close my door against the world, close my mind against the day's news. But unless the writing returns me to the life of family, friends, and neighbors with renewed energy and insight, then it has failed. My writing is an invitation to community, an exploration of what connects us to one another and to the earth.

I love words, yet I love the world more. I do not think of language as thread for a private game of cat's cradle, but as a web flung out, attaching me to the creation. Of course the medium is constantly debased. Television, advertising, government, and schools have so cheapened or inflated language that many writers doubt whether it can still be used in the search for understanding. But knowledge has never been handed to us like pebbles or potatoes; we have always had to dig it up for ourselves. All of culture, writing included, is a struggle over how we should imagine our lives.

Stories are containers in which we carry some of those imaginings. They are the pots and bowls and baskets we use for preserving and sharing our discoveries. Whether in fiction, film, poetry, drama, or essays, stories tell about human character and action, and the consequences of character and action; by making stories and reading them, we are testing ways of being human. It seems idle to protest, as many critics do, that stories are artificial, since everything we make is shot through with artifice. To protest that experience is scattered, not gathered neatly as in stories, is no more than to say that seeds and berries are scattered, not gathered as in the bowl we have filled for supper.

Without venturing into metaphysics, where I would soon get lost, I need to declare that I believe literature is more than self-regarding play. It gestures beyond itself toward the universe, of which you and I are vanishingly small parts. The moves in writing are not abstract, like those in algebra or chess, for words cannot be unhooked from the world. They come freighted with memory and feeling. Linguists describe our ordinary speech as a "natural" language, to distinguish it from the formal codes of mathematics or computers or logic. The label is appropriate, a reminder that everyday language is *wild;* no one defines or controls it. You can never force words to mean only and exactly what you wish them to mean, for they escape every trap you lay for them.

Insofar as my writing is important, it gains that importance from what it witnesses to. I have written from the outset with a pressing awareness of the world's barbarities—the bombing of cities, oppression of the poor, extinction of species, exhaustion of soil, pollution of water and air, murder, genocide, racism, war. If I stubbornly believe that nature is resilient, that love is potent, that humankind may be truly kind, I do so in the face of this cruelty and waste. Without denying evil, literature ought to reduce the amount of suffering, in however small a degree, and not only human suffering but that of all creatures. Although we cannot live without causing harm, we could cause much less harm than we presently do.

The desire to articulate a shared world is the root impulse of literature as it is of science. Individual scientists, like writers, may be cutthroat competitors, out for their own glory; but science itself, the great cathedral of ideas slowly rising, is a common enterprise. Perhaps the symbol for literature should be a rambling library, to which each of us adds a line, a page, a few books. Whether one is a scientist or a writer, the universe outshines those of us who glimpse a bit of it and report what we see. Right now we urgently need to rethink our place on earth, to discover ways of living that do not devour the planet, and this need is far more important than the accomplishments of all writers put together. The health of our land and our fellow creatures is the ultimate measure of the worth and sanity of our lives.

I am forty-eight as I compose this letter to you. I have been writing seriously for twenty-five years, skillfully for about fifteen. Given decent luck, I might continue making books for another twenty-five years. So I think of myself as being midway in my journey as a writer. My steady desire has been to wake up, not to sleepwalk through this brief, miraculous life. I wish to go about with mind and senses alert to the splendor of the world. I wish to see the burning bush.

Writing is hard labor, shot through with intervals of joy. If there were no pleasure in the sinewy turns of a sentence, the bubbling up of an idea, the finding of a path through the maze, who would keep going? I feel the need to tell you many things for which there is no room in a letter, even a long letter. Nothing I have told you here can replace my books, which live or die in the minds of readers like you, and which bear on their current of words more meanings than I know.

Double Take

1. Scott Russell Sanders writes in "Letter to a Reader" that to write this essay he must "also tell you something of my life, for writing is to living as grass is to soil." Considering what Sanders says about the act of introducing the personal, what rhetorical choices does he make in deciding what part of himself he should reveal? Is this an effective strategy? Why or why not?

2. Sanders says he thinks of writing as manual labor. What might he mean by this? Do his essays manifest a quality of manual labor? That is, how does the construction of his writing evoke the very sense of construction, of the labor of making a product?

3. In "Letter to a Reader" Sanders frequently writes about the authors he read and who influenced him as a writer. This suggests that essays are parts of larger conversations with other writers and other texts. What value and effect do you see in making such acknowledgments in one's writing?

4. What effect is created by calling this piece a "letter"? What, then, makes this letter an essay?

Seeing for Yourself

At First Glance

Unlike his other essays in this section, Scott Russell Sanders does not address in "Buckeye" the activity of writing per se. Rather, Sanders narrates a deeply intimate story. As you read this powerful essay, reflect upon what Sanders has written in his other selections about writing. Note how he utilizes those same rhetorical strategies even when he is not writing about writing.

Buckeye

Years after my father's heart quit, I keep in a wooden box on my desk the two buckeyes that were in his pocket when he died. Once the size of plums, the brown seeds are shriveled now, hollow, hard as pebbles, yet they still gleam from the polish of his hands. He used to reach for them in his overalls or suit pants and click them together, or he would draw them out, cupped in his palm, and twirl them with his blunt carpenter's fingers, all the while humming snatches of old tunes.

"Do you really believe buckeyes keep off arthritis?" I asked him more than once.

He would flex his hands and say, "I do so far."

My father never paid much heed to pain. Near the end, when his worn knee often slipped out of joint, he would pound it back in place with a rubber mallet. If a splinter worked into his flesh beyond the reach of tweezers, he would heat the blade of his knife over a cigarette lighter and slice through the skin. He sought to ward off arthritis not because he feared pain but because he lived through his hands, and he dreaded the swelling of knuckles, the stiffening of fingers. What use would he be if he could no longer hold a hammer or guide a plow? When he was a boy he had known farmers not yet forty years old whose hands had curled into claws, men so crippled up they could not tie their own shoes, could not sign their names.

"I mean to tickle my grandchildren when they come along," he told me, "and I mean to build doll houses and turn spindles for tiny chairs on my lathe."

So he fondled those buckeyes as if they were charms, carrying them with him when our family moved from Ohio at the end of my childhood, bearing them to new homes in Louisiana, then Oklahoma, Ontario, and Mississippi, carrying them still on his final day when pain a thousand times fiercer than arthritis gripped his heart.

The box where I keep the buckeyes also comes from Ohio, made by my father from a walnut plank he bought at a farm auction. I remember the auction, remember the sagging face of the widow whose home was being sold, remember my father telling her he would prize that walnut as if he had watched the tree grow from a sapling on his own land. He did not care for pewter or silver or gold, but he cherished wood. On the rare occasions when my mother coaxed him into a museum, he ignored the paintings or porcelain and studied the exhibit cases, the banisters, the moldings, the parquet floors.

I remember him planing that walnut board, sawing it, sanding it, joining piece to piece to make foot stools, picture frames, jewelry boxes. My own box, a bit larger than a soap dish, lined with red corduroy, was meant to hold earrings and pins, not buckeyes. The top is inlaid with pieces fitted so as to bring out the grain, four diagonal joints converging from the corners toward the center. If I stare long enough at those converging lines, they float free of the box and point to a center deeper than wood.

I learned to recognize buckeyes and beeches, sugar maples and shagbark hickories, wild cherries, walnuts, and dozens of other trees while tramping through the Ohio woods with my father. To his eyes, their shapes, their leaves, their bark, their winter buds were as distinctive as the set of a friend's shoulders. As with friends, he was partial to some, craving their company, so he would go out of his way to visit particular trees, walking in a circle around the splayed roots of a sycamore, laying his hand against the trunk of a white oak, ruffling the feathery green boughs of a cedar.

"Trees breathe," he told me. "Listen."

I listened, and heard the stir of breath.

He was no botanist; the names and uses he taught me were those he had learned from country folks, not from books. Latin never crossed his lips. Only much later would I discover that the tree he called ironwood, its branches like muscular arms, good for axe handles, is known in the books as hophornbeam; what he called tulip-tree or canoewood, ideal for log cabins, is officially the yellow poplar; what he called hoop ash, good for barrels and fence posts, appears in books as hackberry.

When he introduced me to the buckeye, he broke off a chunk of the gray bark and held it to my nose. I gagged.

"That's why the old-timers called it stinking buckeye," he told me. "They used it for cradles and feed troughs and peg legs."

"Why for peg legs?" I asked.

"Because it's light and hard to split, so it won't shatter when you're clumping around."

He showed me this tree in late summer, when the fruits had fallen and the ground was littered with prickly brown pods. He picked up one, as fat as a lemon, and peeled away the husk to reveal the shiny seed. He laid it in my palm and closed my fist around it so the seed peeped out from the circle formed by my index finger and thumb. "You see where it got the name?" he asked.

I saw: what gleamed in my hand was the eye of a deer, bright with life. "It's beautiful," I said.

"It's beautiful," my father agreed, "but also poisonous. Nobody eats buckeyes, except maybe a fool squirrel."

I knew the gaze of deer from living in the Ravenna Arsenal, in Portage County, up in the northeastern corner of Ohio. After supper we often drove the Arsenal's gravel roads, past the munitions bunkers, past acres of rusting tanks and wrecked bombers, into the far fields where we counted deer. One June evening, while mist rose from the ponds, we counted three hundred and eleven, our family record. We found the deer in herds, in bunches, in amorous pairs. We came upon lone bucks, their antlers lifted against the sky like the bare branches of dogwood. If you were quiet, if your hands were empty, if you moved slowly, you could leave the car and steal to within a few paces of a grazing deer, close enough to see the delicate lips, the twitching nostrils, the glossy, fathomless eyes.

The wooden box on my desk holds these grazing deer, as it holds the buckeyes and the walnut plank and farm auction and the munitions bunkers and the breathing forests and my father's hands. I could lose the box, I could lose the polished seeds, but if I were to lose the memories I would become a bush without roots, and every new breeze would toss me about. All those memories lead back to the northeastern corner of Ohio, the place where I came to consciousness, where I learned to connect feelings with words, where I fell in love with the earth.

It was a troubled love, for much of the land I knew as a child had been ravaged. The ponds in the Arsenal teemed with bluegill and beaver, but they were also laced with TNT from the making of bombs. Because the wolves and coyotes had long since been killed, some of the deer, so plump in the June grass, collapsed on the January snow, whittled by hunger to racks of bones. Outside the Arsenal's high barbed fences, many of the farms had failed, their barns caving in, their topsoil gone. Ravines were choked with swollen couches and junked washing machines and cars. Crossing fields, you had to be careful not to slice your feet on tin cans or shards of glass. Most of the rivers had been dammed, turning fertile valleys into scummy playgrounds for boats.

One free-flowing river, the Mahoning, ran past the small farm near the Arsenal where our family lived during my later years in Ohio. We owned just enough land to pasture three ponies and to grow vegetables for our table, but those few acres opened onto miles of woods and creeks and secret meadows. I walked that land in every season, every weather, following animal trails. But then the Mahoning, too, was doomed by a government decision; we were forced to sell our land, and a dam began to rise across the river.

If enough people had spoken for the river, we might have saved it. If enough people had believed that our scarred country was worth defending, we might have dug in our heels and fought. Our attachments to the land were all private. We had no shared lore, no literature, no art to root us there, to give us courage, to help us stand our ground. The only maps we had were those issued by the state, showing a maze of numbered lines stretched over emptiness. The Ohio landscape never showed up on postcards or posters, never unfurled like tapestry in films, rarely filled even a paragraph in books. There were no mountains in that place, no waterfalls, no rocky gorges, no vistas. It was a country of low hills, cut over woods, scoured fields, villages that had lost their purpose, roads that had lost their way.

"Let us love the country of here below," Simone Weil urged. "It is real; it offers resistance to love. It is this country that God has given us to love. He has willed that it should be difficult yet possible to love it." Which is the deeper truth about buckeyes, their poison or their beauty? I hold with the beauty; or rather, I am held by the beauty, without forgetting the poison. In my corner of Ohio the gullies were choked with trash, yet cedars flickered up like green flames from cracks in stone; in the evening bombs exploded at the ammunition dump, yet from the darkness came the mating cries of owls. I was saved from despair by knowing a few men and women who cared enough about the land to clean up trash, who planted walnuts and oaks that would long outlive them, who imagined a world that would have no call for bombs.

How could our hearts be large enough for heaven if they are not large enough for earth? The only country I am certain of is the one here below. The only paradise I know is the one lit by our everyday sun, this land of difficult love, shot through with shadow. The place where we learn this love, if we learn it at all, shimmers behind every new place we inhabit.

A family move carried me away from Ohio thirty years ago; my schooling and marriage and job have kept me away ever since, except for visits in memory and in flesh. I returned to the site of our farm one cold November day, when the trees were skeletons and the ground shone with the yellow of fallen leaves. From a previous trip I knew that our house had been bulldozed, our yard and pasture had grown up in thickets, and the reservoir had flooded the woods. On my earlier visit I had merely gazed from the car, too numb with loss to climb out. But on this November day, I parked the car, drew on my hat and gloves, opened the door, and walked.

I was looking for some sign that we had lived there, some token of our affection for the place. All that I recognized, aside from the contours of the land, were two weeping willows that my father and I had planted near the road. They had been slips the length of my forearm when we set them out, and now their crowns rose higher than the telephone poles. When I touched them last, their trunks had been smooth and supple, as thin as my wrist, and now they were furrowed and stout. I took off my gloves and laid my hands against the rough bark. Immediately I felt the wince of tears. Without knowing why, I said hello to my father, quietly at first, then louder and louder, as if only shouts could reach him through the bark and miles and years.

Surprised by sobs, I turned from the willows and stumbled away toward the drowned woods, calling to my father. I sensed that he was nearby. Even as I called, I was wary of grief's deceptions. I had never seen his body after he died. By the time I reached the place of his death, a furnace had reduced him to ashes. The need to see him, to let go of him, to let go of this land and time, was powerful enough to summon mirages; I knew that. But I also knew, stumbling toward the woods, that my father was here.

At the bottom of a slope where the creek used to run, I came to an expanse of gray stumps and withered grass. It was a bay of the reservoir from which the water had retreated, the level drawn down by engineers or drought. I stood at the edge of this desolate ground, willing it back to life, trying to recall the woods where my father had taught me the names of trees. No green shoots rose. I walked out among the stumps. The grass crackled under my boots, breath rasped in my throat, but otherwise the world was silent.

Then a cry broke overhead and I looked up to see a red-tailed hawk launching out from the top of an oak. I recognized the bird from its band of dark feathers across the creamy breast and the tail splayed like rosy fingers against the sun. It was a red-tailed hawk for sure; and it was also my father. Not a symbol of my father, not a reminder, not a ghost, but the man himself, right there, circling in the air above me. I knew this as clearly as I knew the sun burned in the sky. A calm poured through me. My chest quit heaving. My eyes dried.

Hawk and father wheeled above me, circle upon circle, wings barely moving, head still. My own head was still, looking up, knowing and being known. Time scattered like fog. At length, father and hawk stroked the air with those powerful wings, three beats, then vanished over a ridge.

The voice of my education told me then and tells me now that I did not meet my father, that I merely projected my longing onto a bird. My education may well be right; yet nothing I heard in school, nothing I've read, no lesson reached by logic has ever convinced me as utterly or stirred me as deeply as did that red-tailed hawk. Nothing in my education prepared me to love a piece of the earth, least of all a humble, battered country like northeastern Ohio; I learned from the land itself.

Before leaving the drowned woods, I looked around at the ashen stumps, the wilted grass, and for the first time since moving from this place I was able to let it go. This ground was lost; the flood would reclaim it. But other ground could be saved, must be saved, in every watershed, every neighborhood. For each home ground we need new maps, living maps, stories and poems, photographs and paintings, essays and songs. We need to know where we are, so that we may dwell in our place with a full heart.

A CLOSER LOOK AT SCOTT RUSSELL SANDERS

1. When writing about the damming of the Mahoning River, Scott Russell Sanders says, "If enough people had spoken for the river, we might have saved it." This brings up the interesting question of who speaks for nature. Write an essay that considers what it means to speak *for* nature. Does Sanders's essay do so? Or does it speak *about* nature? Is there a difference between the two?

2. Like all of the essayists in this collection, Scott Russell Sanders often directs his attention to writing about writing. Self-reflexivity about our own writing often gives us the opportunity carefully and conscientiously to consider our writing and how we think about it. Often writing about our writing helps us to learn more about it specifically. In an essay, respond to Scott Russell Sanders's definitions of writing and offer your readers your own definitions of writing. How has writing been or not been part of your life? And how does your relationship with writing affect your definition of writing and the choices you make as a writer?

3. "Buckeye," the final essay reprinted here, recounts Sanders's memory of his father and of a particular place where he best remembered his father. In many ways, this essay has the characteristics of a short story, but at the same time it is essayistic. Consider the ways that you might relate a personal narrative in essay form. Then write an essay that enmeshes aspects of the personal narrative into your writing.

Looking from Writer to Writer

1. Compare Scott Russell Sanders's approach to activism to Rick Bass's approach to activism. What rhetorical qualities do both essayists use as they attempt to convince readers to protect the environment? In what ways do they differ in their approaches? And which approach do you think works more effectively if you were trying to convince an audience that favored the development rather than the conservation of nature?

2. Like Scott Russell Sanders, several other writers in this collection can be considered "nature writers"—Rick Bass, Annie Dillard, and Barry Lopez, for instance. Looking back through essays by these other writers, do you see any characteristics in the writing, other than subjects that can be considered "natural," that are similar and might be considered part of what makes writing "nature writing"? That is, other than subject matter, are there similar rhetorical characteristics of the essays of these writers?

3. Both Scott Russell Sanders and Edward Hoagland can be described as revealing the personal in their writing, and hence writing what Sanders refers to as "personal essays." Alice Walker also often reveals the personal in her essays. Does that, however, make her essays "personal essays" as defined by Sanders? Why or why not?

Looking Beyond

NONFICTION

Audubon Reader (Editor). Bloomington, IN: Indiana University Press, 1986.

Hunting for Hope: A Father's Journey. Boston: Beacon Press, 1999.

The Paradise of Bombs. Athens, GA: University of Georgia Press, 1987.

Secrets of the Universe: Scenes from the Journey Home. Boston: Beacon Press, 1992.

Staying Put: Making a Home in a Restless World. Boston: Beacon Press, 1994.

Writing from the Center. Bloomington, IN: Indiana University Press, 1995.

FICTION

Fetching the Dead. Urbana, IL: University of Illinois, 1984.

The Invisible Company. New York: Tor Books, 1989.

Terrarium. Bloomington, IN: Indiana University Press, 1995.

Wilderness Plots: Tales about the Settlement of the American Land. New York: Morrow, 1983.

CHILDREN'S BOOKS

Aurora Means Dawn. New York: Aladdin–Simon and Schuster, 1998.

The Floating House. New York: Atheneum, 1995.

Here Comes the Mystery Man. New York: Atheneum, 1993.

Meeting Trees. Washington, DC: National Geographic Society, 1997.

A Place Called Freedom. New York: Aladdin–Simon & Schuster, 2001.

Warm as Wool. New York: Bradbury Press, 1992.

Amy Tan

A daughter of Chinese immigrants, Amy Tan was born in Oakland, California, in 1952. Her father was an electrical engineer and Baptist minister who came to the United States to escape the Chinese civil war. Her mother Daisy barely escaped Shanghai before the Communist takeover in 1949, leaving behind three daughters from a previous marriage. When she was 14 years old, Tan lost her father and, soon afterward, her oldest brother to brain tumors. Following their deaths, Tan's mother moved the family to Switzerland, where Tan finished high school. After returning to the United States, Tan studied English and linguistics (rather than the premed her mother insisted she major in), earning a BA in English and an MA in linguistics at San Jose State University. She later abandoned doctoral work in linguistics in order to work as a language consultant with developmentally disabled children.

Tan began her writing career as a technical and business writer, first in a business writing firm she cocreated, writing speeches for executives of large corporations, and later as a very successful freelance business writer, writing under a pseudonym for companies such as IBM. It was not until her mid-30s, after working herself to exhaustion, that Tan turned to fiction writing for relief. Even though her career as a fiction writer began to take shape when her first story, "Endgame," won her admission to the Squaw Valley Writers Workshop, it was not until she visited China with her mother in 1987 that Tan found her identity as a fiction writer. The visit not only clarified Tan's often difficult and volatile relationship with her mother, it also clarified Tan's own cultural identities. About that visit she writes: "I discovered how American I was. I also discovered how Chinese I was by the kind of family habits and routines that were so familiar. I discovered a sense of finally belonging to a period of history which I never felt with American history." This tension between cultures and between mothers and daughters became the basis for Tan's first novel, *The Joy Luck Club,* published in 1989.

The novel was an enormous success: It spent eight months on the New York Times Bestseller list, emerged as a finalist for the National Book Award and the National Book Critics Circle Award, and was translated into 25 languages. The novel was followed in 1991 by a second successful novel, *The Kitchen God's Wife,* which also examined her family history, this time the story of her grandmother who had been raped, forced into concubinage, and finally committed suicide. In the years since, Tan has written two children's books and two more novels, *The Hundred Secret Senses* (1995) and *The Bonesetter's Daughter* (2001). Along the way her stories and essays have appeared in the *Atlantic Monthly, Grand Street, McCall's, The Threepenny Review, Harper's,* and *Glamour,* as well as in more academic books on language.

Even though the immigrant experience has been a major influence in her life, Tan maintains that she does not see herself as writing about culture and the immigrant experience. Rather, she explains, "what I believe my books are about is relationships and family," subjects that are not only specific to the immigrant experience. Indeed, as she describes it:

> Writing is an extreme privilege but it's also a gift. It's a gift to yourself and it's a gift of giving a story to someone. What better gift can I give my mother than to finally sit down and listen to her story, hour after hour after hour? She's very repetitive. This is hard work, listening to her say the same laments in her life over and over again, but this time asking for more details. Getting this story out, I realized, was a gift that she was giving me. And there was a gift I could give back to her, and it didn't matter what happened to that book [*The Kitchen God's Wife*] afterwards.

As a writer Tan barters in stories, giving and taking. She takes stories from her mother, her family, and her culture, but she also gives stories to her mother, her family, and her culture.

What is most clear in the essays that follow is Amy Tan's awareness of the power of language in this giving and taking of culture and identity. At a young age she had a love for language that may have developed, she speculates, "because I was bilingual at an early age. I stopped speaking Chinese when I was five, but I loved words. Words to me were magic. You could say a word and it could conjure up all kinds of images or feelings or a chilly sensation or whatever. It was amazing to me that words had this power." As you read the essays, think about the power of language and how Tan uses this power to frame arguments and to tell stories. Also, think about the power of language in your own life, especially how you use language to make things happen, to identify with others, and to live in the world.

Tan on Writing

At First Glance

The essay "Lost Lives of Women" appeared in Life *magazine (along with the photograph Tan alludes to) after the huge success of Amy Tan's first novel,* The Joy Luck Club, *and close to the publication of her second novel,* The Kitchen God's Wife. *Within this context, think about why Tan wrote this essay as you read it. Rhetorically, what do you think Tan was trying to tell readers—about herself, her family, her culture, and why she writes? Think about why readers of* Life *would have reacted positively. Pay specific attention to how Tan "speaks" to her readers and the tone she uses to convey her subject matter. From a writer's perspective, do you find her style and approach effective for her audience?*

Lost Lives of Women

When I first saw this photo as a child, I thought it was exotic and remote, of a far-away time and place, with people who had no connection to my American life. Look at their bound feet! Look at that funny lady with the plucked forehead!

The solemn little girl is, in fact, my mother. And leaning against the rock is my grandmother, Jingmei. "She called me Baobei," my mother told me. "It means treasure."

The picture was taken in Hangzhou, and my mother believes the year was 1922, possibly spring or fall, judging by the clothes. At first glance, it appears the women are on a pleasure outing.

But see the white bands on their skirts? The white shoes? They are in mourning. My mother's grandmother, known to the others as Divong, "The Replacement Wife," has recently died. The women have come to this place, a Buddhist retreat, to perform yet another ceremony for Divong. Monks hired for the occasion have chanted the proper words. And the women and little girl have walked in circles clutching smoky sticks of incense. They knelt and prayed, then burned a huge pile of spirit money so that Divong might ascend to a higher position in her new world.

This is also a picture of secrets and tragedies, the reasons that warnings have been passed along in our family like heirlooms. Each of these women suffered a terrible fate, my mother said. And they were not peasant women but big city people, very modern. They went to dance halls and wore stylish clothes. They were supposed to be the lucky ones.

Look at the pretty woman with her finger on her cheek. She is my mother's second cousin, Nunu Aiyi, "Precious Auntie." You cannot see this, but Nunu Aiyi's entire face was scarred from smallpox. Lucky for her, a year or so after this picture was taken, she received marriage proposals from two families. She turned down a lawyer and married another man. Later she divorced her husband, a daring thing for a woman to do. But then, finding no means to support herself or her young daughter, Nunu eventually accepted the lawyer's second proposal—to become his number two concubine. "Where else could she go?" my mother asked. "Some people said she was lucky the lawyer still wanted her."

Now look at the small woman with a sour face. There's a reason that Jyou Ma, "Uncles Wife," looks this way. Her husband, my great-uncle, often complained that his family had chosen an ugly woman for his wife. To show his displeasure, he often insulted Jyou Ma's cooking. One time Great-Uncle tipped over a pot of boiling soup, which fell all over his niece's four-year-old neck and nearly killed her. My mother was the little niece, and she still has that soup scar on her neck. Great-Uncle's family eventually chose a pretty woman for his second wife. But the complaints about Jyou Ma's cooking did not stop.

Doomma, "Big Mother," is the regal-looking woman seated on a rock. (The woman with the plucked forehead, far left, is a servant, remembered only as someone who cleaned but did not cook.) Doomma was the daughter of my great-grandfather and Nu-pei, "The Original Wife." She was shunned by Divong, "The Replacement Wife," for being "too strong," and loved by Divong's daughter, my grandmother. Doomma's first daughter was born with a hunchback—a sign, some said, of Doomma's own crooked nature. Why else did she remarry, disobeying her family's orders to remain a widow forever? And why did Doomma later kill herself, using some mysterious means that caused her to die slowly over three days? "Doomma died the same way she lived," my mother said, "strong, suffering lots."

Jingmei, my own grandmother, lived only a few more years after this picture was taken. She was the widow of a poor scholar, a man who had the misfortune of dying from influenza when he was about to be appointed a vice-magistrate. In 1924 or so, a rich man, who liked to collect pretty women, raped my grandmother and thereby forced her into becoming one of his concubines. My grandmother, now an outcast, took her young daughter to live with her on an island outside of Shanghai. She left her son behind, to save his face. After she gave birth to another son she killed herself by swallowing raw opium buried in the New Year's rice cakes. The young daughter who wept at her deathbed was my mother.

At my grandmother's funeral, monks tied chains to my mother's ankles so she would not fly away with her mother's ghost. "I tried to take them off," my mother said. "I was her treasure. I was her life."

My mother could never talk about any of this, even with her closest friends. "Don't tell anyone," she once said to me. "People don't understand. A concubine was like some kind of prostitute. My mother was a good woman, high-class. She had no choice."

I told her I understood.

"How can you understand?" she said, suddenly angry. "You did not live in China then. You do not know what it's like to have no position in life. I was her daughter. We had no face! We belonged to nobody! This is a shame I can never push off my back." By the end of the outburst, she was crying.

On a recent trip with my mother to Beijing, I learned that my uncle found a way to push the shame off his back. He was the son my grandmother left behind. In 1936 he joined the Communist party—in large part, he told me, to overthrow the society that forced his mother into concubinage. He published a story about his mother. I told him I had written about my grandmother in a book of fiction. We agreed that my grandmother is the source of strength running through our family. My mother cried to hear this.

My mother believes my grandmother is also my muse, that she helps me write. "Does she still visit you often?" she asked while I was writing my second book. And then she added shyly, "Does she say anything about me?"

"Yes," I told her. "She has lots to say. I am writing it down."

This is the picture I see when I write. These are the secrets I was supposed to keep. These are the women who never let me forget why stories need to be told.

Double Take

1. What is the connection between writing and loss? Why, according to Amy Tan, do stories need to be told?
2. On a number of occasions, Tan addresses the reader directly in "Lost Lives of Women." Identify these occasions and reflect on their effect. What sort of relationship does this direct approach create between the writer and reader?
3. Describe the tone of this essay, pointing to specific examples in the text that help create this tone. Do you think the tone is appropriate for the subject matter and Tan's purpose? Why or why not?
4. Tan identifies her grandmother as her muse, the inspiration that helps her write. Who or what is your muse? What influences or guides your writing? Are you driven to write by different "muses" on different writing occasions—for example, writing papers in your English class as opposed to writing letters to friends? How so?

At First Glance

"Mother Tongue" is one of Amy Tan's best-known essays. It first appeared in The Three-penny Review, *a literary magazine that publishes poetry, fiction, literary essays, and book reviews. Knowing this about the magazine, pay attention to how Tan chooses to begin her essay. Like all writers, Tan is making a choice here, a rhetorical choice that creates a certain relationship between herself and her readers. Think about what the choice means in the context of this magazine. Think as well about Tan's other rhetorical choices in the essay and the extent to which they are connected to that first choice. Since Tan writes about the different "Englishes" she uses, try to identify what English she uses most of the time in this essay.*

Mother Tongue

I am not a scholar of English or literature. I cannot give you much more than personal opinions on the English language and its variations in this country or others.

I am a writer. And by that definition, I am someone who has always loved language. I am fascinated by language in daily life. I spend a great deal of my time thinking about the power of language—the way it can evoke an emotion, a visual image, a complex idea, or a simple truth. Language is the tool of my trade. And I use them all—all the Englishes I grew up with.

Recently, I was made keenly aware of the different Englishes I do use. I was giving a talk to a large group of people, the same talk I had already given to half a dozen other groups. The nature of the talk was about my writing, my life, and my book, *The Joy Luck Club.* The talk was going along well enough, until I remember one major difference that made the whole talk sound wrong. My mother was in the room. And it was perhaps the first time she had heard me give a lengthy speech, using the kind of English I have never used with her. I was saying things like, "The intersection of memory upon imagination" and "There is an aspect of my fiction that relates to thus-and-thus"—a speech filled with carefully wrought grammatical phrases, burdened, it suddenly seemed to me, with nominalized forms, past perfect tenses, conditional phrases, all the forms of standard English that I had learned in school and through books, the forms of English I did not use at home with my mother.

Just last week, I was walking down the street with my mother, and I again found myself conscious of the English I was using, the English I do use with her. We were talking about the price of new and used furniture and I heard myself saying this: "Not waste money that way." My husband was with us as well, and he didn't notice any switch in my English. And then I realized why. It's because over the twenty years we've been together I've often used that same kind of English with him, and sometimes he even uses it with me. It has become our language of intimacy, a different sort of English that relates to family talk, the language I grew up with.

So you'll have some idea of what this family talk I heard sounds like, I'll quote what my mother said during a recent conversation which I videotaped and then transcribed. During this conversation, my mother was talking about a political gangster in Shanghai who had the same last name as her family's, Du, and how the gangster in his early years wanted to be adopted by her family, which was rich by comparison. Later, the gangster became more powerful, far richer than my mother's family, and one day showed up at my mother's wedding to pay his respects. Here's what she said in part:

"Du Yusong having business like fruit stand. Like off the street kind. He is Du like Du Zong—but not Tsung-ming Island people. The local people call putong, the river east side, he belong to that side local people. That man want to ask Du Zong father take him in like become own family. Du Zong father wasn't look down on him, but didn't take seriously, until that man big like become a mafia. Now important person, very hard to inviting him. Chinese way, came only to show respect, don't stay for dinner. Respect for making big celebration, he shows up.

Mean give lots of respect. Chinese custom. Chinese social life that way. If too important won't have to stay too long. He come to my wedding. I didn't see, I heard it. I gone to boy's side, they have YMCA dinner. Chinese age I was nineteen."

You should know that my mother's expressive command of English belies how much she actually understands. She reads the *Forbes* report, listens to *Wall Street Week*, converses daily with her stockbroker, reads all of Shirley MacLaine's books with ease—all kinds of things I can't begin to understand. Yet some of my friends tell me they understand 50 percent of what my mother says. Some say they understand 80 to 90 percent. Some say they understand none of it, as if she were speaking pure Chinese. But to me, my mother's English is perfectly clear, perfectly natural. It's my mother tongue. Her language, as I hear it, is vivid, direct, full of observation and imagery. That was the language that helped shape the way I saw things, expressed things, made sense of the world.

Lately, I've been giving more thought to the kind of English my mother speaks. Like others, I have described it to people as "broken" or "fractured" English. But I wince when I say that. It has always bothered me that I can think of no way to describe it other than "broken," as if it were damaged and needed to be fixed, as if it lacked a certain wholeness and soundness. I've heard other terms used, "limited English," for example. But they seem just as bad, as if everything is limited, including people's perceptions of the limited English speaker.

I know this for a fact, because when I was growing up, my mother's "limited" English limited *my* perception of her. I was ashamed of her English. I believed that her English reflected the quality of what she had to say. That is, because she expressed them imperfectly her thoughts were imperfect. And I had plenty of empirical evidence to support me: the fact that people in department stores, at banks, and at restaurants did not take her seriously, did not give her good service, pretended not to understand her, or even acted as if they did not hear her.

My mother has long realized the limitations of her English as well. When I was fifteen, she used to have me call people on the phone to pretend I was she. In this guise, I was forced to ask for information or even to complain and yell at people who had been rude to her. One time it was a call to her stockbroker in New York. She had cashed out her small portfolio and it just happened we were going to go to New York the next week, our very first trip outside California. I had to get on the phone and say in an adolescent voice that was not very convincing, "This is Mrs. Tan."

And my mother was standing in the back whispering loudly, "Why he don't send me check, already two weeks late. So mad he lie to me, losing me money."

And then I said in perfect English, "Yes, I'm getting rather concerned. You had agreed to send the check two weeks ago, but it hasn't arrived."

Then she began to talk more loudly. "What he want, I come to New York tell him front of his boss, you cheating me?" And I was trying to calm her down, make her be quiet, while telling the stockbroker, "I can't tolerate any more excuses. If I don't receive the check immediately, I am going to have to speak to your manager when I'm in New York next week." And sure enough, the following week there we were in front of this astonished stockbroker, and I was sitting there red-faced and quiet, and my mother, the real Mrs. Tan, was shouting at his boss in her impeccable broken English.

We used a similar routine just five days ago, for a situation that was far less humorous. My mother had gone to the hospital for an appointment, to find out about a benign brain tumor a CAT scan had revealed a month ago. She said she had spoken very good English, her best English, no mistakes. Still, she said, the hospital did not apologize when they said they had lost the CAT scan and she had come for nothing. She said they did not seem to have any sympathy when she told them she was anxious to know the exact diagnosis, since her husband and son had both died of brain tumors. She said they would not give her any more information until the next time and she would have to make another appointment for that. So she said she would not leave until the doctor called her daughter. She wouldn't budge. And when the doctor finally called her daughter, me, who spoke in perfect English—lo and behold—we had assurances the CAT scan would be found, promises that a conference call on Monday would be held, and apologies for any suffering my mother had gone through for a most regrettable mistake.

I think my mother's English almost had an effect on limiting my possibilities in life as well. Sociologists and linguists probably will tell you that a person's developing language skills are more influenced by peers. But I do think that the language spoken in the family, especially immigrant families which are more insular, plays a large role in shaping the language of the child. And I believe that it affected my results on achievement tests, IQ tests, and the SAT. While my English skills were never judged as poor, compared to math, English could not be considered my strong suit. In grade school I did moderately well, getting perhaps B's, sometimes B-pluses, in English and scoring perhaps in the sixtieth or seventieth percentile on achievement tests. But those scores were not good enough to override the opinion that my true abilities lay in math and science, because in those areas I achieved A's and scored in the ninetieth percentile or higher.

This was understandable. Math is precise; there is only one correct answer. Whereas, for me at least, the answer on English tests were always a judgment call, a matter of opinion and personal experience. Those tests were constructed around items like fill-in-the-blank sentence completion, such as, "Even though Tom was _____, Mary thought he was _____." And the correct answer always seemed to be the most bland combinations of thoughts, for example "Even though Tom was shy, Mary thought he was charming," with the grammatical structure "even though" limiting the correct answer to some sort of semantic opposites, so you wouldn't get answers like, "Even though Tom was foolish, Mary thought he was ridiculous." Well, according to my mother, there were very few limitations as to what Tom could have been and what Mary might have thought of him. So I never did well on tests like that.

The same was true with word analogies, pairs of words in which you were supposed to find some sort of logical, semantic relationship—for example, "*Sunset* is to *nightfall* as _____ is to _____." And here you would be presented with a list of four possible pairs, one of which showed the same kind of relationship: *red* is to *spotlight, bus* is to *arrival, chills* is to *fever, yawn* is to *boring*. Well, I could never think that way. I knew what the tests were asking, but I could not block out of my mind the images already created by the first pair, *"sunset* is to *nightfall"*—and I would see a burst of colors against a darkening sky, the moon rising, the lowering of a curtain of stars. And all the other pairs of words—red, bus, spotlight, boring—just threw up a mass of confusing images, making it impossible for me to sort out something as logical as saying: "A sunset precedes nightfall" is the same as "a chill precedes a fever." The only way I would have gotten that answer right would have been to imagine an associative situation, for example, my being disobedient and staying out past sunset, catching a chill at night, which turns into feverish pneumonia as punishment, which indeed did happen to me.

I have been thinking about all this lately, about my mother's English, about achievement tests. Because lately I've been asked as a writer, why there are not more Asian Americans represented in American literature. Why are there few Asian Americans enrolled in creative writing programs? Why do so many Chinese students go into engineering? Well, these are broad sociological questions I can't begin to answer. But I have noticed in surveys—in fact, just last week—that Asian students, as a whole, always do significantly better on math achievement tests than in English. And this makes me think that there are other Asian-American students whose English spoken in the home might also be described as "broken" or "limited." And perhaps they also have teachers who are steering them away from writing and into math and science, which is what happened to me.

Fortunately, I happen to be rebellious in nature and enjoy the challenge of disproving assumptions made about me. I became an English major my first year in college, after being enrolled as pre-med. I started writing nonfiction as a freelancer the week after I was told by my former boss that writing was my worst skill and I should hone my talents toward account management.

But it wasn't until 1985 that I finally began to write fiction. And at first I wrote using what I thought to be wittily crafted sentences, sentences that would finally prove I had mastery over the English language. Here's an example from the first draft of a story that later made its way into *The Joy Luck Club*, but without this line: "That was my mental quandary in its nascent state." A terrible line, which I can barely pronounce.

Fortunately, for reasons I won't get into today, I later decided I should envision a reader for the stories I would write. And the reader I decided upon was my mother, because these were stories about mothers. So with this reader in mind—and in fact she did read my early drafts—I began to write stories using all the Englishes I grew up with: the English I spoke to my mother, which for lack of a better term might be described as "simple"; the English she used with me, which for lack of a better term might be described as "broken"; my translation of her Chinese, which could certainly be described as "watered down"; and what I imagined to be her translation of her Chinese if she could speak in perfect English, her internal language, and for that I sought to preserve the essence, but neither an English nor a Chinese structure. I wanted to capture what language ability tests can never reveal: her intent, her passion, her imagery, the rhythms of her speech and the nature of her thoughts.

Apart from what any critic had to say about my writing, I knew I had succeeded where it counted when my mother finished reading my book and gave me her verdict: "So easy to read."

Double Take

1. Why do you think Amy Tan begins the essay "Mother Tongue" by writing, "I am not a scholar of English or literature. I cannot give you much more than personal opinions on the English language and its variations in this country or others"? What rhetorical effect does the statement have on the reader? Why do you think Tan chooses to present herself as a writer in this way? Do you think it is effective?
2. Tan uses very specific examples to support her claims about language, self-identity, and prejudice in this essay. Identify these examples and assess why they are effective. How might you use such examples in your own writing?
3. At one point in the essay, when she describes her conversation with the New York stockbroker, Tan gives us two versions of English side by side, the first her mother's words and the second her "translation" of those words. Why do you think Tan's use of "perfect English" gets results in ways that her mother's "broken English" does not?
4. Describe the different "Englishes" that you have either grown up with or use and hear on a daily basis. How do they differ? Why do they differ? What function do they serve?

At First Glance

"The Language of Discretion" was published in a collection called The State of the Language, *a book, its editors note, that treats English "in its infinite potential to reveal or betray life's infinite variety." Many of the contributors to the book are academics writing about the meaning of language and its relation to art, violence, and politics. Before you read Amy Tan's essay, think about it in this context. Think about what kinds of questions Tan might have asked herself before she began writing the essay, and how these questions might have shaped the decisions she made as a writer. Also, think about Tan's reasons for writing the essay. Writers often write in response to something, frequently identifying what they are responding to early in their writing. What is Tan responding to, and how does she characterize it? As you read the essay, assess whether you think Tan's essay is an adequate response.*

The Language of Discretion

At a recent family dinner in San Francisco, my mother whispered to me: "Sau-sau [Brother's Wife] pretends too hard to be polite! Why bother? In the end, she always takes everything."

My mother thinks like a *waixiao,* an expatriate, temporarily away from China since 1949, no longer patient with ritual courtesies. As if to prove her point, she reached across the table to offer my elderly aunt from Beijing the last scallop from the Happy Family seafood dish.

Sau-sau scowled. *"B'yao, zhen b'yao!"* (I don't want it, really I don't!) she cried, patting her plump stomach.

"Take it! Take it!" scolded my mother in Chinese.

"Full, I'm already full," Sau-sau protested weakly, eyeing the beloved scallop.

"Ai!" exclaimed my mother, completely exasperated. "Nobody else wants it. If you don't take it, it will only rot!"

At this point, Sau-sau sighed, acting as if she were doing my mother a big favor by taking the wretched scrap off her hands.

My mother turned to her brother, a high-ranking communist official who was visiting her in California for the first time: "In America a Chinese person could starve to death. If you say you don't want it, they won't ask you again forever."

My uncle nodded and said he understood fully: Americans take things quickly because they have no time to be polite.

★ ★ ★

I thought about this misunderstanding again—of social contexts failing in translation—when a friend sent me an article from the *New York Times Magazine* (24 April 1988). The article, on changes in New York's Chinatown, made passing reference to the inherent ambivalence of the Chinese language.

Chinese people are so "discreet and modest," the article stated, there aren't even words for "yes" and "no."

That's not true, I thought, although I can see why an outsider might think that. I continued reading.

If one is Chinese, the article went on to say, "One compromises, one doesn't hazard a loss of face by an overemphatic response."

My throat seized. Why do people keep saying these things? As if we truly were those little dolls sold in Chinatown tourist shops, heads bobbing up and down in complacent agreement to anything said!

I worry abut the effect of one-dimensional statements on the unwary and guileless. When they read abut this so-called vocabulary deficit, do they also con-clude that Chinese people evolved into a mild-mannered lot because the language only allowed them to hobble forth with minced words?

Something enormous is always lost in translation. Something insidious seeps into the gaps, especially when amateur linguists continue to compare, one-for-one, language differences and then put forth notions wide open to misinterpretation: that Chinese people have no direct linguistic means to make decisions, assert or deny, affirm or negate, just say no to drug dealers, or behave properly on the witness stand when told, "Please answer yes or no."

Yet one can argue, with the help of renowned linguists, that the Chinese are indeed up a creek without "yes" and "no." Take any number of variations on the old language-and-reality theory stated years ago by Edward Sapir: "Human beings . . . are very much at the mercy of the particular language which has become the medium for their society. . . . The fact of the matter is that the 'real world' is to a large extent built up on the language habits of the group."*

This notion was further bolstered by the famous Sapir-Whorf hypothesis, which roughly states that one's perception of the world and how one functions in it depends a great deal on the language used. As Sapir, Whorf, and new carriers of the banner would have us believe, language shapes our thinking, channels us along certain patterns embedded in words, syntactic structures, and intonation patterns. Language has become the peg and the shelf that enables us to sort out and categorize the world. In English, we see "cats" and "dogs"; what if the language had also specified *glatz,* meaning "animals that leave fur on the sofa," and *glotz,* meaning "animals that leave fur and drool on the sofa"? How would language, the enabler, have changed our perceptions with slight vocabulary variations?

And if this were the case—of language being the master of destined thought—think of the opportunities lost from failure to evolve two little words, *yes* and *no,* the simplest of opposites! Ghenghis Khan could have been sent back to Mongolia. Opium wars might have been averted. The Cultural Revolution could have been sidestepped.

There are still many, from serious linguists to pop psychology cultists, who view language and reality as inextricably tied, one being the consequence of the other. We have traversed the range from the Sapir-Whorf hypothesis to est and neurolinguistic programming, which tell us "you are what you say."

I too have been intrigued by the theories. I can summarize, albeit badly, ages-old empirical evidence: of Eskimos and their infinite ways to say "snow," their ability to *see* the differences in snowflake configurations, thanks to the richness of their vocabulary, while non-Eskimo speakers like myself founder in "snow," "more snow," and "lots more where that came from."

I too have experienced dramatic cognitive awakenings via the word. Once I added "mauve" to my vocabulary I began to see it everywhere. When I learned how to pronounce *prix fixe,* I ate French food at prices better than the easier-to-say *à la carte* choices.

But just how seriously are we supposed to take this?

Sapir said something else about language and reality. It is the part that often gets left behind in the dot-dot-dots of quotes: ". . . No two languages are ever sufficiently similar to be considered as representing the same social reality. The worlds in which

---

*Edward Sapir, *Selected Writings,* ed. D.G. Mandelbaum (Berkeley and Los Angeles, 1949).

different societies live are distinct worlds, not merely the same world with different labels attached."

When I first read this, I thought, Here at last is validity for the dilemmas I felt growing up in a bicultural, bilingual family! As any child of immigrant parents knows, there's a special kind of double bind attached to knowing two languages. My parents, for example, spoke to me in both Chinese and English; I spoke back to them in English.

"Amy-ah!" they'd call to me.

"What?" I'd mumble back.

"Do not question us when we call," they scolded me in Chinese. "It is not respectful."

"What do you mean?"

"Ai! Didn't we just tell you not to question?"

To this day, I wonder which parts of my behavior were shaped by Chinese, which by English. I am tempted to think, for example, that if I am of two minds on some matter it is due to the richness of my linguistic experiences, not to any personal tendencies toward wishy-washiness. But which mind says what?

Was it perhaps patience—developed through years of deciphering my mother's fractured English—that had me listening politely while a woman announced over the phone that I had won one of five valuable prizes? Was it respect—pounded in by the Chinese imperative to accept convoluted explanations—that had me agreeing that I might find it worthwhile to drive seventy-five miles to view a time-share resort? Could I have been at a loss for words when asked, "Wouldn't you like to win a Hawaiian cruise or perhaps a fabulous Star of India designed exclusively by Carter and Van Arpels?

And when this same woman called back a week later, this time complaining that I had missed my appointment, obviously it was my type A language that kicked into gear and interrupted her. Certainly, my blunt denial—"Frankly I'm not interested"—was as American as apple pie. And when she said, "But it's in Morgan Hill," and I shouted, "Read my lips. I don't care if it's Timbuktu," you can be sure I said it with the precise intonation expressing both cynicism and disgust.

It's dangerous business, this sorting out of languages and behavior. Which one is English? Which is Chinese? The categories manifest themselves: passive and aggressive, tentative and assertive, indirect and direct. And I realize they are just variations of the same theme: that Chinese people are discreet and modest.

Reject them all!

If my reaction is overly strident, it is because I cannot come across as too emphatic. I grew up listening to the same lines over and over again, like so many rote expressions repeated in an English phrasebook. And I too almost came to believe them.

Yet if I consider my upbringing more carefully, I find there was nothing discreet about the Chinese language I grew up with. My parents made everything abundantly clear. Nothing wishy-washy in their demands, no compromises accepted: "Of course you will become a famous neurosurgeon," they told me. "And yes, a concert pianist on the side."

In fact, now that I remember, it seems that the more emphatic outbursts always spilled over into Chinese: "Not that way! You must wash rice so not a single grain spills out."

I do not believe that my parents—both immigrants from mainland China—are an exception to the modest-and-discreet rule. I have only to look at the number of Chinese engineering students skewing minority ratios at Berkeley, MIT, and Yale. Certainly they were not raised by passive mothers and fathers who said, "It is up to you, my daughter. Writer, welfare recipient, masseuse, or molecular engineer—you decide."

And my American mind says, See, those engineering students weren't able to say no to their parents' demands. But then my Chinese mind remembers: Ah, but those parents all wanted their sons and daughters to be *pre-med*.

Having listened to both Chinese and English, I also tend to be suspicious of any comparisons between the two languages. Typically, one language—that of the person doing the comparing—is often used as the standard, the benchmark for a logical form of expression. And so the language being compared is always in danger of being judged deficient or superfluous, simplistic or unnecessarily complex, melodious or cacophonous. English speakers point out that Chinese is extremely difficult because it relies on variations in tone barely discernible to the human ear. By the same token, Chinese speakers tell me English is extremely difficult because it is inconsistent, a language of too many broken rules, of Mickey Mice and Donald Ducks.

Even more dangerous to my mind is the temptation to compare both language and behavior *in translation*. To listen to my mother speak English, one might think she has no concept of past or future tense, that she doesn't see the difference between singular and plural, that she is gender blind because she calls my husband "she." If one were not careful, one might also generalize that, based on the way my mother talks, all Chinese people take a circumlocutory route to get to the point. It is, in fact, my mother's idiosyncratic behavior to ramble a bit.

Sapir was right about differences between two languages and their realities. I can illustrate why word-for-word translation is not enough to translate meaning and intent. I once received a letter from China which I read to non-Chinese speaking friends. The letter, originally written in Chinese, had been translated by my brother-in-law in Beijing. One portion described the time when my uncle at age ten discovered his widowed mother (my grandmother) had remarried—as a number three concubine, the ultimate disgrace for an honorable family. The translated version of my uncle's letter read in part:

> In 1925, I met my mother in Shanghai. When she came to me, I didn't have greeting to her as if seeing nothing. She pull me to a corner secretly and asked me why didn't have greeting to her. I couldn't control myself and cried, "Ma! Why did you leave us? People told me: one day you ate a beancake yourself. Your sister in-law found it and sweared at you, called your names. So . . . is it

true?" She clasped my hand and answered immediately, "It's not true, don't say what like this." After this time, there was a few chance to meet her.

"What!" cried my friends. "Was eating a beancake so terrible?"

Of course not. The beancake was simply a euphemism; a ten-year-old boy did not dare question his mother on something as shocking as concubinage. Eating a beancake was his equivalent for committing this selfish act, something inconsiderate of all family members, hence, my grandmother's despairing response to what seemed like a ludicrous charge of gluttony. And sure enough, she was banished from the family, and my uncle saw her only a few times before her death.

While the above may fuel people's argument that Chinese is indeed a language of extreme discretion, it does not mean that Chinese people speak in secrets and riddles. The contexts are fully understood. It is only to those on the *outside* that the language seems cryptic, the behavior inscrutable.

I am, evidently, one of the outsiders. My nephew in Shanghai, who recently started taking English lessons, has been writing me letters in English. I had told him I was a fiction writer, and so in one letter he wrote, "Congratulate to you on your writing. Perhaps one day I should like to read it." I took it in the same vein as "Perhaps one day we can get together for lunch." I sent back a cheery note. A month went by and another letter arrived from Shanghai. "Last one perhaps I hadn't writing distinctly," he said. "In the future, you'll send a copy of your works for me."

I try to explain to my English-speaking friends that Chinese language use is more *strategic* in manner, whereas English tends to be more direct; an American business executive may say, "Let's make a deal," and the Chinese manager may reply, "Is your son interested in learning about your widget business?" Each to his or her own purpose, each with his or her own linguistic path. But I hesitate to add more to the pile of generalizations, because no matter how many examples I provide and explain, I fear that it appears defensive and only reinforces the image: that Chinese people are "discreet and modest"—and it takes an American to explain what they really mean.

Why am I complaining? The description seems harmless enough (after all, the *New York Times Magazine* writer did not say "slippery and evasive"). It is precisely the bland, easy acceptability of the phrase that worries me.

I worry that the dominant society may see Chinese people from a limited—and limiting—perspective. I worry that seemingly benign stereotypes may be part of the reason there are few Chinese in top management positions, in mainstream political roles. I worry about the power of language: that if one says anything enough times—in *any* language— it might become true.

Could this be why Chinese friends of my parents' generation are willing to accept the generalization?

"Why are you complaining?" one of them said to me. "If people think we are modest and polite, let them think that. Wouldn't Americans be pleased to admit they are thought of as polite?"

And I do believe anyone would take the description as a compliment—at first. But after a while, it annoys, as if the only things that people heard one say were phatic remarks: "I'm so pleased to meet you. I've heard many wonderful things about you. For me? You shouldn't have!"

These remarks are not representative of new ideas, honest emotions, or considered thought. They are what is said from the polite distance of social contexts: of greetings, farewells, wedding thank-you notes, convenient excuses, and the like.

It makes me wonder though. How many anthropologists, how many sociologists, how many travel journalists have documented so-called "natural interactions" in foreign lands, all observed with spiral notebook in hand? How many other cases are there of the long-lost primitive tribe, people who turned out to be sophisticated enough to put on the stone-age show that ethnologists had come to see?

And how many tourists fresh off the bus have wandered into Chinatown expecting the self-effacing shopkeeper to admit under duress that the goods are not worth the price asked? I have witnessed it.

"I don't know," the tourist said to the shopkeeper, a Cantonese woman in her fifties. "It doesn't look genuine to me. I'll give you three dollars."

"You don't like my price, go somewhere else," said the shopkeeper.

"You are not a nice person," cried the shocked tourist, "not a nice person at all!"

"Who say I have to be nice," snapped the shopkeeper.

"So how does one say 'yes' and 'no' in Chinese?" ask my friends a bit warily.

And here I do agree in part with the *New York Times Magazine* article. There is no one word for "yes" or "no"—but not out of necessity to be discreet. If anything I would say the Chinese equivalent of answering "yes" or "no" is dis*crete,* that is, specific to what is asked.

Ask a Chinese person if he or she has eaten, and he or she might say *chrle* (eaten already) or perhaps *meiyou* (have not).

Ask, "So you had insurance at the time of the accident?" and the response would be *dwei* (correct) or *meiyou* (did not have).

Ask, "Have you stopped beating your wife?" and the answer refers directly to the proposition being asserted or denied: stopped already, still have not, never beat, have no wife.

What could be clearer?

As for those who are still wondering how to translate the language of discretion, I offer this personal example.

My aunt and uncle were about to return to Beijing after a three-month visit to the United States. On their last night I announced I wanted to take them out to dinner.

"Are you hungry?" I asked in Chinese.

"Not hungry," said my uncle promptly, the same response he once gave me ten minutes before he suffered a low-blood-sugar attack.

"Not too hungry," said my aunt. "Perhaps you're hungry?"

"A little," I admitted.

"We can eat, we can eat," they both consented.

"What kind of food?" I asked.

"Oh, doesn't matter. Anything will do. Nothing fancy, just some simple food is fine."

"Do you like Japanese food? We haven't had that yet," I suggested.

They looked at each other.

"We can eat it," said my uncle bravely, this survivor of the Long March.

"We have eaten it before," added my aunt. "Raw fish."

"Oh, you don't like it?" I said. "Don't be polite. We can go somewhere else."

"We are not being polite. We can eat it," my aunt insisted.

So I drove them to Japantown and we walked past several restaurants featuring colorful plastic displays of sushi.

"Not this one, not this one either," I continued to say, as if searching for a Japanese restaurant similar to the last. "Here it is," I finally said, turning into a restaurant famous for its Chinese fish dishes from Shandong.

"Oh, Chinese food!" cried my aunt, obviously relieved.

My uncle patted my arm. "You think Chinese."

"It's your last night here in America," I said "So don't be polite. Act like an American."

And that night we ate a banquet.

Double Take

1. Why do you think Amy Tan wrote "The Language of Discretion"? What is the essay's rhetorical purpose? What is Tan responding to? What is she trying to accomplish? Do you think she succeeds in creating an exigency (a timeliness and significance) for her subject matter? Why or why not?

2. In the introduction to this essay, we mentioned that Amy Tan's style in "The Language of Discretion" is more "academic" than it is in her other essays, especially "Lost Lives of Women" and "Mother Tongue." Do you agree with this characterization? If so, explain what makes the essay academic. If not, explain why you think it is not academic. In either case, draw upon your experiences as a writer and reader of academic writing and locate examples from the essay—examples of tone, structure, and content—to support your claim.

3. At one point in the essay Tan asks, "Why am I complaining?" Do you think it is fair to characterize this essay as a complaint? Why or why not?

4. As Tan points out, we often stereotype people on the basis of their language. What stereotypes are you familiar with? How do they emerge? How can they be countered?

Seeing for Yourself

At First Glance

"In the Canon for All the Wrong Reasons" contains an excerpt from a larger essay titled *"Required Reading and Other Dangerous Subjects"* that appeared in The Threepenny Review. *Amy Tan published the excerpted version as an independent essay in* Harper's Magazine. *In many ways, this essay is the most assertive in tone of the four we have selected by Tan. As you read it, pay attention to the tone to see whether you agree with this assessment. Pay attention also to her argument, especially to how she develops it, and analyze whether or not you find Tan's stance on the responsibility of the writer convincing.*

In the Canon for All the Wrong Reasons

Several years ago I learned that I had passed a new literary milestone. I had made it to the Halls of Education under the rubric of "Multicultural Literature," also known in many schools as "Required Reading."

Thanks to this development, I now meet students who proudly tell me they're doing their essays, term papers, or master's theses on me. By that they mean that they are analyzing not just my books but me—my grade-school achievements, youthful indiscretions, marital status, as well as the movies I watched as a child, the slings and arrows I suffered as a minority, and so forth—all of which, with the hindsight of classroom literary investigation, prove to contain many Chinese omens that made it inevitable that I would become a writer.

Once I read a master's thesis on feminist writings, which included examples from *The Joy Luck Club.* The student noted that I had often used the number four, something on the order of thirty-two or thirty-six times—in any case, a number divisible by four. She pointed out that there were four mothers, four daughters, four sections of the book, four stories per section. Furthermore, there were four sides to a mahjong table, four directions of the wind, four players. More important, she postulated, my use of the number four was a symbol for the four stages of psychological development, which corresponded in uncanny ways to the four stages of some type of Buddhist philosophy I had never heard of before. The student recalled that the story contained a character called Fourth Wife, symbolizing death, and a four-year-old girl with a feisty spirit, symbolizing regeneration.

In short, her literary sleuthing went on to reveal a mystical and rather Byzantine puzzle, which, once explained, proved to be completely brilliant and precisely logical. She wrote me a letter and asked if her analysis had been correct. How I longed to say "absolutely."

The truth is, if there are symbols in my work they exist largely by accident or through someone else's interpretive design. If I wrote of "an orange moon rising on a dark night," I would more likely ask myself later if the image was a cliché, not whether it was a symbol for the feminine force rising in anger, as one master's thesis postulated. To plant symbols like that, you need a plan, good organizational skills, and a prescient understanding of the story you are about to write. Sadly, I lack those traits.

All this is by way of saying that I don't claim my use of the number four to be a brilliant symbolic device. In fact, now that it's been pointed out to me in rather astonishing ways, I consider my overuse of the number to be a flaw.

Reviewers and students have enlightened me about not only how I write but why I write. Apparently, I am driven to capture the immigrant experience, to demystify Chinese culture, to point out the differences between Chinese and American culture, even to pave the way for other Asian American writers.

If only I were that noble. Contrary to what is assumed by some students, reporters, and community organizations wishing to bestow honors on me, I am not an expert on China, Chinese culture, mahjong, the psychology of mothers and daughters, generation gaps, immigration, illegal aliens, assimilation, acculturation, racial tension, Tiananmen Square, the Most Favored Nation trade agreements, human rights, Pacific Rim economics, the purported one million missing baby girls of China, the future of Hong Kong after 1997, or, I am sorry to say, Chinese cooking. Certainly I have personal opinions on many of these topics, but by no means do my sentiments and my world of make-believe make me an expert.

So I am alarmed when reviewers and educators assume that my very personal, specific, and fictional stories are meant to be representative down to the nth detail not just of Chinese Americans but, sometimes, of all Asian culture. Is Jane Smiley's *A Thousand Acres* supposed to be taken as representative of all of American culture? If so, in what ways? Are all American fathers tyrannical? Do all American sisters betray one another? Are all American conscientious objectors flaky in love relationships?

Over the years my editor has received hundreds of permissions requests from publishers of college textbooks and multicultural anthologies, all of them wishing to reprint my works for "educational purposes." One publisher wanted to include an excerpt from *The Joy Luck Club,* a scene in which a Chinese woman invites her non-Chinese boyfriend to her parents' house for dinner. The boyfriend brings a bottle of wine as a gift and commits a number of social gaffes at the dinner table. Students were supposed to read this excerpt, then answer the following question: "If you are invited to a Chinese family's house for dinner, should you bring a bottle of wine?"

In many respects, I am proud to be on the reading lists for courses such as Ethnic Studies, Asian American Studies, Asian American Literature, Asian American History, Women's Literature, Feminist Studies, Feminist Writers of Color, and so forth.

What writer wouldn't want her work to be read? I also take a certain perverse glee in imagining countless students, sleepless at three in the morning, trying to read *The Joy Luck Club* for the next day's midterm. Yet I'm also not altogether comfortable about my book's status as required reading.

Let me relate a conversation I had with a professor at a school in southern California. He told me he uses my books in his literature class but he makes it a point to lambast those passages that depict China as backward or unattractive. He objects to any descriptions that have to do with spitting, filth, poverty, or superstitions. I asked him if China in the 1930s and 1940s was free of these elements. He said, No, such descriptions are true; but he still believes it is "the obligation of the writer of ethnic literature to create positive, progressive images."

I secretly shuddered and thought, Oh well, that's southern California for you. But then, a short time later, I met a student from UC Berkeley, a school that I myself attended. The student was standing in line at a book signing. When his turn came, he swaggered up to me, then took two steps back and said in a loud voice, "Don't you think you have a responsibility to write about Chinese men as positive role models?"

In the past, I've tried to ignore the potshots. A *Washington Post* reporter once asked me what I thought of another Asian American writer calling me something on the order of "a running dog whore sucking on the tit of the imperialist white pigs."

"Well," I said, "you can't please everyone, can you?" I pointed out that readers are free to interpret a book as they please, and that they are free to appreciate or not appreciate the result. Besides, reacting to your critics makes a writer look defensive, petulant, and like an all-around bad sport.

But lately I've started thinking it's wrong to take such a laissez-faire attitude. Lately I've come to think that I must say something, not so much to defend myself and my work but to express my hopes for American literature, for what it has the potential to become in the twenty-first century—that is, a truly American literature, democratic in the way it includes many colorful voices.

Until recently, I didn't think it was important for writers to express their private intentions in order for their work to be appreciated; I believed that any analysis of my intentions belonged behind the closed doors of literature classes. But I've come to realize that the study of literature does have its effect on how books are being read, and thus on what might be read, published, and written in the future. For that reason, I do believe writers today must talk about their intentions—if for no other reason than to serve as an antidote to what others say our intentions should be.

For the record, I don't write to dig a hole and fill it with symbols. I don't write stories as ethnic themes. I don't write to represent life in general. And I certainly don't write because I have answers. If I knew everything there is to know about mothers and daughters, Chinese and American, I wouldn't have any stories left to imagine. If I had to write about only positive role models, I wouldn't have enough imagination left to finish the first story. If I knew what to do about immigration, I would be a sociologist or a politician and not a long-winded storyteller.

So why do I write?

Because my childhood disturbed me, pained me, made me ask foolish questions. And the questions still echo. Why does my mother always talk about killing herself? Why did my father and brother have to die? If I die, can I be reborn into a happy family? Those early obsessions led to a belief that writing could be my salvation, providing me with the sort of freedom and danger, satisfaction and discomfort, truth and contradiction I can't find in anything else in life.

I write to discover the past for myself. I don't write to change the future for others. And if others are moved by my work—if they love their mothers more, scold their daughters less, or divorce their husbands who were not positive role models— I'm often surprised, usually grateful to hear from kind readers. But I don't take either credit or blame for changing their lives for better or worse.

Writing, for me, is an act of faith, a hope that I will discover what I mean by "truth." I also think of reading as an act of faith, a hope that I will discover something remarkable about ordinary life, about myself. And if the writer and the reader discover the same thing, if they have that connection, the act of faith has resulted in an act of magic. To me, that's the mystery and the wonder of both life and fiction— the connection between two individuals who discover in the end that they are more the same than they are different.

And if that doesn't happen, it's nobody's fault. There are still plenty of other books on the shelf. Choose what you like.

A CLOSER LOOK AT AMY TAN

1. As she describes it, Amy Tan had a difficult time writing her second novel, *The Kitchen God's Wife*. She started it seven times, along the way throwing out 100 pages here, 200 pages there. Anxious about following up on the success of her first novel, Tan kept asking herself, "What will people think of me for writing something like this?" Reflecting on your own writing habits and experiences, write an essay that describes your writing processes. What makes you anxious as a writer? What challenges you the most as a writer? What questions do you most frequently ask yourself when you write?

2. Reread the four essays by Amy Tan, then write an essay examining what patterns in her writing emerge. What rhetorical strategies do you notice Tan using in all her essays? What do these strategies reveal about Tan as a writer? About the way she makes decisions? About how you as a reader respond to these decisions?

3. In "Mother Tongue" Tan describes the various Englishes she heard her mother use as she was growing up, and explains that she uses all these Englishes in her writing. Looking over the four essays reprinted here, write an essay that addresses what English or Englishes Tan uses to write her essays. Does she use mainly one—standard academic English—or does she combine various Englishes? To what extent does each essay use a different English, if indeed such differences exist?

4. In her essay "In the Canon for All the Wrong Reasons," Tan makes certain claims about the responsibilities of the writer, arguing that it is not her intention or job as a writer to represent Chinese culture in positive ways, or to be a representative for all Chinese people. In reading Amy Tan's essays in this chapter, do you see support for this claim in her own writing? Write an essay in which you argue whether or not Tan practices what she claims. Does Tan practice what she claims? If not, why not? If yes, explain why you agree or disagree with her stance.

Looking from Writer to Writer

1. Both Amy Tan and Alice Walker write about their relationships with their mothers and other women, describing these relationships as influential on their own writing. Reading over their essays, compare the way each essayist portrays this relationship. What is the connection for each between women, creativity, and writing? Why do you think women play such an important role in Tan's and Walker's essays? To what extent do their cultural experiences shape these relationships similarly? How do they shape them differently?

2. Joseph Epstein is known as a guardian of language and calls himself a "language snob." He claims that "the duty of everyone who considers himself educated is to keep language alive by using it with respect and precision." Many of Epstein's essays reflect a running theme that suggests that standards of language excellence, correctness, and clarity must be preserved. Compare Epstein's views on language with Amy Tan's as she presents them in "Mother Tongue" and "The Language of Discretion." How would Tan respond to Epstein's claims about the "correctness" of language? What arguments would she make against such an elitist view of language? Make your case by drawing in particular on Tan's idea of multiple "Englishes."

3. At the end of his essay on writing, "No Reconciliation Allowed," Edward Said cites Theodor Adorno, who writes, "the writer sets up house . . . For a man who no longer has a homeland, writing becomes a place to live." Explain what Adorno means in this statement. Then think about how it applies to the writing of Edward Said and Amy Tan. How does writing for each of them become a place to live? In what ways are the "imaginary homelands" that they create in words similar and different?

Looking Beyond

FICTION

The Bonesetter's Daughter. New York: G. P. Putnam, 2001.
The Hundred Secret Senses. New York: G.P. Putnam, 1995.
The Joy Luck Club. New York: G.P. Putnam, 1989.
The Kitchen God's Wife. New York: G.P. Putnam, 1991.

CHILDREN'S BOOKS

The Chinese Siamese Cat. New York: Maxwell Macmillan International, 1994.
The Moon Lady. New York: Maxwell Macmillan International, 1992.

John Updike

John Hoyer Updike was born on March 18, 1932, in Reading, Pennsylvania, a town that was to serve as the model for the fictional Brewer of some of his later novels. At an early age, he became fascinated by writing—what he calls the "miracle of printer's ink." By the age of 12, he was already aspiring to become a contributor to *The New Yorker,* an aspiration that became a reality nearly 10 years later. In high school Updike contributed drawings, articles, and poetry to the school newspaper, an involvement with school publications that was to continue when he attended Harvard in 1950. At Harvard he served as a cartoonist, then as a poet and prose writer, and finally as president at the *Lampoon,* the university's literary magazine. After getting married in 1953 and graduating from Harvard as an English major in 1954, Updike achieved "the ecstatic breakthrough of my literary life" when he published a poem and a story in *The New Yorker.*

After a year spent at the Ruskin School of Drawing and Fine Art in Oxford, England, Updike returned to the United States where he worked as a staff writer for *The New Yorker* for two years, leaving in 1957 to pursue his fiction and poetry writing. It was during the following years spent living in Ipswich, Massachusetts (the setting for the fictional town of Tarbox; see "The Tarbox Police" reprinted here), with his growing family, that Updike earned his reputation as a poet, short story writer, and novelist. His first book of poems, *The Carpentered Hen and Other Tame Creatures,* was published in 1958, and his first novel, *The Poorhouse Fair,* in 1959. Since then Updike has published a number of best-selling novels, short story and poetry collections, essay collections, book reviews, and critical essays. His many accolades include the Pulitzer Prize (twice, for *Rabbit Is Rich* and *Rabbit at Rest;* the National Book Award for Fiction, the O. Henry Prize, the National Book Critics Circle Award for Criticism, and the National Medal of Arts. His novels have been turned into movies, most recently *The Witches of Eastwick,* and he has appeared twice on the cover of *Time* magazine. As a professional writer, one who is able to sustain himself through his writing, Updike has become an international celebrity, traveling and lecturing extensively—from Venezuela to Africa. His work confirms his reputation as one of America's premier fiction writers.

There is a strong connection to place in Updike's writing. Much of his work is about places he has lived and people he has known. His first novel is based upon an actual poorhouse, and the fictional towns he creates are often based on towns where he lived. Similarly, many of his essays are focused around places: cemeteries, golf courses, baseball games, and so on. "We must write where we stand," he explains, "wherever we do stand, there is life; and an imitation of the life we know, however narrow, is our only ground." It is perhaps the grounded nature of his writing that accounts for its pictorial quality. As he explains in his essay "Why Write?" Updike writes visually and spatially; his books are conceived as "objects in space, with events and persons composed within them like shapes on a canvas." This pictorial quality may well be the result of his early interest in and training in drawing.

Reflecting on his writing, Updike once said, "my work is meditation, not pontification." As you read the essays, consider what Updike means by this statement. Look for the meditative quality in Updike's writing, especially how he creates it rhetorically through his use of subordination and parenthesis. Look also at the pictorial quality of his writing. Many of his essays seem to be constructed of a collection of scenes or snapshots related to a single idea or place, yet Updike manages to hold these snapshots together. Pay attention to how Updike does this, both at the organizational and at the sentence level.

Updike on Writing

At First Glance

The essay "Why Write?" was originally given as a speech at the Festival of Arts in Adelaide, South Australia, and later published in the Southern Review *in Australia. As you read it, consider what Updike has to say about writing and think about it in terms of your own writing. How much, for example, does what Updike say about his writing apply to the writing situations you experience as a student? In addition, consider what Updike has to say in response to the charge that his writing lacks a social agenda. Some critics would say that Updike's writing is visually stunning, extremely pictorial, but that it lacks a political edge. Keep this in mind as you read what Updike says about writing.*

Why Write?

My title offers me an opportunity to set a record of brevity at this Festival of Arts; for an adequate treatment would be made were I to ask, in turn, "Why not?" and sit down.

But instead I hope to explore, for not too many minutes, the question from the inside of a man who, rather mysteriously to himself, has earned a livelihood for close to twenty years by engaging in the rather selfish and gratuitous activity called "writing." I do *not* propose to examine the rather different question of what use is writing to the society that surrounds and, if he is fortunate, supports the writer. The ancients said the purpose of poetry, of writing, was to entertain and to instruct; Aristotle put forward the still fascinating notion that a dramatic action, however terrible and piteous, carries off at the end, in catharsis, the morbid, personal, subjective impurities of our emotions. The enlargement of sympathy, through identification with the lives of fictional others, is frequently presented as an aim of narrative; D.H. Lawrence, with characteristic fervor, wrote, "And here lies the vast importance of the novel, properly handled. It can inform and lead into new places the flow of our sympathetic consciousness, and can lead our sympathy away in recoil from things that are dead." Kafka wrote that a book is an ax to break the frozen sea within us. The frozen sea within himself, he must have meant; though the ax of Kafka's own art (which, but for Max Brod's posthumous disobedience, Kafka would taken with him into the grave), has served as an analogous purpose for others. This note of pain, of saintly suffering, is a modern one, far removed from the serene and harmonious bards and poets of the courts of olden time. Listen to Flaubert, in one of his letters to Louise Colet:

I love my work with a love that is frenzied and perverted, as an ascetic loves the hair shirt that scratches his belly. Sometimes, when I am empty, when words don't come, when I find I haven't written a single sentence after scribbling whole pages, I collapse on my couch and lie there dazed, bogged in a swamp of despair, hating myself and blaming myself for this demented pride which makes me pant after a chimera. A quarter of an hour later everything changes; my heart is pounding with joy. Last Wednesday I had to get up and fetch my handkerchief; tears were streaming down my face. I had been moved by my own writing; the emotion I had conceived, the phrase that rendered it, and satisfaction of having found the phrase—all were causing me to experience the most exquisite pleasure.

Well, if such is the writer at work, one wonders why he doesn't find a pleasanter job; and one also wonders why he appears himself to be the chief market for his own product.

Most people sensibly assume that writing is propaganda. Of course, they admit, there is bad propaganda, like the boy-meets-tractor novels of socialist realism, and old-fashioned propaganda, like Christian melodrama and the capitalist success stories of Horatio Alger or Samuel Smiles. But that some message is intended, wrapped in the story like a piece of crystal carefully mailed in cardboard and excelsior, is not doubted. Scarcely a day passes in my native land that I don't receive some letter from a student or teacher asking me *what I meant to say* in such a book, asking me to elaborate more fully on some sentence I deliberately whittled into minimal shape, or inviting me to speak on some topic, usually theological or sexual, on which it is pleasantly assumed I am an expert. The writer as hero, as Hemingway or Saint-Exupéry or D'Annunzio, a tradition of which Camus was perhaps the last example, has been replaced in America by the writer as educationist. Most writers teach, a great many teach writing; writing is furiously taught in the colleges even as the death knell of the book and the written word is monotonously tolled; any writer, it is assumed, can give a lecture, and the purer products of his academic mind, the "writings" themselves, are sifted and, if found of sufficient quality, installed in their places on the assembly belt of study, as objects of educational contemplation.

How dare one confess, to the politely but firmly inquiring letter-writer who takes for granted that as a remote but functioning element of his education you are duty-bound to provide the information and elucidating essay that will enable him to complete his term paper, or his Ph.D. thesis, or his critical *opus*—how dare one confess that the absence of a swiftly expressible message is, often, *the* message; that reticence is as important a tool to the writer as expression; that the hasty filling out of a questionnaire is not merely irrelevant but *inimical* to the writer's proper activity; that this activity is rather curiously private and finicking, a matter of exorcism and manufacture rather than of toplofty proclamation; that what he makes is ideally as ambiguous and opaque as life itself; that, to be blunt, the social usefulness of writing matters to him primarily in that it somehow creates a few job opportunities—in Australia, a few government grants—a few opportunities to live as a writer.

Not counting journalists and suppliers of scripts to the media, hardly a hundred American men and women earn their living by writing, in a wealthy nation of two hundred million. Does not then, you ask, such a tiny band of privileged spokesmen owe its country, if not the trophy of a Nobel Prize,★ as least the benign services of a spiritual aristocracy? Is not the writer's role, indeed, to speak for humanity, as conscience and prophet and servant of the billions not able to speak for themselves? The conception is attractive, and there are some authors, mostly Russian, who have aspired to such grandeur without entirely compromising their gifts. But in general, when a writer such as Sartre or Faulkner becomes a great man, a well-intentioned garrulity replaces the specific witness that has been theirs to give.

The last time I dared appear on a platform in a foreign land, it was in Kenya, where I had to confess, under some vigorous questioning from a large white man in the audience, that the general betterment of mankind, and even the improvement of social conditions within my own violently imperfect nation, were *not* my basic motivation as a writer. To be sure, *as a citizen* one votes, attends meetings, subscribes to liberal pieties, pays or withholds taxes, and contributes to charities even more generously than—it turns out—one's own President. But as a writer, for me to attempt to extend my artistic scope into all the areas of my human concern, to substitute nobility of purpose for accuracy of execution, would certainly be to forfeit whatever social usefulness I *do* have. It has befallen a Solzhenitsyn to have experienced the Soviet labor camps; it has befallen Miss Gordimer and Mr. Mtshali† to suffer the tensions and paradoxes and outrages of a racist police state; social protest, and a hope of reform, is in the very fiber of their witness. But a writer's witness, surely, is of value in its circumstantiality. Solzhenitsyn's visible and brave defiance of the Soviet state is magnificent; but a novel like *The First Circle* affords us more than a blind flash of conditioned and—let's face it—chauvinistic indignation; it affords us entry into an unknown world, it offers a complex and only implicitly indignant portrait of how human beings live under a certain sort of political system. When I think of the claustrophobic and seething gray world of *The First Circle,* I am reminded in texture of Henry Miller's infamous Paris novels. Here, too, we have truth, and an undeniable passion to proclaim the truth—a seedy and repellent yet vital truth—though the human conditions Miller describes are far removed from any hope of political cure. And Miller, in his way, was also a martyr: as with Solzhenitsyn, his works could not be published in his native land.

We must write where we stand; wherever we do stand, there is life; and an imitation of the life we know, however narrow, is our only ground. As I sat on that stage in Kenya, a symbolic American in a corner of that immense range of peoples symbolically called The Third World, I felt guilty and bewildered that I could not hear in my formidable accuser's orotund phrases anything that had to do with my

---

★That year awarded to Australia's Patrick White.

†Oswald Mtshali, Zulu poet. Both he and Nadine Gordimer were present at the Adelaide Festival.

practice of the writer's profession; I was discomfited that my concerns—to survive, to improve, to make my microcosms amusing to me and then to others, to fail, if fail I must, through neither artistic cowardice nor laziness, to catch all the typographical errors in my proofs, to see that my books appear in jackets both striking and fairly representative of the contents, to arrange words and spaces and imagined realities in patterns never exactly achieved before, to be able to defend any sentence I publish—I was embarrassed that my concerns were so ignoble, compared to his. But, once off the stage (where a writer should rarely be), I tend to be less apologetic, and even to believe that my well-intentioned questioner, and the silent faces in the same audience looking to me to atone for America's sins real and supposed, and the touching schoolchildren begging me by letter to get them through the seventh grade—that none of these people have any felt comprehension of my vocation.

Why write? As soon ask, why rivet? Because a number of personal accidents drift us toward the occupation of riveter, which pre-exists, and, most importantly, the riveting-gun exists, and we love it.

Think of a pencil. What a quiet, nimble, slender and then stubby wonderworker he is! At his touch, worlds leap into being; a tiger with no danger, a steamroller with no weight, a palace at no cost. All children are alive to the spell of pencil and crayons, of making something, as it were, from nothing; a few children never move out from under this spell, and try to become artists. I was once a rapturous child drawing at the dining-room table, under a stained-glass chandelier that sat like a hat on the swollen orb of my excitement. What is exciting that child, so distant from us in time and space? He appears, from the vantage of this lectern unimaginable to him, to be in the grip of two philosophical perceptions.

One, mimesis demands no displacement; the cat I drew did not have to fight for food or love with the real cat that came to the back porch. I was in drawing *adding* to the world rather than rearranging the finite amount of goods within it. We were a family struggling on the poverty edge of the middle class during the Depression; I was keen to avoid my father's noisy plight within the plague of competition; pencil and paper were cheap, unlike most other toys.

And, Two, the world called into being on the pencilled paper admitted of connections. An early exercise, whose pleasure returns to me whenever I assemble a collection of prose or poetry or whenever, indeed, I work several disparate incidents or impressions into the shape of a single story, was this: I would draw on one sheet of paper an assortment of objects—flowers, animals, stars, toaster, chairs, comic-strip creatures, ghosts, noses—and connect them with lines, a path of two lines, so that they all became the fruit of a single impossible tree. The exact age when this creative act so powerfully pleased me I cannot recall; the wish to make collections, to assemble sets, is surely a deep urge of the human mind in its playful, artistic aspect. As deep, it may be, as the urge to hear a story from beginning to end, or the little ecstacy of extracting resemblances from different things. Proust, of course, made simile the cornerstone of his theory of aesthetic bliss, and Plato, if I understand him right, felt that that which a set of like objects have in common *must* have a separate existence in itself, as the *idea* which delivers us, in our perception of the world, from the nightmare of nominalism. At any rate, to make a man of pencil and paper is as much a magical act as painting a bison with blood on the wall of a cave; a child, frail and overshadowed, and groping for his fare, herein *captures* something and, further, brings down praise from on high.

I have described the artistic transaction as being between the awakening ego and the world of matter to which it awakes; but no doubt the wish to please one's parents enters early, and remains with the artist all his life, as a desire to please the world, however displeasing his behavior may seem, and however self-satisfying the work pretends to be. We are surprised to discover, for instance, that Henry James hoped to make lots of money, and that James Joyce read all of his reviews. The artist's personality has an awkward ambivalence: he is a cave dweller who yet hopes to be pursued into his cave. The need for privacy, the need for recognition: a child's vulnerability speaks in both needs, and in my own reaction to, say, the beseeching mail just described, I detect the live ambiguity—one is avid to receive the letters, and loath to answer them. Or (to make some reference to the literary scene I know best) consider the striking contrast between the eager, even breathless warmth of Saul Bellow's fiction, inviting our love and closeness with every phrase, and Bellow's own faintly haughty, distinctly edgy personal surface Again, J.D. Salinger wrote a masterpiece, *The Catcher in the Rye,* recommending that readers who enjoy a book call up the author; then he spent his next twenty years avoiding the telephone. A writer, I would say, out of no doubt deficiencies of character, has constructed a cave-shaped organ, hollow more like a mouth than like an ear, through which he communicates with the world at one remove. Somewhat, perhaps, as his own sub-conscious communicates with him through dreams. Because the opportunities for feedback have been reduced to letters that need not be answered and telephones that can be unlisted, to an annual gauntlet of reviews and non-bestowal of prizes, the communication can be more honest than is any but the most trusting personal exchange; yet also great opportunities for distortion exist unchecked. For one more of these rather subterranean and reprehensible satisfactions of writing that I am here confessing is that the world, so balky and resistant and humiliating, can in the act of mimesis be rectified, adjusted, chastened, purified. Fantasies defeated in reality can be fully indulged; tendencies deflected by the cramp of circumstance can be fol-lowed to an end. In my own case I have noticed, so often it has ceased to surprise me, a prophetic quality of my fictions, even to the subsequent appearance in my life of originally fictional characters. We write, that is, out of latency as much as mem-ory; and years later our laggard lives in reality act out, often with eerie fidelity, the patterns projected in our imaginings.

But we have come too far, too fast, from that ambitious child making his pencil move beneath the stained-glass chandelier. In my adolescence I discovered one could write with a pencil as well as draw, without the annoying need to consult reality so frequently. Also, the cave beneath the written page holds many more kinds of space than the one beneath the drawing pad. My writing tends, I think, to be pic-torial, not only in its groping for visual precision but in the way the books are con-ceived, as objects in space, with events and persons composed within them like shapes on a canvas. I do not recommend this approach; it is perhaps a perversion of the primal narrative urge. Storytelling, for all its powers of depiction, shares with music the medium of time, and perhaps its genius, its most central transformation, has to do with time, with rhythm and echo and the sense of time not frozen as in a painting but channelled and harnessed as in a symphony.

But one can give no more than what one has received, and we try to create for others, in our writings, aesthetic sensations we have experienced. In my case, some of these would be: the graphic precision of a Dürer or a Vermeer, the offhand-and-backwards-feeling verbal and psychological accuracy of a Henry Green, the wonderful embowering metaphors of Proust, the enigmatic concreteness of Kafka and Joyce, the collapse into components of a solved mathematical problem, the unriddling of a scrupulous mystery story, the earth-scorning scope of science fiction, the tear-producing results of a truly humorous piece of writing. Writing, really, can do rather few substantial things: it can make us laugh, it can make us weep, and if is pornography and we are rather young, it can make us come. It can also, of course, make us sleep; and though in the frequent discussion of the writer's social purpose this soporific effect is unfailingly ignored, I suspect it is the most widespread practical effect of writing—a book is less often a flaming sword or a beam of light than a bedtime toddy. Whatever the use, we hope that some members of society will find our product useful enough to purchase; but I think it would be a hypocrisy to pretend that these other people's welfare, or communication with them, or desire to ennoble or radicalize or terrify or lull them, is the primary reason why one writes.

No, what a writer wants, as every aspiring writer can tell you, is to *get into print*. To transform the changing shadows of one's dimly and fitfully lived life into print—into metal or, with the advent of offset printing, into rather mysteriously electrified rubber—to lift through the doubled magic of language and mechanical reproduction our own impressions and dreams and playful constructions into another realm of existence, a multiplied and far-flung existence, into a space far wider than that which we occupy, into a time theoretically eternal: *that* is the siren song that holds us to our desks, our dismal revisions, our insomnia panics, our dictionaries and encyclopedias, our lonely and, the odds long are, superfluous labor. "Of making many books there is no end; and much study is a weariness of the flesh." A weariness one can certainly feel entering even a modestly well-stocked bookstore. Yet it is just this involvement in the world of commerce and industry, this imposition of one's otherwise evanescent fancies upon the machinery of manufacture and distribution, that excites the writer's ego, and gives an illusion of triumph over his finitude.

Although, as a child, I lived what was to become my material and message, my wish to write did not begin with that material and message: rather, it was a wish to escape from it, into an altogether better world. When I was thirteen, a magazine came into the house, *The New Yorker* by name, and I loved that magazine so much I concentrated all my wishing into an effort to make myself small and inky and intense enough to be received into its pages. Once there, I imagined, some transfigured mode of being, called a "writer's life," would begin for me. My fantasy was not entirely fantastic, as my domineering position on this platform and the first-class airplanes tickets that brought me halfway around the world testify. But what I would not altogether insincerely ask you to accept is something shabby, precarious, and even craven about a writer's life.

Among artists, a writer's equipment is least out-of-reach—the language we all more or less use, a little patience at grammar and spelling, the common adventures of blundering mortals. A painter must learn to paint; his studio is redolent of alchemic substances and physical force. The musician's arcanum of specialized knowledge and personal dexterity is even more intimidating, less accessible to the untrained, and therefore somehow less corruptible than the writer's craft. Though some painters and musicians go bad in the prime of their lives, far fewer do, and few so drastically, as writers. Our trick is treacherously thin; our art is so incorrigibly amateur that novices constantly set the world of letters on its ear, and the very phrase "professional writer" has a grimy sound. Hilaire Belloc said that the trouble with writing was that it was never meant to be a profession, it was meant to be a hobby. An act of willful play, as I have described it.

So I have not spoken up to now of language, of the joys of using it well, of the role of the writer as a keeper of the keys of language, a guardian of usage and enforcer of precision. This does not seem to me a very real notion, however often it is put forward.★ Language goes on evolving in the street and in the spoken media, and well-written books are the last places it looks for direction. The writer follows after the spoken language, usually timidly. I see myself described in reviews as a doter upon words. It is true, I am grateful to have been born into English, with its polyglot flexibility and the happy accident, in the wake of two empires, of its worldwide currency. But what I am conscious of doting on is not English *per se,* its pliable grammar and abundant synonyms, but its potential, for the space of some phrases or paragraphs, of becoming reality, of engendering out of imitation another reality, infinitely lesser but thoroughly possessed, thoroughly human.

Pascal says, "When a natural discourse paints a passion or an effect, one feels within oneself the truth of what one reads, which was there before, although one did not know it. Hence one is inclined to love him who makes us feel it, for he has not shown us his own riches, but ours." The writer's strength is not his own; he is a conduit who so positions himself that the world at his back flows through to the readers on the other side of the page. To keep this conduit scoured is his laborious task; to be, in the act of writing, anonymous, the end of his quest for fame.

Beginning, then, with cunning private ambitions and a childish fascination with the implements of graphic representation, I find myself arrived, in this audible search for self-justification, at an embarrassed altruism. Beginning with the wish to make an impression, one ends wishing to erase the impression, to make of it a perfect transparency, to make of oneself a point of focus purely, as selfless as a lens. One begins by seeking celebrity and ends by feeling a terrible impatience with

---

★As, say, by Iris Murdoch, in the 1972 Blashfield Address.

everything—every flattering attention, every invitation to speak and to impersonate a wise man, every hunger of the ego and of the body—an impatience with everything that clouds and clots our rapt witness to the world that surrounds and transcends us. A writer begins with his personal truth, with that obscure but vulnerable and, once lost, precious life that he lived before becoming a writer; but, those first impressions discharged—a process of years—he finds himself, though empty, still posed in the role of a writer, with it may be an expectant audience of sorts and certainly a habit of communion. It is then that he dies as a writer, and becomes an inert cultural object merely, or is born again, by re-submitting his ego, as it were, to fresh drafts of experience and refined operations of his mind. *To remain interested*—of American novelists, only Henry James continued in old age to advance his art; most indeed, wrote their best novels first, or virtually first. Energy ebbs as we live; success breeds disillusion as surely as failure; the power of hope to generate action and vision lessens. Almost alone the writer can reap profit from this loss. An opportunity to sing louder from within the slackening ego is his. For his song has never been all his own: he has been its excuse as much as its source. The little tyrant's delight in wielding a pencil always carried with it an empathy into the condition of *being* a pencil; more and more the writer thinks of himself as an instrument, a means whereby a time and a place make their mark. To become less and transmit more, to replenish energy with wisdom—some such hope, at this more than mid-point of my life, is the reason why I write.

Double Take

1. What is John Updike's answer to the question, why write? Do you agree with his answer? Explain, drawing from your own assumptions about the purpose of writing.
2. In "Why Write?" Updike says, "Writing, really, can make us do rather few substantial things: it can make us laugh, it can make us weep, and if it is pornography and we are rather young, it can make us come. It can also, of course, make us sleep." In your opinion, what else, if anything, can writing make us do? What do you think writing should make us do? While answering these questions, consider how writing can make us "do" anything.
3. How much does what Updike says about writing in this essay apply to fiction writing, especially the novel, and how much does it apply to nonfiction, especially essay-writing? How much of an overlap do you see? At what point do his claims about fiction no longer apply to essayistic writing, to the kind of writing you will most likely do in school?

At First Glance

First published in the Transatlantic Review, *"Cemeteries" provides a good example of the pictorial quality of John Updike's writing. The essay itself is a series of vignettes revolving around the central image of cemeteries. Pay attention to the imagistic qualities of the essay and examine how Updike creates these verbal images. What is his technique? What effects do these images produce for the reader? Also, think about whether or not this essay makes some kind of argument and, if so, what this argument is. Does it matter that the argument might not be direct?*

Cemeteries

"Personal relationships must have been very strange," the tall young State Department man said to me. We were speaking of Russia in the 1930's; we had just turned from the tomb of Stalin's wife, a square stone column the height of a woman, capped by a sculptured female head with something touchingly vivid about the nape of the marble neck. Along tight paths we walked among the heavy tombstones of generals, scientist, commissars, engineers. Many bore inset photographs of the departed; a miniature iron tank adorned the tomb of a tank commander famous in World War II. A ballerina's slippers had been carved on a stone block as if casually set there, creased and warm from use. It was a sunny October Sunday years before Svetlana's memoirs had clarified the mysterious death of her mother; my escort had been describing to me the rumors of poisoning, of murderous Kremlin concubinage, of intricate betrayals.

"Even more than usual," I agreed, and tried to picture men and women rearing children, honoring parents, and seeking each other's love in a decade like a low-ceilinged subway tunnel where the lights are flickering off and the air is suffocatingly stale. I couldn't picture it, life continuing, but here was proof, here were the survivors, Soviet citizens honored in death, standing erect, in close order, in the open, enjoying the pale sunshine and late flowers of the day and season. Life-sized, with faces and trinkets, the tombs conveyed a cheerful substantial impression, as if this atheist state, like ancient Egypt, considered death a short and eminently practical voyage. I felt happy here; I am usually happy in cemeteries.

In Highgate Cemetery—the old, neglected section above the famous monument to Karl Marx—the English journalist asked me about oral love. He was short and middle-aged and had cleverly sensed I would like a cemetery. It was again a warm October day. Intensely green overgrowth narrowed the paths and all but smothered the tombs. Some vaults had been burst open by flourishing saplings; there was a kind of mews of tombs, an arcade of green vault doors so rusted and silted shut no Judgment Day, one felt, could ever crack them open, though there were keyholes and doorknobs and numbers and knockers, as on any genteel, if shady, street.

I discovered I had no opinion on oral love. I ventured that, all other things being equal, I was as much for it as not. In irritation the journalist tucked his note-book away and began to rail at the dead. Their pretensions to immortality enraged him. He rattled at the door of a grenadiers colonel interred in 1903 and invited me, where vandals had smashed a grating, to peer in and see how a burrowing crea-ture, a rat or badger, had penetrated the coffin, adding sawdust to the rubble of bricks and powdered mortar. The pious mottoes—"From strength to strength in the everlasting." "Love shines yet more brightly above"—abraded against my escort like supercilious assertions at a party where he was socially insecure. And indeed he came, with his cleverness, from a Midlands working-class family, and the tombs represented Victorian gentry. "The fools!" he shouted. "'Honor perisheth never.' Well, Mr. Nevil Cunninghame-Wright Esq., O.M., M.B.E., it bloody well has!" He kicked at the black drift of rustflakes and leafmold clogging the Cunninghame-Wright portal, and read the next motto. "'Earth's shadows testify to radiance eter-nal.' Oh, my buggering God! Oh, my dear old Eustace Pickering, you poor old sodden mouse-nest of agglutinated bones, how do you like your radiance eter-nal now?"

He was most affronted by the immense mausoleum of a man called Julius Beer. Chinks in its cupola had admitted generations of pigeons; their excrement, feathers, and corpses covered the marble floor. The mosaic murals of pre-Raphaelite angels were clouded with lime. The journalist, when I had satisfied his desire that I look in, put his mouth against the crusty grating and shouted, "Hooh!" Nothing happened. He bellowed louder, "HOOH!" Evidently, the pigeons were supposed to fly out. He squinted into the depths of the befouled and forgotten memorial. "Damn," he said. "I think they've cleaned it up a bit." He backed off, and his face brightened. "But can you catch that smell, that evil stench? It's a pigeon Dachau. You ass, Julius, you absolutely silly puffed-up old capitalist ass, you were so full of yourself we don't even know what you *did!*" It was true; no identification, not even dates, qualified the high carved name of Julius Beer, the emperor of doveshit.

The cemetery had been private and fashionable. An outward-spreading cypress, now obscured by deciduous trees that had grown up, was to have been the center of a symmetrical system of vault lanes and individual tombs. One tomb, of a "menagerist," had a smiling lion carved upon it. Deep in the woods—elm and oak and ailanthus that had taken root, perhaps, at the outset of World War II—a stone angel lifted her weather-blurred face, vague as Anglican theology, toward green leaves. We were far from the urban compactness of Novodyevichi Cemetery. I was impressed by England's tropical luxuriance; the force so decisively tamed in the parks was here, untended, shattering marble and swallowing crypts whole. Yet I felt that these genteel 19th-century dead, who to judge from the novels about them had loved a country wildness, were not as overthrown as my escort believed. They were merely immersed, much as the living are immersed. A wild sapling grafts onto the spirit no less snugly than a toy tank.

Both of my escorts—the State Department man tacitly, obliquely; the journalist boisterously, indignantly—disapproved of the dead, implying that they were still alive. A cemetery, which like a golf course bestows the gift of space, also touches us with the excitement, the generalized friction, of a party.

The Chemin du Puy steeply climbed the hill from Antibes and on the long gradual downslope, before the farmhouse with the sign MÉCHANTS CHIENS, passed a cemetery of bright plaster, where things twirled to discourage birds. Though lonesome, I never dared enter; the dead were speaking French.

In Mayrhofen, at Christmas, candles glowed and guttered in the snow, before strict upright stones of black marble. The faces of Tyrolean burghers alternated with that of an anguished Jesus. *Hier ruben in Gott,* the stones said.

And in Peredelkino, in the village graveyard where Pasternak is buried, scrolling iron crosses spoke of an Orthodox Russia where burial took place in springtime, and metal echoed the burgeoning shape of the flowers.

In Prague, the tombstones of the Jewish cemetery were squeezed together like cards, conjuring up a jumble of bodies underneath. Visitors left pebbles on them instead of flowers. Was it an ancient custom, or something forced upon the Jews by Hitler? A kind of chapel here had walls gray with the names, six hundred thousand of them, of Jews whose death-dates were 1943, 1944, 1945. Years whose smoke permanently stained the ceiling of Heaven.

And the mass graves of the Siege dead near Leningrad, acres of hummocks, like giant bulb beds in winter, marked with stones tablets 1941, 1942, 1943.

And the Pyramids, and the gaily painted corridors leading into the robbed chambers of Ramses, and the even gayer cells of the nobles, into which light is shuttled by a set of mirrors held by silent brown guides. In Cairo, the necropolis is inhabited by children and beggars, and is a slum.

The Long Island necropolis seen from an airplane: a pegboard that abruptly yields to the equally regular avenues of the living, each gray rooftop companioned by a green backyard pool, like a wide-awake eye.

Also from the air, descending I think into Cleveland, I saw a little triangular family cemetery, precious soil spared from the corner of a field, like the book page whose corner I had turned down to mark my place.

And the stingy clusters of markers, too many of them children, in rocky abandoned places once farmed, like Star Island off Portsmouth, or the mountainsides of Vermont north of Montpelier.

In Marigot, on St. Martin's, one noon, my wife and I walked a mile to a restaurant that was closed, along the shimmering white road, and came back along the beach to cool our feet, and came to a cemetery that was being nibbled away by the sea. There were no signs of an attempt to halt the gentle erosion; one tombstone was teetering, another had fallen upside down, and fragments of a third were being washed and ground into sand. We went up into the cemetery, and there, amid the French *colons* and the tessellated patterns suggestive of voodoo and the conch-shell borders and the paper flowers and the real flowers that looked like paper, my wife, starved and weary, sat on a crypt and dried her feet with her bandana and put on her shoes. I took her picture; I have the slide.

Years before, when we were at college, a girl whose major was biology and whose hobby was fungi used to make me bicycle with her to ancient burying-grounds in Cambridge and Concord. There, on the tipping old Puritan slate tomb-stones half sunk in the earth and sometimes wearing artfully shaped weatherproof hats of lead, she would show me lichen, in a surprising variety of colors, each round specimen, scarcely thicker than a stain, somehow an individual creature or, rather, two creatures—a fungus living symbiotically with an alga. Whitish, brownish, bluish, the lichens enforced their circles upon the incised, uniquely graceful Puritan lettering and the winged skulls which, as the 17th century softened into the 19th, became mere angels, with human faces. She was, perhaps because she majored in biology, wonderful at sex—talk of oral love!—and the lichen, the winged skulls, the sweaty ache in my calves from bicycling, and her plump cleavage as she bent low for a determined inspection and scraping all merged in a confused lazy anticipation of our return and my reward, her round mouth. Cemeteries, where women make themselves at home, are in one sense dormitories, rows of beds.

"But the *view* is so lovely," my mother said to me. We were standing on the fam-ily burial plot, in Pennsylvania. Around us, and sloping down the hill, were the red sandstone markers of planted farmers, named and dated in the innocent rectangular lettering that used to be on patent-medicine labels. My grandfather's stone, rough-hewn granite with the family name carved in the form of bent branches, did not seem very much like him. My grandmother's Christian name, cut below his, was longer and, characteristically, dominated while taking the subservient position. Else-where on the plot were his parents, and great-aunts and uncles I had met only at spicy-smelling funerals in my remotest childhood. My mother paced off two yards, saying, "Here's Daddy and me. See how much room is left?"

"But she"—I didn't have to name my wife—"has never *lived* here." I was again a child at one of those dreaded family gatherings on dark holiday afternoons—awk-ward and stuffed and suffocating under the constant need for tact. Only in Pennsyl-vania, among my kin, am I pressured into such difficult dance-steps of evasion and placation. Every buried coffin was a potential hurt feeling. I tried a perky sideways jig, hopefully humorous, and added, "And the children would feel crowded and keep everybody awake."

She turned her face and gazed downward at the view—a lush valley, a white-washed farmhouse, a straggling orchard, and curved sections of the highway leading to the city whose glistening tip, a television relay, could just be glimpsed five ridges in the distance. She had expected my evasion—she could hardly have expected me to pace off my six feet greedily and plant stakes—but had needed to bring me to it, to breast my refusal and the consequence that, upon receiving her and my father, the plot would be closed, would cease to be a working piece of land. Why is it that nothing that happens to me is as real as these dramas that my mother arranges around herself, like Titania calling Peaseblossom and Mustardseed from the air? Why is it that everyone else lacks the sanguine, corporeal, anguished reality of these farmers, these people of red sandstone? When was Pennsylvania an ocean, to lay down all this gritty rock, that stains your palms pink when you lift it?

Placatory, I agreed, "The view *is* lovely."

"Think of poor Daddy," she said, turning away, Mustardseed dismissed. "He has no sense of landscape. He says he wants to be buried under a sidewalk."

The cemetery of the town where I live, like many, has climbed a hill, and the newest graves are on the top, arranged along ample smooth roadways of asphalt. Some friends of ours have buried children here. But I had stayed away until it was time to teach my son to ride a bicycle. It is safe; on weekdays few cars visit the fresh graves, with their plastic-potted morning glories and exotic metal badges from veterans' organizations. The stones are marble, modernly glossy and simple, though I suppose that time will eventually reveal them as another fashion, dated and quaint. Now, the sod is still raw, the sutures of turf are unhealed, the earth still humped, the wreaths scarcely withered. Sometimes we see, my son and I, the strained murmurous breakup of a ceremony, or a woman in mourning emerge from an automobile and kneel, or stand nonplussed, as in a social gap. I remember my grandfather's funeral, the hurried cross of sand the minister drew on the coffin lid, the whine of the lowering straps, the lengthening, cleanly cut sides of clay, the thought of air, the lack of air forever in the close dark space lined with pink satin, the foreverness, the towering foreverness—it does not bear thinking about, it is too heavy, like my son's body as he wobbles away from me on his bicycle. "Keep moving," I shout, the words turning chalky in my mouth, as they tend to do when I seek to give instruction—"the essence of the process is to keep moving!"

Double Take

1. In "Cemeteries" John Updike uses a great deal of picturesque writing: the decade that looks like a subway, the family cemetery in Cleveland that looks like a folded book page, and the Puritan tombstones overgrown with lichens ("whitish, brownish, bluish, the lichens enforced their circles upon the incised, uniquely graceful Puritan lettering and the winged skulls which . . . became mere angels with human faces"), to name a few. What is the rhetorical effect of such images? In what ways do they contribute to the meaning of this essay?

2. Updike covers a range of topics in this essay: politics, death, family, love, sex, and so forth. Structurally and thematically, what holds this essay together? What is the point of the essay?

3. Like the essay "Why Write?" this essay contains a sexual reference, this time to a college girl majoring in biology who bicycled with the writer to cemeteries. Why do you think Updike includes this reference? What function does it serve? Is it merely gratuitous? Is it sexist?

4. What is the effect of the phrase "my son and I" in the following sentence: "Sometimes we see, my son and I, the strained murmurous breakup of the ceremony . . ." How would the effect change if the sentence was revised as follows: "Sometimes my son and I see the strained murmurous breakup of the ceremony . . ."?

At First Glance

This essay, written about the 1979 Masters golf tournament, held annually in Augusta, Georgia, was originally published in Golf *magazine. Before you begin reading "Thirteen Ways of Looking at the Masters," think about the readers of* Golf *magazine. What sort of individuals do you think read* Golf*? Does the essay demonstrate an awareness of these readers? Also, contemplate John Updike's use of numbered sections and what these sections do for the overall effect of the essay. As a writer, what can you learn about the use of transitions from reading this essay?*

Thirteen Ways of Looking at the Masters

1. AS AN EVENT IN AUGUSTA, GEORGIA

In the middle of downtown Broad Street a tall white monument—like an immensely heightened wedding cake save that in place of the bride and groom stands a dignified Confederate officer—proffers the thought that

> *No nation rose so white and fair;*
> *None fell so pure of crime.*

Within a few steps of the monument, a movie theater, during Masters Week in 1979, was showing *Hair,* full of cheerful miscegenation and anti-military song and dance.

This is the Deep/Old/New South, with its sure-enough levees, railroad tracks, unpainted dwellings out of illustrations to Joel Chandler Harris, and stately homes ornamented by grillework and verandas. As far up the Savannah River as boats could go, Augusta has been a trading post since 1717 and was named in 1735 by James Oglethorpe for the Mother of George III. It changed hands several times during the Revolutionary War, thrived on tobacco and cotton, imported textile machinery from Philadelphia in 1828, and during the Civil War housed the South's largest powder works. Sherman passed through here, and didn't leave much in the way of historical sites.

The Augusta National Golf Club is away from the business end of town, in a region of big brick houses embowered in magnolia and dogwood. A lot of people retire to Augusta, and one of the reasons that Bobby Jones wanted to build a golf course here, instead of near his native Atlanta, was the distinctly milder climate. The course, built in 1931–32 on the site of the Fruitlands Nursery property, after designs by Dr. Alister Mackenzie (architect of Cypress Point) and Jones himself, has the venerable Augusta Country Club at its back, and at its front, across Route 28, an extensive shopping-center outlay. At this point the New South becomes indistinguishable from New Jersey.

2. AS AN EVENT NOT IN AUGUSTA, GEORGIA

How many Augusta citizens are members of the Augusta National Golf Club? The question, clearly in bad taste, brought raised eyebrows and a muttered "Very few" or, more spaciously, "Thirty-eight or forty." The initial membership fee is rumored to be $50,000, there is a waiting list five years' long, and most of the members seem to be national Beautiful People, Golfing Subspecies, who jet in for an occasional round during the six months the course is open. When Ike, whose cottage was near the clubhouse, used to show up and play a twosome with Arnold Palmer, the course would be cleared by the Secret Service. Cliff Roberts, chairman of the tournament from its inception in 1934 until his death in 1977, was a Wall Street investment banker; his chosen successor, William H. Lane, is a business executive from faraway Houston.

A lot of Augusta's citizens get out of town during Masters Week, renting their houses. The lady in the drugstore near the house my wife and I were staying in told me she had once gone walking on the course. *Once:* the experience seemed unrepeatable. The course had looked deserted to her, but then a voice shouted "Fore" and a ball struck near her. The ghost of Lloyd Mangrum, perhaps. The only Augustans conspicuous during the tournament are the black caddies, who know the greens so well they can call a putt's break to the inch while standing on the fringe.

3. AS A STUDY IN GREEN

Green grass, green grandstands, green concession stalls, green paper cups, green folding chairs and visors for sale, green-and-white ropes, green-topped Georgia pines, a prevalence of green in the slacks and jerseys of the gallery, like the prevalence of red in the crowd in Moscow on May Day. The caddies' bright green caps and Sam Snead's bright green trousers. If justice were poetic, Hubert Green would win it every year.

4. AS A RITE OF SPRING

"It's become a rite of spring," a man told me with a growl, "like the Derby." Like Fort Lauderdale. Like Opening Day at a dozen ballparks. Spring it was, especially for us Northerners who had left our gray skies, brown lawns, salt-strewn highways, and plucky little croci for this efflorescence of azaleas and barefoot *jeunes filles en fleurs.* Most of the gallery, like most of the golfers, had Southern accents. This Yankee felt a little as if he were coming in late on a round of equinoctial parties that had stretched from Virginia to Florida. A lot of young men were lying on the grass betranced by the memories of last night's libations, and a lot of matronly voices continued discussing Aunt Earlene's unfortunate second marriage, while the golf balls floated overhead. For many in attendance, the Masters is a ritual observance; some of the old-timers wore sun hats festooned with over twenty years' worth of admission badges.

Will success as a festival spoil the Masters as a sporting event? It hasn't yet, but the strain on the tournament's famous and exemplary organization can be felt. Ticket sales are limited, but the throng at the main scoreboard is hard to squeeze by. The acreage devoted to parking would make a golf course in itself. An army of over two thousand policemen, marshals, walkway guards, salespersons, trash-gleaners, and other attendants is needed to maintain order and facilitate the pursuit of happiness. To secure a place by any green it is necessary to arrive at least an hour before there is anything to watch.

When, on the last two days, the television equipment arrives, the crowd itself is watched. Dutifully, it takes its part as a mammoth unpaid extra in a national television spectacular. As part of it, patting out courteous applause at a good shot or groaning in chorus at a missed putt, one felt, slightly, *canned.*

5. AS A FASHION SHOW

Female fashions, my wife pointed out, came in three strata. First, young women decked out as if going to a garden party—makeup, flowing dresses, sandals. Next, the trim, leathery generation of the mothers, dressed as if they themselves were playing golf—short skirts, sun visors, cleated two-toned shoes. Last, the generation of the grandmothers, in immaculately blued hair and amply filled pants suits in shades we might call electric pastel or Day-Glo azalea.

6. AS A DISPLAY CASE FOR SAM SNEAD AND ARNOLD PALMER

Though they no longer are likely to win, you wouldn't know it from their charismas. Snead, with his rakishly tilted panama and slightly pushed-in face—a face that has known both battle and merriment—swaggers around the practice tee like the Sheriff of Golf County, testing a locked door here, hanging a parking ticket there. On the course, he remains a golfer one has to call beautiful, from the cushioned roll of his shoulders as he strokes the ball to the padding, panther-like tread with which he follows it down the center of the fairway, his chin tucked down while he thinks apparently rueful thoughts. He is one of the great inward golfers, those who wrap the dazzling difficulty of the game in an impassive, effortless flow of movement. When, on the green, he stands beside his ball, faces the hole, and performs the curious obeisance of his "side-winder" putting stroke, no one laughs.

And Palmer, he of the unsound swing, a hurried slash that ends as though he is snatching back something hot from a fire, remains the monumental outward golfer, who invites us into the game to share with him its heady turmoil, its call for constant courage. Every inch an agonist, Palmer still hitches his pants as he mounts the green, still strides between the wings of his army like Hector on his way to yet more problematical heroism. Age has thickened him, made him look almost musclebound, and has grizzled his thin, untidy hair; but his deportment more than ever expresses vitality, a love of life and of the game that rebounds to him, from the multitudes, as fervent gratitude. Like us golfing commoners, he risks looking bad for the sake of some fun.

Of the younger players, only Lanny Wadkins communicates Palmer's reckless determination, and only Fuzzy Zoeller has the captivating blitheness of a Jimmy Demaret or a Lee Trevino. The Masters, with its clubby lifetime qualification for previous winners, serves as an annual exhibit of Old Masters, wherein one can see the difference between the reigning, college-bred pros, with their even teeth, on-camera poise, and abstemious air, and the older crowd, who came up from caddie sheds, drove themselves in cars along the dusty miles of the Tour, and hustled bets with the rich to make ends meet. Golf expresses the man, as every weekend foursome knows; amid the mannerly lads who dominate the money list, Palmer and Snead loom as men.

7. AS AN EXERCISE IN SPECTATORSHIP

In no other sport must the spectator move. The builders and improvers of Augusta National built mounds and bleachers for the crowds to gain vantage from, and a gracefully written pamphlet by the founder, Robert Jones, is handed out as instruction in the art of "letting the Tournament come to us instead of chasing after it." Nevertheless, as the field narrows and the interest of the hordes focuses, the best way to see anything is to hang back in the woods and use binoculars. Seen from within the galleries, the players become tiny walking dolls, glimpsable, like stars on a night of scudding clouds, in the gaps between heads.

Examples of Southern courtesy in the galleries: (1) When my wife stood to watch an approach to the green, the man behind her mildly observed, "Ma'am, it was awful nice when you were sittin' down." (2) A gentleman standing next to me, not liking the smell of a cigar I was smoking, offered to buy it from me for a dollar.

Extraordinary event in the galleries: on the fourth hole a ball set in flight by Dow Finsterwald solidly struck the head of young man sitting beside the green. The sound of a golf ball on a skull is remarkably like that of two blocks of wood knocked together. *Glock.* Flesh hurts; bone makes music.

Single instance of successful spectatorship by this reporter: I happened to be in the pines left of the seventh fairway on the first day of play, wondering whether to go for another of the refreshment committee's standardized but economical ham sandwiches, when Art Wall, Jr. hooked a ball near where I was standing. Only a dozen or so gathered to watch his recovery; for a moment, then, we could breathe with a player and experience with him—as he waggled, peered at obtruding branches, switched clubs, and peered at the branches again—that quintessential golfing sensation, the loneliness of the bad-ball hitter.

Sad truth, never before revealed: by sticking to a spot in the stands or next to the green, one can view the field coming through, hitting variants of the same shots and putts, and by listening to the massed cheers and grunts from the other greens, one can guess at dramas unseen; but the unified field, as Einstein discovered in a more general connection, is unapprehensible, and the best way to witness a golf tournament is at the receiving end of a television signal. Many a fine golf reporter, it was whispered to me, never leaves the set in the press tent.

The other sad truth about golf spectatorship is that for today's pros it all comes down to the putting, and that the difference between a putt that drops and one that rims the cup, though teleologically enormous, is intellectually negligible.

8. AS A STUDY IN TURF-BUILDING

A suburban lawn-owner can hardly look up from admiring the weedless immensity of the Augusta National turf. One's impression, when first admitted to this natural Oz, is that a giant putting surface has been dropped over acres of rolling terrain, with a few apertures for ponds and trees to poke through. A philosophy of golf is expressed in Jones's pamphlet: "The Augusta National has much more fairway and green area than the average course. There is little punishing rough and very few bunkers. The course is not intended so much to punish severely the wayward shot as to reward adequately the stroke played with skill—and judgment."

It is an intentional paradox, then, that this championship course is rather kind to duffers. The ball sits up on Augusta's emerald carpet looking big as a baseball. It was not always such; in 1972, an invasion of *Poa annua,* a white-spiked vagabond grass, rendered conditions notoriously bumpy; in remedy a fescue called Pennlawn and a rye called Pennfine were implanted on the fairways and greens respectively and have flourished. Experimentation continues; to make the greens even harder and slicker, they are thinking of rebuilding them on a sand base—and have already done so on the adjacent par-three course.

From May to October, when the course is closed to play, everything goes to seed and becomes a hayfield, and entire fairways are plowed up: a harrowing thought. The caddies, I was solemnly assured, never replace a divot; they just sprinkle grass seed from a pouch they carry. Well, this is a myth, for I repeatedly saw caddies replace divots in the course of the tournament, with the care of tile-setters.

9. AS DEMOGRAPHY

One doesn't have to want to give the country back to the Indians to feel a nostalgic pang while looking at old photos of the pre-World War II tournaments, with their hatted, necktied galleries strolling up the fairways in the wake of the baggy-trousered players, and lining the trees and greens only one man deep.

The scores have grown crowded, too. The best then would be among the best now—Lloyd Mangrum's single-round 64 in 1940 has not been bettered, though for the last two years it has been equalled. But the population of the second-best has increased, producing virtually a new winner each week of the Tour, and stifling the emergence of stable constellations of superstars like Nelson-Hogan-Snead and Palmer-Player-Nicklaus. In the 1936 and 1938 Masters, only seven players made the thirty-six-hole score of 145 that cut the 1979 field to forty-five players. Not until 1939 did the winner break 280 and not again until 1948. The last total over 280 to win it came in 1973. In 1936, Craig Wood had a first-day round of 88 and finished in the top two dozen. In 1952, San Snead won the Masters in spite of a third-round 77. That margin for intermittent error has been squeezed from tournament golf. Johnny Miller chops down a few trees, develops the wrong muscles, and drops like a stone on the lists. Arnold Palmer, relatively young and still strong and keen, can no longer ram the putts in from twenty feet, and becomes a father figure. A cruel world, top-flight golf, that eats its young.

10. AS RACE RELATIONS

A Martian skimming overhead in his saucer would have to conclude that white Earthlings hit the ball and black Earthlings fetch it, that white men swing the sticks and black men carry them. The black caddies of Augusta, in their white coveralls, are a tradition that needs a symbolic breaking, the converse of Lee Elder's playing in the tournament.

To be fair, these caddies are specialists of a high order, who take a cheerful pride in their expertise and who are, especially during Masters Week, well paid for it. Gary Player's caddie for his spectacular come-from-nowhere victory of 1978 was tipped $10, 000—a sum that, this caddie assured an impudent interrogator, was still safe in the bank. In the New South, blacks work side by side with whites in the concession stands and at the fairway ropes, though I didn't see any in a green marshal's coat. I was unofficially informed that, at the very time when civil rightists were agitating for a black player to be invited to play even if one did not earn qualification—as Elder did in 1975—blacks were not being admitted to the tournament *as spectators.* I wonder about this. On pages 26–27 of the green souvenir album with a text by Cliff Roberts, one can see a photograph of Henry Picard hitting out of a bunker; behind him in the scattering of spectators are a number of ebony gentlemen not dressed as caddies. At any rate, though golf remains a white man's game, it presents in the Masters player and caddie an active white-black partnership in which the white man is taking the advice and doing the manual work. Caddies think of the partnership as "we," as in "We hit a drive down the center and a four-iron stiff to the pin, but then *he* missed the putt."

11. AS CLASS RELATIONS

Though the Augusta National aspires to be the American St. Andrews, there is a significant economic difference between a Scottish golf links thriftily pinked out on a wasteland—the sandy seaside hills that are "links"—and the American courses elaborately, expensively carved from farmland and woods. Though golf has plebeian Scottish roots, in this country its province is patrician. A course requires capital and flaunts that ancient aristocratic prerogative, land. In much of the world, this humbling game is an automatic symbol of capitalist-imperialist oppression; a progressive African novelist, to establish a character as a villain, has only to show him coming off a golf course. And in our nation, for all the roadside driving ranges and four o'clock factory leagues, golf remains for millions something that happens at the end of a long driveway, beyond the MEMBERS ONLY sign.

Yet competitive golf in the United States came of age when, at The Country Club, in Brookline, Massachusetts, a twenty-year-old ex-caddie and workingman's son, Francis Ouimet, beat the British legends Vardon and Ray in a playoff for the U.S. Open. And ever since, the great competitors have tended to come from the blue-collar level of golf, the caddies and the offspring of club pros. Rare is the Bobby Jones who emerges from the gentry with the perfectionistic drive and killer instinct that makes a champion in this game which permits no let-up or loss of concentration, yet which penalizes tightness also. Hagen acted like a swell and was called Sir Walter, but he came up from a caddie's roost in Rochester. The lords of golf have been by and large gentlemen made and not born, while the clubs and the management of the Tour remain in the hands of the country-club crowd. When genteel Ed Sneed and Tom Watson fell into a three-way playoff for the 1979 Masters title, you knew in your bones it was going to be the third player, a barbarian called Fuzzy with a loopy all-out swing, who would stroll through the gates and carry off the loot.

12. AS A PARADE OF LOVELY GOLFERS, NO TWO ALIKE

Charles Coody, big-beaked bird. Billy Casper, once the king of touch, now sporting the bushy white sideburns of a turn-of-the-century railroad conductor, still able to pop them up from a sand-trap and sink the putt. Trevino, so broad across he looks like a reflection in a funhouse mirror, a model of delicacy around the greens and a model of affable temperament everywhere. Player, varying his normal black outfit with white slacks, his bearing so full of fight and muscle he seems to be restraining himself from breaking into a run. Nicklaus, Athlete of the Decade, still golden but almost gaunt and faintly grim, as he feels a crown evaporating from his head. Gay Brewer, heavy in the face and above the belt, nevertheless uncorking a string-straight mid-iron to within nine inches of the long seventh hole in the par-three tournament. Miller Barber, Truman's Capote's double, punching and putting his way to last year's best round, a storm-split 64 in two installments. Bobby Clampett, looking too young and thin to be out there. Andy Bean, looking too big to be out there, and with his perennially puzzled expression seeming to be searching for a game more his size. Hubert Green, with a hunched flicky swing that would make a high-school golf coach scream. Tom Weiskopf, the handsome embodiment of pained near-perfection. Hale Irwin, the picture-book golfer with the face of a Ph.D. candidate. Johnny Miller, looking heavier than we remember him, patiently knocking them out on the practice tee, wondering where the lightning went. Ben Crenshaw, the smiling Huck Finn, and Tom Watson, the more pensive Tom Sawyer, who, while the other boys were whitewashing fences, has become, politely but firmly, the best golfer in the world.

And many other redoubtable young men. Seeing them up close, in the dining room or on the clubhouse veranda, one is struck by how young and in many cases how slight they seem, with their pert and telegenic little wives—boys, really, anxious to be polite and to please even the bores and boors that collect in the interstices of all well-publicized events. Only when one sees them at a distance, as they walk alone or chatting in twos down the great green emptiness of the fairway, does one sense that each youth is the pinnacle of a buried pyramid of effort and investment, of prior competition from pre-teen level up, of immense and it must be at times burdensome accumulated hopes of parents, teachers, backers. And with none of the group hypnosis and exhilaration of team play to relieve them. And with the difference between success and failure so feather-fine.

13. AS A RELIGIOUS EXPERIENCE

The four days of 1979's Masters fell on Maundy Thursday, Good Friday, Holy Saturday, and Easter Sunday. On Good Friday, fittingly, the skies darkened, tornadoes were predicted, and thousands of sinners ran for cover. My good wife, who had gone to divine services, was prevented from returning to the course by the flood of departing cars, and the clear moral is one propounded from many a pulpit: golf and churchgoing do not mix. Easter Sunday also happened to be the anniversary of the assassination of Abraham Lincoln and the sinking of the *Titanic,* and it wasn't such a good day for Ed Sneed either.

About ninety-nine percent of the gallery, my poll of local vibes indicated, was rooting for Sneed to hold off disaster and finish what he had begun. He had played splendidly for three days, and it didn't seem likely he'd come this close soon again. When he birdied the fifteenth and enlarged his once huge cushion back to three strokes, it seemed he would do it. But then, through no flagrant fault of his own, he began "leaking." We all knew how it felt, the slippery struggle to nurse a good round back to the clubhouse. On the seventeenth green, where I was standing, his approach looked no worse than his playing partner's; it just hit a foot too long, skipped onto the sloping back part of the green, and slithered into the fringe. His putt back caught the cup but twirled away. And his putt to save par, which looked to me like a gimme, lipped out, the same way my two-footers do when I lift my head to watch them drop, my sigh of relief all prepared. Zoeller, ten minutes before, had gently rolled in a birdie from much farther away. Sneed's fate seemed sealed then: the eighteenth hole, a famous bogey-maker, waited for him as ineluctably as Romeo's missed appointment with Juliet.

He hadn't hit bad shots, and he hadn't panicked; he just was screwed a half-turn too tight to get a par. The gallery of forty thousand felt for him, right to the pits of our golf-weary stomachs, when his last hope of winning it clean hung on the lip of the seventy-second hole. It so easily might have been otherwise. But then that's life, and that's golf.

Double Take

1. Given that this essay first appeared in *Golf* magazine, in what ways is it rhetorically appropriate for its intended audience? Specifically, what strategies does John Updike use to relate to his readers? How can you tell what these strategies are?
2. On a significant level, this essay resembles a piece of sports reporting, something you might find in a newspaper. In what ways, however, is it different from the genre of the newspaper sports report? That is, what makes this an essay?
3. Unlike the other three essays by John Updike reprinted here, "Thirteen Ways of Looking at the Masters" uses numbered sections as transitions. How do these 13 numbered sections, as opposed to the more subtle transitions in the other essays, affect the movement and meaning of this essay?
4. Rewrite a portion of this essay, but remove the numbered sections and use narrative transitions instead. What sorts of challenges do you find in doing this?

Seeing for Yourself

At First Glance

Like John Updike's "Cemeteries," "The Tarbox Police" (originally published in Esquire *magazine) is an extremely visual essay, almost to the point of resembling a painting. Reading it, one gets the impression of seeing something rather than reading about it. As you experience this visual impression, try to examine how Updike creates it and what kinds of effect it has on you as a reader. How can writers use such images to get the attention of their readers? Like "Thirteen Ways of Looking at the Masters," this essay also uses swift transitions from one scene to the next, but this time Updike does not use section headings. As you move from one scene to the next, what do you think holds this essay together? What is its point or argument?*

The Tarbox Police

Cal.

Hal.

Sam.

Dan.

One has known them since they were boys in the high school. Good-natured boys, not usually among the troublemakers, going out for each sport as its season came along, though not usually among the stars.

Indeed, they are hard to tell apart, without a close look. Cal is an inch taller than Hal, and Dan has a slightly wistful set to his jaw that differentiates him from Sam, who until you see him smile looks mean. Downtown, they don't smile much; if they started, they would never stop, since almost everybody passing by they know. If you look them in the eye for a second they will nod, however. A bit bleakly, but a nod. In the summer they wear sunglasses and their eyes are not there. In their short-sleeved shirts they would melt into the summer crowd of barefooted girls and bare-chested easy riders but for the knobby black armor of equipment, strapped and buckled to their bodies in even the hottest weather: the two-way radio in its perforated case, the billy club dangling overripe from their belts, the little buttoned-up satchel of Mace, and the implausible, impossible gun, its handle peeking from the holster like the metal-and-wood snout of an eyeless baby animal riding backward on its mother's forgetful hip.

They not only know everybody, they know everything. When dear Maddy Frothingham, divorced since she was twenty-two and not her fault, upped and married the charmer she met on some fancy island down East, it was the Tarbox police who came around and told her her new husband was a forger wanted in four states, and took him away. When Janice Tugwell fell down the cellar stairs and miscarried, it was the police who knew what house down by the river Morris's car was parked in front of, and who were kind enough not to tell her where their knock brought him to the door, fumbling with his buttons. It is the police who lock up Squire Wentworth Saturday nights so he won't disgrace himself; it is the police, when there's another fatal accident on that bad stretch of 84, who put the blanket over the body, so nobody else will have to see. Chief Chad's face, when the do-good lawyers come out from Boston to get our delinquents off, is a study in surprise, that the court should be asked to doubt things everybody *knows*. We ask them, the police, to know too much. It hardens them. Young as they are, their faces get cold, cold and prim. When in summer they put on their sunglasses, little is hidden that showed before.

They want to be invisible.

In an ideal state, they would wither away.

My wife and I had an eerie experience a year ago. Our male pup hadn't come back for his supper, and the more my wife thought about it the less she could sleep, so around midnight she got up in her nightie and we put on raincoats and went out in the convertible to search. It was a weekday night, the town looked dead. It looked like a fossil of itself, pressed white into black stone. Except downtown—the blank shop fronts glazed under the blue arc lamps, the street wide as a prairie without parked cars—there was this cluster of shadows. I thought of a riot, except that it was quiet. I thought of witchcraft, except that it was 1971. Cal was there. His blue uniform looked purple under the lights. The rest were kids, the kids that hang around on the green, the long hair and the Levis making the girls hard to distinguish. Half in the street, half on the pavement, they were having a conversation, a party in the heart of our ghostly town.

My wife found her voice and asked Cal about the dog and he answered promptly that one had been hit but not badly by a car up near around the shopping center around four that afternoon, without a collar or a license, and we apologized about the license and explained how our little girl keeps dressing the dog in her old baby clothes and taking his collar off, and, sure enough, found the animal in the dogcatcher's barn, shivering and limping and so relieved to see us he fainted in the driveway and didn't eat for two days; but the point is the strangeness of those kids and that policeman in the middle of nowhere, having what looked like a good time. What do they talk about? Does it happen every night? Is something brewing between them? Nobody can talk to these kids, except the police. Maybe, in the world that's in the making, they're the only real things to one another, kids and police, and the rest of us, me in my convertible and my wife in her nightie, are the shadows. As we pulled away, we heard laughter.

But they have lives too. The Sunday evening the man went crazy on Prudence Street, Hal arrived in a suit as if fresh from church, and Dan wore a checked shirt and bowling shoes that sported a big number 8 on their backs. Dainty feet. Chief Chad had to feather his siren to press the cruiser through the crowd that had collected—sunburned young mothers pushing babies in strollers, a lot of old people from the nursing home up the street. All through the crowd people were telling one another stories. The man had moved here three weeks ago from Detroit. He was crazy on three days of gin. He was an acidhead. He went crazy because his wife had left him. He was a queer. He was a Vietnam veteran. His first shot from the upstairs window had hit a fire hydrant—ka-*zing!*—and the second kicked up dust under the nose of the fat beagle that sleeps by the curb there.

The crazy man was in the second story of the old Cushing place, which the new owners had fixed up for rental with that aluminum siding that looks just like clapboards unless you study the corners. The Osborne house next door, without a front yard, juts out to the pavement, and most of the crowd stayed more or less behind that, though the old folks kept pushing closer to see, and the mothers kept running into the line of fire to fetch back their toddlers, and the dogs raced around wagging the way they do at festivities.

It was strange, coming up the street, to see the cloud of gunsmoke drifting toward the junior high school, just like on television, only in better color. The police crouched down behind the cruiser, trading shots. Chief Chad was huddled behind the corner of the Osbornes', shouting into his radio. The siege lasted an hour. The crazy man, a skinny fellow in a tie-dyed undershirt, was in plain slight in the window above the porch roof, making a speech you couldn't understand and alternately reloading the two rifles he had. One of the old folks hobbled out across the asphalt to the police car and screamed, "*Kill* him! I paid good taxes for fifty years. What's the problem, he's right up there, *kill* him!" Even the crazy man went quiet to hear the old man carry on: the old guy was trembling; his face shone with tears; he kept yelling the word "taxes." Dan shielded him with his body and hustled him back to the crowd, where a nurse from the home wrestled him quiet.

The plan, it turned out, wasn't to kill anybody. The police were aiming around the window, making a sieve of that new siding, until the state police arrived with the tear gas. While the crazy man was being entertained out front, Chief Chad and a state cop sneaked into the back yard and plunked the canisters into the kitchen. The shooting died. The police went in the front door wearing masks and brought out on a stretcher a man swaddled like a newborn baby. A thin sort of baby with a sleeping green face. Though they say that at the hospital when he got his crazy consciousness back he broke all the straps and it took five men to hold him down for the injection.

"Go home!" Chief Chad shouted, shaking his rifle at the crowd.

"The show's over! Damn you all, go home!"

Most people forgave him, he was overwrought.

Bits of the crowd clung to the neighborhood way past dark, telling one another what they saw or knew or guessed, giving it all a rerun. Experience is so vicarious these days, only reminiscence makes it real. One theory was that the crazy man hadn't meant to hurt anybody, or he could have winged a dozen old folks. Yes, but on the corner of the Osbornes', you can still see where a bullet came through one side and out the other, right where Chief Chad's ear had been a second before. Out of all that unreality, the bullet holes remained to be mended. It took weeks before the aluminum man showed up.

And then this March, in town meeting, the moderator got rattled and ejected a citizen. He was the new sort of citizen who have moved into the Marshview development, a young husband with a big honey-colored beard; they appear to feel the world owes them an explanation. We were on the sewer articles. We've been passing these sewer articles for years and the river never smells any better, but you pass them because the town engineer is president of Rotary and doing the best he can. Anyway, young Honeybeard had raised four or five objections, and had the selectmen up and down at the microphone like jack-in-the-boxes, and Bud Perley, moderator ever since he came back from Japan with his medals, got weary of recognizing him, and overlooked his waving hand. The boy—taxpayer, just like the old cuss at the shoot-out—had smuggled in a balloon and enough helium to float it up toward the gym ceiling.

LOVE, the balloon said.

"Eject that man," Perly said.

Who'll ever forget it? Seven hundred of us there, and we'd seen a lot of foolishness on the town-meeting floor, but we'd never seen a man ejected. Hal was over by the water bubbler, leaning against the wall, and Sam was on the opposite side joking with a bunch of high-school students up on the tumbling horses observing for their civics class. The two policemen moved at once, together. They sauntered, almost, across the front of the hall toward the center aisle.

And you saw they had billy clubs, and you saw they had guns, and nobody else did.

Actually, young Honeybeard was a friend of Sam's—they had gone smelt-fishing together that winter—and both smiled sheepishly as they touched, and the boy went out making a big "V" with his arms and people laughed and cheered and no doubt will vote him in for selectman if he runs.

But still. The two policemen had moved in unison, carefully, crabwise-cautious under their load of equipment, and you saw they were real; blundering old Perley had called them into existence, and not a mouth in that hall held more than held breath. This was it. This was power, our power hopefully to be sure, but this was *it*.

A CLOSER LOOK AT JOHN UPDIKE

1. What is the role of place in John Updike's essays? Is there a difference between "place" and "location"? Write an essay that defines these terms and compares and contrasts their meanings. Be sure to turn to Updike's essays in setting up your own definitions.

2. Updike explains that "we must write where we stand; wherever we do stand, there is life; and an imitation of the life we know, however narrow, is our only ground." Given Updike's essays along with the other essays you have read in this book, how accurately does this formulation apply to essay-writing in general? To what extent should essays be grounded in a place where one stands? To what extent is your own writing grounded in the place where you are? Write an essay that addresses these questions.

3. John Updike is famous as a novelist. Speaking in the role of novelist, he writes: "The novelist is of interest only for what he does through empathy and image-producing, image-arranging; the more consciously a theorist he is the more apt he is to become impotent or cranky or both." What about the essayist? Is the essayist "of interest" for the same reasons the novelist is? If so, how? If not, what makes an essayist of interest? Write an essay that considers why an essayist might be of interest. Consider Updike and some of the other essayists you have read as you write this essay.

4. In the essays reprinted here but also in his other work, Updike writes about women and sexuality. To what extent would you characterize his writing as "masculine"? What is masculine abut it? Write a critique of Updike's essays that is directed toward the "masculinity" of his writing.

Looking from Writer to Writer

1. Compare John Updike's more visual and less directly argumentative approach to the more direct activism of Henry Louis Gates, Jr., in his essays. Gates's essays have a social agenda, while Updike prefers to create impressions or scenes free of political underpinnings. Which approach (or some combination of the two) do you consider more important in an essay? To what extent does the approach depend on the audience?

2. Clearly, place plays an important role in Updike's writing. He writes, "We must write where we stand. . . .wherever we do stand, there is life; and an imitation of the life we know, however narrow, is our only ground." Compare this view of writing and place to the view of Edward Said. Place is important to both, and yet

each writer has a different relationship with it. What happens to notions of place when, as in Said's case, he is not permitted to write where he stands?

3. John Updike's essays often depict women in what some readers would call a "sexist" or masculinist manner. Examining critically the way Updike depicts women, compare his depictions to the depiction of women in the essays of Amy Tan, bell hooks, or Alice Walker. As you examine the differences, try to locate how the essayists use language to construct women.

Looking Beyond

Essays
Assorted Prose. New York: Knopf: 1965.
Hugging the Shore: Essays and Criticism. New York: Knopf, 1983.
Just Looking: Essays on Art. New York: 1989.
More Matter: Essays and Criticism. New York: Knopf, 1999.
Odd Jobs: Essays and Criticism. New York: Knopf, 1991.
Picked-Up Pieces. New York: Knopf, 1975.

Fiction
Brazil. New York: Knopf, 1994.
The Centaur. New York: Knopf, 1963.
Gertrude and Claudius. New York: Knopf, 2000.
The Poorhouse Fair. New York: Knopf, 1958.
Problems and Other Stories. New York: Knopf, 1979.
Rabbit at Rest. New York: Knopf, 1990.
Rabbit Is Rich. New York: Knopf, 1981.
Rabbit Redux. New York: Knopf, 1971.
The Same Door: Short Stories. New York: Knopf, 1959.
Trust Me: Short Stories. New York: Knopf, 1987.
The Witches of Eastwick. New York: Knopf, 1984.

Poetry
The Carpentered Hen and Other Tame Creatures. New York: Knopf, 1958.
Collected Poems: 1953–1993. New York: Knopf, 1993.
Tossing and Turning: Poems. New York: Knopf, 1977.

Alice Walker

In a 1973 interview, Alice Walker explains, "I am preoccupied with the spiritual survival, the survival *whole* of my people. But beyond that, I am committed to exploring the oppressions, the insanities, the loyalties, and the triumphs of black women." In much of her writing, Walker explores these oppressions, insanities, loyalties, and triumphs from the perspective of her own experiences as a black woman who grew up poor in the rural South. Walker's life is often her subject matter, especially in her essays, not because she is only interested in herself, but because her life and her experiences are an embodiment of the issues that concern black people, southern black people, and particularly southern black women. "I believe in listening," she writes, "to a person, the sea, the wind, the trees, but especially to young black women whose rocky road I am still traveling."

Alice Walker was born on February 9, 1944, in the small rural town of Eatonton, Georgia, the eighth and youngest child of Minnie Grant and Willie Lee Walker, sharecroppers. Although she "loved the Georgia countryside where I fished and swam and walked through fields of black-eyed Susans," she felt "exiled" in her own town, suffering the degradation not so much of poverty but of segregation and the threat of racial violence. In a later essay, she recalls how, on hot Saturday afternoons, she would gaze into the corner drugstore where white children sat comfortably eating ice cream while black people were not allowed to eat inside. She also recalls the misery of "going to a shabby segregated school that was once the state prison and that had, on the second floor, the large circular print of the electric chair that had stood there." Yet because of such experiences, Walker was able to develop a capacity—shared, she claims, by other black southern writers—"of knowing, with remarkably silent accuracy, the people who make up the larger world that surrounds and suppresses [one's] own."

After graduating from high school in 1961, Walker received a scholarship to attend Spelman College in Atlanta, where she participated in civil rights demonstrations. At the end of her freshman year at Spelman, she attended the World Youth Peace Festival in Helsinki, Finland. Later that year, she got the opportunity to visit the house of Dr. Martin Luther King, Jr. and to meet with Coretta Scott King. In 1964 Walker received a scholarship and transferred to Sarah Lawrence College, a prestigious and predominantly white girls' school in New York. At Sarah Lawrence, Walker found the freedom and leisure to read, write, and live as she pleased. There she also enjoyed the mentoring of poet Muriel Rukeyser and writer Jane Cooper, both of whom nurtured her interest and talent in writing. She read Russian and American writers—the latter including e.e. cummings, Emily Dickinson, William Carlos Williams, and Flannery O'Conner—but the exclusion of black writers such as Gwendolyn Brooks, Arna Bontemps, Jean Toomer, and Zora Neale Hurston from her education and from the "comprehensive" anthologies of literature constituted a "blind spot" for her "that needed desperately to be cleared if I expected to be a whole woman, a full human being, a black woman full of self-awareness and pride." In her teaching—Walker may have been the first to teach a course on black women writers at Wellesley College—and in many of her essays, Walker has commemorated the work of black writers, especially Hurston and Toomer, to help erase this blind spot.

After an intense period of writing poetry in her senior year at Sarah Lawrence, Walker, with the assistance of Rukeyser and the encouragement of Langston Hughes, had her poems accepted for publication (they would eventually be published as *Once* in 1968). After graduating in 1965, Walker returned to Georgia to help register poor black voters. Then, between 1965 and 1967, she attended the Bread Loaf Writers' Conference and worked with the New York Welfare Department. In the winter of 1966–1967, while living in New York with Mel Leventhal, a young Jewish civil rights lawyer who would later become her husband, Walker published her first essay, "The Civil Rights Movement: What Good Was It?" which won first prize in the annual *American Scholar* essay contest.

Despite threats of violence because of their interracial marriage, Walker and Leventhal moved to Jackson, Mississippi, where Leventhal pursued civil rights litigation and Walker taught, first at local Head Start programs and then at Jackson State University. There Walker's daughter was born and Walker published her first novel, *The Third Life of George Copeland* (1970). In 1971, supported by a fellowship from the Radcliffe Institute and teaching part-time at Wellesley College, Walker and her daughter moved to Boston, where Walker published her first collection of short stories, *In Love and Trouble: Stories of Black Women* (1973), and her second volume of poetry, *Revolutionary Petunias and Other Poems* (1973). Then, in 1974, while living in New York, Walker became an editor for *Ms.* magazine, an association that would continue after Walker's divorce from Leventhal and her subsequent move to northern California. In the coastal town of Mendocino, she completed her third and most acclaimed novel, *The Color Purple* (1982). The novel won the Pulitzer Prize and the American Book Award for fiction in 1983, and was made into a motion picture.

The novel escalated Walker to worldwide fame, but it also brought heavy criticism from what some black writers saw as a harsh portrayal of black men.

Walker has continued to publish at a prolific rate: essays, poems, stories, and novels. Her subjects range from political activism to nuclear war to genital mutilation to compassion for animals to bisexuality. Her writing, however, continues to be driven by what Walker has called a "womanist" ideology, an ideology that describes a black feminist who "appreciates and prefers women's culture, emotional flexibility, and women's strength," but who also is "committed to survival and wholeness of entire people, male *and* female." The pursuit of wholeness and survival marks much of Walker's work, as does her belief that the power of writing can give voice and identity to those who are silent or who have been silenced—to capture the culture, rituals, history, imagination, indeed, "the accumulated collective reality of the people themselves."

In her writing Walker states, "I am trying to arrive at that place where black music already is; to arrive at that unself-conscious sense of collective oneness; that naturalness, that (even when anguished) grace." As you read the following essays, pay attention to how Walker arrives at this "unself-conscious sense of collective oneness." In particular, pay attention to how she achieves this while at times writing about very personal, self-conscious experiences. Look at how she rhetorically and thematically weaves the personal and the collective in order to come to an understanding of herself and others.

Walker on Writing

At First Glance

In this essay, published in the New South, *Alice Walker describes both the inheritance and the responsibility of the black southern writer. As you read "The Black Writer and the Southern Experience," try to understand the argument Walker is making in light of the situation that Walker is responding to in the essay. Consider why she is writing the essay (why she is making the argument that she does) and whom she is writing it for—who Walker imagines is her audience. Also, think about how Walker develops her argument. Think about what strategies Walker uses to build her argument and whether or not her audience would find it convincing.*

The Black Writer and the Southern Experience

My mother tells of an incident that happened to her in the thirties during the Depression. She and my father lived in a small Georgia town and had half a dozen children. They were sharecroppers, and food, especially flour, was almost impossible to obtain. To get flour, which was distributed by the Red Cross, one had to submit vouchers signed by a local official. On the day my mother was to go into town for flour she received a large box of clothes from one of my aunts who was living in the North. The clothes were in good condition, though well worn, and my mother needed a dress, so she immediately put on one of those from the box and wore it into town. When she reached the distribution center and presented her voucher she was confronted by a white woman who looked her up and down with marked anger and envy.

"What'd you come up here for?" the woman asked.

"For some flour," said my mother, presenting her voucher.

"Humph," said the woman, looking at her more closely and with unconcealed fury. "Anybody dressed up as good as you don't need to come here *begging* for food."

"I ain't begging," said my mother; "the government is giving away flour to those that need it, and I need it. I wouldn't be here if I didn't. And these clothes I'm wearing was given to me." But the woman had already turned to the next person in line, saying over her shoulder to the white man who was behind the counter with her, "The *gall* of niggers coming in here dressed better than me!" This thought seemed to make her angrier still, and my mother, pulling three of her small children behind her and crying from humiliation, walked sadly back into the street.

"What did you and Daddy do for flour that winter?" I asked my mother.

"Well," she said, "Aunt Mandy Aikens lived down the road from us and she got plenty of flour. We had a good stand of corn so we had plenty of meal. Aunt Mandy would swap me a bucket of flour for a bucket of meal. We got by all right."

Then she added thoughtfully, "And that old woman that turned me off so short got down so bad in the end that she was walking on *two* sticks." And I knew she was thinking, though she never said it: Here I am today, my eight children healthy and grown and three of them in college and me with hardly a sick day for years. Ain't Jesus wonderful?

In this small story is revealed the condition and strength of a people. Outcasts to be used and humiliated by the larger society, the Southern black sharecropper and poor farmer clung to his own kind and to a religion that had been given to pacify him as a slave but which he soon transformed into an antidote against bitterness. Depending on one another, because they had nothing and no one else, the share-croppers often managed to come through "all right." And when I listen to my mother tell and retell this story I find that the white woman's vindictiveness is less important than Aunt Mandy's resourceful generosity or my mother's ready stand of corn. For their lives were not about that pitiful example of Southern womanhood, but about themselves.

What the black Southern writer inherits as a natural right is a sense of *community*. Something simple but surprisingly hard, especially these days, to come by. My mother, who is a walking history of our community, tells me that when each of her children was born the midwife accepted as payment such home-grown or homemade items as a pig, a quilt, jars of canned fruits and vegetables. But there was never any question that the midwife would come when she was needed, whatever the eventual payment for her services. I consider this each time I hear of a hospital that refuses to admit a woman in labor unless she can hand over a substantial sum of money, cash.

Nor am I nostalgic, as a French philosopher once wrote, for lost poverty. I am nostalgic for the solidarity and sharing a modest existence can sometimes bring. We knew, I suppose, that we were poor. Somebody knew; perhaps the landowner who grudgingly paid my father three hundred dollars a year for twelve months' labor. But we never considered ourselves to be poor, unless, of course, we were deliber-ately humiliated. And because we never believed we were poor, and therefore worthless, we could depend on one another without shame. And always there were the Burial Societies, the Sick-and-Shut-in Societies, that sprang up out of sponta-neous need. And no one seemed terribly upset that black sharecroppers were ignored by white insurance companies. It went without saying, in my mother's day, that birth and death required assistance from the community, and that the magni-tude of these events was lost on outsiders.

As a college student I came to reject the Christianity of my parents, and it took me years to realize that though they had been force-fed a white man's palliative, in the form of religion, they had made it into something at once simple and noble. True, even today, they can never successfully picture a God who is not white, and that is a major cruelty, but their lives testify to a greater comprehension of the teach-ing of Jesus than the lives of people who sincerely believe a God *must* have a color and that there can be such a phenomenon as a "white" church.

The richness of the black writer's experience in the South can be remarkable, though some people might not think so. Once, while in college, I told a white middle-aged Northerner that I hoped to be a poet. In the nicest possible language, which still made me as mad as I've ever been, he suggested that a "farmer's daughter" might not be the stuff of which poets are made. On one level, of course, he had a point. A shack with only a dozen or so books is an unlikely place to discover a young Keats. But it is narrow thinking, indeed, to believe that a Keats is the only kind of poet one would want to grow up to be. One wants to write poetry that is understood by one's people, not by the Queen of England. Of course, should she be able to profit by it too, so much the better, but since that is not likely, catering to her tastes would be a waste of time.

For the black Southern writer, coming straight out of the country, as Wright did—Natchez and Jackson are still not as citified as they like to think they are— there is the world of comparisons: between town and country, between the ugly crowding and griminess of the cities and the spacious cleanliness (which actually seems impossible to dirty) of the country. A country person finds the city confining, like a too tight dress. And always, in one's memory, there remain all the rituals of one's growing up: the warmth and vividness of Sunday worship (never mind that you never quite believed) in a little church hidden from the road, and houses set so far back into the woods that at night it is impossible for strangers to find them. The daily dramas that evolve in such a private world are pure gold. But this view of a strictly private and hidden existence, with its triumphs, failures, grotesqueries, is not nearly as valuable to the socially conscious black Southern writer as his double vision is. For not only is he in a position to see his own world, and its close community ("Homecomings" on First Sundays, barbecues to raise money to send to Africa—one of the smaller ironies—the simplicity and eerie calm of a black funeral, where the beloved one is buried way in the middle of a wood with nothing to mark the spot but perhaps a wooden cross already coming apart), but also he is capable of knowing, with remarkably silent accuracy, the people who make up the larger world that surrounds and suppresses his own.

It is a credit to a writer like Ernest J. Gaines, a black writer who writes mainly about the people he grew up with in rural Louisiana, that he can write about whites and blacks exactly as he sees them and *knows* them, instead of writing of one group as a vast malignant lump and of the other as a conglomerate of perfect virtues.

In large measure, black Southern writers owe their clarity of vision to parents who refused to diminish themselves as human beings by succumbing to racism. Our parents seemed to know that an extreme negative emotion held against other human beings for reasons they do not control can be blinding. Blindness about other human beings, especially for a writer, is equivalent to death. Because of this blindness, which is, above all, racial, the works of many Southern writers have died. Much that we read today is fast expiring.

My own slight attachment to William Faulkner was rudely broken by realizing, after reading statements he made in *Faulkner in the University,* that he believed whites superior morally to blacks; that whites had a duty (which at their convenience they would assume) to "bring blacks along" politically, since blacks, in

Faulkner's opinion, were "not ready" yet to function properly in a democratic society. He also thought that a black man's intelligence is directly related to the amount of white blood he has.

For the black person coming of age in the sixties, where Martin Luther King stands against the murderers of Goodman, Chaney, and Schwerner, there appears no basis for such assumptions. Nor was there any in Garvey's day, or in Du Bois's or in Douglass's or in Nat Turner's. Nor at any other period in our history, from the very founding of the country; for it was hardly incumbent upon slaves to be slaves and saints too. Unlike Tolstoy, Faulkner was not prepared to struggle to change the structure of the society he was born in. One might concede that in his fiction he did seek to examine the reasons for its decay, but unfortunately, as I have learned while trying to teach Faulkner to black students, it is not possible, from so short a range, to separate the man from his works.

One reads Faulkner knowing that his "colored" people had to come through "Mr. William's" back door, and one feels uneasy, and finally enraged that Faulkner did not burn the whole house down. When the provincial mind starts out *and continues* on a narrow and unprotesting course, "genius" itself must run on a track.

Flannery O'Connor at least had the conviction that "reality" is at best superficial and that the puzzle of humanity is less easy to solve than that of race. But Miss O'Connor was not so much of Georgia, as in it. The majority of Southern writers have been too confined by prevailing social customs to probe deeply into mysteries that the Citizens Councils insist must never be revealed.

Perhaps my Northern brothers will not believe me when I say there is a great deal of positive material I can draw from my "underprivileged" background. But they have never lived, as I have, at the end of a long road in a house that was faced by the edge of the world on one side and nobody for miles on the other. They have never experienced the magnificent quiet of a summer day when the heat is intense and one is so very thirsty, as one moves across the dusty cotton fields, that one learns forever that water is the essence of all life. In the cities it cannot be so clear to one that he is a creature of the earth, feeling the soil between the toes, smelling the dust thrown up by the rain, loving the earth so much that one longs to taste it and sometimes does.

Nor do I intend to romanticize the Southern black country life. I can recall that I hated it, generally. The hard work in the fields, the shabby houses, the evil greedy men who worked my father to death and almost broke the courage of that strong woman, my mother. No, I am simply saying that Southern black writers, like most writers, have a heritage of love and hate, but that they also have enormous richness and beauty to draw from. And, having been placed, as Camus says, "halfway between misery and the sun," they, too, know that "though all is not well under the sun, history is not everything."

No one could wish for a more advantageous heritage than that bequeathed to the black writer in the South: a compassion for the earth, a trust in humanity beyond our knowledge of evil, and an abiding love of justice. We inherit a great responsibility as well, for we must give voice to centuries not only of silent bitterness and hate but also neighborly kindness and sustaining love.

Double Take

1. The word "community" appears in a number of places in Alice Walker's essay "The Black Writer and the Southern Experience." What does it mean to Walker? Why is community so important to the black writer? According to Walker, what is the relationship between community and writing? Why is community important for any writer, including you?
2. Discuss what Walker means by the socially conscious black writer's "double vision." Why does Walker say it is important for a black writer to possess such a "double vision"?
3. Walker begins the essay with a personal story. What is the rhetorical effect of using such a story? How does it work to set up her central point about black writers? As a writer, to what extent do you think personal stories are effective in writing? To what extent do you think they could be overused?
4. What, according to Walker, is the role of the southern black writer? What is her or his responsibility? Do you agree with her view? Why or why not? What do you think is *your* responsibility as a writer?

At First Glance

Before you begin to read "In Search of Our Mother's Gardens," one of Alice Walker's best-known essays, keep in mind that it was first published in Ms. *magazine. What is significant about this? What would Walker herself most likely have been considering about her context and her audience as she began to write this essay? As you read the essay, consider if Walker's choices as a writer reflect her context and audience and, if so, how. Specifically, try to grasp the argument Walker is making and why this argument would be compelling to her audience. Look, for example, at how Walker addresses her audience, how she shifts from the pronouns "you," "we," and "I."*

In Search of Our Mothers' Gardens

MOTHEROOT

Creation often
needs two hearts
one to root
and one to flower
One to sustain
in time of drouth

and hold fast
against winds of pain
the fragile bloom
that in the glory
of its hour
affirms a heart
unsung, unseen.
—MARILOU AWIAKTA,
ABIDING APPALACHIA

I described her own nature and temperament. Told how they needed a larger life for their expression. . . . I pointed out that in lieu of proper channels, her emotions had overflowed into paths that dissipated them. I talked, beautifully I thought, about an art that would be born, an art that would open the way for women the likes of her. I asked her to hope, and build up an inner life against the coming of that day. . . . I sang, with a strange quiver in my voice, a promise song.

JEAN TOOMER, *"AVEY,"* CANE

The poet speaking to a prostitute who falls asleep while he's talking—

When the poet Jean Toomer walked through the South in the early twenties, he discovered a curious thing: black women whose spirituality was so intense, so deep, so *unconscious,* that they were themselves unaware of the richness they held. They stumbled blindly through their lives: creatures so abused and mutilated in body, so dimmed and confused by pain, that they considered themselves unworthy even of hope. In the selfless abstractions their bodies became to the men who used them, they became more than "sexual objects," more even than mere women: they became "Saints." Instead of being perceived as whole persons, their bodies became shrines: what was thought to be their minds became temples suitable for worship. These crazy Saints stared out at the world, wildly, like lunatics—or quietly, like suicides; and the "God" that was in their gaze was as mute as a great stone.

Who were these Saints? These crazy, loony, pitiful women?

Some of them, without a doubt, were our mothers and grandmothers.

In the still heat of the post-Reconstruction South, this is how they seemed to Jean Toomer: exquisite butterflies trapped in an evil honey, toiling away their lives in an era, a century, that did not acknowledge them, except as "the *mule* of the world." They dreamed dreams that no one knew—not even themselves, in any coherent fashion—and saw visions no one could understand. They wandered or sat about the countryside crooning lullabies to ghosts, and drawing the mother of Christ in charcoal on courthouse walls.

They forced their minds to desert their bodies and their striving spirits sought to rise, like frail whirlwinds from the hard red clay. And when those frail whirlwinds fell, in scattered particles, upon the ground, no one mourned. Instead, men lit candles to celebrate the emptiness that remained, as people do who enter a beautiful but vacant space to resurrect a God.

Our mothers and grandmothers, some of them: moving to music not yet written. And they waited.

They waited for a day when the unknown thing that was in them would be made known; but guessed, somehow in their darkness, that on the day of their revelation they would be long dead. Therefore to Toomer they walked, and even ran, in slow motion. For they were going nowhere immediate, and the future was not yet within their grasp. And men took our mothers and grandmothers, "but got no pleasure from it." So complex was their passion and their calm.

To Toomer, they lay vacant and fallow as autumn fields, with harvest time never in sight: and he saw them enter loveless marriages, without joy; and become prostitutes, without resistance; and become mothers of children, without fulfillment.

For these grandmothers and mothers of ours were not Saints, but Artists; driven to numb and bleeding madness by the springs of creativity in them for which there was no release. They were Creators, who lived lives of spiritual waste, because they were so rich in spirituality—which is the basis of Art—that the strain of enduring their unused and unwanted talent drove them insane. Throwing away this spirituality was their pathetic attempt to lighten the soul to a weight their work-worn, sexually abused bodies could bear.

What did it mean for a black woman to be an artist in our grandmothers' time? In our great-grandmothers' day? It is a question with an answer cruel enough to stop the blood.

Did you have a genius of a great-great-grandmother who died under some ignorant and depraved white overseer's lash? Or was she required to bake biscuits for a lazy backwater tramp, when she cried out in her soul to paint watercolors of sunsets, or the rain falling on the green and peaceful pasturelands? Or was her body broken and forced to bear children (who were more often than not sold away from her)—eight, ten, fifteen, twenty children—when her one joy was the thought of modeling heroic figures of rebellion, in stone or clay?

How was the creativity of the black woman kept alive, year after year and century after century, when for most of the years black people have been in America, it was a punishable crime for a black person to read or write? And the freedom to paint, to sculpt, to expand the mind with action did not exist. Consider, if you can bear to imagine it, what might have been the result if singing, too, had been forbidden by law. Listen to the voices of Bessie Smith, Billie Holliday, Nina Simone, Roberta Flack, and Aretha Franklin, among others, and imagine those voices muzzled for life. Then you may begin to comprehend the lives of our "crazy," "Sainted" mothers and grandmothers. The agony of the lives of women who might have been Poets, Novelists, Essayists, and Short-Story Writers (over a period of centuries), who died with their real gifts stifled within them.

And, if this were the end of the story, we would have cause to cry out in my paraphrase of Okot p'Bitek's great poem:

O, my clanswomen
Let us cry together!
Come,
Let us morn the death of our mother,
The death of a Queen
The ash that was produced
By a great fire!
O, this homestead is utterly dead
Close the gates
With lacari *thorns,*
For our mother
the creator of the Stool is lost!
And all the young women
Have perished in the wilderness!

But this is not the end of the story, for all the young women—our mothers and grandmothers, *ourselves*—have not perished in the wilderness. And if we ask ourselves why, and search for and find the answer, we will know beyond all efforts to erase it from our minds, just exactly who, and of what, we black American women are.

One example, perhaps the most pathetic, most misunderstood one, can provide a backdrop for our mothers' work: Phillis Wheatley, a slave in the 1700s.

Virginia Woolf, in her book *A Room of One's Own,* wrote that in order for a woman to write fiction she must have two things, certainly: a room of her own (with key and lock) and enough money to support herself.

What then are we to make of Phillis Wheatley, a slave, who owned not even herself? This sickly, frail black girl who required a servant of her own at times—her health was so precarious—and who, had she been white, would have been easily considered the intellectual superior of all the women and most of the men in the society of her day.

Virginia Woolf wrote further, speaking of course not of our Phillis, that "any woman born with a great gift in the sixteenth century [insert "eighteenth century," insert "black woman," insert "born or made a slave"] would certainly have gone crazed, shot herself, or ended her days in some lonely cottage outside the village, half witch, half wizard [insert "Saint"], feared and mocked at. For it needs little skill and psychology to be sure that a highly gifted girl who had tried to use her gift for poetry would have been so thwarted and hindered by contrary instincts [add "chains, guns, the lash, the ownership of one's body by someone else, submission to an alien religion"], that she must have lost her health and sanity to a certainty."

The key words, as they relate to Phillis, are "contrary instincts." For when we read the poetry of Phillis Wheatley—as when we read the novels of Nella Larson or the oddly false-sounding autobiography of that freest of all black women writers, Zora Hurston—evidence of "contrary instincts" is everywhere. Her loyalties were completely divided, as was, without question, her mind.

But how could this be otherwise? Captured at seven, a slave of wealthy, doting whites who instilled in her the "savagery" of the Africa they "rescued" her from . . .

one wonders if she was even able to remember her homeland as she had known it, or as it really was.

Yet, because she did try to use her gift for poetry in a world that made her a slave, she was "so thwarted and hindered by . . . contrary instincts, that she . . . lost her health. . . ." In the last years of her brief life, burdened not only with the need to express her gift but also with a penniless, friendless "freedom" and several small children for whom she was forced to do strenuous work to feed, she lost her health, certainly. Suffering from malnutrition and neglect and who knows what mental agonies, Phillis Wheatley died.

So torn by "contrary instincts" was black, kidnapped, enslaved Phillis that her description of "the Goddess"—as she poetically called the Liberty she did not have—is ironically, cruelly humorous. And, in fact, has held Phillis up to ridicule for more than a century. It is usually read prior to hanging Phillis's memory as that of a fool. She wrote:

> *The Goddess comes, she moves divinely fair,*
> *Olive and laurel binds her golden hair.*
> *Wherever shines this native of the skies,*
> *Unnumber'd charms and recent graces rise.[My emphasis]*

It is obvious that Phillis, the slave, combed the "Goddess's" hair every morning; prior, perhaps, to bringing in the milk, or fixing her mistress's lunch. She took her imagery from the one thing she saw elevated above all others.

With the benefit of hindsight we ask, "How could she?"

But at last, Phillis, we understand. No more snickering when your stiff, struggling, ambivalent lines are forced on us. We know now that you were not an idiot or a traitor; only a sickly little black girl, and snatched from your home and country and made a slave; a woman who still struggled to sing the song that was your gift, although in a land of barbarians who praised you for your bewildered tongue. It is not so much what you sang, as that you kept alive, in so many of our ancestors, *the notion of song.*

Black women are called, in the folklore that so aptly identifies one's status in society, "the *mule* of the world," because we have been handed the burdens that everyone else—*everyone* else— refused to carry. We have also been called "Matriarchs," "Superwomen," and "Mean and Evil Bitches." Not to mention "Castraters" and "Sapphire's Mama." When we have pleaded for understanding, our character has been distorted; when we have asked for simple caring, we have been handed empty inspirational appellations, then stuck in the farthest corner. When we have asked for love, we have been given children. In short, even our plainer gifts, our labors of fidelity and love, have been knocked down our throats. To be an artist and a black woman, even today, lowers our status in many respects, rather than raises it: and yet, artists we will be.

Therefore we must fearlessly pull out of ourselves and look at and identify with our lives the living creativity some of our great-grandmothers were not allowed to know. I stress *some* of them because it is well known that the majority of our great-grandmothers knew, even without "knowing" it, the reality of their spirituality, even if they didn't recognize it beyond what happened in the singing at church—and they never had any intention of giving it up.

How they did it—those millions of black women who were not Phillis Wheatley, or Lucy Terry or Frances Harper or Zora Hurston or Nella Larsen or Bessie Smith; or Elizabeth Catlett, or Katherine Dunham, either—brings me to the title of this essay, "In Search of Our Mothers' Gardens," which is a personal account that is yet shared, in its theme and its meaning, by all of us. I found, while thinking about the far-reaching world of the creative black woman, that often the truest answer to a question that really matters can be found very close.

In the late 1920s my mother ran away from home to marry my father. Marriage, if not running away, was expected of seventeen-year-old girls. By the time she was twenty, she had two children and was pregnant with a third. Five children later, I was born. And this is how I came to know my mother: she seemed a large, soft, loving-eyed woman who was rarely impatient in our home. Her quick, violent temper was on view only a few times a year, when she battled with the white landlord who had the misfortune to suggest to her that her children did not need to go school.

She made all the clothes we wore, even my brothers' overalls. She made all the towels and sheets we used. She spent the summers canning vegetables and fruits. She spent the winter evenings making quilts enough to cover all our beds.

During the "working" day, she labored beside—not behind—my father in the fields. Her day began before sunup, and did not end until late at night. There was never a moment for her to sit down, undisturbed, to unravel her own private thoughts; never a time free from interruption—by work or the noisy inquiries of her many children. And yet, it is to my mother—and all our mothers who were not famous—that I went in search of the secret of what has fed that muzzled and often mutilated, but vibrant, creative spirit that the black woman has inherited, and that pops out in wild and unlikely places to this day.

But when, you will ask, did my overworked mother have time to know or care about feeding the creative spirit?

The answer is so simple that many of us have spent years discovering it. We have constantly looked high, when we should have looked high—and low.

For example: in the Smithsonian Institution in Washington, D.C., there hangs a quilt unlike any other in the world. In fanciful, inspired, and yet simple and identifiable figures, it portrays the story of the Crucifixion. It is considered rare, beyond price. Though it follows no known pattern of quilt-making, and though it is made of bits and pieces of worthless rags, it is obviously the work of a person of powerful imagination and deep spiritual feeling. Below this quilt I saw a note that says it was made by "an anonymous Black woman in Alabama, a hundred years ago."

If we could locate this "anonymous" black woman from Alabama, she would turn out to be one of our grandmothers—an artist who left her mark in the only materials she could afford, and in the only medium her position in society allowed her to use.

As Virginia Woolf wrote further, in *A Room of One's Own:*

Yet genius of a sort must have existed among women as it must have existed among the working class. [Change this to "slaves" and "the wives and daughters of sharecroppers."] Now and again an Emily Brontë or a Robert Burns [change this to "a Zora Hurston or a Richard Wright"] blazes out and proves its presence. But certainly it never got itself on to paper. When, however, one reads of a witch being ducked, of a woman possessed by devils [or "Sainthood"], of a wise woman selling herbs [our root workers], or even a very remarkable man who had a mother, then I think we are on the track of a lost novelist, a suppressed poet, of some mute and inglorious Jane Austen. . . .
Indeed, I would venture to guess that Anon, who wrote so many poems without signing them, was often a woman. . . .

And so our mothers and grandmothers have, more often than not anonymously, handed on the creative spark, the seed of the flower they themselves never hoped to see: or like a sealed letter they could not plainly read.

And so it is, certainly, with my own mother. Unlike "Ma" Rainey's songs, which retained their creator's name even while blasting forth from Bessie Smith's mouth, no song or poem will bear my mother's name. Yet so many of the stories that I write, that we all write, are my mother's stories. Only recently did I fully realize this: that through years of listening to my mother's stories of her life, I have absorbed not only the stories themselves, but something of the manner in which she spoke, something of the urgency that involves the knowledge that her stories—like her life—must be recorded. It is probably for this reason that so much of what I have written is about characters whose counterparts in real life are so much older than I am.

But the telling of these stories, which came from my mother's lips as naturally as breathing, was not the only way my mother showed herself as an artist. For stories, too, were subject to being distracted, to dying without conclusion. Dinners must be started, and cotton must be gathered before the big rains. The artist that was and is my mother showed itself to me only after many years. This is what I finally noticed:

Like Mem, a character in *The Third Life of Grange Copeland,* my mother adorned with flowers whatever shabby house we were forced to live in. And not just your typical straggly country stand of zinnias, either. She planted ambitious gardens—and still does—with over fifty different varieties of plants that bloom profusely from early March until late November. Before she left home for the fields, she watered her flowers, chopped up the grass, and laid out new beds. When she returned from the fields she might divide clumps of bulbs, dig a cold pit, uproot and replant roses, or prune branches from her taller bushes or trees—until night came and it was too dark to see.

Whatever she planted grew as if by magic, and her fame as a grower of flowers spread over three counties. Because of her creativity with her flowers, even my memories of poverty are seen through a screen of blooms—sunflowers, petunias, roses, dahlias, forsythia, spirea, delphiniums, verbena . . . and on and on.

And I remember people coming to my mother's yard to be given cuttings from her flowers; I hear again the praise showered on her because whatever rocky soil she landed on, she turned into a garden. A garden so brilliant with colors, so original in its design, so magnificent with life and creativity, that to this day people drive by our house in Georgia—perfect strangers and imperfect strangers—and ask to stand or walk among my mother's art.

I notice that it is only when my mother is working in her flowers that she is radiant, almost to the point of being invisible—except as Creator: hand and eye. She is involved in work her soul must have. Ordering the universe in the image of her personal conception of Beauty.

Her face, as she prepares the Art that is her gift, is a legacy of respect she leaves to me, for all that illuminates and cherishes life. She has handed down respect for the possibilities—and the will to grasp them.

For her, so hindered and intruded upon in so many ways, being an artist has still been a daily part of her life. This ability to hold on, even in very simple ways, is work black women have done for a very long time.

This poem is not enough, but it is something, for the woman who literally covered the holes in our walls with sunflowers:

> *They were women then*
> *My mama's generation*
> *Husky of voice—Stout of*
> *Step*
> *With fists as well as*
> *Hands*
> *How they battered down*
> *Doors*
> *And ironed*
> *Starched white*
> *Shirts*
> *How they led*
> *Armies*
> *Headragged Generals*
> *Across mined*
> *Fields*
> *Booby-trapped*
> *Kitchens*
> *To discover books*
> *Desks*
> *A place for us*
> *How they knew what we*
> *Must know*
> *Without knowing a page*
> *Of it*
> *Themselves.*

Guided by my heritage of a love of beauty and a respect for strength—in search of my mother's garden, I found my own.

And perhaps in Africa over two hundred years ago, there was just such a mother; perhaps she painted vivid and daring decorations in orange and yellows and greens on the walls of her hut; perhaps she sang—in a voice like Roberta Flack's—*sweetly* over the compounds of her village; perhaps she wove the most stunning mats or told the most ingenious stories of all the village storytellers. Perhaps she was herself a poet—though only her daughter's name is signed to the poems that we know.

Perhaps Phillis Wheatley's mother was also an artist.

Perhaps in more than Phillis Wheatley's biological life is her mother's signature made clear.

Double Take

1. In her essay "In Search of Our Mothers' Gardens," Alice Walker at times addresses the reader directly using the pronoun "you." Who, specifically, is implied in this "you"? How is Walker addressing the audience, this "you"? Is it effective? Why or why not? Walker also shifts between the pronouns "you" and "we" and "I." Locate where she does this and think about what effect this shift in pronoun has on the way the reader relates to the writer.
2. Describe with specific examples taken from the essay how Walker builds her argument on behalf of the creativity of black women. What sorts of examples does she use? Why are these examples effective? What can you learn about argument-building from this essay?
3. What is Alice Walker's tone in this essay? Describe it with examples and then explain whether or not you think it is appropriate for the subject she is writing about and for the audience she is writing to.
4. How does Walker define creativity in this essay? What challenges does the creative black woman face? Does Walker's view of creativity match your own?

At First Glance

"My Daughter Smokes" was first published under the title "Slavery on Tobacco Road" in These Times *magazine. The essay remains unchanged, but as you read it think about what the change of title does to the overall effect of the essay. Do you find that you read it differently under its present title? How much persuasive power over a piece of writing does a title have? Think about this question when you write your own essays and titles. Think also, as you read "My Daughter Smokes," about the way Walker weaves the personal and the political, the present and the past, and the balance she creates between these. Do you find this a productive balance? Consider the extent to which this balance contributes to the effectiveness of this essay.*

My Daughter Smokes

My daughter smokes. While she is doing her homework, her feet on the bench in front of her and her calculator clicking out answers to her algebra problems, I am looking at the half-empty package of Camels tossed carelessly close at hand. Camels. I pick them up, take them into the kitchen, where the light is better, and study them—they're filtered, for which I am grateful. My heart feels terrible. I want to weep. In fact, I do weep a little, standing there by the stove holding one of the instruments, so white, so precisely rolled, that could cause my daughter's death. When she smoked Marlboros and Players I hardened myself against feeling so bad; nobody I knew ever smoked these brands.

She doesn't know this, but it was Camels that my father, her grandfather, smoked. But before he smoked "ready-mades"—when he was very young and very poor, with eyes like lanterns—he smoked Prince Albert tobacco in cigarettes he rolled himself. I remember the bright-red tobacco tin, with a picture of Queen Victoria's consort, Prince Albert, dressed in a black frock coat and carrying a cane.

The tobacco was dark brown, pungent, slightly bitter. I tasted it more than once as a child, and the discarded tins could be used for a number of things: to keep buttons and shoelaces in, to store seeds, and best of all, to hold worms for the rare times my father took us fishing.

By the late forties and early fifties no one rolled his own anymore (and few women smoked) in my hometown, Eatonton, Georgia. The tobacco industry, coupled with Hollywood movies in which both hero and heroine smoked like chimneys, won over completely people like my father, who were hopelessly addicted to cigarettes. He never looked as dapper as Prince Albert, though; he continued to look like a poor, overweight, overworked colored man with too large a family; black, with a very white cigarette stuck in his mouth.

I do not remember when he started to cough. Perhaps it was unnoticeable at first. A little hacking in the morning as he lit his first cigarette upon getting out of bed. By the time I was my daughter's age, his breath was a wheeze, embarrassing to hear; he could not climb the stairs without resting every third or fourth step. It was not unusual for him to cough for an hour.

It is hard to believe there was a time when people did not understand that cigarette smoking is an addiction. I wondered aloud once to my sister—who is perennially trying to quit—whether our father realized this. I wondered how she, a smoker since high school, viewed her own habit.

It was our father who gave her her first cigarette, one day when she had taken water to him in the fields.

"I always wondered why he did that," she said, puzzled, and with some bitterness.

"What did he say?" I asked.

"That he didn't want me to go to anyone else for them," she said, "which never really crossed my mind."

So he was aware it was addictive, I thought, though as annoyed as she that he assumed she would be interested.

I began smoking in eleventh grade, also the year I drank numerous bottles of terrible sweet, very cheap wine. My friends and I, all boys for this venture, bought our supplies from a man who ran a segregated bar and liquor store on the outskirts of town. Over the entrance there was a large sign that said COLORED. We were not permitted to drink there, only to buy. I smoked Kools, because my sister did. By then I thought her toxic darkened lips and gums glamorous. However, my body simply would not tolerate smoke. After six months I had a chronic sore throat. I gave up smoking, gladly. Because it was a ritual with my buddies—Murl, Leon, and "Dog" Farley—I continued to drink wine.

My father died from "the poor man's friend," pneumonia, one hard winter when his bronchitis and emphysema had left him low. I doubt he had much lung left at all, after coughing for so many years. He had so little breath that, during his last years, he was always leaning on something. I remember once, at a family reunion, when my daughter was two, that my father picked her up for a minute—long enough for me to photograph them—but the effort was obvious. Near the very end of his life, and largely because he had no more lungs, he quit smoking. He gained a couple of pounds, but by then he was so emaciated no one noticed.

When I travel to Third World countries I see many people like my father and daughter. There are large billboards directed at them both: the tough, "take-charge," or dapper older man, the glamorous, "worldly" young woman, both puffing away. In these poor countries, as in American ghettos and on reservations, money that should be spent for food goes instead to the tobacco companies; over time, people starve themselves of both food and air, effectively weakening and addicting their children, eventually eradicating themselves. I read in the newspaper and in my gardening magazine that cigarette butts are so toxic that if a baby swallows one, it is likely to die, and that the boiled water from a bunch of them makes an effective insecticide.

My daughter would like to quit, she says. We both know the statistics are against her; most people who try to quit smoking do not succeed.★

There is a deep hurt that I feel as a mother. Some days it is a feeling of futility. I remember how carefully I ate when I was pregnant, how patiently I taught my daughter how to cross a street safely. For what, I sometimes wonder; so that she can wheeze through most of her life feeling half her strength, and then die of self-poisoning, as her grandfather did?

But, finally, one must feel empathy for the tobacco plant itself. For thousands of years, it has been venerated by Native Americans as a sacred medicine. They have used it extensively—its juice, its leaves, its roots, its (holy) smoke—to heal wounds and cure diseases, and in ceremonies of prayer and peace. And though the plant as most of us know it has been poisoned by chemicals and denatured by intensive mono-cropping and is therefore hardly the plant it was, still, to some modern

---

★Three months after reading this essay my daughter stopped smoking.

Indians it remains a plant of positive power. I learned this when my Native American friends, Bill Wahpepah and his family, visited with me for a few days and the first thing he did was sow a few tobacco seeds in my garden.

Perhaps we can liberate tobacco from those who have captured and abused it, enslaving the plant on large plantations, keeping it from freedom and its kin, and forcing it to enslave the world. Its true nature suppressed, no wonder it has become deadly. Maybe by sowing a few seeds of tobacco in our gardens and treating the plant with the reverence it deserves, we can redeem tobacco's soul and restore its self-respect.

Besides, how grim, if one is a smoker, to realize one is smoking a slave.

There is a slogan from a battered women's shelter that I especially like: "Peace on earth begins at home." I believe everything does. I think of a slogan for people trying to stop smoking: "Every home a smoke-free zone." Smoking is a form of self-battering that also batters those who must sit by, occasionally cajole or complain, and helplessly watch. I realize now that as a child I sat by, through the years, and literally watched my father kill himself: surely one such victory in my family, for the rich white men who own the tobacco companies, is enough.

Double Take

1. The essay "My Daughter Smokes" is an argument against smoking, but what makes it an essay rather than, say, an editorial or a research paper? What is essayistic about it? Be specific in your response.
2. Why do you think Alice Walker's daughter found this essay persuasive enough to stop smoking after reading it? How does the essay achieve its persuasive power?
3. Compared to the other essays by Alice Walker you have read in this section, in what ways is "My Daughter Smokes" Walkeresque? What features and qualities—in terms of tone, content, structure, and so on—does it share with the other essays?
4. Given what Walker says are the responsibilities of the southern black writer in "The Black Writer and the Southern Experience," to what extent does this essay fulfill that responsibility? Why? How?

Seeing for Yourself

At First Glance

"Beyond the Peacock: The Reconstruction of Flannery O'Connor," like "In Search of Our Mothers' Gardens," was first published in Ms. *magazine. Structurally, it is perhaps the most complex of Alice Walker's essays collected here, having many dimensions that are each inter-locked in one another in a stream-of-consciousness, almost mazelike, pattern. As you read it, think about why Walker might have chosen such a structure and how it might convey the meaning of the essay. Also, try to capture the experience of reading it; that is, try to describe the feeling you have while reading through its different parts: part biography of O'Connor, part autobiography, part literary history, part dialogue. What do you think Walker expects you as a reader to do with these parts? What demands does she place on you in constructing the meaning of the essay? And what can you apply to your own writing from the experience of reading this essay?*

Beyond the Peacock: The Reconstruction of Flannery O'Connor

It was after a poetry reading I gave at a recently desegregated college in Georgia that someone mentioned that in 1952 Flannery O'Connor and I had lived within minutes of each other on the same Eatonton-to-Milledgeville road. I was eight years old in 1952 (she would have been 28) and we moved away from Milledgeville after less than a year. Still, since I have loved her work for many years, the coincidence of our having lived near each other intrigued me, and started me thinking of her again.

As a college student in the sixties I read her books endlessly, scarcely conscious of the difference between her racial and economic background and my own, but put them away in anger when I discovered that, while I was reading O'Connor—Southern, Catholic, and white—there were other women writers—some Southern, some religious, all black—I had not been allowed to know. For several years, while I searched for, found, and studied black women writers, I deliberately shut O'Connor out, feeling almost ashamed that she had reached me first. And yet, even when I no longer read her, I missed her, and realized that though the rest of America might not mind, having endured it so long, I would never be satisfied with a segregated litera-ture. I would have to read Zora Hurston *and* Flannery O'Connor, Nella Larsen *and* Carson McCullers, Jean Toomer *and* William Faulkner, before I could begin to feel *well* read at all.

I thought it might be worthwhile, in 1974, to visit the two houses, Flannery O'Connor's and mine, to see what could be learned twenty-two years after we moved away and ten years after her death. It seemed right to go to my old house first—to set the priorities of vision, so to speak—then to her house, to see, at the very least, whether her peacocks would still be around. To this bit of nostalgic exploration I invited my mother, who, curious about peacocks and abandoned houses, if not about literature and writers, accepted.

In her shiny new car, which at sixty-one she has learned to drive, we cruised down the wooded Georgia highways to revisit our past.

At the turnoff leading to our former house, we face a fence, a gate, a NO TRES-PASSING sign. The car will not fit through the gate and beyond the gate is muddy pasture. It shocks me to remember that when we lived here we lived, literally, in a pasture. It is a memory I had repressed. Now, for a moment, it frightens me.

"Do you think we should enter?" I ask.

But my mother has already opened the gate. To her, life has no fences, except, perhaps, religious ones, and these we have decided not to discuss. We walk through pines rich with vines, fluttering birds, and an occasional wild azalea showing flashes of orange. The day is bright with spring, the sky cloudless, the road rough and clean.

"I would like to see old man Jenkins [who was our landlord] come bothering me about some trespassing," she says, her head extremely up. "He never did pay us for the crop we made for him in fifty-two."

After five minutes of leisurely walking, we are again confronted with a fence, fastened gate, POSTED signs. Again my mother ignores all three, unfastens the gate, walks through.

"He never gave me my half of the calves I raised that year either," she says. And I chuckle at her memory and her style.

Now we are facing a large green rise. To our left calves are grazing; beyond them there are woods. To our right there is the barn we used, looking exactly as it did twenty-two years ago. It is high and weathered silver and from it comes the sweet scent of peanut hay. In front of it, a grove of pecans. Directly in front of us over the rise is what is left of the house.

"Well," says my mother, "it's still standing. And," she adds with wonder, "just look at my daffodils!"

In twenty-two years they have multiplied and are now blooming from one side of the yard to the other. It is a typical abandoned sharefarmer shack. Of the four-room house only two rooms are left; the others have rotted away. These two are filled with hay.

Considering the sad state of the house it is amazing how beautiful its setting is. There is not another house in sight. There are hills, green pastures, a ring of bright trees, and a family of rabbits hopping out of our way. My mother and I stand in the yard remembering. I remember only misery: going to a shabby segregated school that was once the state prison and that had, on the second floor, the large circular print of the electric chair that had stood there; almost stepping on a water moccasin on my way home from carrying water to my family in the fields; losing Phoebe, my cat, because we left this place hurriedly and she could not be found in time.

"Well, old house," my mother says, smiling in such a way that I almost see her rising, physically, above it, "one good thing you gave us. It was right here that I got my first washing machine!"

In fact, the only pleasant thing I recall from that year was a field we used to pass on our way into the town of Milledgeville. It was like a painting by someone who loved tranquillity. In the foreground near the road the green field was used as pasture for black-and-white cows that never seemed to move. Then, farther away, there was a steep hill partly covered with kudzu—dark and lush and creeping up to cover and change fantastically the shapes of the trees. . . . When we drive past it now, it looks the same. Even the cows could be the same cows—though now I see that they *do* move, though not very fast and never very far.

What I liked about this field as a child was that in my life of nightmares about electrocutions, lost cats, and the surprise appearances of snakes, it represented beauty and unchanging peace.

"Of course," I say to myself, as we turn off the main road two miles from my old house, "that's Flannery's field." The instructions I've been given place her house on the hill just beyond it.

There is a garish new Holiday Inn directly across Highway 441 from Flannery O'Connor's house, and, before going up to the house, my mother and I decide to have something to eat there. Twelve years ago I could not have bought lunch for us at such a place in Georgia, and I feel a weary delight as I help my mother off with her sweater and hold out a chair by the window for her. The white people eating lunch all around us—staring though trying hard not to—form a blurred backdrop against which my mother's face is especially sharp. *This* is the proper perspective, I think, biting into a corn muffin; no doubt about it.

As we sip iced tea we discuss O'Connor, integration, the inferiority of the corn muffins we are nibbling, and the care and raising of peacocks.

"Those things will sure eat up your flowers," my mother says, explaining why she never raised any.

"Yes," I say, "but they're a lot prettier than they'd be if somebody human had made them, which is why this lady liked them." This idea has only just occurred to me, but having said it, I believe it is true. I sit wondering why I called Flannery O'Connor a lady. It is a word I rarely use and usually by mistake, since the whole notion of ladyhood is repugnant to me. I can imagine O'Connor at a Southern social affair, looking very polite and being very bored, making mental notes of the absurdities of the evening. Being white she would automatically have been eligible for ladyhood, but I cannot believe she would ever really have joined.

"She must have been a Christian person then," says my mother. "She believed He made everything." She pauses, looks at me with tolerance but also as if daring me to object: "And she was *right*, too."

"She was a Catholic," I say, "which must not have been comfortable in the Primitive Baptist South, and more than any other writer she believed in everything, including things she couldn't see."

"Is that why you like her?" she asks.

"I like her because she could *write*," I say.

"'Flannery' sounds like something to eat," someone said to me once. The word always reminds me of flannel, the material used to make nightgowns and winter shirts. It is very Irish, as were her ancestors. He first name was Mary, but she seems never to have used it. Certainly "Mary O'Connor" is short on mystery. She was an Aries, born March 25, 1925. When she was sixteen, her father died of lupus, the disease that, years later, caused her own death. After her father died, O'Connor and her mother, Regina O'Connor, moved from Savannah, Georgia, to Milledgeville, where they lived in a townhouse built for Flannery O'Connor's grandfather, Peter Cline. This house, called "the Cline house," was built by slaves who made the bricks by hand. O'Connor's biographers are always impressed by this fact, as if it adds the blessed sign of aristocracy, but whenever I read it I think that those slaves were some of my own relatives, toiling in the stifling middle-Georgia heat, to erect her grandfather's house, sweating and suffering the swarming mosquitoes as the house rose slowly, brick by brick.

Whenever I visit antebellum homes in the South, with their spacious rooms, their grand staircases, their shaded back windows that, without the thickly planted trees, would look out onto the now vanished slave quarters in the back, this is invariably my thought. I stand in the backyard gazing up at the windows, then stand at the windows inside looking down into the backyard, and between the me that is on the ground and the me that is at the windows, History is caught.

O'Connor attended local Catholic schools and then Georgia Women's College. In 1945 she received a fellowship to the Writer's Workshop at the University of Iowa. She received her M.A. in 1947. While still a student she wrote stories that caused her to be recognized as a writer of formidable talent and integrity of craft. After a stay at Yaddo, the artist's colony in upstate New York, she moved to a furnished room in New York City. Later she lived and wrote over a garage at the Connecticut home of Sally and Robert Fitzgerald, who became, after her death, her literary executors.

Although, as Robert Fitzgerald states in the preface to O'Connor's *Everything That Rises Must Converge,* "Flannery was out to be a writer on her own and had no plans to go back to live in Georgia," staying out of Georgia for good was not possible. In December of 1950 she experienced a peculiar heaviness in her "typing arms." On the train home for the Christmas holidays she became so ill she was hospitalized immediately. It was disseminated lupus. In the fall of 1951, after nine wretched months in the hospital, she returned to Milledgeville. Because she could not climb the stairs at the Cline house her mother brought her to their country house, Andalusia, about five miles from town. Flannery O'Connor lived there with her mother for the next thirteen years. The rest of her life.

The word *lupus* is Latin for "wolf," and is described as "that which eats into the substance." It is a painful, wasting disease, and O'Connor suffered not only from the disease—which caused her muscles to weaken and her body to swell, among other things—but from the medicine she was given to fight the disease, which caused her hair to fall out and her hipbones to melt. Still, she managed—with the aid of crutches from 1955 on—to get about and to write, and left behind more than three dozen superb short stories, most of them prizewinners, two novels, and a dozen or so brilliant essays and speeches. Her book of essays, *Mystery and Manners,* which is primarily concerned with the moral imperatives of the serious writer of fiction, is the best of its kind I have ever read.

"When you make these trips back south," says my mother, as I give the smiling waitress my credit card, "just what is it exactly that you're looking for?"

"A wholeness," I reply.

"You look whole enough to me," she says.

"No," I answer, "because everything around me is split up, deliberately split up. History split up, literature split up, and people are split up too. It makes people do ignorant things. For example, one day I was invited to speak at a gathering of Mississippi librarians and before I could get started, one of the authorities on Mississippi history and literature got up and said she really *did* think Southerners wrote so well because 'we' lost the war. She was white, of course, but half the librarians in the room were black."

"I bet she was real old," says my mother. "They're the only ones still worrying over that war."

"So I got up and said no, 'we' didn't lose the war. '*You* all' lost the war. And you all's loss was our gain."

"Those old ones will just have to die out," says my mother.

"Well," I say, "I believe that the truth about any subject only comes when all the sides of the story are put together, and all their different meanings make one new one. Each writer writes the missing parts to the other writer's story. And the whole story is what I'm after."

"Well, I doubt if you can ever get the *true* missing parts of anything away from the white folks," my mother says softly, so as not to offend the waitress who is mopping up a nearby table; "they've sat on the truth so long by now they've mashed the life out of it."

"O'Connor wrote a story once called 'Everything That Rises Must Converge.'"

"What?"

"Everything that goes up comes together, meets, becomes one thing. Briefly, the story is this: an old white woman in her fifties—"

"That's not old! I'm older than that, and I'm not old!"

"Sorry. This middle-aged woman gets on a bus with her son, who likes to think he is a Southern liberal . . . he looks for a black person to sit next to. This horrifies his mother, who, though not old, has old ways. She is wearing a very hideous, very expensive hat, which is purple and green."

"Purple and *green?*"

"Very expensive. *Smart.* Bought at the best store in town. She says, 'With a hat like this, I won't meet myself coming and going.' But in fact, soon a large black woman, whom O'Connor describes as looking something like a gorilla, gets on the bus with a little boy, and she is wearing the same green-and-purple hat. Well, our not-so-young white lady is horrified, out*done*."

"I *bet* she was. Black folks have money to buy foolish things with too, now."

"O'Connor's point exactly! Everything that rises, must converge."

"Well, the green-and-purple-hats people will have to converge without me."

"O'Connor thought that the South, as it became more 'progressive,' would become just like the North. Culturally bland, physically ravished, and, where the people are concerned, well, you wouldn't be able to tell one racial group from another. Everybody would want the same things, like the same things, and everybody would be reduced to wearing, symbolically, the same green-and-purple hats."

"And do you think this is happening?"

"I do. But that is not the whole point of the story. The white woman, in an attempt to save her pride, chooses to treat the incident of the identical hats as a case of monkey-see, monkey-do. She assumes she is not the monkey, of course. She ignores the idiotic-looking black woman and begins instead to flirt with the woman's son, who is small and black and *cute*. She fails to notice that the black woman is glowering at her. When they all get off the bus she offers the little boy a 'bright new penny.' And the child's mother knocks the hell out of her with her pocketbook."

"I bet she carried a large one."

"Large, and full of hard objects."

"Then what happened? Didn't you say the white woman's son was with her?"

"He had tried to warn his mother. 'These new Negroes are not like the old,' he told her. But she never listened. He thought he hated his mother until he saw her on the ground, then he felt sorry for her. But when he tried to help her, she didn't know him. She'd retreated in her mind to a historical time more congenial to her desires. 'Tell Grandpapa to come get me,' she says. Then she totters off, alone, into the night."

"Poor *thing*," my mother says sympathetically of this horrid woman, in a total identification that is *so* Southern and *so* black.

"That's what her son felt, too, and *that* is how you know it is a Flannery O'Connor story. The son has been changed by his mother's experience. He understands that, though she is a silly woman who has tried to live in the past, she is also a pathetic creature and so is he. But it is too late to tell her about this because she is stone crazy."

"What did the black woman do after she knocked the white woman down and walked away?"

"O'Connor chose not to say, and that is why, although this is a good story, it is, to me, only half a story. *You* might know the other half. . . ."

"Well, I'm not a writer, but there *was* an old white woman I once wanted to strike . . ." she begins.

"Exactly," I say.

I discovered O'Connor when I was in college in the North and took a course in Southern writers and the South. The perfection of her writing was so dazzling I never noticed that no black Southern writers were taught. The other writers we studied—Faulkner, McCullers, Welty—seemed obsessed with a racial past that would not let them go. They seemed to beg the question of their characters' humanity on every page. O'Connor's characters—whose humanity if not their sanity is taken for granted, and who are miserable, ugly, narrow-minded, atheistic, and of intense racial smugness and arrogance, with not a graceful, pretty one anywhere who is not, at the same time, a joke— shocked and delighted me.

It was for her description of Southern white women that I appreciated her work at first, because when she set her pen to them not a whiff of magnolia hovered in the air (and the tree itself might never have been planted), and yes, I could say, yes, these white folks without the magnolia (who are indifferent to the tree's existence), and these black folks without melons and superior racial patience, these are like Southerners that I know.

She was for me the first great modern writer from the South, and was, in any case, the only one I had read who wrote such sly, demythifying sentences about white women as: "The woman would be more or less pretty—yellow hair, fat ankles, muddy-colored eyes."

Her white male characters do not fare any better—all of them misfits, thieves, deformed madmen, idiot children, illiterates, and murderers, and her black characters, male and female, appear equally shallow, demented, and absurd. That she retained a certain distance (only, however, in her later, mature work) from the inner workings of her black characters seems to me all to her credit, since, by deliberately limiting her treatment of them to cover their observable demeanor and actions, she leaves them free, in the reader's imagination, to inhabit another landscape, another life, than the one she creates for them. This is a kind of grace many writers do not have when dealing with representatives of an oppressed people within a story, and their insistence on knowing everything, on being God, in fact, has burdened us with more stereotypes than we can ever hope to shed.

In her life, O'Connor was more casual. In a letter to her friend Robert Fitzgerald in the mid-fifties she wrote, "as the niggers say, I have the misery." He found nothing offensive, apparently, in including this unflattering (to O'Connor) statement in his Introduction to one of her books. O'Connor was then certain she was dying, and was in pain; one assumes she made this comment in an attempt at levity. Even so, I do not find it funny. In another letter she wrote shortly before she died she said: "Justice is justice and should not be appealed to along racial lines. The problem is not abstract for the Southerner, it's concrete: he sees it in terms of persons, not races— which way of seeing does away with easy answers." Of course this observation, though grand, does not apply to the racist treatment of blacks by whites in the South, and O'Connor should have added that she spoke only for herself.

But *essential* O'Connor is not about race at all, which is why it is so refreshing, coming, as it does, out of such a *racial* culture. If it can be said to be "about" anything, then it is "about" prophets and prophecy, "about" revelation, and "about" the impact of supernatural grace on human beings who don't have a chance of spiritual growth without it.

An indication that *she* believed in justice for the individual (if only in the corrected portrayal of a character she invented) is shown by her endless reworking of "The Geranium," the first story she published (in 1946), when she was twenty-one. She revised the story several times, renamed it at least twice, until, nearly twenty years after she'd originally published it (and significantly, I think, after the beginning of the Civil Rights Movement), it became a different tale. Her two main black characters, a man and a woman, underwent complete metamorphosis.

In the original story, Old Dudley, a senile racist from the South, lives with his daughter in a New York City building that has "niggers" living in it too. The black characters are described as being passive, self-effacing people. The black woman sits quietly, hands folded, in her apartment; the man, her husband, helps Old Dudley up the stairs when the old man is out of breath, and chats with him kindly, if condescendingly, about guns and hunting. But in the final version of the story, the woman walks around Old Dudley (now called Tanner) as if he's an open bag of garbage, scowls whenever she sees him, and "didn't look like any kind of woman, black or white, he had ever seen." Her husband, whom Old Dudley persists in calling "Preacher" (under the misguided assumption that to all black men it is a courtesy title), twice knocks the old man down. At the end of the story he stuffs Old Dudley's head, arms, and legs through the banisters of the stairway "as if in a stockade," and leaves him to die. The story's final title is "Judgment Day."

The quality added is rage, and, in this instance, O'Connor waited until she saw it *exhibited* by black people before she recorded it.

She was an artist who thought she might die young, and who then knew for certain she would. Her view of her characters pierces right through to the skull. Whatever her characters' color or social position she saw them as she saw herself, in the light of imminent mortality. Some of her stories, "The Enduring Chill" and "The Comforts of Home" especially, seem to be written out of the despair that must, on occasion, have come from this bleak vision, but it is for her humor that she is most enjoyed and remembered. My favorites are these:

> Everywhere I go I'm asked if I think the universities stifle writers. My opinion is that they don't stifle enough of them. There's many a best-seller that could have been prevented by a good teacher.
>
> —MYSTERY AND MANNERS

> "She would of been a good woman, if it had been somebody there to shoot her every minute of her life."
>
> —"*THE MISFIT*,"
> A GOOD MAN IS HARD TO FIND

> There are certain cases in which, if you can only learn to write poorly enough, you can make a great deal of money.
>
> —MYSTERY AND MANNERS

> It is the business of fiction to embody mystery through manners, and mystery is a great embarrassment to the modern mind.
>
> —MYSTERY AND MANNERS

It mattered to her that she was a Catholic. This comes as a surprise to those who first read her work as that of an atheist. She believed in all the mysteries of her faith. And yet, she was incapable of writing dogmatic or formulaic stories. No religious tracts, nothing haloed softly in celestial light, not even any happy endings. It has puzzled some of her readers and annoyed the Catholic church that in her stories not only does good not triumph, it is not usually present. Seldom are there choices, and God never intervenes to help anyone win. To O'Connor, in fact, Jesus was God, and he won only by losing. She perceived that not much has been learned by his death by crucifixion, and that it is only by his continual, repeated dying—touching one's own life in a direct, searing way—that the meaning of that original loss is pressed into the heart of the individual.

In "The Displaced Person," a story published in 1954, a refugee from Poland is hired to work on a woman's dairy farm. Although he speaks in apparent gibberish, he is a perfect worker. He works so assiduously the woman begins to prosper beyond her greatest hopes. Still, because his ways are not her own (the Displaced Person attempts to get one of the black dairy workers to marry his niece by "buying" her out of a Polish concentration camp), the woman allows a runaway tractor to roll over and kill him.

"As far as I'm concerned," she tells the priest, "Christ was just another D.P." He just didn't fit in. After the death of the Polish refugee, however, she understands her complicity in a modern crucifixion, and recognizes the enormity of her responsibility for other human beings. The impact of this new awareness debilitates her; she loses her health, her farm, even her ability to speak.

This moment of revelation, when the individual comes face to face with her own limitations and comprehends "the true frontiers of her own inner country," is classic O'Connor, and always arrives in times of extreme crisis and loss.

There is a resistance by some to read O'Connor because she is "too difficult," or because they do not share her religious "persuasion." A young man who studied O'Connor under the direction of Eudora Welty some years ago amused me with the following story, which may or may not be true:

"I don't think Welty and O'Connor understood each *other,*" he said, when I asked if he thought O'Connor would have liked or understood Welty's more conventional art. "For Welty's part, wherever we reached a particularly dense and symbolic section of one of O'Connor's stories she would sigh and ask 'Is there a Catholic in the class?'"

Whether one "understands" her stories or not, one knows her characters are new and wondrous creations in the world and that not one of her stories—not even the earliest ones in which her consciousness of racial matters had not evolved sufficiently to be interesting or to differ much from the insulting and ignorant racial stereotyping that preceded it—could have been written by anyone else. As one can tell a Bearden from a Keene or a Picasso from a Hallmark card, one can tell an O'Connor story from any story laid next to it. Her Catholicism did not in any way limit (by defining it) her art. After her great stories of sin, damnation, prophecy, and revelation, the stories one reads casually in the average magazine seem to be about love and roast beef.

Andalusia is a large white house at the top of a hill with a view of a lake from its screened-in front porch. It is neatly kept, and there are, indeed, peacocks strutting about in the sun. Behind it there is an unpainted house where black people must have lived. It was, then, the typical middle-to-upper-class arrangement: white folks up front, the "help," in a far shabbier house, within calling distance from the back door. Although an acquaintance of O'Connor's has told me no one lives there now—but that a caretaker looks after things—I go up to the porch and knock. It is not an entirely empty or symbolic gesture: I have come to this vacant house to learn something about myself in relation to Flannery O'Connor, and will learn it whether anyone is home or not.

What I feel at the moment of knocking is fury that someone is paid to take care of her house, though no one lives in it, and that her house still, in fact, stands, while mine—which of course we never owned anyway—is slowly rotting into dust. Her house becomes—in an instant—the symbol of my own disinheritance, and for that instant I hate her guts. All that she has meant to me is diminished, though her diminishment within me is against my will.

In Faulkner's backyard there is also an unpainted shack and a black caretaker still lives there, a quiet, somber man who, when asked about Faulkner's legendary "sense of humor" replied that, as far has he knew, "Mr. Bill never joked." For years, while reading Faulkner, this image of the quiet man in the backyard shack stretched itself across the page.

Standing there knocking on Flannery O'Connor's door, I do not think of her illness, her magnificent work in spite of it; I think: it all comes back to houses. To how people live. There are rich people who own houses to live in and poor people who do not. And this is wrong. Literary separatism, fashionable now among blacks as it has always been among whites, is easier to practice than to change a fact like this. I think: I would level this country with a sweep of my hand, if I could.

"Nobody can change the past," says my mother.

"Which is why revolutions exist," I reply.

My bitterness comes from a deeper source than my knowledge of the difference, historically, race has made in the lives of white and black artists. The fact that in Mississippi no one even remembers where Richard Wright lived, while Faulkner's house is maintained by a black caretaker is painful, but not unbearable. What comes close to being unbearable is that I know how damaging to my own psyche such injustice is. In an unjust society the soul of the sensitive person is in danger of deformity from just such weights as this. For a long time I will feel Faulkner's house, O'Connor's house, crushing me. To fight back will require a certain amount of energy, energy better used doing something else.

My mother has been busy reasoning that, since Flannery O'Connor died young of a lingering and painful illness, the hand of God has shown itself. Then she sighs. "Well, you know," she says, "it is true, as they say, that the grass is always greener on the other side. That is, until you find yourself over there."

In a just society, of course, clichés like this could not survive.

"But grass *can* be greener on the other side and not be just an illusion," I say. Grass on the other side of the fence might have good fertilizer, while grass on your side might have to grow, if it grows at all, in sand."

We walk about quietly, listening to the soft sweep of the peacocks' tails as they move across the yard. I notice how completely O'Connor, in her fiction, has described just this view of the rounded hills, the tree line, black against the sky, the dirt road that runs from the front yard down to the highway. I remind myself of her courage and of how much—in her art—she has helped me to see. She destroyed the last vestiges of sentimentality in white Southern writing; she caused white women to look ridiculous on pedestals, and she approached her black characters—as a mature artist—with unusual humility and restraint. She also cast spells and worked magic with the written word. The magic, the wit, and the mystery of Flannery O'Connor I know I will always love; I also know the meaning of the expression "Take what you can use and let the rest rot." If ever there was an expression designed to protect the health of the spirit, this is it.

As we leave O'Connor's yard the peacocks—who she said would have the last word—lift their splendid tails for our edification. One peacock is so involved in the presentation of his masterpiece he does not allow us to move the car until he finishes with his show.

"Peacocks are inspiring," I say to my mother, who does not seem at all in awe of them and actually frowns when she sees them strut, "but they sure don't stop to consider they might be standing in your way."

And she says, "Yes, and they'll eat up every bloom you have, if you don't watch out."

A CLOSER LOOK AT ALICE WALKER

1. As quoted in the introduction to this section, Alice Walker has written: "I am trying to arrive at that place where black music already is; to arrive at that unself-conscious sense of collective oneness; that naturalness, that (even when anguished) grace." Given that her work is so often personal in nature,

write an essay in which you explain how Walker achieves this "unself-conscious sense of collective oneness" through personal reflection. How does she arrive at the collective while focusing on the personal?

2. In an interview, Walker explains: "Langston Hughes wrote in his autobiography that when he was sad, he wrote his best poems. When he was happy he didn't write anything. This is true of me, where poems are concerned. When I am happy (or neither happy nor sad), I write essays, short stories, and novels. Poems—even happy ones—emerge from an accumulation of sadness." In an essay, address why poems might require sadness but essays do not. What does this statement reveal about essays as a genre? Do you agree with Walker?

3. Alice Walker has written, "One wants to write poetry that is understood by one's people, not by the Queen of England." What about essays? In what ways are Walker's essays suited to her audience? What rhetorical strategies does she use to make her essays appropriate to her subject matter and her audience? Considering Walker's statement, write an essay that compares and contrasts what you see as the primary similarities and differences between essays and poems. Pay specific attention to the role audience plays in each of these genres.

4. Walker often reflects on the power of language, "for it is language more than anything else that reveals and validates one's existence, and if the language we actually speak is denied us, then it is inevitable that the form we are permitted to assume historically will be one of caricature, reflecting someone else's literary or social fantasy." Write an essay in which you reflect on the power of language in your own life. In particular, think about the way language has been used to define you and how you have used language to define others. Think also about recent controversies such as the ebonics debate and the English Only movement.

Looking from Writer to Writer

1. Compare what Alice Walker calls her "womanist" ideology and writing to what one might call the "masculine" ideology and writing of John Updike or even Rick Bass. In what ways are these ideologies reflected in the writing style, choice of subject, voice and other rhetorical strategies of each writer? Which ideology and style speaks most to you? Why?

2. In her essay "Black Women Writing," bell hooks describes the political climate that often fails to support black women writers. Speaking of her work, hooks's biographer wrote that "it is the unheard voice of black women which drives her

overall work." In what ways can the same be said of Alice Walker's writing? In particular, in what ways do the views of hooks and Walker about black women and writing connect? To what extent do they differ?

3. In his essay "The Singular First Person," Scott Russell Sanders defines the personal essay. Write an essay in which you examine the extent to which Alice Walker's essays can be described as "personal essays." Turn to Sanders's essay to support your argument.

Looking Beyond

ESSAYS

In Search of Our Mothers' Gardens: Womanist Prose. New York: Harcourt Brace Jovanovich, 1982.

Living By The Word: Selected Writings 1973–1987. New York: Harcourt Brace Jovanovich, 1988.

The Same River Twice: Honoring the Difficult. New York: Washington Square Press, 1996.

FICTION

By the Light of My Father's Smile. New York: Random House, 1998.

In Love and Trouble: Stories of Black Women. New York: Harcourt Brace Jovanovich, 1973.

Meridian. New York: Harcourt Brace Jovanovich, 1976.

Possessing the Secret of Joy. New York: Harcourt Brace Jovanovich, 1992.

The Color Purple. New York: Harcourt Brace Jovanovich, 1982.

The Temple of My Familiar. New York: Harcourt Brace Jovanovich, 1989.

The Third Life of Grange Copeland. New York: Pocket Books, 1970.

You Can't Keep a Good Woman Down: Stories. New York: Harcourt Brace Jovanovich, 1981.

POETRY

Good Night Willie Lee, I'll See You in the Morning: Poems. New York: Dial Press, 1979.

Her Blue Body Everything We Know: Earthling Poems. New York: Harcourt Brace Jovanovich, 1992.

Horses Make a Landscape Look More Beautiful: Poems. New York: Harcourt Brace Jovanovich, 1984.

Once: Poems. New York: Harcourt Brace Jovanovich, 1968.

Revolutionary Petunias and Other Poems. New York: Harcourt Brace Jovanovich, 1973.

Edward O. Wilson

Edward O. Wilson was born in Birmingham, Alabama, in 1929. During his childhood, he lived in different cities and towns around the South. He explains that as he grew up he became increasingly introverted. His time was spent alone, exploring the natural world that surrounded his home. His adventures as a boy left him with a never-ending love for the natural sciences; as he grew older and formalized his studies beyond catching butterflies with homemade nets, he became not only one of the world's foremost experts on ants, but one of the most renowned scientists of the 20th century, particularly in the area of entomology, the study of insects. As he explains in *Naturalist,* his autobiography, "most children have a bug period. I never outgrew mine."

Wilson's formal education includes a BS and MA in biology from the University of Alabama and a PhD from Harvard. Wilson remained at Harvard as a professor of biology, and is currently Pellegrino University Research Professor and Honorary Curator in Entomology of the Museum of Comparative Zoology. He has been awarded both of Harvard's most prestigious teaching awards. Despite Wilson's active academic career, he often writes that his true passion lies in field research, being out in wild places studying the indigenous organisms, particularly insects. His fascinating autobiography recounts numerous exciting adventures Wilson had in remote places around the world and the discoveries he made in those places that changed the way we think about insects, biology, evolution, and science in general. There is little question that Wilson's discoveries are some of the most important in contemporary science.

In 1978 Wilson was awarded the Pulitzer Prize for his groundbreaking book *On Human Nature,* which explores the relationship between biology and behavior. Critics of this book argued that it reduced human behavior to simple, uncontrollable biological processes. Many others, though, saw the value in what Wilson was teaching. He won a second Pulitzer Prize for *The Ants,* which he coauthored with Bert Holldobler in 1990—an intensive study of ants, as well as insect life in general. These two prizes signified not only Wilson's contribution to science, but his contribution to the writing world. Throughout his writing, Wilson has tried both in his rhetoric and the message of his work to overcome the bifurcation between sciences and literature. His books are ripe with personal narrative and argue that sciences and literature could benefit much from each other. He has posited that "the linkage of science and literature is the premier challenge of the 21st century." For those interested in the craft of writing, Wilson's statement is one of exciting potential. His writing stands as an award-winning example of what such connections might produce in terms of texts.

In 1998 Wilson published his acclaimed book *Consilience,* in which he claims that all life is governed by a few biological laws that ultimately answer all questions about biological life. The book received a good deal of positive and negative criticism, with some of the most severe critiques coming from religious leaders who argued that Wilson's reduction of all life's questions to biology dismissed the possibility of religion. Wilson addresses the debate between theology and science in an essay in *Consilience,* which is included here. Ultimately, Wilson admits he may be wrong about his position and has written about the critique of *Consilience,* "I may be wrong. I say that clearly in my book. Twice. The spirit of science is to say you may be wrong. I've never heard the religious say they may be wrong."

As you read the selections gathered here as representative of Wilson's work, pay close attention to his ability to tell fascinating stories while also giving scientific information. Also, think about how Wilson represents the roles of writing and the roles of science, not only in his specific statements about the two subjects, but in the choices he makes in conveying information about each.

Wilson on Writing

At First Glance

In this essay, Edward O. Wilson makes the claim that sciences and literature would benefit from one another, though bringing the two together is a difficult task. He writes, "To wring literature from science is to join two radically different modes of thought." As you read "The Writing Life," consider how Wilson approaches this subject in what he argues for and how his own writing serves as an example of the kind of writing he calls for. Think about what makes this essay "literary" and what makes it "scientific."

The Writing Life

In 1954, as a newly minted 25-year-old Ph.D. in Biology, my dream was to hunt for ants in remote, unexplored rain forests. The dream—scientific thema might be the better phrase—was an extension of my experience as a teenage entomologist in the forest and swamps of my native Alabama. To trek across wide, unmapped terrain searching for new species was for me the greatest imaginable adventure. The tropical forests were the wildlands of Alabama writ large. That image was fixed in my mind; it still is. I have followed many goals in my professional life, many of them sublimations of the dream, but if I were given free reign in an afterworld, that is what I would choose to do forever.

It all began in my childhood bug period. My first excursion was in 1939 in Washington, D.C., where my father, a federal employee, had been called for a brief tour of duty. With an excitement I can still summon, I went forth one day from our apartment on Fairmont Street, bottle in hand, to explore the wilderness of nearby Rock Creek Park and bring back specimens of ants, beetles, spiders, anything that moved, for my first collection. Soon I discovered the National Zoo, also within walking distance, and the National Museum of Natural History, a five-cent streetcar ride away, and began to haunt both. Then I narrowed my focus to butterflies, and with a homemade net began a pursuit of the red admiral, the great spangled fritillary, the tiger swallowtail and the elusive and prized mourning cloak. At this time, thanks to a National Geographic article on the subject, I also acquired a fascination for ants.

Returning to Alabama, I escalated my bug period by shifting to snakes. Now I hunted the black racer, the ribbon snake, the coachwhip, and the pygmy rattlesnake. In time I caught, studied and released nearly all of the 40 species native to southern

Alabama, though a few I kept for a while in cages I constructed in the back yard. In my senior year in high school, I switched to ants, to my parents' undoubted relief. I had always wanted to be an entomologist. College is coming, I thought. Now is the time to get serious.

At the University of Alabama and later, in graduate studies at Harvard University, I continued to spend as much time as possible outdoors. Then came the golden opportunity that turned dream into reality. I was elected to Harvard's Society of Fellows for a three-year term, with full (well, reasonable) financial support to go anywhere, pursue any subject. So off I went and was rarely seen thereafter at Harvard. At last I could reach the tropical forests—my Louvre, my Library of Congress! After trips to Cuba and Mexico, I departed for a lengthy tour of the South Pacific: Fiji, New Caledonia, Vanuatu, Australia, and finally the splendid naturalist paradise of New Guinea.

In the mid-1950's very few young biologists had the means to undertake such a distant expedition. I liked being alone. I savored pristine wilderness, climbed the unexplored center of a mountain range (on the Huon Peninsula of New Guinea), discovered scores of new species, and filled my journal with notes on the behavior and ecology of ants. Returning to Harvard, I converted the information into a stream of technical articles. Most were strictly factual or theoretical, their data squeezed into the mandatory straitjacket of scientific writing.

Descriptive field research is sometimes dismissed by laboratory scientists as "stamp collecting." There is truth in the label. Natural history is primitive and simple, motivated, I believe, by an innate human urge to find, name and classify, going back to Aristotle and beyond. The naturalist is a civilized hunter. But there is much more to the science than muddy boots, mosquito bites and new species. While I was in the South Pacific, my mind was turning over the rich theories of ecology and evolution I had learned in reading and formal study. I was especially fascinated by the idea of faunal dominance. That sweeping concept was developed during the first half of the 20th century, first by the paleontologists William Diller Matthew and George G. Simpson and then, most thoroughly, by Harvard's curator of entomology Philip J. Darlington—whose position I was eventually to inherit.

The theory of faunal dominance holds that while evolution occurs everywhere, certain land masses generate disproportionately more terrestrial and aquatic groups, such as the familiar murid rodents and ranid frogs, which are able to colonize and dominate other land masses. To Matthew and Simpson, who worked on mammals, this staging area was the circumpolar north temperate regions. To Darlington, who worked on the cold-blooded reptiles, amphibians and fishes, it was the tropics of the Old World.

Here, I thought, is a truly Homeric scenario, the stuff of great scientific adventure. The questions it posed were obvious: Why are some kinds of animals dominant, and why do they arise with probability in certain parts of the world? Those are mysteries that seem to be soluble from the fossil record and contemporary natural history. Matthew, Simpson and Darlington had worked with entire groups and a broad brush. I chose to take the study down to the species level, using ants to focus on the region from Asia to Australia and the Pacific archipelagoes. I also brought to bear the ecological data I had accumulated during my field research, something else that had not been done to that time. In a nutshell, I was able to show that tropical Asia is the center of faunal dominance.

Species spread out from there to Australia and the Pacific, with little reverse flow. The pioneer species are generally those adapted to marginal habitats, such as shorelines and riverbanks, from which overseas dispersal is easiest. But once they reach outer archipelagoes, they tend to adapt to the inland forests, where they split into daughter species. Eventually these decline, giving way to new colonists.

In the 1960s this "taxon cycle," as I called it, became part of the inspiration for the theory of island biography developed by Robert H. MacArthur of Princeton and myself. Our conception, which helps to explain the equilibrium and turnover of plant and animal species generally, played a useful later role in general ecology and conservation planning.

None of my reports and theory hinted of motivation, and very little emotion was expressed beyond the occasional "I was interested in the problem of . . ." or "It turned out, to my surprise, that . . ." I played by the aforementioned rules: Humanistic excursions are not relevant; confession is a sign of weakness and self-indulgence. The audience of a scientific communication is other scientists, and not just any other scientists but fellow specialists working in and around a narrowly defined topic. I doubt that more than a dozen fellow entomologists read my article announcing the discovery of cerapachyine ants on New Caledonia, although the data are still used. The taxon cycle and island biogeography became familiar to a wider circle of biologists but still are unknown to the lay public, and for that matter a majority of scientists, who are preoccupied with their own sectors of the frontier.

Only later did it occur to me to write about these early efforts as a personal history, in a narrative that includes motive and emotion. When I decided to try it, in *Biophilia* (1984) and *Naturalist* (1994), I discovered how difficult it is to compose this form of literature. Not only difficult but risky, opening the author to the indignity of being all too clearly understood. The vast majority of scientists would rather stay inside the guild, so that attempts to cross over from their own research directly to the arts (as opposed to merely playing the cello or admiring modern art) are correspondingly rare.

But the rewards to the broader culture, if the effort has quality, are potentially great. I hope others will try. Thanks to the continuing exponential growth of scientific knowledge as well as the innovative thrust of the creative arts, the bridging of the two cultures is now in sight as a frontier of its own. Among its greatest challenges, still largely unmet, is the conversion of the scientific creative process and world view into literature.

To wring literature from science is to join two radically different modes of thought. The technical reports of pure science are not meant to be and cannot be reader-friendly. They are humanity's tested factual knowledge, open to verification, framed by theory, couched in specialized language for exactitude, trimmed for brevity, and delivered raw. Metaphor is unwelcome except in cautious, homeopathic doses. Hyperbole, no matter how brilliant, is anathema. In pure science, discovery counts for everything, and personal style next to nothing.

In literature metaphor and personal style are, in polar contrast, everything. The most successful innovator is an honest illusionist: His product, as Picasso said of visual art, is the lie that helps us see the truth. Imagery, phrasing and analogy in literature are not crafted to establish empirical facts, and even less are they meant to be put into a general theory. Rather, they are the vehicles by which the writer conveys his feelings directly to his audience.

The central role of literature is the transmission of the details of human experience by artifice that intensifies aesthetic and emotional response. Originality and power of metaphor are coin of the realm. Their source is an intuitive understanding of human nature, not an accurate knowledge of the material world; in this respect literature is the exact opposite of pure science.

The linkage of science and literature is a premier challenge of the 21st century, for the following reason: The scientific method has expanded our understanding of life and the universe in spectacular fashion across the entire scale of space and time, in every sensory modality, and beyond the farthest dreams of the pre-scientific mind. It is as though humanity, after wandering for millennia in a great dark cavern with only the light of a candle (to use a metaphor!), can now find its way with a searchlight.

No matter how much we see, or how beautifully theory falls out to however many decimal places, all of experience is still processed by the sensory and nervous systems peculiar to our species, and all of knowledge is still evaluated by our idiosyncratically evolved emotions. Both the research scientist and the creative writer are members of the Homo sapiens, in the family Hominidae of the order Primates, and a biological species exquisitely adapted to planet Earth. Art is in our bones: We all live by narrative and metaphor.

The successful scientist is a poet who works like a bookkeeper. When his bookkeeper's work is done and duly registered in peer-reviewed technical journals, he can if he wishes return to the poetic mode and pour human life into the freeze-dried database. But chastely so, taking care never to misstate facts, never to misrepresent theory, never to betray Nature.

Double Take

1. The title of this essay is "The Writing Life," which might imply that Edward O. Wilson is going to talk about his life as a writer or about writing in general. Yet Wilson doesn't mention writing until the final paragraphs of the essay; the majority of the essay is about his life as a naturalist. Why might Wilson have adopted the strategy of addressing the crux of his position in the final moments of the essay rather than throughout the piece?
2. Wilson characterizes a difference between "scientific writing" and "literature." Gathering what Wilson says about these two genres, what might be some rhetorical aspects or characteristics of scientific writing and literature? How might they be different?

3. Wilson writes, "Only later did it occur to me to write about these early efforts as a personal history, in a narrative that includes motive and emotion. When I decided to try it, in *Biophilia* (1984) and *Naturalist* (1994), I discovered how difficult it is to compose this form of literature. Not only difficult, but risky, opening the author to the indignity of being all too clearly understood." What might Wilson mean by difficulty and risk in writing? How do authors' choices add to or protect from these difficulties and risks?
4. Wilson writes of technical, scientific writing that it is "not meant to be and cannot be reader-friendly." What does Wilson mean by "reader-friendly"? What facets of scientific writing might lend to this characterization? Can you find parts of this essay that are not "reader-friendly"?

At First Glance

The essay "The Serpent" was first printed in 1984 as a chapter in Edward O. Wilson's book Biophilia *where it served as part of Wilson's larger argument about a conservation ethic. The version reprinted here appeared in Wilson's collection of essays,* In Search of Nature, *published 12 years later. In the 1996 version, Wilson mentions how the essay originally fit in* Biophilia *in order to clarify some points made in the later version. As you read this essay, consider how Wilson might have considered the two different versions of the piece: one as an integral part of a larger work and one as an independent text. Also, consider how the difference of 12 years in publication dates might affect how an audience receives the piece. Have political situations changed? Might new research affect what is conveyed in an essay like this?*

The Serpent

Science and the Humanities, biology and culture, are bridged in a dramatic manner by the phenomenon of the serpent. Fabricated from symbols and bearing portents of magic, the snake's image enters the conscious and unconscious mind with ease during reverie and dreams. It appears without warning and departs abruptly, leaving behind not a specific memory of any real snake but the vague sense of a more powerful creature, the serpent, surrounded by a mist of fear and wonderment.

These qualities are dominant in a dream I have experienced often through my life, for reasons that will soon become clear.

I find myself in a locality that is wooded and aquatic, silent and drawn wholly in shades of gray. As I walk into this somber environment I am gripped by an alien feeling. The terrain before me is mysterious, on the rim of the unknown, at once calm and forbidding. I am required to be there but in the dream state cannot grasp the reasons. Suddenly, the Serpent appears. It is not an ordinary, literal reptile, but much more, a threatening presence with unusual powers. It is protean in size and shape, armored, irresistible. The poisonous head radiates a cold, inhuman intelligence. While I watch, its muscular coils slide into the water, beneath prop roots, and back onto the bank. The Serpent is somehow both the spirit of that shadowed place and the guardian of the passage into deeper reaches. I sense that if I could capture or control or even just evade it, an indefinable but great change would follow. The anticipation of that transformation stirs old and nameless emotions. The risk is also vaguely felt, like that emanating from a knife blade or high cliff. The Serpent is life-promising and life-threatening, seductive and treacherous. It now slips close to me, turning importunate, ready to strike. The dream ends uneasily, without clear resolution.

The snake and the serpent, flesh-and-blood reptile and demonic dream-image, reveal the complexity of our relation to nature and the fascination and beauty inherent in all organisms. Even the deadliest and most repugnant creatures are endowed with magic in the human mind. Human beings have an innate fear of snakes; more precisely, they have an innate propensity to learn such fear quickly and easily past the age of five. The images they build out of this peculiar mental set are both powerful and ambivalent, ranging from terror-stricken flight to the experience of power and male sexuality. As a consequence the serpent has become an important part of cultures around the world.

There is a highly complex principle to consider here, one that extends well beyond the ordinary concerns of psychoanalytic reasoning about sexual symbols. Life of any kind is infinitely more interesting than almost any conceivable variety of inanimate matter. The latter is valued chiefly to the extent that it can be metabolized into live tissue, accidentally resembles it, or can be fashioned into a useful and properly animated artifact. No one in his right mind looks at a pile of dead leaves in preference to the tree from which they fell.

What is it exactly that binds us so closely to living things? The biologist will tell you that life is the self-replication of giant molecules from lesser chemical fragments, resulting in the assembly of complex organic structures, the transfer of large amounts of molecular information, ingestion, growth, movement of an outwardly purposeful nature, and the proliferation of closely similar organisms. The poet-in-biologist will add that life is an exceedingly improbable state, metastable, open to other systems, thus ephemeral—and worth any price to keep.

Certain organisms have still more to offer because of their special impact on mental development. In 1984, in a book titled *Biophilia,* I suggested that the urge to affiliate with other forms of life is to some degree innate. The evidence for the proposition is not strong in a formal scientific sense: the subject has not been studied enough in the scientific manner of hypothesis, deduction, and experimentation to let us be certain about it one way or the other. Nevertheless the biophilic tendency is so clearly evinced in daily life and so widely distributed as to deserve serious attention. It unfolds in the predictable fantasies and responses of individuals from early childhood onward. It cascades into repetitive patterns of culture across most or all societies, a consistency often noted in the literature of anthropology. These processes appear to be part of the programs of the brain. They are marked by the quickness and decisiveness with which we learn particular things about certain kinds of plants and animals. They are too consistent to be dismissed as the result of purely historical events etched upon a mental blank slate.

Perhaps the most bizarre of the biophilic traits is awe and veneration of the serpent. The dreams from which the dominant images arise are known to exist in all societies whose mental life has been studied. At least 5 percent of the people at any given time remember experiencing them, while many more would probably do so if they recorded their waking impressions over several months. The images described by urban New Yorkers are as detailed and emotional as those of Australian aboriginals and Zulus. In all cultures the serpents are prone to be mystically transfigured. The Hopi know Palulukon, the water serpent, a benevolent but frightening godlike being. The Kwakiutl fear the *sisiutl,* a three-headed serpent with both human and reptile faces, whose appearance in dreams presages insanity or death. The Sharanahua of Peru summon reptile spirits by taking hallucinogenic drugs and stroking their faces with the severed tongues of snakes. They are rewarded with dreams of brightly colored boas, venomous snakes, and lakes teeming with caimans and anacondas. Around the world serpents and snakelike creatures are the dominant elements of dreams in which animals of any kind appear. They are recruited as the animate symbols of power and sex, totems, protagonists of myths, and gods.

These cultural manifestations may seem at first detached and mysterious, but there is a simple reality behind the ophidian archetype that lies within the experience of ordinary people. The mind is primed to react emotionally to the sight of snakes, not just to fear them but to be aroused and absorbed in their details, to weave stories about them. This distinctive predisposition played an important role in an unusual experience of my own, a childhood encounter with a large and memorable snake, a creature that actually existed.

I grew up in the panhandle of northern Florida and the adjacent counties of Alabama. Like most boys in that part of the country set loose to roam the woods, I enjoyed hunting and fishing and made no clear distinction between these activities and life at large. But I also cherished natural history for its own sake and decided very early to become a biologist. I had a secret ambition to find a Real Serpent, a snake so fabulously large or otherwise different that it would exceed the bounds of imagination, let alone existing fact.

Certain circumstances encouraged this adolescent fantasy. First of all, I was an only child with indulgent parents, encouraged to develop my own interests and hobbies, however farfetched; in other words, I was spoiled. Second, the physical surroundings inclined youngsters toward an awe of nature. Four generations earlier, that part of the country had been covered by a wilderness as formidable in some respects as the Amazon. Dense thickets of cabbage palmetto descended into meandering spring-fed streams and cypress sloughs. Carolina parakeets and ivory-billed woodpeckers flashed overhead in the sunlight, and wild turkeys and passenger pigeons still counted as game. On soft spring nights after heavy rains a dozen varieties of frogs croaked, rasped, bonged, and trilled their love songs in mixed choruses. Much of the Gulf Coast fauna derived from species that had spread north from the tropics over millions of years and adapted to the warm local temperate conditions.

Columns of miniature army ants, close replicas of the large marauders of South America, marched mostly unseen at night over the forest floor. *Nephila* spiders the size of saucers spun webs as wide as garage doors across the woodland clearings.

From the stagnant pools and knothole sinks, clouds of mosquitoes rose to afflict the early immigrants. They carried the Confederate plagues, malaria and yellow fever, which periodically flared into epidemics and reduced the populations along the coastal lowlands. This natural check is one of the reasons the strip between Tampa and Pensacola remained sparsely settled well into the twentieth century and why even today, long after the diseases have been eradicated, it is still the relatively natural "other Florida."

Snakes abounded. The Gulf Coast has a greater variety and denser populations than almost any other place in the world, and they are frequently seen. Striped ribbon snakes hang in gorgonlike clusters on branches at the edge of ponds and streams. Poisonous coral snakes root through the leaf litter, their bodies decorated with warning bands of red, yellow, and black. They are easily confused with their mimics, the scarlet kingsnakes, banded in a different sequence of red, black, and yellow. The simple rule recited by woodsmen is: "Red next to yellow will kill a fellow, red next to black is a friend of Jack." Hognoses, harmless thick-bodied sluggards with upturned snouts, are characterized by an unsettling resemblance to venomous African gaboon vipers and a habit of swallowing toads live. Pygmy rattlesnakes two feet long contrast with diamondbacks of seven feet or more. Watersnakes are a herpetologist's medley distinguished by size, color, and the arrangement of body scales, encompassing ten species of *Natrix, Seminatrix, Agkistrodon, Liodytes, and Farancia.*

Of course limits to the abundance and diversity exist. Because snakes feed on frogs, mice, fish, and other animals of similar size, they are necessarily scarcer than their prey. You can't just go out on a stroll and point to one individual after another. An hour's careful search will often turn up none at all. But I can testify from personal experience that on any given day you are ten times more likely to meet a snake in Florida than in Brazil or New Guinea.

There is something oddly appropriate about the abundance of snakes. Although the Gulf wilderness has been largely converted into macadam and farmland, and the sounds of television and company jets are heard in the land, a remnant of the old rural culture remains, as if the population were still pitted against the savage and the unknown. "Push the forest back and fill the land" remains a common sentiment, the colonizer's ethic and tested biblical wisdom (the very same that turned the cedar groves of Lebanon into the barrens they are today). The prominence of snakes lends symbolic support to this venerable belief.

In the back country during a century and half of settlement, the common experience of snakes was embroidered into the lore of serpents. Cut off a rattlesnake's head, one still hears, and it will live on until sundown. If a snake bites you, open the puncture wounds with a knife and wash them with kerosene to neutralize the poison (if there are any survivors of this cure, I have never met them). If you believe with all your heart in Jesus, you can hang rattlers and copperheads around your neck without fear. If one strikes you just the same, accept it as a sign from the Lord and find peace in whatever follows. The hognose snake, on the other hand, is always death in the shape of a slithery **S**. Those who get too close to one will have venom sprayed in their eyes and be blinded; the very breath from the snake's skin is lethal. This species is the beneficiary of its dreadful legend: I have never heard of any being killed.

Deep in the woods live creatures of startling power. (*That* is what I most wanted to hear.) Among them is the hoopsnake. Skeptics, who used to be found hunkered down in a row along the county courthouse balustrade on a Saturday morning, say it is only mythical; on the other hand it might be the familiar coachwhip racer turned vicious by special circumstances. Thus transformed, it puts its tail in its mouth and rolls down hills at great speed to attack its terrified victims. Then there are reports of the occasional true monsters: a giant snake believed to live in a certain swamp (used to be there anyway, even if no one's seen it in recent years); a twelve-foot diamondback rattler a farmer killed on the edge of town a few years back; some unclassified prodigy recently glimpsed as it sunned itself along the river's edge.

It is a wonderful thing to grow up in southern towns where animal fables are taken half-seriously, breathing into the adolescent mind a sense of the unknown and the possibility that something extraordinary might be found within a day's walk of where you live. No such magic exists in the environs of Schenectady, Liverpool, and Darmstadt, and for all children dwelling in such places where the options have finally been closed, I feel a twinge of sadness. I found my way out of Mobile, Pensacola, and Brewton to explore the surrounding woods and swamps with a languorous intensity. I formed the habit of quietude and concentration into which I still pass my mind during field excursions, having learned to summon the old emotions as part of the naturalist's technique.

Some of these feelings must have been shared by my friends. In the mid-1940s during the hot season between spring football practice and the regular schedule of games in the fall, working on highway cleanup gangs and poking around outdoors were about all we had to do. But there was some difference: I was hunting snakes with passionate commitment. On the Brewton High School football team of 1944–45 most of the players had nicknames leaning toward the infantilisms and initials favored by southerners: Bubba Joe, Flip, A. J., Sonny, Shoe, Jimbo, Junior, Snooker, Skeeter. As the underweight third-string left end, allowed to play only in the fourth quarter when the foe had been crushed beyond any hope of recovery, mine was Snake. But although I was inordinately proud of this measure of masculine acceptance, my main hopes and energies had been invested elsewhere. There are an incredible forty species of snakes native to that region, and I managed to capture almost all of them.

One kind became a special target just because it was so elusive: the glossy watersnake *Natrix rigida*. The adults lay on the bottom of shallow ponds well away from the shore and pointed their heads out of the alga-green water in order to breath and to scan the surface in all directions. I waded out toward them very carefully, avoiding the side-to-side movements to which snakes are most alert. I needed to get within three or four feet in order to manage a diving tackle, but before I could cover the distance they always pulled their heads under and slipped silently away into the opaque depths. I finally solved the problem with the aid of the town's leading slingshot artist, a taciturn loner my age, proud and quick to anger, the sort of boy who in an earlier time might have distinguished himself at Antietam or Shiloh. Aiming pebbles at the heads of the snakes, he was able to stun several long enough for me to grab them underwater. After recovering, the captives were kept for a while in homemade cages in our backyard, where they thrived on live minnows placed in dishes of water.

Once, deep in a swamp miles from home, half lost and not caring, I glimpsed an unfamiliar brightly colored snake disappearing down a crayfish burrow. I sprinted to the spot, thrust my hand after it, and felt around blindly. Too late: the snake had squirmed out of reach into the lower chambers. Only later did I think about the possibilities: suppose I had succeeded and the snake had been poisonous? My reckless enthusiasm did catch up with me on another occasion when I miscalculated the reach of a pygmy rattlesnake, which struck out faster than I thought possible and hit me with startling authority on the left index finger. Because of the small size of the reptile, the only results were a temporarily swollen arm and a fingertip that still grows a bit numb at the onset of cold weather.

I found my Serpent on a still July morning in the swamp fed by the artesian wells of Brewton, while working toward higher ground along the course of a weed-choked stream. Without warning a very large snake crashed away from under my feet and plunged into the water. Its movement especially startled me because so far that day I had encountered only modestly proportioned frogs and turtles silently tensed on mudbanks and logs. This snake was more nearly my size as well as violent and noisy—a colleague, so to speak. It sped with wide body undulations to the center of the shallow watercourse and came to rest on a sandy riffle. Though not quite the monster I had envisioned, it was nevertheless unusual, a water moccasin (*Agkistrodon piscivorus*), one of the poisonous pit vipers, more than five feet long with a body as thick as my arm and a head the size of a fist. It was the largest snake I had ever seen in the wild. I later calculated it to be just under the published size record for the species. The snake now lay quietly in the shallow clear water completely open to view, its body stretched along the fringing weeds, its head pointed back at an oblique angle to watch my approach. Moccasins are like that. They don't always keep going until they are out of sight, in the manner of ordinary watersnakes. Although no emotion can be read in the frozen half-smile and staring yellow cat's eyes, their reactions and posture make them seem insolent, as if they see their power reflected in the caution of human beings and other sizable enemies.

I moved through the snake handler's routine: pressed the snake stick across the body in back of the head, rolled it forward to pin the head securely, brought one hand around to grasp the neck just behind the swelling masseteric muscles, dropped the stick to seize the body midway back with the other hand, and lifted the entire animal clear of the water. The technique almost always works. The moccasin, however, reacted in a way that took me by surprise and put my life in immediate danger. Throwing its heavy body into convulsions, it twisted its head and neck slightly forward through my gripped fingers, stretched its mouth wide open to unfold the inch-long fangs and expose the dead-white inner lining in the intimidating "cottonmouth" display. A fetid musk from its anal glands filled the air. At that moment the morning heat became more noticeable, the episode turned manifestly frivolous, and at last I wondered what I was doing in that place alone. Who would find me? The snake began to turn its head far enough to clamp its jaws on my hand. I was not very strong for my age, and I was losing control. Without thinking I heaved the giant out into the brush, and this time it thrashed frantically away until it was out of sight and we were rid of each other.

I sat down and let the adrenaline race my heart and bring tremors to my hand. How could I have been so stupid? What is there in snakes anyway that makes them so repellent and fascinating? The answer in retrospect is deceptively simple: their ability to remain hidden, the power in their sinuous limbless bodies, and the threat from venom injected hypodermically through sharp hollow teeth. It pays in elementary survival to be interested in snakes and to respond emotionally to their generalized image, to go beyond ordinary caution and fear. The rule built into the brain in the form of a learning bias is: become alert quickly to any object with the serpentine gestalt. *Overlearn* this particular response in order to keep safe.

Other primates have evolved similar rules. When guenons and vervets, the common monkeys of the African forest, see a python, cobra, or puff adder, they emit a distinctive chuttering call that rouses other members in the group. (Different calls are used to designate eagles and leopards.) Some of the adults then follow the intruding snake at a safe distance until it leaves the area. The monkeys in effect broadcast a dangerous-snake alert, which serves to protect the entire group and not solely the individual who encountered the danger. The most remarkable fact is that the alarm is evoked most strongly by the kinds of snakes that can harm them. Somehow, apparently through the routes of instinct, the guenons and vervets have become competent herpetologists.

The idea that snake aversion is inborn in man's relatives is supported by studies of rhesus macaques, the large brown monkeys of India and surrounding Asian countries. When adults see a snake of any kind, they react with the generalized fear response of their species. They variously back off and stare (or turn away), crouch, shield their faces, bark, screech, and twist their faces into the fear grimace—lips retracted, teeth bared, and ears flattened against the head. Monkeys raised in the laboratory without previous exposure to snakes show the same response to them as those brought in from the wild, though in weaker form. During control experiments designed to test the specificity of the response, the rhesus failed to react to other, nonsinuous objects placed in their cages. It is the form of the snake and perhaps also its distinctive movements that contain the key stimuli to which the monkeys are innately tuned.

Grant for the moment that snake aversion does have a hereditary basis in at least some kinds of nonhuman primates. The possibility that immediately follows is that the trait evolved by natural selection. In other words, individuals who respond leave more offspring than those who do not, and as a result the propensity to learn fear quickly spreads through the population—or, if it was already present, is maintained there at a high level.

How can biologists test such a proposition about the origin of behavior? They turn natural history upside down: they search for species historically free of forces in the environment believed to favor the evolutionary change, to see if in fact the organisms do *not* possess the trait. Lemurs, primitive relatives of monkeys, offer such an inverted opportunity. They are indigenous inhabitants of Madagascar, where no large or poisonous snakes exist to threaten them. Sure enough, lemurs presented with snakes in captivity fail to display anything resembling the automatic fear responses of the African and Asian monkeys. Is this adequate proof? In the chaste idiom of scientific discourse, we are permitted to conclude only that the evidence is "consistent with the proposition." Neither this nor any comparable hypothesis can be settled by a single case. Only further examples can raise confidence in it to a level beyond potential challenge by determined skeptics.

Another line of evidence comes from studies of the chimpanzee, a species thought to have shared a common ancestor with prehumans as recently as 5 million years ago. Chimps raised in the laboratory become apprehensive in the presence of snakes, even if they have had no previous experience. They back off to a safe distance and follow the intruder with a fixed stare while alerting companions with the *Wah!* warning call. More important, the response becomes gradually more marked during adolescence.

This last quality is especially interesting because human beings pass through approximately the same developmental sequence. Children under five years of age feel no special anxiety over snakes, but later they grow increasingly wary. Just one or two mildly bad experiences, such as the sight of a garter snake writhing away in the grass, having a rubber model thrust at them by a playmate, or hearing a counselor tell scary stories at the campfire, can make children deeply and permanently fearful. The pattern is unusual if not unique in the ontogeny of human behavior. Other common fears, notably of the dark, strangers, and loud noises, start to wane after seven years of age. In contrast, the tendency to avoid snakes grows stronger with time. It is possible to turn the mind in the opposite direction, to learn to handle snakes without apprehension or even to like them in some special way, as I did—but the adaptation takes a special effort and is usually a little forced and self-conscious. The special sensitivity is just as likely to lead to full-blown ophidiophobia, the pathological extreme in which the mere appearance of a snake brings on a feeling of panic, cold sweat, and waves of nausea. I have witnessed these events.

At a campsite in Alabama, on a Sunday afternoon, a four-foot-long black racer glided out from the woods across the clearing and headed for the high grass along a nearby stream. Children shouted and pointed. A middle-aged woman screamed and collapsed to the ground sobbing. Her husband dashed to his pickup truck to get a shotgun. But black racers are among the fastest snakes in the world, and this one made it safely to cover. The onlookers probably did not know that the species is non-venomous and harmless to any creature larger than a cotton rat.

Halfway around the world, in the village of Ebabaang in New Guinea, I heard shouting and saw people running down a path. When I caught up with them they had formed a circle around a small brown snake that was essing leisurely across the front yard of a house. I pinned the snake and carried it off to be preserved in alcohol for the museum collections at Harvard. This seeming act of daring earned either the admiration or the suspicion of my hosts—I couldn't be sure which. The next day children followed me around as I gathered insects in the nearby forest. One brought me an immense orb-weaving spider gripped in his fingers, its hairy legs waving and the evil-looking black fangs working up and down. I felt panicky and sick. It so happens that I suffer from mild arachnophobia. To each his own.

Why should serpents have such a strong influence during mental development? The direct and simple answer is that throughout the history of mankind a few kinds have been a major cause of sickness and death. Every continent except Antarctica has poisonous snakes. Over large stretches of Asia and Africa the known death rate from snakebites is 5 persons per 100,000 each year or higher. The local record is held by a province in Burma, with 36.8 deaths per 100,000 a year. Australia has an exceptional abundance of deadly snakes, a majority of which are relatives of the cobra. Among them the tiger snake is especially feared for its large size and tendency to strike without warning. In South and Central America live the bushmaster, fer-de-lance, and jaracara, among the largest and most aggressive of the pit vipers. With backs colored like rotting leaves and fangs long enough to pass through a human hand, they lie in ambush on the floor of the tropical forest for the small warm-blooded animals that constitute their major prey. Few people realize that a complex of dangerous snakes, the "true" vipers, are still relatively abundant throughout Europe. The common adder *Viperus berus* ranges to the Arctic Circle. The number of people bitten in such improbable places as Switzerland and Finland is still high enough, running into the hundreds annually, to keep outdoorsmen on a sort of yellow alert. Even Ireland, one of the few countries in the world lacking snakes altogether (thanks to the last Pleistocene glaciation and not Saint Patrick), has imported the key ophidian symbols and traditions from other European cultures and preserved the fear of serpents in art and literature.

Here, then, is the sequence by which the agents of nature appear to have been translated into the symbols of culture. For hundreds of thousands of years, time enough for the appropriate genetic changes to occur in the brain, poisonous snakes have been a significant source of injury and death to human beings. The response to the threat is not simply to avoid it, in the way that certain berries are recognized as poisonous through a process of trial and error. People also display the mixture of apprehension and morbid fascination characterizing the nonhuman primates. They inherit a strong tendency to acquire the aversion during early childhood and to add to it progressively, like our closest phylogenetic relatives, the chimpanzees. The mind then adds a great deal more that is distinctively human. It feeds upon the emotions to enrich culture. The tendency of the serpent to appear suddenly in dreams, its sinuous form, and its power and mystery are the natural ingredients of myth and religion.

Consider how sensation and emotional states are elaborated into stories during dreams. The dreamer hears a distant thunderclap and changes an ongoing episode to end with the slamming of a door. He feels a general anxiety and is transported to a schoolhouse corridor, where he searches for a classroom he does not know in order to take an examination for which he is unprepared. As the sleeping brain enters its regular dream periods, marked by rapid eye movement beneath closed eyelids, giant fibers in the lower brainstem fire upward into the cortex. The awakened mind responds by retrieving memories and fabricating stories around the sources of physical and emotional discomfort. It hastens to recreate the elements of past real experience, often in a jumbled and antic form. And from time to time the serpent appears as the embodiment of one or more of these feelings. The direct and literal fear of snakes is foremost among them, but the dream-image can also be summoned by sexual desire, a craving for dominance and power, and the apprehension of violent death.

We need not turn to Freudian theory in order to explain our special relationship to snakes. The serpent did not originate as the vehicle of dreams and symbols. The relation appears to be precisely the other way around and correspondingly easier to study and understand. Humanity's concrete experience with poisonous snakes gave rise to the Freudian phenomena after it was assimilated by genetic evolution into the brain's structure. The mind has to create symbols and fantasies from something. It leans toward the most powerful preexistent images or at least follows the learning rules that create the images, including that of the serpent. For most of this century, perhaps overly enchanted by psychoanalysis, we have confused the dream with the reality and its psychic effect with the ultimate cause rooted in nature.

Among prescientific people, whose dreams are conduits to the spirit world and snakes a part of ordinary experience, the serpent has played a central role in the building of culture. There are magic incantations for simple protection, as in the hymns of the Atharva Veda: "With my eye do I slay thy eye, with poison do I slay thy poison. O Serpent, die, do not live; back upon thee shall thy poison turn."

"Indra slew thy first ancestors, O Serpent," the chant continues, "and since they are crushed, what strength forsooth can be theirs?" And so the power can be controlled and even diverted to human use through iatromancy and the casting of magic spells. Two serpents entwine the caduceus, which was first the winged staff of Mercury as messenger of the gods, then the safe-conduct pass of ambassadors and heralds, and finally the universal emblem of the medical profession (by whom it was confused with the staff of Asclepius, Greek god of medicine, which was entwined with a single serpent).

Balaji Mundkur has shown how the inborn awe of snakes matured into rich productions of art and religion around the world. Serpentine forms wind across stone carvings from paleolithic Europe and are scratched into mammoth teeth found in Siberia. They are the emblems of power and ceremony for the shamans of the Kwakiutl, the Siberian Yakut and Yenisei Ostyak, and many tribes of Australian aboriginals. Stylized snakes have often served as the talismans of the gods and spirits who bestow fertility: Ashtoreth of the Canaanites, the demons Fu-Hsi and Nu-kua of the Han Chinese, and the powerful goddesses Mudammā and Manasā of Hindu India. The ancient Egyptians venerated at least thirteen ophidian deities ministering to various combinations of health, fecundity, and vegetation. Prominent among them was the triple-headed giant Nehebkau, who traveled widely to inspect every part of the river kingdom. Amulets in gold inscribed with the sign of a cobra god were placed in Tutankhamen's funeral wrappings. Even the scorpion goddess Selket bore the title "mother of serpents." Like her offspring she prevailed simultaneously as a source of evil, power, and goodness.

The Aztec pantheon was a phantasmagoria of monstrous forms among whom serpents were given pride of place. The calendrical symbols included the ophidian *olin nahui* and *cipactli,* the earth crocodile that possessed a forked tongue and rattlesnake's tail. The rain god Tlaloc consisted in part of two coiled rattlesnakes whose heads met to form the god's upper lip. *Coatl,* serpent, is the dominant element in the names of Aztec divinities. Coatlicue was a threatening chimera of snake and human parts, Cihuacoatl the goddess of childbirth and mother of the human race, and Xiuhcoatl the fire serpent over whose body fire was rekindled every fifty-two years to mark a major division in the religious calendar. Quetzalcoatl, the plumed serpent with a human head, reigned as god of the morning and evening stars and thus of death and resurrection. As inventor of the calendar, deity of books and learning, and patron of the priesthood, he was revered in the schools where nobles and priests were taught. His reported departure over the eastern horizon upon a raft of snakes must have been the occasion of consternation for the intellectuals of the day, something like the folding of the Guggenheim Foundation.

Contradictory ophidian images were a feature of ancient Greek religion as well. Among the early forms of Zeus was the serpent Meilichios, at once god of love, gentle and responsive to supplication, and god of vengeance, whose sacrifice was offered at night. Another great serpent protected the lustral waters at the spring of Ares. He coexisted with the Erinyes, avenging spirits of the underworld so horrible that they could not be pictured in early mythology. Euripides depicted them as serpents in his *Iphigeneia in Tauris:* "Dost see her, her the Hades-snake who gapes/To slay me, with dread vipers, openmouthed?"

Slyness, deception, malevolence, betrayal, the implicit threat of a forked tongue flicking in and out of the mask-like head, all qualities tinged with miraculous powers to heal and guide, forecast and empower, became the serpent's prevailing image in western cultures. The serpent in the Garden of Eden, appearing as in a dream to serve as Judaism's evil Prometheus, gave humankind knowledge of good and evil and with it the burden of original sin, in return for which God ordained:

> *I will put enmity between you and the woman,*
> *between your brood and hers.*
> *They shall strike at your head,*
> *and you shall strike at their heel.*

To summarize the relation between human and snake: life becomes part of us. Culture transforms the snake into the serpent, a far more potent creation than the literal reptile. Culture, as a product of the mind, can be interpreted as an image-making machine that recreates the outside world through symbols arranged into maps and stories. But the mind does not have the capacity to grasp reality in its full chaotic richness; nor does the body last long enough for the brain to process information piece by piece like an all-purpose computer. Rather, consciousness races ahead to master certain kinds of information with enough efficiency to survive. It submits to a few biases easily, while automatically avoiding others. A great deal of evidence has accumulated in genetics and physiology to show that the controlling devices are biological in nature, built into the sensory apparatus and brain by particularities in cellular architecture.

The combined biases are what we call human nature. The central tendencies, exemplified so strikingly in fear and veneration of the serpent, are the wellsprings of culture. Hence simple perceptions yield an unending abundance of images with special meaning while remaining true to the forces of natural selection that created them.

How could it be otherwise? The brain evolved into its present form over a period of about 2 million years, from the time of *Homo habilis* to the late Stone Age of *Homo sapiens,* during which people existed in hunter-gatherer bands in intimate contact with the natural environment. Snakes mattered. The smell of water, the hum of a bee, the directional bend of a plant stalk mattered. The naturalist's trance was adaptive: the glimpse of one small animal hidden in the grass could make the difference between eating and going hungry in the evening. And a sweet sense of horror, the shivery fascination with monsters and creeping forms that so delights us today even in the sterile hearts of the cities, could keep you alive until the next morning. Organisms are the natural stuff of metaphor and ritual. Although the evidence is far from all in, the brain appears to have kept its old capacities, its channeled quickness. We stay alert and alive in the vanished forests of the world.

Double Take

1. Why does Edward O. Wilson begin "The Serpent" with the account of his dream? What role does the dream play in the rest of the essay?
2. How does Wilson go about teaching his readers about snakes and serpents? What elements of this essay are designed to give the audience specific facts that assist Wilson in his ultimate comparison of snakes and serpents? What can you learn as a writer about ways of comparing facts and ideas from this essay?
3. What rhetorical effect does Wilson gain in recounting stories about his childhood and his encounters with snakes? What specifically is Wilson conveying when he writes about the incident with the large water moccasin and the incident when he reaches his hand into the hole after the brightly colored snake?

At First Glance

In this essay, Edward O. Wilson takes on the difficult task of placing ethics and religion in conversation with each other. In doing so, he creates two distinct positions: the transcendentalist and the empiricist. Before positioning his own argument, Wilson places these two positions in debate with one another. As you read this piece, examine how Wilson frames his own statements by analyzing the argument he creates for the sake of debate. That is, think about the rhetorical strength of Wilson's own argument once he frames and analyzes it in relation to the larger debate.

Ethics and Religion

Centuries of debate on the origin of ethics come down to this: Either ethical precepts, such as justice and human rights, are independent of human experience or else they are human inventions. The distinction is more than an exercise for academic philosophers. The choice between the assumption makes all the difference in the way we view ourselves as a species. It measures the authority of religion, and it determines the conduct of moral reasoning.

The two assumptions in competition are like islands in sea of chaos, immovable, as different as life and death, matter and the void. Which is correct cannot be learned by pure logic; for the present only a leap of faith will take you from one to the other. But the true answer will eventually be reached by the accumulation of objective evidence. Moral reasoning, I believe, is at every level intrinsically consilient with the natural sciences.

Every thoughtful person has an opinion on which of the premises is correct. But the split is not, as popularly supposed, between religious believers and secularists. It is between transcendentalists, those who think that moral guidelines exist outside the human mind, and empiricists, who think them contrivances of the mind. The choice between religious or nonreligious conviction and the choice between ethically transcendentalist or empiricist conviction are cross-cutting decisions made in metaphysical thought. An ethical transcendentalist, believing ethics to be independent, can either be an atheist or else assume the existence of a deity. In parallel manner, an ethical empiricist, believing ethics to be a human creation only, can either be an atheist or else believe in a creator deity (though not in a law-giving God in the traditional Judeo-Christian sense). In simplest terms the option of ethical foundation is as follows:

I believe in the independence of moral values, whether from God or not,

versus

I believe that moral values come from humans alone; God is a separate issue.

Theologians and philosophers have almost always focused on transcendentalism as the means to validate ethics. They seek the grail of natural law, which comprises freestanding principles of moral conduct immune to doubt and compromise. Christian theologians, following St. Thomas Aquinas' reasoning in *Summa Theologiae,* by and large consider natural law to be the expression of God's will. Human beings, in this view, have the obligation to discover the law by diligent reasoning and weave it into the routine of their daily lives. Secular philosophers of transcendental bent may seem to be radically different from theologians, but they are actually quite similar, at least in moral reasoning. They tend to view natural law as a set of principles so powerful as to be self-evident to any rational person, whatever the ultimate origin. In short, transcendentalism is fundamentally the same whether God is invoked or not.

For example, when Thomas Jefferson, following John Locke, derived the doctrine of natural rights from natural law, he was more concerned with the power of transcendental statements than in their divine or secular origin. In the Declaration of Independence he blended the secular and religious presumptions in one transcendentalist sentence, thus deftly covering all bets: "We hold these Truths to be self-evident, that all Men are created equal, that they are endowed by their Creator with certain unalienable Rights, that among these are Life, Liberty, and the Pursuit of Happiness." That assertion became the cardinal premise of America's civil religion, the righteous sword wielded by Lincoln and Martin Luther King, and it endures as the central ethic binding together the diverse peoples of the United States.

So compelling are such fruits of natural law theory, especially when the deity is also invoked, that they may seem to place the transcendentalist assumption beyond question. But to its noble successes must be added appalling failures. It has been perverted many times in the past, used for example to argue passionately for colonial conquest, slavery, and genocide. Nor was any great war ever fought without each side thinking its cause transcendentally sacred in some manner or other. "Oh how we hate one another," observed Cardinal Newman, "for the love of God."

So perhaps we can do better, by taking empiricism more seriously. Ethics, in the empiricist view, is conduct favored consistently enough throughout a society to be expressed as a code of principles. It is driven by hereditary predispositions in mental development—the "moral sentiments" of the Enlightenment philosophers—causing broad convergence across cultures, while reaching precise form in each culture according to historical circumstance. The codes, whether judged by outsiders as good or evil, play an important role in determining which cultures flourish, and which decline.

The importance of the empiricist view is its emphasis on objective knowledge. Because the success of an ethical code depends on how wisely it interprets the moral sentiments, those who frame it should know how the brain works, and how the mind develops. The success of ethics also depends on the accurate prediction of the consequence of particular actions as opposed to others, especially in cases of moral ambiguity. That too takes a great deal of knowledge consilient with the natural and social sciences.

The empiricist argument, then, is that by exploring the biological roots of moral behavior, and explaining their material origins and biases, we should be able to fashion a wiser and more enduring ethical consensus than has gone before. The current expansion of scientific inquiry into the deeper processes of human thought makes this venture feasible.

The choice between transcendentalism and empiricism will be the coming century's version of the struggle for men's souls. Moral reasoning will either remain centered in idioms of theology and philosophy, where it is now, or it will shift toward science-based material analysis. Where it settles will depend on which world view is proved correct, or at least which is more widely *perceived* to be correct.

The time has come to turn the cards face up. Ethicists, scholars who specialize in moral reasoning, are not prone to declare themselves on the foundations of ethics, or to admit fallibility. Rarely do you see an argument that opens with the simple statement: *This is my starting point, and it could be wrong.* Ethicists instead favor a fretful passage from the particular into the ambiguous, or the reverse, vagueness into hard cases. I suspect that almost all are transcendentalists at heart, but they rarely say so in simple declarative sentences. One cannot blame them very much; it is difficult to explain the ineffable, and they evidently do not wish to suffer the indignity of having their personal beliefs clearly understood. So by and large they steer around the foundation issue altogether.

That said, I will of course try to be plain about my own position: I am an empiricist. On religion I lean toward deism but consider its proof largely a problem in astrophysics. The existence of a cosmological God who created the universe (as envisioned by deism) is possible, and may eventually be settled, perhaps by forms of material evidence not yet imagined. Or the matter may be forever beyond human reach. In contrast, and of far greater importance to humanity, the existence of a biological God, one who directs organic evolution and intervenes in human affairs (as envisioned by theism) is increasingly contravened by biology and the brain sciences.

The same evidence, I believe, favors a purely material origin of ethics, and it meets the criterion of consilience: Causal explanations of brain activity and evolution, while imperfect, already cover the most facts known about moral behavior with the greatest accuracy and the smallest number of freestanding assumptions. While this conception is relativistic, in other words dependent on personal viewpoint, it need not be irresponsibly so. If evolved carefully, it can lead more directly and safely to stable moral codes than transcendentalism, which is also, when you think about it, ultimately relativistic.

And yes—lest I forget—I may be wrong.

In order to sharpen the distinction between transcendentalism and empiricism, I have constructed a debate between defenders of the two world views. To add passionate conviction, I have also made the transcendentalist a theist, and the empiricist a skeptic. And to be as fair as possible, I have drawn their arguments from the most closely reasoned sources in theology and philosophy of which I am aware.

THE TRANSCENDENTALIST

"Before taking up ethics, let me affirm the logic of theism, because if the existence of a law-giving God is conceded, the origin of ethics is instantly settled. So please consider carefully the following argument in favor of theism.

"I challenge your rejection of theism on your own empiricist grounds. How can you ever hope to disprove the existence of a personal God? How can you explain away the three thousand years of spiritual testimony from the followers of Judaism, Christianity, and Islam? Hundreds of millions of people, including a large percentage of the educated citizens of industrial countries, *know* there is an unseen sentient power guiding their lives. The testimony is overwhelming. According to recent polls, nine in ten Americans believe in a personal God who can answer prayers and perform miracles. One in five has experienced His presence and guidance at least once during the year previous to the poll. How can science, the underwriting discipline of ethical empiricism, dismiss such widespread testimony?

"The nucleus of the scientific method, we are constantly reminded, is the rejection of certain propositions in favor of others in strict conformity to fact-based logic. Where are the facts that require the rejection of a personal God? It isn't enough to say that the idea is unnecessary to explain the physical world, at least as scientists understand it. Too much is at stake for theism to be dismissed with that flip of the hand. The burden of proof is on you, not on those who believe in a divine presence.

"Looked at in proper perspective, God subsumes science, science does not subsume God. Scientists collect data on certain subjects and build hypotheses to explain them. In order to extend the reach of objective knowledge as far as they can, they provisionally accept some hypotheses while discarding others. That knowledge, however, can cover only part of reality. Scientific research in particular is not designed to explore all of the wondrous varieties of human mental experience. The idea of God, in contrast, has the capacity to explain *everything,* not just measurable phenomena, but phenomena personally felt and subliminally sensed, including revelations that can be communicated solely through spiritual channels. Why should all mental experience be visible in PET scans? Unlike science, the idea of God is concerned with more than the material world given us to explore. It opens our minds to what lies outside that world. It instructs us to reach out to the mysteries that are comprehensible through faith alone.

"Confine your thoughts to the material world if you wish. Others know that God encompasses the ultimate causes of the Creation. Where do the laws of nature come from if not a power higher than the laws themselves? Science offers no answer to that sovereign question of theology. Put another way, why is there something rather than nothing? The ultimate meaning of existence lies beyond the rational grasp of human beings, and therefore outside the province of science.

"Are you also a pragmatist? There is an urgently practical reason for belief in ethical precepts ordained by a supreme being. To deny such an origin, to assume that moral codes are exclusively man-made, is a dangerous creed. As Dostoyevsky's Grand Inquisitor observed, all things are permitted when there is no ruling hand of God, and freedom turns to misery. In support of that caveat we have nothing less than the authority of the original Enlightenment thinkers themselves. Virtually all believed in a God who created the universe, and many were devout Christians to boot. Almost none was willing to abandon ethics to secular materialism. John Locke said that 'those who deny the existence of the Deity are not to be tolerated at all. Promises, covenants and oaths, which are the bonds of human society, can have no hold upon or sanctity for an atheist; for the taking away of God, even only in thought, dissolves all.' Robert Hooke, a great physicist of the seventeenth century, in composing a brief on the newly created Royal Society, wisely cautioned that the purpose of this quintessential Enlightenment organization should be 'To improve the knowledge of naturall things, and all useful Arts, Manufactures, Mechanick practises, Engynes and Inventions by Experiments—(not meddling with Divinity, Metaphysics, Moralls, Politicks, Grammar, Rhetorick or Logick).'

"These sentiments are just as prevalent among leading thinkers of the modern era, as well as a large minority of working scientists. They are reinforced by queasiness over the idea of organic evolution as espoused by Darwin. This keystone of empiricism presumes to reduce the Creation to the products of random mutations and environmental circumstance. Even George Bernard Shaw, an avowed atheist, responded to Darwinism with despair. He condemned its fatalism and the demoting of beauty, intelligence, honor, and aspiration to an abstract notion of blindly assembled matter. Many writers have suggested, not unfairly in my opinion, that such a sterile view of life, which reduces human beings to little more than intelligent animals, gave intellectual justification to the genocidal horrors of Nazism and communism.

"So surely there is something wrong with the reigning theory of evolution. Even if some form of genetic change occurs within species in the manner proclaimed by the new Darwinism, the full, stupendous complexity of modern organisms could not have been created by blind chance alone. Time and again in the history of science new evidence has overturned prevailing theories. Why are scientists so anxious to stay with autonomous evolution and to discount the possibility of an intelligent design instead? It is all very curious. Design would seem to be a simpler explanation than the random self-assembly of millions of kinds of organisms.

"Finally, theism gains compelling force in the case of the human mind and—I won't shrink from saying it—the immortal soul. Little wonder that a quarter or more of Americans reject totally the idea of any kind of human evolution, even in anatomy and physiology. Science pushed too far is science arrogant. Let it keep its proper place, as the God-given gift to understand His physical dominion."

THE EMPIRICIST

"I'll begin by freely acknowledging that religion has an overwhelming attraction for the human mind, and that religious conviction is largely beneficent. Religion rises from the innermost coils of the human spirit. It nourishes love, devotion, and, above all, hope. People hunger for the assurance it offers. I can think of nothing more emotionally compelling than the Christian doctrine that God incarnated himself in testimony of the sacredness of all human life, even of the slave, and that he died and rose again in promise of eternal life for everyone.

"But religious belief has another, destructive side, equaling the worst excesses of materialism. An estimated one hundred thousand belief systems have existed in history, and many have fostered ethnic and tribal wars. Each of the three great Western religions in particular expanded at one time or another in symbiosis with military aggression. Islam, which means 'submission,' was imposed by force of arms on large portions of the Middle East, Mediterranean perimeter, and southern Asia. Christianity dominated the New World as much by colonial expansion as by spiritual grace. It benefited from a historical accident: Europe, having been blocked to the East by the Muslim Arabs, turned west to occupy the Americas, whereupon the cross accompanied the sword in one campaign of enslavement and genocide after another.

"The Christian rulers had an instructive example to follow in the early history of Judaism. If we are to believe the Old Testament, the Israelites were ordered by

God to wipe the promised land clean of heathen. 'Of these peoples which the LORD your God gives you as an inheritance, you shall let nothing that breathes remain alive, but you shall utterly destroy them: the Hittite and the Amorite and the Canaanite and the Perizzite and the Hivite and the Jebusite, as the LORD your God has commanded you,' thus reports Deuteronomy, 20:16–17. Over a hundred cities were consumed by fire and death, beginning with Joshua's campaign against Jericho and ending with David's assault on the ancient Jebusite stronghold of Jerusalem.

"I bring up these historical facts not to cast aspersions on present-day faiths but rather to cast light on their material origins and those of the ethical systems they sponsor. All great civilizations were spread by conquest, and among their chief beneficiaries were the religions validating them. No doubt membership in state-sponsored religions has always been deeply satisfying in many psychological dimensions, and spiritual wisdom has evolved to moderate the more barbaric tenets obeyed in the days of conquest. But every major religion today is a winner in the Darwinian struggle waged among cultures, and none ever flourished by tolerating its rivals. The swiftest road to success has always been sponsorship by a conquering state.

"To be fair, let me now put the matter of cause and effect straight. Religious exclusion and bigotry arise from tribalism, the belief in the innate superiority and special status of the in-group. Tribalism cannot be blamed on religion. The same causal sequence gave rise to totalitarian ideologies. The pagan *corpus mysticum* of Nazism and the class-warfare doctrine of Marxism-Leninism, both essentially dogmas of religions without God, were put to the service of tribalism, not the reverse. Neither would have been so fervently embraced if their devotees had not thought themselves chosen people, virtuous in their mission, surrounded by wicked enemies, and conquerors by right of blood and destiny. Mary Wollstonecraft correctly said, of male domination but extensible to all human behavior, 'No man chooses evil because it is evil; he only mistakes it for happiness, which is the good he seeks.'

"Conquest by a tribe requires that its members make sacrifices to the interests of the group, especially during conflict with competing groups. That is simply the expression of a primal rule of social life throughout the animal kingdom. It arises when loss of personal advantage by submission to the needs of the group is more than offset by gain in personal advantage due to the resulting success of the group. The human corollary is that selfish, prosperous people belonging to losing religions and ideologies are replaced by selfless, poor members of winning religions and ideologies. A better life later on, either an earthly paradise or resurrection in heaven, is the promised reward that cultures invent to justify the subordinating imperative of social existence. Repeated from one generation to the next, submission to the group and its moral codes is solidified in official doctrine and personal belief. But it is not ordained by God or plucked from the air as self-evident truth. It evolves as a necessary device of survival in social organisms.

"The most dangerous of devotions, in my opinion, is the one endemic to Christianity: *I was not born to be of this world.* With a second life waiting, suffering can be endured—especially in other people. The natural environment can be used up. Enemies of the faith can be savaged and suicidal martyrdom praised.

"Is it all an illusion? Well, I hesitate to call it that or, worse, a noble lie, the harsh phrase sometimes used by skeptics, but one has to admit that the objective evidence supporting it is not strong. No statistical proofs exist that prayer reduces illness and mortality, except perhaps through a psychogenic enhancement of the immune system; if it were otherwise the whole world would pray continuously. When two armies blessed by priests clash, one still loses. And when the martyr's righteous forebrain is exploded by the executioner's bullet and his mind disintegrates, what then? Can we safely assume that all those millions of neural circuits will be reconstituted in an immaterial state, so that the conscious mind carries on?

"The smart money in eschatology is on Blaise Pascal's wager: Live well but accept the faith. If there is an afterlife, the seventeenth-century French philosopher reasoned, the believer has a ticket to paradise and the best of both worlds. 'If I lost,' Pascal wrote, 'I would have lost little; if I won I would have gained eternal life.' Now think like an empiricist for a moment. Consider the wisdom of turning the wager around as follows: If fear and hope and reason dictate that you must accept the faith, do so, but treat this world as if there is none other.

"I know true believers will be scandalized by this line of argument. Their wrath falls on outspoken heretics, who are considered at best troublemakers and at worst traitors to the social order. But no evidence has been adduced that nonbelievers are less law-abiding or productive citizens than believers of the same socioeconomic class, or that they face death less bravely. A 1996 survey of American scientists (to take one respectable segment of society) revealed that 46 percent are atheists and 14 percent doubters or agnostics. Only 36 percent expressed a desire for immortality, and most of those only moderately so; 64 percent claimed no desire at all.

"True character arises from a deeper well than religion. It is the internalization of the moral principles of a society, augmented by those tenets personally chosen by the individual, strong enough to endure through trials of solitude and adversity. The principles are fitted together into what we call integrity, literally the integrated self, wherein personal decisions feel good and true. Character is in turn the enduring source of virtue. It stands by itself and excites admiration in others. It is not obedience to authority, and while it is often consistent with and reinforced by religious belief, it is not piety.

"Nor is science the enemy. It is the accumulation of humanity's organized, objective knowledge, the first medium devised able to unite people everywhere in common understanding. It favors no tribe or religion. It is the base of a truly democratic and global culture.

"You say that science cannot explain spiritual phenomena. Why not? The brain sciences are making important advances in the analysis of complex operations of the mind. There is no apparent reason why they cannot in time provide a material account of the emotions and ratiocination that compose spiritual thought.

"You ask where ethical precepts come from if not divine revelation. Consider the alternative empiricist hypothesis, that precepts and religious faith are entirely material products of the mind. For more than a thousand generations they have increased the survival and reproductive success of those who conformed to tribal faiths. There was more than enough time for epigenetic rules—hereditary biases of mental development—to evolve that generate moral and religious sentiments. Indoctrinability became an instinct.

"Ethical codes are precepts reached by consensus under the guidance of the innate rules of mental development. Religion is the ensemble of mythic narratives that explain the origin of a people, their destiny, and why they are obliged to subscribe to particular rituals and moral codes. Ethical and religious beliefs are created from the bottom up, from people to their culture. They do not come from the top down, from God or other nonmaterial source to the people by way of culture.

"Which hypothesis, transcendentalist or empiricist, fits the objective evidence best? The empiricist, by a wide margin. To the extent that this view is accepted, more emphasis in moral reasoning will be placed on social choice, and less on religious and ideological authority.

"Such a shift has in fact been occurring in Western cultures since the Enlightenment, but the pace has been very slow. Part of the reason is a gross insufficiency of knowledge needed to judge the full consequences of our moral decisions, especially for the long term, say a decade or more. We have learned a great deal about ourselves and the world in which we live, but need a great deal more to be fully wise. There is a temptation at every great crisis to yield to transcendental authority, and perhaps that is better for a while. We are still indoctrinable, we still are easily god-struck.

"Resistance to empiricism is also due to a purely emotional shortcoming of the mode of reasoning it promotes: It is bloodless. People need more than reason. They need the poetry of affirmation, they crave an authority greater than themselves at rites of passage and other moments of high seriousness. A majority desperately wish for the immortality the rituals seem to underwrite.

"Great ceremonies summon the history of a people in solemn remembrance. They showcase the sacred symbols. That is the enduring value of ceremony, which in all high civilizations has historically assumed a mostly religious form. Sacred symbols infiltrate the very bones of culture. They will take centuries to replace, if ever.

"So I may surprise you by granting this much: It would be a sorry day if we abandoned our venerated sacral traditions. It would be a tragic misreading of history to expunge *under God* from the American Pledge of Allegiance. Whether atheists or true believers, let oaths be taken with hand on the Bible, and may we continue to hear *So help me God*. Call upon priests and ministers and rabbis to bless civil ceremony with prayer, and by all means let us bow our heads in communal respect. Recognize that when introits and invocations prickle the skin we are in the presence of poetry, and the soul of the tribe, something that will outlive the particularities of sectarian belief, and perhaps belief in God itself.

"But to share reverence is not to surrender the precious self and obscure the true nature of the human race. We should not forget who we are. Our strength is in truth and knowledge and character, under whatever sign. Judaeo-Christians are told by Holy Scripture that pride goeth before destruction. I disagree; it's the reverse: Destruction goeth before pride. Empiricism has turned everything around in the formula. It has destroyed the giddying theory that we are special beings placed by a deity in the center of the universe in order to serve as the summit of Creation for the glory of the gods. We can be proud as a species because, having discovered that we are alone, we owe the gods very little. Humility is better shown to our fellow humans and the rest of life on this planet, on whom all hope really depends. And if any gods are paying attention, surely we have earned their admiration by making that discovery and setting out alone to accomplish the best of which we are capable."

The argument of the empiricist, to repeat my earlier confession, is my own. It is far from novel, having roots that go back to Aristotle's *Nicomachean Ethics* and, in the beginning of the modern era, to David Hume's *A Treatise of Human Nature* (1739–40). The first clear evolutionary elaboration of it was by Darwin in *The Descent of Man* (1871).

The argument of the religious transcendentalist, on the other hand, is the one I first learned as a child in the Christian faith. I have reflected on it repeatedly since, and am by intellect and temperament bound to respect its ancient traditions.

It is also the case that religious transcendentalism is bolstered by secular transcendentalism, with which it has fundamental similarities. Immanuel Kant, judged by history the greatest of secular philosophers, addressed moral reasoning very much as a theologian. Human beings, he argued, are independent moral agents with a wholly free will capable of obeying or breaking moral law: "There is in man a power of self-determination, independent of any coercion through sensuous impulses." Our minds are subject to a categorical imperative, he said, of what our actions ought to be. The imperative is a good in itself alone, apart from all other considerations, and it can be recognized by this rule: "Act only on that maxim through which you wish also it become a universal law." Most important, and transcendental, *ought* has no place in nature. Nature, Kant said, is a system of cause and effect, while moral choice is a matter of free will, for which there is no cause and effect. In making moral choices, in rising above mere instinct, human beings transcend the realm of nature and enter a realm of freedom that belongs to them exclusively as rational creatures.

Now this formulation has a comforting feel to it, but it makes no sense at all in terms of either material or imaginable entities, which is why Kant, even apart from his tortured prose, is so hard to understand. Sometimes a concept is baffling not because it is profound but because it is wrong. It does not accord, we know now, with the evidence of how the brain works.

In *Principia Ethica* (1903) G. E. Moore, the founder of modern ethical philosophy, essentially agreed with Kant. Moral reasoning in his view cannot dip into psychology and the social sciences in order to locate ethical principles, because they yield only a causal picture and fail to illuminate the basis of moral justification. So to pass from the factual *is* to the normative *ought* commits a basic error of logic, which Moore called the naturalistic fallacy. John Rawls, in *A Theory of Justice* (1971), once again traveled the transcendental road. He offered the very plausible premise that justice be defined as fairness, which is to be accepted as an intrinsic good. It is the imperative we would follow if we had no starting information about our own status in life. But in making such an assumption, Rawls ventured no thought on where the human brain comes from or how it works. He offered no evidence that justice-as-fairness is consistent with human nature, hence practicable as a blanket premise. Probably it is, but how can we know except by blind trial-and-error?

I find it hard to believe that had Kant, Moore, and Rawls known modern biology and experimental psychology they would have reasoned as they did. Yet as this century closes, transcendentalism remains firm in the hearts not just of religious believers but also of countless scholars in the social sciences and humanities who, like Moore and Rawls before them, have chosen to insulate their thinking from the natural sciences.

Many philosophers will respond by saying, But wait! What are you saying? Ethicists don't need that kind of information. You really can't pass from *is* to *ought*. You are not allowed to describe a genetic predisposition and suppose that because it is part of human nature, it is somehow transformed into an ethical precept. We must put moral reasoning in a special category, and use transcendental guidelines as required.

No, we do not have to put moral reasoning in a special category, and use transcendental premises, because the posing of the naturalistic fallacy is itself a fallacy. For if *ought* is not *is,* what is? To translate *is* into *ought* makes sense if we attend to the objective meaning of ethical precepts. They are very unlikely to be ethereal messages outside humanity awaiting revelation, or independent truths vibrating in a nonmaterial dimension of the mind. They are more likely to be physical products of the brain and culture. From the consilient perspective of the natural sciences, they are no more than principles of the social contract hardened into rules and dictates, the behavioral codes that members of a society fervently wish others to follow and are willing to accept themselves for the common good. Precepts are the extreme in a scale of agreements that range from casual assent to public sentiment to law to that part of the canon considered unalterable and sacred. The scale applied to adultery might read as follows:

> *Let's not go further; it doesn't feel right, and it would lead to trouble. (We probably ought not.)*
>
> *Adultery not only causes feelings of guilt, it is generally disapproved of by society, so these are other reasons to avoid it. (We ought not.)*
>
> *Adultery isn't just disapproved of, it's against the law. (We almost certainly ought not.)*
> *God commands that we avoid this mortal sin. (We absolutely ought not.)*

In transcendental thinking the chain of causation runs downward from the given *ought* in religion or natural law through jurisprudence to education and finally to individual choice. The argument from transcendentalism takes the following general form: *There is a supreme principle, either divine or intrinsic in the order of nature, and we will be wise to learn about it and find the means to conform to it.* Thus John Rawls opens *A Theory of Justice* with a proposition he regards as irrevocable: "In a just society the liberties of equal citizenship are taken as settled; the rights secured by justice are not subject to political bargaining or to the calculus of social interests." As many critiques have made clear, that premise can lead to many unhappy consequences when applied to the real world, including the tightening of social control and decline of personal initiative. A very different premise therefore is suggested by Robert Nozick in *Anarchy, State, and Utopia* (1974): "Individuals have rights, and there are things no person or group may do to them (without violating their rights). So strong and far-reaching are these rights that they raise the question of what, if anything, the state and its officials may do." Rawls would point us toward egalitarianism regulated by the state, Nozick toward libertarianism in a minimalist state.

The empiricist view in contrast, searching for an origin of ethical reasoning that can be objectively studied, reverses the chain of causation. The individual is seen as predisposed biologically to make certain choices. By cultural evolution some of the choices are hardened into precepts, then laws, and if the predisposition or coercion is strong enough, a belief in the command of God or the natural order of the universe. The general empiricist principle takes this form: *Strong innate feeling and historical experience cause certain actions to be preferred; we have experienced them, and weighed their consequences, and agree to conform with codes that express them. Let us take an oath upon the codes, invest our personal honor in them, and suffer punishment for their violation.* The empiricist view concedes that moral codes are devised to conform to some drives of human nature and to suppress others. *Ought* is not the translation of human nature but of the public will, which can be made increasingly wise and stable through the understanding of the needs and pitfalls of human nature. It recognizes that the strength of commitment can wane as a result of new knowledge and experience, with the result that certain rules may be desacralized, old laws rescinded, and behavior that was once prohibited freed. It also recognizes that for the same reason new moral codes may need to be devised, with the potential in time of being made sacred.

If the empiricist world view is correct, *ought* is just shorthand for one kind of factual statement, a word that denotes what society first chose (or was coerced) to do, and then codified. The naturalistic fallacy is thereby reduced to the naturalistic dilemma. The solution of the dilemma is not difficult. It is this: *Ought* is the product of a material process. The solution points the way to an objective grasp of the origin of ethics.

A few investigators are now embarked on just such a foundational inquiry. Most agree that ethical codes have arisen by evolution through the interplay of biology and culture. In a sense they are reviving the idea of moral sentiments developed in the eighteenth century by the British empiricists Francis Hutcheson, David Hume, and Adam Smith.

By moral sentiments is now meant moral instincts as defined by the modern behavioral sciences, subject to judgment according to their consequences. The sentiments are thus derived from epigenetic rules, hereditary biases in mental development, usually conditioned by emotion, that influence concepts and decisions made from them. The primary origin of the moral instincts is the dynamic relation between cooperation and defection. The essential ingredient for the molding of the instincts during genetic evolution in any species is intelligence high enough to judge and manipulate the tension generated by the dynamism. That level of intelligence allows the building of complex mental scenarios well into the future, as I described in the earlier chapter on the mind. It occurs, so far as known, only in human beings and perhaps their closet relatives among the higher apes.

A way of envisioning the hypothetical earliest stages of moral evolution is provided by game theory, particularly the solutions to the famous Prisoner's Dilemma. Consider the following typical scenario of the Dilemma. Two gang members have been arrested for murder and are being questioned separately. The evidence against them is strong but not compelling. The first gang member believes that if he turns state's witness, he will be granted immunity and his partner will be sentenced to life in prison. But he is also aware that his partner has the same option. That is the dilemma. Will the two gang members independently defect so that both take the hard fall? They will not, because they agreed in advance to remain silent if caught. By doing so, both hope to be convicted on a lesser charge or escape punishment altogether. Criminal gangs have turned this principle of calculation into an ethical precept: Never rat on another member; always be a stand-up guy. Honor does exist among thieves. If we view the gang as a society of sorts, the code is the same as that of a captive soldier in wartime obliged to give only name, rank, and serial number.

In one form or another, comparable dilemmas that are solvable by cooperation occur constantly and everywhere in daily life. The payoff is variously money, status, power, sex, access, comfort, and health. Most of these proximate rewards are converted into the universal bottom line of Darwinian genetic fitness: greater longevity and a secure, growing family.

And so it has likely always been. Imagine a Paleolithic hunter band, say composed of five men. One hunter considers breaking away from the others to look for an antelope on his own. If successful he will gain a large quantity of meat and hide, five times greater than if he stays with the band and they are successful. But he knows from experience that his chances of success alone are very low, much less than the chances of a band of five working together. In addition, whether successful alone or not, he will suffer animosity from the others for lessening their own prospects. By custom the band members remain together and share the animals they kill equitably. So the hunter stays. He also observes good manners while doing so, especially if he is the one who makes the kill. Boastful pride is condemned because it rips the delicate web of reciprocity.

Now suppose that human propensities to cooperate or defect are heritable: Some members are innately more cooperative, others less so. In this respect moral aptitude would simply be like almost all other mental traits studied to date. Among traits with documented heritability, those closest to moral aptitude are empathy to the distress of others and certain processes of attachment between infants and their caregivers. To the heritability of moral aptitude add the abundant evidence of history that cooperative individuals generally survive longer and leave more offspring. It is to be expected that in the course of evolutionary history, genes predisposing people toward cooperative behavior would have come to predominate in the human population as a whole.

Such a process repeated through thousands of generations inevitably gave birth to the moral sentiments. With the exception of stone psychopaths (if any truly exist), these instincts are vividly experienced by every person variously as conscience, self-respect, remorse, empathy, shame, humility, and moral outrage. They bias cultural evolution toward the conventions that express the universal moral codes of honor, patriotism, altruism, justice, compassion, mercy, and redemption.

The dark side to the inborn propensity to moral behavior is xenophobia. Because personal familiarity and common interest are vital in social transactions, moral sentiments evolved to be selective. And so it has ever been, and so it will ever be. People give trust to strangers with effort, and true compassion is a commodity in chronically short supply. Tribes cooperate only through carefully defined treaties and other conventions. They are quick to imagine themselves victims of conspiracies by competing groups, and they are prone to dehumanize and murder their rivals during periods of severe conflict. They cement their own group loyalties by means of sacred symbols and ceremonies. Their mythologies are filled with epic victories over menacing enemies.

The complementary instincts of morality and tribalism are easily manipulated. Civilization has made them more so. Only ten thousand years ago, a tick in geological time, when the agricultural revolution began in the Middle East, in China, and in Mesoamerica, populations increased in density tenfold over those of hunter-gatherer societies. Families settled on small plots of land, villages proliferated, and labor was finely divided as a growing minority of the populace specialized as craftsmen, traders, and soldiers. The rising agricultural societies, egalitarian at first, became hierarchical. As chiefdoms and then states thrived on agricultural surpluses, hereditary rulers and priestly castes took power. The old ethical codes were transformed into coercive regulations, always to the advantage of the ruling classes. About this time the idea of law-giving gods originated. Their commands lent the ethical codes overpowering authority, once again—no surprise—to the favor of the rulers.

Because of the technical difficulty of analyzing such phenomena in an objective manner, and because people resist biological explanations of their higher cortical functions in the first place, very little progress has been made in the biological exploration of the moral sentiments. Even so, it is an astonishing circumstance that the study of ethics has advanced so little since the nineteenth century. As a result the most distinguishing and vital qualities of the human species remain a blank space on the scientific map. I think it an error to pivot discussions of ethics upon the freestanding assumptions of contemporary philosophers who have evidently never given thought to the evolutionary origin and material functioning of the human brain. In no other domain of the humanities is a union with the natural sciences more urgently needed.

When the ethical dimension of human nature is at last fully opened to such exploration, the innate epigenetic rules of moral reasoning will probably not prove to be aggregated into simple instincts such as bonding, cooperativeness, or altruism. Instead, the rules most probably will turn out to be an ensemble of many algorithms whose interlocking activities guide the mind across a landscape of nuanced moods and choices.

Such a prestructured mental world may at first seem too complicated to have been created by autonomous genetic evolution alone. But all the evidence of biology suggests that just this process was enough to spawn the millions of species of life surrounding us. Each kind of animal is furthermore guided through its life cycle by unique and often elaborate sets of instinctual algorithms, many of which are beginning to yield to genetic and neurobiological analyses. With all these examples before us, it is not unreasonable to conclude that human behavior originated the same way.

Meanwhile, the mélanges of moral reasoning employed by modern societies are, to put the matter simply, a mess. They are chimeras, composed of odd parts stuck together. Paleolithic egalitarian and tribalistic instincts are still firmly installed. As part of the genetic foundation of human nature, they cannot be replaced. In some cases, such as quick hostility to strangers and competing groups, they have become generally ill-adapted and persistently dangerous. Above the fundamental instincts rise superstructures of arguments and rules that accommodate the novel institutions created by cultural evolution. These accommodations, which reflect the attempt to maintain order and further tribal interests, have been too volatile to track by genetic evolution; they are not yet in the genes.

Little wonder, then, that ethics is the most publicly contested of all philosophical enterprises. Or that political science, which at foundation is primarily the study of applied ethics, is so frequently problematic. Neither is informed by anything that would be recognizable as authentic theory in the natural sciences. Both ethics and political science lack a foundation of verifiable knowledge of human nature sufficient to produce cause-and-effect predictions and sound judgments based on them. Surely it will be prudent to pay closer attention to the deep springs of ethical behavior. The greatest void in knowledge in such a venture is the biology of the moral sentiments. In time this subject can be understood, I believe, by paying attention to the following topics.

- *The definition of the moral sentiments:* first by precise descriptions from experimental psychology, then by analysis of the underlying neural and endocrine responses.

- *The genetics of the moral sentiments:* most easily approached through measurements of the heritability of the psychological and physiological processes of ethical behavior, and eventually, with difficulty, by identification of the prescribing genes.

- *The development of the moral sentiments as products of the interactions of genes and environment.* The research is most effective when conducted at two levels: the histories of ethical systems as part of the emergence of different cultures, and the cognitive development of individuals living in a variety of cultures. Such investigations are already well along in anthropology and psychology. In the future they will be augmented by contributions from biology.

- *The deep history of the moral sentiments:* why they exist in the first place, presumably by their contributions to survival and reproductive success during the long periods of prehistoric time in which they genetically evolved.

From a convergence of these several approaches, the true origin and meaning of ethical behavior may come into focus. If so, a more certain measure can then be taken of the strength and flexibility of the epigenetic rules composing the various moral sentiments. From that knowledge, it should be possible to adapt the ancient moral sentiments more wisely to the swiftly changing conditions of modern life into which, willy-nilly and largely in ignorance, we have plunged ourselves.

Then new answers might be found for the truly important questions of moral reasoning. How can the moral instincts be ranked? Which are best subdued and to what degree, which validated by law and symbol? How can precepts be left open to appeal under extraordinary circumstances? In the new understanding can be located the most effective means for reaching consensus. No one can guess the form the agreements will take. The process, however, can be predicted with assurance. It will be democratic, weakening the clash of rival religions and ideologies. History is moving decisively in that direction, and people are by nature too bright and too contentious to abide anything else. And the pace can be confidently predicted: Change will come slowly, across generations, because old beliefs die hard even when demonstrably false.

The same reasoning that aligns ethical philosophy with science can also inform the study of religion. Religions are analogous to superorganisms. They have a life cycle. They are born, they grow, they compete, they reproduce, and, in the fullness of time, most die. In each of these phases religions reflect the human organisms that nourish them. They express a primary rule of human existence, that whatever is necessary to sustain life is also ultimately biological.

Successful religions typically begin as cults, which then increase in power and inclusiveness until they achieve tolerance outside the circle of believers. At the core of each religion is a creation myth, which explains how the world began and how the chosen people—those subscribing to the belief system—arrived at its center. There is often a mystery, a set of secret instructions and formulas available only to hierophants who have worked their way to a higher state of enlightenment. The medieval Jewish cabala, the trigradal system of Freemasonry, and the carvings on Australian Aboriginal spirit sticks are examples of such arcana. Power radiates from the center, gathering converts and binding followers to the group. Sacred places are designated where the gods can be importuned, rites observed, and miracles witnessed.

The devotees of the religion compete as a tribe with those of other religions. They harshly resist the dismissal of their beliefs by rivals. They venerate self-sacrifice in defense of the religion.

The tribalistic roots of religion and those of moral reasoning are similar and may be identical. Religious rites, as evidenced by burial ceremonies, are very old. In the Paleolithic period of Europe and the Middle East, it appears that bodies were sometimes placed in shallow graves sprinkled with ochre or blossoms, and it is easy to imagine ceremonies performed there that invoked spirits and gods. But, as theoretical deduction and the evidence suggest, the primitive elements of moral behavior are far older than Paleolithic ritual. Religion arose on an ethical foundation, and it has probably always been used in one manner or another to justify moral codes.

The formidable influence of the religious drive is based on far more, however, than just the validation of morals. A great subterranean river of the mind, it gathers strength from a broad spread of tributary emotions. Foremost among them is the survival instinct. "Fear," as the Roman poet Lucretius said, "was the first thing on earth to make gods." Our conscious minds hunger for a permanent existence. If we cannot have everlasting life of the body, then absorption into some immortal whole will serve. *Anything* will serve, as long as it gives the individual meaning and somehow stretches into eternity that swift passage of the mind and spirit lamented by St. Augustine as the short day of time.

The understanding and control of life is another source of religious power. Doctrine draws on the same creative springs as science and the arts, its aim being the extraction of order from the mysteries of the material world. To explain the meaning of life it spins mythic narratives of the tribal history, populating the cosmos with protective spirits and gods. The existence of the supernatural, if accepted, testifies to the existence of that other world so desperately desired.

Religion is also empowered mightily by its principal ally, tribalism. The shamans and priests implore us, in somber cadence, *Trust in the sacred rituals, become part of the immortal force, you are one of us. As your life unfolds, each step has mystic significance that we who love you will mark with a solemn rite of passage, the last to be performed when you enter that second world free of pain and fear.*

If the religious mythos did not exist in a culture, it would be quickly invented, and in fact it has been everywhere, thousands of times through history. Such inevitability is the mark of instinctual behavior in any species. That is, even when learned, it is guided toward certain states by emotion-driven rules of mental development. To call religion instinctive is not to suppose any particular part of its mythos is untrue, only that its sources run deeper than ordinary habit and are in fact hereditary, urged into birth through biases in mental development encoded in the genes.

I have argued in previous chapters that such biases are to be expected as a usual consequence of the brain's genetic evolution. The logic applies to religious behavior, with the added twist of tribalism. There is a hereditary selective advantage to membership in a powerful group united by devout belief and purpose. Even when individuals subordinate themselves and risk death in common cause, their genes are more likely to be transmitted to the next generation than are those of competing groups who lack equivalent resolve.

The mathematical models of population genetics suggest the following rule in the evolutionary origin of such altruism. If the reduction of survival and reproduction of individuals due to genes for altruism is more than offset by the increased probability of survival of the group due to the altruism, the altruism genes will rise in frequency throughout the entire population of competing groups. Put as concisely as possible: The individual pays, his genes and tribe gain, altruism spreads.

Let me now suggest a still deeper significance of the empiricist theory of the origin of ethics and religion. If empiricism is disproved, and transcendentalism is compellingly upheld, the discovery would be quite simply the most consequential in human history. That is the burden laid upon biology as it draws close to the humanities. If the objective evidence accumulated by biology upholds empiricism, consilience succeeds in the most problematic domains of human behavior and is likely to apply everywhere. But if the evidence contradicts empiricism in any part, universal consilience fails and the division between science and the humanities will remain permanent all the way to their foundations.

The matter is still far from resolved. But empiricism, as I have argued, is well supported thus far in the case of ethics. The objective evidence for or against it in religion is weaker, but at least still consistent with biology. For example, the emotions that accompany religious ecstasy clearly have a neurobiological source. As least one form of brain disorder is associated with hypperreligiosity, in which cosmic significance is given to almost everything, including trivial everyday events. Overall it is possible to imagine the biological construction of a mind with religious beliefs, although that alone does not dismiss transcendentalism or prove the beliefs themselves to be untrue.

Equally important, much if not all religious behavior could have arisen from evolution by natural selection. The theory fits—crudely. The behavior includes at least some aspects of belief in gods. Propitiation and sacrifice, which are near-universals of religious practice, are acts of submission to a dominant being. They are one kind of a dominance hierarchy, which is a general trait of organized mammalian societies. Like humans, animals use elaborate signals to advertise and maintain their rank in the hierarchy. The details vary among species but also have consistent similarities across the board, as the following two examples will illustrate.

In packs of wolves the dominant animal walks erect and "proud," stiff-legged, deliberately paced, with head, tail, and ears up, and stares freely and casually at others. In the presence of rivals, the dominant animal bristles its pelt while curling its lips to show teeth, and it takes first choice in food and space. A subordinate uses opposite signals. It turns away from the dominant individual while lowering its head, ears, and tail, and it keeps its fur sleeked and teeth covered. It grovels and slinks, and yields food and space when challenged.

In troops of rhesus monkeys, the alpha male of the troop is remarkably similar in mannerisms to a dominant wolf. He keeps his head and tail up, walks in a deliberate, "regal" manner while casually staring at others. He climbs nearby objects to maintain height above his rivals. When challenged he stares hard at the opponent with mouth open—signaling aggression, not surprise—and sometimes slaps the ground with open palms to signal his readiness to attack. The male or female subordinate affects a furtive walk, holding its head and tail down, turning away from the alpha and other higher-ranked individuals. It keeps its mouth shut except for a fear grimace, and when challenged makes a cringing retreat. It yields space and food and, in the case of males, estrous females.

My point is the following. Behavioral scientists from another planet would notice immediately the semiotic resemblance between animal submissive behavior on the one hand and human obeisance to religious and civil authority on the other. They would point out that the most elaborate rites of obeisance are directed at the gods, the hyperdominant if invisible members of the human group. And they would conclude, correctly, that in baseline social behavior, not just in anatomy, *Homo sapiens* has only recently diverged in evolution from a nonhuman primate stock.

Countless studies of animal species, with instinctive behavior unobscured by cultural elaboration, have shown that membership in dominance orders pays off in survival and lifetime reproductive success. That is true not just for the dominant individuals, but for the subordinates as well. Membership in either class gives animals better protection against enemies and better access to food, shelter, and mates than does solitary existence. Furthermore, subordination in the group is not necessarily permanent. Dominant individuals weaken and die, and as a result some of the underlings advance in rank and appropriate more resources.

It would be surprising to find that modern humans had managed to erase the old mammalian genetic programs and devise other means of distributing power. All the evidence suggests that they have not. True to their primate heritage, people are easily seduced by confident, charismatic leaders, especially males. That predisposition is strongest in religious organizations. Cults form around such leaders. Their power grows if they can persuasively claim special access to the supremely dominant, typically male figure of God. As cults evolve into religions, the image of the supreme being is reinforced by myth and liturgy. In time the authority of the founders and their successors is graven in sacred texts. Unruly subordinates, known as "blasphemers," are squashed.

The symbol-forming human mind, however, never stays satisfied with raw apish feeling in any emotional realm. It strives to build cultures that are maximally rewarding in every dimension. In religion there is ritual and prayer to contact the supreme being directly, consolation from coreligionists to soften otherwise unbearable grief, explanations of the unexplainable, and the oceanic sense of communion with the larger whole that otherwise surpasses understanding.

Communion is the key, and hope rising from it eternal; out of the dark night of the soul there is the prospect of a spiritual journey to the light. For a special few the journey can be taken in this life. The mind reflects in certain ways in order to reach ever higher levels of enlightenment until finally, when no further progress is possible, it enters a mystical union with the whole. Within the great religions, such enlightenment is expressed by the Hindu samadhi, Buddhist Zen satori, Sufi fana, Taoist wu-wei, and Pentecostal Christian rebirth. Something like it is also experienced by hallucinating preliterate shamans. What all these celebrants evidently feel (as I once felt to some degree as a reborn evangelical) is hard to put in words, but Willa Cather came as close as possible in a single sentence. "That is happiness," her fictional narrator says in *My Ántonia,* "to be dissolved into something complete and great."

Of course that is happiness, to find the godhead, or to enter the wholeness of Nature, or otherwise to grasp and hold on to something ineffable, beautiful, and eternal. Millions seek it. They feel otherwise lost, adrift in a life without ultimate meaning. Their predicament is summarized in an insurance advertisement of 1997: *The year is 1999. You are dead. What do you do now?* They enter established religions, succumb to cults, dabble in New Age nostrums. They push *The Celestine Prophecy* and other junk attempts at enlightenment onto the best-seller lists.

Perhaps, as I believe, it can all eventually be explained as brain circuitry and deep, genetic history. But this is not a subject that even the most hardened empiricist should presume to trivialize. The idea of the mystical union is an authentic part of the human spirit. It has occupied humanity for millennia, and it raises questions of utmost seriousness for transcendentalists and scientists alike. What road, we ask, was traveled, what destination reached by the mystics of history?

No one has described the true journey with greater clarity than the great Spanish mystic St. Teresa of Avila, who in her 1563–65 memoir describes the steps she took to attain divine union by means of prayer. At the beginning of the narrative she moves beyond ordinary prayers of devotion and supplication to the second level, the prayer of the quiet. There her mind gathers its faculties inward in order to give "a simple consent to become the prisoner of God." A deep sense of consolation and peace descends upon her when the Lord supplies the "water of grand blessings and graces." Her mind then ceases to care for earthly things.

In the third state of prayer the saint's spirit, "drunk with love," is concerned only with thoughts of God, who controls and animates it.

> *O my King, seeing that I am now, while writing this, under the power of this heavenly madness . . . grant, I beseech Thee, that all those with whom I may have to converse may become mad through Thy love, or let me converse with none, or order it that I may have nothing to do in the world, or take me away from it.*

In the fourth state of prayer St. Teresa of Avila attains the mystical union:

> *There is no sense of anything, only fruition . . . the senses are all occupied in this function in such a way that not one of them is at liberty. . . . The soul, while thus seeking after God, is conscious, with a joy excessive and sweet, that it is, as it were, utterly fainting away in a trance; breathing, and all the bodily strength fail it. The soul is dissolved into that of God, and with the union at last comes comprehension of the graces bestowed by Him.*

For many the urge to believe in transcendental existence and immortality is overpowering. Transcendentalism, especially when reinforced by religious faith, is psychically full and rich; it feels somehow *right*. In comparison empiricism seems sterile and inadequate. In the quest for ultimate meaning, the transcendentalist route is much easier to follow. That is why, even as empiricism is winning the mind, transcendentalism continues to win the heart. Science has always defeated religious dogma point by point when the two have conflicted. But to no avail. In the United States there are fifteen million Southern Baptists, the largest denomination favoring literal interpretation of the Christian Bible, but only five thousand members of the American Humanist Association, the leading organization devoted to secular and deistic humanism.

Still, if history and science have taught us anything, it is that passion and desire are not the same as truth. The human mind evolved to believe in the gods. It did not evolve to believe in biology. Acceptance of the supernatural conveyed a great advantage throughout prehistory, when the brain was evolving. Thus it is in sharp contrast to biology, which was developed as a product of the modern age and is not underwritten by genetic algorithms. The uncomfortable truth is that the two beliefs are not factually compatible. As a result those who hunger for both intellectual and religious truth will never acquire both in full measure.

Meanwhile, theology tries to resolve the dilemma by evolving sciencelike toward abstraction. The gods of our ancestors were divine human beings. The Egyptians, as Herodotus noted, represented them as Egyptian (often with body parts of Nilotic animals), and the Greeks represented them as Greeks. The great contribution of the Hebrews was to combine the entire pantheon into a single person, Yahweh—a patriarch appropriate to desert tribes—and to intellectualize His existence. No graven images were allowed. In the process, they rendered the divine presence less tangible. And so in biblical accounts it came to pass that no one, not even Moses approaching Yahweh in the burning bush, could look upon His face. In time the Jews were prohibited even from pronouncing His true full name. Nevertheless, the idea of a theistic God, omniscient, omnipotent, and closely involved in human affairs, has persisted to the present day as the dominant religious image of Western culture.

During the Enlightenment a growing number of liberal Judaeo-Christian theologians, wishing to accommodate theism to a more rationalist view of the material world, moved away from God as a literal person. Baruch Spinoza, the preeminent Jewish philosopher of the seventeenth century, visualized the deity as a transcendent substance present everywhere in the universe. *Deus sive natura,* God or nature, he declared, they are interchangeable. For his philosophical pains he was banished from Amsterdam under a comprehensive anathema, combining all curses in the book. The risk of heresy notwithstanding, the depersonalization of God has continued steadily into the modern era. For Paul Tillich, one of the most influential Protestant theologians of the twentieth century, the assertion of the existence of God-as-person is not false; it is just meaningless. Among many of the most liberal contemporary thinkers, the denial of a concrete divinity takes the form of process theology. Everything in this most extreme of ontologies is part of a seamless and endlessly complex web of unfolding relationships. God is manifest in everything.

Scientists, the roving scouts of the empiricist movement, are not immune to the idea of God. Those who favor it often lean toward some form of process theology. They ask this question: When the real world of space, time, and matter is well enough known, will that knowledge reveal the Creator's presence? Their hopes are vested in the theoretical physicists who pursue the goal of the final theory, the Theory of Everything, T.O.E., a system of interlocking equations that describe all that can be learned of the forces of the physical universe. T.O.E. is a "beautiful" theory, as Steven Weinberg has called it in his important essay *Dreams of a Final Theory.* Beautiful because it will be elegant, expressing the possibility of unending complexity with minimal laws, and symmetric, because it will hold invariant through all space and time. And inevitable, meaning that once stated no part can be changed without invalidating the whole. All surviving subtheories can be fitted into it permanently, in the manner in which Einstein described his own contribution, the general theory of relativity. "The chief attraction of the theory," Einstein said, "lies in its logical completeness. If a single one of the conclusions drawn from it proves wrong, it must be given up; to modify it without destroying the whole structure seems to be impossible."

The prospect of a final theory by the most mathematical of scientists might seem to signal the approach of a new religious awakening. Stephen Hawking, yielding to the temptation in *A Brief History of Time* (1988), declared that this scientific achievement would be the ultimate triumph of human reason, "for then we would know the mind of God."

Well—perhaps, but I doubt it. Physicists have already laid in place a large part of the final theory. We know the trajectory; we can see roughly where it is headed. But there will be no religious epiphany, at least none recognizable to the authors of Holy Scripture. Science has taken us very far from the personal God who once presided over Western civilization. It has done little to satisfy our instinctual hunger so poignantly expressed by the psalmist:

> *Man liveth his days like a shadow, and he disquieteth himself in vain with prideful delusions; his treasures, he knoweth not who shall gather them. Now, Lord, what is my comfort? My hope is in thee.*

The essence of humanity's spiritual dilemma is that we evolved genetically to accept one truth and discovered another. Is there a way to erase the dilemma, to resolve the contradictions between the transcendentalist and empiricist world views?

No, unfortunately, there is not. Furthermore, a choice between them is unlikely to remain arbitrary forever. The assumptions underlying the two world views are being tested with increasing severity by cumulative verifiable knowledge about how the universe works, from atom to brain to galaxy. In addition, the harsh lessons of history have made it clear that one code of ethics is not as good—at least, not as durable—as another. The same is true of religions. Some cosmologies are factually less correct than others, and some ethical precepts are less workable.

There is a biologically based human nature, and it is relevant to ethics and religion. The evidence shows that because of its influence, people can be readily educated to only a narrow range of ethical precepts. They flourish within certain belief systems, and wither under others. We need to know exactly why.

To that end I will be so presumptuous as to suggest how the conflict between the world views will most likely be settled. The idea of a genetic, evolutionary origin of moral and religious beliefs will be tested by the continuance of biological studies of complex human behavior. To the extent that the sensory and nervous systems appear to have evolved by natural selection or at least some other purely material process, the empiricist interpretation will be supported. It will be further supported by verification of gene-culture coevolution, the essential linking process described in earlier chapters.

Now consider the alternative. To the extent that ethical and religious phenomena do *not* appear to have evolved in a manner congenial to biology, and especially to the extent that such complex behavior cannot be linked to physical events in the sensory and nervous systems, the empiricist position will have to be abandoned and a transcendentalist explanation accepted.

For centuries the writ of empiricism has been spreading into the ancient domain of transcendentalist belief, slowly at the start but quickening in the scientific age. The spirits our ancestors knew intimately first fled the rocks and trees, then the distant mountains. Now they are in the stars, where their final extinction is possible. *But we cannot live without them.* People need a sacred narrative. They must have a sense of larger purpose, in one form or other, however intellectualized. They will refuse to yield to the despair of animal mortality. They will continue to plead in company with the psalmist, *Now, Lord, what is my comfort?* They will find a way to keep the ancestral spirits alive.

If the sacred narrative cannot be in the form of a religious cosmology, it will taken from the material history of the universe and the human species. That trend is in no way debasing. The true evolutionary epic, retold as poetry, is as intrinsically ennobling as any religious epic. Material reality discovered by science already possesses more content and grandeur than all religious cosmologies combined. The continuity of the human line has been traced through a period of deep history a thousand times older than that conceived by the Western religions. Its study has brought new revelations of great moral importance. It has made us realize that *Homo sapiens* is far more than a congeries of tribes and races. We are a single gene pool from which individuals are drawn in each generation and into which they are dissolved the next generation, forever united as a species by heritage and a common future. Such are the conceptions, based on fact, from which new intimations of immortality can be drawn and a new mythos evolved.

Which world view prevails, religious transcendentalism or scientific empiricism, will make a great difference in the way humanity claims the future. During the time the matter is under advisement, an accommodation can be reached if the following overriding facts are realized. On the one side, ethics and religion are still too complex for present-day science to explain in depth. On the other, they are far more a product of autonomous evolution than hitherto conceded by most theologians. Science faces in ethics and religion its most interesting and possibly humbling challenge, while religion must somehow find the way to incorporate the discoveries of science in order to retain credibility. Religion will possess strength to the extent that it codifies and puts into enduring, poetic form the highest values of humanity consistent with empirical knowledge. That is the only way to provide compelling moral leadership. Blind faith, no matter how passionately expressed, will not suffice. Science for its part will test relentlessly every assumption about the human condition and in time uncover the bedrock of the moral and religious sentiments.

The eventual result of the competition between the two world views, I believe, will be the secularization of the human epic and of religion itself. However the process plays out, it demands open discussion and unwavering intellectual rigor in an atmosphere of mutual respect.

Double Take

1. Now that you have read Edward O. Wilson's "Ethics and Religion," do you see his playing out the argument between the transcendentalist and the empiricist as an effective strategy? Why or why not?
2. By addressing ethics and religion, Wilson is taking on two fairly broad and demanding subjects. What are his goals in addressing these large subjects? What sort of audience do you suppose he is addressing? Who is Wilson writing to? For?
3. Wilson has a single paragraph that reads: "And yes—lest I forget—I may be wrong." What is his reason for writing this? What effect does making such a concession have on his overall argument?

Seeing for Yourself

At First Glance

In this essay, Edward O. Wilson creates an anthropomorphized world of termites in order to articulate the difficult idea that "human beings possess a species-specific nature and morality, which occupy only a tiny section of the space of all possible social and moral conditions." In "Humanity Seen from a Distance," Wilson is trying to explain a difficult scientific concept to an audience much larger than the scientific community—an audience that might not have the scientific background to understand the concept as a scientific hypothesis. Think about how the "termitocentric fantasy" affects your understanding of the essay and why Wilson might have decided to use this example while writing to an audience of nonscientists.

Humanity Seen from a Distance

All man's troubles arise from the fact
that we do not know what we are
and do not agree on what we want to be.

VERCORS (JEAN BRULLER),
You Shall Know Them (1953)

Here is the commencement address of the distinguished dean of the faculty of the International Termite University:

> On one thing we can surely agree! We are the pinnacle of 3 billion years of evolution, unique by virtue of our high intelligence, employment of symbolic language, and diversity of cultures evolved over hundreds of generations. Our species alone has sufficient self-awareness to perceive history and the meaning of personal mortality. Having largely escaped the sovereignty of our genes, we now base social organization mostly or entirely upon culture. Our universities disseminate knowledge from the three great branches of learning: the natural sciences, the social sciences, and the termitities. Since our ancestors, the macrotermitine termites, achieved 10-kilogram weight and larger brains during their rapid evolution through the later Tertiary period and learned to write with pheromone script, termitistic scholarship has refined ethical philosophy. It is now possible to express the deontological imperatives of moral behavior with precision. These imperatives are mostly self-evident and universal. They are the very essence of termity. They include the love of darkness and of the deep, saprophytic, basidiomycetic penetralia of the soil; the central-

ity of colony life amidst a richness of war and trade among colonies; the sanctity of the physiological caste system; the evil of personal reproduction by worker castes; the mystery of deep love for reproductive siblings, which turns to hatred the instant they mate; rejection of the evil of personal rights; the infinite aesthetic pleasures of pheromonal song; the aesthetic pleasure of eating from nestmates' anuses after the shedding of the skin; the joy of cannibalism and surrender of the body for consumption when sick or injured (it is more blessed to be eaten than to eat); and much more . . .

Some termitistically inclined scientists, particularly the ethologists and sociobiologists, argue that our social organization is shaped by our genes and that our ethical precepts simply reflect the peculiarities of termite evolution. They assert that ethical philosophy must take into account the structure of the termite brain and the evolutionary history of the species. Socialization is genetically channeled and some forms of it all but inevitable. This proposal has created a major academic controversy. Many scholars in the social sciences and termitities, refusing to believe that termite nature can be better understood by a study of fishes and baboons, have withdrawn behind the moat of philosophical dualism and reinforced the crenellated parapets of the formal refutation of the naturalistic fallacy. They consider the mind to be beyond the reach of materialistic biological research. A few take the extreme view that conditioning can alter termite culture and ethics in almost any direction desired. But the biologists respond that termite behavior can never be altered so far as to resemble that of, say, human beings. There is such a thing as a biologically based termite nature . . .

I have concocted this termitocentric fantasy to illustrate a generalization strangely difficult to explain by conventional means: that human beings possess a species-specific nature and morality, which occupy only a tiny section in the space of all possible social and moral conditions. If intelligent life exists on other planets (and the consensus of astronomers and biochemists is that it does, in abundance), we cannot expect it to be hominoid, mammalian, eucaryotic, or even DNA based. We should rescue the contemplation of other civilizations from science fiction. Real science tries to characterize not just the real world but all possible worlds. It identifies them within the much vaster space of all conceivable worlds studied by philosophers and mathematicians.

The social sciences and humanities have been blinkered by a steadfastly nondimensional and nontheoretical view of mankind. They focus on one point, the human species, without reference to the space of all possible species natures in which it is embedded. To be anthropocentric is to remain unaware of the limits of human nature, the significance of biological processes underlying human behavior, and the deeper meaning of long-term genetic evolution. That larger perspective can be gained only by moving back from the species, step by step, and taking a deliberately more distanced view.

In order to see the significance of multidimensionality, consider human social behaviors as a frequency-distribution function. The sociologist is perhaps closest of all to the array described by the function. Immersed in minute details of local culture, the typical sociologist fills the role of the local naturalist among the social scientists. He is not much concerned with the limits and ultimate meaning of human behavior. Indeed, he is likely to be oblivious to such distant matters, for the intricacy of detail seen in literate cultures is more than sufficiently important and absorbing to hold the attention of a first-rate scholar. The anthropologist and primatologist take a more distant view and are the equivalent of biogeographers. They have an interest in gobal patterns in the distribution of social traits, and they search for rules and laws to explain these peculiarities. The zoologist is the most removed. His concern is the tens of thousands of social species among the colonial invertebrates, social insects, and nonhuman vertebrates. The diversity he sees is enormous, but there is sufficient convergence in some categories of behavior among otherwise disparate taxonomic groups to raise in his mind the hope that general laws governing their genetic evolution might be adduced, just as studies of rats, fruit flies, and colon bacteria have yielded principles of genetics and physiology that could then be extended to human beings.

Of course, human social behavior has unique qualities unlikely to be predicted from a general, animal-based sociobiology. It cannot be compared to the purely mechanical behavior of human chromosomes and neuron membranes, which function almost exactly like those of rodents and insects. The human social repertoire now evolves along a dual track of inheritance: conventional genetic transmission, which is altered by conventional Darwinian natural selection; and cultural transmission, which is Lamarckian (traits acquired by the individual's adaptation are passed directly to offspring) and much swifter. Furthermore, unique features of organization exist: fully symbolic, endlessly productive language; long-remembered contracts based on convention; a complex materials-based culture; and religion. But the fact that humankind has entered a new zone of evolution is not evidence that the species has shed genetic constraint. Nor does sublimity necessarily elevate a species above biology. Traits that intelligent beings regard as transcendent may have arisen as biological adaptations while remaining obedient to genetic programs. The migratory flight of the golden plover from the Yukon to Patagonia and back is a marvel, but its brain and wings are made from organic polymers, and the 10,000-mile route of its journey is as necessary to the completion of its life cycle as its daily meal of beach fleas and insects. Substantial evidence exists that human behavior as a whole, including the most complex forms subject to the greatest cultural variation, is both genetically constrained and to some degree ultimately adaptive in the strict Darwinian sense. Thus social theory can be regarded as continuous with evolutionary biology.

If the perspective of the social sciences and humanities has been nondimensional in space, it has been equally restricted in time. This may seem a strange statement given that the examination of historical change is undeniably at the heart of each of the major disciplines. But all the analysis is based on a single species and, beyond that, on what is assumed to be a single genotype—the principle of the psychic unity of humankind. This conception of human sociality, though comforting, is inadequate for the needs of social theory. The evidence is strong that human populations vary to a degree typical of animal populations in behavioral traits, in particular in the genetic components of number ability, word fluency, memory, perceptual skill, psychomotor skill, extroversion–introversion, proneness to homosexuality, proneness to alcoholism, susceptibility to certain forms of neurosis and psychosis, timing of language acquisition and other major steps in cognitive development, age at first sexual activity, and other individual phenotypes that affect social organization. There is also evidence of geographic variation across human populations, in other words "racial" differences, in the earliest motor and temperament development of newborns.

Although genetic evolution is slow, it can occur rapidly enough to differ in rate from cultural evolution by only one or two orders of magnitude. Under only moderate selection pressures, one gene can be mostly substituted for another throughout an entire population in as few as ten generations, a period of only 200 or 300 years in the case of human beings. A single gene can profoundly alter behavior, especially when it affects the threshold of response or level of excitability. However, new, complex patterns of behavior are based on multiple genes, which can be assembled only over much longer periods, perhaps hundreds or even thousands of generations. For this reason we do not expect to find that human nature has been altered greatly during historical times, or that people in industrial societies differ basically from those in preliterate, hunter-gatherer societies. But the possibility that some genetic change has occurred has not been eliminated, and it cannot be assumed that small amounts of genetic change are easily washed out by the effects of socialization during the lifetimes of individuals.

If these elementary estimates are correct, significant elements of behavior might have originated within the past 100,000 years. In fact, contemporary human nature need not be the product of the history of the ancestral *Australopithecus afarensis–Homo habilis* line 2 to 4 million years ago. It is more likely a biogram shaped gradually throughout the history of *Homo,* up to and including the historic period. Thus social theory could profit by extending its reach just beyond the historical period dominated by cultural evolution to the near prehistoric period during which more nearly balanced combinations of genetic and cultural change occurred.

A CLOSER LOOK AT EDWARD O. WILSON

1. In each of these essays, Edward O. Wilson discusses some rather grand and important topics: culture, science, religion, human nature, and so on. Write an essay explaining how Wilson validates his authority to speak and write on these subjects. Why would a reader be receptive to Wilson's points? What gives him the credibility to write about such issues?

2. In "The Writing Life," Wilson makes the argument for linking scientific writing with more personal, literary narrative. He specifically identifies the absence of metaphor in scientific writing and the artistic use of metaphor in literature. In Wilson's other essays gathered here, in which he is not writing about writing, does he act out his desire to blend more metaphoric writing with scientific information? In what ways? What effect does such a strategy have on our reading of these pieces? Write an essay in which you analyze these other essays based on Wilson's own claim about scientific writing and more literary writing.

3. Wilson's agenda to link scientific writing with "literary" writing is not a simple task. Many issues such as vocabulary, audience, content, form, style, and so on affect how he bridges these discourses. The same would hold true for any convergence of discourses. Write an essay that addresses how other kinds of writing (e.g., business writing, technical writing, legal writing, medical writing) might also work (or not work) in more literary forms. What problems or advantages might arise in linking these genres?

Looking from Writer to Writer

1. Edward O. Wilson is a scientist, as is Stephen J. Gould. Yet each has taken upon himself the task of sharing scientific study with as large an audience as possible through his writing, making science a popular subject. Each of these two scientists is known as much for his writing as for his scientific discoveries. Compare the essays in this book by these scientist-writers and consider how they write about science and how they make that science accessible to their readers. Do you find one more accessible than the other? Why?

2. In his essay "The Writing Life," Edward O. Wilson characterizes a difference between "scientific writing" and "literature." Likewise, Barry Lopez, in his essay "We Are Shaped by the Sound of the Wind, the Slant of Sunlight," offers a characterization of "nature writing." Looking at both of these essays, construct a set of definitions that explains the differences and similarities between scientific writing and nature writing. Can nature writing be scientific? Are there examples

of other writers in this book whose work exemplifies the characteristics of either nature writing or scientific writing as Wilson and Lopez have described them?

3. In his essay "The Serpent," Edward O. Wilson offers a few anecdotes about his childhood and snakes. Several other writers in this book also use anecdotes about childhood, notably those provided in Henry Louis Gates, Jr.'s essays. Each of these writers certainly has distinctively different styles of writing, yet each finds the personal anecdote an effective strategy. Compare the ways that Wilson and Gates use the personal anecdote and consider how each uses this similar strategy in different ways and the effect of doing so on their writing.

Looking Beyond

NONFICTION

The Ants (with Bert Holldobler). Cambridge, MA: Belknap-Harvard University Press, 1990.

Biophilia. Cambridge, MA: Harvard University Press, 1984.

Caste and Ecology in the Social Insects (with George F. Oster). Princeton, NJ: Princeton University Press, 1978.

Consilience: The Unity of Knowledge. New York: Random House, 1998.

The Diversity of Life. Cambridge, MA: Belknap-Harvard University Press, 1992.

In Search of Nature. Washington, DC: Island Press, 1996.

The Insect Societies. Cambridge, MA: Belknap-Harvard University Press, 1971.

Journey to the Ants: A Story of Scientific Exploration (with Bert Holldobler). Cambridge, MA: Belknap-Harvard University Press, 1994.

Naturalist. Washington DC: Island Press, 1994.

On Human Nature. Cambridge, MA: Harvard University Press, 1978.

Sociobiology: The New Synthesis. 1980. Twenty-Fifth Anniversary Edition. Cambridge, MA:Belknap-Harvard University Press, 2000.

rew up in a place
ere the truth is in the
dows—which is to say
re is none, and one
kes it up. I grew up
h so many things that
e, well, not quite
; but when people
them enough, they
ame true, or were
epted as true. •
o's afraid of Virginia
olf? Every little
ho dodo, from Hem-
way to Mailer. There
o more subversive act
1 the act of writing
n a woman's experi-
e of life using a
nan's judgment. •
nclude nature in our
ies is to return to an
r form of human
reness in which
re is not scenery, not
arehouse of natural
urces, not real estate,
a possession, but a
tinuation of commu-
• If permission to
e (and for a writer
is exactly equal to
power to write) is a
then what of the lack
ermission? • A few
s ago I revisited
bay, which is my lost
after an absence of
thing like half my
• What concerned
ow was how a sub-

THE STUDENT WRITERS

Essays about Writing

Sarah Huntley

Sarah Huntley, 20, studies English and religion at the University of Florida. She has volunteered with Young Life, a nondenominational Christian youth ministry, and works during the summer at a girl's camp. Her favorite color is blue, and she enjoys mint chocolate chip ice cream. She likes to spend time outdoors and takes part in activities such as camping, hiking, and playing in the rain.

Huntley on Writing

At First Glance

Sarah Huntley's essay "Before Beginning" addresses issues that new writers face and considers what writers must think about before they become writers. One of the interesting links that Huntley makes here is the relationship between reading and writing, between being a reader and being a writer. As you read this essay, you assume the role of reader to Huntley's writer. Consider how Huntley sees the act of reading, and ask yourself if you are fulfilling that role. At the same time, notice the tone with which Huntley constructs her argument. Her position is powerful, yet her writing expresses that power with a subtle complacence. What rhetorical choices has Huntley made regarding the tone and voice of her essay that allow her to make such a powerful, yet calming, argument? Does that calming tone affect how you, as reader, approach the essay? Notice also Huntley's view of the essay. She claims, "the essay lends itself as more available than fiction or poetry." Consider how available and accessible her own essay is.

Before Beginning

There are questions, so it seems, that authors ask themselves about the nature of their chosen craft. Their answers are many and varied in results, but common in their quest—how do I, as an author, write. Orwell's "Why I Write," Dillard's *The Writing Life,* Stephen King's *On Writing,* Kerouac's dashed-off "Belief and Technique for Modern Prose," bell hooks's *Remembered Rapture,* and many other contemplations on writing provide insights into the minds of established authors. To ask myself the question of why I write or how I write seems premature, though. As a student of writing, and a young one at that, the world of writing is not yet under my belt, and certainly not mastered enough to have any authority on the subject. The question of writing becomes for me, then, a sort of mission statement—a gathering of thoughts and a deep breath before beginning. Writing pulls on me, undeniable and unsatisfied. Why I write is a question left for the future. The question that presses now: Why *will* I write?

Who writes? Many people write, but very few of them would consider themselves writers. Business letters, journals, research papers, e-mails to friends and acquaintances, car manuals, or texts on the backs of shampoo bottles or cereal boxes—these are all writings that require a knowledge of the audience, word choice, and a basic understanding of composition, but something in the term "writer" implies a more deliberate approach. This deliberate approach is specific in the crafting of sentences, in word choice and arrangement for effectiveness and aesthetic appeal, in understanding the power and seductiveness of certain ideas or story lines. The writer should understand her audience; she should lure the reader in.

There are, no doubt, many readers out there. The corporate successes of giant bookstores, housed in warehouse-sized storefronts with overstuffed armchairs and accompanying cafes, and even larger Internet-based booksellers may strike blows against those little friendly neighborhood bookstores, but they are perhaps indicative of a culture that reads—or at least needs over a million titles to choose from. For some readers, a bookshelf may amount to little more than a trophy case. The increasing influence of a television book club that pushes issues of literacy and even turns authors into celebrities also points to the widening popularization of literature.

What makes a reader among all those that read? Is it enough to have a shelf full of books read and displayed as trophies of accumulated knowledge? Perhaps a reader's taste should be dynamic and up with the times. The telling sense of urgency—always a new book waiting to be read while the other is pulled out at the breakfast table, on coffee breaks, or at bedtime—often accompanies those who consider themselves avid readers. Is a reader one who is genuinely affected by what one reads?

My mother read *The Lion, The Witch, and The Wardrobe* to me when I was still a young girl, and for what I remember as being months afterwards, I would check the backs of our closets. At an age when I was probably too old to really believe that I might find a snowy wood and Mr. Tumnus behind my family's winter coats, I still wanted to believe. Even at that young age, I had become a reader.

Perhaps part of the attraction of being a reader lies in having an emotion articulated for you. In light of the work it can take to understand it, the popularity of *Romeo and Juliet* to an adolescent audience astounds me. A recent Hollywood version, with then teen heartthrobs Leonardo DiCaprio and Claire Danes, grossed over $46 million. I am sure that much of that film's success came out of its all-star cast and highly stylized filming, but teenagers were still affected by something written four centuries earlier. Maybe teens still enjoy reading Shakespeare because they feel like the plays understand them. Pining after the boy that her parents will not let her date, young Suzy Teenager clutches her pillow and reads, with the help of footnotes, a lament over forbidden love. Suzy Teenager, at this moment, is affected by the power of words over emotion.

Why will I write? To understand something by being able to articulate it, to pin down a feeling with words and have it in my grasp? No. If the only purpose for writing is to understand our lives a little better, then that attempt is better left for diaries and journals, and one has to be pretty famous and probably dead to have their journals published. Writers, then, must have something to offer, something to share with their proposed audience.

Questions must sometimes be asked before something can begin. Why should I train for a triathlon? Why would I want to get married? The question of why I will write seems just as drastic an undertaking as the other questions. So many writers, in fact, come across as dead set against their own profession. In a recent lecture, Dr. Elie Wiesel commented briefly on the profession of writing. "If you can live without writing," he advised an auditorium full of students, professors, and interested public, "do it." Similarly, in *The Writing Life,* Annie Dillard wrote, "Why people want to be writers, I will never know, unless it is that their lives lack a material footing." With prospects looking so daunting and even bleak, the question should be weighed carefully. I have, after all, sat down to try my hand at essays before. Information and short quotes written on Post-it notes stick to my walls and then are later taped for durability as I struggle at my computer for hours. As a student and someone with an admittedly young voice, trying to flesh out lofty thoughts and connections can be heart wrenching. Still, the pull toward writing gets to me. Maybe I lack that material footing—the common sense to preserve my sanity. Maybe part of the drive toward writing is that challenge itself. Mountain climbers don't head toward Everest because the snow is prettier there or life more dazzling when one's oxygen is coming from a can. Climbers are after the challenge. Of course, the ardor of college-level essay writing (or maybe any writing for that matter) should not be compared to climbing Mount Everest. After all, I have never heard of anyone dying of a difficult essay.

I am encouraged that writing is a skill, something to work at. Jack Kerouac, in a later essay, speculated on the question of whether great writers are born or made. He answered straightforwardly: "Writers are made, for anybody who isn't illiterate can write; but geniuses of the writing art like Melville, Whitman, or Thoreau are born." I think that most of us speculating on the handling of words would be willing to settle for less than genius. Geniuses are so often misunderstood anyway, right?

We write and rewrite; we study other writers; we take classes on writing; we read books about writing. I recently searched Amazon.com and found 19,582 titles of books about writing. They ranged from the indispensable *Elements of Style* to more existential topics of spirit and writing, from junior high creative writing teachers to established and renowned authors. There is an economy built around the craft of writing. Certainly, writers are made and not born. Many authors have admitted to either being terrible writers when they first began or having begun only out of necessity. William Kennedy said that a "retarded orangutan could write a better story" than his first short story. What a relief that writing develops with work, fine-tuning, and even the hard-learned lesson of rejection. Why will I brave writing? I can write because I don't have to be perfect the first time around and it is something to get good at, something to work hard for.

Why would a writer choose the essay as his or her medium of choice? The essay lends itself as more available than fiction or poetry. John Loughery writes in the introduction to *The Eloquent Essay* that the essay has "an elasticity of form that has the advantage of appealing to a world of different tastes. The essay as a letter, review, story, appreciation, parody, portrait, travelogue, reminiscence, diatribe, dialogue, oration, dissection, debate, or as the seemingly ingenuous act of thinking aloud piques every literate person's curiosity at some time or other." In the introduction to *1989, The Best American Essays,* Geoffrey Wolff lamented that he had once been taught that the role of the writer is to "take facts in, quietly manipulate them behind an opaque scrim, and display them as though the arranger never arranged." One of the beauties of the modern essay is that the voice of the narrator can quietly hide itself, as in a John McPhee essay, or glaringly present itself, as in

Martin Luther King, Jr.'s, "Letter from a Birmingham Jail." The essay can be long or short, persuasive or undecided, pragmatic or poetic. Essays can present a straightforward line of thought, without readers having to "find the hidden meaning," an element of fiction that Dillard explores in *Living by Fiction*.

I will write, sharing what I have to offer with other readers. I will write, understanding the gravity of such an undertaking. I will write, but *why?* What do I have to share? I believe in appreciating life—in paying careful attention to air and soil, sunlight and shadow, beauty and pain. Appreciation comes with a noticing, a watching of fine details. I first read *The Color Purple* during my freshman year in college. Although the story was powerful, it is the implications of the title that affect me daily. I have passed fields of purple and have had to stop and take notice. I have come into the habit of pointing out the colors of wildflowers—the fall and play of shadows and light. This habit is more than a reminder of literature, more than a reminder of beauty; it is a code for living, a code for appreciation.

Appreciation stems from understanding as well as noticing. In *A Natural History of the Senses*, Diane Ackerman examines the fine workings and implications of smell, touch, taste, hearing, and vision. After reading that book, the world fairly comes alive, and one has to try and shut two or three senses out, so that one sense can prevail and be reveled in. I will write for appreciation.

There are spring-fed rivers near my town. On hot summer days we can drive down to the spring sources and go swimming. The springs themselves run a deep blue-green, and the water feels clean and cold as it pushes with purity and force into the river. The river runs cold—a stark contradiction against the heat of the day. While no plants grow close to the spring source, the river is alive with long and slick river weeds that are a deep green; the appearance of the river is mottled with the play of shadows from the trees above with light and the dark plants against the sandy bottom. One particular afternoon, the air was so hot and the water so cold that it took my breath away, but my friends and I stayed in all afternoon. We swam against the current; we pushed each other into the weeds; we did flips in the water and jumped from trees along the side. We floated on our backs and laughed and played and swam until we were too tired to do anything but drag ourselves onto the bank and lay out of breath and slightly shivering in the sun.

"This is why," I leaned over and confidently told my friend.

"This is why, what?" he asked.

"This is why we like Florida."

I gained a new appreciation for my home state that day. I learned to appreciate it by enjoying it.

I read John McPhee's *Oranges*. I visited south Florida, and a friend's small grove of orange trees was more alive in my mind than it could have ever been before. I noticed the sharp smell of orange blossoms; I understood why one of the trees grew oranges on one side, grapefruit on the other; I savored glass after glass of freshly squeezed orange juice. I first read Annie Dillard's *Pilgrim at Tinker Creek* by flashlight, camped only a few miles from Tinker Mountain itself. I noticed the light that played off each leaf in the trees; I understood a little about the dragonfly nymphs that hovered above the ponds; I swam and played in the river that rushed by our campsite.

We make this world our home by appreciating it. Whether we are in Florida, Virginia, or halfway across the globe, we should notice the fine details, understand some of the workings of where we are, and, above all, enjoy our surroundings. I will write because I want other people, that potentially small audience that will listen, to feel the surprising joy of really appreciating wherever they are. Braving rejection and the tortuous process of crafting an essay, I will write to share what I have to offer.

We can grasp the world and make it home by learning to savor it—to enjoy it and understand it. Dillard writes, "The writer looking for subjects inquires not after what he loves best, but after what he alone loves at all." What, then, is my proposed role of writer? Am I the street-corner preacher on the proverbial soapbox— ranting of truth, of something so worth sharing that even a small crowd of listeners makes a difference? So the writer raises his or her thoughts in one hand and waves to a small crowd gathering—this is life; this is the way to see it. This seems a romanticized view, I know, but I suppose that most mission statements are romanticized. After all, writing is a challenge and my deep breath before beginning had better be a big breath indeed.

Double Take

1. The title of Sarah Huntley's essay is "Before Beginning." What do you do before you begin to write?
2. What sort of relationship does Huntley set up between the reader and writer? To what extent are readers and writers compatible? To what extent are they or can they be at odds?
3. In this essay, Huntley shifts her discussion from reading to writing to Florida. How does she manage this movement? Pay attention to her use of transitions and other rhetorical strategies.

Monique Fournier

Monique Fournier graduated with a BA in English from the University of Hawaii at Hilo in 2001. She spent her formative years in northern Virginia, but has lived all over the country. A four-year break between her sophomore and junior years—during which time she enlisted in the United States Coast Guard—convinced Fournier that perhaps college isn't all that bad. *Kanilehua,* the University of Hawaii, Hilo's art and literary magazine, awarded her work second and third place in fall 2000 and first place in spring 2001. Fournier has yet to admit that she wants to be a writer when she grows up.

Fournier on Writing

At First Glance

Monique Fournier writes about voice, particularly about finding her own voice in her writing, even her college writing. As you read her essay, "Bees and Fears: Why I Write," you may notice that Fournier has developed a very distinct voice. As you read and become familiar with her voice, think about the ways that she has carefully constructed that voice for her audience. Also, consider how her construction of that voice lends to making this a personal essay.

Bees and Fears: Why I Write

Much of what I have written is never seen by anyone but me. I have notebooks full of poems and unfinished stories dating back to high school. Breaking them out when I'm feeling melancholy, I flip through each work and study it as if it is an artifact from a particular era in my life. And I suppose each one is. It's a shame that my fears keep me from sharing these pieces of my past. I share the fact that I write—that I'm a writer—with few of the people close to me. I've often felt that I internalize too much—analyze every little word and action I come in contact with. I think about these little things for so long that they begin to take on a life of their own, and I become scared to ever share them with anyone else. Does anyone ever *truly* understand another? Sometimes I fool myself into believing the answer is yes, but then I see that slight glaze in the eyes of the listener and I redecide to never share these overanalyzed little thoughts again. After especially frustrating nights of feeling that no one is interested, I return home and pound out my feelings into my hard drive. Or I wake up minutes after falling asleep, a few words linked perfectly together in my head. I frantically scratch them down on whatever is convenient—scrap paper, tissues, backs of books.

I agree with George Orwell when he reports that sheer egoism is the first reason why writers write. It is the first motive of four from his "Why I Write" essay. I think I do write out of sheer egoism. I want to be seen as clever, to be known, to be talked about. None of which will ever happen if I insist on never showing anyone anything personal I have written. I took small steps recently, entering some of my work in my university's literary magazine. Winning a prize two of the times I entered did nothing to bolster my opinion of my writing. Instead, I've convinced myself that it must not be a very good magazine. Or perhaps there were very few entries. Maybe the judges chose randomly, and I just got lucky. Sheer egoism can exist, I suppose, right alongside poor self-image.

762

I write because people confuse me. The egoist in me can never understand why others don't look at the world the same way as I do. I become disappointed, for example, with every person who thinks it silly that I didn't take my husband's last name. And I think they in turn are disappointed that my reasons have little to do with feminism. I kept my own name simply because I'm confounded why so many people do not question why they don't. They just sign their marriage license with a new last name as if it is the natural order of things and aberrant to do otherwise. (I also find it unfair that if I had taken my husband's name, I would've had to change every card I carry in my wallet and call every agency that bills me while he would have to do nothing.) My brain is made crazy by not understanding why people tend to insist on accepting the status quo without question. I deal with my internal reactions to people and society by writing them down.

I write because I am closer to finding my writing voice than I ever have been before. Six years ago, I dropped out of college after completing my sophomore year. I assumed that it was because college wasn't for me, that I just wasn't meant for the classroom. It turns out that I wasn't ready for college writing. I now believe that once a writer finds her voice, she can easily apply it to any college level writing assignment. Writing those first two years was difficult for me because I was simply plugging chains of words into every paper without any "me" glue to hold them together. Realizing I have a voice, and taking steps to uncover it, has helped me (and my grade point average) immensely during my undergraduate career. The professors who have influenced me the most are great voice guides. Intentionally or not, they rein in the urge to beat a student's natural voice into submitting to their own. They instead provide the environment in which a voice is allowed to be discovered and developed by the student. Beyond teaching students the tools and skills needed in the mechanics of writing, the best thing a professor can do is be a nonintrusive guide.

I write because I have to. A few weeks ago I saw a special on The Learning Channel or The Discovery Channel (one of those channels that make me feel smarter only because it's rare that I have the willpower to flip past MTV and watch informative programming). The special was all about killer bees. I've heard random things about killer bees . . . a bit of news brief here and there. It wasn't the special that became so interesting to me. It was one little side story within the special.

Included within killer bee facts was a short aside concerning the uses of bee colonies. Apparently, trucks carrying boxes of beehives drive all around various parts of the world and stop at orchards to pollinate the fields. Said boxed beehives usually have special grids in front of the openings so that only the worker bees can escape. The worker bees always return to the hive, to their queen, who can't fit through the grids because of her larger size. So the bees escape. They pollinate the crop, and return to the boxed hive—where, if I remember correctly, the grids are covered for the trip—and the truck carrying the beehives drives on to the next field. Stops can be extremely far apart, separated sometimes by hundreds or even thousands of miles.

For hours, all I could think about was the bees that might be left behind. I don't mean to anthropomorphize them too much—but can you imagine? You're just this little bee, and the only life you know is one in which you live in a manmade beehive with a big grid your only escape. All you want to do is what nature meant you to do—fly forth and pollinate, bringing back what you can to the hive so that the cycle of life will continue. So you go out, and you do your job, and then you fly back to see your manmade grilled hive moving away from you. Maybe you think you didn't do your job well enough, or fast enough, and this is your punishment. Or maybe you're just confused, and can't figure out in your little bee brain why your hive is moving. But there you are, in some strange field, doing what you're supposed to be doing, and coming to grips with the fact that you will never see your hive or your queen again. I assume that this little bee can only live for a limited amount of time outside of her structured bee society. She might fly around a bit more, pollinating until her pockets are full. But what does the bee really have to look forward to anymore?

And this made me sad. I felt the need to tell someone else this story. But who to tell? Chances are that my listener's eyes would glaze over with disinterest. (Chances are also good that I perceive a glaze of disinterest in others that does not exist—some self-created result stemming from a fear of rejection. Disinterest, to me, is one of the worst forms of rejection, no matter whether it is true or simply perceived.)

So I write. I write this now, getting it out of my system so I won't feel the need to share it vocally. And I feel a little bad about everything else I have ever written, because at this moment I feel that nothing can ever be as important as that bee coming home from work to find her whole life driving away from her at 70 miles an hour.

I write because I am a writer, regardless of whether I ever admit so aloud.

Double Take

1. Describe Monique Fournier's tone in "Bees and Fears: Why I Write." How would you characterize it? What does it sound like? How does she create this tone? Look for specific examples.
2. In this essay, Fournier reflects on what it means to be a writer. What is your sense of what it means to be a writer? Do you think of yourself as a writer? Why or why not?
3. Fournier begins her essay by disclosing her vulnerabilities as a writer. What effect does such disclosure have on you as a reader? How does it shape the way you read the essay? What are the merits and drawbacks of beginning this way?

Melvin Sterne

Before returning to college, Melvin Sterne spent 25 years working union construction, traveling, and writing. While completing his BA in English at the University of Washington, he volunteered as a creative writing teacher working with at-risk high school students. He is currently pursuing an MFA in creative writing at the University of California, Davis, where he also teaches writing.

Sterne on Writing

At First Glance

In this essay, Melvin Sterne makes an argument about the need to respect and preserve a writer's identity. As you read the essay, think about the choices he makes in constructing his argument—from his organization to his claims to his examples to his word choices and to his tone—and their effects. Think also about how these choices might have different effects on different readers. How, for example, would professors perceive these choices compared to how other students might perceive them? Who do you think is Sterne's target audience? Along the way, consider what Sterne means when he claims that writing is a process of socialization.

Untitled

It is almost eight o'clock on a Monday morning. I've done my yoga, made my coffee, and now I'm sitting in front of my computer writing. Today I'm writing an essay about writing, but I could just as easily be editing the short story I wrote yesterday, working on a new story, my novel-in-progress, writing a poem, or working on the final paper for my lit class. It doesn't really matter to me because I *love* writing and given time, and nothing else to do, I write.

I remember when I was a boy my father gave me the "What are you going to do with your life?" speech. I replied that I wanted to be a writer. This wasn't a flippant remark inspired by juvenile imagination. I was dead serious. I believe I was lucky enough to know that early in life *exactly* what I wanted to do.

My father, of course, warned me that writers don't make any money—that I should become a doctor or a lawyer. So I entered college as a premed student, was miserable, and dropped out after my freshman year. I traveled around the country working union construction for years before returning to college. I carried a pencil and a 3 × 5 pad with me on the job, and if things got slow, or an idea popped into my head, I found a quiet corner to hide in and wrote it down. Some of my best work started out this way.

Twenty years later I returned to school. People ask me if school has helped my writing and the answer is not as much as they might think. When I worked construction, I worked on a job until it was finished, then moved on to another one. I would work for three months, get "moneyed-up," as they say, and then hang out and write for three months. And if I didn't feel like writing I could read. I've read thousands of short stories—not just read them, but thought about them. Asked myself questions like: *Why does this work? What are the author's goals, and how does he/she achieve them? What fictive choices does the author make? Why?* and *To what effect?* I talked to other writers, editors, and read books and articles about writing. I suppose you could say I put myself through a school of my own making. To me, that will always be the way to learn to write.

In college there is so much other work to do—books to read, essays to write, classes, labs, meetings to attend, and if you really want to stand out from the crowd you will find extracurricular activities to pursue. If you're young and want a social life—forget it! This is why so much college writing gets done at five o'clock in the morning on the day that it is due. I've pulled all-nighters more often than I would have liked. We don't like to admit it, but it's true. This is not the best way to write.

But writing is tough in college for more reasons than the lack of time. Professors complain that students coming out of high school don't know how to write. What they mean is that students coming out of high school don't know how to write *academically*. There is a difference. Granted I'm no expert, but I've taken enough composition and rhetoric to know that writing is largely a process of *socialization,* and the academic writing is about learning to *play the game.* Worse yet, the rules of the game are different for different departments. Different conventions apply to different writings. This can make learning to write very confusing for the student. Differences can be as trivial as citations in a bibliography, or as significant as stating your argument in passive or assertive form.

On some levels I understand and concur with the need to establish conventions. Academics must read, analyze, and digest large amounts of information in limited periods of time. To do that, they need to work efficiently, and organization is essential to the task. On the other hand, when educators become obsessed with details of convention, something is lost for the student. For instance, I have always questioned the wisdom of using writing as a test of subject knowledge. A student writes a history paper about the French Revolution and finds he or she has had points deducted for using passive language, too many commas, or beginning a sentence with a conjunction. Their final grade is not indicative of their knowledge of French history, but of their ability to communicate within the established convention. Worse yet, they may be judged by their instructor's understanding (or lack thereof) of that convention. Even university professors carry prejudices, their own opinions about what constitutes *good* writing.

I suppose the situation is tolerable—if our stated goal is to socialize students into a given field. But if our goal is to impart knowledge to as many students as possible, perhaps this strategy should be rethought. And make no mistake about it, most students see the process for what it is. While some respond by playing the game, others withdraw, fearing that their *identity* is at risk in the socialization process.

This is what is most disturbing to me—the feeling that writing to conventions squeezes the life out of young writers. You might say that a side effect of convention is to remove the person from the paper. Call it the great equalizer—the linguistic equivalent of school uniforms. The problem is that with younger writers, the more concerned they are likely to be with developing an identity and how they are being perceived by others. There is something inherently frightening about committing ideas to paper. It is impossible to write without imparting something of one's self to what is written. What students fear most is that they will be judged for *who they are,* not *what they say.* For the majority of students, writing is not a natural act; but as writing relates to identity, it is a sacred act. Teachers need to remember that behind the paper is a personality. Forcing students into conventions serves the discipline, not the person. And teachers should be mindful that writing can and should be *fun;* that participating in the dialogue of academia ought to be a rewarding experience in itself.

The funny thing is, "immutable" rules of grammar, punctuation, and spelling are relatively recent inventions. We know that languages change, and will continue to change, over time and geographic divides. The determination of "right" and "wrong" usage is arbitrary at best, racist at worst. Nonstandard varieties of English are demonstrated to be superior to "standard" English in many ways. In the worst application of language conventions, students from nonmainstream backgrounds are penalized for using what is, in effect, their own language.

I have been able to adapt tolerably well to academic writing conventions. Mostly. I must confess that I enjoy breaking rules when I think I can get away with it. My age and life's experiences have been assets to me. I am secure in who I am and focused on my academic goals. I am eager to acquire the writing skills I need to succeed in school. Most importantly, I am able to work enough in fiction (where conventions are less restrictive) so that I never felt my soul was in jeopardy.

Next year I will begin work on my master's degree in English. How far will I advance in academia? Who knows? My goal is to spend the rest of my life writing and teaching writing, hopefully at the college level. At the end of my career I would like to look back and say that I did some good work, wrote some good stories, and that my students learned in my classroom. Most importantly, I would like to know that my students emerged from my classroom more secure in themselves and confident in their abilities. I believe most students can become good writers. It is more important that they become good people. Conventions, like languages, are bound to change. The students in your class today will make those changes tomorrow.

Thanks for sharing this time with me. I think I'll make another cup of coffee now, then go back to work on my next short story.

Double Take

1. Early in the essay, Melvin Sterne describes how he learned to write. How did you learn to write? What do you remember most about when you were first taught to write? What rules or habits have stuck with you?
2. Using the very questions Sterne asks of other writers—What are the author's goals? How does he or she achieve them? What fictive choices does the author make? Why? Why do they work?—ask yourself: What are Sterne's goals in this essay, and how does he achieve them? Be specific in your response, drawing examples from the essay.
3. Sterne mentions the different writing conventions found in different disciplines. As a student writer, what differences in conventions and expectations have you experienced in writing for different disciplines and teachers?

Kathe McAllister

Kathe McAllister completed her MA in English, with an emphasis on creative writing, at Kansas State University in May 2001. She writes fiction, poetry, and nonfiction. In the future she plans to follow in the footsteps of Toni Morrison, who said of her early days: "I just kept on writing."

McAllister on Writing

At First Glance

In many ways, Kathe McAllister's essay "Blue Sky and Gravel: Where There Is No Plot" is both an argument and a demonstration. As you read it, watch for how McAllister practices what she preaches, paying special attention to the unconventional qualities of the writing and whether these qualities, in form and content, satisfactorily reflect her goals as a writer. In addition, think about how McAllister moves from one section of the essay to another while maintaining the meaning she is trying to convey. Finally, consider what McAllister might mean when she claims that the way we write reflects the way we see the world.

Blue Sky and Gravel: Where There Is No Plot

In my memory there walks a tangled line of people. Each person clutches the hand of the one in front as the line moves slowly, with little purpose—seemingly with no conscious volition. The people are easily distracted, they have difficulty walking in only one direction, their feet stumble. There is a woman, or perhaps sometimes it is a man, in the lead. I still see that white uniform marching before as they trail behind, though it is little more than a blur to me now. Those in the line have mostly become ciphers, a vague human squiggle on the lens of my mind's eye. Only one can I still see even somewhat clearly, she was a woman, and she walked at the end of the line. What I remember is the Kewpie doll she always carried suspended from loose fingers, which trailed in her wake like some mysterious bald fetish.

Madison Smart Bell's *Narrative Design* is one of the few writing guides I have come across that makes a useful distinction between what he terms "linear" design, or what we might term "conventional" narrative, and what he terms "modular" design, or what some like to call "post-modern" narrative. "I see two different ways, he writes, "quite distinct if not opposed, of thinking about the raw material of which narratives are made—two ways of contemplating original experience, whether real, imagined, or some blend of the two, to which the work will give form. You may think of the primary experience as a single amorphous mass of information. Or you may conceive of it as a grab bag of unassembled components—something like a jumble of unsnapped Legos, say." A writer with the first view, he states "sees the artifact [the raw material of experience] singly, as an integrated whole," this linear type of writer is most concerned with "the overall movement of the principal narrative vector from its start to its finish, all other issues being subordinate to this overarching concern." By contrast, he tells us that artists who see their raw material in the second way work to "assemble the work out of small component parts. This breed of artist is . . . [like a] mosaicist, assembling fragments of glass and tile to form what can be understood, at a greater distance, as a coherent, shapely image."

"Two different ways of writing," says Bell. "Quite distinct, if not *opposed*," he says. As a developing creative writer, I have found this distinction very important. I am currently writing a book about the loss of my mother. It's episodic, moving from the present to the past of 10 years ago, to the past of 12 years ago, to an imagined past, and then back again, sometimes within the space of several pages. There is no plot to speak of, only what writers often refer to as "voice." It's a book of fragments, of moments, of tiny understandings. It's a book composed of shards. There is no overarching narrative and no intricately grand plot. In other words, I've been approaching my work like the mosaicist Bell describes. While I certainly hope that when done, the book will be understood "at a greater distance, as a coherent, shapely image," what I do not foresee is a "principal narrative vector." I first read Bell's definition a year ago. It's comforting to me that he describes and understands how I approach my work. It's distressing to me that he also seems to be in the minority.

As I write this, I have just completed my master's degree in English and am the veteran of numerous workshops attended at my undergraduate institution, at summer writing programs, and during my graduate education. I have also facilitated informal community workshops of my own. In other words, I consider myself a veritable cesspool of workshopping information (OK, so not really, but suffice it to say that I've had my share of workshop experiences). On numerous occasions over the years I have turned in either parts of the novel I am working on or other creative pieces that do not conform to a conventional, overarching narrative form. The consternation this causes many of my readers has been remarkable. "Why do you keep on jumping around?" they ask, and "Why can't you just put all of the scenes in the order that they happened?" or, best of all, "Why is there no plot?" I should preface my remarks here by saying that I am not trying to defend what may truly be bad writing by slapping the label "post-modern" on it. I should also point out that much of the early work I was putting up for workshops did indeed have problems, as might be expected. However, those issues aside, what I have noticed all too often in workshops is a basic objection to any kind of writing that is not in conventional, linear narrative form. Many teachers and students of writing—at least those I have encountered—seem to operate from the basic assumption that good writers are writers who have approached their writing with a conventional narrative design in mind.

But this bias toward a conventional or "traditional" approach to narrative is understandable. After all, something doesn't get labeled traditional unless there is a tradition attached to it. Most of the writing in our Western world *is* linear. We are taught from the time we are small that stories ought to have a clear beginning, middle, and end. Things ought to happen for reason and, of course, it "makes sense" that events should follow logically from one another. Discussions and definitions of "plot" figure prominently in most writing guides, and it's likely that every school child in the United States has been in a classroom where the teacher sketched

Frietag's pyramid on the blackboard and explained the necessity of exposition, followed by complication, then the all-important crisis, leading to falling action, which results, finally, in the long-awaited resolution. Janet Burroway, in *Writing Fiction,* an extremely popular text used in beginning fiction classes, points out that the main trouble with Frietag's "useful diagram" is that "it visually suggests that a crisis comes in the middle," but as she goes on to outline, the crisis normally occurs closer to the end. While it's nice that Burroway doesn't think Frietag's model is perfect, the applicability of the model to creation of *all* narrative is never questioned. The traditional approach to writing is further reinforced by the majority of books that are a part of school curriculums. I still remember my own high school literature classes, which I spent slogging through such plot-heavy works as Thomas Hardy's *Tess of the D'Urbervilles,* and George Eliot's *Silas Marner.* We read linear texts, just as we are trained to write linear texts.

Of course, Western society's marked preference for logic and order is nothing new. We *like* our narratives nice and neat. Stray ends are messy; we like it better when things make sense. I certainly can write this way in certain contexts. For instance, I generally cannot write critical papers without an outline. I have also been known to write effective introductions, to develop well-reasoned arguments, and to conclude them nicely. However, when I turn to creative writing this approach falls apart. The attempts I've made to write more traditional narratives (and believe me, I've made them) have had lackluster results. My plotbound stories contain nothing but dull, one-dimensional characters valiantly lurching their way up the rising action to the climax so they can slink off shamefaced into the denouement. Conventional narrative simply doesn't work for me. Any emotional resonance my work may have results from my ability to allow who I am to come through that work. And my creative mind does not move in a linear way.

But what difference does any of this really make? Who cares if some writers approach their work in a way that is "opposed" to conventional narrative? What does it matter if some well-intentioned teacher tries to help them "straighten" things out? And besides, wouldn't it be easier if writers like me stopped all of this nonsense and just learned to create a proper plot? And if I can't, whose problem is it besides my own?

Memoirist Patricia Hampl has this to say in *I Could Tell You Stories:* "Memoir must be written because each of us must have a created version of the past. Created: that is, real, tangible, made of the stuff of a life lived in place and in history . . . We must acquiesce to our experience and our gift to transform experience into meaning and value. You tell me your story, I'll tell you my story." While Hampl is talking specifically about memoir, her point is clear. Telling stories is important. It is through narrative that we come to understand our lives, and that others come to understand us. It is through hearing others' voices that we come to understand them. What happens then, when a voice is stilled because traditional narrative forms do not sustain it? Hampl writes that "what is remembered [i.e., written] is what *becomes* reality." If what I, as a writer, need to say goes unsaid because I am struggling to write the way I "should" write, rather than the way I must, then my reality is diminished. So too, is the reality of many other voices that can't authentically speak through conventional linear forms. So too, is the reality of each one of us.

August 3rd, 1987. It was a hot day in Green Bay, Wisconsin. As that hot day deepened into warm darkness, my mother drove to Good Times, the little blue-collar tavern where she tended bar on the weekends. She poured beer and washed glasses, talked with the regulars, and sold two six-packs of Miller early in the evening to two men already well on their way to drunk. One of these men would later return with his brother. The brothers were angry. They believed she'd overcharged for the beer (she hadn't) and they were going to get even. In that cooling humid night they forced open the door, took the money from the till, and strangled my mother to death.

I was 15 on that hot day in August, the day she was killed, the day my world shattered. If I am to understand how that happened, and replicate the experience of trying to understand that for a reader, then I cannot write something whole—there is nothing whole to be written. There are only the shattered pieces. How does one make a plot, how does one make sense, of what makes no sense? Of what cannot make sense.

I write the way I write because it's the only way I can in this world—the same world through which that tangled line of people I still see in my memory walked. I was a child when I first watched that line from my mother's bedroom window, my face pressed up against the window screen. They were the "crazies" who lived in a home across the street from the trailer park where we lived. Several times a week they appeared to tour the drive that wound between the trailers. Once aired out, they disappeared back across the street.

And all I really remember of them is that Kewpie doll. I understand that doll. I know how it is—how it's difficult to see the world as a place with a beginning, a middle, and an end when you're dangling from the fingers of a crazy person, bumping along, seeing blue sky one minute, gravel road the next.

Double Take

1. Given the different ways of writing that Kathe McAllister, citing Madison Smart Bell, describes, how would you describe your writing style? What design best describes your approach to writing? How much of that design depends on the kind of writing you are doing and the readers you are writing for?
2. To what extent is "Blue Sky and Gravel" unconventional? How does this unconventionality contribute to the essay's meaning?
3. To what extent is the essay conventional? That is, to what extent does it conform to what McAllister describes as Western society's preference for logic and order? How would you describe the essay's logic and order?

Heidi Beck

Heidi Beck is a graduate student at the University of Washington. She received her master's degree in teaching English as a second language (ESL) in June 2001. Beck's interest in communication between people has taken various tangents throughout the years, but expression of ideas has always been the underlying theme.

A Seattle native, Beck also received her bachelor of arts degree from the University of Washington. As a drama major, she soon realized that to make a living in her undergraduate field, she would have to keep her day job. Although she still loves the theater, she felt the opportunity to act in meaningful works was limited; in addition, she realized she lacked the necessary talents to be a successful waitress. Soon to enter the world of ESL, she now realizes that to survive in this profession, she will have to keep her night job. Still, she is excited about the future. In addition, Beck has discovered how well her areas of study complement each other and loves using drama in the ESL classroom. She finds this approach both satisfying and successful, and has presented workshops on its use. This also provides her the opportunity to remind her family that her drama degree was good for something after all.

Future dreams for Beck include researching historical language policy in Poland, restoring her '64 Rambler, converting the world to vegetarianism, and writing a screenplay.

Beck on Writing

At First Glance

This essay is Heidi Beck's response to the statement: "why write." Of all the student essays in this section, it is perhaps the most direct, offering a list of reasons and explanations. At the same time, the essay has a conversational feel to it, a quality that gives the impression that Beck is exploring her reasons as she writes. As you read the essay, pay attention to how Beck achieves this balance between directness and exploration; look particularly for those places in the essay that reflect its searching quality. Also, as you read, think about how Beck's reasons for writing compare to yours.

Why I Write

If you asked me why I write, my reply would be simple, straightforward—and similar to the answers with which other writers, renown and unknown, respond. For me, to write is to communicate ideas, to influence others, to create beauty with language. It is also so much more. Sometimes, to write is to exist. Writing also allows me to express myself, to deal with emotion, to evoke a sense of permanence, to reach out toward greatness . . . and sometimes I write because I have to. Interestingly, if asked why I read, my response would be the same. In fact, I often find it difficult to separate the two; it's the same sharing of ideas, just approached from different ends. Each encourages and inspires the other.

These answers reveal that my writing reflects how I perceive and project myself as a human being. I want to communicate, and influence, and create, and do all these things. Perhaps most of all, I want to experience greatness and be forever changed by it. For me, writing has two kinds of greatness: technical skill and creative ability. It's the latter that touches the human spirit. In reading I reach greatness by crossing the bridge the author has built. In writing however, I construct the bridge. Now . . . think back to the first time you read *A Tale of Two Cities*. Could you imagine how Dickens was going to end his story, uniting such a multitude of details and characters spanning languages, countries, and class? I couldn't. In fact, I was so caught up in his skill at weaving together time and place that when I reached the end, I had to read the book all over again just so I could concentrate on the beauty of the language and the power of the story. Even greater than his mastery of words and storytelling was his capacity to envision the human spirit at its most noble. In a period of history dripping with hatred and death, Dickens showed us a human soul capable of making the ultimate sacrifice for another; one whose only reward was to know "it is a far, far better thing that I do, than I have ever done; it is a far, far better rest that I go to, than I have ever known." Dickens built a bridge that even today is a masterpiece in both construction and destination. It is also an inspiration; could I ever write in such a profoundly moving way? Perhaps yes, perhaps no . . . but of the greatest importance is that this writing inspires me to try.

I often reread well-loved classics or see movies that have profoundly affected me a second, a third, or a fourth time. It's as if I discover something new about the characters and about the gift and skill of their creator each time. As a child I used to read some of my favorite books over and over; it was like visiting old friends. I couldn't imagine getting through summer vacation without them. That's what good writing is to me: familiar not stale, timely not dated, comfortable and welcoming—no matter how often we return. Or perhaps it's the opposite: uncomfortable and challenging. What makes it great in my mind, and what makes me want to achieve this in my own writing is the feeling that something timeless is being communicated. I find great satisfaction in reading a good book; therein lies the reason I love to create through writing—that provides me great satisfaction as well. Sometimes I feel afraid to look too closely. What if I examine it so thoroughly the magic disappears? Still, I'm beginning to think that it's worth the risk, especially now as I am about to leave graduate school and embark on a new career as an ESL teacher. Already I've taught writing classes and wondered how I could foster an environment in which my students believe that they have the potential to create magic too. Perhaps a closer look at my other motivations will provide some additional clues.

I write to communicate ideas. I used to love to act. In fact, I still find performing very enjoyable. However, it didn't take long to realize that as an actor, you have very little control over the message you convey. Furthermore, I found out that unless I truly believed in the message, I wasn't that interested in conveying it! Professional actors can't afford to be that choosy. Later I learned that there are other ways of communicating ideas that can be just as satisfying. I became especially intrigued by foreign languages, and how understanding and reading works in an author's native tongue allows a more authentic experience of the writer's thoughts. When I read something in its original language, I'm getting a clear view into a world different than mine, without the barriers that translation can sometimes erect. It allows me special insight into the authors and the cultures that have created them. When I write, I know that I am directly offering others my opinions and ideas, and indirectly providing them a glimpse into the culture and world from which I come.

I write to influence others. Understanding what seems right to us, and working to change what doesn't, can give us a sense of empowerment. Before I joined the Peace Corps, I worked for a national nonprofit organization that focused on fitness and families. Although I worked in an administrative capacity and had little contact with the public, it seemed like I was contributing to the general good, and I felt I was getting a sense of worth from what I was doing. However, as the years passed and I was unable to advance because I lacked a degree in an area deemed valuable by the organization, I became frustrated. What initially seemed a mere division between professional staff and the rest of us became a chasm, and even though I had an understanding boss who offered me challenging opportunities, the position of the national organization continued to bother me. Through my boss, I became a member of the national professional organization—and not just a member, but a board member for the Northwest chapter and its newsletter editor. Producing a quarterly letter and an editorial column that called for the organization to treat its staff with the same dignity and respect that it did its members allowed me to work toward changing what I saw as an unfair situation. Did it change then? No. Has it changed now? Probably not. But I know that because of my writing, more people became aware of something previously unnoticed. At board meetings and conferences I was sometimes approached and told about individual staff and association changes that were being implemented. Did I enlighten some people to evaluate situations among staff that could be perceived as unfair? Yes. Did I influence some staff to make changes that were within their power? I like to think so.

I write to create beauty. In a composition class I took recently, we students would go round and round discussing the relative merits of correct grammar versus freedom of expression. Maybe because my mother was an English teacher (who as a child was raised in a strict parochial school where bad grammar was punishable by a few raps on the knuckles), the use of traditional grammar has been so ingrained in me that by now it has become automatic and just feels right. Perhaps, as a foreign language student, it makes sense to me because the same sort of traditional grammar patterns are found in many other Western languages. For example, informal English *who/what/where* questions permit prepositions to be left dangling, stranded alone at the end of a sentence; the rules of many other Indo-European languages will not allow this. Perhaps as an English language teacher, I know that for students coming from a related language background, my adherence to traditional grammatical forms allows them to recognize similarities to their first language, which can make learning English less stressful. Most of all, using traditional grammar forms for me is beauty in motion; it makes ordinary writing poetry. Fitting words together is similar to working an intricate jigsaw puzzle; doing it correctly provides me the same feeling of accomplishment. My written world would be a much less expressive, much less lovely place without old-fashioned relative clauses: "and therefore never send to know for whom the bell tolls . . ." Donne's world was much different than ours, but could his thoughts be expressed more beautifully today? I think not. That said, I do admit to seeing a certain kind of beauty in nontraditional forms, but I don't get goose bumps the way I do when I read or produce writing in which the words just flow down the page like a river. I can neither draw nor paint. I'm not able to create beauty with colors and images, but I can create it with words. Mike Rose, scholar and teacher of writing, said it so well in an essay describing the important elements in the teaching of writing. One of those elements was "insisting on the importance of craft and grace." If we can write gracefully, if we can inspire others to "continue struggling for graceful written language" we are creating beauty.

I write to exist. Writing defines who I am. Sometimes in life that becomes not only important but absolutely essential. As a Peace Corps volunteer in a small town in rural Poland, I often felt the only definition of my existence was through my writing: articles for our country newsletter and U.S. newspapers; letters to other volunteers and friends and family back home. Although I knew the language fairly well, it was difficult to become a member of my community; the pervasive Eastern European suspicion of strangers was hard to overcome. Village mind-sets, communist politics—many factors old and new worked together to cause a distrust of outsiders. It was easy to understand, but not so easy to adapt. Whole weekends could go by without me speaking to anyone. At those times I existed through my writing, as I detailed the latest challenge or shared the rare success story.

I write to express myself. Peter Elbow, professor of writing and advocate of personal writing, would be proud. Ever since childhood I have been writing in my own "voice" and I never even knew it. I have always loved to write and have never seemed to experience the writer's block about which so many professionals and college students complain. Still, I understand its origins: If I couldn't write what and how I wanted, I could still put words down on paper, but I wouldn't be happy with what I wrote. Although I rarely have trouble writing, if I'm not in the mood, I can't produce a piece of writing I want to share. Mood, motivation, freedom—that's what voice is all about. To really be effective, I believe it's necessary for writers at any level to say what they want to say, and to use their voice to do so.

If you can just figure out the angle from which to approach it, you can put your voice into anything, from academic discourse to journal writing, from personal letters on flowery stationery to e-mail on a computer screen. Voice is a funny thing; it can exist all along and you can never know you have it—you just know when you don't! That feeling of satisfaction is missing. It wasn't until my composition course that I learned the formal definition of voice. Even after reading Elbow's essays and listening to lengthy class discussions, I still wasn't sure I had grasped the concept. And then one day, while communicating with a classmate about a writing assignment (and complaining about the overall volume of work in the process), she replied that she laughed out loud when she read my message, and that I certainly had no trouble letting my voice shine through. That was my voice? Why didn't somebody say so? Voice is just me being me! It's why if I can't say in a letter to a friend what I really want to say, on stationery that matches my mood, with ink that matches my stationery and a stamp that matches both, it's better for me not to write at all. It's why I respond to an e-mail of one or two sentences with an e-mail of one or two paragraphs. Hemingway, I'm not; I couldn't possibly die in the rain as succinctly as he. But the secret is to express our thoughts in our own unique style and individual voice, which Hemingway did so heartbreakingly well. That's what makes his works so real and such a pleasure to read. Or to write. No matter how many words.

I write to release joy or anesthetize pain. To plagiarize (uh, I mean paraphrase!) T. H. White, the only cure for being sad is to write something. I've inherited the ability to write schmaltzy poems and humorous limericks from my father. I love his poems and stories. More remarkable than what he produces, however, is that even for this no-nonsense left-brain, retired aerospace engineer, writing is an outlet for emotion: joy, celebration, grief, loss. Sometimes I write when I'm feeling happy or adventurous. A few years ago, everyone on my Valentine list, including a couple of new additions, got a personalized rhyme. My old friends appreciated the humor, my nephews loved Tante Heidi's silliness, and my new friends, well—can you think of a better way to meet somebody? So all right, the surgeon was married. And the physical therapist was an unattached sports addict who wanted to stay that way. What counts is that through writing I made two new friends, and friendship is always an occasion for joy.

When I'm sad, writing can be a release from pain. Sometimes it is the only release—and it doesn't give you a hangover. I've written songs and poems to help me endure separation and cope with death. I've written when I felt I couldn't bear the pain of loss and longing any longer. When I write I'm alone, not lonely. There are times I think I surely would have died had I not been able to write.

I write to make things last. It has never been clear to me why so many good things in my life have come tainted with a sense of loss. Endings are a part of the circle of life; without them there are no beginnings. Regardless, they have always made me very sad. As a child growing up in a rural neighborhood, except for the occasional summer slumber party or birthday get-together, summers were a lonely time for me populated mostly by animals, books, and Disney albums. (No videos back then!) Even so, I hated the last day of summer vacation. Although I couldn't wait to see my friends again, and wear my new school clothes, the very last day of summer always felt sad. I would stay up all night, trying to make it last, and to be awake to say good-bye. Usually to keep awake, I would write down all the great moments of the summer, as if putting them down on paper would make the memories last forever. This habit of writing to hold on to the past has extended well into my adult life. One magical summer about 15 years ago I attended a study session in Poland. It was a summer that was to change the course of my life. One reason for this was that I fell in love. At that time I was accustomed to keeping a weekly journal; however, from my first step in Poland I felt absolutely compelled to record daily every single event of the summer school. And that was before I learned his name! Once we both knew how we felt about each other, there was no time to spend writing about it. At the end of the summer, when we were at the airport and about to be separated, I felt I could barely breathe. As soon as I got on the plane, I sat down to write every detail in my journal that I hadn't yet recorded. Luckily, it was a long flight; I had weeks and weeks to catch up. Somewhere over the Atlantic I finished the last entry, got a drink, and began to cry. Finally, my memories were safe. It helped me, to record the past, but unfortunately, I wasn't able to write the future. He did propose, I did return—but somehow our timing was off and we did not end up together. This fairy tale had no happily ever after. Today, even after all this time, occasional images of that summer return to me with such crystal clarity that I wonder why it seemed so necessary back then to put them down on paper. Or was it the very act of writing them down that etched them permanently in my brain?

I write because I have to. As a soon-to-graduate graduate student (ah. . . English!), I am looking forward to the day when I can read books and journals and not be required to produce an 8- to 10-page double-spaced analysis of them. And yet, because writing normally is such a joy for me, remembering what the "because I have to" feels like is perhaps one of the best tools I can possess to help me teach students who write because they have to—in a second language. What have I learned to do when I feel I just cannot crank out one more opinion essay or research paper? Oh, there are all kinds of tricks, but for me as a writer and a teacher of writing skills, the most important one is this: If somehow I can frame the assignment in parameters that allow individual expression, I can write and write well no matter how tired, drained, and uncreative I am feeling. I can even make it 8 to 10 pages.

When I received my teaching assistantship, I swore I'd never be like those TAs I had as an undergraduate: calculus TAs who couldn't understand my lack of understanding, science TAs who couldn't provide another perspective, even foreign language TAs who couldn't sympathize with my need for alternative explanations. It all came so effortlessly to them, they couldn't fathom my difficulty. Even though I love languages, learning them has never come easily to me; I thought that qualification alone was going to make me one of the finest instructors ever. However, when I found myself teaching writing and responding to questions about writing assignments by saying "just write," I realized I needed something more. Becoming aware of the composition process has certainly helped, as have the concepts that just as people learn language differently, so do they approach writing differently. I can teach basic skills on how to write, but what I really want to do is to help students discover what makes them want to write. By understanding why writing means so much to me, perhaps I can help make it more meaningful to them.

I may never write the great American novel or create the timeless screenplay. Perhaps what I have learned from life is of benefit only to me. There are eternal values that cross cultural and temporal boundaries, but I may not be the one to share them. Do I have the gift? I don't know and perhaps it doesn't matter. What does matter is that I offer what I have to say in my voice, and that I do so with grace and beauty. If I do that, then however others judge my work, I will always continue the struggle. I will always write.

Double Take

1. Notice that many of Heidi Beck's paragraphs begin with the simple retort "I write to . . ." as a listed response to her title "Why I Write." That is, Beck's paragraphs are carefully constructed to list and explain why she writes. Do you find this strategy effective—of listing the reasons she writes as she explains those reasons? What does such a strategy do to enhance (or detract) from the essay?
2. Locate the places in this essay where you think Beck's voice is most distinct. What makes them so? What effects do they have on you as a reader?
3. Of the eight reasons Beck gives for why she writes, which most reflect your reasons for writing? Which least reflect your reasons? Explain why.

Spencer Schaffner

Spencer Schaffner was initiated into the cult of the five-paragraph essay during his junior year at Boulder High School. He went on to the University of Colorado at Boulder and has an MA in English from Boston College. Currently working on an MA in secondary education and a PhD in rhetoric and composition at the University of Washington, Schaffner's main research interests involve the language that composition instructors use to teach writing. In his spare time Schaffner makes furniture and handmade books, and maintains a website at http://students.washington.edu/spiegel.

Schaffner on Writing

At First Glance

One thing you will notice about Spencer Schaffner's essay "The Five-Paragraph Essay: Friend or Foe?" is his running outline in superscripted text which indicates what part of the essay each sentence and paragraph is. In many ways Schaffner's use of the superscripted indicators helps define the five-paragraph essay and the formula for writing one. In many ways, too, the superscripted guidelines serve as a metaconversation about the five-paragraph essay. As you read this interestingly crafted essay, consider why Schaffner decided to use these tags and what effect they have on your reading of the essay. Consider also how creativity can emerge from working within even the most regimented constraints.

The Five-Paragraph Essay: Friend or Foe?

Intro ¶: Thesis In this five-parragraph essay about *the* five-paragraph essay,TM? I will argue (aided/constrained by one of the stricter form[ula]s for the five-paragraph essay—five paragraphs made up of five sentences each) that the five-paragraph essay is a writing appliance that is at once useful for writers and readers and mind-numbing to fill with words. Intro ¶: Point A But by now you're probably already saying *yawn;* people who pay attention to such things know that the five-paragraph essay is out-moded, which is why it has been more or less dispensed with already (though versions of its former self still creep around American high schools)—so why I am returning to the site of the five-paragrapher will be my first topic paragraph: This will include some personal moments about my relationship with the five-paragraph essay, but I also want to say that the five-paragraph essay could be given a sort of makeover (much like what happened in the recent Volkswagen Bug restyling) to benefit some writers and writing occasions. Intro ¶: Point B I'm willing to admit that one of the more unfortunate things about the five-paragraph essay is its inherent inflexibility—but this need not be the case! So after I discuss my own personal relationship with the five-paragraph essay (and engage in ensuing proclamations about recycling this old beast), I'll illustrate the potential for flexibility within the five-paragraph essay by dedicating a five-sentence paragraph to reflecting on the writing of the five-paragraph essay that you're reading and I'm writing right now: What is it like writing a five-paragraph essay? Intro¶: Point C Because you know, the thing is, even if you get away from the regimentation of one formally delineated five-by-five stylistic apparatus, most written discourse (and a good deal of our speech) is as laid out for us in advance as a TV dinner. Intro ¶: Conclusion Why all this matters will be

784

got at in my conclusion, where I also hope to touch on how the five-paragraph essay is a sort of Parthenon in the polytheistic world of essay writing; an icon to one of the many gods of composition, it can be a place to revisit and explore what can be learned from writing by numbers.

¶2: Intro To return to this Parthenon that is the five-paragraph essay, and then to explore its inner workings, is to return to a monument to our ongoing cultural regime of Mandated Scholastic Composition, a learning culture in which the five-pargrapher is but one example of a container for student ideas—only with the five-paragraph essay, of course, it is always the same container each time, a container equipped with Plexiglas walls that are as easy for the assessor (read: overworked, underpaid language arts instructor) to see into as they are for the student to fill up with language. ¶2: Point A Inasmuch as this is a fair characterization of the five-paragraph essay, the fact that it has generally been scrapped (along with the type-writer; these are rigid, outmoded writing technologies) can be seen, generally, as a good thing for students of writing everywhere: The clunky old technology has been dispensed with and replaced by *word processing* and *flexible* essays that allow students to express their ideas in ways that respond to and are appropriately constituted by the ideas themselves—I mean, this essay is a perfect example of how difficult it is to write in the old way: My prose (if you can call it that) is being made exceedingly wacky as I grammatically contort and dislocate and squeeze my ill-fitting thoughts into this form—and as I cobble and slice together ideas that become increasingly hard to follow, there's a great deal I want to say that's left out. ¶2: Point B However, what I really want to relate in this paragraph is what happened to me when, thanks to Ms. Mitchell (my high school composition teacher and Staunch Advocate of the five-by-five five-paragraph essay), I was schooled, nay, *drilled,* in the practices of five-paragraphing. ¶2: Point C Once a blank slate without the slightest idea of what an essay was or how to write one, I learned the five-paragraph essay well, and then took my new knowledge with me to college ("you tell 'em what you're going to tell 'em, tell 'em, then tell 'em what you told 'em," Ms. Mitchell used to repeat)—where "my writing" was received with resounding cheers of adoration from my professors; I mean, they ate the stuff up; it was *that* easy for them to figure out what I was saying. ¶2: Conclusion/Transition So I suppose my point is that while in many ways the five-paragraph essay is a cantankerous beast that no writer should be forced to grapple with (reminder: in case you hadn't noticed, I really am *struggling* here to make this thing work!), it can serve as both a pair of training wheels for starting writers and as a way to, at least in my own experience, help keep the red pens at bay in college.

¶3: Intro Though rigid by nature, the five-paragraph essay can be tweaked and modified to serve various writers' specific needs; I mean come on, in a very real sense, most published academic journal articles (the ones written by those professors of mine who wrote "good" and "well put" and "nicely said" in the margins of my papers in college) are merely modified, tricked-out versions of the five-paragraph essay I learned to write in high school: For an academic article in the humanities, start by establishing the relevant academic conversation the essay will be concerned with (introduction), then establish the place the article has within that conversation (introduction antechamber), then, having told 'em what you're going to tell 'em, say what you're going to say (body paragraphs), and finish with a conclusion. ¶3: Point A My first reflection, then, on the composition of this essay you're reading right now is twofold: first of all, in the writing of it, I've had to make a lot of sentences (like this one) two- and three- and even fourfold in order to fit everything I want to say into this size-two essay; but at the same time, because of the five-paragraph mandate of the form, it's been both fun and wonderfully straightforward to plug away at the keyboard since, on this multiply semicoloned and em-dashed-to-the-max journey, the good old introduction (read: road map) tells me where to go every step of the way. ¶3: Point B The challenge, of course, is making my thoughts about the five-paragraph essay fit into itself, and having only written three paragraphs so far, I'm starting to understand why all those dopey topics—"Should Uniforms Be Worn in School?" or "Handgun: Friend or Foe?"—coexist alongside the five-paragraph essay in American secondary education: they practically require one another. ¶3: Point C But some writers and teachers of writing live by the old adage that "you've gotta start somewhere," and for a lot of starting writers (this was the case for me), the five-paragraph essay can work as an instrument. ¶3: Conclusion/Transition Not only that, but inasmuch as the five-paragraph essay is a form (like sonnets, villanelles, and academic journal articles), there can be something gained from using and manipulating and mastering a form that has as much cultural currency as this one does: struggling over how to carefully construct a mere five paragraphs consisting of a mere five sentences each, and then making that coalesce into a word structure that coherently means something—all this can amount to an ecstatic set of mental calisthenics . . . yielding even better results when the form, the training wheels, the scaffolding—whatever you want to call it—is finally abandoned.

¶4: Intro But is this possible? ¶4: Point A First of all, it's important to remember how rule-governed language and discourse are already (though linguists and discourse analysts fight like mad about how much this is true), so when students start becoming indoctrinated into container-based models specifying how to write (like the five-paragraph essay), residues from these writing practices are merely added to an already substantial accretion of rules. ¶4: Point B As productive as being an able practitioner of the five-paragraph essay was for me in college, it was a disaster when I got to graduate school: big whomping essays running 30 pages and employing multiple theoretical models required innovative structures to support all that ~~fluff~~ weight. ¶4: Point C At some point (for me it was in grad school; for others it might come sooner), five paragraphs fail to help anymore, becoming a hindrance not only to the way an essay can work, but to the thinking that goes on during the actual writing. ¶4: Conclusion/Transition So what I'm arguing for is that in some applications, or at the very least as a model to help show the formal structures underlying even the highly celebrated fare of academic journals, the five-paragraph essay should not be forgotten: Let's not throw it out; it might teach us something.

Concluding ¶: Thesis The you-tell-'em-what-you're-going-to-tell-'em model of writing might not encourage innovation, it might not address all the needs of struggling writers, but inasmuch as the five-paragraph essay (1) represents the structure and form implicit in most writing (even the very-super-most innovative, wacky, totally out-there essays), and (2) can be a relatively easy, democratic way for students to get writing and thinking work done—it's not that bad. ^{Concluding ¶: Point A} As I said in the second paragraph of this essay (sentences 3–4; isn't this nifty?), revisiting the relic of the five-paragraph essay is to return to a piece of writing equipment that made a lot of struggling writers and graders of writing feel safe. ^{Concluding ¶: Point B} Are non-five-paragraph essayists, from the fledgling to the skilled professional, really less constrained by formal, stylistic, and genre requirements? ^{Concluding ¶: Point C} Sure. ^{Concluding ¶: Final Point} But inasmuch as the five-paragraph essay loudly advertises the rigid formality of its structure, and inasmuch as a fledgling writer can exist within that structure (and indeed, for some of us at one time or another, thrive!), learning to perform the five-paragrapher can be an important exercise in adapting to the varying and sometimes absurd-seeming constraints of all writing, an exercise that can serve all writers who move on to navigate the various other forms and requirements embedded in the writing we do.

Double Take

1. Chances are, you too have had some training in the five-paragraph essay. If so, describe your experiences. To what extent has the five-paragraph essay served you as a writer? To what extent has it hindered you?
2. In the conclusion to "The Five-Paragraph Essay: Friend or Foe?" Spencer Schaffner claims that the five-paragraph essay can be democratic. What do you think he means by that? How could something so constraining be democratic?
3. Even though this is a formally constructed five-paragraph essay about the five-paragraph essay, Schaffner is able to make a number of creative choices within these constraints. Describe some of these creative choices. What makes them creative? And what can we learn about creativity as a result?

Marianne Rasmussen

Marianne Rasmussen was born in Bountiful, Utah, in 1978. Her passion for both language and music became apparent when, at 19 months old, she began inventing songs and incorporating the art of cliché into her developing vocabulary. She is currently a senior at the University of Utah, pursuing a bachelor of arts degree in English and a bachelor of music degree in composition. Her English studies emphasize creative writing, particularly poetry, and journalism. Rasmussen is a staff writer for *RED Magazine,* a local arts and entertainment publication affiliated with the University of Utah. She completed a three-month internship with the Salt Lake Organizing Committee, where she was involved in planning Arts Festival events for the 2002 Winter Olympic Games. Areas of academic interest include the influence of art in shaping identity and the interchangeability of musical and poetic forms. Rasmussem plans to continue graduate study in both music and literature, and hopes one day to become a rock star or an English teacher, "whichever comes first."

At First Glance

Marianne Rasmussen's "The Selfish Art: Exploring Identity through Writing" is a densely woven essay which examines the varied and complex dimensions involved in the act of writing. It includes tensions and contradictions as Rasmussen works through what writing means to her. As you read, try to keep track of these tensions and contradictions, and see how together they might comprise a richer view of writing. Pay attention also to those places in the essay where the tensions and contradictions might actually prevent readers from understanding what writing is.

The Selfish Art: Exploring Identity through Writing

I have always been a selfish writer. In junior high, I used to write joke poems in geometry class to keep from falling asleep (I found that sonnets worked best, since the punchline is already written into the final couplet). One day my teacher caught me and warned me that if I didn't knock it off I wouldn't pass the class. Shortly thereafter, I discovered the art of note writing. Soon my best friend and I spent more time sending each other notes than we did working on homework. Through our writing, we could elevate the dramas of eighth grade to hyperbolic proportions, satirize the authority figures that arbitrarily governed our lives, and in general wreak havoc on the otherwise inconsequential space we occupied. For me, writing was a way to make life seem more interesting than it truly was. Before I was even aware of it, I had become a writer.

In high school, I began to recognize the value of writing as a mode of understanding. I used it as a way of pulling the disparate parts of life together into something controllable. Writing became a tool for exploring who I was and trying to make sense of the world around me. I was still writing for fun, but I was also writing as a way of coming to terms with my own identity. It was about this time that I was introduced to authors like Toni Morrison, Charles Dickens, Albert Camus, and Joseph Conrad. These writers had something important to say—not just about themselves—but about all of us. They possessed the ability to use language not only to capture truth, but also to create it in meaningful ways. I remember sitting on a train, reading T. S. Eliot, and sensing that something entirely new had opened itself up to me. I hardly knew where to find myself in relation to what I was reading. I then became aware of the possibilities of writing as a way of accessing a different kind of understanding—through characters, histories, places, ideas, and cultures outside of my own. Where writing was a way of understanding myself, reading became a way of understanding others. The recognition of the familiar among the unfamiliar made the truths these authors shared seem most resonant. It was then that I recognized that good writing, serious writing, should look further than the narrow frame of one's own front window. Good writing challenges identity and, in doing so, allows us access to greater truths than we could ever teach ourselves.

The process of writing is ultimately the search for understanding. In this pursuit, it is often the case that the end justifies the means. Science, for example, examines the laws of nature. It relies on empirical evidence, recorded data, and observable facts to uncover universal laws. Religion, by contrast, seeks to understand the nature of God through faith. It insists that believing in unobservable truths reveals insight beyond human reason. The work of writing lies somewhere between these two extremes. It uses tangible details to access intangible truths. It demands equal parts experimentation and faith. A writer hopes to achieve understanding through the careful construction of parts into a meaningful whole. In this endeavor, process is often as important as product. There is no one particular method of approach or a single, definable end. Unlike science or religion, writing is not limited by fixed values. Language is the appropriate "means" for the exploration of human experience because it is not restricted by the boundaries of the corporeal world. Good writing does not present absolute truths, but suggests potential solutions among an infinite number of possibilities. Whether fiction or nonfiction, poetry or prose, writing is a way of both marking our spot on the globe and mapping out its unfamiliar landscapes. It allows us to explore our own existence and our existence in relation to others. The common ground where the individual meets the collective is where we find the truth of human experience.

I recently read several personal journal entries that I wrote during my senior year of high school. To read one's own journal is to experience the anguish of personal writing at its finest. Viewed under the illuminating light of retrospect, these entries capture both the seeming immediacy and ultimate narrowness of present perspective. Journals are an important reminder of who we were, which has inevitably influenced who we now are. Each page is distinctly different, but I like to think that no one entry is less or more true than another. They are all true in the moment, and that moment is always moving to a newer moment where a new truth will be born. Two years from now, when I look back on the journal entry I wrote yesterday, I will probably cringe, chuckle, and move on to the next blank page. Life is like a journal. In order to capture it we must be willing to accept the past and look to the future. The purpose of this type of writing is to capture the self. It's like a photograph. It doesn't create objects—it merely preserves them.

Serious writing, on the other hand, requires an active form of creation. The nature of human existence and the consistency of inconsistency make writing an effective tool for exploring our ever-changing social and cultural landscape. Just as journals chronicle personal progression, literature chronicles collective human progression. The distinction between the two is significant. The importance of a private work is tied directly to its author. The life of that author is the context, and any meaning within it is influenced by a reader's familiarity with that context (i.e., the person who wrote it). Literature or poetry is unlike this because, as a deliberate work, it must create its own context apart from its author. Reading is a form of discovery, and to supplement it with an explanation is to cheat readers of the discovery process. Writers must be conscious of art as a living entity: one that will continually be evaluated apart from their personal existence. Thus, the success of a text is ultimately dependent on its ability to stand on its own. That said, I must confess that I personally don't believe you can ever entirely separate authors from their writing. Even as they exist apart from one another, they are linked by mutual influence. What is important is that the person doesn't get in the way of the work, or vice versa. When I begin writing a poem, I generally start with a free-write exercise: a continuous, uncensored collection of images, emotions, or ideas. These exercises are often prompted by personal experience. Sometimes they come easily. More often I have to work for them. While my own experience serves as a point of departure for my writing, I do not consider my poems to be purely private works. An enormous amount of rewriting, revising, rethinking, and restructuring must take place in order to make an actual poem. A delicate balance between the role of author as individual and the individuality of the work must be achieved. Somewhere in the back of my mind there is this odd sense that the writing somehow shapes itself, and writers are merely the instruments for that shaping. In actuality, I think it is a mutual effort. The result is art that moves beyond its origins to take on a life of its own.

Poets love to talk about their work in terms of familial relationships. In *The Author to Her Book,* Anne Bradstreet addresses her writing as, "Thou ill-form'd offspring of my feeble brain." It is an apt metaphor, since in many ways writing is like raising a child. It involves giving birth, nourishing, guiding, and eventually learning to let go of whatever it has created. It's a process I have often heard referred to in workshops as "baby killing." Killing a baby is the sacrificial act of removing some element of a draft that a poet is particularly in love with. It is often the result of the painful awareness that our own words are hindering our work as a whole. It sounds terrible, but I think that, deep down, poets secretly delight in killing their babies. They sit around, ordering each other to kill their babies, talking about how they killed their babies. In sick Abrahamic rituals, they sacrifice their poems on the altar of art, hoping that in the end someone will smile down and say "just kidding." The more I write, the more I find myself required to perform this act. I must segregate my own needs as a writer from the needs of my writing. Personal truth must be abandoned in the search for connective truth. It is necessary, since connective truths bring us closer to understandings that we are incapable of attaining alone. The truth in writing, then, is not the way it reenacts reality, but the way it interacts with reality. Writing becomes a sort of mediator between seemingly opposing forces. It is an organizing principle between the chaotic and the structured, a link between the real and the imagined, a bridge between the expressed and the inexpressible. In shaping a work, a writer is forced to continually question the conventions of understanding, push the parameters of reality, and expand the limits of possibility. By blurring established boundaries, the writer enables language to create rare moments when readers encounter something so true, they wonder why they didn't find the words to express it themselves. The instructive and connective potential of these moments is, I believe, the true possibility of writing. It is the recognition of self in the work of others that first draws us into a text. Hopefully, it is the desire to understand others that keeps us there. Good writing challenges who we are by both establishing and displacing our sense of identity. In the end, it is our ability to share truth that defines our humanity.

There is a passage in Conrad's *Heart of Darkness* where Marlow, frustrated with his own inability to communicate, exclaims, "No, it is impossible, it is impossible to convey the life-sensation of any given epoch of one's existence—that which makes its truth, its meaning— its subtle and penetrating essence. We live, as we dream— alone." Fortunately, this is not entirely true. Writing gives us the words to express our dreams. It reminds us not only of who we are, but who we might become. Each individual contribution to the project of writing adds to the ever-shifting context of humanity, making each one of us active participants in shaping existence. Writing allows us to expand our understanding, and thanks to it, we never have to live—or dream—alone.

Double Take

1. Marianne Rasmussen begins her essay by describing herself as a selfish writer. What do you think she means by that, and what indications of that selfishness do you notice in the essay?
2. At the end of "The Selfish Art: Exploring Identity through Writing," Rasmussen declares that writing allows us to never have to live alone, while earlier she describes writing as a selfish act. A tension seems to emerge here between a view of the writer as an individual and a view of the writer as a social participant. How does Rasmussen make sense of this tension? How do you make sense of this tension?
3. Much of this essay explores the relationship between the writer and his or her writing. As a writer, how do you relate to and identify with your own writing?

A CLOSER LOOK AT THE STUDENT WRITERS

1. Choose two or more student essays from this section and in an essay compare their writers' "voices." First describe each writer's voice as it emerges in the essay and then analyze how it shapes the way you as a reader relate to the essay. Along the way, think about the power of "voice" as a rhetorical device for making meaning.

2. Melvin Sterne and Kathe McAllister both argue on behalf of the writer's freedom of choice, especially regarding form, voice, and style. Spencer Schaffner, on the other hand, recognizes at least some value in regulating a writer's freedom through the constraint of form. As a writer, where do you see yourself in this debate? Write an essay that positions your view of writing in relationship with Stern, McAllister, and Schaffner.

3. All the student essayists in this section describe themselves as writers, but throughout their essays, they also subtly describe themselves as readers. Look closely at two or more of the essays, and pay attention to how the essayists describe themselves as readers. Then in an essay compare and analyze the way they define the act of reading. Is there a connection between the way they define themselves as readers and the way they define themselves as writers?

Looking from Writer to Writer

1. Heidi Beck's essay shares the same title as Annie Dillard's "Why I Write." Looking at the two essays together, do you see any similarities other than the title? The other essays gathered in this chapter also answer the question "why I write." Are there any essays other than Beck's that seem more similar to Dillard's? What characteristics do they share?

2. All of the writers in this collection make statements concerning how they envision writing; some, like Joseph Epstein, Edward Hoagland, and Scott Russell Sanders, make specific comments about the role of the essay. Looking at those three writers' ideas of the role of the essay, in what ways do the essays in this student writers chapter fit or not fit those discussions of the essay?

3. Several of the essays gathered in this chapter address the places where the writers write. Sarah Huntley, for instance, writes specifically about how living in Florida affects her writing. Kathe McAllister locates part of her essay in Green Bay, Wisconsin. Likewise, other writers in this book—including Scott Russell Sanders, Annie Dillard, Rick Bass, Barry Lopez, André Aciman, Salman Rushdie, bell hooks, Ursula Le Guin, and Jamaica Kincaid—address issues of place. In what ways do the writers in this chapter address place that are comparable or in contrast to other writers in this collection?

Credits

ANDRÉ ACIMAN
"A Literary Pilgrim Progresses to the Past" by André Aciman from *The New York Times*, August 28, 2000. Copyright © 2000 The New York Times Co. Reprinted by permission; "Alexandria: The Capital of Memory" from *False Papers: Essays on Exile and Memory* by André Aciman. Copyright © 2000 by André Aciman. Reprinted by permission of Farrar, Straus and Giroux, LLC; "A Late Lunch" from *False Papers: Essays on Exile and Memory* by André Aciman. Copyright © 2000 by André Aciman. Reprinted by permission of Farrar, Straus and Giroux, LLC; "Shadow Cities" from *False Papers: Essays on Exile and Memory* by André Aciman. Copyright © 2000 by André Aciman. Reprinted by permission of Farrar, Straus and Giroux, LLC.

RICK BASS
"Without Safety: Writing Nonfiction" by Rick Bass as appeared in *Columbia*, 1990. Copyright © 1990 Rick Bass. Reprinted by permission of the author; "On Willow Creek" by Rick Bass as appeared in *Los Angeles Times Magazine*, November 28, 1993. Copyright © 1993 Rick Bass. Reprinted by permission of Rick Bass; "Why I Hunt: A Predator's Meditation" by Rick Bass as appeared in *Esquire*, October 1990. Copyright © 1990 Rick Bass. Reprinted by permission of the author; "Thunder and Lightning" by Rick Bass as appeared in *Sierra*, January 1995. Copyright © 1995 Rick Bass. Reprinted by permission of the author.

JOAN DIDION
"Why I Write" by Joan Didion. Copyright © 1976 by Joan Didion. Originally published in *The New York Times Book Review*. Reprinted by permission of the author; "The Women's Movement" from *The White Album* by Joan Didion. Copyright © 1979 by Joan Didion. Reprinted by permission of Farrar, Straus and Giroux, LLC; "In Bogota" from *The White Album* by Joan Didion. Copyright © 1979 by Joan Didion. Reprinted by permission of Farrar, Straus and Giroux, LLC; "Girl of the Golden West" by Joan Didion. Reprinted with the permission of Simon & Schuster from *After Henry* by Joan Didion. Copyright © 1992 by Joan Didion.

ANNIE DILLARD
"A Line of Words" from *The Writing Life* by Annie Dillard. Copyright © 1989 by Annie Dillard. Reprinted by permission of HarperCollins Publishers Inc.; "Total Eclipse" and

"Teaching a Stone to Talk" from *Teaching A Stone To Talk: Expeditions and Encounters* by Annie Dillard. Copyright © 1982 by Annie Dillard. Reprinted by permission of Harper-Collins Publishers Inc.; "Spring" from *Pilgrim At Tinker Creek* by Annie Dillard. Copyright © 1974 by Annie Dillard. Reprinted by permission of HarperCollins Publishers Inc.

BARBARA EHRENREICH
Introduction to "The Snarling Citizen" from *The Snarling Citizen* by Barbara Ehrenreich. Copyright © 1995 by Barbara Ehrenreich. Reprinted by permission of Farrar, Straus and Giroux, LLC.; "Stamping Out a Dread Scourge" by Barbara Ehrenreich from *Time,* February 17, 1992, Vol. 13, No. 7, p. 88. Copyright © 1992 Time Inc. Reprinted by permission; "Premature Pragmatism" by Barbara Ehrenreich as appeared in *Ms.* Magazine, October 1986. Copyright © 1986 by Barbara Ehrenreich. Reprinted by permission of International Creative Management, Inc.; "Oh, Those Family Values" by Barbara Ehrenreich from *Time,* July 18, 1994, Vol. 144, No. 3, p. 62. Copyright © 1994 Time Inc. Reprinted by permission.

JOSEPH EPSTEIN
"Compose Yourself" from *With My Trousers Rolled* by Joseph Epstein, W.W. Norton & Co. Reprinted with permission from the publisher; "A Mere Journalist" from *Once More Around the Block,* by Joseph Epstein. Copyright © 1987 by Joseph Epstein. Used by permission of W.W. Norton & Company, Inc.; "The Art of the Nap" by Joseph Epstein. Copyright © 1996 by Joseph Epstein. Reprinted by permission of Georges Borchardt, Inc; "Penography" from *The Middle of My Tether: Familiar Essays* by Joseph Epstein. Copyright © 1983 by Joseph Epstein. Used by permission of W.W. Norton & Company, Inc.

HENRY LOUIS GATES, JR.
"Writing, 'Race,' & the Difference It Makes" by Henry Louis Gates, Jr. from *Critical Inquiry,* Autumn 1985, Vol. 12, No. 1, pp. 1–20. Reprinted by permission of The University of Chicago Press; "Sunday" from *In Short* by Henry Louis Gates, Jr., W.W. Norton & Co. Reprinted with permission from the publisher; "In the Kitchen" and "Prime Time" from *Colored People: A Memoir* by Henry Louis Gates, Jr. Copyright © 1994 by Henry Louis Gates, Jr. Used by permission of Alfred A. Knopf, a division of Random House, Inc.

STEPHEN JAY GOULD
"Pieces of Eight: Confession of a Humanistic Naturalist," "A Cerion for Christopher," and " The Great Western and the Fighting Temeraire" from *Leonardo's Mountain of Clams and the Diet of Worms* by Stephen Jay Gould. Copyright © 1998 by Turbo, Inc. Used by permission of Harmony Books, a division of Random House, Inc.; "The Creation Myths of Cooperstown" from *Bully for the Brontosaurus: Reflections in Natural History* by Stephen Jay Gould. Copyright © 1991 by Stephen Jay Gould. Used by permission of W.W. Norton & Company, Inc.

EDWARD HOAGLAND
"To the Point: Truth Only Essays Can Tell" by Edward Hoagland. Copyright © 1993 by *Harper's Magazine.* All rights reserved. Reproduced from the March issue by special permission; "The Courage of Turtles" from *The Courage of Turtles* by Edward Hoagland. Published

by Lyons & Burford. Copyright © 1968, 1970, 1993 by Edward Hoagland. Reprinted by permission of Lescher & Lescher, Ltd. All rights reserved; "Learning to Eat Soup" from *Balancing Acts* by Edward Hoagland. Published by The Lyons Press. Copyright © 1988, 1992, 1999 by Edward Hoagland. Reprinted by permission of Lescher & Lescher, Ltd; "In Okefenokee" from *Balancing Acts* by Edward Hoagland. Published by The Lyons Press. Copyright © 1985, 1992, 1999 by Edward Hoagland. Reprinted by permission of Lescher & Lescher, Ltd.

BELL HOOKS

"Women Who Write Too Much" and "Black Women Writing" from *Remembered Rapture* by bell hooks. Copyright © 1999 by Gloria Watkins. Reprinted by permission of Henry Holt and Company, LLC; "Touching the Earth" from *Sisters of the Yam* by bell hooks. Reprinted by permission of South End Press; "Justice: Childhood Love Lessons" from *All About Love* by bell hooks. Copyright © 2000 by Gloria Watkins. Reprinted by permission of HarperCollins Publishers, Inc.

JAMAICA KINCAID

"Writing = Life," interview with Jamaica Kincaid by Brad Goldfarb, *Interview,* October 1997. Reprinted by permission of Brant Publications, Inc.; "In History" by Jamaica Kincaid. Copyright © 1997 by Jamaica Kincaid. Reprinted with the permission of The Wylie Agency; "Alien Soil" by Jamaica Kincaid. Copyright © 1993 by Jamaica Kincaid. Reprinted with the permission of The Wylie Agency; "Garden of Envy" by Jamaica Kincaid. Copyright © 1998 by Jamaica Kincaid. Reprinted with the permission of The Wylie Agency.

URSULA K. LE GUIN

"Prospects for Women in Writing" and "The Carrier Bag Theory of Fiction" from *Dancing at the Edge of the World* by Ursula K. Le Guin. Copyright © 1986 by Ursula K. Le Guin. Used by permission of Grove/Atlantic, Inc; "The Fisherwoman's Daughter" from *Dancing at the Edge of the World* by Ursula K. Le Guin. Copyright © 1988 by Ursula K. Le Guin. Used by permission of Grove/Atlantic, Inc; "Along the Platte" from *Dancing at the Edge of the World* by Ursula K. Le Guin. Copyright © 1983 by Ursula K. Le Guin. Used by permission of Grove/Atlantic, Inc.

BARRY LOPEZ

"We Are Shaped by the Sound of the Wind, the Slant of Sunlight," published as "The Language of Animals" by Barry Holstun Lopez. Reprinted by permission of Sterling Lord Literistic, Inc. Copyright © 1998 by Barry Holstun Lopez; "The Stone Horse" and "A Presentation of Whales" from *Crossing Open Ground* by Barry Holstun Lopez. Reprinted by permission of Sterling Lord Literistic, Inc. Copyright © 1988 by Barry Holstun Lopez.; "A Passage of Hands" from *About This Life* by Barry Lopez. Copyright © 1998 by Barry Holstun Lopez. Used by permission of Alfred A. Knopf, a division of Random House, Inc.

CYNTHIA OZICK

"On Permission to Write" from *Metaphor and Memory* by Cynthia Ozick. Copyright © 1989 by Cynthia Ozick. Used by permission of Alfred A. Knopf, a division of Random House,

Inc.; "The Hole/Birth Catalog" and "A Drugstore in Winter" from *Art and Ardor* by Cynthia Ozick. Copyright © 1983 by Cynthia Ozick. Used by permission of Alfred A. Knopf, a division of Random House, Inc.; "Rushdie in the Louvre" from *Fame & Folly* by Cynthia Ozick. Copyright © 1996 by Cynthia Ozick. Used by permission of Alfred A. Knopf, a division of Random House, Inc.

SALMAN RUSHDIE

"Imaginary Homelands," "The New Empire Within Britain," "In Good Faith," and "Censorship" from *Imaginary Homelands* by Salman Rushdie, Penguin Putnam Inc., 1991. Reprinted with permission from the publisher.

EDWARD SAID

"No Reconciliation Allowed" from *Letters of Transit* by Edward Said, W.W. Norton & Co. Reprinted with permission from the publisher; "The Mind of Winter: Reflections on Life in Exile" by Edward Said. Copyright © 1984 by Edward Said. Reprinted with permission of The Wylie Agency, Inc.; "Palestine, Then and Now: An Exile's Journey through Israel and the Occupied Territories" by Edward Said. Copyright © 1992 by Edward Said. Reprinted with permission of The Wylie Agency, Inc.; "Jungle Calling" by Edward Said. Copyright © 1989 by Edward Said. Reprinted with permission of The Wylie Agency, Inc.

SCOTT RUSSELL SANDERS

"The Singular First Person" from *Secrets of the Universe: Essays on Family, Community, Spirit, and Place* by Scott Russell Sanders. Reprinted with permission from Beacon Press, Boston; "Writing from the Center" by Scott Russell Sanders. Copyright © 1994 by Scott Russell Sanders. First published in *Georgia Review*, collected in *Writing from the Center* by Scott Russell Sanders, Indiana University Press. Reprinted by permission of the author; "Letter to a Reader" by Scott Russell Sanders. Copyright © 1992 by Scott Russell Sanders. First published in *My Poor Elephant: 27 Male Writers at Work*, ed. Eve Shelnut, collected in *Writing from the Center* by Scott Russell Sanders, Indiana University Press. Reprinted by permission of the author; "Buckeye" by Scott Russell Sanders. Copyright © 1995 by Scott Russell Sanders. First published in *Orion*, collected in *Writing from the Center* by Scott Russell Sanders, Indiana University Press. Reprinted by permission of the author.

AMY TAN

"Snapshot: Lost Lives of Women" by Amy Tan. Copyright © 1991 by Amy Tan. First appeared in *Life* Magazine. Reprinted by permission of the author and the Sandra Dijkstra Literary Agency; "Mother Tongue" by Amy Tan. Copyright © 1990 by Amy Tan. First appeared in *The Threepenny Review*. Reprinted by permission of the author and the Sandra Dijkstra Literary Agency; "Language of Discretion" by Amy Tan. Copyright © 1990 by Amy Tan. Reprinted by permission of the author and the Sandra Dijkstra Literary Agency; "In the Canon for All the Wrong Reasons" by Amy Tan. Copyright © 1996 by Amy Tan. First appeared in *The Threepenny Review*. Reprinted by permission of the author and the Sandra Dijkstra Literary Agency.

JOHN UPDIKE

"Why Write?" and "Cemeteries" from *Picked-Up Pieces* by John Updike. Copyright © 1975 by John Updike. Used by permission of Alfred A. Knopf, a division of Random House, Inc.; "Thirteen Ways of Looking at the Masters" and "The Tarbox Police" from *Hugging the Shore* by John Updike. Copyright © 1983 by John Updike. Used by permission of Alfred A. Knopf, a division of Random House, Inc.

ALICE WALKER

"The Black Writer and the Southern Experience" from *In Search of Our Mother's Gardens: Womanist Prose.* Copyright © 1983 by Alice Walker. Reprinted by permission of Harcourt, Inc.; "In Search of Our Mothers' Gardens" from *In Search of Our Mother's Gardens: Womanist Prose.* Copyright © 1974 by Alice Walker. Reprinted by permission of Harcourt, Inc., "Women" from *Revolutionary Petunias and Other Poems.* Copyright © 1970, 1998 by Alice Walker. Reprinted by permission of Harcourt, Inc.; "My Daughter Smokes" from *Living by the Word: Selected Writings 1973–1987.* Copyright © 1987 by Alice Walker. Reprinted by permission of Harcourt, Inc.; "Beyond the Peacock: The Reconstruction of Flannery O'Connor" from *In Search of Our Mother's Gardens: Womanist Prose.* Copyright © 1975 by Alice Walker. Reprinted by permission of Harcourt, Inc.

EDWARD O. WILSON

"The Writing Life" by Edward O. Wilson as appeared in *The Washington Post,* June 25, 2000. Reprinted with the permission of Edward O. Wilson; Reprinted by permission of the publisher from "The Serpent" in *Biophelia* by Edward O. Wilson, Cambridge, Mass.: The Belknap Press of Harvard University Press. Copyright © 1984 by the President and Fellows of Harvard College; "Ethics and Religion" from *Concilience* by Edward O. Wilson. Copyright © 1998 by Edward O. Wilson. Used by permission of Alfred A. Knopf, a division of Random House, Inc.; "Humanity Seen from a Distance" by Edward O. Wilson from *In Search of Nature,* The Tanner Lectures on Human Values, The University of Utah. Reprinted with permission.

PHOTO CREDITS

p. 13, © Bassouls Sophie/Corbis Sygma; p. 41, © Bassouls Sophie/Corbis Sygma; p. 77, © Robert Birnbaum; p. 107, © Richard Howard/Timepix; p. 147, © Kimberly Butler/Timepix; p. 165, © 2002 Matthew Gilson; p. 213, © Shawn Henry/Corbis Sygma; p. 249, © Arnold Newman/Getty Images; p. 287, © Oscar White/Corbis; p. 329, © Jill Krementz; p. 357, © AFP/Corbis; p. 383, © Bettmann/Corbis; p. 419, © Galen Rowell/Corbis; p. 459, © Rick Maiman/Corbis Sygma; p. 489, © Matthew Mendelsohn/Corbis; p. 527, © Bettmann/Corbis; p. 573, Courtesy Scott Russell Sanders; p. 617, © Reuters NewMedia, Inc./Corbis; p. 641, © Frank Capri/SAGA/Getty Images; p. 671, © Roger Ressmeyer/Corbis; p. 705, © Douglas McFadd/Getty Images

Index of Authors and Titles

★ Student writers and works are indicated by an asterisk.